TAXATION OF ESTATES, GIFTS AND TRUSTS

Twenty-Third Edition

By

Regis W. Campfield

Professor of Law and Marilyn Jeanne Johnson
Distinguished Law Faculty Fellow,
Southern Methodist University

Martin B. Dickinson

Robert A. Schroeder Professor of Law, University of Kansas

William J. Turnier

W. P. Mangum Professor of Law, University of North Carolina

AMERICAN CASEBOOK SERIES®

Mat # 40339547

American Casebook Series and West Group are trademarks
registered in the U.S. Patent and Trademark Office.

COPYRIGHT © 1997 WEST PUBLISHING CO.
© West, a Thomson business, 1999, 2002
© 2006 Thomson/West
     610 Opperman Drive
     P.O. Box 64526
     St. Paul, MN 55164–0526
     1–800–328–9352
Printed in the United States of America

ISBN–13: 978–0–314–15931–1
ISBN–10: 0–314–15931–2

TEXT IS PRINTED ON 10% POST CONSUMER RECYCLED PAPER

For Mary, Allison and Claire
and Mother and Dad

R.W.C.

For my granddaughter, Olivia Dickinson

M.B.D.

For my grandchildren, Alexander, Ethan and others yet to come

W.J.T.

*

Preface

This volume has its roots in the Study of Federal Tax Law series first published under the leadership of Professors Willard Pedrick and Vance Kirby almost thirty years ago. Publication of annual new editions then assured that it was the most up to date set of teaching materials available. In 1997 the West Group took over publication of the series with a commitment that users would always be provided with up to date materials. This is the fourth edition to be published by the West Group.

This volume provides the materials essential for a basic course in federal estate and gift taxation. It also provides the materials required for the study of the closely related topic of the income taxation of trusts and estates. The materials begin with the taxation of lifetime gifts, proceed on to the principles of valuation for gift and estate tax purposes and move on to cover the estate tax and the generation skipping transfer tax. Finally the materials explore the principles involved in the income taxation of estates and trusts as well as related matters such as the taxation of income in respect of a decedent.

We recognize that teachers vary widely in the sequence of coverage of the topics in this volume. Therefore, each major portion of the text has been written so as to stand alone, and it is entirely feasible to begin with income taxation of estates and trusts, then move to the estate tax, or adopt some other order. In fact, we vary in our own coverage of the material.

Consistent with our practice in former editions we have included a significant number of problems to assist students in checking their understanding of materials covered in each of the chapters. We have also included materials that employ a planning perspective so that students attain some degree of understanding of how estate planners deal with the issues as they cope with their clients' estate planning goals.

We have continued most previous editing practices. Most footnotes are omitted from edited materials without indication. Those that appear bear their original numbers. Asterisks have been used to show major deletions. Minor deletions, such as dropping "of the Code" following a reference to a section of the Internal Revenue Code, have been made without indication. Where multiple authorities within a sentence are given in support of a statement or series of statements, we have chosen not to indicate each deleted authority and have indicated the presence of such deletions with only one set of asterisks within or at the end of a sentence. Back to back deletions from different paragraphs are shown with only one set of asterisks, and deletions of dissenting or concurring opinions are not always indicated. Editorial additions to opinions are placed within brackets. With the exception of these minor editorial liberties, the edited materials are as close as possible to the officially reported versions. For example, we have italicized no materials which were not italicized in the original, and have left parenthetical comments in the form chosen by the authors of the original materials.

We have continued to use paragraph numbers to separate materials in the book. We believe that this serves several purposes. First, it facilitates the preparation of a professor's assignment without including materials that he or she would prefer neither to assign nor to discuss. Second, it facilitates cross references. Finally, because we intend to continue the practice of publishing updated supplements and editions whenever developments warrant, the use of paragraph numbers facilitates integration of new materials.

Over the years we have benefited from the assistance of many fine editors, research assistants, secretaries and other support staff. In completing this edition we were fortunate to have the assistance of a number of extremely able individuals. Roxanne Birkel of West Group provided cheerful and able editorial assistance. Lori Farmer and Julie Lynch of the University of Kansas and Bonita Summers of the University of North Carolina all provided exceptional word processing assistance in the preparation of this manuscript. Sean Patrick O'Bryan and Jillian Hekmati provided Professor Dickinson with important research assistance. John Veazey provided valued research and editorial assistance to Professor Turnier. Gregory Ivy, Associate Director of the Southern Methodist University Law Library provided Professor Campfield with important research and technical support. Professor Campfield also acknowledges support for his research provided by Dean John Attanasio of SMU School of Law in the form of a grant.

Although this volume represents a true collaborative effort, each of us assumed primary editorial responsibility for various individual chapters. Professor Campfield assumed primary responsibility for chapters 22, 27, 30, 31 and 32. Professor Dickinson assumed primary responsibility for chapter 2 through 14, 21, 25, 28 and 29, and Professor Turnier assumed primary responsibility for chapter 1, 15 through 20, 23, 24 and 26. This and prior editions have benefited from the comments of users, both teachers and students, and we invite the reactions of those who use these materials.

REGIS W. CAMPFIELD
MARTIN B. DICKINSON
WILLIAM J. TURNIER

February 2006

Summary of Contents

PART I. INTRODUCTION TO FEDERAL TRANSFER TAX SYSTEM

PART II. GIFT TAX (CHAPTER 12 OF THE INTERNAL REVENUE CODE)

*

Table of Contents

PART I.   INTRODUCTION TO FEDERAL TRANSFER TAX SYSTEM

*

Table of Cases

The principal cases are in bold type. Cases cited or discussed in the text are roman type. References are to paragraphs. Cases cited in principal cases and within other quoted materials are not included.

*

Table of Statutes

1

TABLE OF STATUTES

UNITED STATES CODE ANNOTATED
26 U.S.C.A.—Internal Revenue Code

Sec.	This Work Par.
7872(d)	3037
7872(d)(1)(A)	3037
7872(d)(1)(B)	3037
7872(d)(1)(E)(ii)	3037
7872(e)(2)	3037
7872(f)(2)	3037
7872(f)(2)(A)	3037
7872(f)(2)(B)	3037
7872(f)(3)	3037

STATUTES AT LARGE

Year	This Work Par.
1981, P.L. 97–34	23013
2001, P.L. 107–16	25007

POPULAR NAME ACTS

ECONOMIC GROWTH AND TAX RELIEF RECONCILIATION ACT OF 2001

Sec.	This Work Par.
901	28005
901	29001
901(a)	2005

REVENUE ACT OF 1916

Sec.	This Work Par.
202(b)	20001

REVENUE ACT OF 1926

Sec.	This Work Par.
302(d)	19007
302(d)	19037

REVENUE RECONCILIATION ACT OF 1990

Sec.	This Work Par.
11602(e)(1)(A)(ii)	11091
11602(e)(1)(A)(iii)	3091
11602(e)(1)(A)(iii)	11107

TAX REFORM ACT OF 1986

Sec.	This Work Par.
1402(c)(1)	31223

STATE STATUTES

ALABAMA CODE

Sec.	This Work Par.
26–1–2.1	19103

ALASKA STATUTES

Sec.	This Work Par.
34.40.110	18085

WEST'S ANNOTATED CALIFORNIA PROBATE CODE

Sec.	This Work Par.
21552	27285

DELAWARE CODE

Ch.	This Work Par.
12, § 3571	18085

NEVADA REVISED STATUTES

Sec.	This Work Par.
166.040(1)(b)	18085

RHODE ISLAND GENERAL LAWS

Sec.	This Work Par.
18–19.2–2 to 18–9.2–5	18085

UTAH CODE ANNOTATED

Sec.	This Work Par.
25–6–14	18085

VIRGINIA CODE

Sec.	This Work Par.
11–9.5	3079
11–9.5	19103

UNIFORM PROBATE CODE

Sec.	This Work Par.
Pt. 9A	28073

*

Table of Treasury Regulations

lv

*

Table of Technical Advice Memoranda

*

Table of Private Letter Rulings

*

Table of Revenue Rulings

Table of Revenue Procedures

*

Table of Internal Revenue Service Notices

---

*

Table of Internal Revenue Service Actions on Decisions

———

*

TAXATION OF ESTATES, GIFTS AND TRUSTS

Twenty-Third Edition

*

Part I

INTRODUCTION TO FEDERAL TRANSFER TAX SYSTEM

Chapter 1

ORIENTATION

A. CONSTITUTIONAL ISSUES

[¶ 1001]

1. NOT A DIRECT TAX

The transfer of wealth at death has long been a favorite taxable event. Such a levy prevailed in ancient Rome. In the United States a federal stamp tax on legacies and shares in intestate estates was first adopted in 1797 although it was repealed in 1802. The Civil War federal inheritance tax was repealed in 1870. It is notable that the federal income tax of 1894—held unconstitutional in Pollock v. Farmers' Loan and Trust Co., 157 U.S. 429 (1895)—provided that property acquired by gift or inheritance should be taxed as income. A federal graduated inheritance tax adopted in 1898 was repealed in 1902, but its validity was sustained in Knowlton v. Moore, 178 U.S. 41 (1900). In Knowlton v. Moore, the Supreme Court held that an inheritance tax is an excise imposed on the act of passing property at death, and not a direct tax. Therefore, an inheritance tax is not subject to the requirements of Sections 2 and 9 of Article I that direct taxes be apportioned according to population.

[¶ 1007]

2. THE MODERN ESTATE AND GIFT TAXES

The modern federal estate tax, in its earliest form, dates back to 1916, and that revenue measure was sustained against constitutional challenge in New York Trust Co. v. Eisner, 256 U.S. 345 (1921), in which Justice Holmes, relying on the earlier decision in Knowlton v. Moore, observed that "a page of history is worth a volume of logic." As will be seen from some of the older cases in this course book, other constitutional attacks were launched against the federal estate tax with absolutely no success.

In 1924 Congress, concerned about the erosion of the estate tax base presented by inter vivos gifts, adopted the first gift tax. Only two years later, a different Congress repealed the nation's first gift tax. Several taxpayers who were unfortunate enough to have had their gifts taxed in this two-year period challenged the constitutionality of the 1924 gift tax. In Bromley v. McCaughn, 280 U.S. 124 (1929), the Supreme Court upheld the constitutionality of a gift tax. Thus, when Congress enacted the present gift tax in 1932, it did so confident of its constitutionality.

B. LEGISLATIVE HISTORY

[¶ 1013]

1. FEDERAL ESTATE AND GIFT TAXATION BEFORE 1976

Prior to the Tax Reform Act of 1976, the trend of the estate and gift tax rates had been upward, so much so that in 1970 Professor Willard Pedrick used the term "fierce" to describe the estate tax rate schedule. At the time, the estate tax rates went up to a maximum of 77 percent for taxable estates over $10 million, and the exemption from estate taxes was only $60,000. The gift tax rates were 75 percent of the estate tax rates, each donor was entitled to a $30,000 lifetime gift tax exemption, and a donor could give $3,000 to each person in the world each year without gift tax cost and without using any of his or her $30,000 gift tax lifetime exemption.

However, Congress, after embracing rates which as Professor Pedrick indicated would "strike terror into the heart of the clients, conveniently provided a number of toll free roads open to those with accredited guides." Pedrick, Extra Sensory Perception and Estate Planning—Change and the Estate Planner's Art, 4th Inst. Est. Plan. ¶ 203,300 (1970). The combination of dramatically progressive rates with a less than comprehensive gift and estate tax base and a number of generous deductions typically resulted in the imposition of transfer tax burdens which were at marked variance with those "fierce" statutory marginal rates.

In his widely known article, "A Voluntary Tax? New Perspectives on Estate Tax Avoidance," 77 Colum. L. Rev. 161 (1977), Professor George Cooper demonstrated how, with the assistance of competent counsel, those stated rates could be dramatically at variance with actual effective rates on gratuitous transfers. Cooper noted that with respect to the DuPont fortune "There has been a cumulative effective tax rate of 5% for two generations." In the article, Professor Cooper catalogued many of the devices then in use to minimize the burden of the estate tax.

In the hearings on the Tax Reform Act of 1976, Professor James Casner before the House Ways and Means Committee exclaimed: "In fact we haven't got an estate tax, what we have, you pay an estate tax if you want to; if you don't want to, you don't have to." In a similar vein, economist Professor Lester Thurow observed that: "In practice, loopholes have become so large that inheritance taxes have virtually ceased to exist: collections amount to an annual wealth tax of less than 0.2 percent. For all practical purposes, gift and inheritance taxes do not exist in the United States. They do not stop wealth from being transferred from generation to generation." Professor Thurow then asked, "Are effective inheritance taxes zero because a democratic society decides they should be zero? Or are zero inheritance taxes merely the best example of the political power that wealth can buy?" Thurow, Generating Inequality, at 197 (1975).

The movement for reform was almost glacially slow. In 1942, Erwin Griswold, then Professor of Law at the Harvard Law School, published an article in the Harvard Law Review calling for correlation of the federal estate and gift taxes. In 1947, an Advisory Committee to the Treasury Department called for integration of the gift and estate taxes. A project of the American Law Institute developed proposals for structural reform of the federal estate and gift taxes in 1969—after more than five years of intensive study. That same year the Federal Treasury published its recommended revision of the two levies—with no action then forthcoming.

2. RESTRUCTURING BEGINNING IN 1976

[¶ 1019]

a. The 1976 Changes

In 1976, proposals to revise the federal estate and gift levies were incorporated into the Tax Reform Act of 1976. The structural changes made by this legislation were truly sweeping. The prime structural change was the effective consolidation of the estate tax and the gift tax into one. Though the two names continue, and nominally there is both an estate tax and a gift tax, in substance there is now one levy on the transfer of capital by gift or by inheritance. The British accomplished much the same reform in 1975. Their system is accurately labeled as the "Capital Transfer Tax." That, too, in principle, is the United States system—in all but name. The importance of recognizing that the United States has one integrated, unitized levy on the transfer of capital by gift and inheritance cannot be overemphasized.

The prime structural changes effected by the Tax Reform Act of 1976, applicable generally to events transpiring after January 1, 1977, were: (1) establishment of one unitary tax table with cumulation of lifetime and death transfers for transfer tax computation; (2) establishment of one unitary credit (which in a phasing-in process was designed to shelter by 1981 a total of $175,625 from the estate and gift taxes combined) in lieu of the separate exemptions of $30,000 and $60,000, respectively, for the old gift and estate taxes; and (3) provision of a new chapter taxing "terminations" or "distributions" from "generation-skipping trusts."

The explanatory report on the Tax Reform Act of 1976, Estate and Gift Tax Provisions, prepared by the Staff of the Joint Committee on Taxation at 13–14 provides the following explanation of the reasons for the changes:

> Two features of prior law which give rise to considerable variations in estate and gift tax burdens for people who transfer the same amount of wealth were the separate rate schedule and exemption provision for estates and gifts. There were several tax advantages to lifetime gifts. The gift tax rates were 75 percent of estate tax rates; and, unlike the estate tax, the amount of the gift tax itself was not included in the tax base. Also, someone who split his total transfers between gifts and bequests achieved the advantage of "rate splitting," since the first dollar of taxable bequests was taxed at the bottom estate tax rate even where there had been substantial lifetime gifts. These opportunities for reducing the

¶ 1013

overall burden by lifetime giving were inequitable, especially since many people are not wealthy enough to make lifetime gifts. The Act unified the estate and gift taxes—both the exemptions (which have been converted into a credit) and the rates—to deal with these inequities.

Another cause of unequal treatment of taxpayers with the same amount of wealth transfers had been the ability to use "generation-skipping" trusts. When wealth is bequeathed from the parent to his child, then from the child to a grandchild and finally from the grandchild to a great-grandchild, the estate tax is imposed three times. However, if the parent places the wealth in a trust in which the child and then the grandchild has the right to the income from the trust, with the principal going to the great-grandchild, the parent will achieve virtually the same result and, in effect, skip two generations of estate tax. In these cases, the estate tax could be avoided for 100 years or more under prior law. Since such trust arrangements have been used largely by wealthier people, this failure to tax generation-skipping trusts has undermined the progressivity of the estate and gift taxes. The Act significantly limited estate tax avoidance through generation-skipping trusts by imposing a tax at the time of the death of the child or grandchild, [subject to a limited exemption available in specified circumstances].

[¶ 1025]

b. Economic Recovery Tax Act of 1981 (ERTA)

President Ronald Reagan's discomfort with the federal estate and gift tax system, often expressed during the presidential campaign of 1980, bore fruit in the Economic Recovery Tax Act of 1981. The principal instruments for dramatic reduction in the ranks of prospective estate taxpayers were: (1) an increase in the unified credit, scheduled in a gradual phasing-in process, to reach a level of $192,800 in 1987 (the equivalent of an exemption then of $600,000); (2) an increase in the per donee per annum gift tax exclusion from $3,000 to $10,000; (3) an unlimited marital deduction so that property, without monetary limits, can pass from one spouse to the other without being subjected to any federal transfer tax at all; and (4) also as noted earlier, a reduction in the top rate from 70 percent to 50 percent by 1985. Subsequent legislation froze the top rate at 55 percent through 1992 and in 1993 the top rate was permanently set at 55 percent.

[¶ 1031]

c. Revenue Act of 1987 and Revenue Reconciliation Act of 1993

The Tax Reform Act of 1986, bringing about the Internal Revenue Code of 1986, did not effect major changes in federal estate and gift taxes. But the Revenue Act of 1987 did bring some changes: notably the continuation of the top rate of 55 percent through 1992 and a phaseout of the benefits of graduated rates and unified credit in estates over $10 million. The phaseout was accomplished by imposing a supplementary tax of 5 percent on estates valued between $10 million and $21,040,000. The Revenue Reconciliation Act of 1993 permanently reinstated the top rate of 55 percent but, otherwise, did little to affect estate and gift taxation.

d. Taxpayer Relief Act of 1997

The Taxpayer Relief Act of 1997 made several significant changes. The amount excludible from estate and gift tax over one's lifetime by the unified credit was increased from $600,000 (which had prevailed since 1987) to $625,000 in 1998 with phased-in additional increases scheduled. The statute refers to the sum so excluded from tax as "the applicable exclusion amount." The 1997 Act also provided an inflation adjustment mechanism for the $10,000 per donee per annum gift tax exclusion and for the $1,000,000 generation skipping transfer tax exclusion.

Moreover, the Act also provided that the 5% supplementary tax no longer applied when the average aggregate tax rate equals 55%, thereby restoring to the super rich the benefit of the unified credit although still depriving them of the advantage of the progressive rate structure. The result was that the 5% supplementary tax would no longer be imposed on estates in excess of $17,184,000.

3. THE SCHEDULED DEATH AND RESURRECTION OF THE DEATH TAX

Central to George W. Bush's 2000 presidential campaign was the promise of substantial tax cuts and central to his tax cut program was elimination of the gift tax and the estate tax, which he characterized as the "death tax." Consequently, the Economic Growth and Tax Relief Reconciliation Act of 2001 provided for repeal of the estate tax for those dying after December 31, 2009 and for repeal of the generation skipping transfer tax for generation skipping transfers taking place after December 31, 2009. The Act also contained a number of other significant changes: (1) the 5 percent supplementary tax that applied to estates between $10 million and $17,184,000 was repealed and the maximum marginal rates of the estate, gift and generation skipping taxes were to be reduced to 50 percent and phased down over the remaining life of the estate tax; (2) the lifetime exclusions for the estate and generation skipping transfer taxes were raised to $1,000,000 and over those taxes remaining lives were to be phased up reaching $3,500,000 by 2009; and (3) credit for state death taxes against federal estate tax liability was to be phased out by 2005 to be replaced by a deduction for such taxes.

Awareness that the gift tax performed a critical role in backstopping the income tax against massive revenue losses led to a decision that its retention was necessary even after the estate tax saw its last days. Consequently, the Act retained the gift tax and provided for no increase in its lifetime exclusion amount beyond $1,000,000. Also taxable gifts made after December 31, 2009 are to be taxed at the flat rate of 35 percent.

As the price for repeal of the estate tax, the 2001 Act also provides that after December 31, 2009 property passing at death will no longer have a step up or fresh start basis. Instead, such property will have a basis in the hands of the estate's heirs equal to the lesser of its basis in the hands of the decedent or its date of death fair market value. However, the executor will be allowed to increase (but not above fair market) basis of appreciated property passing to other than a surviving spouse by up to $1,300,000 plus any unused capital loss carry forward and the amount of all reductions in basis effected in the case of property where the date of death value of such property was less than its adjusted basis in decedent's hands. The basis of property passing to a surviving spouse may be increased by an additional $3,000,000.

Congress, in exercising its responsibilities under the Congressional Budget Act of 1974, set a maximum estimated cost of $1.35 trillion for the 2001 Act over a ten year period. Despite heavy use of backend loading of many of the cuts, as the legislative process wore on, it was proving impossible to meet the $1.35 trillion target until Congress cynically decided to meet its budgetary goals by providing for repeal in entirety of the 2001 Act on January 1, 2011. This legislative two step also allowed the Act to avoid the so called Byrd rule, named after Senator Robert Byrd a fiscal hawk, which requires a super majority for tax measures having a significant budgetary impact that extends beyond ten years. This built in repeal of the 2001 Act on January 1, 2011 means that absent additional legislation, the repealed estate and generation skipping taxes and all the phased in changes in rates and exemptions as well as all other changes wrought by the 2001 Act, will come back into effect on January 1, 2011. Needless to say, this has led to humorous commentary as to the need for taxpayers to time their deaths with precision to maximize benefits for their heirs with possible roles for artificial respirators and Dr. Kevorkian.

C. FEDERAL TAXES ON TRANSFERS OF WEALTH

[¶ 1037]

1. ESTATE TAX (SECTIONS 2001–2057)

An estate tax return must be filed within nine months after death for each decedent whose estate tax base exceeds "the applicable exclusion amount" (which phases up from $2,000,000 in 2006 through 2008 to $3,500,000 in 2009). See §§ 6018(a) and 6075(a); ¶ 29,007. The estate tax base consists of several elements, principally the decedent's gross estate and the taxable gifts made by the decedent after 1976. See § 6018(a)(4); ¶ 28,001. Property is included (1) at its fair market value on the date of death as to property included in the gross estate and (2) at its fair market value as of the date of the gift in the case of taxable gifts made after 1976.

The estate tax is calculated after deducting the decedent's debts and mortgages, expenses of administering the decedent's estate, the decedent's funeral expenses, losses incurred during administration, gifts to the decedent's spouse (if made in a qualifying way), and gifts to charity and certain interests in closely held family business. ¶ ¶ 1079–1103, 15,001.

¶ 1037

The estate tax was originally a progressive tax but with the changes made in the 2001 Act (¶ 1033) in 2006 a flat rate of 46% will be applied to all taxed property and in 2007, 2008 and 2009 a flat rate of 45% will apply.

[¶ 1043]

2. GIFT TAX (SECTIONS 2501–2524)

Gift tax returns must be filed annually. See § 6075(b)(1). A gift tax return must be filed whenever total gifts to the same donee in the same year exceed the annual per donee exclusion of $10,000 (adjusted for inflation with the figure adjusted to $12,000 in 2006). See § 6019(a). A donor could thus give each person in Ohio, for example, $11,000 each year without filing a gift tax return or paying any gift tax. While a gift tax return is required whenever gifts to a single donee in the same year exceed the annual per donee exclusion, the donor will not pay any gift tax until the donor's lifetime total of gifts (in excess of the per donee per annum exclusion) exceeds one million dollars. See ¶ 1033. Gifts to the donor's spouse are tax free if they are made in a qualifying way—as are gifts to charity.

3. OTHER FEATURES OF THE TAXES

[¶ 1049]

a. Relationship of Estate and Gift Taxes

Although the estate and gift taxes are separate and distinct taxes, they do employ the same rate schedule to determine tax liability. Until passage of the 2001 Act the two taxes had also offered the same tax exemption (in the form of a credit against tax). The 2001 Act provided that in 2002 both taxes would share the same $1,000,000 exclusion from tax although in the case of the estate tax only the exemption would be phased up to $3,500,000 by 2009.

The estate and gift taxes are imposed upon the exercise of the privilege of gratuitously transferring property. See §§ 2001 and 2501. In that sense, both taxes are classified as excise taxes. However, not only must there be a gratuitous transfer of property for the estate or gift tax to apply, but the tax does not apply until the gift is "complete." While "transfer" is the operative term and appears in the portion of the statute imposing the tax, the term "complete" is judge-given.

Example: Bill made a gift of Blackacre, worth $1,000,000, to his son Andrew expressly barring its sale by Andrew and reserving the right to revoke the gift at any time. Because Bill can revoke the gift at any time, the transfer is not complete for gift tax purposes and has no gift tax consequences.

Sometimes the estate tax and gift tax appear to overlap and, in some of those cases, the overlap is reconciled so as to avoid double taxation by crediting the gift tax paid against the estate tax liability.

Example: Maria deeded her farm to her nephew, Pedro, expressly reserving to herself "the right to all of the income from the farm during my life and the right to occupy" the farm for life. For gift tax purposes, Maria has made a transfer to Pedro of a future interest, namely the right to possession and enjoyment of the farm after Maria dies. This transfer is complete for gift tax purposes at the time Maria delivered the deed to Pedro. The gift to Pedro will be valued actuarially, taking into account the prevailing interest rate and Maria's age at the time of the gift. For example, if the gift was made on June 4, 1992, at a time when the farm had a fair market value of $1 million and Maria was 62 years of age, the gift of the future interest to Pedro would have a value of $295,670 (using the valuation techniques prescribed in Reg. § 25.2512–5). The gift tax on the transfer to Pedro is $86,327.80 (using the rate tables found in § 2001 as required by § 2502(a)), but the gift tax can be offset by the unified credit provided to Maria in § 2505 (assuming Maria's prior taxable gifts had not exhausted her unified credit).

While Pedro has neither the possession nor the enjoyment of the farm during Maria's life, his interest in the farm is a valuable property right— so valuable in fact that, if Pedro predeceases Maria, Pedro's future interest in the farm shall be subject to estate tax at his death (and shall pass under his will if he has a will or shall pass under the intestate laws if Pedro does not have a will).

At Maria's death—assuming she died in 2006 when the farm had a value of $2.5 million—the farm will also be included in Maria's estate for estate tax purposes. See § 2036(a)(1). The farm will be included in Maria's estate at its fair market value of $2.5 million. The basis of inclusion is that: (1) Maria retained for her life the use and enjoyment of the farm; and (2) the estate tax would be emasculated if the estate tax could be avoided by lifetime transfers such as Maria has made. Including the farm in Maria's estate would mean a estate tax liability of $1,010,800 (determined by reference to the tax rate table and maximum rate in § 2001) reduced by $780,800, the estate tax version of the phase-down unified credit which prevails in 2006, and which is provided by § 2010, meaning that Maria's estate would pay $230,000 in estate taxes. Had any gift taxes been paid by Maria on the gift to Pedro of the future interest, practically speaking, she would have received a credit against her estate tax liability for that payment.

[¶ 1055]

b. *Unified Credit (Sections 2010 and 2505)*

From 1987 through 1997, each taxpayer was provided with a so called "unified credit" of $192,800 which could be used first against any gift tax otherwise due and to the extent not so used would be available for use against the taxpayer's estate tax liability. This $192,800 in essence translated into an aggregate $600,000 exclusion that was available for use against the gift tax and, to the extent not so used, against the estate tax.

As already noted above, in 1997 Congress decided to increase the amount excludible under the unified credit. In 2001 it revisited the issue and further increased the amount excludible from tax. In the case of the gift tax for gifts made in year 2002 and thereafter the unified credit was frozen at $345,800, which is the equivalent of a $1,000,000 exclusion. In the case of the estate tax, the 2001 Act provided that the exclusion and its unified credit equivalent is to be increased for individuals dying during a given year accordingly:

Year	Exclusion	Unified Credit
2002 and 2003	1,000,000	$345,800
2004 and 2005	1,500,000	555,800
2006, 2007 and 2008	2,000,000	780,800
2009	3,500,000	1,455,800

It must be kept in mind that the above exclusion is in effect applied first to the gift tax and then, to the extent the excluded amount does not exceed $1,000,000, to the estate tax. For example, assume, for simplicity, that the annual per donee gift tax exclusion (¶ 1043) is not available, and that Bonita made no gifts other than a taxable gift of $200,000 in 1998 and died in 2006 with an estate of $2,500,000. In 1998, Bonita would have been able to exclude the entire $200,000 gift from taxation. In 2006, her estate would be left with the equivalent of a $1,800,000 exclusion which could shelter from estate taxation all but $700,000 of her $2,500,000 estate. The actual mechanics whereby this is effected is described at ¶ ¶ 2007 and 15,001.

[¶ 1061]

c. Annual Exclusion (Section 2503(b))

The gift tax—but not the estate tax—provides for an inflation adjusted $10,000 annual exclusion ($12,000 in 2006). That means that an individual could make a gift of the annual exclusion amount each year to every person in the country without gift tax consequences and without having to file a gift tax return.

[¶ 1067]

d. Adjusted Taxable Gifts (Section 2001(b))

As part of the integration of the estate and gift taxes, gifts made after December 31, 1976, are included in the base used for determining the tax rate applicable to transfers made at death by an individual. These post–1976 gifts are referred to as adjusted taxable gifts and are distinguished from earlier gifts (which are not taken into account for estate tax computation purposes).

Example: Melvin made a gift of $100,000 to his son, Jasper, in 1975 and another gift of $210,000 to Jasper in 1983. Melvin died in 2006. He willed all his property to Jasper. At his death in 2006, Melvin's estate was valued at $2,300,000, but the base used in computing his estate tax liability was grossed up to $2,500,000 by including the $200,000 of post–1976 gifts. (Note that the gift tax exclusion allowed $10,000 to escape classification as an adjusted taxable gift.) Using the rate tables given in § 2001, Melvin's tax liability before the unified credit of $780,800 (2006 Unified Credit) is $1,010,800, and, after the credit is taken off, his estate tax liability is $230,000. (Although Melvin had no gift tax to pay in 1983 because his $210,000 transfer to Jasper was sheltered by the gift tax exclusion and the unified credit, he was obligated to file a gift tax return.)

D. GENERATION–SKIPPING TAX (SECTIONS 2601–2663)

[¶ 1073]

The generation-skipping transfer tax (GST) is a flat-rate tax that generally applies to transfers by individuals or distributions from trusts that skip generations. Its purpose is to backstop the estate tax. Congress believed that it was appropriate to impose a wealth transfer tax each generation and where very wealthy families managed to avoid imposition of a transfer tax every generation by arranging for transfers that skipped generations, Congress decided to impose a special supplementary generation-skipping tax to compensate for the revenues which were thereby otherwise lost. In general the tax is imposed at a rate equal to the maximum estate tax rate. Transferors who are subject to the GST are entitled to a lifetime exemption equal to the estate tax exclusion for the year in question.

Example: In 2006 Maria transferred $300,000 to an irrevocable trust for the benefit of her grandson Alexander and his issue and allocated, as she is permitted to do, $300,000 of her then available $2,000,000 GST exemption to the trust. Because the amount placed in the trust is completely sheltered by the GST exemption allocated to the trust, distributions from the trust to anyone will be forever free of the GST. (The GST is independent of federal estate and gift taxes, which means that Maria may still have incurred gift tax liability when she placed $300,000 in the trust.)

Example: In 2006 Albert transferred $3,000,000 to an irrevocable trust for the benefit of his daughter Betty and his grandson Cleve and allocated all his then available $2,000,000 GST exemption to the trust. (The GST is independent of federal estate and gift taxes, which means that Albert incurred gift tax liability when the $3,000,000 was placed in the trust.) The GST will apply to distributions from the trust to persons at the generational level of grandson Cleve and younger (but not to distributions to Betty and persons at or above her generational level). Because the amount of the GST exemption allocated to the trust was equal to two-thirds of the amount transferred to the trust ($2,000,000/$3,000,000) two-thirds of all distributions from the trust to Cleve (and others of his generation and younger) will effectively be forever exempt from the GST.

E. BASIC COMPUTATIONAL MODEL

[¶ 1079]

1. INTEGRATION OF ESTATE AND GIFT TAXES

The estate and gift tax computational scheme is quite complex, in part because the two separate taxes are to be integrated to limit each taxpayer to the equivalent of a coordinated single lifetime exemption with the exemption for the gift tax capped at a lower level than that for the estate tax. Additional complication results from the need to integrate the tax rules applicable to gifts made before 1977 with those made after 1976. In sum, the complication results from the fact that gifts made any time by a taxpayer are aggregated to determine the tax rate applicable to the most recent gift. However, in determining the tax rate applicable to property subject to the estate tax, only gifts made after 1976 are aggregated with the property from the taxpayer at death. These post–1976 gifts are referred to as "adjusted taxable gifts," a term that is important only for estate tax purposes. See ¶ 1067.

[¶ 1082]

2. THE TAX–EXCLUSIVE GIFT TAX AND THE TAX–INCLUSIVE ESTATE TAX

Although the same nominal rate applies under the gift tax as applies under the estate tax, there is an important difference in computing each of the taxes which results in a lower effective tax burden being imposed on gifts than on estates. The estate tax is computed on a tax-inclusive basis. In other words, the tax is imposed on all that one transfers at death, including the estate tax itself. The gift tax, on the other hand, is calculated on a tax-exclusive basis, which means that only the gift going to private parties and not the gift tax paid with respect to it forms the base of the tax. This difference in the method of calculating the two taxes dates back to the first days of the gift tax. It means that in the right circumstances there may be significant tax advantages in making gifts. This critical difference between the two taxes will be dealt with in greater detail in Chapter 2.

[¶ 1085]

3. UNIFIED CREDIT SUBSTITUTED FOR EXEMPTION (SECTIONS 2010 AND 2505)

As one of the steps which it took toward unifying the estate and gift taxes, Congress, in 1976, eliminated the $30,000 lifetime gift tax exemption and the $60,000 estate tax exemption. It substituted for them a single lifetime credit against estate and gift tax liability. Since the credit is "unified" to the extent a taxpayer has not used it during life to offset gift tax liability, it is available to shelter the estate from taxation. See ¶ 1055. Awareness that an exemption or an exclusion from tax available to all taxpayers was the economic equivalent of a credit led Congress to restate the estate and gift tax credit provisions of §§ 2010 and 2505 in terms of an exclusion. In 2001 Congress chose to create a lower exemption amount for the gift tax ($1 million) than that which would eventually be available under the estate tax while still retaining unification. For example, in 2006 when the estate tax exemption is $2,000,000, if a taxpayer had used $700,000 of his gift tax exclusion, he would still have $1,300,000 remaining as an estate tax exclusion were he to die in 2006. On the other hand, if he had made $1,200,000 of taxable gifts, he would have used the full $1 million gift tax exclusion and paid tax on $200,000 of gifts. Were he to die in 2006 possessing $3,000,000 in

¶ 1079

additional assets, he would have $1,000,000 of exemption remaining to use against his estate tax liability and could use all or some portion of the gift tax paid on the $200,000 of taxed gifts as a credit against his estate tax liability. The actual mechanics whereby this occurs is described at ¶¶ 2007 and 15,001.

[¶ 1091]

4. DEDUCTION FOR STATE DEATH TAXES PAID (SECTION 2011)

In early 20th century America, death taxes had traditionally been a major source of revenue for the states. To reassure the states that the federal government did not intend to elbow them out of this important source of revenue, Congress in 1924 provided a statutory credit mechanism whereby a portion of the federal estate tax could be offset by state death taxes paid.

In 2001 Congress decided to break with tradition and provided that the amount that qualifies for credit shall be reduced by 25 percent each year commencing in 2002, resulting in complete repeal of the credit for taxpayers dying after December 31, 2004, after which state death taxes are allowed as a deduction in determining the amount subject to federal tax. Congress apparently decided to substitute a deduction for a credit to raise revenue to pay for part of the cost of much of the liberalized treatment of transfer taxes implemented by the 2001 Act. This change will offset about one-quarter of the cost of all other changes in transfer taxes wrought by the 2001 Tax Act and in some states actually increase the combined state/federal effective marginal tax rate on large estates.

[¶ 1097]

5. STATE DEATH TAX SYSTEMS

Not to be ignored are the death tax systems that exist in the various states. (A few states even have gift taxes, but there never has been a federal credit or deduction for state gift taxes paid.) The death tax systems in some of the states are patterned after the federal estate tax, while other states have another form of death tax commonly referred to as an inheritance tax. An inheritance tax differs from an estate tax in that the available exemption and the applicable tax rates are determined by the relationship of the decedent and the beneficiaries of the decedent's estate. That is, property passing to a surviving spouse will be subject to lower rates and enjoy a higher exemption than property passing from the decedent to a nonrelative. In recent years many states had abandoned their formal inheritance tax systems and substituted what could be called a "soak up" or a "sponge" tax. That is, these states had imposed an inheritance tax exactly equal to the maximum federal credit that had been available when computing the estate tax liability of the decedent for state death taxes paid by that decedent. A few states which imposed an inheritance tax, out of caution, also had imposed a supplementary "soak up" or "sponge" tax to guard against the possibility that for a given estate their inheritance tax might have resulted in a creditable state death tax which was less than the maximum amount allowable as a credit under the federal estate tax.

Depending on the wording of state "sponge" or "soak up" tax legislation, repeal of the credit for state death taxes resulted in de facto repeal of state death taxes in many states that imposed only "soak up" or "sponge" taxes. Given the tight financial picture for many of the states, it should come as no surprise that some of the states that imposed only a "soak up" or "sponge" tax have broken the link between their estate taxes and the federal credit mechanism. For example, some states have produced this result by providing that their sponge tax is equal to the maximum amount allowed as a credit under federal law as it then prevailed at a historic date such as 1987 or 2000.

F. DETERMINING TRANSFERS AND OWNERSHIP OF PROPERTY—THE APPLICABILITY OF STATE LAW

[¶ 1103]

In Morgan v. Commissioner, 309 U.S. 78 (1940), the Supreme Court stated that, "State law creates legal interests and rights. The federal revenue acts designate what interests or rights, so created, shall be taxed." Accordingly, the federal estate tax statute must normally turn to the state law to determine the existence of the interests in property that may be held by the decedent at the time of death. For example, the life beneficiary of a trust may die and the question arises whether certain property, such as crops and livestock on the farm held in the trust, belongs to the life beneficiary or to the trust (and, in turn, the remainderman). The answer to such issues would depend on state law. If the issue of ownership is directly presented to the state court and decided conclusively as far as the contending parties are concerned, should such a decision bind the IRS for tax purposes? Pursuing the situation of the life beneficiary of the farm held in trust: if the issue of ownership of the crops and livestock had been brought to the probate court for resolution and if the probate court had held that the life beneficiary did not own such property, must the IRS accept the court's decision as determining the includibility of such property in the life beneficiary's gross estate? The IRS might have serious doubts about the propriety of its being bound by state court litigation in which it was not represented and in which the ownership issue was not actively contested. In our example, if the life beneficiary's heir was also the remainderman of the trust, the ownership issue tried before the probate court would not be important except for estate tax purposes, and the contest between the estate of the life beneficiary and the remainderman in probate court would be unreal.

For some time, the test for determining which state decisions were conclusive for the Internal Revenue Service had not been wholly clear; however, the Supreme Court, in Commissioner v. Estate of Bosch, 387 U.S. 456 (1967), resolved the issue.

¶ 1097

[¶ 1107]

COMMISSIONER v. ESTATE OF BOSCH

Supreme Court of the United States, 1967.
387 U.S. 456.

MR. JUSTICE CLARK delivered the opinion of the Court.

[In 1930 decedent conveyed property to a revocable trust from which his wife was to be paid income for her life. Under the terms of the trust wife had a general power of appointment. Provision was made for disposition of trust assets to the extent that at termination wife had failed to appoint property from the trust. In 1951 wife executed an instrument purporting to release the general power and convert it into a special power. Decedent died in 1957. Under § 2056(b)(5) of the Code, the entire trust corpus would have been excluded from taxation if at decedent's death his wife had held a general, rather than a special, power of appointment. Decedent's executor brought an action in state court seeking to have wife's 1951 release of the general power declared invalid, hoping thereby to in essence exclude trust corpus from taxation. All parties at the proceeding argued that wife's 1951 release was invalid and the trial court judge made a finding that the release was invalid. The issue before the United States Supreme Court was the degree of deference, if any, which should be accorded to state court determinations in such situations. The following explanation was offered for the Court's disposition of the case.]

First, the Commissioner was not made a party to either of the same proceedings here and neither had the effect of *res judicata*, nor did the principle of collateral estoppel apply. It can hardly be denied that both state proceedings were brought for the purpose of directly affecting federal estate tax liability. Next, it must be remembered that it was a federal taxing statute that the Congress enacted and upon which we are here passing. Therefore, in construing it, we must look to the legislative history surrounding it. We find that the report of the Senate Finance Committee recommending enactment of the marital deduction used very guarded language in referring to the very question involved here. It said that "proper regard," not finality, "should be given to interpretations of the will" by state courts and then only when entered by a court "in a bona fide adversary proceeding." * * * These restrictive limitations clearly indicate the great care that Congress exercised in the drawing of the Act and indicate also a definite concern with the elimination of loopholes and escape hatches that might jeopardize the federal revenue. This also is in keeping with the long-established policy of the Congress, as expressed in the Rules of Decision Act, 28 U.S.C. § 1652. There it is provided that in the absence of federal requirements such as the Constitution or Acts of Congress, the "laws of the several states ... shall be regarded as rules of decision in civil actions in the courts of the United States, in cases where they apply." This Court has held that judicial decisions are "laws of the ... state" within the section. Erie R. Co. v. Tompkins, [304 U.S. 64 (1938)]; Cohen v. Beneficial Loan Corp., 337 U.S. 541 (1949); King v. Order of Travelers, 333 U.S. 153 (1948).

¶ 1107

Moreover, even in diversity cases this Court has further held that while the decree of "lower state courts" should be "attributed some weight ... the decision [is] not controlling ..." where the highest court of the State has not spoken on the point. King v. Order of Travelers, supra, at 160–161. And in West v. A.T. & T. Co., 311 U.S. 223 (1940), this Court further held that "an intermediate appellate state court ... is a datum for ascertaining state law which is not to be disregarded by a federal court *unless it is convinced by other persuasive data that the highest court of the state would decide otherwise.*" At 237. (Emphasis supplied.) Thus, under some conditions, federal authority may not be bound even by an intermediate state appellate court ruling. It follows here then, that when the application of a federal statute is involved, the decision of a state trial court as to an underlying issue of state law should *a fortiori* not be controlling. This is but an application of the rule of Erie R. Co. v. Tompkins, supra, where state law as announced by the highest court of the State is to be followed. This is not a diversity case but the same principle may be applied for the same reasons, *viz.*, the underlying substantive rule involved is based on state law and the State's highest court is the best authority on its own law. If there be no decision by that court then federal authorities must apply what they find to be the state law after giving "proper regard" to relevant rulings of other courts of the State. In this respect, it may be said to be, in effect, sitting as a state court. Bernhardt v. Polygraphic Co., 350 U.S. 198 (1956).

We believe that this would avoid much of the uncertainty that would result from the "non-adversary" approach and at the same time would be fair to the taxpayer and protect the federal revenue as well.

* * *

Note

[¶ 1108]

Mary E. Scott v. Commissioner, 226 F.3d 871 (7th Cir. 2000) provides a good example of the need for Federal courts to be vested with the power to disregard lower state court decisions. Lucille Horstmeier and Mary Scott had lived together for 19 years. During that time Horstmeier had earned almost all of the couple's income while Scott tended to their household maintenance and financial management. A home in Glenview, Illinois was purchased by Horstmeier and placed in her name. She effected the purchase by putting $50,000 down and taking out a mortgage of $55,000 in her name alone. No evidence was provided to indicate that Scott ever provided any consideration for the home. Shortly thereafter the couple fully displayed that they knew how to create a co-tenancy when they intended to do so by purchasing a second home in Skokie which was titled in both names and for which Scott made financial contributions. After Horstmeier's death in 1993, Scott, who was the executor of Horstmeier's estate (and her sole beneficiary under a revocable trust), sought and obtained an uncontested determination in Illinois probate court that Scott actually owned one-half of the Glenview home under a resulting trust theory. On the basis of the probate court's finding of a resulting trust, Scott only included one-half of the value of the Glenview home. Both the Tax Court (77 T.C.M. (CCH) 1940, T.C.M. (RIA) ¶ 99,145 (1999)) and the Eleventh Circuit Court of Appeals disregarded the Illinois probate court's determination in finding that the full value of the Glenview home should be included in Horstmeier's estate.

G. SOME STATISTICAL INFORMATION ON THE REACH OF THE TRANSFER TAXES

[¶ 1109]

1. ESTATE AND GIFT TAXES

In 2004, the federal estate and gift taxes combined raised about $24.8 billion up from $20.4 billion in 1997, a rather significant rate of growth when one factors in the enlargement of the exemption and reduction in maximum rates wrought by the 2001 Act. While this is a considerable sum, it is relatively unimportant when compared to the $809 billion in federal individual income tax and the $189 billion in corporate income tax raised in that year. Economic Report of the President, "Federal Receipts, Outlays, Surplus or Deficit, and Debt, Fiscal Years 2001–2006," Table B–81 (2005) and Economic Report at the President, "Federal Receipts, Outlays, Surplus or Deficit, and Debt, Fiscal Years 1995–2001" Table B–79 (2000).

For several reasons, the relative importance to the legal establishment and the Treasury of the gift and estate taxes cannot be gauged by comparing the revenue raised by the two income taxes and the estate and gift tax. First, the type of individual whose death results in the collection of estate or gift tax typically represents an important client for a law firm; only a very small minority of income taxpayers are in this category. Second, given the relative ease with which competent estate planners and determined taxpayers can significantly reduce gift and estate taxes which would otherwise be due, the relative amounts of tax raised by the individual and corporate income taxes and the estate and gift taxes are far from indicative of the career opportunities for lawyers represented by these various taxes. Third, the phasing-in of changes, temporary repeal of the estate and generation skipping transfer taxes and sunset of changes wrought by the 2001 Act have all vastly complicated the task of estate planners and have necessitated that clients frequently "check-in" with their attorneys on a periodic basis, thereby generating even more legal work for the bar.

[¶ 1115]

2. PERSONAL WEALTH

According to a recent study by Federal Reserve Board Senior Economist Arthur Kennickell, based on Federal Reserve surveys of consumer finances, in the period between 1989 and 2001, the richest one percent of all Americans, the next nine percent and the bottom ninety percent have each held about one third of national net worth. Within the lowest ninety percent, the lowest one-half held only about three percent of the total. According to Kennickell, during this period, most changes in the relative ownership of the various groups were primarily dependent on the economic cycle. For example, the fate of the top one percent tended to rise and fall with the economy, rising to 34.6% of national net worth in 1995 and dropping to 30.2% in 1992. Also of interest is the fact that from 1989 to 2001, the percentage of families with net wealth over $1,000,000 (stated in terms of 2001 inflation adjusted dollars) rose from 4.7 percent of all families to 7 percent of all families. Kennickell, A Rolling Tide: Changes in the Distribution of Wealth in the United States, 1989–2001 (2003).

Recent data indicates that as of 2004 there were 7.5 millionaire households in the U.S. and that the country lead the world in creating super rich families with the number of households possessing $20 million or more in liquid assets going up at the rate of 3,000 per year. Robert Frank, Millionaire Ranks Hit New High, Wall Street Journal, D1, May 25, 2005.

"The very rich are different from you and me," wrote Ernest Hemingway in The Snows of Kilimanjaro, "they have more money." The very rich are different not merely in terms of having more but are also different in their admixture of wealth. Consider that in 1998 the top one percent of American households owned 49.4% of all stocks and mutual funds held by households, 54% of all assets held in trust, 19.5% of all business equity, 35.8% of all non-home realty, 9% of the value of principal residences, 11.3% of all money on deposit, 11.3% of the value of all life insurance and 19.7% of the value of all pension accounts. See Wolff, Recent Trends in Wealth Ownership, 1983–1998.

H. THE CASE FOR AND AGAINST ESTATE AND GIFT TAXATION

[¶ 1120]

1. COMPARATIVE DATA

In 2003 the Joint Committee on Taxation conducted a study of the tax laws of most OECD countries as well as notorious tax haven jurisdictions to determine, among other things, whether the countries imposed either an estate or an inheritance tax. The 39 countries studied were, Australia, Austria, Bahamas, Belgium, Belize, Bermuda, Canada, Cayman Islands, Costa Rica, Denmark, Dominican Republic, Finland, France, Germany, Greece, Hong Kong, Iceland, Ireland, Israel, Italy, Japan, Korea, Luxembourg, Mexico, Netherlands, New Zealand, Norway, Philippines, Portugal, Seychelles, Singapore, South Africa, Spain, Sweden, Switzerland, Taiwan, Turkey, United Kingdom and the United States. The study revealed that all of the jurisdictions imposed either an estate or an inheritance tax with the exception of Australia, Bahamas, Cayman Islands, Costa Rica, Israel, Italy, Mexico, New Zealand, Seychelles and one of the twenty-six Swiss cantons. Even among the ranks of this group of ten, Australia, which does impose a tax on transfers to strangers, and Canada compensate for lack of such a tax by taxing unrealized gains at death, Mexico and Italy impose modest real estate transfer taxes and the Bahamas imposes a 4% probate fee. When one drops out the tax haven jurisdictions of Seychelles and Cayman Islands, the only true tax free opportunities for dying in the group of 39 are presented by New Zealand, Israel, Costa Rica and one of the twenty-six Swiss cantons. Joint Committee on Taxation, Review of the Present Tax and Immigration Treatment of Relinquishment of Citizenship and Termination of Long–Term Residency (2003).

Despite much political rhetoric to the contrary, the American citizen is not, at least from a relative standpoint, dramatically overtaxed. For 1998, the United States ranked 25th out of the 29 OECD member nations (followed only by Turkey, Japan, Korea and Mexico) in respect to total (federal, state and local) tax revenue as a percentage of gross domestic product. Taxes amounted to 28 percent of GDP for the United States as against 53 percent for Sweden (ranking first) and 37.9 percent for Canada (ranking 14th). Organization for Economic Cooperation and Development, Revenue Statistics of OECD Member Countries 1965–1999, at 88 (2000).

[¶ 1125]

2. TO TAX OR NOT TO TAX

The very notion of a tax on the transfer of wealth has drawn its fair share of strong support and criticism. No less a capitalist than Andrew Carnegie called for the enactment of a federal estate tax on the ground that:

> Of all forms of taxation this seems the wisest. Men who continue hoarding great sums all their lives, the proper use of which for public ends would work good to the community from which it chiefly came, should not be made to feel that the community, in the form of the State, cannot thus be deprived of its proper share. By taxing estates heavily at death the State marks its condemnation of the selfish millionaire's unworthy life. Carnegie, "The Gospel of Wealth," reprinted in The Gospel of Wealth and Other Timely Essays, 14, at 22 (Kirkland ed. 1965).

Andrew Mellon who served as Secretary of the Treasury from 1921 to 1932 and like Carnegie was one of the wealthiest men of his generation, on the other hand, saw transfer taxes as inevitably leading to the "destruction of the total capital of the country" which would "destroy the very source from which revenue is to flow." Mellon, Taxation: The People's Business, 114, at 122 (1924).

In recent years there has been renewed interest in debating the role, if any, that a tax on gratuitous transfers should play in our federal tax system. The debate has ranged from proposals to do away completely with all transfer taxes and to replace them and the present income tax with one form or another of a tax on consumption to a proposal to, after providing for certain exclusions, confiscate all wealth at death.

Professor Edward McCaffrey in The Uneasy Case for Wealth Transfer Taxation, 104 Yale L.J. 283 (1994), urged repeal of both the income, estate and gift taxes and replacement of all three with a progressive tax on consumption. Under such a tax, individuals would presumably be taxed on income but would be given a deduction for all savings and investments. Taxpayers would also be taxed on withdrawals from savings where spent on consumption. This would be true whether the savings which were withdrawn to finance consumption were the fruit of the consumer's past efforts or represented wealth that had been given to or inherited by the consumer. McCaffrey opposes wealth transfer taxes on the ground that they punish behavior (principally work and saving) that a liberal society ought to encourage and encourage behavior (principally leisure and consumption) which such a society ought to discourage. The values that McCaffrey identifies with a liberal society as they impact on the issue of tax structure design are efficiency, fairness, rewarding productivity, discouragement of private, and especially large-scale, preclusive use of resources and encouragement of use of resources for productive purposes in the economy of the larger society. Professor McCaffrey summarizes his arguments in favor of terminating all wealth transfer taxes (along with the income tax) and replacing them with a progressive consumption tax as follows:

> The five arguments can now be summarized and related as follows. (1) The current estate tax is porous, ineffective, and counterproductive on purely liberal grounds. (2) No stronger version is popular or practical, in part because (3) the liberal theory supporting an estate tax does not fit in a nonideal world where individual earnings lack presumptive, decisive moral weight, and in part because (4) our objective, political values, even under ideal conditions, lead liberal society to approve of work and savings and only or at least especially to disapprove of the wanton private use of resources, and any wealth tax is perverse on these scores. (5) Therefore, our practices have been moving, at least inchoately, toward a progressive consumption-without-estate tax. If we more consciously and consistently implemented what our practices suggest, we would have a better liberal egalitarian system than any featuring a wealth transfer tax. By meeting our objective values and changing the very meaning and hence the dangers of the private possession of wealth, we achieve in the end a happy convergence between liberal egalitarian theory and our actual practices. Id. at 297.

On the other extreme is Professor Mark Ascher who in Curtailing Inherited Wealth, 89 Mich. L. Rev. 69, 73–75 (1990), advocates something that closely resembles confiscation of wealth at death:

> My proposal views inheritance as something we should tolerate only when necessary—not something we should always protect. My major premise is that all property owned at death, after payment of debts and administration expenses, should be sold and the proceeds paid to the United States government. There would be six exceptions. A marital exemption, potentially unlimited, would accrue over the life of a marriage. Thus, spouses could continue to provide for each other after death. Decedents would also be allowed to provide for dependent lineal descendants. The amount available to any given descendant would, however, depend on the descendant's age and would drop to zero at an age of presumed independence. A separate exemption would allow generous provision for disabled lineal descendants of any age. Inheritance by lineal

¶ 1125

ascendants (parents, grandparents, etc.) would be unlimited. A universal exemption [$250,000] would allow a moderate amount of property either to pass outside the exemptions or to augment amounts passing under them. Thus, every decedent would be able to leave something to persons of his or her choice, regardless whether another exemption was available. Up to a fixed fraction of an estate could pass to charity. In addition, to prevent circumvention by lifetime giving, the gift tax would increase substantially.

My proposal strikes directly at inheritance by healthy, adult children. And for good reason. We cannot control differences in native ability. Even worse, so long as we believe in the family, we can achieve only the most rudimentary successes in evening out many types of opportunities. And we certainly cannot control many types of luck. But we can—and ought to—curb one form of luck. Children lucky enough to have been raised, acculturated, and educated by wealthy parents need not be allowed the additional good fortune of inheriting their parents' property. In this respect, we can do much better than we ever have before at equalizing opportunity. This proposal would leave "widows and orphans" essentially untouched. The disabled, grandparents, and charity would probably fare better than ever before. But inheritance by healthy, adult children would cease immediately, except to the extent of the universal exemption.

Professors Charles Davenport, Jay Soled and Willard Pedrick have provided good examples of the conventional case which can be made for retention of a gratuitous transfer tax. Charles Davenport and Jay A. Soled, Enlivening the Death–Tax Death–Talk, 84 Tax Notes 591 (1999); Willard Pedrick, Through the Glass Darkly: Transfer Taxes Tomorrow, 19 Inst. Est. Plan. ¶ 1902 (1985). Traditional defenders typically make the following case for retention of taxes on gratuitous transfers.

First, the estate and gift taxes make a significant contribution to the Treasury, a contribution which is even more marked when one factors into the calculus the role they play in backstopping the income tax. For example, a 2001 Joint Committee on Taxation study estimated that immediate repeal of the estate and gift taxes would result in a revenue loss from estate, gift and income taxes in excess of $600 billion over a ten year period.

Second, proponents of transfer taxes note that they enhance the overall progressivity of our federal tax system. For example, Professor Michael Graetz notes that the estate and gift taxes have accounted for as much as one-third of the progressivity in the federal tax system. To appreciate this point consider that the Social Security Tax is a moderately regressive tax, imposed only on wage and self employed income, the Medicare tax is a proportional tax imposed only on wage and self employed income, and the federal income tax ranks only as a moderately progressive tax after one makes allowance for capital gains preferences and deferral of taxation on many such gains due to the realization principle (the increase in the value of property is not taxed until disposition of appreciated property).

Third, transfer taxes contribute to the break up of large concentrations of personal wealth that provide wealthy families and individuals with disproportionate influence on political, cultural and social affairs at both the national and local levels. Leading political proponents of this argument Republican Theodore Roosevelt and his Democratic cousin Franklin. It is argued that transfer taxes have thereby made our society and economy more dynamic.

Fourth, the transfer tax concentrates the attention of the wealthy on the need to engage in estate planning. Absent the tax, most households would defer confronting the issue of disposition of wealth until death was imminent. In a good number of cases it is likely that, absent the tax, the issue might never be addressed leaving the family without a well developed plan for the devolution of property at death.

Fifth, the alleged need to liquidate assets to pay the federal estate tax has the economic benefit of forcing assets to the market where they will presumably pass to those who can make the economically most efficient use of those assets. For example, an estate strapped for cash to pay the estate tax will sell those assets which produce the lowest return for it. The marketplace will insure that the property so sold passes to those who can make the most efficient use of it.

Sixth, presence of the estate tax and its deduction for bequests to charities provides substantial incentive for wealthy decedents to bestow some significant portion of their wealth on philanthropic institutions. Some economists have estimated that repeal of the estate tax with result in a decline of twelve percent in bequests to charities.

Seventh, the tax satisfies the moral imperative that the affluent come to the aid of the poor. It guarantees that even miserly multi-millionaires embrace this obligation, albeit entirely unwillingly.

Note

[¶ 1135]

To the foregoing litany of justifications for a wealth transfer tax we might add a consideration provided by multi-billionaire Warren Buffett, one of America's wealthiest individuals. Buffett finds it curious that while many of the rich worry about the debilitating effects of food stamps and welfare on the work ethic of the poor, they themselves live off a boundless supply of "privately funded food stamps" and fret about an estate tax which stands in the way of providing the same opportunity for their descendants. Buffett's version of an ideal tax system is a markedly progressive tax on personal consumption and an enormous wealth transfer tax, with the latter presumably intended to spare the children of the wealthy from the corruption of their work ethic. Buffett says that when he dies he intends to leave his children enough so that they can do anything but not do nothing. Roger Lowenstein, Buffett, 334–350 (1995).

¶ 1125

I. TRUST AND ESTATE INCOME
(SECTIONS 641–678)

[¶ 1145]

The taxation of the income of trusts and estates is not much different from the taxation of the income of individuals. One of the differences is the distribution deduction available to trusts and estates. That is, trusts and estates, unlike corporations, enjoy a deduction for certain distributions made to the beneficiary of the trust or estate. Much of the discussion of trust and estate income taxation relates to implementation of this scheme. Furthermore, rules have been developed to discourage, if not eliminate, the use of the trust and the estate as tax shelters, i.e., entities to be used for warehousing income: (1) to avoid or postpone taxing that income to the beneficiaries who might be in higher income tax brackets; or (2) to keep that warehoused income out of the estates of the beneficiaries for federal estate tax purposes. These rules relate to distributions of accumulated income, multiple trusts for the same beneficiary, etc. Also, the income tax rates applicable to trusts and estates are "compressed" relative to the income tax rates applicable to individuals, e.g., the maximum income tax rate applies to trust and estate income that exceeds $10,050 in 2006 while, in the case of married individuals filing joint income tax returns, the top tax bracket begins at $336,550. The materials in this course book develop these and other issues related to the income taxation of estates and trusts.

J. INCOME FROM DECEDENTS (SECTION 691)

[¶ 1151]

Income from decedents, technically referred to as "income in respect of a decedent" (IRD) presents several issues. Examples of IRD include commissions paid a salesman after his death which are attributable to sales made before death. Such commissions are subject to both the federal estate tax and the federal income tax when received. Reconciling this and other issues presented by IRD is considered in this course book.

K. TAX COMPLIANCE AND CONTROVERSIES

[¶ 1157]

The federal estate tax and the federal gift tax, are plainly rather small potatoes in the garden patch of federal taxation. Nevertheless, they do affect the course of living and dying, do yield significant revenue and do, as well, generate some tax controversies. Compliance with the requirements of the estate tax and gift tax rules is the subject of later chapters.

The procedural setting for resolving controversies arising out of federal estate and gift tax cases is essentially the same as for the federal income tax. When the audit of the estate tax or gift tax return results in a claim for additional tax by the Treasury, essentially the same administrative and judicial remedies are available for resolving the dispute. Treasury regulations and Treasury rulings in the estate and gift tax field are subject to challenge and sometimes come off the loser in court.

L. ON TO SUBSTANCE

[¶ 1163]

The materials in this course book are intended to start the student in an acquaintance with the substantive provisions of the federal transfer tax system, together with some of the most significant interpretations by the courts and the Treasury. A beginning acquaintance with the federal transfer tax is enough in most to kindle a relatively keen interest in planning, i.e., arrangements to minimize the federal levies on intergenerational transfers of property. The many options provided by the system in its present configuration mean that there are planning opportunities. The 2001 Act, with its phasing down of rates, phasing up of the estate tax exemption, repeal of the estate tax followed by its reinstitution, change in basis rules and continued role for the gift tax, adds further complexity to the process of estate planning. The matter of planning to minimize exposure to federal transfer taxes, moreover, is a challenging activity. This course book is not designed as a planning book as such, but recognition is given from time to time to the planning possibilities offered by particular features of the system.

M. REFERENCE MATERIAL

[¶ 1169]

There are a number of sources of varying length to assist the beginning student in getting started with the federal transfer tax system. This volume offers considerable text material for student use. Short student texts are McNulty and McCouch, Federal Estate and Gift Taxation (6th ed. 2003) (West, Nutshell Series) and Willbanks, Federal Estate and Gift Taxation: An Analysis and Critique (3d ed. 2004) (American Casebook Series). Of similar length is the CCH publication, U.S. Master Estate and Gift Tax Guide 2005 (2005 ed.). Two standard full length texts are Bittker and Lokken, Federal Taxation of Income, Estates and Gifts (3d ed. 1999) and Stephens, Maxfield, Lind and Calfee, Federal Estate and Gift Taxation: Including the Generation–Skipping Transfer Tax (8th ed. 2002).

¶ 1157

Part II

GIFT TAX

(Chapter 12 of the Internal Revenue Code)

Chapter 2

INTRODUCTION

A. EVOLUTION OF THE GIFT TAX

[¶ 2001]

Our present gift tax dates back only to 1932 and is now incorporated in Chapter 12 of the 1986 Internal Revenue Code, §§ 2501 through 2524. A gift tax was enacted in 1924, but it proved so ineffective that it was repealed in 1926.

In concept the gift tax is simple enough: § 2501(a) imposes a tax "on the transfer of property by gift ... by any individual." At the time of its enactment, the gift tax was designed to plug the principal loophole in the estate tax system: without the gift tax, an individual could simply transfer property to the objects of her bounty during her life. If the individual retained no strings or powers over the property, the federal estate tax could be avoided altogether.

Despite the enactment of the gift tax in 1932, important advantages of lifetime gifts over death transfers remained in effect until 1976. The gift tax rates were only 75 percent of the estate tax rates, and in all cases a lifetime gift removed from the donor's prospective estate not only the property given, but also the funds used to pay the gift tax imposed on the transfer.

Enactment of the unified transfer tax system in 1976 eliminated most of the advantages of lifetime giving as compared to death transfers. Beginning in 1976 it could be said that in most cases the total transfer tax burden would be approximately the same whether the decedent's property was transferred during the decedent's lifetime, at the decedent's death, or some combination of the two. The 2001 Act, however, tilted the balance markedly in favor of death transfers as compared to lifetime gifts—at least to the extent any gift tax must be paid.

This is true for two reasons. First, a transfer by gift may cause taxation of amounts that could have been sheltered by the estate tax unified credit at death. The applicable exclusion amount under the gift tax was "frozen" at $1,000,000 beginning in 2002, while the applicable exclusion amount for estate tax purposes rises to $3,500,000 by 2009. A taxpayer who makes a taxable gift of $3,500,000 in 2006 has to pay a gift tax of $1,125,000. If the taxpayer simply held the property until her death in 2009, the entire

$3,500,000 would pass free of tax. Second, if the estate tax is repealed in 2010, as scheduled, all transfer taxes could be avoided by deferring the transfer until death—regardless of the size of the estate.

B. THE GIFT TAX AFTER 2009

[¶ 2005]

After 2009 the purpose and nature of the gift tax will change radically. Under § 2210(a) as added by the 2001 Act, the estate tax will not apply to estates of decedents dying after December 31, 2009. At that point there will be no need to prevent avoidance of the estate tax through lifetime gifts, and it would seem that the gift tax should be repealed as well.

Congress, however, concluded that the absence of a gift tax would open the door to substantial *income* tax avoidance. For example, it was feared that taxpayers in high income tax brackets would transfer property by gift to low bracket family members, or to entities that could avoid the income tax in a variety of ways. Therefore, Congress concluded that it was necessary to deter such efforts by imposing a penalty on substantial lifetime transfers.

After 2009 there will be a credit against gift tax available in the amount of the tax on $1,000,000 of gifts. § 2505(a)(1) as in effect after December 31, 2009. There will be a new rate structure that begins at 18% and rises to 35% on cumulative gifts over $500,000. § 2502(a) as in effect after December 31, 2009. The practical effect for most taxpayers is that all gifts over a cumulative lifetime total of $1,000,000 will be taxed at 35%. The 35% rate was chosen because this was the top individual income tax rate after the rate reductions imposed by the 2001 Act were fully phased in. § 1(i)(2).

The § 2503(b) annual exclusion remains in effect, but a new provision will apparently have the effect of denying the exclusion for any transfer that is in trust, rather than outright. § 2511(c) as in effect after December 31, 2009. Section 2503(b) is explored at ¶ 7013.

The entirety of the 2001 Act is subject to a sunset provision, which states that no provision of the 2001 Act will apply to taxable years, deaths, or gifts after December 31, 2010. Section 901(a), Economic Growth and Tax Relief Reconciliation Act of 2001. If no contrary action is taken by Congress prior to December 31, 2010, the provisions of the 2001 Act will disappear, and the estate and gift tax law will take the form that was in effect prior to enactment of the 2001 Act. Therefore, it is possible that the gift tax regime described above could exist for only one year (2010) and then be supplanted on January 1, 2011, by restoration of the system as it existed prior to the 2001 Act amendments.

C. MECHANICS OF THE GIFT TAX

[¶ 2007]

Determination of the gift tax—and ultimately the estate tax as well—involves the following procedure:

1. The initial step is imposition of a gift tax on transfers during the donor's lifetime. The tax is imposed on all taxable gifts in each calendar year.

   (a) First, a tentative gift tax is determined under the § 2001(c) rate schedule on the total of all taxable gifts made by the donor at any time after June 6, 1932, including the calendar year in question. §§ 2502(a)(1), 2502(b).

   (b) From the tentative tax determined in (a) there is subtracted another tentative tax computed under the § 2001(c) rate schedule on the total of all taxable gifts made after June 6, 1932, and *prior* to the calendar year in question. § 2502(a)(2).

   (c) The excess of the (a) tentative tax (the tax on all gifts) over the (b) tentative tax (the tax on all gifts prior to the year in question) is the gift tax imposed on the taxable gifts made during the year. § 2502(a).

   (d) The unified credit specified in §§ 2505(a)(1), less the amount of credit previously used (§ 2502(a)(2)), is then available to offset the gift tax so imposed. The tax payable is the gift tax, if any, in excess of the available credit.

2. With respect to gifts in later years, the computations in 1 are repeated each year a gift is made, with the effect of putting subsequent gifts in progressively higher tax brackets. The unified credit available in a later year is reduced by the amount of credit actually used in prior years. § 2505(a)(2).

   [handwritten: Prof says wo "allowable," not "used"]

3. The final step in the unified tax system is determination of the individual's estate tax under Chapter 11 of the Code (§§ 2001–2210) at the time of the individual's death. The estate tax is imposed on the "taxable estate." The taxable estate consists of the gross estate (which includes all property owned at death as well as certain transfers that are considered testamentary in character), less various deductions. § 2051.

   (a) All taxable gifts made by the decedent after 1976 (other than gifts that are already included in the gross estate because of their testamentary character) are added to the taxable estate for the purpose of determining a tentative estate tax using the § 2001(c) rate schedule. § 2001(b)(1).

   (b) From the tentative estate tax determined in (a) there is subtracted the total of gift taxes that were payable with respect to gifts made by the decedent after 1976. (Note that the amount deducted is not the gift tax actually paid, but the hypothetical amount that would have been paid if the gift tax rate structure for the year of gift had been the same as the actual rate structure for the year of death.) The excess of the tentative estate tax over the gift taxes payable is the estate tax before credits. § 2001(b).

¶ 2007

    (c) The unified credit amount specified in § 2010(c) is allowed against the estate tax computed in (b).

The last step described above—application of the full unified credit amount specified in § 2010(c)—sometimes causes confusion. The credit is meant to be truly "unified", i.e., a single credit amount to be used against both lifetime and death transfers. Therefore, it may seem incongruous to allow the full credit amount at death if the decedent used a portion of the credit to shelter lifetime gifts from tax.

The answer to this conundrum lies in the arithmetic required by § 2001(b)(2), the effect of which is that the estate tax payable is reduced by the gift tax that was payable by the decedent. To the extent the decedent used a portion of her unified credit to eliminate payment of gift tax, the gift tax payable is thereby decreased, resulting in a concomitant *decrease* in the § 2001(b)(2) deduction for gift tax payable. This produces a concomitant *increase* in the estate tax payable under § 2001(b). The net effect is to *increase* the estate tax payable by the amount of the unified credit used to shelter lifetime gifts. Therefore, the estate tax due is increased on a dollar-for-dollar basis in the amount of the credit used to reduce gift tax liability. The result is that all the benefits of the gift tax credit are eliminated when the estate tax is computed. Therefore it is appropriate to allow the full estate tax unified credit at death, regardless of the amount of gift tax credit used during life.

For example, assume that the decedent made a lifetime taxable gift of $100,000, thereby creating a gift tax liability, before the unified credit, of $23,800. The decedent used $23,800 of her unified credit to offset the gift tax otherwise due, so that she actually paid no gift tax. The taxable gift of $100,000 will be added to the decedent's taxable estate for purposes of determining the tax due at her death under § 2001(b)(2). If the decedent had actually paid the $23,800 in gift tax during her life, this would have reduced the estate tax due under § 2001(b) by $23,800. Because the decedent used $23,800 of unified credit to avoid payment of tax, however, the § 2001(b)(2) reduction is zero. As a result, the decedent's estate tax is $23,800 higher than it would have been had $23,800 of credit not been used to shelter lifetime gifts.

If the taxpayer made gifts in years prior to 1987, it is necessary to consult the prior versions of §§ 2505 and 2010 to determine the unified credit amount available each year gifts were made. During the period 1987 through 1997, the unified credit was $192,800, producing an exemption equivalent, or applicable exclusion amount, of $600,000. The applicable exclusion amount rose after 1997, reaching $1,000,000 in 2002. The applicable exclusion amount for gift tax purposes remains capped at $1,000,000 after 2002.

Problem

[¶ 2013]

Alice Jones made taxable gifts of $60,000 in 1998, $40,000 in 1999, and $700,000 in 2000. She dies in 2006 with a taxable estate of $2,500,000. How much gift tax, if any, did Alice owe for 1998, 1999, and 2000, and how much estate tax, if any, is imposed at her death? For purposes of this problem, ignore all credits except the unified credit. The term "taxable gifts" refers to gifts after application of the § 2503(b) annual per donee exclusion.

D. BASIS IN GIFT TRANSFERS

[¶ 2015]

The general rule applicable to gift transfers is that the donee takes the donee's basis for income tax purposes. § 1015(a). For example, assume that Mother buys stock for $6,000. The stock appreciates to a value of $10,000, at which point Mother transfers the stock to Son by gift. Son's basis for the stock is $6,000. If he later sells the stock for $11,000, he will have a taxable gain of $5,000.

This "carryover basis" rule is dramatically different from the "step-up in basis" rule that applies to transfers at death. In the above example, assume that Mother, rather than transferring the stock by gift, holds the stock until her death, and she bequeaths the stock, then worth $10,000, to Son. Son has a basis for the stock equal its value on the date of Mother's death—$10,000. § 1014(a). If Son later sells the stock for $11,000, he will have a taxable gain of only $1,000. The $4,000 appreciation that occurred before Mother's death escapes taxation entirely. If the alternate valuation date provided by § 2032 and explained below at ¶ 9013 is elected for Mother's estate, Son's basis will be the value of the stock on the alternate valuation date. § 1014(a)(2). Section 1014(a) can also produce a "step down in basis" if the value of the stock at Mother's death is lower than her basis for the stock.

A special rule applies to gift transfers if the property has depreciated in the donor's hands, i.e., the value at the date of gift is lower than the donor's basis. In this case, for purposes of determining loss, but not gain, the basis to the donee is the value on the date of the gift. § 1015(a). For example, assume that Mother buys a stock for $20,000. It drops in value to $13,000, at which point Mother gives the stock to Son. If the stock value declines further, and Son ultimately sells the stock for $10,000, he will have a deductible loss of only $3,000. If however, the stock appreciates to $25,000 and Son then sells the stock, he will have taxable gain of only $5,000. If Son sells the stock for a price between $13,000 and $20,000, there is neither gain nor loss. Reg. § 1.1015–1(a)(2). The purpose of this special rule is to prevent a donor from transferring a prospective loss to a family member who is in a higher tax bracket, or is otherwise better positioned to use the loss. For example, the donor may have no capital gains against which to offset the loss, while the donee may have substantial capital gains.

If the gift is between spouses or incident to divorce, the donee spouse take's the donor's spouse's basis in all cases, even if the donor's spouse's basis is higher than the value of the property at the time of the gift. §§ 1015(e), 1041(b)

¶ 2013

The donee is permitted to increase the donee's basis by a portion of any gift tax paid by the donor with respect to the transfer. § 1015(d). Assume that Father gives land worth $100,000 to Daughter at a time when the § 2503(b) exclusion amount is $12,000. Father's basis for the land is $60,000, and Father pays $20,000 of gift tax with respect to the transfer. The general rule of § 1015(a) is that Daughter takes Father's basis of $60,000. Section 1015(d), however, permits Daughter to increase the basis in the amount of the portion of the $20,000 gift tax that is allocable to the portion of the taxable value of the gift that constitutes unrealized appreciation. § 1015(d)(6). In this case, the unrealized appreciation portion is $100,000 less $60,000, or $40,000. The taxable amount, after deducting the annual per donee exclusion, is $100,000 less $12,000, or $88,000. The appreciation portion is therefore $40,000/$88,000, or 45%. Daughter can therefore increase her basis for the property by 45% of $20,000, or $9,000. Daughter's basis for the property is $60,000 plus $9,000, or $69,000. Reg. § 1.1015–5(c).

Chapter 3

WHAT CONSTITUTES A GIFT

[¶ 3001]

It is well established that Congress intended an expansive definition of what constitutes a "gift" so as to be subject to the gift tax. Section 2511(a) provides that the gift tax is to apply "whether the transfer is in trust or otherwise, whether the gift is direct or indirect, and whether the property is real or personal, tangible or intangible ..." Reg. § 25.2511–1(c)(1) states that "any transaction in which an interest in property is gratuitously passed or conferred upon another, regardless of the means or device employed, constitutes a gift subject to tax." In Commissioner v. Wemyss, ¶ 3007, the Supreme Court described Congress as intending "to hit all the protean arrangements which the wit of man can devise that are not business transactions within the meaning of ordinary speech." 324 U.S. 303, 306 (1945).

A. IS DONATIVE INTENT NECESSARY?

[¶ 3005]

One might assume that Congress intended the term "gift" to connote the common-law concept of a transfer made gratuitously and with donative intent. The Regulations, however, take a very expansive view, refusing to follow the path of the common law: "Donative intent on the part of the transferor is not an essential element in the application of the gift tax to the transfer." Reg. § 25.2511–1(g)(1). Even more explicitly, Reg. § 25.2512–8 states:

> Transfers reached by the gift tax are not confined to those only which, being without a valuable consideration, accord with the common law concept of gifts, but embrace as well sales, exchanges, and other dispositions of property for a consideration to the extent that the value of the property transferred by the donor exceeds the value in money or money's worth of the consideration given therefor. However, a sale, exchange, or other transfer of property made in the ordinary course of business (a transaction which is bona fide, at arm's length, and free from any donative intent), will be considered as made for adequate and full consideration in money or money's worth.

[¶ 3007]

COMMISSIONER v. WEMYSS

Supreme Court of the United States, 1945.
324 U.S. 303.

FRANKFURTER, J.: In 1939 taxpayer proposed marriage to Mrs. More, a widow with one child. Her deceased husband had set up two trusts, one half the income of which was for the benefit of Mrs. More and the other half for that of the child with provision that, in the event of Mrs. More's remarriage, her part of the income ceased and went to the child. The corpus of the two trusts consisted of stock which brought to Mrs. More from the death of her first husband to her remarriage, about five years later, an average income of $5,484 a year. On Mrs. More's unwillingness to suffer loss of her trust income through remarriage the parties on May 24, 1939, entered upon an agreement whereby taxpayer transferred to Mrs. More a block of shares of stock. Within a month they married. The Commissioner ruled that the transfer of this stock, the value of which, $149,456.13, taxpayer does not controvert, was subject to the Federal Gift Tax, §§ 501 and 503 of the Revenue Act of 1932. Accordingly, he assessed a deficiency which the Tax Court upheld, 2 T.C. 876, but the Circuit Court of Appeals reversed the Tax Court, 144 F.2d 78. We granted certiorari to settle uncertainties in tax administration engendered by seemingly conflicting decisions. 324 U.S. 308.

The answer to our problem turns on the proper application of §§ 501 (a) [1986 Code § 2501(a)(1)] and 503 [1986 Code § 2512(b)] supra to the immediate facts. These provisions are as follows:

Sec. 501. Imposition of Tax.

(a) For the calendar year 1932 and each calendar year thereafter a tax, computed as provided in section 502, shall be imposed upon the transfer during such calendar year by any individual ... of property by gift.

Sec. 503. Transfers for less than adequate and full consideration.

Where property is transferred for less than an adequate and full consideration in money or money's worth, then the amount by which the value of the property exceeded the value of the consideration shall, for the purpose of the tax imposed by this title, be deemed a gift, and shall be included in computing the amount of gifts made during the calendar year.

In view of the major role which the Tax Court plays in federal tax litigation, it becomes important to consider how that court dealt with this problem. Fusing, as it were, §§ 501 and 503, the Tax Court read them as not being limited by any common law technical notions about "consideration." And so, while recognizing that marriage was of course a valuable consideration to support a contract, the Tax Court did not deem marriage to satisfy the requirement of § 503 in that it was not a consideration reducible to money value. Accordingly, the Court found the whole value of the stock transferred to Mrs. More taxable under the statute and the relevant Treas. Reg. 79 (1936 ed.) Art. 8: "A consideration not reducible to a money value, as love and affection, promise of marriage, etc., is to be wholly disregarded, and the entire value of the property transferred constitutes the amount of the gift." In the alternative, the Tax Court was of the view that if Mrs. More's loss of her trust income rather than the marriage was consideration for the taxpayer's transfer of his stock to her, he is not relieved from the tax because he did not receive any money's worth from Mrs. More's relinquishment of her trust income, and, in any event, the actual value of her interest in the trust, subject to fluctuations of its stock earnings, was not proved. One member of the Tax Court dissented, deeming that the gift tax legislation invoked ordinary contract conceptions of "consideration."

The Circuit Court of Appeals rejected this line of reasoning. It found in the marriage agreement an arm's length bargain and an absence of "donative intent" which it deemed essential: "A donative intent followed by a donative act is essential to constitute a gift; and no strained and artificial construction of a supplementary statute should be indulged to tax as a gift a transfer actually lacking donative intent." 144 F.2d 78, 82.

Sections 501 and 503 are not disparate provisions. Congress directed them to the same purpose, and they should not be separated in application. Had Congress taxed "gifts" simpliciter, it would be appropriate to assume that the term was used in its colloquial sense, and a search for "donative intent" would be indicated. But Congress intended to use the term "gifts" in its broadest and most comprehensive sense. H. Rep. No. 708, 72d Cong., 1st Sess., p. 27; Rep. No. 665, 72d Cong., 1st Sess., p. 39 * * * Congress chose not to require an ascertainment of what too often is an elusive state of mind. For purposes of the gift tax it not only dispensed with the test of "donative intent." It formulated a much more workable external test, that where "property is transferred for less than an adequate and full consideration in money or money's worth," the excess in such money value "shall, for the purpose of the tax imposed by this title, be deemed a gift...." And Treasury Regulations have emphasized that common law considerations were not embodied in the gift tax.

To reinforce the evident desire of Congress to hit all the protean arrangements which the wit of man can devise that are not business transactions within the meaning of ordinary speech, the Treasury Regulations make clear that no genuine business transaction comes within the purport of the gift tax by excluding "a sale, exchange, or other transfer of property made in the ordinary course of business (a transaction which is bona fide, at arm's length, and free from any donative intent)." Treas. Reg. 79 (1936 ed.) Art. 8. [Reg. § 25.2512–8.] Thus on finding that a transfer in the circumstances of a particular case is not made in the ordinary course of business, the transfer becomes subject to the gift tax to the extent that it is not made "for an adequate and full consideration in money or money's worth." See 2 Paul, Federal Estate and Gift Taxation (1942) p. 1113.

The Tax Court in effect found the transfer of the stock to Mrs. More was not made at arm's length in the ordinary course of business. It noted that the inducement was marriage, took account of the discrepancy between what she got and what she gave up, and also of the benefit that her marriage settlement brought to her son. These were considerations the Tax Court could justifiably heed, and heeding, decide as it did. * * *

If we are to isolate as an independently reviewable question of law the view of the Tax Court that money consideration must benefit the donor to relieve a transfer by him from being a gift, we think the Tax Court was correct. * * * To be sure, the Revenue Act of 1932 does not spell out a requirement of benefit to the transferor to afford relief from the gift tax. Its forerunner, § 320 of the 1924 Act, 43 Stat. 253, 314, was more explicit in that it provided that the excess of the transfer over "the consideration received shall ... be deemed a gift." It will hardly be suggested, however, that in reimposing the gift tax in 1932 Congress meant to exclude transfers that would have been taxed under the 1924 Act. The section taxing as gifts transfers that are not made for "adequate and full [money] consideration" aims to reach those transfers which are withdrawn from the donor's estate. To allow detriment to the donee to satisfy the requirement of "adequate and full consideration" would violate the purpose of the statute and open wide the door for evasion of the gift tax. See 2 Paul, supra, at 1114.

Reversed.

B. INTEREST–FREE AND LOW–INTEREST LOANS

1. JUDICIAL RESPONSE

[¶ 3019]

DICKMAN v. COMMISSIONER

Supreme Court of the United States, 1984.
465 U.S. 330.

CHIEF JUSTICE BURGER delivered the opinion of the Court:

We granted certiorari to resolve a conflict among the Circuits as to whether intrafamily, interest-free demand loans result in taxable gifts of the value of the use of the money lent.

I

A

Paul and Esther Dickman were husband and wife; Lyle Dickman was their son. Paul, Esther, Lyle, and Lyle's wife and children were the owners of Artesian Farm, Inc. (Artesian), a closely-held Florida corporation. Between 1971 and 1976, Paul and Esther loaned substantial sums to Lyle and Artesian. Over this five-year interval, the outstanding balances for the loans from Paul to Lyle varied from $144,715 to $342,915; with regard to Paul's loans to Artesian, the outstanding balances ranged from $207,875 to $669,733. During the same period, Esther loaned $226,130 to Lyle and $68,651 to Artesian. With two exceptions, all the loans were evidenced by demand notes bearing no interest.

Paul Dickman died in 1976, leaving a gross estate for federal estate tax purposes of $3,464,011. The Commissioner of Internal Revenue audited Paul Dickman's estate and determined that the loans to Lyle and Artesian resulted in taxable gifts to the extent of the value of the use of the loaned funds.[1] The Commissioner then issued statutory notices of gift tax deficiency both to Paul Dickman's estate and to Esther Dickman.[2]

Esther Dickman and the estate, petitioners here, sought redetermination of the deficiencies in the Tax Court. Reaffirming its earlier decision in Crown v. Commissioner, 67 T.C. 1060 (1977), aff'd, 585 F.2d 234 (C.A.7 1978), the Tax Court concluded that intrafamily, interest-free demand loans do not result in taxable gifts. 41 TCM 620, 623 (1980). Because the Tax Court determined that all the loans to Lyle and Artesian were made payable on demand, it held that the loans were not subject to the federal gift tax. Id., at 624.

B

The United States Court of Appeals for the Eleventh Circuit reversed, holding that gratuitous interest-free demand loans give rise to gift tax liability. 690 F.2d 812, 819 (1982). Reviewing the language and history of the gift tax provisions of the Internal Revenue Code of 1954 (Code), 26 U.S.C. § 2501 et seq., the Court of Appeals concluded that Congress intended the gift tax to have the broadest and most comprehensive coverage possible. The court reasoned that the making of an interest-free demand loan constitutes a "transfer of property by gift" within the meaning of 26 U.S.C. § 2501(a)(1), and accordingly is subject to the gift tax provisions of the Code. In so holding, the Court of Appeals squarely rejected the contrary position adopted by the United States Court of Appeals for the Seventh Circuit in Crown v. Commissioner, 585 F.2d 234 (1978). We granted certiorari to resolve this conflict * * *; we affirm.

II

A

The statutory language of the federal gift tax provisions purports to reach any gratuitous transfer of any interest in property. Section 2501(a)(1) of the Code imposes a tax upon "the transfer of property by gift." 26 U.S.C. § 2501(a)(1). Section 2511(a) highlights the broad sweep of the tax imposed by § 2501, providing in pertinent part:

> Subject to the limitations contained in this chapter, the tax imposed by section 2501 shall apply whether the transfer is in trust or otherwise, whether the gift is direct or indirect, and whether the property is real or personal, tangible or intangible. . . .

1. In valuing the gifts, the Commissioner multiplied the loan balances outstanding at the end of each taxable quarter by interest rates ranging from six percent to nine percent per annum. These interest rates were taken from § 6621 of the Internal Revenue Code of 1954, 26 U.S.C. § 6621, made applicable by Code § 6601 to under payments of tax.

2. The Commissioner asserted a $42,212.91 deficiency against Paul Dickman's estate and a $41,109.78 deficiency against Esther Dickman.

¶ 3019

Id., at § 2511(a). The language of these statutes is clear and admits of but one reasonable interpretation: transfers of property by gift, by whatever means effected, are subject to the federal gift tax.

The committee reports accompanying the Revenue Act of 1932, 47 Stat. 169, which established the present scheme of federal gift taxation, make plain that Congress intended the gift tax statute to reach all gratuitous transfers of any valuable interest in property. Among other things, these reports state:

> The terms "property," "transfer," "gift," and "indirectly" are used in the broadest and most comprehensive sense; the term "property" reaching every species of right or interest protected by law and having an exchangeable value.

The words "transfer ... by gift" and "whether ... direct or indirect" are designed to cover and comprehend all transactions ... whereby, and to the extent ... that, property or a property right is donatively passed to or conferred upon another, regardless of the means or the device employed in its accomplishment.

H.R. Rep. No. 708, 72d Cong., 1st Sess., 27–28 (1932); S. Rep. No. 665, 72d Cong., 1st Sess., 39 (1932). The plain language of the statute reflects this legislative history; the gift tax was designed to encompass all transfers of property and property rights having significant value.

On several prior occasions, this Court has acknowledged the expansive sweep of the gift tax provisions. In Commissioner v. Wemyss, 324 U.S. 303, 306 (1945), the Court explained that:

> Congress intended to use the term "gifts" in its broadest and most comprehensive sense.... [in order] to hit all the protean arrangements which the wit of man can devise that are not business transactions within the meaning of ordinary speech.

The Court has also noted that the language of the gift tax statute "is broad enough to include property, however conceptual or contingent," Smith v. Shaughnessy, 318 U.S. 176, 180 (1943), so as "to reach every kind and type of transfer by gift," Robinette v. Helvering, 318 U.S. 184, 187 (1943). Thus, the decisions of this Court reinforce the view that the gift tax should be applied broadly to effectuate the clear intent of Congress.

B

In asserting that interest-free demand loans give rise to taxable gifts, the Commissioner does not seek to impose the gift tax upon the principal amount of the loan, but only upon the reasonable value of the use of the money lent. The taxable gift that assertedly results from an interest-free demand loan is the value of receiving and using the money without incurring a corresponding obligation to pay interest along with the loan's repayment.[3] Is such a gratu-

---

3. The Commissioner's tax treatment of interest-free demand loans may perhaps be best understood as a two-step approach to such transactions. Under this theory, such a loan has two basic economic components: an arm's length loan from the lender to the borrower, on which the borrower pays the lender a fair rate of interest, followed by a gift from the lender to the borrower in the amount of that interest. See Crown v. Commissioner, 585 F.2d 234, 240 (C.A.7 1978).

itous transfer of the right to use money a "transfer of property" within the intendment of § 2501(a)(1)?

We have little difficulty accepting the theory that the use of valuable property—in this case money—is itself a legally protectible property interest. Of the aggregate rights associated with any property interest, the right of use of property is perhaps of the highest order. One court put it succinctly:

> "Property" is more than just the physical thing—the land, the bricks, the mortar—it is also the sum of all the rights and powers incident to ownership of the physical thing. Property is composed of constituent elements and of these elements the right to use the physical thing to the exclusion of others is the most essential and beneficial. Without this right all other elements would be of little value.... Passailaigue v. United States, 224 F.Supp. 682, 686 (M.D.Ga.1963).

What was transferred here was the use of a substantial amount of cash for an indefinite period of time. An analogous interest in real property, the use under a tenancy at will, has long been recognized as a property right. E.g., Restatement (Second) of Property § 1.6 (1977); G. Thompson, Commentaries on the Modern Law of Real Property § 1020 (J. Grimes ed. 1980). For example, a parent who grants to a child the rent-free, indefinite use of commercial property having a reasonable rental value of $8000 a month has clearly transferred a valuable property right. The transfer of $100,000 in cash, interest-free and repayable on demand, is similarly a grant of the use of valuable property. Its uncertain tenure may reduce its value, but it does not undermine its status as property. In either instance, when the property owner transfers to another the right to use the object, an identifiable property interest has clearly changed hands.

The right to the use of $100,000 without charge is a valuable interest in the money lent, as much so as the rent-free use of property consisting of land and buildings. In either case, there is a measurable economic value associated with the use of the property transferred. The value of the use of money is found in what it can produce; the measure of that value is interest—"rent" for the use of the funds. We can assume that an interest-free loan for a fixed period, especially for a prolonged period, may have greater value than such a loan made payable on demand, but it would defy common human experience to say that an intrafamily loan payable on demand is not subject to accommodation; its value may be reduced by virtue of its demand status, but that value is surely not eliminated.

* * *

Against this background, the gift tax statutes clearly encompass within their broad sweep the gratuitous transfer of the use of money. Just as a tenancy at will in real property is an estate or interest in land, so also is the right to use money a cognizable interest in personal property. The right to use money is plainly a valuable right, readily measurable by reference to current interest rates; the vast banking industry is positive evidence of this reality.

¶ 3019

Accordingly, we conclude that the interest-free loan of funds is a "transfer of property by gift" within the contemplation of the federal gift tax statutes.

C

Our holding that an interest-free demand loan results in a taxable gift of the use of the transferred funds is fully consistent with one of the major purposes of the federal gift tax statute: protection of the estate tax and the income tax. The legislative history of the gift tax provisions reflects that Congress enacted a tax on gifts to supplement existing estate and income tax laws. H.R. Rep. No. 708, supra, at 28; S. Rep. No. 665, supra, at 40; see also 65 Cong. Rec. 3119–3120, 8095–8096 (1924); Harriss, Legislative History of Federal Gift Taxation, 18 Taxes 531, 536 (1940). Failure to impose the gift tax on interest-free loans would seriously undermine this estate and income tax protection goal.

A substantial no-interest loan from parent to child creates significant tax benefits for the lender quite apart from the economic advantages to the borrower. This is especially so when an individual in a high income tax bracket transfers income-producing property to an individual in a lower income tax bracket, thereby reducing the taxable income of the high-bracket taxpayer at the expense, ultimately, of all other taxpayers and the government. Subjecting interest-free loans to gift taxation minimizes the potential loss to the federal fisc generated by the use of such loans as an income tax avoidance mechanism for the transferor. Gift taxation of interest-free loans also effectuates Congress' desire to supplement the estate tax provisions. A gratuitous transfer of income-producing property may enable the transferor to avoid the future estate tax liability that would result if the earnings generated by the property—rent, interest, or dividends—became a part of the transfer-or's estate. Imposing the gift tax upon interest-free loans bolsters the estate tax by preventing the diminution of the transferor's estate in this fashion.

III

Petitioners contend that administrative and equitable considerations require a holding that no gift tax consequences result from the making of interest-free demand loans. In support of this position, petitioners advance several policy arguments; none withstands studied analysis.

A

Petitioners first advance an argument accepted by the Tax Court in Crown v. Commissioner, supra:

> [O]ur income tax system does not recognize unrealized earnings or accumulations of wealth and no taxpayer is under any obligation to continuously invest his money for a profit. The opportunity cost of either letting one's money remain idle or suffering a loss from an unwise investment is not taxable merely because a profit *could have been made* from a wise investment. 67 T.C., at 1063–1064.

Thus, petitioners argue, an interest-free loan should not be made subject to the gift tax simply because of the possibility that the money lent might have

¶ 3019

enhanced the transferor's taxable income or gross estate had the loan never been made.

This contention misses the mark. It is certainly true that no law requires an individual to invest his property in an income-producing fashion, just as no law demands that a transferor charge interest or rent for the use of money or other property. An individual may, without incurring the gift tax, squander money, conceal it under a mattress, or otherwise waste its use value by failing to invest it. Such acts of consumption have nothing to do with lending money at no interest. The gift tax is an excise tax on transfers of property; allowing dollars to lie idle involves no transfer. If the taxpayer chooses not to waste the use value of money, however, but instead transfers the use to someone else, a taxable event has occurred. That the transferor himself could have consumed or wasted the use value of the money without incurring the gift tax does not change this result. Contrary to petitioners' assertion, a holding in favor of the taxability of interest-free loans does not impose upon the transferor a duty profitably to invest; rather, it merely recognizes that certain tax consequences inevitably flow from a decision to make a "transfer of property by gift." 26 U.S.C. § 2501(a)(1).

B

Petitioners next attack the breadth of the Commissioner's view that interest-free demand loans give rise to taxable gifts. Carried to its logical extreme, petitioners argue, the Commissioner's rationale would elevate to the status of taxable gifts such commonplace transactions as a loan of the proverbial cup of sugar to a neighbor or a loan of lunch money to a colleague. Petitioners urge that such a result is an untenable intrusion by the government into cherished zones of privacy, particularly where intrafamily transactions are involved.

Our laws require parents to provide their minor offspring with the necessities and conveniences of life; questions under the tax law often arise, however, when parents provide more than the necessities, and in quantities significant enough to attract the attention of the taxing authorities. Generally, the legal obligation of support terminates when the offspring reach majority. Nonetheless, it is not uncommon for parents to provide their adult children with such things as the use of cars or vacation cottages, simply on the basis of the family relationship. We assume that the focus of the Internal Revenue Service is not on such traditional familial matters. When the government levies a gift tax on routine neighborly or familial gifts, there will be time enough to deal with such a case.

Moreover, the tax law provides liberally for gifts to both family members and others; within the limits of the prescribed statutory exemptions, even substantial gifts may be entirely tax free. First, under § 2503(e) of the Code, 26 U.S.C. § 2503(e), amounts paid on behalf of an individual for tuition at a qualified educational institution or for medical care are not considered "transfer[s] of property by gift" for purposes of the gift tax statutes. More significantly, section 2503(b) of the Code provides an annual exclusion from the computation of taxable gifts of $10,000 per year, per donee; this provision

¶ 3019

allows a taxpayer to give up to $10,000 annually to each of any number of persons, without incurring any gift tax liability. The "split gift" provision of Code § 2513(a), which effectively enables a husband and wife to give each object of their bounty $20,000 per year without liability for gift tax, further enhances the ability to transfer significant amounts of money and property free of gift tax consequences. Finally, should a taxpayer make gifts during one year that exceed the § 2503(b) annual gift tax exclusion, no gift tax liability will result until the unified credit of Code § 2505 has been exhausted. These generous exclusions, exceptions, and credits clearly absorb the sorts of de minimis gifts petitioners envision and render illusory the administrative problems that petitioners perceive in their "parade of horribles."

* * *

IV

As we have noted, * * * Congress has provided generous exclusions and credits designed to reduce the gift tax liability of the great majority of taxpayers. Congress clearly has the power to provide a similar exclusion for the gifts that result from interest-free demand loans. Any change in the gift tax consequences of such loans, however, is a legislative responsibility, not a judicial one. Until such a change occurs, we are bound to effectuate Congress' intent to protect the estate and income tax systems with a broad and comprehensive tax upon all "transfer[s] of property by gift." Cf. Diedrich v. Commissioner, 457 U.S. 191, 199 (1982).

We hold, therefore, that the interest-free demand loans shown by this record resulted in taxable gifts of the reasonable value of the use of the money lent. Accordingly, the judgment of the United States Court of Appeals for the Eleventh Circuit is

Affirmed.

[JUSTICE POWELL, joined by JUSTICE REHNQUIST, dissented.]

[¶ 3037]

2. STATUTORY RESPONSE

Although *Dickman* (¶ 3019) eliminated the advantageous gift tax treatment of interest-free loans, the IRS continued to view interest-free or low-interest loans as significant income tax avoidance devices, and especially so in times of high interest rates. For example, a parent in a high income tax bracket could make an interest-free loan to a child who could then invest the funds—perhaps in the very same investment the parent would have chosen. The income from the investment would be taxed at the child's low income tax bracket rather than the parent's high bracket. IRS attempts to impute income to the recipient of such an interest-free loan were consistently rebuffed. Martin v. Commissioner, 649 F.2d 1133 (5th Cir.1981); Beaton v. Commissioner, 664 F.2d 315 (1st Cir.1981); Baker v. Commissioner, 677 F.2d 11 (2d Cir.1982); Suttle v. Commissioner, 625 F.2d 1127 (4th Cir.1980); Parks v. Commissioner, 686 F.2d 408 (6th Cir.1982); Hardee v. United States, 708 F.2d 661 (Fed.Cir.1983).

¶ 3037

Interest-free or low-interest loans grew rapidly in popularity in the early 1980's, encouraged by the unprecedented high interest rates of that time. Such loans became a favorite device for intra-family income shifting, principally to children. An interest-free loan could effectively shift the burden of taxation on income for any period the parent might choose—whether months or years—an approach that proved especially popular for accumulation of college expense funds.

Confronted with a growing tax avoidance threat, Congress responded aggressively, incorporating in the Tax Reform Act of 1984 a very broad provision—§ 7872—that forcefully addresses both the gift and income tax aspects of interest-free or low-interest loans.

A simple example using current income tax rates will illustrate the application of § 7872. Assume that Mother, whose marginal income tax bracket is 35 percent, wishes to finance Daughter's college education in part with earnings from funds invested in United States Treasury Bills. Mother lends $50,000 to Daughter on January 1, receiving in return a no-interest note, payable on demand. The loan is outstanding throughout the year. Daughter invests the $50,000 in Treasury Bills and earns interest on the $50,000 at 6 percent—totaling $3,000. The results before and after § 7872 are as follows:

1. Prior to enactment of § 7872, the results were very favorable for Mother and Daughter. Although use of the $50,000 constituted a gift under *Dickman*, the use value of the $50,000 was well within the annual per donee exclusion, with the result that no gift tax return was required. The $3,000 in Treasury Bill income was taxed entirely to Daughter, at a total tax cost that would probably not exceed 10 percent, even if Daughter had income from other sources as well. Therefore, the earnings available for Daughter's college education after income taxes were $3,000 less income taxes of $300, or $2,700. By contrast, if Mother had earned the same income herself and paid income tax at a 35 percent rate, only $1,950 would be available for college expenses.

2. Section 7872 radically changes the treatment of the transaction. First, § 7872 assigns a definite value to use of the $50,000 for both gift and income tax purposes. This is determined by the "applicable Federal rate," which is typically higher than the rate obtainable on Treasury Bills. If the applicable Federal rate throughout the year is 7 percent, the value of the loan for both gift and income tax purposes is $3,500. The $3,500 amount is treated for all tax purposes as an imputed gift from Mother to Daughter, followed by an imputed interest payment from Daughter to Mother, with these results:

    (a) Mother is treated as making a $3,500 gift to Daughter. This amount is excluded from Daughter's gross income by § 102(a). However, there is a $3,500 gift by Mother for gift tax purposes. If Mother has exhausted the § 2503(b) annual per donee exclusion for Daughter with other gifts, the $3,500 is a taxable gift.

¶ 3037

(b) Mother is treated as receiving $3,500 in interest, and she must pay income tax on this amount. Therefore, Mother pays more in income tax than she would had she herself invested the funds in 6% Treasury Bills, yielding interest income of $3,000.

(c) Daughter is treated as paying $3,500 in interest to Mother and may be entitled to a $3,500 interest deduction for income tax purposes. Because her only income may be the $3,000 of interest actually earned on the Treasury Bills, the interest deduction may provide little tax benefit.

Although the application of § 7872 to the transaction described above is relatively simple, the complexities involved in applying the same principles more broadly are formidable. A few of the more important aspects of § 7872 are described below:

1. The section applies to any "gift loan," which is defined as a loan as to which "the forgoing of interest is in the nature of a gift." § 7872(c)(1)(A) and (f)(3).

2. The section also applies to a loan that in fact constitutes compensation to an employee or a dividend to a shareholder or that has a tax avoidance purpose. § 7872(c)(1). If the loan falls in the compensation or dividend category, the imputed transfer of $3,500 from lender to borrower is treated as payment of salary or a dividend rather than a gift.

3. The section applies to both demand and term loans and provides complex rules for valuation of term loans. § 7872(a) and (b).

4. The section applies not just to interest-free loans, but to any loan that bears interest at a rate below the applicable Federal rate. In the case of a low-interest gift loan, the amount of the gift (and imputed interest) is the difference between the applicable Federal rate and the interest actually paid. § 7872(e)(2).

5. The crucially important minimum required interest rate—the applicable Federal rate—is determined by reference to the average yield on United States government obligations. §§ 7872(f)(2) and 1274(d)(1)(C). For demand instruments the rate is the average market interest rate on government obligations having a maturity of three years or less. §§ 7872(f)(2)(B) and 1274(d)(1)(A). For term loans of more than three years, the market interest rates for longer-term government obligations are used, depending on the term of the loan. The applicable Federal rates are redetermined each month. § 1274(d)(1)(B). In the case of a term loan, the applicable Federal rate for the entire period of the loan is determined by the rate for the month in which the loan is made. § 7872(f)(2)(A). In the case of a demand loan, the rate varies from month to month as the Federal rates are redetermined. § 7872(f)(2)(B).

¶ 3037

Because loans between family members may have legitimate purposes other than tax avoidance, Congress has provided exceptions for circumstances in which tax avoidance is not present. However, the exceptions are narrow:

1. A general de minimis exception is provided for gift loans between individuals not exceeding $10,000 outstanding at any one time. § 7872(c)(2)(A). This exception, however, is not available if the loan is "directly attributable to the purchase or carrying of income-producing assets." § 7872(c)(2)(B). Therefore, if the borrower directly or indirectly invests the borrowed funds in an asset that produces income, (such as Treasury Bills or a certificate of deposit) the $10,000 exception will not apply. As a result, the de minimis exception will not be available for the typical income-shifting interest-free loan. However, the de minimis exception will apply if the borrower does not invest the borrowed funds but rather expends them immediately, e.g., for tuition and other college expenses. It is uncertain how the de minimis rule would be applied to circumstances in which the borrower temporarily invests a portion of the borrowed funds in income-producing assets before expending them.

2. A more important exception applies to loans up to $100,000. § 7872(d). This exception is designed for circumstances such as a loan by a parent to a child to enable the child to make a down payment on a personal residence. If the loan arrangements do not "have as 1 of their principal purposes the avoidance of any Federal tax" (§ 7872(d)(1)(B)), the amount of interest imputed is limited to the borrower's net investment income from all sources—not just the earnings investment of the borrowed funds. § 7872(d)(1)(A). Note that this exception eliminates only the imputed interest—not the imputed gift. Note also that any investment income earned by the borrower will automatically be imputed to the lender if the borrower's net investment income exceeds $1,000. § 7872(d)(1)(E)(ii). This produces the strange result that in years when the loan is outstanding, interest earned by a borrower child from a bank account or other investment is immediately attributed to the lender parent, so that the parent in effect pays tax on income that is earned by the child. "Tax avoidance" is defined so broadly in the proposed regulations that it may be difficult for many taxpayers to qualify for the § 7872(d) exception. Prop. Reg. § 1.7872–4(e).

The practical effect of § 7872 is to largely eliminate the tax advantages of interest-free or low-interest loans, making such loans attractive only under limited circumstances. One such case is a family that has investment alternatives producing a yield substantially greater than the applicable Federal rate. If an investment available to the family yields 12 percent and the applicable Federal rate is 7 percent, a loan at 7 percent permits shifting of the income tax burden on the additional 5 percent to the child. Another possible application involves the child's investment of demand loan funds in a long-term investment that produces a yield higher than the applicable Federal rate for demand instruments. Again, the income tax on the difference between the

¶ 3037

long-term rate and the applicable Federal rate for demand instruments is shifted to the child. Finally, interest-free loans to eliminate or reduce the child's need to borrow for purchase of a residence may be attractive, at least until the child begins to have significant investment income. For example, if the parent would earn an after-tax rate of only 4 percent on the invested funds and the child would have to pay interest on mortgage debt at 8 percent, with little offsetting tax benefit because of the child's low tax bracket, the parent's provision of an interest-free loan to reduce the need for borrowing by the child may be attractive. However, once the child's net investment income exceeds $1,000, the entirety of the investment income will be imputed to the parent, and the advantages of the loan will be diminished.

Problems

[¶ 3043]

1. Jane Brown entered Enormous State University in the fall of Year 1. Her tuition and other expenses for the fall of Year 1, a total of $12,000, were paid by her mother, Alma. Late in Year 1 Alma, who has high income from a retail business as well as from various investments, was advised that she could save a substantial amount of income tax by making an interest-free loan to Jane, so that Jane could use the earnings to pay her college expenses directly.

    On January 1 of Year 2, Alma lent $200,000 in cash to Jane, without interest, to be repaid upon Alma's demand. Jane invested the $200,000 in United States Treasury bills throughout Year 2 at an average yield of 6 percent, producing $12,000 of income, which Jane used to pay her college expenses for the spring of Year 2. Alma did not demand repayment of the loan during Year 2. Assume that throughout Year 2 the applicable Federal rate for demand instruments under Section 1274(d), compounded semiannually, was 7 percent.

    How should Alma and Jane treat this transaction for gift and income tax purposes in Year 2?

2. Would the result in Problem 1 be changed if the amount lent were only $10,000?

3. Assume the same facts as in Problem 1. Jane repaid the entire $200,000 to Alma on December 31 of Year 4.

    Jane graduated from Enormous State University in Year 5 and moved to Granite City, where she wished to purchase a residence. On July 1 of Year 5, Alma lent $50,000 in cash, without interest, to Jane to be repaid on Alma's demand. Jane used the entirety of the funds to make a down payment on a home on July 1 of Year 5. During Year 5 Jane had no investment income.

    During Year 6 Jane's salary increased, and she began to put some money aside in a money market account. During Year 6 she received interest of $1,800 on the money market account, and all of this constituted investment income as defined in § 163(d)(3). Alma did not demand repayment of the loan at any time during Year 5 or Year 6. Assume that throughout Year 5 and Year 6 the applicable Federal rate for demand instruments under Section 1274(d), compounded semiannually, was 8 percent.

How should Alma and Jane treat these transactions for gift and income tax purposes in Year 5 and Year 6?

4. George, a first-year law student, was so exhausted by his studies that his parents became worried about his health. Thinking that George needed rest and recreation, George's parents arranged for George and his friends to use the parents' condominium at Vail, Colorado, during the week of George's spring vacation.

George and his friends used the condominium without charge. The usage occurred at a popular time for skiing, and George's parents could have readily rented the condominium to others for $3,000 for the week.

Did George's parents make a taxable gift to him? If so, what is the amount of the gift? *No gift; not commercial*

C. GIFTS OF SERVICES

[¶ 3049]

1. IN GENERAL

Section 2501 states that the gift tax is to be imposed on the "transfer of property by gift." Does the word "property" include personal services? The Commissioner has not, in fact, pressed for an expansive interpretation of the word "property" to include personal services. A gift of a right to income, however, is clearly taxable as a gift, making the timing of a gift of services crucial. If the taxpayer waits until after the services have been performed to manifest donative intent, the services may have already earned him a right to income, and a transfer of that right will be subject to the gift tax.

The issue arises often in the context of decedents' estates. An executor who is a family member may prefer to forego a fee in order to maximize the amount that will go to the beneficiaries of the estate. Alternatively, the executor could claim his fee as executor. In that event, the fee would be taxable to the executor as income, and the amount the beneficiaries receive would be reduced accordingly.

An executor who decides that it is preferable to forego the fee must be sure to avoid being treated as having made a gift to the beneficiaries in the amount of the executor's entitlement to compensation. The following ruling provides the Commissioner's guidance as to how that can be accomplished.

[¶ 3061]

REVENUE RULING 66–167

1966–1 C.B. 20.

* * *

In the instant case, the taxpayer served as the sole executor of his deceased wife's estate pursuant to the terms of a will under which he and his adult son were each given a half interest in the net proceeds thereof. The laws of the state in which the will was executed and probated impose no limitation on the use of either principal or income for the payment of compensation to an executor and do not purport to deal with whether a failure to withdraw any particular fee or commission may properly be considered as a waiver thereof.

The taxpayer's administration of his wife's estate continued for a period of approximately three full years during which time he filed two annual accountings as well as the usual final accounting with the probate court, all of which reported the collection and disposition of a substantial amount of estate assets.

At some point within a reasonable time after first entering upon the performance of his duties as executor, the taxpayer decided to make no charge for serving in such capacity, and each of the aforesaid accountings accordingly omitted any claim for statutory commissions and was so filed with the intention to waive the same. The taxpayer-executor likewise took no other action which was inconsistent with a fixed and continuing intention to serve on a gratuitous basis.

The specific questions presented are whether the amounts which the taxpayer-executor could have received as fees or commissions are includible in his gross income for Federal income tax purposes and whether his waiver of the right to receive these amounts results in a gift for Federal gift tax purposes.

In Revenue Ruling 56-472, the executor of an estate entered into an agreement to serve in such capacity for substantially less than all of the statutory commissions otherwise allowable to him and also formally waived his right to receive the remaining portion thereof. The basic agreement with respect to his acceptance of a reduced amount of compensation antedated the performance of any services and the related waiver of the disclaimed commissions was signed before he would otherwise have become entitled to receive them. Under these circumstances, the ruling held that the difference between the commissions which such executor could have otherwise acquired an unrestricted right to obtain and the lesser amount which he actually received was not includible in his income and that his disclaimer did not effect any gift thereof.

In Revenue Ruling 64-225, the trustees of a testamentary trust in the State of New York waived their rights to receive one particular class of statutory commissions. This waiver was effected by means of certain formal instruments that were not executed until long after the close of most of the years to which such commissions related. This circumstance, along with all the other facts described therein, indicated that such trustees had not intended to render their services on a gratuitous basis. The Revenue Ruling accordingly held that such commissions were includible in the trustees' gross income for the taxable year when so waived and that their execution of the waivers also effected a taxable gift of these commissions.

The crucial test of whether the executor of an estate or any other fiduciary in a similar situation may waive his right to receive statutory commissions without thereby incurring any income or gift tax liability is whether the waiver involved will at least primarily constitute evidence of an intent to render a gratuitous service. If the timing, purpose, and effect of the waiver make it serve any other important objective, it may then be proper to conclude that the fiduciary has thereby enjoyed a realization of income by means of controlling the disposition thereof and, at the same time, has also effected a taxable gift by means of any resulting transfer to a third party of his contingent beneficial interest in a part of the assets under his fiduciary control. See the above cited Revenue Rulings and the authorities therein cited, as well as section 25.2511–1(c) of the Gift Tax Regulations.

The requisite intention to serve on a gratuitous basis will ordinarily be deemed to have been adequately manifested if the executor or administrator of an estate supplies one or more of the decedent's principal legatees or devisees, or of those principally entitled to distribution of decedent's intestate estate, within six months after his initial appointment as such fiduciary, with a formal waiver of any right to compensation for his services. Such an intention to serve on a gratuitous basis may also be adequately manifested through an implied waiver, if the fiduciary fails to claim fees or commissions at the time of filing the usual accountings and if all the other attendant facts and circumstances are consistent with a fixed and continuing intention to serve gratuitously. If the executor or administrator of an estate claims his statutory fees or commissions as a deduction on one or more of the estate, inheritance, or income tax returns which are filed on behalf of the estate, such action will ordinarily be considered inconsistent with any fixed or definite intention to serve on a gratuitous basis. No such claim was made in the instant case.

Accordingly, the amounts which the present taxpayer-executor would have otherwise become entitled to receive as fees or commissions are not includible in his gross income for Federal income tax purposes, and are not gifts for Federal gift tax purposes.

[¶ 3067]

2. INVESTMENT COUNSEL, BUSINESS OPPORTUNITIES, AND LOAN GUARANTEES

A parent with expertise, contacts, and substantial resources may be in a position to provide valuable assistance to a son or daughter undertaking business or investment activities. The parent can provide expertise that would cost the child a great deal if obtained through a compensated consultant. The parent can refer promising business opportunities to the child. The IRS has shown little inclination to tax such transfers as gifts and has generally been unsuccessful when it has tried.

In Commissioner v. Hogle, 165 F.2d 352 (10th Cir.1947), the IRS sought to tax as a gift the value of a parent's investment counsel, which provided substantial profits and income for his children. The Tenth Circuit declined to treat this as a taxable transfer. In Estate of Blass v. Commissioner, 11 T.C.M. (CCH) 622, T.C.M. (P–H) ¶ 52,194 (1952), the taxpayer identified business opportunities, brought those opportunities to the attention of trusts benefitting other family members, and provided services and expertise making possible the trusts' profitable purchase and sale of property. The Tax Court, following *Hogle*, held that there was no taxable gift, despite the fact that the income from the transactions would be taxed to the taxpayer for income tax purposes.

Another mechanism a prosperous parent can employ is to guarantee loans to her children, thereby making available to the children sources of credit the children could not otherwise obtain. In Priv. Ltr. Rul. 9113009 the IRS asserted that a parent's guarantee of a loan made by a bank to a child of the parent would be treated as a taxable gift to the extent of the market value of the guarantee. In Priv. Ltr. Rul. 9409108, however, the IRS withdrew Priv. Ltr. Rul. 9113009 because of a change in the IRS position on another issue and stated the IRS "express[es] no opinion at this time" on the other issues involved in Priv. Ltr. Rul. 9113009, presumably including treatment of a loan guarantee as a gift. There remains the possibility that the IRS might someday reassert the principle that a loan guarantee can be taxed as a gift. However, the difficulty of determining and valuing the parent's guarantee may prove an insurmountable obstacle.

D. GIFTS BY AGENTS

[¶ 3073]

ESTATE OF CASEY v. COMMISSIONER

United States Court of Appeals, Fourth Circuit, 1991.
948 F.2d 895.

PHILLIPS, Circuit Judge:

The Commissioner of Internal Revenue (Commissioner) appeals a decision of the Tax Court that gifts of decedent Olive Casey's assets made during her lifetime by her attorney-in-fact were authorized by a durable power of attorney held by the attorney, hence were not revocable at the time of her death, and therefore were not includible in her gross estate for federal estate tax purposes. Because we agree with the Commissioner that the Tax Court erred in finding the gifts authorized, hence not revocable, we reverse.

I

As stipulated under the Tax Court's rules, the relevant facts are these.

Olive Casey (Olive) died testate, a resident of Virginia, in September of 1989. Until his death in June of 1982, she had been married to Carlton C. Casey (Carlton), and of this marriage there were three sons, Carlton D. Casey, C. Lewis Casey, and Robert T. Casey (Robert), all of whom survived Olive's death.

* * *

In December of 1973, Olive executed a power of attorney appointing Robert her attorney-in-fact. The power of attorney was a "durable" one executed pursuant to then recently enacted Va. Code Ann. § 11–9.1. The principal feature of such a power of attorney—one not allowed by the common law—is that it is not revoked by the principal's disability, incompetence, or incapacity, but endures until her death unless revoked by the principal or a duly appointed guardian.

This power of attorney authorized Robert, "to lease, sell, grant, convey, assign, transfer, mortgage and set over to any person, firm or corporation and for such consideration as he may deem advantageous, any and all of my property . . ." and "to accept and receive any and all consideration payable to me on account of any such lease, sale, conveyance, transfer or assignment and to invest and reinvest the proceeds derived therefrom." And it followed this conferral of specific powers with the general power

> [t]o do, execute and perform all and every other act or acts, thing or things as fully and to all intents and purposes as I myself might or could do if acting personally, it being my intention by this instrument to give my attorney hereby appointed, full and complete power to handle any of my business or to deal with any and all of my property of every kind and description, real, personal, or mixed, wheresoever located and howsoever held in his full and absolute discretion.

J.A. at 29–30. Critically for our purposes, the instrument nowhere expressly conferred any power "to make gifts," or "to convey with or without consideration," or the like.

In December of 1974, a year after Olive executed the power of attorney, Carlton embarked upon an estate plan designed to minimize his estate tax by taking advantage of the annual gift tax exclusion. From 1974 through 1977, following this plan, he made yearly transfers of property to the Caseys' three children and to seven trusts established for their grandchildren. Olive joined in these conveyances to release her dower interests, and filed gift tax returns consenting to being treated as having made one-half of each conveyance.

At some time between 1977 and 1980, Olive became incompetent to manage her affairs due to Alzheimer's disease, and she remained so until her death in 1989. Accordingly, when Carlton made additional conveyances of real estate to his estate plan donees in 1980 and 1981, Robert joined in their execution to convey Olive's dower interest, signing as her attorney-in-fact.

After Carlton's death in June of 1982, Robert, as attorney-in-fact for Olive, later that year transferred $14,000 to the estate plan donees, including himself, from Olive's bank account. And in 1983, in similar fashion he conveyed to the estate plan donees, including himself, real estate owned by Olive valued at $47,360, and transferred to the same donees $50,000 in cash from Olive's bank accounts.

In both 1982 and 1983, Olive had available income that exceeded the amounts required for her support. After the various gifts had been made by Robert, Olive had assets in excess of $426,000.

Following Olive's death in 1989, the federal estate tax return filed on behalf of her estate did not include in [her] gross estate the gifts made by Robert as attorney-in-fact in 1982 and 1983. Taking the position that in the absence of an express grant of authority, a general power of attorney does not authorize gifts of a principal's assets by an attorney-in-fact, the Commissioner determined that Robert's 1982 and 1983 gifts were voidable transfers of Olive's assets. Accordingly, he concluded that they constituted revocable transfers includible in Olive's gross estate under § 2038(a)(1) of the IRC.

Upon the estate's petition in the Tax Court challenging the resulting deficiency assessment that court rejected the Commissioner's position and held the gifts not includible in Olive's gross estate.

Looking to Virginia law as controlling on the issue, the Tax Court (Korner, J.) concluded that under that law, as it would be applied by the state's highest court, the gifts would be found authorized by the power of attorney. The court's analysis was brief. Conceding "the general proposition that broad, general language in a power of attorney should be carefully scrutinized," the court opined, however, that "a construction which faithfully reflects the intent of the grantor of the power is equally important." Believing that Virginia's highest court "would closely scrutinize the circumstances under which Robert Casey was granted the power of attorney," the court held that this would lead that court to the conclusion "that the power to make gifts to family members in order to minimize [estate taxes] and to carry out an established estate plan, was within the scope of the power granted." J.A. at 72–73. The court did not identify the particular power expressed in the instrument within whose scope it thought the specific power of gift would be found. Though it spoke in the plural of "circumstances" supporting such a finding, the only circumstance specifically identified by the court was Olive's having joined her husband, both before and after execution of the power of attorney, in making comparable gifts "in order to make use of the annual gift tax exclusion." The court summed up:

> Based on the broad grant of authority in the power of attorney itself and on the particular circumstances under which it was granted, as well as decedent's established pattern of giving, we hold that Robert Casey was authorized to make the gifts in question on the decedent's behalf.

J.A. at 73.

From the resulting decision disallowing the deficiency, the Commissioner took this appeal.

II

The Tax Court rightly recognized that Virginia law controlled on the dispositive issue of the power of attorney's interpretation, Morgan v. Commissioner, 309 U.S. 78, 80 (1940), and that in the absence of direct Virginia authority on the point, it must seek to determine how Virginia's highest court would decide the issue, Commissioner v. Estate of Bosch, 387 U.S. 456, 465 (1967).

Following the same path, we conclude that the Tax Court erred in its determination that the Virginia Supreme Court would find the gifts in issue authorized by the power of attorney. We conclude to the contrary that the most relevant Virginia decisions dealing with the interpretation of powers of attorney in general and with the particular problem of self-dealing transactions by attorneys-in-fact point in the other direction.

A

First off, we believe that the Virginia Supreme Court might well adopt, as a matter of policy, a flat rule that the unrestricted power to make gifts will not be found in any formally drawn, comprehensive, durable power of attorney that does not expressly grant it. Such a rule—which would make the gifts here revocable ones—would be but a special application of an assumption generally made in the interpretation of such instruments. As expressed in the Restatement (Second) of Agency:

> Formal instruments which delineate the extent of authority, such as powers of attorney . . . , giving evidence of having been carefully drawn by skilled persons, can be assumed to spell out the intent of the principal accurately with a high degree of particularity. Such instruments are interpreted in light of general customs and the relations of the parties, but since such instruments are ordinarily very carefully drawn and scrutinized, the terms used are given a technical rather than a popular meaning, and it is assumed that the document represents the entire understanding of the parties.

Id. § 34, comment h.

A sister state in this circuit recently has adopted such a flat rule applicable to powers of attorney generally. In Fender v. Fender, 329 S.E.2d 430, 431 (S.C.1985), the Supreme Court of South Carolina, invalidating gifts by a familial attorney-in-fact, announced that "[i]n order to avoid fraud and abuse, we adopt a rule barring a gift by an attorney-in-fact to himself or a third party *absent clear intent to the contrary in writing*" (emphasis added).

When one considers the manifold opportunities and temptations for self-dealing that are opened up for persons holding general powers of attorney—of which outright transfers for less than value to the attorney-in-fact herself are the most obvious—the justification for such a flat rule is apparent. And its justification is made even more apparent when one considers the ease with which such a rule can be accommodated by principals and their draftsmen.

Virginia has not, so far as we are advised, adopted any such flat rule, else our task here would be quickly done. Neither, however, has it rejected such a rule, and we think there are significant intimations in Virginia decisions interpreting powers of attorney and assessing the self-dealing conduct of attorneys-in-fact that strongly suggest the likely attractiveness of such a rule to that Court.

* * *

Every factor that suggests the attractiveness of such a flat rule for powers of attorney in general is increased where the power is a durable one. In conferring a non-durable power, a principal has the assurance that so long as it is in effect she will have the ability to protect herself against the exercise of particular powers even if expressly conferred, and that the power will not survive her incapacity so to protect her interests. The special quality of the durable power—that it survives incapacity—removes the most critical basis for that assurance, making post-capacity protection wholly dependent upon the care with which powers are expressly conferred in the instrument. It makes special sense, therefore, to assume that such powers of attorney will have been drafted with particular care to enumerate expressly all the powers intended to be conferred.

B

The Virginia Court may not be disposed to go so far as to adopt such a flat rule, even if confined to durable powers. If not, we believe that the court would nevertheless decline, looking to the complete text of this particular instrument, and possibly to the circumstances of its execution, to infer in it a power, though unexpressed, to make the gifts here in issue.

The Virginia Court's traditional approach to interpreting such instruments is the approach generally taken by courts. The guiding principle is that in determining whether an attorney-in-fact has certain powers, courts should first seek the principal's intent as manifest in the instrument itself, and look to surrounding circumstances only to clarify ambiguity in the instrument. See Hotchkiss v. Middlekauf, 32 S.E. 36 (Va.1899).

When one looks to the relevant language of the instrument here to discern Olive Casey's intent on the power at issue, the most powerful indicator of her intent is a glaring omission. Of the four principal purposes for asset transfer—sale, lease, mortgage, and gift—all but gift are expressly authorized, *in specific terms*, by the power of attorney. When one ponders the care with which this instrument enumerates these specific legal purposes for asset transfer, the omission of gift strongly suggests a positive intent rather than oversight or any opposing intent with respect to that power. And when one considers the feature that distinguishes gift from all the other purposes— the lack of value in exchange—a validating reason for the omission is obvious. The omitted power of transfer by gift is by all odds the most potentially "dangerous" to any principal, hence, the one to be most cautiously inferred where not expressly granted. See Restatement (Second) of Agency, § 34 comment h.

The estate seeks to avoid the force of this critical omission by pointing to two instances of more general conferrals of power in the instrument that it claims should be interpreted to embrace gift-power. The first is the inclusion, along with the specific legal modes of asset transfer above noted, of the more general terms "grant, convey, assign, transfer, . . . and set over." The other involves the use of traditional boiler-plate authorizations: to "do and perform all things and acts relating to my property * * * which I might personally do," and even more generally—

> (11) To do, execute and perform all and every other act or acts, thing or things as fully and to all intents and purposes as I myself might or could do if acting personally, it being my intention by this instrument to give my attorney hereby appointed, full and complete power to handle any of my business or to deal with any and all of my property of every

¶ 3073

kind and description, real, personal or mixed, wheresoever located and howsoever held, in his full and absolute discretion.

As to the inclusion, along with the specific powers to sell, lease, and mortgage, of the more general powers to "grant, convey, assign, transfer, * * * and set aside," the estate has two problems. First, this enumeration of specific and general powers of asset transfer is immediately qualified in its entirety by the phrase "for such consideration as [the attorney-in-fact] may deem advantageous." Second, it is followed by an express authorization to "accept and receive any and all considerations payable on account of any such lease, sale, conveyance, transference * * * and to invest and reinvest the proceeds * * *." In combination, these two provisions suggest most strongly that the only asset transfer powers intended to be conferred by the enumeration of the specific and general powers were transfers for value.

* * *

We think it most likely therefore that the Virginia Court, following its general rule of holding attorneys-in-fact to the letter of their instructions, would stop with the language of this instrument, finding no intrinsic ambiguity in it respecting gift power, but only a glaring omission to include such a power where its inclusion, if it had been intended, was most appropriate. On this basis, we believe that Court most likely would find the omission of a specific gift power in the power of attorney dispositive of the principal's intent on the subject, and hold the gifts here not authorized without resorting to any extrinsic circumstances for guidance as to the principal's intent.

* * *

III

Compelling policy considerations counsel great care by courts asked to infer powers not expressly authorized by powers of attorney. This is especially so when the power is a "dangerous" one such as a gift-power. And it may be even more so when the power of attorney is a durable one which survives a principal's personal ability to monitor its exercise. Where the instrument is a formal one, with comprehensively enumerated powers, the traditional rule that its author's intent is to be sought entirely in the language of the instrument unless ambiguity makes that impossible, is complemented by the rule that courts may properly assume that such an instrument expresses the principal's entire intent. In interpreting such an instrument, the issue is the principal's actual intent at the time of its execution, not what it might or should have been. This may or may not coincide with the best interests of, or justice to, particular parties affected by the instrument as circumstances later develop. When they do not coincide, remedy to avoid perceived injustice or to serve unanticipated interests should be sought elsewhere than in a departure from or wrenching of the traditional rules of interpretation. Their maintenance is necessary to predictability in the counseling and drafting of these important instruments and in litigation of disputes over their intended meaning.

¶ 3073

In this case, all of these rules point away from finding in the power of attorney here in issue an unexpressed power to make gifts of this principal's assets. We believe that the highest court of Virginia, whose law controls on this issue, would in applying these basic rules so hold, and on that basis we so hold. By this we determine, contrary to the Tax Court's decision, that the gifts here in issue were revocable ones properly includible in Olive Casey's gross estate for estate tax purposes.

The decision of the Tax Court is reversed.

Planning Note

[¶ 3079]

As explained at ¶ 7013, there are important advantages to § 2503(b) annual exclusion gifts that entirely avoid gift and estate tax. For example, if the donor has four children and eight grandchildren, and the § 2503(b) exclusion amount is $12,000, $12,000 can be transferred entirely tax-free to each descendant—a total of $144,000. If the principal's marginal estate tax bracket is 45 percent, the saving in prospective estate tax would be at least $64,800. And this can be repeated each year.

A donor who is still competent can make such transfers himself. However, if the donor's capacity is in doubt, there will arise the question whether an agent under a power of attorney has authority to make such gifts for the donor. If transfers by the agent are binding on the principal under local law, the gifts will be treated as complete prior to the principal's death, and the $144,000 will not be included in the principal's gross estate. On the other hand, if the transfers are not binding on the principal, with the result that the decedent's executor has legal power to void the gifts and reclaim the funds, the gifts are not treated as complete prior to death, and the $144,000 will be included in the principal's gross estate, fully subject to estate tax. The same principles would be applied to each year in which gifts are made by an agent.

Two separate issues are involved. The first is whether the decedent has executed a power of attorney that authorizes the agent to act after the principal loses legal capacity. Under the traditional common-law rule, the principal's incapacity terminated the agency. Many states, however, have adopted the Uniform Durable Power of Attorney Act or similar statutes creating powers that are "durable" in the sense of surviving the principal's incapacity. Typically, specific language is required to assure "durability" of the power. Failure to include the required language makes the power "non-durable," and the principal—or his successor—has power to void the agent's actions. In that event, gifts by the agent will not be treated as completed during the principal's life, and the transferred property will be included and taxed in the decedent's gross estate. However, if the power includes the requisite durability language, the agent will have authority to act despite the principal's legal incapacity.

The second issue is whether the power of attorney—even if valid despite the principal's incapacity—confers authority for the agent to make gifts on behalf of the principal. This is the issue addressed in *Casey*, above. In order to assure a favorable result, the planner should draft the power of attorney so as to expressly and specifically assure the necessary gift authority. In some states statutory provisions may be helpful. For example, shortly after the *Casey* decision, Virginia added to its durable power statute a provision giving the attorney-in-fact authority to make gifts if the power "evidences the principal's intent to give the attorney-in-fact or agent full power to handle the principal's affairs." The gifting power, however, is limited to gifts "in accordance with the principal's personal history of making or joining in the making of gifts." Va. Code Ann. § 11–9.5 (Michie 1999).

Typically the principal will not be comfortable granting an unfettered power to make gifts. Usually the primary tax objectives can be obtained by authorizing gifts not exceeding the § 2503(b) exclusion amount for each donee each year within certain categories of family members, such as descendants. If the principal is willing, it may be desirable in some cases to go further and authorize more substantial transfers, e.g., up to the applicable exclusion amount under the gift tax unified credit.

Because gratuitous transfers are unusual and by definition do not benefit the donor, gifts by agents will inevitably be carefully scrutinized. The planner who contemplates a need for such gifts should take care to assure both durability of the power and express authority for all gifts that might prove desirable.

Additional decisions reaching the same result as *Casey*, as well as cases reaching the contrary result, are cited at ¶ 19,103 in connection with taxation of retained powers under § 2038.

Problem

[¶ 3081]

Jane Wilson, a widow, has a substantial estate that will be subjected to a marginal estate tax rate of 45% at her death. Jane has 3 children and 6 grandchildren, and in recent years she has made annual gifts to each of these descendants each year in the amount of the maximum Section 2503(b) annual per donee exclusion.

One month ago Jane suffered a stroke. She is now in a coma, is not expected to revive, and will probably die within a month. Jane has not yet made any gifts during the current year. The maximum Section 2503(b) exclusion amount is $12,000.

Jane's children have consulted Jane's estate planner to inquire about the possibility that an agent, acting on behalf of Jane, could make additional $12,000 transfers to each of the 9 descendants prior to Jane's death, thereby saving more than $48,000 in prospective estate taxes.

How would you respond to the children's query under each of the following alternative circumstances:

1. Jane has not executed a power of attorney.
2. Jane has executed a power of attorney, but it is not "durable," i.e., it does not survive incapacity of the principal.

3. Jane has executed a durable power of attorney that includes the language required by local law to make the power survive incapacity of the principal. The power of attorney does not expressly authorize gifts. However, it does state that it grants to the attorney-in-fact "general power" to act for Jane "with respect to all lawful subjects and purposes."

4. Jane has executed a durable power of attorney that includes the language required by local law to make the power survive incapacity of the principal. In addition to the language set forth in Problem 3, the power authorizes the attorney-in-fact "to make gifts to any one or more of my descendants as determined by my attorney-in-fact in his absolute discretion, provided that the total value of the gifts to any donee during any calendar year shall not exceed the maximum amount that can be excluded from taxable gifts for purposes of the United States Gift Tax pursuant to § 2503(b) of the Internal Revenue Code, as in effect at the time of the gift."

E. INDIRECT GIFTS

[¶ 3085]

A gift can occur without a direct transaction between donor and donee. Typically, this occurs in the context of a closely held business.

For example, if Mother provides all the capital for a newly formed corporation but takes only part of the stock herself and causes the remainder of the stock to be issued to Daughter, there will be a taxable gift by Mother to Daughter. For both income and gift tax purposes, the transaction will be treated as if the entirety of the stock had first been issued to Mother, followed by a gratuitous transfer of part of the stock by Mother to Daughter. § 351(g)(3); Reg. § 1.351–1(b); D'Angelo Associates, Inc. v. Commissioner, 70 T.C. 121 (1978).

There may be a gift even if Daughter contributes property as well, provided the value received by Mother is less than the value Mother contributes. A good example is Estate of Trenchard, 69 T.C.M. (CCH) 2164, T.C.M. (RIA) ¶ 95,121 (1995). Here both parents and children contributed property to capitalize a newly formed corporation. The parents received preferred stock, the children received common stock, and both parents and children received debentures. The court determined that the value of the property contributed by the parents was greater than the value of the preferred stock and debentures received by them, with the result that the parents were treated as making a gift of the difference to their children.

Similarly, a recapitalization of a corporation that changes the relative values of the ownership interests among family members without consideration can constitute a taxable gift. § 356(g)(1); Rev. Ruls. 86–39, 1986–1 C.B. 301 and 89–3, 1989–1 C.B. 278.

Typically, the crucial issue in indirect gift cases is valuation. A good example is Estate of Maggos, 79 T.C.M. (CCH) 1861, T.C.M. (RIA) ¶ 2000–129

¶ 3085

(2000). Here a mother and her son owned all the stock of a corporation. In 1987 the mother's 567 shares were redeemed for $3,000,000. The Tax Court undertook a thorough analysis of the value of the corporation, employing the various valuation techniques and discounts discussed in Chapter 11. The court concluded that the 567 shares were in fact worth $4,900,000 at the time of the redemption. Therefore, the mother had made a gift of $1,900,000 in 1987. The Tax Court determination occurred in 2000, with the result that interest on the unpaid gift tax had presumably accrued for more than 12 years. As explained at ¶ 8013, filing a gift tax return with the necessary disclosures and appraisals can initiate the three-year statute of limitations under § 6501(a), with the result that such a transaction could not be questioned for either gift or estate tax purposes after three years. The *Maggos* circumstances demonstrate the wisdom of filing such gift tax returns for any substantial transaction that might conceivably be viewed as incorporating a value disparity.

If a contribution, redemption, recapitalization or other change in the capital structure of a corporation or partnership has the effect of giving one family member liquidation or distribution rights different from those held by other family members, the transaction may be treated as a gift. § 2701(e)(5). Furthermore, the strict valuation rules of § 2701(a) may be applied, with the result that the magnitude of the gift may be greatly expanded, as explained at ¶ 12,037.

Indirect gifts can occur by inaction. If one shareholder gratuitously waives or fails to exercise legal rights in such a way as to benefit other shareholders, a gift may occur. For example, if a shareholder controlling a closely held corporation foregoes the opportunity to require the corporation to pay noncumulative dividends on preferred stock held by the controlling shareholder, there is a taxable gift to the common shareholders whose interests are thereby enhanced. Tech. Adv. Mem. 8723007. Likewise, if a shareholder fails to exercise a right to convert preferred stock to common, thereby causing the fruits of growth in the value of the corporation to accrue entirely to the benefit of the existing holders of common stock, a taxable gift to the common shareholders may occur. Tech. Adv. Mem. 8726005.

In Snyder v. Commissioner, 93 T.C. 529 (1989), stock in a closely held corporation was held primarily by a mother and her children. The mother held Class A preferred, which had a noncumulative seven percent dividend right. The Class A preferred could be converted at any time to Class B preferred, which had a cumulative seven percent dividend right. Several years passed when dividends were not paid on the Class A preferred, yet the mother did not convert to Class B, which would have assured her of entitlement to cumulative dividend payments. The Tax Court held that the mother made a gift each year in the amount of the missed dividend by failing to exercise her conversion right.

The IRS, relying on *Snyder*, carried the gift-by-inaction doctrine to an even more sophisticated level in Tech. Adv. Mem. 9301001. Here, a father held 55 percent of the corporation voting rights and under local law could dictate any corporate action he wished, including liquidation. The father arranged for issuance to himself of preferred stock that paid a dividend of only 0.38 percent of the liquidation value of the stock, at a time when the going market yield for preferred dividends was 11.55 percent. Common stock was issued to the children. The father acquiesced in continuation of this arrangement over the years as the corporation grew in value, thereby enhancing the value of the common. The IRS concluded that the father had made an indirect gift to the children each year because the father could have liquidated the corporation at any time and invested the liquidation proceeds in other assets that would have produced a return much greater than 0.38 percent. Apparently the IRS viewed the value of the annual gift as being the reasonable preferred dividend the father should have received, less the tiny amount actually paid.

Where a corporation is involved in a gift, the gift tax is generally applied by looking through the corporation and treating the shareholders as the real parties in interest. If a corporation makes a gift, the gift is treated as if made by the shareholders. Reg. § 25.2511–1(h)(1). Likewise, if a gift is made to a corporation, the gift is treated as if made to the shareholders, and the gift will be treated as a future interest for purposes of the § 2503(b) annual exclusion. Georgia L. Ketteman Testamentary Trust v. Commissioner, 86 T.C. 91 (1986).

A special rule, however, is applied to gifts to charitable and other entities in which members do not have traditional economic interests. Reg. § 25.2511–1(h)(1). In these cases the entity is treated as the donee. In Priv. Ltr. Rul. 200533001, for example, a gift was made to a social club exempt from income tax under § 501(c)(7). The IRS ruled that the social club was not formed for the economic benefit of the members. Therefore, the gift was treated as made to the entity, not the members. Because the gift was available for immediate expenditure, it was treated as a present interest qualifying for the § 2503(b) annual per donee exclusion.

As with direct transfers, an indirect transfer will not constitute a gift unless the transferor receives less than adequate and full consideration in money or money's worth from the person receiving the benefit. § 2512(b). See ¶ 3097, below.

F. PAYMENT OF TAXES ON TRUST INCOME

[¶ 3087]

The IRS has ruled that the grantor's payment of income taxes imposed on the income of a "grantor trust" does not constitute a gift to the trust or to the beneficiaries who receive the trust income.

The "grantor trust" concept is explored in Chapter 31. Under the grantor trust rules set forth in §§ 671–677, the grantor is taxed on the income of a trust if the grantor retains certain powers or benefits with respect to the trust. Such a trust is called a "grantor trust" because the grantor is taxed on the income. For example, a mother might establish a grantor trust that would provide income to her son. The son would receive the income, but the mother would have to pay the taxes on the trust income. This leads to the question whether the mother's payment of taxes on the income might be treated as a gift from the mother to the son. The son receives all the benefits, while the mother bears the tax burden.

The IRS has ruled unequivocally that there is no gift of the income tax paid by the grantor. Rev. Rul. 2004–64, 2004–27 I.R.B. 7. The IRS recognizes that the gratuitous payment of tax for which another person is liable constitutes a gift by the payor. Doerr v. United States, 819 F.2d 162 (7th Cir. 1987). The IRS distinguished the *Doerr* rule, however, because, in the case of a grantor trust, neither the trustee nor the beneficiary has any obligation to pay tax on trust income. Hence the grantor's payment of tax does not relieve either the trustee or the beneficiary of a legal obligation.

Rev. Rul. 2004–64 provides a significant opportunity for untaxed transfers. The grantor can give the beneficiary the benefit of entirely untaxed income, while the grantor's prospective gross estate is diminished to the extent of the tax payments.

G. GIFTS BY TRUSTEES

[¶ 3088]

Trustees make "gratuitous" transfers every day, in the sense that the beneficiary receiving the transfer gives no consideration. For example, if the Tenth National Bank is trustee of a trust that gives the Bank discretion to distribute property to Sam or Alice, the Bank's decision to distribute property to Sam rather than Alice is certainly "gratuitous," and might be viewed as a "gift" in the sense that Sam is enriched, while the Bank receives nothing in return.

It is important to remember, though, that the gift tax is not a tax on property, but an excise imposed on the transferor for the privilege of transferring the transferor's property to another person. The gift tax cannot apply unless the transferor makes herself poorer while making the transferee richer. In the example above, the Tenth National Bank has no beneficial interest in the property. Hence it gives up nothing when it transfers property to Sam, and the gift tax has no application. This principle is stated explicitly in the Regulations: "A transfer by a trustee of trust property in which he has no beneficial interest does not constitute a gift ..." Reg. § 25.2511–1(g)(1).

There are two important exceptions to the rule that a distribution by a trustee is not treated as a gift for gift tax purposes.

First, if the trustee was the grantor of the trust, the transfer may constitute a gift because the transfer *completes* a gift that was initiated when the grantor transferred property to the trust. Under principles that will be explored in Chapter 4, a transfer to a trust is not a completed gift if the transferor retains the power to direct the beneficial enjoyment of the property transferred. Reg. § 25.2511–2(b). When the grantor, acting as trustee, exercises that power by transferring property to a beneficiary of her choice, the gift is complete, and therefore taxable at that time (rather than when the original transfer was made to the trust).

¶ 3087

Second, if the trustee has a beneficial interest in the property, the general rule is that a distribution that diminishes the trustee's beneficial interest but benefits the distributee constitutes a gift by the trustee to the beneficiary. For example, if the trustee is herself a permissible beneficiary, her decision as trustee to distribute property to another beneficiary is clearly a gift. There is an exception, however, if the trustee, although holding a beneficial interest, makes the distribution pursuant to a power "the exercise or nonexercise of which is limited by a reasonably fixed or ascertainable standard which is set forth in the trust instrument." Reg. § 25.2511–1(g)(2). For example, if the instrument directs the trustee to distribute to the beneficiary amounts "necessary for medical care," this would constitute a "fixed or ascertainable standard," with the result that a distribution for medical care would not be a gift. By contrast, a power to distribute for the beneficiary's "pleasure, desire, or happiness" would not be viewed as subject to a fixed or ascertainable standard. Reg. § 25.2511–1(g)(2).

H. LAPSING RIGHTS

[¶ 3091]

A gift may occur by operation of law where certain rights in a partnership or corporation lapse, in effect producing a transfer of value between partners or stockholders.

For example, assume that Mother owns all the stock of a corporation. Only voting common stock is outstanding. Mother gives one-third of the stock to Daughter. For gift tax purposes, the transfer to Daughter will be valued taking into account Mother's retention of two-thirds of the voting power, thereby reducing the value assigned to the gift of a minority interest to Daughter, as explained at ¶ 11,043. Assume further that at the time of the gift the corporation's articles of incorporation are changed to provide that on November 1, 2012, Mother's stock will cease to have voting rights.

Section 2704(a)(1) requires that the lapse of voting rights on November 1, 2012, be treated as a gift by Mother to Daughter. The gift consists of the difference between the value of Mother's stock with voting rights and the value of Mother's stock without voting rights. § 2704(a)(2).

If the rule of § 2704(a)(1) were not imposed, Mother and Daughter could accomplish a transfer of the controlling voting rights, which may have very substantial value, without imposition of gift or estate tax. This would occur because, after the lapse of voting rights, the value of Mother's stock would be discounted to reflect the lack of voting rights. This was the result prior to adoption of § 2704 in 1990. Estate of Harrison v. Commissioner, 52 T.C.M. (CCH) 1306, T.C.M. (P–H) ¶ 87,008 (1987).

Section 2704 is effective only as to lapses of rights or restrictions created after October 8, 1990. In other words, the rule of § 2704 would not apply to the above example if the change in the articles of incorporation were made prior to October 9, 1990. Revenue Reconciliation Act of 1990, section 11602(e)(1)(A)(iii). The Conference Committee Report on the 1990 Act states the Committee's intention that "no inference be drawn regarding the transfer tax effect of restrictions and lapsing rights under present law." H.R. Conf. Rep. No. 964, 101st Cong., 2d Sess. at 157 (1990).

Section 2704 applies to lapsing rights in both corporations and partnerships and to voting, liquidation, and similar rights. § 2704(a)(1) and (3). Section 2704 applies only if the family of the person holding the lapsing right controls the corporation or partnership. § 2704(a)(1) and (c).

I. CONSIDERATION

[¶ 3097]

Because the principal function of the gift tax is to backstop the estate tax by levying a toll on lifetime transfers that would not otherwise be taxed, the concept of "consideration" naturally plays an important role in the gift tax. If the transfer is made for full consideration, the transferor is not making herself poorer by the transfer; no tax is being avoided, because the transferor's estate, by reason of the consideration received, is just as large as before the transfer. Thus lack of full consideration becomes the acid test in determining whether a "gift" is present for gift tax purposes. The consideration test is stated succinctly in § 2512(b):

> Where property is transferred for less than an adequate and full consideration in money or money's worth, then the amount by which the value of the property exceeded the value of the consideration shall be deemed a gift * * *

This statement of the consideration rule introduces two central concepts. First, only consideration in "money or money's worth" counts. This reflects a hard-headed, even cynical, approach that, in the interest of certainty and administrative convenience, disregards nonmonetary items, such as a promise to marry, despite the great value the parties might actually assign to such a promise.

The second concept involves the requirement of "adequate and full consideration." There will be a gift to the extent the monetary value of the consideration received is less than the monetary value of the consideration given. A mother who gives a parcel of land worth $100,000 to her son in exchange for $25,000 in cash is treated as making a $75,000 gift to her son. Of course, this principle could be carried to great extremes if the IRS sought to tax the gift implicit in any "bad bargain," e.g., where the buyer has through ignorance paid too much, or the seller has for similar reasons accepted too little. The IRS has disavowed any such intent, stating in its Regulations that "a sale, exchange, or other transfer of property made in the ordinary course of business (a transaction which is bona fide, at arm's length, and free from any donative intent) will be considered as made for an adequate and full consideration in money or money's worth." Reg. § 25.2512–8.

¶ 3091

[¶ 3103]

1. WHAT CONSTITUTES CONSIDERATION?

The gift tax provisions of the Code provide little assistance in determining what might constitute "money or money's worth" consideration for purposes of § 2512(b). At an early date the courts were required to interpret § 2512(b) in the context of the typical antenuptial agreement providing that one spouse will surrender future marital rights in return for an immediate transfer of cash or property.

In Merrill v. Fahs, below, the Supreme Court resolved the issue by looking to the estate tax law, which from 1932 forward had expressly addressed this issue in the form of § 2043(b). Section 2043(b)(1) expressly denies marital rights the status of consideration for purposes of determining whether a death transfer is made for consideration.

[¶ 3109]

MERRILL v. FAHS

Supreme Court of the United States, 1945.
324 U.S. 308.

FRANKFURTER, J.:

This is a companion case to Commissioner v. Wemyss, No. 629, just decided.

On March 7, 1939, taxpayer, the petitioner, made an antenuptial agreement with Kinta Desmare. Taxpayer, a resident of Florida, had been twice married and had three children and two grandchildren. He was a man of large resources, with cash and securities worth more than $5,000,000, and Florida real estate valued at $135,000. Miss Desmare's assets were negligible. By the arrangement entered into the day before their marriage, taxpayer agreed to set up within ninety days after marriage an irrevocable trust for $300,000, the provisions of which were to conform to Miss Desmare's wishes. The taxpayer was also to provide in his will for two additional trusts, one, likewise in the amount of $300,000, to contain the same limitations as the inter vivos trust, and the other, also in the amount of $300,000, for the benefit of their surviving children. In return Miss Desmare released all rights that she might acquire as wife or widow in taxpayer's property, both real and personal, excepting the right to maintenance and support. The inducements for this agreement were stated to be the contemplated marriage, desire to make fair requital for the release of marital rights, freedom for the taxpayer to make appropriate provisions for his children and other dependents, the uncertainty surrounding his financial future and marital tranquility. That such an antenuptial agreement is enforceable in Florida is not disputed, North v. Ringling, 149 Fla. 739, nor that Florida gives a wife an inchoate interest in all the husband's property, contingent during his life but absolute upon death. Florida Statutes (1941) § 731.34; Smith v. Hines, 10 Fla. 258; Henderson v. Usher, 125 Fla. 709. The parties married, and the agreement was fully carried out.

On their gift tax return for 1939, both reported the creation of the trust but claimed that no tax was due. The Commissioner, however, determined a deficiency of $99,000 in taxpayer's return in relation to the transfer of the $300,000. Upon the Commissioner's rejection of the taxpayer's claim for refund of the assessment paid by him, the present suit against the Collector was filed. The District Court sustained the taxpayer, 51 F.Supp. 120, but was reversed by the Circuit Court of Appeals for the Fifth Circuit, one judge dissenting. 142 F.2d 651. We granted certiorari in connection with Commissioner v. Wemyss [¶ 3007] and heard the two cases together. 323 U.S. 703.

* * * [L]ike the *Wemyss* case, this case turns on the proper application of § 503 of the Revenue Act of 1932 [1986 Code § 2512(b)]. In the interest of clarity we reprint it here: "Where property is transferred for less than an adequate and full consideration in money or money's worth, then the amount by which the value of the property exceeded the value of the consideration shall, for the purpose of the tax imposed by this title, be deemed a gift, and shall be included in computing the amount of gifts made during the calendar year." Taxpayer claims that Miss Desmare's relinquishment of her marital rights constituted "adequate and full consideration in money or money's worth." The Collector, relying on the construction of a like phrase in the estate tax, contends that release of marital rights does not furnish such "adequate and full consideration."

We put to one side the argument that in any event Miss Desmare's contingent interest in her husband's property had too many variables to be reducible to dollars and cents, and that any attempt to translate it into "money's worth" was "mere speculation bearing the delusive appearance of accuracy." Humes v. United States, 276 U.S. 487, 494. We shall go at once to the main issue.

The guiding light is what was said in Estate of Sanford v. Commissioner, 308 U.S. 39: "The gift tax was supplementary to the estate tax. The two are in pari materia and must be construed together." The phrase on the meaning of which decision must largely turn—that is, transfers for other than "an adequate and full consideration in money or money's worth"—came into the gift tax by way of estate tax provisions. It first appeared in the Revenue Act of 1926. Section 303(a)(1) of that Act, 44 Stat. 9, 72, allowed deductions from the value of the gross estate of claims against the estate to the extent that they were bona fide and incurred "for an adequate and full consideration in money or money's worth." It is important to note that the language of previous Acts which made the test "fair consideration" was thus changed after courts had given "fair consideration" an expansive construction.

The first modern estate tax law had included in the gross estate transfers in contemplation of, or intended to take effect in possession or enjoyment at, death, except "a bona fide sale for a fair consideration in money or money's worth." Section 202(b), Revenue Act of 1916 [1986 Code § 2053(c)(1)(A)]. Dower rights and other marital property rights were intended to be included in the gross estate, since they were considered merely an expectation, and in 1918 Congress specifically included them. Section 402(b), 40 Stat. 1057, 1097 [1986 Code § 2034]. This provision was for the purpose of clarifying the

¶ 3109

existing law. H. Rep. No. 767, 65th Cong., 2d Sess., p. 21. In 1924 Congress limited deductible claims against an estate to those supported by "a fair consideration in money or money's worth", § 303(a)(1), 43 Stat. 253, 305, employing the same standard applied to transfers in contemplation of death, H. Rep. No. 179, 68th Cong. 1st Sess., pp. 28, 66. Similar language was used in the gift tax, first imposed by the 1924 Act, by providing, "Where property is sold or exchanged for less than a fair consideration in money or money's worth" the excess shall be deemed a gift. Section 320, 43 Stat. 253, 314.

The two types of tax thus followed a similar course, like problems and purposes being expressed in like language. In this situation, courts held that "fair consideration" included relinquishment of dower rights. * * * Congress was thus led, as we have indicated, to substitute in the 1926 Revenue Act, the words "adequate and full consideration" in order to narrow the scope of tax exemptions. When the gift tax was reenacted in the 1932 Revenue Act, the restrictive phrase "adequate and full consideration" as found in the estate tax was taken over by the draftsman.

To be sure, in the 1932 Act Congress specifically provided that relinquishment of marital rights for purposes of the estate tax shall not constitute "consideration in money or money's worth." The Committees of Congress reported that if the value of relinquished marital interests "may, in whole or in part, constitute a consideration for an otherwise taxable transfer (as has been held so), or an otherwise unallowable deduction from the gross estate, the effect produced amounts to a subversion of the legislative intent.* * * "H. Rep. No. 708, 72d Cong., 1st Sess., p. 47; S. Rep. No. 665, 72d Cong., 1st Sess., p. 50. Plainly, the explicitness was one of cautious redundancy to prevent "subversion of the legislative intent." Without this specific provision, Congress undoubtedly intended the requirement of "adequate and fair consideration" to exclude relinquishment of dower and other marital rights with respects to the estate tax.

We believe that there is every reason for giving the same words in the gift tax the same reading. Correlation of the gift tax and the estate tax still requires legislative intervention. * * * But to interpret the same phrases in the two taxes concerning the same subject matter in different ways where obvious reasons do not compel divergent treatment is to introduce another and needless complexity into this already irksome situation. Here strong reasons urge identical construction. To hold otherwise would encourage tax avoidance. Commissioner v. Bristol, supra at 136; 2 Paul, Estate and Gift Taxation (1942) p. 1118. And it would not fulfill the purpose of the gift tax in discouraging family settlements so as to avoid high income surtaxes. H. Rep. No. 708, 72d Cong., 1st Sess., p. 28; S. Rep. No. 665, 72d Cong., 1st Sess., p. 40. There is thus every reason in this case to construe the provisions of both taxes harmoniously. * * *

Affirmed.

¶ 3109

Note

[¶ 3116]

Note that the transfer in *Merrill v. Fahs* was made in 1939—long before enactment of the marital deduction in 1948. Today the gift tax marital deduction, explored at ¶ 7163, would in appropriate circumstances shelter this transfer from gift tax.

[¶ 3121]

2. DIVORCE TRANSFERS

Application of the consideration rule to divorce transfers is controlled by § 2516. This section is founded on the premise that property transfers incident to divorce are fundamentally arm's-length transactions in which consideration of equal monetary value flows to each party. Therefore, the gift tax should not apply.

Section 2516 requires both a written agreement and a divorce decree. The divorce decree must occur during the three-year period beginning one year before the date of the agreement and ending two years after the agreement. If this test is met, all transfers pursuant to the agreement, whenever made, that are intended to either settle property rights or provide reasonable support for minority issue of the marriage, are treated as made for full and adequate consideration. Therefore, none of the qualifying payments will be treated as gifts for gift tax purposes.

If § 2516 is not satisfied, e.g., the divorce occurs outside the 3-year window, treatment of the transfers for gift tax purposes is less certain. Under language and reasoning adopted from the estate tax, there will not be full and adequate consideration if the payments are founded solely on a "promise or agreement." §§ 2043(b) and 2053(c)(1)(A). In the typical case, however, the property settlement agreement will be incorporated in the divorce decree, with the result that the payments will be viewed as founded not only on a "promise or agreement," but also on the decree. In that event §§ 2043(b) and 2053(c)(1)(A) will be inapplicable, and the transfers will generally be treated as made for full and adequate consideration. As a result, the transfers will not constitute gifts. Harris v. Commissioner, 340 U.S. 106 (1950). This rule, however, applies only if the divorce court has power to modify the divorcing parties' settlement agreement. Estate of Barrett v. Commissioner, 56 T.C. 1312 (1971).

The correlative estate tax provision—§ 2043(b)(2)—likewise treats transfers that satisfy § 2516(1) as made for adequate and full consideration. Therefore, an amount owed to a former spouse pursuant to a divorce decree is deductible from the decedent's gross estate pursuant to § 2053(a)(3) if the requirements of § 2516 are satisfied.

[¶ 3125]

3. DISCHARGE OF SUPPORT OBLIGATIONS

When a parent provides food and shelter for a minor child, is there a gift? The answer should be "no" on the ground that the parent receives full and adequate consideration in the form of discharge of a support obligation that could otherwise be enforced against the parent. Curiously, there is no authority directly stating this principle. Strong support, however, is provided by Rev. Rul. 68–379, 1968–2 C.B. 414, in which the IRS, in pre–§ 2516 days, ruled that a divorcing husband did not make a taxable gift when he transferred funds to his wife in settlement of her support rights.

The rule becomes less clear when the payments move beyond support to discretionary expenditures that might not be considered a part of the parent's support obligation, e.g., automobiles, recreational travel, and private school expenses. Because the extent of the support obligation is a matter of state law, the result can vary widely across the country.

Similarly unclear is the extent to which there is a support obligation after a child attains the age of majority, typically at age 18. The traditional view is that there is no such obligation if the child is competent. That would produce the result that any transfer to a child age 18 or over would constitute a gift. In many states, however, divorce courts have power to order divorcing parents to provide support, especially education, after majority. This responsibility is explored in Braun v. Commissioner, below at ¶ 31,097. If there is such a potential obligation after the age of majority, at least some transfers for the benefit of adult children might not constitute gifts.

The issue of what constitutes support necessarily arises under §§ 677(b) and 678(c), involving the grantor trust rules. Resolution of the issue in that context is explored below at ¶¶ 31,085–31,109.

With the age of majority typically at eighteen and college tuition at high levels in many cases, parents funding higher education for their children could be viewed as making substantial taxable gifts. Two exclusions, however, tend to prevent this. The first is the § 2503(b) annual per donee exclusion, which permits husband and wife collectively to make substantial transfers entirely free of the gift tax. See ¶ 7013, below. The other is the § 2503(e) exclusion for tuition and medical expenses, which permits tax-free direct payment of tuition, over and above the § 2503(b) exclusion, without limit as to amount. See ¶ 7157, below.

[¶ 3127]

4. ADEQUACY OF CONSIDERATION

Under § 2512, the presence of consideration for purposes of contract law does not assure that the transfer will escape the gift tax. The value of the consideration must equal the value of the property transferred. If the consideration received has less value than the consideration given, the difference will be taxable as a gift. Reg. § 25.2512–8 adds that the consideration must be reducible to money or money's worth. For example, the value of living expenses furnished for the family of a taxpayer's adult son was a taxable gift because the son's family returned nothing but love and affection. Rev. Rul. 54–343, 1954–2 C.B. 318.

Regulation § 25.2512–8 softens this rule by stating that even if the consideration is not objectively equal in value to the property transferred, the

IRS will not assert gift tax liability if the transfer was made in the ordinary course of business. This alleviates the possibility of imposing the gift tax on a seller who, in a bad bargain, has not received the full value of the property sold, a result that would only compound the seller's misfortune.

[¶ 3133]

5. PAYMENT OF GIFT TAX AS CONSIDERATION

Sometimes a donor is willing to make a gift on the condition that the donee pay the gift tax. For example, a donor parent may wish to transfer stock in a closely held family corporation to a son or daughter, but may not wish to give up the cash necessary to pay the gift tax on such a transfer. In that event, the son or daughter may agree to pay the tax.

Because the primary obligation to pay the gift tax is imposed on the donor by § 2502(c), the donee's payment of the tax must be viewed as an offsetting benefit to the donor. Therefore, the "net gift" that is taxable is the difference between the value of the property transferred and the amount of the donor's gift tax obligation discharged by the donee. The net gift rule is fully developed in Rev. Rul. 75–72, 1975–1 C.B. 310. This ruling describes the algebraic formula that may be necessary to determine both the amount of the gift and the gift tax due. Such a formula is necessary because the donee's commitment to pay the tax reduces the amount of the gift, which in turn reduces the tax due, and so on.

A net gift may have income tax consequences as well. The income tax issue arises if the amount of gift tax discharged by the donee exceeds the donor's basis for the property transferred. The Supreme Court addressed this issue in Diedrich v. Commissioner, 457 U.S. 191 (1982). In one of the two cases addressed in *Diedrich*, the donor's basis for the stock transferred was only $8,742, and the gift tax liability discharged by the donee was $232,630. The Supreme Court, relying on Old Colony Trust Co. v. Commissioner, 279 U.S. 716 (1929), concluded that for income tax purposes there was a sale, and the amount realized by the donor was the amount of the donor's tax obligation discharged by the donee, or $232,630. Therefore, the donor realized a taxable gain of $232,630 less $8,742, or $223,888.

[¶ 3151]

6. GIFTS OF ENCUMBERED PROPERTY

The possibility that a gift may cause imposition of income tax liability on the donor seems a strange result. Nevertheless, it is an important principle that must be borne in mind as a donor chooses the property to be given to the objects of her bounty.

Although *Diedrich*, discussed at ¶ 3133, directly addresses only the circumstance in which the benefit to the donor is the donee's payment of gift tax, there is equivalent benefit to the donor if the transfer has the effect of relieving the donor of any other liability with respect to the property transferred. This result is founded on the Supreme Court's holding in Crane v. Commissioner, 331 U.S. 1 (1947), that a party who conveys property subject

¶ 3127

to a liability must be treated as receiving consideration in the amount of the liability because the transferee can be expected to discharge the debt.

For example, assume that a mother owns farmland with a fair market value of $350,000 and a basis to her of $120,000, but encumbered by a mortgage securing an indebtedness of $170,000. If the mother transfers the land to her son as an inter-vivos gift, the annual per donee exclusion and unified credit may prevent the imposition of any gift tax. The transfer, however, will cause a realized taxable gain to the mother of $50,000—the amount by which the $170,000 mortgage exceeds the mother's $120,000 basis for the property. Estate of Levine v. Commissioner, 634 F.2d 12 (2d Cir.1980).

Sometimes gain can be avoided by selecting for the transfer property that is not encumbered by a mortgage in excess of the donor's basis. Alternatively, it may be possible to shift the encumbrance to other property that is not to be transferred.

Note that the "mortgage over basis" problem has no application to transfers between spouses or pursuant to divorce. Section 1041 provides nonrecognition treatment for all such transfers except those in trust. Reg. § 1.1041–1T(d), Q–12; § 1041(e).

[¶ 3169]

7. POLITICAL CONTRIBUTIONS

Application of the consideration test to contributions to political parties and candidates could raise interesting questions. That inquiry, however, is obviated by § 2501(a)(4), which provides that any transfer to a "political organization" is excluded from taxable gifts. Section 2501(a)(4) refers to § 527(e), which defines "political organization" as any committee, fund, or organization organized and operated primarily for the nomination, election, or appointment of an individual to a federal, state, or local office. There is no limitation on the amount excluded by § 2501(a)(4).

¶ 3169

Chapter 4

WHEN A GIFT OCCURS

A. INTRODUCTION

[¶ 4001]

Usually, it is easy to determine when a gift occurs. A mother hands $100 in cash to her daughter. A father delivers to his son an executed deed conveying real estate to the son.

In other cases, the timing of the gift is less clear. If the donor retains control over the property—either directly or indirectly—completion of the gift may be prevented because the donor has the power to recall the property. More difficult questions arise if the donor retains not the power to revoke the gift, but only a power to modify the terms of the gift.

Timing questions also arise when multiple steps are necessary to place full ownership in the donee. In the case of a gift by check, for example, does the gift occur when the check is delivered to the donee, when the donee deposits the check in his or her account, or when the check is ultimately paid by the drawee bank?

Timing questions have obvious importance in determining when—or if— the gift tax applies. Often such questions arise at death, in circumstances in which the decedent made an arguably incomplete transfer prior to death. If the transfer did not constitute a completed gift during the decedent's life, the asset purportedly transferred during life will generally remain a part of the decedent's gross estate for estate tax purposes and will therefore be subject to the estate tax. On the other hand, if the transfer was a completed gift during life, the usual result is that the estate tax does not apply to the asset.

The timing of a gift can be important even if death does not intervene. Assume that in both Year 1 and Year 2 the § 2503(b) annual exclusion amount is $12,000. Further assume that Grandmother transfers a check for $12,000 to Grandson in December of Year 1, followed by another $12,000 check in January of Year 2. If Grandson holds the Year 1 check and does not deposit it until Year 2, and this causes the Year 1 transfer to be treated as not completed until Year 2, Grandmother may have lost the availability of the $12,000 annual per donee exclusion in Year 1, and her gifts to Grandson will total $24,000 in Year 2. Only $12,000 of this amount can be sheltered by the

$12,000 annual per donee exclusion. Grandmother will have made a $12,000 taxable gift in Year 2.

The time of completion of the gift also has valuation ramifications. Assume that the donor purports to transfer real estate by gift in Year 1, when the real estate is worth $200,000. Assume further, however, that the gift is treated as incomplete because the donor has retained control over the property, and the donor does not surrender control until Year 4, when the real estate is worth $500,000. The gift is not complete until Year 4, and the value of the gift is determined at that time. For gift tax purposes there is a gift of $500,000—not $200,000.

B. RETAINED CONTROL

[¶ 4007]

The most difficult questions involving timing of the gift arise when the donor retains control of some kind over the gift. If the donor retains an unlimited power to revoke the gift, it is clear that no gift has occurred. If the retained power is less extensive, however, the timing question becomes more difficult.

1. THE CONTROL CONCEPT

[¶ 4013]

ESTATE OF SANFORD v. COMMISSIONER

Supreme Court of the United States, 1939.
308 U.S. 39.

MR. JUSTICE STONE delivered the opinion of the Court:

This and its companion case, No. 37, Rasquin v. Humphreys, present the single question of statutory construction whether in the case of an inter vivos transfer of property in trust, by a donor reserving to himself the power to designate new beneficiaries other than himself, the gift becomes complete and subject to the gift tax imposed by the federal revenue laws at the time of the relinquishment of the power. Co-relative questions, important only if a negative answer is given to the first one, are whether the gift becomes complete and taxable when the trust is created or, in the case where the donor has reserved a power of revocation for his own benefit and has relinquished it before relinquishing the power to change beneficiaries, whether the gift first becomes complete and taxable at the time of relinquishing the power of revocation.

In 1913, before the enactment of the first gift tax statute of 1924, decedent created a trust of personal property for the benefit of named beneficiaries, reserving to himself the power to terminate the trust in whole or in part, or to modify it. In 1919 he surrendered the power to revoke the trust by an appropriate writing in which he reserved "the right to modify any or all of the trusts" but provided that this right "shall in no way be deemed or

¶ 4013

construed to include any right or privilege" in the donor "to withdraw principal or income from any trust." In August, 1924, after the effective date of the gift tax statute, decedent renounced his remaining power to modify the trust. After his death in 1928, the Commissioner following the decision in Hesslein v. Hoey, 91 F. (2d) 954, in 1937, ruled that the gift became complete and taxable only upon decedent's final renunciation of his power to modify the trusts and gave notice of a tax deficiency accordingly.

The order of the Board of Tax Appeals sustaining the tax was affirmed by the Court of Appeals for the Third Circuit, 103 F.2d 81, which followed the decision of the Court of Appeals for the second circuit in Hesslein v. Hoey, supra, in which we had denied certiorari, 302 U.S. 756. In the *Hesslein* case, as in the *Humphreys* case now before us, a gift in trust with the reservation of a power in the donor to alter the disposition of the property in any way not beneficial to himself, was held to be incomplete and not subject to the gift tax under the 1932 Act so long as the donor retained that power.

We granted certiorari in this case May 15, 1939, and in the *Humphreys* case May 22, 1939, upon the representation of the Government that it has taken inconsistent positions with respect to the question involved in the two cases and that because of this fact and of the doubt of the correctness of the decision in the *Hesslein* case decision of the question by this Court is desirable in order to remove the resultant confusion in the administration of the revenue laws.

It has continued to take these inconsistent positions here, stating that it is unable to determine which construction of the statute will be most advantageous to the Government in point of revenue collected. It argues in this case that the gift did not become complete and taxable until surrender by the donor of his reserved power to designate new beneficiaries of the trusts. In the *Humphreys* case it argues that the gift upon trust with power reserved to the donor, not afterward relinquished, to change the beneficiaries was complete and taxable when the trust was created. It concedes by its brief that "a decision favorable to the government in either case will necessarily preclude a favorable decision in the other."

In ascertaining the correct construction of the statutes taxing gifts, it is necessary to read them in the light of the closely related provisions of the revenue laws taxing transfers at death, as they have been interpreted by our decisions. Section 319 of the Revenue Act of 1924, 43 Stat. 253, reenacted as Sec. 501 of the 1932 Act, 47 Stat. 169, imposed a graduated tax upon gifts. It supplemented that laid on transfers at death, which had long been a feature of the revenue laws. When the gift tax was enacted Congress was aware that the essence of a transfer is the passage of control over the economic benefits of property rather than any technical changes in its title. Following the enactment of the gift tax statute, this Court in Reinecke v. Northern Trust Company, 278 U.S. 339 (1929) held that the relinquishment at death of a power of revocation of a trust for the benefit of its donor was a taxable transfer. * * * and * * * the relinquishment by a donor at death of a reserved power to modify the trust except in his own favor is likewise a transfer of the property which could constitutionally be taxed under the

¶ 4013

provisions of § 302(d) of the 1926 Revenue Act (reenacting in substance 302(d) of the 1924 Act) [1986 Code § 2036(a)] although enacted after the creation of the trust. * * *

The rationale of decision in both cases is that "taxation is not so much concerned with the refinements of title as it is with the actual command over the property taxed" * * * and that a retention of control over the disposition of the trust property, whether for the benefit of the donor or others, renders the gift incomplete until the power is relinquished whether in life or at death. The rule was thus established, and has ever since been consistently followed by the Court, that a transfer of property upon trust, with power reserved to the donor either to revoke it and recapture the trust property or to modify its terms so as to designate new beneficiaries other than himself is incomplete, and becomes complete so as to subject the transfer to death taxes only on relinquishment of the power at death.

There is nothing in the language of the statute, and our attention has not been directed to anything in its legislative history to suggest that Congress had any purpose to tax gifts before the donor had fully parted with his interest in the property given, or that the test of the completeness of the taxed gift was to be any different from that to be applied in determining whether the donor has retained an interest such that it becomes subject to the estate tax upon its extinguishment at death. The gift tax was supplementary to the estate tax. The two are in *pari materia* and must be construed together. * * * An important, if not the main, purpose of the gift tax was to prevent or compensate for avoidance of death taxes by taxing the gifts of property inter vivos which, but for the gifts, would be subject in its original or converted form to the tax laid upon transfers at death.

Section 322 of the 1924 Act provides that when a tax has been imposed by § 319 upon a gift, the value of which is required by any provision of the statute taxing the estate to be included in the gross estate, the gift tax is to be credited on the estate tax. The two taxes are thus not always mutually exclusive as in the case of gifts made in contemplation of death which are complete and taxable when made, and are also required to be included in the gross estate for purposes of the death tax. But § 322 is without application unless there is a gift inter vivos which is taxable independently of any requirement that it shall be included in the gross estate. Property transferred in trust subject to a power of control over its disposition reserved to the donor is likewise required by § 302(d) to be included in the gross estate. But it does not follow that the transfer in trust is also taxable as a gift. The point was decided in the *Guggenheim* case where it was held that a gift upon trust, with power in the donor to revoke it is not taxable as a gift because the transfer is incomplete, and that the transfer whether inter vivos or at death becomes complete and taxable only when the power of control is relinquished. We think, as was pointed out in the Guggenheim case, supra, 285, that the gift tax statute does not contemplate two taxes upon gifts not made in contemplation of death, one upon the gift when a trust is created or when the power of revocation, if any, is relinquished, and another on the transfer of the same property at death because the gift previously made was incomplete.

¶ 4013

It is plain that the contention of the taxpayer in this case that the gift becomes complete and taxable upon the relinquishment of the donor's power to revoke the trust cannot be sustained unless we are to hold, contrary to the policy of the statute and the reasoning in the *Guggenheim* case, that a second tax will be incurred upon the donor's relinquishment at death of his power to select new beneficiaries, or unless as an alternative we are to abandon our ruling in the *Porter* case. The Government does not suggest, even in its argument in the *Humphreys* case, that we should depart from our earlier rulings, and we think it clear that we should not do so both because we are satisfied with the reasoning upon which they rest and because departure from either would produce inconsistencies in the law as serious and confusing as the inconsistencies in administrative practice from which the Government now seeks relief.

There are other persuasive reasons why the taxpayer's contention cannot be sustained. By §§ 315(b), 324 and more specifically by § 510 of the 1932 Act [1986 Code § 6324(b)], the donee of any gift is made personally liable for the tax to the extent of the value of the gift if the tax is not paid by the donor. It can hardly be supposed that Congress intended to impose personal liability upon the donee of a gift of property, so incomplete that he might be deprived of it by the donor the day after he had paid the tax. Further, § 321(b)(1) [1986 Code § 2522(a)] exempts from the tax, gifts to religious, charitable, and educational corporations and the like. A gift would seem not to be complete, for purposes of the tax, where the donor has reserved the power to determine whether the donees ultimately entitled to receive and enjoy the property are of such a class as to exempt the gift from taxation. Apart from other considerations we should hesitate to accept as correct a construction under which it could plausibly be maintained that a gift in trust for the benefit of charitable corporations is then complete so that the taxing statute becomes operative and the gift escapes the tax even though the donor should later change the beneficiaries to the non-exempt class through exercise of a power to modify the trust in any way not beneficial to himself.

The argument of petitioner that the construction which the Government supports here, but assails in the *Humphreys* case, affords a ready means of evasion of the gift tax is not impressive. It is true, of course, that under it gift taxes will not be imposed on transactions which fall short of being completed gifts. But if for that reason they are not taxed as gifts they remain subject to death taxes assessed at higher rates, and the Government gets its due, which was precisely the end sought by the enactment of the gift tax.

* * *

Affirmed.

Note

[¶ 4019]

The *Sanford* result is now codified in Reg. § 25.2511–2(c).

In *Sanford* the Court implied that the test of completeness for gift tax purposes is the same as that applied under the estate tax. If that were the

¶ 4013

case, the gift tax and estate tax would always be mutually exclusive. In other words, a gift treated as complete for gift tax purposes would never be included in the gross estate for estate tax purposes, and an incomplete gift would never be subject to the gift tax, but would be included in the gross estate. Four years after *Sanford*, however, the Supreme Court retreated from this position and squarely held that the gross estate may include an asset that was taxed as a completed gift during life. Smith v. Shaughnessy, 318 U.S. 176 (1943).

For example, assume that a mother transfers property to a trust for her son and daughter. The trust instrument provides that the daughter is to receive the trust income until she attains age 25, at which time the son is to receive the principal. The mother reserves the power, with the consent of the son and daughter, to pay income or principal to the mother's sister. This would be treated as a completed gift of the entire trust property for gift tax purposes because the son and daughter have interests adverse to the mother's exercise of her retained power. Reg. § 25.2511–2(e). Nevertheless, if the mother dies prior to the daughter's attainment of age 25, the entire value of the trust property at the time of the mother's death will be included in the mother's gross estate for estate tax purposes. See § 2038(a)(1) and Reg. § 20.2038–1(a), discussed in Chapter 19.

This scenario appears to impose double taxation on the same trust property—once under the gift tax and a second time under the estate tax. That is not the result, however, because double taxation is prevented by two provisions. First, the last sentence of § 2001(b) prohibits the inclusion in "adjusted taxable gifts" of property that is includible in the decedent's gross estate. In other words, at mother's death only the current value of the trust property is taxed, and there is no double inclusion. Second, § 2001(b)(2) permits the mother's executor to deduct from the estate tax due at death any gift tax allocable to the inter-vivos transfer. In other words, to the extent the mother paid gift tax on the original transfer in trust, she will be fully credited with that payment.

[¶ 4037]

2. THE SUBSTANTIAL ADVERSE INTEREST CONCEPT

If the grantor learns that her retention of control over a trust will have the effect of including the trust in her gross estate, she might seek to avoid this rule by requiring that another person acquiesce in the grantor's exercise of control. Naturally, the grantor is likely to confer such a power on a friend or a bank that the grantor expects to be compliant. The result is that the requirement of acquiescence by a third party may have little or no effect on the grantor's retained control.

Avoidance of estate tax in these circumstances is prevented by §§ 2036(a)(2) and 2038(a)(1), which, under certain circumstances, require inclusion of an asset in the decedent's gross estate if, at the date of death, the asset is subject to a power of disposition exercisable by the decedent either alone or in conjunction with any other person. See Chapters 18 and 19.

A corollary is applied to gifts: a gift is neither complete nor taxable if the donor has retained a power over the property, either alone or in conjunction with any other person. Under the gift tax, however, there is an important exception not found in the estate tax. The gift will be considered complete and therefore taxable if the person holding power jointly with the donor has a "substantial adverse interest in the disposition of the transferred property or the income therefrom." Reg. § 25.2511-2(e). The problem is what constitutes a "substantial adverse interest."

[¶ 4043]

COMMISSIONER v. PROUTY

United States Court of Appeals, First Circuit, 1940.
115 F.2d 331.

MAGRUDER, J.:

In 1923 Olive H. Prouty, the taxpayer herein, set up three trusts. Between 1923 and 1931 the grantor, by virtue of power reserved to her, made various amendments to the trust instruments. The Commissioner ruled that the gifts were not complete in 1931; that under Section 501 of the Revenue Act of 1932 (47 Stat. 245), as amended by Section 511 of the Revenue Act of 1934 (48 Stat. 758) [1986 Code § 2501(a)(1)], gift taxes became due upon amendment of each of the trusts on January 2, 1935, whereby the grantor finally relinquished all reserved power to revoke or amend the trust instruments. Upon petition for redetermination of the deficiency, the Board of Tax Appeals held with the taxpayer that the gifts had been completed prior to the enactment of the gift tax in 1932, and decided that there was no deficiency in gift taxes for the year 1935. The correctness of this decision by the Board is now before us on petition for review.

After the amendments in 1931 each of the three trust instruments contained a provision reserving to the grantor a power to revoke or amend, with the written consent of her husband, Lewis I. Prouty, during his lifetime, and thereafter, alone. As a condition precedent to the exercise of this power in a given calendar year, the grantor had to serve upon the trustee, during the preceding year, a formal notification of intention to revoke or amend.

* * *

If, therefore, Lewis Prouty is determined to be a person not having a substantial adverse interest in the disposition of the trust corpus or income therefrom, the gifts were not complete in 1931 and gift taxes accrued in 1935 upon the grantor's unqualified relinquishment of her power to revoke or amend.

We shall refer first to Trusts Nos. 2 and 3, because in them we think it clear that Lewis did not have a substantial adverse interest as of 1931.

In Trust No. 2 the grantor declared herself trustee of certain securities, with direction to the trustee to pay out of the net income the sum of $2,500 a year to Lewis I. Prouty during his lifetime, "and to add the balance of the net income to the principal and invest it as a part thereof during the lifetime of Lewis I. Prouty, with full power and authority in the sole and uncontrolled discretion of said Olive Higgins Prouty as long as she shall be the Trustee hereunder from time to time to pay to said Lewis I. Prouty and said Jane Prouty [a daughter], or either of them, in such proportions as the said Trustee may see fit the whole or any part of the principal of the trust fund if said Trustee deems it necessary or advisable for the maintenance, support and welfare of said Lewis I. Prouty and said Jane Prouty or either of them. . . ." It was provided that Lewis would succeed as trustee if he outlived the grantor; but in that event Lewis as trustee would not be empowered to make any payments to himself, other than the annuity, though he could in his "sole and uncontrolled discretion" make payments of the whole or any part of the principal to Jane Prouty if he deemed it advisable for her maintenance, support and welfare. At Lewis' death the property was to pass to Jane, with various remainders over. The power in the grantor to amend or revoke the trust, with the consent of Lewis, has already been mentioned.

Trust No. 3 was the same as Trust No. 2, except that Richard Prouty, a son, was substituted for Jane.

So far as the annuity is concerned, the Commissioner conceded that an effective gift thereof in each trust had been made prior to the passage of the Revenue Act of 1932. Accordingly, in determining the deficiency, he subtracted the value of the annuities, calculated on the basis of Lewis' life expectancy, and subjected the remaining value of the corpus of each trust to the gift tax. This method of apportionment might be objected to on the ground that if the annuity constituted a substantial adverse interest, it was an interest in the whole of the corpus out of the net income of which the annuity was payable, so that the gift should be treated as having been completed in 1931 as to all the trust res. But such an interpretation would afford an obvious facility for tax evasion, particularly with respect to the grantor's income tax in the application of the comparable provisions of Section 166 dealing with revocable trusts. To the extent that a proposed partial revocation would leave Lewis' annuity intact, he would have no substantial countervailing interest tending to induce him to withstand the grantor's wishes. We think that the Commissioner was justified in deducting the capital value of the annuity and in treating the transfer in 1935 upon relinquishment of the power as being a gift merely of the remainder of the corpus after such deduction. Therefore, in considering whether Lewis had a substantial adverse interest in Trusts Nos. 2 and 3, we may leave out of account the annuities to him provided in these trusts. * * *

The only other interest which Lewis had in the corpus of Trusts Nos. 2 and 3 was the possibility that, under the provision previously quoted, his wife, as trustee, might in her "sole and uncontrolled discretion" pay over to him such portions of the principal as she might deem advisable for his maintenance, support and welfare. But the main purpose of the trust was to accumulate the income during Lewis' lifetime, and the record does not suggest the existence of circumstances indicating any likelihood that Lewis would ever receive anything by virtue of this provision. Certainly Lewis, while receiving

¶ 4043

aggregate annuities of $7,500 from the three trusts, could never obtain a court decree compelling the trustee to give him something under this discretionary power. That such a remote and speculative possibility of gain does not constitute a "substantial adverse interest" was ruled by this court on quite similar facts in Fulham v. Commissioner, 110 F. (2d) 916, 918.

Another point was stressed by the Board in connection with Trusts Nos. 2 and 3, namely, that in each case the corpus at the death of Lewis was to go to his children. "It is natural to assume," said the Board, "that his desire and concern for the support, maintenance, and welfare of his children after his death would prompt him to resist any effort on the part of the grantor of the trust to alter, amend or revoke that part of the trust so as to revest in her title to such property." No doubt this is an interest of a sort. But we think the phrase "substantial adverse interest," as it was used in Section 501 (c) of the Revenue Act of 1932 and as it is used in Sections 166 and 167, means a direct legal or equitable interest in the trust property, and not merely a sentimental or parental interest in seeing the trust fulfilled for the advantage of other beneficiaries. Loeb v. Commissioner, 113 F. (2d) 664, 666.

Trust No. 1 presents a different situation. We may lay to one side the annuity of $2,500 payable to Lewis; and also the possibility that Lewis might receive something through the exercise by the grantor as trustee of her discretion to pay to Lewis such part of the principal as she might deem advisable for his maintenance, support and welfare. Under this trust instrument Lewis had, in addition, two important interests affecting the whole of the corpus, interests which were lacking in the other two trusts. (1) If he should outlive the grantor, the corpus was to pass at his death as he should by his last will direct and appoint. The prospect of acquiring this power of disposition certainly would furnish a pecuniary motive, far from negligible, tending to induce Lewis to stand out against any desire of the grantor to revoke the trust. Cf. Curry v. McCanless, 307 U.S. 357, 371. (2) If he should outlive the grantor, he would succeed as trustee and, as such trustee, would have full discretion to pay to himself the whole or any part of the principal should he deem it advisable for his own maintenance, support and welfare. In Cox v. Commissioner, 110 F. (2d) 934, such a power held by a grantor-trustee was held to be so substantial as to amount in effect to a power in the grantor to revest in himself the corpus of the trust estate and hence to subject the grantor to an income tax under Section 166; this despite the fact that the power may have been technically a fiduciary one.

Examining these intimate family trusts, one must recognize an element of unreality in the inquiry whether a beneficiary's interest is substantially adverse to the grantor. The supposition is that, given a sufficient stake in the trust, the beneficiary is not likely to yield to a wish of the grantor to revoke the trust. In many cases the grantor may have full confidence in the compliant disposition of the member of the family he selects to share his power of revocation, even though such member is named as beneficiary of a handsome interest in the trust. The very fact that the grantor reserved a power to revoke indicates a mental reservation on his part as to the finality of the gift; and if the grantor wishes to hold on to a power of recapture, * * * it

¶ 4043

stands to reason he will vest the veto power in someone whose acquiescence he can count on. However, we cannot read into the gift tax, any more than into Sections 166 and 167, the proposition that a member of the grantor's immediate family can never be deemed to have "a substantial adverse interest." So far as the gift tax is concerned, it is fair enough to take the grantor at his word. As to the income tax, it might be rational for Congress to tax all family income as a unit. But as the law now stands—both gift tax and income tax—we must give weight to the formal rights conferred in the trust instrument in determining whether a given beneficiary has a substantial adverse interest, bearing in mind the admonition of Helvering v. Clifford, 309 U.S. 331, 335, that "where the grantor is the trustee and the beneficiaries are members of his family group, special scrutiny of the arrangement is necessary. * * *"

The present case is on the border line, but considering the aggregate of Lewis' interests under the terms of Trust No. 1, we are not persuaded that the Board was in error in its conclusion that Lewis had a "substantial adverse interest." It is true that Lewis will have to outlive the grantor to reap the benefits, but in the normal vicissitudes of life the chance of his survival is substantial. Lewis has a contingent interest in the whole of the current income, for if the trustee does not pay it to him under her discretionary power, it must be added to the corpus and thus becomes subject to Lewis' testamentary power of appointment. A substantial chance of coming into a good thing may constitute a "substantial adverse interest"; especially where, as here, it is a chance to control the disposition of the entire corpus of a large estate. It is a chance one would not lightly relinquish. The interest need not be presently vested in possession and enjoyment. See Jane B. Shiverick, 37 B. T. A. 454.

The Commissioner further contends, however, that a gift is not complete even where the grantor's reserved power to revoke is subject to the veto of a person who does have a substantial adverse interest; and that therefore a gift tax became payable in 1935 when the grantor relinquished this power. * * * It is pointed out that when such a power so restricted is extinguished by death of the grantor, the corpus is treated as part of the gross estate of the grantor for purposes of the estate tax. * * * And in Estate of Sanford v. Commissioner, 308 U.S. 39, the court said that the gift tax is supplementary to the estate tax; that the two are in pari materia and must be construed together; that "There is nothing in the language of the statute, and our attention has not been directed to anything in its legislative history to suggest that Congress had any purpose to tax gifts before the donor had fully parted with his interest in the property given, or that the test of the completeness of the taxed gift was to be any different from that to be applied in determining whether the donor has retained an interest such that it becomes subject to the estate tax upon its extinguishment at death." Nevertheless, as the court pointed out (308 U.S. at 45), the two taxes * * * are not always mutually exclusive.

[W]e conclude that since Lewis had a substantial adverse interest in Trust No. 1 as of 1931, the gift was complete at that time, despite the power

¶ 4043

of revocation reserved to the grantor in conjunction with Lewis. As a result, Trust No. 1 escapes both the gift tax and the estate tax. However, our decision is not a precedent endangering the revenue. The tax is avoided here only because the gift was made before the gift tax was enacted. These family trusts, created since 1932, will inevitably be subject to the gift tax, or the estate tax, or in some instances, both. The Commissioner's argument, advanced to meet the exigencies of the case at bar, if accepted and applied in future cases, would only result in postponing the incidence of the tax.

We have not overlooked an additional argument advanced by the Commissioner. Leaving aside the question whether Lewis had a substantial adverse interest in Trust No. 1, the Commissioner contends that the "bundle of rights and powers" retained by Mrs. Prouty as of 1931 was such that she remained in substance the owner of the corpus, and that the income of the trust was then taxable to her under Section 22 (a) by the doctrine of Helvering v. Clifford, 309 U.S. 331; that the gift being regarded as incomplete for purposes of the income tax should be similarly regarded for purposes of the gift tax. The answer is twofold. In the first place, it is far from clear that the premise is correct as to the applicability of Helvering v. Clifford. Cf. Commissioner v. Branch, decided by this court October 23, 1940. Second, the gift tax does not seem to be so closely integrated with the income tax that decisions like the Clifford case extending the applicability of Section 22 (a) to the grantor of a trust, must necessarily be read as holding that no gift tax was payable upon the creation of the trust. It may be frankly recognized, however, that the interrelation of the income, estate, and gift taxes presents many puzzling problems which deserve the attention of Congress.

The decision of the Board of Tax Appeals is affirmed as to Trust No. 1 and reversed as to Trusts Nos. 2 and 3; and the case is remanded to the Board for further proceedings not inconsistent with this opinion.

Note

[¶ 4049]

Regulation § 25.2511–2(e) does not entirely solve the problem of collusion. A beneficiary with a substantial adverse interest could make a secret bargain with the donor to agree to any exercise of power the donor might desire. But such arrangements would be stricken down as shams. See, e.g., Camp v. Commissioner, 195 F.2d 999 (1st Cir.1952). Further explication of the "substantial adverse interest" concept for gift tax purposes is found in *Camp*, where the following observations are offered:

1. If the trust instrument gives a designated beneficiary any interest in the corpus of the trust property or of the income therefrom, which is capable of monetary valuation, and the donor reserves no power to withdraw that interest, in whole or in part, except with the consent of such designated beneficiary, then the gift of that particular interest will be deemed to be complete, for the purposes of the gift tax. See accord, our discussion in Commissioner v. Prouty, 115 Fed. (2d) 331, 334 (1940), with reference to the annuities to the husband in Trusts 2 and 3. * * *

¶ 4043

2. If the only power reserved by the donor is a power to revoke the entire trust instrument (not a power to modify the trust in any particular), and this power may be exercised only in conjunction with a designated beneficiary who is given a substantial adverse interest in the disposition of the trust property or the income therefrom, then the transfer in trust will be deemed to be a present gift of the entire corpus of the trust, for purposes of the gift tax. In such cases, the gift of the entire corpus will be deemed to have been "put beyond recall" by the donor himself.

3. If the trust instrument reserves to the donor a general power to alter, amend or revoke, in whole or in part, and this power is to be exercised only in conjunction with a designated beneficiary who has received an interest in the corpus or income capable of monetary valuation, then the transfer in trust will be deemed to be a completed gift, for purposes of the gift tax, only as to the interest of such designated beneficiary having a veto over the exercise of the power. As to the interests of the other beneficiaries, the gifts will be deemed to be incomplete, for as to such interests the donor reserves the power to take them away in conjunction with a person who has no interest in the trust adverse to such withdrawal. * * *

195 F.2d at 1004.

[¶ 4055]

3. INFORMAL RESERVATIONS

In most cases, the presence of a completed gift is determined by the documents executed by the parties. However, if the actual disposition of the property is in fact controlled by oral understandings or other directions contrary to the documents, the facts—not the documents—will determine taxability.

In Warner v. Commissioner, 49 T.C.M. (CCH) 5, T.C.M. (P–H) ¶ 84,582 (1984), the donor, seeking to shelter his assets from his wife's divorce claims, transferred property to a bank as trustee of an ostensibly irrevocable trust. However, the responsible bank officer orally agreed to dispose of the trust assets as dictated by the donor and agreed to return the assets to the donor upon the donor's request. The bank did in fact honor the donor's directions. The Tax Court held that the donor had not in fact relinquished control; hence there was no completed gift.

[¶ 4059]

4. RETENTION OF POWER TO CHANGE THE TRUSTEE

The donor may transfer property to a trustee (other than himself) who has power to modify beneficial enjoyment. If the donor can replace the trustee with himself, it seems clear that the trustee's powers must be imputed to the donor, necessarily making the gift incomplete. A similar doctrine is applied to include the trust property in the decedent's estate under §§ 2036 and 2038. See ¶ 18,184 and ¶ 19,139.

At one time the IRS sought to expand this rule to circumstances in which the donor retains a power to replace the trustee, not with the donor, but with another person or entity of the donor's choosing. The IRS reasoned that the donor could search among trustee candidates and ultimately find one willing to do the donor's bidding, thereby giving the donor effective control over the trustee's exercise of discretion. Under this rationale, the transfer in trust would not be a completed gift, and the trust property would be included in the donor's gross estate for estate tax purposes. The IRS view was rejected for purposes of both the gift tax (Estate of Vak v. Commissioner, 973 F.2d 1409 (8th Cir.1992)) and the estate tax (Estate of Wall, ¶ 18,185). Ultimately, the IRS conceded defeat and acknowledged that, if the donor retains power to replace the trustee with a person who is neither the grantor nor a person related or subordinate to the grantor (as defined in § 672(c)), the retention of such a power will neither cause the transfer in trust to be an incomplete gift nor require inclusion of the trust property in the donor's gross estate. See the further exploration of this issue beginning at ¶ 18,183.

Problems

[¶ 4061]

The problems below provide an opportunity to apply the tests for a completed gift set forth in Reg. § 25.2511–2 and the materials in ¶ 4001 through ¶ 4059. In each case, assume that the donor is not the trustee unless otherwise indicated. Further assume that the grantor has not retained any power over the trust unless otherwise indicated.

In each case, determine whether and when there is a completed gift and the interest that constitutes the gift.

1. Donor places $100,000 in trust for 11 years, income to be paid to A, remainder to donor.

2. Donor places $100,000 in trust for 11 years, income to be paid to A and B in such proportions as the trustee designates, remainder to donor.

3. Donor places $100,000 in trust for 11 years with the donor named as trustee, income to be paid to A, remainder to C.

4. Donor places $100,000 in trust for 11 years with the donor named as trustee, and with income to be paid to A and B in such proportions as the trustee in his uncontrolled discretion designates, remainder to C.

5. Donor places $100,000 in trust for 11 years with the donor named as trustee, and with income to be paid to A and/or B "as necessary for medical care," remainder to C.

6. Donor places $100,000 in trust for 11 years, with the donor and E named as trustees, and with income to be paid to A and B in such proportions as the trustees in their uncontrolled discretion designate, remainder to C. E has no beneficial interest in the trust.

¶ 4059

7. Donor places $100,000 in trust for 11 years, income to be paid to A, remainder to C. Donor reserves the right to revoke the trust during the first five years.

8. Donor places $100,000 in trust for 11 years, income is to be paid to A, who is to receive the remainder as well. However, the donor reserves the power to require that the income be accumulated and added to principal during the 11 years.

C. PROMISSORY NOTES

[¶ 4067]

REVENUE RULING 84–25

1984–1 C.B. 191.

Issue

What are the gift and estate tax consequences if a donor/decedent gratuitously transfers a legally binding promissory note that has not been satisfied at the decedent's death?

Facts

On August 1, 1977, D gratuitously transferred to A a promissory note in which D promised to pay A a sum of money on December 31, 1982. The note was legally enforceable under state law.

On May 30, 1982, D died. The note had not been satisfied at D's death.

Law and Analysis

In the case of a legally enforceable promise for less than an adequate and full consideration in money or money's worth, the promisor makes a completed gift under section 2511 of the Internal Revenue Code on the date when the promise is binding and determinable in value rather than when the promised payment is actually made. In such a case, the amount of the gift is the fair market value of the contractual promise on the date it is binding. Section 25.2512–4 of the Gift Tax Regulations.

Section 2053(a)(3) of the Code provides for an estate tax deduction for the amount of claims against the estate as are allowable by the laws of the state under which the estate is being administered. These deductions, when founded on a promise or agreement, are limited by section 2053(c)(1) to the extent that the obligations are contracted bona fide and for an adequate and full consideration in money or money's worth.

Under section 2001(b) of the Code, the estate tax is computed by determining a tentative tax on the sum of the taxable estate and the adjusted taxable gifts (section 2001(b)(1)) and subtracting from that amount the tax payable, calculated as provided in section 2001(b)(2), with respect to gifts made after 1976. The adjusted taxable gifts include only the value of the

¶ 4067

taxable gifts made by the decedent after 1976 that are not includible in the decedent's gross estate.

In this case, D made a completed gift under section 2511 of the Code on August 1, 1977, the date on which D's promise was legally binding and determinable in value. Compare, Rev. Rul. 67–396, 1967–2 C.B. 351, which provides that the transfer of a promissory note that is unenforceable under state law is not a completed gift.

No deduction is allowable under section 2053 of the Code for A's claim as promisee on D's note, because the note was not contracted for an adequate and full consideration in money or money's 0worth. Section 2053(c)(1).

Since the note has not been paid, the assets that are to be used to satisfy D's promissory note are a part of D's gross estate. Therefore, D's 1977 gift to A is deemed to be includible in D's gross estate for purposes of section 2001 of the Code. Thus, D's 1977 gift is not an adjusted taxable gift as defined in section 2001(b) of the Code. Consequently, the value of D's 1977 gift is not added under section 2001(b)(1)(B) to D's adjusted taxable gifts in computing the tentative estate tax under section 2001(b)(1).

Of course, a different situation would be presented had the note been partially satisfied prior to D's death. To the extent that the note had been paid, the assets used to satisfy the note would not be included in D's estate and hence there would be no reason not to treat the satisfied portion of the note as an adjusted taxable gift. Therefore, the holding of this ruling applies only to the extent the promissory note remains unsatisfied at D's death.

HOLDING

The gratuitous transfer of a legally binding promissory note is a completed gift under section 2511 of the Code. If the note has not been satisfied at the promisor's death, no deduction is allowable under section 2053(a)(3) for the promisee's claim with respect to the note. The completed gift is not treated as an adjusted taxable gift in computing the tentative estate tax under section 2001(b)(1).

* * *

D. CHECKS

[¶ 4073]

A gift by check raises especially difficult questions in determining when the gift is complete. Under typical state law the donor has power to stop payment of the check at any time until the check is actually accepted and paid by the drawee bank. Reg. § 25.2511–2(b) provides that a gift is complete only when the donor has put the property beyond the donor's "dominion and control." It would seem that that does not occur until the check is actually accepted and paid by the drawee bank. Nevertheless, there are some circumstances in which the gift may be treated as complete when the check is transferred to the donee, depending on the nature of the gift and the reason for determining the time of completion.

¶ 4067

If the check is transferred to a charity, the gift is treated as relating back to the time the charity receives the check, even though the check may not be accepted and paid until after the donor's death. This conclusion is based on the premise that the giving of the check evidences a binding commitment to a charitable subscription that could be enforced against the donor even if payment is stopped on the check. Estate of Spiegel v. Commissioner, 12 T.C. 524 (1949)

If the check is transferred to a noncharitable donee, however, the time of completion depends on several factors.

If the donor remains alive until the check is paid by the drawee bank, the time of the gift may relate back to the transfer of the check to the donee if certain conditions are met. In Estate of Metzger v. Commissioner, 100 T.C. 204 (1993), aff'd, 38 F.3d 118 (4th Cir.1994), the Tax Court held that the gift relates back to the delivery of the check to the donee if (1) there is an unconditional delivery to the donee, (2) the check is deposited in the donee's bank account within a reasonable time, (3) the donor's account has a sufficient balance to permit payment when the check is delivered to the donee, and (4) the check is ultimately paid by the drawee bank.

In Rev. Rul. 96–56, 1996–2 C.B. 161, the IRS acquiesced in *Metzger,* but imposed more stringent conditions. The IRS stated that delivery of a check to a noncharitable donee will be deemed a completed gift "on the earlier of (i) the date on which the donor has so parted with dominion and control under local law as to leave in the donor no power to change its disposition, or (ii) the date on which the donee deposits the check (or cashes the check against available funds of the donee) or presents the check for payment, if it is established that: (1) the check was paid by the drawee bank when first presented to the drawee bank for payment; (2) the donor was alive when the check was paid by the drawee bank; (3) the donor intended to make a gift; (4) delivery of the check by the donor was unconditional; and (5) the check was deposited, cashed, or presented in the calendar year for which completed gift treatment is sought and within a reasonable time of issuance." Note that requirement (2) has the effect of denying the benefit of Rev. Rul. 96–56 if the donor dies before the check is paid by the drawee bank. More significantly, requirement (5) grants relation back treatment only if the check is deposited or cashed within the calendar year in which the donee received the check.

In cases where the donor dies before presentment of the check to the drawee bank, the courts support the IRS position stated in requirement (2) of Rev. Rul. 96–56. The relation back treatment is not allowed if the donee is not a charity and the check is not paid by the drawee bank until after the donee's death. McCarthy v. United States, 806 F.2d 129 (7th Cir.1986); Estate of Dillingham v. Commissioner, 903 F.2d 760 (10th Cir.1990). Rosano v. United States, 245 F.3d 212 (2d Cir. 2001); Estate of Newman v. Commissioner, 203 F.3d 53 (D.C.Cir. 1999). In these cases the result was to include the amount of the check in the decedent's gross estate, thereby depriving the decedent of the benefit of the § 2503(b) exclusion for checks transferred prior to death.

Planning Note

[¶ 4079]

Donors making year-end gifts or gifts during a serious illness should be alert to the ramifications of the above rules. Where a serious illness is not present, and the objective is optimum utilization of the § 2503(b) annual per donee exclusion each year, donors should bear in mind the requirement of Rev. Rul. 96–56 that the check be deposited within a reasonable time and in any event within the year for which an exclusion is to be claimed. Recipients of traditional holiday gifts made late in December should be instructed as to the importance of prompt deposit. Where a serious illness is present, the rule is even stricter, and actual payment by the drawee bank must be achieved before death. In this situation prompt deposit is even more important.

E. CO–OWNERSHIP

[¶ 4085]

If title to property is conveyed to the transferor and another person as co-owners, treatment of the transfer under the gift tax depends on both the nature of the ownership and the type of property involved.

If the transfer is to another person as tenant in common with the donor, there is a completed gift of one-half of the property. The donee co-owner has an immediate right to dispose of one-half of the property as she wishes. Therefore, the donor has surrendered all dominion and control over that one-half of the property, and treatment as a completed gift is consistent with the "dominion and control" test expressed in Reg. § 25.2511–2(b).

The result is the same for a transfer to joint tenancy with right of survivorship if the property is something other than a bank account or a United States savings bond. For example, if the property transferred to joint tenancy is real estate, most states give the donee joint tenant an immediate right to sever the property and dispose of one-half as the donee wishes. Therefore, there is a completed gift as to one-half of the property. Reg. § 25.2511–1(h)(5).

If the property transferred to joint tenancy is a bank account (or any similar property that could be retrieved in its entirety by the donor), there is not a completed gift. This is so because the entirety of the funds could be withdrawn from the account by the donor, thereby restoring the entire property to the donor. A completed gift occurs only when and if the donee actually withdraws funds from the account. The same principle is applied to United States savings bonds registered to "A or B" (Reg. § 25.2511–1(h)(4)) and to joint brokerage accounts (Rev. Rul. 69–148, 1969–1 C.B. 226).

Although the gift tax rules relating to co-ownership are simple, the estate tax rules are more complex. As explained below in Chapter 16, special estate tax rules are applied so as to recognize the survival aspect of joint tenancy, with the result that part or all of joint tenancy property may be included in the decedent joint tenant's gross estate, depending on the circumstances. In the case of a tenancy in common, the inclusion is always the decedent's proportionate share of the property, e.g., one-half in the case of two tenants in common.

F. GIFTS BY CONTRACT

[¶ 4097]

REVENUE RULING 79–384

1979–2 C.B. 344.

ISSUE

What are the federal gift tax consequences of the payment of $10,000 as a result of a judgment against the payer, who promised to make the payment if the payee graduated from college?

FACTS

In 1972, A promised in writing to pay B, A's child, $10,000 if B graduated from college. At that time B was 16 years old. B graduated from college on June 1, 1977. B promptly demanded payment of the $10,000 in accordance with A's promise. A refused to pay the money and B brought suit in the local courts. On September 25, 1978, a judgment was issued by the local court against A on the contract with B in the amount of $10,000. A paid the money to B on the same day.

LAW AND ANALYSIS

* * *

In Estate of Copley v. Commissioner, 15 T.C. 17 (1950), affirmed, 194 F.2d 364 (7th Cir.1952), acq., 1965–2 C.B. 4, the petitioner entered into an antenuptial agreement in which the petitioner promised to give the future spouse a sum of money in consideration of the marriage and in lieu of all of the spouse's marital rights in the petitioner's property. The agreement became legally enforceable under state law on the date of the marriage in 1931. The petitioner transferred part of the sum in 1936 and the remainder in 1944. The court concluded that a gift tax would have been due in 1931 if there had been a gift tax law in effect at that time.

In Harris v. Commissioner, 178 F.2d 861 (2d Cir.1949), reversed on other grounds, 340 U.S. 106 (1950), 1950–2 C.B. 77, the Court of Appeals held that a promise to make a gift becomes taxable in the year in which the obligation becomes binding and not when the discharging payments are made. See, also, Rosenthal v. Commissioner, 205 F.2d 505 (2d Cir.1953); Rev. Rul. 69–347, 1969–1 C.B. 227.

Therefore, where one promises to transfer property in the future, the gift tax consequences of the promise are judged as of the first date on which it is

¶ 4097

possible to determine that the transfer must be made and that the transfer will be of a determinable amount. See also Rev. Rul. 69–347, 1969–1 C.B. 227.

In the present case, the fact that B graduated from college is not consideration, in money or money's worth, received by A. Even if A had received some benefit from B's graduation from college, it is not possible to place a monetary value on that benefit. Therefore, under section 25.2512–8 of the regulations, discussed above, A received no consideration, for federal gift tax purposes, in exchange for A's promise to pay $10,000 even though B's graduating from college may have been "consideration" under state law. See Hamer v. Sidway, 27 N.E. 256, (Ct.App.1891); Restatement of Contracts § 76 (1932); 1 A. L. Corbin, Corbin on Contracts 132 (1963).

In the present case, as in the Copley case, discussed above, A's promise to pay became binding on A before the subject of the promise was transferred. As in Rev. Rul. 69–346, discussed above, it was not possible to determine, as of the date when the donor's promise was made, whether a gift would actually result.

Such a determination could be made only when B graduated from college. Since B properly fulfilled the condition of A's obligation, A became bound to make the payment on B's graduation. It is thus on that date that A's gift was made, for federal gift tax purposes.

The fact that B found it necessary to obtain the assistance of the local courts in order to compel A to comply with the terms of the agreement and that A did not actually transfer the $10,000 until more than a year after B reached age 21 does not alter the conclusion in the present case. In Copley, discussed above, the donor's promise became binding in 1931, although payment was not made until 1936 and 1944. It was held that the gift was made in 1931 when the promise became enforceable.

HOLDING

The donor, A, made a gift of $10,000 on the day B graduated from college, the date when A's promise became enforceable and determinable in value, notwithstanding the fact that A did not actually make the payment of $10,000 until a later date when judgment was rendered against A.

G. JOINT AND MUTUAL WILLS

[¶ 4109]

Under the law of many states, two or more persons (typically spouses) may make "joint and mutual" wills that become binding and irrevocable upon the death of the first of the persons to die. For example, Husband and Wife execute identical wills that are stated to be joint and mutual. Each will provides that the property is to go outright to the couple's children upon the death of the second spouse to die. Wife dies first, bequeathing a life estate in her property to Husband, remainder to the children. The IRS takes the position that at the moment of Wife's death there is a completed gift by Husband of a remainder interest (after Husband's life) in his property to the children. This is founded on local law, which makes Husband's bequest of his property to the children binding and irrevocable immediately upon Wife's death. In Grimes v. Commissioner, 851 F.2d 1005 (7th Cir.1988), the Seventh Circuit upheld the IRS position, reasoning that this was like any other gift by contract, i.e., completion of performance by Mother makes the contract—and hence the Husband's transfer to the children—binding and irrevocable. The taxpayer sought to prevent this result by arguing that local law (Illinois) permitted the surviving spouse to consume the property subject to the joint and mutual wills, but the court construed Illinois law as prohibiting such consumption.

H. INSTALLMENT TRANSFERS

[¶ 4111]

Timing issues often arise because of the dollar limit on the annual per donee exclusion provided by § 2503(b), discussed below beginning at ¶ 7013. Because the exclusion is available for gifts to each donee in each separate calendar year, it is often important that a gift be treated as occurring in the calendar year that will provide optimum benefit from the exclusion.

This may be especially difficult if the property to be transferred is a single asset having a value greater than the § 2503(b) exclusion amount. For example, a grandparent may wish to transfer to a grandchild a parcel of land worth $60,000. Assume that the annual per donee exclusion maximum is $12,000. In order to assure full availability of the annual per donee exclusion, the gift must somehow be divided into five separate gifts of $12,000 in each of five years. Such a division may be cumbersome because of changes in value of the land, necessitating annual appraisals. Also, gifts of partial interests create an awkward divided ownership situation.

The case and rulings below illustrate some of the mechanisms used to address this problem, as well as the IRS responses. These authorities relate to an earlier time when the § 2503(b) exclusion amount was only $3,000.

[¶ 4115]

HAYGOOD v. COMMISSIONER

Tax Court of the United States, 1964.
42 T.C. 936.

SCOTT, Judge:

[The taxpayer transferred properties to each of her two sons and in return took a vendor's lien note from each for the full value of the properties, payable $3,000 per year, the first payments being due the day after the deeds were executed. Each vendor's lien note was secured by a deed of trust on the properties transferred. In accordance with her intention when she transferred the properties, the taxpayer canceled the $3,000 payments due the day after the execution of the deeds and in subsequent years canceled the other $3,000 payments.]

¶ 4115

OPINION

It is respondent's position that in addition to the property of a value of $28,180 given by petitioner to her sons in December 1961 with respect to which no issue is here involved, petitioner made total gifts in the year 1961 of property to her sons of $32,500. Respondent takes the position that since the value of the pieces of city property which petitioner deeded to her sons, taking back a non-interest-bearing vendor's lien note in the amount of $16,500 from one son and a similar note in the amount of $16,000 from the other, was $32,500, this represents the amount of petitioner's gifts to her sons since the notes executed by her sons and the liens given as security therefor were without substance. It is respondent's position that petitioner's sons owed her nothing for the property in 1961 and were vested with ownership thereof and that such gifts constituted transfers subject to tax.

It is petitioner's position that she gave the rural property valued at $28,180 to her sons in 1961, and in addition gave them $6,000 of the value of the city property in that year. It is eminently clear from the testimony that it was petitioner's intent to give only a $3,000 interest to each of her sons in the city property deeded to them in the year 1961. Had petitioner in 1961 deeded only a 3/16.5 interest to C. Gerald Haygood in the portion of the city property which she intended to give to him and only a 3/16 interest to F. Donald Haygood in the portion of the city property she intended to give to him, which was apparently the procedure her accountant intended for her to follow, and in subsequent years deeded similar interests until the entire property was transferred, respondent apparently would not question the transaction as being a gift of a value of only $3,000 to each son in the year 1961. In fact respondent's regulations specifically provide for such a transfer.

It is respondent's position that petitioner transferred all of her interest in the property and in return therefor received nothing of value. Respondent does not consider there to be any substance to the notes and deeds of trust signed by petitioner's sons. Respondent states that his position is supported by the provisions of section 2501 of the Internal Revenue Code of 1954 imposing a tax for years after 1954 on the transfer of property by gift, section 2511 providing that the tax shall apply whether the transfer is in trust or otherwise and whether the gift is direct or indirect, and section 2512 providing that where the gift is made in property the value of the property at the date of the gift and when property is transferred for less than an adequate and full consideration in money or money's worth, that the amount by which the value of the property exceeds the value of the consideration shall be deemed a gift. Respondent contends that it is immaterial whether petitioner intended to give the entire value of the property in 1961 since she in that year actually did part with dominion and control over the property without receiving any valuable consideration in return therefor, relying on his regulations which he contends so state.

Respondent cites in support of his position the case of Minnie E. Deal, 29 T.C. 730 (1958). *Minnie E. Deal* involved a conveyance by the taxpayer there involved of real property to a trust for the benefit of her four daughters. The property was conveyed to the trust unencumbered. On the same date that the

¶ 4115

real property was conveyed by the taxpayer in *Minnie E. Deal*, supra, to the trust, each of her four daughters gave her a non-interest-bearing note which they would have been, with one exception, financially able to pay. The taxpayer forgave a $3,000 portion of each note to each daughter in the year of the transfer of the property, and a similar portion of each note in the 2 subsequent years, and the remaining balance of the note in the following year. In *Minnie E. Deal*, supra, we stated at page 736:

> After carefully considering the record, we think that the notes executed by the daughters were not intended to be enforced and were not intended as consideration for the transfer by the petitioner, and that, in substance, the transfer of the property was by gift. * * *

In conclusion we stated:

> * * * We have found, and held, that these notes were not given as a part of the purchase price of the property which petitioner conveyed to the trust and did not serve to reduce the amount of the gift. Therefore, even if we assume, as petitioner argues, that the daughters were legally liable on the notes to petitioner, that fact has no effect on the question we have here to decide. The Commissioner has not included as part of the gifts made by petitioner in 1952 the cancellation of the 4 notes for $3,000 each [of] which had been executed by the daughters to petitioner. Since no such gifts were included by respondent in his determination of the deficiency, the cancellation cannot be made the basis for the exclusions in the amount of $12,000 which petitioner claimed on her return and which she still contends should be granted.

The *Minnie E. Deal* case is clearly distinguishable on its facts from the instant case. Here the notes were vendor's lien notes given for the property. Clearly as a matter of law, they would have been enforceable and respondent does not contend otherwise. Respondent's position is, and the record shows, that it was not petitioner's intention to enforce payment of the notes. Respondent points out that petitioner's sons were not able to pay the $3,000 payments on the notes due on December 31, 1961, on that date since they did not have the funds with which to make the payments. There is a stipulated fact that the sons were not financially able to make the $3,000 payments due on December 31, 1961. This stipulation must imply without considering the rural property given to petitioner's sons the preceding day since this property had a value of $28,180. However, the ability of the sons to pay $3,000 on December 31, 1961, is academic since it was petitioner's intention to and she did forgive the payment due on that day. It is stipulated that at the time these notes were given, the fair market value of the properties conveyed was $16,000 and $16,500, respectively. In view of the agreed value of the properties, the deeds of trust to the properties further securing the vendor's lien notes would obviously have some value.

* * *

We hold that the value of the property transferred by petitioner did not exceed the value of the vendor's lien notes and deeds of trust received in return therefor by more than the $3,000 in the case of each son, which amounts petitioner has reported as gifts in the year 1961.

Decision will be entered for petitioner.

[¶ 4121]

REVENUE RULING 77–299
1977–2 C.B. 343.

Advice has been requested with respect to the Federal gift tax consequences of a transfer of property under the circumstances described below.

G had given A and B, G's grandchildren, $3,000 per year at Christmas since each grandchild was 10 years old. When A and B were, respectively, 21 and 22 years old and enrolled in graduate school, G proposed to give Blackacre, with a fair market value of $27,000, to A and Whiteacre, with a fair market value of $24,000, to B. Both Blackacre and Whiteacre were unimproved tracts of nonincome-producing real property. A and B had spent the money previously given them by G, did not have any other funds, and did not have an independent source of income. When informed of G's intent, G's attorney, in order to minimize G's Federal gift tax on the transfer, suggested a sale of the property to each grandchild in return for installment notes that would be payable in yearly amounts equal to the annual gift tax exclusion.

The plan was implemented in July 1972, at which time A and B each received a package of instruments in the mail from G's attorney. A's package contained a check from G for $50, a deed to Blackacre, a mortgage on the property, one note with a face amount of $2,950 and eight notes each in the amount of $3,000. B's package contained a check from G for $50, a deed to Whiteacre, a mortgage on the property, one note with a face amount of $2,950 and seven notes each in the amount of $3,000. A letter also accompanied each package explaining the transaction to A and B and indicating that G did not intend to collect on the notes, but intended to forgive each payment as it became due. A and B did not have prior knowledge of the transaction. There were no negotiations concerning the transaction, and G's attorney represented all of the parties to the transaction.

The notes were noninterest-bearing and nonnegotiable. The notes provided that A owed $26,950 on Blackacre and B owed $23,950 on Whiteacre. The first note of each grandchild in the amount of $2,950 matured on January 1, 1973, and each additional note in the amount of $3,000 matured on January 1 of each succeeding year. Each of the deeds recited that it was given in consideration of a cash payment of $50 and the notes. Additionally, each deed described the notes and recited that the mortgages on the property were taken to secure the payment of the notes. The deeds, mortgage, and notes were executed on July 15, 1972, and at the same time A and B each transferred $50 to G. Thereafter, the deeds (but not the mortgages) were recorded with the proper county authorities.

¶ 4115

On December 25, 1972, G forgave the $2,950 due from A and B on January 1, 1973. On December 25 of 1973 and 1974, G forgave the $3,000 due from A and B on January 1 of the following years.

The specific question presented is whether the transfer of the property in return for the notes secured by a purchase money mortgage was a bona fide sale between the parties or whether the transaction was in substance a gift of the transferor's entire interest in the property structured to avoid the Federal gift tax.

Section 2501 of the Internal Revenue Code of 1954 imposes a tax on the transfer of property by gift. The gift tax applies, under the provisions of section 2511 of the Code and section 25.2511–1(a) of the Gift Tax Regulations, whether the transfer is in trust or otherwise and whether the gift is direct or indirect. Thus, the gift tax applies to all transactions whereby property or property rights or interests are gratuitously passed or conferred upon another, regardless of the means or device employed. See section 25.2511–1(c) of the regulations.

In the case of present interests, section 2503 of the Code excludes $3,000 of gifts per calendar year for each donee from gifts subject to the gift tax.

Section 2512 of the Code provides that when property is transferred for less than an adequate and full consideration in money or money's worth, the amount by which the value of the property exceeds the value of the consideration shall be deemed a gift and shall be included in computing the amount of gift made during the calendar year.

Section 25.2512–8 of the regulations states:

Transfers reached by the gift tax are not confined to those only which, being without a valuable consideration, accord with the common law concept of gifts, but embrace as well sales, exchanges, and other dispositions of property for a consideration to the extent that the value of the property transferred by the donor exceeds the value in money or money's worth of the consideration given therefor. However, a sale, exchange, or other transfer of property made in the ordinary course of business (a transaction which is bona fide, at arm's length, and free from any donative intent), will be considered as made for an adequate and full consideration in money or money's worth.

In Minnie E. Deal, 29 T.C. 730 (1958), the taxpayer transferred in trust a remainder interest in unimproved, nonincome-producing property to the taxpayer's children in return for noninterest-bearing, unsecured demand notes. The taxpayer canceled $3,000 of each child's indebtedness each year until the balance due was completely canceled. The Tax Court held the notes executed by the children were not intended as consideration for the transfer and, rather than a bona fide sale, the taxpayer made a gift of the remainder interest to the children. * * *

Thus, in the instant case, whether the transfer of property was a sale or a gift depends upon whether, as part of a pre-arranged plan, G intended to forgive the notes that were received when G transferred the property.

¶ 4121

It should be noted that the intent to forgive notes is to be distinguished from donative intent, which, as indicated by section 25.2511–1(g)(1) of the regulations, is not relevant. A finding of an intent to forgive the note relates to whether valuable consideration was received and, thus, to whether the transaction was in reality a bona fide sale or a disguised gift. Therefore, such an inquiry is necessary in situations such as the one described here. "Nothing can be treated as consideration that is not intended as such by the parties." Fire Insurance Association v. Wickham, 141 U.S. [564,] 579 (1891). Donative intent, on the other hand, rather than relating to whether a transaction was actually a sale or a gift, relates to whether the donor intended the transaction to be a sale or a gift. Although the same facts would be used in determining either type of intent, they relate to two entirely different inquiries.

In the instant case, the facts clearly indicate that G, as part of a prearranged plan, intended to forgive the notes that were received in return for the transfer of G's land. Therefore, the transaction was merely a disguised gift rather than a bona fide sale.

The Service will not follow the decisions in Selsor R. Haygood, 42 T.C. 936 (1964), acq. in result, 1965–1 C.B. 4, nonacq., 1977–32 I.R.B. 5, and J.W. Kelley, 63 T.C. 321 (1974), nonacq., 1977–32 I.R.B. 5, that held that forgiveness of notes constituted a gift of a present interest, under circumstances similar to the present ruling.

Accordingly, for Federal gift tax purposes, G made a transfer by gift to A in 1972 in the amount of $27,000. In addition, G made a transfer by gift to B in 1972 in the amount of $24,000.

[¶ 4127]

REVENUE RULING 83–180

1983–2 C.B. 169.

ISSUE

What are the gift tax consequences where, under the circumstances described below, the donor transfers specified portions of real property equal in value to the annual gift tax exclusion allowable under section 2503 of the Internal Revenue Code in effect for the years of the transfers?

FACTS

In 1980, A owned 10 acres of income producing real estate and transferred 3 of those acres to B. At that time the land was correctly appraised at $1,000 per acre. In 1981, A transferred 2 of A's remaining 7 acres to D. The land was correctly valued at $1,500 per acre. In 1982, A transferred to B the remaining 5 acres which were appraised at $2,000 per acre. Because the value of each transfer was equal to the annual exclusion available in the respective years of transfer, A did not file federal gift tax returns for the transfers, and consequently paid no gift tax.

LAW AND ANALYSIS

Section 2501 of the Code imposes a tax on the transfer of property by gift. Section 25.2511–2(b) of the Gift Tax Regulations provides that the gift is complete to the extent that the donor has parted with dominion and control over the property. Section 25.2511–2(a) of the regulations states that the gift tax is not imposed upon the receipt of the property by the donee but rather is an excise upon the donor's act of transfer.

Section 2503(b) of the Code as in effect for 1980 and 1981 provided that the first $3,000 may be excluded from the value of gifts of present interests in property made by a donor to any donee during the calendar year. For gifts of present interests made after December 31, 1981, section 2503(b) now provides that the annual exclusion is $10,000. Under section 25.2503–3 of the regulations, a "present interest" in property is defined as an unrestricted right to the immediate use, possession, or enjoyment of property or the income from property.

In Rev. Rul. 77–299, 1977–2 C.B. 343, in a purported sale transaction, G deeded nonincome producing land to G's grandchildren in exchange for a series of noninterest bearing notes that were payable annually, each note maturing in a succeeding year. Each note was equal in amount to the annual gift tax exclusion. In a letter to the transferees G stated that each note would be forgiven as the payment became due. Rev. Rul. 77–299 holds that in view of G's intent to forgive the notes as they matured, the notes received were not valuable consideration for the transfer. Rev. Rul. 77–299 concludes that the transaction was a disguised gift of the donor's entire interest in the property. In view of the fact that G deeded G's entire interest in the property to the grandchildren, and received less than adequate consideration for the transfer, a single gift of G's entire interest in the property occurred at the time of the "sales" transaction.

In the present case, unlike the situation presented in Rev. Rul. 77–299, A made separate completed gifts to B in separate taxable years. Each annual gift consisted of a portion of A's interest in the real property. A retained ownership and control of the remaining portions. Because A made a completed gift of only a portion of the property each year, only that portion transferred to B each year is subject to the gift tax. Each of the gifts qualifies for the annual exclusion under section 2503 of the Code because under the terms of the transfers, B received the present unrestricted right to the immediate use, possession, and enjoyment of an ascertainable interest in the real property. Because separate annual gifts are involved, and the value of each gift equals the annual gift tax exclusion in effect for the year of transfer, A, unlike the donor in Rev. Rul. 77–299, can use the exclusion for each annual gift.

HOLDING

Where a donor transfers, on an annual basis, a specified portion of real property, the donor has made a completed gift each year of the portion transferred, and each gift qualifies for the annual exclusion under section

¶ 4127

2503 of the Code. It is not relevant that the value of each portion transferred equals the annual gift tax exclusion in effect for the year of the transfer.

Planning Note

[¶ 4133]

As explained above, a donor is often confronted with the need to make a series of gifts of portions of a single larger property. Typically this occurs because the donor wishes to keep the value of each gift within the § 2503(b) annual exclusion amount. Several alternatives are available to the donor, as described below. Each has its advantages and disadvantages.

The simplest approach is to transfer a portion of the property itself each year. For example, the donor might transfer by deed a specific number of acres of land, as was done in Rev. Rul. 83–180, ¶ 4127. Alternatively, the donor might give a percentage tenancy in common interest. Either approach assures qualification for the § 2503(b) exclusion if the value of the property given does not exceed the § 2503(b) limit, but these methods have significant disadvantages. The most troublesome is uncertainty as to value. If the transferred acreage is later determined to have a value greater than the § 2503(b) limit, a portion of the donor's unified credit will have been consumed. This danger can be minimized by obtaining an appraisal, but the appraisal would have to be repeated each year as subsequent gifts are made.

The second disadvantage of a gift of a portion of the property is the divided ownership that necessarily results. The donor and donee become co-owners (either as tenants in common or as owners of separate parcels) of a single tract as to which unified management may be desirable. The donor will thereby surrender some of his control over the property, and conflict between donor and donee may result.

Another approach is the installment sale technique that was used in *Haygood*, ¶ 4115. This has the advantage of requiring only one appraisal. It also provides assurance that each year's transfer will not exceed the § 2503(b) limit, and it assures unified ownership and control of the land by the purchaser-donee. A major disadvantage is the possibility of a contention by the IRS, in accord with Rev. Rul. 77–299, ¶ 4121, that the donor did not intend to enforce the notes given by the buyer, with the result that the entire gift is treated as occurring in the year of the alleged sale. The installment sale approach also triggers taxable gain to the seller and brings into play complex income tax issues related to installment reporting under §§ 453 and 453B, as well as the time value of money rules imposed by §§ 483 and 1272. If the sale contract provides that the remaining installments due are to be canceled in the event of the transferor's death, there are immediate income tax consequences when the transferor dies. The income inherent in the canceled installments is taxed to the transferor's estate as if it were realized immediately upon the transferor's death. Rev. Rul. 86–72, 1986–1 C.B. 253.

A third approach is contribution of the property to an entity such as a corporation, partnership, or limited liability company. The donor can transfer the property to a newly formed corporation, partnership, or limited liability

¶ 4127

company without recognition of gain pursuant to § 351 or § 721. The donor can then give shares of stock or interests in the partnership or limited liability company to the donee each year. The need for annual appraisals is not avoided, but the entity approach permits the donor to keep control of the property as long as the donor retains ownership of a majority of the interests in the entity. In addition, gifts of interests in the entity may qualify for minority discounts, as explained below at ¶ 11,037.

Problem

[¶ 4139]

Wilma Merced, age 76, is a widow. She is in good health but is worried about estate tax exposure because the value of her property is well in excess of the amount that can be sheltered by the unified credit. She has few liquid assets, and her property consists almost entirely of land she actively farms. She wants to continue to farm this land, but is willing to give one parcel, the "Back 80," worth $120,000, to her son, Tad. Wilma believes the Back 80 may appreciate substantially in value in the years ahead. Wilma's basis for the Back 80 is $40,000.

What methods could you offer to Wilma for transferring the Back 80 to Tad at minimum tax cost? What would be the advantages or disadvantages of each?

How would your advice be changed if Wilma expressed strong interest in keeping control of farming on the Back 80 for as long as possible despite the transfer to Tad?

I. EFFECT OF A REVERSION

[¶ 4151]

The gift tax can be imposed only on the property actually transferred by the donor. If the donor gives only a life estate to the donee, and the remainder is to revert to the donor, the taxable gift consists only of the life estate.

In the life estate example, the value of the gift can be readily computed by reference to the life expectancy of the donee. See Chapter 10. The issue becomes more complex, however, if there is uncertainty as to whether the reversion will in fact return to the donor. For example, assume that the reversion to the donor is to be effective only if the donor is married at the time of the donee's death. This cannot be predicted with actuarial certainty, and the value of the reversion is not determinable. In that event, the reversion is assigned a zero value for gift tax purposes, and the donor is treated as having made a completed gift of all interests in the property at the time of the transfer. Robinette v. Helvering, 318 U.S. 184 (1943), which appears at ¶ 14,007.

Chapter 5

POWERS OF APPOINTMENT

(Section 2514)

[¶ 5001]

The history of the tax treatment of powers of appointment and the current complexities are fully explored in Chapter 22 in the context of the estate tax. Therefore, this chapter provides only a general description of the major principles applicable to powers of appointment for purposes of the gift tax.

Both the gift tax and the estate tax distinguish sharply between "general" and nongeneral powers. "General power" is carefully defined in § 2514(c) and (subject to certain exceptions) includes any power that permits the property to be appointed to *any one or more* of the following: the powerholder, the powerholder's creditors, the powerholder's estate, or creditors of the powerholder's estate. A taxpayer who holds a general power is viewed as having rights essentially equivalent to full ownership. Therefore, if the taxpayer exercises such a power by appointing the property to another, the exercise is taxable to the same extent as if the taxpayer had transferred property owned outright. § 2514(a) and (b).

For example, assume that Husband creates a trust, granting a life estate to Wife, remainder to the couple's children. Husband gives Wife a power to appoint the principal of the trust to herself or to anyone else at any time within the first ten years after the trust is created. Wife holds a general power, and her exercise of that power to appoint trust property to a person other than herself constitutes a taxable gift.

But the law goes further. If a taxpayer holds such a general power but releases it or permits it to lapse, a taxable transfer occurs, subject to certain exceptions. § 2514(b) and (e). The taxpayer is viewed as having effectively dictated the disposition of the property by releasing the power or by permitting it to lapse. By voluntarily forgoing exercise of the power, the taxpayer has caused the property to go to others. It should be noted that this extension of the rule, i.e., taxing releases and lapses in the same way as exercises, applies only to powers created after October 21, 1942. Powers created on or before October 21, 1942, are taxed only if actually exercised. § 2514(a).

If the power described in the example above was created after October 21, 1942, and Wife voluntarily releases the power, she is treated as making a taxable gift of the remainder to the children at the time of the release. Similarly, if Wife lets the ten years expire without exercising the power, so that the power lapses at the end of that period, Wife is treated as making a taxable gift of the remainder to the children on the date of the lapse, subject to the exception noted below. In either case, because the children will receive the property if the power is not exercised, the children are referred to as the "takers in default of appointment."

If the power is exercised or released, the amount of the gift is the value of the property subject to the power. In the case of Wife's release described above, the gift would consist of the actuarial value, at the time of the release, of the remainder after Wife's life estate.

A special rule applies to lapses, however. A lapse is treated as a taxable transfer only to the extent that the value of the property subject to the lapse exceeds the greater of $5,000 or five percent of the aggregate value of the property out of which the power could have been satisfied. § 2514(e). For example, if the powerholder has a general power to appoint $25,000 out of a trust that has a total value of $200,000, and the powerholder permits the power to lapse, the powerholder is treated as having made a transfer in the amount of $15,000—the excess of $25,000 over $10,000 (five percent of the $200,000 value of the trust). There is a taxable gift of $15,000 if the powerholder has no other interests in the trust.

A power designed to take maximum advantage of this rule is called a "5 and 5 power." Typically such a power permits the powerholder to withdraw the greater of $5,000 or 5 percent of the trust fund each year, and the power lapses at the end of each year if not exercised. Each annual lapse of such a power is fully covered by the $5,000 or 5 percent exception expressed in § 2514(e), and no taxable gifts will occur unless the powerholder actually exercises the power.

The $5,000 limit applies to the total of all powers held by the powerholder, regardless of the number of trusts involved. The limit cannot be multiplied by giving the powerholder a "5 and 5 power" in each of multiple trusts. Rev. Rul. 85–88, 1985–2 C.B. 202.

By contrast, nongeneral powers escape taxation entirely—even if exercised. For example, assume that in the circumstances above, Wife has power to appoint the principal only to her descendants—not to herself. This is not a general power, and Wife's exercise or release of the power—or its lapse—is not a taxable transfer.

[¶ 5007]

SELF v. UNITED STATES

United States Court of Claims, 1956.
142 F.Supp. 939.

LITTLETON, Judge:

This is a suit to recover gift taxes paid by plaintiff for the year 1951, in the amount of $918.23. The facts have been stipulated and may be summarized as follows:

On November 23, 1948, plaintiff's father transferred a block of common stock of a corporation called Greenwood Mills in trust, with the income from the trust fund to be paid to plaintiff for life, with remainders to plaintiff's descendants, if any, and if none, to a charitable foundation. By this trust instrument plaintiff was given the right at any time during his life to appoint by deed all or part of the trust property to or among his descendants. The plaintiff's father paid a gift tax upon the entire value of the property transferred in trust on November 23, 1948.

On October 2, 1951, plaintiff exercised the limited power of appointment given him under the trust instrument by executing 2 deeds appointing 100 shares of the Greenwood Mills common stock to a trust for his son and 100 shares of the same stock to a trust for his daughter. The 200 shares were, pursuant to the terms of the trust, separated and transferred to the 2 trusts for the benefit of plaintiff's children. The plaintiff filed a gift tax return for 1951, and paid, inter alia, a gift tax on the value of the right to receive the income for life from the 200 shares of Greenwood Mills common stock. The plaintiff filed a timely claim for refund. No action has been taken on the claim and this suit was timely filed.

The issue before the court is whether in exercising his limited power of appointment the plaintiff made a taxable gift equal to the value of the right to receive the income for life from the trust property transferred.

* * *

At common law, the transfer of property under a power of appointment was considered to have been made directly from the donor to the appointee. The donor's instrument effected the transfer and the property did not belong to the donee. Prior to 1942, the common law concept of powers of appointment was followed by the courts in gift tax cases and it was held that the appointment by the donee of the power did not constitute a taxable gift on the part of the donee. Section 452 of the Revenue Act of 1942, 56 Stat. 798, and section 3(a) of the Powers of Appointment Act of 1951, 65 Stat. 91, amended section 1000 of the 1939 Internal Revenue Code to provide that the exercise or release of a general power of appointment is taxable, with certain limitations relative to effective dates.

The defendant concedes that the transfer of an interest in property pursuant to the exercise of a limited or special power of appointment is not subject to the gift tax. It is defendant's position that the plaintiff's power

¶ 5007

related only to the trust corpus, not to the trust income, and that the transfer of the income interest was not made pursuant to a limited power and is therefore subject to the gift tax. The defendant argues that plaintiff transferred two separate interests when he exercised his limited power of appointment. First, he transferred 200 shares of stock in which he had no interest or vested right. Second, he transferred his vested right to the income from those 200 shares for his life. The plaintiff contends that because of the inherent nature of the income-producing property, such as the stock, it was impossible to transfer the property pursuant to the power of appointment without transferring the fruits from the property.

We believe that when the donee exercises a power of appointment over a corpus consisting of income-producing property by transferring part of the income-producing property to the appointee, the income to be earned from the property thus transferred automatically and necessarily goes with the legal title to the property, unless provision is specifically made for the contrary. In fact, the terms of the provision granting the power of appointment to plaintiff indicate that plaintiff's right to the income from the part of the corpus transferred pursuant to the power was to terminate upon the exercise of the power. The first sentence of this article provides that the "entire net income of the trust fund" should be paid to plaintiff during his life. The second sentence provides that, nevertheless, plaintiff should have the power by deed to appoint any or all of the corpus to his descendants. The third sentence provides that upon the exercise of the power the "trustees shall separate from the trust fund the portion or portions appointed and pay over such portions" as instructed by plaintiff.

The defendant admits that the right to the income to be earned from the shares was transferred automatically pursuant to the exercise of the power of appointment by the imposition of a gift tax on the value of the income when the power was exercised. The plaintiff did not purport to make an independent gift of the right to the income and the deeds of appointment by their terms related only to the shares of stock.

The defendant makes a general argument, the essence of which is that a gift tax should be imposed on the donee of a limited power of appointment upon the exercise of the power when the donee has a beneficial interest in the property transferred pursuant to the power. This argument is based on the theory that such a donee is giving up an economic interest when he exercises the power. This same argument and precise question were presented to the court in Commissioner v. Walston, 4 Cir., 168 F.2d 211. In that case, the taxpayer's father left a share of his estate in trust with the income to the taxpayer for life with remainders over. The taxpayer was also given the power to appoint the principal or income of the trust to or among her father's descendants by deed during her lifetime and/or to appoint the property to anyone by will at her death. In 1938, the taxpayer appointed by deed to her brother one-half of the trust corpus and the income for his life from the remaining half of the trust corpus. The Commissioner of Internal Revenue contended that the taxpayer made a taxable gift of her right to the income from the trust for her life. The Tax Court and the Court of Appeals held that

¶ 5007

the right to the income was transferred under the power of appointment and not by the taxpayer in her independent capacity and therefore the transfer was not taxable. Each court pointed out that where the income beneficiary had a life estate subject to a power of appointment, the income beneficiary had a temporary interest which might last for life, but which was subject to termination if and when the power of appointment was exercised. Consequently, to the extent the power is exercised, the income beneficiary's estate is terminated by reason of the power and not by a desire on the part of the income beneficiary to give up the life estate irrespective of the power.

The donor of the power of appointment is considered the transferor of the gift and the donee merely acts as his agent and gives direction to the gift pursuant to the donor's wishes. Unless the power of appointment concept is ignored, there is no difference between making the income beneficiary the donee of the special or limited power of appointment and making a third person who has no beneficial interest in the income or corpus the donee of the power. In the latter event no one would suggest that a gift tax should be imposed when the life estate of the income beneficiary is terminated by the transfer of the corpus pursuant to the exercise of the power.

The Congress has chosen to ignore this concept insofar as general powers of appointment are concerned and therefore has specifically subjected them to tax under section 1000(e) [1986 Code § 2514]. However, as defendant concedes, this concept is still applicable to property or interest that is transferred under a special or limited power of appointment.

The defendant refers us to Treasury Regulations 108, sec. 86.2(b)(2)(as amended by T.D. 6077, 1954–2 C.B. 308) as authority for its position. Congress has chosen not to impose a gift tax on property transferred under a special or limited power of appointment and if the property was transferred under a special or limited power of appointment, as it was in this case, it is not taxable. We do not deem this portion of the regulation necessarily inconsistent with our decision because the plaintiff in the instant case did not have, in addition to his special power, a general power to appoint by will, as is the case in the example given in the regulation. However, to the extent that the example given in the regulation implies that a donee, who has only the right to the income from the corpus subject to a special or limited power of appointment, is subject to a gift tax on the exercise of the special or limited power of appointment, we disagree with it.

Plaintiff is entitled to recover and judgment will be entered in the amount of $918.23, with interest as provided by law.

It is so ordered.

Note

[¶ 5009]

The IRS is unwilling to follow the *Self* decision. Rev. Rul. 79–327, 1979–2 C.B. 342. The Commissioner's position is also embodied in the regulations: Reg. §§ 25.2514–1(b)(2) and 25.2514–3(e) Example (3).

¶ 5007

The Commissioner's opposition to the *Self* result was implemented in Tech. Adv. Mem. 9419007. Here the taxpayer, under age 30, was entitled to the income from a trust until attaining age 30, at which time the entire trust principal was to be paid to the taxpayer if the taxpayer was then living. The instrument also granted to the taxpayer a power to appoint her interest in the trust to certain family members. The taxpayer, before attaining age 30, exercised the power by appointing both her remaining income interest and the remainder to one of the designated family members. Clearly, the taxpayer's power was nongeneral for purposes of § 2514(c), and the taxpayer argued that § 2514 prevented taxation of the exercise. The Commissioner, however, ruled that the taxpayer had made a taxable gift of the remaining income interest as well as the remainder. In the Commissioner's view, the taxpayer had full ownership and enjoyment of the property transferred, i.e., the income interest and the remainder. Had the taxpayer so chosen, she could have continued to receive the income and ultimately receive the remainder upon attaining age 30. Therefore, the taxpayer transferred property in which she had full ownership, not just a power of appointment, and the § 2514 power of appointment rules did not control.

Problems

[¶ 5013]

1. In January of Year 1, Tamara Rodriguez died. She bequeathed $400,000 of her estate to the Rodriguez Trust, naming the Seventh National Bank as trustee. Tamara's son, Diego, is to receive all income from the trust throughout his life. Until January 10 of year 10, Diego has a power to appoint part or all of the trust property to anyone, including himself. Upon Diego's death the remaining trust property goes outright to Diego's then living grandchildren.

   only important thing in chap. 5

   (a) As to each alternative event described below, state the gift tax results, assuming the value of the trust property is $700,000 on the date when each event occurs.

      (i) On March 10 of Year 2, Diego appoints the entire trust property to his son, Luis.

      (ii) On November 10 of Year 8, Diego irrevocably releases the power of appointment. On November 10 of Year 8, the actuarial value of Diego's life estate is $200,000.

      (iii) Diego does not exercise the power. At midnight on January 10 of Year 10, the power lapses. On January 10 of Year 10, the actuarial value of Diego's life estate is $150,000.

   (b) Assume the same facts, except that Diego's power of appointment permits him to appoint the property only to his wife and children. How would this change the results in part (a)?

2. Alfred Brown died in Year 1. He bequeathed most of his estate to the Tenth National Bank as trustee of the Brown Trust, which was created by Alfred's will. The will provides that the income of the Brown Trust is to be paid to Alfred's wife, Sylvia, throughout her life. Upon Sylvia's death the trust principal is to be distributed to the children of Alfred and Sylvia.

The will also provides that Sylvia has power to appoint a maximum of $40,000 of principal each calendar year to herself or to her children, all adults. If the power is not exercised, it lapses at the end of each calendar year. The value of the property transferred to the Brown Trust was $1,000,000, and the value of the trust property has increased since then.

The trust was funded in Year 1. Sylvia did not exercise her invasion power during Year 1, Year 2, or Year 3. Did Sylvia make taxable gifts during Year 1, Year 2, or Year 3? If so, what was the value of each gift?

¶ 5013

Chapter 6

DISCLAIMERS

(Section 2518)

[¶ 6001]

In considering the transfer tax treatment of disclaimers or renunciations of property that otherwise would have been received by the person disclaiming, one starting place is the traditional rule that is applied to intestate property absent enactment of state or federal disclaimer legislation. At common law, an intestate taker was prohibited from disclaiming. An heir who renounced her interest was treated as having received the property immediately upon her ancestor's death and as having then made a gift to the person who took the property as a result of the heir's relinquishment of her interest. "The general rule as to intestate succession is that the title to the property of an intestate passes by force of rules of law [referring to the general laws of intestate succession of the relevant jurisdiction], and that those so entitled by law have no power to prevent the vesting of title in themselves." Hardenbergh v. Commissioner, 198 F.2d 63 (8th Cir.1952), cert. denied, 344 U.S. 836 (1952). That is the law of most states, except to the extent they have legislated to the contrary. Accordingly, as held in *Hardenbergh*, and absent federal or state legislation changing this result, an heir who is entitled to the property by intestacy would find it impossible to renounce the property and thereby escape treatment of the transfer of the property to another as a gift by the heir.

On the other hand, the common law rule is to the contrary as to a legatee or devisee under a will. The decedent is viewed as having gratuitously transferred property to the legatee or devisee, who should be entitled to reject the transfer. Therefore, a legatee or devisee is generally entitled under local law to refuse a testamentary gift. Brown v. Routzahn, 63 F.2d 914 (6th Cir.1933), cert. denied, 290 U.S. 641 (1933).

In most states the common law rules have been supplanted by statutes that expressly authorize disclaimer of a wide variety of property interests. Because of the diversity of local statutory and case law, there was an extended period of uncertainty as to the efficacy of a disclaimer for United States estate and gift tax purposes. Relief came in the form of § 2518, adopted in 1976. This provision provides definitive and uniform national rules dictating the effect of disclaimers for purposes of the gift tax, estate tax, and tax on generation-skipping transfers.

If a disclaimer qualifies under the § 2518 rules, the interest disclaimed is treated as though it had never been transferred to the individual making the disclaimer. Therefore, the transfer of property that occurs by virtue of the disclaimer is not treated as a gift for purposes of the gift tax. Similarly, the disclaimer is not treated as a transfer for purposes of the estate tax or the tax on generation-skipping transfers. § 2518(a); Reg. § 25.2518–1(b). For example, if a child of the decedent disclaims a bequest, with the result that under local law the property goes to the decedent's surviving spouse, the bequest will be treated as a transfer directly from the decedent spouse to the surviving spouse; therefore, it will qualify for the marital deduction with respect to the decedent's estate. Reg. § 20.2056(d)–2(b).

To qualify under § 2518, the disclaimer must be irrevocable and unconditional. In addition, the following requirements must be met:

1. The disclaimer must be in writing.

2. The disclaimer must be received by the transferor or the holder of title to the property not later than nine months after the transfer that creates the interest in the disclaimant. However, if the disclaimant is under age 21 when the interest is created, the period for making the disclaimer is extended until nine months after the disclaimant has reached age 21.

3. The disclaimant must not have accepted any interest or benefit with respect to the property disclaimed.

4. The interest disclaimed must pass to another person without any direction or control by the disclaimant.

The Treasury's regulations on disclaimers construe the requirements of § 2518 very strictly. For example, any "affirmative act which is consistent with ownership of the property," such as acceptance of dividends, interest, or rent, can be treated as a disqualifying acceptance of benefits. Reg. § 25.2518–2(d). Similarly, it the disclaimer causes property to pass to a trust over which the disclaimant has discretionary power to determine beneficial enjoyment by others, the property may be treated as having passed with direction by the disclaimant. In that event the disclaimer will not meet the test of § 2518(b)(4) and will be treated as a taxable gift by the disclaimant. Reg. § 25.2518–2(e). The idea is that the disclaimant must truly renounce any and all dominion over the property. The one exception to this rule involves the decedent's surviving spouse. A disclaimer by the surviving spouses qualifies even though the result of the disclaimer is to give the benefits of the property to the surviving spouse in another form. § 2518(b)(4)(A); Reg. § 25.2518–2(e)(2).

As noted in the preceding paragraph, and as specifically provided in § 2518(b)(3), a disclaimer is not qualified under § 2518 if, as of the time of the disclaimer, the disclaimant has "accepted the interest or any of its benefits." This rule creates a special problem with IRA's and qualified retirement plan interests, because the relevant income tax rules require that certain minimum distributions be made in each calendar year. § 401(a)(9). If the decedent dies before the distribution for the calendar year of death has been made, the distribution must be made in that calendar year to the named beneficiary. Depending on the date of death, the distribution may be made shortly after the date of death, and long before the expiration of the 9–month period § 2518 provides for disclaimers. This raises the question whether the beneficiary's receipt of such a required distribution violates § 2518(b)(3), thereby barring the beneficiary from disclaiming his or her remaining interest in the IRA or qualified plan. The IRS resolved this problem in Rev. Rul. 2005–36, 2005–26 I.R.B. 1368. The IRS ruled that receipt of a required distribution would not prevent the beneficiary from disclaiming the remaining value of the IRA. Although the ruling literally applies only to IRA's, the rationale should apply with equal force to qualified plans in general.

Special rules are applied to disclaimers of joint tenancy interests. As to property other than bank accounts and brokerage and investment accounts, application of § 2518 is premised on the concept that a two-step transfer is involved. First, one-half the property is deemed to be transferred when the transferor creates the joint tenancy. Second, the other one-half of the property is deemed to be transferred when the decedent joint tenant dies. In the typical case the decedent joint tenant dies more than nine months after the creation of the joint tenancy, so that a disclaimer of the first one-half after the decedent joint tenant's death would not be timely. But the surviving joint tenant can disclaim the second one-half within nine months after the death of the decedent joint tenant. This rule applies regardless of which joint tenant originally contributed the property, and regardless of whether local law permits each tenant to unilaterally sever the joint tenancy. Reg. § 25.2518–2(c)(4)(i). This rule, as stated in the Regulations, confirms and follows several court decisions: Kennedy v. Commissioner, 804 F.2d 1332 (7th Cir.1986); Estate of Dancy v. Commissioner, 872 F.2d 84 (4th Cir.1989); McDonald v. Commissioner, 853 F.2d 1494 (8th Cir.1988), cert. denied, 490 U.S. 1005 (1989).

A different rule is applied to joint bank, brokerage, and investment accounts. If under local law a transferor may unilaterally regain her contributions without the consent of the other joint tenant, with the result that under Reg. § 25.2511–1(h)(4) the transfer into joint tenancy is not a completed gift, the entire transfer to the surviving joint tenant is viewed as occurring upon the death of the first joint tenant to die. Therefore, the surviving joint tenant may disclaim the entirety of the joint tenancy property until nine months after the death of the decedent joint tenant. The surviving joint tenant, however, cannot disclaim any portion of the account attributable to consideration furnished by her. Reg. § 25.2518–2(c)(4)(iii). For example, if Alice contributed 70% of the property and Betty contributed 30%, a disclaimer of the entire account by Betty within nine months after Alice's death would be treated as follows. There would be a valid disclaimer as to 70%, and this amount would be treated as going directly from Alice to the persons entitled to the property under local law in the event Betty predeceased Alice. The remaining 30%, however, would not be treated as having been disclaimed, and Betty would be treated as making a gift of 30% of the property to the persons receiving that 30%.

A disclaimer of joint tenancy property can be very helpful in estates in which excessive joint tenancy is used. For example, assume that Mother and Father's assets are embodied entirely in their farm, which they own in joint tenancy, and that the estate tax applicable exclusion amount is $2,000,000. If the farm is worth $4,000,000 when Mother dies, and joint tenancy causes the farm to go in its entirety to Father, the estate tax results can be very expensive. If Mother has no other property, she will have failed to use any of her unified credit, and Father's unified credit will shelter only a portion of his estate from tax at his death. The remedy is a disclaimer by Father of one-half of the farm held in joint tenancy, with the result that one-half goes to the children, who are mother's heirs-at-law if father does not survive. The $2,000,000 portion of the farm going to the children is sheltered by unified credit, and Father's $2,000,000 portion may be sheltered by his unified credit at his death.

Disclaimers can be dangerous. A disclaimer that is valid for purposes of local property law may nevertheless be invalid for federal gift, estate, and generation-skipping tax purposes. Imagine, for example, a circumstance in which Father bequeaths property to Son. Son disclaims the property, with the result that the property goes to Father's widow. Although the disclaimer might be invalid for federal tax purposes because it violates one of the requirements of § 2518, it would nevertheless be valid for local property law purposes. As a result the property would go to the widow, with two unfortunate results: First, the property would be treated as transferred from Son to Mother as a taxable gift. Second, Son would no longer have any interest in the property and therefore might not have funds for payment of the gift tax.

Section 2518 is applicable only where the transfer creating an interest in the person disclaiming is made after 1976. In the case of transfers made before 1977, the rules relating to disclaimers in effect prior to 1977 remain applicable. In that event, under Reg. § 25.2511–1(c)(2), the disclaimer will be treated as a taxable gift unless it is made "within a reasonable time after knowledge of existence of the transfer." This rule applies to all pre–1977 transfers, including those that took place before the gift tax was adopted. United States v. Irvine, 511 U.S. 224 (1994).

Planning Note

[¶ 6013]

Disclaimers play an important role in tax-oriented estate planning. Three factors contribute to this phenomenon. First, the presence of § 2518 and of disclaimer statutes in most states permits certainty as to the property law and tax law results of a disclaimer. Second, the unlimited estate tax marital deduction, discussed in Chapter 27, makes it attractive to transfer all of the decedent spouse's property to the surviving spouse, giving the surviving

¶ 6001

spouse the opportunity to reduce the transfer by disclaimer if desired. Third, the substantial and growing size of the estate tax unified credit makes optimum use of the credit an important objective, and a disclaimer may be important in achieving that goal.

The typical plan relying on a disclaimer involves a bequest of most or all of the decedent spouse's property outright to the surviving spouse. This transfer qualifies for the unlimited estate tax marital deduction under § 2056. However, the decedent's will also creates a "bypass trust" that provides substantial economic benefits for the surviving spouse without causing inclusion of any of the bypass trust assets in the surviving spouse's gross estate. For example, the bypass trust may provide life income and limited principal invasion rights for the surviving spouse. The will may provide only a modest bequest or perhaps no bequest at all to the bypass trust.

The will further provides that, should the surviving spouse disclaim any of the property bequeathed to the surviving spouse, the property disclaimed will go to the bypass trust. This permits the surviving spouse to evaluate the family's financial circumstances during the nine months after the decedent spouse's death and then determine the best allocation of assets between the surviving spouse and the bypass trust. The optimum division is then accomplished by a partial or total disclaimer by the surviving spouse.

For example, assume that Wife dies with a gross estate of $3,500,000 when the estate tax applicable exclusion amount is $2,000,000. She bequeaths $500,000 outright to her children and the remaining $3,000,000 outright to Husband. However, Wife's will also creates a bypass trust and provides that any property disclaimed by Husband will go to the bypass trust. This arrangement permits Husband to evaluate the family's circumstances after Wife's death and decide how best to divide the estate. In most cases, it will be best for Husband to disclaim $1,500,000 to the bypass trust. This amount, together with the $500,000 bequest to the children, will fully utilize the $2,000,000 unified credit available at Wife's death.

The advantage of this disclaimer arrangement is great flexibility in adjusting the family's tax planning after Wife's death, providing an important opportunity for postmortem tax planning. This opportunity is especially important in times of uncertainty as to the time when one of the spouses might die, or as to the law that might be in effect at that time.

Problems

[¶ 6025]

1. Sallie Wilson signed her will in 1994. At that time she owned 100 shares of Tech Corp. stock, which were then worth only $5,000. In her will she bequeathed all shares of Tech Corp. stock she owned at her death to her daughter, Alice. Sallie's will provided that, in the event Alice did not survive Sallie, the Tech Corp. stock would go to Sallie's husband, Alan. Sallie bequeathed all the rest of her estate to Alan. Under § 2056(a), the general rule is that any property that goes outright to the spouse of a decedent qualifies for the marital deduction, with the result that the marital deduction property is excluded from the decedent's taxable estate.

¶ 6025

Sallie died on February 2, 2006. Tech Corp. prospered greatly in the 12 years prior to Sallie's death. By the time of Sallie's death, after numerous stock splits, the original 100 shares had grown to 3,000 shares, with a total value of $2,500,000. The remainder of Sallie's assets had a value of $500,000.

By the time of Sallie's death Alice had become very prosperous. Also, she was concerned about Alan, who owned few assets. Finally, she was concerned about the estate taxes that would be imposed on Sallie's estate if Alice received the Tech Corp. stock.

As a result, on September 20, 2006, Alice disclaimed all rights to the Tech Corp. stock. The disclaimer was delivered to Sallie's executor, a bank, which then distributed all 3000 shares of Tech Corp. stock to Alan. Under local law the disclaimer is valid, with the result that the Tech Corp. stock is disposed of as if Alice had predeceased Sallie.

How much estate tax is owed at Sallie's death? Does Alice owe any gift tax? If so, how much?

2. Assume the same facts as in Part A, except that Alice does not execute the disclaimer until November 20, 2006. Under local law the disclaimer is valid, with the result that the Tech Corp. stock goes to Alan.

How much estate tax is owed at Sallie's death? Does Alice owe any gift tax? If so, how much?

¶ 6025

Chapter 7

UNIFIED CREDIT, EXCLUSIONS AND DEDUCTIONS

A. UNIFIED CREDIT

[¶ 7001]

As explained in Chapter 2, § 2505 provides a credit against the gift tax. In 2002 the credit amount reached $345,800—equivalent to the tax imposed on taxable gifts totaling $1,000,000. The practical effect is to shelter the first $1,000,000 of taxable gifts from tax. The $1,000,000 amount is referred to in the statute as the "applicable exclusion amount." § 2505(a)(1). Although the applicable exclusion amount for estate tax purposes rose above $1,000,000 after 2003, the applicable exclusion amount for gift tax purposes remains permanently capped at $1,000,000. §§ 2010(c) and 2505(a)(1).

The credit is referred to as "unified" because it is available only once to each taxpayer and applies to both inter-vivos transfers and transfers at death. To the extent the gift tax credit is used to shelter lifetime transfers, the benefit of the credit against the estate tax will be concomitantly reduced. This is not achieved by reducing the estate tax credit as such, but through the § 2001(b) estate tax computation process. Although the statutory provisions incorporating the unified credit appear to permit double use of the credit, once during life and again at death, the mechanics of the tax computation under § 2001(b) are such that each individual can obtain the benefit of only a single unified credit, the maximum credit being the estate tax credit applicable in the year of the individual's death. This phenomenon is explained at ¶ 2007 and is illustrated by the problem at ¶ 2013.

The objective of Congress in adopting the unified credit was to exempt modest estates from tax. Congress chose a credit approach rather than a deduction approach so that the economic benefit of the credit would be the same regardless of the size of the estate. If Congress had granted a deduction, the benefit of the deduction would have varied depending on the size of the estate. For example, in 2006 a deduction of $2,000,000 would produce a tax saving of $780,800 for an estate having a value of $2,000,000. But for an estate having a value of $12,000,000, and therefore subject to a marginal tax rate of 46%, the tax saving would be $920,000.

By contrast, the credit approach reduces the tax burden of any estate valued at $2,000,000 or more—regardless of size—by exactly $780,800. The practical effect is to shelter the "first" $2,000,000 of the taxable estate from tax. If the taxpayer makes taxable gifts, the same sheltering effect occurs as to the first $1,000,000 of taxable gifts.

The credit and deduction approaches, respectively, will produce this difference in results if implemented without changing the underlying rate structure. The effect of either the credit or deduction approach can be dramatically changed if adoption of the credit or deduction is accompanied by a change in the rate structure. See Turnier & Kelly, "The Economic Equivalence of Standard Tax Credits, Deductions and Exemptions," 36 Fla. L. Rev. 1003 (1984).

Planning Note

[¶ 7007]

The continuing increases in the unified credit give the credit a central role in tax planning. With proper planning, a married couple dying in 2006 can pass a total of $4,000,000 to their descendants (or others) entirely tax free. However, the requirement of "proper planning" cannot be taken lightly. As described in fuller detail in connection with the estate tax, maximum use of the unified credit at the death of each spouse requires a careful pattern of division and disposition of property to assure the overall optimum result.

For example, assume the case of Husband and Wife, both of whom die in 2006. Wife owns property worth $4,000,000, while Husband owns no property. If Wife dies first, no tax will be imposed at her death if the entirety of her property is bequeathed to Husband. The § 2056 estate tax unlimited marital deduction will shelter the entire $4,000,000 transfer from tax.

When Husband dies later in 2006 and bequeaths the $4,000,000 to the couple's children, there will be a taxable estate of $4,000,000, only $2,000,000 of which will be sheltered from tax by Husband's unified credit. The § 2001 tax before application of the unified credit is $1,700,800, and the unified credit is only $780,800. Therefore, a tax of $920,000 must be paid. In effect, failure of the couple to use any of Wife's unified credit imposes an unnecessary tax cost on the children in the amount of $920,000.

The remedy for this problem is a transfer by Wife at her death of $2,000,000 to the children or to a "bypass trust," i.e., a trust that provides income and other benefits for Husband without causing inclusion of the trust assets in Husband's gross estate. If Wife dies first, this approach limits Husband's prospective estate to $2,000,000—an amount that can be fully sheltered by his unified credit. Therefore, the entire $4,000,000 is ultimately passed to the children free of any tax, producing a tax saving for the family of $920,000. (Of course, appreciation of Husband's assets above $2,000,000 would cause payment of tax at Husband's death unless Husband can reduce his estate through nontaxable or other means.)

The only remaining problem is the possibility that Husband might predecease Wife, so that Husband's unified credit would go unused and Wife

¶ 7001

would have a taxable estate of $4,000,000, again costing the family $920,000 in estate tax. The remedy for this is an inter-vivos transfer by Wife to Husband of $2,000,000, a transfer that will be entirely free of gift tax by virtue of the § 2523 gift tax marital deduction. This permits Husband to bequeath $2,000,000 to the children or a bypass trust, thereby using the entirety of his unified credit should he predecease. This assures no tax regardless of the order of deaths. The family thereby saves $920,000 in taxes.

Note that the above example relates to deaths in 2006, when the estate tax applicable exclusion amount is $2,000,000. Under current law, the estate tax applicable exclusion amount is scheduled to rise to $3,500,000 in 2009. This will dramatically raise the amount a couple can shelter from tax in this way. For example, if the couple described above own assets worth $7,000,000 and die in 2009 (when the applicable exclusion amount is $3,500,000), the entire $7,000,000 can be sheltered from tax if proper planning, as described above, is employed.

As noted above, the gift tax applicable exclusion amount is permanently capped at $1,000,000. For that reason taxpayers wishing to minimize taxes in this way may need to defer until death a portion of their transfers to their children. For example, if Wife makes a taxable gift of $2,000,000 to the children rather than deferring the transfer until her death, the gift tax applicable exclusion amount would shelter only $1,000,000 of the gift, and a gift tax of $435,000 would be payable. This tax could be entirely avoided if Wife transferred only $1,000,000 by gift and deferred the remaining $1,000,000 transfer until death.

B. ANNUAL PER DONEE EXCLUSION

[¶ 7013]

1. IN GENERAL

A provision of central importance to the gift tax is § 2503(b), which provides an annual per donee exclusion. The exclusion is "annual" because the specified amount is available anew each year. The exclusion is "per donee" because gifts of the specified amount to each and every donee, without limitation as to number, may be excluded by a single donor. The exclusion is not limited to donees who are family members.

The exclusion was originally set at $5,000 in 1932 and then reduced to $4,000 in 1939 and $3,000 in 1942. It remained at $3,000 until 1981, when it was raised to $10,000 for gifts after 1981. The exclusion remained fixed at $10,000 through 1998 but was indexed for inflation thereafter. Under the indexing regime set forth in § 2503(b)(2), the exclusion amount is not increased until indexation requires an additional amount of at least $1,000. Therefore, several years pass between increases in the exclusion. The exclusion amount was raised to $11,000 effective in 2002, and to $12,000 effective in 2006. Several of the cases referred to in this chapter were decided when the exclusion amount was only $3,000.

The exclusion occupies an important position in gift and estate planning. Continued and carefully planned use of the exclusion provides a ready vehicle for transfer of substantial amounts to younger generations without a tax burden of any kind.

For example, assume that parents with substantial wealth have three children and seven grandchildren, and that the exclusion amount is $12,000. Ten donees are available, and the husband and wife together may give $24,000 to each donee each year tax free. As a result, $240,000 can be transferred entirely tax free to the children and grandchildren each year. Continuation of this pattern over a ten-year period would permit tax-free transfer of $2,400,000.

This method of avoiding transfer taxes is especially convenient and attractive if each spouse makes one-half of the gifts from his or her own funds, so that § 2513 gift-splitting (see ¶ 8007 below) need not be used. In that event no gift tax return will be required for any of the gifts. § 6019(a)(1). The same no-return result can be achieved even if only one spouse will provide the gift property. If the spouse from whose assets the gifts are to be made transfers one-half of the intended gift property outright to the other spouse, followed by independent gifts of that amount by the transferee spouse, no return is necessary. The transfer between spouses is covered by the § 2523 gift tax marital deduction, and no return need be filed with respect to transfers that qualify for the deduction. § 6019(a)(2).

If only one spouse is to make the gifts, and that spouse is unwilling to make an outright transfer to the other spouse as described in the preceding paragraph, the full benefit of the annual per donee exclusion is nevertheless available through gift-splitting under § 2513. As explained at ¶ 8007, below, if both spouses agree to treat the gifts of either spouse as if made one-half by each spouse, each gift is treated as split between the spouses for all purposes of the gift tax. If Wife gives $24,000 to Son, and Husband agrees to split gifts, Wife and Husband are each treated as giving $12,000 to Son. Gift splitting is available only if gift tax returns are filed by both spouses. § 2513(b); Reg. § 25.2513-2.

A further attraction of annual per donee exclusion gifts is the zero inclusion ratio assigned to most such gifts for purposes of the tax on generation-skipping transfers. § 2642(c). As a result, such gifts may entirely escape the generation-skipping tax, regardless of the number of generations skipped. See Chapter 29.

2. PRESENT INTEREST REQUIREMENT

[¶ 7019]

a. *Limitation on Annual Exclusion*

The most important limitation on the annual exclusion is that it does not apply to gifts of future interests. A gift of a future interest is fully subject to tax except to the extent sheltered by deductions or the unified credit. Reg. § 25.2503-3(a) states:

¶ 7013

"Future interests" is a legal term, and includes reversions, remainders, and other interests or estates, whether vested or contingent, and whether or not supported by a particular interest or estate, which are limited to commence in use, possession, or enjoyment at some future date or time. The term has no reference to such contractual rights as exist in a bond, note (though bearing no interest until maturity), or in a policy of life insurance, the obligations of which are to be discharged by payments in the future.

By contrast, the Regulations define a present interest as "an unrestricted right to the immediate use, possession, or enjoyment of property or the income from property (such as a life estate or term certain)." Reg. § 25.2503–3(b). Thus, an unrestricted gift of an immediate income interest in a trust is a gift of a present interest for which an exclusion is available to the extent of the actuarial value of the income interest.

If an income interest is given, the exclusion is available only if the donor transfers the unrestricted right to receive all or some identifiable part of the income, beginning immediately. If the donor transfers the right to a fixed percentage of the income the gift constitutes a present interest in the amount of that percentage multiplied by the actuarial value of the entire income interest.

If the beneficiary's right to income is restricted or deferred in any way, the income right is a future interest and does not qualify for the exclusion. For example, if the trustee is to distribute to the beneficiary only such income as the trustee determines to be desirable, there is no present interest. Similarly, if the beneficiary has an unrestricted right to income but will not begin receiving income until the end of a significant period of time after the transfer, there is no present interest. Reg. § 25.2503–3. The deferral rule is applied strictly. For example, in Estate of Jardell v. Commissioner, 24 T.C. 652 (1955), the donor transferred on October 2, 1949, the right to receive royalties from mineral production occurring after December 31, 1949. The Tax Court held that the delay of less than three months prevented the transfer from qualifying as a present interest.

An indirect gift (discussed at ¶ 3085) may or may not constitute a present interest. If the donor transfers property to a corporation, thereby gratuitously benefitting its shareholders, an indirect gift to the shareholders has occurred. The gift, however, is not a present interest because the shareholders have no immediate right to the benefits of the gift. Estate of Stinson v. United States, 214 F.3d 846 (7th Cir. 2000); Georgia L. Ketteman Testamentary Trust v. Commissioner, 86 T.C. 91 (1986); Rev. Rul. 71–443, 1971–2 C.B. 337. By contrast, if the donor gratuitously transfers property to a general partnership, thereby making a gift to the partners, the result is different. Under the Uniform Partnership Act, the partners have an immediate right to withdraw the amounts in their respective capital accounts. Therefore, a gift that increases a partner's capital account constitutes a present interest. Wooley v. United States, 736 F.Supp. 1506 (S.D.Ind.1990).

A gift to a limited partnership, or a gift consisting of a limited partnership interest, may or may not qualify as a present interest. In Tech. Adv.

¶ 7019

Mem. 9751003, the IRS concluded that gifts of limited partnership interests did not constitute present interests. The donee limited partners had no certain entitlement to an income stream, but would receive only such distributions as the general partner thought appropriate. Furthermore, the donee limited partners could not freely sell their interests, but were subject to significant restrictions.

If a gift is made to an entity that is charitable, public, or political, with the result that the members or owners have no economic interest in the entity, the gift is treated as made to the entity rather than the members. Reg. § 25.2511–1(h)(1). For example, in Priv. Ltr. Rul. 9818042, the taxpayer made a gift to a social club exempt from income taxation under § 501(c)(7). The IRS concluded that no individual member had an economic interest in the gift, with the result that the gift was treated as made to the club, not the members. Because the club had the right to immediate and unrestricted use of the gift, the gift qualified for the § 2503(b) exclusion.

It is important to remember that the present interest question is secondary to, and entirely apart from, the question whether a gift is complete. One first determines whether a gift is complete, using the principles explored in Chapter 4. Only if the gift is complete does one then ask whether the gift constitutes a present interest. A conclusion that the gift is not a present interest has no effect whatever on the prior conclusion that the gift is complete.

Problem

[¶ 7021]

Fred is very generous. During the current year he made gifts as described below. In the case of each gift, state whether any portion of the gift constitutes a present interest for purposes of § 2503(b), thereby qualifying for the annual per donee exclusion.

(a) Fred gave $10,000 in cash to Artemis.

(b) Fred gave to Betty an insurance policy on Fred's life. The amount payable upon Fred's death is $100,000. Betty has an insurable interest in Fred's life, and at the time of the gift the policy had a market value of $5,000.

(c) Fred paid the annual premium of $3,000 under a $100,000 insurance policy on Fred's life owned by Carl, who has an insurable interest in Fred's life.

(d) Fred contributed $30,000 to Powell Corporation, a manufacturing business. The stock of Powell Corporation is owned in equal one-third amounts by Dalton, Dewey, and Doris. Fred has no interest in the corporation.

(e) Fred transferred $40,000 to the Wilfong Trust. A bank is the trustee, and the trust is to last for 12 years. The trust instrument provides that one-half of the trust income must be paid to Ernest each year. The trustee has discretion to distribute to Ernest the other one-half of the income, as well as any or all of the principal. Upon termination of the trust, the principal and accumulated income are to be paid to Edgar.

(f) Fred transferred $50,000 to the Fargo Trust. A bank serves as trustee, and the trust is to last for 12 years. The income for the first eight months of the trust is to be accumulated. The trustee is to pay all trust income earned after the first eight months to Felipe on an annual basis. Upon termination of the trust all trust property is to be paid to Alice.

(g) Fred transferred $30,000 to the Patterson Partnership, a general partnership in which Pat, Paul, and Pedro are each equal, one-third partners. Fred has no interest in the Patterson Partnership.

(h) Fred transferred $30,000 to the Ignatius Trust. A bank serves as trustee, and the trust is to last for 12 years. Each year the entirety of the income is to be paid to Ichabod, Irene, and Isadore in such shares as the trustee in its discretion determines.

(i) Fred transferred $20,000 to the Jewell Trust. A bank serves as trustee, and the trust is to last for 12 years. Jordan is to receive all income of the trust annually, and upon termination of the trust the trust property is to be paid to Jarboe. The trustee has power to distribute principal to Jennifer at any time.

[¶ 7025]

b. Trusts: Requirement of Income–Producing Property

If property is transferred outright, and the donee is free to sell or otherwise dispose of the property, the transfer constitutes a present interest whether or not the property produces income. For example, an outright gift of unproductive land is a present interest because the donee could sell the land and realize an immediate cash benefit.

If property is transferred in trust, however, the income producing capacity of the property has a direct bearing on availability of the annual per donee exclusion for an income interest. Although the donee may be entitled to any income produced by the property, the right to income is meaningless if there is no realistic expectation that income will in fact be produced. As evidenced by the following case, the IRS, with considerable success, has taken the position that the annual per donee exclusion is not available for a gift of closely held stock to a trust if the stock cannot realistically be expected to produce dividend income.

[¶ 7031]

STARK v. UNITED STATES

United States Court of Appeals, Eighth Circuit, 1973.
477 F.2d 131, cert. denied, 414 U.S. 975 (1973).

PER CURIAM:

We are presented with the question whether, in order to claim the $3,000 gift tax exclusion pursuant to 26 U.S.C. § 2503(b), a taxpayer might satisfy his burden of proving that an income interest in a trust has "ascertainable value,"[1] by reference to the actuarial tables found in Treas. Reg. 26 CFR § 25.2512–5(c).

The taxpayer made gifts of the stock of a closely held corporation to three trusts, for the benefit of each of the taxpayers' three minor grandchildren. The beneficiaries were to receive the net income from the trusts until each reached the age of 30, at which time the beneficiaries could terminate the trusts and receive the trust corpus. The parties agree that the gifts of the shares of stock to the trusts constitute gifts of future interests and thus are not subject to the annual exclusion, but the taxpayers claim that their making the gifts of the income from the stock entitles each to the annual exclusion of $3,000 for each beneficiary of the trusts pursuant to § 2503(b). The taxpayers based their asserted right to the exclusions on the argument that the right of the beneficiaries to the net income of the trusts was a present interest and was capable of valuation by the use of the actuarial tables prepared by the Commissioner in Treas. Reg. § 25.2512–5(c). The Government argued that since the stock of the corporation had never publicly traded and since no dividends had been paid on the stock since 1950, the taxpayers had not established an "ascertainable value" for the right to the income from the stock held in trust.

The undisputed evidence indicates, and the district court specifically found, that there was little possibility that any income would be forthcoming to the beneficiaries from the trusts in question. Under these circumstances, we hold that the income interest had no ascertainable value, and that the taxpayers cannot be allowed to assert a value for the income interest simply by using the actuarial tables of Treas. Reg. § 25.2512–5(c). * * *

Note

[¶ 7037]

The requirement of income production in the case of trust interests has been applied to assets other than closely held stock. In Calder v. Commissioner, 85 T.C. 713 (1985), the donor transferred Alexander Calder paintings to trusts that required payment to the beneficiaries of any income earned by the

---

1. In order for a gift to be subject to the § 2503(b) exclusion, two requirements must be satisfied. First, the gift must not be a gift of a future interest, as that term is defined in Treas. Reg. 26 C.F.R. § 25.2503–3(a). Second, the gift must have an "ascertainable value." This requirement of ascertainable value is one judicially imposed. * * *

trust. In addition, the trust instruments permitted the trustees to convert the paintings to income-producing property. The Tax Court nevertheless denied annual per donee exclusions for the gifts because there was no showing that the paintings were likely to produce income.

The rule enunciated in *Stark* applies only to gifts in trust. If the property is given outright, and the donee is free to sell or otherwise transfer the property, its income-producing capacity is irrelevant because the donee could sell the property for its fair market value and reinvest the proceeds. Also, the *Stark* rule does not apply "to such contractual rights as exist in a bond, note (though bearing no interest until maturity), or in a policy of life insurance, the obligations of which are to be discharged by payments in the future." Reg. § 25.2503–3(a). Presumably this exception is based on the assumption that bonds, notes, and the like are readily marketable for cash, thereby giving the donee immediate access to cash if desired. It could be argued that similar interests in trusts should likewise be treated as present interests, at least if readily marketable. But the IRS has consistently and successfully rejected this argument in the case of trust interests.

c. *Restrictions on Transfer*

[¶ 7038]

HACKL v. COMMISSIONER

United States Court of Appeals, Seventh Circuit, 2003.
335 F.3d 664.

TERENCE T. EVANS, Circuit Judge.

Most post-retirement hobbies don't involve multi-million dollar companies or land retirees in hot water with the IRS, but those are the circumstances in this case. Albert J. (A.J.) and Christine M. Hackl began a tree-farming business after A.J.'s retirement and gave shares in the company to family members. The Hackls believed the transfers were excludable from the gift tax, but the IRS thought otherwise. The Tax Court agreed with the IRS, *Hackl v. Comm'r,* 118 T.C. 279, 2002 WL 467117 (2002), resulting in a gift tax deficiency of roughly $400,000 for the couple. The Hackls appeal.

Our story begins with A.J. Hackl's retirement and subsequent search for a hobby that would allow him to keep his hand in the business world, diversify his investments, and provide a long-term investment for his family. Tree-farming fit the bill and, in 1995, A.J. purchased two tree farms (worth around $4.5 million) and contributed them, as well as about $8 million in cash and securities, to Treeco, LLC, a limited liability company that he set up in Indiana * * *

A.J. and his wife, Christine, initially owned all of Treeco's stock (which included voting and nonvoting shares), with A.J. serving as the company's manager. Under Treeco's operating agreement, the manager served for life (or until resignation, removal, or incapacity), had the power to appoint a successor, and could also dissolve the company. In addition, the manager controlled any financial distributions, and members needed his approval to withdraw from the company or sell shares. If a member transferred his or her shares without consent, the transferee would receive the shares' economic rights but not any membership or voting rights. Voting members could run Treeco during any interim period between managers, approve any salaries or bonuses paid by the company, and remove a manager and elect a successor. With an 80–percent majority, voting members could amend the Articles of Organization and operating agreement and dissolve the company after A.J.'s tenure as manager. Both the voting and the nonvoting members had the right to access Treeco's books and records and to decide whether to continue Treeco following an event of dissolution (such as the death, resignation, removal, retirement, bankruptcy, or insanity of the manager). During A.J.'s watch, Treeco has operated at a loss and not made any distributions to its stockholders. While Treeco has yet to turn a profit, A.J. was named "Tree Farmer of the Year" in Putnam County, Florida, in 1999.

Shortly after Treeco's creation, A.J. and Christine began annual transfers of Treeco voting and nonvoting shares to their children, their children's spouses, and a trust set up for the couple's grandchildren. After January 1998, 51 percent of the company's voting shares were in the hands of the couple's children and their spouses. The Hackls attempted to shield the transfers from taxation by treating them as excludable gifts on their gift tax returns. While the Internal Revenue Code imposes a tax on gifts, 26 U.S.C. § 2501(a), a donor does not pay the tax on the first $10,000 of gifts, "other than gifts of future interests in property," made to any person during the calendar year, 26 U.S.C. § 2503(b)(1). Unfortunately for the Hackls, the IRS thought that the transfers were future interests and ineligible for the gift tax exclusion. The Hackls took the dispute to the Tax Court which, as we said, sided with the IRS.

* * *

The crux of the Hackls' appeal is that the gift tax doesn't apply to a transfer if the donors give up all of their legal rights. In other words, the future interest exception to the gift tax exclusion only comes into play if the donee has gotten something less than the full bundle of legal property rights. Because the Hackls gave up all of their property rights to the shares, they think that the shares were excludable gifts within the plain meaning of § 2503(b)(1). The government, on the other hand, interprets the gift tax exclusion more narrowly. It argues that any transfer without a substantial present economic benefit is a future interest and ineligible for the gift tax exclusion.

The Hackls' initial argument is that § 2503(b)(1) automatically allows the gift tax exclusion for their transfers. The Hackls argue that their position reflects the plain—and only—meaning of "future interest" as used in the statute, and that the Tax Court's reliance on materials outside the statute (such as the Treasury regulation definition of future interest and case law) was not only unnecessary, it was wrong. We disagree. Calling any tax law "plain" is a hard row to hoe, and a number of cases (including our decision in *Stinson Estate v. United States,* 214 F.3d 846 (7th Cir.2000)) have looked

¶ 7038

beyond the language of § 2503(b)(1) for guidance. *See, e.g., United States v. Pelzer,* 312 U.S. 399, 403–04, 61 S.Ct. 659, 85 L.Ed. 913 (1941), and *Comm'r v. Disston,* 325 U.S. 442, 446, 65 S.Ct. 1328, 89 L.Ed. 1720 (1945) (stating that regulatory definition of future interest has been approved repeatedly). The Hackls do not cite any cases that actually characterize § 2503(b)(1) as plain, and the term "future interest" is not defined in the statute itself. Furthermore, the fact that both the government and the Hackls have proposed different—yet reasonable—interpretations of the statute shows that it is ambiguous. Under these circumstances, it was appropriate for the Tax Court to look to the Treasury regulation and case law for guidance.

Hedging their bet, the Hackls say that the applicable Treasury regulation supports the conclusion that giving up all legal rights to a gift automatically makes it a present interest. The applicable Treasury regulation states that a "future interest" is a legal term that applies to interests "which are limited to commence in use, possession, or enjoyment at some future date or time," Treas. Reg. § 25.2503–3. The regulation also provides that a present interest in property is "[a]n unrestricted right to the immediate use, possession, or enjoyment of property or the income from property (such as a life estate or term certain)." We don't think that this language automatically excludes all outright transfers from the gift tax. *See also Hamilton v. United States,* 553 F.2d 1216, 1218 (9th Cir.1977).

We previously addressed the issue of future interests for purposes of the gift tax exclusion in *Stinson Estate.* In that case, forgiveness of a corporation's indebtedness was a future interest outside the gift tax exclusion because shareholders could not individually realize the gift without liquidating the corporation or declaring a dividend—events that could not occur upon the actions of any one individual under the corporation's bylaws. *See* 214 F.3d at 848. We said that the "sole statutory distinction between present and future interests lies in the question of whether there is postponement of enjoyment of specific rights, powers or privileges which would be forthwith existent if the interest were present." *Id.* at 848–49 (quoting *Howe v. United States,* 142 F.2d 310, 312 (7th Cir.1944)). In other words, the phrase "present interest" connotes the right to substantial present economic benefit. *See Fondren v. Comm'r,* 324 U.S. 18, 20, 65 S.Ct. 499, 89 L.Ed. 668 (1945).

In this case, Treeco's operating agreement clearly foreclosed the donees' ability to realize any substantial present economic benefit. Although the voting shares that the Hackls gave away had the same legal rights as those that they retained, Treeco's restrictions on the transferability of the shares meant that they were essentially without immediate value to the donees. Granted, Treeco's operating agreement did address the possibility that a shareholder might violate the agreement and sell his or her shares without the manager's approval. But, as the Tax Court found, the possibility that a shareholder might violate the operating agreement and sell his or her shares to a transferee who would then not have any membership or voting rights can hardly be called a substantial economic benefit. Thus, the Hackls' gifts—while outright—were not gifts of present interests.

¶ 7038

The Hackls protest that Treeco is set up like any other limited liability corporation and that its restrictions on the alienability of its shares are common in closely held companies. While that may be true, the fact that other companies operate this way does not mean that shares in such companies should automatically be considered present interests for purposes of the gift tax exclusion. As we have previously said, Internal Revenue Code provisions dealing with exclusions are matters of legislative grace that must be narrowly construed. *See Stinson Estate,* 214 F.3d at 848. The onus is on the taxpayers to show that their transfers qualify for the gift tax exclusion, a burden the Hackls have not met.

The decision of the Tax Court is AFFIRMED.

[¶ 7039]

3. GIFTS TO MINORS

As explained above, the annual per donee exclusion is not available unless the donee receives either outright ownership or an unrestricted and immediate right to income from the property. This requirement impairs the practical utility of the exclusion if the gift is to be made to a minor.

For example, assume that Grandmother, who has a substantial estate, wishes to make gifts to each of several grandchildren. The grandchildren vary in age from 4 to 16, and Grandmother intends that the gifts be used to fund college educations for the grandchildren. Grandmother fears that outright gifts would not accomplish this purpose because the grandchildren might use the property for other purposes. For the same reason, she is uncomfortable with gifts to trusts that would require distribution of income to the grandchildren.

The situation is frustrating for Grandmother because the annual per donee exclusion offers such an attractive opportunity to transfer substantial amounts to her descendants without any tax burden. Planners have responded to such circumstances with efforts to devise vehicles that will accomplish Grandmother's purposes. As demonstrated below, Congress has done its part through enactment of §§ 529 and 2503(c), and creative lawyering has played an important role as well.

a. Outright Gifts

[¶ 7041]

REVENUE RULING 54–400
1954–2 C.B. 319.

Advice is requested whether a gift of shares of stock to a minor is a gift of a present or a future interest where the shares are issued in the name of minor (1) before the appointment of a legal guardian, (2) after the appointment of a legal guardian, or (3) if no legal guardian is appointed.

Section 86.11 of Regulation 108 provides that no part of the value of a gift of a future interest may be excluded in determining the total amount of gifts

¶ 7038

made during the calendar year. "Future interests" is a legal term, and includes reversions, remainders, and other interests or estates, whether vested or contingent, and whether or not supported by a particular interest or estate, which are limited to commence in use, possession, or enjoyment at some future date or time.

An unqualified and unrestricted gift to a minor, with or without the appointment of a legal guardian, is a gift of a present interest; and disabilities placed upon minors by State statutes should not be considered decisive in determining whether such donees have the immediate enjoyment of the property or the income therefrom within the purport of the Federal gift tax law. See John E. Daniels v. Commissioner, Tax Court Memorandum Opinion entered February 13, 1951. In the case of an outright and unrestricted gift to a minor, the mere existence or nonexistence of a legal guardianship does not of itself raise the question whether the gift is of a future interest. Cf. Rev. Rul. 54–91, C. B. 1954–1, 207 involving a gift in trust for the benefit of a minor. It is only where delivery of the property to the guardian of a minor is accompanied by limitations upon the present use and enjoyment of the property by the donee, by way of a trust or otherwise, that the question of a future interest arises. See Kathryn Schuhmacher, 8 T.C. 453.

In view of the foregoing, it is held that a gift of the type involved herein to a minor is a gift of a present interest unless the use and enjoyment of the property is in some manner limited or restricted by the terms of the donor's conveyance. The exclusion authorized by section 1003(b) of the Internal Revenue Code of 1939 [1986 Code § 2503(b)] may be applied against such gift.

b. *Trust Gifts in General*

[¶ 7049]

At an early date the Supreme Court confronted the issue of trust gifts benefitting minors. Fondren v. Commissioner, 324 U.S. 18 (1945); Commissioner v. Disston, 325 U.S. 442 (1945). In each case the donor created a trust for the benefit of a minor. In *Fondren* the trustee had discretionary power to distribute principal and income for the support, maintenance, and education of the minor. In *Disston* the trustee was specifically directed to apply for the minor's benefit such income "as may be necessary for the education, comfort, and support" of the minor. In both cases the Supreme Court concluded that the minor had no entitlement to a specific and identifiable income stream. Therefore, there was no present interest. This was true despite the "education, comfort, and support" mandate in *Disston* because it was not possible to identify a specific amount of income that would be distributed for those purposes. Hence the annual per donee exclusion was denied in both cases.

Planners then turned to another approach. As explained at ¶ 7025, above, an outright gift always constitutes a present interest. Planners reasoned that if the minor (or the minor's guardian) is given an unfettered right to demand the trust property, the minor should be viewed as having the equivalent of outright ownership; that should certainly constitute a present interest. The result was creation of trusts for the benefit of minors, with provision for discretionary distributions of principal and income to the minor, and with the added element that the minor or the minor's guardian could demand and receive the trust property at any time.

This "right of withdrawal" approach was successful in the Seventh Circuit, which concluded that the minor, regardless of age, regardless of the extent of need for funds, and regardless of whether a guardian had in fact been appointed, must be viewed as possessing a withdrawal right tantamount to outright ownership. Hence the annual per donee exclusion was allowed for the entire transfer in trust. Kieckhefer v. Commissioner, 189 F.2d 118 (7th Cir.1951).

The Second Circuit was less hospitable. It concluded that under *Fondren* the minor's access to the property must be evaluated in realistic terms, taking into account the probability that the minor would in fact need funds and whether a guardian had in fact been appointed. Stifel v. Commissioner, 197 F.2d 107 (2d Cir.1952). The practical effect of the Second Circuit view was to deny or severely limit the exclusion in most cases.

c. *Crummey Trusts: General Rule*

[¶ 7071]

The split between *Kieckhefer* and *Stifel* regarding withdrawal rights left the estate planning community uncertain as to whether providing a withdrawal right could assure availability of the annual per donee exclusion. Even if the *Kieckhefer* view should prevail, there remained the problem that the withdrawal right remained extant indefinitely, posing the threat that the minor might actually exercise the right and thereby thwart the donor's intent.

Both issues were resolved in the case that follows, which has given its name to a widely used technique that can now assure availability of the annual per donee exclusion while minimizing the minor's access to the funds.

[¶ 7073]

CRUMMEY v. COMMISSIONER

United States Court of Appeals, Ninth Circuit, 1968.
397 F.2d 82.

BYRNE, District Judge:

* * *

On February 12, 1962, the petitioners executed, as grantors, an irrevocable living trust for the benefit of their four children. The beneficiaries and their ages at relevant times are as follows:

	Age 12/31/62	Age 12/31/63
John Knowles Crummey	22	23
Janet Sheldon Crummey	20	21
David Clarke Crummey	15	16

¶ 7049

	Age 12/31/62	Age 12/31/63
Mark Clifford Crummey	11	12

Originally the sum of $50 was contributed to the trust. Thereafter, additional contributions were made by each of the petitioners in the following amounts and on the following dates:

$4,267.77 .... 6/20/62
49,550.00 .... 12/15/62
12,797.81 .... 12/19/63

The dispute revolves around the tax years of 1962 and 1963. Each of the petitioners filed a gift tax return for each year. Each petitioner claimed a $3,000 per beneficiary tax exclusion under the provisions of 26 U.S.C. 2503(b). The total claimed exclusions were as follows:

D.C. Crummey .... 1962—$12,000 1963—$12,000
E.E. Crummey .... 1962—$12,000 1963—$12,000

The Commissioner of Internal Revenue determined that each of the petitioners was entitled to only one $3,000 exclusion for each year. This determination was based upon the Commissioner's belief that the portion of the gifts in trust for the children under the age of 21 were "future interests" which are disallowed under § 2503(b). The taxpayers contested the determination of a deficiency in the Tax Court. The Commissioner conceded by stipulation in that proceeding that each petitioner was entitled to an additional $3,000 exclusion for the year 1963 by reason of Janet Crummey having reached the age of 21.

The Tax Court followed the Commissioner's interpretation as to gifts in trust to David and Mark, but determined that the 1962 gift in trust to Janet qualified as a gift of a present interest because of certain additional rights accorded to persons 18 and over by California law. Thus, the Tax Court held that each petitioner was entitled to an additional $3,000 exclusion for the year 1962.

The key provision of the trust agreement is the "demand" provision which states:

> THREE *Additions*. The Trustee may receive any other real or personal property from the Trustors (or either of them) or from any other person or persons, by lifetime gift, under a Will or Trust or from any other source. Such property will be held by the Trustee subject to the terms of this Agreement. A donor may designate or allocate all of his gift to one or more Trusts, or in stated amounts to different Trusts. If the donor does not specifically designate what amount of his gift is to augment each Trust, the Trustee shall divide such gift equally between the Trust then existing, established by this Agreement. The Trustee agrees, if he accepts such additions, to hold and manage such additions in trust for the uses and in the manner set forth herein. *With respect to such additions, each child of the Trustors may demand at any time (up to and*

¶ 7073

including December 31 of the year in which a transfer to his or her Trust has been made) the sum of Four Thousand Dollars ($4,000) or the amount of the transfer from each donor, whichever is less, payable in cash immediately upon receipt by the Trustee of the demand in writing and in any event, not later than December 31 in the year in which such transfer was made. Such payment shall be made from the gift of that donor for that year. If a child is a minor at the time of such gift of that donor for that year, or fails in legal capacity for any reason, the child's guardian may make such demand on behalf of the child. The property received pursuant to the demand shall be held by the guardian for the benefit and use of the child. (Emphasis supplied.)

The whole question on this appeal is whether or not a present interest was given by the petitioners to their minor children so as to qualify as an exclusion under § 2503(b). The petitioners on appeal contend that each minor beneficiary has the right under California law to demand partial distribution from the Trustee. In the alternative they urge that a parent as natural guardian of the person of his minor children could make such a demand. As a third alternative, they assert that under California law a minor over the age of 14 has the right to have a legal guardian appointed who can make the necessary demand. The Commissioner, as cross petitioner, alleges as error the Tax Court's ruling that the 1962 gifts in trust to Janet (then age 20) were present interests.

It was stipulated before the Tax Court in regard to the trust and the parties thereto that at all times relevant all the minor children lived with the petitioners and no legal guardian had been appointed for them. In addition, it was agreed that all the children were supported by petitioners and none of them had made a demand against the trust funds or received any distribution from them.

The tax regulations define a "future interest" for the purposes of § 2503(b) as follows:

"Future interests" is a legal term, and includes reversions, remainder, and other interests or estates, whether vested or contingent, and whether or not supported by a particular interest or estate, which are limited to commence in use, possession or enjoyment at some future date or time. Treasury Regulations of Gift Tax, § 25.2503–3.

This definition has been adopted by the Supreme Court. Fondren v. Commissioner, 324 U.S. 18 (1945); Commissioner v. Disston, 325 U.S. 442 (1945). In *Fondren* the court stated that the important question is when enjoyment begins. There the court held that gifts to an irrevocable trust for the grantor's minor grandchildren were "future interests" where income was to be accumulated and the corpus and the accumulations were not to be paid until designated times commencing with each grandchild's 25th birthday. The trustee was authorized to spend the income or invade the corpus during the minority of the beneficiaries only if need were shown. The facts demonstrated that need had not occurred and was not likely to occur.

¶ 7073

Neither of the parties nor the Tax Court has any disagreement with the above summarization of the basic tests. The dispute comes in attempting to narrow the definition of a future interest down to a more specific and useful form.

The Commissioner and the Tax Court both placed primary reliance on the case of Stifel v. Commissioner, 197 F.2d 107 (2d Cir.1952). In that case an irrevocable trust was involved which provided that the beneficiary, a minor, could demand any part of the funds not expended by the Trustee and, subject to such demand, the Trustee was to accumulate. The trust also provided that it could be terminated by the beneficiary or by her guardian during minority. The court held that gifts to this trust were gifts of "future interests." They relied upon Fondren for the proposition that they could look at circumstances as well as the trust agreement and under such circumstances it was clear that the minor could not make the demand and that no guardian had ever been appointed who could make such a demand.

The leading case relied upon by the petitioners is Kieckhefer v. Commissioner, 189 F.2d 118 (7th Cir.1951). In that case the donor set up a trust with his newly born grandson as the beneficiary. The trustee was to hold the funds unless the beneficiary or his legally appointed guardian demanded that the trust be terminated. The Commissioner urged that the grandson could not effectively make such a demand and that no guardian had been appointed. The court disregarded these factors and held that where any restrictions on use were caused by disabilities of a minor rather than by the terms of the trust, the gift was a "present interest." The court further stated that the important thing was the right to enjoy rather than the actual enjoyment of the property.

The *Kieckhefer* case has been followed in several decisions. In Gilmore v. Commissioner, 213 F.2d 520 (6th Cir.1954) there was an irrevocable trust for minors. It provided that all principal and accumulated income would be paid on demand of the beneficiary. The trust was to terminate on the beneficiary's death. Anything remaining in the trust at the time of death would go to the beneficiary's estate.

The Tax Court stated that the demand provision would have made the advancements "present interests" but for spendthrift provisions and the authority of the Trustee to invest in nonincome producing properties. The Circuit agreed that the demand provision made the advancements "present interests" and further held that the other provisions did not change that character. Reliance was placed on the "right to enjoy" language of *Kieckhefer*.

* * *

Although there are certainly factual distinctions between the *Stifel* and *Kieckhefer* cases, it seems clear that the two courts took opposing positions on the way the problem of defining "future interests" should be resolved. As we read the *Stifel* case, it says that the court should look at the trust instrument, the law as to minors, and the financial and other circumstances of the parties. From this examination it is up to the court to determine whether it is likely that the minor beneficiary is to receive any present enjoyment of the property.

¶ 7073

If it is not likely, then the gift is a "future interest." At the other extreme is the holding in *Kieckhefer* which says that a gift to a minor is not a "future interest" if the only reason for a delay in enjoyment is the minority status of the donee and his consequent disabilities. The *Kieckhefer* court noted that under the terms there present, a gift to an adult would have qualified for the exclusion and they refused to discriminate against a minor. The court equated a present interest with a present right to possess, use or enjoy. The facts of the case and the court's reasoning, however, indicate that it was really equating a present interest with a present right to possess, use or enjoy except for the fact that the beneficiary was a minor. In between these two positions there is a third possibility. That possibility is that the court should determine whether the donee is legally and technically capable of immediately enjoying the property. Basically this is the test relied on by the petitioners. Under this theory, the question would be whether the donee could possibly gain immediate enjoyment and the emphasis would be on the trust instrument and the laws of the jurisdiction as to minors. It was primarily on this basis that the Tax Court decided the present case, although some examination of surrounding circumstances was apparently made. This theory appears to be the basis of the decision in George W. Perkins, 27 T.C. 601 (1956). There the Tax Court stated that where the parents were capable of making the demand and there was no showing that the demand could be resisted, the gift was of a present interest. This approach also seems to be the basis of the "right to enjoy" language in both *Kieckhefer* and *Gilmore*.

Under the provisions of this trust the income is to be accumulated and added to the corpus until each minor reaches the age of 21, unless the trustee feels in his discretion that distributions should be made to a needy beneficiary. From 21 to 35 all income is distributed to the beneficiary. After 35 the trustee again has discretion as to both income and corpus, and may distribute whatever is necessary up to the whole thereof. Aside from the actions of the trustee, the only way any beneficiary may get at the property is through the "demand" provision, quoted above.

One question raised in these proceedings is whether or not the trust prohibits a minor child from making a demand on the yearly additions to the trust. The key language from paragraph three is as follows:

> If a child is a minor at the time of such gift of that donor for that year, or fails in legal capacity for any reason, the child's guardian may make such demand on behalf of the child.

The Tax Court interpreted this provision in favor of the taxpayers by saying that "may" is permissive and thus that the minor child can make the demand if allowed by law, or, if not permitted by law, the guardian may do it. Although, as the Commissioner suggests, this strains the language somewhat, it does seem consistent with the obvious intent in drafting this provision. Surely, this provision was intended to give the minor beneficiary the broadest demand power available so that the gift tax exclusion would be applicable.

There is very little dispute between the parties as to the rights and disabilities of a minor accorded by the California statutes and cases. The problem comes in attempting to ascertain from these rights and disabilities

¶ 7073

the answer to the question of whether a minor may make a demand upon the trustee for a portion of the trust as provided in the trust instrument.

It is agreed that a minor in California may own property. Estate of Yano, 188 Cal. 645, 206 Pac. 995 (1922). He may receive a gift. De Levillain v. Evans, 39 Cal. 120. A minor may demand his own funds from a bank (Cal. Fin. Code §§ 850 & 853), a savings institution (Cal. Fin. Code §§ 7600 & 7606), or a corporation (Cal. Corp. Code §§ 2221 & 2413). A minor of the age of 14 or over has the right to secure the appointment of a guardian and one will be appointed if the court finds it "necessary or convenient." Cal. Prob. Code § 1406; Guardianship of Kentera, 41 Cal.2d 639, 262 P.2d 317 (1953).

It is further agreed that a minor cannot sue in his own name (Cal. Civ. Code § 42) and cannot appoint an agent. (Cal. Civ. Code § 33). With certain exceptions a minor can disaffirm contracts made by him during his minority. Cal. Civ. Code § 35. A minor under the age of 18 cannot make contracts relating to real property or personal property not in his possession or control. Cal. Civ. Code § 33.

The parent of a child may be its natural guardian, but such a guardianship is of the person of the child and not of his estate. Kendall v. Miller, 9 Cal. 591; Cal. Civ. Code § 202.

After examining the same rights and disabilities, the petitioners, the Commissioner, and the Tax Court each arrived at a different solution to our problem. The Tax Court concentrated on the disabilities and concluded that David and Mark could not make an effective demand because they could not sue in their own name, nor appoint an agent and could disaffirm contracts. The court, however, concluded that Janet could make an effective demand because Cal. Civ. Code § 33 indirectly states that she could make contracts with regard to real and personal property.

The Commissioner concentrated on the inability to sue or appoint an agent and concluded that none of the minors had anything more than paper rights because he or she lacked the capacity to enforce the demand.

The petitioners urge that the right to acquire and hold property is the key. In the alternative they argue that the parent as a natural guardian could make the demand although it would be necessary to appoint a legal guardian to receive the property. Finally, they urge that all the minors over 14 could make a demand since they could request the appointment of a legal guardian.

The position taken by the Tax Court seems clearly untenable. The distinction drawn between David and Mark on the one hand, and Janet on the other, makes no sense. The mere fact that Janet can make certain additional contracts does not have any relevance to the question of whether she is capable of making an effective demand upon the trustee. We cannot agree with the position of the Commissioner because we do not feel that a lawsuit or the appointment of an agent is a necessary prelude to the making of a demand upon the trustee. As we visualize the hypothetical situation, the child would inform the trustee that he demanded his share of the additions up to $4,000. The trustee would petition the court for the appointment of a legal guardian and then turn the funds over to the guardian. It would also seem possible for

¶ 7073

the parent to make the demand as natural guardian. This would involve the acquisition of property for the child rather than the management of the property. It would then be necessary for a legal guardian to be appointed to take charge of the funds. The only time when the disability to sue would come into play, would be if the trustee disregarded the demand and committed a breach of trust. That would not, however, vitiate the demand.

All this is admittedly speculative since it is highly unlikely that a demand will ever be made or that if one is made, it would be made in this fashion. However, as a technical matter, we think a minor could make the demand.

Given the trust, the California law, and the circumstances in our case, it can be seen that very different results may well be achieved, depending upon the test used. Under a strict interpretation of the *Stifel* test of examining everything and determining whether there is any likelihood of present enjoyment, the gifts to minors in our case would seem to be "future interests." Although under our interpretation neither the trust nor the law technically forbid a demand by the minor, the practical difficulties of a child going through the procedures seem substantial. In addition, the surrounding facts indicate the children were well cared for and the obvious intention of the trustors was to create a long term trust. No guardian had been appointed and, except for the tax difficulties, probably never would be appointed. As a practical matter, it is likely that some, if not all, of the beneficiaries did not even know that they had any right to demand funds from the trust. They probably did not know when contributions were made to the trust or in what amounts. Even had they known, the substantial contributions were made toward the end of the year so that the time to make a demand was severely limited. Nobody had made a demand under the provision, and no distributions had been made. We think it unlikely that any demand ever would have been made.

All exclusions should be allowed under the *Perkins* test or the "right to enjoy" test in *Gilmore*. Under *Perkins*, all that is necessary is to find that the demand could not be resisted. We interpret that to mean legally resisted and, going on that basis, we do not think the trustee would have any choice but to have a guardian appointed to take the property demanded.

Under the general language of *Kieckhefer* which talked of the "right to enjoy", all exclusions in our case would seem to be allowable. The broader *Kieckhefer* rule which we have discussed is inapplicable on the facts of this case. That rule, as we interpret it, is that postponed enjoyment is not equivalent to a "future interest" if the postponement is solely caused by the minority of the beneficiary. In *Kieckhefer*, the income was accumulated and added to the corpus until the beneficiary reached the age of 21. At that time everything was to be turned over to him. This is all that happened unless a demand was made. In our case, on the contrary, if no demand is made in any particular year, the additions are forever removed from the uncontrolled reach of the beneficiary since, with the exception of the yearly demand provision, the only way the corpus can ever be tapped by a beneficiary, is through a distribution at the discretion of the trustee.

¶ 7073

We decline to follow a strict reading of the *Stifel* case in our situation because we feel that the solution suggested by that case is inconsistent and unfair. It becomes arbitrary for the I.R.S. to step in and decide who is likely to make an effective demand. Under the circumstances suggested in our case, it is doubtful that any demands will be made against the trust—yet the Commissioner always allowed the exclusion as to adult beneficiaries. There is nothing to indicate that it is any more likely that John will demand funds than that any other beneficiary will do so. The only distinction is that it might be easier for him to make such a demand. Since we conclude that the demand can be made by the others, it follows that the exclusion should also apply to them. In another case we might follow the broader *Kieckhefer* rule, since it seems least arbitrary and establishes a clear standard. However, if the minors have no way of making the demand in our case, then there is more than just a postponement involved, since John could demand his share of yearly additions while the others would never have the opportunity at their shares of those additions but would be limited to taking part of any additions added subsequent to their 21st birthdays.

We conclude that the result under the *Perkins* or "right to enjoy" tests is preferable in our case. The petitioners should be allowed all of the exclusions claimed for the two year period.

The decision of the Tax Court denying the taxpayers' exclusions on the gifts to David and Mark Crummey is reversed. The decision of the Tax Court allowing the taxpayers' exclusions on the 1962 gift to Janet Crummey is affirmed.

[¶ 7079]

PRIVATE LETTER RULING 8004172

November 5, 1979.

This is in response to your letter of * * * in which you request rulings on the gift tax consequences of a proposed inter-vivos trust, under sections 2503 and 2514 of the Internal Revenue Code of 1954.

According to your letter, A intends to establish an irrevocable trust for the benefit of his minor grandchildren.

By the terms of the trust agreement, the income and principal are payable to the grandchildren at the trustee's discretion. When B's oldest child reaches age 21, a separate trust will be created for each of B's children (A's grandchildren). The income and principal of these separate trusts will be payable to the grandchildren in the trustee's discretion. The principal will be distributed (or held in further trust) as each grandchild reaches the age of 35.

The proposed trust agreement provides in part as follows:

Item IV

Dispositive Provisions

Section 1. Withdrawal Rights. Within seven (7) days of receipt of any and all property placed in this trust as a gift, the Trustee shall notify each of the living children of the Settlor's son, * * * (hereinafter referred to as the "Settlor's grandchildren"), of the nature and value of the property received. From the time of the transfer to the trust, each such grandchild shall have the unrestricted right until thirty (30) days after the date of notification to demand and immediately receive from the trust a share of the additional contribution equal to one (1) divided by the number of such grandchildren living at the time of the transfer to the trust. The maximum value of property that may be received by a grandchild at any time shall be an amount which when added to all other amounts received by such grandchild during the calendar year pursuant to this provision shall not exceed the greater of Five Thousand Dollars ($5,000.00) or five percent (5%) of the value of the additional contribution. Should any of the Settlor's grandchildren be a minor, this power of withdrawal may be exercised by his or her natural or legal guardian.

LAW

Section 2511 of the Code provides that the gift tax applies to a transfer by way of gift, whether the transfer is in trust or otherwise, whether the gift is direct or indirect and whether the property is real or personal, tangible or intangible.

Section 2503(b) of the Code provides that each citizen of the United States in computing gifts for the calendar quarter may exclude the first $3,000 of gifts (other than future interest in property) made to any one person during the calendar year in determining the total amount of gifts for the calendar quarter. The $3,000 annual exclusions may be applied to all gifts of a present interest in the order in which they are made until the exclusion is exhausted. * * *

Section 2514(e) of the Code provides that the lapse of a non-cumulative power of appointment is a release of that power. Such a release is a taxable gift to the extent that the lapse exceeds the greater of $5,000 or 5 percent of the value of the assets over which the lapsed power could be exercised.

ANALYSIS

Item IV, section 1, of the trust agreement provides that the grandchild has 30 days from the date of notification to demand the additional contributions to the trust (subject to the $5,000 or 5 percent limit). The grandchild can compel immediate distribution of those additional contributions. Accordingly, provided that there is no impediment under the trust or local law to the appointment of a guardian, annual exclusions under section 2503(b) of the Code will be allowable for additional contributions to the original trust. Crummey v. Commissioner, 397 F.2d 82 (9th Cir.1968). Such annual exclusions are available to the grantor or to any other donor who makes a completed gift in accordance with the terms of the trust agreement.

In future years, when a grandchild fails to exercise his power of appointment over annual contributions, there will be a lapse of that power under section 2514(e) of the Code. Item IV, section 1, of the trust agreement limits the contributions that can be transferred to an amount which, when added to

¶ 7079

all other amounts received by such grandchild during the year, will not exceed the greater of $5,000 or 5 percent of the value of the additional contribution. Thus, any annual lapse in future years cannot exceed the greater of $5,000 or 5 percent of the value of the assets out of which the exercise of the lapsed powers could be satisfied. Under section 2514(e) of the Code, this will not result in a taxable lapse for the year or years in which the demand right is unexercised.

* * *

Note

[¶ 7085]

Private Letter Ruling 8004172 evidences the Commissioner's acquiescence in the *Crummey* approach. The *"Crummey* withdrawal" language quoted from the trust in question is routinely used in approximately this form.

The trust described in Priv. Ltr. Rul. 8004172 demonstrates the flexibility available in a *Crummey* trust. Note that once the 30–day withdrawal period has passed, the beneficiary has no right whatever to income or principal until age 35. Until then the beneficiary receives only such amounts as the trustee decides to distribute.

There are limits on the extent to which the withdrawal right can be restricted. The Commissioner has taken the position that the beneficiary must be given a realistic and meaningful right to withdraw. For example, in Rev. Rul. 81–7, 1981–1 C.B. 474, the Service denied the annual exclusion because the beneficiary had only two days in which to exercise the right to withdraw and, furthermore, was not informed of the withdrawal right. Another effort to restrict the withdrawal right failed in Tech. Adv. Mem. 9532001. There the donor included the customary withdrawal language, but when the trust was created he obtained from each beneficiary a document whereby the beneficiary irrevocably waived any right to withdraw subsequent contributions and also waived any right to be informed of subsequent contributions. The IRS ruled that no exclusion would be allowed as to any contribution after the initial transfer. The IRS reasoned that there is a present interest only if the beneficiary has an immediate right to possession at the time of each gift—a right that was prospectively destroyed by the waiver.

[¶ 7087]

d. *Crummey Trusts: Contingent Beneficiaries*

Once the *Crummey* withdrawal right became established, it occurred to planners that the number of donees holding such rights, and therefore the number of § 2503(b) exclusions allowed, could be expanded indefinitely by giving such withdrawal rights to numerous contingent beneficiaries. Although the donor would not expect any of the contingent beneficiaries to exercise their withdrawal rights, and although the interests of the contingent beneficiaries might be quite remote, the rationale of the *Crummey* opinion suggested that each beneficiary's withdrawal right could qualify for an additional exclusion.

The IRS addressed this issue in Tech. Adv. Mem. 8727003, in which the donor created a trust that provided a life estate and general power of appointment for the donor's son. The son's wife and six descendants were to receive the trust property in default of appointment by the son, but they had no other interests in the trust. The donor gave *Crummey* withdrawal rights to the wife and each of the six descendants as well as the son, thereby generating a total of eight annual per donee exclusions. The IRS ruled that no exclusion would be allowed for the withdrawal rights held by the wife and the descendants, who had only "remote contingent interests." The IRS reasoned that Congress intended the annual exclusion to be allowed only as to donees having a "continuing interest" in the trust.

Subsequently, the Tax Court addressed the issue in the case that follows.

[¶ 7091]

ESTATE OF CRISTOFANI v. COMMISSIONER

United States Tax Court, 1991.
97 T.C. 74, acq., 1992–1 C.B. 1.

RUWE, Judge:

Respondent determined a deficiency in petitioner's Federal estate tax in the amount of $49,486. The sole issue for decision is whether transfers of property to a trust, where the beneficiaries possessed the right to withdraw an amount not in excess of the section 2503(b) exclusion within 15 days of such transfers, constitute gifts of a present interest in property within the meaning of section 2503(b).

FINDINGS OF FACT

Petitioner is the Estate of Maria Cristofani, deceased, Frank Cristofani, executor. Maria Cristofani (decedent) died testate on December 16, 1985. * * *

Decedent has two children, Frank Cristofani and Lillian Dawson. Decedent's children were both born on July 9, 1948. They were in good health during the years 1984 and 1985.

Decedent has five grandchildren. Two of decedent's five grandchildren are Frank Cristofani's children. They are Anthony Cristofani, born July 16, 1975, and Loris Cristofani, born November 30, 1978. Decedent's three remaining grandchildren are Lillian Dawson's children. They are Justin Dawson, born December 1, 1972, Daniel Dawson, born August 9, 1974, and Luke Dawson, born November 14, 1981. During 1984 and 1985, the parents of decedent's grandchildren were the legal guardians of the person of their respective minor children. There were no independently appointed guardians of decedent's grandchildren's property.

* * *

On June 12, 1984, decedent executed an irrevocable trust entitled the Maria Cristofani Children's Trust I (children's trust). Frank Cristofani and Lillian Dawson were named the trustees of the children's trust.

In general, Frank Cristofani and Lillian Dawson possessed the following rights and interests in the children's trust corpus and income. Under Article Twelfth, following a contribution to the children's trust, Frank Cristofani and Lillian Dawson could each withdraw an amount not to exceed the amount specified for the gift tax exclusion under section 2503(b). Such withdrawal period would begin on the date of the contribution and end on the 15th day following such contribution. Under Article Third, Frank Cristofani and Lillian Dawson were to receive equally the entire net income of the trust quarter-annually, or at more frequent intervals. After decedent's death, under Article Third, the trust estate was to be divided into as many equal shares as there were children of decedent then living or children of decedent then deceased but leaving issue. Both Frank Cristofani and Lillian Dawson survived decedent, and thus the children's trust was divided into two equal trusts. Under Article Third, if a child of decedent survived decedent by 120 days, that child's trust would be distributed to the child. Both Frank Cristofani and Lillian Dawson survived decedent by 120 days, and their respective trusts were distributed upon the expiration of the 120–day waiting period. During the waiting period, Frank Cristofani and Lillian Dawson received the entire net income of the separate trusts as provided for in Article Third.

In general, decedent's five grandchildren possessed the following rights and interests in the children's trust. Under Article Twelfth, during a 15–day period following a contribution to the children's trust, each of the grandchildren possessed the same right of withdrawal as described above regarding the withdrawal rights of Frank Cristofani, and Lillian Dawson. Under Article Twelfth, the trustee of the children's trust was required to notify the beneficiaries of the trust each time a contribution was received. Under Article Third, had either Frank Cristofani or Lillian Dawson predeceased decedent or failed to survive decedent by 120 days, his or her equal portion of decedent's children's trust would have passed in trust to his or her children (decedent's grandchildren).

Under Article Third, the trustees, in their discretion, could apply as much of the principal of the children's trust as necessary for the proper support, health, maintenance, and education of decedent's children. In exercising their discretion, the trustees were to take into account several factors, including ''The settlor's desire to consider the settlor's children as primary beneficiaries and the other beneficiaries of secondary importance.''

* * *

[In each of the taxable years 1984 and 1985 the decedent transferred property worth $70,000 to the trust.]

Decedent did not report the two $70,000 transfers on Federal gift tax returns. Rather, decedent claimed seven annual exclusions of $10,000 each under section 2503(b) for each year 1984 and 1985. These annual exclusions were claimed with respect to decedent's two children and decedent's five grandchildren.

There was no agreement or understanding between decedent, the trustees, and the beneficiaries that decedent's grandchildren would not exercise their withdrawal rights following a contribution to the children's trust. None of decedent's five grandchildren exercised their rights to withdraw under Article Twelfth of the children's trust during either 1984 or 1985. None of decedent's five grandchildren received a distribution from the children's trust during either 1984 or 1985.

Respondent allowed petitioner to claim the annual exclusions with respect to decedent's two children. However, respondent disallowed the $10,000 annual exclusions claimed with respect to each of decedent's grandchildren claimed for the years 1984 and 1985. Respondent determined that the annual exclusions that decedent claimed with respect to her five grandchildren for the 1984 and 1985 transfers ... were not transfers of present interests in property. Accordingly, respondent increased petitioner's adjusted taxable gifts in the amount of $100,000.

OPINION

* * *

In the instant case, petitioner argues that the right of decedent's grandchildren to withdraw an amount equal to the annual exclusion within 15 days after decedent's contribution of property to the children's trust constitutes a gift of a present interest in property, thus qualifying for a $10,000 annual exclusion for each grandchild for the years 1984 and 1985. Petitioner relies upon Crummey v. Commissioner, 397 F.2d 82 (9th Cir.1968), revg. on this issue T.C. Memo. 1966–144.

* * *

In deciding whether the minor beneficiaries received a present interest, the Ninth Circuit specifically rejected any test based upon the likelihood that the minor beneficiaries would actually receive present enjoyment of the property. Instead, the court focused on the legal right of the minor beneficiaries to demand payment from the trustee. The Ninth Circuit, relying on Perkins v. Commissioner, 27 T.C. 601 (1956), and Gilmore v. Commissioner, 213 F.2d 520 (6th Cir.1954), revg. 20 T.C. 579 (1953), stated:

> All exclusions should be allowed under the Perkins test or the "right to enjoy" test in *Gilmore*. Under *Perkins*, all that is necessary is to find that the demand could not be resisted. We interpret that to mean legally resisted, and going on that basis, we do not think the trustee would have any choice but to have a guardian appointed to take the property demanded. [Crummey v. Commissioner, 397 F.2d at 88.]

The court found that the minor beneficiaries had a legal right to make a demand upon the trustee, and allowed the settlors to claim annual exclusions, under section 2503(b), with respect to the minor trust beneficiaries.

¶ 7091

The Ninth Circuit recognized that there was language in a prior case, Stifel v. Commissioner, 197 F.2d 107 (2d Cir.1952), affg. 17 T.C. 647 (1951), that seemed to support a different test.

As we read the *Stifel* case, it says that the court should look at the trust instrument, the law as to minors, and the financial and other circumstances of the parties. From this examination it is up to the court to determine whether it is likely that the minor beneficiary is to receive any present enjoyment of the property. If it is not likely, then the gift is a "future interest." [Crummey v. Commissioner, supra at 85.]

As previously stated, the Ninth Circuit rejected a test based on the likelihood that an actual demand would be made. Respondent does not rely on or cite *Stifel* in his brief. We believe that the test set forth in Crummey v. Commissioner, supra, is the correct test.

Subsequent to the opinion in *Crummey*, respondent's revenue rulings have recognized that when a trust instrument gives a beneficiary the legal power to demand immediate possession of corpus, that power qualifies as a present interest in property. * * *

In the instant case, respondent has not argued that decedent's grandchildren did not possess a legal right to withdraw corpus from the children's trust within 15 days following any contribution, or that such demand could have been legally resisted by the trustees. In fact, the parties have stipulated that "following a contribution to the children's trust, each of the grandchildren possessed the *same right of withdrawal* as * * * the withdrawal rights of Frank Cristofani and Lillian Dawson." (Emphasis added.) The legal right of decedent's grandchildren to withdraw specified amounts from the trust corpus within 15 days following any contribution of property constitutes a gift of a present interest. Crummey v. Commissioner, *supra*.

On brief, respondent attempts to distinguish *Crummey* from the instant case. Respondent argues that in *Crummey* the trust beneficiaries not only possessed an immediate right of withdrawal, but also possessed "substantial, future economic benefits" in the trust corpus and income. Respondent emphasizes that the children's trust identified decedent's children as "primary beneficiaries," and that decedent's grandchildren were to be considered as "beneficiaries of secondary importance."

Generally, the beneficiaries of the trust in *Crummey* were entitled to distributions of income. Trust corpus was to be distributed to the issue of each beneficiary sometime following the beneficiary's death. See Crummey v. Commissioner, T.C. Memo. 1966–144. Aside from the discretionary actions of the trustee, the only way any beneficiary in *Crummey* could receive trust corpus was through the demand provision which allowed each beneficiary to demand up to $4,000 in the year in which a transfer to the trust was made. The Ninth Circuit observed:

In our case * * * if no demand is made in any particular year, the additions are forever removed from the uncontrolled reach of the beneficiary since, with exception of the yearly demand provision, the only way the corpus can ever be tapped by a beneficiary, is through a distribution at the discretion of the trustee. [Crummey v. Commissioner, 397 F.2d at 88.]

In the instant case, the primary beneficiaries of the children's trust were decedent's children. Decedent's grandchildren held contingent remainder interests in the children's trust. Decedent's grandchildren's interests vested only in the event that their respective parent (decedent's child) predeceased decedent or failed to survive decedent by more than 120 days. We do not believe, however, that *Crummey* requires that the beneficiaries of a trust must have a vested present interest or vested remainder interest in the trust corpus or income, in order to qualify for the section 2503(b) exclusion.

As discussed in *Crummey*, the likelihood that the beneficiary will actually receive present enjoyment of the property is not the test for determining whether a present interest was received. Rather, we must examine the ability of the beneficiaries, in a legal sense, to exercise their right to withdraw trust corpus, and the trustee's right to legally resist a beneficiary's demand for payment. Crummey v. Commissioner, 397 F.2d at 88. Based upon the language of the trust instrument and stipulations of the parties, we believe that each grandchild possessed the legal right to withdraw trust corpus and that the trustees would be unable to legally resist a grandchild's withdrawal demand. We note that there was no agreement or understanding between decedent, the trustees, and the beneficiaries that the grandchildren would not exercise their withdrawal rights following a contribution to the children's trust.

Respondent also argues that since the grandchildren possessed only a contingent remainder interest in the children's trust, decedent never intended to benefit her grandchildren. Respondent contends that the only reason decedent gave her grandchildren the right to withdraw trust corpus was to obtain the benefit of the annual exclusion.

We disagree. Based upon the provisions of the children's trust, we believe that decedent intended to benefit her grandchildren. Their benefits, as remaindermen, were contingent upon a child of decedent's dying before decedent or failing to survive decedent by more than 120 days. We recognize that at the time decedent executed the children's trust, decedent's children were in good health, but this does not remove the possibility that decedent's children could have predeceased decedent.

In addition, decedent's grandchildren possessed the power to withdraw up to an amount equal to the amount allowable for the 2503(b) exclusion. Although decedent's grandchildren never exercised their respective withdrawal rights, this does not vitiate the fact that they had the legal right to do so, within 15 days following a contribution to the children's trust. Events might have occurred to prompt decedent's children and grandchildren (through their guardians) to exercise their withdrawal rights. For example, either or both of decedent's children and their respective families might have suddenly and unexpectedly been faced with economic hardship; or, in the event of the insolvency of one of decedent's children, the rights of the grandchildren might have been exercised to safeguard their interest in the trust assets from their parents' creditors. In light of the provisions in decedent's trust, we fail to see how respondent can argue that decedent did not intend to benefit her grandchildren.

Finally, the fact that the trust provisions were intended to obtain the benefit of the annual gift tax exclusion does not change the result. As we stated in Perkins v. Commissioner, supra,

> regardless of the petitioners' motives, or why they did what they in fact did, the legal rights in question were created by the trust instruments and could at any time thereafter be exercised. Petitioners having done what they purported to do, their tax-saving motive is irrelevant. [Perkins v. Commissioner, 27 T.C. at 606.]

Based upon the foregoing, we find that the grandchildren's right to withdraw an amount not to exceed the section 2503(b) exclusion, represents a present interest for purposes of section 2503(b). Accordingly, petitioner is entitled to claim annual exclusions with respect to decedent's grandchildren as a result of decedent's transfers of property to the children's trust in 1984 and 1985.

Note

[¶ 7095]

The Commissioner acquiesced in *Cristofani*, but only "in result." 1992–1 C.B. 1. The Commissioner's position on withdrawal rights held by contingent beneficiaries is illustrated by the following ruling.

[¶ 7096]

TECHNICAL ADVICE MEMORANDUM 9731004

April 21, 1997.

ISSUE:

Whether transfers of property to trusts granting each of 16, or in some cases 17, named individuals the right to withdraw a specified portion of the trust corpus at any time during the year following the transfer constitute gifts of present interests in property and therefore qualify for 16, or 17, annual exclusions under § 2503(b) of the Internal Revenue Code.

FACTS:

* * * In 1981, 1982, 1983, 1984, 1985, 1986, and 1992, Donor established a total of eight irrevocable trusts and transferred to each trust a portion of her tenancy in common interest in the real estate and cash.

* * *

The term of each trust was for the life of the Donor. Article III of each trust provides that any income realized by the trust during the Donor's lifetime shall (subject to the withdrawal provisions of the trust) be distributed annually to the son or daughter of Donor who is the primary beneficiary of that trust. In the event the Donor's child (the primary beneficiary) is deceased with children surviving, then such income is to pass equally to his or her children, *per stirpes*. In the event the Donor's son or daughter is deceased without children surviving him or her, then the income is to pass to the Donor's remaining children, *per stirpes*.

Article III of each trust also provides that during the Donor's lifetime each beneficiary named in Exhibit B of each trust has a non-cumulative power to withdraw a specified amount at all times during a one year period commencing on the date of a contribution made on the beneficiary's behalf during the calendar year. If the withdrawal right has not been exercised by the end of such year, it shall lapse. If the withdrawal right is not fully exercised, the amount subject to the power and not withdrawn is to be held in further trust and administered in accordance with the terms of the trust. * * *

The individuals named in Exhibit B of each trust are the Donor's four children, the spouses of those children, and all of the Donor's grandchildren. A total of 16 individuals are named in each Exhibit B of the trusts created in 1981–1986. A total of 17 individuals are named in Exhibit B of the 1991 and 1992 trusts.

* * *

The total value of Donor's transfers to these trusts was $835,950. No gift tax returns were filed with respect to any transfers made to these trusts.

LAW AND ANALYSIS:

* * *

The Service generally does not contest gift tax annual exclusions for transfers subject to withdrawal powers that are held by current income beneficiaries and persons with vested remainder interests. These individuals have current or long term economic interest in the trust and in the value of the corpus. It is understandable that in weighing these interests, they decide not to exercise their withdrawal rights. However, where nominal beneficiaries enjoy only discretionary income interests, contingent rights to the remainder, or no rights whatsoever in the income or remainder, their non-exercise of the withdrawal rights indicates that there was some kind of prearranged understanding with the donor that these rights were not meant to be exercised or that their exercise would result in undesirable consequences, or both.

The facts and circumstances of the instant case indicate that Donor was attempting to obtain multiple exclusions to eliminate the gift tax on the transfers to the trusts. In substance, however, the Donor did not make *bona fide* gifts of present interests when she granted withdrawal rights in Trusts #1–#6 and Trusts #7 and #8 to 15 or 16 individuals other than the primary beneficiary.

We do not dispute that, with respect to transfers initially funding each trusts and the subsequent transfer in 1993 to Trust #7, each donee of a withdrawal right received timely notice of the existence of the right and had adequate time in which to exercise the right. (There is no indication, however, that notice was received by the donees of the withdrawal rights with respect to the transfer to Trust #6 that occurred on January 6, 1987.)

However, only the primary beneficiary of each trust had a vested income or vested remainder interest in that trust. This fact is evident upon an examination of the terms of Trust #1, which is similar to the other seven trusts except for the identity of the primary beneficiary and the contingent beneficiaries.

Trust #1 was established on December 28, 1981, with a transfer of an interest in real property. Under the terms of Trust #1, B, the primary beneficiary and daughter of the Donor, was to receive the income realized by the trust on an annual basis during the life of Donor. In the event that B died during the Donor's life, the income of the trust was to pass equally to B's surviving children, *per stirpes*, if any, or if none to Donor's remaining children, *per stirpes*.

Each of the 16 individuals named in Exhibit B (a group consisting of the Donor's children and their spouses, and the Donor's grandchildren) had the non-cumulative power to withdraw an amount specified at all times during a one-year period commencing on the date of a contribution to the trust.

Upon Donor's death, subject to the withdrawal powers, the trustee was to distribute the trust property to B. In the event [B] predeceased D, the trust property was to pass equally to B's surviving children, *per stirpes*. In the event B had no children surviving her, the trust property was to pass equally to the Donor's remaining children, *per stirpes*

Because B's sons were entitled to income of Trust #1 only in the event that they survived B while the Donor lived they had a contingent income interest in Trust #1. Because B's sons were entitled to receive the corpus of Trust #1 only in the event that the Donor died, predeceased by B, the sons had a contingent remainder interest in Trust #1.

Donor's other children, A, C, and D, had only remote contingent remainder interests in Trust #1. In the event that B and all B's children died, while the Donor survived, the Donor's children were entitled to the income from Trust #1. In the event that at the time the Donor died neither [B] nor any of B's children survived, the trust corpus would pass to the Donor's remaining children.

The children of A, C, and D had even more remote contingent income and remainder interests in Trust #1 because they would receive income or corpus only if B, all of B's children, and their own parent died before the Donor. For example, A's children would receive income from the trust only if B, all of B's children, and A died before the Donor. Similarly, the trust corpus would pass to A's children only if at the time Donor died B, all of B's children, and A were deceased.

Neither the spouse of B nor the spouses of B's siblings, (A, C, and D) had any interest in Trust #1 aside from his or her withdrawal right.

Each of the other seven trusts had substantially similar dispository terms.

* * *

¶ 7096

The substantive effect of all these trusts and all these transfers was to carry out the Donor['s] intention that upon her death the farm property comprising the corpus of the eight trusts would be transferred outright in four approximately equal shares to the Donor's four children. Such a purpose could not be accomplished if any of the 15 or 16 individuals (other than the primary beneficiary) had exercised his or her withdrawal right to remove property from the trust.

In fact, none of the individuals ever exercised a withdrawal right with respect to any of the ten transfers to the trusts. The individuals (other than the primary beneficiary of the trust) had only a contingent interest, a remotely contingent interest, or no possible interest in any property left in the trust upon the expiration of the withdrawal rights. The children of the primary beneficiary would receive trust property only if their parent died before their grandmother. The siblings of the primary beneficiary would receive trust property only if the primary beneficiary and all the primary beneficiary's children died before the siblings' mother. The grandchildren of the Donor, other than those who are children of the primary beneficiary, would receive trust property only if the primary beneficiary, and the grand-children's parent died before their grandmother. The spouses of the donor's children would never receive any interest in the trust property.

The fact that none of the withdrawal rights was ever exercised, even by those who had no other interests in the trusts, leads to the conclusion that as part of a prearranged understanding, all of the individuals (other than the primary beneficiary) knew that their rights were paper rights only, or that exercising them would result in unfavorable consequences. There is no other logical reason why these individuals would choose not to withdraw the amount specified in each trust as a gift which would neither be includible in their income nor subject the Donor to the gift tax.

Having considered the facts and circumstances surrounding the creation, funding, and purpose of each trust, we conclude that Donor did not [intend] to make *bona fide* gifts of present interests to any of the trusts' beneficiaries other than the primary beneficiary of each trust.

Note

[¶ 7097]

In Estate of Kohlsaat v. Commissioner, 73 T.C.M. (CCH) 2732, T.C.M. (RIA) ¶ 97,212 (1997), sixteen descendants of the trust grantor, all contingent beneficiaries of the trust, were given *Crummey* withdrawal rights. The IRS argued that there were "understandings" between the grantor and the beneficiaries that the withdrawal rights would not be exercised. Although the opinion does not describe the evidence presented, the Tax Court concluded that the evidence did not establish the existence of such understandings. Also, the Tax Court noted that several credible reasons were offered by the trust beneficiaries as to why they did not exercise the withdrawal rights. The court refused to infer the existence of "understandings" simply because there were no withdrawals, and § 2503(b) exclusions were allowed as to all contingent beneficiaries.

¶ 7096

[¶ 7102]

e. *Crummey Trusts: Planning*

The *"Crummey* withdrawal right" has become an accepted and frequently used method of making gifts to minors in such a way as to qualify for the annual per donee exclusion. This approach permits greater flexibility than is provided by use of either a § 2503(c) trust or a gift to a custodian under the Uniform Transfers to Minors Act, both discussed below. Care must be exercised, however, to assure adequate notice to the donee as well as a reasonable time for exercise of the withdrawal right, as explained at ¶ 7085, above.

Many taxpayers are tempted to use *Crummey* withdrawal rights to shelter the maximum amount excludable under § 2503(b). It should be recognized, however, that hidden dangers lie in granting any right to withdraw more than $5,000 per year per donee. If the donee fails to exercise such a withdrawal right, it is clear that the donee has thereby made a transfer to the beneficiaries of the trust (if other than herself) in the amount that could have been withdrawn. This is so because the donee has permitted a general power of appointment to lapse. § 2514(e). See Chapter 5. Section 2514(e) further provides that such a lapse is considered a transfer only to the extent that the amount as to which lapse occurs exceeds the greater of $5,000 or five percent of the amount subject to the power.

If a transfer of $12,000 subject to withdrawal is made and the assets of the trust do not exceed $100,000, the result is that the "$5,000 or 5 percent" rule of § 2514(e) will apply only to the first $5,000 subject to the withdrawal right. Lapse of the withdrawal right as to any amount in excess of $5,000 will constitute a taxable gift to the extent the beneficiaries of the trust are persons other than the holder of the withdrawal right. Because this will be a gift in trust, it will ordinarily not qualify as a present interest gift and thus will not be sheltered by the annual per donee exclusion. In that event a taxable gift will result, a portion of the unified credit of the holder of the withdrawal right will be consumed, and a gift tax return will be required.

The result is that a *Crummey* gift greater than $5,000 per donee may cause an unintended secondary gift by the holder of the *Crummey* power, requiring a gift tax return and use of a portion of the donee's unified credit. The problem is exacerbated because all of the donee's withdrawal rights are aggregated for purposes of the § 2514(e) $5,000 or five percent exclusion. In other words, the holder of a withdrawal right can annually apply only one $5,000 or five percent exclusion against all the withdrawal rights held by her, even if the withdrawal rights relate to separate trusts and separate donors. Rev. Rul. 85–88, 1985–2 C.B. 202.

The secondary gift problem can be avoided–regardless of the amount subject to withdrawal–if the holder of the withdrawal right holds all beneficial interests in the trust. In that event the lapse of the power constitutes a transfer by the power holder for his or her own benefit, and there is no gift.

Another way to avoid the secondary gift problem is through use of "hanging powers." Under this approach, the trust instrument provides that failure to exercise the withdrawal power causes a lapse of the power only to the extent of the greater of $5,000 or 5% of the fund subject to withdrawal. The remaining portion of the power "hangs" in suspense to be used in later years—or to lapse in subsequent years if the donor ceases or diminishes contributions to the trust. For example, assume that the donor transfers $8,000 to the trust, and the donee has a power to withdraw the entirety of this amount within 30 days. The donor can use the § 2503(b) exclusion to shelter the entire transfer from tax. When the 30 days pass without exercise, the power lapses only as to $5,000, and the donee retains a power to withdraw $3,000 in later years. Because the lapse falls within the "5 and 5" exception provided by § 2514(e), there is no gift by the donee. If the donor transfers $2,000 or less to the trust during the subsequent year, lapse of the withdrawal right as to the remaining $3,000 is again covered by the § 2514(e) exception, and there is no taxable gift by the donee in the subsequent year. The only catch is that, if the donee dies while holding the "hanging" power to withdraw $3,000, that amount will be included in the donee's gross estate. § 2041(a)(2).

Even if the amount subject to the withdrawal right is limited to $5,000 per donee, so that the gift tax problems described above are avoided, income tax complications remain. A holder of the *Crummey* power who does not exercise the power may be taxed on the income from the property subject to the power, at least during the period the property is subject to the power, and perhaps afterwards as well, all pursuant to § 678, explored at ¶ 31,229, below.

Problems

[¶ 7103]

1. At the beginning of Year 1 Charles, who is not married, transferred $13,000 in cash to a trust that gives Alice, Charles' daughter, the right to withdraw within 30 days any amount transferred to the trust. The $13,000 is the only trust asset. Alice did not exercise her withdrawal right. The trust provides that one-half of the income of the trust is to be paid each year to Alice or her estate, and the other one-half is to be paid to Alice's brother, Sam, or his estate. The trust is to terminate at the end of Year 12, when the entire corpus is to be transferred to Sam's daughter, Gertrude. Assume for purposes of this problem that the value of a 12–year term certain is .681369 of the principal and that the value of the remainder after a 12–year certain is .318631 of the principal. Further assume that the § 2503(b) exclusion amount is $12,000.

    Has Charles or Alice made a taxable gift? If so, what is the amount of each taxable gift?

2. Assume the same facts as in *Cristofani*, ¶ 7091, with these additions: The trust provides that if no descendant of Maria is living 120 days after Maria's death, the trust property is to be distributed to Eloise Gantry and Nancy Nearing, friends of Maria. The trust also provides that Eloise and Nancy are to have immediate withdrawal rights of the same kind Maria's descendants possess. Eloise and Nancy, good friends of Maria, are both prosperous, and Maria feels sure neither will exercise her withdrawal

right. Each year Maria contributes $108,000 to the trust. Assume that the § 2503(b) exclusion amount is $12,000.

To what extent are exclusions available under § 2503(b)?

3. Assume the same facts as in *Cristofani*, ¶ 7091, with these additions: The trust provides that each of Janet Wilson, Ruth Neville, Sally Branson, Alice Newt, Helen Gutbohl, and Irma Wilson are to have withdrawal rights of the same kind Maria's descendants possess. However, none of these persons has any other interest in the trust. All of these persons are prosperous and good friends of Maria, who feels sure that none will exercise the withdrawal right. Each year Maria contributes $156,000 to the trust. Assume that the § 2503(b) exclusion amount is $12,000.

To what extent are exclusions available under § 2503(b)?

[¶ 7109]

f. § 2503(c) Trusts

The confusion that resulted from the early conflict between the Seventh Circuit in *Kieckhefer* and the Second Circuit in *Stifel*, referred to in *Crummey* (¶ 7073), caused Congress, in its enactment of the 1954 Code, to include a new provision granting a "safe harbor" for donors who wanted to use a trust vehicle without providing for withdrawal privileges by the minor (whether through a guardian or not). For those donors who do not choose the *Crummey* approach, an assured, although less flexible, alternative is available under § 2503(c).

[¶ 7121]

HEIDRICH v. COMMISSIONER

Tax Court of the United States, 1971.
55 T.C. 746, acq., 1974–1 C.B.2.

FORRESTER, Judge:

* * *

Petitioners argue that the gifts were gifts of present interests in the traditional common-law sense, and that, in any event, by virtue of the legislatively created exception delineated in section 2503(c) the trust arrangements "[should not] be considered a gift of a future interest in property for purposes of subsection (b)." We agree with petitioner that the gifts here qualify as transfers for the benefit of minors in accordance with the provisions of section 2503(c).

Respondent argues that each trust imposes "substantial restrictions" on the trustee's discretion to pay over the income or property of the trust to the named beneficiary, and therefore fails to satisfy the conditions of section 25.2503–4(b)(1) of the Gift Tax Regulations, a provision which we recently approved in James T. Pettus, Jr., 54 T.C. 112 (1970). Respondent points specifically to the language of the trust agreements which provides that:

> The Trustee shall pay to the beneficiary, [name of beneficiary] or apply on said beneficiary's behalf such income from the Trust and so much of

the principal thereof as may be necessary for the education, comfort and support of the beneficiary, and shall accumulate for such beneficiary all income not so needed. * * * [Emphasis supplied.]

The Commissioner concedes that "education, comfort and support" are purposes broad enough not to constitute "substantial restrictions" upon the trustee's discretion. Cf. Rev. Rul. 67–270, 1967–2 C.B. 349. However, he contends that the phrases as may be necessary and not so needed impose "a substantial obstacle to the exercise of the trustee's discretionary power" because "where a trustee's power is exercisable only in the event of need (as so clearly required by the terms of this trust), there is a substantial restriction on the power within the meaning of § 25.2503–4(b) of the Regulations."

A perusal of the recent cases dealing with restrictions on trusts for the benefit of minors would show that the allegedly restrictive language of the instruments here does not significantly affect the trustee's normal discretionary power to expend the trust's income or property. * * * A discretionary trust power conditioned upon a general requirement of need is not so restricted that it will cause the trust to be ineligible for treatment under section 2503(c). Mueller v. United States, supra. Indeed, as we recognized in James T. Pettus, Jr., 54 T.C. 112, 120 (1970):

> The section appears to contemplate that the trustee or other person authorized to administer the gift may have discretion from the time the gift is made until the donee reaches 21 years of age to expend the property for the benefit of the minor to the extent that it is needed. * * * [Emphasis supplied.]

Here, respondent admits that the purposes "education, comfort and support" do not themselves constitute "substantial restrictions" upon the trustee's discretionary power. The additional phrase, *"as may be necessary,"* embodies no more than the settlor's gratuitous directive to the trustee to do what would have been required had the phrase been omitted. The phrase neither adds to nor detracts from what would otherwise have been the trustee's discretionary power to distribute trust funds for the purposes "education, comfort and support" because the purposes are so broad that to determine what may be necessary to accomplish them is to determine how to accomplish them. Similarly, the use of the phrase *"as not needed,"* in referring back to the phrase *"as may be necessary,"* reflects only the draftsman's desire to achieve an internally consistent sentence.

The *Pettus* case itself is distinguishable because the actual purposes of the trust there were so narrow that they constituted a substantial restraint upon the trustee's discretion. Furthermore, respondent's reliance on such cases as Commissioner v. Disston, 325 U.S. 442 (1945); Fondren v. Commissioner, 324 U.S. 18 (1945); Jennings v. Smith, 161 F.2d 74 (C.A.2, 1947); and Camiel Thorrez, 31 T.C. 655 (1958), aff'd. 272 F.2d 945 (C.A.6, 1959); is misplaced. None of these early cases dealt with the "substantial restrictions" language of section 25.2503–4(b)(1), Gift Tax Regs.[10]

---

10. Nor does Rev. Rul. 69–345, 1969–1 C.B. 226 apply to the factual situation here. The trust in question there provided that:

"The trustee shall distribute to or for the benefit of the beneficiary, until he attains the age of twenty-one years, so much of the

Therefore, we find that the terms of the instant trusts "when read as a whole approximate the scope of the term 'benefit,' as used in section 2503(c)." Rev. Rul. 67–270, 1967–2 C.B. 349.

Respondent also contends that the terms of the trust agreement fail to satisfy section 2503(c)(2)(A). A transfer in trust for a minor does not meet the requirements of section 2503(c)(2)(A) unless the trust arrangement provides that the trust's unexpended income and property will "pass to the donee on his attaining the age of 21 years." * * *

The trust terms themselves must require that the unexpended trust funds will pass to the donee upon his attaining the age of 21; it does not suffice that the trustee acted upon a mistaken interpretation that the trust provided for passing at the age of 21. Laura M. Hutchinson, 47 T.C. 680, 688, 689 (1967).

Respondent relies upon Rev. Rul. 60–218, 1960–1 C.B. 378, superseding Rev. Rul. 59–144, 1959–1 C.B. 249. That ruling held that a trust would not satisfy the requirements of section 2503(c) if, upon the donee's attaining the age of 21, the trust instrument provided alternatively that: (1) the donee might compel immediate distribution of the trust; (2) the donee might elect to extend the duration of the trust so that he would receive a distribution of one-third of the trust upon attaining 25, one-third upon attaining 29, and the balance upon attaining 33; or (3) if the donee failed to make the election, the trust would continue upon its own terms. Under the facts presented by respondent's ruling if the donee failed to make an affirmative election, he would be bound by the terms of the trust instrument until the final distribution of the trust property at age 33.

In the instant case, however, each donee, after attaining the age of 21, will have a continuing right to immediate possession of the trust property. At any time after attaining 21, each donee may make a simple written demand which, upon receipt by the trustee, will require both termination of the trust and delivery of the trust property to the donee. While making such a written demand might constitute a "positive act" (to borrow from the language of Rev. Rul. 60–218, supra), some sort of positive action, whether it be signing a check or physically grasping a corporate bond, is almost always necessary to place property within one's absolute and immediate possession. Here, where the only impediment to the donee's use and possession of the unexpended trust funds will be the submission of a written demand to the trustee and where the written demand will be purely within the donee's power to make, we must conclude that the trust funds will pass to the donee at the time the right to make the written demand accrues. Since each donee may make

income and principal of the trust estate as may be necessary in the sole discretion of the trustee for the care, support, education, and welfare of the beneficiary. In determining whether such need exists, the trustee shall take into consideration other resources available to the beneficiary and other payments made to him or for his benefit."

While we express neither approval nor disapproval of respondent's ruling that such a provision would impose a substantial restriction upon the trustee's discretionary power, we note that the second sentence of the quoted provision establishes an explicit restrictive standard not present in the case before us.

written demand upon attaining the age of 21, the trust arrangement conforms to the requirement of section 2503(c)(2)(A).

* * * [W]e find and hold entirely for petitioners on the issue presented for decision * * *

Note

[¶ 7124]

As explained below at ¶ 7136, Congress adopted § 529 in 1996, thereby creating a vehicle that has important advantages over § 2503(c) trusts in terms of both tax benefits and flexibility, assuming the purpose of the funds is to provide the cost of higher education. Therefore, Section 2503(c) trusts now have limited utility, primarily involving circumstances in which (1) the purpose of the funds is not to provide education costs, (2) the purpose is to provide funds for elementary or secondary education, or (3) it is important to the donor to retain control over investment of the funds.

g. Uniform Gifts to Minors Act and Uniform Transfers to Minors Act

[¶ 7127]

REVENUE RULING 59–357

1959–2 C.B. 212.

The Internal Revenue Service has been requested to clarify its position in regard to the income, gift, and estate tax consequences of gifts to minors under both the Uniform Gifts to Minors Act and the Model Gifts of Securities to Minors Act.

Uniform laws have been adopted in many states to facilitate gifts to minors. Generally, these laws eliminate the usual requirement that a guardian be appointed or a trust set up when a minor is to be the donee of a gift. Under the Model Gifts of Securities to Minors Act, a donor may appoint either himself or a member of the minor's family as custodian to manage a gift of securities. The Uniform Gifts to Minors Act provides that money as well as securities may be the subject of a gift to a minor and that a bank, trust company, or any adult may act as custodian. When a gift is made pursuant to the model or uniform act the property vests absolutely in the minor. The custodian is authorized to apply as much of the income or principal held by him for the benefit of the minor as he may deem advisable in his sole discretion. Income and principal not so applied are to be delivered to the donee when he reaches the age of 21 or, in event of his prior death, to his estate.

Revenue Ruling 56–86, C.B. 1956–1, 449, holds that a transfer of securities to a minor donee, pursuant to a statute similar to the Model Gifts of Securities to Minors Act, constitutes a completed gift for Federal gift tax purposes at the time the transfer was made. Such a gift qualifies for the annual gift tax exclusion authorized by section 2503(b) of the Internal Revenue Code of 1954.

Revenue Ruling 56–484, C.B. 1956–2, 23, holds that income, which is derived from property transferred under the Model Gifts of Securities to Minors Act and which is used in the discharge or satisfaction, in whole or in part, of a legal obligation of any person to support or maintain a minor, is taxable to such person to the extent so used, but is otherwise taxable to the minor donee.

Revenue Ruling 57–366, C.B. 1957–2, 618, holds that the value of property transferred to a minor donee under the Model Gifts of Securities to Minors Act is includible in the gross estate of the donor for Federal estate tax purposes if the donor appoints himself custodian and dies while serving in that capacity and before the donee attains the age of 21 years.

The provision of the Uniform Gifts to Minors Act regarding the powers of the custodian as to distributions differs from the comparable provision of the Model Gifts of Securities to Minors Act in only three respects. First, the "model" act authorizes the custodian to apply so much of the income from the securities "as he may deem advisable for the support, maintenance, general use and benefit of the minor in such manner, at such time or times, and to such extent as the custodian in his absolute discretion may deem suitable and proper, without court order, without regard to the duty of any person to support the minor and without regard to any funds which may be applicable or available for the purposes." The "uniform" act does not use the term "absolute discretion," but this provision is otherwise virtually identical.

Second, the "uniform" act differs from the "model" act in that, in lieu of the latter part of the language quoted above, it provides that the income can be applied by the custodian for the minor's support without regard to the duty of himself or of any other person to support the minor or his ability to do so. Thus, the custodian, who may be legally obligated to support the minor, has power to use custodianship income for such support even though he may have adequate funds for this purpose.

Third, the "uniform" act contains a provision not found in the "model" act which gives a parent or guardian of the minor, or the minor himself after he reaches the age of 14, the right to petition the court to order the custodian to spend custodial property for the minor's support, maintenance or education. This provision, coupled with the "uniform" act's omission of the term "absolute" with reference to the discretion vested in the custodian, suggests the existence of a limitation on the custodian's otherwise uncontrolled power to withhold enjoyment of the custodial property from the minor, at least as to a portion of such property. Nevertheless, the custodian's power to withhold enjoyment is not substantially affected by such limitation.

In view of the foregoing, it is the opinion of the Internal Revenue Service that neither these nor other variations between the "model" act and the "uniform" act warrant any departure from the position previously published in Revenue Ruling 56–86, supra, Revenue Ruling 56–484, supra, and Revenue Ruling 57–366, supra, in regard to gifts made under the "model" act.

¶ 7127

Therefore, any transfer of property to a minor under statutes patterned after either the Model Gifts of Securities to Minors Act or the Uniform Gifts to Minors Act constitutes a completed gift for Federal gift tax purposes to the extent of the full fair market value of the property transferred. Such a gift qualifies for the annual gift tax exclusion authorized by section 2503(b) of the Code. See Rev. Rul. 56–86, C.B. 1956–1, 449; and section 25.2511–2(d) of the Gift Tax Regulations. No taxable gift occurs for Federal gift tax purposes by reason of a subsequent resignation of the custodian or termination of the custodianship.

Income derived from property so transferred which is used in the discharge or satisfaction, in whole or in part, of a legal obligation of any person to support or maintain a minor is taxable to such person to the extent so used, but is otherwise taxable to the minor donee. See Rev. Rul. 56–484, C.B. 1956–2, 23.

The value of property so transferred is includible in the gross estate of the donor for Federal estate tax purposes if * * * (2) the donor appoints himself custodian and dies while serving in that capacity. See Rev. Rul. 57–366, C.B. 1957–2, 618; and section 20.2038–1(a) of the Estate Tax Regulations. In all other circumstances custodial property is includible only in the gross estate of the donee.

Note

[¶ 7133]

During the late 1960s and early 1970s many states lowered the age of majority to 18 and simultaneously lowered to 18 the age for full possession by the donee of property held under the Uniform Gifts to Minors Act. This raised the question whether a Uniform Act transfer would continue to comply with § 2503(c). The Commissioner so ruled on the ground that § 2503(c) sets forth the "maximum restrictions that may be attached to minors and still have such gifts considered as present interests ..." Rev. Rul. 73–287, 1973–2 C.B. 321, 322.

Although Rev. Rul. 59–357 addresses only the Uniform Gifts to Minors Act and the Model Gifts of Securities to Minors Act, the ruling's conclusions should apply with equal force to the Uniform Transfers to Minors Act, promulgated by the National Conference of Commissioners on Uniform State Laws in 1986, and now adopted in most states.

As explained below at ¶ 7136, Congress adopted § 529 in 1996, thereby creating a vehicle that has important advantages over Uniform Transfers to Minors Act gifts in terms of both tax benefits and flexibility, assuming the purpose of the funds is to provide the cost of higher education.

4. QUALIFIED TUITION PROGRAMS

[¶ 7136]

Qualified tuition programs are authorized by § 529 and are often referred to as "529 Plans." Although § 529 is included in Subtitle A of the Internal

Revenue Code, relating to income taxes, § 529 includes provisions that have important gift and estate tax effects as well.

Since enactment of § 529 in 1996, 529 Plans have become a popular vehicle for accumulation of college expenses. These plans offer a combination of multiple tax benefits and flexibility that often make 529 Plans superior to both § 2503(c) trusts (¶ 7109) and Uniform Transfers to Minors Act gifts (¶ 7127) as a means of providing financing for future higher education.

The benefits of a 529 Plan can be illustrated by describing the circumstances of Grandmother, who wishes to establish a fund that will provide the cost of future college education for a recently born grandchild, Samuel. It is assumed that the § 2503(b) exclusion amount is $12,000.

1. Grandmother transfers $12,000 to a 529 Plan sponsored by the state in which she lives, naming Samuel as the beneficiary.

2. The $12,000 transfer qualifies for the § 2503(b) exclusion and therefore is not subject to gift tax. § 529(c)(2)(A)(i).

3. In many states, Grandmother's contribution to the plan is partially or wholly deductible for state income tax purposes.

4. If Grandmother dies while the 529 Plan is in effect, none of the plan assets are included in her gross estate for estate tax purposes. § 529(c)(4)(A).

5. Neither Grandmother nor Samuel is taxed on the earnings of the 529 Plan. § 529(c)(1). Nor is the plan itself subject to income tax. § 529(a).

6. Grandmother determines the timing, amount, and purpose of any distribution from the 529 Plan.

7. If a distribution is used for Samuel's "qualified higher education expenses," the distribution is not taxed to either Samuel or Grandmother. For this purpose, "qualified higher education expenses" includes expenditures for tuition, fees, books, supplies and equipment. In most cases "qualified higher education expenses" also includes room and board costs up to the standard room and board allowance fixed by the educational institution Samuel attends. § 529 (e)(3).

8. Grandmother's contribution to the 529 Plan does not impair her ability to make direct tuition payments excludable for gift tax purposes under § 2503(e) (¶ 7157, below), (whether in the year of contribution or in years when distributions are made from the 529 Plan. § 529(c)(2)(A)(ii). Also, in years in which 529 Plan contributions are not made (or deemed made, under § 529(c)(2)(B)), Grandmother can make § 2503(b) annual per donee exclusion gifts to Sam.

9. At any time she wishes, Grandmother can without tax cost change the beneficiary from Samuel to another member of Samuel's family, as broadly defined in § 529(e)(2), provided the new beneficiary is not in a generation below Samuel. § 529(c)(3)(C)(ii) and 529(c)(5)(B).

¶ 7136

10. If Grandmother falls into financial difficulty, she can withdraw funds from the 529 Plan for her own use. Grandmother will be taxed on the portion of the distribution allocable to the untaxed earnings of the plan, and Grandmother must pay a 10% penalty on this portion as well. §§ 529(c)(3)(A) and 529(c)(6).

11. Grandmother is not limited to her own state's plan. She can use the 529 Plan offered by any state.

12. Without tax consequences, Grandmother can transfer the funds in the existing 529 Plan to a 529 Plan offered by another state. § 529(c)(3)(C)(i)(I).

13. Under virtually all 529 Plans, expenditures from the 529 Plan are not limited to educational institutions in the Grandmother's state or to educational institutions in the state sponsoring the plan; the funds can be used at any qualifying institution of higher education.

The favorable gift tax treatment described in Item 2 is further expanded by a rule that permits spreading of a larger transfer over as many as 5 years for purposes of the § 2503(b) exclusion. For example, Grandmother could transfer $60,000 to the 529 Plan. Assuming the § 2503(b) limit is $12,000, she could elect to treat the contribution as spread over 5 years for gift tax purposes, using the five $12,000 exclusions to shelter the entire gift. § 529(c)(2)(B). If Grandmother dies within five years, however, the portion of the transfer allocable to the post-death period is included in her gross estate. § 529(c)(4)(B).

Section 529(b)(5) prohibits the owner of a 529 account from directing investment of the assets in the account. Nevertheless, the IRS has stated that it intends to issue regulations that will permit the owner to change the investment once each calendar year, or upon a change in the designated beneficiary. The owner, however, must select among "broad-based investment strategies designed exclusively by the program" holding the funds. Notice 2001–55, 2001–39 I.R.B. 299.

Although each 529 plan is nominally offered by a state, typically the funds are actually invested with a financial institution (often a family of mutual funds) that has contracted with the state. The costs and investment results vary widely. A comparison of all 529 plans is available at *www.saving-forcollege.com.*

5. RECIPROCAL AND SHAM TRANSFERS

[¶ 7139]

Many taxpayers find the § 2503(b) dollar limit frustrating. Section 2503(b) transfers provide a "free ride" in the sense that none of the donor's unified credit is used, and § 2503(b) transfers can be made to the same individuals year after year. There is great allure in finding additional donees, so that the benefits of § 2503(b) can be multiplied. The Commissioner is alert to circumstances in which taxpayers have succumbed to the temptation to multiply donees through artificial transfers.

¶ 7136

[¶ 7141]

SATHER v. COMMISSIONER

United States Court of Appeals, Eighth Circuit, 2001.
251 F.3d 1168.

HANSEN, Circuit Judge.

The Internal Revenue Service (IRS) imposed gift tax deficiencies and accuracy-related penalties on Larry Sather, Kathy Sather, John Sather, Sandra Sather, Duane Sather, and Diane Sather related to gifts made by each of them in 1993, * * * [T]he tax court found that the transactions at issue involved cross-gifts, denied claimed annual exclusions, and upheld the tax deficiencies and a portion of the penalties. We affirm the imposition of gift tax deficiencies but reverse the accuracy-related penalties.

I.

This case involves the transfer of stock in a closely-held family business from one generation to the next. The Sather brothers, Larry, John, Duane, and Rodney (collectively the "brothers"), along with Larry's, John's, and Duane's wives, Kathy, Sandra, and Diane, respectively (collectively the "wives"), owned 100% of the stock in Sather, Inc., which they previously received from the brothers' parents. At the time of the transfers at issue, Rodney was unmarried and had no children. Larry, John, and Duane each had three children. In an effort to transfer the stock of Sather, Inc., to the next generation of Sathers, the brothers consulted their accountant for advice on structuring the transfer. Upon their accountant's advice, Larry, John, and Duane and each of their respective wives transferred $9,997 worth of stock to each of their children and to each of their nieces and nephews on December 31, 1992. Larry, John, and Duane also transferred additional shares to their own children to effect the full transfer of Sather, Inc., stock to the next generation of Sathers. On January 5, 1993, Larry, John, and Duane each transferred $19,994 worth of stock to each of their nieces and nephews and approximately $15,000 worth of stock to each of their own children. The wives each transferred $3,283 worth of stock to each of their own children.[2] The transfers were made to irrevocable trusts for each set of children (Larry's, John's, and Duane's).

Each donor filed a separate gift tax return for 1992, claiming nine $10,000 gift tax exclusions, one for each donee (each individual's own three children and six nieces and nephews, or nine nieces and nephews in Rodney's case). Each donor likewise filed a gift tax return for 1993, again claiming nine $10,000 gift tax exclusions and electing to have each gift treated as made one-half by each spouse, as allowed under the Internal Revenue Code (I.R.C.) § 2513, 26 U.S.C. § 2513 (1994). * * * The IRS allowed only three $10,000

---

2. Rodney also made transfers of approximately $10,000 worth of stock to each of his nieces and nephews on both dates and made transfers to the other brothers, but those transfers are not at issue here. Rodney was not assessed any additional tax as the transfers to his nieces, nephews, and brothers were all bona fide transfers; neither he nor his immediate family (he had none) received anything in exchange.

¶ 7141

exclusions per year for each of the donors—Larry, Kathy, John, Sandra, Duane, and Diane—and assessed gift taxes and penalties based on the remaining transfers. The IRS reasoned that the gifts to each of the donors' own children were valid gifts, but that the gifts to each niece and nephew were constructive gifts to the donors' own children.

* * *

II. Reciprocal Gifts

The Internal Revenue Code imposes a tax "on the transfer of property by gift," I.R.C. § 2501(a), "whether the gift is direct or indirect," I.R.C. § 2511(a). The first $10,000 worth of gifts of a present interest made to any person in a calendar year is excluded from the definition of a taxable gift. I.R.C. § 2503(b). Thus, it is not uncommon for taxpayers to avoid the gift tax by structuring gifts just below the $10,000 exclusion limit. This case requires us to determine whether the gifts in this case, similar gifts made by the donors to each other's children, are really cross-gifts, that is, indirect gifts to their own children.

The tax court found that the cumulative transfers at issue lacked economic substance, relying on the reciprocal trust doctrine. The Sathers argue that there is economic substance to the transactions as a whole when Rodney's gifts to the nieces and nephews are considered, as is required by the step-transaction doctrine. Whether a transaction lacks economic substance, and whether several transactions should be considered integrated steps of a single transaction, are both fact questions which we review for clear error. * * *

The reciprocal trust doctrine, a variation of the substance over form concept, * * * was developed in the context of trusts to prevent taxpayers from transferring similar property in trust to each other as life tenants, thus removing the property from the settlor's estate and avoiding estate taxes, while receiving identical property for their lifetime enjoyment that would likewise not be included in their estate. See United States v. Grace's Estate, 395 U.S. 316, 320, 89 S.Ct. 1730, 23 L.Ed.2d 332 (1969). The Supreme Court held that the reciprocal trust doctrine applies to multiple transactions when the transactions are interrelated and, "to the extent of mutual value, leave the settlors in approximately the same economic position as they would have been in had they created trusts naming themselves as life beneficiaries." Id. at 324, 89 S.Ct. 1730. The doctrine seeks to discern the reality of the transaction; " 'the fact that the trusts are reciprocated or 'crossed' is a trifle, quite lacking in practical or legal significance.' " * * *

Substance over form analysis applies equally to gift tax cases. * * * It is impliedly included in the gift tax statute itself—including indirect transfers within the definition of a taxable gift. See I.R.C. § 2511(a). "The terms 'property,' 'transfer,' 'gift,' and 'indirectly' are used in the broadest and most comprehensive sense;.... The words 'transfer ... by gift' and 'whether ... direct or indirect' are designed to cover and comprehend all transactions ... whereby ... property or a property right is donatively passed....' " Dickman v. Comm'r, 465 U.S. 330, 334, 104 S.Ct. 1086, 79 L.Ed.2d 343 (1984) (quoting H.R.Rep. No. 708, 72nd Cong., 1st Sess., 27–28 (1932) and S.Rep. No. 665,

¶ 7141

72nd Cong., 1st Sess., 39 (1932)) (some alterations in original). Application of the reciprocal trust doctrine[4] is likewise appropriate in the gift tax context as a method for discerning the substance of gift transfers. " 'The purpose of the doctrine is merely to identify the transferor of property.' " Exchange Bank, 694 F.2d at 1267 (quoting Bischoff v. Comm'r, 69 T.C. 32, 45–46, 1977 WL 3667 (1977)). Once the transferor is identified, the tax code determines whether the transfer is subject to tax. Id.

Applying the reciprocal trust doctrine to this case, there can be no doubt that the gifts were interrelated. The Sather brothers together sought advice on how to transfer the stock to the next generation of Sathers. The transfers to all the children were made on the same days and were for the same amounts of stock. We cannot say that the tax court erred—clearly or otherwise—in determining that the transfers were interrelated.

The second prong of the Grace's Estate analysis requires that "the settlors [be left] in approximately the same economic position as they would have been in had they created trusts naming themselves as life beneficiaries." Grace's Estate, 395 U.S. at 324, 89 S.Ct. 1730. We do not believe that the Supreme Court meant to limit the doctrine to cases involving life estate trusts, or even to cases where the donor retains an economic interest, but used that language in the context of the specific facts of the case. * * * In this case, the parents transferred stock to their nieces and nephews in exchange for transfers to their own children by the nieces' and nephews' parents. Though the Sathers received no direct economic value in the exchange, they did receive an economic benefit by indirectly benefitting their own children. The donors were in the same economic position—the position of passing their assets to their children—by entering the cross-transactions as if they had made direct gifts of all of their stock to their own children.

Applying the analysis of the reciprocal trust doctrine, we hold that these interrelated gifts were reciprocal transactions that must be uncrossed to reach the substance of the transactions. * * *

* * *

The purpose of the second Grace's Estate prong is to discern the taxability of the transactions as uncrossed in the context of a particular set of facts. * * * Uncrossing the gifts in the present case, the tax court made the factual finding that each immediate family was in the same position as if each donor had made gifts only to the donor's own children. Thus, using the reciprocal trust doctrine to identify the actual transferor, each donor made transfers to each of his or her own children but no gifts to any of the nieces and nephews. * * * We cannot say that the tax court clearly erred in making this factual finding. Under I.R.C. § 2503(b), each transferor—Larry, Kathy, John, Sandra, Duane, and Diane—was entitled to one $10,000 exclusion for gifts made to each uncrossed donee, their own children, for each year in which gifts were made. Because each transferor has only three children but claimed nine

---

4. The tax court has taken to calling it the "reciprocal transaction doctrine" in the con- text of reciprocal indirect transfers outside the trust arena. * * *

exclusions, the IRS correctly determined that the transferors understated their gift tax liabilities.

The Sathers argue that the step-transaction doctrine requires us to consider the gifts made by Rodney to each of his nieces and nephews, and that in so doing, we will find economic substance in the whole transaction. Each of Larry's, John's, and Duane's immediate families had a net increase in economic value, while Rodney's immediate family (consisting only of himself) had a net decrease in economic value. True as this may be, it does not change the fact that uncrossing the reciprocal gifts leaves each of the transferors in the same position as if he or she had transferred stock only to his or her own children. The purpose of the reciprocal trust doctrine is to discern the actual transferor—Rodney's transfers do not affect the reality of the other transferors' gifts, which amounted to a transfer of their own stock to their own children.

* * *

V. Conclusion

The transfers of stock to each donor's nieces and nephews were reciprocal transfers, or cross-gifts, made in exchange for identical transfers from the nieces and nephew's parents to the donor's own children. As such, the transfers must be uncrossed and the tax code applied to the substance of the transactions. The IRS correctly determined that each donor was entitled to three $10,000 exclusions. The signed returns prepared by the accountant, found by the tax court to be a reliable advisor, provide sufficient evidence of Kathy's, Sandra's, and Diane's reliance and afford them the protection of the reasonable cause exception to the accuracy-related penalties. We therefore affirm in part and reverse in part the tax court's decision.

Note

[¶ 7143]

The opinion in *Estate of Grace*, on which the *Sather* opinion relies, is set forth at ¶ 18,109.

The attractions of the § 2503(b) exclusion have proved too tempting to other taxpayers as well. In Heyen v. United States, 945 F.2d 359 (10th Cir. 1991), the donor transferred a $10,000 block of stock in a closely held corporation to each of 27 friends unrelated to the donor. At the donor's behest, each friend then transferred her stock to a member of the donor's family, and the amount ultimately received by each family member far exceeded $10,000. The donor nevertheless claimed a $10,000 exclusion for each of the 27 transfers. The Tenth Circuit concluded that the retransfer to the family members had been prearranged by the donor, and that the gifts were actually made to the family members. No exclusions were allowed for the transfers to friends.

6. ADJUSTMENT CLAUSES

[¶ 7145]

REVENUE RULING 86–41

1986–1 C.B. 300.

ISSUE

What are the federal gift tax consequences in the two situations described below where a donor transfers a specified portion of real property under terms that provide for an adjustment to the portion transferred depending on the determination by the Internal Revenue Service of the value of the property for federal gift tax purposes?

FACTS

Situation 1. In 1982, A transferred an interest in a tract of income producing real property to B. Under the deed of transfer, B received a one-half undivided interest in the tract. However, the deed further provided that if the one-half interest received by B were ever determined by the Internal Revenue Service to have a value for federal gift tax purposes in excess of $10,000, then B's fractional interest would be reduced so that its value equaled $10,000. Under local law the adjustment clause operated as a condition subsequent. Thus, if the Service determined that a gift was made in excess of $10,000, the adjustment clause would effectively reconvey to A a fractional share of the tract of real property sufficient to reduce the value of B's interest to $10,000 as of the date of the gift.

On A's federal gift tax return, A reported that the fair market value of the one-half interest transferred by gift to B was $10,000 (one-half the value of the entire tract), and applied the annual exclusion against the gift. On examination of A's 1982 federal gift tax return, it was determined that the fair market value of a one-half interest in the tract subject to the transfer to B was $15,000 rather than $10,000.

Situation 2. The facts are the same as in *Situation 1*, except that B was not required to reconvey any property to A. Rather, the transfer contained the condition that if the Internal Revenue Service determined that B received a gift in excess of $10,000, B would transfer to A consideration equal to the amount of the excess.

LAW AND ANALYSIS

Section 2501 of the Internal Revenue Code imposes a tax on the transfer of property by gift. Section 2511(a) provides that the gift tax applies whether the transfer is in trust or otherwise, whether the gift is direct or indirect, and whether the property is real or personal, tangible, or intangible. Section 25.2511–2(a) of the Gift Tax Regulations states that the gift tax is not imposed upon the receipt of the property by the donee but rather is an excise upon the donor's act of transfer.

¶ 7145

Section 2503(b) of the Code provides that a donor may exclude from his or her taxable gifts the first $10,000 of gifts of present interest in property made to each donee during the calendar year. Under § 25.2503 of the regulations, a "present interest" in property is defined as an unrestricted right to the immediate use, possession, or enjoyment of property or the income from property.

Rev. Rul. 65–144, 1965–1 C.B. 442, holds that if the terms of a trust provide that the trust terms will be substantially modified to the extent necessary to qualify the transfer in trust for the gift tax charitable deduction under section 2522 of the Code, those terms providing for modification are considered ineffective for federal gift tax purposes. Gifts subject to conditions subsequent of the kind considered in Rev. Rul. 65–144 tend to discourage the enforcement of federal gift tax provisions, because operation of the provisions would either defeat the gift or otherwise render examination of the return ineffective. See also Commissioner v. Procter, 142 F.2d 824 (4th Cir.1944), cert. denied, 323 U.S. 756 (1944). The Service, accordingly, will not give effect to such clauses and will consider the terms of the gift as unmodified for federal tax purposes.

In *Situations 1* and *2*, the facts demonstrate that A intended to make a gift to B of a present one-half interest in the property. In both cases, the purpose of the adjustment clause was not to preserve or implement the original, bona fide intent of the parties, as in the case of a clause requiring a purchase price adjustment based on an appraisal by an independent third party retained for that purpose. Rather, the purpose of the clause was to recharacterize the nature of the transaction in the event of a future adjustment to A's gift tax return by the Service. As in Rev. Rul. 65–144, the terms of the deed of transfer to B providing for the reduction of the portion transferred would tend to discourage the examination of returns and the collections of tax and therefore are ineffective for federal gift tax purposes. Because the reduction provision is ineffective for federal gift tax purposes, A has made a gift of a present one-half interest in the property, the first $10,000 of which qualifies for the annual exclusion under section 2503 of the Code. The value of the gift is $15,000, the fair market value of a one-half interest in the tract as determined on examination. The fact that, in *Situation 2*, the adjustment of the gift was to be made by recharacterizing the transfer as a part-gift/part-sale is irrelevant.

HOLDING

In both *Situations 1* and *2*, if the donor transfers a specified portion of real property under terms that provide for a recharacterization of the transaction depending on the Service's valuation of the property for federal gift tax purposes, the adjustment clause will be disregarded for federal tax purposes. Consequently, in both cases the value of the gift will be determined without regard to the adjustment clause and the first $10,000 in the value of the gift, as so determined, will qualify for the annual exclusion from gift tax.

¶ 7145

Note

[¶ 7151]

The Tax Court upheld the Commissioner's position on adjustment clauses in Ward v. Commissioner, 87 T.C. 78 (1986), where the donor provided for revocation of the gift to the extent the stock transferred was determined to have a value greater than $2,000 per share.

The invalidity of "condition subsequent" adjustment clauses is well established. In Commissioner v. Procter, 142 F.2d 824 (4th Cir.), cert. denied, 323 U.S. 756 (1944), the instrument of gift purported to revoke the transfer to the extent it was determined to be subject to the gift tax, and this clause was held invalid for tax purposes. Therefore, the gift tax was imposed on the entire gift, without regard to what the actual gift might be for local property law purposes.

C. EXCLUSION FOR EDUCATIONAL AND MEDICAL EXPENSES

[¶ 7157]

An exclusion is provided for direct payment of certain educational and medical expenses. § 2503(e).

This exclusion is unlimited in amount and is available over and above the annual per donee exclusion provided by § 2503(b). The § 2503(e) exclusion, however, is subject to important limitations. In the case of educational expenses, the exclusion is available only for tuition. In the case of both educational and medical expenses, the exclusion is available only for payments made directly by the donor to the educational institution or medical care provider. A transfer to the donee, who then remits the funds to the educational institution or medical care provider, is not excluded. Reg. § 25.2503–6.

In Tech. Adv. Memo. 199941013, the Commissioner ruled that prepaid tuition qualifies for the § 2503(e) exclusion. Here the donor transferred funds to a private elementary-secondary school for payment of tuition for the donor's two grandchildren. The payments covered tuition for as many as seven years in the future. In one year the payments totaled $94,000. The payments were nonrefundable, and if the grandchildren did not attend the school as expected, the funds would be forfeited to the school. This ruling is especially significant because there is no limit on the amount that can be excluded under § 2503(e).

Another advantage of § 2503(e) gifts is the zero inclusion ratio applied to such gifts for purposes of the tax on generation-skipping transfers. § 2642(c). The result is that such gifts entirely escape the tax on generation-skipping transfers. See Chapter 29.

¶ 7157

Problem

[¶ 7159]

Your client is Mildred Irving, an 80-year-old widow who owns property worth $4 million. Mildred is growing increasingly concerned about estate taxes and wishes to reduce the tax that would be imposed in the event of her death.

Mildred believes strongly in education, and she would like to provide funding to assure that all her grandchildren will have access to higher education. Mildred is willing to make gifts for the benefit of her grandchildren of as much as one-third of her assets for this purpose. Mildred has seven grandchildren, ranging in age from two to 22 years.

What alternatives would you recommend to Mildred for accomplishing her purposes?

D. MARITAL DEDUCTION

[¶ 7163]

The gift tax marital deduction, embodied in § 2523(a), provides an unlimited deduction for transfers between spouses during their lives. This reflects a policy judgment that spouses should be free to transfer their property between themselves as they think best, without unnecessary tax obstacles. In fact, so long as the transfer is between spouses, they need not even file a gift tax return. § 6019(a)(2). Only when the property moves outside the marriage partners—typically to the children—is a tax imposed.

The unlimited marital deduction is of relatively recent vintage, having been adopted in 1981. From 1948 through 1981 the marital deduction was in general limited to one-half of the property transferred. This arrangement was originally adopted in 1948, when the similar estate tax marital deduction and the income tax joint return for married couples were adopted. The common purpose of all three measures was to provide a rough kind of equality between married couples in common-law states and married couples in community property states.

In community property states, property covered by the community property law is treated as owned one-half by each spouse. Therefore, community property spouses have a built-in tax benefit in that their estates (at least to the extent of their community property) are split equally between the spouses by operation of law. Under the progressive tax rates imposed by the gift, estate, and income tax laws, the result of such a splitting of assets or income is a lower overall tax burden than if only one spouse had all the income or owned all the assets. The purpose of the marital deductions adopted in 1948 was to permit spouses in common law states to enjoy similar tax benefits.

The adoption of the unlimited marital deduction in 1981, however, reflected a purpose entirely different from that of the 1948 enactment. In

1981 Congress fully embraced the idea that no tax should be imposed until the property leaves the spouses.

Even after 1981, however, not every transfer between spouses qualifies for the marital deduction. Although a transfer in fee will always qualify, many transfers of less than fee interests will not qualify because of violation of the terminable interest rule that is embodied in § 2523(b) and discussed in greater detail at ¶ 27,115 in the context of the estate tax.

The terminable interest rule reflects the fear that some transfers between spouses could be used to evade the estate tax. For example, assume that a wife bequeaths to her surviving husband a life estate in certain property, with remainder to the children. Assume further that the husband's life estate has a current actuarial value equal to 90 percent of the full value of the property. If the transfer of the life estate to the husband qualifies for the marital deduction, only 10 percent of the property is subject to tax at the wife's death; yet none of the property will be subject to tax at the husband's death, because the husband's ownership will cease at his death.

To prevent such avoidance, § 2523(b) treats the husband's life estate as a "terminable interest" that does not qualify for the marital deduction. Hence, the entire property transferred by the wife is subject to tax. The husband's interest is nondeductible because it meets the tests stated in § 2523(b): (1) The husband's interest will fail upon the occurrence of a contingency (his death). (2) The wife has transferred an interest in the property (the remainder) to persons other than the husband (the children). (3) The persons other than the husband (the children) will receive the property upon the occurrence of the contingency described in (1)(the husband's death).

A major exception to the nondeductibility rule is the life estate with power of appointment, which has its counterpart in § 2056(b)(5) of the estate tax provisions. The gift tax exception permits property to be placed in trust (or a similar arrangement) for the benefit of the donor's spouse, provided the spouse has an income interest for life and a power to appoint the property to herself or her estate exercisable by will or during her life, and under all conditions and events. § 2523(e). See ¶ 27,199 et seq. for a full examination of the life estate-power of appointment arrangement.

Another exception to the terminable interest rule is available on an elective basis. If the donee spouse is entitled to all the income from the property throughout the donee spouse's life (payable no less frequently than annually) and no one has power to appoint any part of the property to a person other than the donee spouse, the donor may elect to treat the transfer as "qualified terminable interest property" ("QTIP") that will qualify for the marital deduction. § 2523(f). If such an election is made, the property will be included in the donee spouse's gross estate at her death (§ 2044) unless the donee spouse gives away her interest in the property during her lifetime, in which case there will be a taxable gift (§ 2519). The QTIP provision is important for an individual who may want his or her spouse to have the income benefits of the property without the right to determine the disposition of the property upon the donee spouse's death. This is especially useful in successive marriage situations. For example, a woman might wish to give the

¶ 7163

income from her property to her second husband while assuring that upon his death the corpus would go to the children of her first marriage. The QTIP rules are examined more fully at ¶ 27,275 et seq. in the context of the estate tax.

The gift tax statute also provides an exception to the terminable interest rule for gifts made between spouses in joint tenancy or in tenancy by the entirety. § 2523(d). For example, a husband may get the benefit of the deduction when he buys stock and places it in joint tenancy with his wife; the fact that he retains the right of severance or survivorship does not deprive the gift of the marital deduction.

In general, the gift tax marital deduction is not available if the transfer is to a spouse who is not a citizen of the United States. § 2523(i)(1). The § 2503(b) annual per donee exclusion amount, however, is raised to $100,000 (indexed) if the donee spouse is not a citizen. § 2523(i)(2). The indexed exclusion amount for 2006 is $120,000. Rev. Proc. 2005–70, 2005–47 I.R.B. 979.

E. CHARITABLE DEDUCTION

[¶ 7169]

Like the income tax and the estate tax, the gift tax has a generous deduction for contributions to charity. § 2522(a). The deductions for gifts to charity under the two transfer taxes are unlimited, whereas the charitable deduction for income taxes (§ 170) has specific percentage limitations correlated to adjusted gross income. Nevertheless, all three taxes define the eligible charitable recipients in virtually identical language. §§ 170(c)(2), 2055(a)(2), and 2522(a)(2).

If property is given outright to charity, the gift tax charitable deduction is allowed for the entire value of the property. However, if less than all interests in the property are given to charity, the deduction will be limited to the value of the charity's interest and in some cases may be entirely disallowed.

Partial interest gifts provide a fruitful opportunity for tax avoidance. For example, assume that the donor gives a life estate in certain property to his son while giving the remainder interest in the same property to charity. Under ordinary valuation principles the donor would be permitted to deduct the current actuarial value of the charitable remainder. However, the property may be a wasting asset, such as a mineral property. In that event the son may receive substantially all the value of the property as income during his lifetime, leaving little or nothing for the charity.

The remedy is a very tightly defined set of requirements that must be met to obtain a gift tax deduction for a gift of a partial interest gift to charity; no deduction is allowed unless one of the specified arrangements is used. § 2522(c). These rules are designed to assure that the charity will in fact receive value equivalent to the deduction allowed to the donor. These limitations are more fully explored in Chapter 26, which addresses the similar limitation on charitable deductions for estate tax purposes.

Chapter 8

GIFT TAX RETURNS AND ADMINISTRATIVE REQUIREMENTS

A. RETURN REQUIREMENTS

[¶ 8001]

The gift tax is imposed on a calendar-year basis. The return must be filed by April 15 of the calendar year after the year in which a gift occurs, and the tax must be paid in full with the return. §§ 6075(b)(1) and 6151(a). During the period 1971–1981, gift tax returns were required to be filed quarterly. Prior to 1971 returns were filed annually.

The general rule is that a return must be filed if any "transfer by gift" is made during the calendar year. However, there are four broad exceptions. § 6019. No return is required if all transfers fall within one or more of the following categories:

1. Annual per donee exclusion gifts within § 2503(b).

2. Educational and medical expense gifts within § 2503(e).

3. Transfers for which the § 2523 marital deduction is allowed.

4. Certain transfers for which the § 2522 charitable deduction is allowed.

The donor has primary liability for payment of the gift tax. § 2502(c). The donee, however, is secondarily liable if the donor does not pay. §§ 6324(b) and 6901(a)(1)(A)(iii).

Form 709, United States Gift (and Generation–Skipping Transfer) Tax Return, must be used to report gifts.

B. SPOUSAL GIFT SPLITTING

[¶ 8007]

Section 2513 permits spouses to treat gifts by one spouse as if made one-half by each spouse. This permits spouses to take full advantage of the exclusions and unified credits available to each of them, although only one spouse actually makes gifts. For example, assume that the § 2503(b) annual exclusion amount is $12,000, and that Wife has substantial property and Husband has little property. Wife gives $24,000 to daughter, but Husband gives nothing to daughter. Wife and Husband can elect to treat the transfer as a $12,000 gift by each of them, for purposes of the gift tax. This qualifies the transfer for the annual per donee exclusion available to each spouse and eliminates any consumption of the Wife's unified credit. Gifts cannot be split unless a return is filed. § 2513(b); Reg. § 25.2513–2. Therefore, a return must be filed even if the annual per donee exclusion will cover all gifts after splitting.

Gift-splitting and filing of a return may be avoided if one spouse makes an outright transfer of money or property to the other spouse, followed by the donee spouse's transfer of the money or property to another person. If the donee spouse has unrestricted dominion over the property and the donee spouse's transfer to a third party is in fact independent of the transfer from the donor spouse, each spouse can use his or her annual per donee exclusion to shelter the transfer. The unlimited gift tax marital deduction prevents any tax liability with respect to the gift between the spouses. § 2523(a).

The benefits of gift-splitting are not limited to the annual per donee exclusion. Gifts that are split under § 2513(b) are treated as split for all purposes of the gift tax. § 2513(a)(1). For example, gift-splitting can be used to take advantage of the nonpropertied spouse's § 2505 unified credit. Gift-splitting can likewise be used to cause one-half of the transfer to be taxed at the gift tax brackets applicable to the nonpropertied spouse, which may be lower than those that would be applicable if the gift were attributed entirely to the propertied spouse.

In addition, gift-splitting under § 2513(b) is honored for purposes of the tax on generation-skipping transfers, discussed in Chapter 29. § 2652(a)(2). Therefore, gift-splitting can be used to take full advantage of the generation-skipping tax exemption available to each spouse. § 2631(a).

Gift-splitting is not without cost. A nontransferring spouse who consents to split gifts undertakes joint and several liability for the entire gift tax liability of the transferring spouse for the year as to which gifts are split. § 2513(d).

C. STATUTE OF LIMITATIONS

[¶ 8013]

As with other taxes, the general statute of limitations requires that the United States assess additional gift tax within three years after the return is filed. § 6501(a). Likewise, the tax may be assessed at any time if no return is filed, the return is false or fraudulent with intent to evade tax, or there is a willful attempt to defeat or evade the tax. § 6501(c)(1), (2), and (3).

A stricter and special rule, however applies only to the gift tax. If a gift required to be shown on a return is not so shown, gift tax may be imposed at any time. This special rule, however, does not apply to any item that is disclosed on the return or an attachment "in a manner adequate to apprise the Secretary of the nature of such item." § 6501(c)(9). This rule gives great importance to full disclosure of gifts. First, if there is adequate disclosure, the three-year statute of limitations *will* apply, and the IRS cannot seek to impose additional tax after that time. Second, if there is adequate disclosure, with the result that the three-year statute applies, the IRS cannot after three years increase the value of the gift for other purposes, such as raising the bracket at which gifts in subsequent years are taxed, or raising the bracket at which the donor's taxable estate is taxed under § 2001(b). Even if there is not adequate disclosure, the value established by a "final determination," such as a settlement agreement with the IRS, is likewise binding for all purposes. §§ 2001(f), 2504(c), 6501(c)(9).

Because adequate disclosure is necessary to assure the benefit of the three-year statute of limitations, the required level of disclosure is a crucial issue. The Treasury expectations in this regard are set forth in Reg. § 301.6501(c)–1(f). Typically, the central issue is that of valuation. If an independent appraisal is not provided, the donor must provide extensive information on the method used to value the asset transferred, including a full explanation of any discounts taken. Reg. § 301.6501(c)–1(f)(2)(iv). If an independent appraisal is provided, there will be adequate disclosure if the appraisal provides the extensive valuation data described in Reg. § 301.6501(c)–1(f)(3)(ii).

As explained in Chapter 3, the IRS may seek to treat as a gift any transaction in which a disparity of value is present. For example, as noted at ¶ 3085, if a parent's stock is redeemed by a corporation in which a child has substantial ownership, the IRS may argue that the redemption price is lower than the true value of the stock redeemed, creating an indirect gift from parent to child. The Regulations state that in the case of a transaction "in the ordinary course of operating a business," such as payment of salary to a family member, adequate disclosure is provided through simple reporting of the transaction on the *income* tax return. As to other transactions, however, fuller disclosure is required. § 301.6501(c)–1(f)(4). It seems likely that the redemption described above would not be regarded as being "in the ordinary course of business". Therefore, although the redemption could be reported on the income tax (rather than gift tax) return, disclosure should be made at the level that would be required on a gift tax return, as described above.

D. GIFT TAX PROBLEM

[¶ 8019]

This year Wilma Brown, who lives at 42 Rock Chalk Lane, Lawrence, Kansas, made the following transfers:

1. On July 3 she gave $224,000 in cash to her daughter, Alice Brown, of 224 Longview, Atlanta, Georgia.

2. On August 10 she gave $24,000 in cash to her son, Arthur, who is a law student at the University of Kansas. His address is 2101 Ranger,

Lawrence, Kansas. In addition, she paid directly to the University of Kansas $8,000 for Arthur's tuition and $5,000 for his room and board in a University dormitory.

3. On September 10 she gave a painting to the Spencer Art Museum, a part of the University of Kansas. She obtained an appraisal valuing the painting at $30,000. Wilma's basis for the painting was $10,000.

4. On October 1 she transferred $2,300,000 in cash to the Ninth National Bank of Nashville, Tennessee, as trustee of the Georgia Smith Trust. The instrument creating the Georgia Smith Trust provides that Georgia Smith, of 310 Placer Court, Juneau, Alaska, is to receive all income from the trust until Georgia's death, at which time the corpus is to be returned to Wilma. Georgia is not related to Wilma. Wilma created the Georgia Smith Trust in 1990, when she transferred $500,000 in cash to it, and she was not married at that time. She filed a gift tax return in Wichita, Kansas, with respect to the 1990 gift. Georgia, who is not related to Wilma, was born in 1930. Wilma was born in 1935. The trust's Employer Identification Number is 48–1203123. Wilma had made no gifts prior to 1990. (Assume that in 1990 Georgia's life estate in the $500,000 was worth .67876 of the principal, or $339,380, determined under Reg. §§ 25.2512–5A and 20.2031–7A. Further assume that the value of Georgia's life income interest in the $2,300,000 gift made this year is .55544 of the principal of $2,300,000, or $1,277,512, pursuant to Reg. §§ 25.2512–5 and 20.2031–7.) In 1990 the § 2503(b) annual exclusion amount was $10,000.

5. On October 12 she gave a parcel of real estate to her husband, Nestor. She had bought the land in 1987 for $30,000, and its value at the time of the gift was $140,000.

Determine Wilma's gift tax liability, if any, for this year. Assume that Nestor is willing to split gifts with Wilma. Wilma is a United States citizen, and her Social Security Number is 495–42–8036. Nestor is also a United States citizen, and his Social Security Number is 302–21–4211.

Form 709, reproduced in Appendix C, may be used. Note, however, that the Form 709 reproduced in Appendix C is for 2005. More recent versions of Form 709, as well as other IRS forms, may be obtained on the Internet at the IRS website: www.irs.ustreas.gov.

¶ 8019

Part III

VALUATION

¶ 8019

Chapter 9

GENERAL PRINCIPLES
OF VALUATION

A. GENERAL RULES

[¶ 9001]

The valuation process is crucial to determination of the estate, gift, and generation-skipping taxes. It is the value of the property (or the interest in the property) transferred (or deemed to be transferred) that is subjected to the tax rates imposed by the three taxes, i.e., § 2001 for the estate tax, § 2502 for the gift tax, and §§ 2621, 2622, and 2623 for the generation skipping tax. Surprisingly, the statute itself is not helpful in addressing the valuation issue; the statute appears to be written on the assumption that the term "value" is self-defining. See, for example, how the term "value" is used in § 2031(a) for the estate tax, § 2512(a) for the gift tax, and §§ 2621, 2622, and 2623 for the generation-skipping tax.

Fortunately, the Regulations are much more specific. The Regulations equate "value" to "fair market value," which in turn is defined as "the price at which the property would change hands between a willing buyer and a willing seller, neither being under any compulsion to buy or to sell and both having reasonable knowledge of relevant facts." Reg. §§ 20.2031–1(b) and 25.2512–1. The Regulations then present special rules for the valuation of certain types of property; for example, stocks and bonds (Reg. §§ 20.2031–2 and 25.2512–2), interests in businesses (Reg. §§ 20.2031–3 and 25.2512–3), household effects (Reg. § 20.2031–6), annuities, life estates, terms for years, remainders and reversions (Reg. §§ 20.2031–7 and 25.2512–5), and life insurance contracts (Reg. §§ 20.2031–8 and 25.2512–6). If the special rules of valuation are not applicable, the general principles of valuation set forth in Reg. § 20.2031–1 or 25.2512–1 govern.

The valuation principles under the generation-skipping tax are the same as those employed under the gift and estate taxes. The generation-skipping tax regulations incorporate the gift and estate tax valuation principles by reference. Reg. § 26.2642–2(a).

Valuation principles and techniques developed for purposes other than the gift and estate tax are often employed. For example, the concept of valuation based on "highest and best use" is applied. Although land may be used exclusively for agricultural purposes at the time of the decedent's death, the presence of residential development potential requires that the land be valued at its residential development price rather than the lower agricultural value (unless the special valuation method described in Chapter 13 is available). Estate of Pattison v. Commissioner, 60 T.C.M. (CCH) 471, T.C.M. (P–H) ¶ 90,428 (1990).

The "willing buyer-willing seller" concept forms the foundation for all transfer tax valuation. Although numerous special rules have been developed for application to specific types of property, all are necessarily founded on a free market approach: how would independent actors value the property for purposes of purchase or sale? As more fully explained in Chapter 11, this inevitably leads to their conclusion that the hypothetical buyer and seller are anonymous, i.e., entirely unrelated to the transferor and transferee.

The hypothetical "willing buyer" is assumed to have full knowledge of the relevant facts, which may increase or decrease the fair market value. In Estate of Crossmore v. Commissioner, 56 T.C.M. (CCH) 483, T.C.M. (P–H) ¶ 88,494 (1988), a major asset of the decedent's estate was a legacy from the decedent's aunt, whose will had not yet been admitted to probate when the decedent died. Because the aunt bequeathed her entire residuary estate to the decedent and the decedent had acted as a close personal adviser to the aunt during the aunt's declining years, it appeared likely that the aunt's will and the legacy to the decedent would be contested. The Tax Court concluded that the value of the legacy to the decedent should be discounted accordingly.

The "willing buyer-willing seller" rule has the effect of giving value for gift or estate tax purposes to rights that have accrued but are not yet realized. In this sense, the gift and estate taxes apply an accrual accounting approach, without regard to whether the donor or decedent is a cash or accrual taxpayer for income tax purposes. For example, if the decedent owns a bond, the estate tax value of the bond at the date of death includes interest accrued to the date of death because that is how the marketplace would value the bond if it were sold on that date. The accrued interest is added to the principal value of the bond although the interest may not be payable until well after the decedent's death. Priv. Ltr. Rul. 9047062.

The same accrual principle applies to compensation for services. Assume that the decedent receives a monthly salary of $5,000 paid at the end of each month, and that the decedent dies after one-half of a month has elapsed. The accrued right to $2,500 is included as an asset of the decedent's gross estate for estate tax purposes. This is so without regard to the accounting method the decedent used for income tax purpose. The treatment of the accrued salary for income tax purposes, however, is entirely different. If the decedent is a cash basis taxpayer, none of the accrued salary is includible in the decedent's income for the period ending with his death; this is so because the decedent did not actually receive the salary prior to his death. Instead, the $2,500 will constitute income to the decedent's estate when actually received by the estate. Under § 691 the $2,500 will constitute "income in respect of a decedent" and will be treated as salary income when received by the estate. This rule is explored in Chapter 32.

¶ 9001

The gift and estate taxes reach far, and the courts have supported the IRS in taxing any asset to which the real world would attach economic value. The extent to which this principle has been carried is illustrated by Estate of Andrews v. United States, 850 F.Supp. 1279 (E.D.Va.1994), in which the decedent's very name was taxed. The decedent's name was Virginia Andrews, and she was an internationally known, best-selling author. Andrews' publisher proposed to continue publication of books that would be attributed to Andrews, while in fact ghostwritten by others. This required that Andrews' executor and legatees consent to use of Andrews' name. The executor had not treated Andrews' name as an asset of the estate for estate tax purposes, but the IRS did so. The court agreed with the IRS, finding that the amount to be received under a book contract signed by Andrews several weeks before her death could be used as evidence of the amount a publisher would pay for the right to use Andrews' name. The IRS argued that Andrews' name had a value of $1,244,910, but the court concluded that the realistic value was only $703,500—the amount on which the estate was ultimately taxed. See the further discussion of *Andrews* at ¶ 15,027.

B. VALUATION DATE

[¶ 9007]

For gift tax purposes, the valuation date is the date of transfer without any exceptions; this rule is set forth in the statute. § 2512(a). For estate tax purposes, all property is valued at the date of death, pursuant to § 2031(a), unless the alternate valuation date is elected. See ¶ 9013, below.

The date of death valuation rule applies not only to property owned outright by the decedent but also to property that is included in the decedent's gross estate but not in fact owned by the decedent at death. For example, assume that ten years prior to her death the decedent transferred property to a trust as to which she retained a right to control beneficial enjoyment, thereby causing inclusion of the trust assets in her gross estate under § 2038, discussed in Chapter 19. The trust assets will be included in the decedent's gross estate at their value on the date of the decedent's death—not the value at the time the assets were originally transferred to the trust. Reg. § 20.2031–1(b).

Although it is clear that valuation is to be determined as of the date of gift (for purposes of the gift tax) or the date of death (for purposes of the estate tax), the statute does not state whether subsequent events can be considered. The Supreme Court addressed this issue at an early date in Ithaca Trust Co. v. United States, 279 U.S. 151 (1929). The decedent husband had granted a life estate to his wife, followed by a remainder to charity. The wife died before the estate tax return for the husband's estate was filed, and the executor of the husband's estate sought to value the charitable remainder in light of the wife's premature death—rather than according to the Commissioner's actuarial tables, which forecast a longer life for the wife. Mr. Justice Holmes, writing for the Court, resoundingly repudiated consideration of subsequent events:

¶ 9001

[T]he value of the thing to be taxed must be estimated as of the time when the act is done. But the value of property at a given time depends upon the relative intensity of the social desire for it at that time, expressed in the money that it would bring in the market. ...Like all values, as the word is used by the law, it depends largely on more or less certain prophecies of the future, and the value is no less real at that time if later the prophecy turns out false than when it comes out true. ...Tempting as it is to correct uncertain probabilities by the now certain fact, we are of the opinion that it cannot be done, but that the value of the wife's life interest must be estimated by the mortality tables. 279 U.S. at 155.

The *Ithaca Trust* rule, however, does not prevent consideration of all subsequent events. For example, in Morrissey v. Commissioner, 243 F.3d 1145, (9th Cir. 2001), the decedent's stock was sold one and two months after the alternate valuation date, which the estate had elected. The Ninth Circuit viewed these sales as credible evidence of the value on the alternate valuation date. In Estate of Scull v. Commissioner, 67 T.C.M. (CCH) 2953, T.C.M. (RIA) ¶ 94,211 (1994), the decedent owned art work that was auctioned nearly 11 months after death. The court concluded that the auction prices provided the best evidence of value, but the court reduced the auction prices by 15%, representing appreciation that had occurred in the art market during the 11 months. Finally, in Gettysburg National Bank v. United States, 92–2 USTC ¶ 60,108 (M.D. Pa. 1992), the property in question was sold 16 months after death. The court held that the sale price was relevant in proving fair market value on the date of death because there had been no material change in the property or the market during the sixteen months after the death.

The distinction between *Ithaca Trust* on the one hand, and *Morrissey, Scull,* and *Gettysburg* on the other, is crucial. In *Ithaca Trust* an independent and unforeseen event—the wife's death—had occurred to change the value of the life estate after the death of the decedent. In *Morrisey, Scull,* and *Gettysburg*, by contrast, the post-death sales were not events that changed the value of the assets. The sales were, instead, simply *evidence* of value. Such evidence must of course be considered in the light of events that occur after the date of death and before the date of sale. For example, if the general market for similar assets rises significantly between the date of death and the sale, the value indicated by the sale price will be too high and should be adjusted downward. This is exactly what the court did in *Scull*, taking into account an independent event–the 15% percent appreciation in the art market between the date of death and the sale.

C.   ALTERNATE VALUATION DATE

[¶ 9013]

In the case of the estate tax, § 2032 permits election of an alternate valuation date. This provision permits the executor to elect on the original estate tax return to value the gross estate assets as of the date exactly six months after the date of death. The purpose of this section when originally enacted in 1935 was to permit estates that had shrunk in value during the Great Depression to use the lower values that might prevail one year after the date of death. With the 1970 revenue legislation, which accelerated the payment of the estate and gift taxes, the optional date was changed to six months from the date of death.

Although the alternate valuation date was designed to prevent imposition of an excessively high estate tax, some taxpayers sought to use it instead to reduce income taxes. If the alternate valuation date is elected, the estate's basis for the assets is the value on that date, not the date of death. § 1014(a)(2). An executor might well wish to elect the alternate valuation date because of higher values on that date if the income tax advantages of a higher basis more than offset the increase in estate tax caused by the election. For example, if the election of the alternate valuation date raises the estate tax payable by only $50,000, but the result is an increase in the basis of estate assets by $400,000, the prospective income tax saving may be greater than the estate tax cost of the election. Such a strategy is especially attractive if the executor expects the major estate assets to be sold soon and if the estate tax liability would be low in any event.

Because Congress viewed this tactic as a perversion of the purpose of § 2032, it adopted a rule limiting the alternate valuation date election to circumstances in which the election produces both a decrease in the value of the gross estate and a decrease in the sum of the estate tax and the generation-skipping tax that will be imposed with respect to the decedent's estate. § 2032(c). Although this change restricts the election to circumstances in which estate values decline, the executor should nevertheless continue to weigh both the income and estate tax effects of the election. While electing the alternate valuation date may lower the estate tax liability, the estate tax saving may be less than the additional income tax liability caused by the resulting lower basis.

The alternate valuation date election, if made, applies to all assets of the estate; one cannot "pick and choose" the assets to be valued on the alternate date. Nor does the election provide an opportunity to redetermine what property is includible in the gross estate; inclusion of property in the gross estate is invariably made as of the date of death and is unaffected by subsequent events, whether or not the optional date has been elected. The election of the alternate date merely allows a different time for valuation of the property that is a part of the gross estate as determined at the date of death.

If the election is made, property sold, distributed, or otherwise disposed of prior to the alternate valuation date is valued as of the date of sale, distribution, or other disposition. § 2032(a)(1).

A special rule applies to property the value of which is affected by the mere lapse of time. § 2032(a)(3). An example of such property is a patent, which by its nature has a limited life under patent law. A term for years is a further example. Valuing such items on the alternate date without adjustment would allow the natural and inevitable decline in value of such properties to reduce the estate tax even though there is no general decline in market

¶ 9013

valuation of the underlying property. Accordingly, the section requires that such property be valued as of the date of death, with adjustment for any difference in value on the alternate date not attributable to mere lapse of time. Reg. § 20.2032–1(f) provides illustrations of the treatment of such property, such as life estates, remainders, and patents, under the "mere lapse of time" rule. But there remain difficult valuation issues, as illustrated by the following authority.

[¶ 9025]

REVENUE RULING 63–52
1963–1 C.B. 173.

Advice has been requested whether the increase in the value of certain life insurance policies, by reason of the death of the insured during the alternate valuation period, would constitute "included property" for purposes of valuing the gross estate of the deceased beneficiary under the alternate valuation provisions of section 2032 of the Internal Revenue Code of 1954.

Among the assets of a decedent, at the time of his death, were several insurance policies on the life of another person. The decedent was the owner and beneficiary of these policies. Within one year after the decedent's death, the insured also died. The estate of the decedent, to which his interest in these policies had passed, became entitled to and thereafter collected the death proceeds of the policies. The value of the policies following the death of the insured substantially exceeded their value at the date of the decedent's death.

* * *

Section 20.2032–1(d) of the Estate Tax Regulations provides that all property interests existing at the date of a decedent's death which form a part of his gross estate are "included property" for the purpose of valuing the gross estate under the alternate valuation method. Such property remains "included property" for the purpose of valuing the gross estate even though the property interests change in form during the alternate valuation period by being actually received, or disposed of, in whole or in part, by the estate. On the other hand, the regulations provide that property earned or accrued (whether received or not) after the date of the decedent's death and during the alternate valuation period with respect to any property interest existing at the date of the decedent's death, which does not represent a form of "included property" itself or the receipt of "included property," is excluded in valuing the gross estate under the alternate valuation method.

In Herbert H. Maass v. Higgins, 312 U.S. 443 (1941), Ct. D. 1494, C.B. 1941–1, 434, the Supreme Court of the United States held that ordinary rents, dividends, and interest received during the year following the decedent's death are not to be included in the value of the gross estate, if such estate is valued under the optional (alternate) valuation provisions of section 302(j) of the Revenue Act of 1926, as amended (corresponding to section 2032(a) of the 1954 Code). The Court stated as follows:

It is not denied that, in common understanding, rents, interest, and dividends are income. Under the Revenue Acts, if such items are collected by a decedent's estate, the executors are bound to return them and pay tax upon them as income.

The decision of the Supreme Court as to rents, dividends, and interest, however, does not preclude the inclusion in the gross estate of the appreciation in the value of an insurance policy resulting from the death of the insured within the alternate valuation period.

In the instant case, the death of the insured was the precise event which caused the increase in the value of the insurance policies as of the alternate valuation date. The increase in value occasioned by the death of the insured was not due to "mere lapse of time," within the meaning of section 2032(a)(3) of the Code. See Estate of John A. Hance v. Commissioner, 18 T.C. 499 (1952), acquiescence, C.B. 1953–1,4. The increase in value of the policies cannot, therefore, be attributed to a "mere lapse of time."

An insurance policy is not, in common understanding, income producing property, and the appreciation in value of an insurance policy by reason of the death of the insured is not income in the statutory sense. Accordingly, the appreciation in value of the life insurance policies in the instant case, which occurred when the insured died is not "property earned or accrued" as in the case of ordinary interest, rents and dividends. Rather, the termination of the insurance contracts, brought about by the death of the insured, constitutes a disposition of the property interest in the contracts, within the meaning of section 2032(a)(1) of the Code.

The increase in value of the insurance contracts is, therefore, "included property," for purposes of valuing the gross estate under the alternate valuation method.

This interpretation is supported by H.R. Report No. 1885, on the Revenue Act of 1935, 74th Cong., 1st Sess., C.B. 1939–1 (Part 2), 660, at 664, which gives an example showing how the calculation of the value of property included in the gross estate should be made during the one-year period following the decedent's death. In this example, the appreciation and depreciation in the value of stocks and bonds and other assets, occurring during the year after death, are shown in the values of those assets as of one year after the date of the decedent's death or as of the date of sale, distribution, or other disposition of such assets (maturity in the case of foreign bonds). This example negatives a construction that the appreciation in value of the insurance policies, resulting from the death of the insured during the alternate valuation period, was "property earned or accrued" within the meaning of the Estate Tax Regulations.

Accordingly, it is held that for Federal estate tax purposes, the appreciation in value of the life insurance policies which matured by reason of the death of the insured during the alternate valuation period is not property earned or accrued. Therefore, no part of the proceeds of the insurance is excluded property, but is "included property," within the meaning of the

¶ 9025

Estate Tax Regulations, so that the entire value of the proceeds of the policies is includible in the gross estate.

Compare Revenue Ruling 55–379, C.B. 1959–1, 449, which holds that the increase in value of a policy of insurance, such as one owned by a decedent who was not the insured, which increase is attributable to the payment of premiums, or any interest earned, during the year following date of death, is deemed to be "excluded property." Note, however, that ruling involved the valuation of a policy in the estate of a person other than the insured where the policy did not mature during the alternate valuation period by reason of the death of the insured.

Problems

[¶ 9035]

1. Arnold Wilson died on February 10. At his death Arnold owned the right to receive income from the Murphy Trust until the death of Jonas Murphy. If Arnold should die prior to the death of Jonas, Arnold's estate would become entitled to the income until Jonas' death. Upon the death of Jonas Murphy the trust property was to be paid to Jonas' children, Zachariah and Melba.

   On February 10 the Murphy Trust had a value of $1,000,000 and was invested largely in technology stocks. On May 5 Jonas Murphy died in an automobile accident. On May 5 the value of the Murphy Trust was only $700,000.

   Arnold's executor filed the United States estate tax return for Arnold's estate on November 3. Arnold's executor elected use of the alternate valuation date (August 10) under § 2032(a).

   How should the right to income from the Murphy Trust be valued for purposes of determining Arnold's gross estate?

2. Emily Turnbull died on March 4 of Year 1. At her death she owned a patent on an industrial chemical process. The patent was to expire on March 4 of Year 2. On March 4 of Year 1 the patent was worth $500,000. On September 4 of Year 1 the patent was worth only $250,000. Emily's executor elected the alternate valuation date (September 4 of Year 1).

   How should the patent be valued in Emily's gross estate?

Chapter 10

ACTUARIAL VALUATION

A. GENERAL PRINCIPLES

[¶ 10,001]

Many property rights must be valued by use of actuarial principles. For example, if a donor transfers a remainder that will become possessory upon the death of a person whose age is 74, the value of the remainder depends on the probable longevity of the life tenant. As explained below, the general rule is that the probable longevity of the life tenant is determined actuarially, i.e., by reference to the average longevity of all persons age 74, rather than by reference to the health or circumstances of the life tenant individually. Currently the Treasury uses Life Table 90CM, set forth at the end of Reg. § 20.2031–7(d)(7), to determine life expectancy. The Life Table 90CM expectancy figures are used to determine the remainder values set forth in Reg. § 20.2031–7(d)(7) Table S.

Once the probable longevity of the life tenant is determined, discounting principles must be used to determine the value of the remainder interest, as provided in Reg. §§ 20.2031–7 and 25.2512–5. For example, if the age of the life tenant is 74 and a discount rate (prevailing interest rate) of 10% per annum is assumed, the present value of the remainder interest is .40479 of the fair market value of the entire property. If the entire property is worth $100,000, the remainder interest is assigned a present value of $40,479. Reg. § 20.2031–7(d)(7) Table S. Derivation of the discount rate used by the Treasury is explained below.

A similar approach is used if the interest to be valued is a right to income rather than a remainder interest. For example, if the donor gives to a donee the right to receive the income from property until the death of a person age 74, and a discount rate of 10% is assumed, the present value of the income interest is .59521. If the entire property is worth $100,000, the income interest is assigned a value of $59,521. As explained in Reg. § 20.2031–7(d)(2)(iii), the value of the income interest is derived by subtracting the value of the remainder interest (.40479) from the value of the entire property (1.00000), producing a .59521 value for the income interest.

The $40,479 value for the remainder and $59,521 for the income interest are the "present values" of those interests, i.e., what a buyer would theoretically pay right now for each interest. In a market where the prevailing interest rate is 10%, a buyer would pay $40,479 for the remainder, i.e., the right to receive $100,000 at the death of person currently age 74. The present value is far below the prospective $100,000. This is so because until the death occurs, the buyer will be deprived of the use value of the $100,000, i.e., the opportunity to invest and earn income from the $100,000. When interest rates are high, the lost use value is greater, with the result that the present value is a smaller portion of the $100,000. Likewise, when interest rates are low, the lost use value is lower, with the result that the present value is a larger portion of the $100,000.

A similar approach underlies valuation of the income interest. In a market where the prevailing interest rate is 10%, a buyer would pay $59,521 for the right to receive the income from $100,000 until the death of a person age 74. Under normal economic circumstances, when interest rates are high the income right will have a greater value relative to $100,000, and when interest rates are low, the income right will have a smaller value relative to $100,000.

Because the values of the remainder and income interests, respectively, vary with interest rates, the Treasury tables set forth at Reg. § 20.2031–7(d)(7) provide values based on a variety of interest rate levels, ranging from 4.2% to 14%. Values for interest rates below 4.2% and above 15% are provided in IRS Publication 1457. The determination of the rate to be used for any given transfer is explained below.

Note that under the Regulations approach the total of the present value of the income interest ($59,521) and the present value of the remainder ($40,479) is $100,000, the exact present value of the entire property. The Regulations are based on the assumption that the total of all values for partial interests will be 100% of the current value of the entire property. This is a logical result, based on the premise that "the whole must equal the sum of its parts." In the real world, however, the marketplace may evaluate the remainder and income interests differently, producing a cumulative value less or more than 100%. In the interest of administrability, however, the Regulations ignore this possibility.

Section 7520 establishes the guidelines for actuarial valuation, delegating to the Commissioner the authority to promulgate specific formulas and tables. Section 7520 authorizes the Commissioner to issue tables that incorporate current actuarial data, and the tables must be updated at least every 10 years. The Commissioner has implemented this mandate as to the estate tax through tables set forth in Reg. § 20.2031–7(d)(7). The estate tax tables are applied as well to lifetime gifts pursuant to Reg. § 25.2512–5(d). The tables apply to gifts and deaths after April 30, 1999.

The interest rate to be applied is 120 percent of the § 1274(d)(1) Federal midterm rate as determined and published by the Treasury each month. § 7520(a). This rate—commonly referred to as the "§ 7520 rate"—determines the discount rate to be applied under Regulation §§ 20.2031–7 and 25.2512–5. For example, if the § 7520 rate for the month in which the gift occurs is 8 percent, the donor transfers a remainder interest that becomes

¶ 10,001

possessory after the life of a person age 70, and the property involved is worth $100,000, Table S of Reg. § 20.2031–7(d)(7) indicates that the value of the remainder is .40540 of the total value, or $40,540. The life estate value is therefore $100,000 less $40,540, or $59,460.

If a term certain (i.e., a specific time period) is involved, Table B of Regulation § 20.2031–7(d)(6) is used. Reg. § 20.2031–7(d)(2)(iii). For example, if the § 7520 rate is 9.2% and the interest to be valued consists of the right to receive income from property for 20 years, Table B indicates that the remainder after the income interest is worth .172007 of the total value. Therefore, the term certain value is 1.0 less .172007, or .827993. If the entire property is worth $100,000, the 20–year term certain is worth $82,799.

The value of an annuity must be interpolated from the tables using a method explained in Reg. § 20.2031–7(d)(2)(iv). For example, assume that a donor transfers $200,000 to a trust. The trust provides that Alice (or her estate) is to receive a payment of $15,000 from the trust each year for 12 years. The payments are to be made at the end of each quarter. After 12 years the entire trust principal is to be paid to Edward. The § 7520 rate is 11 percent. Table B of Reg. § 20.2031–7(d)(6) indicates that the value of the remainder after a 12–year term certain at 11% is .285841. Therefore, the value of the income interest is 1.0 less .285841, or .714159. The "annuity factor" is then computed by dividing the income interest value of .714159 by the § 7520 interest rate (.11 in this case), producing an annuity factor of 6.49235. The tentative value of the 12–year annuity interest is therefore $15,000 x 6.49235, or $97,385. Because payments are to be made at the end of each quarter rather than annually, the tentative value of the annuity must be multiplied by 1.0404 to produce a final value for Alice's annuity of $101,320. Regulation §§ 20.2031–7(d)(2)(iv)(B) and 20.2031–7(d)(6) Table K. The value of the remainder is the amount that remains after subtracting the value of the annuity from the value of the entire property. Therefore, Edward's remainder is worth $200,000 less $101,320, or $98,680.

In the above example the payments are to be made at the *end* of each quarter. Therefore, Reg. § 20.2031–7(d)(6) Table K is used. If the payments are to be made at the *beginning* of each quarter, each payment will be received earlier and will therefore have a slightly higher value. Table J provides the values for payments to be made at the beginning of each period.

Further explanation of use of the actuarial tables is provided in Reg. §§ 20.2031–7 and 25.2512–5.

In the case of gifts and deaths prior to May 1, 1999, actuarial valuation is determined by Reg. § 20.2031–7A. Reg. §§ 20.2031–7(c) and 25.2512–5(c).

B. EXCEPTIONS

[¶ 10,007]

Valuation under § 7520 and the Commissioner's tables is based on the assumption of average mortality and an average income return from the property. It is of course understood that individual cases may vary widely from these assumptions and incorporate a shorter or longer actual life expectancy or a lower or higher actual income return. In the vast majority of cases, such variances are ignored, and the tables are applied to derive the actuarial value.

In extreme cases, however, the real world facts may be so different from the assumptions incorporated in the tables that reliance on the tables becomes inappropriate. The Regulations specify circumstances in which the tables are to be disregarded for this reason. §§ 20.7520–3 and 25.7520–3. The breadth of these Regulations may stretch the bounds of statutory authority. Section 7520(a) decrees that the § 7520 rate and the tables "shall" be used for valuation of "any annuity, any interest for life or a term of years, or any remainder or reversionary interest." The only exception to this mandate is § 7520(b), which specifies that § 7520 rate is not to be applied to qualified retirement plans (Part I of Subchapter D of Chapter 1 of the Code), or to "any other provision specified in regulations." This exception seems designed to permit the Commissioner to exempt designated areas of the tax law from the operation of § 7520. It does not seem to encompass the Commissioner's exclusion of certain types of property interests, as is done in Reg. §§ 20.7520–3 and 25.7520–3.

Nevertheless, the Regulations delineate several circumstances in which the tables are not to be applied. If the tables are not applied, the value of the interest "is based on all of the facts and circumstances." Reg. §§ 20.7520–3(b)(1)(iii) and 25.7520–3(b)(1)(iii).

One issue addressed in these Regulations is longevity. The tables are conclusive despite the health or probable longevity of the specific individual involved, unless the individual is "terminally ill" at the time of the transfer. For this purpose, an individual is considered terminally ill if he or she has "an incurable illness or other deteriorating physical condition" and "there is at least a 50 percent probability that the individual will die within 1 year." Reg. §§ 20.7520–3(b)(3)(i) and 25.7520–3(b)(3). If there is a terminal illness, the "actual life expectancy" must be used in valuing the transfer. Reg. §§ 20.7520–3(b)(4) Example 1 and 25.7520–3(b)(4).

The Treasury also takes the position that § 7520 and the tables are not applicable if the value of the interest may be impaired. For example, if the trustee or another party has discretion to invade principal, thereby reducing the amount producing income for the holder of an income interest, the income interest is considered impaired, and the tables are not to be used. Reg. § 20.7520–3(b)(2)(ii)(B) and 25.7520–3(b)(2)(ii)(B). The Regulations further assert the broader rule that the tables are not to be used unless the governing instrument provides for the income beneficiary "that degree of beneficial enjoyment of the property during the term of the income interest that the principles of the law of trusts accord to a person who is unqualifiedly designated as the income beneficiary of a trust for a similar period of time." Reg. §§ 20.7520–3(b)(2)(ii)(A) and 25.7520–3(b)(2)(ii)(A). This rule is specifically applied to unproductive property. If the principal of the trust consists of closely held stock on which no dividends have been paid for a number of years, there is no expectation that dividends will be paid, and the income beneficiary has no right to demand that the trust property be made productive, the income beneficiary is not viewed as having the full beneficial rights of a trust income beneficiary; hence the tables are not applicable. However, if the beneficiary has a right to require that the trust property be made productive, the income interest will be valued under the tables without regard to the historic or prospective productivity of the property. Reg. §§ 20.7520–3(b)(2)(v) Examples 1 and 2; Reg. § 25.7520–3(b)(2)(v) Examples 1 and 2.

Application of the § 7520 rate in the context of the tables raises more difficult questions if the income from the property transferred is far above or below the rate mandated by § 7520. The result of using the § 7520 rate may be a dramatically unrealistic valuation of either the income interest or the remainder interest. The Regulations appear to accept this possibility, provided the income beneficiary has the right to require the trustee to make the property productive, i.e., invest in assets producing a reasonable yield. The Regulations expressly allow use of the tables even though the minimum rate of income that the beneficiary can require under local law is below the § 7520 rate. Reg. §§ 20.7520–3(b)(2)(v) Example 2 and 25.7520–3(b)(2)(v) Example 2. However, if the beneficiary has no right to demand productivity and the property is unlikely to produce income, the income and remainder interests will be valued in light of the probable actual return rather than the § 7520 rate. Reg. §§ 20.7520–3(b)(2)(v) Example 1 and 25.7520–3(b)(2)(v) Example 1.

Even if the beneficiary has the right to require that the property be made productive, there remains the possibility of tax avoidance through use of the tables. For example, a donor parent may transfer a remainder interest to a child while retaining an income interest in circumstances in which the actual income is likely to be very low. In this circumstance use of the § 7520 rate may dramatically overstate the value of the income interest and understate the value of the remainder, effectively permitting the parent to transfer the property to the donee child at a substantially discounted value for gift tax purposes.

Exploitation of the tables in intra-family transfers is effectively prevented by § 2702, discussed at ¶ 12,079. In transfers between family members, § 2702 assigns a zero value to the retained interest unless there is a required payment, at least annually, of a fixed dollar amount or a fixed percentage of the value of the trust. §§ 2702(a)(2)(A) and 2702(b). For example, if a parent transfers a remainder interest to a child, and the parent retains a right to the "income" from the property, the income interest is treated as valueless. As a result, the entire value of the property is assigned to the remainder, and the parent is treated as making a gift to the child of the entire value of the property. This prevents exploitation of the tables by transferring property that will produce income far below the level assumed in the tables.

By contrast, if the parent retains a right to receive a fixed dollar payment from the property each year, or a right to a payment equal to the value of a fixed percentage of the property, the tables are used to value the remainder that is given to the child. § 2702(b)(1) and (2). In this case the payment to the parent is fixed and cannot be manipulated.

¶ 10,007

[¶ 10,019]

SHACKLEFORD v. UNITED STATES

United States Court of Appeals, Ninth Circuit, 2001.
262 F.3d 1028.

THOMAS, Circuit Judge:

This appeal presents the question of whether a statutory anti-assignment restriction on lottery payments justifies departure from the Department of Treasury's annuity tables when determining the asset's present value in calculating estate tax. Under the circumstances of this case, we conclude that it does and affirm the judgment of the district court.

I

* * *

Like most lottery winners, retired Air Force officer Thomas J. Shackleford probably wasn't thinking of tax consequences when he hit the $10 million California Lotto in 1987. Nor were his heirs. However, the estate tax problem became abundantly clear upon Shackleford's untimely death after receiving only three of twenty $508,000 annual payments. At that time, California law prohibited any assignment of lottery payments. Cal. Gov't Code § 8880.32(g). On death, future payments were to be made to a deceased winner's estate according to the annuity terms. *Id.* However, the payment of federal estate tax is not similarly structured. Thus, although the estate was limited to receiving annual installments, the estate tax was calculated based on the present value of the income stream, due on a much shorter schedule. Under the present value annuity tables in the Treasury regulations, 26 C.F.R. § 20.2031–7, the present value of the remaining payments was calculated to be $4,023,903. This meant that the estate owed $1,543,397 in federal estate taxes without any concomitant source of revenue to fund the payment.

The estate initially filed a return that reported the federal estate tax liability in accordance with the Treasury regulation tables and paid a total federal estate tax liability in the amount of $1,543,397. After auditing the return, the Internal Revenue Service ("IRS") found no error in the reported tax. Subsequently, the estate filed both amended tax returns and claims for refund, asserting that the value of the future payments was improperly reported. The last of the claims for refund argued that the proper value of the lottery payments was zero. In the alternative, the estate argued that use of the annuity tables to value the payments resulted in an unrealistic and unreasonable value because it did not reflect the fair market value of the asset. The IRS rejected the final refund claim, and the estate filed its claim for refund in district court.

The government filed a motion for summary judgment arguing that the estate was not entitled to a refund because the payments were an annuity for a term of years, the value of which was properly determined under the tables in 26 C.F.R. § 20.2031–7. The district court denied the motion, holding that if the estate could prove that the true value of the interest was substantially below the value attributed by the tables then departure would be warranted. *Shackleford v. United States,* No. 98–105580, 1998 WL 723161 (E.D.Cal. July 29, 1998). After a bench trial, the district court found that the lack of a market must be considered in determining a fair valuation of property for estate tax purposes and that because marketability is not a factor considered by the tables, using them would result in "a substantially unrealistic and unreasonable result." *Shackleford v. United States,* No. Civ. S–96–1370, 1999 WL 744121, (E.D.Cal. August 6, 1999). The court thereupon departed from the tables and valued the payments at $2,012,500. Id. Based on this valuation, the parties stipulated to a judgment for the estate in the amount of $1,622,674.86 ($1,104,156.27 in tax and $518,518.59 in interest).

II

* * *

The "value" of property to be included in the gross estate is the fair market value of the item at the time of the decedent's death. 26 C.F.R. § 20.2031–1(b). The fair market value is the price at which the property would change hands between a willing buyer and a willing seller, neither being under any compulsion to buy or sell and both having reasonable knowledge of relevant facts. The fair market value of a particular item of property includible in the decedent's gross estate is not to be determined by a forced sale price. Nor is the fair market value of an item of property to be determined by the sale price of the item in a market other than that in which such item is most commonly sold to the public, taking into account the location of the item wherever appropriate.... All relevant facts and elements of value as of the applicable valuation date shall be considered in every case. 26 C.F.R. § 20.2031–1(b).

Non-commercial annuities, such as the lottery payments at issue, are valued pursuant to tables promulgated by the Secretary of the Treasury, except when another regulatory provision applies. 26 U.S.C. § 7520. The general "fair market value" regulation quoted above, 26 C.F.R. § 20.2031–1(b), is such a provision, allowing departure from the tables "where they do not produce a value that reasonably approximates the fair market value...." *O'Reilly v. Comm'r,* 973 F.2d 1403, 1407 (8th Cir.1992).

The IRS has explained that the "[v]aluation factors for determining the present value of interests measured by a term certain are based on two components: a term of years component and an interest rate component." Notice 89–24, 1989–1 C.B. 660. Although the tables provide the presumptive valuation of non-commercial annuities, courts have long recognized that a table-produced valuation is not applicable when the result is unrealistic and unreasonable. *See, e.g., Weller v. Comm'r,* 38 T.C. 790, 803, 1962 WL 1155 (1962). In such cases, a modification to the valuation or a complete departure from the tables may be justified.

As the Eighth Circuit explained:

When use of the tables produces a substantially unrealistic and unreasonable result *and* when a more reasonable and realistic valuation technique is available, faith that the tables will "average out" in the long run will not suffice. Compliance with the statute and fairness in the particular case require that the reviewing court use that alternative method to determine the fair market value of the gifted property.

O'Reilly, 973 F.2d at 1409. *See also Estate of Christ v. Comm'r,* 480 F.2d 171, 172 (9th Cir.1973) (approving of tax court's adoption of *Hanley v. United States,* 105 Ct.Cl. 638, 63 F.Supp. 73, 81 (1945), which held that the tables are to apply unless the result would be "substantially at variance with the facts"); *Froh v. Comm'r,* 100 T.C. 1, 3–4, 1993 WL 1869 (1993) ("use of the actuarial tables is presumptively correct unless it is shown that such use is 'unrealistic and unreasonable' ").

For these reasons, although the general rule requires that the tables be used because they provide both certainty and convenience when applied in large numbers of cases, *see Bank of California v. United States,* 672 F.2d 758, 759–60 (9th Cir.1982), exceptions have been made when the tables do not reasonably approximate the fair market value of the asset. However, because the table-produced valuation is presumed correct, the party who desires to use an alternative method to value an estate's interest bears the "considerable burden of proving that the tables produce such an unrealistic and unreasonable result that they should not be used." *O'Reilly,* 973 F.2d at 1408.

III

In this case, the district court concluded that the discount tables did not reasonably approximate the fair market value of the lottery payments because California's statutory anti-assignment restriction reduced the fair market value. The district court's conclusion is consistent with tax theory. Indeed, the reality of a decedent's economic interest in any particular property right is a major factor in determining valuation for estate tax purposes.* * * Each of the characteristics of a property interest must be considered in determining its value for taxing purposes.* * * The right to transfer is "one of the most essential sticks in the bundle of rights that are commonly characterized as property[.]" * * * It is axiomatic that if an asset's marketability is restricted, it is less valuable than an identical marketable asset. * * * We have long recognized that restrictions on alienability reduce value. *See e.g., Bayley v. Comm'r,* 624 F.2d 884, 885 (9th Cir.1980) (holding that stock transfer restrictions affect valuation); *Trust Services of Am., Inc. v. United States,* 885 F.2d 561, 569 (9th Cir.1989) ("[I]f stock is subject to resale restrictions under the federal securities laws which prevent it from being sold freely in the public market, a discount from the mean may be necessary to measure the stock's value accurately." (citation omitted)). *Estate of Jung v. Comm'r,* 101 T.C. 412, 434, 1993 WL 460544 (1993) (because stock of closely held corporations is not publically traded, minority shares ordinarily receive "[a] marketability discount [to reflect] the hypothetical buyer's concern that there will not be a ready market when that buyer decides to sell the stock"); *see also Theophilos v. Comm'r,* 85 F.3d 440, (9th Cir.1996) (minority shareholders in close corporations generally receive a discount to reflect lack of control).

¶ 10,019

In this case, there is little doubt that the statutory restrictions on transfer reduced the fair market value of the right to receive future lottery payments. The district court, after considering expert testimony on the point, reached the same conclusion in finding that the "[u]se of the annuity tables produces a substantially unrealistic and unreasonable result because the table does not reflect the discount which must be taken by virtue of the non-liquidity of the prize." * * *

Contrary to the government's argument, the lack of a market due to the anti-assignment restriction does not mean that the asset cannot be valued except by the tables. Where a willing seller and willing buyer do not exist, we will presume both their presence and a hypothetical sale.* * * Thus, given the expert testimony presented, the district court did not err in analyzing fair market value by assuming a hypothetical market.

The government also contends that allowing consideration of alienability in determining fair market value would undercut the bright line regulatory rule established by employment of the tables. Of course, this "bright line rule" has not deterred the IRS from seeking exceptions when it is the disadvantaged party. In fact, the IRS has often taken advantage of the economic reality rationale for departure from the tables, urging that the table-produced result under-values the particular asset at issue. * * *

More importantly, consideration of transfer restrictions in a fair market analysis does not alter the presumption that the value provided by the tables is correct and subject to revision only if the party seeking departure shows that the tables produce an unrealistic and unreasonable value. In such a case, if the taxpayer proves that a more realistic and reasonable valuation method exists that more closely approximates fair market value, courts are free to employ it. In this case, on the basis of the evidence presented, the district court concluded that strict application of the discount tables did not accurately reflect economic reality and reached an alternate determination of fair market value. We cannot say that the district court erred in this assessment.

As to the floodgates that the government believes to be opened by the injection of economic reality, one must only note the improbability of the confluence of government intervention, untimely death, and the lotto. * * *

       AFFIRMED.

Note

[¶ 10,027]

In a case with virtually identical facts, including a state law (Connecticut) prohibition on assignment of the lottery prize, the Second Circuit reached the same result. Estate of Gribauskas v. Commissioner, 342 F.3d 85 (2d Cir. 2003).

In a split decision, however, the Fifth Circuit reached the opposite conclusion on essentially identical facts involving a nontransferable Texas lottery prize. Cook v. Commissioner, 349 F.3d 850 (5th Cir. 2003). The majority observed that the actuarial tables are routinely applied to other nonmarketable annuities, such as survivor annuities under ERISA, and that "non-marketability of a private annuity is an assumption underlying the annuity tables." The majority also argued that all the nonlottery cases in which application of the tables had been found unreasonable involved circumstances in which the assumptions underlying the tables were in question, e.g., the reliability of the rate of return. Finally, the majority reasoned that there is no rational basis for applying a discount for nonmarketability to a certain, fixed, and secure income stream. The Fifth Circuit therefore affirmed the Tax Court's application of the Treasury tables to determine the value of the lottery prize.

The reference in *Cook* to the inalienability of survivor annuities under ERISA raises interesting possibilities. In *Shackleford*, ¶ 10,019, the court notes that "It is axiomatic that if an asset's marketability is restricted, it is less valuable than an identical marketable asset." If the lottery payments involved in *Shackleford* were appropriately discounted because of inalienability, could not an inalienable survivor annuity under ERISA be similarly discounted?

The usual rules of actuarial valuation are clearly inappropriate for wasting assets, i.e., assets that will necessarily be consumed over time. A good example is Froh v. Commissioner, 100 T.C. 1 (1993), aff'd by unpublished opinion, 46 F.3d 1141 (9th Cir. 1995). In *Froh* the donor created trusts that provided 10–year income interests for the donees, with remainders reserved to the donor. The donor then transferred interests in natural gas reserves to the trusts. The donor contended that the 10–year income interests should be assigned a value of only .614457 of the full value of the reserves, pursuant to the usual rules for valuing term interests, now embodied in Reg. § 25.2512–5(d)(2)(iii). The Commissioner, however, presented evidence that the gas properties were wasting assets and would probably be exhausted within ten years. The Tax Court agreed, concluding that in these circumstances use of the Regulations would be "unrealistic and unreasonable." The result was assignment to the gifted income interests of 100 percent of the value of the gas properties.

Problems

[¶ 10,039]

Assume in each case that all transfers occur after April 30, 1999, and that the § 7520 rate at the time of the transfer is 7% per annum. Assume further that in each case the donee of the interest is not a family member as defined in § 2704(c)(2); therefore, the special valuation principles of § 2702 do not apply.

1. On November 1 of Year 1 Arthur Brown transferred $100,000 to an irrevocable trust. The trust provides that for 12 years the income from the trust is to be paid to Mildred Jones or her estate. At the end of the 12 years the trust is to terminate and the corpus is to be returned to Arthur. How should the gift to Mildred be valued for gift tax purposes?

2. Assume the same facts as in Problem 1. Arthur dies on November 1 of Year 3. At what value would the reversion be included in Arthur's estate for estate tax purposes, assuming that the trust value on November 1 of Year 3 is $120,000?

¶ **10,039**

3. Wilma Brown transferred $100,000 to an irrevocable trust. The trust provides that the income is to be paid to Gladys Jones, age 64, until the death of Gladys. At that time the trust is to terminate, and the corpus is to be transferred to Edward Wilson, or Edward's estate. How should the gifts to Gladys and Edward, respectively, be valued for gift tax purposes?

4. Jane Porter transferred $300,000 to a trust. The trust instrument requires that the trustee pay $1,500 to Alfred Porter on the last day of each month in each year until Alfred's death. Alfred was born 60 years before Jane's transfer. Upon Alfred's death the remaining trust funds are to be paid to Jane. What is the value of the gift to Alfred?

Chapter 11

CLOSELY HELD BUSINESSES AND OTHER ASSETS

A. GENERAL PRINCIPLES

[¶ 11,001]

Closely held businesses raise difficult valuation issues because interests in such businesses are not regularly traded. Although willing buyers and willing sellers determine prices every day for actively traded business interests (such as stock listed on an exchange), the willing buyer-willing seller analysis is essentially hypothetical in its application to nontraded business interests.

The starting point in valuing closely held businesses is § 2031(b), which dictates that nontraded stock and securities be valued by reference to the actual market valuation of similar enterprises, the stock or securities of which are actively traded. The Regulations somewhat expand this mandate by specifying the aspects of a closely held business that are to be given the greatest weight for purposes of comparison with actively traded securities. Reg. §§ 20.2031–2(f) and 20.2031–3.

The Regulations on valuation of closely held businesses are very brief. The general principles set forth in the Regulations are amplified by Rev. Rul. 59–60, below, which remains the landmark IRS pronouncement on valuation of closely held businesses.

[¶ 11,007]

REVENUE RULING 59–60

1959–1 C.B. 237.

SEC. 1. PURPOSE

The purpose of this Revenue Ruling is to outline and review in general the approach, methods and factors to be considered in valuing shares of the capital stock of closely held corporations for estate tax and gift tax purposes. The methods discussed herein will apply likewise to the valuation of corporate stock on which market quotations are either unavailable or are of such scarcity that they do not reflect the fair market value.

SEC. 2. BACKGROUND AND DEFINITIONS

.01 All valuations must be made in accordance with the applicable provisions of the Internal Revenue Code of 1954 and the Federal Estate Tax and Gift Tax Regulations. Sections 2031(a), 2032 and 2512(a) of the 1954 Code (sections 811 and 1005 of the 1939 Code) require that the property to be included in the gross estate, or made the subject of a gift, shall be taxed on the basis of the value of the property at the time of death of the decedent, the alternate date if so elected, or the date of gift.

.02 Section 20.2031–1(b) of the Estate Tax Regulations (section 81.10 of the Estate Tax Regulations 105) and section 25.2512–1, of the Gift Tax Regulations (section 86.19 of Gift Tax Regulations 108) define fair market value, in effect, as the price at which the property would change hands between a willing buyer and a willing seller when the former is not under any compulsion to buy and the latter is not under any compulsion to sell, both parties having reasonable knowledge of relevant facts. Court decisions frequently state in addition that the hypothetical buyer and seller are assumed to be able, as well as willing, to trade and to be well informed about the property and concerning the market for such property.

.03 Closely held corporations are those corporations the shares of which are owned by a relatively limited number of stockholders. Often the entire stock issue is held by one family. The result of this situation is that little, if any, trading in the shares takes place. There is, therefore, no established market for the stock and such sales as occur at irregular intervals seldom reflect all of the elements of a representative transaction as defined by the term "fair market value."

SEC. 3. APPROACH TO VALUATION

.01 A determination of fair market value, being a question of fact, will depend upon the circumstances in each case. No formula can be devised that will be generally applicable to the multitude of different valuation issues arising in estate and gift tax cases. Often, an appraiser will find wide differences of opinion as to the fair market value of a particular stock. In resolving such differences, he should maintain a reasonable attitude in recognition of the fact that valuation is not an exact science. A sound valuation will be based upon all the relevant facts, but the elements of common sense, informed judgment and reasonableness must enter into the process of weighing those facts and determining their aggregate significance.

.02 The fair market value of specific shares of stock will vary as general economic conditions change from "normal" to "boom" or "depression," that is, according to the degree of optimism or pessimism with which the investing public regards the future at the required date of appraisal. Uncertainty as to the stability or continuity of the future income from a property decreases its value by increasing the risk of loss of earnings and value in the future. The value of shares of stock of a company with very uncertain future prospects is highly speculative. The appraiser must exercise his judgment as to the degree of risk attaching to the business of the corporation which issued the stock, but that judgment must be related to all of the other factors affecting value.

¶ 11,007

.03 Valuation of securities is, in essence, a prophecy as to the future and must be based on facts available at the required date of appraisal. As a generalization, the prices of stocks which are traded in volume in a free and active market by informed persons best reflect the consensus of the investing public as to what the future holds for the corporations and industries represented. When a stock is closely held, is traded infrequently, or is traded in an erratic market, some other measure of value must be used. In many instances, the next best measure may be found in the prices at which the stocks of companies engaged in the same or a similar line of business are selling in a free and open market.

Sec. 4. Factors to Consider

.01 It is advisable to emphasize that in the valuation of the stock of closely held corporations or the stock of corporations where market quotations are either lacking or too scarce to be recognized, all available financial data, as well as all relevant factors affecting the fair market value, should be considered. The following factors, although not all-inclusive, are fundamental and require careful analysis in each case:

(a) The **nature of the business** and the history of the enterprise from its inception.

(b) The **economic outlook in** general and the condition and outlook of the specific industry in particular.

(c) The **book value** of the stock and the financial condition of the business.

(d) The **earning capacity** of the company.

(e) The **dividend-paying** capacity.

(f) Whether or not the enterprise has **goodwill** or other intangible value.

(g) **Sales of the stock** and the **size of the block** of stock to be valued.

(h) The **market price** of stocks of corporations engaged in the same or a similar line of business having their stocks actively traded in a free and open market, either on an exchange or over-the-counter.

.02 The following is a brief discussion of each of the foregoing factors:

(a) The history of a corporate enterprise will show its past stability or instability, its growth or lack of growth, the diversity or lack of diversity of its operations, and other facts needed to form an opinion of the degree of risk involved in the business. For an enterprise which changed its form of organization but carried on the same or closely similar operations of its predecessor, the history of the former enterprise should be considered. The detail to be considered should increase with approach to the required date of appraisal, since recent events are of greatest help in predicting the future; but a study of gross and net income, and of dividends covering a long prior period, is highly desirable. The history to be studied should include, but need not be limited to, the nature of the business, its products or services, its operating and investment assets, capital structure, plant facilities, sales records and management, all of which should be considered as of the date of the appraisal,

¶ 11,007

with due regard for recent significant changes. Events of the past that are unlikely to recur in the future should be discounted, since value has a close relation to future expectancy.

(b) A sound appraisal of a closely held stock must consider current and prospective economic conditions as of the date of appraisal, both in the national economy and in the industry or industries with which the corporation is allied. It is important to know that the company is more or less successful than its competitors in the same industry, or that it is maintaining a stable position with respect to competitors. Equal or even greater significance may attach to the ability of the industry with which the company is allied to compete with other industries. Prospective competition which has not been a factor in prior years should be given careful attention. For example, high profits due to the novelty of its product and the lack of competition often lead to increasing competition. The public's appraisal of the future prospects of competitive industries or of competitors within an industry may be indicated by price trends in the markets for commodities and for securities. The loss of the manager of a so-called "one-man" business may have a depressing effect upon the value of the stock of such business, particularly if there is a lack of trained personnel capable of succeeding to the management of the enterprise. In valuing the stock of this type of business, therefore, the effect of the loss of the manager on the future expectancy of the business and the absence of management-succession potentialities are pertinent factors to be taken into consideration. On the other hand, there may be factors which offset, in whole or in part, the loss of the manager's services. For instance, the nature of the business and of its assets may be such that they will not be impaired by the loss of the manager. Furthermore, the loss may be adequately covered by life insurance, or competent management might be employed on the basis of the consideration paid for the former manager's services. These, or other offsetting factors, if found to exist, should be carefully weighed against the loss of the manager's services in valuing he stock of the enterprise.

(c) Balance sheets should be obtained, preferably in the form of comparative annual statements for two or more years immediately preceding the date of appraisal, together with a balance sheet at the end of the month preceding that date, if corporate accounting will permit. Any balance sheet descriptions that are not self-explanatory, and balance sheet items comprehending diverse assets or liabilities, should be clarified in essential detail by supporting supplemental schedules. These statements usually will disclose to the appraiser (1) liquid position (ratio of current assets to current liabilities); (2) gross and net book value of principal classes of fixed assets; (3) working capital; (4) long-term indebtedness; (5) capital structure; and (6) net worth. Consideration also should be given to any assets not essential to the operation of the business, such as investments in securities, real estate, etc. In general, such nonoperating assets will command a lower rate of return than do the operating assets, although in exceptional cases the reverse may be true. In computing the book value per share of stock, assets of the investment type should be revalued on the basis of their market price and the book value adjusted accordingly. Comparison of the company's balance sheets over sever-

¶ 11,007

al years may reveal, among other facts, such developments as the acquisition of additional production facilities or subsidiary companies, improvement in financial position, and details as to recapitalizations and other changes in the capital structure of the corporation. If the corporation has more than one class of stock outstanding, the charter or certificate of incorporation should be examined to ascertain the explicit rights and privileges of the various stock issues including: (1) voting powers, (2) preference as to dividends, and (3) preference as to assets in the event of liquidation.

(d) Detailed profit-and-loss statements should be obtained and considered for a representative period immediately prior to the required date of appraisal, preferably five or more years. Such statements should show (1) gross income by principal items; (2) principal deductions from gross income including major prior items of operating expenses, interest and other expense on each item of long-term debt, depreciation and depletion if such deductions are made, officers' salaries, in total if they appear to be reasonable or in detail if they seem to be excessive, contributions (whether or not deductible for tax purposes) that the nature of its business and its community position require the corporation to make, and taxes by principal items, including income and excess profits taxes; (3) net income available for dividends; (4) rates and amounts of dividends paid on each class of stock; (5) remaining amount carried to surplus; and (6) adjustments to, and reconciliation with, surplus as stated on the balance sheet. With profit and loss statements of this character available, the appraiser should be able to separate recurrent from nonrecurrent items of income and expense, to distinguish between operating income and investment income, and to ascertain whether or not any line of business in which the company is engaged is operated consistently at a loss and might be abandoned with benefit to the company. The percentage of earnings retained for business expansion should be noted when dividend-paying capacity is considered. Potential future income is a major factor in many valuations of closely-held stocks, and all information concerning past income which will be helpful in predicting the future should be secured. Prior earnings records usually are the most reliable guide as to the future expectancy, but resort to arbitrary five-or-ten-year averages without regard to current trends or future prospects will not produce a realistic valuation. If, for instance, a record of progressively increasing or decreasing net income is found, then greater weight may be accorded the most recent years' profits in estimating earning power. It will be helpful, in judging risk and the extent to which a business is a marginal operator, to consider deductions from income and net income in terms of percentage of sales. Major categories of cost and expense to be so analyzed include the consumption of raw materials and supplies in the case of manufacturers, processors and fabricators; the cost of purchased merchandise in the case of merchants; utility services; insurance; taxes; depletion or depreciation; and interest.

(e) Primary consideration should be given to the dividend-paying capacity of the company rather than to dividends actually paid in the past. Recognition must be given to the necessity of retaining a reasonable portion of profits in a company to meet competition. Dividend-paying capacity is a factor that must be considered in an appraisal, but dividends actually paid in the past may not

¶ 11,007

have any relation to dividend-paying capacity. Specifically, the dividends paid by a closely held family company may be measured by the income needs of the stockholders or by their desire to avoid taxes on dividend receipts, instead of by the ability of the company to pay dividends. Where an actual or effective controlling interest in a corporation is to be valued, the dividend factor is not a material element, since the payment of such dividends is discretionary with the controlling stockholders. The individual or group in control can substitute salaries and bonuses for dividends, thus reducing net income and understating the dividend-paying capacity of the company. It follows, therefore, that dividends are less reliable criteria of fair market value than other applicable factors.

(f) In the final analysis, goodwill is based upon earning capacity. The presence of goodwill and its value, therefore, rests upon the excess of net earnings over and above a fair return on the net tangible assets. While the element of goodwill may be based primarily on earnings, such factors as the prestige and renown of the business, the ownership of a trade or brand name, and a record of successful operation over a prolonged period in a particular locality, also may furnish support for the inclusion of intangible value. In some instances it may not be possible to make a separate appraisal of the tangible and intangible assets of the business. The enterprise has a value as an entity. Whatever intangible value there is, which is supportable by the facts, may be measured by the amount by which the appraised value of the tangible assets exceeds the net book value of such assets.

(g) Sales of stock of a closely held corporation should be carefully investigated to determine whether they represent transactions at arm's length. Forced or distress sales do not ordinarily reflect fair market value nor do isolated sales in small amounts necessarily control as the measure of value. This is especially true in the valuation of a controlling interest in a corporation. Since, in the case of closely held stocks, no prevailing market prices are available, there is no basis for making an adjustment for blockage. It follows, therefore, that such stocks should be valued upon a consideration of all the evidence affecting the fair market value. The size of the block of stock itself is a relevant factor to be considered. Although it is true that a minority interest in an unlisted corporation's stock is more difficult to sell than a similar block of listed stock, it is equally true that control of a corporation, either actual or in effect, representing as it does an added element of value, may justify a higher value for a specific block of stock.

(h) Section 2031(b) of the Code states, in effect, that in valuing unlisted securities the value of stock or securities of corporations engaged in the same or a similar line of business which are listed on an exchange should be taken into consideration along with all other factors. An important consideration is that the corporations to be used for comparisons have capital stocks which are actively traded by the public. In accordance with section 2031(b) of the Code, stocks listed on an exchange are to be considered first. However, if sufficient comparable companies whose stocks are listed on an exchange cannot be found, other comparable companies which have stocks actively traded in on the over-the-counter market also may be used. The essential factor is that whether the stocks are sold on an exchange or over-the-counter there is evidence of an active, free public market for the stock as of the valuation date. In selecting corporations for comparative purposes, care should be taken to use only comparable companies. Although the only restrictive requirement as to comparable corporations specified in the statute is that their lines of business be the same or similar, yet it is obvious that consideration must be given to other relevant factors in order that the most valid comparison possible will be obtained. For illustration, a corporation having one or more issues of preferred stock, bonds or debentures in addition to its common stock should not be considered to be directly comparable to one having only common stock outstanding. In like manner, a company with a declining business and decreasing markets is not comparable to one with a record of current progress and market expansion.

Sec. 5. Weight to Be Accorded Various Factors

The valuation of closely held corporate stock entails the consideration of all relevant factors as stated in section 4. Depending upon the circumstances in each case, certain factors may carry more weight than others because of the nature of the company's business. To illustrate:

(a) Earnings may be the most important criterion of value in some cases whereas asset value will receive primary consideration in others. In general, the appraiser will accord primary consideration to earnings when valuing stocks of companies which sell products or services to the public; conversely, in the investment or holding type of company, the appraiser may accord the greatest weight to the assets underlying the security to be valued.

(b) The value of the stock of a closely held investment or real estate holding company, whether or not family owned, is closely related to the value of the assets underlying the stock. For companies of this type the appraiser should determine the fair market values of the assets of the company. Operating expenses of such a company and the cost of liquidating it, if any, merit consideration when appraising the relative values of the stock and the underlying assets. The market values of the underlying assets give due weight to potential earnings and dividends of the particular items of property underlying the stock, capitalized at rates deemed proper by the investing public at the date of appraisal. A current appraisal by the investing public should be superior to the retrospective opinion of an individual. For these reasons, adjusted net worth should be accorded greater weight in valuing the stock of a closely held investment or real estate holding company, whether or not family owned, than any of the other customary yardsticks of appraisal, such as earnings and dividend paying capacity.

Sec. 6. Capitalization Rates

In the application of certain fundamental valuation factors, such as earnings and dividends, it is necessary to capitalize the average or current results at some appropriate rate. A determination of the proper capitalization rate presents one of the most difficult problems in valuation. That there is no ready or simple solution will become apparent by a cursory check of the rates of return and dividend yields in terms of the selling prices of corporate shares listed on the major exchanges of the country. Wide variations will be found even for companies in the same industry. Moreover, the ratio will fluctuate from year to year depending upon economic conditions. Thus, no standard tables of capitalization rates applicable to closely held corporations can be formulated. Among the more important factors to be taken into consideration in deciding upon a capitalization rate in a particular case are: (1) the nature of the business; (2) the risk involved; and (3) the stability or irregularity of earnings.

Sec. 7. Average of Factors

Because valuations cannot be made on the basis of a prescribed formula, there is no means whereby the various applicable factors in a particular case can be assigned mathematical weights in deriving the fair market value. For this reason, no useful purpose is served by taking an average of several factors (for example, book value, capitalized earnings and capitalized dividends) and basing the valuation on the result. Such a process excludes active consideration of other pertinent factors, and the end result cannot be supported by a realistic application of the significant facts in the case except by mere chance.

* * *

[¶ 11,013]

REVENUE RULING 65–193

1965–2 C.B. 370.

Revenue Ruling 59–60, C.B. 1959–1, 237, is hereby modified to delete the statements, contained therein at section 4.02(f), that "In some instances it may not be possible to make a separate appraisal of the tangible and intangible assets of the business. The enterprise has a value as an entity. Whatever intangible value there is, which is supportable by the facts, may be measured by the amount by which the appraised value of the tangible assets exceeds the net book value of such assets."

The instances where it is not possible to make a separate appraisal of the tangible and intangible assets of a business are rare and each case varies from the other. No rule can be devised which will be generally applicable to such cases.

Other than this modification, Revenue Ruling 59–60 continues in full force and effect.

Note

[¶ 11,019]

The principles of Rev. Rul. 59–60 have been applied in hundreds of litigated cases involving a wide variety of businesses. An analysis or summary of those cases is far beyond the scope of this work. However, *Estate of Cook,* which follows, provides a good example of the procedure for using the market valuation of listed securities to derive a value for similar closely held securities.

[¶ 11,025]

ESTATE OF COOK v. UNITED STATES

United States District Court, Western District of Missouri, 1986.
86–2 USTC ¶ 13,678.

BARTLETT, District Judge: Plaintiff the Estate of Howard Winston Cook seeks a refund of a gift tax deficiency assessment resulting from a gift of 1,725 shares of Central Bancompany, Inc. stock on December 24, 1976.

* * *

The sole issue before this Court is the fair market value of the 1,725 shares of Central Bancompany, Inc. stock on December 24, 1976.

On November 6, 1970, Central Bancompany, Inc. was incorporated under the laws of the state of Missouri as a general business corporation. It was inactive until December 30, 1971, when it acquired the Central Trust Bank and became an operating bank holding company with its principal place of business in Jefferson City, Missouri. * * *

At all times since its incorporation, Central Bancompany, Inc. had 200,000 shares of authorized common stock. In 1976, there were 194,329 shares outstanding. The 1,725 shares at issue represent .89% of the outstanding common stock of Central Bancompany, Inc. on December 24, 1976. On December 24, 1976, Howard Winston Cook, Sam Cook and their children owned approximately 59% of the outstanding shares of Central Bancompany, Inc.

On December 24, 1976, Howard Winston Cook created the Howard Winston Cook Irrevocable Trust by transferring to the trust, 1,725 shares of common stock of Central Bancompany, Inc. The beneficiaries of the trust were Cook's children, Mary Blair Cook, Laura Winston Cook and Steven Winston Cook. On January 12, 1977, Howard Winston Cook filed a Form 709 United States Gift Tax Return reporting a gift tax liability of $2,250 based on a $40 per share valuation. Howard Winston Cook died on May 8, 1978. On March 2, 1982, the Internal Revenue Service sent the Howard Winston Cook Estate a notice of gift tax deficiency in the amount of $84,063 based on an asserted fair market value of $257 per share. The Estate of Howard Winston Cook paid the assessment plus interest and filed this claim for refund.

* * *

Because neither expert opinion offered by the parties was persuasive, the Court will analyze the evidence presented in light of the applicable standard for determining fair market value when market sales do not present fair market value.

OUTLOOK FOR THE BANKING INDUSTRY IN 1976

The national economy was coming out of a recession in 1976. There was uncertainty in the banking industry because the effects of deregulation were unknown. Interest rates were fluctuating rapidly. Although the industry outlook may have been uncertain in 1976, the Court is not convinced that this uncertainty affected Central Bancompany, Inc. more dramatically than other Missouri bank holding companies.

Central Bancompany, Inc.'s Position in the Industry

In December 1976, Central Bancompany, Inc. was the seventh largest bank holding company in Missouri. Central Bancompany, Inc. was the largest multibank holding company with its principal office and primary trade area located outside a metropolitan area.

Central Bancompany, Inc.'s single largest depositor was the State of Missouri. In December 1976, there was some uncertainty whether Central Bancompany, Inc. would continue to serve as the main depositor for state government because a new administration had just been elected. There was discussion about opening the state's banking business to competitive bidding. In order to satisfy the security requirements for being a state depositor, Central Bancompany, Inc. had to maintain a higher level of retained earnings than other banks of comparable size. Nevertheless, Central Trust Bank was the dominant bank in central Missouri and had by location and experience a strong claim on a substantial portion of the state of Missouri's banking business.

Evidence of Other Sales

There were several sales of Central Bancompany, Inc. stock between January 4, 1973, and February 12, 1982, at prices ranging from $36 per share to $68.18. * * * Standing alone, these prices do not establish the fair market value of the shares at issue because the sales were sporadic and persons intimately involved in the ownership and management of Central Bancompany, Inc. set the price. For the reasons stated in the April 3, 1985, Memorandum Opinion and Order, these sales transactions are entitled to little evidentiary weight on the question of fair market value.

Central Bancompany, Inc.'s Financial Information

Based on the admissions of the parties and the audited consolidated financial statements of Central Bancompany, Inc., the following financial information about Central Bancompany, Inc. has been established:

Year	1973	1974	1975	1976
Total Assets	296,630,326	389,778,687	404,479,530	421,409,327
Total Liabilities	265,034,534	355,692,750	366,656,079	380,332,297
Stockholders' Equity	29,685,313	34,085,937	37,823,451	41,077,030
Book Value	150.17	175.09	194.64	211.38
Net Income	3,798,398	4,267,159	4,022,635	3,603,371
Net Income Per Share	19.45	21.60	20.68	18.54
Dividends Paid Per Share	1.20	1.40	1.40	1.80

The book value of Central Bancompany, Inc.'s stock had increased approximately $61 per share from $150.17 to $211.38 per share over the four year period from 1973 to 1976. During this same period, Central Bancompany,

Inc. had substantial earnings with 1976 earnings per share of $18.54. Further, due to the corporation's conservative dividend policy, a high percentage of net income was retained each year.

COMPARISON TO MISSOURI BANK HOLDING COMPANIES

Comparing the financial data pertaining to Central Bancompany, Inc. with the financial data of other publicly traded Missouri bank holding companies as set forth in Plaintiff's Exhibit 16 demonstrates that the actual sales prices of Central Bancompany, Inc. between January 4, 1973, and February 12, 1982, did not reflect accurately the fair market value of Central Bancompany, Inc. on December 24, 1976.

For instance, the ratio of bid price (market value) to book value of the stock of comparable Missouri bank holding companies in 1976 ranged from 51% (lowest) to 92% (highest). The Missouri bank holding companies most comparable to Central Bancompany, Inc. in location of principal bank and service area (hereafter "rural Missouri bank holding companies") had an average market value to book value ratio of 67%. The average market value to book value ratio of all publicly traded Missouri bank holding companies was 74%. However, assuming a market value of $40 per share, Central Bancompany, Inc's market value to book value ratio was only 19% ($40/$21/1.38=18.92%). For Central Bancompany, Inc. to have a market value to book value ratio comparable to the lowest market value to book value ratio of the publicly traded Missouri bank holding companies, Central Bancompany, Inc. stock would have to sell for at least $107.80. For Central Bancompany, Inc. to have a market value to book value ratio comparable to the average of all Missouri bank holding companies, Central Bancompany, Inc. stock would have to sell for $156.42 per share. For Central Bancompany, Inc. to have a market value to book value ratio comparable to the average of the rural Missouri bank holding companies, the stock would have to sell for $141.62. For Central Bancompany, Inc. to have a market value to book value ratio comparable to the highest market value to book value ratio of any Missouri bank holding company, Central Bancompany, Inc. stock would have to sell for $194.47 per share.[4]

A comparison of price/earnings ratios of Missouri bank holding companies confirms that the actual sales prices of Central Bancompany, Inc. stock are significantly lower than its fair market value. The price/earnings ratio of comparable Missouri bank holding companies ranges from 4.9 (lowest), to 5.9 (the average of the rural Missouri bank holding companies), to 6.6 (the average of all other Missouri bank holding companies), to 8.4 (highest).

4. Projected Fair Market Value of Central Bancompany, Inc. Stock Applying Market/Book Value Ratio of Comparable Missouri Bank Holding Companies

Market value/ book ratios		Projected market value of CBI stock	Calculation
92%	Highest	$194.47	$211.38 × 92% = $194.47
74%	Average	$156.42	$211.38 × 74% = $156.42
51%	Lowest	$107.80	$211.38 × 51% = $107.80
67%	Rural	$141.62	$211.38 × 67% = $141.62

However, the price/earnings ratio of Central Bancompany, Inc.'s stock in 1976 (assuming a market price of $40) is only 2.16 ($40.00/$18.54=2.16). For Central Bancompany, Inc. to have a price/earnings ratio comparable to the lowest price/earnings ratio of any Missouri bank holding company, it would have to sell for at least $90.85 per share. To have a price/earnings ratio comparable to the average of all Missouri bank holding companies, Central Bancompany, Inc. stock would have to sell for $122.36 per share. To have a price/earnings ratio comparable to the average of the rural Missouri bank holding companies, the stock would have to sell for $109.39 per share. To have a price/earnings ratio comparable to the highest price/earnings ratio of any Missouri bank holding company, Central Bancompany, Inc. stock would have to sell for $155.74 per share.[6]

A comparison of dividend yield and dividend paying capacity demonstrates that at $40 per share the stock of Central Bancompany, Inc. stock was substantially undervalued. The dividend paid/earnings per share ratio of other Missouri bank holding companies ranged from 21% (lowest), to 26.3% (the average of rural Missouri bank holding companies), to 37.9% (the average of all Missouri bank holding companies), to 57% (highest). In 1976, the dividend paid/earnings per share ratio of Central Bancompany, Inc. stock was 9.7% ($1.80/$18.54=9.7%). Therefore, Central Bancompany, Inc. is paying out in dividends a substantially lower percentage of its earnings than other Missouri bank holding companies.

However, at a price per share of $40, the dividend yield of Central Bancompany, Inc. stock in 1976 was 4.5% ($1.80/$40). This dividend yield was comparable to the yields of other Missouri bank holding companies. However, since the dividend yield is based on the artificially low dividend paid, the comparison of dividend yield with other Missouri bank holding companies is not meaningful.

If Central Bancompany, Inc. paid a comparable percentage of its earnings as a dividend as other Missouri bank holding companies, the Central Bancompany, Inc. dividend would range from $3.89 (applying the lowest dividend paid/earnings per share ratio of any Missouri bank holding company), to $4.88 (applying the average dividend paid/earnings per share ratio of the rural Missouri bank holding companies), to $7.03 (applying the average dividend paid/earnings per share ratio of all other comparable Missouri bank holding companies), to $10.56 (applying the highest earnings per share/dividends paid ratio of any publicly traded Missouri bank holding company).[9]

6. Projected Fair Market Value of Central Bancompany, Inc. Stock Applying Price/Earnings Ratios of Comparable Missouri Bank Holding Companies

Price/earnings ratio		Projected FMV of CBI stock	Earnings/share in 1976 × price/earnings ratios of other Missouri Banks		Value of CBI stockholding
4.9	Lowest	$ 90.85	$18.54 × 4.9	=	$ 90.85
[6.6]	Average	$122.36	$18.54 × 6.6	=	$122.36
8.4	Highest	$155.74	$18.54 × 8.4	=	$155.74
5.9	Rural	$109.39	$18.54 × 5.9	=	$109.39

¶ 11,025

Assuming Central Bancompany, Inc. paid a percentage of earnings as a dividend comparable to other publicly traded Missouri bank holding companies, a corresponding price per share of its stock can be computed using the average dividend yields of comparable Missouri bank holding companies. The average dividend yield of other Missouri bank holding companies (5.8%) produces a price per share of $121.21 assuming Central Bancompany, Inc. paid a dividend of $7.03 per share. The average dividend yield of the rural Missouri bank holding companies (4.5%) produces a price per share of $108.44 assuming Central Bancompany, Inc. paid a dividend of $4.88 per share. The lowest dividend yield of comparable Missouri bank holding companies (3.8%) produces a price per share of $102.37 assuming Central Bancompany, Inc. paid a dividend of $3.89 per share. The highest dividend yield of comparable Missouri bank holding companies (8.4%) produces a price per share of $125.71 assuming Central Bancompany, Inc. paid a dividend of $10.56 per share.[10]

After carefully considering each of the factors set forth in 26 C.F.R. § 26.2512–2(f), the fair market value of Central Bancompany, Inc. stock on December 24, 1976, was $130 per share.

B. PREMIUM FOR CONTROL

[¶ 11,031]

ESTATE OF CHENOWETH v. COMMISSIONER

United States Tax Court, 1987.
88 T.C. 1577.

KÖRNER, Judge:

Respondent determined a deficiency of Federal estate tax against petitioner in the amount of $232,227.50. The sole issue between the parties is

9. Calculation of CBI Dividend if CBI Paid a Percentage of Earnings to Dividend Comparable to Other Missouri Bank Holding Companies

Dividend Paid/ Earnings Per Share		Dividend	Calculation
21%	Lowest	$ 3.89	$ 3.89 = $18.54 × 21%
57%	Highest	$10.56	$10.56 = $18.54 × 57%
37.9%	Average	$ 7.03	$ 7.03 = $18.54 × 37.9%
26.3%	Rural	$ 4.88	$ 4.88 = $18.54 × 26.3%

10. Fair Market Value of CBI Stock Assuming CBI Paid a Dividend Based on Percentage of Its Earnings Comparable to Other Publicly Traded Missouri Bank Holding Companies

Dividend Paid/ Earnings Per Share		Comparable Dividend Yield	Assumed CBI Dividend if Same % of Net Income Paid	Projected Mkt. Value CBI Stock if Same % of Earnings Paid	Calculation
26.3	Rural	4.5%	$ 4.88	$108.44	$ 4.88/4.5% = $108.40
37.9	Average	5.8%	$ 7.03	$121.21	$ 7.03/5.8% = $121.21
21	Lowest	3.8%	$ 3.89	$102.37	$ 3.89/3.8% = $102.37
57	Highest	8.4%	$10.56	$125.71	$10.56/8.4% = $125.71

whether, in computing the marital deduction to which it is entitled under the provisions of section 2056, petitioner may value certain stock passing to decedent's surviving spouse by taking into account an alleged additional element of value because of the control which such block of stock has over the company involved.

* * *

Petitioner herein is the Estate of Dean A. Chenoweth (hereinafter "decedent"), acting by and through Julia Jenilee Chenoweth (hereinafter "Jenny"), the duly appointed personal representative of the estate. At the time of filing of the petition herein, petitioner's residence was in Tallahassee, Florida.

Decedent died on July 31, 1982. A timely Federal estate tax return was thereafter filed for his estate by the personal representative. The principal asset of decedent's gross estate was all of the outstanding common voting stock of Chenoweth Distributing Company, Inc. (hereinafter the "company"), which was owned by decedent at the date of his death and which was valued in the Federal estate tax return at $2,834.033. For purposes of arriving at the value of the gross estate under section 2031, respondent has accepted this valuation.

Under decedent's will, duly probated, decedent left 255 shares, or 51 percent, of the company's stock to his surviving wife, Jenny, and 245 shares, or 49 percent, of the company's stock to his daughter by a prior marriage, Kelli Chenoweth. So far as the bequest to Jenny is concerned, there is no dispute between the parties that the bequest was outright and qualifies for the marital deduction provided by section 2056. The parties are likewise in agreement that under Florida law, which governs here, the 51 percent stock interest passing to Jenny gives her complete control of the company.

As filed with respondent, decedent's estate tax return claimed a marital deduction with respect to the stock interest in the company passing to Jenny in the amount of $1,445,356, which was precisely 51 percent of the date of death value of $2,834,033 for all the stock. In the petition filed herein, however, petitioner now claims that the value of the company's stock passing to Jenny for marital deduction purposes should be $1,996,038, arrived at by adding a "control premium" of 38.1 percent to the value of such stock as originally reported.

Respondent contests this claim, and, in his motion for summary judgment, takes the position that, as a matter of law, petitioner is not entitled to increase the value of the controlling interest in the company, and claimed as a marital deduction, above a strict 51 percent share of the value of all the stock of the company, as reported in the gross estate. Petitioner, opposing respondent's motion, contends that there is no such prohibition as a matter of law.
* * *

The issue presented here is a novel one, and does not seem to have been directly addressed until now, at least by this Court. It requires us to consider the fundamental nature of the Federal estate tax, as a basis for how assets are to be valued for purposes of inclusion in the gross estate under section 2031. At the same time, we must also consider the nature of the marital deduction provided by section 2056, the valuation of assets qualifying for deduction under that section, and the moment in time when such assets are to be valued.

* * *

We may accept as a first step, then, that for purposes of inclusion in the decedent's gross estate under section 2031, his assets are to be valued at their worth at the moment of death. In this context, and for these purposes, respondent recognizes that a block of stock which represents the controlling interest in a company may be worth more than a block of stock in the same company which does not carry with it the control of the company. Thus, respondent's regulations provide, in part:

> On the other hand, if the block of stock to be valued represents a controlling interest, either actual or effective, in a going business, the price at which other lots change hands may have little relation to its true value. [Sec. 20.2031–2(e), Estate Tax Regs.]

* * *

The courts have likewise recognized that an additional element of value may be present in a block of shares representing a controlling interest, for valuation purposes under section 2031. * * * By the same token, a block of shares in a closely held corporation which is a noncontrolling minority interest may call for a reduction of its fair market value.

In the instant case, there is no dispute between the parties as to the value of the stock of the company. It was all owned by decedent at the moment of his death, and the value of that 100 percent interest was included in decedent's gross estate at a value which respondent has accepted. Certainly ownership of 100 percent of the outstanding stock of the company constitutes control. Whether the value used in this case for purposes of section 2031 included an element of value because of the control factor is not clear from this record, but we assume that it did.

* * *

This brings us to a consideration of the marital deduction provisions of section 2056.

* * *

The regulations * * * provide:

> The value, for the purpose of the marital deduction, of any deductible interest which passed from the decedent to his surviving spouse is to be determined as of the date of the decedent's death, * * *. The marital deduction may be taken only with respect to the net value of any deductible interest which passed from the decedent to his surviving spouse, * * * [Sec. 20.2056(b)–4(a), Estate Tax Regs.]

At this point, the focus of our inquiry has changed. For purposes of section 2031, we were concerned only with the value of the assets to be included in the decedent's gross estate as a whole, and without reference to

¶ 11,031

the destination of those assets under decedent's will or through the laws of descent and distribution. Under section 2056, however, a somewhat different question is presented: What is the asset that passes to the decedent's surviving spouse, and what is the value of it? Here, for the first time, we are concerned with the destination of the asset and the nature and the value of that interest which passes.

Under decedent's will, 255 shares of the company's stock, representing a controlling interest in the company, was broken off from the total stock ownership of decedent, as reflected for gross estate purposes under section 2031, and was bequeathed to his surviving spouse Jenny. That 51 percent share of the stock of the company carried with it the element of control and the additional element of value which inheres in such a controlling interest. For the first time, then, we must consider the total stock interest of decedent as composed of two pieces: the 51 percent share passing to decedent's surviving spouse, including the control element, and the 49 percent interest representing a minority share of the company which passed to decedent's child Kelli. As we have indicated above herein, it is clear to us that these two blocks of stock have different values. As we said in Estate of Salsbury v. Commissioner, supra:

> The payment of a premium for control is based on the principle that the per share value of minority interests is less than the per share value of a controlling interest. * * * A premium for control is generally expressed as the percentage by which the amount paid for a controlling block of shares exceeds the amount which would have otherwise been paid for the shares if sold as minority interests and is not based on a percentage of the value of the stock held by all or a particular class of minority shareholders. * * *

* * * In the instant case, it is clear to us that the block of the company's stock passing under decedent's will to his surviving widow was the controlling interest in the company, and was entitled to be valued for purposes of section 2056 so as to include an additional element of value because of that control. Thus, simply valuing the 51 percent share of the company's stock qualifying for the marital deduction at a mechanical 51 percent of the total value ascribed to the stock for purposes of inclusion in the gross estate would not give effect to the additional element of value for control which inheres in that block of stock. The amount of such control premium presents a material issue of fact which is not resolved in the present record and therefore requires that respondent's motion for summary judgment be denied.

* * * While we would tend to agree that the sum of the parts cannot equal more than the whole—that is, that the majority block together with the control premium, when added to the minority block of the company's stock with an appropriate discount for minority interest, should not equal more than the total 100 percent interest of the decedent, as reported for purposes of section 2031—it might well turn out that the sum of the parts can equal less than the whole—that is, that the control premium which is added to the majority block passing to decedent's surviving spouse might be less than the

proper minority discount to be attributed to the shares passing to decedent's daughter Kelli.

In any event, this question is not before us at this time. We are not required to determine at this point whether the minority block of shares passing to Kelli requires that a discount be assigned to it, nor the amount of such discount, nor that such discount must precisely equal the amount of control premium which is properly assignable to the majority block of shares qualifying for marital deduction under section 2056. All we decide here is that such majority block may be entitled to an extra element of value because of the control over the company which such block possesses; that such additional element of value can properly be considered in computing the amount of the marital deduction; and that this presents a material question of fact which has not been resolved between the parties and as to which petitioner must have an opportunity to present its proof.

* * *

Note

[¶ 11,033]

In theory, the magnitude of the control premium should vary from case to case, depending on the nature of the business and the realistic economic advantages offered by control, such as power to determine (1) salaries and other expenditures, (2) the extent of dividend or other distributions, (3) the extent to which earnings are reinvested and the business expanded, and (4) participation in mergers, liquidations, and substantial asset sales. Although a controlling owner has a theoretical duty to deal fairly with minority owners, in the real world a majority owner has a great deal of latitude.

In Estate of Salsbury v. Commissioner, 34 T.C.M. (CCH) 1441, T.C.M. (P–H) ¶ 75,333 (1975), the Tax Court assigned a 38.1% control premium to a 51.8% ownership interest. In Estate of Trenchard v. Commissioner, 69 T.C.M. (CCH) 2164, T.C.M. (RIA) ¶ 95,121 (1995), the Tax Court assigned a 40% control premium to a 61% ownership interest. Although the magnitude of the premium varies from case to case, these two cases, decided 20 years apart, are typical.

C. MINORITY DISCOUNTS

[¶ 11,037]

ESTATE OF BRIGHT v. UNITED STATES

United States Court of Appeals, Former Fifth Circuit, 1981.
658 F.2d 999.

ANDERSON III, Circuit Judge:

This case presents to the en banc court an important question involving the principles of federal estate tax valuation. Mary Frances Smith Bright died

¶ 11,037

on April 3, 1971. During her lifetime, she and her husband, Mr. Bright, owned 55% of the common stock of East Texas Motor Freight Lines, Inc., 55% of the common stock of twenty-seven affiliated corporations, and 55% of the common and preferred stock of Southern Trust and Mortgage Company (the stock of all such corporations is hereinafter referred to collectively as the "stock").

During her lifetime, Mr. and Mrs. Bright held the 55% block of stock as their community property under the laws of the State of Texas. The remaining forty-five percent is owned by parties unrelated to the Brights; a thirty percent block of stock is owned by H.G. Schiff, and the remaining fifteen percent is owned by two or three other individuals. None of the stock was publicly traded and no market existed for any of the stock on the date of Mrs. Bright's death. Mr. Bright is executor under the will of his wife. The will devised Mrs. Bright's interest in the stock to Mr. Bright as trustee of a trust for the primary benefit of Mrs. Bright's four children.

After audit of the estate tax return, the government assessed a deficiency, which was paid by the estate, and the instant suit for a refund of over $3 million in federal estate taxes and assessed interest was brought in the district court. The sole issue before the district court was the value of the estate's stock. Before the bench trial on the fair market value issue, the district judge ruled as a matter of law that "no element of control can be attributed to the decedent in determining the value of the decedent's interest in the stock ... for estate tax purposes. The parties are hereby ordered to proceed with preparation for trial and trial of this case on that basis." At the trial the district court found that the value of the stock was consistent with the testimony of the estate's expert witnesses, and entered judgment for the estate. The government filed a timely notice of appeal. A panel of this court vacated the judgment of the district court and remanded with instructions, holding that the district court erred in entering the pretrial order relating to the element of control. 619 F.2d 407 (June 18, 1980). The estate's petition for rehearing en banc was granted, and the panel opinion was vacated. 628 F.2d 307 (Oct. 2, 1980). We now affirm the judgment of the district court.

The only issue facing the en banc court is whether the district court erred in entering the above quoted pretrial order relating to the element of control. We reject the heart of the government's arguments, and also reject a secondary government argument because it was raised for the first time on appeal.

Two principal arguments constitute the heart of the government's case, the first based on its description of the property transferred as an undivided one-half interest in the control block of 55% of the stock, and the second based on family attribution between the estate's stock interest and the stock interest held individually by Mr. Bright.[1]

---

1. The government also argued in the court below, and argues on appeal, that the district court's pre-trial order held as a matter of law that a minority discount should be applied. The government argues that a minority discount should be allowed only if evidence supporting a discount is adduced. We do not disagree with the government's statement of the law, but we reject the government's characterization of the district court's pretrial order. The order did not mandate a minority discount: it held only that the interest to be valued was in fact a 27 1/2% interest, which of course left open for proof at trial whether or not the taxpayer would in fact adduce proof to

First, the government argues that the property to be valued for estate tax purposes is an undivided one-half interest in the control block of 55% of the stock, and that the proper method of valuation would be to value the 55% control block, including a control premium, and then take one-half thereof. Both parties agree that the estate tax is an excise tax on the transfer of property at death, and that the property to be valued is the property which is actually transferred, as contrasted with the interest held by the decedent before death or the interest held by the legatee after death. * * * Both also agree that state law, Texas in this case, determines precisely what property is transferred. * * * Both parties agree that, under Texas law, the stock at issue was the community property of Mr. and Mrs. Bright during her life, that Mrs. Bright's death dissolved the community, that upon death the community is divided equally, that each spouse can exercise testamentary disposition over only his or her own half of the community, and that "only the decedent's half is includable in his gross estate for federal tax purposes." Commissioner v. Chase Manhattan Bank, 259 F.2d at 239. Under Texas law, upon the division of the community at death, each spouse owns an undivided one-half interest in each item of community property. Caddell v. Lufkin Land & Lumber Co., 255 S.W. 397 (Tex.Com.App., 1923).

In its brief the government argued that, because the interest to be valued was an undivided one-half interest in the full 55% control block, the proper method would be to value the whole, including its control premium, and then take one-half thereof to establish the value of the estate's undivided one-half interest. The estate points out that the government's argument overlooks the fact that the block of stock is subject to the right of partition under Texas law at the instance of either the surviving spouse or the estate of the deceased spouse. Tex. Prob. Code Ann. § 385 (Vernon 1980). The government has not argued that partition would not be freely granted in a case involving fungible shares, such as this case. Thus, the estate has no means to prevent the conversion of its interest into shares representing a 27 1/2% block, and we conclude that the estate's interest is the equivalent of a 27 1/2% block of the stock. Accordingly, we reject the government's approach of valuing the 55% control block, with its control premium, and then taking one-half thereof. Accord Estate of Lee v. Commissioner, 69 T.C. 860 (1978).

Having determined that the property which is to be valued for estate tax purposes is the 27 1/2% block of stock owned by the estate, we turn to the government's second argument, which is based on the doctrine of family attribution[2] between the successive holders of interest to be taxed, the decedent, the executor, and the legatee, on the one hand, and the related

support a minority discount. Accordingly, there is no merit in the government's argument.

2. At several points, the government's brief seems to disavow any attempt to import family attribution into this area. A close reading of the government's brief reveals, however, that the government shuns only the argument that family attribution requires or mandates that the stock of related parties be valued as a unit. The government's position is that the relation-ship between the decedent, executor or legatee, on the one hand, and another stockholder, on the other hand, is a fact relevant to value. When we refer in this opinion to family attri-bution, we refer to this non-mandatory ver-sion. Similarly, our opinion deals only with family attribution based on the identity of the decedent, the executor or the legatee. It is this identity which is irrelevant under the case law and reasoning which this opinion will develop.

party, Mr. Bright, on the other. The government argues that the following facts are relevant and should have been considered by the district court in valuing the 27 1/2% block: the fact that Mr. and Mrs. Bright were husband and wife and held their stock during her lifetime as a control block of 55%; the fact that Mr. Bright held the estate's 27 1/2% block after her death as executor and subsequently as trustee of the testamentary trust for their children, while he simultaneously held another 27 1/2% block in his individual capacity, thus continuing the control block after death; and the fact that the government might be able to adduce evidence that Mr. Bright, as executor or trustee, would not be willing to sell the estate's 27 1/2% block as a minority interest, but would be willing to sell it only as part of the block of 55% including his individually-owned stock so that a substantial control premium could be realized.[3] Such facts and evidence, the government argues, would have formed the basis of expert testimony that the value of the estate's stock includes some control premium. For several reasons, we reject the government's attempt to import into this area of the estate tax law this kind of family attribution, and we hold that the foregoing evidence proffered by the government is not admissible to prove the value of the stock at issue.

First, we reject any family attribution to the estate's stock because established case law requires this result. A recent case directly in point is Estate of Lee v. Commissioner, supra. There Mr. and Mrs. Lee held as community property 4,000 of the 5,000 outstanding shares of the common stock of a closely held corporation. They also held all 50,000 shares of the preferred stock. Upon the death of Mrs. Lee, the community was dissolved, leaving Mr. Lee and the estate of Mrs. Lee each with an undivided one-half interest in each item of the community property. 69 T.C. at 873. The Tax Court held that this was the equivalent of 2,000 shares of common stock and 25,000 shares of preferred stock, and that the estate's interest was a minority interest. 69 T.C. at 874.

In United States v. Land, supra, this court held that a restrictive agreement, which depressed the value of a partnership interest but which by its terms expired at decedent's death, did not affect value for estate tax purposes because the estate tax is an excise tax on the transfer of property at death and accordingly valuation is to be made at the time of the transfer, i.e., at death, and the valuation is to be measured by the interest that actually passes. 303 F.2d at 172. It follows necessarily from our *Land* holding that the fact that Mr. and Mrs. Bright held their stock during her lifetime as a control block of 55% is an irrelevant fact. It is a fact which antedates her death, and no longer exists at the time of her death. Dictum in *Land* also suggests that the post-death fact—that the estate's 27 1/2% will pass to Mr. Bright as trustee of the testamentary trust—is also irrelevant:

3. This opinion will show that all three facts are irrelevant to the proper valuation formula because they depend upon the family relationship between the decedent, the executor or the legatee, on the one hand, and another stockholder, i.e., Mr. Bright in his capacity as an individual stockholder, on the other hand. The third factor is inadmissible also because it assumes an unwillingness to sell in direct contradiction to the established valuation formula which assumes a willing seller.

Brief as is the instant of death, the court must pinpoint its valuation at this instant—the moment of truth, when the ownership of the decedent ends and the ownership of the successors begins. It is a fallacy there, therefore, to argue value before—or—after death on the notion that valuation must be determined by the value either of the *interest that ceases or of the interest that begins*. Instead, the valuation is determined by the interest that passes, and the value of the interest before or after death is pertinent only as it serves to indicate the value at death.

303 F.2d at 172. (Emphasis added.)

Beginning at least as early as 1940, the Tax Court has uniformly valued a decedent's stock for estate tax purposes as a minority interest when the decedent himself owned less than 50%, and despite the fact that control of the corporation was within the decedent's family. * * * Similarly, many district courts have either expressly or impliedly rejected the application of family attribution to an estate's stock in the valuation process for estate tax purposes. * * * Our research has uncovered no cases, and the government has cited none, which have attributed family-owned stock to the estate's stock in determining the value thereof for estate tax purposes.

* * *

We conclude that the case law reflects long established precedent that family attribution should not apply to lump a decedent's stock with that of related parties for estate tax valuation purposes. This constitutes our first reason for rejecting family attribution in the instant context.

Our second reason for rejecting this kind of family attribution is our conclusion that the doctrine is logically inconsistent with the willing buyer-seller rule set out in the regulations. Reg. § 20.2031–1(b) provides in pertinent part:

The fair market value is the price at which the property would change hands between a willing buyer and a willing seller, neither being under any compulsion to buy or to sell and both having reasonable knowledge of relevant facts.

This cardinal rule for determining value has been universally applied, both by the Internal Revenue Service and the courts.

It is apparent from the language of the regulation that the "willing seller" is not the estate itself, but is a hypothetical seller. In Revenue Ruling 59–60, the Internal Revenue Service has so held:

Court decisions frequently state in addition that the hypothetical buyer and seller are assumed to be able, as well as willing, to trade and to be well informed about the property and concerning the market for such property.

1959–1 C.B. at 237 (emphasis added). Courts also have so held. In United States v. Simmons 346 F.2d 213, 217 (5th Cir.1965), this court said that "the 'willing buyer and seller' are a hypothetical buyer and seller having a reasonable knowledge of relevant facts." In Rothgery v. United States 475 F.2d 591 (Ct.Cl.1973), the Court of Claims said:

[I]t is necessary to begin the resolution of any valuation problem by presupposing a "willing seller." In the present case, therefore, we must begin with the assumption that the decedent's 125 shares of stock in the corporation were not bequeathed by the decedent to his son, the plaintiff, and that such shares were available for sale by the decedent's estate as a "willing seller."

475 F.2d at 594.

The notion of the "willing seller" as being hypothetical is also supported by the theory that the estate tax is an excise tax on the transfer of property at death and accordingly that the valuation is to be made as of the moment of death and is to be measured by the interest that passes, as contrasted with the interest held by the decedent before death or the interest held by the legatee after death. Earlier in this opinion, we noticed that our United States v. Land, supra, decision logically requires a holding that the relationship between Mr. and Mrs. Bright and their stock is an irrelevant, before death fact. Thus, it is clear that the "willing seller" cannot be identified with Mrs. Bright, and therefore there can be no family attribution with respect to those related to Mrs. Bright. Similarly the dictum in *Land*—that valuation is not determined by the value of the interest in the hands of the legatee—means that the "willing seller" cannot be identified with Mr. Bright as executor or as trustee of the testamentary trust. Therefore, there can be no family attribution based on identity of the executor and trustee, Mr. Bright. The *Land* dictum is established law. Edwards v. Slocum, 264 U.S. at 62, 44 S.Ct. at 293 (Holmes, J. saying, "It [the tax] comes into existence before, and is independent of, the receipt of the property by the legatee."); Ithaca Trust Co. v. United States, 279 U.S. at 155, 49 S.Ct. at 292 (Holmes, J. saying, "The tax is on the act of the testator, not on the receipt of the property by the legatees."); Walter v. United States, 341 F.2d 182, 185 (6th Cir.1965)("[T]he estate tax is imposed upon the *transfer* of property by a decedent, and not the *receipt* of property by a beneficiary. . . . " (emphasis in original)). The *Land* dictum also comports with common sense. It would be strange indeed if the estate tax value of a block of stock would vary depending upon the legatee to whom it was devised.

* * *

Accordingly, we affirm the district court's ruling to the extent that it defined the interest to be valued as equivalent to 27 1/2% of the stock, to the extent that it excluded as evidence of value the fact that the estate's stock had, prior to decedent's death, been held jointly with Mr. Bright's interest as community property, and the fact that, after death, the particular executor (Mr. Bright) and legatee (Mr. Bright as trustee) was related to another stock holder (Mr. Bright individually), and to the extent that it excluded any evidence that Mr. Bright, as executor or trustee, would have refused to sell the estate's 27 1/2% block except in conjunction with his own stock and as part of a 55% control block. We hold that family attribution cannot be applied to lump the estate's stock to that of any related party, but rather that the stock is deemed to be held by a hypothetical seller who is related to no one.

* * *

¶ **11,037**

For the foregoing reasons, we AFFIRM.

DISSENTING OPINION

Alvin B. RUBIN, Circuit Judge, with whom VANCE, Frank M. JOHNSON, Jr., POLITZ and HATCHETT, Circuit Judges, join, dissenting:

It requires my brethren twenty pages of manuscript to explain why they affirm the valuation for estate tax purposes of stock at an amount that is but 27% of the value that the taxpayer's own experts placed on that stock's pro rata share of the corporation's "public value." Thus, stock that, according to the bearish view of the taxpayer's appraisers, would have a "public value" of $4.4 million is valued at $1.2 million for tax purposes. The estate tax law imposes a tax based on fair market value and the majority affirms a tax refund on the basis of a record from which evidence relevant to the determination of that value was excluded. I, therefore, respectfully dissent from the result reached. I would remand the case so that all of the admissible evidence can be weighed.

Like the majority, I reject many of the government's contentions. The time for evaluation of donated stock is the moment of transfer. Whether stock transferred either inter vivos or upon death was, before its transfer, held in community with the owner's spouse is, of course, irrelevant to its value at the moment of transfer. So, too, is the kinship of the decedent with other stockholders.

While my colleagues discuss at length why the value of the 27.5% interest should not be enhanced because it is part of a majority block and thus controls the corporation, they do not discuss why it should be discounted to one-half its public value because it is a minority interest. An appraisal based on "public value" of $4.4 million might be increased if control-value is considered. It does not necessarily follow that, because the control-value premium cannot be added, a subtraction because the stock represents a minority interest is correct.

The value that must be determined is the "price at which the property would change hands between a willing buyer and a willing seller, neither being under any compulsion to buy or to sell and both having reasonable knowledge of relevant facts." Reg. § 20.2031–1(b). This classic formulation assumes shrewd traders on both sides. Such traders would know that Mr. Bright owned 27.5% of the stock, Mr. Schiff owned 30%, and that the 27.5% available from the willing seller would give control to Bright or to Schiff or could be used to maneuver a course between them. My colleagues agree that these facts would be admissible evidence and that the facts at least "might" affect the fair market value of the 27.5% interest.

* * *

Insofar as the pre-trial order ruled that the stock should not be valued as part of the community, it was correct. Insofar as it went further, it was premature and it foreclosed evidence plainly admissible. Because this barrier excluded light that might have revealed the fair market value of the stock

¶ 11,037

and, indeed, the possible gross injustice of valuing it at 27% of its "public value," I respectfully dissent.

Note

[¶ 11,039]

As indicated by *Bright*, a central issue is that of aggregation—whether minority interests can be combined for valuation purposes. In *Bright* the court declined to aggregate the respective 27.5% interests of husband and wife, with the result that the decedent wife's 27.5% interest was treated separately, and therefore qualified for a minority discount. Had the two interests been aggregated to total 55%, not only would a minority discount have been denied, but a control premium would have been added. Thus the *Bright* rule negating aggregation among family members is crucially important in many situations.

In Estate of Bonner v. United States, 84 F.3d 196 (5th Cir.1996), the *Bright* rule was extended so as to deny aggregation in the case of separate interests included in the same decedent's gross estate. The principle is best illustrated by the court's treatment of what it refers to as the "New Mexico property." The wife died first, bequeathing to a trust benefitting her husband a 50% interest in the New Mexico property. The husband was entitled to all income from the trust throughout his life. The wife's executor made the election described in § 2056(b)(7) as to the trust, thereby qualifying the trust's 50% interest for the marital deduction in the wife's estate, but requiring inclusion of the trust's 50% interest in the husband's gross estate at his death pursuant to § 2044. (See ¶ 27,275 regarding this arrangement, referred to as Qualified Terminable Interest Property, or QTIP.) At his death the husband owned the other 50% of the New Mexico property outright, and this was included in his gross estate under § 2033. Although 100% of the New Mexico property was therefore included in the husband's gross estate, the court nevertheless concluded that each 50% must be viewed separately, and each qualified for a fractional interest discount, discussed below at ¶ 11,081. A fuller analysis of *Bonner* is provided at ¶ 27,360, in the context of the marital deduction.

In Estate of Mellinger v. Commissioner, 112 T.C. 26 (1999), the Tax Court reached the same result—again declining to combine the decedent's own stock with stock held in a QTIP trust for his benefit (and therefore included in the decedent's gross estate under § 2044). The Commissioner acquiesced in this decision. 1999–35 I.R.B. 35.

In Estate of Fontana v. Commissioner, 118 T.C. 318 (2002), however, the Tax Court reached the contrary result in the case of a § 2056(b)(5) life estate-power of appointment trust. Here the wife had predeceased the husband, transferring 44% of the stock to a trust that provided a life estate for the husband and gave him a general power to appoint the stock to anyone (including himself) at his death. (As explained below at ¶ 27,199, this arrangement qualified for the marital deduction in the wife's estate.) Upon the husband's later death, he owned 50% of the stock outright. The Tax Court

¶ 11,037

concluded that the two blocks should be treated as combined to produce 94% ownership in the husband, thereby denying any minority discount. The court observed that a general power of appointment is viewed as "essentially identical to outright ownership." Therefore, the husband could dispose of the entire 94% collectively, and aggregation was appropriate. The court distinguished the *Bonner* and *Mellinger* cases on the ground that in those cases the surviving spouse did not have power to dictate the disposition of the trust property after the surviving spouse's death.

Like control premiums, minority discounts can vary widely, depending on the circumstances, such as the nature of the business and the pattern of ownership. Nevertheless, many planners have come to expect a minority discount of 30% or more in routine situations. This view is based on such cases as Carr v. Commissioner, 49 T.C.M. (CCH) 507, T.C.M. (P–H) ¶ 85,019 (1985), in which a 25% discount was allowed, and Ward v. Commissioner, 87 T.C. 78 (1986), in which a 50% discount was allowed. Both the IRS and the courts, however, take the position that a substantial minority discount will be allowed only if the taxpayer can offer persuasive evidence in support of the discount. For example, in Knight v. Commissioner, 115 T.C. 506 (2000), the Tax Court reduced the claimed total discounts of 44% to only 15%. The court viewed the evidence offered in support of the discounts as insufficient to support the higher levels claimed. Still, the converse is equally valid. If the taxpayer can effectively document the reasons why a prospective buyer would discount the purchase price substantially, a large discount should be achieved.

[¶ 11,043]

REVENUE RULING 93–12

1993–1 C.B. 202.

ISSUE

If a donor transfers shares in a corporation to each of the donor's children, is the factor of corporate control in the family to be considered in valuing each transferred interest, for purposes of section 2512 of the Internal Revenue Code?

FACTS

P owned all of the single outstanding class of stock of X corporation. P transferred all of P's shares by making simultaneous gifts of 20 percent of the shares to each of P's five children, A, B, C, D, and E.

LAW AND ANALYSIS

* * *

Section 25.2512–2(a) of the regulations provides that the value of stocks and bonds is the fair market value per share or bond on the date of the gift. Section 25.2512–2(f) provides that the degree of control of the business represented by the block of stock to be valued is among the factors to be considered in valuing stock where there are no sales prices or bona fide bid or asked prices.

Rev. Rul. 81–253, 1981–1 C.B. 187, holds that, ordinarily, no minority shareholder discount is allowed with respect to transfers of shares of stock between family members if, based upon a composite of the family members' interests at the time of the transfer, control (either majority voting control or de facto control through family relationships) of the corporation exists in the family unit. The ruling also states that the Service will not follow the decision of the Fifth Circuit in Estate of Bright v. United States, 658 F.2d 999 (5th Cir.1981).

In *Bright*, the decedent's undivided community property interest in shares of stock, together with the corresponding undivided community property interest of the decedent's surviving spouse, constituted a control block of 55 percent of the shares of a corporation. The court held that, because the community-held shares were subject to a right of partition, the decedent's own interest was equivalent to 27.5 percent of the outstanding shares and, therefore, should be valued as a minority interest, even though the shares were to be held by the decedent's surviving spouse as trustee of a testamentary trust. See also, Propstra v. United States, 680 F.2d 1248 (9th Cir.1982). In addition, Estate of Andrews v. Commissioner, 79 T.C. 938 (1982), and Estate of Lee v. Commissioner, 69 T.C. 860 (1978), nonacq., 1980–2 C.B. 2, held that the corporation shares owned by other family members cannot be attributed to an individual family member for determining whether the individual family member's shares should be valued as the controlling interest of the corporation.

After further consideration of the position taken in Rev. Rul. 81–253, and in light of the cases noted above, the Service has concluded that, in the case of a corporation with a single class of stock, notwithstanding the family relationship of the donor, the donee, and other shareholders, the shares of other family members will not be aggregated with the transferred shares to determine whether the transferred shares should be valued as part of a controlling interest.

In the present case, the minority interests transferred to A, B, C, D, and E should be valued for gift tax purposes without regard to the family relationship of the parties.

HOLDING

If a donor transfers shares in a corporation to each of the donor's children, the factor of corporate control in the family is not considered in valuing each transferred interest for purposes of section 2512 of the Code. For estate and gift tax valuation purposes, the Service will follow *Bright, Propstra, Andrews*, and *Lee* in not assuming that all voting power held by family members may be aggregated for purposes of determining whether the transferred shares should be valued as part of a controlling interest. Consequently, a minority discount will not be disallowed solely because a transferred interest, when aggregated with interests held by family members, would be a part of a controlling interest. This would be the case whether the donor held

¶ 11,043

100 percent or some lesser percentage of the stock immediately before the gift.

* * *

[¶ 11,061]

TECHNICAL ADVICE MEMORANDUM 9436005

May 26, 1994.

ISSUE

Should the fact that each of three 30 percent blocks of stock transferred has "swing vote" attributes be taken into account as a factor in determining the fair market value of the stock?

FACTS

The donor owned all of [the] outstanding common stock of Corporation, totaling 28,975 shares. On December 18, 1989, the donor transferred 8,592 shares (approximately 30 percent of the outstanding common stock in Corporation) to each of three children. The donor also transferred 1,509 shares (approximately 5 percent of the stock) to his spouse. The donor retained 1,510 shares or approximately 5 percent of the stock. The transfers to the children were reported on a timely filed federal Gift Tax Return, Form 709. The donor's spouse consented to the gift-splitting provisions of § 2513 of the Internal Revenue Code.

The ownership of the stock before and after the transfer may be summarized as follows:

Summary of Stock Holdings

	Donor	Child 1	Child 2	Child 3	Spouse
Before	100%	0	0	0	0
After	5%	30%	30%	30%	5%

With respect to each gift, the stock was valued at approximately $50 per share representing the net asset value of Corporation, less a 25 percent discount characterized as a discount for "minority interest and marketability."

APPLICABLE LAW AND ANALYSIS

* * *

In general, in determining the value of shares of stock that represent a minority interest, a discount may be allowed in appropriate circumstances to reflect the fact that the holder of a minority interest lacks control over corporate policy, and thus for example, cannot compel the payment of dividends or the liquidation of the corporation. Ward v. Commissioner, 87 T.C. 78, 106 (1986). Where a donor makes simultaneous gifts of multiple shares of securities to different donees, each gift is valued separately in determining fair market value for gift tax purposes. See, e.g., Whittemore v. Fitzpatrick, 127 F.Supp. 710 (D.C.Conn.1954); Avery v. Commissioner, 3 T.C. 963 (1944); § 25.2512–2(e).

In Rev. Rul. 93–12, 1993–1 C.B. 202, a donor transferred 20 percent of the outstanding shares of a closely-held corporation to each of his five children. The ruling concludes that, if a donor transfers shares in a corporation to each of the donor's children, the factor of corporate control in the family is not considered in valuing each transferred interest for purposes of § 2512. Thus, in valuing the shares, a minority discount will not be disallowed solely because a transferred interest, when aggregated with interests held by other family members, would be a part of a controlling interest.

In Estate of Winkler v. Commissioner, TCM 1989–[231], the decedent, Clara Winkler, owned 10 percent of the voting stock of a closely-held corporation. Of the balance of the voting stock, 40 percent was owned by other members of the Winkler family and 50 percent was owned by members of the Simmons family. The court recognized that the decedent's block constituted a minority interest in the corporation. However, the court found that, in view of the fact that neither family possessed a controlling interest in the corporation, the decedent's minority block had special characteristics that enhanced its value. The court described these "swing vote" characteristics as follows:

> This 10 percent voting stock could become pivotal in this closely held corporation where members of one family held 50 percent and members of another family held 40 percent. By joining with the Simmons family a minority shareholder could effect control over the corporation and by joining the Winkler family, such a minority shareholder could block action.... Looking at this even split between the two families, the 10 percent block of voting stock, in the hands of a third party unrelated to either family could indeed become critical. While it is difficult to put a value on this factor, we think it increases the value of the Class A voting stock by at least the 10 percent that [respondent's appraiser] found.

The court went on to find that, under the facts presented, the increased value attributable to the swing vote characteristics of the stock offset any minority discount otherwise available. See also, Glenn Desmond and Richard Kelley, Business Valuation Handbook, § 11.01 (1991)("Likewise, if a minority block would enable another minority holder to achieve a majority with control or if the minority were needed to reach the percentage ownership needed to merge or file consolidated statements, the stock would have added value."); Shannon P. Pratt, Valuing Small Businesses and Professional Practices, 527 (2d ed. 1994)("[I]f two stockholders own 49 percent [of the stock] and a third owns 2 percent, the 49 percent stockholders may be on a par with each other.... The 2 percent stockholder may be able to command a considerable premium over the pro-rata value for that particular block because of the swing vote power."); Estate of Bright v. United States, 658 F.2d 999, 1007 and 1009 n. 9 (5th Cir.1981), where the court discussed swing vote analysis in detail.

¶ 11,061

In the instant case, immediately before the transfers, the donor owned 100 percent of the outstanding stock of Corporation. The donor simultaneously transferred 3 blocks of stock, each constituting 30 percent of the outstanding stock, to each of his three children.[8] As discussed above, the three transfers are valued separately for gift tax purposes. As is evident, each gift, viewed separately, possesses the same swing vote characteristics described by the court in Estate of Winkler. That is, as a result of the simultaneous transfer, three individuals each owned a 30 percent block of stock. The owner of any one of the transferred blocks could join with the owner of any of the other transferred blocks and control the corporation. Thus, any one of these 30 percent blocks, whether owned by an individual related or unrelated to the family, could be critical in controlling the corporation. As the court concluded in Estate of Winkler, this swing vote attribute of each of the transferred blocks enhances the value of each block and is properly taken into account in determining the fair market value of each block transferred.

The donor argues that attributing a swing vote value to each transferred block in this case produces an arbitrary result. That is, if the donor had not made a simultaneous transfer, but rather had transferred each 30 percent block at different times, the valuation of each block would be different. For example, the first 30 percent block transferred might have no swing vote attributes, since after the initial transfer, the donor would continue to possess control of the corporation through his ownership of the retained 70 percent block.

However, the objection raised by the donor is inapposite. First, donor's assumption that the value of none of the three seriatim gifts would reflect swing vote attributes is incorrect. We agree that the value of the first 30 percent transfer would not reflect any swing vote value. However, the second transfer of 30 percent of the stock would possess swing vote value. Further, as a result of this second transfer, the value of the 30 percent interest held by the first transferee would increase, because that block would acquire enhanced voting control in the form of swing vote value as a result of the second transfer. After that transfer, the value of each of the three blocks would have been equalized, because no one stockholder would possess control of the corporation. This enhancement of value with respect to the first transferee's block at the time of the second transfer would constitute an indirect gift to that transferee at the time of the second transfer. Finally, the third 30 percent block would also have swing vote value both before and after the third transfer. Thus, we believe that, even if the three transfers were made at different times, the total value of the gifts would ultimately be the same as if the three transfers were made simultaneously.

Further, under established case law, gift tax valuation results are often dependent on the nature and timing of the gift. For example, a single transfer of a large block of stock to an individual might be valued differently for gift tax purposes than several independent transfers of smaller blocks at different

---

8. For valuation purposes, the focus is on shares actually transferred by the donor, notwithstanding that the transfers were treated as made one-half by the donor's spouse under § 2513.

times. On the other hand, the result might not differ with respect to the swing value approach, or any other valuation principles, in the case of an integrated series of transfers. See, e.g., Citizens Bank and Trust Co. v. Commissioner, 839 F.2d 1249 (7th Cir.1988); Estate of Murphy v. Commissioner, T.C.M. 1990–472. Accordingly, we do not believe the donor's objections in any way mitigate against applying swing vote analysis to the facts presented here.

As discussed above, all relevant factors are to be considered when valuing closely held stock. As the court concluded in *Estate of Winkler,* swing block potential is one such factor. In this case, each 30 percent block of stock has swing vote characteristics. The extent to which the swing vote potential enhances the value of each block transferred is a factual determination. However, all relevant factors including the minority nature of each block, any marketability concerns, and swing vote potential, should be taken into account in valuing each block.

Conclusion

In determining the fair market value of three 30 percent blocks of stock transferred by the donor, the swing vote attributes of each block are factors to be taken into consideration in determining the value of each block.

* * *

Note

[¶ 11,065]

There are significant impediments to qualification for a minority discount. One is the "swing vote" rationale set forth in Tech. Adv. Mem. 9436005 (¶ 11,061, above). If the IRS can show that the minority status of the interest is offset by a "swing vote" value that hypothetical buyers would assign to the minority interest, the minority discount otherwise available may be negated.

Another obstacle to qualification for a discount is the possibility that a buyer of a minority interest would have a right to demand liquidation of the enterprise, thus ending his minority status and entitling him to receive a portion of the enterprise assets outright. Although the taxpayer might still be entitled to a fractional interest discount, as explained at ¶ 11,081, below, the fractional interest discount would usually be smaller than a minority interest discount.

Typically the owner of minority stock in a corporation has no entitlement to demand liquidation, so that the liquidation issue does not arise. This makes corporate stock the most reliable vehicle for achieving a minority discount. At the other extreme, the buyer of a general partnership minority interest may have an unfettered right to demand liquidation at any time. Under these circumstances a minority discount would not be appropriate, although a lesser fractional interest discount would probably be allowed.

¶ 11,061

The liquidation issue becomes more complex with entities that lie between these extremes—such as limited partnerships and limited liability companies. Depending on local law and the governing instrument, the purchaser of a minority interest may or may not have an effective right to demand liquidation. If there is an effective right to demand liquidation, the IRS will probably oppose allowance of a minority discount and permit only a smaller fractional interest discount. On the other hand, if there is no effective liquidation right, a minority discount should be allowed in the absence of swing vote value. See ¶ 11,111.

D. MARKETABILITY DISCOUNTS

[¶ 11,071]

Discounts are often allowed in order to reflect the lack of marketability of an asset. The willing buyer-willing seller approach can produce unrealistically high values if the market is thin, buyers are few, or the asset has unusual infirmities.

Such discounts, which can be as high as 35 percent, are often applied to interests in closely held businesses, even if a minority discount is not available. The valuation initially assigned to the business under Rev. Rul. 59–60 (¶ 11,007) is derived by analogy from publicly traded interests. Buyers will not pay as much for investments for which there is no ready market.

The IRS often resists or seeks to reduce marketability discounts, especially in circumstances in which the assets held by the entity are readily marketable. An example is McCord v. Commissioner, 120 T.C. 358 (2003). The entities involved were two limited partnerships, and one-third and two-thirds, respectively, of their assets were marketable securities or interests in real estate holding partnerships. The taxpayer claimed a 35% marketability discount, but the Tax Court reduced the discount to 20%.

Historically, there was some confusion between minority discounts and marketability discounts. Courts often granted a single discount percentage, such as 40%, without segregating the discount between that attributable to minority status and that attributable to lack of marketability. The distinction between the two is important because even a controlling interest can qualify for a marketability discount if interests in the entity are not regularly traded. In recent years, the courts have properly tended to segregate the minority, marketability, and other discounts described below, specifying a percentage for each discount.

As indicated above, a modest marketability discount is routinely allowed if the stock is not listed on an exchange. If the marketability of the stock is subject to specific restrictions on sale, the marketability discount may be substantially greater. For example, in Estate of McClatchy v. Commissioner, 147 F.3d 1089 (9th Cir.1998), the Ninth Circuit faced the difficult issue of determining value where the securities laws restricted sale of the decedent's stock. In *McClatchy* the decedent owned two million shares of a publicly traded stock. Because the decedent was an "affiliate" of the corporation for securities law purposes, sale of the shares by him would have been importantly restricted. For that reason the executor contended that the shares should be valued at only $25 million, as compared to the $36 million value that would be applied (according to the IRS) if no such restrictions were present. The executor of the decedent's estate, however, was not an "affiliate." Therefore, the executor was free to sell the stock without securities law restrictions. The IRS argued that because the decedent's death had the effect of eliminating the securities law restrictions, the stock should be valued for estate tax purposes at $36 million.

A divided Ninth Circuit rejected the IRS position and held that the proper valuation was $25 million. The court reasoned that the securities law restrictions were eliminated, not by the death of the owner, but by the ownership of stock by a nonaffiliate, i.e., the executor. The court cited well established law, including *Bright*, ¶ 11,037, to the effect that for estate tax purposes assets must be valued without regard to the identity of the recipient. The majority proved its point by observing that if the executor were an affiliate, the restrictions would remain in place, and the stock would then be worth only $25 million. Therefore, the increase in value to $36 million was not attributable to the death of the decedent, but to the nonaffiliate status of the executor. Permitting the nonaffiliate status of the executor to control would directly violate the rule that, for estate tax purposes, the identity of the recipient of the property is irrelevant to valuation.

E. PORTFOLIO DISCOUNTS

[¶ 11,072]

A "portfolio discount" may be available where the asset to be valued is an interest in an entity that holds disparate assets. The idea is that while there might be a strong market for particular assets, few buyers would be willing to purchase a mixture of both attractive and unattractive properties. The same principle applies to a "conglomerate" entity owning properties in different industries.

In Knight v. Commissioner, 115 T.C. 506 (2000), the taxpayer sought a portfolio discount, and the Tax Court described the discount as applying to "a company that owns two or more operations or assets, the combination of which would not be particularly attractive to a buyer." The court, however, held that the taxpayer's expert "gave no convincing reason why the partnership's mix of assets would be unattractive to a buyer." Hence no portfolio discount was allowed. 115 T.C. 506, 516–518.

In Bennett v. Commissioner, 65 T.C.M. (CCH) 1816, T.C.M. (RIA) ¶ 93,034 (1993), however, the taxpayer was successful in achieving a significant portfolio discount. In *Bennett* the estate included all the stock of a real estate investment corporation. The corporation held a wide variety of real estate interests. Some were desirable properties, while others had serious problems, including delinquent tenants. The Commissioner sought to value the corporation stock at the total of the aggregate fair market values of the

¶ 11,071

individual parcels. The Tax Court, however, reasoned that the asset to be valued was the stock, not the real estate, and that there were few buyers who would be willing and able to undertake the burdens of such a varied conglomeration of assets. A 15% portfolio discount was allowed.

F. ABSORPTION DISCOUNTS

[¶ 11,073]

In some cases—typically involving real estate—an "absorption discount" has been allowed. This discount originates in the concept of "blockage." As explained at ¶ 14,001, the blockage principle permits a reduction in value if the property transferred could not be marketed within a reasonable period of time without reducing the price. A typical example would involve a decedent holding 1,000,000 shares of listed stock the average daily trading of which is only 40,000 shares. The same concept has been applied to real estate that may be difficult to sell within a reasonable period in a local market because of the unique character of the properties or the small number of buyers interested in properties of this kind.

In Estate of Rodgers v. Commissioner, 77 T.C.M. (CCH) 1831, T.C.M. (RIA) ¶ 99,129 (1999), the decedent owned an interest in a closely held real estate development company. The company owned undeveloped real estate, and the decedent's share was valued at $20,366,470 without discounting. The estate was successful in persuading the court that the quantity of undeveloped real estate was so substantial relative to the market that it could not be sold within a year without depressing the price. The court allowed a discount of $1,700,000–approximately 8.3%.

The *Rodgers* decision is especially significant because the Commissioner argued that an absorption discount should be allowed only for assets owned directly by the decedent—not assets owned indirectly through an entity. The Commissioner argued that the estate could sell the decedent's interest in the company in order to obtain cash for payment of estate taxes, and that there was no evidence that it would be necessary for the company to sell its assets. The court rejected this argument and applied the absorption discount to the underlying real estate, which accordingly reduced the value of the decedent's interest in the company.

Estate of Auker v. Commissioner, 75 T.C.M. (CCH) 2321, T.C.M. (RIA) ¶ 98,185 (1998), involved similar facts, except that the properties involved were apartment houses. The court followed the same approach as in *Rodgers*, but gave more specific attention to what constitutes a reasonable period for disposition of the properties. The court concluded that the appropriate time period for disposition of the apartment houses was six months, and that an absorption discount should be allowed if it could be proved that the properties could not be sold within six months without reducing the price. Following this approach, the court allowed a 6.189% absorption discount.

G. DISCOUNTS FOR PROSPECTIVE
TAX LIABILITY

[¶ 11,075]

If the asset to be valued is corporation stock, and the corporation owns appreciated assets, a buyer of the stock might well take into account the prospective tax that would have to be paid upon the corporation's sale of the appreciated assets, or upon distribution of the corporate assets to the buyer (as shareholder). Hence it is arguable that the value of the stock should be discounted to take into account the prospective tax liability that would be incurred on such a sale or distribution.

Under current corporation tax rules, it is generally not possible for a corporation to get appreciated corporation assets into the hands of shareholders without paying tax on the appreciation. The gain will be taxed to the corporation whether the transfer of the asset to the shareholders occurs in the form of a distribution, redemption of stock, or liquidation. §§ 311(b)(1), 336(a) (If the corporation has elected to be taxed under Subchapter S, however, it may be possible to effectively avoid taxation of the gain embodied in the corporation's appreciated property.)

In Eisenberg v. Commissioner, 155 F.3d 50 (2d Cir.1998), Acq., 1999–1 C.B. xix, the Second Circuit held that the prospective tax liability inherent in appreciated corporation assets can be taken into account in valuing stock in the corporation. In *Eisenberg* the taxpayer made gifts of stock in a corporation the only substantial asset of which was a commercial office building. The corporation's basis for the building was only $69,500, while the value of the building on the date of the first gift was $600,000. The court concluded that the taxable gain that would be recognized upon sale of the building, or upon distribution of the building to the shareholders, would be $530,500. The court concluded that the value of the corporation at the time of the gift should be reduced to reflect the prospective tax liability. The court allowed the discount although there was no plan for sale or distribution of the building, or for liquidation of the corporation. The court rejected earlier precedents to the contrary because those decisions antedated the 1986 repeal of the *General Utilities* doctrine, which had permitted distribution of appreciated property to shareholders without recognition of gain to the corporation. General Utilities & Operating Co. v. Helvering, 296 U.S. 200 (1935).

In *Eisenberg* the IRS argued that the most productive use of the building would consist of continued ownership by the corporation (rather than sale or distribution of the building), and that any tax liability was too speculative to consider. The court rejected these arguments, reasoning that at least some buyers would view the prospective tax liability as impairing the buyer's flexibility in exploiting the corporation's assets to best advantage, necessarily reducing the amount the buyer would be willing to pay. At the same time, the court conceded that some buyers might be able to avoid or defer the tax. The court remanded the matter to the Tax Court, providing this commentary regarding determination of an appropriate discount:

¶ 11,075

"Where there is a relatively sizable number of potential buyers who can avoid or defer the tax, the fair market value of the shares might well approach the pre-tax market value of the real estate. Potential buyers who could avoid or defer the tax would compete to purchase the shares, albeit in a market that would include similar real estate that was not owned by a corporation. However, where the number of potential buyers who can avoid or defer the tax is small, the fair market value of the shares might be only slightly above the value of the real estate net of taxes. In any event, all of these circumstances should be determined as a question of valuation for tax purposes."

155 F.3d at 59, footnote 16.

The Tax Court had earlier reached the same conclusion. Davis v. Commissioner, 110 T.C. 530 (1998). In *Davis* the corporation owned assets worth approximately $80,000,000. Of this total, $70,043,204 was attributable to stock in Winn–Dixie Stores, Inc. for which the corporation's basis was only $338,283. There was no evidence that sale of the Winn–Dixie stock by the corporation was contemplated. Nevertheless, the court examined the applicable income tax law and concluded that under the law in effect since 1986 there would be no effective way for the corporation or the shareholders to sell or distribute the Winn–Dixie stock without incurring income tax on the large gain involved. The court reasoned that a buyer of the decedent's stock would necessarily take into account the impact income taxes would have on any attempt to realize the cash value of the corporation's principal assets. The court ultimately granted a marketability discount of $29 million, which expressly included $9 million of discount attributable to the potential income tax liability.

As noted above, the Commissioner acquiesced in the Second Circuit's *Eisenberg* decision, expressly stating that the acquiescence related to "whether a discount for potential capital gains tax liability may be applied in valuing closely-held stock." 1999–1 C.B. xix. In Estate of Welch v. Commissioner, 208 F.3d 213 (6th Cir. 2000) (unpublished), the Sixth Circuit concluded that the Commissioner's acquiescence in *Eisenberg* mandated consideration of the tax liability discount and remanded the case to the Tax Court with directions to apply the discount if supported by the evidence.

An important application of the tax liability discount occurred in Estate of Dunn v. Commissioner, 301 F.2d 339 (5th Cir. 2002). In *Dunn* the decedent owned a controlling interest in a construction company. The IRS relied in part on an asset-based approach to valuation. In other words, the IRS sought to value the stock by determining the aggregate value for which the company's underlying assets could be sold. The 5th Circuit held that, to the extent the IRS relied on an asset-based approach, the value would have to be reduced by the full 34% tax that would be imposed upon sale of the company's assets.

The discount for prospective tax liability is sometimes referred to as the "BIG discount," with BIG referring to "built in gain."

Efforts to expand the BIG discount beyond C corporation stock have been unsuccessful. In Estate of Smith v. Commissioner, 391 F.3d 621 (5th Cir.

2004), the executor argued that retirement accounts owned by the decedent should be discounted to reflect the tax liability that distributees would incur upon distribution of the account funds to them. Such distributions would be fully taxable to the distributees because the distribution would constitute income in respect of a decedent (IRD). (IRD is discussed in Chapter 32.) The court denied any discount, reasoning that a hypothetical buyer of the accounts would not be one of the beneficiaries and hence would not be concerned with tax liability. The court's more convincing rationale, however, was that Congress has already granted relief against double taxation (both estate and income) in these circumstances through the special IRD deduction allowed by § 691(c), discussed below at ¶ 32,109.

The Tax Court applied the same rationale in denying a discount for the prospective tax liability inherent in an IRA owned by the decedent. Estate of Kahn v. Commissioner, 125 T.C. No. 11 (2005). Similarly, the IRS denied a discount for the prospective tax liability that would be imposed upon any distribution of accrued interest under Series E United States Savings Bonds. Tech. Adv. Mem. 200303010.

H.   FRACTIONAL INTEREST DISCOUNTS

[¶ 11,081]

A discount may be available if the decedent owns a fractional interest in an asset—especially real estate—even if the decedent's interest is greater than 50 percent. The theory is that the full value may be obtainable only with integrated disposition and development of the entire property. At the very least, a buyer unwilling to acquiesce in the desires of co-owners would have to bear the cost of a partition action. Even if partition could be achieved inexpensively, the potential development value of a fractional portion might be significantly diminished when separated from the remainder of the property.

For these reasons, significant discounts have been allowed where there is convincing evidence that a severed partial interest would have a value less than its proportionate share of the entire property value. Propstra v. United States, 680 F.2d 1248 (9th Cir.1982)(15 percent discount on real estate); Estate of Pillsbury v. Commissioner, 64 T.C.M. (CCH) 284, T.C.M. (RIA) ¶ 92,425 (1992)(15 percent discount on commercial real estate); Estate of Youle v. Commissioner, 56 T.C.M. (CCH) 1594, T.C.M. (P–H) ¶ 89,138 (1989) (20–25 percent discount on farmland).

In Estate of Williams v. Commissioner, 75 T.C.M (CCH) 1758, T.C.M. (RIA) ¶ 98,059 (1998), the taxpayer achieved a total discount of 44%. The taxpayer transferred undivided one-half interests in timberland as a gift. The taxpayer's experts were persuasive, and the court accepted their valuation approach: first a 20% discount for marketability, lowering the net value to 80%. Then a 30% discount from this figure for lack of control, lowering the value by an additional 24% to 56% of the original, undiscounted value.

I. RESTRICTIVE AGREEMENTS

[¶ 11,091]

If sale of a security is restricted, its value may be dramatically affected. For example, if a shareholder cannot sell the security to an outsider without first offering it to other shareholders or the issuing corporation for $100 per share, it is difficult to view the value of the security as exceeding $100 per share. Certainly if a buyer would be subject to the same restriction, no prospective buyer would pay more than $100 per share. Hence the "willing buyer-willing seller" analysis naturally produces a value equivalent to the restriction price.

Although the principle is sound, it has sometimes been exploited to produce unrealistically low valuations in circumstances in which the restriction had little purpose other than tax avoidance. The Treasury and the courts long sought to differentiate between restrictions that legitimately fix values for nontax reasons and those that should be disregarded as tax motivated.

Because of continuing litigation involving restrictive agreements, Congress in 1990 adopted legislation aimed squarely at the use of restrictive agreements to fix valuation for transfer tax purposes. Section 2703(a) states the general rule that all such restrictions are to be disregarded in determining valuation of the restricted property.

Nevertheless, the restriction will be given effect for valuation purposes if the restriction meets the following requirements enumerated in Section 2703(b):

1. The restriction must be a "bona fide business arrangement."

2. The restriction must not be "a device to transfer such property to members of the decedent's family for less than full and adequate consideration in money or money's worth."

3. The terms of the restriction must be "comparable to similar arrangements entered into by persons in an arms' length transaction."

Requirements 1 and 2 were already well established prior to adoption of § 2703 and are expressly stated in Reg. § 20.2031–2(h). However, the Senate Committee Report states that § 2703 is designed to strengthen requirement 2:

> [Section 2703] clarifies that the business arrangement and device requirements are independent tests. The mere showing that the agreement is a bona fide business arrangement would not give the agreement estate tax effect if other facts indicated that the agreement is a device to transfer property to members of the decedent's family for less than full and adequate consideration. In making this clarification, it adopts the reasoning of St. Louis County Bank v. United States, 674 F.2d 1207 (8th Cir.1982), and rejects the suggestions of other cases that the maintenance of family control standing alone assures the absence of a device to transfer wealth.

S. Rep. No. 3209, 101st Cong., 2d Sess. 67–68 (1990).

Requirement 3 was new with § 2703 and imposes the additional requirement that the agreement must conform to industry valuation practices that would be applied if unrelated parties were involved.

Section 2703 is effective as to restrictions or agreements entered into or "substantially modified" after October 8, 1990. Revenue Reconciliation Act of 1990, section 11602(e)(1)(A)(ii). The Treasury has taken a very expansive view of what might constitute a "substantial modification" of a pre-October 9, 1990, agreement. Under the Treasury interpretation, even minor changes or the addition of new parties could be treated as "substantial modifications," triggering application of § 2703 rather than the more liberal case law rules that controlled prior to adoption of § 2703. Reg. § 25.2703–1(c). Therefore, caution should be exercised in amending or adding parties to any pre-October 9, 1990, agreement.

J. LAPSING RIGHTS

[¶ 11,107]

Special valuation rules are applied to lapsing rights involving closely held businesses. The lapse of certain rights is treated as a gift if the lapse occurs during the lifetime of the person holding the rights. If the lapse occurs at the death of the person holding the rights, that person's gross estate is increased by the value of the lapsing rights. § 2704 (a).

For example, assume that Mother and Daughter control a corporation, and that Mother's stock has voting rights that lapse upon Mother's death. Under § 2704, when Mother dies, her gross estate will include the value of the lapsed voting rights. Similarly, if Mother's voting rights lapsed prior to her death, Mother would be treated as making a taxable gift, on the date of lapse, in the amount of the value of the lapsed voting rights. § 2704(a)(1).

The § 2704 treatment of a lapse of rights as a taxable transfer applies only to rights created after October 8, 1990. Revenue Reconciliation Act of 1990, section 11602(e)(1)(A)(iii). Section 2704 is intended to overrule Estate of Harrison v. Commissioner, 52 T.C.M. (CCH) 1306, T.C.M. (P–H) ¶ 87,008 (1987), in which the Tax Court held that liquidation rights lapsing at death are not included in the gross estate of the decedent. H.R. Conf. Rep. No. 964, 101st Cong., 2d Sess. 157 (1990). See ¶ 3091.

Treatment of a lapse as a taxable transfer applies only to voting or liquidation rights in a corporation or partnership, and only if the family of the person holding the lapsing right controls the entity. § 2704(a)(1). The value of the transfer consists of the difference between the value of the interests held by the person whose right has lapsed, including the lapsed right, and the value of those interests without the lapsed right. § 2704(a)(2).

K. RESTRICTIONS ON LIQUIDATION

[¶ 11,111]

As explained above in connection with minority discounts (¶ 11,065) and fractional interest discounts (¶ 11,081), the power of the owner of an interest in an entity to force liquidation of the entity may be important in determining the value of the interest. If the owner of the interest is "locked in," in the sense that she cannot force liquidation, then she may not be able to gain the full benefits of her interest without the cooperation of her fellow owners. This is especially damaging to owners of minority interests. Any buyer of the interest would be similarly limited; therefore, the value of the interest should be discounted accordingly.

By contrast, if the owner of the interest has legal power to force liquidation, she can thereby obtain her pro rata share of the underlying assets. She would then become the sole owner of those assets and could dispose of them as she wishes. Under these circumstances, a minority discount would not be appropriate, although a fractional interest discount might be available.

Many taxpayers have tried to take advantage of these rules by creating artificial restrictions limiting liquidation of the entity involved. A substantial discount is then claimed on the ground that a buyer of the interest could not compel liquidation.

Section 2704(b) addresses this problem. It applies only in circumstances in which the transferor (the decedent or donor) and her family control the entity. § 2704(b)(1)(B). In the case of a corporation, control means ownership of at least 50% (by vote or value) of the stock. In the case of a partnership, control means ownership of at least 50% of the capital or profits interest, or, in the case of a limited partnership, ownership of any general partner interest. §§ 2704(c)(1) and 2701(b)(2).

Section 2704 applies only if there is a transfer (by gift or at death) of an interest to a member of the transferor's family, as defined in § 2704(c)(2). § 2704(b)(1)(A).

Finally, Section 2704 applies only to an "applicable restriction." § 2704(b)(1). A restriction is an "applicable restriction only if it limits the ability of the entity to liquidate and (1) the restriction lapses after the transfer described in the prior paragraph or (2) the family has power to remove the restriction after the transfer. § 2704(b)(2)(B).

The practical effect of these rules is that virtually any restriction on liquidation is disregarded in valuing an intra-family transfer because the family controlling the entity has power to eliminate the restriction. Congress, however, thought this result too extreme. Therefore, it provided an exception honoring restrictions imposed by federal or state law. § 2704(b)(3)(B). The Regulations implementing this exception state that a restriction imposed by the documents governing the entity will be disregarded for purposes of

§ 2704(b) only if the restriction is "more restrictive than the limitations that would apply under the State law general applicable to the entity in the absence of the restrictions." Reg. § 25.2704–2(b).

An example will illustrate this principle. Assume that the Wilson family owns all interests in Wilson LLC, a limited liability company. Wilson LLC owns investment real estate. Dad Wilson dies owning 60% of the membership interests. The operating agreement of Wilson LLC requires that owners of 75% of the membership interests consent to a liquidation and concur in major decisions. If this restriction is considered in valuing Dad's interest, his interest might be significantly reduced in value because of Dad's inability to liquidate the LLC and obtain 60% of the assets. Without liquidation, Dad must obtain the consent of owners of an additional 15% of the membership interests in order to control the operations of the business. A hypothetical buyer would take this limitation into account and discount the price he would offer for Dad's 60% interest.

Further assume that the limited liability company statute governing Wilson LLC requires that 51% of the owners concur in any liquidation, but permits limited liability companies to impose a higher percentage. Because the 75% requirement imposed by the operating agreement of Wilson LLC is more restrictive that the general state law, § 2704(b) applies, and the 75% liquidation requirement is ignored in valuing Dad's interest. For estate and gift tax valuation purposes, therefore, Dad is treated as having power to liquidate the entity whenever he wishes and thereby obtain direct ownership of the entity's assets. As a result, no discount should be allowed for Dad's 60% interest. Reg. § 25.2704–2(d) Example 1.

By contrast, assume that state law requires that owners of 80% of the membership interests in any limited liability company concur in a liquidation. In that event, the Wilson LLC 75% requirement would not be more restrictive than general state law, and the restriction on liquidation would not be disregarded for purposes of valuation. In other words, § 2704(b) would not apply, and the restriction on liquidation would be considered in valuing Dad's interest. As a result, Dad's interest might be substantially discounted because of his inability to compel liquidation and thereby obtain direct ownership of the entity's assets.

L. FAMILY LIMITED PARTNERSHIPS

[¶ 11,115]

In Rev. Rul. 93–12, ¶ 11,043, the IRS acquiesced in the holding in *Bright*, ¶ 11,037, to the effect that there is no attribution among family members for purposes of determining whether a minority discount will be allowed. This was a crucial turning point because it was now possible to obtain minority and other discounts while maintaining family ownership and control. The key lay in creation of an entity to hold the assets, because the principal discounts are available only as to interests in an entity, such as a corporation or partnership.

The entity of choice has become the limited partnership. Where members of a family are the sole or principal owners, such an entity is referred to as a "family limited partnership" or "FLP." (Limited liability companies and S corporations are sometimes used as well.)

The strategy is elegantly simple. Mom and Dad Wilson transfer their assets to Wilson Limited Partnership. Mom and Dad then transfer minority interests in the partnership to their children, leaving each of Mom and Dad with minority interests. Furthermore, the partnership agreement provides for restrictions that prevent Mom and Dad from forcing liquidation. Although Mom and Dad may not have a legal right to control the operation of Wilson Limited Partnership, in practice the children permit Mom and Dad to make the important management decisions.

The minority interests initially transferred to the children qualify for substantial discounts, and Mom and Dad can make gifts of additional discounted minority interests in later years. At the death of Mom and Dad, each owns a minority interest that likewise qualifies for substantial discounts. The result is that all the interests in Wilson Limited Partnership are valued at substantial discounts for gift and estate tax purposes. For example, although the Wilson Limited Partnership might hold assets worth $5,000,000, the aggregate value of the partnership interests for gift and estate tax purposes might be only $3,000,000, producing a dramatic reduction in gift and estate tax liability.

Ultimately, after the death of Mom and Dad, all interests in Wilson Limited Partnership are held by the children. At that point the children, if they so wish, can liquidate Wilson Limited Partnership and distribute the assets outright among themselves. The overall result is simply passage of Mom and Dad's assets to their children. But the interim creation of a partnership "wrapper" permits passage of the assets at substantial discounts for gift and estate tax purposes.

The IRS views such arrangements as artificial tax avoidance devices, and especially so in cases in which the FLP holds passive investment assets that could just as well be held outright. IRS acceptance of the principle that ownership by different family members cannot be aggregated, however, has made it difficult for the IRS to attack FLP's. Over the years the IRS made strenuous efforts to defeat FLP's, but with only limited success.

By the time this edition was being prepared, the IRS had finally achieved significant success by applying § 2036 to FLP's. Section 2036, the subject of Chapter 18 of this book, is an estate tax provision that includes in the decedent's gross estate (and therefore subjects to estate tax) any asset as to which the decedent retains until his death a right to the income from the property or a right to control disposition of the income. If it is determined that the decedent in fact retained such rights in an FLP, the result is to include the underlying FLP assets in the decedent's gross estate, as if the decedent owned those assets directly. In effect, the partnership "wrapper" is ignored, and no discounts are available.

In Estate of Thompson v. Commissioner, 382 F.3d 367 (3d Cir. 2004), the IRS achieved exactly this result. In *Thompson* the FLP was formed only two years before the decedent's death and consisted largely of marketable securities. There was no business purpose (other than tax avoidance) for creation of the FLP. The decedent retained only modest assets in his own hands and necessarily relied on income distributions from the FLP for his support. Finally, the transfers to the FLP occurred when the prospective decedent was 95 years old, giving a testamentary feel to the transaction. These circumstances led the court to conclude that there was a de facto understanding that the decedent would continue to benefit from the FLP assets throughout his life.

In Strangi v. Commissioner, 417 F.3d 468 (5th Cir. 2005), the Fifth Circuit reached the same result on facts similar to those in *Thompson*. In *Strangi* the transfers were made only two months before the decedent's death. The decedent transferred $10 million of assets, primarily cash and securities. There was no realistic business purpose for the transfer, and the transfer left the decedent with insufficient funds for his needs, necessitating distributions from the FLP for his support. The court therefore concluded that there was an implied agreement that the decedent would retain the enjoyment of the FLP property.

In another case, however, the Fifth Circuit reached the contrary result. Estate of Kimbell v. United States, 371 F.3d 257 (5th Cir. 2004). As in *Thompson* and *Strangi*, the decedent had transferred property to a newly created FLP not long before his death. But there were good business reasons for placing the assets (which included oil and gas working interests) in a partnership, and the decedent retained ample property to provide for his own support. Hence the court concluded that the decedent should not be viewed as having retained the benefits of the transferred property. The court reached this result despite the advanced age of the decedent—96.

Surely future developments will provide many more chapters in this saga. For the present, though, it does seem possible to identify factors that will tend to protect an FLP against IRS attack. The prospects for success will be greater to the extent most or all of these elements are present: (1) the FLP is not created shortly before the death of the decedent, (2) there is a business purpose (other than tax avoidance) for creation of the FLP, (3) the assets transferred to the FLP are operating assets requiring management, rather than passive investment assets, such as marketable securities, (4) the decedent retains adequate assets to support himself without receiving income from the FLP; (5) there is not a pattern of distributions from the FLP to the decedent for his support; (6) all the formalities of partnership existence and operation are carefully observed. The application of § 2036 to FLP's is more fully discussed at ¶ ¶ 18,257 and 24,051.

Problems

[¶ 11,135]

1. At his death Luis Ortega owned 1000 shares of General Motors stock. On the date of his death, the high price for the stock on the New York Stock

¶ 11,115

Exchange was 40, and the low was 39. How will the stock be valued in Luis' gross estate?

2. At his death Arnold Porter owned all 10,000 shares of stock of Porter, Inc. Porter, Inc. is engaged in manufacturing paint. None of the stock has ever been traded. A comparison of Porter, Inc. with similar paint companies the shares of which are listed on exchanges, using the approach described in Rev. Rul. 59–60, produces a fair market value of $60 per share. How will the stock be valued in Arnold's estate?

3. Assume the same facts as in Problem 2, except that Arnold owned 60% of the Porter, Inc. stock, and the remaining 40% was owned by an unrelated party. What principles should be applied in valuing the stock in Arnold's gross estate?

4. Assume the same facts as in Problem 2, except that Arnold owned only 40% of the Porter, Inc. stock, and the remaining 60% was owned by a single unrelated party.

5. Assume the same facts as in Problem 4, except that the 60% of the stock not owned by Arnold was spread among 5 other owners.

6. Assume the same facts as in Problem 3, except that Arnold does not die, but instead during his life gives all his stock to his three children—20% to each. How will the stock be valued for gift tax purposes?

7. Jason Brown created Brown Corp. in 1945. Brown Corp. prospered over the years, and Jason strongly desired to keep ownership of Brown Corp. stock among his descendants.

   Jason Brown died fifteen years ago, owning 60% of the stock of Brown Corp., which Jason bequeathed to his only child, Armella. Twelve years ago Jason's wife, Rita, died, owning the remaining 40% of the Brown Corp. stock. Rita bequeathed her stock to Armella, with the result that Armella then owned 100% of the stock.

   Ten years ago Armella gave 12% of the stock to each of her four children.

   Seven years ago Armella gave 5% of the stock to her husband, Robert.

   Describe the principles that should be applied in valuing the Brown Corp. stock involved in each transfer described above. Assume that current law applies to all transfers.

¶ 11,135

Chapter 12

RETAINED INTERESTS AND VALUE FREEZES

(Sections 2701 and 2702)

A. INTRODUCTION

[¶ 12,001]

Special valuation problems are created if a donor transfers to a donee only a portion of the donor's interest in an asset. Both Congress and the Commissioner have taken steps to assure that the transferred interest and the retained interest, respectively, are realistically valued for gift and estate tax purposes.

Historically, transfers of partial interests were often exploited for tax avoidance purposes. A parent might transfer a partial interest in property to a child while retaining an interest in the same property. For gift tax purposes, the parent might treat the retained interest as having a value equal to a large portion of the value of the entire property. That would imply a modest value for the transferred interest and little gift tax liability. It often turned out later that the true value of the transferred interest was much higher than the value originally determined by the parent, with the result that the parent had successfully transferred a large part of the value of the property at little or no gift tax cost.

The most dramatic example of this technique is "value freezing." A typical value freeze would be undertaken in circumstances such as these: Dad owns all the common stock issued by a corporation through which Dad operates his business. The common stock (the only class outstanding) is worth $1,000,000. Dad believes the enterprise will grow in value. Dad has other substantial assets and is concerned about future estate tax exposure. He would like to involve Daughter in management and wants to give her a stake in the business, while retaining for himself much of the income produced by the enterprise.

Dad effects a value freeze as follows. First, Dad completes an income tax-free recapitalization of the corporation whereby his $1,000,000 of common stock is exchanged for $980,000 of preferred stock and $20,000 of common stock. The preferred shares have voting rights that assure Dad of continued control. The preferred pays a cumulative dividend at a market rate and is entitled to the first $980,000 of assets if the corporation is liquidated. Dad gives the $20,000 of common to Daughter. If Dad splits the gift with Mom under § 2513, the entire gift can be sheltered by the § 2503(b) annual exclusion.

Dad dies 10 years later, when the value of the corporation has risen to $3,000,000. Assuming no change in interest rates or creditworthiness of the corporation, the value of Dad's preferred is "frozen" at $980,000, and only this amount—perhaps augmented by a modest premium for control—is included in Dad's gross estate. No estate tax is imposed at Dad's death on Daughter's common stock, which is now worth $3,000,000 less $980,000, or $2,020,000. In effect, $2,020,000 of enterprise value has passed to Daughter entirely tax free. The key to this result lies in the "freezing" of Dad's interest. The value of Dad's preferred is determined by the dividend and liquidation preference. The growth in value of the corporation has little or no effect on the value of Dad's preferred.

Value freezes of this kind represent only one type of tax avoidance made possible by use of retained interests. However, because corporation value freezes present the most dramatic and readily understood avoidance opportunity, the "Dad–Daughter" value freeze described above will be used as a universal example throughout the discussions in ¶¶ 12,007–12,061, which explore the efforts of the Commissioner and Congress to prevent such avoidance in the context of corporations and partnerships. As explained at ¶ 12,079–12,097, similar principles have been applied to retained interest transactions involving trusts and other assets.

B. RESPONSES BY COMMISSIONER & CONGRESS

[¶ 12,007]

1. LITIGATION AND REVENUE RULING 83–120

The Commissioner's initial efforts to combat value freezes proved unsuccessful. The Commissioner argued that the value of Dad's retained preferred stock at his death should include most of the enterprise value because Dad retained control of the corporation. The Commissioner was singularly unsuccessful in this effort and typically achieved only the addition of a modest control premium to the preferred stock value, as in Estate of Salsbury v. Commissioner, 34 T.C.M. (CCH) 1441, T.C.M. (P–H) ¶ 75,333 (1975).

The Commissioner then shifted to an effort to assure proper valuation of the common when it was transferred to Daughter. This approach was embodied in Rev. Rul. 83–120, 1983–2 C.B. 170. Rev. Rul. 83–120 established valuation rules designed to assure that the preferred and common, respectively, are properly valued when Dad gives the common to Daughter. For example, Rev. Rul. 83–120 dictated that if the preferred dividend is at a level below market or is not cumulative, the value of the preferred must be reduced accordingly, causing a concomitant increase in the value of the common for gift tax purposes.

[¶ 12,013]

2. SECTION 2036(c)

Rev. Rul. 83–120 proved difficult to enforce and generally ineffective in preventing widespread value-freezing transactions spawned by the highly inflationary early 1980s. It became clear that the Commissioner could not defeat value freezes through administrative action alone, and that legislation would be necessary. The result was adoption in 1987 of § 2036(c).

Section 2036(c) attacked value freezes aggressively by requiring inclusion in Dad's gross estate of the full value ($2,020,000) of Daughter's common at Dad's death despite Dad's completed transfer of the common ten years earlier. This result was achieved by treating Dad as having retained "enjoyment" of the common until his death for purposes of § 2036(a).

The § 2036(c) solution was extremely complex and appeared to endanger a wide variety of otherwise innocuous transactions involving closely held businesses and property. In addition, § 2036(c) imposed prospective liability that was unlimited in both duration and amount. Under § 2036(c), Dad's gross estate would include the full value of Daughter's common regardless of whether the common had been transferred one year or 40 years before Dad's death, provided the transfer occurred after the effective date of § 2036(c). Furthermore, Dad's estate would include the entire value of Daughter's common whether that value was $2,020,000 or $100,000,000.

For these reasons, § 2036(c) was vigorously attacked by small business advocates and by many lawyers and accountants involved in estate planning. Ultimately, Congress retroactively repealed § 2036(c).

[¶ 12,019]

3. SECTIONS 2701 AND 2702

In 1990, Congress replaced § 2036(c) with §§ 2701 and 2702, part of a new Chapter 14 of the Code. Chapter 14 also includes § 2703, relating to restrictive agreements (discussed at ¶ 11,091), and § 2704, relating to certain lapsing rights (discussed at ¶ 3091 and ¶ 11,107). Chapter 14 represents an attempt to defeat a wide variety of gift and estate tax avoidance devices involving valuation of closely held businesses and other property. Sections 2701 and 2702 are aimed squarely at value-freezing strategies involving retained interests.

In adopting § 2701, Congress abandoned the § 2036(c) effort to include Daughter's common in Dad's gross estate. Instead, § 2701 focuses on proper valuation of the common stock for gift tax purposes at the time the common stock is transferred by Dad to Daughter. Section 2702 applies similar principles to transfers involving trusts and other property, as discussed beginning at ¶ 12,079.

Section 2701 applies stringent rules to valuation of Dad's preferred stock for gift tax purposes at the time Dad transfers the common stock to Daughter. These rules may dramatically decrease the value assigned to Dad's preferred stock, necessarily increasing the value of the common stock transferred to Daughter. However, the § 2701 valuation rules do not apply unless specific circumstances are present, as explained at ¶ 12,067. If § 2701 is not applicable, the general principles of valuation (including Rev. Rul. 83–120, discussed at ¶ 12,007) will be applied to value the common. S. Rep. No. 3209, 101st Cong., 2d Sess. at 63 (1990). If § 2701 is applicable, the common stock may be assigned a value much higher than $20,000. In certain instances the entire $1,000,000 enterprise value will be assigned to the common stock for gift tax purposes.

The remainder of this Chapter 12 describes the valuation rules imposed by § 2701 and 2702. Section 2701 (¶ 12,025–12,073) applies to interests in corporations and partnerships. Section 2702 (¶ 12,079–12,097) applies to interests in trusts and other property.

C.   SECTION 2701 VALUATION RULES

[¶ 12,025]

Section 2701 mandates application of special valuation rules to transfers of interests in corporations or partnerships. The starting point is the general rule that any interest transferred will be valued according to the usual fair market value standard, i.e., willing buyer-willing seller, discussed at ¶ 9001. This approach includes all the valuation principles applicable to closely held businesses (¶ 11,001 et seq.), including marketability, minority, and other discounts. S. Rep. No. 3209, 101st Cong., 2d Sess. at 61 (1990). The special valuation rules of § 2701 apply only if (1) the transferor transfers an interest in a corporation or partnership to a member of his family (as defined in § 2701(e)(1)), and (2) the transferor or an applicable family member (as defined in § 2701(e)(2)) retains an interest in the same corporation or partnership. § 2701(a)(1). If § 2701 applies, one or both of two special valuation rules, described below, must be used to value the transfer for gift tax purposes.

[¶ 12,031]

1.   MINIMUM VALUE RULE FOR TRANSFERRED INTERESTS

If common stock is transferred, all issued common stock, including that transferred, must be assigned a value equal to at least 10 percent of the total enterprise value. § 2701(a)(4)(A). For this purpose the enterprise value includes not only all equity interests, but also the amount of any debt owed by the corporation to the transferor or a family member. § 2701(a)(4)(A)(ii). However, certain short-term debt is excluded. Reg. § 25.2701–3(c)(3)(i)(A).

¶ 12,031

In the example of Dad and Daughter, the common transferred to Daughter would be assigned a minimum value of $100,000—10 percent of the $1,000,000 enterprise value. This minimum value rule "is intended to reflect the 'option value' of the right of the [common] to future appreciation." S. Rep. No. 3209, 101st Cong., 2d Sess. at 65 (1990). If Dad transferred only one-half of the issued common to Daughter, the transferred common would be assigned a minimum value of $50,000. The 10% minimum value is assigned collectively to all common stock, not just the stock transferred to Daughter. Note that this rule sets only a minimum value, which may be raised by application of the usual valuation principles or by operation of the zero-value rule described in ¶ 12,037, which follows.

[¶ 12,037]

2. ZERO VALUE RULE FOR RETAINED INTERESTS

The second rule mandates a zero value for the transferor's retained interest if certain conditions are present. § 2701(a)(3)(A). A "subtraction" method is then used in valuing the transferred interest. Reg. § 25.2701–3(a)(1). If the transferor owns all interests in the corporation before the transfer, the value of the retained interest is subtracted from the entire enterprise value to produce the value of the transferred interest. If the retained interest is valued at zero, the entire enterprise value will necessarily be assigned to the transferred interest. If persons other than the transferor and the transferee hold interests in the enterprise, determination of the value of the interest becomes more complex. See Reg. § 25.2701–3(b) and (d).

In the Dad–Daughter example, the result of assigning a zero value to Dad's preferred stock would be to assign the entire enterprise value of $1,000,000 to Daughter's common stock, so that Dad would be treated as making a taxable gift of $1,000,000 when he transfers the common to Daughter.

The zero value rule may be applied to two types of rights:

1. Any liquidation, put, call, or conversion right retained by the transferor is assigned a zero value unless that right must be exercised at a specific time and at a specific amount. § 2701(a)(3)(A), (b)(1)(B), (c)(2)(A), and (c)(2)(B)(i). Therefore, the typical preferred stock entitlement to a set dollar amount upon liquidation of the corporation is treated as worthless because there is no fixed time for liquidation. The rationale for assigning a zero value to such rights is that if the family controls the business, and there is no requirement that the liquidation or conversion right be exercised at a specified date and time, the family will, in its own best interest, arrange for the right never to be exercised. In the example above, Dad should not be permitted to subtract the value of his preferred stock liquidation entitlement in determining the value of the common transferred to Daughter because, as a practical matter, it is unlikely that the family will ever liquidate the corporation.

2. The general rule is that a right to receive distributions (such as dividends) from a corporation is assigned a zero value if the transferor and the transferor's family control the corporation. § 2701(a)(3)(A) and (b)(1)(A). However, the zero value rule does not apply if a dividend of a fixed amount must be paid at stated intervals and the dividend is cumulative. A dividend of this kind, i.e., a dividend that escapes the zero value rule, is called a "qualified payment." § 2701(a)(3)(A) and (c)(3)(A). For this purpose, a dividend is regarded as fixed in amount if it bears a fixed relationship to a specified market interest rate. § 2701(c)(3)(B). In the Dad–Daughter example, if the dividend on the preferred stock is fixed in amount, payable periodically, and cumulative, the dividend right will not be assigned a zero value. However, if the dividend is not cumulative, does not have fixed dates, or does not have a fixed payment amount, the dividend right will be assigned a zero value. The rationale for this distinction again derives from family control of the corporation. If there is no requirement that dividends be paid regularly, the family is unlikely to cause payment of dividends that would simply increase the assets to be taxed in Dad's estate at his death. For that reason, the dividend right should be regarded as essentially valueless. On the other hand, if dividends are required to be paid, Dad's estate will necessarily be enhanced by the dividend payments, and the right to dividends should be valued accordingly.

A zero value will typically be assigned to the liquidation preference embodied in preferred stock because there is no requirement that liquidation occur at a specific time. A zero value will be assigned to the distribution (dividend) right if the dividend is not cumulative. The resulting zero value for the preferred stock in such circumstances is appropriate because the preferred has only an illusory value—a value that can be entirely controlled by the family. Liquidation may never occur, with the result that the liquidation right may have no practical value. Furthermore, the family may choose to forgo payment of preferred dividends. If the dividends are not cumulative, the dividend right will be rendered meaningless. As a result, the family can effectively shift all the future growth in enterprise value to the holders of the common. Under these circumstances, § 2701 produces the right result: Dad's transfer of common stock to Daughter is tantamount to transfer of all meaningful economic interests in the business.

In some cases the preferred will be assigned a zero value, but the distribution (dividend) right will escape the zero value rule because the dividend is fixed in amount and cumulative. This triggers a special valuation rule. First, the fair market value of the distribution right is determined without regard to § 2701. Under Rev. Rul. 83–120, 1983–2 C.B. 170, this would include such factors as the dividend yield relative to that of comparable publicly traded preferred stock and the extent to which corporation earnings provide adequate funding to pay the dividend. Once the dividend value is determined, a special "lower of" rule is applied to value the dividend and liquidation right in conjunction with one another. § 2701(a)(3)(B); Reg. § 25.2701–2(a)(3). Under this rule the value of the entire interest, i.e., the preferred stock, is the "lower of" the value of the distribution right or the value of the liquidation right, assuming exercise of the liquidation right in such a way as to produce the lowest possible value.

For example, assume that preferred stock has a par value of $1,000,000, but that the holder has the right to require the corporation to redeem the stock at any time for $900,000. Further assume that the preferred pays a fixed, cumulative dividend, and that the market value of the right to receive the dividend is $1,000,000. In determining the value of the preferred, it is assumed that the liquidation right will be exercised so as to produce the lowest possible value, i.e., redemption for $900,000. Because this is lower than the $1,000,000 value of the distribution right, the value of the preferred stock is $900,000 for purposes of § 2701. If the value of the distribution right were only $850,000, that value would be lower and would prevail. Reg. § 25.2701–2(a)(5).

If the retained interest consists only of a qualified payment right, without any liquidation right, the qualified payment is valued without regard to § 2701. § 2701(a)(3)(C). In other words the usual valuation rules, including those enunciated in Rev. Rul. 83–120, are applied.

D. OTHER ASPECTS OF THE SECTION 2701 VALUATION RULES

[¶ 12,055]

If, in the Dad–Daughter example at ¶ 12,001, both the liquidation preference and the dividend right are assigned a zero value, the result is that the entire $1,000,000 enterprise value is assigned to the common stock given to Daughter. There remains the question of how Dad's preferred should be valued at Dad's later death. Double taxation would result if Dad's preferred were valued at $980,000 at Dad's death. This result is avoided by § 2701(e)(6), which requires that "appropriate adjustments" be made at Dad's death "to reflect the increase in the amount of any prior taxable gift" the valuation of which was affected by § 2701. The purpose of the adjustment is "to prevent the double taxation of rights that were given a zero value" under Section 2701. S. Rep. No. 3209, 101st Cong., 2d Sess. at 65 (1990).

For example, if § 2701 was applied to increase the gift tax value of the common given to Daughter by $980,000, the value assigned to Dad's retained preferred would be reduced by $980,000 at Dad's death or upon a subsequent gift of the preferred by Dad. Reg. § 25.2701–5. This adjustment, however, is subject to a number of limitations specified in the Regulation.

On the other hand, § 2701 can increase the value included in Dad's gross estate if the dividend right is a qualified payment and the corporation fails to timely pay the required dividends on the preferred stock. In that event, any dividend not paid is added back to Dad's gross estate at his death, together with an increment representing imputed earnings that would have accrued from investment of timely paid dividends. A similar increase in value applies for gift tax purposes if Dad gives the preferred stock away during his life. § 2701(d)(1).

Application of the § 2701 valuation rules can transform a sale into a gift, and § 2701 expressly provides that the rules of the section are used not just to determine valuation but to determine whether a gift has occurred. § 2701(a)(1). Assume, for example, that Dad's preferred has a fixed, cumulative dividend supporting a market value of $980,000, and that Dad sells the common to Daughter for $20,000 rather than simply giving the common to Daughter as a gift. The valuation rules discussed at ¶ 12,037 would produce a value of $980,000 for the preferred and therefore $20,000 for the common, but the minimum value rule of § 2701(a)(4) would dictate a value of $100,000 for the common. Therefore, Dad would be viewed as having transferred $100,000 of value to Daughter in exchange for $20,000 of cash, resulting in a $80,000 gift from Dad to Daughter.

Section 2701 can transform other transactions into gifts. Any transaction that has the effect of giving one type of interest to Dad and another type of interest to Daughter can have this effect. Obvious examples are contributions to capital, redemptions and recapitalizations. § 2701(e)(5). For example, if Dad and Daughter together capitalize a new corporation, with Dad contributing $980,000 and receiving preferred stock, while Daughter contributes $20,000 and receives common stock, the transaction may be treated as a § 2701 transfer. Reg. § 25.2701–1(b)(2)(i). It appears that, under § 2701(e)(5), Dad would be treated as purchasing all interests in the corporation, followed by a sale of all the common to Daughter for $20,000. If the common is valued at $1,000,000 because § 2701 assigns a zero value to the preferred, the result is a net gift by Dad of $980,000. S. Rep. No. 3209, 101st Cong., 2d Sess. at 64, Example 6 (1990).

E. PRACTICAL EFFECTS OF THE SECTION 2701 VALUATION RULES

[¶ 12,061]

The practical effects of the § 2701 valuation rules may be illustrated in the context of the Dad–Daughter example at ¶ 12,001. Because Dad has transferred common stock to Daughter, the minimum value for transferred interests rule will apply, resulting in assignment of a minimum value of $100,000 to the common stock. This will raise the minimum value of Dad's gift of common stock from $20,000 to $100,000.

Whether or not the zero value for retained interests rule will apply depends on the nature of the preferred Dad retains. If the preferred is not required to be redeemed at a fixed date, and the dividend is either not cumulative or not fixed in amount, the preferred is assigned a zero value. The full enterprise value will be assigned to the common, and Dad will be treated as having made a gift of $1,000,000.

Dad and Daughter will likely seek to avoid this result by making the dividend cumulative and fixed in amount—therefore a qualified payment.

¶ 12,061

§ 2701(c)(3). If the dividend supports valuation of the dividend right at $980,000 pursuant to Rev. Rul. 83–120, the "lesser of" rule will produce a value of $980,000 for the preferred, leaving a value of only $20,000 for the common. Because this is less than the $100,000 dictated by the minimum value rule, the $100,000 value will apply, and Dad will be treated as making a gift of $100,000.

Assuming no change in interest rates or creditworthiness, at Dad's death his preferred will be valued at $980,000, presumably less a $80,000 adjustment pursuant to § 2701(e)(6), representing the amount by which § 2701 increased the value of Dad's gift. If the preferred dividends are paid timely, there will be no addition to Dad's gross estate pursuant to § 2701(d).

The bottom line is that Dad and Daughter can escape the most damaging effects of § 2701 and achieve the most important benefits of traditional value freezing. If the preferred dividend is cumulative and can support a valuation of $980,000, the only effect of § 2701 will be to raise the value of the gift of common stock from $20,000 to $100,000. Dad's preferred will be included in his gross estate at $980,000, less a reduction under § 2701(e)(6) in the amount of $80,000. The result is that $2,000,000 of value will have been transferred to Daughter at the cost of the gift tax on a gift of $100,000 and a gross estate inclusion of $900,000. In effect, $2,000,000 of the $3,000,000 enterprise value will have passed to Daughter tax free.

Nevertheless, § 2701 creates significant impediments to value freezes. In order to avoid § 2701, Dad will have to make the preferred dividend cumulative and assure that the dividend rate and coverage support a $980,000 valuation. If the value of the dividend right is below $980,000, this will lower the value of the preferred and raise the value of the common. If the dividend is cumulative but the corporation fails to actually pay the dividend, Dad's gross estate will be increased accordingly.

The practical result is that the value-freezing objective will be fully achieved only if the preferred carries an adequate cumulative dividend that is actually paid. The dividends will not be deductible by the corporation for income tax purposes, will be taxed as income to Dad, (albeit at a favorable rate of 15%), and may constitute such a corporation cash drain that Dad will find it difficult to achieve the growth in corporation value that he anticipates. The net result is to limit the benefits of value freezing to enterprises that can achieve a growth in enterprise value more rapid than the requisite preferred dividend rate.

Consequently, Congress has achieved part but not all of its objectives in combating value freezes. Taxpayers can no longer "play games" by creating illusory retained interests, such as noncumulative dividends and redemption rights that might or might not be exercised. If the retained interest is to be assigned any value, it must be a real preferred or a similar interest with finite and certain economic rights. However, if the taxpayer can meet those tests and the enterprise can afford to pay an adequate dividend, much of the benefit of value freezing can still be achieved.

¶ 12,061

F. TRANSACTIONS NOT SUBJECT TO THE SECTION 2701 VALUATION RULES

[¶ 12,067]

The general rule is that any transfer of an interest in a corporation or partnership to a family member is subject to the § 2701 valuation rules if the donor (or a member of the donor's family) retains an interest in the same corporation. However, there are exceptions that exclude many transactions from application of § 2701.

The "minimum value for transferred interests" rule applies only to transfers of common stock. § 2701(a)(4)(A) and (B)(i). Also, it does not apply if market quotations for the common stock are readily available on an established securities market. § 2701(a)(1).

The "zero value rule for retained interests" does not apply if any one of the following circumstances is present:

1. The corporation has issued only one class of stock. § 2701(a)(2)(B).

2. The corporation has issued more than one class of stock, but the only difference between the classes relates to voting rights. § 2701(a)(2)(C).

3. The corporation has issued more than one class of stock, but all interests transferred by the donor are in the same proportion as the donor's retained interest. § 2701(a)(2)(C). For example, if the donor owns both preferred stock and common stock and transfers one-third of his holding of each to the donee, the zero value rule does not apply. Reg. § 25.2701–1(c)(4). Similarly, if the transferor owns only one class of stock, the zero value rule will not apply to a gift of a portion of that stock to a family member.

4. Market quotations are readily available for the retained interest on an established securities market. § 2701(a)(2)(A).

5. Market quotations are readily available for the transferred interest on an established securities market. § 2701(a)(1).

These exceptions have great practical importance and permit a variety of typical stock dispositions among family members without triggering § 2701. If only one class of stock is outstanding, Exception 1 permits any and all transfers of stock among family members without application of the zero value rule. Parents in these circumstances can continue a regular program of annual per donee exclusion gifts of stock to children or other descendants but still maintain control of the corporation. Although the "minimum value for transferred interests" will technically apply, it will have no practical effect. The minimum value rule requires that all issued common stock be assigned a minimum value of 10 percent of the enterprise value. If only common stock is outstanding, the common will have a value equal to 100 percent of enterprise value even without application of the minimum value rule.

Exception 2 allows even greater flexibility because it permits creation of voting and nonvoting stock without triggering application of § 2701. Thus, parents may transfer to descendants rights to future appreciation, in the form of nonvoting common stock, while retaining full voting control. Exception 2 is especially significant because it has the practical effect of excluding S corporations from the operation of § 2701. An S corporation is permitted to have only one class of stock, but differences in voting rights are permissible. § 1361(b)(1)(D) and (c)(4).

Exception 3 is important because it permits multiple classes of stock without application of the zero value rule, provided all transfers are proportionate. This is sometimes called the "vertical slice" rule. However, the minimum value rule for common stock remains operative even if all transfers are proportionate.

G. PARTNERSHIPS

[¶ 12,073]

If the transfer involves a partnership, principles similar to those applicable to corporations are applied. § 2701(a)(1) and (4). Several definitions and rules specifically applicable to partnerships are provided. §§ 2701(a)(2), (a)(4)(B)(i), (b)(2)(B) and (c)(1)(A)(ii).

H. CORPORATION RETAINED INTEREST PROBLEMS

[¶ 12,075]

1. Mom has worked hard to build the manufacturing business she operates through Dynamic Corporation. The business now has a fair market value of $2,000,000. Mom owns all the stock—100 shares of common. Dynamic Corporation has no indebtedness to Mom. Mom wants to bring Son into the business and is concerned about the estate tax liability that her death would cause. Mom has proposed to you a number of alternative dispositions of stock described below. As to each proposed disposition, Mom wants to know whether the transaction would be treated as a gift for gift tax purposes and, if so, the principles that would be applied to value the interest transferred.

    (a) Mom transfers 20 shares of common to Son.

    (b) Dynamic Corporation is recapitalized, with the result that Mom holds 50 shares of Class A common and 50 shares of Class B common. The only difference between the classes is that Class A common shares have voting rights, while Class B common shares do not. Mom transfers 20 shares of Class B common to Son.

    (c) Dynamic Corp. is recapitalized, with the result that Mom owns 80 shares of preferred stock and 20 shares of common stock. The preferred has a preference right of $20,000 per share in the event of liquidation, and a cumulative dividend of $2,000 per share must be paid on the preferred annually. Mom gives all 20 shares of common stock to Son. The 10 percent dividend on the preferred is consistent with current preferred yields. As a result, the dividend right has a market value of $20,000 per share. The earnings are fully adequate to cover the preferred dividend.

(d) The facts are the same as in (c), except that the preferred dividend is not cumulative.

2. Dad and Daughter decide to pool their resources and create Synergistic Corporation for the development of computer software. Dad contributes $800,000 and receives 80 shares of preferred stock. Each share of preferred has a $10,000 preference on liquidation and a 14 percent ($1,400) annual noncumulative dividend. Daughter contributes $200,000 and receives common stock. Does this transaction have gift tax consequences?

I. TRUSTS

[¶ 12,079]

1. GENERAL PRINCIPLES: GRITS, GRATS, AND GRUTS

Trusts offer opportunities for overvaluation of retained interests, resulting in artificially reduced valuation of transferred interests. For this reason, if an interest in a trust is transferred, § 2702 imposes certain rules for valuation of retained interests similar to those that are applicable to retained interests in corporations and partnerships under § 2701.

An example will illustrate the kind of tax avoidance § 2702 is intended to prevent. Assume that Mom transfers to a trust a parcel of investment real estate worth $100,000 that produces an annual income of only $2,000. Mom retains the right to receive the income from the trust for 15 years. At that time the trust is to terminate, and the real estate is to be distributed outright to Son.

In the absence of § 2702, the actuarial valuation principles described at ¶ 10,001 would be used to value Son's remainder for gift tax purposes. If the § 7520 rate at the time the trust is created were 10 percent, the remainder would be assigned a value of .239392, or $23,939. Reg. §§ 25.2512–5(d)(2) and 20.2031–7(d)(6), Table B. Therefore, the remaining value of .760608, or $76,061 would be assigned to Mom's retained income interest. Mom would be treated as making a taxable gift of only $23,939. Mom, however, will in fact receive far less than $76,061 over the life of the trust because the actual income yield is only 2 percent, or $2,000 per year.

If Mom lives longer than 15 years, the trust will terminate, Son will receive the real estate outright, and nothing will be included in Mom's gross estate at her death. As a result, $100,000 will have been transferred to Son at the cost of a gift tax on only $23,939, and the 15 years of income will augment Mom's gross estate very little. Furthermore, Son may receive much more than $100,000 if the property appreciates substantially during the 15–year period.

This avoidance technique, known as a "grantor retained income trust," or "GRIT," was frequently employed prior to adoption of § 2702.

The Commissioner could attack Mom's valuation of the remainder by arguing that use of the 10 percent interest rate is "unrealistic and unreasonable" in light of the actual 2 percent return, relying on the principle discussed in *Shackleford* (¶ 10,019). However, it is by no means clear when the actual return becomes so low that use of the § 7520 rate is "unrealistic and unreasonable." Furthermore, this approach requires the Commissioner to litigate the issue on a case-by-case basis. As a result, § 2702 was adopted to provide a clear, definitive, and easily administered solution.

Section 2702 prevents tax avoidance of this kind by applying strict valuation rules to both the retained interest and the transferred interest if the transfer is between members of the same family. Section 2702(a)(2)(A) requires that any trust interest retained by the grantor be valued at zero unless it constitutes a "qualified interest." An interest is a qualified interest only if annual payments are required and those payments consist of (1) a fixed dollar amount or (2) an amount equal to a fixed percentage of the trust value, determined annually. § 2702(b)(1) and (2). In the above example, Mom is entitled merely to the "income," not a fixed dollar amount or a percentage of trust assets. Therefore, her retained income right is not a "qualified interest." As a result, Mom's income right is assigned a zero value, and the entire $100,000 value of the trust is assigned to Son's remainder. Mom is treated as making a taxable gift of $100,000 when she transfers the remainder to Son.

If the retained right is a "qualified interest," i.e., a right to annual payments of a fixed dollar amount or a fixed percentage of trust value, § 2702 does not apply, and the retained interest is valued according to the usual rules of § 7520. Because the payments are fixed in amount or percentage, they will be made without regard to the income actually produced. Under these circumstances the usual § 7520 rules will necessarily produce an accurate valuation of the retained income interest.

For example, if the trust described above provides for payment to Mom of $2,000 at the end of each year (rather than payment of the "income") and the § 7520 rate at the time the trust is created is 10 percent, Mom's right to the $2,000 annual payments is valued at only $15,212.16 under the method described at ¶ 10,001. Therefore, the remainder given to Son is valued at $100,000 less $15,212, or $84,788. Mom is treated as making a taxable gift of $84,788. This should be compared with the taxable gift value of $23,939 that obtained under the pre–§ 2702 valuation of the remainder, assuming Mom retained the right to "income." In this manner, § 2702 requires that the remainder interest be realistically valued, preventing a greatly undertaxed transfer of value to Son.

The Regulations impose strict requirements as to what constitutes a "qualified interest," including specific provisions that must be included in the granting instrument. Reg. § 25.2702–3.

Trust interests providing "qualified interests" that meet the requirements of § 2702 have commonly accepted names. A "grantor retained annuity

¶ 12,079

trust," or "GRAT," is a trust that provides for the grantor a retained right to annual payments of a specific dollar amount. A "grantor retained unitrust," or "GRUT," is a trust that provides for the grantor a retained right to annual payments equal to a fixed percentage of the total value of the trust assets, determined annually.

Although § 2702 is aimed primarily at transfers of remainder interests, it also applies to a transfer of an income interest if the transferor retains a remainder interest. Such transactions provide similar opportunities for tax avoidance if the return from the property exceeds the yield assumed under § 7520. A similar valuation approach is therefore applied to transfers of income interests. If the transferor retains a remainder, that remainder is treated as having a zero value unless the transferred interest is a right to annual payments of a fixed dollar amount or a fixed percentage of trust assets. § 2702(a)(1) and (b)(3). If the transferred interest is a right merely to "income," the remainder will be treated as valueless, and the entire value of the trust property will be assigned to the transferred income interest.

Section 2702 does not apply to every transfer of a trust remainder interest. Section 2702 applies only if the transfer is to a member of the transferor's family (as defined in § 2704(c)(2)), and the retained interest is held by the transferor or a member of the transferor's family as defined in § 2701(e)(2). § 2702(a)(1). Section 2702 does not apply to a transfer that is not yet complete for gift tax purposes. § 2702(a)(3)(A)(i).

[¶ 12,085]

2. QUALIFIED PERSONAL RESIDENCE TRUSTS

An important exception to the rules of § 2702 is that for personal residences. Section 2702(a)(3)(A)(ii) provides that § 2702 does not apply to a trust if the sole trust property is an interest in a personal residence that is occupied by the holder of a term interest in the trust. This gives rise to a frequently used vehicle–the qualified personal residence trust, or QPRT.

A typical QPRT operates as follows. Mom, a widow age 70, owns a home worth $400,000. She wants to continue to reside in the home but is concerned about estate tax exposure because she expects the home to appreciate substantially in the years ahead. The solution is a QPRT. Mom transfers the home to a trust. The trust instrument provides that Mom is entitled to occupy the home for 10 years. After 10 years the home will pass outright to Son, but Mom will continue to occupy the home upon payment of market level rent. Because the sole trust asset is a personal residence, § 2702 does not apply. § 2702(a)(3)(A)(ii). The remainder given to Son is therefore valued under Reg. §§ 25.2512–5(d)(2) and 20.2031–7(d) Table B. If the § 7520 rate at the time of the transfer is 9%, the value of the remainder is .422411 of the $400,000 total value, or $168,964. This is the value of Mom's gift to Son for gift tax purposes. (In practice, the trust instrument often includes a provision requiring reversion of the entire property to Mom if she dies within 10 years. This reversion possibility has an actuarial value that substantially reduces the value of the remainder below $168,964, further lowering the amount of the taxable gift.)

If Mom dies within 10 years, the entire value of the home at the time of Mom's death is included in her gross estate under § 2036(a), explored in Chapter 18. Under § 2001(b), last sentence, the $168,964 gift is not treated as an adjusted taxable gift and is not added to the amount taxed at Mom's death. Hence the value of the home is not double taxed.

If Mom survives for 10 years, nothing is included in her gross estate, and the home passes tax free to Son. In addition, Mom's gross estate will be reduced by her rental payments to Son after 10 years. If, for example, the home has appreciated in value to $700,000 by the time of Mom's death, the family will have succeeded in passing a $700,000 asset to Son at the cost of gift tax on only $168,964. A crucial element in assuring this result is payment by Mom to Son of rent at a market level after 10 years. If Mom pays less than market rent, she could be viewed as having retained enjoyment of the home for purposes of § 2036, thereby causing inclusion of the home in her estate, under principles discussed in Chapter 18.

A QPRT may be used for two personal residences, so that a vacation home may be transferred in this way as well. Reg. § 25.2702–5(b)(2)(i). The Regulations include many specific requirements for a QPRT. Reg. § 25.2702–5.

[¶ 12,091]

3. PRACTICAL EFFECTS OF SECTION 2702

Section 2702 effectively prevents donors from using the customary rules of actuarial valuation to achieve tax avoidance in intrafamily transfers. In the case of transfers of remainder interests, the retained income right must be "tied down" to a specific dollar figure or a specific percentage of trust value—without regard to the actual income to be generated. This assures realistic valuation of both the retained income right and the transferred remainder.

Still, retained income transfers can offer significant tax savings, especially when viewed as value-freezing devices. Assume, for example, that Mom creates a grantor retained annuity trust, or GRAT, retaining a right to payments of $10,000 annually for 10 years, with remainder outright to Son. If the value of the trust property is $100,000 and the Section 7520 rate is 10 percent, the retained right will be valued at $61,446, and the transferred remainder will be valued at only $38,554.

If Mom survives beyond 10 years the property goes to Son without further payment of tax, and the property will not be included in Mom's gross estate. If the property appreciates in value at a rate faster than 10 percent, the family will achieve substantial tax savings because Mom's estate will be augmented only by the annual $10,000 payments. If the property is worth $300,000 at Mom's death, that amount will have passed to Son at the cost of only (1) the gift tax on transfer of the $38,554 remainder to Son and (2) estate tax on any of the $10,000 income payments Mom still holds at her death.

A more extreme use of a GRAT or GRUT to achieve a value-freezing objective is explained in the following material.

¶ 12,085

[¶ 12,095]

4. ZEROED–OUT GRATS AND GRUTS

In a GRAT, if the retained right to payments is set at a high enough level, the actuarial value of the gifted remainder can be reduced essentially to zero. This is referred to as a "zeroed-out GRAT." The same strategy can be employed with a GRUT. The purpose of such an arrangement is to "freeze" the value of the property transferred, so that much of the appreciation during the period of the GRAT or GRUT benefits the remainderman rather than the transferor who has retained a right to periodic payments.

A dramatic example of this technique was involved in Walton v. Commissioner, 115 T.C. 589 (2000), Acq., Notice 2003–72, 2003–2 C.B. 964. The donor was Audrey Walton, and the donees were Audrey's two daughters. On April 7, 1993, Audrey transferred 7.2 million shares of Wal–Mart Stores, Inc. stock to trusts for her daughters. The value of the stock transferred to each trust was $100,000,000. The trusts were to terminate in two years, at which time the remaining principal was to be transferred to Audrey's daughters. The trusts provided that during the first year Audrey would receive a payment equal to 49.35% of the initial trust value, and that during the second year Audrey would receive a payment equal to 59.22% of the value of the trust at the beginning of the second year. The payments could be made in kind using Wal–Mart stock, and in fact most of the payments did consist of Wal–Mart stock. Under the § 7520 rate in effect for April of 1993, the actuarial value of each daughter's remainder was $6,195. Audrey filed a gift tax return reporting a taxable gift of $6,195 to each daughter.

As of the inception of the trust, the value of the total payments to be made to Audrey from each trust was $109,000,000. Any amount in excess of this value at the termination of the trust would go tax-free to the daughter. If, for example, the Wal–Mart stock in each trust rose in value to $129,000,000 by the time the trust terminated, each daughter would receive $129,000,000 less $109,000,000 or $20,000,000. In that event Audrey would have succeeded in transferring $20,000,000 of Wal–Mart stock to each daughter at the cost of the gift tax on a transfer of only $6,195.

As it turned out, the price of Wal–Mart stock declined, with the result that the payments to Audrey exhausted all the Wal–Mart stock, and the daughters received nothing. Although nothing was accomplished, the cost to Audrey was only the gift tax on two remainder transfers of $6,195 each, plus the modest cost of creating and administering the trusts. If Wal–Mart stock had risen in value, however, a great deal of value might have been passed at minimal tax cost.

In order to achieve the very low remainder value of $6,195, it was necessary to provide that, in the event of Audrey's death prior to termination of the trust, her estate would receive the remaining payments. The IRS argued that under this approach, the retained interest should be valued as an annuity payable for the shorter of two years or the period ending with Audrey's death. This analysis would reduce the value of the retained interest and therefore increase the value of the remainder. The result would be value for the gifted remainder interest in each trust of $1.9 million, rather than the $6,195 value reported by Audrey. The IRS position on valuation was based on Reg. § 25.2702–3(e) Example 5. The Tax Court, examining the legislative history of § 2702 and concluded that Reg. § 25.2702–3(e) Example 5 is an "unreasonable interpretation and invalid extension" of § 2702. 115 T.C. 589, 604. Therefore, the correct value of each remainder interest was $6,195, as asserted by Audrey.

The Commissioner has since acquiesced in *Walton* and has issued Regulations affirming the *Walton* result. Notice 2003–72, 2003–2 C.B. 964; Reg. § 25.2702–3(e) Examples 5, 6, and 8.

J. INTERESTS IN OTHER PROPERTY

[¶ 12,097]

Retained interests in property other than corporations, partnerships, and trusts offer similar tax avoidance possibilities. For example, assume that Dad transfers a parcel of real estate to Son, while retaining a right to income from the real estate for 15 years. The usual rules for valuation of income interests might greatly overstate the true value of the income interest, thereby unjustifiably reducing the value assigned to the remainder for gift tax purposes.

Section 2702(c)(1) addresses this problem by treating any transfer of an interest in property as if it were a transfer of a trust interest. This triggers the valuation rules of § 2702(a), and the interest retained by the transferor will be valued at zero unless it is a "qualified interest" as defined in § 2702(b). If the retained interest is expressed as an annual payment of a fixed dollar amount or a fixed percentage of the value of the property, determined annually, the usual rules of valuation under § 7520 will apply. If the retained interest is not so expressed, however, the retained interest will be assigned a zero value, and the entire value of the property will be assigned to the remainder.

It might appear that § 2702 could be readily avoided by a joint purchase of property, so that no "transfer" is present. For example, Dad and Son might jointly purchase a parcel of real estate. Dad would buy an income interest, and Son would buy the remainder interest. Technically, there would be no "transfer" triggering application of § 2702(c).

This loophole is closed by § 2702(c)(2), which treats any joint purchase by two members of the same family as if the person acquiring the income interest had first acquired the entire property and then transferred the remainder to the other family member in exchange for the consideration provided by the other family member. This triggers the § 2702(c)(1) rule calling for treatment of the transaction as if it were a transfer of an interest in a trust. If the retained income interest is not a qualified interest, the retained interest will be valued at zero. Therefore, the transferor will be treated as having transferred the entire property to the holder of the remainder interest in exchange for the consideration provided by the transferee. The difference in value will be a taxable gift. Reg. § 25.2702–4(d) Example 1.

Problems

[¶ 12,107]

1. Dad, age 60, transfers $2,000,000 to an irrevocable trust. The trust provides that Dad (or his estate) is to receive at the end of each year a payment of $50,000 from the trust, regardless of the amount of income. The trust is to terminate in 20 years, at which time all principal and accumulated income, if any, is to be distributed to Daughter. At the time the trust is created the § 7520 rate is 10 percent. How should Dad treat this transfer for gift tax purposes?

2. Assume the same facts as in Problem 1, except that the trust provides that Dad is to receive all "income" from the trust each year for 20 years. How should Dad treat this transfer for gift tax purposes?

3. Mom and Daughter decide to pool their resources and purchase an office building. Mom contributes $400,000 and Daughter contributes $100,000. Mom purchases the right to receive the income from the property for 15 years, and Daughter purchases all other interests in the property. How should Mom treat the purchase for gift tax purposes?

Chapter 13

SPECIAL USE VALUATION

(Section 2032A)

[¶ 13,001]

As explained at ¶ 9001, the general rule is that fair market value is determined by the "willing buyer—willing seller" rule set forth in Reg. §§ 20.2031–1(b) and 25.2512–1. This approach requires that property be valued at the "highest and best use" to which the property could be put, rather than the actual use at the time of valuation. Furthermore, in the case of real estate, fair market value is typically derived from prices actually paid for comparable properties in recent sales. If agricultural land near a city is valued at its urban development potential, the estate tax burden may make continuation of farm use impossible. The economic return from farm use may be far below the level necessary to pay the high estate tax based on urban development valuation.

Estate tax valuation based on comparable sales may have dramatic consequences even if no urban development potential is present. Since the Nineteenth Century there has been a consistent reduction in the number of farms, and a concomitant rise in the acreage per farm. Economies of scale require ever larger assemblages of land. As a result, when parcels become available, there is often strong demand from neighboring farm owners who can benefit from spreading high fixed costs of equipment over a larger enterprise. Often the result is artificially high prices for parcels that are actually sold.

Even without this aggregation phenomenon, the general valuation rules could result in especially onerous estate tax liabilities for farm families. Since World War II farm land has consistently sold at prices that incorporate a lower return from invested capital than is customary in other industries. There is disagreement as to the reason for this phenomenon. It probably relates to both the bidding up of prices for available acreage in a time of aggregation, as explained above, and the strong desire of farm families to retain the life style implicit in farm ownership.

The result is that many farm families tend to be "land poor." Their land may have very substantial value, but the actual income produced tends to be relatively low. This can result in heavy estate tax liability without income sufficient to pay the tax, even if payment of the tax is deferred, as explained at ¶ 28,033. As a result, many farm families fear that they may have no choice but to sell substantial acreage in order to pay estate taxes. This may lower the farm size below an economically sustainable level and ultimately force the family out of farming.

Congress responded to this concern in 1976, adopting § 2032A. Section 2032A is designed to alleviate the problem by permitting valuation of farmland by reference to its income producing potential rather than its hypothetical sale value. In other words, under § 2032A the value for estate tax purposes is a reasonable multiple of hypothetical farm earnings, not the higher price the farm land might actually bring on the market. Although § 2032A can apply to any real estate used in a trade or business, its practical use is limited almost entirely to farming. The total reduction in value for any individual's estate was limited to $750,000 through 1998, but indexed in subsequent years. § 2032A(a)(2) and (3). In 2006, for example, the maximum value reduction permissible under § 2032A is $900,000. Rev. Proc. 2005–70, 2005–47 I.R.B. 979.

Section 2032A is intended to benefit only families that retain the land in the family and continue to use it for farming purposes. Therefore, the availability of § 2032A is tightly restricted, and estate planners who seek to use § 2032A must give careful attention to the eligibility requirements before, at, and after death.

The first requirement for § 2032A qualification is that farm assets must constitute a substantial portion of the decedent's estate. The real and personal property of the farm or other closely held business included in the decedent's gross estate must have an aggregate value equal to 50 percent or more of the decedent's gross estate, and the real property must have an aggregate value equal to 25 percent or more of the decedent's gross estate. § 2032A(b)(1)(A) and (B). These computations are made using the "adjusted value" of each asset, i.e., the fair market value less debt encumbering the asset. § 2032A(b)(3).

The farm or other business must pass from the decedent to a "qualified heir," defined as (1) an ancestor or spouse of the decedent, (2) a lineal descendant of the decedent, the decedent's spouse, or a parent of the decedent, or (3) a spouse of such lineal descendant. § 2032A(b)(1) and (e)(1) and (2). In addition, during five of the eight years preceding the decedent's death, the decedent or a member of his family must have owned the land and used it for a qualified use, and the decedent or a member of his family must have materially participated in the operation of the farm or other closely held business. § 2032A(b)(1)(C). The material participation issue is crucial in the many cases in which farm ownership is relatively passive. Reg. § 20.2032A–3(e)(2) states the following general rules: "No single factor is determinative of the presence of material participation, but physical work and participation in management decisions are the principal factors to be considered. As a minimum, the decedent and/or a family member must regularly advise or consult with the other managing party on the operation of the business."

The five-of-eight-year material participation test period may end prior to the death of the decedent if he became disabled or began receiving and continued to receive Social Security retirement benefits until his death. § 2032A(b)(4). This important provision permits an older person to retire and receive Social Security benefits without endangering § 2032A qualification.

The five-of-eight-year "qualified use" requirement is even more rigorous than the material participation requirement because qualified use must exist at the date of the decedent's death as well as during the five-of-eight-year period preceding death. § 2032A(b)(1). "Qualified use" means an "equity interest" in the operation. The decedent or a member of his family must, both at the time of death and during five of the eight years preceding death, receive a return from the land that is dependent on the economic productivity of the farm or business. Reg. § 20.2032A–3(b)(1). For example, if the decedent (or a family member) receives rent that consists of an agreed percentage of the crop production less expenses, this is regarded as an equity interest that constitutes qualified use. However, if the decedent (or a family member) receives a fixed rent of an agreed number of dollars per acre, regardless of production, qualified use is not present. Estate of Abell v. Commissioner, 83 T.C. 696 (1984).

The election to make use of § 2032A must be made no later than the time for filing the estate tax return (including any extensions) and must be joined with an agreement, signed by each person who has an interest in the property, consenting to the recovery by the United States of any tax that was saved by the election if, within a period of 10 years after death, the qualified heir disposes of the property or ceases to use it for the qualified purpose. § 2032A(d)(1) and (2).

The recapture provision (§ 2032A(c)), which is referred to in the above described agreement, is directed at the estate tax saving attributable to the election. If the qualified heir, within 10 years after the decedent's death but before the death of the qualified heir, disposes of the property to a nonfamily member or ceases to use the property for a qualified purpose, he must repay all or a portion of the tax savings obtained by virtue of the reduced valuation under the § 2032A election. In the case of a disposition of the farmland, the amount of the recapture tax imposed is the lesser of (1) the tax benefit attributable to the special use valuation or (2) the excess of the amount realized upon the disposition of the property over the value of the property as determined under special use valuation. If the disqualification occurs other than by a disposition (e.g., a change to nonfarming use), the amount of the recapture tax is the lesser of (1) the tax benefit attributable to the special use valuation or (2) the excess of the fair market value of the land over the value determined under special use. § 2032A(c)(2)(A). If the qualified heir dies without having disposed of the farmland or ceasing the qualified use, recapture is no longer applicable to the farmland owned by the qualified heir. § 2032A(c)(1).

¶ 13,001

The qualified heir is expressly made liable for the recapture amount, and a special lien is imposed upon the land to support the possible recapture. §§ 2032A(c)(5) and 6324B.

There are two valuation methods available under a § 2032A election:

1. The farm method, which involves capitalization of the average annual cash rent for comparable land used for farming in the same locality (reduced by state and local real estate taxes). The rate of capitalization is the average interest rate for all new Federal Land Bank (now Farm Credit System) loans. § 2032A(e)(7). Each number used is the average amount for the five most recent calendar years preceding the decedent's death. For example, in the case of decedents dying in 2005, the capitalization rate for land in the Texas Farm Credit Bank District was 6.11%. Rev. Rul. 2005–41, 2005–28 I.R.B. 69.

2. The multiple factor method. For those farms where no comparable cash rent may be determined, or where the executor elects not to use the farm method, and for other closely held businesses, the statute provides for use of the following factors in arriving at the value of the qualified land (§ 2032A(e)(8)):

    (a) Capitalization of the income reasonably expected to be derived from the property;

    (b) Capitalization of the fair rental value of the property;

    (c) Assessed land values in a state that provides a differential or use value assessment law for farmland or closely held business;

    (d) Comparable sales in the same geographical area sufficiently removed from an urban or resort area that a nonqualified use would not be a significant factor in the price; and

    (e) Any other factor that fairly values the qualified use of the property.

Section 2032A can have a dramatic impact on valuation of property for estate tax purposes, especially in circumstances where sale prices greatly exceed the value justified by the income produced by the property. For example, assume the case of a ranch consisting of 1,000 acres of grassland suitable for grazing cattle. Because of the financial structure of agriculture, such land might be selling at $500 per acre at a time when, for the preceding five years, the average market rental value was only $30 per acre, the property taxes averaged $4 per acre, and the applicable Farm Credit System loan rate averaged 10 percent. In the absence of § 2032A, the Commissioner might well be successful in fixing the estate tax value of the land at a figure near the price it could command in the market—$500 per acre. However, under § 2032A(e)(7) a much lower value would be produced: the rental value ($30) less the property taxes ($4), or $26, would be divided by the Farm Credit System loan rate of 10 percent to produce a value of only $260 per acre. Thus, the total value of the 1,000 acres for estate tax purposes would be lowered from $500,000 to $260,000.

¶ 13,001

A § 2032A election has an important downside: the post-death basis of the property will be the reduced value under § 2032A, not the full fair market value. § 1014(a)(3). If the land is later sold, the lower basis will increase the amount of gain—and consequently the income tax due—on the sale. Many families, however, have no expectation of selling, with the result that the basis is viewed as having little importance. In any event, the prospect of certain and immediate estate tax savings will likely be viewed as outweighing a speculative and perhaps long-delayed income tax cost.

If the executor transfers the § 2032A land to a qualified heir in satisfaction of a pecuniary bequest, a sale or exchange occurs for income tax purposes. Because the basis of the land to the executor will be artificially lowered by § 1014(a)(3), there would typically be taxable gain to the executor in the amount of the difference between the true fair market value and the § 2032A valuation. This result is prevented by § 1040(a), which limits recognition of the gain to the difference between the true value on the date of transfer and the true value on the death of death (or alternative valuation date).

Problem

[¶ 13,007]

Ralph Brown's wife, Wilma, died 15 years ago. Ralph has only one child, Tom. Ralph farmed until his death and hoped that Tom might continue the farm enterprise. Ralph bequeathed his entire estate to Tom.

Ralph dies in the year 2006. The state of his domicile, where all the land is located, does not impose a death tax. Ralph's estate consists of six assets: four parcels of farmland, a collection of equipment used in farming, and a substantial holding of Microsoft stock. At the date of his death and at the alternate valuation date the six assets have fair market values as follows:

Asset	Date of Death	Alternate Valuation Date
Microsoft Stock	$ 1,200,000	$ 1,240,000
Equipment	400,000	380,000
Land parcel A	200,000	200,000
Land parcel B	200,000	240,000
Land parcel C	400,000	440,000
Land parcel D	600,000	660,000
Total	$3,000,000	$3,160,000

Each land parcel consists of 400 acres. There are no encumbrances on any of the assets at the time of Ralph's death.

During the years 1999 through 2004 and during 2006 until his death, Ralph leased Parcel A to Sally Jones, who is the daughter of Ralph's sister, Gertrude. The lease to Sally Jones required a fixed cash rental payment of $40 per acre per year. Sally used the land in her own farming enterprise, in which she materially participated.

During the years 1999 through 2006, Ralph leased Parcel B to William Roundtree, who was not related to Ralph. Under the lease, Ralph was to receive a fixed rent of $50 per acre per year. The lease provided that Ralph would materially participate in farming decisions as to Parcel B, and Ralph did so throughout the period 1999 through 2006.

During the years 2000 through 2006 Ralph leased Parcel C to Leta Turner, who is not related to Ralph. The lease provided that Ralph was to receive rent consisting of one-half of the gross proceeds from crop production, less one-half of fertilizer and seed costs. The lease provided that Ralph was to participate fully in farm management decisions, and Ralph did so throughout the period 2000 through 2006.

Ralph used Parcel D for his own farming operations from 1994 through 2006. He used the equipment described above for this purpose as well.

For the five calendar years preceding Ralph's death the average annual gross cash rental rates per acre for farmland in the vicinity of Ralph's land and of the same quality as Ralph's parcels, were as follows:

Parcel A	$39
Parcel B	$39
Parcel C	$51
Parcel D	$87

Property taxes for all the parcels averaged $3 per acre during the five years preceding Ralph's death. For the five years preceding Ralph's death, the average annual Farm Credit System interest rate for new loans for Ralph's region was 10 percent.

Could the value of Ralph's gross estate be reduced by an election under Section 2032A? If so, what would be the amount of the reduction?

¶ 13,007

Chapter 14

OTHER VALUATION MATTERS

A. BLOCKAGE

[¶ 14,001]

In the case of listed securities, the quoted trading price may not accurately represent the price the decedent could have obtained for the securities at the time of death. This will often be the case if the decedent's holdings were large relative to the usual trading volume in the security. For example, if the decedent held 300,000 shares of a security with an average daily trading volume of only 20,000 shares, it is obvious that the market would be depressed if the decedent put all his stock on the market at the same time.

This phenomenon is called "blockage," and the Treasury has recognized that blockage may dictate a lower price for the stock than the quoted trading price on the date of death. Reg. §§ 20.2031–2(e) and 25.2512–2(e). Under these circumstances the value for estate tax purposes is the price at which the decedent's stock could hypothetically be sold as one block outside the usual market, e.g., through an underwriter.

The blockage concept has been applied to property other than securities. The estate of Alexander Calder included 1292 gouache (opaque watercolor) paintings executed by Calder. At the time of his death, the average number of gouaches sold each year did not exceed 61. Therefore, the Commissioner permitted a blockage discount of 60 percent, lowering the value of the gross estate by almost two million dollars. Shortly after the artist's death, his widow, to whom he bequeathed the gouaches, transferred almost all of the paintings to six separate trusts for family members, so that each trust had from 153 to 306 gouaches. The widow took the position that the 60–percent blockage discount permitted for estate tax purposes should likewise be allowed for gift tax purposes. The Commissioner took issue with this, arguing that each trust should be viewed separately, so that the determining factor would be the number of years each trust would require to liquidate its gouaches without taking into account sales by other trusts. The court accepted this argument, and also took into account the actual rate of sales of the gouaches by the trusts. The result for gift tax purposes was a smaller discount than that employed for estate tax purposes. Calder v. Commissioner, 85 T.C. 713 (1985).

Substantial discounts were likewise allowed as to works of art still held by sculptor David Smith and artist Georgia O'Keeffe at their deaths. Estate of O'Keeffe v. Commissioner, 63 T.C.M. (CCH) 2699, T.C.M. (RIA) ¶ 92,210 (1992); Estate of Smith v. Commissioner, 57 T.C. 650 (1972), aff'd, 510 F.2d 479 (2d Cir.1975), cert. denied, 423 U.S. 827 (1975).

The blockage concept has been further extended to other assets, especially real estate, and sometimes characterized as an "absorption discount." Absorption discounts are discussed at ¶ 11,073.

B. UNASCERTAINABLE VALUE

[¶ 14,007]

ROBINETTE v. HELVERING

Supreme Court of the United States, 1943.
318 U.S. 184.

Mr. Justice BLACK delivered the opinion of the Court.

This is another case under the gift tax provisions of the Revenue Act of 1932, §§ 501, 506 [1986 Code §§ 2501(a)(1), 2512 (a)], which, while presenting certain variants on the questions decided today in Smith v. Shaughnessy, No. 429, is in other respects analogous to and controlled by that case.

In 1936, the petitioner, Elise Biddle Robinson, was thirty years of age and was contemplating marriage; her mother, Meta Biddle Robinette, was 55 years of age and was married to the stepfather of Miss Robinson. The three, daughter, mother and stepfather, had a conference with the family attorney, with a view to keeping the daughter's fortune within the family. An agreement was made that the daughter should place her property in trust, receiving a life estate in the income for herself, and creating a second life estate in the income for her mother and stepfather if she should predecease them. The remainder was to go to her issue upon their reaching the age of 21, with the further arrangement for the distribution of the property by the will of the last surviving life tenant if no issue existed. Her mother created a similar trust, reserving a life estate to herself and her husband and a second or contingent life estate to her daughter. She also assigned the remainder to the daughter's issue. The stepfather made a similar arrangement by will. The mother placed $193,000 worth of property in the trust she created, and the daughter did likewise with $680,000 worth of property.

The parties agree that the secondary life estates in the income are taxable gifts, and this tax has been paid. The issue is whether there has also been a taxable gift of the remainders of the two trusts. The Commissioner determined that the remainders were taxable, the Board of Tax Appeals reversed the Commissioner, and the Circuit Court of Appeals reversed the Board of Tax Appeals. 129 F.2d 832.

The petitioner argues that the grantors have not relinquished economic control and that this transaction should not be subject both to the estate and to the gift tax. What we have said in the Smith case determines these

¶ 14,007

questions adversely to the petitioner. However, the petitioners emphasize certain other special considerations.

First. Petitioner argues that since there were no donees in existence on the date of the creation of the trust who could accept the remainders, the transfers cannot be completed gifts. The gift tax law itself has no such qualifications. It imposes a tax "upon the transfer . . . of property by gift." And Treasury Regulations provide that "The tax is a primary and personal liability of the donor, is an exercise upon his act of making the transfer, is measured by the value of the property passing from the donor, and attaches regardless of the fact that the identity of the donee may not then be known or ascertainable." We are asked to strike down this regulation as being invalid because inconsistent with the statute. We do not think it is. As pointed out in the *Smith* case, the effort of Congress was to reach every kind and type of transfer by gift. The statute "is aimed at transfers of the title that have the quality of a gift." Burnet v. Guggenheim, 288 U.S. 280, 286. The instruments created by these grantors purported on their face wholly to divest the grantors of all dominion over the property; it could not be returned to them except because of contingencies beyond their control. Gifts of future interests are taxable under the Act, § 504(b), and they do not lose this quality merely because of the indefiniteness of the eventual recipient. The petitioners purported to give the property to someone whose identity could be later ascertained and this was enough.

Second. It is argued that the transfers were not gifts but were supported by "full consideration in money or money's worth." This contention rests on the assumption that an agreement between the parties to execute these trusts was sufficient consideration to support the transfers. We need not consider or attempt to decide what were the rights of these parties as among themselves. Petitioners think that their transaction comes within the permissive scope of Article 8 of Regulation 79 (1936 edition) which provides that "a sale, exchange or other transfer of property made in the ordinary course of business (a transaction which is bona fide at arm's length and free from any donative intent) will be considered as made for an adequate and full consideration in money or money's worth." The basic premise of petitioner's argument is that the moving impulse for the trust transaction was a desire to pass the family fortune on to others. It is impossible to conceive of this as even approaching a transaction "in the ordinary course of business."

Third. The last argument is that "in any event, in computing the value of the remainders herein, allowance should be made for the value of the grantor's reversionary interest." Here unlike the Smith case the government does not concede that the reversionary interest of the petitioner should be deducted from the total value. In the Smith case, the grantor had a reversionary interest which depended only upon his surviving his wife, and the government conceded that the value was therefore capable of ascertainment by recognized actuarial methods. In this case, however, the reversionary interest of the grantor depends not alone upon the possibility of survivorship but also upon the death of the daughter without issue who should reach the age of 21 years. The petitioner does not refer us to any recognized method by

¶ 14,007

which it would be possible to determine the value of such a contingent reversionary remainder. It may be true as the petitioner argues that trust instruments such as these before us frequently create "a complex aggregate of rights, privileges, powers and immunities and that in certain instances all these rights, privileges, powers and immunities are not transferred or released simultaneously." But before one who gives this property away by this method is entitled to deduction from his gift tax on the basis that he had retained some of these complex strands it is necessary that he at least establish the possibility of approximating what value he holds. Factors to be considered in fixing the value of this contingent reservation as of the date of whether or not the daughter would marry; whether she would have children; whether they would reach the age of 21; etc. Actuarial science may have made great strides in appraising the value of that which seems to be unappraisable, but we have no reason to believe from this record that even the actuarial art could do more than guess at the value here in question. Humes v. United States, 276 U.S. 487, 494.

The judgment of the Circuit Court of Appeals is *affirmed*.

[¶ 14,013]

LOCKARD v. COMMISSIONER

United States Court of Appeals, First Circuit, 1948.
166 F.2d 409.

MAGRUDER, Circuit Judge.:

Barbara M. Lockard petitions for review of a decision of the Tax Court of the United States determining that there is a deficiency in gift tax of $5,517.39 for the year 1941. (7 T.C. 1151.)

* * *

We come now to the remaining question in the case, as to the valuation of the gift made by petitioner in 1941.

On December 31, 1941, petitioner, having meanwhile resigned as cotrustee, executed an instrument in which she undertook to assign to the remaining trustee all her reversionary interest in the trust and directed the trustee to continue from and after April 1, 1944, if Mr. Lockard should then be living, to hold the trust property in trust for the following purposes:

2. Until the death of my said husband, Derwood W. Lockard, to pay the entire net income thereof to him, and to pay to him such amounts from principal, not in excess of $3,000 in any calendar year, as the trustee in his uncontrolled discretion shall think necessary for the comfortable maintenance and support of the said Derwood W. Lockard.

3. Upon the death of said Derwood W. Lockard to transfer the principal then held to me if I shall then be living, and if I shall not then be living, to my executors, administrators or assigns free of trust.

¶ **14,013**

Since petitioner had reserved no power to amend the terms of the original trust, this instrument of December 31, 1941, was perhaps technically the creation of a new trust rather than an extension of the term of the old one. In any case, the instrument constituted a new taxable gift to Mr. Lockard. Since he already had the irrevocable right to receive the income up to March 31, 1944, the new gift was of the right to receive the income from and after April 1, 1944, for the remainder of his life, plus the right to receive such amounts from principal, not in excess of $3,000 in any calendar year, as the trustee might in his uncontrolled discretion think necessary for the life beneficiary's comfortable maintenance and support.

In her gift tax return for 1941, petitioner valued this new gift to Mr. Lockard at $55,000. The Commissioner ruled that this valuation should be increased to the amount of $99,459.37, which amount, according to the stipulation, is the "value as of December 31, 1941, of the right of the beneficiary to receive each year after March 30, 1944, the amount of $3,000 from the principal of the trust together with the income of the diminishing trust fund, for the remainder of his life." Part of the deficiency determined by the Commissioner was attributable to this increase in the valuation of the gift. The Tax Court upheld the Commissioner.

Petitioner challenges this ruling on the ground that it treats the discretionary power in the trustee to make payments out of principal up to a maximum of $3,000 a year as a completed gift to the beneficiary of the absolute right to receive such payments, disregarding the limitations imposed on the trustee's power to invade the principal. It is argued that, since the corpus may never be invaded, the gift in 1941 should be valued at the sum of $84,535.90, which is the stipulated "value as of December 31, 1941, of the right of the beneficiary to receive the trust income after March 30, 1944, for the remainder of his life"; and that, if and when invasion of the corpus may become necessary, gifts of principal will then become complete and subject to the gift tax in the years in which principal is actually distributed. This argument of petitioner, as the Tax Court conceded, "is an impressive one and has a strong practical appeal." Nevertheless, we feel obliged to sustain the Tax Court in rejecting it.

By the transfer in 1941, there was a gift of something more than a right to future income; there was also a gift of another intangible interest of a contingent nature, a right to receive payments out of principal, to a maximum of $3,000 in any calendar year, to the extent that the trustee should deem such payments necessary for the comfortable maintenance and support of the beneficiary.[1] This interest, which will be protected by a court of equity, is certainly worth something, despite its contingent nature; in fact the donee

---

1. It might be suggested that the gift of this contingent interest in corpus should be regarded as not "complete" for gift tax purposes, because it is subject to the discretionary power of the trustee, a person who has no interest in the trust estate adverse to the settlor. But this suggestion, however intrinsically reasonable, is inadmissible in view of the legislative history of the gift tax with reference to the closely analogous power of revocation, for it there clearly appears "that Congress intended the gift tax to fall on transfers in trust where the power to revoke is held solely by others, regardless of their complete lack of interest." 2 Paul, Federal Estate and Gift Taxation, § 17.11 (1942), and id. 1946 Supplement. * * *

¶ 14,013

could hardly fail to regard its existence as a valuable assurance against future adversity, and it certainly is a property interest within the broad terms of the gift tax law. The gift in its entirety must be valued as of the date of the gift. I.R.C. § 1005 [1986 Code § 2512(a)]. If it be objected that the valuation fixed by the Commissioner ignores the limitations upon the trustee's power to invade corpus, it is equally true that petitioner's suggested valuation of the 1941 gift ignores the beneficiary's contingent interest in the principal conferred upon him by the transfer in trust executed by petitioner on December 31, 1941.

The government argues that, by the transfer of December 31, 1941, "the taxpayer relinquished completely her right to have the corpus to the extent of $3,000 annually returned to her"; that she "parted completely with the reversion to, and dominion over corpus to this extent"; and that, since so much of the corpus as will be necessary to pay such annuity of $3,000 per year for the remainder of the beneficiary's life "cannot be returned to her except because of contingencies beyond her control," she must be deemed to have made a taxable gift of corpus to this extent under the authority of Robinette v. Helvering, 318 U.S. 184 (1943), and Smith v. Shaughnessy, 318 U.S. 176 (1943). We would not put the matter quite this way. The taxpayer did not relinquish completely the right to have the corpus returned to her intact at the termination of the trust. She retained the right to have the corpus so return to her, except in so far as the trustee might find it necessary, within the limits of his discretionary power, to invade the corpus. It is true, as the government says, that the corpus cannot be returned to her intact "except because of contingencies beyond her control"; but that is not the test of her taxability for a gift in 1941 of an interest in corpus. This is apparent from Smith v. Shaughnessy, supra, where there was an irrevocable transfer of property in trust, the income to be paid to the settlor's wife for life, and upon her death the corpus to go to the settlor if living, or if not, to the wife's heirs. The government conceded "that the right of reversion to the donor in case he outlives his wife is an interest having value which can be calculated by an actuarial device, and that it is immune from the gift tax" (318 U.S. at 178). This concession was made notwithstanding the fact that the corpus could not be returned to the donor except upon a contingency beyond the donor's control, namely, the predecease of the donor's wife.

The real difficulty with the petitioner's case here is that the Commissioner's determination is presumptively correct; and petitioner has not suggested, and cannot suggest, any reliable actuarial method of computing the value of her reserved right to receive the corpus back intact in case the trustee should not find it necessary to invade the corpus, to the extent permitted, for the comfortable maintenance and support of Mr. Lockard during the remainder of his life. Robinette v. Helvering, supra. * * * Indeed, the stipulation of facts does not even furnish a sufficient basis for an informed guess, as of December 31, 1941; with respect to the likelihood of an invasion of corpus. No facts appear as to Mr. Lockard's accustomed scale of living, nor as to his other sources of income, if any. Considering Mr. Lockard's age (thirty-four, in 1941), the trust might well last for twenty or thirty years; and on the facts of record it could not be assumed to be unlikely that the trustee would find it necessary

¶ 14,013

to invade the corpus for the beneficiary's "comfortable maintenance and support", in view of the modest income that might be expected from a trust estate of not over $140,000. It appears from the stipulation that, up to October 1, 1945, the trustee had in fact not made any payment to Mr. Lockard from the principal of the trust. But events subsequent to the date of the transfer have no bearing on the value of the gift as of the date it was made. Cf. Ithaca Trust Co. v. United States, 279 U.S. 151 (1929).

A judgment will be entered affirming the decision of the Tax Court.

Note

[¶ 14,015]

The Seventh Circuit adopted a different approach to the valuation of an interest subject to trustee discretion in Estate of Gokey v. Commissioner, 735 F.2d 1367 (7th Cir.1984)(unpublished opinion). In *Gokey* the issue was the valuation for estate tax purposes of a remainder after a life estate under a trust instrument that permitted the trustee to make corpus distributions to the life tenant if the trustee "deems such use necessary for her care, comfort, support or welfare." In its original opinion, the Tax Court held that the remainder should be valued in accord with the ordinary actuarial principles for remainder interests as set forth in the Regulations under § 2031, ignoring the possible reduction of the remainder value that would be caused by invasion to benefit the life tenant. 72 T.C. 721 (1979). The Seventh Circuit reversed, holding that "the expected value of the remainder interest must reflect the probability" that the trustee will in fact invade corpus. On remand, the Tax Court examined the resources and needs of the life tenant and concluded that the probability of invasion of corpus was such that the remainder should be valued at only 25 percent of its actuarial value without consideration of the invasion possibility. 49 T.C.M. (CCH) 368, T.C.M. (P–H) ¶ 84,665 (1984). See further discussion of Gokey at ¶ 18,145.

C. DISCOVERY OF COMMISSIONER'S VALUATION METHOD

[¶ 14,019]

The rapid inflation of the 1970s, especially in real estate, gave greater importance to the valuation issue and produced even wider disparities between the values determined by taxpayers and those determined by the Commissioner. The problem was compounded because many taxpayers experienced difficulty in obtaining information as to the Commissioner's valuation method. Congress responded to this problem in 1976 by enacting § 7517, which permits the taxpayer to obtain information from the Commissioner as to the basis for any value determination made for estate or gift tax purposes. The Commissioner must respond within 45 days, must explain the basis for the value determination, including computations, and must provide a copy of any expert appraisal obtained by the Commissioner. The taxpayer's request is filed with the district director. Reg. § 301.7517–1(a).

¶ 14,013

D. BURDEN OF PROOF

[¶ 14,020]

The general rule in Tax Court cases is that the taxpayer has the burden to prove the Commissioner's asserted deficiency to be invalid. If the taxpayer proves that the Commissioner's deficiency is invalid, the burden shifts to the Commissioner to prove that there is a deficiency. Cohen v. Commissioner, 266 F.2d 5, 11 (9th Cir. 1959).

Under certain circumstances, however, § 7491, added to the Code in 1998, imposes the initial burden of proof on the IRS. This provision applies only to factual issues and may prove important in some valuation cases. Section 7491 has its greatest impact in cases in which the court must choose between two conflicting positions, and cannot split the difference. In valuation cases, however, it appears that a court can still adopt a value between those proposed by the IRS and the taxpayer, respectively, with the result that the burden of proof may have little practical impact.

A taxpayer seeking to take advantage of § 7491 must satisfy all of several requirements: (1) the taxpayer must present credible evidence for the taxpayer's position, (2) the taxpayer must comply with all substantiation requirements, and (3) the taxpayer must comply with all "reasonable" IRS requests for documents, witnesses, and other information. § 7491(a).

E. DECLARATORY JUDGMENT
BY THE TAX COURT

[¶ 14,021]

Section 7477 permits a donor to obtain a declaratory judgment from the Tax Court as to the value of a gift, provided the donor has exhausted all available administrative remedies within the IRS. Without § 7477, Tax Court jurisdiction would not be available in many cases. Ordinarily, the Tax Court has jurisdiction only if a deficiency in tax has been asserted by the IRS. If the IRS seeks to raise the value to be assigned to a gift, but the available unified credit fully shelters the IRS-asserted value from tax, there would be no deficiency and hence no Tax Court jurisdiction without § 7477. Yet assigning a higher value to the gift would consume more of the donor's unified credit and accelerate the point at which later transfers become taxable. Section 7477 permits the Taxpayer to petition the Tax Court to determine the valuation.

F. PENALTY FOR UNDERVALUATION

[¶ 14,025]

Often it appears that a taxpayer has little to lose and much to gain from a substantial understatement of value on a gift or estate tax return. If the return should escape careful audit and the value not be questioned, the taxpayer will have gained a saving in tax. If the valuation should be ques-

¶ 14,025

tioned by the IRS and adjusted upward, the only loss to the taxpayer from the understatement of value would appear to be the interest imposed on the late payment of tax.

Section 6662 deters such an approach by imposing a penalty of 20 percent of the underpayment if the understatement of value is substantial. §§ 6662(a) and (b)(5). The penalty does not apply unless the value stated on the return is one-half or less of the value finally determined. § 6662(g)(1). If the reported value is 25 percent or less of the finally determined value the penalty is 40 percent of the tax deficiency attributable to the undervaluation. § 6662(h)(2)(C). The penalty does not apply if there is reasonable cause for the underpayment and the taxpayer acted in good faith. § 6664(c).

Problems

[¶ 14,027]

1. Lois Olson died on January 10 of Year 1, when the applicable exclusion amount under § 2010 was $2,000,000. Her estate included closely held stock that was difficult to value. Because the Olson family wished to hold estate tax liability to the lowest amount possible, they persuaded the executor to value the stock at only $2,000,000, with the result that no estate tax was payable. The executor filed a return on the October 10 due date, reporting no tax due.

   More than two years later, the Internal Revenue Service questioned the value assigned to the stock. After extended negotiations, an agreement was reached whereby the stock would be valued at $9,000,000 for estate tax purposes. This raised the total estate tax liability to $3,220,000. The executor paid the additional $3,220,000 on October 10 of Year 4.

   What penalties and interest would be payable on October 10 of Year 4? (Assume that the § 6621(a)(2) rate was 10 percent per annum throughout Years 1 through 4, and ignore compounding, including § 6622.)

2. Assume the same facts, except that on the original return the stock was valued at $4,600,000, with the result that $1,196,000 of estate tax was payable. The executor paid the $1,196,000 with the return, which was filed on the return due date of October 10 of Year 1. Answer the same question as in Problem 1.

G. PENALTY FOR OVERVALUATION

[¶ 14,031]

There are circumstances in which overvaluation on the federal estate tax return may lead to imposition of the § 6662(e) penalty for overstatement of value with respect to the income tax. The Commissioner takes the position that adoption by a legatee of the value used for federal estate tax purposes as the basis for property received at death, pursuant to § 1014, is not a defense to imposition of the § 6662(e) penalty if the estate tax value is unreasonably high. Rev. Rul. 85–75, 1985–1 C.B. 376.

Typically, overvaluation poses such a problem in circumstances in which most or all of the estate is sheltered from tax by the marital deduction and unified credit, so that the legatees have an incentive to assign high values to estate property. In these circumstance the high valuation may trigger little or no estate tax liability, but the high valuation will increase the § 1014 basis for the property, thereby decreasing the amount of gain on a later sale.

Part IV

ESTATE TAX

(Chapter 11 of the Internal Revenue Code)

¶ 14,031

Chapter 15

PROPERTY OWNED

(Sections 2033 and 2034)

A. INTEGRATION OF GIFT TAX WITH ESTATE TAX

[¶ 15,001]

Upon the death of an individual, the taxable estate is determined under Chapter 11 (§ 2051) by including all property owned at death (§ 2033) and not subject to an exclusion from the estate tax (§§ 2031 (c) and 2032A), and certain additional property transferred during life under testamentary circumstances (§§ 2035 through 2042), and subtracting certain deductions for administration expenses and debts, casualty losses, charitable gifts, marital bequests and family owned business interests (§§ 2053 through 2057). Four additional steps are then undertaken to determine the actual dollar amount of the tax due from the estate.

1. The taxable estate is then aggregated with all the taxable gifts made during the individual's lifetime since the effective date of the integration, i.e., December 31, 1976. Any taxable gifts that have already been included in the taxable estate by virtue of one of the transfer sections of Chapter 11 (i.e., §§ 2035 through 2040) will not be included again (§ 2001(b)). Note that only taxable gifts are used.

2. A tentative estate tax is computed on the aggregate amount in step 1, above, using the uniform rate schedule provided in § 2001(c).

3. From the tentative tax determined under step 2, above, there is subtracted the total amount of gift tax payable under Chapter 12 with respect to gifts made by the individual since December 31, 1976, using the rate structure applicable under § 2001 (c) at the time of decedent's death. This requires a computation of the gift tax on gifts made after the effective date of the integrated system as if those gifts had been made in the year of death.

4. The excess of the tentative estate tax computed as in step 2, above, over the total amount of gift tax computed in step 3, above, is the estate tax imposed on the estate. Against this estate tax, the unified credit (§ 2010) is allowed on a dollar-for-dollar basis.

In the foregoing computation of the final estate tax payable, it may seem that the unified credit is taken twice, once in the gift tax determination and then again in computing the estate tax. However, this is not true; the unified credit taken for gift tax purposes is washed out in computing the estate tax imposed in step 4, above, and the credit is then allowed against the estate tax so imposed. Thus, the benefit of only a single unified credit is allowed to each individual for the individual's lifetime and upon death. Moreover because the gift tax determined in step 3 is allowed as a deduction against the estate tax, the fact that there is a lesser credit amount allowed under the gift tax will mean that in the case of sufficiently large taxable estates, the lower gift tax credit available will result in little if any additional aggregate tax.

There are three circumstances where gift taxes paid will not be available in full as a credit against estate taxes. First, where death occurs after repeal of the estate tax there will be no opportunity to use any gift tax paid as a credit against the estate tax as none will be due. Moreover, because gift tax paid but not used as a credit is not refundable, the taxpayer's estate will derive no financial benefit from any such gift taxes paid. Second, where the taxpayer dies with insufficient assets in his estate to enable the full amount of the gift tax paid to act as an offset against the estate tax, full potential use of the credit for gift taxes will not be made. For example, assume that X makes $1.5 million in taxable gifts in 2002 that (ignoring the annual per donee exclusion) will result in a gift tax of $210,000. If X dies in 2006, when the estate tax exemption is $2 million, possessed of $600,000 in assets, his estate tax before reducing it for gift taxes paid under § 2001 (b)(2) will only total $46,000. His estate will not be able to obtain full use of the $210,000 in gift taxes paid as a credit. Only $46,000 of gift taxes paid will serve to offset estate taxes of $46,000. Third, when gifts were taxed at a higher rate than they would have been taxed in the year of death had they been made then, full use of gift taxes paid as a credit may not occur. The reason for this is that § 2001(b) (2) only allows for a reduction of the tentative tax, on estate assets and gifts combined, by an amount equal to the gift tax which would have been due on all post 1976 gifts based on the rate structure "in effect at the decedent's death." If gift taxes were, for example, paid in 2002 at the 50% maximum rate then in effect and the taxpayer died in 2008 when the maximum rate was 45%, the full amount of the gift taxes paid in 2002 could not be used as a credit in 2008, when a lower maximum rate would be used to calculate the amount which is to be subtracted (under § 2001 (b)(2)) from the tentative tax on all combined estate assets and gifts to determine final tax liability.

It might also appear that some gifts of property that were made subject to the gift tax are being taxed twice when these same property interests are also included in the taxable estate under provisions that will be examined in the upcoming chapters. For example, take the case of an individual who creates a

¶ 15,001

trust, reserving to herself a life estate and conveying to her son the remainder interest following on her life estate. On creation of the trust, she will be required to treat the gift of the remainder as a taxable gift. Under § 2036, which we will examine in Chapter 18, at the death of the life tenant, the value of the remainder interest passing to the life tenant's son will be included in her estate. Double taxation does not occur, because, as mentioned in step 1, above, under § 2001(b) any previously taxable gift that is subsequently included in the estate is ignored when the aggregation of the taxable estate and taxable gifts described in step 1, above, occurs.

B. INTRODUCTORY BACKGROUND

[¶ 15,007]

Excise taxes are taxes imposed on specified privileged activities that are made subject to taxation. The estate tax is a tax levied on the privilege of being able to transfer gratuitously title to property at death and, as such, is classified as an excise tax. In keeping with the excise nature of the estate tax, § 2001(a) states that "A tax is hereby imposed on the transfer of the taxable estate * * *." Because of the excise nature of the tax, the courts, when dealing with other than direct transfers at death, often find it difficult to distinguish privileged, and consequently taxed, activities from similar non-privileged, and consequently untaxed, activities.

What is now § 2033 of the Internal Revenue Code of 1986 (and previously of the 1954 Code) was once known as § 811(a) of the Code of 1939. Its nature as a provision aimed at the property owned by the decedent in the probate sense, i.e., property reachable by the deceased's creditors in the probate proceeding, was set out in the statute itself for many years. Thus from 1916 to 1926 the section prescribed that property should be included in the gross estate "to the extent of the interest therein of the decedent at the time of his death which after his death is subject to the payment of the charges against his estate and the expenses of its administration and is subject to distribution as part of his estate." Under this language the Supreme Court, in United States v. Field, 255 U.S. 257 (1921), held that exercise of a general power of appointment did not subject the appointive property to the estate tax under this section because the donee did not own the property in the conventional sense.

In its original form § 2033, thus, was certainly limited to property owned by the decedent in the conventional sense, i.e., property owned within the meaning of the state law of property and estate administration. There are arrangements such as employee pension and death benefit plans that leave the grantor feeling no poorer than if the fund were in the grantor's bank account, yet it may be difficult in the extreme to claim that under the local law of property the decedent died owning an interest in the property. Is there a prospect that § 2033 can burst the bonds of its antecedents? Could § 2033 reach interests that might be deemed sufficiently significant to be taxable for federal estate tax purposes even though not considered interests in property

¶ 15,001

within the meaning of the local law of property? The cases and rulings in this chapter will shed some light on this question.

Before examining those authorities, it might be worthwhile noting that federal courts have considerable discretion in determining the precise nature of an individual taxpayer's interest in property under state property law. The need for such flexibility is apparent when one considers that, without this power, cooperating, unethical heirs could attain favorable tax results by, in essence, redefining the nature and extent of the deceased's property interests at a proceeding in a local probate court at which no truly adverse parties were present. The nature of the legal doctrine under which this is done was discussed at ¶ 1107.

[¶ 15,013]

HELVERING v. SAFE DEPOSIT AND TRUST CO. OF BALTIMORE

Supreme Court of the United States, 1942.
316 U.S. 56.

MR. JUSTICE BLACK:

* * *

Zachary Smith Reynolds, age 20, died on July 6, 1932. At the time, he was beneficiary of three trusts: one created by his father's will in 1918, one by deed executed by his mother in 1923, and one created by his mother's will in 1924. From his father's trust, the decedent was to receive only a portion of the income prior to his twenty-eighth birthday, at which time, if living, he was to become the outright owner of the trust property and all accumulated income. His mother's trusts directed that he enjoy the income for life, subject to certain restrictions before he reached the age of 28. Each of the trusts gave the decedent a general testamentary power of appointment over the trust property; in default of exercise of the power the properties were to go to his descendants, or if he had none, to his brother and sisters and their issue *per stirpes*.

The Commissioner included all the trust property within the decedent's gross estate for the purpose of computing the Federal Estate Tax. The Board of Tax Appeals and the Circuit Court of Appeals, however, held that no part of the trust property should have been included.

The case presents two questions, the first of which is whether the decedent at the time of his death had by virtue of his general powers of appointment, even if never exercised, such an interest in the trust property as to require its inclusion in his gross estate under [§ 2033].* * *

The Government argues that at the time of his death the decedent had an "interest" in the trust properties that should have been included in his gross estate, because he, to the exclusion of all other persons, could enjoy the income from them; would have received the corpus of one trust upon reaching the age of 28; and could alone decide to whom the benefits of all the trusts would pass at his death. These rights, it is said, were attributes of ownership substantially equivalent to a fee simple title, subject only to specified restrictions on alienation and the use of income. The respondents deny that the rights of the decedent with respect to any of the three trusts were substantially equivalent to ownership in fee, emphasizing the practical importance of the restrictions on alienation and the use of income, and arguing further that the decedent never actually had the capacity to make an effective testamentary disposition of the property because he died before reaching his majority.

We find it unnecessary to decide between these conflicting contentions on the economic equivalence of the decedent's rights and complete ownership.[1] For even if we assume with the Government that the restrictions upon the decedent's use and enjoyment of the trust properties may be dismissed as negligible and that he had the capacity to exercise a testamentary power of appointment, the question still remains: Did the decedent have "at the time of his death" such an "interest" as Congress intended to be included in a decedent's gross estate under § 302(a) of the Revenue Act of 1926 [now § 2033]? It is not contended that the benefits during life which the trusts provided for the decedent, terminating as they did at his death, made the trust properties part of his gross estate under the statute. And viewing § 302(a) in its background of legislative, judicial, and administrative history, we cannot reach the conclusion that the words "interest ... of the decedent at the time of his death" were intended by Congress to include property subject to a general testamentary power of appointment unexercised by the decedent.

The forerunner of § 302(a) of the Revenue Act of 1926 [now § 2033] was § 202(a) of the Revenue Act of 1916, 39 Stat. 777. In United States v. Field, 255 U.S. 257, this Court held that property passing under a general power of appointment *exercised* by a decedent was not such an "interest" of the decedent as the 1916 Act brought within the decedent's gross estate. While the holding was limited to *exercised* powers of appointment, the approach of the Court, the authorities cited, and certain explicit statements in the opinion left little doubt that the Court regarded property subject to *unexercised* general powers of appointment as similarly beyond the scope of the statutory phrase "interest of the decedent."

* * *

When it was held in the *Field* case that property subject to an *exercised* general testamentary power of appointment was not to be included in the decedent's gross estate under the Revenue Act of 1916, this Court referred to an amendment passed in 1919 which specifically declared property passing under an *exercised* general testamentary power to be part of the decedent's gross estate. The passage of this amendment, said the Court, "indicates that

---

1. In declining to pass upon this issue, we do not reject the principle we have often recognized that the realities of the taxpayer's economic interest, rather than the niceties of the conveyancer's art, should determine the power to tax. See Curry v. McCanless, 307 U.S. 357, 371, and cases there cited. Nor do we deny the relevance of this principle as a guide to statutory interpretation where, unlike here, the language of a statute and its statutory history do not afford more specific indications of legislative intent. Helvering v. Clifford, 309 U.S. 331.

¶ 15,013

Congress was at least doubtful whether the previous act included property passing by appointment." In the face of such doubts, which cannot reasonably be supposed to have been less than doubts with respect to *unexercised* powers, Congress nevertheless specified only that property subject to exercised powers should be included. From this deliberate singling out of *exercised* powers alone, without the corroboration of the other matters we have discussed, a Congressional intent to treat *unexercised* powers otherwise can be deduced. At the least, § 302(f) of the 1926 Act,[7] the counterpart of the 1919 amendment referred to in the *Field* case, represents a course of action followed by Congress, since 1919, entirely consistent with a purpose to exclude from decedents' gross estates property subject to unexercised general testamentary powers of appointment.

In no judicial opinion brought to our attention has it been held that the gross estate of a decedent includes, for purposes of the Federal Estate Tax, property subject to an unexercised general power. On the contrary, as the court below points out, "the courts have been at pains to consider whether property passed under a general power or not so as to be taxable under Section 302(f), a consideration which would have been absolutely unnecessary if the estate were taxable under 302 (a) [now § 2033] because of the mere existence of a general power whether exercised or not." 121 F.2d 307, 312. In addition, the uniform administrative practice until this case arose appears to have placed an interpretation upon the Federal Estate Tax contrary to that the Government now urges. No regulations issued under the several revenue acts, including those in effect at the time this suit was initiated, prescribe that property subject to an unexercised general testamentary power of appointment should be included in a decedent's gross estate. Because of the combined effect of all of these circumstances, we believe that a departure from the long-standing, generally accepted construction of § 302 (a), now contested for the first time by the Government, would override the best indications we have of Congressional intent.

[The portion of the opinion relating to a second issue has been omitted.]

Notes

[¶ 15,019]

1. Because of the narrow reading given to § 2033 in *Safe Deposit and Trust Co. of Baltimore* and other similar cases, it became necessary for Congress to pass a number of special provisions including in the taxable estate several items that might have been included under § 2033 had the courts given it a broader reach. These provisions will be treated extensively in a

---

7. "The value of the gross estate of the decedent shall be determined by including the value at the time of his death of all property, real or personal, tangible or intangible, wherever situated—

* * *

"(f) To the extent of any property passing under a general power of appointment exer-

cised by the decedent (1) by will, or (2) by deed executed in contemplation of, or intended to take effect in possession or enjoyment at or after, his death, except in case of a bona fide sale for an adequate and full consideration in money or money's worth;" 44 Stat. 9, 70–71.

number of subsequent chapters. The narrow reading given to § 2033 might profitably be contrasted with the broad reading given to § 61, which under the income tax constitutes the basic starting point for defining income. Much of the study of the estate tax in subsequent chapters will involve statutory provisions that sweep into the gross estate items excluded under the narrow readings given to § 2033, the basic starting point for a study of the estate tax. By contrast, much of the study of income tax typically involves an examination of provisions that narrow the scope of § 61, the basic starting point for a study of that tax.

The Supreme Court's restrictive reading of § 2033 in the above case should be contrasted with the Fifth Circuit's more liberal reading of that section in the case that follows at ¶ 15,025.

2. Generally, state and municipal bonds that are exempt from federal income taxation are nevertheless subject to estate and gift taxation because estate and gift taxes are levied on the privilege of transferring property and not on the property itself. In United States v. Wells Fargo Bank, 485 U.S. 351 (1988), the U.S. Supreme Court held that the same rule of taxability applied to the Public Housing Agency bonds exempted from "all taxes" by Congress because a transfer tax exemption was not intended.

[¶ 15,025]

FIRST VICTORIA NATIONAL BANK v. UNITED STATES

United States Court of Appeals, Fifth Circuit, 1980.
620 F.2d 1096.

GOLDBERG, Circuit Judge:

[Under the rice allotment program as it operated in Texas (decedent's domicile), the Secretary of Agriculture, with help of local officials, assigns to producers acreage on which rice may be grown under the Agricultural Assistance Act of 1938. Allotments that may be of significant value and are sold in local markets, are annually assigned to producers based on their history of rice production. Under certain circumstances, production history can be transferred to others. Since this history can carry with it the right to rice allotments, it, in itself, may be viewed as a thing of value. By federal law, the rice history of a producer can be transferred to the producer's heirs or devisees under limited circumstances and subject to certain requirements. This favorable history can then be used by the transferee to qualify for allotments in a given year. At issue in the case was whether the rice history of the decedent could be included in the estate.]

* * * The decedent, T. J. Babb, died on July 4, 1973. He had been engaged for many years in the production of rice, and had annually been granted rice allotments under the Act since at least 1958. By notices dated December 1, 1972, and May 1, 1973, Babb was issued producer rice allotments of 1208.3 acres. Prior to the deadline of May 1, 1973, in compliance with the applicable regulations, Babb allocated his 1973 allotment to farms on which he intended to produce rice for the crop year 1973.

¶ 15,019

At the time of his death, no producer rice allotment for 1974 had been determined for or issued to Babb. After Babb's death, by notice dated March 28, 1974, a producer rice allotment of 1142.6 acres was issued to his estate.

The estate tax return filed by the First Victoria National Bank, appellee here, as executor included no amount for either the value of decedent's interests in the rice allotment program or the value of the rice crop growing on July 4, 1973. After examination of the return by an agent of the Internal Revenue Service, the Service determined that items of $50,000, representing the value of crops growing on July 4, 1973, and $285,600, representing the value of decedent's rice producer allotment and rice production history, were includable in the gross estate.

* * *

The trial court granted appellee's motion, ruling that (1) on July 4, 1973, decedent's 1973 rice allotment was "used up" and its value merged with the growing crops (which were valued at $50,000), (2) decedent's history of rice production did not constitute property for estate tax purposes, and (3) there was no transfer of rice history upon Babb's death because any transfer was conditional upon subsequent events; to wit, that the transferees continue the rice farming operations. * * *

Is the value of "rice history acreage" includable in decedent's estate?

The proper resolution of this appeal turns on whether "rice history acreage" is "property" within the contemplation of I.R.C. §§ 2031 and 2033, n.1 supra. * * *

The attempt to define "property" is an elusive task. There is no cosmic synoptic definiens that can encompass its range. The word is at times more cognizable than recognizable. It is not capable of anatomical or lexicographical definition or proof. It devolves upon the court to fill in the definitional vacuum with the substance of the economics of our time.

* * *

The precise question before us is whether "rice acreage history" is "property" for purposes of the estate tax laws. In deciding this question, we start with the basic principle that "unless there is some special reason intrinsic to the particular provision [under consideration] ... , the general word 'property' has a broad reach in tax law." Du Pont de Nemours & Co. v. United States, 471 F.2d 1211, 1218, 200 Ct.Cl. 391 (1973). * * *

We find the analogy to the good will of a business to be * * * apt. No one can seriously doubt that good will is an asset whose value is includable in its owner's estate. Yet good will is an intangible asset which, like "rice history acreage," has value only because it carries the expectancy of receiving future assets of more concrete value. Like "rice history acreage," good will is an asset whose value may evaporate overnight. Like "rice history acreage" good will can be sold or devised. Like "rice history acreage," good will is ordinarily transferred along with other assets (in the case of good will, a business; in the case of rice acreage history, a rice farm).

¶ 15,025

Moreover, such expectancies as a right to compensation under a contingent fee contract, and a promise to return property to an estate if other property is insufficient to meet the estate's tax obligations, have been held to be "property" includable in a decedent's estate. "Rice history acreage" is no less certain an interest than these.

* * *

We also fail to find convincing appellee's strained attempt to analogize "rice history acreage" to an interest created after death, like a cause of action for wrongful death * * *. We note the crucial distinction that neither a cause of action for wrongful death nor Social Security survivors' benefits can ever be transferred by a decedent prior to his death. Each of these interests is "created" only upon a decedent's death, whereas Babb possessed rice acreage history prior to this death.

"Rice acreage history" is not only devisable and descendible, but also transferable *inter vivos*. Those heirs who inherited Babb's rice farming operations, by filing the requisite document with the county commission, were able to retain possession of the "rice history acreage" possessed by Babb the moment before his death. They could have converted the value of the rice acreage history into cash by selling it to others by early 1974, if not earlier. When an interest possesses these attributes, there can be no doubt that its value must be included in the owner's estate, for the focus of the estate tax is on the passage of an interest at death.

* * *

Note

[¶ 15,027]

In Estate of Andrews v. United States, 850 F.Supp. 1279 (E.D.Va.1994), (also discussed at ¶ 9001) the court included the value of the name of a well-known author in her taxable estate. Virginia Andrews was the predominant author in the "children in jeopardy" genre. At her death, Andrews' publisher proposed that her estate permit it to obtain ghostwriters for future works which would bear her name. The estate agreed and several highly successful books were figuratively, if not literally, ghostwritten. The decedent's executor had failed to include the value of Andrews' name on the estate tax return. The IRS assessed a deficiency and the court agreed with the IRS that, under these circumstances, the decedent's name was a valuable commercial asset, the value of which should be included in her taxable estate.

[¶ 15,029]

TECHNICAL ADVICE MEMORANDUM 9152005

August 30, 1991.

[In this Technical Advice Memorandum, the IRS was called upon to indicate the proper tax treatment for stolen property held by the decedent, a

¶ 15,025

resident of Texas, who had stolen valuable works of art during 1945 while serving with the US Army in Europe. At his death in 1980, the decedent bequeathed these items to his sister and brother and some of their children, who retained them for six years before attempting to sell them first in the legitimate art market and then in the illegal art market. Under the law of Texas, a holder of stolen property has title to such property which is superior to that of all potential claimants other than that of the person from whom the property was stolen. Borrowing from the line of income tax cases which holds that thieves and other criminals are taxable on the income from their criminal ventures, the IRS reached the following conclusion.]

Similarly, for federal estate tax purposes, no distinction should be drawn between a decedent's property that has been obtained by theft and decedent's property that has been lawfully obtained. If the decedent, at death, possessed the use and economic benefits of the stolen property that are equivalent to ownership, the decedent's lack of title to the stolen property does not affect its inclusion in the decedent's gross estate under § 2033 when the decedent can successfully transfer the property to his heirs. See also Burnet v. Wells, 289 U.S. at 678; Sanford's Estate v. Commissioner, 308 U.S. at 43.

Estate of Bluestein, 15 T.C. 770 (1950), a case cited by the taxpayer's representative in support of his contentions, is distinguishable from the present case because, in *Estate of Bluestein*, the property that had been converted was restored to its rightful owner immediately after the decedent's death during the course of the administration of the decedent's estate. In contrast, in the present case, the art objects were distributed to the Decedent's heirs, who held the property under their complete dominion and control for more than a decade.

* * *

The art objects that the Decedent stole during and immediately after World War II, and that he possessed at his death, are includible in his gross estate under § 2033 of the Code. [The IRS also held that since most stolen art is sold in the illicit market, that market should be employed in assigning a value to decedent's art for estate tax purposes.]

Notes

[¶ 15,031]

1. Under Texas law, after the one-year period for making claims against the estate has expired, the true owners can recover possession of stolen property in an action brought against the heirs. The potential result in this situation is to leave the thief's heirs without the stolen property and his estate with a substantial tax bill.

2. In Tech. Adv. Mem. 9207004, the IRS further pursued the estate tax treatment of the proceeds of crime, this time in the case of a drug dealer whose marijuana-laden plane crashed, killing the drug dealer pilot. The IRS, consistent with its analysis in Tech. Adv. Mem. 9152005, held that the seized illegal drugs were includible in the decedent's estate at their street value in

the locus of the crash. Moreover, despite the fact that the drugs were seized by Florida officials, the IRS held that to allow a deduction under either § 2053 (claims against the estate) or § 2054 (casualty losses by the estate) to reflect this fact "would violate the sharply defined public policy against drug trafficking." See, Turnier, *The Pink Panther Meets the Grim Reaper: The Estate Taxation of the Fruits of Crime*, 72 N.C. L.Rev. 163 (1993).

C. INTERESTS AT DEATH

[¶ 15,037]

1. GENERATION SKIPPING

Even a careless reading of §§ 2001 and 2033 would lead to the conclusion that one who dies holding only a life estate would not be subjected to estate tax under these sections. This is so because the decedent died possessing no interest which he could transfer. On this principle rested much of the tax-minimization estate planning of bygone years. A life estate to a child with remainder to the grandchildren, embroidered perhaps with a nontaxable power of appointment, which is discussed more fully in Chapter 22, gave the child much of the substance of ownership without requiring the child to pay the rate that would have been exacted had the property been left to the child outright. But the old order has changed. Generation skipping transfers are now subject (after allowance of a generous exclusion) to special supplementary tax, imposed under Chapter 13 of the Code. That subject is complex; it is treated in this book in Chapter 29.

[¶ 15,043]

2. EFFECT OF DEATH ON INTERESTS HELD

At death, interests in property that are potentially includible in the estate are often affected in a fashion that may have significant tax consequences. For example, on some occasions such interests have their values dramatically enhanced and on others they are terminated or voided—all with dramatic results for the estate of the decedent.

In Estate of Riegelman v. Commissioner, 253 F.2d 315 (2d Cir.1958) the court included in the gross estate of a deceased attorney amounts to which his estate was entitled pursuant to the firm's partnership agreement. The agreement called for the estate of the taxpayer to be paid an amount which reflected the value of: (1) the deceased's partner's share of undistributed profits realized and collected by the partnership prior to death; (2) the deceased's share of profits realized and collected after his death attributable to work performed before his death; and (3) a share, for a limited period of time, of post death fees and profits attributable to work completed after the deceased's death on matters in process in the firm at his death as well as certain matters upon which work was commenced and completed by the firm after death. While the decedent's executor conceded that items (1) and (2) were properly includible in his gross estate, the executor objected to including in decedent's gross estate item (3) payments received for work done subsequent to decedent's death. The court in including this item in decedent's gross estate noted:

> The right of Riegelman's estate to share in the profits of the partnership for the stipulated period after his death was a chose in action, in lieu of that to which it would have succeeded in the absence of an agreement, which passed from Riegelman to his estate as a part of his wealth and hence was properly includible in his gross estate for the purpose of computing an estate tax.

While death can create or fix the value of items of wealth that are includible in decedent's gross estate, as was done in *Riegelman,* it can also, as the case which follows demonstrates, extinguish wealth possessed during life.

[¶ 15,061]

ESTATE OF MOSS v. COMMISSIONER

United States Tax Court, 1980.
74 T.C. 1239.

IRWIN, Judge:

[John A. Moss, prior to his death, sold his interest in a mortuary and related realty to his employees under a contract that provided for monthly installment payments which were characterized by the court as "adequate and full consideration," and which were spread out over nine years and seven months. The note for the stock was referred to in the contract as Note B and the note for the related realty was referred to as Note C. The contract provided that: "Unless sooner paid, all sums, whether principal or interest, shall be deemed canceled and extinguished as though paid upon death of J.A. Moss." When the parties entered into the contract, Moss, who was 72 years old, was of good health and there was no indication that he would die prior to his collecting all payments under the contract. Monthly payments were made under the contract until Moss unexpectedly died about 16 months later. Pursuant to the contract, no further payments were made.

The principal issue presented for consideration by the court was whether the remaining payments under Notes B and C, which were extinguished at his death, are includible in Moss's gross estate.]

In *Estate of Buckwalter*, decedent's son was indebted to a bank on a 20–year note due in 1971 bearing 4 1/2 percent interest. Decedent proposed that he and his son enter into an arrangement whereby decedent would pay off the unamortized principal of his son's note on December 31, 1954. The son would pay him the identical monthly amounts which would have been due the bank, except that interest would be computed at 2 1/2 percent so that the entire loan would be repaid in 1968 rather than in 1971. The son was instructed to keep the transaction secret, the payments were to be a "matter of honor" and the decedent stated that it was [his] intention not to show "in any way that [the son was] in any way indebted to me, otherwise [decedent] would be required to pay in Penna. a personal property tax each year." Decedent recognized that he probably would not be alive at the end of the amortization period, and stated that his son was to be entirely free of any obligation to his estate. He added a long postscript to the letter setting forth a summary schedule of 30–day payments, showing components of interest and principal in each such payment in December of each year as well as "balance of amortized principal" until final payment in 1968. He also stated that his son might "cut away" the schedule and "destroy the rest of the letter after all details are consummated."

In a second letter to his son about a week later, after the proposal had been accepted, decedent stated that he was sending his son a schedule for payments and credits for the period January 1, 1955, to May 23, 1962, and that for the period thereafter he had "a schedule made up to show complete amortization of an honor loan," which he intended to seal and enclose in his lock box with a legend on the envelope in his son's handwriting reading "Personal Property of Abraham L. Buckwalter, Jr." In a single sentence, decedent informed his son that he could "consider the proposition on my part as a form of annuity at 2 and 1/2%."

We held that decedent had an interest in a debt owed to him by his son at the time of his death and that the unpaid principal was includable in his gross estate under section 2033. The taxpayer there argued that in substance, decedent merely had purchased an annuity from his son which terminated with his death, and therefore, nothing should be included in his gross estate. We disagreed with the contention that the substance of the transaction was an annuity and held that decedent had an interest in the loan at the time of his death.

Respondent contends that decedent, in this case, simply chose to pass the funeral home business to his employees under the guise of the notes which were canceled upon death rather than through his will as he had planned prior to 1972 and, therefore, this case is no different than the situation in *Buckwalter*.

Petitioner argues that the case at bar is factually distinguishable. We agree. In *Buckwalter*, the decedent retained control of the entire debt until his death. The son was not relieved of the debt until he removed the evidence of the loan after the decedent's death. Therefore, at any time prior to his death, decedent could have revoked his decision to cancel the debt at his death and required the son to be obligated to his estate. The decedent sought to achieve the same result as a bequest in a will by keeping the details of the loan contained in a sealed envelope in his own lock box and permitting the son to cancel the debt at his death.

This is not the case here. The parties have stipulated that decedent's sale of stock for which the notes were issued was a bona fide sale for adequate and full consideration. The cancellation provision was part of the bargained for consideration provided by decedent for the purchase price of the stock. As such, it was an integral provision of the note. We do not have a situation, therefore, where the payee provided in his will or endorses or attaches a statement to a note stating that the payor is to be given a gift by the cancellation of his obligation on the payee's death.

¶ 15,061

We believe there are significant differences between the situation in which a note contains a cancellation provision as part of the terms agreed upon for its issue and where a debt is canceled in a will. The most significant difference for purposes of the estate tax is, as petitioner points out, that a person can unilaterally revoke a will during his lifetime, and, therefore, direct the transfer of his property, at his death. All interest that decedent had in the notes lapsed at his death.

Respondent next contends that the cancellation provision can be considered an assignment of the notes by the decedent to his employees to become effective upon his death. We believe that this is simply a variation of his argument that the cancellation provision is similar to a bequest in a will, and we reject it for the same reasons that we rejected that argument.

* * * [T]he situation here is analogous to that of an annuity or an interest or estate limited for decedent's life. Since there is not [an] interest remaining in decedent at his death, we hold that the notes are not includable in his gross estate.

Respondent also relies on Stewart v. United States, 158 F.Supp. 25 (N.D.Cal.1957), affd. in part and revd. in part 270 F.2d 894 (9th Cir.1959), cert. denied 361 U.S. 960 (1960), as presenting an analogous situation. In that case, the decedent purchased annuities providing for the payment of monthly sums to her for life, beginning when she reached a designated age. The policies also provided that in the event the decedent died before payment of any annuities or before the amount paid in had been returned, payment was to be made to certain named beneficiaries. A few months prior to her death, the decedent exercised an option in the policy under which the companies would pay her a designated sum for 240 months, and decedent relinquished her right to make payment contingent on her life. In the event of her death prior to the expiration of the 240 months, payment was to be made to her grandchildren. The decedent, either solely or with her husband, had the right to change the beneficiaries. The Court held that the annuities were includable in the decedent's estate under section 811(a) of the Internal Revenue Code of 1939, the predecessor to section 2033.

Stewart is obviously distinguishable. In that case, the decedent had the right to receive 240 monthly payments. If she died prior to receiving all the payments, the payments continued to be paid to named third parties. The payor was obligated, therefore, to continue making payments under the contract. Moreover, the decedent retained the right to designate the beneficiaries under the contract.

Even should we consider the payments to decedent as an "annuity" the value of the notes would still not be includable in his gross estate. In Estate of Bergan v. Commissioner, 1 T.C. 543 (1943), the decedent had made an inter vivos transfer to her sister of her interest in an estate in exchange for her sister's promise to care for and support the decedent for the remainder of the decedent's life. We held therein that the decedent did not retain a life interest in the income from the transferred property under the predecessor of section 2036 because no trust was created to secure the "annuity" nor did the decedent reserve to herself the right to the income from the transferred property. The decedent merely contracted with her sister for her support and her share of the estate was transferred as the consideration for such contract. Similarly, in the present case, decedent transferred his stock and the * * * property as full consideration for Note B and Note C. While the notes were secured by a stock pledge agreement, this fact, alone, is insufficient to include the value of the notes in decedent's gross estate. * * *

Note

[¶ 15,063]

A SCIN involving sale of a family restaurant by a father to a son passed judicial scrutiny in Estate of Constanza v. Commissioner, 320 F.3d 595 (6th Cir. 2003). The Court of Appeals did note that a SCIN involving family members is presumed to be a gift, with the presumption rebuttable by an affirmative showing which it found present.

Planning Note

[¶ 15,073]

Lest visions of sugar plums dance in your head as a result of the *Moss* case, you should understand that it is uniformly agreed that, if a self-cancelling installment note (SCIN) is employed, the purchasers must pay a premium that reflects the economic advantage to them which results from the cancellation privilege. Failure to provide for a premium would result in the vendor being deemed to have made a taxable gift to the vendee equal to the fair market value of the premium which should have been created. (¶ 3097 and ¶ 3127) The premium must be in the form of either a purchase price premium, an interest rate premium or a combination of the two. Given this premium consideration, in the law of large numbers, the Treasury should lose no revenue because of the use of such devices. For every taxpayer who, like Moss, dies earlier than expected, there should be a sufficient number of taxpayers who use a SCIN to sell a business and collect in full on their SCIN and who, because of the use of premiums, die with estates which are larger than they would have been had a SCIN not been employed.

In addition to being required to develop the value of the premium component based on actuarial factors, the authorities also agree that the taxpayer must then adjust the premium to reflect added considerations regarding the vendor's projected life span. For example, a seventy-year old vendor with a history of heart disease would be expected to employ a SCIN with a premium significantly in excess of the premium which a septuagenarian of normal health might be expected to employ.

Taking some of the bloom off the SCIN rose is Estate of Frane v. Commissioner, 998 F.2d 567 (8th Cir.1993), (¶ 32,043), in which the court held that, under §§ 453B and 691, where vendor and vendee are related, cancellation, at death, of the installment notes should give rise to income in respect of a decedent equal to the thus far unrecognized gain despite the fact that it reflects sales proceeds that will never be received. Should this negative

¶ 15,061

tax result be considered in assigning a lower premium to a SCIN with related parties?

[¶ 15,079]

3. LAPSING RIGHTS IN FAMILY CONTROLLED BUSINESSES (SECTION 2704)

Suppose that a parent seeks to affect the value of property that the parent owns with a child by providing that some of the parent's rights lapse at death, thereby enhancing the value of the child's rights in the property. Because the parent has not formally transferred property to the child, the parent hopes to escape the reach of § 2033. Congress has added § 2704 to the Code to cope with such ploys in a limited context. That section deals with the estate and gift tax ramifications of lapsing rights involving closely held businesses. The gift tax discussion of these rights is found at ¶ 11,091. If death triggers a lapse of voting or liquidation rights in a corporation or partnership, the lapse is deemed to result in a transfer of the lapsed rights for estate tax purposes if the individual holding the lapsing rights and that person's family, both before and after death, hold control of the business. For these purposes, control is defined as 50 percent of voting rights in a corporation or 50 percent of the capital or profits in a partnership.

Under § 2704(a)(2) the value included in the estate of the holder of the lapsing rights is the value of all interests in the business entity owned by the holder before lapse over the value of all such interests immediately after the lapse. Where restrictions to liquidate a corporation or partnership are present and are either the product of an arm's-length commercial arrangement with a lender or are imposed by law, they are to be ignored in determining the value of the transferred interest. In addition to the value determined under § 2704(a)(2), there is also included in the estate of the deceased under § 2033 or other relevant sections the value of the property owned by the deceased with respect to which lapsing rights existed.

For example, assume that Father owned all 100 shares of class A common stock of Ajax Inc., that Daughter owned all 900 shares of class B common stock of Ajax and that no other class of Ajax stock existed. The class A and class B stock are identical except that class A stock is entitled to 10 votes per share and the class B stock is entitled to one vote per share. Moreover, in the event that Ajax is liquidated, the holders of class A stock are entitled to receive, on a per share basis, nine times the amount of property that the holders of class B stock are entitled to receive. Both the super voting rights of the class A stock and its liquidation preference lapse at Father's death. Assume further that before Father's death the Ajax common stock, held by him was worth $1.2 million and that after his death it was worth $200,000. Under § 2704(a)(2) there is to be included in Father's estate the $1 million decline in the value of his stock attributable to the lapse. Furthermore, the $200,000 value assigned to the Ajax common stock held by Father's estate after lapse is to be included in his taxable estate under § 2033.

D. CONTINGENT INTERESTS

[¶ 15,085]

Under § 6163 the executor may elect to postpone the portion of the estate tax generated by inclusion in the gross estate of "a reversionary or remainder interest" until six months after the termination of the precedent interest. If undue hardship would result the Commissioner can extend the date for payment for an additional period of up to three years. Section 6163 plainly contemplates that remainder and reversionary interests are includable in the gross estate under § 2033. But what if the future interest is contingent—one that may fail upon an event distant in time, e.g., death of a named person without issue? Are such contingent interests subject to estate taxation, and, if so, at what valuation? What are the competing considerations and how are they to be reconciled?

[¶ 15,091]

IN RE ESTATE OF HILL

United States Court of Appeals, Second Circuit, 1952.
193 F.2d 724.

SWAN, Chief Judge.

[Walter J. Hill, the decedent, at the time of his death possessed three distinct contingent interests under an inter vivos trust that he had established. The issue before the court was the degree to which, in each of those three cases, contingent interests should give rise to includible property.]

The taxpayer contends that each of the decedent's three interests in the trust property is so speculative as to be incapable of valuation and therefore nothing whatever should have been included in the gross estate because of the trust. This contention, however, is not seriously pressed with respect to the right to receive annually excess net income during the life of the trust, and obviously could not be supported if it were. During the years 1919 to 1943 inclusive the settlor had received from this source an aggregate of more than $228,000; and for the years 1944 to 1947 inclusive he or his estate received $42,000 additional. At the date of his death the annual income requirements of the trust were $5,000 to the wife and $12,000 to the daughter, while the net income of the trust for 1944 and the three succeeding years has averaged better than $27,000. Actuarially the trust might be expected to continue for about 32 years after the settlor's death. The annual payments are known, the earnings of the trust can be estimated, and the difference will be the surplus returnable to the settlor's estate. Discounted to present worth, that surplus should be included in the taxable estate. The taxpayer estimates that on the assumption that excess income maintains the previous average rate over the remainder of the trust, the value on March 4, 1944 of the right to receive it would be $176,000, using a discount factor of 4 per cent. We do not pass upon the validity of the taxpayer's assumption or discount factor, for the case must be remanded for reasons hereafter explained and the valuation of the right to excess income is for the Tax Court's determination in the first instance. Appellant further argues that in terms of what this right would sell for in the market, a prospective purchaser would require the actuarial value of so uncertain a right to be drastically discounted. This is also a matter for the Tax Court's consideration upon which we express no opinion.

Next to be considered is the decedent's right during the continuance of the trust to have returned to him or his estate upon the happening of certain contingencies such portions of the trust corpus as the trustees in their discretion should determine to be not needed for the subsequent administration of the trust. * * * [C]ontingencies upon which portions of the corpus may be returned to the settlor or his estate are the death of the wife or the daughter during the life of the trust. If the wife dies before the daughter the trustees are to select such portion of the trust property "as shall in their judgment, which shall be final in the premises, be sufficient in amount and character safely to produce such amount of income as shall be reasonably necessary for the subsequent administration of the trust." This portion they shall retain as trust property and the balance they shall deliver to the settlor or his estate. If the daughter dies before the wife the portion retained as trust property must be sufficient in the judgment of the trustees, "which shall be final in the premises" safely to produce "a net income, after the payment of taxes thereon," of $12,000 per year. The taxpayer argues that because the decedent's expectancy of having returned to him or his estate some part of the corpus during the life of the trust depended upon the exercise of discretionary powers conferred upon the trustees, it was not a judicially enforceable right and therefore was not an "interest" in property within the meaning of section 811(a) [now § 2033]. In this the taxpayer is in error. The case upon which he particularly relies, Commissioner v. Irving Trust Co., 147 F.2d 946 (2d Cir.1945), is distinguishable. There the trustees had absolute discretion in the return of corpus, without any standard having been set up to guide them. Here the settlor has directed that they return so much of the corpus as they determine not "reasonably necessary for the subsequent administration of the trust." At the date of death the trust property was worth $786,569.60 and produced an annual income $10,000 in excess of the amount needed to pay the wife and daughter. If the wife shall die before the daughter, as is actuarially probable, the trustees will be relieved of the annual $5,000 payment to her and it seems likely that they would exercise their discretion to return some part of the corpus as they had previously done when her share of the income was reduced by her remarriage. If they refused to do so we cannot doubt, even though the trustees' judgment is declared "final in the premises," that a court of equity would intervene to enforce the settlor's mandate that they retain only so much as is reasonably necessary safely to produce the income needed for their subsequent administration. The amount of corpus returnable to the decedent's estate under these provisions of the trust is somewhat speculative and admits of no accurate determination, but we cannot doubt that the right had value at the date of the settlor's death. As this court said in Bankers Trust Co. v. Higgins, 136 F.2d 477, 479, " * * * we should not demand certainty; better a fair guess than the one answer sure to be wrong."

¶ 15,091

The decedent's other interest in the corpus was a contingent reversion upon termination of the trust. This was conditional upon the complete failure of the daughter's issue. Actuarially it is most unlikely that the estate will receive anything under this provision. At the settlor's death there was alive an infant granddaughter who might marry and have children before the trust terminated. Also the daughter aged 35 survived; she was married and the prospect that she might have additional children was not improbable. We agree with the taxpayer's contention that the possibility of enjoyment by the decedent's estate of this contingent reversion was so remote at the date of death that the reversion had no ascertainable value. Commissioner v. Cardeza's Estate, 173 F.2d 19, 23; see also Robinette v. Helvering, 318 U.S. 184, 189 (1943).

* * *

We agree with the taxpayer that under section 811(a) [now § 2033] the proper method of computation in the case of a trust is to determine as of the date of death the values of the decedent's rights in the trust property and to include in the gross estate the sum of such values.

The case is remanded for further proceedings consistent with this opinion.

Notes

[¶ 15,097]

1.   The Treasury adopts a realistic attitude on the subject of fertility. Thus, in Rev. Rul. 61–88, 1961–1 C.B. 417, where the life tenant was a married woman aged 44 at the time of the decedent's death and the decedent's remainder was conditioned on the death without issue of the life tenant, the ruling takes the position that the remainder is one of substantial value—to be valued by the usual principles unless it is shown by medical evidence that birth of issue is impossible. An earlier ruling dealing with the problem of the deductibility of a charitable remainder contingent on death without issue of two childless women of 55 and 59 years of age generously ruled that the contingent bequest to charity was sufficiently assured to warrant allowance of the deduction. Rev. Rul. 59–143, 1959–1 C.B. 247.

2.   Though not to be classified as a contingent interest in the property sense, what of a deceased attorney's claim for a contingent fee? Suppose the attorney dies in midstream; should the executor include something in the attorney's gross estate with respect to this item, and, if so, how is a value to be placed on the property right? The Treasury's position on the question should not occasion surprise. Consider this extract from Rev. Rul. 55–123, 1955–1 C.B. 443:

> In the instant case, the decedent's right to receive payment for services rendered in cases completed in his lifetime, was fixed by contract. After the decedent's death, his personal representatives had a right to recover on a *quantum meruit* basis the reasonable value of the services rendered by him on a contingent fee basis in the cases in which settle-

ments or judgments were obtained after his death. This right of the personal representatives is a chose in action, a species of personal property.

A determination of the fair market value as of the date of decedent's death or other applicable valuation date, of the right of the personal representatives of a deceased attorney to recover for services rendered on a contingent fee basis in cases remaining unsettled as of such date may present a difficult problem, but it is possible to fairly appraise or estimate the value of such right. * * *

In the instant case, the executor elected to have the property of the estate valued in accordance with Section 811(j) [now § 2032 which now provides an alternate valuation date of six months] of the Internal Revenue Code of 1939; that is, one year after the date of death or as of the date of sale, exchange, or other disposition in the interim. The amount realized by the estate during the year following the decedent's death for his services constitutes a disposition of the claim for compensation and the amount received therefor represents the fair market value of the property as of the date of such disposition. In view of the foregoing, it is held that the fair market value as of the applicable valuation date of the right of the executor to receive compensation for legal services performed by the decedent on a contingent fee basis is includible in his gross estate as an interest in property within the purview of [§ 2033].

3. If the contingency is resolved within six months after the decedent's death, the option under § 2032 to value the property as of six months after the date of death (or the disposition date if that is earlier) averts the horrible prospect of paying an estate tax on a value that later evaporates. But what if the event that saps all value from the contingent interest takes place six months and a day after the decedent's death? Why not tax at full value when the interest falls in—and wholly exempt from tax when the interest fails?

E. EMPLOYEE DEATH BENEFITS

[¶ 15,103]

Death benefits that an employer pays to the estate or survivors of an employee can often be of significant value. Typically these benefits are paid to individuals designated by the employee, but on occasion they are payable to persons designated by the employer. Two principal issues arise in this area. First, under what circumstances are such benefits included in the estate and, second, when so included, what is the proper amount to be included?

[¶ 15,109]

1. ISSUE OF INCLUSION

Employee death benefits payable to the decedent's estate under an existing plan that had granted these rights to the employee before his or her death, or which rather than being payable to his or her estate are payable to

individuals designated by the employee, are includible in the taxable estate of
the deceased. See Rev. Rul. 65–217, 1965–2 C.B. 214, and authorities cited
therein. Benefits provided at the discretion of the employer, after death, to
individuals designated by the employer are treated differently. Revenue Ruling 65–217 indicates that such benefits are to be excluded from the estate on
the ground that, because no right to such property existed at death, the
benefits may not be deemed to be passing from the decedent. A similar result
prevails where, although the benefits were not discretionary at death, they
were, under the terms of the employer's plan, payable to a class of individuals
designated by the employer, such as the surviving spouse or lineal issue. Since
tax consequences of vast magnitude revolve around whether designation of
the class of beneficiaries has been made by the employer or the employee, it is
not surprising to discover that the IRS occasionally takes the position that, for
purposes of § 2033, designations of beneficiaries by employers should be
imputed to employee-shareholders.

[¶ 15,115]

ESTATE OF TULLY

United States Court of Claims, 1976.
528 F.2d 1401.

KUNZIG, Judge.

The single issue presented in this estate tax case is the includability in
decedent Edward A. Tully, Sr.'s gross estate of death benefits paid directly to
Tully's widow by his employer. Plaintiffs (coexecutors) move for partial
summary judgment claiming that no estate tax provision compels such treatment. Defendant's cross-motion counters that the death benefits must be
added to the gross estate as required either by section 2038(a)(1) or section
2033 of the Internal Revenue Code of 1954. We agree with plaintiffs and hold
the sum at issue not includable in Tully's gross estate.

The facts in this case are uncontested. Before his death, Tully was
employed by Tully and DiNapoli, Inc. (T & D), a company owned 50% by
decedent and 50% by Vincent P. DiNapoli. On July 1, 1959, Tully, DiNapoli
and T & D entered into a contract whereby T & D promised to pay death
benefits to the Tully and DiNapoli widows. Later, in October 1963, the same
parties amended the 1959 agreement to limit the maximum amount of death
payments to $104,000. On March 7, 1964, Tully died. T & D paid his widow
the $104,000 called for in the contract.

Because the death benefits were paid directly by T & D to the widow,
plaintiffs did not include this sum in Tully's gross estate when they filed the
estate tax return. On audit, the Internal Revenue Service (IRS) concluded
that the $104,000 was part of Tully's gross estate and assessed an estate tax
deficiency. Plaintiffs paid the deficiency, filed a refund claim and by timely
petition filed in this court, brought the present action after the IRS disallowed
their claim.

* * *

The Government relies only on sections 2038(a)(1) and 2033, and no others, in its argument that the death benefits at issue here are includable in Tully's gross estate.

Defendant's contentions, specifically its argument that sections 2038(a)(1) and 2033 must be treated as virtually identical, suggest at the outset that we consider the basic philosophy of estate tax law. As enacted by Congress, the primary purpose of the estate tax is to tax "the transfer of property at death." C. Lowndes & R. Kramer, Federal Estate and Gift Taxes § 2.2 (3d Ed. 1974). If sufficient incidents of ownership in an item of property are given away before death, no tax will be imposed. Since all estate tax statutes are direct[ed] at taxing property transferred at death, it can become easy to confuse their operation or to apply them in an overlapping fashion.

Within this context, the two estate tax sections involved in the instant case, 2038(a)(1) and 2033, both impose a tax on property transferred at death. However, they are directed at two different situations. Section 2038(a)(1) is specific in its terms. It taxes property which an individual has given away while retaining enough "strings" to change or revoke the gift. Section 2033 is more general in its approach, and taxes property which has never really been given away at all.

Certain of defendant's arguments misconstrue this basic difference between section 2038(a)(1) and section 2033. By suggesting that the same "controls" over property which might represent a section 2038(a)(1) "power" can also be viewed as a section 2033 "interest," the Government attempts to turn section 2033 into an estate tax "catch all." This was not the intent of Congress in enacting section 2033. Congress has provided a "catch all" in the income tax statutes. It has not done so in the estate tax area. Therefore, defendant's efforts to treat the two sections as virtually identical by the "catch all" method are misplaced.

In accordance with this analysis, our inquiry takes two avenues. First, did Tully transfer the death benefits but keep a power to change or revoke them until the time of his death? If so, section 2038(a)(1) applies. Second, did Tully have an "interest" in the benefits at his death? If he had an "interest," section 2033 applies.

[The Court's explanation as to why § 2038 is not applicable is reproduced in Chapter 19, ¶ 19,055.]

Nor does section 2033 require addition of the benefits to Tully's gross estate. The Government argues that corporate control, "pegging" the benefits to Tully's salary, and naming "widow" as beneficiary constituted section 2033 "interests" kept by Tully until his death. We found above that these facts did not give rise to a section 2038(a)(1) "power." We also determine that they did not create a section 2033 "interest."

Having found that Tully transferred the death benefits to his wife and that he could not reach them for his own use, he could not have kept a section 2033 "interest." The *de minimis* associations Tully may have still had with

¶ 15,115

the benefits are not strong enough to force a conclusion that decedent never transferred his interests in the benefits to his wife.

* * *

Defendant would use section 2033 as a "catch all." The simple answer to this is that section 2033 is not a "catch all," but applies to situations where decedent kept so much control over an item of property that in substance he still owns the property. "Interest" as used in section 2033 connotes a stronger control than "power" as used in section 2038(a)(1). If controls over property cannot rise to the dignity of section 2038(a)(1) "powers" they equally cannot create section 2033 "interests." In the instant case, having failed to establish that corporate stock ownership, "pegging" the benefits to Tully's salary and naming the "widow" as beneficiary created section 2038(a)(1) "powers," defendant equally fails to demonstrate that the same facts create section 2033 "interests."

In summary, we have considered an employee plan in which the employee transferred death benefits to his wife, but kept until his death certain tangential associations with the plan. These *de minimis* associations did not rise to the level of section 2038(a)(1) "powers" to "alter, amend, revoke or terminate" the transfer, and did not constitute "interests" sufficient to force the conclusion that section 2033 applies. Therefore, the death benefits at issue here were not includable in Tully's gross estate.

Note

[¶ 15,121]

In Rev. Rul. 55–83, 1955–1 C.B. 112, the IRS ruled that there is no inclusion in the estate with respect to social security lump-sum death benefits, which under social security rules are payable to a surviving spouse, because the deceased has no control over the designation of the beneficiary. To the same effect is Rev. Rul. 67–277, 1967–2 C.B. 322 and Rev. Rul. 75–145, 1975–1 C.B. 298, which deals with the tax treatment of uncashed benefit checks.

Planning Note

[¶ 15,124]

Since, in the absence of a showing of employee control of the employer, we do not include employee death benefits in the taxable estate unless such benefits are paid to the estate of the employee or to individuals designated by the employee, corporate counsel might often be expected to advise against establishment of plans under which benefits are payable to beneficiaries designated by the employee or are payable to the employee's estate.

In structuring a death benefit plan, care must also be exercised to consider nontax factors such as the impact of the different types of plans on employee morale. The employer might quite possibly decide that the benefit, in terms of employee morale, derived with respect to most employees from a taxable plan that allows the employee to designate beneficiaries, outweighs the detriment that the employer suffers with respect to a few wealthy employees as a result of establishing a plan that has a negative tax impact on a handful of highly compensated employees. By creating a plan that pays death benefits for lowly compensated individuals to their estates and pays death benefits for highly compensated individuals to an employer-designated class of individuals, the employer might be able to maximize its credits with each group of employees.

[¶ 15,127]

2. AMOUNT INCLUDIBLE

Where an inclusion is appropriate with respect to a death benefit because, for example, the benefit was payable to the employee's estate or the employee had the right to designate beneficiaries, the issue still remains as to the amount properly includible. Is the value included the estimated fair market value of the benefit before death or is it the fair market value of the benefit transferred? For example, presume that under a death benefit plan $100,000 is to be transferred to the estate of a 52–year-old male employee if he is employed at death. The employee and his insurance agent, moments before the employee's fatal heart attack at the nineteenth hole at the country club, might consider the right to be worth only $5,000 and the employer's actuary might have asked him to set aside only that amount to meet the employer's responsibilities to this employee under the plan. At death, do we include this value in the employee's estate on the ground that it is the value of what he owned, or do we include the fair market value of the rights transferred to the estate, i.e., $100,000? The following case addresses that issue.

[¶ 15,133]

GOODMAN v. GRANGER

United States Court of Appeals, Third Circuit, 1957.
243 F.2d 264, cert. denied, 355 U.S. 835 (1957).

KALODNER, Circuit Judge.

When does the federal estate tax attach?

More specifically stated, when does such tax attach to a decedent-employee's contractual right to annual deferred compensation payments from his employer, payable to his estate after his death?

That problem, of first impression, is presented by this appeal by the government from a judgment in favor of the taxpayer, Eleanor D. Goodman, administratrix of the estate of Jacques Blum, deceased, in a suit brought by her in the District Court for the Western District of Pennsylvania to recover estate taxes and interest alleged to have been erroneously assessed and collected.

The District Court, subscribing to the taxpayer's contention, concluded as a matter of law that the decedent's contractual right was to be " * * * valued during decedent's lifetime and *at the moment before death* * * * " and made the factual finding that at such moment the contractual right was "value-less", for reasons which will subsequently be discussed. In its opinion the District Court stated "It must be admitted that if the value in the contracts is to be fixed *the moment after death*, then the Government is correct in its contention in this case." [Emphasis in original.]

* * *

The decedent, Jacques Blum, for several years prior to his sudden death of a heart attack at the age of 52 on May 2, 1947, was executive vice-president of Gimbel Brothers, Inc. ("Gimbels") in charge of its Pittsburgh store.

On October 19, 1944, June 1, 1945 and May 26, 1946, decedent entered into identical contracts of employment with Gimbel Brothers covering the years ending January 31, 1945, January 31, 1946 and January 31, 1947, respectively. Each contract provided for a basic salary of $50,000 per year, and for additional "contingent benefits" of $2,000 per year for fifteen years "after the employee ceases to be employed by the employer" by reason of death or otherwise. The post-employment "contingent payments" were to be made only if the employee duly performed the services agreed upon and did not engage in a competing business within a specified period after termination of his employment; and they were to be reduced if his post-employment earnings from a non-competing business plus the contingent payments exceeded seventy-five percent of his yearly average compensation under the contracts. Any of the fifteen annual contingent payments which fell due after the employee's death were to be paid to his estate, or to a nominee designated in his will.

The third contract for the period of employment ending January 31, 1947 was, by its terms, renewed on a month-to-month basis and was in effect at the time of decedent's death. At the latter time there was every prospect that he would continue to advance in his highly successful career in retailing.

After the decedent's death Gimbels paid the $6,000 annual installments provided by the three separate contracts ($2,000 each) to the taxpayer in her capacity as administratrix as they became due. She filed with the Collector a timely federal estate tax return and included the three contracts at a value of $15,000. Upon audit of the return the Internal Revenue Agent in Charge, Pittsburgh, increased the value of the three contracts from $15,000 to $66,710.34, the present worth of $90,000, payable in equal annual installments of $6,000 a year over a period of fifteen years. The increase in the value of the contracts resulted in a deficiency of $15,958.18, including interest, which was assessed against and paid by the taxpayer, and for the recovery of which she brought the suit here involved.

* * *

The sum of the taxpayer's position is (1) what is taxed is "the value" of the decedent's interest in his contract that "ceased by reason of death," not the value of what is received by the recipient (the administratrix); otherwise stated, "the value" of the decedent's interest in his contract was to be determined as "of the moment before death."

¶ 15,133

The government's position may be summarized as follows: (1) the estate tax is measured by the value of property transferred by death and here an absolute right to the fifteen deferred compensation payments passed by decedent's death to the taxpayer inasmuch as the possibility of forfeiture was extinguished by decedent's death; (2) the government properly valued the right to the deferred compensation payments in the same manner as an annuity for a term certain, i.e. at the commuted value in accordance with the applicable Treasury Regulations.

As earlier noted, the District Court agreed with the taxpayer's view. In doing so it stated:

> It seems clear under the authorities and the statute and the regulations that the value of the contract rights *is limited to the interest of the decedent during his lifetime.* That interest * * * is valueless. There was no fair market value on which to base a deficiency assessment." [Emphasis in original.]

It may be noted parenthetically that the taxpayer's testimony as to lack of value, adverted to by the District Court, was premised on the circumstance that the employment contracts specified four contingencies which, if any of them had occurred, would have forfeited the decedent's right to the deferred compensation payments.

It is clear that the decedent's interest in the employment contracts was "property" includible in his gross estate under Section 811(a) of the Internal Revenue Code of 1939 [now § 2033]. Determination of the time when that interest is to be valued is the crux of the dispute.

We have had the benefit of thorough discussions by both the government and the taxpayer of the nature of the federal estate tax. Both parties cited Knowlton v. Moore, 178 U.S. 41 (1900); Young Men's Christian Association v. Davis, 264 U.S. 47 (1924); and Edwards v. Slocum, 264 U.S. 61 (1924). The government cited them for the proposition that the subject of the tax is neither the property of the decedent, nor the property of the legatee, but rather the transfer of assets affected by death. The taxpayer emphasizes the language in these cases which supports the theory that what is taxed is the value of the interest that ceased by reason of death, not the value of what is received by the recipient. We are in accord with both of these general axioms which aid in clarifying the nature of the federal estate tax. However, the cases cited and the principles drawn therefrom are not decisive of the question posed by this case. While the nature of the tax has been discussed in numerous Supreme Court cases, the question of the proper time to determine the nature of a decedent's interest and the value thereof requires a more particularized analysis.

The taxpayer has ignored the very nature of the tax which it is urged is dispositive of this case. True, the tax reaches the " ' * * * interest which ceased by reason of the death' ", Knowlton v. Moore, supra at 49, but the reference there was to the distinction between an estate tax and an inheritance tax. The inheritance tax is levied upon the individual shares of the decedent's estate after distribution to the legatees; the estate tax is imposed upon the total estate of the decedent which is transferred to the legatees. The estate tax has been characterized as "an excise imposed upon the transfer of or shifting in relationships to property at death." United States Trust Co. v. Helvering, 307 U.S. 57, 60 (1939). The estate and inheritance taxes have the common element of being based upon the transmission of property from the dead to the living. In Knowlton v. Moore, supra, the Supreme Court recognized this basic principle when it said:

> " * * * tax laws of this nature in all countries rest in their essence upon the principle that death is the generating source from which the particular taxing power takes its being, and that it is the power to transmit, or the transmission from the dead to the living, on which such taxes are more immediately rested."

Since death is the propelling force for the imposition of the tax, it is death which determines the interests to be includible in the gross estate. Interests which terminate on or before death are not a proper subject of the tax. Assets may be acquired or disposed of before death, possibilities of the loss of an asset may become actualities or may disappear. Upon the same principle underlying the inclusion of interests in a decedent's gross estate, valuation of an interest is neither logically made nor feasibly administered until death has occurred. The taxpayer's theory of valuing property before death disregards the fact that generally the estate tax is neither concerned with changes in property interests nor values prior to death. The tax is measured by the value of assets transferred by reason of death, the critical value being that which is determined as of the time of death.

As was so succinctly stated by Judge Hartshorne in Christiernin v. Manning, 138 F.Supp. 923, 925 (D.N.J.1956):

> "There cannot be a decedent, till death has occurred. A decedent's estate is not transferred either by his will or by intestacy, till death has occurred. * * * And the decedent's interest in the property taxable is to be such interest 'at the time of his death' * * *."

Here the employment contracts provided for additional "contingent" compensation of $6,000 per year for fifteen years to be paid to Blum or his estate after the termination of his employment by reason of death or otherwise. True, the right to these payments was forfeitable upon the occurrence of any of the specified contingencies. However, forfeiture as a result of the contingencies never occurred during Blum's lifetime, and any possibility of their occurrence was extinguished by his death. Gimbels has been making and the estate has been collecting the payments provided by the contracts. Valuation of the right to these payments must be determined as of the time of Blum's death when the limiting factor of the contingencies would no longer be considered. Death ripened the interest in the deferred payments into an absolute one, and death permitted the imposition of the tax measured by the value of that absolute interest in property.

In Mearkle's Estate v. Commissioner, 129 F.2d 386 (3d Cir.1942), we considered the proper method of valuing an annuity upon the death of the decedent which by its terms was payable to the decedent during his life and to

¶ 15,133

his wife for her life. The criterion adopted was the purchase price of an annuity contract upon the life of the wife measured by her life expectancy on the date of her husband's death. There is no reference in this test to the husband's life expectancy upon the date of his death or to the joint expectancies of the decedent and his wife. See Christiernin v. Manning, supra. The value of decedent's interest in the annuity up to the time of his death is not considered, and, as in the situation here involved, death cuts off prior limiting factors.

For the reasons stated the judgment of the District Court will be reversed with directions to proceed in accordance with this opinion.

F.   CLAIMS UNDER WRONGFUL DEATH AND SURVIVAL STATUTES

[¶ 15,145]

In this country, when death results from intentional or negligent action, damages are awarded in most cases under two different statutory theories of recovery. Under the pure wrongful death statute, a right to sue is created in a class of beneficiaries who have a statutorily defined familial relationship with the deceased. These parties are allowed a recovery for their economic losses resulting from death. Under the survival type statute, the executor or administrator of the estate sues as the representative of the deceased and is awarded damages based on the economic loss and pain and suffering inflicted on the deceased. In recent years, states have been creating wrongful death statutes that draw on both types of statutes.

In Rev. Rul. 54–19, 1954–1 C.B. 179, the IRS indicated that damages under a pure wrongful death statute were not includible in the estate of the deceased. Since under the wrongful death statute the decedent never possessed any interest in property transferred at his death, the IRS indicated that there was no basis for including any awarded damages in the deceased's estate.

An action under a survival-type statute presents a situation that offers the potential to produce a different result. The following case deals with the taxability of damages under a survival-type statute.

[¶ 15,151]

CONNECTICUT BANK AND TRUST CO. v. UNITED STATES

United States Court of Appeals, Second Circuit, 1972.
465 F.2d 760.

ROBERT P. ANDERSON, Circuit Judge:

[Warren and Virginia Horton, as well as a passenger in their automobile, were killed when the car was struck by a tractor trailer on the Chesapeake Bay Bridge Tunnel. Since plaintiffs were domiciled in Connecticut, suit was brought under that state's survival-type statute. Prior to trial, the suits were settled for $320,000 with nothing paid with respect to antemortem pain and suffering.]

The crucial issue to be decided under § 2033 is whether or not the value of an action for wrongful death is "property . . . of the decedent at the time of his death." Much of the Government's argument and the opinion of the court below rest on the differences between the Connecticut statutory scheme for wrongful death recovery and the more common pattern of recovery in the majority of the states based upon "Lord Campbell's Act," which provides for a direct right of action on behalf of designated beneficiaries of the decedent to recover for his wrongful death, with damages to be measured by the loss to the survivors. The Connecticut statutes, on the other hand, provide for a right of action in the executor or administrator, with damages to be measured on the basis of the loss of the decedent's ability to carry on life's activities. In addition, by recent amendments, the wrongful death proceeds in Connecticut are distributed according to the terms of the decedent's will, if there is one, and are subject to the general claims of the estate. The differences in results under the two types of statutes may be more theoretical than real, but in any event, these differences have little relevance concerning the question of whether or not the right of action for wrongful death was *property owned at death*.

Simple logic mandates the conclusion that an action for wrongful death cannot exist until a decedent has died, at which point, he is no longer a person capable of owning any property interests. The Government's reply to this is that at the very instant of death the right of action arose which the decedent was then capable of owning at death. The only authorities cited for this position, however, are cases where *preexisting* property interests were *valued* as of the instant of death, but valuation at time of death of prior existing interests is a far different concern from that in this case where the property interest itself has sprung from the fact that the death has taken place.

While it is true that Congress may constitutionally place an excise tax on property created by death, as well as upon property transferred by death, § 2033 does not read so broadly. In a discussion of the estate tax the Supreme Court described the scope of § 2033: "What this law taxes is not the interest to which the legatees and devisees succeeded on death, but the interest which ceased by reason of death," Y.M.C.A. v. Davis, 264 U.S. 47, 50 (1924); see also, Nichols v. Coolidge, 274 U.S. 531, 537 (1927). Where, as here, there was no property interest in the decedent which passed by virtue of his death, but rather one which arose after his death, such an interest is not property owned at death and not part of the gross estate under § 2033 * * *.

The Treasury Department has issued three Revenue Rulings concerning the inclusion of wrongful death proceeds under § 2033, all of which hold that the proceeds are not part of the gross estate. In this case, the Government tries to distinguish them because they concerned rights of action arising under New Jersey and Virginia state law and the federal Death on the High Seas Act; however, the rationale of those rulings is fully applicable here. In Rev. Rul. 54–19, 1954–1 Cum.Bull. 179, 180, the Department stated: "Inasmuch as the decedent had no right of action or interest in the proceeds at the time of his death, nothing 'passed' from the decedent to the beneficiaries. Accordingly, the amounts recovered by the beneficiaries would not be includible in the decedent's gross estate for Federal estate tax purposes." It held that such proceeds were not part of the gross estate in Rev. Rul. 68–88, 1968–1 Cum.Bull. 397, 398, because "[t]he right of action for wrongful death does not accrue until death occurs," and in Rev. Rul. 69–8, 1969–1 Cum.Bull. 219, because "[t]he decedent in his lifetime never had an interest in either the right of action or the proceeds." See also Rev. Rul. 55–581, 1955–2 Cum.Bull. 381, holding that an allotment paid by the armed services to designated beneficiaries of servicemen who die in active duty is not part of the gross estate; and Rev. Rul. 55–87, 1955–1 Cum.Bull. 112, holding that a lump sum payment for funeral expenses to social security recipients is not taxable under § 2033.

[The portion of the opinion on a second point relating to § 2041, power of appointment, has been reprinted in Chapter 22 at ¶ 22,022.]

Note

[¶ 15,157]

In Rev. Rul. 75–127, 1975–1 C.B. 297, the IRS indicated that it would, in general, abide by the result of *Connecticut Bank and Trust Co.*; however, where the damages awarded represent damages to which the decedent had become entitled during his or her life (such as pain and suffering and medical expenses), the IRS indicated that it would persist in attempting to include these amounts in the estate of the deceased. What does this suggest to you regarding the allocation of damages in settlement of a tort claim? Woe be to malpractice insurance carriers of those trial attorneys who feel that they can remain ignorant of the tax laws. It might be helpful to reread the summary of facts in *Connecticut Bank and Trust* to observe how the attorney in that case settled the claims so that no part of the damage award was ultimately made subject to estate taxation.

G.   COMMUNITY PROPERTY IN GROSS ESTATE

[¶ 15,169]

REVENUE RULING 54–89
1954–1 C.B. 181.

Advice is requested relative to the extent real property acquired in the manner set forth below is to be included in the decedent's gross estate for Federal estate tax purposes.

A married man, a resident of Texas, a community property State, purchased with the community funds of himself and his wife real property situated in New Mexico [a community property state] and Kansas [a common law property state]. The husband took title to the purchased property in his own name. He died survived by his wife.

¶ 15,169

The respective rights of the husband and wife in real property are governed by the law of the place where such property is situated rather than by the law of the domicile of the parties.

The law of descent and distribution contained in chapter 31 of the New Mexico Statutes, annotated, 1941, provides that upon the death of the husband one-half of the community estate goes to the wife and the other half is subject to the testamentary disposition of the husband. (Sec. 31–109.) Accordingly, it is held that the value of only one-half of the New Mexico real estate is includible in the deceased husband's gross estate.

The general rule in a community property State is that where a husband, as manager and business agent of the community, purchases real property in a common law State with community funds and takes title thereto in his own name, he holds a one-half interest in the property as trustee for his wife.

Section 67–406 of General Statutes of Kansas, Annotated, reads as follows:

> Conveyance to one person when consideration paid by another. When a conveyance for a valuable consideration is made to one person and the consideration therefor is paid by another, no use or trust shall result in favor of the latter; but the title shall vest in the former, subject to the provisions of the next two sections.

Section 67–407 provides that every such conveyance shall be presumed fraudulent as against the creditors of the person paying the consideration.

Section 67–408 provides as follows:

> The provisions of the section next before the last shall not extend to cases where the alienee shall have taken any absolute conveyance in his own name without the consent of the person with whose money the consideration was paid; or where such alienee in violation of some trust shall have purchased the land with moneys not his own; or where it shall be made to appear that by agreement and without any fraudulent intent the party to whom the conveyance was made, or in whom the title shall vest, was to hold the land or some interest therein in trust for the party paying the purchase money or some part thereof.

In construing the provisions of sections 67–406 and 408 of the General Statutes of Kansas, the Supreme Court of Kansas has consistently held that where the husband purchases land in Kansas in part or in whole with his wife's money, a trust is impressed on the land in favor of the wife to the extent the purchase price was paid with her funds, unless the wife intended to make a gift to her husband. Accordingly, it is held that the value of only one-half of the Kansas real property is includible in the deceased husband's gross estate.

Note

[¶ 15,173]

In Rev. Rul. 72–443, 1972–2 C.B. 531, the decedent, a resident of Norway, a community property jurisdiction, purchased realty in a U.S. common law property state using community assets. The Treasury indicated that the general rule in such situations is that the property rules of the state or country where the realty is located determine its character as separate or community property, whereas in the case of movable property, the law of domicile of the owners will be used to determine its character. The common law property state in which the purchased realty was located provided that when a domiciliary of a community property jurisdiction uses community funds to purchase realty in the state in question, the party holding title to the property will be deemed to hold it as trustee for the other spouse to the extent that the other spouse's assets were used to effect the purchase. The ruling concluded with the observation that: "In light of the above, the decedent is considered, under the laws of the state in which that property is located, to own one-half the property as trustee for his wife. Accordingly, it is held that only one-half the value of the real property is includible in his gross estate under section 2033 of the Code."

Problems

[¶ 15,175]

1. Anne–Marie transfers Blackacre to Alice for life, remainder to Alice's issue, gift over to the Red Cross on failure of issue. When Alice dies, how much will be included in her taxable estate?

2. Andrew transfers Blackacre to Christine for life, remainder to Ted in fee simple. Ted dies while Christine is living. At his death, what is includible in Ted's taxable estate?

3. Paul gave his 53–year-old, childless daughter, Jane, a term of years for 20 years in income of a trust, with remainder to Jane's issue. Jane died five years after establishment of the trust. At her death, what is includible in her estate?

4. In the prior problem, assume that Paul, rather than Jane had died. At his death, is anything includible in his estate?

5. In an arm's-length transaction, Mary sold her business to her employees for $1 million, to be paid in 10 annual payments of $100,000 bearing interest at a fair market rate. Under the terms of the contract of sale, Mary's death will result in cancellation of all remaining payments. The interest rate on the notes contained premium to reflect the potential loss to Mary's estate due to the cancellation provision. At her death two years after the sale, will anything be included in her estate?

6. Nancy is a vice president at Apex, Inc. Under the company's death benefit plan, one full year's salary is to be paid to "the surviving spouse of any deceased employee and in absence of a surviving spouse to the surviving issue of such employee." At Nancy's death $250,000 was paid to her husband Paul. What, if anything, is includible in Nancy's estate?

7. John died in a plane crash and at his death $800,000 was paid by the airline's insurer in settlement of all claims. The $800,000 consisted of $600,000 paid to John's dependents under the state wrongful death statute to compensate them for their economic losses and $200,000 paid to

compensate for pain and suffering inflicted on John. What, if anything, is includible in John's estate?

8. At Sally's death she owned Blackacre, worth $500,000, and Whiteacre, worth $800,000. Sally was married to Phil for 20 years, and they spent their entire lives as residents of a community property state. Sally inherited Blackacre from her father two years earlier when it was worth $300,000. Whiteacre was purchased eight years prior to her death for $200,000, which came from savings from her job accumulated over the six years prior to the purchase. What amount, if any, is includible in Sally's estate?

¶ 15,175

Chapter 16

JOINT TENANCIES

(Section 2040)

A. INTRODUCTION

[¶ 16,001]

At the outset, the student must have clearly in mind the distinction between joint tenancies and tenancies by the entirety, on the one hand, and tenancies-in-common, on the other. Tenancies-in-common are merely the co-ownership of property, with the usual incidents that accompany property interests held outright; a tenant-in-common has a separate, undivided interest in the property, which is descendible at death and transferable by deed or will. Accordingly, tenancies-in-common are fully covered by the provisions of § 2033, which is directed generally at interests in property held by the decedent at death.

Joint tenancies and tenancies by the entirety have as their distinguishing feature the right of survivorship; upon the death of a joint tenant or a tenant by the entirety, individual's right to share in the possession and enjoyment of the property terminates. Nothing passes to the heirs or devisees of the joint tenant or tenant by the entirety, but the interest in the property continues on with the surviving tenant. The last survivor winds up with the full possession and ownership in the entire property.

Historically, joint tenancies required at their creation the co-existence of the mystical four unities of time, title, interest, and possession; without all these unities existing for the tenants, the joint tenancy with its survivorship rights cannot arise. Failing these requirements, the tenancy would be an ordinary co-ownership of the tenancy-in-common variety. A joint tenancy, with its four unities, is a rather fragile thing which may readily be destroyed by an act of one of the joint tenants breaking one or more of the unities. For example, a sale of a joint tenant's interest destroys the unity of title and results in a tenancy-in-common between the purchaser and the other tenant.

While the tenancy by the entirety also requires the four unities and has the right of survivorship as its characteristic feature, it differs from the joint tenancy in that it can arise only where the tenants are husband and wife and only for the duration of their marriage. Moreover, it cannot be destroyed, as in the case of a joint tenancy, merely by the unilateral act of one of the tenants; it terminates only upon divorce, death or mutual agreement.

B. STATUTORY PROVISIONS OF SECTION 2040

[¶ 16,007]

Without special provisions designed to deal with the peculiar common law estates of joint tenancy and tenancy by the entirety, it is not at all clear how a decedent's interest in such property would be treated for estate tax purposes. In view of the property law concept that nothing passes from a joint tenant upon death, but rather the full title continues to reside in the survivor, it might have been difficult to include any part of the joint tenancy property in the gross estate. In considering the possible reach of § 2033, one should explore the arguments available to the Commissioner in supporting a position that at least the proportionate share of the deceased joint tenant should be includible in the gross estate by virtue of § 2033 alone.

In any event, Congress, in enacting the first estate tax statute in 1916, included a provision governing joint tenancies and tenancies by the entirety that has been retained as § 2040 of the 1986 Code without material change except for the addition of subsection (b), prescribing that only one-half a spousal joint tenancy is includible in the estate—and even that half is subject to the new unlimited marital deduction under § 2056. The result of this is that the value of one-half of the spousal joint tenancy is includible in the estate of the first spouse who dies but that value, because it passes to a surviving spouse, then qualifies for the marital deduction in computing the taxable estate. See Chapter 28.

Though the language of the section is tortured and indirect, its purpose and meaning are basically clear. Indeed, the Regulations (§ 20.2040–1) have done much to implement the turgid wording of the statute. Basic rules are provided under § 2040 for three types of situations under which joint tenancies and tenancies by the entirety are found:

> *Situation 1*: Where the interest in the tenancy property has been acquired by the decedent and the other tenant or tenants by gift, bequest, devise, or inheritance, the value of the property will be includible in the deceased tenant's gross estate to the extent of the deceased's fractional share.

> *Situation 2:* In all other cases, except joint tenancies between spouses, the entire value of the tenancy property will be includible in the deceased tenant's gross estate except such portion thereof as is allocable to the part of the consideration furnished by the other tenant or tenants for the acquisition of the property. For example, when two persons purchase property in joint tenancy and each pays a portion of the purchase price, the fraction which each pays determines the fraction of the value of the property at the date of death which is includible in the

gross estate of the first to die. It is to be particularly noted that the statute, in this type of transaction, requires the inclusion of the entire joint tenancy property except such portion thereof "as may be shown" to have originated with the surviving tenant; thus, this has the effect of a presumption of inclusion no matter which tenant may die first, leaving the burden of rebuttal to the estate.

Situation 3: For joint tenancies between spouses only, a straightforward rule was provided in § 2040(b) by the Economic Recovery Tax Act of 1981 prescribing that for such spousal joint tenancies one-half of the value of the joint tenancy property is includible in the estate of the deceased spouse.

This rule of half includibility of § 2040(b) supersedes the consideration furnished rule of § 2040(a) and in some cases will give a more favorable result and in other cases a less favorable result. In any event, the rule for spousal joint tenancies is now simple. Moreover, as pointed out earlier, the includibility of half a spousal joint tenancy in the estate of the deceased spouse exacts no estate tax price because joint tenancy property qualifies for the marital deduction which, by virtue of the 1981 Act, is now an unlimited marital deduction in respect to amount. Consequently, spousal joint tenancy property will not be subject to estate tax in the estate of the first spouse to die.

One significant consequence of the spousal joint tenancy rule is that only one-half such joint tenancy property will qualify for a step-up (or step-down) in basis presently prescribed by § 1014. By contrast and as something of an anomaly, community property under the terms of § 1014(b)(6) qualifies for a step-up basis at date of death for both halves of the community property. Accordingly, while the law remains in this curious posture, community property spouses are well advised to stick with community property as against conversion to joint tenancies in light of the income tax basis rules.

Disquieting disruptions to the relatively straightforward treatment of spousal joint tenancies outlined above are provided by: (1) Gallenstein v. United States, 975 F.2d 286 (6th Cir.1992); and (2) § 2056(d)(1)(B). In *Gallenstein*, the court held that because of statutory language about the effective dates of several changes in § 2040, the one-half inclusion rule of § 2040(b) with respect to spousal joint tenancies did not apply to spousal joint tenancies created before 1977. These would follow the old rule—in the absence of proof that the surviving joint tenant had provided any of the consideration used to purchase the joint tenancy there would be a full inclusion of the joint tenancy in the estate of the first to die. Given the unlimited marital deduction which was added in 1981, this full inclusion, for joint tenancies purchased prior to 1977, is without adverse estate tax consequences and results in the surviving spouse taking a step-up (or step-down) basis in the entire joint tenancy. It is important to remember that *Gallenstein* applies only to spousal joint tenancies created before 1977, and that the IRS is unwilling to accept the result in *Gallenstein* and continues to litigate the issue although it has met with no success to date. See, e.g., Patten v. United States, 116 F.3d 1029 (4th Cir. 1997); Hahn v. Commissioner, 110 T.C. 140 (1998) Acq. 2001–2 C.B. xv. Section 2056(d)(1)(B) provides that the half includibility

¶ 16,007

rule of § 2040(b) with respect to spousal joint tenancies shall not apply in certain cases where the surviving spouse is not a US citizen. In such cases the spousal joint tenancy is treated as a non-spousal joint tenancy. Assuming that the surviving non-citizen spouse cannot establish that he or she provided consideration for the purchase of the joint tenancy, full includibility is the proper result, thereby, avoiding the possibility that property which constituted the joint tenancy will never be taxed, even at the death of the surviving non-citizen who may not be subject to US estate taxation at his or her death. The special treatment accorded to property passing from one spouse to a non-citizen spouse is discussed at length at ¶ 27,055.

The cases in this chapter will deal predominantly with tenancies by the entireties where one owner died prior to the Economic Recovery Tax Act of 1981 which, as noted, dramatically changed the tax treatment of joint interests with rights of survivorship held by married couples. They are included because the legal principles articulated by the cases are still valid for non-spousal joint tenancies with rights of survivorship.

C. SECTION 2040(a)

[¶ 16,013]

1. HISTORY

In United States v. Jacobs, 306 U.S. 363 (1939), the Supreme Court passed on the constitutionality of the estate taxation of joint tenancies. The Court held the statutory predecessor to § 2040 to be constitutional even when applied to a joint tenancy with rights of survivorship that was created prior to the enactment of the estate tax but where the decedent died after enactment. In so holding, the Court emphasized that Congress has the power to tax the occasion of a joint tenant's acquiring the status of survivor at the death of the co-tenant. Since that event occurred after enactment of the predecessor of § 2040, no failure of due process existed.

The Court in *Jacobs* also held that, where the deceased spouse had previously given the survivor the funds, which she used to purchase her portion of a joint tenancy with rights of survivorship, the full value of the jointly held property should be included in the estate of the decedent. Since the survivor had satisfied the statute's requirement that she had "received" or "acquired" from the decedent her share in (or contribution to) the jointly held property, the Court had little difficulty in deciding that the full value of the property was taxable at the death of the first joint tenant to die.

Jacobs thus not only dealt with the constitutionality of the joint tenancy provision but also served to focus attention on the more difficult issue of exactly what constitutes qualifying consideration provided by the surviving joint tenant. This is an extremely important issue inasmuch as the "consideration furnished" rule is the premise underlying estate taxation of joint property held by joint tenants who are not married to each other.

[¶ 16,019]

2. SERVICES AS CONSIDERATION

Survivors, who succeed in establishing that their labor constituted consideration for the purchase of jointly held assets, find themselves having to establish the existence of a business partnership for the operation of the jointly owned enterprise. See, e.g., United States v. Neel, 235 F.2d 395 (10th Cir.1956)(court found partnership based on course of conduct and pattern of behavior); Singer v. Shaughnessy, 198 F.2d 178 (2d Cir.1952)(formal understanding later supplemented by written agreement). Less fortunate are those survivors who are not able to establish the presence of a business partnership and find their dedicated services characterized as the product of love and affection. See, e.g., Estate of Kjorvestad v. United States, 81–1 USTC ¶ 13,401, 47 AFTR 2d 81–1635 (D.N.D.1981); Loveland's Estate v. Commissioner, 13 T.C. 5 (1949).

Often joint tenants work with each other in the operation of a jointly held farm or business. If they labored together on the understanding that some or all of the fruits of the labor of the survivor were to be invested in the jointly held property, this provides the survivor with the opportunity to claim that the survivor provided a portion of the consideration for purchase of at least some of the jointly held assets.

Many of the cases, such as *Neel*, involve husbands and wives. After the addition of § 2040(b) to the Code in 1981, which makes the whole issue of the relative value of consideration provided by spousal joint tenants irrelevant, there has been a marked decrease of cases in which the issue of services as consideration has been raised under § 2040. In the future one will typically encounter the issue in the context of a parent and child, or unmarried couples, who operate a jointly held business or farm together. For example, in Estate of Anderson v. Commissioner, 58 T.C.M. (CCH) 840, T.C.M. (P–H) ¶ 89,643 (1989), the Tax Court found that in one mother-son joint enterprise the son, through his performance of substantial uncompensated services, had provided full and adequate consideration so that only one-half of a joint tenancy with rights of survivorship was to be included in his mother's estate at her death. In a second venture, where the son performed no services, full inclusion resulted. Similarly in Fratini v. Commissioner, 76 T.C.M. (CCH) 342, T.C.M. (RIA) ¶ 98,308 (1998) the court, in the case of joint tenancies involving life partners, determined the value of managerial, maintenance and janitorial services provided by the surviving joint tenant.

¶ 16,019

3. INCOME AND PROFITS ON GIFT PROPERTY

[¶ 16,031]

ESTATE OF GOLDSBOROUGH v. COMMISSIONER

United States Tax Court, 1978.
70 T.C. 1077, aff'd, 673 F.2d 1310 (4th Cir.1982).

FEATHERSTON, Judge.

* * *

Section 2040 provides in general that the decedent's gross estate includes the entire value of jointly held property but that section "except[s] such part thereof as may be shown to have originally belonged to * * * [the surviving joint tenant(s)] and never to have been received or acquired by the latter from the decedent for less than an adequate and full consideration in money or money's worth." Section 2040 further provides that if the decedent owned property jointly with another, the amount to be excluded from the decedent's gross estate is "only such part of the value of such property as is proportionate to the consideration furnished by * * * [the surviving joint tenant(s)]." Mathematically this "consideration furnished" exclusion can be expressed as follows:

$$\text{Amount excluded} = \begin{array}{c}\text{Entire value of property}\\\text{(on the date of death}\\\text{or alternate valuation}\\\text{date)}\end{array} \times \frac{\text{Survivor's consideration}}{\text{Entire consideration paid}}$$

In the instant case, the decedent (Goldsborough) acquired on May 12, 1937, real property (St. Dunstans) in her individual name. On April 4, 1946, decedent transferred St. Dunstans, valued at $25,000 on that date, to her two daughters (Eppler and O'Donoghue) as a gift. On July 17, 1949, the daughters sold St. Dunstans to H.W. Ford and his wife for $32,500. Sometime in that same year, each daughter invested her share of the proceeds from the sale of St. Dunstans in various stocks and securities; each daughter took title to her respective stocks and securities in joint tenancy with decedent. These stocks and securities remained in joint tenancy until December 21, 1972, the date of decedent's death, and during the period of joint tenancy the stocks and securities appreciated in value to $160,383.19, the value on the alternate valuation date.

Thus, the section 2040 exclusion depends on the amount, if any, of the consideration Eppler and O'Donoghue, the surviving joint tenants, furnished toward the $32,500 purchase price of the jointly held stocks and securities.

Respondent contends that all the funds used to purchase the stocks and securities in question were derived from decedent and thus the entire value of the jointly held property ($160,383.19) is includable in her gross estate.

Petitioners Buppert and Eppler argue that only the value of St. Dunstans at the time the gift was made to decedent's two daughters (i.e., $25,000) is

¶ 16,019

includable in decedent's gross estate. In the alternative, petitioner Eppler contends that the gain of $7,500, measured by the appreciation in value from the time St. Dunstans was given to the two daughters in 1946 until that property was sold by them in 1949, constitutes consideration furnished by the daughters toward the $32,500 purchase price of the jointly held stocks and securities. Thus Eppler argues that $37,011.50 ($7,500/$32,500 of $160,383.19), the value of the jointly held property on the alternate valuation date, should be excluded from decedent's gross estate. We agree with this alternative argument.

To be sure, section 2040 is not a paragon of clarity, and the courts and Internal Revenue Service have wrestled with the question of whether a contribution made out of gain representing appreciation in value of property received gratuitously from decedent is attributable to the decedent or, instead, is to be treated as income from the property and thus separate funds of the surviving tenant.[5] The law, as we perceive it, recognizes two distinct situations and treats the two differently. In one situation, the surviving joint tenant receives property gratuitously from the decedent; the property thereafter appreciates, and the property itself is contributed in an exchange for jointly held property. In this circumstance section 20.2040–1(c)(4),[6] Estate Tax Regs., treats all the property as having been paid for by the decedent, and the entire value of the property is included in the decedent's gross estate. See Estate of Kelley v. Commissioner, 22 B.T.A. 421, 425 (1931).

In the second situation, the surviving joint tenant receives property gratuitously from the decedent; the property thereafter appreciates or produces income and is sold, and the income or the sales proceeds are used as consideration for the acquisition of the jointly held property. In this situation, the income or the gain, measured by the appreciation from the time of receipt of the gift to the time of sale, has been held to be the surviving joint tenant's income and a part of that joint tenant's contribution to the purchase price. Harvey v. United States, 185 F.2d 463, 467 (7th Cir.1950); First National Bank of Kansas City v. United States, 223 F.Supp. 963, 967 (W.D.Mo.1963); Swartz v. United States, 182 F.Supp. 540, 542 (D.Mass.1960). Thus, in the words of the statute, "such part of the value of such property as is proportionate to the consideration furnished by [the surviving joint tenant]" is excluded.

The facts of the instant case fall precisely within this second situation. In Harvey v. United States, supra at 465, the court characterized the facts and framed the issue as follows:

> The jointly held property is not the gift property itself, in either its original or transmuted form, but property traceable to (1) the profits

---

5. It is clear that income from property acquired gratuitously from the decedent constitutes a contribution from a surviving joint tenant's separate funds. Sec. 20.2040–1(c)(5), Estate Tax Regs.

6. Sec. 20.2040–1(c)(4), Estate Tax Regs., provides as follows:

"If the decedent, before the acquisition of the property by himself and the other joint owner, gave the latter a sum of money or other property which thereafter became the other joint owner's entire contribution to the purchase price, then the value of the entire property is so included, notwithstanding the fact that the other property may have appreciated in value due to market conditions between the time of the gift and the time of the acquisition of the jointly held property."

made through sales of the original gift property and successive reinvestments of the proceeds of such sales or (2) the rents, interest and dividends produced by such property in its original or converted form, while title thereto was in the wife. The question presented by this appeal, then, is whether such profits and income, realized from property originally received by the wife as a gift from her husband and traceable into property which was held by them as joint tenants at the time of the husband's death, came within the exception to the requirement of Section 811(e) [predecessor to sec. 2040] that the entire value of property held in joint tenancy shall be included in the decedent's gross estate.

The Government in *Harvey* argued that the full value of the jointly held property should be included in the decedent's gross estate, and the court dealt with that argument in the following manner (185 F.2d at 467):

> It seems clear that none of the cases cited contains any support for the novel proposition that income produced by gift property, after the gift has been completed, belongs to the donor and is property received or acquired from him by the donee; nor is there, in these cases, anything to impeach the conclusion of the trial court, or that of the Tax Court in the *Howard* case,[7] that the income produced by property of any kind belongs to the person who owns the property at the time it produces such income and does not originate with a donor who has made a completed gift of that property prior to its production of the income. * * *

> * * * Moreover, no reason is suggested for holding that one form of income, i.e., "profit gained through a sale or conversion of capital assets," * * * is outside the exception, whereas other forms of income, such as dividends, rentals and interest, fall within its terms. It follows that the government's contention that the full value of the property held in joint tenancy by decedent and his wife at the time of his death should have been included in decedent's gross estate must be rejected. [Citations omitted.]

Thus we conclude that Eppler and O'Donoghue furnished $7,500 toward the $32,500 purchase price paid for the stocks and securities they held in joint tenancy with decedent until her death on December 21, 1972. Under the terms of the statute, such part of the value of the property, i.e., $160,383.19 on the alternate valuation date, as is proportionate to the $7,500 of consideration Eppler and O'Donoghue furnished is excluded from decedent's gross estate. Under the mathematical formula, set out above, the amount of the exclusion is $37,011.50.

* * *

Note

[¶ 16,037]

In English v. United States, 270 F.2d 876 (7th Cir.1959), the court was confronted with how it should treat stock dividends received with respect to

---

7. Estate of Howard v. Commissioner, 9 T.C. 1192, 1202–1203 (1947).

stock held by joint tenants with rights of survivorship where the decedent joint tenant had provided all the consideration for the purchase of the original jointly held stock. The court concluded that such dividends were not to be considered income from jointly held property that could qualify as adequate consideration under the line of cases referred to in *Goldsborough*. The court viewed the dividended stock as representing the same interest as the original jointly held stock, with the result that both were included in the decedent's estate at his death.

D. CONTRIBUTIONS AND CHANGING VALUES

[¶ 16,049]

Section 2040(a) permits exclusion from the gross estate of such part of the value of the joint tenancy property "as is proportionate to the consideration furnished" by the surviving joint tenant. This exclusion contemplates the determination of a ratio or fraction by reference to the total consideration furnished and the portions thereof contributed by the joint tenants, all at values at the time of acquisition. The fraction representing the surviving tenant's contribution so ascertained is then applied to the value of the property at the date of death for the purpose of excluding the portion of the joint tenancy attributable to the surviving tenant. However, suppose that the contributions towards the acquisition of the joint tenancy were made at separate times when the property may have changed substantially in value. For example, in 1970, F purchased a lot for $10,000 of his own funds, taking title in joint tenancy with daughter D; in 1975, when the lot had increased in value to $20,000, D built on the lot a house costing $40,000, which D paid out of her own funds. Upon F's death in 2006, when the house and lot were worth $180,000, what portion is to be treated as originating with F and what portion should be excluded from his estate as being allocable to D?

There is scant authority on what the answer should be. There are three possible results. First, we could tax the full $180,000 minus only the $40,000 consideration paid by D. This should be rejected as inconsistent with the proportionate consideration language of § 2040. Second, we could ignore the fact that the property had increased in value by the time the improvement had been made and allow D to exclude 4/5 of the value of the house and lot, since her $40,000 investment reflected 4/5 of the total of $50,000 invested by F and D. This result should be rejected since it would theoretically allow a party who made a modest investment in improvements in vastly appreciated joint property dramatically to alter tax results. For example, assume that no improvement had been made in the land which shortly before F's death had appreciated to $90,000. A $10,000 investment by D in modest improvements should not be allowed to exclude $50,000 from taxation at F's death. Third, at each new investment in improvements, we could recalculate the relative value of each holder's contribution. For example, until 1975 F could be deemed to have provided all the consideration for the lot. In 1975, after D's $40,000 investment in the joint tenancy, F could be deemed to have provided 1/3 of the consideration and D to have provided 2/3 of the consideration for the tenancy.

Estate of Peters v. Commissioner, 386 F.2d 404 (4th Cir.1967), provides some authority for concluding that this is the proper result.

Although the third approach is probably the correct one to follow, it does not take much imagination to realize how difficult it would be to apply this rule in an environment where little is typically known of the value of the property each time one of the joint tenants makes an improvement.

E.   MORTGAGES AND CONTRIBUTIONS

[¶ 16,067]

An interesting problem arises in connection with purchase money mortgages. Where the property is acquired in joint tenancy partially for cash and partially for mortgaged indebtedness in which the tenants are jointly and severally liable, with either joint tenant being entitled to contribution from the other in the event that he or she is compelled to satisfy more than one-half of the debt, each tenant is treated as contributing toward the purchase price his or her share of the debt, as well as the cash which each contributes. See Bremer v. Luff, 7 F.Supp. 148 (N.D.N.Y.1933).

Assume that A and B purchased a joint tenancy in Whiteacre for $100,000 with A and B each contributing $10,000 in cash toward the purchase price and the balance funded with an $80,000 mortgage on which A and B were jointly and severally liable. No payments on the principal of the mortgage were made and at A's death Whiteacre was worth $120,000. This will result in one-half of the value of Whiteacre, or $60,000, being included in A's estate at A's death.

Whenever one of the joint tenants makes payment on the principal of the mortgage debt, this operates to increase that party's contribution to the purchase price and reduce the contribution of the other joint tenant. For example, assume that A had retired $20,000 of the mortgage debt, A's contribution toward the purchase price of Whiteacre would be $60,000. That sum would be comprised of: (1) $10,000 cash payment; (2) $20,000 of retired debt; and (3) $30,000, one-half of the remaining $60,000 mortgage. B would be treated as having provided $40,000 toward the purchase of Whiteacre consisting of: (1) $10,000 cash payment; and (2) $30,000, one-half of the remaining mortgage debt. Assuming Whiteacre was worth $120,000 on A's death, this would result in 60 percent of its value, $72,000, being included in A's estate. See Rev. Rul. 79–302, 1979–2 C.B. 328. For additional refinements of the law in this area, see Rev. Ruls. 81–183, 1981–2 C.B. 180, and 81–184, 1981–2 C.B. 181, which deal with the consequences of second mortgages and refinancings.

F.   SIMULTANEOUS DEATHS OF JOINT TENANTS

[¶ 16,079]

Not important

In Rev. Rul. 76–303, 1976–2 C.B. 266, the IRS indicated how jointly held property was to be taxed where one of the joint tenants (X) provided all the consideration, and the parties (X and Y) died in a common accident in a jurisdiction which had adopted the Uniform Simultaneous Death Act, which provides that "[w]here there is no sufficient evidence that two joint tenants or tenants by the entirety have died otherwise than simultaneously the property so held shall be distributed one-half as if one had survived and one-half as if the other had survived." The IRS indicated that in such circumstance, since there is no evidence to indicate that Y had provided any consideration for purchase of the property, the value of the one-half with respect to which Y is considered to have survived X is includible in X's estate under § 2040. Since X provided all the consideration, none of the one-half of the property with respect to which X is considered to have survived Y is includible in Y's estate. Moreover, since X and Y are each deemed to have survived as to one-half of the property, each is considered to have acquired absolute ownership in one-half of the property, which will be included in their gross estates under § 2033. The net result is that the entire value of the jointly held property will be taxed in X's estate and one-half of its value will be taxed in Y's estate.

If X and Y are married, the marital deduction (Chapter 27) will effectively exclude from X's estate the one-half which passes to Y. However, if they are not, the only relief will come from § 2013 which provides a decedent's estate with a credit for all or some of the estate tax paid on property transferred to the decedent by the estate of another within 10 years before or 2 years after the decedent's death. Since the credit is not necessarily total, this presents special challenges for estate planners who represent unmarried couples that desire to hold property as joint tenants with rights of survivorship.

G. UNSCRAMBLING THE JOINT TENANCY OMELET

[¶ 16,091]

In nonspousal situations, § 2040 provides the IRS with a "heads I win, tails I still may win" rule. It does that by basically including all joint property with survivorship rights in the estate of the first to die unless the survivor can shoulder the burden of establishing the portion of the purchase price provided by the survivor, in which case, based on the relative amount of consideration provided by the survivor, some or all of the property will be excluded from the deceased's estate. When one adds to this taxpayer disadvantage the complexity of dealing with simultaneous deaths, improvements, mortgages and rules regarding the source of consideration, it readily becomes apparent that, from a tax standpoint, nonspouses typically should not establish joint tenancies with rights of survivorship and should terminate most such estates which already exist. Moreover, due to the limited availability of the "step-up" basis under § 1014 (see ¶ 16,007), spouses also may wish to minimize the creation of such estates or to terminate some or all which do exist. Fortunately, it is not at all difficult to transmute a joint tenancy into another form of property ownership beyond the reach of § 2040. By simply severing a joint interest with rights of survivorship or by transforming it into a tenancy in common, property can be removed from the clutches of § 2040.

When studying § 2035 (Chapter 23), it may be desirable to reread this section and notice that § 2035(a) does not deal with jointly held property, the result being that a deathbed transformation of a joint tenancy with rights of survivorship into a tenancy in common or severance of the joint interest could remove vast amounts from the estate where the soon-to-die individual provided all consideration for purchase of the original joint tenancy.

In United States v. Chandler, 410 U.S. 257 (1973), the Supreme Court considered whether a registered owner of a US Savings Bond, Series E, who made physical delivery to a donee has thereby eliminated the joint bond from the donor's estate. The Treasury regulations provided that the only way to convey ownership of the bond was to have it reissued; the Court held that the regulation by the Treasury was valid and, accordingly, the property was still in the estate of the deceased bond owner.

H. COMMUNITY PROPERTY

[¶ 16,103]

Prior to 1942, community property, which exists in a number of states, was taxed only under the predecessor provision of § 2033 (then § 811(a)). This type of ownership is quite distinct from joint tenancies and tenancies by the entirety, and the courts had held, without specific legislation, that the interest of each spouse in community property was includible in each spouse's gross estate for estate tax purposes to the extent that the interest was vested in the spouse under state law. See Greenwood v. Commissioner, 134 F.2d 915 (9th Cir.1943).

In an attempt to equalize the estate tax treatment of married couples in community property states with that of married couples residing in the common-law states, Congress enacted in 1942, over the heated opposition of representatives of the community property states, legislation designed to bring all the community property within the gross estate of the spouse whose personal services or investments earned it. The constitutionality of this legislation was questioned in due course, but was sustained in Fernandez v. Wiener, 326 U.S. 340 (1945). The Court concluded:

> This redistribution of powers and restrictions upon power is brought about by death notwithstanding that the rights in the property subject to these powers and restrictions were in every sense "vested" from the moment the community began. It is enough that death brings about changes in the legal and economic relationships to the property taxed, and the earlier certainty that those changes would occur does not impair the legislative power to recognize them, and to levy a tax on the happening of the event which was their generating force.

By 1948, the pressure of the community property states was combined with tax counsel and others from the common-law states to push through compromise legislation that would restore to the community property couples their former tax advantage of dividing their estates automatically and would accord to couples in the common-law states a comparable privilege in the form of a marital deduction under § 2056, which will be fully considered in Chapter 28.

As noted at ¶ 16,007, one aspect of the favoritism shown to community property is found in the income tax basis provision of § 1014(b)(6), which prescribes that, on death of one of the spouses in a community property jurisdiction, both halves of the community property acquire a "stepped-up" new income tax basis equivalent to the value of both halves of the community property as of the date of the death of one of the community property spouses. This sharp differential in favor of community property as compared to joint tenancy property is difficult to rationalize as a matter of policy.

Problems

[¶ 16,109]

1. Five years ago Brad and his wife, Maria, purchased a lot as tenants by the entireties with rights of survivorship, with Brad providing the full $50,000 purchase price. At his death four years later, the lot was worth $80,000. What value is included in Brad's estate, and what is Maria's adjusted basis in the lot after Brad's death?

2. What would your answer be in the prior problem if Brad and Maria were not married but were sister and brother and the property was held by them as a joint tenancy with rights of survivorship?

3. Bob purchased 1,000 shares of stock for $20 per share, with Bob providing the full $20,000 consideration. He took title in joint tenancy with rights of survivorship with himself, his wife, Alice, and their daughter, Gabriella. Two years later when the stock was worth $30,000, Bob died. What amount is includible in his estate?

4. Bill provided the full $5,000 purchase price for ABC stock to which he and his son, Angelo, took title as joint tenants with rights of survivorship. The stock was sold several years later for $10,000. Bill and Angelo placed their shares of the sale proceeds in separate bank accounts. They subsequently used their full share of the sale proceeds to purchase, as joint tenants with rights of survivorship, an unimproved lot. At Bill's death the lot was worth $16,000. What is the value of the property includible in Bill's estate at his death?

5. Carol and her son, Bill, purchased Sunny Valley Farm as joint tenants with rights of survivorship for $100,000. Carol provided $20,000 in cash as a down payment on the property, and both Carol and Bill assumed personal liability for an $80,000 mortgage taken out on the property. No payments other than interest were made on the mortgage, and, at Carol's death, Sunny Valley was worth $200,000. What are the estate tax consequences?

6. Would the analysis in the prior problem change if it were discovered that, while the farm was operated during Carol's lifetime, $10,000 in payments on the principal of the mortgage had been made from income produced by the operation of Sunny Valley? What if, rather than coming from income of the joint enterprise, the full $10,000 in payments on principal had been provided by Carol?

Chapter 17

LIFE INSURANCE

(Section 2042)

A. INTRODUCTION

[¶ 17,001]

Insurance is a device whereby a group of individuals or enterprises, typically with the aid of a corporate intermediary referred to as the insurer, share or spread a risk of loss.

Although there are hundreds of different types of life insurance products available, there are two basic categories, term and whole or cash value. Under term insurance, the holder or owner of the policy pays a premium to the insurer sufficient to enable the insurer, in the event of death of the insured, to pay to the policy's beneficiaries the face amount of the policy. Term insurance is sometimes described as "pure" insurance in that the premium charged reflects only the risk of death for the insured, the cost of administering the insurance program and profit for the insurer. As the insured increases in age, the premium increases or the coverage (face amount) of the policy declines.

Under whole or cash value life insurance, the holder of the policy in essence acquires two separate interests, an insurance policy and a savings account. The annual premium paid for such a policy is typically several times that charged for a term policy but unlike term insurance, the premium for this form of life insurance normally does not increase (nor does coverage decline) with the age of the insured. The surplusage in premiums over that needed to cover risk of death, administration expenses and profits for the insurer forms the basis for creation of a savings component in the policy. The value of this savings component is often referred to as the cash surrender value because the owner of the policy can surrender her rights in the policy to the insurer, in exchange for this sum. Typically the owner of such a policy can "borrow" the cash value of the policy from the insurer, in which case, in the event of death of the insured, the amount so withdrawn will not be available for distribution to the policy's beneficiaries. Earnings on cash value typically are used to: (1) pay all or part of the higher premium necessitated by increasing mortality risk as the insured ages; (2) add coverage to keep up with inflation; or (3) enhance the cash value through reinvestment. For a more thorough discussion of these and other life insurance products, see Jerry, Understanding Insurance Law § 13A (3d ed., 2002).

Under state law, for a party to be able to acquire a life insurance policy that party must have what is defined by statute or judicial decision as an "insurable interest" in the life of the insured. In general, for a party to have an insurable interest in the life of another he must have an economic interest in the continued existence of the insured. The reason for this is understandable once we step back into history. Prior to the development of the insurable interest doctrine in eighteenth century England, it was common for people to wager on the outcomes of trials involving capital offenses by purchasing insurance on the life of the accused. It was also fashionable to use insurance to place wagers on the lives of prominent personages, such as the King or the Duke of Norfolk. Not unexpectedly, this led to lively coverage in the financial press of every detail of the state of health of those favored by individuals who fancied gambling in this fashion. See Jerry, Id. at § 40.

It was to eliminate this unsavory form of gambling, as well as to foil plots for enrichment based on schemes to insure and then murder strangers that the insurable interest doctrine was developed. In addition to being able to insure one's own life, the insurable interest rule permits insurance of the lives of close relatives, key employees and business associates. The actual parties covered will vary from state to state. Occasionally the insurable interest rule will impact tax planning involving life insurance.

The estate tax as originally enacted in 1916 contained no specific provision for the inclusion of life insurance in the gross estate, with the result that only insurance payable to the estate was subject to taxation. In 1918 Congress reacted by passing a specific provision which included in the decedent's estate the proceeds of policies on the life of the deceased payable: (1) to the deceased's executor; or (2) to "all other beneficiaries as insurance under policies taken out by the decedent."

Few serious problems ever arose with respect to the taxation of the first category, insurance payable to the executor, although the courts and the IRS have made clear that encompassed by that language is life insurance which, while not designated as payable to the estate, financially benefits the estate. See Reg. § 20.2042–1(b); Bintliff v. United States, 462 F.2d 403 (5th Cir. 1972). For example, a life insurance policy payable to a creditor of the deceased as collateral for a loan to the deceased is considered to be payable to the estate of the deceased. Given its uncontroversial history, it is not surprising that a provision which includes in the estate life insurance payable to the deceased's executor has remained in the Code virtually unchanged since 1918. See § 2042(1).

With respect to the second category of insurance—that payable to "all other beneficiaries"—the statute has gone through a number of changes. In 1942 Congress decided to tax the proceeds of such insurance on the life of the decedent if the decedent: (1) directly or indirectly paid the premiums; or (2) possessed any of the incidents of ownership with respect to the policy.

In 1954, Congress, doubtless not without some prompting from the life insurance industry, decided to drop the premiums payment test on the ground that no other property which is owned by others is included in the estate of the deceased because the deceased purchased it for others. In 1954 the statute was also amended to indicate that possession by a decedent of a reversionary interest in a policy on his or her life would give rise to inclusion of policy proceeds in his or her estate if the value of the reversionary interest exceeds five percent of the value of the policy immediately before death.

Since 1954 there has been no change of substance to § 2042 and proceeds of a policy are now includible in the estate of the insured decedent under § 2042 if: (1) payable to the decedent's executor; or (2) payable to others if the decedent retained with respect to the policy "any of the incidents of ownership, exercisable either alone or in conjunction with any other person."

[¶ 17,005]

1. INCIDENTS OF OWNERSHIP

The report of the House Ways and Means Committee that accompanied the 1942 legislation, which added the "incidents of ownership" language to the Code, contains the following statement on the meaning of the phrase:

> There is no specific enumeration of incidents of ownership, the possession of which at death forms the basis for inclusion of insurance proceeds in the gross estate as it is impossible to include an exhaustive list. Examples of such incidents are the right of the insured or his estate to the economic benefits of the insurance, the power to change the beneficiary, the power to surrender or cancel the policy, the power to assign it, the power to revoke an assignment, the power to pledge a policy for a loan, or the power to obtain from the insurer a loan against the surrender value of the policy. Incidents of ownership are not confined to those possessed by the decedent in a technical legal sense. For example, a power to change the beneficiary reserved to a corporation of which the decedent is the sole stockholder is an incident of ownership in the decedent. * * * H.R. Rep. No. 2333, 77th Cong., 2d Sess. 57, at 163.

Regulation § 20.2042–1(c)(2) contains examples of incidents of ownership which are fundamentally the same as those provided in the legislative history of the 1942 legislation.

[¶ 17,010]

2. APPLICATION OF OTHER CODE SECTIONS

While § 2042 sets forth the principal rules for taxation of life insurance on the decedent's life, other sections may also cause an inclusion of policy proceeds in the estate of the insured. For example, under § 2035, which covers transfers within three years of death, if the decedent transferred the incidents of ownership in a policy on his life to other parties and died within

¶ 17,001

three years of the transfer, there would be an inclusion, under § 2035, in the decedent's estate of the amount paid to beneficiaries under the policy. See Chapter 23, ¶ 23,025 et seq.

Also, note that § 2042 applies only to policies on the life of the decedent. Section 2042 does not apply where the decedent owned a policy of insurance on the life of another person and that other person, the insured, survives the deceased owner of the policy. Instead, the policy is included in the deceased policy owner's estate (rather than that of the insured) under § 2033. Generally speaking, the value of the policy thereby included is its interpolated terminal reserve, i.e., roughly its cash value plus unearned premium. The basic valuation rules are provided in Reg. § 20.2031–8(a)(1) and (2).

[¶ 17,015]

3. LIABILITY FOR TAX ON LIFE INSURANCE

In most states, if there is no will or if the will is silent on the issue, taxes will be borne by those who receive taxable property. If, as form wills commonly do, the will directs that all taxes and debts be borne by the probate residue, this could result in little or nothing of value passing to the residual legatee, especially in a case where there is a large non-probate estate. Aware of this potential for unintended injustices, Congress has selectively attempted to deal with this issue for a number of non-probate assets which are included in the taxable estate. See ¶ 28,073. In the case of life insurance, unless the decedent clearly directs otherwise in his will, under § 2206, the executor is entitled to collect from the beneficiaries of taxable life insurance on the life of decedent "such portion of the total tax paid as the proceeds of such policies bear to the taxable estate."

B. LIFE INSURANCE BROADLY DEFINED

[¶ 17,020]

In order for benefits paid at death to be taxable as life insurance under § 2042 there must be a spreading of a risk of loss of life among a larger group. It is unimportant precisely what label is placed on the contract or arrangement. For example, death benefits paid by fraternal beneficial societies, flight insurance, accidental death insurance and double indemnity riders on conventional life insurance policies all constitute life insurance for purposes of § 2042. See Commissioner v. Estate of Noel, 380 U.S. 678 (1965); Estate of Ackerman v. Commissioner, 15 B.T.A. 635 (1929); Reg. § 20.2042–1(a)(1); & Rev. Rul. 65–222, 1965–2 C.B. 374. In Commissioner v. Treganowan, 183 F.2d 288 (2d Cir.1950), the court, perhaps operating at the outer limits of the law, ruled that death benefits paid to designated beneficiaries of deceased members of the New York Stock Exchange constituted life insurance since the fund from which such benefits were paid had its origins in levies on the 1,374 members of the Exchange.

The following ruling demonstrates not only how less than garden variety life insurance can be subject to tax under § 2042 but also demonstrates a situation in which §§ 2042(1) and 2033 could be applied in the context of an accidental death.

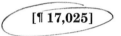

[¶ 17,025]

REVENUE RULING 83–44

1983–1 C.B. 228.

ISSUE

Is the value of death benefits receivable under a policy issued pursuant to State Y's no-fault insurance statute by the executor of D, the operator of the insured vehicle, and C, a passenger in the vehicle, includible in the respective gross estates of D and C under section 2042 of the Internal Revenue Code?

FACTS

D, a resident of State Y, died as a result of an injury incurred when the automobile that D owned and was driving was involved in a collision. C, a passenger in the automobile, died in the collision. Under State Y's no-fault motor vehicle insurance statute, an owner of a motor vehicle registered in State Y must carry no-fault insurance or maintain another form of financial security, such as a cash bond, for the payment of benefits specified in the statute. * * *

D carried the required no-fault insurance policy. The policy provided for the payment of up to $50x$ dollars as a "basic economic loss benefit" covering D's medical expenses and loss of income arising from D's injury while operating the insured vehicle. In addition, in the event of D's accidental death while operating the insured vehicle, a $10x$ dollar "death benefit" was paid to D's estate. The policy also provided that a "death benefit" of $10x$ dollars was to be paid to the estate of any passenger killed in the insured vehicle. Payment of the death benefit did not preclude the recipient estates, or heirs of the decedents, from pursuing any right of action for additional damages arising on account of the accident. D's estate and C's estate each received a $10x$ dollar death benefit payment under the policy, and $20x$ dollars was paid to D's estate as a basic economic loss benefit covering D's medical expenses incurred as a result of the accident.

LAW AND ANALYSIS

Section 2042(1) of the Code provides that the gross estate includes the proceeds of insurance receivable by the executor under policies on the life of the decedent. Section 20.2042–1(a)(1) of the Estate Tax Regulations provides that the term "insurance" refers to life insurance of every description, including death benefits paid by fraternal beneficial societies operating under the lodge system.

In Helvering v. LeGierse, 312 U.S. 531 (1941), 1941–1 C.B. 430, the Court, in defining what constitutes life insurance for purposes of the predecessor of section 2042 of the Code, stated that the essential elements of life insurance are risk-shifting and risk-distributing in the event of loss because of death.

In Rev. Rul. 57–54, 1957–1 C.B. 298, an airplane owner carried insurance which provided for payments to passengers or their representatives in the event of accidental death. The ruling holds that the payments made to a decedent's estate are not life insurance proceeds under section 2042 of the Code even though they are paid without regard to the legal liability of the insured because, under the facts of the ruling, the proceeds were payable only if the insured were released from liability by those persons having a cause of action arising out of the accident. The ruling holds that payments are includible under section 2042 if an insurer unconditionally agrees to make payments in the event of the insured's death and the executor accepts the payments.

In Rev. Rul. 68–88, 1968–1 C.B. 397, amounts were payable under an uninsured motorists endorsement in an automobile liability policy. This endorsement provided that the insurer would pay to a deceased insured's estate all amounts which the insured's estate would have been legally entitled to recover as damages from the operator of an uninsured automobile in an action for wrongful death. The ruling holds that the payments originated under the state's wrongful death statute since, after payment of the claim, the decedent's executor was foreclosed from instituting a wrongful death action and the insurer became subrogated to the rights of the insured against the uninsured motorist. Thus, in that situation, the payments were not life insurance proceeds for purposes of section 2042 of the Code.

In this case, the no-fault insurance policy purchased by D is a contract under which D shifted the risk of deaths to the insurer, and the insurer distributed the risk of loss among those participating in the no-fault insurance program. The payment of a death benefit to D's executors is conditioned only upon D's loss of life and is not a substitute for a wrongful death suit. The death benefit, which is payable regardless of the existence of a wrongful death claim, flows from the insurance policy and is similar to the unconditional payment discussed in Rev. Rul. 57–54, cited above. Consequently, the death benefit payable under the policy to D's executor is proceeds of insurance on the life of D. Since the proceeds are payable to the executor, the proceeds are includible in D's gross estate under section 2042(1) of the Code.

Similarly, the death benefit payable to C's executor also represents the proceeds of insurance on the life of C, includible in C's gross estate under section 2042(1) of the Code. See Rev. Rul. 57–54, cited above.

The basic economic loss benefit of $20x$ dollars was paid to D's estate to cover medical expenses incurred by D, and not on account of D's loss of life. Consequently, the $20x$ dollars is not includible in D's gross estate under section 2042(1) of the Code. However, the benefit is includible under section 2033 of the Code. See Rev. Rul. 75–127, 1975–1 C.B. 297.

Holding

The value of death benefits receivable under a policy issued pursuant to State Y's no-fault insurance statute by the executors of D, the operator of the insured vehicle, and *C*, a passenger in the vehicle, is includible in the respective gross estates of *D* and *C* under section 2042(1) of the Code.

C. POSSESSION OF THE INCIDENTS OF OWNERSHIP

[¶ 17,030]

UNITED STATES v. RHODE ISLAND HOSPITAL TRUST CO.

United States Court of Appeals, First Circuit, 1966.
355 F.2d 7.

COFFIN, Circuit Judge.

This appeal presents the question whether the proceeds of a life insurance policy on decedent's life are properly includable in the gross estate of the decedent by reason of the alleged possession at his death of "any of the incidents of ownership, exercisable either alone or in conjunction with any other person," under Section 2042 of the Internal Revenue Code of 1954, 26 U.S.C. § 2042.

* * *

The facts, undisputed, are of two kinds: "intent facts"—those relating to the conduct and understanding of the insured and his father, who was the instigator, premium payer, and primary beneficiary of the policy; and the "policy facts"—those revealed by the insurance contract itself.

Decedent's father, Charles A. Horton, was a textile executive, a prominent businessman in his community, and, according to the testimony, "a man with strong convictions and vigorous action." Charles and his wife, Louise, had two sons, decedent and A. Trowbridge Horton. In 1924, when decedent was 18 and Trowbridge 19, their father purchased an insurance policy on the life of each boy from Massachusetts Mutual Life Insurance Company. The policies were identical, each having the face amount of $50,000, the proceeds being payable to Charles and Louise, equally, or to the survivor.

Charles Horton's purpose was to assure that funds would be available for his wife, should he and either son die. Charles kept the policies in his safe deposit box and paid all premiums throughout his life. Under the policies, however, the right to change beneficiaries had been reserved to the sons. In January, 1952, the boys' mother, Louise, died. In March, 1952, Charles told each of his sons to go to the insurance company's office and sign a change of beneficiary form. The amendment executed by decedent named his father as primary beneficiary, with decedent's wife, brother, and the executors or administrators of the last survivor being the successive beneficiaries. After this amendment, decedent continued to retain the right to make further changes, but none was made. Decedent died on April 1, 1958, survived by his wife and father. His father died on October 2, 1961.

¶ 17,025

The father, Charles, regarded the policies as belonging to him, saying at one point that it would be "out of the question" for the sons to claim them. Decedent's brother never discussed the policies with his father, never asked for a loan based on the policies, obediently signed the change of beneficiary form at his father's request, and considered the policy on his life as the property of his father. Decedent's widow recalled only that decedent had once told her that his father had a policy on himself and his brother but that "in no way did it mean anything to us or would it ever. It was completely his." She added that her husband, the decedent, had wanted more insurance of his own, but was not able to obtain it.

Coming to what we call "policy facts", a careful reading of the policy, captioned "Ordinary Life Policy—Convertible", reveals the following rights, privileges, or powers accorded to the decedent.

—Right to change beneficiary. In the application, an unrestricted change of beneficiary provision was elected by striking out two alternative and more limited provisions. The policy itself indicated reservation of "the right successively to change the beneficiary" by the insertion of typewritten dashes where, otherwise, the word "not" would have been inserted.

—Assignment. No assignment would be recognized until the original assignment, a duplicate, or a certified copy was filed with the company. The company did not assume responsibility for the validity of an assignment.

—Dividends. The insured had the option to have dividends paid in cash, used to reduce premiums, used to purchase paid-up additions, or accumulate subject to withdrawal on demand.

—Loans. On condition that the unlimited right to change the beneficiary was reserved, as in this case, the company would "loan on the signature of the insured alone".

—Survival. Should no beneficiary survive the insured, the proceeds were payable to his executors and administrators.

—Alteration. The policy could be altered only on the written request of the insured and of "other parties in interest".

—Discharge of company's obligations. The company would not be responsible for the conduct of any trustee or for the determination of the identity or rights of beneficiaries. Payment at the direction of a trustee or in good faith to a beneficiary would discharge the company of its contractual obligations. Beneficiaries were advised by the policy that they need hire no firm or person to collect the amount payable under the policy, but that they would save time and expense by writing to the company directly.

The plaintiffs contend that the district court properly held that decedent possessed no incidents of ownership in the policy; that the term "incidents of ownership" refers to the rights of insured or his estate to the economic benefits of the policy; that the question of possession of such incidents is one of fact; that such possession depends upon all relevant facts and circumstances, including the intention of the parties; and that these facts and circumstances clearly establish that decedent's father was the real owner of

¶ 17,030

the policy, while decedent was merely the nominal owner, having no real economic interest in it.

The government asserts that, as a matter of law, the facts bring this case squarely within the reach of Section 2042, as applied by the cases, notwithstanding the evidence as to the intentions and extra-policy circumstances of the parties, and the lack of economic benefit to decedent.

* * *

Taking the subsidiary facts as presented to the district court, we differ with its conclusion that "the decedent's father was actually the real owner of the various incidents of ownership in said policy." But in differing we recognize that early holdings and occasional dicta, early and late, have invited litigation. This is the kind of case where the government enters, appearing to seek its pound of flesh on the basis of petty technicality, while the taxpayer's decedent generally appears as a person who had very little to do with the insurance policy which is causing so much trouble to his estate. If such hard cases have not made bad law, they have at least made bad dicta. * * * [W]e think it appropriate to set forth the considerations of fact, law, and policy which have persuaded us.

To begin, the statute which bears on this case has a reason for being, is part of a general rationale and tax law pattern, and is deliberately precise. Before the Revenue Act of 1942, the tax criterion governing cases in this area was "policies taken out" by the decedent on his own life. Section 302(g), Revenue Act of 1926, ch. 27, 44 Stat. 9. This led to difficult problems of interpretation, which the courts resolved by creating two criteria: "payment of premiums" and possession of "incidents of ownership." The Revenue Act of 1942, ch. 619, 56 Stat. 798, Section 404, eliminated the "policies taken out" language, and sanctified the judicial gloss, with Congress, in its committee reports, including an illustrative list of the kinds of rights included under "incidents of ownership." These included decedent's right to change beneficiaries, to borrow, to assign, to revoke an assignment, and to surrender or cancel. H.Rep.No.2333, 77th Cong., 2d Sess., p. 164, 1942–2 Cum.Bull. 372, 491.

In acting this way, Congress was, we think, trying to introduce some certitude in a landscape of shifting sands. In the provision which was the predecessor of Section 2042, it was not trying to tax the *extent* of the interest of the decedent. That it knew how to do this is evident, for example, from a reading of Section 2033 * * * which includes in the gross estate of the decedent "the value of all property * * * to the extent of the interest therein * * *." What it was attempting to reach in Section 2042 and some other sections was the *power* to dispose of property * * *. Power can be and is exercised by one possessed of less than complete legal and equitable title. The very phrase "incidents of ownership" connotes something partial, minor, or even fractional in its scope. It speaks more of possibility than of probability.

Plaintiffs seize on Section 20.2042–1(c)(2) of the Treasury Regulations on Estate Tax, which says " * * * the term 'incidents of ownership' is not limited in its meaning to ownership of the policy in the technical legal sense.

¶ 17,030

Generally speaking, the term has reference to the right of the insured or his estate to the economic benefits of the policy." Plaintiffs urge that there must be "a real control over the economic benefits." To this there are two answers. First, it is clear that the reference to ownership in the "technical legal sense" is not abandoned and supplanted by reference to "economic benefits." Second, the regulation goes on to list illustrative powers referred to by Congress in its reports. All of these are powers which may or may not enrich decedents' estate, but which can affect the transfer of the policy proceeds.

Viewed against this background, what power did decedent possess? This is the relevant question—not how did he feel or act. Did he have a capacity to do something to affect the disposition of the policy if he had wanted to? Without gaining possession of the policy itself, he could have borrowed on the policy. He could have changed the method of using dividends. He could have assigned the policy. He could have revoked the assignment. Should he have gained possession of the policy by trick (as by filing an affidavit that the policy was lost), force, or chance, he could have changed the beneficiary, and made the change of record irrevocable. Other such possibilities might be imagined. We cite these only to evidence the existence of some power in decedent to affect the disposition of the policy proceeds. In addition, he always possessed a negative power. His signature was necessary to a change in beneficiary, to a surrender for cash value, to an alteration in the policy, to a change in dividend options. Even with this most limited power, he would be exercising an incident of ownership "in conjunction with" another person.

The existence of such powers in the decedent is to be distinguished from such rights as may have existed in decedent's father or duties owed the father by decedent. It is, therefore, no answer that decedent's father might have proceeded against him at law or in equity. The company made it clear in the contract that it bore no responsibility for the validity of an assignment, that it could pay a beneficiary without recourse, and that it was under no obligation to see to the carrying out of any trust. It even made clear that a beneficiary need only write to the home office to receive payment. Should a third party— for example, an innocent creditor who had given valuable consideration to decedent—receive the proceeds of the policy, the proceeds of a loan on the policy, or the cash value, it could not be said that the transaction between decedent and such third person would in all such cases be nugatory. For decedent had some powers—perhaps not rights, but powers—which could, if exercised alone or in conjunction with another, affect the disposition of some or all of the proceeds of the policy.

Nor is it a compelling argument that decedent lacked physical possession of the policy. Moreover, as we have noted, some rights could be exercised without physical possession of the policy.

* * *

To the principle of heavy predominance of the "policy facts" over the "intent facts" there must be added the caveat that, where the insurance contract itself does not reflect the instructions of the parties, as where an agent, on his own initiative, inserts a reservation of right to change a beneficiary contrary to the intentions which had been expressed to him, no incidents of ownership are thereby created. The case before us presents no such issue, for the right in decedent to change beneficiaries was recognized on the one occasion when it was exercised and this right continued thereafter.

* * *

In any event, the statute has been on the books since the Revenue Act of 1942. This is only one of a number of cases applying it in the face of considerable external evidence of intent. Charles Horton, who caused the policy to be taken out, saw fit to vest decedent with rights in the policy and to allow such rights to continue for thirty-four years. Charles was a successful businessman and with as much incentive, opportunity, and capacity to be aware of the laws of the land as most people. It is difficult to speculate what purpose he thought was being served by his son's retention of rights in the policy. Had he wished to deprive his son of all incidents of ownership in the policy, this result could easily have been accomplished. But the step was not taken. We find that the decedent died, possessing at least an incident of ownership in the policy on his life.

* * *

[¶ 17,035]

MORTON v. UNITED STATES

United States Court of Appeals, Fourth Circuit, 1972.
457 F.2d 750.

CRAVEN, Circuit Judge:

* * * The district judge concluded * * * the Commissioner erroneously included in the gross estate the proceeds of a policy of life insurance. We affirm. We think that the decedent did not possess any of the incidents of ownership of this insurance policy at the time of his death so as to require inclusion of the proceeds in the decedent's gross estate under Section 2042(2) of the Internal Revenue Code of 1954.

* * * [T]he policy was taken out in 1932 by the decedent at the instigation of his father-in-law, who wanted to provide financial security for his daughter. The decedent paid none of the premiums on this insurance policy and it is clear that he never considered that he "owned" it. The premiums were paid by his father-in-law, then by a corporation owned by the decedent's wife and her sister, and finally by the decedent's wife until the decedent's death in 1963. The policy was kept in the office safe of another corporation owned by the decedent's wife and her sister.

The provisions of the policy which have a bearing on whether or not the proceeds should be included in the decedent's gross estate have been summarized correctly by the district court as follows:

1. *Assignments.* No assignment of the policy would be binding upon the Company until filed at its home office, and the Company assumed no responsibility as to the validity or effect of any assignment.

2. *Premium loans.* The insured and assignees, if any, could request the insurer for a premium loan provided the request was made prior to default and the cash surrender value was sufficient to cover the premium then due.

3. *Cash surrender value.* Upon receipt of the policy and a full and valid surrender of all claims thereunder, and "without the consent or participation of any Beneficiary not irrevocably designated or any Contingent Beneficiary" the Company would pay the cash surrender value of the policy.

4. *Policy loans.* At any time after premiums for two full years had been paid and while the policy was in force except as extended-term insurance, without the consent or participation of any beneficiary not irrevocably designated or any contingent beneficiary, a policy loan could be obtained by properly assigning the policy and forwarding it to the Company at its home office. The amount of the policy loans was limited to the amount secured by the cash surrender value of the policy.

5. *Dividend options.* At the option of the insured, dividends could be (a) withdrawn in cash; (b) applied toward the payment of premiums; (c) applied toward the purchase of a participating paid-up addition to the policy; (d) left to accumulate with interest. Dividends were subject to withdrawal in cash at any time or could be paid with the proceeds of the policy.

6. *Endowment option.* Whenever the reserve on the policy at the end of a policy year, together with the reserve on the existing dividend additions, should be equal to or in excess of the face amount of the policy, the insured could upon surrender of the policy, as well as a full and valid surrender of all claims thereunder, without consent or participation of any beneficiary not irrevocably designated or any contingent beneficiary, obtain the face amount of the policy.

7. *Full paid participating insurance.* The insured could obtain full paid participating insurance provided certain specified conditions were met.

8. *Paid-up insurance.* The insured and assigns, if any, upon written request to the Company, could obtain participating paid-up life insurance instead of automatic extended-term insurance, if such request was made prior to default in premium payment or within the grace period.

9. *Beneficiaries.* The insured could (1) designate one or more beneficiaries either with or without reservation of the right to revoke such designation; (2) designate one or more contingent beneficiaries; (3) change any beneficiary not irrevocably designated; and (4) change any contingent beneficiary.

10. *Method of payment.* The insured could designate the method by which the proceeds of the policy would be paid to the beneficiaries.

11. *Reinstatement.* The insured could have the policy reinstated at any time within five years after default in payment of premiums by paying all premium arrears, with interest, and any indebtedness which might exist, with interest, upon evidence satisfactory to the Company of his insurability.

In 1938 the decedent executed an endorsement of the policy effecting an irrevocable designation of beneficiaries and mode of settlement. It is the effect of this endorsement upon the other terms of the policy which is determinative of the issue raised.

* * *

It is clear that before the execution of the irrevocable designation of beneficiaries and mode of settlement the policy conferred upon the decedent, as the insured, many, if not all of the powers which Congress had in mind as being incidents of ownership sufficient to cause the proceeds to be included in his gross estate. Ordinarily the possession by the insured of the power to cash the policy in, to elect the endowment option, to get a loan on the policy or to change the beneficiary is sufficient to cause the proceeds to be included in his gross estate. However, we think that the irrevocable designation of beneficiaries and mode of settlement, coupled with payment of premiums by persons other than the insured, made it legally impossible for the decedent to exercise other powers purportedly given him as insured by the policy in such a way that any economic benefit would accrue to him or his estate or so that he could subsequently control the transfer of the proceeds of the policy.

The government concedes that the endorsement of April 7, 1938, divested the decedent of the right to change beneficiaries and to select another method of payment. However, it maintains that other provisions of the policy were left unaffected and there remained in the decedent some incidents of ownership.

It is well established that if the insured retains no right to change the beneficiary of a life insurance policy or, as here, gives up that right, the beneficiary stands in the position of a third party beneficiary to the insurance contract with indefeasibly vested rights in the proceeds. * * * Most authorities are also in agreement that the insured cannot deal with the policy in such a way as to defeat the irrevocably designated third party beneficiaries' interest in the proceeds, by, for example, surrendering the policy for its cash surrender value, without the consent of the beneficiaries, and we think the district court was clearly correct that this result would obtain in [the state of decedent's domicile].

The inquiry is not ended here, however. The district court rejected the government's secondary contention that even if the insured had no independent power he nevertheless had the power to act "in conjunction with" the beneficiaries in exercising incidents of ownership and thus the proceeds of the policy would be includable in the decedent's gross estate under the express language of Section 2042(2) of the Code. We agree that the decisive factor is the existence of the *power* to exercise incidents of ownership either alone or in conjunction with any other person. If both the decedent and the beneficiaries were legally required to act in conjunction in order to affect any of the options of the policy which could be called incidents of ownership, and even if these options could only be exercised in the best financial interest of the beneficiaries and with the approval of a court, the decedent nevertheless possessed the power to exercise the incidents of ownership "in conjunction with any other person." That would suffice under Section 2042(2) to bring the proceeds of the policy within the gross estate. But we are convinced the beneficiaries could effectively act alone to exercise the incidents of ownership. Participation

¶ 17,035

by the decedent "in conjunction with" the beneficiaries was not required, we think, on the facts of this case.

The law of [the state of decedent's domicile] with regard to the right of irrevocably designated beneficiaries to exercise options of a life insurance policy without the consent of the insured is unclear at best. Other courts which have considered analogous insurance problems have done so in light of earlier revenue acts which did not make the proceeds taxable if any incident of ownership was exercisable in conjunction with another person, and hence did not fully consider whether the consent of the insured would be a prerequisite to the exercise of a particular power by an irrevocably designated beneficiary. We think that whether or not an irrevocably designated beneficiary would have the right to obtain a loan on the policy, cash it in, or elect the endowment option when the *insured* had paid the premiums is doubtful. The indefeasibly vested right to the proceeds by the beneficiary probably would not extend to the right to the use of the premiums which these options represent when the premiums were contributed by another. However, when the irrevocably designated beneficiary has also paid the premiums, we think that he has the legal power to exercise the options in the insurance contract which pertain to the use of these premiums without participation of the insured.

Full paid participating insurance, dividends, paid-up insurance, cash surrender value, premium loans and the endowment option all represent use of the premiums with the consent of the insurance company. We think that general principles of equity and contract law strongly suggest that exercise of such premium payment derived rights properly belong to the irrevocably designated beneficiary who has paid the premiums to the exclusion of the insured who contributed nothing. It is not necessary to ignore the policy facts in order to recognize that with respect to premium derived options it is clear that the decedent never considered the policy his, and had the question come up, that all parties would have doubtless agreed that the decedent's wife should be entitled to exercise these options.

The options for premium loans and reinstatement provide for methods of keeping the policy alive in the event of nonpayment of premiums, and the insured's participation would not be necessary where the beneficiary has a vested right to the proceeds. To hold otherwise would allow the insured to indirectly defeat this vested interest. We hold that where an insured has never paid a premium and has never for any purpose treated the policy as his own that his irrevocable designation of beneficiaries and mode of payment of proceeds is an effective assignment of all of his incidents of ownership in the policy.

The judgment of the district court will be

Affirmed.

Note

[¶ 17,040]

How do you reconcile *Rhode Island Hospital Trust* and *Morton*? Could the attorney in *Rhode Island Hospital Trust* have attempted to save the day by establishing that under state law the insured decedent held the policy as a nominee or agent for the benefit of his father whom the court characterized as "the instigator, premium payer, and primary beneficiary of the policy?"

D. AVOIDING POSSESSION OF THE INCIDENTS OF OWNERSHIP

[¶ 17,043]

An insured who wishes to avoid having proceeds of a policy on her life included in her estate has two fundamental options. First, she can avoid purchasing a policy on her life and leave that task to others making sure that the policy so acquired vests her with no incidents of ownership. Second, she can assign to others all incidents of ownership held by her in policies on her life and can then hope to live at least three additional years thereafter. See Chapter 23, ¶ 23,025 *et seq.* The materials below deal with these alternatives in a variety of contexts.

[¶ 17,045]

1. INTRODUCTION

Obviously one of the best ways of avoiding inclusion of life insurance proceeds in the estate of the insured, in addition to not making it payable to the executor, is avoiding the insured's ever possessing any incidents of ownership by having others with an insurable interest purchase the policy on the life of the insured and make sure that the policy vests no incidents of ownership in the insured. Often the beneficiary of a policy will be a spouse or child, and it is simple enough for that party acquire out the policy. Moreover, since there is no longer a premium payment test, it matters little if the insured financially assists the holder of the policy. Where this strategy is employed, care must be taken in planning the estate of the holder of the policy so that an unanticipated sequence of deaths and failure to draft carefully the will of the holder of the policy do not combine to produce unintended undesirable tax consequences. For example, assume that a wife acquires a policy on the life of her husband payable to their children and predeceases her husband with a will which leaves her entire estate to the husband, thereby transferring to him the incidents of ownership on a policy on his life. The husband's only means of avoiding possession of the incidents of ownership on the policy would seem to be a timely disclaimer of all interest in the policy. See Chapter 6.

Where the intended beneficiary is a party without an insurable interest, for example a son-in-law, a niece or a companion, there are two alternatives. First, the insured could apply for and acquire a policy on her life and assign the policy to the intended beneficiary. This strategy has several problems: (1) the insurable interest rules of a minority of states will allow insurers to void such policies; and (2) under § 2035 unless the insured lives three years after assignment of the policy, the policy proceeds will be included in her estate. See Chapter 23, ¶ 23,025 *et seq.* A second strategy which works in some cases

¶ 17,040

and which avoids the § 2035 problem is to arrange to have a party (other than the insured) who has an insurable interest acquire the policy on the life of the insured. For example, if a woman, as part of her estate plan, wished to have a policy payable to her niece or son-in-law, it would be simple enough to arrange for the woman's husband or daughter to acquire the policy, naming the niece or son-in-law as beneficiary. If state insurable interest rules permit, the policy could then be assigned to the beneficiary although this step is not essential to exclude the policy from the estate of the insured.

There can be unexpected and costly gift tax consequences where someone other than the insured or the beneficiary of a policy purchases a policy from an insurer and continues to hold the incidents of ownership with designation of the beneficiary remaining revocable until death of the insured. In such a circumstance the holder of the revocable power to designate beneficiaries may be deemed to have made an incomplete or revocable gift of the policy which becomes complete at the death of the insured. At this moment there will be a completed gift by the holder to the beneficiary of the value of the proceeds of the policy.

For example, were a mother to acquire from an insurer a policy on her husband's life payable to a child as a revocable beneficiary and were she not to designate irrevocably the child as the beneficiary prior to her husband's death, at the moment of her husband's death the mother would be deemed to be making a gift of the policy proceeds to the child. See Goodman v. Commissioner, 156 F.2d 218 (2d Cir.1946). What was saved from the estate tax could be lost to the gift tax. To guard against such losses, it is wise to consider designating irrevocably both beneficiaries and contingent beneficiaries when policies are acquired and then held by other than the beneficiary.

Where spouses seek to avoid the impact of the incidents of ownership test by acquiring from an insurer policies on each other's life, at least two potential problems are present. First, as previously mentioned, unless the first to die transfers to a person other than the surviving spouse all ownership of the policy on the life of the survivor, or by will bequeaths all interest in this policy to someone other than the surviving spouse, the survivor will find himself or herself with an unintended estate planning problem which can be solved with a timely disclaimer of all interest in the policy. Second, there is some possibility that the IRS could employ the reciprocal trust doctrine, which you will study in Chapter 18 (¶ 18,103 *et seq.*), to include all or some of the insurance proceeds on the life of the first to die in that party's estate despite Rev. Rul. 56–397, 1056–2 C.B. 599 (reciprocal trust doctrine does not apply where partners insure each other to fund buy-sell agreement).

[¶ 17,050]

2. POSSESSION OF UNRETAINED INCIDENTS HELD AS A FIDUCIARY

In Estate of Skifter v. Commissioner, 468 F.2d 699 (2d Cir.1972), the decedent who owned a policy on his life, more than three years prior to his death, assigned all incidents of ownership in the policy to his wife who predeceased her husband and left the policy in question to a trust for the benefit of third parties with her husband as trustee. When the husband subsequently died the IRS sought to include the policy proceeds in his estate on the ground that he possessed the incidents of ownership in the policy in question. The Second Circuit refused to include the policy proceeds in husband's estate on the ground that based on analogy to §§ 2036 and 2038 (Chapters 18 and 19) he had not *retained* the incidents of ownership which after their reconveyance to him he only held in a fiduciary capacity with no possibility of self-benefit. Three years later in Terriberry v. United States, 517 F.2d 286 (5th Cir.1975), cert. denied, 424 U.S. 977 (1976) the IRS was able to get the Fifth Circuit to reach a contrary result on virtually identical facts. Moreover, shortly before deciding *Terriberry* the Fifth Circuit had repudiated the Second Circuit's *Skifter* analysis in Rose v. United States, 511 F.2d 259 (5th Cir.1975). In *Rose* the decedent's brother had created three separate trusts for each of decedent's children funding each with $100 and naming decedent as trustee. Decedent applied, as trustee for each trust, for three separate policies on his life. At his death twelve years later, decedent still held the policies as a trustee under each of the trusts. The Fifth Circuit rejected the reasoning of the Second Circuit in *Skifter* that § 2042(2) applied only to *retained* incidents of ownership noting that the statute specifically refers only to "possessed" incidents and included the proceeds from each of the policies in decedent's taxable estate.

Nine years after its resounding victories in *Rose* and *Terriberry*, the IRS indicated in the ruling which follows below that, on rethinking the issue, it had come to agree with the Second Circuit's opinion in *Skifter*.

[¶ 17,055]

REVENUE RULING 84–179

1984–2 C.B. 195.

Issue

For purposes of section 2042(2) of the Internal Revenue Code, does an insured decedent possess incidents of ownership in an insurance policy if the decedent transferred all incidents of ownership to another person who, in an unrelated transaction, transferred all incidents of ownership to another person who, in an unrelated transaction, transferred the policy in trust and, at death, the decedent was a trustee with discretionary powers which, although broad, could not be exercised for *D*'s personal benefit?

Facts

In 1960, *D*, the decedent, purchased an insurance policy on *D*'s life and transferred all incidents of ownership to *D*'s spouse. The spouse designated their adult child as the policy beneficiary.

The spouse died in 1978 and, by will, established a residuary trust for the benefit of the child. *D* was designated as trustee. The insurance policy on *D*'s life was included in the spouse's residuary estate and was transferred to the testamentary trust. The drafting of the spouse's will to provide for the residuary trust and the appointment of *D* as trustee were unrelated to *D*'s transfer of the policy to the spouse.

As trustee, *D* had broad discretionary powers in the management of the trust property and the power to distribute or accumulate income. Under the terms of the policy, the owner could elect to have the proceeds made payable according to various plans, use the loan value to pay the premiums, borrow on the policy, assign or pledge the policy, and elect to receive annual dividends. The terms of the old will did not preclude *D* from exercising these rights, although *D* could not do so for *D*'s own benefit. *D* paid the premiums on the policy out of other trust property.

D was still serving as trustee when *D* died in 1984.

LAW AND ANALYSIS

Section 2042(2) provides that the value of the gross estate includes the value of all property to the extent of the amount receivable as insurance under policies on the life of the decedent by beneficiaries (other than the executor), with respect to which the decedent possessed at date of death any of the incidents of ownership in the policies, exercisable either alone or in conjunction with any other person.

Section 20.2042–1(c)(2) of the Estate Tax Regulations provides that the meaning of the term "incidents of ownership" is not confined to ownership of the policy in the technical legal sense. The term includes the power to change the beneficiary, to surrender or cancel the policy for a loan, or to obtain from the insurer a loan against the surrender value of the policy, etc.

Section 20.2042–1(c)(4) of the regulations provides that a decedent is considered to have an incident of ownership in a policy held in trust if under the terms of the policy the decedent (either alone or in conjunction with another person) has the power (as trustee or otherwise) to change the beneficial ownership in the policy or its proceeds, or the time or manner of enjoyment thereof, even though the decedent has no beneficial interest in the trust.

The legislative history of section 2042 indicates that Congress intended section 2042 to parallel the statutory scheme governing those powers that would cause other types of property to be included in a decedent's gross estate under other Code sections, particularly sections 2036 and 2038. S. Rep. No. 1622, 83rd Cong., 2d Sess. 124 (1954). See Estate of Skifter v. Commissioner, 468 F.2d 699 (2d Cir.1972).

Sections 2036(a)(2) and 2038(a)(1) concern lifetime transfers made by the decedent. Under these sections, it is the decedent's power to affect the beneficial interests in, or enjoyment of, the transferred property that required inclusion of the property in the gross estate. Section 2036 is directed at those powers retained by the decedent in connection with the transfer. See, for example, United States v. O'Malley, 383 U.S. 627 (1966), 1966–2 C.B. 526. Section 2038(a)(1) is directed at situations where the transferor-decedent sets the machinery in motion that purposefully allows fiduciary powers over the property interest to subsequently return to the transferor-decedent, such as by an incomplete transfer. See Estate of Reed v. United States, Civil No. 74–543 (M.D. Fla., May 7, 1975); Estate of Skifter v. Commissioner, above cited, at 703–05.

In accordance with the legislative history of section 2042(2), a decedent will not be deemed to have incidents of ownership over an insurance policy on decedent's life where decedent's powers are held in a fiduciary capacity, and are not exercisable for decedent's personal benefit, where the decedent did not transfer the policy or any of the consideration for purchasing or maintaining the policy to the trust from personal assets, and the devolution of the powers on decedent was not part of a prearranged plan involving the participation of decedent. This position is consistent with decisions by several courts of appeal. See *Estate of Skifter*; Estate of Fruehauf v. Commissioner, 427 F.2d 80 (6th Cir.1970); Hunter v. United States, 624 F.2d 833 (8th Cir.1980). But see Terriberry v. United States, 517 F.2d 286 (5th Cir.1975), cert. denied, 424 U.S. 977 (1976); Rose v. United States, 511 F.2d 259 (5th Cir.1975), which are to the contrary. Section 20.2042–1(c)(4) will be read in accordance with the position adopted herein.

The decedent will be deemed to have incidents of ownership over an insurance policy on the decedent's life where decedent's powers are held in a fiduciary capacity and the decedent has transferred the policy or any of the consideration for purchasing and maintaining the policy to the trust. Also, where the decedent's powers could have been exercised for decedent's benefit, they will constitute incidents of ownership in the policy, without regard to how those powers were acquired and without consideration of whether the decedent transferred property to the trust. *Estate of Fruehauf*; *Estate of Skifter*, above cited at 703. Thus, if the decedent reacquires powers over insurance policies in an individual capacity, the powers will constitute incidents of ownership even though the decedent is a transferee.

In the present situation, *D* completely relinquished all interest in the insurance policy on *D*'s life. The powers over the policy devolved on *D* as a fiduciary, through an independent transaction, and were not exercisable for *D*'s own benefit. Also, *D* did not transfer property to the trust. Thus, *D* did not possess incidents of ownership over the policy for purposes of section 2042(2) of the Code.

HOLDING

An insured decedent who transferred all incidents of ownership in a policy to another person, who in an unrelated transaction transferred powers over the policy in trust to the decedent, will not be considered to possess incidents of ownership in the policy for purposes of section 2042(2) of the Code, provided that the decedent did not furnish consideration for maintaining the policy and could not exercise the powers for personal benefit. The result is the same where the decedent, as trustee, purchased the policy with trust assets, did not contribute assets to the trust or maintain the policy with personal assets, and could not exercise the powers for personal benefit.

Note

[¶ 17,060]

Given Congressional rejection of the premiums payment test in 1954, it is curious to see non-payment of premiums mentioned by the IRS as a critical factor in Rev. Rul. 84–179. The premiums payment test seems to have as much resiliency with the IRS and selected members of the judiciary as does Elvis with the dirt track racing crowd.

[¶ 17,065]

3. IRREVOCABLE LIFE INSURANCE TRUSTS

Often because of unforeseeable changes in family situations, such as the birth of additional children or a shift in economic status among dependents, irrevocably assigning a policy to an individual or group of individuals or having such parties purchase and hold such a policy prove to be less than optimal solutions to accommodating both tax minimization and changing family financial needs.

An individual who holds, or is about to purchase, life insurance on her life and who wishes to avoid inclusion of the policy proceeds in her estate at death, but at the same time wishes to ensure the insurance will be available to benefit the insured's family in a flexible fashion, frequently seeks to attain these goals by effecting a transfer of the policy to an irrevocable trust or by arranging for the trustee to purchase the policy. Although with the demise of the premium payment test it is unnecessary, the trust is sometimes funded with property, the income from which will be used to pay policy premiums. A trusted family friend, attorney or financial institution is often appointed as trustee to provide for responsive treatment of the family. Since, at his or her death, the insured will not possess any of the incidents of ownership, the policy proceeds will typically be excluded from the estate of the insured. In establishing the trust, care must be taken so that the insured does not retain any rights or powers with respect to the trust that could result in its inclusion in the estate under not only § 2042, but also §§ 2036, 2037, or 2038 (Chapters 18, 19 and 20).

Moreover, if an existing policy on which the insured holds the incidents of ownership is transferred into the trust, unless the insured lives for at least three years after effecting the transfer, the proceeds of the policy will be included in the taxable estate of the insured decedent under § 2035. See Salyer v. United States, 98–2 USTC ¶ 60,326, 82 AFTR 2d ¶ 98,5967 (E.D. Ky.1998).

The following ruling, while impliedly indicating IRS acceptance of the principle of the irrevocable life insurance trust as an effective estate planning device, also indicates the need for the estate planner to pay attention to detail when employing such a device.

[¶ 17,070]

REVENUE RULING 79–129

1979–1 C.B. 306

ISSUE

To what extent are the proceeds of a life insurance policy on a decedent's life includible in the decedent's gross estate under section 2042 of the Internal Revenue Code of 1954, in the circumstances described below?

FACTS

In 1973, D obtained an ordinary life insurance policy on D's life. The policy had a face amount of $150,000. Simultaneously, D created an irrevocable funded insurance trust and named the X Trust Company as trustee.

The insurance policy designated the trustee of the insurance trust as owner of the policy. Under the terms of the policy, D possessed the right to borrow against the cash surrender value in an amount not to exceed the total amount of the policy premiums paid by D. However, the policy had no cash surrender value during the first year.

The policy designated D's estate as the beneficiary of the policy proceeds to the extent of an amount equal to the cash surrender value of the policy immediately prior to D's death, less any outstanding indebtedness against the policy. The policy designated the X Trust Company, as trustee of the insurance trust, as the beneficiary of the balance of the proceeds.

With the exception of D's right to borrow against the cash surrender value, noted above, all other contract rights with respect to the policy were exercisable by the trustee of the insurance trust, as owner of the policy. These contract rights included the right to assign and surrender the policy, to elect paid up insurance, and to change the beneficiary of the policy proceeds to the extent they exceeded the cash surrender value, which was payable to D's estate.

The terms of the trust provide that, on D's death, the trustee is to hold the insurance proceeds for the benefit of D's spouse and children. The trust agreement further provides that D would be responsible for payment of the portion of the annual premium that is equal to the increase in the cash surrender value of the policy during the year. The trustee would be responsible for the payment of the balance of the annual premium.

D died in 1977, more than three years after D obtained the insurance policy and created the insurance trust. Between 1973 and 1977, D paid a total of $12,000 in premiums on the policy, in accordance with D's obligations under the terms of the trust agreement. During the period, D did not exercise the power to borrow against the cash surrender value. At the time of D's death, the cash surrender value of the policy was $12,000. Consequently, $12,000 of the policy proceeds was paid to D's estate. The balance of the proceeds, $138,000, was paid to the X Trust Company in accordance with the terms of the policy.

¶ 17,070

On the Federal estate tax return filed for D's estate, the executor included the $12,000 in policy proceeds payable to the decedent's estate under section 2042(1). The executor excluded the $138,000 balance of the proceeds, which was payable to a beneficiary other than the decedent's estate, on the ground that this portion of the proceeds was not includible under section 2042(2), because the incidents of ownership in the policy possessed by D could not be exercised to affect this portion of the policy proceeds.

LAW AND ANALYSIS

Section 2042(1) provides for the inclusion in the gross estate of the proceeds of insurance on the decedent's life receivable by the decedent's estate. Section 2042(2) of the Code includes in the gross estate proceeds of insurance on the decedent's life receivable by beneficiaries other than the decedent's estate under policies with respect to which the decedent possessed at his death any incidents of ownership, exercisable either alone or in conjunction with any other person.

Section 20.2042–1(c)(2) of the Estate Tax Regulations describes "incidents of ownership" as follows:

"For purposes of this paragraph, the term 'incidents of ownership' is not limited in its meaning to ownership of the policy in the technical legal sense. Generally speaking, the term has reference to the right of the insured or his estate to the economic benefits of the policy. Thus, it includes the power to change the beneficiary, to surrender or cancel the policy, to assign the policy, to revoke an assignment, to pledge the policy for a loan, or to obtain from the insurer a loan against the surrender value of the policy, etc. . . . . "

The right of an insured to obtain a loan against the surrender value of the policy is specified in the regulations as an incident of ownership. The courts have recognized that this power furnishes grounds for including the entire policy proceeds in the gross estate, even in situations where the decedent's power to borrow is limited to the amount of the policy premiums.

In the situation presented in the instant case, $12,000 in policy proceeds were paid to D's estate, under the terms of the policy. Since this $12,000 in proceeds is payable to D's estate, this amount is includible in D's gross estate pursuant to section 2042(1).

The balance of the proceeds, $138,000, was paid to the X Trust Company, a beneficiary other than the decedent's estate. Consequently, the estate taxation of these proceeds is governed by section 2042(2).

Under the terms of the insurance contract, D possessed the right to borrow against the cash surrender value of the policy to the extent of the premiums paid by D and not recovered. In accordance with section 20.2042–1(c)(2) of the regulations, and [reported cases], this power qualifies as an incident of ownership for purposes of section 2042(2), even though the amount D could borrow against the surrender value was limited. If the decedent possessed an incident of ownership in the policy, then the entire policy proceeds payable to a beneficiary other than the decedent's estate are

¶ 17,070

includible in the decedent's gross estate regardless of the fact that a portion of the proceeds subject to inclusion could not be affected by the exercise of the incident of ownership.

HOLDING

1) Pursuant to section 2042(1), $12,000 of the policy proceeds are includible in D's gross estate.

2) The balance of the proceeds, $138,000, is includible in D's gross estate pursuant to section 2042(2).

The same Federal estate tax consequences would obtain regardless of the source of premium payments, or the portion of proceeds payable to the trustee and the decedent's estate.

Further, if D had died within the first year after the policy was issued, then the policy would have had no cash surrender value at the time of D's death. Under the terms of the policy the entire policy proceeds, $150,000, would have been paid to the trustee. Under these circumstances, $150,000 would be includible in D's gross estate under section 2042(2) of the Code, representing the proceeds payable to a beneficiary other than the decedent's estate under an insurance policy with respect to which the decedent possessed incidents of ownership. No amount of the proceeds would be includible under section 2042(1), since no portion of the proceeds would be payable to D's estate.

Note

[¶ 17,072]

The Internal Revenue Service has given its blessing to the following. A married couple purchased a joint policy payable on the death of the survivor, commonly called a "last to die" policy. The policy was held by an irrevocable life insurance trust which, by its terms, did not require the trust to use the policy proceeds to pay the estate tax due on the death of the survivor (or any other debts of the parties) but merely authorized the trust to do so. Because the trust was not obligated, but was merely authorized, to satisfy the estate tax debts of the estate of the survivor with the policy proceeds, the I.R.S. ruled that the proceeds were not to be included in the estate of the survivor under § 2042(1) as proceeds payable to the estate of the survivor. Priv. Ltr. Rul. 200147039.

[¶ 17,075]

4. ASSIGNING GROUP TERM LIFE INSURANCE

Employment, or membership in a professional association, union or alumni association often brings with it an opportunity to participate in a group term life insurance program. Typically after coverage is extended under the group policy, as long as the insured remains a member of the group and premiums are paid, the policy remains in effect. To remove the proceeds of such policies from their estates, insureds will often assign all interests in the group policy to family members or an irrevocable life insurance trust if this is permitted under the group contract.

The IRS had initially contended that because of the ability of the insured to terminate membership in the organization which entitled the insured to continued coverage, the insured, even after assignment of all interest in the policy, had effectively retained a key incident of ownership, ability to cancel the policy. See Rev. Rul. 69–54, 1969–1 C.B. 221 (Situation 1)(termination of employment). While this might make considerable sense in the case of an alumni association or American Bar Association group policy, it makes considerably less sense where the insured could only terminate the group policy by resigning from employment or from membership in a union or an integrated bar association where termination of membership might mean loss of a means of livelihood. In Rev. Rul. 72–307, 1972–1 C.B. 307, the IRS abandoned the position taken in Rev. Rul. 69–54 that the power to terminate a group policy by resigning one's employment constituted possession of an incident of ownership with respect to an assigned employment based group life insurance policy. The IRS observed that the significant collateral consequence of termination of employment had caused the Commissioner to reverse the position taken in Rev. Rul. 69–54 on this issue.

Occasionally employment based group term policies, in order to avoid leaving retired or terminated employees uninsured or underinsured, provide that on termination of employment the insured can convert the group policy into an individual policy. In Rev. Rul. 69–54, 1969–1 C.B. 221 (Situation 2), the IRS initially indicated that where an employee insured had assigned all interests in a group policy but had retained such a conversion privilege, the proceeds of the policy were includible in the employee's taxable estate on the ground that the employee had retained an incident of ownership.

In the following ruling the IRS indicated that it had also reconsidered and changed its opinion on this issue.

[¶ 17,080]

REVENUE RULING 84–130

1984–2 C.B. 194.

ISSUE

If a decedent transferred all the incidents of ownership in a noncontributory group-term life insurance policy on decedent's life, but retained the right to convert the policy to an individual policy should the decedent cease employment, are the proceeds includible in the decedent's gross estate under section 2042(2) of the Internal Revenue Code?

FACTS

D died in March 1982. At the time of death, D was employed by Y Corporation which made all the payments on a group term life insurance policy on D's life. Under the terms of the policy, D owned all the incidents of ownership. In 1977, D transferred all the ownership rights to A. However, D retained the right to convert the policy to an individual policy in the event *D*'s employment with *Y* was terminated.

LAW AND ANALYSIS

Section 2042(2) provides that the value of the gross estate includes the value of proceeds from insurance policies on the life of the decedent receivable by beneficiaries other than the executor where the decedent possessed incidents of ownership in the policy exercisable either alone or in conjunction with any other person.

Section 20.2042–1(c)(2) of the Estate Tax Regulations provides that the term "incidents of ownership," in general, means the right of the insured or the insured's estate to the economic benefits of the policy. Examples of incidents of ownership include the power to change the beneficiary, to surrender or cancel the policy, to assign the policy, to revoke an assignment, to pledge the policy for a loan, and to obtain from the insurer a loan against the surrender value of the policy.

These examples contained in section 20.2042–1(c)(2) of the regulations concern powers that directly affect the insurance policy rather than powers that are collateral consequences of potentially costly related actions of the decedent. An example of a power exercisable only as a result of potentially costly related action, and thus not an incident of ownership for purposes of section 2042(2), is the power to cancel a group-term policy by termination of employment. The power of cancellation is considered a collateral consequence of the power that every employee has to terminate employment. Similarly, a power to convert a group-term policy that is exercisable only by the voluntary termination of employment is a collateral consequence of a potentially costly action. That is, * * * the power to convert is a collateral consequence of the power that every employee has to terminate employment.

Although termination of employment may occur either at the complete discretion of the employer or by the decedent's voluntary action, for purposes of section 2042(2) of the Code, the Service will not distinguish between conversion rights exercisable upon voluntary termination of employment and such rights exercisable upon involuntary termination.

Accordingly, the insurance proceeds payable to *A* under the group insurance policy are not includible in *D*'s gross estate because *D*'s retained conversion privilege is not an incident of ownership for purposes of section 2042(2). * * *

HOLDING

If a decedent transferred all the incidents of ownership in a noncontributory group-term life insurance policy on the decedent's life, but retained the right to convert the policy to an individual policy should the decedent's employment be terminated, the proceeds are not includible in the decedent's gross estate under section 2042(2).

* * *

¶ 17,080

Notes

[¶ 17,085]

1. Why does the IRS limit its ruling to a noncontributory life insurance policy? Is this appropriate in a post premiums payment test world? Could the IRS be concerned about the fact that many employee group policies are contributory, with the employee signing up for the desired level of coverage which is to be paid for by salary deduction, and the employee by revoking salary deduction authorization could effectively revoke an assigned group life insurance policy? What if the group policy provided for payment by a means other than salary deduction; would there then be any need to bar an insured from effectively removing the policy from his or her estate through assignment on the ground that the policy is contributory?

2. Occasionally employers will have death benefit plans which provide benefits payable to a designated group of individuals such as a surviving spouse and issue. Since the employee has no right to designate beneficiaries, benefits paid under the plan are not included in the employee's estate under § 2033. See ¶ 15,109. If the employee has any other right with respect to the death benefit, the IRS may attempt to assert that the right constitutes an incident of ownership with respect to employer provided life insurance, the proceeds of which are includible in the employee's estate at death. For example, in Estate of Lumpkin, 474 F.2d 1092 (5th Cir.1973), the Fifth Circuit included in the estate of a deceased employee under § 2042(2) death benefits paid to an employer (Humble Oil Co., now Exxon) designated class of beneficiaries under a plan which gave the employee only the right to designate whether benefits were to be paid out in a lump sum or in installments over a period of years. The Third Circuit in Estate of Connelly v. United States, 551 F.2d 545 (3d Cir.1977), reached a contrary result on the identical plan with the identical employer on the ground that a right which was so ethereal could not constitute an incident of ownership. Since the IRS in Rev. Rul. 81–128, 1981–1 C.B. 469, has indicated that, in all Circuits other than the Third, it will not follow *Connelly*, estate planners should make sure that employee insureds who wish to remove death benefits from their estates assign even ethereal rights in such benefits.

E. THE UNIFORM SIMULTANEOUS DEATH ACT

[¶ 17,090]

Under the general rule of the 1953 version of the Uniform Simultaneous Death Act (which prevails in most states) , absent clear evidence that two parties died other than simultaneously, it is presumed that each survived the other for inheritance purposes. The Act contains a special rule where the insured and the primary beneficiary under a life insurance policy die simultaneously. In such a circumstance the insured is deemed to have survived the beneficiary. Consequently, in such a situation benefits under the policy will be paid to the policy's contingent beneficiary. The impact of the Act in a classic life insurance cross ownership situation is illustrated by the following ruling.

¶ 17,090

[¶ 17,095]

REVENUE RULING 77–181

1977–1 C.B. 272.

Advice has been requested whether the full value of certain life insurance policies is includible in the gross estates of the decedents under the circumstances described below. If the full value of the insurance policies is not includible, advice has been further requested as to how they should be valued.

A and *B*, residents of State *Y*, each owned insurance policies on the other's life with the proceeds payable to the owner or the owner's estate. In 1973, *A* and *B* were killed under circumstances that led a court to decree that no order of death could be estimated, thus bringing into operation State *Y*'s Uniform Simultaneous Death Act in the administration of their property. The State *Y* statute provides the presumption that for purposes of life or accident insurance policy proceeds, the insured will be presumed to have survived the beneficiary. Accordingly, the proceeds of each policy were paid to the contingent beneficiary, which in each case was the estate of the owner. Thus, the proceeds of life insurance on the life of *A* were paid to the estate of *B*, and the proceeds on the life of *B* were paid to the estate of *A*.

Section 2033 provides that "The value of the gross estate shall include the value of all property to the extent of the interest therein of the decedent at the time of his death."

Section 20.2033–1(a) of the Estate Tax Regulations provides:

In general. The gross estate of a decedent who was a citizen or resident of the United States at the time of his death includes under section 2033 the value of all property, whether real or personal, tangible or intangible, and wherever situated, beneficially owned by the decedent at the time of his death. * * *

Section 20.2031–8(a)(2) of the Estate Tax Regulations provides:

As valuation of an insurance policy through sale of comparable contracts is not readily ascertainable when, at the date of the decedent's death, the contract has been in force for some time and further premium payments are to be made, the value may be approximated by adding to the interpolated terminal reserve at the date of the decedent's death the proportionate part of the gross premium last paid before the date of the decedent's death which covers the period extending beyond that date. If, however, because of the unusual nature of the contract such an approximation is not reasonably close to the full value of the contract, this method may not be used.

State law governs what the decedent owns for purposes of estate taxation. The Federal taxing statutes merely determine how that interest shall be taxed. Rogers v. Helvering, 320 U.S. 410 (1943); Morgan v. Commissioner, 309 U.S. 78 (1940). Federal estate tax liability attaches to the value of the property at the instant of the decedent's death. United States v. Land, 303 F.2d 170 (5th Cir.1962), cert. denied, 371 U.S. 862. At the moment of death in the instant case, both *A* and *B* possessed valuable ownership rights in the life insurance policies they owned, properly includible in their respective gross estates under section 2033. Chown v. Commissioner, 428 F.2d 1395 (9th Cir.1970); Old Kent Bank & Trust Co. v. United States, 430 F.2d 392 (6th Cir.1970); Meltzer v. Commissioner, 439 F.2d 798 (4th Cir.1971); Wien v. Commissioner, 441 F.2d 32 (5th Cir.1971). Hence the instant problem is solely one of valuation.

In *Chown* and the related cases cited above, which also involved the taxability of life insurance proceeds in a simultaneous death situation, the courts held that the full value of policy proceeds was improperly included in the decedent-beneficiary's gross estate. However, since in the instant case, the policy proceeds were in fact paid to each decedent-beneficiary's estate as contingent beneficiary, whereas in *Chown* and the related cases the proceeds did not flow to the estate of the decedent-beneficiary but instead passed directly to the decedent's children as secondary beneficiaries, the question arises whether the Federal estate tax is properly due and owing on the full value of the proceeds since *A* and *B* each had a transmittable interest in the insurance proceeds paid to their estates.

To tax the decedent's estate on the full value of the policy proceeds when at the moment of the decedent's death, the decedent, by law, retains only the ownership interest in a yet unmatured policy negates the effect of the simultaneous death statutes, as well as the fundamental estate taxation concept, that estate tax liability attaches to the value of the property at the *instant* of the deceased's death. The fact that the decedent-beneficiary's estate has, subsequent to the decedent's death, received the policy proceeds is without legal significance for estate tax purposes since estate tax liability is fixed as of the instant of death.

Chown and the related cases have decided that in a simultaneous death situation only the interpolated terminal reserve value of a life insurance policy is to be included in the estate of the owner. As set forth in section 20.2031–8(a)(2) of the regulations, the interpolated reserve value provides a stable method of estimating the value of an ordinary life insurance policy. "To allow either the taxpayers' or the government's method to prevail would destroy this certainty and replace it with fluctuating individual imponderables with which no court could cope and which the Supreme Court rejected in [Commissioner v. Noel, 380 U.S. 678 (1965)(1965–2 C.B. 371)]." Wien v. Commissioner, 441 F.2d 32, 41 (1971).

Accordingly, in a simultaneous death and cross-owned insurance situation where the local law establishes the presumption that the insured survived the beneficiary, the value of the proceeds to be included in the gross estate of each of the owners is the sum of the interpolated terminal reserve of the policy at the date of the insured decedent's death and the proportionate part of the gross premium last paid before the date of the insured's death which covers the period extending beyond that date.

Note

[¶ 17,097]

There are two versions of the Uniform Simultaneous Death Act. The first version which was adopted in 1940 and amended in 1953 is the version of the Act referred to in Rev. Rul. 77–181. It is commonly called the Uniform Simultaneous Death Act and by 2005 had been adopted in 32 states and the Virgin Islands. A second version of the Act which was adopted in 1991 and amended in 1993 is officially referred to as the Uniform Simultaneous Death Act (1993). By 2005 it had been adopted by 16 states and the District of Columbia. Unlike the original Act, the 1993 Act does not specifically refer to life insurance but the reporter's comments indicate that no change in treatment of life insurance was intended by this change in language. Given appropriate facts the IRS could therefore be expected to reach the same conclusion under the 1993 Act as it reached under the original Act in Rev. Rul. 77–181.

F. ATTRIBUTION OF INCIDENTS OF OWNERSHIP TO SHAREHOLDERS AND PARTNERS

[¶ 17,100]

The question sometimes arises whether incidents of ownership are to be attributed to the principal shareholder of a closely held corporation which has taken out a policy on the life of the shareholder. Regulation § 20.2042–1(c)(6) meets this issue head-on by specifically providing that, with respect to proceeds of corporate-owned life insurance payable to either the corporation or a third party for a valid business purpose, incidents of ownership held by the corporation will not be attributed to the decedent (insured) through his stock ownership, whether or not the decedent is the sole or controlling stockholder. However, to the extent that the corporate-owned life insurance is not payable to the corporation or to a third party for a valid business purpose, the incidents of ownership will be attributed to the insured decedent who is a sole or controlling shareholder. Generally, a decedent will not be deemed a controlling shareholder unless "he owned stock possessing more than 50 percent of the total combined voting power of the corporation."

The proper treatment of insurance held by a partnership in which the insured is a partner is somewhat more murky, although it, in general, is similar to the treatment of insurance held by a corporation. In Estate of Knipp v. Commissioner, 25 T.C. 153 (1955), acq. 1959–1 C.B. 4, aff'd on another issue, 244 F.2d 436 (4th Cir.1957), cert. denied, 355 U.S. 827 (1957), the Tax Court refused to find that a 40 percent partner possessed incidents of ownership in a policy on his life held by the partnership. The Tax Court reasoned that it would result in unfair double taxation to conclude otherwise since the proceeds of the policy were to be considered in valuing the decedent's partnership interest. In Rev. Rul. 83–147, 1983–2 C.B. 158, the IRS indicated that it agrees with the result in *Knipp* as long as the policy proceeds

¶ 17,097

are payable to or for the benefit of the partnership. Where, as in Rev. Rul. 83–147, the policy held by a partnership in which the decedent insured was a one-third general partner was payable to a third party (the decedent's child) for a purpose unrelated to partnership activities, the IRS indicated the incidents of ownership on the policy would be attributed to the deceased partner. In Rev. Rul. 83–148, 1983–2 C.B. 153, the IRS ruled on a situation involving a partner in a large law firm who assigned to a trust all the partner's interest in a group term life insurance policy on the partner's life held by the partnership. The IRS held that in this case the proceeds of the assigned policy were not includible in decedent's estate despite the fact that decedent's partnership, even after the assignment, retained the right to cancel the group policy and § 2042(2) indicates that possession by the insured at death of incidents of ownership "exercisable either alone or in conjunction with any other person" warrants inclusion of policy proceeds in the estate of the insured.

G. BUY–SELL AGREEMENTS FUNDED WITH LIFE INSURANCE

[¶ 17,110]

When one co-owner in a business dies, the survivors commonly wish to carry on the business by themselves, without the heirs of the deceased who often know nothing of the enterprise. Similarly, surviving spouses and issue of deceased often would rather not participate in the business enterprise and would rather sell their newly inherited interests for a fair price.

To meet these concerns co-owners often enter into two types of arrangements whereby the interest of the deceased co-owner is purchased at her or his death for its fair market value: (1) the cross purchase; and (2) the entity purchase. On occasion the purchase is structured as a combination of cross purchase and entity purchase.

Under the cross purchase the co-owners agree that the surviving co-owners shall purchase the deceased's interest for its fair market value, whereas under the entity purchase they agree that the business enterprise itself shall effect such a purchase. Where the co-owners, or the enterprise, anticipate that they will lack sufficient assets to enable them to comply with the buy-sell agreement, they commonly use life insurance to enable them to satisfy their contractual obligations.

Under the cross purchase arrangement, as properly structured, each co-owner will obtain life insurance on the life of the other co-owners payable to the co-owner taking out the policy, and on the death of one of his partners or fellow shareholders will use the policy proceeds to help him satisfy his obligation to purchase the deceased partner's interest in the business enterprise. Since, under the arrangement as outlined, the surviving co-owner holds all the incidents of ownership on the life insurance policy on the deceased co-owner payable to the surviving co-owner, there will be no inclusion of the policy proceeds in the estate of the deceased co-owner. Occasionally co-owners who attempt to structure cross purchases without the aid of estate planners make the error of each co-owner taking out a policy on his life payable to fellow co-owners to enable them to carry out their purchase obligations. This has the disastrous result of the policy proceeds being included in the deceased co-owner's estate since he died possessed of the incidents of ownership on the policy on his life. In addition there will be included in the deceased co-owner's estate the value of the business interest purchased by his surviving co-owners with the policy proceeds, thereby in essence resulting in a double inclusion under the defectively structured arrangement.

Under the entity purchase arrangement the business enterprise, to enable it to purchase the interest of a deceased investor, will take out and hold a life insurance policy, frequently a so-called renewable first-to-die policy, under which the insurer pays the policy proceeds to the entity as soon as any one of the entity co-owners dies. As in the case of the cross-purchase arrangement, all the incidents of ownership rules previously discussed in this chapter apply in determining whether the policy proceeds, or any portion thereof, will be included in the estate of the deceased co-owner under § 2042.

Although the entity purchase seems preferable to the cross-purchase, especially in the case of a business with a number of co-owners where a stupefying number of policies might have to be issued to provide for a cross purchase, it is not without its problems. For example, in the case of a partnership which holds a life insurance policy, as required under *Knipp* (¶ 17,100), there will be an increase (modest for a small minority partner) in the value of the partnership interest of the deceased partner when the policy proceeds are included in valuing her partnership interest to avoid the incidents of ownership on the policy from being attributed to her. In the case of C corporations there may be alternative minimum tax problems, with the annual internal build up in value of the policy and the excess of death benefits over basis in the policy both considered to be part of the corporation's alternative minimum tax base. See § 56(g)(4)(B)(ii) and Reg. § 1.56(g)–1(c)(5)(v). Moreover, while surviving co-owners who purchase interests from the deceased under a cross purchase acquire basis in the interest thus acquired, a purchase of a deceased shareholder's stock by the corporation or a deceased partner's interest by the partnership provides the surviving co-owners with no additional basis in their ownership interests in the enterprise, a not inconsequential consideration if they are considering selling out in the not too distant future.

H. INSURANCE PURCHASED WITH COMMUNITY FUNDS

[¶ 17,120]

The regulations provide fairly basic guidance as to the estate tax treatment of life insurance in community property states. If proceeds of a life insurance policy which is community property are payable to the deceased spouse's estate and under local community property law one-half of the proceeds belongs to the decedent's spouse, only one-half will be considered receivable for the benefit of the decedent's estate and subject to tax under § 2042(1). See Reg. § 20.2042–1(b)(2). Where, however, the policy calls for payment at decedent's death not to the decedent's estate but to a third party such as a child, and the decedent has retained incidents of ownership as agent for the other spouse or as manager of the community assets, the decedent is deemed to possess incidents of ownership only with respect to one-half of the policy on his life and consequently only one-half of the policy proceeds will be included in his estate at his death under § 2042(2). See Reg. § 20.2042–1(c)(5). Assuming that the policy remained revocable as to designation of the beneficiary, at decedent's death the surviving spouse will be deemed to have made a gift to the beneficiary equal to the other one-half of the proceeds. See Reg. § 25.2511–1 (h)(9). If the uninsured spouse were to die first only one-half of the interpolated terminal reserve value of the policy would be included in her estate under § 2033. See Reg. § 20.2042–1(c)(5); Rev. Rul. 75–100, 1975–1 C.B. 303.

Problems

[¶ 17,130]

1. Six years ago Alice purchased from Granite Insurance Co. a $100,000 policy on her life payable to her only child and heir, Franklin, who her will also designated as the executor of her estate. One month after taking out the policy Alice irrevocably assigned all incidents of ownership in the policy to Franklin. Alice annually gave $10,000 to Franklin who, after the first year paid the $1,000 annual premium on the policy. At Alice's death $100,000 was paid to Franklin by Granite. What are the estate tax consequences of the above?

2. Judy last year acquired a $200,000 policy on the life of her husband, Charles, payable to their son, Scott. Until Charles death last month, Judy continued to hold all incidents of ownership in the policy which included the ability to change beneficiaries. What are the estate and gift tax consequences of the above to Judy, Scott and Charles' estate?

3. In the prior problem assume that two months after acquiring the policy Judy assigned all incidents of ownership in the policy to Scott.

4. In problem (2) assume that Scott rather than Judy had acquired the policy on his father's life.

5. Michael was appointed guardian of the property of his four year old daughter, Sandy, and acting in his capacity as guardian purchased a $400,000 policy on his life payable to Sandy. Michael, as guardian of the property, continued to hold all incidents of ownership in the policy until his death five years later. What are the estate tax consequences for Michael's estate?

6. Pat had held all incidents of ownership on a $500,000 policy on her life payable to her daughter, Maria. On advice from her attorney, Pat, six years ago, assigned all incidents of ownership on the policy to an irrevocable trust for the benefit of Maria with her attorney serving as trustee. On

Pat's death earlier this month $500,000 was paid to Maria. What are the estate tax consequences?

7. Sam and Emma, who are married, each took out a $300,000 policy on the other's life payable equally to their children, Andrew and Gabriella. Until Sam's death six weeks ago they each had retained all incidents of ownership in the policies acquired by them, including the ability to change beneficiaries. What are the gift and estate tax consequences of the above?

8. Al and his son Bill were equal partners in a construction company which was worth $2 million. Al's interest in the partnership was the principal asset which he owned and Al, who was a widower, wished at his death to benefit equally Bill and Bill's sister, Libby, who is a successful doctor and has no interest in being a partner in a construction company. Bill and Al are considering solving this problem with a buy-sell arrangement but Bill does not have much by way of liquid assets available to him. What suggestions do you have?

Chapter 18

RETAINED LIFE ESTATES

(Section 2036)

A. BACKGROUND AND GENERAL APPLICATION

[¶ 18,001]

As originally enacted in 1916, the Internal Revenue Code contained a provision including in the estate all transfers "intended to take effect in possession or enjoyment at or after death." It was originally thought that the types of transfers presently taxed under §§ 2036, 2037 and 2038 would be taxed under this provision. Due to several Supreme Court decisions of questionable quality, which dramatically limited the scope of the old "possession or enjoyment" provision, Congress found it necessary to pass §§ 2036, 2037 and 2038 in much their present form for the purpose of unequivocally indicating the proper tax treatment of the types of transactions that it intended to tax under the "possession or enjoyment" standard. This little bit of legislative history will explain why, on occasion, this older language is employed in state death tax statutes and why state courts occasionally construe the language in these statutes by resorting to federal court decisions under §§ 2036, 2037 and 2038. This history also explains why all three of these sections have some reference to either "possession" or "enjoyment" and why the courts will occasionally stress these terms in their decisions.

Section 2036, in general, includes within the estate two types of transfers: (1) those under which the transferor retains income from property for life; and (2) those under which the transferor retains the right for life to designate the persons who are to enjoy the transferred property or the income from it. Needless to say, the statute is not so simple, and, as this chapter will reveal, § 2036, like much of the Code, has grown in length and complexity.

Several observations are in order before proceeding to learn more about this section. First, were it not for § 2036, avoidance of estate taxes would be child's play for all but a handful of the nation's wealthiest. For example, assume that an individual, upon reaching adulthood, established a trust under which she retained income for life with remainder to a class such as surviving issue per stirpes or heirs under a state intestate statute. Because of the donor's age, enormous discounts would be employed in determining the value of the taxable gift, the remainder interest transferred to the trust. A gift tax would then be imposed only on this amount. Moreover, the unified credit would certainly bar taxation of such gifts in all but a few cases. Furthermore, all subsequent appreciation of trust corpus would escape taxation and, absent § 2036, at death no estate tax would be due since § 2033, in the prevailing judicial environment, could hardly be expected to reach such property (see ¶ 15,007 et seq.). Thus, it is apparent that the Treasury needs § 2036 if the estate tax is to be expected to be more than a leaky sieve for the legally sophisticated.

Second, the inclusion within the sweep of § 2036 of not only situations involving retained possession or enjoyment but also of the right to designate possession or enjoyment of property or income is indicative of the fact that Congress deems retention of this incident of ownership sufficient to warrant taxation. For the dynastically wealthy, riches provide more than mere personal pleasure. Vast material wealth, for example, brings with it the power to control the lives of others by granting or withholding the opportunity to participate in the enjoyment of that wealth.

In closing this introductory discussion, we call attention to the issue of who is liable for the estate tax that results from inclusion under § 2036. Over the years Congress has become concerned that the beneficiaries of nonprobate assets were often not shouldering any of the tax burden resulting from inclusion of such interests in the taxable estate. The response to this has been the inclusion of a number of remedial provisions requiring such beneficiaries, in the absence of clear language to the contrary in decedent's will, to pay their fair share of estate tax resulting from inclusion of their interests in the taxable estate. In 1988, § 2207B was added to the Code with respect to interests taxable under § 2036, requiring the beneficiaries of interests following on the decedent's life estate to pay, in the absence of direction in the will to the contrary, a proportionate share of the estate tax that results from inclusion of their interests in the decedent's taxable estate. For discussion of this and other comparable provisions see ¶ 28,073.

B. INFORMAL RESERVATIONS

[¶ 18,007]

It should come as no surprise that taxpayers will attempt to avoid the reach of § 2036 by making conveyances absolute on their face but with understandings that the donor will still reap some benefit, such as retaining rental income from or use of the property in question. For example, in Estate of McNichol v. Commissioner, 265 F.2d 667 (3d Cir.1959), a father conveyed rental property to his children pursuant to an oral understanding that he continue to receive rents from the property during his life. Understandably, the court allowed the oral agreement to characterize the nature of decedent's interest in the conveyed property and included the property in his estate under § 2036(a)(1). See also Estate of Whitt v. Commissioner, 751 F.2d 1548 (11th Cir.1985); Estate of Trotter v. Commissioner, 82 T.C.M. (CCH) 633, TCM (RIA) ¶ 2001–250 (2001). Where the taxpayers transfer properties to a limited partnership and make gifts of interests in the partnership to family members but still proceed to collect income from the transferred properties as if they were sole owners or live rent free in a residence contributed to the partnership, the courts are able to infer the presence of an informal reservation of income and include the value of the transferred properties in the taxpayer's estate. See ¶ 18,257. A clever attempt to reach a higher level of obfuscation is examined in the case that follows.

[¶ 18,009]

ESTATE OF MAXWELL v. COMMISSIONER

United States Court of Appeals, Second Circuit, 1993.
3 F.3d 591.

LASKER, Senior District Judge:

This appeal presents challenges to the tax court's interpretation of section 2036(a) of the Internal Revenue Code, relating to "Transfers with retained life estate." The petitioner, the Estate of Lydia G. Maxwell, contends that the tax court erred in holding that the transaction at issue (a) was a transfer with a retained life estate within the meaning of 26 U.S.C. § 2036 and (b) was not a bona fide sale for adequate and full consideration under that statute.

The decision of the tax court is affirmed.

I.

On March 14, 1984, Lydia G. Maxwell (the "decedent") conveyed her personal residence, which she had lived in since 1957, to her son Winslow Maxwell, her only heir, and his wife Margaret Jane Maxwell (the "Maxwells"). Following the transfer, the decedent continued to reside in the house until her death on July 30, 1986. At the time of the transfer, she was eighty-two years old and was suffering from cancer.

The transaction was structured as follows:

(1) The residence was sold by the decedent to the Maxwells for $270,000;[1]

(2) Simultaneously with the sale, the decedent forgave $20,000 of the purchase price (which was equal in amount to the annual gift tax exclusion to which she was entitled);

(3) The Maxwells executed a $250,000 mortgage note in favor of decedent;

(4) The Maxwells leased the premises to her for five years at the monthly rental of $1800; and

---

1. The parties have stipulated that the fair market value of the property on the date of the purported sale was $280,000.

¶ 18,009

(5) The Maxwells were obligated to pay and did pay certain expenses associated with the property following the transfer, including property taxes, insurance costs, and unspecified "other expenses."

While the decedent paid the Maxwells rent totaling $16,200 in 1984, $22,183 in 1985 and $12,600 in 1986, the Maxwells paid the decedent interest on the mortgage totaling $16,875 in 1984, $21,150 in 1985, and $11,475 in 1986. As can be observed, the rent paid by the decedent to the Maxwells came remarkably close to matching the mortgage interest which they paid to her. In 1984, she paid the Maxwells only $675 less than they paid her; in 1985, she paid them only $1,033 more than they paid her, and in 1986 she paid the Maxwells only $1,125 more than they paid her.

Not only did the rent functionally cancel out the interest payments made by the Maxwells, but the Maxwells were at no time called upon to pay any of the principal on the $250,000 mortgage debt; it was forgiven in its entirety. As petitioner's counsel admitted at oral argument, although the Maxwells had executed the mortgage note, "there was an intention by and large that it not be paid." Pursuant to this intention, in each of the following years preceding her death, the decedent forgave $20,000 of the mortgage principal, and, by a provision of her will executed on March 16, 1984 (that is, just two days after the transfer), she forgave the remaining indebtedness.

The decedent reported the sale of her residence on her 1984 federal income tax return but did not pay any tax on the sale because she elected to use the once-in-a-lifetime exclusion on the sale or exchange of a principal residence provided for by 26 U.S.C. § 121.

She continued to occupy the house by herself until her death. At no time during her occupancy did the Maxwells attempt to sell the house to anyone else, but, on September 22, 1986, shortly after the decedent's death, they did sell the house for $550,000.

Under I.R.C. § 2036(a), where property is disposed of by a decedent during her lifetime but the decedent retains "possession or enjoyment" of it until her death, that property is taxable as part of the decedent's gross estate, unless the transfer was a bona fide sale for an "adequate and full" consideration. 26 U.S.C. § 2036.

* * *

There are two questions before us: Did the decedent retain possession or enjoyment of the property following the transfer. And if she did, was the transfer a bona fide sale for an adequate and full consideration in money or money's worth.

II.

Section 2036(a) provides in pertinent part:

The value of the gross estate shall include the value of all property to the extent of any interest therein of which the decedent has at any time made a transfer (except in case of a bona fide sale for an adequate and full consideration in money or money's worth), by trust or otherwise, under

¶ 18,009

which he has retained for his life or for any period not ascertainable without reference to his death or for any period which does not in fact end before his death—

(1) the possession or enjoyment of, or the right to the income from, the property, . . .

26 U.S.C. § 2036(a). In the case of real property, the terms "possession" and "enjoyment" have been interpreted to mean "the lifetime use of the property." United States v. Byrum, 408 U.S. 125, 147 (1972).

In numerous cases, the tax court has held, where an aged family member transferred her home to a relative and continued to reside there until her death, that the decedent-transferor had retained "possession or enjoyment" of the property within the meaning of § 2036. * * *

[T]he tax court found as a fact that the decedent had transferred her home to the Maxwells "with the understanding, at least implied, that she would continue to reside in her home until her death." This finding was based upon the decedent's advanced age, her medical condition, and the overall result of the sale and lease. The lease was, in the tax court's words, "merely window dressing"—it had no substance.

* * *

[The tax] court held, on the basis of all the facts described above, that the decedent's use of the house following the transfer depended not on the lease but rather on an implied agreement between the parties that the decedent could and would continue to reside in the house until her death, as she actually did. It found that the lease "represented nothing more than an attempt to add color to the characterization of the transaction as a bona fide sale." The tax court did not rely on the tenancy alone to establish "possession or enjoyment."

Just as petitioner argues that the decedent's tenancy alone does not justify inclusion of the residence in her estate, so it argues that the decedent's payment of rent sanctifies the transaction and renders it legitimate. Both arguments ignore the realities of the rent being offset by mortgage interest, the forgiveness of the entire mortgage debt either by gift or testamentary disposition, and the fact that the decedent was eighty-two at the time of the transfer and actually continued to live in the residence until her death which, at the time of the transfer, she had reason to believe would occur soon in view of her poor health.

The Estate relies primarily on Barlow v. Commissioner, 55 T.C. 666 (1971). In that case, the father transferred a farm to his children and simultaneously leased the right to continue to farm the property. The tax court held that the father did not retain "possession or enjoyment," stating that

"one of the most valuable incidents of income-producing real estate is the rent which it yields. He who receives the rent in fact enjoys the property."

¶ 18,009

Barlow, 55 T.C. at 671 (quoting McNichol's v. Commissioner, 265 F.2d 667, 671 (3d Cir.), cert. denied, 361 U.S. 829 (1959)). However, *Barlow* is clearly distinguishable on its facts: In that case, there was evidence that the rent paid was fair and customary and, equally importantly, the rent paid was not offset by the decedent's receipt of interest from the family lessor.

* * *

For the reasons stated above, we conclude that the decedent did retain possession or enjoyment of the property for life and turn to the question of whether the transfer constituted "a bona fide sale for adequate and full consideration in money or money's worth."

III.

Section 2036(a) provides that even if possession or enjoyment of transferred property is retained by the decedent until her death, if the transfer was a bona fide sale for adequate and full consideration in money or money's worth, the property is not includible in the estate. Petitioner contends that the Maxwells paid an "adequate and full consideration" for the decedent's residence, $270,000 total, consisting of the $250,000 mortgage note given by the Maxwells to the decedent, and the $20,000 the decedent forgave simultaneously with the conveyance.[3]

The tax court held that neither the Maxwells' mortgage note nor the decedent's $20,000 forgiveness constituted consideration within the meaning of the statute.

$250,000 Mortgage Note

As to the $250,000 mortgage note, the tax court held that:

> Regardless of whether the $250,000 mortgage note might otherwise qualify as "adequate and full consideration in money or money's worth" for a $270,000 or $280,000 house, the mortgage note here had no value at all if there was no intention that it would ever be paid.

> The conduct of decedent and the Maxwells strongly suggest that neither party intended the Maxwells to pay any part of the principal of either the original note or any successor note.

There is no question that the mortgage note here is a fully secured, legally enforceable obligation on its face. The question is whether it is actually what it purports to be—a bona fide instrument of indebtedness—or whether it is a facade. The petitioner argues not only that an allegedly unenforceable intention to forgive indebtedness does not deprive the indebtedness of its status as "consideration in money or money's worth" but also that "[t]his is true even if there was an implied agreement exactly as found by the Tax Court." (Petitioner's Memorandum of Law at 3).

---

3. As noted above, the parties have stipulated that the fair market value of the property on the date of the purported sale was $280,000. The Estate contends that $270,000 was full and adequate consideration for the sale, with a broker, for a house appraised at $280,000. We assume this fact to be true for purposes of determining whether the transaction was one for "an adequate and full consideration in money or money's worth."

We agree with the tax court that where, as here, there is an implied agreement between the parties that the grantee would never be called upon to make any payment to the grantor, as, in fact, actually occurred, the note given by the grantee had "no value at all." We emphatically disagree with the petitioner's view of the law as it applies to the facts of this case. As the Supreme Court has remarked,

> the family relationship often makes it possible for one to shift tax incidence by surface changes of ownership without disturbing in the least his dominion and control over the subject of the gift or the purposes for which the income from the property is used.

Commissioner v. Culbertson, 337 U.S. 733, 746 (1949). There can be no doubt that intent is a relevant inquiry in determining whether a transaction is "bona fide." As another panel of this Court held recently, construing a parallel provision of the Internal Revenue Code, in a case involving an intrafamily transfer:

> when the bona fides of promissory notes is at issue, the taxpayer must demonstrate affirmatively that "there existed at the time of the transaction a real expectation of repayment and an intent to enforce the collection of the indebtedness." Estate of Van Anda v. Commissioner, 12 T.C. 1158, 1162 (1949), aff'd per curiam, 192 F.2d 391 (2d Cir.1951). See also Estate of Labombarde v. Commissioner, 58 T.C. 745, 754–55 (1972), aff'd, 502 F.2d 1158 (1st Cir.1973).

Flandreau v. Commissioner, [994 F.2d 91, 93 (2d Cir.1993)] (case involving I.R.C. § 2053(c)(1)). In language strikingly apposite to the situation here, the court stated:

> it is appropriate to look beyond the form of the transactions and to determine, as the tax court did here, that the gifts and loans back to decedent were "component parts of single transactions."

Id. (citation omitted).

The tax court concluded that the evidence "viewed as a whole" left the "unmistakable impression" that

> regardless of how long decedent lived following the transfer of her house, the entire principal balance of the mortgage note would be forgiven, and the Maxwells would not be required to pay any of such principal.

Id.

The petitioner's reliance on Haygood v. Commissioner, 42 T.C. 936 (1964), not followed by Rev. Rul. 77–299, 1977–2 CB 343 (1977), Kelley v. Commissioner, 63 T.C. 321 (1974), not followed by Rev. Rul. 77–299, 1977–2 C.B. 343 (1977), and Wilson v. Commissioner, 64 T.C.M. (CCH) 583 (1992),[4] is misplaced. Those cases held only that intent to forgive notes in the future does not *per se* disqualify such notes from constituting valid consideration. In contrast, in the case at hand, the decedent did far more than merely

---

4. Apart from all of the other distinctions outlined below, *Wilson* is not a tax court opinion but a tax court memorandum; moreover, the decision in *Wilson* succeeded the Tax Court decision in this case.

"indicate[] an intent to forgive the indebtedness in the future." *Wilson*, 64 T.C.M. (CCH) 583, 584 (1992).

In *Haygood*, *Kelley*, and *Wilson*, the question was whether transfers of property by petitioners to their children or grandchildren in exchange for notes were completed gifts within the meaning of the Internal Revenue Code. None of the notes was actually paid by the grantees; instead the notes were either forgiven by petitioners at or about the time they became due (*Haygood* and *Kelley*) or the petitioner died prior to the date when the note was due (*Wilson*). In those circumstances, the tax court held that the notes received by petitioners, secured by valid vendor's liens or by deeds of trust on the property, constituted valuable consideration for the transfer of the property.

The *Kelley* court made no finding as to intent to forgive the notes. In *Haygood*, although the court did find that the "petitioner had no intention of collecting the debts but did intend to forgive each payment as it became due," it also found that the transfer of the property to the children had been a mistake.[5] And, the *Wilson* court found that:

> The uncontradicted testimony in this case establishes that petitioner and her children intended that the children would sell the property and pay the note with the proceeds.

Wilson, 64 T.C.M. (CCH) at 584.

By contrast, in the case at hand, the tax court found that, at the time the note was executed, there was "an understanding" between the Maxwells and the decedent that the note would be forgiven.

> In our judgment, the conduct of decedent and the Maxwells with respect to the principal balance of the note, when viewed in connection with the initial "forgiveness" of $20,000 of the purported purchase price, strongly suggests the existence of an understanding between decedent and the Maxwells that decedent would forgive $20,000 each year thereafter until her death, when the balance would be forgiven by decedent's will.

If *Haygood* is read as holding that the intent to forgive notes has no effect on the question of whether the notes constitute valid consideration, it appears to be inconsistent with controlling tax principles and tax court decisions. For example, in Deal v. Commissioner, 29 T.C. 730 (1958),[6] the tax court held that the notes executed by the children were not intended as consideration for the transfer, holding that:

---

5. The court stated that it was "eminently clear from the testimony that it was petitioner's intent to give only a $3,000 interest [in the property] to each of her sons" that year but her lawyer accidentally structured the transaction to give the entire property to the petitioner's sons. Haygood v. Commissioner, 42 T.C. 936, 942 (1964).

6. *Deal* involved a conveyance by the taxpayer of a remainder interest in real property to a trust for the benefit of her four daughters. The taxpayer forgave a $3,000 portion of each note to each daughter in the year of the trans-

fer of the property, and a similar portion of each note in the two subsequent years, and the remaining balance of the note in the following year. The tax court held that the taxpayer had made a gift of the remainder interest to the children.

The petitioner claims that *Deal* "may have been wrongly decided." However, *Deal* is still good law. Although *Haygood* reached a different conclusion, the court was careful not to overrule *Deal* but to distinguish it on its facts. Haygood v. Commissioner, 42 T.C. 936, 944 (1964).

¶ 18,009

After carefully considering the record, we think that the notes executed by the daughters were not intended to be enforced and were not intended as consideration for the transfer by the petitioner, and that, in substance, the transfer of the property was by gift.

29 T.C. at 746, quoted by *Haygood*. See also Rev. Rul. 77–299, 1977–2 C.B. 343 (1977). Even *Kelley* stated that notes "in proper legal form and regular on their face" are only "prima facie" what they purport to be. *Kelley*, 63 T.C. at 324–25.

$20,000 Initial Forgiveness

We also agree with the tax court that, as to the $20,000 which was forgiven simultaneously with the conveyance,

In the absence of any clear and direct evidence that there existed an obligation or indebtedness capable of being forgiven . . .

the $20,000 item had "no economic substance."

To conclude, we hold that the conveyance was not a bona fide sale for an adequate and full consideration in money or money's worth.

* * *

Section 2043

The petitioner argues finally that the tax court should be reversed because, under 26 U.S.C. § 2043, if there was any consideration in money or money's worth paid to the decedent, even if the payment was inadequate, the Estate is at least entitled to an exclusion pro tanto. The argument has no merit in the circumstances of this case. The tax court held, and we do also, that the transfer was without *any* consideration. Section 2043 applies only where the court finds that some consideration was given.

The decision of the tax court is affirmed.

Notes

[¶ 18,013]

1. For years the Treasury attacked informal arrangements by which an individual parts with the legal title but continues to enjoy the property in fact. Thus, a husband may deed the house to his wife without any assurance that he will not be thrown out into the cold but without any expectation that it will happen. Is the house still includible in his gross estate? Should only a half be includible, even on the government's theory? The question has thus far produced several district court and Tax Court decisions—almost all rejecting the government's theory. See e.g. Estate of Gutchess v. Commissioner, 46 T.C. 554 (1966)(acq.). But the Treasury's acquiescence in *Gutchess* does not reach a parent's gift of the home to the children—at least where they do not move in with the parent. See Estate of Honigman v. Commissioner, 66 T.C. 1080 (1976)(where mother remained in the house after transfer, in fact, § 2036 applies by its terms); Rev. Rul. 78–409, 1978–2 C.B. 234 (where decedent lived

in the house, it is taxable under § 2036 despite an absolute deed); Estate of Trotter, 82 T.C.M. (CCH) 633, T.C.M. (RIA) ¶ 2001–250 (2001) (taxpayer deeded condo to trust for benefit of children and continued to live there paying only occupancy expenses, taxable under § 2036). But see Estate of Roemer v. Commissioner, 46 T.C.M. (CCH) 1176, T.C.M. (P–H) ¶ 83,509 (1983), reviewing the "live together" cases and dealing the Treasury a defeat in a situation in which a mother gave her house to her daughter who had lived with her for five years prior to the gift and the two remained together in the house after the gift.

Somewhat related is Estate of Wyly v. Commissioner, 610 F.2d 1282 (5th Cir.1980). A gift by husband to wife of his community property does not result in the inclusion of one-half the gift in his taxable estate under § 2036 though Texas law treats income from separate property during marriage as community property. The fact that husband did not reserve any interest was of controlling importance. It was the local law that provided half ownership of income from the transferred interest.

2. In Rev. Rul. 79–109, 1979–1 C.B. 297, the IRS ruled that, where a parent conveyed a vacation home to children, expressly reserving the right to use the home for one month, only that portion of the value of the home represented by the retained use need be included in the estate. Although this might have been deemed an overly generous concession in another era, the result is hardly shocking to a Bar familiar with the concept of interval ownership. Although Rev. Rul. 79–109 involved an express reservation, its embrace of segmented ownership has potential application in the area of informal reservations.

3. In Estate of du Pont v. Commissioner, 63 T.C. 746 (1975), the Tax Court saw through a rather complicated manipulation involving formation of a corporation and transfer to the corporation of residential property with a lease back at a substantially less than fair market value rent. The Tax Court found this to be a reserved life estate under § 2036. The decision demonstrates that having your cake and eating it too under § 2036 is not all that simple.

4. In a number of cases the Tax Court has used § 2036 and the informal retention doctrine to fully tax to a decedent the value of family limited partnerships. In each of the cases a wealthy parent created a limited partnership and contributed most of his or her assets to the partnership. Limited partnership interests were given directly or indirectly to children with the donees claiming large discounts (¶ 11,115 et seq.). Again at the death of the donor, a large discount was claimed for the value of any general partnership interest retained by donor. In such cases, the donor general partners (as well as the donees) treated all assets formally transferred to the partnership as if they had still been the property of the donor general partners. These individuals continued to use personal assets such as a home as their own without payment of rent and to comingle partnership funds with their funds or to use partnership income to meet the donor decedent's living expenses. In such cases the court has routinely held that under § 2036 all partnership assets were to be taxed as assets of the estate of the donor decedent. See, e.g., Estate

of Reichardt, 114 T.C. 144 (2000); Estate of Schauerhamer, 73 T.C.M. (CCH) 2855, T.C.M. (RIA) ¶ 97,242 (1997) and the cases discussed at ¶ 18,257.

C. CONTINGENT RETAINED LIFE ESTATES—SECTION 2036(a)(1)

[¶ 18,025]

When the decedent transfers the property to pay the income for life to the beneficiary and then to pay the income back to the transferor if he is still living at the beneficiary's death, is such a transfer within the reach of the language of § 2036?

Consider the following extract from Commissioner v. Estate of Nathan, 159 F.2d 546 (7th Cir.1947), cert. denied, 334 U.S. 843 (1948):

> The doubt, if any exists in this case, is over the question, was the property which was transferred and in which deceased retained a contingent life interest, terminable by his death or by that of his sister? Stated differently, was the period during which his contingent estate therein existed ascertainable without reference to his death or did the period of the contingent estate which decedent retained in the trust he created have a possible ending before his death?

> Notwithstanding some doubt (in view of the discussion in the *Curie* case) we hold the language of the statute must be so construed as to impose an estate tax on the property covered by this trust less the value of the life estate of the sister. Our decision is not predicated on the Regulation [Reg. § 20.2036–1(a)]. It is made necessary by the statute which, without the Regulation, imposes the tax.

> The Commissioner could not have found or held otherwise. The transfer in which the deceased retained a contingent estate was held by him for a period which did not in fact end before his death. It was his death, not his sister's death, which terminated his contingent interest.

> * * *

> The factual difference between the instant case and the usual trust agreement which may be called testamentary has not been ignored. The decedent here retained only a contingent estate which became effective in case he survived his sister. Notwithstanding this rather important fact so far as enjoyment is concerned, it did not take the transfer out of the reach of the language of Section 811(c) [now § 2036] which controls our decision. We cannot lessen the effect or the meaning of the words because the settlor's interest was less certain or the enjoyment of the estate reserved more remote. We feel we must give the words used their fair, rightful meaning and we can not make them depend on the size or nature of the settlor's reservation appearing in his transfer. The vital test of said reservation in settlor's favor necessitates an answer to the query—was the transfer one which was for a period not ascertainable without reference to his death?

¶ 18,025

Further support for the view expressed in *Estate of Nathan* is found in the Report of the Conference Committee on the Revenue Act of 1949 (H.R. Report No. 1412, 81st Cong., 1st Sess., reported in 49–2 C.B. 300):

> The expression "not ascertainable without reference to his death" as used in section 811(c)(1)(B) [now § 2036 (a)] and elsewhere in the conference amendments includes the right to receive the income from transferred property after the death of another person who in fact survived the transferor; but in such a case the amount to be included under section 811(c)(1)(B) in the transferor's gross estate does not include the value of the outstanding income interest in such other person.

Consistent with the foregoing authorities is Reg. § 20.2036–1(a), which indicates that, where a donor has retained a contingent life estate in property, the estate is to include the full value of the property in question minus only the value of an income interest which precedes that of the donor and which is actually being enjoyed. A question arises as to whether this might not, on occasion, result in the inclusion in the estate of more value than is called for by § 2036. For example, consider the following case. Assume that the decedent had established a trust with income to his wife for her life, then to his son for the son's life, and then to himself for his life, with remainder to a granddaughter (or her estate). Under the regulations, at the donor's death only the value of the wife's life estate is subtracted from the value of the trust in determining the amount includible. Since the donor's death does not transfer anything of value to the son, it seems inappropriate also not to exclude the value of the son's contingent life estate. That result, however, is inconsistent with the regulations.

D. INTERRELATIONSHIP OF TRANSFERRED PROPERTY AND RETENTION OF INCOME

[¶ 18,055]

Occasionally a question arises with respect to situations where the decedent is receiving a stream of payments from a party as a result of having conveyed property to this party as part of either a gift or sale.

1. PRIVATE ANNUITIES

[¶ 18,061]

RAY v. UNITED STATES

United States Court of Appeals, Ninth Circuit, 1985.
762 F.2d 1361.

SCHROEDER, Circuit Judge.

* * *

The decedent, David Ray, and his former wife, Frances Ray, entered into a Property Settlement Agreement and Trust Agreement in 1959 as part of their divorce proceedings. The Trust Agreement provided that David Ray was to receive $400 a month for life, and Frances Ray was to receive $300 a month for life. These amounts were to be reduced by any sums the parties received from retirement and social security benefits or salary. If the net income from the trust was insufficient to maintain the monthly payments, the trustee was authorized to invade principal as necessary to maintain the payments. Additionally, the trustee, in his discretion, could distribute additional funds from the principal "for the care, maintenance and health of either . . . party." On the death of the last to die, the trustee was to distribute the trust corpus to the parties' children.

Frances died before David, who died testate in 1975. The Inventory and Appraisement filed in probate listed as property of the estate one-half of the assets of the trust; however, the Estate Tax Return failed to list this interest as property of the estate. The IRS audited the return, determined that one-half of the value of the trust was includable in the estate, and assessed $10,138.11 in estate tax and $994.78 in interest against the estate. The estate paid the amount and filed a claim for a refund which the IRS disallowed. The estate then filed this action in the district court.

The estate argued in the district court that no part of the trust was includable in the estate because the decedent received full and adequate consideration for the transfer, i.e., release from his marital support obligations. The district court rejected the argument. On appeal, the estate has abandoned it. The estate now primarily asserts that the Trust Agreement is equivalent to an annuity contract for a specified monthly payment, and, therefore, the value of the trust corpus should be excluded from the decedent's gross estate.

* * *

Substance, not form, governs our determination of whether this transaction should be regarded as a trust with a reserved life estate or a sale in exchange for an annuity. Lazarus v. Commissioner, 513 F.2d 824, 828 (9th Cir.1975). We have addressed this issue in several cases arising under a related statute, section 677 of the Internal Revenue Code, 26 U.S.C. § 677. See Stern v. Commissioner, 747 F.2d 555 (9th Cir.1984); LaFargue v. Commissioner, 689 F.2d 845 (9th Cir.1982); Lazarus, 513 F.2d 824. Although section 677 deals with the taxation of income paid from a trust to its grantor, the court's analysis in those cases applies to our analysis under section 2036.

In Lazarus, we held that although the taxpayers had labeled the transaction a sale in exchange for an annuity, it was reasonable to characterize it in substance as a transfer to a trust with a retained life estate; therefore, the taxpayers, as owners of the trust, were liable for tax on the trust income. 513 F.2d at 829. The following factors supported the court's conclusion: (1) the property the taxpayers transferred to the trust was, in effect, the only source for their "annuity" payments; (2) since the trust's income was designed to equal the annual payments to the taxpayers, the "annuity" payments would not be paid from the trust corpus; and (3) the trust corpus would be available for "ultimate distribution to the trust beneficiaries." Id. at 829.

¶ 18,061

In *LaFargue*, on the other hand, we held that both the formal structure of the transaction and its substance supported the taxpayer's characterization of it as a sale in exchange for an annuity. 689 F.2d at 846. We emphasized that not only was the formal structure of the transaction that of an annuity obligation, but also that the amount of the annuity was not calculated to bear a "mathematical relationship" to the income of the trust. Id. Further, the taxpayer did not control the property transferred. Id. Distinguishing *Lazarus*, we noted that the trust corpus was available and partially used to pay the annuity. Id. The annuity payments were not simply a conduit for the trust income. Id. at 848. "As with any annuity taken in exchange for property, the risk of Taxpayer's early death lay with the taxpayer, whereas the risk of Taxpayer's late demise lay with the trust and its trustees." Id. at 850.

In *Stern*, we analyzed the transaction in light of *Lazarus* and *LaFargue* and held, as in *LaFargue*, that the taxpayers' characterization of the transaction as creating an annuity should be upheld. 747 F.2d at 558. The amount of the annuity was not tied to the trust's income.

Applying the factors we examined in *Stern*, *LaFargue* and *Lazarus*, we must conclude that this transaction was not an annuity arrangement. First, the parties did not formally structure it as one. On its face, the Trust Agreement purported to be a transfer to a trust with a retained income interest, not the purchase of an annuity. Nothing in the record indicates that the parties intended a sale in exchange for an annuity.

Second, the substance of this transaction reflects its form. Were this an annuity arrangement, one would expect the exhaustion of both income and principal over the life of the annuitant. See *Lazarus*, 513 F.2d at 829 n.11. Here, however, the payments to the Rays closely approximated the trust's income. The parties apparently calculated the payments so that the trust corpus would remain intact because the trust operated at a break even point from its inception until Mr. Ray's death, at which time the trustee used principal to pay Mr. Ray's funeral expenses. This "tie" between the amount of the payments and the trust income is the most important characteristic which distinguishes this transaction from an annuity purchase. *Stern*, 747 F.2d at 558; *LaFargue*, 689 F.2d at 848 & n.5; *Lazarus*, 513 F.2d at 829–30.

* * *

The estate's reliance on language in Fidelity–Philadelphia Trust Co. v. Smith, 356 U.S. 274 (1958), is similarly misplaced since there the Court stressed that payments of income from transferred property were excludable where they were "personal obligations of the transferee." The Court stated:

> Where a decedent, not in contemplation of death, has transferred property to another in return for a promise to make periodic payments to the transferor for his lifetime, it has been held that these payments are not income from the transferred property so as to include the property in the estate of the decedent. In these cases the promise is a personal obligation of the transferee, the obligation is usually not chargeable to the transferred property, and the size of the payments is not determined by the

size of the actual income from the transferred property at the time the payments are made.

Id. at 280 n.8 (citations omitted). Here, the payments were chargeable solely to the transferred property and income therefrom; they were not personal obligations of the trustee. Moreover, it appears that the size of the payments was initially determined to approximate the expected income from the trust property. See *Lazarus*, 513 F.2d at 830.

* * *

The estate did not carry its burden of proving that the assessment was incorrect. The district court's judgment is AFFIRMED.

Note

[¶ 18,067]

The federal estate tax difference between a true annuity and a retained life estate is just one of the matters to be pondered in contemplating an annuity arrangement as an estate planning tool. On the income tax side, see Rev. Rul. 69–64, 1969–1 C.B. 85 (basis and exclusion ratio); Rev. Rul. 62–136, 1962–2 C.B. 12 (closed transaction when annuity contract issued by corporation); Estate of Bell v. Commissioner, 60 T.C. 469 (1973)(closed transaction where escrow and cognovit judgment note); and Rev. Rul. 55–119, 1955–1 C.B. 352 (basis of transferee buying property with annuity payments).

With an annuity arrangement, compare a sale for note cancellable on the death of the note-holder/seller. It should be recalled that in Estate of Moss v. Commissioner, ¶ 15,061, the Tax Court held the estate of the seller nontaxable on such cancellable at death notes.

Planning Note

[¶ 18,073]

The private annuity is occasionally used by family members to achieve both gift and estate tax savings in situations where a family desires to retain an income-producing asset or business. If properly structured, the initial transfer of the income-producing or business asset in exchange for the private annuity, a promise by the purchaser to provide the vendor with periodic payments for the vendor's life, does not give rise to immediate significant income or gift tax consequences. In order to avoid a taxable gift, care must be taken to assure that the actuarially determined value of the stream of payments under the annuity equals the value of the purchased asset. The income tax treatment of the annuitant is relatively simple if cash or unappreciated property is used to purchase the annuity. In this case, under § 72, a portion of each payment is treated as an untaxed recovery of capital and the balance is treated as income. If the annuitant dies prior to recovering all the capital, a loss is allowed for the unrecovered amount. Moreover, once an annuitant exceeds his or her projected lifespan, all annuity payments subsequently received are taxed as income. Where appreciated property is sold in exchange for a private annuity, the income tax treatment of the annuitant becomes more complicated. Since concerns about creditworthiness of the purchaser prevent accurate determination of the real fair market value of the annuity, so long as the annuity is not secured, the purchaser need not pay tax on any profit derived from the sale until payments are received. See Commissioner v. Estate of Kann, 174 F.2d 357 (3d Cir.1949).

Assuming a profit on the sale of appreciated property for a private annuity, the vendor, for tax reporting purposes, breaks down each payment into three components: recovery of capital, profit on the sale, and income on the annuity. See § 453 and Rev. Rul. 69–74, 1969–1 C.B. 43. As in the case of an annuity acquired for cash, an annuitant who outlives the projected lifespan is no longer allowed to exclude a portion of the annuity as a recovery of capital, and if an early death occurs a loss will be allowed.

The income tax treatment of the purchaser is somewhat murky. The purchaser initially takes the fair market value of the property as his basis in the purchased asset. After this the tax treatment becomes more arcane. Although one might expect that a portion of each payment to the annuitant would be treated as interest for which the purchaser would be entitled to an income tax deduction, under the generally prevailing (and to at least one author's mind erroneous) view, this is not the case and no interest deduction is allowed. See, e.g., Dix v. Commissioner, 392 F.2d 313 (4th Cir.1968)(may turn on failure to designate interest). Even after the total of the payments under the annuity exceeds the fair market value of the purchase at the time of sale, a number of courts have been reluctant to allow any interest deduction. Apparently, at this point, the added payments are allowed to increase the adjusted basis of the purchased asset.

Because of the unsatisfactory income tax treatment of the purchaser and the annuitant's fears about the necessarily unsecured nature of an annuity contract that *Kann* mandates, private annuities are employed far less than, at first blush, might be expected. Moreover, if the annuity is properly structured, in the law of large numbers, annuitants should have returned to their estates, as a return of capital alone, an amount equal to the fair market value of the assets that they sold. Unless employed with respect to sales of appreciating assets, there should, on the average, be no estate tax benefit to annuitants under most private annuity arrangements.

[¶ 18,079]

2. ANNUITY–LIFE INSURANCE COMBINATIONS

What if a taxpayer who simultaneously purchases from the same insurance company an annuity and a single premium life insurance policy promptly gives the latter to the beneficiaries and lives for at least three years; can the two investments be combined and can the proceeds of the insurance policy be included in the taxpayer's estate under § 2036(a)(1)?

Two Supreme Court decisions bear on the issue. In Helvering v. Le Gierse, 312 U.S. 531 (1941), the Court included in the estate of an octogenarian the proceeds of a recently purchased annuity-life insurance combination with a death benefit of $25,000. The law at the time did not include the proceeds of life insurance policies in the estate unless they exceeded $40,000. All but one paragraph of the eight-page decision of the Court was dedicated to establishing that, since there was no shifting of risk, a principal feature of insurance, the $25,000 proceeds of the life policy would not be deemed to be proceeds of a life insurance policy and thus would not be able to qualify for the then-existing exemption. In the one sentence of its opinion dedicated to the issue of the inclusion of the life insurance proceeds in the estate, the Court stated that "We hold that they are taxable under § 302(c) [the predecessor to §§ 2036, 2037 and 2038] * * * as a transfer to take effect in possession or enjoyment at or after death."

Seventeen years later in Fidelity–Philadelphia Trust Co. v. Smith (F.R.), 356 U.S. 274 (1958), the Court again confronted the issue of the proper tax treatment of an annuity-life insurance combination purchased by a 76–year old who was allowed to purchase both policies without obtaining a medical examination. Shortly after purchasing the life insurance policies, the decedent assigned all interests in them to her children and lived for 12 more years. Since the $40,000 life insurance exclusion had been repealed in 1942, four years prior to the taxpayer's death, the Court focused its attention solely on the issue of inclusion under the 1939 Code's version of § 2036(a)(1). It distinguished *Le Gierse* on the ground that the taxpayer in that case had retained the life insurance policy, whereas the taxpayer in *Fidelity-Philadelphia Trust* had conveyed it to her children. In rejecting the Commissioner's contention that the two policies should be taken as a whole, with the retention of the annuity resulting in inclusion of the "combined" life insurance proceeds, the Court stated:

> To establish its contention, the Government must aggregate the premiums of the annuity policies with those of the life insurance policies and establish that the annuity payments were derived as income from the entire investment. This proposition cannot be established. Admittedly, when the policies were purchased, each life insurance-annuity combination was the product of a single, integrated transaction. However, the parties neither intended that, nor acted as if, any of the transactions would have a quality of indivisibility. Regardless of the considerations prompting the insurance companies to hedge their life insurance contracts with annuities, each time an annuity-life insurance combination was written, two items of property, an annuity policy and an insurance policy, were transferred to the purchaser. The annuity policy could have been acquired separately, and the life insurance policy could have been, and was, conveyed separately. The annuities arose from personal obligations of the insurance companies which were in no way conditioned on the continued existence of the life insurance contracts. These periodic payments would have continued unimpaired and without diminution in size throughout the life of the insured even if the life insurance policies had been extinguished. Quite clearly the annuity payments arose solely from the annuity policies. The use and enjoyment of the annuity policies were entirely independent of the life insurance policies. Because of this independence, the Commissioner may not, by aggregating the two types

¶ 18,079

of policies into one investment, conclude that by receiving the annuities, the decedent had retained income from the life insurance contracts.

Before visions of sugar plums dance too vividly in the tax-planning mind, see § 2039 and *Estate of Montgomery*, ¶ 21,055. In addition to shattered dreams on the estate tax front as respects the annuity-life insurance package, there turned out to be income tax woes as well. See Rev. Rul. 65–57, 1965–1 C.B. 56, in which the IRS refused to see any insurance element in the package, resulting in the loss of the income tax exclusion for life insurance proceeds. Sometimes it is better not to have schemed at all!

Moreover, in other settings the courts may not be able to see two separate items of property. In Estate of Cooper v. Commissioner, 74 T.C. 1373 (1980), detachment of interest coupons from bonds was viewed as a simple reservation of income with the bonds still taxable under § 2036.

E. THE DECEDENT–TRANSFEROR

[¶ 18,085]

Section 2036 includes within the estate only property that was the object of a "retained" life estate or power and does not include life estates given to the taxpayer by third parties. Consequently, taxpayers will stumble into the grasp of § 2036 because they unartfully retained a life interest. For example, in several situations settlors have established trusts designating themselves as beneficiaries but granting the trustee complete discretion as to whether any income is to be paid to the settlor-beneficiary. Because the law in most states, based on public policy considerations, prohibits settlors from so putting property beyond the reach of their creditors, the corpus of such self-settled spendthrift trusts are deemed includible in the estate of the settlor-beneficiaries based on their ability to thereby obtain economic access to such funds to satisfy the claims of their creditors. See, e.g. Tech. Adv. Mem. 19991700 (California state law); Estate of Paxton, 86 T.C. 785 (1986) (Washington state law). Exploiting choice of law principles, estate planners recently started creating self-settled spendthrift trusts in off-shore tax havens whose laws did not allow creditors to reach such assets thereby hoping to put these trusts beyond the reach of creditors and the IRS. Joining the race to the bottom, Alaska, Delaware, Nevada, Rhode Island and Utah recently changed their property laws to meet the foreign competition. See, Alaska Stat. § 34.40.110 (2004); Del. Code. Ch. 12, § 3571 (2005); Nev. Rev. Stat. § 166.040(1)(b) (2005); R.I. Gen. Laws §§ 18–9.2–2 to 18–9.2–5 (2005) & Utah Code Ann. § 25–6–14 (2005). Ponder whether a resident of a state such as California should be allowed to place property beyond the reach of the IRS by merely creating a Delaware discretionary trust. It is also worth asking if even the citizens of Delaware should be able to do so. What of possible application of the informal reservation theory?

Taxpayers may, of course, attempt, with varying degrees of success, to avoid the reach of § 2036 by arranging for others to create or hold the critical interests.

¶ 18,079

1. GENERAL ISSUE

[¶ 18,091]

IN RE ESTATE OF PYLE

United States Court of Appeals, Third Circuit, 1963.
313 F.2d 328.

HASTIE, Circuit Judge.

[Decedent, Ida Pyle, applied for and obtained a policy on the life of her husband, Wallace. Ida was initially designated as the beneficiary of the policy. Some time later while her husband was alive, as owner of the policy, Mrs. Pyle entered into an agreement with the insurer that at her husband's death, it would retain the policy proceeds and would pay Mrs. Pyle 3% interest thereon, plus dividends, for her life. At her death the policy proceeds and any additional earnings thereon were to be paid to the Pyle children. This arrangement was made revocable as long as Mr. Pyle was alive. Upon Mr. Pyle's death, benefits were paid to Ida until her death. The IRS took the position that the sum paid to the children by the insurer at Mrs. Pyle's death was taxable in her estate under § 2036. The executor of Mrs. Pyle's estate brought suit in the Tax Court which resolved the issue in favor of the Commissioner. The executor appealed from that decision.]

Section 2036 of the 1954 Code requires that there shall be included in the gross estate of a decedent the value of "any interest [in property] * * * of which the decedent has at any time made a transfer * * * under which he has retained for his life * * * the right to income from, the property * * *." The Tax Court concluded that, in the circumstances outlined above, Mrs. Pyle's action during the lifetime of her husband in changing the disposition to be made of the proceeds of the life insurance policy upon maturity constituted a transfer of property under which she retained a life estate.

Challenging this conclusion, the petitioner argues that it was the death of the insured husband rather than the earlier action of Mrs. Pyle which in legal contemplation effected the transfer of property. The fact that Mrs. Pyle's election as to the disposition of proceeds at maturity was revocable until her husband died and that interests in such proceeds were contingent or inchoate until her husband's death are thought to support this contention.

We think petitioner's argument is unsound. The only transfer of property with which we are concerned is the transfer of the right to receive proceeds upon maturity. That transfer could be accomplished only through the exercise of ownership rights created by the terms of the policy and vested exclusively in Mrs. Pyle from the date of issuance until her husband's death. The fact that the husband's death was the event which caused the policy to mature and made Mrs. Pyle's election as to changes in the disposition of the proceeds irrevocable did not make him a transferor. For he had no power over the disposition of the proceeds during his lifetime and no interest in them which could pass to another at his death. An instructive analogy is provided by Goodnow v. United States, Ct.Cl.1962, 302 F.2d 516, where a wife was held not to have been the transferor of the proceeds of a policy on her husband's life because he was the legal owner of the policy, with a vested right to elect among optional dispositions of the proceeds. As concerns the proceeds, the position of the husband there was essentially the position of the wife here.

Petitioner also points out that some of the premiums on the policy were paid by the husband. But certainly this gave him no interest in and no power over the disposition to be made of the proceeds upon his death. That is the only transfer which is relevant here. There are other cases, notably Estate of Susie C. Haggett, 1950, 14 T.C. 325, acq., 1950–2 Cum. Bull. 2, upon which petitioner relies, in which the original purchase of insurance or an annuity was a transaction constituting a transfer of property which was to become effective in some degree only upon the purchaser's death. The present case is different because it was neither the original purchase of insurance nor the payment of premiums which in fact or in law accomplished the decisive shifting of the right to proceeds. Those transactions are simply irrelevant.

Here again, Goodnow v. United States, supra, is helpful. For in that case the wife paid certain premiums on policies on her husband's life, but the husband was vested with ownership rights in the policies, including control over the disposition of proceeds. In these circumstances, the wife's payment of premiums did not make her a transferor of any property interest in the policies.

It remains only to consider whether Mrs. Pyle's election of an alternative disposition of the proceeds was such a transaction as amounts to a transfer of property with a retained life estate, within the meaning of section 2036. Mrs. Pyle was the beneficiary originally named in the policy and as such was entitled to receive the entire proceeds of the policy on her husband's death. Then, as was her right under the terms of the policy, she caused the dispositive provisions of the policy to be changed so that she would receive only interest on the proceeds during her life, with ownership and enjoyment of this property passing to other designated persons upon her death. If it had been after maturity that Mrs. Pyle gave up her absolute right to the proceeds of the policy and elected instead to receive income for life with remainder to others, the transaction would clearly have been a transfer of property within section 2036. This case is different only in two respects. Mrs. Pyle acted while enjoyment of her right to the proceeds was still prospective and contingent upon her husband's death. Thereafter, so long as her husband lived, she could have revoked her action. While such circumstances may affect the time when in legal contemplation the transfer is accomplished, they do not make the actor any less a transferor of an interest in property. * * *

The decision of the Tax Court will be affirmed.

Notes

[¶ 18,097]

1. Compare *Estate of Pyle* with Goodnow v. United States, 302 F.2d 516 (Ct.Cl.1962) which was discussed by the court in *Estate of Pyle*. In *Goodnow* the husband applied for the policies and placed them in a trust that, by its

terms, would pay the income from the trust corpus to the wife following the death of the husband. The husband retained the incidents of ownership in the policies during his life and the right to revoke the trust but the wife paid all the premiums on the policies. When the husband died the insurance proceeds were included in his taxable estate—naturally. When the wife later died, the government asserted that the insurance proceeds, now the trust corpus, were taxable to her estate under § 2036 on the theory that by paying the premiums the wife made retained life estate transfers. The Court of Claims rejected this theory on the ground that the husband as the applicant for the insurance policies and the holder of the incidents of ownership thereon was the true settlor of the trust and further that the wife did not literally retain the income from the property she transferred, i.e., the premium payments. Is this decision consistent with *Pyle*? Is the approach to the interpretation of the term "transfer" consistent with the approach taken with respect to transfers in contemplation of death by payment of insurance premiums in contemplation of death?

2. A simple gambit intended to disguise the role of the transferor-decedent failed in Estate of Shafer v. Commissioner, 749 F.2d 1216 (6th Cir.1984). There, on purchase of a lot, the buyer, Arthur Shafer, instructed the seller to convey only a life estate to the buyer with a remainder to his son and the son's wife. The Court of Appeals affirmed a Tax Court decision penetrating the disguise and recognizing the arrangement for what it was—a transfer with a reserved life estate. An extract from the opinion is instructive:

> * * * Arthur did not receive Lot No. 463 in fee and then, while retaining a life estate, transfer a remainder interest in the property to Chase and Resor. Rather, accepting the Tax Court's factual findings, Arthur had the grantors execute the deed so as to convey a remainder interest to Chase and Resor as tenants in common while retaining a life estate for himself and Eunice. In form, therefore, only one transfer occurred: Whidden and Flanders conveyed a life estate to Arthur and Eunice with a remainder to Chase and Arthur as tenants in common. In substance, however, Arthur achieved in one step what might ordinarily take two. The effect of the transaction in the present case is merely to eliminate the intermediate step of Arthur receiving the land in fee; Arthur still retained the possession and enjoyment of the property while conveying a remainder interest to Chase and Resor. We believe that this constitutes a "transfer" under Section 2036(a); the inclusion or circumvention of the intermediate step should not make a difference in the estate tax consequences of the transaction.

3. Another "grantor, grantor, who is the grantor" question was presented in Commissioner v. Estate of Vease, 314 F.2d 79 (9th Cir.1963), where the daughter was held to be the grantor of a retained life estate trust established when she and other family members agreed before having knowledge of its contents to implement her deceased father's unexecuted will. The court rejected an argument based on the income tax rule that a compromise of a will contest passes property by "inheritance" for income tax purposes and held that the daughter had agreed to make a transfer to carry out her father's

unexecuted will. What of the possibility that the agreement made before knowledge of the will's contents might be based on a valuable consideration?

2. RECIPROCAL TRUSTS

Taxpayers and their counsel are inventive and often seem to underrate the Treasury's capability for recognizing the substance of a transaction. Over the years a variety of unsuccessful attempts to disguise retained life estate transfers have perished in court. In a "reciprocal trust" device each of the parties, (commonly spouses), creates a trust for the other with income for life to the other and remainder to third parties (typically children) subject perhaps to a power of appointment of some sort. The substance, of course, is that the result is precisely the same as though each grantor had created his or her own trust, which plainly would then be subject to § 2036. In *Estate of Grace* the Supreme Court decided that such devices offered the taxpayer little salvation.

[¶ 18,109]

UNITED STATES v. ESTATE OF GRACE

Supreme Court of the United States, 1969.
395 U.S. 316.

MR. JUSTICE MARSHALL delivered the opinion of the Court.

This case involves the application of § 811(c)(1)(B) of the Internal Revenue Code of 1939 [1986 Code § 2036] to a so-called "reciprocal trust" situation. After Joseph P. Grace's death in 1950, the Commissioner of Internal Revenue determined that the value of a trust created by his wife was includible in his gross estate. A deficiency was assessed and paid, and, after denial of a claim for a refund, this refund suit was brought. The Court of Claims, with two judges dissenting, ruled that the value of the trust was not includible in decedent's estate under § 811(c)(1)(B) and entered judgment for respondent. * * *

Decedent was a very wealthy man at the time of his marriage to the late Janet Grace in 1908. Janet Grace had no wealth or property of her own, but, between 1908 and 1931, decedent transferred to her a large amount of personal and real property, including the family's Long Island estate. Decedent retained effective control over the family's business affairs, including the property transferred to his wife. She took no interest and no part in business affairs and relied upon her husband's judgment. Whenever some formal action was required regarding property in her name, decedent would have the appropriate instrument prepared and she would execute it.

On December 15, 1931, decedent executed a trust instrument, hereinafter called the Joseph Grace trust. Named as trustees were decedent, his nephew, and a third party. The trustees were directed to pay the income of the trust to Janet Grace during her lifetime, and to pay to her any part of the principal which a majority of the trustees might deem advisable. Janet was given the power to designate, by will or deed, the manner in which the trust estate remaining at her death was to be distributed among decedent and their children. The trust properties included securities and real estate interests.

On December 30, 1931, Janet Grace executed a trust instrument, hereinafter called the Janet Grace trust, which was virtually identical to the Joseph Grace trust. The trust properties included the family estate and corporate securities, all of which had been transferred to her by decedent in preceding years.

The trust instruments were prepared by one of decedent's employees in accordance with a plan devised by decedent to create additional trusts before the advent of a new gift tax expected to be enacted the next year. Decedent selected the properties to be included in each trust. Janet Grace, acting in accordance with this plan, executed her trust instrument at decedent's request.

Janet Grace died in 1937. The Joseph Grace trust terminated at her death. Her estate's federal estate tax return disclosed the Janet Grace trust and reported it as a nontaxable transfer by Janet Grace. The Commissioner asserted that the Janet and Joseph Grace trusts were "reciprocal" and asserted a deficiency to the extent of mutual value. Compromises on unrelated issues resulted in 55% of the smaller of the two trusts, the Janet Grace trust, being included in her gross estate.

Joseph Grace died in 1950. The federal estate tax return disclosed both trusts. The Joseph Grace trust was reported as a nontaxable transfer and the Janet Grace trust was reported as a trust under which decedent held a limited power of appointment. Neither trust was included in decedent's gross estate.

The Commissioner determined that the Joseph and Janet Grace trusts were "reciprocal" and included the amount of the Janet Grace trust in decedent's gross estate. A deficiency in the amount of $363,500.97, plus interest, was assessed and paid.

* * *

The doctrine of reciprocal trusts was formulated in response to attempts to draft instruments which seemingly avoid the literal terms of § 811(c)(1)(B) [now § 2036], while still leaving the decedent the lifetime enjoyment of his property. The doctrine dates from Lehman v. Commissioner, 109 F.2d 99 (C.A. 2d Cir.), cert. denied, 310 U.S. 637 (1940). In *Lehman*, decedent and his brother owned equal shares in certain stocks and bonds. Each brother placed his interest in trust for the other's benefit for life, with remainder to the life tenant's issue. Each brother also gave the other the right to withdraw $150,000 of the principal. If the brothers had each reserved the right to withdraw $150,000 from the trust that each had created, the trusts would have been includible in their gross estates as interests of which each had made a transfer with a power to revoke. When one of the brothers died, his estate argued that neither trust was includible because the decedent did not have a power over a trust which he had created.

¶ 18,109

The Second Circuit disagreed. That court ruled that the effect of the transfers was the same as if the decedent had transferred his stock in trust for himself, remainder to his issue, and had reserved the right to withdraw $150,000. The court reasoned:

> "The fact that the trusts were reciprocated or 'crossed' is a trifle, quite lacking in practical or legal significance. . . . The law searches out the reality and is not concerned with the form." 109 F.2d, at 100.

The court ruled that the decisive point was that each brother caused the other to make a transfer by establishing his own trust.

The doctrine of reciprocal trusts has been applied numerous times since the *Lehman* decision. It received congressional approval in § 6 of the Technical Changes Act of 1949, 63 Stat. 893. The present case is, however, this Court's first examination of the doctrine.

The Court of Claims was divided over the requirements for application of the doctrine to the situation of this case. Relying on some language in *Lehman* and certain other courts of appeals' decisions, the majority held that the crucial factor was whether the decedent had established his trust as consideration for the establishment of the trust of which he was a beneficiary. The court ruled that decedent had not established his trust as a *quid pro quo* for the Janet Grace trust, and that Janet Grace had not established her trust in exchange for the Joseph Grace trust. Rather, the trusts were found to be part of an established pattern of family giving, with neither party desiring to obtain property from the other. Indeed, the court found that Janet Grace had created her trust because decedent requested that she do so. It therefore found the reciprocal trust doctrine inapplicable.

The court recognized that certain cases had established a slightly different test for reciprocity. Those cases inferred consideration from the establishment of two similar trusts at about the same time. The court held that any inference of consideration was rebutted by the evidence in the case, particularly the lack of any evidence of an estate tax avoidance motive on the part of the Graces. In contrast, the dissent felt that the majority's approach placed entirely too much weight on subjective intent. Once it was established that the trusts were interrelated, the dissent felt that the subjective intent of the parties in establishing the trusts should become irrelevant. The relevant factor was whether the trusts created by the settlors placed each other in approximately the same objective economic position as they would have been in if each had created his own trust with himself, rather than the other, as life beneficiary.

We agree with the dissent that the approach of the Court of Claims majority places too much emphasis on the subjective intent of the parties in creating the trusts and for that reason hinders proper application of the federal estate tax laws. It is true that there is language in *Lehman* and other cases that would seem to support the majority's approach. It is also true that the results in some of those cases arguably support the decision below.

¶ 18,109

Nevertheless, we think that these cases are not in accord with this Court's prior decisions interpreting related provisions of the federal estate tax laws.

Emphasis on the subjective intent of the parties in creating the trusts, particularly when those parties are members of the same family unit, creates substantial obstacles to the proper application of the federal estate tax laws. As this Court said in Estate of Spiegel v. Commissioner, 335 U.S. 701, 705–706 (1949):

> "Any requirement ... [of] a post-death attempt to probe the settlor's thoughts in regard to the transfer, would partially impair the effectiveness of ... [section 811(c)] as an instrument to frustrate estate tax evasions."

We agree that "the taxability of a trust corpus ... does not hinge on a settlor's motives, but depends on the nature and operative effect of the trust transfer." Id., at 705.

We think these observations have particular weight when applied to the reciprocal trust situation. First, inquiries into subjective intent, especially in intrafamily transfers, are particularly perilous. The present case illustrates that it is, practically speaking, impossible to determine after the death of the parties what they had in mind in creating trusts over 30 years earlier. Second, there is a high probability that such a trust arrangement was indeed created for tax-avoidance purposes. And, even if there was no estate-tax-avoidance motive, the settlor in a very real and objective sense did retain an economic interest while purporting to give away his property. Finally, it is unrealistic to assume that the settlors of the trusts, usually members of one family unit, will have created their trusts as a bargained-for exchange for the other trust. "Consideration," in the traditional legal sense, simply does not normally enter into such intrafamily transfers.

For these reasons, we hold that application of the reciprocal trust doctrine is not dependent upon a finding that each trust was created as a *quid pro quo* for the other. Such a "consideration" requirement necessarily involves a difficult inquiry into the subjective intent of the settlors. Nor do we think it necessary to prove the existence of a tax-avoidance motive. As we have said above, standards of this sort, which rely on subjective factors, are rarely workable under the federal estate tax laws. Rather, we hold that application of the reciprocal trust doctrine requires only that the trusts be interrelated, and that the arrangement, to the extent of mutual value, leaves the settlors in approximately the same economic position as they would have been in had they created trusts naming themselves as life beneficiaries.

Applying this test to the present case, we think it clear that the value of the Janet Grace trust fund must be included in decedent's estate for federal estate tax purposes. It is undisputed that the two trusts are interrelated. They are substantially identical in terms and were created at approximately the same time. Indeed, they were part of a single transaction designed and carried out by decedent. It is also clear that the transfers in trust left each party, to the extent of mutual value, in the same objective economic position as before.

¶ 18,109

Indeed, it appears, as would be expected in transfers between husband and wife, that the effective position of each party *vis-a-vis* the property did not change at all. It is no answer that the transferred properties were different in character. For purposes of the estate tax, we think that economic value is the only workable criterion. Joseph Grace's estate remained undiminished to the extent of the value of his wife's trust and the value of his estate must accordingly be increased by the value of that trust.

The judgment of the Court of Claims is reversed and the case is remanded for further proceedings consistent with this opinion.

It is so ordered.

Notes

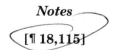

[¶ 18,115]

1. In Estate of Levy v. Commissioner, 46 T.C.M. (CCH) 910, T.C.M. (P–H) ¶ 83,453 (1983), the Tax Court declined to apply the "reciprocal trust" doctrine on the ground that a special power to appoint either the income or the corpus of the trust established by the husband for the wife with no such power in the wife's trust for the husband meant that the trusts were so substantially different as to preclude the operation of the doctrine. Consistent with this approach is Priv. Ltr. Rul. 9643013 in which the IRS ruled that the reciprocal trust doctrine did not apply to a situation in which a husband and wife each established trusts which were not mirror images of the other. Each of the trusts named the couple's children as beneficiaries, but one of the trusts also named the settlor's spouse as a beneficiary. Moreover, the two trusts varied somewhat in vesting special powers of appointment in different parties with the holder in one case being an independent party. See also Priv. Ltr. Rul. 200426008.

2. In Revenue Ruling 74–533, 1974–2 C.B. 293, the IRS confronted the issue of the proper amount to be included in the estate where parties establish reciprocal trusts of different value. Husband transferred $400,000 to a trust with income to his wife for her life, remainder to their issue. Wife, on the same day, contributed $300,000 to a trust with income to her husband for his life, remainder to their issue. At husband's death more than 10 years later, the principal of the trust established by wife had grown from $300,000 to $500,000 and was paid over to the children at that moment. The value of the trust established by husband had grown from $400,000 to $600,000 by the time wife died six months after her husband. The IRS indicated that, since it deemed the trusts to be reciprocal trusts, at husband's death it was appropriate to include in his estate the full value of the $500,000 principal of the trust established by his wife. However, since only three-quarters of the $400,000 trust that husband established for wife's benefit could be deemed to have been established in exchange for the $300,000 trust that wife established for her husband, only three-quarters of its value at wife's death, or $450,000, should be included in wife's estate at her death.

F. SUPPORT OF DEPENDENTS AND OTHER BENEFICIAL RETENTIONS

[¶ 18,121]

1. BASIC PARAMETERS OF THE PROBLEM

As the regulations make clear, the retention of income in a form that assures that it will be used to meet the legal obligations of the transferor, such as to pay the transferor's taxes or grocery bills, is surely a retention of the income by the transferor. Suppose the relation between the prescribed use of the income and the legal obligation of the transferor is not so clear? In Estate of Hays v. Commissioner, 181 F.2d 169 (5th Cir.1950), the decedent transferred mortgaged property in trust and provided that the trust income should be used to retire the mortgage on which the decedent was personally liable. To the government's claim that this amounted to a retention of the income by the transferor, the court responded in part as follows:

> The indebtedness secured by liens on the land conveyed by decedent to the trust, although originally incurred by her, constituted no charge upon her capital assets after the conveyance. Thereafter, the decedent's liability for said indebtedness was contingent, not only upon the failure of the trust to pay the same, but upon the existence of a deficiency after a foreclosure sale of the land and the application of the proceeds of the sale to the payment of the indebtedness. The possibility of decedent's liability for said debts was so remote that her direction that the trust pay the same did not constitute a reservation of income by her from the land conveyed in trust. Such possibility of liability was too remote to come within the meaning of the statute. 26 U.S.C.A. § 811(d)(1) [now § 2036(a)].

* * *

> It is not a general or indefinite benefit but a pecuniary benefit that is necessary for a transaction to constitute a reservation of income, and in this case no pecuniary benefit resulted to the decedent by the trustee's payment of the mortgage notes. A pecuniary benefit means an increase in one's net worth by the receipt of money or property. The payment of the mortgage notes did not and could not increase the decedent's net worth; she received no money; she received no property; none of her property was thereby enhanced in value or released from liens or encumbrances. The payment of the mortgage debts resulted in pecuniary benefit to the trust alone, in that the net worth of its land was increased to the extent of the payments made. There was no legal obligation upon the decedent to discharge this debt except in case of a deficiency being due after there had been a sale of the land upon foreclosure of the mortgage.

[¶ 18,127]

2. SUPPORT OF DEPENDENTS

Since state law imposes an obligation on parents to support their minor issue, it should come as no surprise that the IRS views trusts established by parents to support their minor issue as happy hunting grounds in the search for fair game for inclusion under § 2036(a)(1). Before reading the materials that follow, it would be helpful to read Reg. § 20.2036–1(b)(2).

[¶ 18,133]

ESTATE OF CHRYSLER v. COMMISSIONER

Tax Court of the United States, 1965.
44 T.C. 55.

ARUNDELL, Judge:

* * *

By trust indenture dated June 16, 1945, under which Nicholas Kelley, John W. Drye, Jr., and Harry C. Davis were trustees, decedent created an irrevocable trust for the benefit for life of his daughter, Helen F. Chrysler, who was born on February 2, 1944.

By trust indenture dated December 6, 1946, under which Nicholas Kelley, John W. Drye, Jr., and Harry C. Davis were trustees, decedent created an irrevocable trust for the benefit for life of his son Jack F. Chrysler, Jr., who was born on May 31, 1946.

The provisions of each trust were identical in all material respects except for the language necessary to make one trust pertain to the decedent's infant daughter and the other trust to his infant son. The corpus of each trust was $115,000 in cash. The trust for the daughter provided in part:

1. A. The Trustees shall hold, manage, invest and from time to time reinvest the trust estate and shall collect the income therefrom and shall pay over the net annual income therefrom to Helen Forker Chrysler, daughter of the Grantor, during her life; provided, however, that as long as Helen Forker Chrysler shall be a minor, the Trustees shall use and apply so much of the net annual income and any accumulated income of the trust estate as the Trustees shall deem advisable for the maintenance, education and support of said Helen Forker Chrysler; or instead of making personal application of such income, the Trustees may transfer, assign and pay over so much of such income as they deem advisable to either parent or the guardian of the person or property of said Helen Forker Chrysler, or the person with whom she resides, to be by such parent, guardian or person so used and applied (and the receipt of such parent, guardian or person shall be full acquittance and discharge to the Trustees in respect of any such sum or sums so paid over, and the Trustees shall have no duty or responsibility in supervising the application of any such income) and the Trustees shall accumulate the balance of such income during the minority of said Helen Forker Chrysler, and upon her attaining the age of twenty-one years, the Trustees shall transfer, assign and pay over to her all accumulations of income on the trust estate; or if said Helen Forker Chrysler shall die before attaining the age of twenty-one years, all accumulations of income on the trust estate shall

be transferred, assigned and paid over to the executor or administrator of the estate of said Helen Forker Chrysler.

In the management, administration and investment of any accumulated income, the Trustees shall have all the powers, authority and discretion given to them with respect to the trust estate by any provisions of this trust indenture.

Each trust provided for the complete disposition of the remainder after the termination of the respective life estate.

The fair market value on November 7, 1958, of the principal of each of the two trusts was $534,920.37 and $698,120.83, respectively, which amounts were included in the decedent's gross estate as items 2 and 3, respectively.

Decedent was never a trustee under either trust. None of the income of either trust collected by the trustees was used for the maintenance, education or support of the respective beneficiary during decedent's lifetime and all such income of both trusts was taxed to the trustees and the net income of both trusts was accumulated by them.

* * *

Respondent contends that the values of the corpora of the two trusts (items 2 and 3) created by decedent on June 16, 1945, and December 6, 1946, are includable in the decedent's gross estate under the provisions of section 2036(a), I.R.C. 1954. In so contending, the respondent, in effect *assumes* that the two trusts were created for the maintenance, education and support of his two minor children. In his brief he argues thus:

> Decedent established each of the trusts shortly after the respective births of his two children. The purpose for which the trusts were created was for the maintenance, education and support of his children. These trusts were an effective instrumentality through which the decedent could discharge his legal obligation to support his children. Since both of decedent's children were minors at the date of decedent's death, decedent was under a duty imposed by law to support them (Sec. 32, Domestic Relations Law of New York). Decedent could have availed himself at any time until his death to have the income applied for the support of his children.

The above argument, except for the part that decedent was under a duty imposed by law to support his minor children, is not supported by the facts. Decedent could *not* have availed himself at any time until his death of having the income applied for the support of his children. This could only be done in the discretion of the three trustees. Decedent was not one of the trustees. The trusts were irrevocable. They created life estates with remainders over. When decedent created the trusts he parted forever with all right to the income or principal of the trusts, or the right, either alone or in conjunction with any person, to designate the persons who shall possess or enjoy the property or the income therefrom.

The facts in the cases principally relied upon by the respondent involve facts entirely different from the facts in the instant case. In the first case cited in the footnote the decedent there created a trust, the income of which was payable to his wife with the provision that she should use it for their family and joint living expenses and for her own maintenance and support. In Commissioner v. Dwight's Estate, 205 F.2d 298 (C.A.2, 1953), reversing and remanding 17 T.C. 1317, the husband decedent had created two trusts to pay the income to his wife and children for their "support and maintenance." And in Estate of William H. Lee, 33 T.C. 1064, our syllabus is as follows:

> *Held*: Decedent, in making transfers of property in trust with income to be paid to his wife "for her maintenance and support," retained the right to have the income used to fulfill his legal obligation of support, and the trust corpus is to be included in the valuation of his gross estate. Commissioner v. Dwight's Estate, 205 F.2d 298 (C.A.2), followed.

In the instant case, the decedent could not direct the trustees to apply any of the income for the maintenance, education and support of the minor beneficiaries. Sole discretion as to whether any income of the trusts was to be so applied rested and remained in the trustees. The trust instruments specifically provided that only "so much" of such income "as the Trustees shall deem advisable" shall be so used, and the balance accumulated.

We think the facts in the instant case are more like those in Commissioner v. Douglass' Estate, 143 F.2d 961 (C.A.3, 1944), affirming 2 T.C. 487, cited and relied upon by petitioner. The decedent in that case created a trust for the benefit of his four children. Neither decedent nor any of the beneficiaries was among the three trustees named. Decedent died in 1938. In the trust instrument decedent gave the trustees permission to apply the income of the minor's share to the extent that the trustees "may deem necessary for the education, support and maintenance of said minor." In denying the Commissioner's claim that one-fourth of the value of the principal of the trust was to be included in the decedent's gross estate, the court said in part:

> In addition to the theory thus advanced the Commissioner's argument cites Helvering v. Mercantile–Commerce Bank & Trust Co. et al., 8 Cir., 111 F.2d 224, certiorari denied, 1940, 310 U.S. 654. This involved a trust for a wife created by a husband in his lifetime. The income was to be paid to her for family expenses and her own maintenance and support. The Eighth Circuit held that the corpus of the trust was to be included as part of his estate for estate tax purposes. The decision is, obviously, not an authority on the question before us in this litigation. *There is certainly an important difference of fact between the trust set up for the very purpose of providing for the settlor's legal obligation to his wife and the one in which disinterested trustees have an option to apply a portion of the income for the support of the settlor's minor child.*

Under the section of the estate tax law already quoted, the settlor's estate is subject to the tax if he retained the possession or enjoyment of the income from the property or the right to designate the persons who should enjoy it. But he did neither. *He granted the property to trustees, retaining nothing.* The Commissioner's argument that these trustees would be likely to do what he asked of them about assigning income for the support of a minor child departs from the "practical" and "realistic" approach we are asked, in the same

¶ 18,133

argument, to take. We have no notion what the trustees would have done had such a request been made. *It is apparent, from the terms of the instrument, that the settlor could not direct or control the matter, once the trust settlement had become effective.* [Emphasis supplied.]

We hold that the respondent erred in including items 2 and 3 in the decedent's gross estate.

Planning Note

[¶ 18,139]

If a donor establishes a trust like the trust in *Chrysler* and makes herself or himself the trustee with discretionary disbursement powers, such trust will, of course, be included in the donor's estate under § 2036(a)(2). The key to *Chrysler* rests in granting discretion to a third party.

The trust in *Chrysler* was prepared by what, at the time, were some of the nation's best estate planners. If a responsive third party trustee is selected, the granting of discretion to that trustee to make disbursements to income beneficiaries who are minor issue of the settlor and whom the settlor is obliged to support provides an excellent means whereby the corpus of the trust can be put beyond the reaches of § 2036. Care must be taken, however, to avoid the reciprocal trust doctrine (¶ 18,103). The dynastically wealthy should have little interest in this device since, in such families, settlors seldom would wish, or need, to have trust resources used to satisfy their support obligations. Among the "marginal millionaire" crowd, the device used in *Chrysler* should have strong appeal.

The case that follows demonstrates the degree to which care must be exercised when trying to squeeze through the opening given to the taxpayer by *Chrysler*.

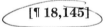

[¶ 18,145]

ESTATE OF GOKEY v. COMMISSIONER

Tax Court of the United States, 1979.
72 T.C. 721, aff'd in part and rev'd in part, 735 F.2d 1367 (7th Cir.1984).

WILES, Judge:

[The deceased, Joseph Gokey, on October 1, 1961, established three trusts, one each for the benefit of his then minor children, Bridget, Gretchen and Patrick. He then also created a trust for the benefit of his wife, Mildred. Under the terms of her trust she was to receive income for her life and the trustee was vested with discretion to invade corpus for her care, comfort, support or welfare. On her death, the corpus of that trust was to be distributed equally to the three trusts established for the benefit of the children. The trusts for benefit of the children each contained the following provision:]

Section 2: Until each beneficiary becomes twenty-one (21) years of age, the Trustee shall use such part or all of the net income of his or her trust for the support, care, welfare, and education of the beneficiary thereof, payments from such net income to be made to such beneficiary or in such other manner as the Trustee deems to be in the best interest of the beneficiary, and any unused income shall be accumulated and added to the principal of such beneficiary's trust. After each beneficiary becomes twenty-one (21) years of age, the Trustee shall pay to him or her, in convenient installments, the entire net income of his or her trust. In the Trustee's discretion, said income payments may be supplemented at any time with payments of principal from a beneficiary's share whenever the Trustee deems any such payments necessary for the support, care, welfare, or education of the beneficiary thereof.

[The decedent died on October 20, 1969. Bridget had reached majority so no effort was made to effect an inclusion under her trust. Gretchen and Patrick were then 15 and 13 years old, respectively. The Commissioner sought to include the full value of their trusts, $797,583.66. On the theory that if Gretchen's and Patrick's trusts were deemed to satisfy Joseph's support obligation with respect to them, the Commissioner sought to include in Joseph's taxable estate the value of their remainder interests in their mother's trust. His theory for doing so was that Joseph, through Gretchen's and Patrick's trusts, had retained a contingent life estate (satisfaction of his support obligation with respect to Gretchen and Patrick) in this trust subject to Mildred's life estate which was presently being enjoyed.]

The first issue is whether decedent retained the possession or enjoyment of, or the right to the income from, property transferred by him to irrevocable trusts for the benefit of Gretchen and Patrick. If so, the value of the property in those trusts is properly includable in decedent's gross estate under section 2036. The resolution of this issue depends upon whether, within the meaning of section 20.2036–1(b)(2), Estate Tax Regs., the income or property of the trusts was to be applied toward the discharge of the decedent's legal obligation to support Gretchen and Patrick during his lifetime.

Respondent contends that under Illinois law, decedent was under a legal duty to support his minor children, Gretchen and Patrick; that the terms of the children's trusts clearly require the trustees to use the trusts' income and property for their support; and that, therefore, the value of the trust property is includable in decedent's gross estate.

Petitioners do not dispute decedent's obligation to support Gretchen and Patrick under Illinois law; however, they contend that the use of the property or income therefrom for the children's support was within the unrestricted discretion of the trustees; that even if trusts did not give the trustees any discretion in this matter, the decedent nevertheless intended to grant them this discretion; that the use of the term "welfare" in the trusts creates an unascertainable standard which, even if ascertainable, is much broader than the standard for support; and that, therefore, the value of the trust property is not includable in decedent's gross estate. We agree with respondent on this issue.

Respondent relies upon section 20.2036–1(b)(2), Estate Tax Regs., which states that the use, possession, right to the income, or other enjoyment of the transferred property is considered as having been retained by or reserved to the decedent within the meaning of section 2036(a)(1) to the extent that the use, possession, right to the income, or other enjoyment *is to be applied* toward the discharge of a legal obligation of decedent which includes an obligation to support a dependent. "Is to be applied" is not to be read as "may be applied," which exists where an independent trustee is vested with discretion over distributions. Estate of Mitchell v. Commissioner, 55 T.C. 576, 580 (1970). This creates a factual question as to whether the income from the trust property must be restricted or confined to fulfilling the settlor's obligation to support his dependents. Estate of Lee v. Commissioner, 33 T.C. 1064, 1067 (1960).

We believe the language of the children's trusts found in section 2 of the 1961 trust agreement which relates "shall use such part or all of the net income * * * for the support, care, welfare, and education of the beneficiary" clearly manifests decedent's intent to require the trustees to apply the income for the stated purpose. In our view, it is impossible to construe the instrument as one which gives the trustees discretion as to whether or not income shall be used for "support, care, welfare, and education." That standard completely controls the application of the trusts' funds. If those needs exceed the trusts' income, principal may be utilized. If those needs do not absorb all the trusts' income, the remaining income is accumulated and added to principal. Moreover, the section 2 phrase "payments from such net income to be made to such beneficiary or in such other manner as the Trustee deems to be in the best interest of the beneficiary" does not alter our interpretation. Clearly, this phrase only grants the trustee discretion in the method of payment adopted. Since we find decedent's intent clearly expressed in the trust instrument, we need not look beyond the four corners of the instrument to determine intent.

Petitioners next argue that the use of the word "welfare" within the phrase "the Trustee shall use such part or all of the net income of his or her trust for the support, care, welfare, and education of the beneficiary thereof" in section 2 of the 1961 trust instrument, gives the trustee authority to make nonsupport expenditures which, in turn, violates the "is to be applied" language of section 20.2036–1(b)(2), Estate Tax Regs. They support this theory by arguing that the standard "support, care, welfare, and education" is not ascertainable under, among others, sections 2036(a)(2) and 2041; and even if ascertainable, "welfare" is broader than "support" under Illinois law.

In determining whether "support, care, welfare, and education" is subject to an ascertainable external standard, we must rely upon Illinois law. In Estate of Wood v. Commissioner, 39 T.C. 919, 923–924 (1963), we held that the phrase "support, maintenance, welfare, and comfort" was subject to an ascertainable standard:

> We think that these four somewhat overlapping nouns were intended in the aggregate to describe the life beneficiary's standard of living in all its aspects * * *

> Admittedly, the words "support," and "maintenance" are regarded as referable to a standard of living, and the addition of the naked words

"comfort" and "welfare" in the context of the instrument before us merely rounds out the standard of living concept.

In Estate of Bell v. Commissioner, 66 T.C. 729, 734–735 (1976), we found that the phrase "well being and maintenance in health and comfort" was subject to an ascertainable standard in Illinois:

> Although providing a modicum of discretion to the trustees, this language created a standard enforceable in a court of equity. Under Illinois law, a court of equity would look to the beneficiary's accustomed living standard in compelling compliance by the trustees, either to require income distributions for the stated purposes or to restrain distributions for unauthorized purposes. In re Whitman, 22 Ill. 511 (1859)("support, education, and maintenance"); French v. Northern Trust Co., 197 Ill. 30, 64 N.E. 105, 106 (1902)("properly maintained and comfortably provided for out of such property"); Burke v. Burke, 259 Ill. 262, 102 N.E. 293, 294 (1913)("the comforts and necessities of life").

We similarly believe that under Illinois law, a court of equity would look to Gretchen's and Patrick's accustomed living standard in compelling compliance by the trustee to require income distributions for the stated purposes. As a result, we find that the terms "support, care, welfare, and education," when viewed in the aggregate, were intended to describe the children's standard of living and are, therefore, subject to an external ascertainable standard. Having found that the phrase in the aggregate created an ascertainable standard requiring the trustee to make expenditures for the children's accustomed living standard, we must reject petitioners' argument that the term "welfare" in the phrase allows the trustee to make nonsupport payments because "welfare" is broader than "support" under Illinois law.

* * * [After further examining Illinois law, the Court concluded] that, under Illinois law, support is equivalent to accustomed standard of living. We are satisfied that the instrument before us provides an ascertainable standard under Illinois law. Accordingly, we find that decedent's gross estate includes the value of Gretchen's and Patrick's trusts since we find them to be support trusts within the meaning of section 2036(a)(1) and section 20.2036–1(b)(2), Estate Tax Regs.

[Having thus included in Joseph's estate the aggregate value of the assets in Gretchen's and Patrick's trusts, the Court then turned its attention to the values of the remainders which both Gretchen's and Patrick's trusts were entitled to be paid under the terms of Mildred's trust upon the expiration of her life estate.]

Having determined that the value of the assets in the children's trusts is includable in decedent's gross estate, we must now determine the value of the assets in each trust; specifically, what is the value of the children's trusts' one-third remainder interests in a trust decedent created for the benefit of Mrs. Gokey in the October 1, 1961, trust agreement. Article I, sections 1 and 2 of that trust, grants Mrs. Gokey a life estate with remainder over equally to decedent's three children. Relying upon section 20.2031–7, Estate Tax Regs., respondent values Mrs. Gokey's life estate at $215,040.17 with a resulting remainder interest of $66,245.78 to each of the children. He then included $66,245.78, separately, in the value of assets held in Gretchen's and Patrick's trusts. Petitioners do not dispute the existence of the remainder interests, but, nevertheless, value them at zero because of the trustee's power of invasion in favor of Mrs. Gokey's life estate and the spendthrift clause prohibiting the children from alienating their remainder interests. Petitioners agree that if we hold for respondent on this issue, the proper value of each remainder interest is $66,245.78. Thus, we must only decide whether the value of each remainder interest is zero or $66,245.78. We find the value of each to be $66,245.78.

Petitioners' argument essentially suggests that under the "willing buyer and seller test" of section 20.2031–1(b), Estate Tax Regs., the remainder interests have no value since no one would buy a remainder interest that could not be alienated because of a spendthrift provision or a remainder interest subject to a power of invasion of principal in favor of the life tenant. This argument is without merit.

Valuation questions are primarily factual and although alienability and powers of invasion affect value, we do not believe they destroy it as a matter of law. In United States v. Simmons, 346 F.2d 213, 216–217 (5th Cir.1965), the court found that even a tax refund claim which could not be lawfully sold or assigned because of a Federal anti-assignment statute, had some value: "The 'willing buyer and seller' are a *hypothetical* buyer and seller having a reasonable knowledge of relevant facts." (Emphasis added.) With regard to petitioners' second point, we do not question the difficulties associated with valuing an interest subject to a power of invasion. However, life estates coupled with a power to invade have been valued in the past. Moreover, the fact that this power of invasion is limited by the ascertainable standard "care, comfort, support or welfare" relating to Mrs. Gokey's accustomed standard of living assists in determining a value for her life estate interest. Since we have already found that the phrase "support, care, welfare, and education" constituted an ascertainable standard under Illinois law, we believe this standard is similarly ascertainable, since only "comfort" is substituted for "education" and Rock Island Bank & Trust Co. v. Rhoads, [353 Ill. 131, 187 N.E. 139 (1933)], held that comfort means support. Of course, if the life estate may be valued, so may the remainder interests. Accordingly, we find that, under the record before us, the remainder interests have some value. As a result, pursuant to the agreement of the parties and petitioners' burden of proof to overcome the correctness of respondent's determined value, we find the value of Gretchen's and Patrick's remainder interests to be $66,245.78 each.

We have considered the parties' other arguments and find them unpersuasive.

To reflect the foregoing,

Decisions will be entered under Rule 155.

¶ 18,145

Notes

[¶ 18,151]

1. On appeal, the Seventh Circuit affirmed most parts of the decision of the Tax Court but reversed with respect to the value of the remainder interests in Mildred's trust that were to be included in Joseph's estate. See 735 F.2d at 1367. The Seventh Circuit determined that the actuarially determined value of the includible remainder interests in Mildred's trust should be discounted by the value of the probability that an invasion of corpus for Mildred's benefit, as permitted by the terms of the trust, would take place. On remand, the Tax Court allowed a discount of 75 percent due to consideration of this element. Estate of Gokey, 49 T.C.M. (CCH) 368, T.C.M. (P–H) ¶ 84,665 (1984). See added discussion of this issue under ¶ 14,015.

2. Most of the decided cases, like *Gokey*, involve families that were intact up until the moment of death. In such circumstances, establishment by the settlor of a trust under which income is to be used to satisfy the settlor's legal support obligation with respect to a minor child results in the finding that a retained life estate is present if the settlor dies prior to the child's legal emancipation.

3. Where a support trust for the child of a broken marriage is present, a new wrinkle is added. In these circumstances, if the settlor retains custody of the minor, the courts have been willing to find the presence of a retained life estate if the settlor dies prior to legal emancipation. See National Bank of Commerce v. Henslee, 179 F.Supp. 346 (M.D.Tenn.1959). A different result is obtained where the settlor does not have legal custody of the minor and pursuant to a separation agreement with the spouse agrees to establish, in satisfaction of the support obligation to spouse and child, a trust with income to both. In such circumstances, discharge of the support obligation is deemed to provide the consideration that places the trust beyond the reach of § 2036. See Estate of McKeon v. Commissioner, 25 T.C. 697 (1956). For a case involving a support trust entered into during days of marital bliss and subsequently referred to in a divorce decree, see Estate of Pardee v. Commissioner, 49 T.C. 140 (1967).

4. In Rev. Rul. 59–357, 1959–2 C.B. 212, the IRS ruled that where a parent, who has a legal support obligation with respect to a minor child, makes a gift to his child under the Uniform Gifts to Minors Act (UGMA), appointing himself as custodian for the gift, and dies while the child is still a minor, the property which is the subject of the gift shall be included in the parent's estate. The ruling bases its rationale on the fact that the donor parent under the UGMA has the right to use income from the gifted property to support the minor. The ruling goes on to state that "In all other circumstances custodial property is includible only in the gross estate of the donee." This has been interpreted as indicating that a parent can avoid the reach of § 2036 (a)(1) on gifts to minor children by simply appointing a spouse as custodian. Exchange Bank and Trust Co. of Florida v. United States, 694 F.2d 1261 (Fed.Cir.1982) (dictum).

¶ 18,151

Parents who have support obligations with respect to minor children and who appoint each other as custodians with respect to gifts under the UGMA or the Uniform Transfers to Minors Act (UTMA) will find the IRS asserting that application of the reciprocal trust doctrine (¶ 18,109) results in an inclusion in the estate if one of the parents dies while a child is still in minority.

The issue of the application of §§ 2036 and 2038 to gifts under UGMA and UTMA is discussed at greater length elsewhere (¶ 18,181; 18,190; 19,073; and 19,133).

[¶ 18,157]

3. SUPPORT OF SPOUSE

Where a donor establishes a trust for support of a spouse, the same basic issues arise since each spouse has a legal obligation to support the other. Critical to a determination of whether an inclusion is present are: (1) whether the trust requires, or as in *Chrysler* merely permits, income to be used for support and maintenance; and (2) whether the beneficiary spouse is given discretion as to how the income is to be used. Where income must be used to meet a legal support obligation with respect to a spouse, inclusion in the estate is required. See, e.g., Richards v. Commissioner, 375 F.2d 997 (10th Cir.1967)(inclusion despite fact that decedent supported spouse and trust income was never so used). Where, as in *Chrysler*, the trustee is given discretion as to use of the income, no inclusion results under § 2036. See, e.g., Estate of Mitchell v. Commissioner, 55 T.C. 576 (1970). Where the beneficiary spouse has discretion to use income as he or she wishes, no inclusion results. See, e.g., Estate of Sessoms v. Commissioner, 8 T.C.M. (CCH) 1056, T.C.M. (P–H) ¶ 49,286 (1949); Estate of Sherman v. Commissioner, 9 T.C. 594 (1947).

In Estate of Sullivan v. Commissioner, 66 T.C.M. (CCH) 1329, T.C.M. (RIA) ¶ 93,531 (1993), the court held that, where the settlor of a trust effectively reserved the right to distribute corpus for support and maintenance of his wife, an inclusion in the estate of decedent-settlor should be made of an amount equal to a portion of the trust which, given the couple's standard of living, would be needed to support decedent's widow.

Where a donor establishes a trust incident to a divorce to support an ex-spouse or soon to be ex-spouse, a special rule prevails. In 1984, § 2043(b)(2) was added to the Code providing that a transfer incident to a divorce, which meets the requirements of § 2516, shall be considered made for full and adequate consideration. The impact of § 2043(b)(2) on alimony trusts is illustrated by the following private letter ruling.

[¶ 18,159]

PRIVATE LETTER RULING 9235032
May 29, 1992.

[A and B entered into a settlement agreement pursuant to their obtaining a divorce. Under paragraph 10 of the agreement, B was obliged monthly to pay A a fixed sum of money as alimony. The agreement authorized B to meet this obligation by making direct payments to A, purchasing an annuity, or establishing an alimony trust. Sometime later B chose the latter course of action and the IRS ruled that at B's death, the alimony trust was to be taxed in the following manner.]

Section 2036(a) provides that the value of the gross estate shall include the value of all property to the extent of any interest therein of which the decedent has at any time made a transfer (except in a case of a bona fide sale for adequate and full consideration in money or money's worth), by trust or otherwise, under which he has retained for his life or for any period not ascertainable without reference to his death or for any period that does not in fact end before his death (1) the possession or enjoyment of, or the right to the income from, the property, or (2) the right, either alone or in conjunction with any person, to designate the persons who shall possess or enjoy the property or the income therefrom.

Section 20.2036–1(b)(2) of the Estate Tax Regulations provides that the term "use, possession, right to income, or other enjoyment of the transferred property" is considered to have been retained by or reserved to the decedent to the extent that the use, possession, right to income, or other enjoyment is to be applied toward the discharge of a legal obligation of the decedent, or otherwise for his pecuniary benefit. The term "legal obligation" includes a legal obligation to support a dependent during the decedent's lifetime.

Section 2053(a) provides for a deduction in determining the amount of the taxable estate for amounts that are paid in satisfaction of claims against the estate. Under section 2053(c), the deduction for claims against the estate is allowed only to the extent that the claim is contracted bona fide for an adequate consideration in money or money's worth.

Section 2043(b)(2) provides that for purposes of section 2053, a transfer of property which satisfies the requirements of section 2516(1) is considered as made for an adequate and full consideration in money or money's worth.

In the instant case, under the terms of Paragraph 10 of the agreement, a personal obligation is imposed on the taxpayer to pay A the monthly amount. The taxpayer's transfer to the trust does not relieve the taxpayer, or his estate, of this personal obligation because, under the terms of the agreement, the taxpayer, or his estate, is required to discharge the maintenance obligation, in the event the trust does not generate sufficient funds. Rather, the taxpayers transfer to the trust enabled the taxpayer to satisfy that obligation if and to the extent that each payment is in fact made from the trust. If any trust payment were to fall short of the obligation, then the taxpayer would be required to pay the difference from other funds. Accordingly, in the instant case, the taxpayer has retained the use, possession, enjoyment or right to income from the property under section 2036(a)(1) of the Code and section 20.2036–1(b)(2) of the regulations, since the trust income and corpus is to be applied to discharge the taxpayer's continuing legal obligation under the agreement. Accordingly, the value of the trust corpus on the date of the taxpayer's death will be includible in his gross estate under section 2036(a)(1). In this regard, we note that section 2516(1) does not apply to satisfy the full and adequate consideration exception contained in section 2036. Estate of Nelson v. Commissioner, 47 T.C. 279, 287 (1966), rev'd. on other grounds, 396 F.2d 519 (2d Cir.1968).

However, the value of *A*'s remaining maintenance right on the date of the taxpayer's death would be treated as a claim contracted for adequate consideration under section 2043(b)(2) and therefore, would be deductible under section 2053(a)(3). Cf. Rev. Rul. 76–113, 1976–1 C.B. 276.

Notes

[¶ 18,161]

1. Presumably, under the IRS position as set forth in Priv. Ltr. Rul. 9235032, the amount deductible under § 2053(a)(3) will not equal the amount included under § 2036(a)(1). For example, assume that an alimony trust contains $800,000 and requires that all income is to be paid to a former spouse who at decedent's death is age 67. If we assume that the value of the ex-spouse's income interest is $480,000, under the theory of the ruling, this will result in a net inclusion of $320,000 ($800,000—$480,000). Do you agree with this result?

2. Suppose that rather than the settlor designating who shall enjoy the remainder interest, the recipient of alimony, as part of the divorce proceedings, was allowed to designate the remainder person. What should then follow?

G. RETENTION OF CONTROL— SECTION 2036(a)(2)

[¶ 18,163]

Clearly, § 2036(a)(2) requires that a donor's estate include property with respect to which the donor retained the right to designate which one of several beneficiaries is to enjoy the use of, or the income from, property. Occasionally, the donor, by retaining a power that under certain circumstances effectively retains this privilege, finds that an interest has been retained that will make the property subject to inclusion in the estate. Also at issue under § 2036(a)(2) is whether inclusion in the estate of the donor is appropriate when the donor has retained not the right to determine who is to enjoy the income from property but rather the right to determine when, or under what circumstances, the beneficiary will enjoy the income from the property.

1. CONTROL OVER TIMING OF ENJOYMENT

[¶ 18,169]

STRUTHERS v. KELM

United States Court of Appeals, Eighth Circuit, 1955.
218 F.2d 810.

COLLET, Circuit Judge:

The question for determination is whether the creator of three trusts, Mrs. Mary Case Barney, reserved the right, in conjunction with other persons, to designate the persons who should possess or enjoy the property constituting the trusts or the income therefrom. If she did so, the property constituting the trusts was subject to estate tax on her estate under [1939 Code] § 811(c)(1)(B)(ii), 26 U.S.C.A. § 811(c)(1)(B)(ii), 1953 Supp. [The 1939 Code section involved in this case is the same in all material respects as § 2036 of the 1986 Code.] * * *

The facts are not in dispute. The trust indenture was executed February 18, 1937. By it Mrs. Barney created three separate [irrevocable] trusts in favor of her three children, Hadwen C. Barney, Mary B. Struthers, and Elizabeth B. Wesbrook. With the exception of the named beneficiary, the terms of the three trusts were for present purposes identical. In each Mrs. Barney was designated as one of the three trustees.

The trust instrument in which Mary B. Struthers is the beneficiary is typical of the three trust agreements. The pertinent portions thereof are as follows:

* * *

"3. The Trustees shall collect and receive all interest, income and profits earned by said Trust Fund. The net income from said Trust Fund, or so much thereof as the Trustees shall deem advisable, may be accumulated by said Trustees and invested for the benefit of Mary B. Struthers, daughter of said Mary Case Barney, or the Trustees may in their discretion pay the net income or so much thereof as they deem advisable to the said Mary B. Struthers at such times and in such amounts as in their sole judgment they deem advisable. In addition thereto the Trustees may use such amounts out of the principal from time to time as in their judgment and discretion they may deem necessary and advisable for the care, comfort, support and maintenance of said Mary B. Struthers.

"4. Upon the death of the said Mary Case Barney, the Trust hereby created shall cease and terminate and the entire Trust Fund and all accumulated or unpaid net income shall be paid over and distributed to the said Mary B. Struthers.

* * *

"7. The Trustor declares that she has been fully advised as to the legal effect of the execution of this agreement and informed as to the character and amount of the property hereby transferred and conveyed; and further that she has given consideration to the question whether the trust hereby created shall be revocable or irrevocable, and she now declares that it shall be irrevocable and that she shall hereafter be without power at any time, either alone or in conjunction with any other person, or persons, to revoke, change, amend, alter, annul, or terminate the trust hereby created or any of the provisions herein contained.''

* * *

The Government's position is that the value of the three trusts should be included in Mrs. Barney's estate and taxed as a part of her estate because she retained the right, in conjunction with the other trustees, to designate the persons who should possess or enjoy the property or the income therefrom. That position is based upon the wording of the trust instruments which provide that the net income of the trust, or so much thereof as the trustees shall deem advisable, may be accumulated and invested for the benefit of the named beneficiary, or the net income, or such portion of it as the trustees deem advisable, may be paid to the beneficiary, or that the trustees may use such amount of the principal from time to time for the care, support and maintenance of the beneficiary as they in their judgment and discretion may determine.

At the time the case was heard the trial court, applying the law of Minnesota as declared in First & American National Bank of Duluth v. Higgins, 208 Minn. 295, 293 N.W. 585, concluded that Mrs. Barney retained no possibility of a reverter; that since the trust instruments made no provision as to the disposition of the trust income or the trust fund in the event the beneficiary predeceased Mrs. Barney, and since the beneficiary's interest in the estate was vested in the manner declared by the law of Minnesota and not susceptible to change by Mrs. Barney or by her and the trustees acting jointly or severally, as trustees, that no control of the remainder was retained by or was vested in Mrs. Barney and that the mere control of the time when the beneficiary or the beneficiary's possible devisees might enjoy the fund did not constitute such a substantial control over the trusts contemplated by the statute as would require the treatment of the trusts as part of Mrs. Barney's estate. Reliance for that conclusion was placed upon Hays' Estate v. Commissioner, 181 F.2d 169. Taking cognizance, however, of Lober v. United States, 108 F.Supp. 731, 124 Ct. Cl. 44, and the pendency of that case before the Supreme Court on certiorari, the trial court reserved formal judgment pending final disposition of the *Lober* case. When the latter was decided by the Supreme Court, Lober v. United States, 346 U.S. 335, the trial court, being convinced that this case was controlled by the *Lober* case, entered judgment for the Government, dismissing the complaint. We are convinced that the *Lober* case is determinative of this.

Appellant undertakes to distinguish this from the *Lober* case upon two grounds. First, that in this case the right of control over the disposition of the trusts vested entirely in the beneficiaries at the time the trusts were established, that the beneficiary might have subjected the entire trust to the payment of the beneficiary's debts or by devise designated another as the recipient in event the beneficiary predeceased Mrs. Barney, or, in the event neither occurred, that the law of descents and distribution of the State of Minnesota fixed with certainty the recipient of the trust fund beyond the power of any person to change. For that reason it is said that Mrs. Barney could not have had the power, acting alone or in conjunction with the other trustees, to designate the persons who should possess or enjoy the trusts or the income therefrom. The further argument is advanced that the facts in this case distinguish it from the *Lober* case because of paragraph 7 of the trust instrument, heretofore quoted, wherein Mrs. Barney stated that—"She shall hereafter be without power at any time, either alone or in conjunction with any other person or persons, to revoke, change, amend, or terminate the trust hereby created or any of the provisions herein contained."

The *Lober* case was decided under [1939 Code] § 811(d)(1), 26 U.S.C.A. § 811(d)(2) [substantially the same as § 2038 of the 1986 Code], which made trusts taxable as part of the donor's estate " 'where the enjoyment thereof was subject at the date of his death to any change through the exercise of a power * * * to alter, amend, or revoke * * *.' " Lober v. United States, 346 U.S. 335, 336. But the gravamen of both [1939 Code] § 811(d)(2) and 811(c)(1)(B)(ii) is the same. Both deal, in regard to the question before us, with the "enjoyment" or "possession" of the trust. Both sections adopt as the factor determinative of whether the trust shall be treated as a part of the donor's estate the existence or nonexistence of the power of the donor to "alter, amend or revoke", [1939 Code] § 811(d)(2), or, to designate the person who shall "possess or enjoy" the property or its income (§ 811(c)(1)(B)(ii)). The *Lober* opinion, quoting from Commissioner v. Holmes' Estate, 326 U.S. 480, states that [1939 Code] § 811(d)(2) "was more concerned with 'present economic benefit' than with 'technical vesting of title or estates.' " In the *Lober* case the fact relied on as distinguishing this case from the *Lober* case was assumed, i.e., that the trust instrument gave Lober's children a vested interest under state law so that if they had died after creation of the trusts their interests would have passed to their estates. But that fact was held undeterminative and Lober's estate was charged with the estate tax because Lober's children, as beneficiaries of the trust, were granted no "present right to immediate enjoyment of either income or principal" without Lober's consent. In this case the beneficiary under Mrs. Barney's trust instrument was not granted the present right to immediate enjoyment of the income or principal without Mrs. Barney's permission, acting "in conjunction with" the other trustees. Since the *Holmes' Estate* case and the *Lober* case give controlling emphasis and effect to the present right of enjoyment of the trust by the beneficiary, rather that [sic] when the title to the trust property technically vested under state law, or the absence of power on the part of the donor to alter or amend that title, this case may not be distinguished from Lober v. United States and Commissioner v. Holmes' Estate, supra. It must follow that the judgment is correct and is affirmed.

¶ 18,169

Notes

[¶ 18,175]

1. In Estate of Alexander v. Commissioner, 81 T.C. 757 (1983), the doctrine of *Struthers v. Kelm* was applied in uncompromising fashion to a trust where the grantor-decedent could only distribute or accumulate income for eventual distribution to the beneficiary or her estate and even that would have required that he exercise his authority to remove the trustee and name himself, which he had not done. Still, the application of the *Struthers v. Kelm* doctrine does seem indicated on such facts.

Other cases reaching the conclusion that retention by the donor of control over merely the timing of a designated beneficiary's enjoyment of income results in an inclusion in the donor's gross estate under § 2036(a)(2) are Estate of Sulovich v. Commissioner, 587 F.2d 845 (6th Cir.1978); Rott v. United States, 321 F.Supp. 654 (E.D.Mo.1971) and Deaktor v. Commissioner, 25 T.C.M. (CCH) 992, T.C.M. (P–H) ¶ 66,194 (1966). Both *Rott* and *Deaktor* involved a version of the spendthrift trust in which the donor had retained the right to withhold from the income beneficiary annual income which was added to corpus. In both cases the income beneficiary, her estate or designees were the remaindermen of the trusts. Had the donor in these cases or in *Struthers* been willing to vest control over timing of enjoyment in an independent party, estate taxation could have been easily avoided.

2. Some commentators have objected to the holding of *Struthers* and its progeny on the ground that since § 2036(a)(2) speaks in terms of a retained right to designate the "persons" who shall enjoy income, § 2036(a)(2) should not apply in a situation such as that involved in *Struthers* where the beneficiary could, at her death, by will finally obtain enjoyment of the income by conveying her interest in it to others. This they believe is a sufficient guarantee of the beneficiary being assured that she alone will enjoy the income and since the decedent could not pick and chose among various beneficiaries, § 2036(a)(2) by its terms does not apply. This argument, to date, has had little appeal to the judiciary or to the IRS and perhaps also to beneficiaries who, deprived of enjoyment of income during their life, find the power to control its enjoyment at their death by will to be a poor substitute.

3. In Reg. § 20.2036–1(b)(3), the Treasury indicates that the phrase the "right ... to designate the person or persons who shall possess or enjoy the transferred property or the income therefrom" does not include a power over the transferred property itself that does not affect the enjoyment of the income received or earned during the decedent's life. As a result of this language, there is no inclusion under § 2036 in the decedent's estate in the following circumstance. Assume that X established a trust under which income goes to A for 10 years, after which corpus of the trust is to be distributed to A. Assume that X also retained the right to terminate the trust at any moment and vest A in complete immediate ownership of the corpus. Since X's actions can never deprive A of the income, there is no inclusion in X's estate under § 2036, even if X dies possessed of the power to terminate.

Although retention of such a power does not result in taxation under § 2036, it can result in taxation under § 2038, which is discussed below. For present purposes, consideration should be confined to how this language in the regulations relates to the result in *Struthers v. Kelm*.

Planning Note

[¶ 18,181]

Gifts to minors under either the Uniform Gifts to Minors Act (UGMA) or the Uniform Transfers to Minors Act (UTMA) may result in inclusion under § 2036 or § 2038 if the donor appoints himself or herself as custodian and dies before the donee reaches the age at which the custodianship ends. See, e.g., Prudowsky's Estate v. Commissioner, 55 T.C. 890 (1971), aff'd, 465 F.2d 62 (7th Cir.1972)(gift with donor-parent as custodian taxable under §§ 2036(a)(1) and 2038); see also Rev. Ruls. 59–357, 1959–2 C.B. 212, and 57–366, 1957–2 C.B. 618 (gifts under UGMA and Uniform Gifts of Securities to Minors Act with donor as custodian taxable under § 2038); cf. Estate of Sulovich v. Commissioner, 587 F.2d 845 (6th Cir. 1978)(Totten Trust accounts result in taxation under §§ 2036 & 2038).

The favored way of avoiding this problem is for the donor to designate a trusted third party as the custodian under the UGMA or the UTMA. Married couples who wish to make gifts to their minor children might instinctively be tempted to designate each other as the custodian for their gifts. The estate planner must be concerned with the possibility that the IRS might seek to resort to the reciprocal trust doctrine to effect an inclusion in the estate of the first such spouse to die. For a discussion of possible application of the reciprocal trust doctrine to this and other situations under the UGMA and the UTMA, see ¶¶ 18,151; 18,190; 19,073; and 19,133.

2. CONTINGENT RETAINED POWERS TO DETERMINE ENJOYMENT

As established at ¶ 18,025, a retained contingent life estate will give rise to an inclusion in the estate under § 2036(a)(1). The principal issue here under consideration is whether anything is to be included within the estate under § 2036(a)(2) where the donor-decedent had, under certain circumstances, retained the right to determine the conditions of enjoyment for other beneficiaries.

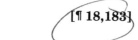

[¶ 18,183]

ESTATE OF FARREL v. UNITED STATES

United States Court of Claims, 1977.
553 F.2d 637.

DAVIS, Judge.

[In 1961 Marian Farrel established an irrevocable trust with her grandchildren (and their issue) as beneficiaries. Two independent individuals were named as trustees and were given discretionary power to pay income and principal out among the trust beneficiaries. At some time in the future, trust assets were to be divided among the beneficiaries or contributed to a new trust over which the trustees were to have discretionary powers. No provision was made for any distribution to Mrs. Farrel.

The trust called for two trustees at all times and gave Mrs. Farrel the power to fill any vacancy. Mrs. Farrel did not have the power, either under the deed of trust or Connecticut law, to remove a trustee. The instrument was silent as to whether Mrs. Farrel could appoint herself to fill a vacancy, but this would be permitted under state law. On two separate occasions when vacancies occurred Mrs. Farrel appointed independent third parties as successor trustees.

After Mrs. Farrel died in 1969, the IRS sought to include trust corpus in her estate under § 2036(a)(2).]

Both parties agree that (a) the trustees had "the right, either alone or in conjunction with any person, to designate the persons who shall possess or enjoy the property or the income therefrom" within the meaning of Section 2036(a)(2); (b) Mrs. Farrel, the decedent settlor, could lawfully designate herself (under the trust and Connecticut law) as successor trustee if a vacancy occurred during her life; (c) the occurrence of a vacancy in the office of trustee was a condition which Mrs. Farrel could not create and which was beyond her control; and (d) Mrs. Farrel had the opportunity, before her 1969 death, to appoint a successor trustee only during the two periods in 1964 and 1965 mentioned above. The legal conflict is whether the right of the trustees (as to who should enjoy or possess the property or income) should in these circumstances be attributed to the decedent under § 2036(a) for any of the three periods designated in that statutory provision—her life; any period not ascertainable without reference to her death; any period which does not in fact end before her death. The Government's answer is yes and the plaintiff of course says no.

Only Section 2036(a) is now before us but, since taxpayer's presentation emphasizes a comparison of that provision with Section 2038 (a cognate but separate part of the estate tax), it is important to set out, at the beginning, the relevant aspects of the latter, as we do in the margin. Plaintiff's primary point is that (i) it is now and has long been settled that Section 2038 does not cover a power or right subject to a conditional event which has not occurred prior to and does not exist at the decedent's death, such as a discretionary power to distribute income or principal under specified conditions which have not occurred before the death, and (ii) the same rule has been and is applicable to Section 2036(a).

There is no question that taxpayer is correct as to the construction of Section 2038. That slant was given by the courts to the provision's predecessor under the 1939 Code * * * and the Treasury has itself adopted the same interpretation for the 1954 Code as well. Treasury Regulations on Estate Tax (1954 Code), Section 20.2038–1 (a) and (b).

The initial and fundamental question we have to face is whether this settled understanding of Section 2038 necessarily governs Section 2036(a), as it now stands. We think not for two reasons which we shall consider in turn: first, that the critical points-of-view of the two provisions differ, and, second, that the regulations governing the two sections take diametrically opposed positions on the narrow issue of contingent rights and powers of the kind involved here.

The two separate provisions appear to diverge sharply in their perspective—the point from which the pertinent powers and rights are to be seen. Section 2038(a) looks at the problem from the decedent's death—what he can and cannot do at that specific moment. Excluded are contingent rights and powers (beyond the decedent's control) which are not exercisable at that moment because the designated contingency does not exist at that time. Section 2036(a), on the other hand, looks forward from the time the decedent made the transfer to see whether he has retained any of the specified rights "for his life or for any period not ascertainable without reference to his death or for any period which does not in fact end before his death." This language makes the transferor's death one pole of the specified time-span but the whole of the time-span is also significant. Because of the statute's reference to the time-span, differences of interpretation are quite conceivable. It is possible for instance, to hold the words to mean that the retained right has to exist at all times throughout one of the periods, but it is also possible to see the language as covering contingencies which could realistically occur at some separate point or points during the designated periods—always including the moment of decedent's death. We take it (from the argument's insistence on the parallel to 2038) that taxpayer would not stand on the former ("at all times") interpretation if a vacancy in the trusteeship existed and had not been filled at Mrs. Farrel's death. But under the language of 2036(a) there is no compelling reason why the moment of death has to be exclusively important. Unlike Section 2038, this provision seems to look forward from the time of transfer to the date of the transferor's death, and can be said to concentrate on the significant rights with respect to the transferred property the transferor retains, not at every moment during that period, but whenever the specified contingency happens to arise during that period (so long as the contingency can still occur at the end of the period).

There is nothing unreasonable about this latter construction, which accords with Congress' over-all purpose to gather into the estate tax all transfers which remain significantly incomplete—on which the transferor still holds a string—during his lifetime. It is hard to believe, for instance that, whatever may be true of 2038, 2036(a) would have to be seen as failing to cover a trust where the trustee, with discretionary powers, could be removed by the settlor, and the settlor substituted as trustee, whenever economic conditions fell below a stated level (e.g., a designated level on a certain stock exchange index or a level of earnings of the trust) even though fortuitously that condition did not happen to exist at the time of death. In a case like that, the lifetime link between the decedent and the trust property (and income) would be so strong as plainly to measure up to both the letter and the spirit of

2036(a) if the Treasury chose to see it that way. This case, though perhaps less clear, falls into the same class of a continuing substantial tie.

The other element which leads us to reject plaintiff's attempt to equate 2036(a) with 2038, for this case, is that the Treasury has affirmatively chosen to separate the two sections—there is a Treasury regulation under the former § 20.2036–1 which, to our mind, clearly covers this decedent's situation (in contrast to the regulation under 2038 which excludes it). Taxpayer urges us to read the regulation otherwise, and if we cannot to hold it invalid.

The regulation says flatly * * * that it is immaterial "(iii) whether the exercise of the power was subject to a contingency beyond the decedent's control which did not occur before his death (e.g., the death of another person during the decedent's lifetime)." This would seem on its surface to blanket this decedent's position under her trust, but plaintiff would read it very literally and narrowly to apply only where the contingency relates to the "exercise" of an already existing power, and conversely, to be inapplicable where the power only springs into existence when a trustee vacancy occurs. Similarly, taxpayer sees in the broad sweep of the last sentence of § 20.2036–1(b)(3) * * * the implied negative pregnant that a restricted power in the decedent to appoint herself a substitute trustee only in the event of a vacancy lies outside 2036(a). We cannot accept these strained (if not casuistic) analyses of the regulation because they go directly counter to its apparent purpose to cover just such contingencies as we have here. If proof of that objective is needed it is fully supplied by the companion regulation under 2038 (Treasury Regulation on Estate Tax (1954 Code), § 20.2038–1(b)) which declares in coordinate terms that "section 2038 is not applicable to a power the exercise of which was subject to a contingency beyond the decedent's control which did not occur before his death (e.g., the death of another person during the decedent's life). *See, however Section 2036(a)(2) for the inclusion of property in the decedent's gross estate on account of such a power*" (emphasis added).

We are required, then, to consider whether § 20.2036–1(b)(3) should be overturned as invalid. Recognizing the deference due Treasury Regulations * * *, we cannot take that step. We have pointed out that 2036 is not the same as 2038 in its wording or in the viewpoint from which it appraises the decedent's link to the transferred property. We have also said that it is not unreasonable to regard 2036(a), in the way the Treasury does, as a blanket overall sweeping-in of property over which the decedent still has at death some significant, though contingent, power to choose those who shall have possession or enjoyment.

To this, plaintiff's ultimate response is double-barreled: (i) the regulation was not contemporaneous with the adoption of the predecessor of 2036 but came years later, and (ii) for taxable years before the regulation was adopted courts applied the same rule to the predecessors of 2036 as they have to 2038 and its predecessors. Both points may be technically correct. The relevant regulation was promulgated in 1958 many years after the first predecessor of 2036 was enacted. And in 1947 Jennings v. Smith, supra, seemed to use, as an alternative holding, the same rule for the forerunner of 2036 that it applied to the predecessor of 2038. To the same effect was Estate of Kasch v. Commissioner, supra (1958)(predecessor section). Nevertheless the Treasury was not foreclosed, in our view, from taking the position it did in 1958. As we have stressed, neither the text nor the purpose of 2036 demands that it be treated the same as 2038. The judicial observations lumping the two predecessor provisions responded to Government arguments treating the two sections as fully parallel on this point. Moreover, *Jennings v. Smith* was the only appellate decision on the point which was outstanding when the 1958 regulations were promulgated, and its statement was, at best, a rather summary alternative holding not truly necessary to the ultimate decision. Thus, the judicial interpretation of Section 2036's predecessor was neither so strong nor so encrusted that Congress may be thought to have embodied it in Section 2036 when it adopted the 1954 Code. On the contrary, we think the Treasury was free to take a new look under that new Code, as it evidently did. In sum, the current regulation under 2036 is a reasonable reading of the text and objective of the statute and the previous contrary judicial interpretation was not such that the Treasury was forced to bow to it despite the *prima facie* acceptability of the administrative stance.

We end by noting that the contingent right of Mrs. Farrel to make herself a trustee in the event of a vacancy—unlike the *de facto* "powers" involved in United States v. Byrum, 408 U.S. 125 (1972) and in Estate of Tully v. United States, 208 Ct. Cl. 596, 528 F.2d 1401 (1976)—was a legally enforceable right, in effect imbedded in the trust instrument, which bore directly on the designation of the persons to possess or enjoy the trust property or income. That the exercise of this right was foreseeable when the trust was created— that it was a real right, neither insignificant nor illusory—is shown by the fact that Mrs. Farrel had two opportunities to exercise it in eight years and, if she had lived, may well have had more.

For these reasons we hold that plaintiff is not entitled to recover and the petition is dismissed.

Notes

[¶ 18,184]

1. It is desirable to retain the power to remove and replace a trustee for several reasons. A trustee may be surcharged for any disbursements or other losses not in accord with the deed of trust. As a consequence, most trustees, but in particular corporate trustees, err on the side of caution when discretionary disbursements are called for both by circumstances and by the terms of the trust. Trustees often seek court approval for all but pedestrian matters, and the cost of such legal action is typically charged to the trust as an expense. Appointment of a stranger or a corporation as trustee can thus result in expensive unresponsiveness. Since most trustees enjoy their fees, it is rare for a trustee, even one with a dreadful record for investments, ever to step down voluntarily. Spending trust corpus to defend their position and reputation, trustees can take on all challengers who seek to have them removed by judicial action. Consequently, settlors have traditionally been advised by their

attorneys to retain some control over trustees by, if allowed by state law, retaining the right to remove the trustee and appoint a new trustee in order to insure their responsiveness and to guard against years of poor investment strategy.

2. In Rev. Rul. 79–353, 1979–2 C.B. 325, the IRS dealt with a situation where a settlor vested a corporate trustee with powers that, had they been retained by the settlor, would have resulted in inclusion of the trust corpus in settlor's estate at settlor's death. Since the settlor had retained the right to remove the corporate trustee and replace it with another corporate trustee, the IRS held that the corpus of the trust was to be included, under § 2036(a)(2), in settlor's estate at death. The decision of the IRS appears to have been based on the theory that the settlor, by threatening the trustee with removal or by finding a compliant replacement, could have caused the trustee to do exactly as settlor wished in exercising discretion regarding distribution of trust income. Howls of protest and disbelief ushered forth from the estate planning Bar to greet Rev. Rul. 79–353. Fourteen years after its issuance Rev. Rul. 79–353 received judicial scrutiny in the case which follows.

[¶ 18,185]

ESTATE OF WALL v. COMMISSIONER

United States Tax Court, 1993.
101 T.C. 300.

NIMS, Judge:

* * *

* * * Mrs. Wall, the grantor, retained the right in each trust indenture to remove the corporate sole trustee and replace it with another corporate trustee which had to be "independent" from the grantor. In each case the trustee was given the authority to distribute principal and income to a beneficiary essentially unrestrained by an ascertainable standard. Did the right to replace the corporate trustee in turn encompass the right to exercise the powers of the trustee? For the following reasons, we think not.

The underlying assumption of Rev. Rul. 79–353 and respondent's argument is that even a corporate trustee will be compelled to follow the bidding of a settlor who has the power to remove the trustee; otherwise the settlor will be able to find another corporate trustee which will act as the settlor wishes. In other words, says respondent, under these circumstances the settlor has the de facto power to exercise the powers vested in the trustee. But the Supreme Court has said in *Byrum* that the section 2036(a)(2) right connotes an ascertainable and legally enforceable power, as exemplified by the facts in United States v. O'Malley, 383 U.S. 627 (1966). As the Supreme Court states in *Byrum*, "*O'Malley* was covered precisely by the statute [§ 2036(a)(2)] for two reasons: (1) there the settlor had reserved a legal right, set forth in the trust instrument; and (2) this right expressly authorized the settlor, 'in conjunction' with others, to accumulate income and thereby 'to designate' the persons to enjoy it." United States v. Byrum, 408 U.S. at 136.

¶ 18,185

In the case before us respondent simply speculates that Mrs. Wall, by merely threatening First Wisconsin to replace it, could indirectly have exercised powers of the trustee similar to, though broader than, those in *O'Malley*. In Estate of Beckwith v. Commissioner, 55 T.C. 242 (1970), the trust indenture explicitly provided for the periodic distribution of trust income to a named beneficiary. Under the terms of the trust indenture the settlor retained no power or right to control the amounts or the timing of the distributions. The Commissioner, however, relied upon certain "practical considerations" which, he contended, enabled the decedent to control the flow of the income. The so-called practical considerations included the authority for the trust to retain stock in the settlor's closely held corporation; the power given the trustee to vote the stock; the settlor's retained right to remove a trustee and appoint a successor other than himself; and the close business relationships between the settlor and the individual trustees. We held that none of the so-called practical considerations nor all of them combined provided a basis for an inference that the settlor, by prearrangement or informal understanding or otherwise, reserved the right to cause the trustees to retain the closely held stock or to give the settlor proxies with respect thereto. Estate of Beckwith v. Commissioner, 55 T.C. at 248–249.

While it is true that First Wisconsin's power to distribute income and principal is not restricted to the extent existing in *Estate of Beckwith*, it is also true that, under established principles of the law governing trusts, a trustee would violate its fiduciary duty if it acquiesced in the wishes of the settlor by taking action that the trustee would not otherwise take regarding the beneficial enjoyment of any interest in the trust, or agreed with the settlor, prior to appointment, as to how fiduciary powers should be exercised over the distribution of income and principal. The trustee has a duty to administer the trust in the sole interest of the beneficiary, to act impartially if there are multiple beneficiaries, and to exercise powers exclusively for the benefit of the beneficiaries. See, e.g., Bogert, Law of Trusts and Trustees, sec. 543, at 217 (2d ed. 1993)("Perhaps the most fundamental duty of a trustee is that he must display throughout the administration of the trust complete loyalty to the interests of the beneficiary and must exclude all selfish interest and all consideration of the interests of third persons."). While the parties and amicus have not briefed the Wisconsin law on this virtually universal rule, it would seem highly unlikely that there is a variance between Wisconsin and other jurisdictions.

In irrevocable trusts such as those under scrutiny, the trustee is accountable only to the beneficiaries, not to the settlor, and any right of action for breach of fiduciary duty lies in the beneficiaries, not in the settlor. Bogert, supra, sec. 42, at 431–433. It also seems incontrovertible that the trustee's duty of sole fidelity to the beneficiary remains the same regardless of whether or not distributions are discretionary and whether or not limited by a standard such as one related to health, education, support in reasonable comfort, and the like.

In the absence of some compelling reason to do so, which respondent has not shown, we are not inclined to infer any kind of fraudulent side agreement

¶ 18,185

between Mrs. Wall and First Wisconsin as to how the administration of these trusts would be manipulated by Mrs. Wall. Instead, since the language of the trust indentures provides maximum flexibility as to distributions of income and principal, the trustee would be expected to look to the circumstances of the beneficiaries to whom sole allegiance is owed, and not to Mrs. Wall, in order to determine the timing and amount of discretionary distributions.

It seems also likely that Mrs. Wall might have conceived that a beneficiary might move to a distant location, making the beneficiary's personal contact with the trust department impractical, or that First Wisconsin might merge with an out-of-state bank in a way that would change the character of its trust department. These motives, if they indeed existed, are not the equivalent of a retained right contemplated by section 2036(a)(2). Nor do they imply arrangements, not previously contemplated, made after a transfer has been completed to permit the transferor to enjoy the benefits of the property. See Estate of Barlow v. Commissioner, 55 T.C. 666, 670 (1971). We therefore apply the Supreme Court's definition of a section 2036(a)(2) retained right; namely, that it must be an ascertainable and legally enforceable power. United States v. Byrum, 408 U.S. at 136. We hold that Mrs. Wall did not retain such an ascertainable and enforceable power to affect the beneficial enjoyment of the trust property.

On brief respondent points out that sections 2036(a)(2) and 2038(a)(1) frequently overlap and urges that in this case both are equally applicable. We agree that these sections frequently overlap, but for reasons stated above we hold that neither is applicable. We have focused essentially on section 2036(a)(2), but for the reasons given, Mrs. Wall's retained power to substitute another independent corporate trustee for First Wisconsin is not the type of power which would affect the "enjoyment" of the trust property contemplated by section 2036(a)(2) or section 2038(a)(1).

To reflect the foregoing.

Decision will be entered for petitioner.

Planning Note

[¶ 18,186]

In Rev. Rul. 95–58, 1995–36 I.R.B. 16, the IRS accepted the results in *Wall* and Estate of Vak v. Commissioner, 973 F.2d 1409 (8th Cir.1992) (retained power to remove trustee with discretionary powers and replace with independent trustee did not result in incomplete gift). The IRS stated that it would no longer claim that a retained power to remove and replace a trustee possessed of discretionary powers results in an inclusion under § 2036 (a)(2) so long as the grantor's power to remove and appoint a new trustee does not permit the grantor to appoint as a replacement trustee: (1) the grantor; or (2) "an individual or corporate successor trustee * * * related or subordinate to the decedent (within the meaning of section 672 (c))." In general this would preclude appointment of a spouse, parent, issue, sibling, employee, or a corporation or employee of a corporation with respect to which the grantor and trust, either alone or combined, have significant voting control. For further discussion of § 672 (c) consult ¶ 31,163.

The best present solution to this problem is for the estate planner to draft a trust document which bars the grantor from appointing as a replacement for a trustee who holds discretionary powers: (1) the grantor; and (2) any party defined as a related or subordinate party under § 672(c).

The IRS focus on § 672(c) is interesting because there is no statutory justification to be found in § 2036 for so restricting the category of potential replacement trustees.

[¶ 18,188]

3. RECIPROCAL TRANSFERS

Assume that Grandpa placed $500,000 in a trust naming his grandson Peter as income beneficiary until Peter was 25, at which time the trust would terminate with the trust corpus and all accumulated income to be then distributed to Peter. Under the deed of trust Grandpa vested his wife, Grandma, with absolute discretionary power to pay each year as much of the income to Peter as she deemed appropriate, with all accumulated income being added to trust corpus. Assume also that Grandma contributed $500,000 to a trust which was the mirror image of Grandpa's trust except that the income beneficiary was granddaughter Sara and that Grandpa was the party vested with discretionary power with respect to this trust. If Grandpa were to die while the second trust was operative, one might conclude, based on the Supreme Court's decision in United States v. Estate of Grace, 395 U.S. 316 (1969) (see ¶ 18,109), that under the reciprocal trust doctrine the value of the trust for the benefit of Sara should be included in Grandpa's estate. In the case which follows, a contrary conclusion was reached on virtually identical facts.

[¶ 18,189]

ESTATE OF GREEN v. UNITED STATES

United States Court of Appeals, Sixth Circuit, 1995.
68 F.3d 151.

KRUPANSKY, Circuit Judge.

Plaintiff–Appellee, the Estate of Jack Green, challenged the ruling of the Internal Revenue Service ("IRS") that the reciprocal trust doctrine required that the property transferred in a trust created by Jack Green for the benefit of his granddaughter be included in his gross estate. The district court concluded that the reciprocal trust doctrine did not apply, and the IRS appealed.

Jack Green and his wife, Norma Green, had two grandchildren, Jennifer Lee Goodman and Greer Elizabeth Goodman. Jennifer and Greer were sisters, and the couple's only grandchildren. On December 20, 1966, Jack and Norma Green executed two trust agreements for the benefit of their grandchildren.

¶ 18,186

As settlor of the "Jennifer" trust, Jack Green designated his wife Norma trustee and Jennifer as its beneficiary. Norma Green, the settlor of the "Greer" trust, named her husband as the trustee and Greer as its beneficiary.

The trusts were substantially identical. The authority vested in each trustee was the same: the trustees could not alter, amend, revoke or terminate their respective trusts. The only retained authority by each trustee was the discretion to reinvest and time the distribution of trust corpus and income until each respective beneficiary reached her 21st birthday. Under the terms and conditions of the trusts, neither Jack or Norma Green, directly or indirectly, retained or reserved any economic benefit from the assets or income of the trusts.

The government posits that the limited discretionary power to reinvest and time the distribution of trust corpus and income to third party beneficiaries invoked the reciprocal trust doctrine to uncross the trusts and subject the trusts to taxation pursuant to 26 U.S.C. §§ 2036(a)(2) and 2038(a)(1). The estate has countered the application of the reciprocal trust doctrine by citing to the Supreme Court decision in United States v. Grace, 395 U.S. 316 (1969), wherein the Court, in a simple one-sentence statement defined, to the exclusion of all other standards, the criteria to be considered in applying the doctrine:

> Rather, we hold that application of the reciprocal trust doctrine requires only that the trusts be interrelated, and that the arrangement, *to the extent of mutual value, leaves the settlors in approximately the same economic position as they would have been in had they created trusts naming themselves as life beneficiaries.*

Id. at 324, (emphasis added).

In the instant case, the government seeks to rewrite *Grace* by a strained and attenuated interpretation of language that needs no interpretation.* * * The government asserts that the only condition precedent required to apply the doctrine and uncross the trusts is a finding of retained settlor/trustee fiduciary powers even if the retained fiduciary powers are not coupled with retained settlor/trustee economic benefits which leave "the settlors in approximately the same economic position as they would have been in had they created trusts naming themselves as life beneficiaries." The Supreme Court in *Grace* explained that "[f]or purposes of the estate tax, we think that economic value is the only workable criterion." *Grace*, 395 U.S. at 325 (emphasis added).* * *

Without considering the district court's findings that the trusts here in issue were not interrelated, this court concludes that the settlor/trustee retained fiduciary powers to reinvest income and time distribution of trust income and corpus until the beneficiaries reach 21 years of age do not constitute a retained economic benefit that satisfies the *core* mandate of *Grace* "that the arrangement, to the *extent of mutual value,* leaves the settlors in *approximately the same economic position as they would have been in had they created trusts naming themselves as life beneficiaries.*" *Grace*, 395 U.S. at 324 (emphasis added).

¶ 18,189

For the foregoing reasons, the decision of the district court is AF-FIRMED.

NATHANIEL R. JONES, Circuit Judge, dissenting.

Because I believe that trusts in this case satisfy the requirements set forth by the Supreme Court in *United States v. Estate of Grace*, 395 U.S. 316 (1969), I dissent.

* * *

In this case, the trusts were simultaneously executed and amended under the same terms and funded with the same amounts of money. The trusts also contained the same operative terms and identical addenda. In addition, the trusts mirrored each other in the sense that each grandparent was a trustee of the trust the other created, and each was a trustee for one grandchild. These factors can point only to the conclusion that the trusts were interrelated.

* * *

In addition to the requirement that trusts be "interrelated" in order to be reciprocal, *Estate of Grace* imposes the requirement that the trusts "leave [] the settlors in approximately the same economic position as they would have been in had they created trusts naming themselves as life beneficiaries." 395 U.S. at 324.* * *

Had Green named himself trustee of the Jennifer trust, he would have retained the powers to deny his granddaughter immediate enjoyment and thus the power to designate. Therefore, the value of the trust would be included in his gross estate. The same would apply to the trust created by Norma Green if she were the named trustee. Instead, Green and his wife named each other as trustees of their respective trusts, and under the majority's holding, were able to avoid the inclusion of the trusts assets in their estates and avoid additional estate taxes.

In *Grace*, the Supreme Court concluded that application of the reciprocal trust doctrine was appropriate because the transactions left the parties in the same economic position as they were before the creation of the trusts. 395 U.S. at 324. The same has occurred with the Greens. The parties in Grace maintained their economic positions through retention of a life estate, where the Greens' maintained their economic positions through retention of the power to designate whom would enjoy the trust assets. Retaining either of these economic interests subjects a party to estate taxes under section 2036.

* * *

The majority holds that the reciprocal trust doctrine does not apply because the Greens' trust arrangement did not leave the parties in the same economic position as they would have been in if they had created trusts naming themselves as life beneficiaries. I do not agree that this is the core mandate of the reciprocal trust doctrine. Rather I find the Court's pronouncement limited to the facts of *Grace*. In *Grace* the Court was presented with a situation in which the parties sought to circumvent the estate tax on their retained life estates. In the present case, we are presented with parties attempting to avoid the estate taxes on their retained powers to designate. This distinction I do not choose to minimize. Thus, instead of looking to the fact specific language requiring the parties to be in the same position if they had named themselves beneficiaries of the estate, I look to the Court's broader pronouncements on economic position.

I find that the Greens' trusts were interrelated and that the trusts arrangements failed to disturb the grandparents economic positions with respect to their granddaughters. I would apply the reciprocal trust doctrine to uncross these trusts and include the value of the trust property in Jack Green's estate. I respectfully dissent.

Notes

[¶ 18,190]

1. *Green* is a case of dubious merit. Not only is it inconsistent with a long standing Tax Court decision on the topic, Estate of Bischoff v. Commissioner, 69 T.C. 32 (1977), but it also is inconsistent with the theory of cases, such as *Estate of Farrel* (¶ 18,183), which construe §§ 2036(a)(1) and 2036(a)(2) as parallel provisions with the former dealing with retained enjoyment and the latter dealing with retained control over enjoyment. Assuming that *Green* was incorrectly decided, was the IRS correct in attempting to include in Jack Green's gross estate, under the reciprocal trust doctrine the value of the trust established by him for Jennifer? Under the authority of *Estate of Grace* (¶ 18,109) and Rev. Rul. 75–533 (¶ 18,115) should the IRS not have been attempting to include the value of the trust established by Norma Green for the benefit of Greer? This could be an important distinction had the trusts varied in investment performance or had the statute of limitations run before the government discovered its error.

2. Problems such as those presented by *Green* are not restricted to trust situations but often commonly arise under the Uniform Transfers to Minors and the Uniform Gifts to Minors Acts where grandparents appoint each other as custodians for gifts to grandchildren.

Planning Note

[¶ 18,191]

Given the dubious nature of the holding in *Green* and the Tax Court's contrary decision in *Bischoff* (¶ 19,073) it is best to avoid possible application of the reciprocal trust doctrine by either: (1) having grantors designate parties other than each other as the holder of a discretionary power with respect to transferred property; or (2) providing considerable substantive differences (other than the identity of beneficiaries) between the two trusts. See *Estate of Levy* and Priv. Ltr. Rul. 9643013 (¶ 18,115).

[¶ 18,192]

4. RETAINED POWER SUBJECT TO STANDARD

Where the deceased retains a power subject to a standard, the issue occasionally arises as to whether the standard in essence has deprived the holder of discretion so that we may safely conclude that the holder in fact does not possess a "power" (as contrasted with a mere ministerial obligation) described in § 2036(a)(2).

[¶ 18,193]

OLD COLONY TRUST CO. v. UNITED STATES

United States Court of Appeals, First Circuit, 1970.
423 F.2d 601.

ALDRICH, Chief Judge.

The sole question in this case is whether the estate of a settlor of an inter vivos trust, who was a trustee until the date of his death, is to be charged with the value of the principal he contributed by virtue of reserved powers in the trust. The executor paid the tax and sued for its recovery in the district court. All facts were stipulated. The court ruled for the government, 300 F.Supp. 1032, and the executor appeals.

The initial life beneficiary of the trust was the settlor's adult son. Eighty per cent of the income was normally to be payable to him, and the balance added to principal. Subsequent beneficiaries were the son's widow and his issue. The powers upon which the government relies to cause the corpus to be includible in the settlor-trustee's estate are contained in two articles. A third article, purporting to limit the personal liability of the trustees for acts of mismanagement, although relied on by the government, has no bearing on the questions in this case because it does not affect the meaning, extent or nature of the trustees' duties and powers. Briggs v. Crowley, 1967, 352 Mass. 194. We will not consider it further.

Article 4 permitted the trustees to increase the percentage of income payable to the son beyond the eighty per cent,

"in their absolute discretion * * * when in their opinion such increase is needed in case of sickness, or desirable in view of changed circumstances."

In addition, under Article 4 the trustees were given the discretion to cease paying income to the son, and add it all to principal,

"during such period as the Trustees may decide that the stoppage of such payments is for his best interests."

Article 7 gave broad administrative or management powers to the trustees, with discretion to acquire investments not normally held by trustees, and the right to determine, what was to be charged or credited to income or principal, including stock dividends or deductions for amortization. It further provided that all divisions and decisions made by the trustees in good faith should be conclusive on all parties, and in summary, stated that the trustees were empowered, "generally to do all things in relation to the Trust Fund which the Donor could do if living and this Trust had not been executed."

The government claims that each of these two articles meant that the settlor-trustee had "the right * * * to designate the persons who shall possess or enjoy the [trust] property or the income therefrom" within the meaning of section 2036(a)(2) of the Internal Revenue Code of 1954, 26 U.S.C. § 2036(a)(2), and that the settlor-trustee at the date of his death possessed a power "to alter, amend, revoke, or terminate" within the meaning of section 2038(a)(1)(26 U.S.C. § 2038(a)(1)).

If State Street Trust Co. v. United States, 1 Cir., 1959, 263 F.2d 635, was correctly decided in this aspect, the government must prevail because of the Article 7 powers. There this court, Chief Judge Magruder dissenting, held against the taxpayer because broad powers similar to those in Article 7 meant that the trustees "could very substantially shift the economic benefits of the trusts between the life tenants and the remaindermen," so that the settlor "as long as he lived, in substance and effect and in a very real sense * * * 'retained for his life * * * the right * * * to designate the persons who shall possess or enjoy the property or the income therefrom; * * *.'" 263 F.2d at 639–40, quoting 26 U.S.C. § 2036(a)(2). We accept the taxpayer's invitation to reconsider this ruling.

It is common ground that a settlor will not find the corpus of the trust included in his estate merely because he named himself a trustee. Jennings v. Smith, 2 Cir., 1947, 161 F.2d 74. He must have reserved a power to himself[2] that is inconsistent with the full termination of ownership. The government's brief defines this as "sufficient dominion and control until his death." Trustee powers given for the administration or management of the trust must be equitably exercised, however, for the benefit of the trust as a whole. The court in *State Street* conceded that the powers at issue were all such powers, but reached the conclusion that, cumulatively, they gave the settlor dominion sufficiently unfettered to be in the nature of ownership. With all respect to the majority of the then court, we find it difficult to see how a power can be subject to control by the probate court, and exercisable only in what the trustee fairly concludes is in the interests of the trust and its beneficiaries as a whole, and at the same time be an ownership power.

The government's position, to be sound, must be that the trustee's powers are beyond the court's control. Under Massachusetts law, however, no amount of administrative discretion prevents judicial supervision of the trustee. Thus in Appeal of Davis, 1903, 183 Mass. 499, a trustee was given "full power to make purchases, investments and exchanges * * * in such manner as to them shall seem expedient; it being my intention to give my trustees * * * the same dominion and control over said trust property as I now have." In spite of this language, and in spite of their good faith, the court charged the trustees for failing sufficiently to diversify their investment portfolio.

---

2. The number of other trustees who must join in the exercise of that power, unless the others have antagonistic interests of a substantial nature is, of course, immaterial. Treas. Reg.   § 20.2036–1(a)(ii),   (b)(3)(i)(1958); § 20.2038–1(a)(1958).

The Massachusetts court has never varied from this broad rule of accountability, and has twice criticized *State Street* for its seeming departure. Boston Safe Deposit & Trust Co. v. Stone, 1965, 348 Mass. 345, 351, n. 8; Old Colony Trust Co. v. Silliman, 1967, 352 Mass. 6, 8–9. See also, Estate of McGillicuddy, 54 T.C. 315 (1970). We make a further observation, which the court in *State Street* failed to note, that the provision in that trust (as in the case at bar) that the trustees could "do all things in relation to the Trust Fund which I, the Donor, could do if * * * the Trust had not been executed," is almost precisely the provision which did not protect the trustees from accountability in *Appeal of Davis,* supra.

We do not believe that trustee powers are to be more broadly construed for tax purposes than the probate court would construe them for administrative purposes. More basically, we agree with Judge Magruder's observation that nothing is "gained by lumping them together." State Street Trust Co. v. United States, supra, at 642. We hold that no aggregation of purely administrative powers can meet the government's amorphous test of "sufficient dominion and control" so as to be equated with ownership.

This does not resolve taxpayer's difficulties under Article 4. Quite different considerations apply to distribution powers. Under them the trustee can, expressly, prefer one beneficiary over another. Furthermore, his freedom of choice may vary greatly, depending upon the terms of the individual trust. If there is an ascertainable standard, the trustee can be compelled to follow it. If there is not, even though he is a fiduciary, it is not unreasonable to say that his retention of an unmeasurable freedom of choice is equivalent to retaining some of the incidents of ownership. Hence, under the cases, if there is an ascertainable standard the settlor-trustee's estate is not taxed, but if there is not, it is taxed.

The trust provision which is uniformly held to provide an ascertainable standard is one which, though variously expressed, authorizes such distributions as may be needed to continue the beneficiary's accustomed way of life. On the other hand, if the trustee may go further, and has power to provide for the beneficiary's "happiness," or "pleasure," or "use and benefit," or "reasonable requirement[s]," the standard is so loose that the trustee is in effect uncontrolled.

In the case at bar the trustees could increase the life tenant's income "in case of sickness, or [if] desirable in view of changed circumstances." Alternatively, they could reduce it "for his best interests." "Sickness" presents no problem. Conceivably, providing for "changed circumstances" is roughly equivalent to maintaining the son's present standard of living. The unavoidable stumbling block is the trustees' right to accumulate income and add it to capital (which the son would never receive) when it is to the "best interests" of the son to do so. Additional payments to a beneficiary whenever in his "best interests" might seem to be too broad a standard in any event. * * * [S]ee Estate of Yawkey, 1949, 12 T.C. 1164, where the court said, at p. 1170,

> "We can not regard the language involved ['best interest'] as limiting the usual scope of a trustee's discretion. It must always be anticipated that trustees will act for the best interests of a trust beneficiary, and an

exhortation to act 'in the interests and for the welfare' of the beneficiary does not establish an external standard.''

Power, however, to decrease or cut off a beneficiary's income when in his "best interests," is even more troublesome. When the beneficiary is the son, and the trustee the father, a particular purpose comes to mind, parental control through holding the purse strings. The father decides what conduct is to the "best interests" of the son, and if the son does not agree, he loses his allowance. Such a power has the plain indicia of ownership control. The alternative, that the son, because of other means, might not need this income, and would prefer to have it accumulate for his widow and children after his death, is no better. If the trustee has power to confer "happiness" on the son by generosity to someone else, this seems clearly an unascertainable standard. Cf. Merchants Nat'l Bank v. Com'r, supra, at 261–263.

The case of Hays' Estate v. Com'r, 5 Cir., 1950, 181 F.2d 169, is contrary to our decision. The opinion is unsupported by either reasoning or authority, and we will not follow it. With the present settlor-trustee free to determine the standard himself, a finding of ownership control was warranted. To put it another way, the cost of holding onto the strings may prove to be a rope burn. State Street Bank & Trust Co. v. United States, supra.

Affirmed.

Planning Note

[¶ 18,199]

Where the settlor of a trust does not wish to retain the right to income from a trust but rather wishes to retain some flexibility with respect to the degree of enjoyment of property or designation of the ultimate beneficiaries, it is often possible to strike some balance that goes a long way toward realizing the settlor's goals. By not personally retaining the § 2036(a)(2) right, but by placing that right in a trusted individual who shares the settlor's values, the planning goals of the settlor can often be accommodated. Siblings of the settlor, a spouse, close friends or even a trusted attorney often prove to be adequate alter egos for settlors who are able to let go at least to this degree. When selecting such individuals three principal concerns exist. First, the settlor should be sure that potential beneficiaries of the power possessed by these individuals are neither the individuals themselves nor include among them the natural objects of the bounty of these individuals. Here, however, an exception may be tolerated if the holder is a spouse without issue from a prior marriage who are potential beneficiaries along with the settlor's own issue. For example, to allow one's brother to designate who among the issue of the settlor's parents will enjoy income from a trust is only asking for trouble. Problems might also be expected to arise if a previously married spouse with issue from both marriages is allowed to designate who among her issue will enjoy income from a trust. Second, care should be taken that the designated individual does not have similar plans for the settlor with the result that reciprocal trusts may be found to be present. Third, care should be taken that the trustee has and functions with sufficient independence from the grantor so as to preclude the IRS from asserting that, based on the trustee's lack of independence, the grantor has retained the powers invested in the trustee. Recall that in Rev. Rul. 95–58 (¶ 18,186) the IRS embraced § 672(c) as a standard. Given the accepted use of relatives as trustees in numerous cases and rulings, § 672(c) is unlikely to become a judicial standard. For example, if § 672(c) had been the standard for an independent trustee, *Estate of Grace* and most reciprocal trust cases could have been resolved against the taxpayer without resorting to the reciprocal trust doctrine. Nonetheless care should be taken that, at a minimum, the chosen party actually functions independently. See ¶ 18,103 et seq.

From the settlor's standpoint, appointment of a trusted attorney as a trustee who possesses discretionary powers may provide a solution to the settlor's tax problems. However, because of significant potential legal liability, it may be wise for the attorney to decline the honor and fee unless the attorney's firm and liability insurance policies are well equipped to cope with all eventualities.

[¶ 18,205]

UNITED STATES v. BYRUM

Supreme Court of the United States, 1972.
408 U.S. 125.

MR. JUSTICE POWELL delivered the opinion of the Court.

[The decedent, Milliken Byrum, created an irrevocable trust, for the benefit of his children and their issue, to which he transferred stock in three Ohio corporations in which he owned at least 71 percent of the stock prior to the transfers. After the transfers and at his death four years later Byrum owned less than 50 percent of the stock in two corporations and 59 percent of the stock in the third corporation. Under the deed of trust, Byrum retained the right to vote the transferred stock (thus giving him voting control), to veto its transfer, to approve all new investments and to remove the corporate trustee. At Byrum's death, the Commissioner sought to effect an inclusion of trust corpus on the theory that Byrum's retained voting privileges and control over retention by the trust of the stock in question allowed him not only to retain the enjoyment of income from the property but also to determine the flow of income from the trust and thereby to designate the persons who will enjoy the income.]

* * *

The Government relies primarily on its claim, made under § 2036(a)(2), that Byrum retained the right to designate the persons who shall enjoy the income from the transferred property. The argument is a complicated one. By retaining voting control over the corporations whose stock was transferred, Byrum was in a position to select the corporate directors. He could retain this position by not selling the shares he owned and by vetoing any sale by the trustee of the transferred shares. These rights, it is said, gave him control over corporate dividend policy. By increasing, decreasing, or stopping dividends completely, it is argued that Byrum could "regulate the flow of income to the trust" and thereby shift or defer the beneficial enjoyment of trust income between the present beneficiaries and the remaindermen. The sum of this retained power is said to be tantamount to a grantor-trustee's power to accumulate income in the trust, which this Court has recognized constitutes the power to designate the persons who shall enjoy the income from transferred property.

At the outset we observe that this Court has never held that trust property must be included in a settlor's gross estate solely because the settlor retained the power to manage trust assets. On the contrary, since our decision in Reinecke v. Northern Trust Co., 278 U.S. 339 (1929), it has been recognized that a settlor's retention of broad powers of management does not necessarily subject an *inter vivos* trust to the federal estate tax. Although there was no statutory analogue to § 2036(a)(2) when *Northern Trust* was decided, several lower court decisions decided after the enactment of the predecessor of § 2036(a)(2) have upheld the settlor's right to exercise managerial powers without incurring estate-tax liability. * * *

[The Court noted that *Northern Trust*, while it was of some value, was not controlling since it was not decided under § 2036(a)(2) or its predecessor. It then went on to discuss the case.] The holding of *Northern Trust*, that the settlor of a trust may retain broad powers of management without adverse estate-tax consequences, may have been relied upon in the drafting of hundreds of *inter vivos* trusts. The modification of this principle now sought by the Government could have a seriously adverse impact, especially upon settlors (and their estates) who happen to have been "controlling" stockholders of a closely held corporation. Courts properly have been reluctant to depart from an interpretation of tax law which has been generally accepted when the departure could have potentially far-reaching consequences. When a principle of taxation requires reexamination, Congress is better equipped than a court to define precisely the type of conduct which results in tax consequences. When courts readily undertake such tasks, taxpayers may not rely with assurance on what appear to be established rules lest they be subsequently overturned. Legislative enactments, on the other hand, although not always free from ambiguity, at least afford the taxpayers advance warning.

* * *

[The Court next addressed the IRS contention that United States v. O'Malley (see ¶ 18,217) compelled inclusion of the donated stock in Byrum's estate under § 2036(a)(2). It noted *O'Malley* was covered by § 2036(a)(2) because in that case the settlor, in the deed of trust, had expressly reserved the legal right, in conjunction with two other parties, to accumulate income and thereby designate the condition of its enjoyment by others.]

It must be conceded that Byrum reserved no such "right" in the trust instrument or otherwise. The term "right," certainly when used in a tax statute, must be given its normal and customary meaning. It connotes an ascertainable and legally enforceable power, such as that involved in *O'Malley*. Here, the right ascribed to Byrum was the power to use his majority position and influence over the corporate directors to "regulate the flow of dividends" to the trust. That "right" was neither ascertainable nor legally enforceable and hence was not a right in any normal sense of that term.

Byrum did retain the legal right to vote shares held by the trust and to veto investments and reinvestments. But the corporate trustee alone, not Byrum, had the right to pay out or withhold income and thereby to designate who among the beneficiaries enjoyed such income. Whatever power Byrum may have possessed with respect to the flow of income into the trust was derived not from an enforceable legal right specified in the trust instrument, but from the fact that he could elect a majority of the directors of the three corporations. The power to elect the directors conferred no legal right to command them to pay or not to pay dividends. A majority shareholder has a fiduciary duty not to misuse his power by promoting his personal interests at the expense of corporate interests. Moreover, the directors also have a fiduciary duty to promote the interests of the corporation. * * *

The Government seeks to equate the *de facto* position of a controlling stockholder with the legally enforceable "right" specified by the statute. Retention of corporate control (through the right to vote the shares) is said to be "tantamount to the power to accumulate income" in the trust which resulted in estate tax consequences in *O'Malley*. The Government goes on to assert that "[t]hrough exercise of that retained power, [Byrum] could increase or decrease corporate dividends ... and thereby shift or defer the beneficial enjoyment of trust income." This approach seems to us not only to depart from the specific statutory language, but also to misconceive the realities of corporate life.

* * * In making decisions with respect to dividends, the board must consider a number of factors. It must balance the expectation of stockholders to reasonable dividends when earned against corporate needs for retention of earnings. The first responsibility of the board is to safeguard corporate financial viability for the long term. This means, among other things, the retention of sufficient earnings to assure adequate working capital as well as resources for retirement of debt, for replacement and modernization of plant and equipment, and for growth and expansion. The nature of a corporation's business, as well as the policies and long-range plans of management, are also relevant to dividend payment decisions. Directors of a closely held, small corporation must bear in mind the relatively limited access of such an enterprise to capital markets. This may require a more conservative policy with respect to dividends than would be expected of an established corporation with securities listed on national exchanges.

Nor do small corporations have the flexibility or the opportunity available to national concerns in the utilization of retained earnings. When earnings are substantial, a decision not to pay dividends may result only in the accumulation of surplus rather than growth through internal or external expansion. The accumulated earnings may result in the imposition of a penalty tax.

These various economic considerations are ignored at the directors' peril. Although vested with broad discretion in determining whether, when, and

¶ 18,205

what amount of dividends shall be paid, that discretion is subject to legal restraints. If, in obedience to the will of the majority stockholder, corporate directors disregard the interests of shareholders by accumulating earnings to an unreasonable extent, they are vulnerable to a derivative suit. They are similarly vulnerable if they make an unlawful payment of dividends in the absence of net earnings or available surplus, or if they fail to exercise the requisite degree of care in discharging their duty to act only in the best interest of the corporation and its stockholders.

Byrum was similarly inhibited by a fiduciary duty from abusing his position as majority shareholder for personal or family advantage to the detriment of the corporation or other stockholders. There were a substantial number of minority stockholders in these corporations who were unrelated to Byrum. Had Byrum and the directors violated their duties, the minority shareholders would have had a cause of action under Ohio law. * * *

We conclude that Byrum did not have an unconstrained *de facto* power to regulate the flow of dividends to the trust, much less the "right" to designate who was to enjoy the income from trust property. His ability to affect, but not control, trust income, was a qualitatively different power from that of the settlor in *O'Malley*, who had a specific and enforceable right to control the income paid to the beneficiaries. Even had Byrum managed to flood the trust with income, he had no way of compelling the trustee to pay it out rather than accumulate it. Nor could he prevent the trustee from making payments from other trust assets, although admittedly there were few of these at the time of Byrum's death. We cannot assume, however, that no other assets would come into the trust from reinvestments or other gifts.

We find no merit to the Government's contention that Byrum's *de facto* "control," subject as it was to the economic and legal constraints set forth above, was tantamount to the right to designate the persons who shall enjoy trust income, specified by § 2036(a)(2).

The Government asserts an alternative ground for including the shares transferred to the trust within Byrum's gross estate. It argues that by retaining control, Byrum guaranteed himself continued employment and remuneration, as well as the right to determine whether and when the corporations would be liquidated or merged. Byrum is thus said to have retained "the . . . enjoyment of . . . the property" making it includable within his gross estate under § 2036(a)(1). The Government concedes that the retention of the voting rights of an "unimportant minority interest" would not require inclusion of the transferred shares under § 2036(a)(1). It argues, however, "where the cumulative effect of the retained powers and the rights flowing from the shares not placed in trust leaves the grantor in control of a close corporation and assures that control for his lifetime, he has retained the 'enjoyment' of the transferred stock."

It is well settled that the terms "enjoy" and "enjoyment," as used in various estate tax statutes, "are not terms of art, but connote substantial present economic benefit rather than technical vesting of title or estates." For example, in Reinecke v. Northern Trust Co., 278 U.S. 339 (1929), in which the critical inquiry was whether the decedent had created a trust "intended . . .

¶ 18,205

'to take effect in possession or enjoyment at or after his death,' " the Court held that reserved powers of management of trust assets, similar to Byrum's power over the three corporations, did not subject an *inter vivos* trust to the federal estate tax. In determining whether the settlor had retained the enjoyment of the transferred property, the Court said:

> "Nor did the reserved powers of management of the trusts save to decedent any control over the economic benefits or the enjoyment of the property. He would equally have reserved all these powers and others had he made himself the trustee, but the transfer would not for that reason have been incomplete. The shifting of the economic interest in the trust property which was the subject of the tax was thus complete as soon as the trust was made. His power to recall the property and of control over it for his own benefit then ceased and as the trusts were not made in contemplation of death, the reserved powers do not serve to distinguish them from any other gift *inter vivos* not subject to the tax." 278 U.S., at 346–347.

* * *

As the Government concedes, the mere retention of the right-to-vote shares does not constitute the type of "enjoyment" in the property itself contemplated by § 2036(a)(1). In addition to being against the weight of precedent, the Government's argument that Byrum *retained* "enjoyment" within the meaning of § 2036(a)(1) is conceptually unsound. This argument implies, as it must under the express language of § 2036(a), that Byrum "retained for his life ... (1) the possession or enjoyment" of the *"property"* transferred to the trust or the *"income"* therefrom. The only property he transferred was corporate stock. He did not transfer "control" (in the sense used by the Government) as the trust never owned as much as 50% of the stock of any corporation. Byrum never divested himself of control, as he was able to vote a majority of the shares by virtue of what he owned and the right to vote those placed in the trust. Indeed, at the time of his death he still owned a majority of the shares in the largest of the corporations and probably would have exercised control of the other two by virtue of being a large stockholder in each. The statutory language plainly contemplates retention of an attribute of the property transferred—such as a right to income, use of the property itself, or a power of appointment with respect either to income or principal.[34]

Even if Byrum had transferred a majority of the stock, but had retained voting control, he would not have retained "substantial present economic benefit." The Government points to the retention of two "benefits." The first of these, the power to liquidate or merge, is not a *present* benefit; rather, it is a speculative and contingent benefit which may or may not be realized. Nor is the probability of continued employment and compensation the substantial "enjoyment of ... [the transferred] property" within the meaning of the statute. The dominant stockholder in a closely held corporation, if he is active

---

34. The interpretation given § 2036(a) by the Government * * * would seriously disadvantage settlors in a control posture. If the settlor remained a controlling stockholder, any transfer of stock would be taxable to his estate. * * *

¶ 18,205

and productive, is likely to hold a senior position and to enjoy the advantage of a significant voice in his own compensation. These are inevitable facts of the free enterprise system, but the influence and capability of a controlling stockholder to favor himself are not without constraints. Where there are minority stockholders, as in this case, directors may be held accountable if their employment, compensation and retention of officers violate their duty to act reasonably in the best interest of the corporation and all of its stockholders. Moreover, this duty is policed, albeit indirectly, by the Internal Revenue Service, which disallows the deduction of unreasonable compensation paid to a corporate executive as a business expense. We conclude that Byrum's retention of voting control was not the retention of the enjoyment of the transferred property within the meaning of the statute.

* * *

Notes

[¶ 18,211]

1.   A case applying the *Byrum* doctrine to dramatic facts was Estate of Gilman v. Commissioner, 547 F.2d 32 (2d Cir.1976). There the decedent set up a voting trust with six shares representing control of a paper company. Though the government claimed that the decedent continued to "enjoy" the six shares, which were valued at $24,500,000 by the Commissioner, the court held the case was governed by *Byrum*.

2.   The Tax Reform Act of 1976 added a so-called anti-*Byrum* provision that, refined by the Revenue Act of 1978, now appears as § 2036(b).

In general, under this section the retention of the right to vote stock of a controlled corporation is deemed to be retention of the enjoyment of the transferred property with the potential for inclusion in the estate under § 2036(a)(1). A corporation is treated as a controlled corporation if, at any time within the three years preceding the transferor's death or after the transfer of its stock, the decedent-donor owned or had the right (either alone or in conjunction with another) to vote stock possessing at least 20 percent of the combined voting power of all classes of stock.

Within a few years after the passage of § 2036(b), its limited potential was amply demonstrated by Revenue Ruling 81–15, 1981–1 C.B. 457. In that ruling the IRS indicated that § 2036(b) would not apply to a situation in which an individual contributed assets to a newly formed corporation in exchange for 10 shares of voting common stock and 990 shares of nonvoting common stock and then proceeded to retain the voting stock and to transfer the nonvoting stock to a trust for the benefit of his children. Since the donor could not vote the transferred stock and since it never was endowed with voting rights, he could not be viewed as having retained voting rights with respect to it. Several private letter rulings have subsequently been issued, which are totally in accord with Revenue Ruling 81–15. See Priv. Ltr. Ruls. 9004017 and 9004009.

More recently the IRS was asked to rule on a situation in which two brothers each transferred an identical amount of stock possessing more than 20% of the voting control in a family corporation to a family limited partnership in which each brother would be a 50% general partner. The partnership agreement provided that in the event the brothers could not agree to how the stock was to be voted, each could vote a proportionate share (50%) of the stock held by the partnership. On the occasion of the death of one brother, the IRS ruled that the shares that he contributed to the partnership were to be included in his estate under § 2036 (b) because under the agreement he would be allowed to vote those shares without the agreement of his sibling. Moreover, the IRS noted that even if acquiescence of the other brother had been required for the stock to be voted, the "either alone or in conjunction with any person" language of § 2036 (b)(2) would have required inclusion of the stock in the estate of the deceased. Tech. Adv. Mem. 199938005.

Typical corporations first confront an income tax on their profits and then must pay their dividends, which are taxable as income to their shareholders from after-tax earnings. Moreover, compensation paid to a corporation's employees, although taxable to them as income, is deductible by the corporation in calculating its income for tax purposes. The result of this is that most owners of small businesses arrange to draw their profits from the enterprise in the form of tax-deductible salaries. Consequently, they typically tend to view corporate offices and employment, and not ownership of stock on which dividends might be paid, as the principal means whereby they are to be provided with a stream of income from the corporate enterprise. They are concerned with maintaining voting control with respect to the corporation for two reasons: (1) to insure their continued employment in the enterprise; and (2) to control the economic future of the enterprise. Revenue Ruling 81–15 provides them with a splendid means whereby they can realize these goals and yet remove from their estates much of the economic value of their companies.

H. AMOUNT INCLUDIBLE

[¶ 18,217]

Significant questions occasionally arise as to the amount of property that is to be included within the estate where an income interest was retained by the donor. As a general rule, the entire corpus of a trust subject to a retained life interest is to be included in the estate at its date of death value (or at its alternate valuation date value). The regulations indicate that several exceptions to this general rule are worthy of consideration. First, Reg. § 20.2036–1(a) indicates that, where the donor retained an income interest in only a portion of an asset (e.g., a one-third interest), just that portion of the trust corpus will be included in the decedent's estate. Moreover, as noted previously, if the decedent retained only a contingent life estate following upon the life estate of another, which life estate was presently being enjoyed, the estate would include the full value of the trust, minus the value of the life estate that was being enjoyed at the decedent's death. See Reg. § 20.2036–1(b)(1)(ii).

¶ 18,211

Another issue of interest involves situations in which income from a trust, with respect to which decedent retained a prohibited interest or power, is retained by the trust and added to corpus. At the decedent's death should the entire trust corpus be included or, as is done under § 2035, should the value represented by the retained income (see ¶ 23,085) be excluded?

In United States v. O'Malley, 383 U.S. 627 (1966), the Supreme Court decided that in such a situation the entire trust corpus, consisting of the original corpus as well as retained income, should be included in the estate of the decedent, Edward Fabrice. The following excerpt from its opinion explains why the Court reached this conclusion.

> * * *At the time Fabrice established these trusts, he owned all of the rights to the property transferred, a major aspect of which was his right to the present and future income produced by that property. With the creation of the trusts, he relinquished all of his rights to income except the power to distribute that income to the income beneficiaries or to accumulate it and hold it for the remaindermen of the trusts. He no longer had, for example, the right to income for his own benefit or to have it distributed to any other than the trust beneficiaries. Moreover, with respect to the very additions to principal now at issue, he exercised his retained power to distribute or accumulate income, choosing to do the latter and thereby adding to the principal of the trusts. All income increments to trust principal are therefore traceable to Fabrice himself, by virtue of the original transfer and the exercise of the power to accumulate. Before the creation of the trusts, Fabrice owned all rights to the property and to its income. By the time of his death he had divested himself of all power and control over accumulated income which had been added to the principal, except the power to deal with the income from such additions. With respect to each addition to trust principal from accumulated income, Fabrice had clearly made a "transfer" as required by § 811(c)(1)(B)(ii) [now § 2036 (a)(2)]. Under that section, the power over income retained by Fabrice is sufficient to require the inclusion of the original corpus of the trust in his gross estate. The accumulated income added to principal is subject to the same power and is likewise includable.

I. RELINQUISHMENT OF RETAINED INCOME INTEREST WITHIN THREE YEARS OF DEATH

[¶ 18,235]

A prospective decedent with a reserved life estate transfer destined for inclusion in the taxable estate under § 2036 might consider relinquishment of the reserved life estate as a method for escaping the reach of § 2036. Because of the express language of § 2035(a)(2), however, it is quite evident that the property will be included in the decedent's gross estate unless she manages to live for at least three years after relinquishing the reserved life estate.

Another possible ploy would be to sell the reserved life estate for adequate and full consideration in money or money's worth, thus providing the basis for an argument that the relinquished life estate would not be subject to § 2035 because it would arguably be a transfer supported by adequate and full consideration in money or money's worth. See § 2035(d).

[¶ 18,241]

UNITED STATES v. ALLEN

United States Court of Appeals, Tenth Circuit, 1961.
293 F.2d 916.

MURRAH, Chief Judge.

This is an appeal from a judgment of the trial court awarding plaintiff-executors a refund for estate taxes previously paid.

The pertinent facts are that the decedent, Maria McKean Allen, created an irrevocable trust in which she reserved 3/5ths of the income for life, the remainder to pass to her two children, who are the beneficiaries of the other 2/5ths interest in the income. When she was approximately seventy-eight years old, the trustor-decedent was advised that her retention of the life estate would result in her attributable share of the corpus being included in her gross estate, for estate tax purposes. With her sanction, counsel began searching for a competent means of divesture [sic], and learned that decedent's son, Wharton Allen, would consider purchasing his mother's interest in the trust. At that time, the actuarial value of the retained life estate, based upon decedent's life expectancy, was approximately $135,000 and her attributable share of the corpus, i.e., 3/5ths, was valued at some $900,000. Upon consultation with his business advisers, Allen agreed to pay $140,000 for the interest, believing that decedent's actual life span would be sufficient to return a profit to him on the investment. For all intents and purposes, he was a bona fide third party purchaser—not being in a position to benefit by any reduction in his mother's estate taxes. The sale was consummated and, upon paying the purchase price, Allen began receiving the income from the trust.

At the time of the transfer, decedent enjoyed relatively good health and was expected to live her normal life span. A short time thereafter, however, it was discovered that she had an incurable disease, which soon resulted in her untimely death. As a result of the death, Allen ceased receiving any trust income and suffered a considerable loss on his investment.

The Internal Revenue Commissioner determined that 3/5ths of the corpus, less the $140,000 purchase money, should be included in decedent's gross estate because (1) the transfer was invalid because made in contemplation of death, and (2) the sale was not for an adequate and full consideration.

Plaintiff-executors paid the taxes in accord with the Commissioner's valuation of the estate, and brought this action for refund, alleging that the sale of the life interest was for an adequate consideration; and that, therefore, no part of the trust corpus was properly includible in the gross estate.

The trial court held for plaintiffs, finding that the transfer was in contemplation of death, but regardless of that fact, the consideration paid for the life estate was adequate and full, thereby serving to divest decedent of any interest in the trust, with the result that no part of the corpus is subject to estate taxes.

Our narrow question is thus whether the corpus of a reserved life estate is removed, for federal estate tax purposes, from a decedent's gross estate by a transfer at the value of such reserved life estate. In other words, must the consideration be paid for the interest transferred, or for the interest which would otherwise be included in the gross estate?

In one sense, the answer comes quite simply—decedent owned no more than a life estate, could not transfer any part of the corpus, and Allen received no more than the interest transferred. And, a taxpayer is, of course, entitled to use all proper means to reduce his tax liability. It would thus seem to follow that the consideration was adequate, for it was in fact more than the value of the life estate. And, as a practical matter, it would have been virtually impossible to sell the life estate for an amount equal to her share in the corpus.

It does not seem plausible, however, that Congress intended to allow such an easy avoidance of the taxable incidence befalling reserved life estates. This result would allow a taxpayer to reap the benefits of property for his lifetime and, in contemplation of death, sell only the interest entitling him to the income, thereby removing all of the property which he has enjoyed from his gross estate. Giving the statute a reasonable interpretation, we cannot believe this to be its intendment. It seems certain that in a situation like this, Congress meant the estate to include the corpus of the trust or, in its stead, an amount equal in value.

The judgment of the trial court is therefore reversed and the case is remanded for further proceedings in conformity with the opinion filed herein.

BREITENSTEIN, Circuit Judge (concurring in result).

* * *

Trustor-decedent in 1932 created an irrevocable trust and received no consideration therefor. She retained for life the right to income from 3/5ths of the property which she placed in the trust. By the plain language of the statute that portion of the property held in the trust and devoted to the payment to her of income for life is includible within her gross estate. Such property is an "interest" of which she made a transfer with the retention of income for life.

The fact that the transfer of the life estate left her without any retained right to income from the trust property does not alter the result. As I read the statute the tax liability arises at the time of the inter vivos transfer under which there was a retention of the right to income for life. The disposition thereafter of that retained right does not eliminate the tax liability. The fact that full and adequate consideration was paid for the transfer of the retained life estate is immaterial. To remove the trust property from inclusion in decedent's estate there must be full and adequate consideration paid for the interest which would be taxed. That interest is not the right to income for life but the right to the property which was placed in the trust and from which the income is produced.

As the 1932 trust was irrevocable, trustor-decedent could thereafter make no unilateral transfer of the trust property. Granting that she could sell her life estate as that was a capital asset owned by her, such sale has no effect on the includibility in her gross estate of the interest which she transferred in 1932 with the retention of the right to income for life.

For the reasons stated I would reverse the judgment with directions to dismiss the case.

Note

[¶ 18,247]

1. What if the taxpayer in *Allen* definitely wished to sell her income interest to a child for good and valid nontax reasons but wished to put the property beyond the reach of § 2035, which, in this particular case, would effect an inclusion in the estate if the retained life interest is transferred for less than adequate consideration? According to the concurring judge's analysis, the taxpayer could accomplish her purpose only if her child transferred to her an amount in excess of the value of her life estate. Would the child then be making a taxable gift to the taxpayer?

2. Settlor established a trust in 1941 retaining a life estate and conveying remainder interests to her children and grandchildren. Settlor later wished to terminate the trust with the consent of all beneficiaries and to distribute, from among trust assets, to each beneficiary the actuarially determined value of each beneficiary's interest. The IRS ruled that, were this to be done and were the settlor to live three years after termination of the trust, nothing would be included in her estate under § 2036. After three years the only sum to be included in settlor's estate as a result of the above would be any trust property remaining in settlor's possession at her death. Moreover, the IRS indicated that the termination would not be subject to § 2702. Priv. Ltr. Rul. 9815023.

3. In 1988 settlor taxpayer established a trust retaining an income interest for ten years. Under the terms of the trust if settlor died before ten years had expired, the trust corpus was to be paid to his revocable trust. The trustee was also given the power to buy out settlor's remaining term of years and the contingent interest of the revocable trust for its actuarial value. In 1995, nineteen days after taxpayer was diagnosed as having terminal cancer, the trustee commuted the value of taxpayer's remaining term of years in the $6.15 million trust by paying him $2.25 million. Taxpayer died the following day. In Tech. Adv. Mem. 199935003 the IRS ruled that the situation was controlled by the *Allen* case and the full value of the corpus of the trust ($6.15 million) was to be included in taxpayer's estate. The vesting of control of the decision to sell in a trustee rather than in the taxpayer was not deemed significant under the facts presented.

¶ 18,241

Planning Note

[¶ 18,253]

A donor who has retained significant rights so that an inclusion results under § 2036 often finds that, as the golden years grow near, it will be greatly to his or her advantage to sever the strings that bind. Because of § 2035(a)(2) a surrender or gift of the string within three years of death will prove ineffectual. Similarly, the *Allen* case offers no hope in the form of a sale of such an interest for adequate consideration within three years of death. The sooner the task of severance of the string is confronted the better.

J. ADEQUATE AND FULL CONSIDERATION

[¶ 18, 256]

Section 2036 provides an exclusion from the decedent's estate in the case of "a bona fide sale for adequate and full consideration." Presumably this language will exclude from § 2036 a situation where parent and child approach an owner of property and the parent purchases a life estate in the property for its actuarially determined value and the child, with her assets, purchases the remainder interest for its actuarially determined value, although the parent will still have to be concerned with the fact that, under § 2702, he might be deemed to be making a gift to the child equal to the value of parent's life estate. This result could be avoided, however, by structuring the parent's interest as a qualified annuity or unitrust interest. See ¶ 12,079–12,103.

Of considerably more interest are situations where owners of property retain life estates in the property in question but sell, to the natural objects of their bounty, remainder interests for their actuarially determined fair value. At the death of the life tenant is the property in question excluded from his estate under the "adequate and full consideration exception?" Several recent cases have held, quite correctly in our opinion, that in such situations there is no inclusion under § 2036 in the life tenant's estate. Estate of Magnin v. Commissioner, 184 F.3d 1074 (9th Cir. 1999), Wheeler v. United States, 116 F.3d 749 (5th Cir.1997), D'Ambrosio v. Commissioner, 101 F.3d 309 (3d Cir.1996), cert. denied 520 U.S. 1230 (1997). This issue as well as the widow's election variation of this estate planning technique, which is employed in community property states, is discussed at greater length at ¶ ¶ 24,031 et seq.

K. FAMILY LIMITED PARTNERSHIPS

[¶ 18,257]

The use of limited partnerships by families to obtain dramatically reduced valuations for assets has been discussed at ¶ 11,115. In brief, members of the senior generation, typically a mother and father, will contribute assets to a partnership, receiving partnership interests in exchange for the contributed assets. The parents will then give each of the children an interest in the partnership, claiming a large valuation discount based on the interposition of an entity (the partnership) between the underlying assets and the ownership interest transferred and will also claim a discount based on the transfer of a minority interest to each of their children. On death, each of the parents will also claim a significant discount (typically in the range of 50%) based on their ownership of a minority interest in an entity that owns the underlying assets. If the taxpayer prefers, he or she can dispense with the lifetime gifts and merely seek a more modest discount based solely on interposition of an entity.

In addition to addressing the legitimacy of the discounts as discussed at ¶ 11,115 et seq., the Internal Revenue Service has also sought to attack such transfers under § 2036 on the ground that the taxpayer has retained either: (1) the enjoyment of the income from property held by the partnership; or (2) the right to control enjoyment of such property. Taxpayers may encounter difficulties under § 2036(a)(1) or § 2036(a)(2). Taxpayers typically encounter problems under § 2036(a)(1) by transferring all, or virtually all, their assets to the family limited partnership (FLP) and leaving themselves reliant on the FLP for housing and funds for their support and maintenance. See, e.g., Estate of Abraham v. Commissioner, 408 F.3d 26 (1st Cir. 2005), Estate of Thompson, 382 F.3d 367 (3d Cir. 2004) & Estate of Reichardt v. Commissioner, 114 T.C. 144 (2000). Relying on either explicit agreements to provide for the support of the donor or implicit understandings (see ¶ 18,007) the courts may include the transferred assets in the estate of the deceased taxpayer. Taxpayers can likely avoid the reach of § 2036(a)(1) by retaining housing and sufficient assets to provide for their support and maintenance and other anticipated needs and pleasures and transferring to the partnership assets employed in the conduct of a business or assets requiring active management. See, Estate of Kimbell v. United States, 371 F.3d 257 (5th Cir. 2004).

FLP cases in which the taxpayer's loss hinges on § 2036(a)(2) are less common. The theory of any such holding would center on the fact that the taxpayer-donor retained the right to control enjoyment by others of income from transferred property based on his control over the distribution of income and assets from the FLP. In Kimbell v. United States, 244 F.Supp.2d 700 (N.D. Texas 2003) the district court held there was an inclusion under § 2036(a)(2), based on taxpayer's ability to control entity decisions with a 50% ownership interest, only to be reversed by the court of appeals, which noted that more than 50% ownership by the taxpayer would be essential to find a controlling interest. More importantly the Court of Appeals also found that, because the taxpayer, pursuant to arrangements set in place as part of establishment of the entity, had obtained the benefit of participation in the management by his son of properties contributed to the FLP, adequate and full consideration (in the form of management services) was present and it was actually irrelevant whether the taxpayer retained any control over transferred assets. Kimbell v. United States, 371 F.3d 257 (5th Cir. 2004). In Estate of Strangi 85 T.C.M. (CCH) 1331, T.C.M. (RIA) ¶ 2003–145 (2003) the Tax Court found an inclusion under both §§ 2036(a)(1) and 2036(a)(2). The court's § 2036(a)(1) finding was based on the fact that the taxpayer had placed ninety-eight percent of his wealth, including his residence, in the FLP.

¶ 18,257

The § 2036(a)(2) finding was based on the fact that, pursuant to the arrangement that the taxpayer had put in place, through his son-in-law/attorney-in-fact the taxpayer held the power to determine distributions of income and other partnership assets. The Tax Court's decision in *Strangi* was affirmed by the Court of Appeals. Estate of Strangi v. Commissioner, 417 F.3d 468 (5th Cir. 2005). Because the Tax Court found a deficiency based on both § 2036(a)(1) and § 2036(a)(2), it is uncertain whether the Court of Appeals fully bought into the Tax Court's § 2036(a)(2) finding or it should be characterized as mere dictum.

Even if the taxpayer comes within the scope of either § 2036(a)(1) or § 2036(a)(2), she still has the opportunity to demonstrate that she has transferred property to her heirs under the FLP "for adequate and full consideration." In general a taxpayer will have a reasonable chance of succeeding under the "adequate and full consideration" exception where she has contributed to the partnership business assets or other assets requiring active management by other than the donor-taxpayer. Where the taxpayer merely contributes to the partnership highly liquid assets or a personal residence, the chance of successfully seeking respite under the consideration exception is greatly diminished. See, Kimbell v. United States, 371 F.3d 257 (5th Cir. 2004) (adequate consideration present due to partner-son's management of partnership's oil leases) Estate of Strangi v. Commissioner, 417 F.3d 468 (5th Cir. 2005) (bona fide sale absent because no "substantial business or other non-tax purpose" present), Estate of Bongard v. Commissioner, 124 T.C. 95 (2005)(a legitimate and significant non-tax reason essential to claim adequate consideration). *Bongard* is excerpted at ¶ 24,052 and discusses both the § 2036(a) issue and the adequate and full consideration issue.

This area of the law is very much in flux and awaits fuller discussion by the courts. For example, how does the Supreme Court's decision in *Byrum* factor into the § 2036(a)(2) analysis? How does one measure adequacy of consideration? Is the value of management provided by the junior generation to be weighed against the diminution in value that results from funding the FLP and transferring away control? Moreover, the holdings in cases are very fact specific. A taxpayer who seeks to form a FLP and thereby obtain a significant valuation discount as well as keeping a good distance from the reaches of § 2036 should be sure that her estate planner has consulted the most recent cases and has paid special attention to the line of cases that will be determinative of the result in her legal forum.

Problems

[¶ 18,259]

1. Grandma gave her beach cottage to her son Paul, but as a result of an understanding with Paul she continued to use the cottage free of any rent for the month of September until her death eight years after the gift. What, if anything, is includible in Grandma's estate?

2. Nick established a trust for the benefit of his grandchildren. Under the terms of the trust, the income was annually distributed to the grandchil-

dren in equal amounts, with the corpus to be divided equally among them when the youngest reached 25 years. Grandpa Nick, who died while the trust was in effect, retained the right to remove the corporate trustee and to replace it with an independent corporate trustee. Does this result in an inclusion in Nick's estate?

3. Would your answer be any different in the prior problem if the corporate trustee had discretion to distribute income among the grandchildren in unequal shares and to withhold income, adding it to corpus?

4. Andrea sold her interest in an apartment house (worth $400,000) to her son Bob for a properly priced private annuity of $50,000 per year. At Andrea's death four years later, the apartment house was worth $600,000. What, if anything, is includible in Andrea's estate?

5. In the prior problem, would your answer be different if the annuity had been secured by a lien on the apartment house and the rents derived from it?

6. Albert made a gift of $50,000 of stock to his minor son, Zack, under the Uniform Transfers to Minors Act, naming himself as custodian. Albert died when Zack was still a minor and the stock was worth $80,000. What, if anything, is includible in Albert's estate?

7. In the prior problem, assume that rather than appointing himself as guardian, Albert had appointed his wife, Noreen. What is the tax result?

8. In the prior problem, assume that Noreen had also made a gift of $50,000 of stock to Zack and that, just as Albert decided to appoint her as custodian for his gift, she also decided to appoint Albert as custodian for her gift. What is the tax result?

9. Marsha and John divorced. John was given custody of their minor son, Bobby, and Marsha was given custody of their minor daughter, Barbara. As part of the divorce settlement, John, to satisfy his support obligation, placed $600,000 in trust with income to Marsha for her life and remainder over to a trust for the children. Also as part of the settlement, in satisfaction of his obligation to support Barbara, he placed $200,000 in trust with income to Barbara for her support until she reaches age 25, at which time corpus is to be distributed to Barbara. In order to protect Bobby's feelings, John established a similar support trust for him, funding it with $200,000. At John's death last month, the children were still in their minority and the trusts had not increased in value. What are the estate tax consequences of the above arrangements?

10. Sally established a trust for the benefit of her three adult children, appointing herself as trustee. Under the terms of the trust, the income was to be divided equally among them, except that Sally retained the right to vary distribution to provide for "medical emergencies, professional education and inability of any beneficiary to support himself or herself." What are the tax consequences of this trust at Sally's death?

11. In the prior problem, assume that the trust also gave Sally the right to vary distributions "for any other valid reason." What are the tax consequences?

¶ 18,259

Chapter 19

POWERS TO ALTER, AMEND, REVOKE, OR TERMINATE

(Section 2038)

A. HISTORICAL INTRODUCTION

[¶ 19,001]

As mentioned in the introduction of Chapter 18, the Internal Revenue Code as originally enacted in 1916 contained a provision that included in the gross estate all transfers "intended to take effect at or after death." The Supreme Court gave a very limited interpretation to this provision, in effect rendering this language impotent. Congress responded by passing several specific sections, among them § 2038, which were intended to sweep within the gross estate those property interests that an unenthusiastic Supreme Court allowed to escape.

Clearly, a taxpayer who once owned property and transferred it while retaining the right to revoke the transfer should be deemed to be the owner of the property at death. It is the death of the taxpayer holding such a right to revoke that effectively transfers the taxpayer's right to the property. Section 2038 insures that all such property will be included in the gross estate of the decedent taxpayer. The Section goes somewhat further and, in general, sweeps into the gross estate property transferred by an individual who retained the power, acting alone or in conjunction with others, to alter, amend, revoke or terminate enjoyment of the property transferred.

In the cases that follow some light is shed on the kinds of powers regarded as taxable under § 2038. The student should be able to achieve some feeling of confidence concerning the taxable status of powers not exercisable in favor of the holder-grantor, narrow powers permitting only a shift as between two beneficiaries, powers to simply speed up distribution to a beneficiary, and perhaps as to the taxability of powers subject to standards as well as the significance for purposes of § 2038 of retained administrative powers.

As you read § 2038 and the materials that follow, consider how the section partially overlaps with § 2036. The extent of the overlap will be addressed elsewhere in this chapter. See ¶ 19,157.

B. BREADTH OF POWER

[¶ 19,007]

Many of the issues that were confronted under § 2036(a)(2) are also issues under § 2038. For example, in defining the breadth of § 2038, it is necessary to consider whether that section encompasses within its sweep retentions of the right to alter enjoyment of property in a personally nonbeneficial manner or the right to determine not who will enjoy the property but merely when the designated beneficiary will enjoy it.

In Porter v. Commissioner, 288 U.S. 436 (1933), the Supreme Court was asked to pass on a situation in which the grantor of a trust for benefit of his issue retained to himself the power to alter or modify the terms of the trust indenture "in any manner but expressly excepting any change in favor of himself or his estate." The executor of his estate argued, to no avail, that, since the retained power could not be exercised in a fashion that would benefit the holder, it should not be included in his estate under § 2038. In finding that inclusion under § 2038 [subdivision (d) of § 302 of the 1926 Revenue Act] requires far less than reservation of the right to revoke enjoyment and revest it in the donor, the Court observed:

> The net estate upon the transfer of which the tax is imposed, is not limited to property that passes from decedent at death. Subdivision (d) [now § 2038] requires to be included in the calculation all property previously transferred by decedent, the enjoyment of which remains at the time of his death subject to any change by the exertion of a power by himself alone or in conjunction with another. Petitioner argues that, as decedent was without power to revoke the transfers or to alter or modify the trusts in favor of himself or his estate, the property is not covered by subdivision (d). But the disjunctive use of the words "alter," "modify" and "amend" negatives that contention. We find nothing in the context or in the policy evidenced by this and prior estate tax laws or in the legislative history of subdivision (d) to suggest that conjunctive use of these words was intended, or that "alter" and "modify" were used as equivalents of "revoke" or are to be understood in other than their usual meanings. We need not consider whether every change, however slight or trivial, would be within the meaning of the clause. Here the donor retained until his death power enough to enable him to make a complete revision of all that he had done in respect of the creation of the trusts even to the extent of taking the property from the trustees and beneficiaries named and transferring it absolutely or in trust for the benefit of others. So far as concerns the tax here involved, there is no difference in principle between a transfer subject to such changes and one that is revocable. The transfers under consideration are undoubtedly covered by subdivision (d).

¶ 19,001

Porter definitively established that property is to be included within the estate of the donor where the donor retains the right to determine the identity of the individual who is to enjoy property or to choose among a class of potential beneficiaries. An issue not decided in *Porter* was whether § 2038 encompassed within its sweep transfers in which only the right to determine the timing of enjoyment is retained by the donor. Lober v. United States, the case that follows, addresses that issue.

[¶ 19,013]

LOBER v. UNITED STATES

Supreme Court of the United States, 1953.
346 U.S. 335.

MR. JUSTICE BLACK delivered the opinion of the Court.

This is an action for an estate tax refund brought by the executors of the estate of Morris Lober. In 1924 he signed an instrument conveying to himself as trustee money and stocks for the benefit of his young son. In 1929 he executed two other instruments, one for the benefit of a daughter, the other for a second son. The terms of these three instruments were the same. Lober was to handle the funds, invest and reinvest them as he deemed proper. He could accumulate and reinvest the income with the same freedom until his children reached twenty-one years of age. When twenty-one they were to be paid the accumulated income. Lober could hold the principal of each trust until the beneficiary reached twenty-five. In case he died his wife was to be trustee with the same broad powers Lober had conveyed to himself. The trusts were declared to be irrevocable, and as the case reaches us we may assume that the trust instruments gave Lober's children a "vested interest" under state law, so that if they had died after creation of the trusts their interests would have passed to their estates. A crucial term of the trust instruments was that Lober could at any time he saw fit turn all or any part of the principal of the trusts over to his children. Thus he could at will reduce the principal or pay it all to the beneficiaries, thereby terminating any trusteeship over it.

Lober died in 1942. By that time the trust property was valued at more than $125,000. The Internal Revenue Commissioner treated this as Lober's property and included it in his gross estate. That inclusion brought this lawsuit. The Commissioner relied on § 811(d)(2) [this section is the predecessor of § 2038 of the 1986 Code] of the Internal Revenue Code, 26 U.S. C. § 811 (1946 ed.). That section, so far as material here, required inclusion in a decedent's gross estate of the value of all property that the decedent had previously transferred by trust "where the enjoyment thereof was subject at the date of his death to any change through the exercise of a power ... to alter, amend, or revoke...." In Commissioner v. Holmes, 326 U.S. 480, we held that power to terminate was the equivalent of power to "alter, amend, or revoke" it, and we approved taxation of the Holmes estate on that basis. Relying on the *Holmes* case, the Court of Claims upheld inclusion of these trust properties in Lober's estate. 108 F.Supp. 731. This was done despite the assumption that the trust conveyances gave the Lober children an indefeasible "vested interest" in the properties conveyed. The Fifth Circuit Court of Appeals had reached a contrary result where the circumstances were substantially the same, in Hays' Estate v. Commissioner, 181 F.2d 169, 172–174. Because of this conflict, we granted certiorari. 345 U.S. 969.

Petitioners stress a factual difference between this and the *Holmes* case. The *Holmes* trust instrument provided that if a beneficiary died before expiration of the trust his children succeeded to his interest, but if he died without children, his interest would pass to his brothers or their children. Thus the trustee had power to eliminate a contingency that might have prevented passage of a beneficiary's interest to his heirs. Here we assume that upon death of the Lober beneficiaries their part in the trust estate would, under New York law, pass to their heirs. But we cannot agree that this difference should change the *Holmes* result.

We pointed out in the *Holmes* case that § 811(d)(2) was more concerned with "present economic benefit" than with "technical vesting of title or estates." And the Lober beneficiaries, like the *Holmes* beneficiaries, were granted no "present right to immediate enjoyment of either income or principal." The trust instrument here gave none of Lober's children full "enjoyment" of the trust property, whether it "vested" in them or not. To get this full enjoyment they had to wait until they reached the age of twenty-five unless their father sooner gave them the money and stocks by terminating the trust under the power of change he kept to the very date of his death. This father could have given property to his children without reserving in himself any power to change the terms as to the date his gift would be wholly effective, but he did not. What we said in the *Holmes* case fits this situation too: "A donor who keeps so strong a hold over the actual and immediate enjoyment of what he puts beyond his own power to retake has not divested himself of that degree of control which § 811(d)(2) requires in order to avoid the tax." Commissioner v. Holmes, supra, at 487.

Affirmed.

Notes

[¶ 19,019]

1.   The *Lober* decision, holding that a power to alter or amend does not require that there be any power to shift benefits between beneficiaries but that a mere acceleration or postponement is enough, has far-reaching implications. There may, for example, be disguised powers to advance corpus. In Walter v. United States, 341 F.2d 182 (6th Cir.1965), a power to remove and replace the trustee subjected the trust to the estate tax where the trustee had power to advance principal and the grantor could theoretically have removed the trustee and replaced him with herself. Compare *Wall v. Commissioner* and Rev. Rul. 95–58 at ¶ ¶ 18,185 and 18,186.

2.   Retention or reacquisition by the donor of an overly broad power to divide income and principal can also result in inclusion under § 2038. See Commissioner v. Estate of Hager, 173 F.2d 613 (3d Cir.1949). Clearly, a

settlor of a trust who retained the right to designate, as he wished, all accretions to the trust as either income or principal, has reserved to himself the power to determine the timing of enjoyment of property and in many circumstances the identification of the beneficiary. Where the settlor retains merely ordinary fiduciary powers to divide income and principal, a contrary result is clearly in order. In *Hager*, the trust was funded equally by a husband and wife and the retained power was held only by the husband. Since the wife had funded one-half of the trust, the Commissioner successfully sought to include only the one-half of the trust funded by the decedent who had retained the power in question.

Planning Note

[¶ 19,025]

As in the case of § 2036(a)(2)(¶ 18,199), where the settlor of a trust wishes to retain some degree of flexibility with respect to the enjoyment of property and yet desires to escape the reach of the estate tax, this goal can be accomplished by vesting the otherwise troublesome powers in a trusted third party. All the basic cautions that were voiced at ¶ 18,199 also apply here. That paragraph should be read now.

C. JOINT POWERS

[¶ 19,031]

Section 2038 clearly states that, even if the prohibited power is exercisable by the decedent in conjunction with another person, an inclusion in the estate will, nonetheless, result. Although clear on its face, there are any number of issues that could be raised about the section. For example, is it relevant that the co-holder of the power has a financial interest that is adversely affected by exercise of the power? Moreover, since common-law trust doctrine allows a trust to be revoked by the settlor and all beneficiaries acting together, are all settlors thereby deemed to be holders of a prohibited joint power? In the case of employee death benefits, is it possible to view a shareholder-employee who has voting control of the corporate employer as a co-holder of the power to alter employee death benefit plans that would otherwise not be taxable? These are the sorts of issues that will be addressed by the cases that follow.

1. BASIC PARAMETERS OF THE PROBLEM

[¶ 19,037]

HELVERING v. CITY BANK FARMERS TRUST CO.

Supreme Court of the United States, 1935.
296 U.S. 85.

Mr. Justice ROBERTS delivered the opinion of the Court.

* * *

The questions for decision are whether [§ 302(d) of the Revenue Act of 1926; now § 2038] requires inclusion in the gross estate of the value of the corpus of a trust established in 1930 where the creator reserved a power to revoke or modify, to be exercised jointly with a beneficiary and the trustee * * *.

By a writing dated February 21, 1930, Gertrude Feldman James, a non-resident citizen, transferred securities to the respondent as trustee, the trust to last during the lives of her two daughters or the survivor of them. The income was to be paid to her until her death, or until the termination of the trust, whichever should first occur. After her death, her husband surviving, the income was to be paid to him. If he did not outlive her, or upon his death, the income was to be distributed amongst their issue per stirpes. At the termination of the trust the corpus was to be delivered to the husband, if he were alive; if not, to the settlor, if living, or, if she were dead, to the beneficiaries at that time entitled to receive the income; if there were none such, to the heirs at law of the husband. The trust was irrevocable save that the settlor reserved the right to modify, alter or revoke it, in whole or in part, or to change any beneficial interest, any such revocation or alteration to be effected with the written consent of the trustee and her husband or, if the husband were dead, of the trustee and her husband's brother. If they could not agree the decision of the husband or of the brother, as the case might be, was to be final. Samuel James, the husband, survived the grantor, whose death occurred before the termination of the trust, and he is in receipt of the income.

The petitioner included the value of the corpus of the trust in Mrs. James' gross estate and determined a deficiency of tax. The Board of Tax Appeals reversed, holding that § 302(d) [now § 2038] did not apply. The Circuit Court of Appeals affirmed the Board's decision. We granted the writ of certiorari because the decision below conflicts with that in another circuit. We hold that the section covers this case and as so applied is valid.

* * *

The respondent insists that a power to recall an absolute and complete gift only with the consent of the donee is in truth no power at all; that in such case the so-called exercise of the power is equivalent to a new gift from the donee to the donor. And so it is claimed that the statute arbitrarily declares that to exist which in fact and law is nonexistent. The position is untenable. The purpose of Congress in adding clause (d) to the section as it stood in an earlier act was to prevent avoidance of the tax by the device of joining with the grantor in the exercise of the power of revocation someone who he believed would comply with his wishes. Congress may well have thought that a beneficiary who was of the grantor's immediate family might be amenable to persuasion or be induced to consent to a revocation in consideration of other expected benefits from the grantor's estate. Congress may adopt a measure reasonably calculated to prevent avoidance of a tax. * * *

In view of the evident purpose of Congress we find nothing unreasonable or arbitrary in the provisions of § 302(d) of the Revenue Act of 1926 [now

¶ 19,037

§ 2038] as applied in the circumstances of this case. It was appropriate for Congress to prescribe that if, subsequently to the passage of that Act, the creator of a trust estate saw fit to reserve to himself jointly with any other person the power of revocation or alteration, the transaction should be deemed to be testamentary in character, that is, treated for the purposes of the law as intended to take effect in possession or enjoyment at the death of the settlor.

The judgment is

Reversed.

Note

[¶ 19,043]

Is it critical to the Court's analysis that a settlor could modify, revoke, or terminate the trust with consent of only one of the beneficiaries? Should the result be different if the deed of trust required the settlor to obtain the consent of all beneficiaries to undertake such action? The answers are provided by a companion case, Helvering v. Helmholz, 296 U.S. 93 (1935), in which the Supreme Court confronted a situation where the settlor, who was also a beneficiary of the trust which she established, merely retained the right to terminate the trust acting together with all beneficiaries. The Court noted that, under the common law, all beneficiaries acting with the consent of the settlor could terminate a trust. Consequently, since the settlor had retained no power beyond that provided her by the common law, the Court concluded that Congress cannot tax such transfers under § 2038.

Note that Reg. § 20.2038–1(a) now incorporates the holdings of the *City Bank Farmers Trust Co.* and *Helmholz* cases.

[¶ 19,049]

2. EMPLOYEE DEATH BENEFITS

As we have seen in Chapter 15, if employee death benefits are paid to individuals designated by the employer, rather than by the employee, these benefits are not included in the deceased employee's estate under § 2033. Unhappy with defeats in the § 2033 arena, the Commissioner has sought victory in the § 2038 arena. These efforts have been predicated on the theory that, where the decedent employee is also a shareholder, director or officer of the employer, he or she, acting in conjunction with others of similar stature, could alter the death benefit plan, thereby resulting in inclusion under the joint holder language of § 2038.

[¶ 19,055]

ESTATE OF TULLY

United States Court of Claims, 1976.
528 F.2d 1401.

KUNZIG, Judge.

[The facts and one issue considered by the court, relating to the application of § 2033, appear at ¶ 15,109, wherein the court concluded that the employee death benefits provided by the decedent's employer were not includible, under § 2033, in his gross estate. The court here addresses itself to the possibility that § 2038 might make the benefits taxable.]

Defendant argues that Tully transferred an interest in the death benefits at some point prior to his death and kept a section 2038(a)(1) power to "alter, amend, revoke or terminate" the enjoyment of the benefits after the transfer until his death. Plaintiffs counter that there was no "transfer" in the 1959 contract or thereafter because decedent never had any interest in the benefits which he could transfer. Even if a transfer is found, plaintiffs claim Tully did not keep a section 2038(a)(1) "power" after such transfer.

Contrary to plaintiffs' position, Tully did transfer an interest in the death benefits to his wife by executing the 1959 contract. In one of the three death benefit plans at issue in Estate of Bogley v. United States, 514 F.2d 1027, 206 Ct. Cl. 695 (1975), the decedent (an employee, officer, director and 34% shareholder) entered into an enforceable contract with his employer. In consideration of decedent's past and future services, the employer promised to pay decedent's *widow* or the estate two years' salary after his death. We found that where decedent was married at the time of the execution of the contract he " * * * did make a transfer of his interest to his wife during his lifetime by making the contract with [the employer]." Bogley, supra, 514 F.2d at 1039, 206 Ct. Cl. at 715. In the instant case, the basic facts are nearly identical. The 1959 agreement looked to Tully's past and future services to T & D for consideration. The benefits here were also payable to the "widow" and decedent was married at the time of the 1959 contract. Tully in substance, if not in form, made a gift of a part of his future earnings to his wife.

However, within the meaning of section 2038(a)(1), Tully did not keep a power to "alter, amend, revoke or terminate" the death benefit transfer after the 1959 contract. There was no express reservation of such power in either the 1959 or 1963 contracts and no indication in the record of any other express agreements in which Tully obtained a section 2038(a)(1) power.

The Government implies that Tully's 50% stock ownership of T & D gave him unfettered power to change the death benefit plan to suit his own tastes. The facts do not bear this out. To the contrary, Tully's every movement could have been blocked by the other 50% shareholder. Tully did not have individual control of T & D and could not by himself, alter the terms of the death benefit, agreement. As stated by the court in Harris v. United States, 29 Am.Fed.Tax R.2d 1558 (C.D.Cal.1972), section 2038(a)(1) powers must be *demonstrable, real, apparent* and *evident,* not speculative. See also Hinze v. United States, 29 Am.Fed.Tax R.2d 1553 (C.D.Cal.1972). We agree with this test and find Tully did not have a section 2038(a)(1) power to "alter, amend, revoke or terminate" through his 50% stock ownership in T & D at the time of his death.

Moreover, the death benefits are not includable in Tully's gross estate despite the fact that Tully *might* have altered, amended, revoked or terminated them in conjunction with T & D and DiNapoli. A power to "alter, amend,

¶ 19,055

revoke or terminate" expressly exercisable in conjunction with others falls within section 2038(a)(1), but "power" as used in this section does not extend to *powers of persuasion*. If section 2038(a)(1) reached the possibility that Tully might convince T & D and DiNapoli to change the death benefit plan, it would apply to *speculative powers*. Section 2038(a)(1) cannot be so construed. *Harris*, supra; *Hinze*, supra. In addition, if section 2038(a)(1) applies to situations where an employee *might* convince an employer to change a death benefit program, it would sweep all employee death benefit plans into the gross estates of employees. It would always be at least possible for an employee to convince the employer that it would be to their mutual benefit to modify the death benefit plan. In light of the numerous cases where employee death benefit plans similar to the instant plan were held not includable in the employee's gross estate, we find that Congress did not intend the "in conjunction" language of section 2038(a)(1) to extend to the mere possibility of bilateral contract modification. Therefore, merely because Tully might have changed the benefit plan "in conjunction" with T & D and DiNapoli, the death benefits are not forced into Tully's gross estate.

Tully also did not obtain a section 2038(a)(1) "power" from the remote possibility that he could have altered the amount of death benefits payable to his widow by changing his compensation scheme. The death benefits here were to be paid based on decedent's annual salary. From this, defendant reasons that up until the time of his death, Tully could have accepted lesser compensation or terminated his employment in order to alter or revoke the death benefits. In practical terms, we reject this *possibility*. This is not a factor which rises to the level of a section 2038(a)(1) "power." An employee might accept lesser compensation or terminate his employment for a myriad of reasons, but to conclude that a motive for such action would be the death benefit plan itself is not only speculative but ridiculous. And we have already made clear that a section 2038(a)(1) "power" cannot be speculative, but must be *demonstrable, real, apparent* and *evident*. *Harris*, supra; *Hinze*, supra. In addition, modification of Tully's employment contract would have required the cooperation of T & D or a breach by Tully. Neither of these two events constitutes a section 2038(a)(1) "power." Further, it is a common practice to "peg" employee death benefit plans to the employee's salary. To our knowledge, no court has ever held that such practice subjects death benefits to inclusion in the employee's gross estate. On the contrary, in Estate of Whitworth v. Commissioner, 22 CCH Tax Ct. Mem. 177 (1963), the court concluded that although the decedent could have terminated his widow's benefits by leaving his employ or by breaching his employment contract, the death benefits at issue were *not* includable in his estate as a section 2038(a)(1) revocable transfer. Due to the practicalities of death benefit contracts and using the rationale of the *Whitworth* case, we hold that no section 2038(a)(1) power was created by the remote possibility that Tully might have changed the amount of death benefits prior to his death.

Finally, Tully did not retain a section 2038(a)(1) "power" to revoke or terminate the transfer to his wife by virtue of the *possibility* that he could have divorced her. The contract called for T & D to make the death benefit payments to Tully's *widow*. It might be argued that Tully could have divorced his wife to terminate her interest in the death benefits, but again such an argument ignores practicalities, reduces the term "power" to the speculative realm, and is not in accord with prior cases. In reality, a man might divorce his wife, but to assume that he would fight through an entire divorce process merely to alter employee death benefits approaches the absurd. Further, in various cases, death benefits payable to the "widow" * * * were not thereby held includable in the gross estate. The possibility of divorce in the instant situation is so *de minimis* and so speculative rather than *demonstrative, real, apparent,* and *evident* that it cannot rise to the level of a section 2038(a)(1) "power." *Harris,* supra; *Hinze,* supra. Thus the use of "widow" in the death benefit contract did not give Tully a real power to revoke or terminate the death benefit transfer to his wife.

In short, in the 1959 contract Tully transferred certain interests to his wife by obtaining T & D's promise to pay death benefits. While it may be argued that Tully kept a certain *de minimis* association with the death benefit plan, such association never rose to the dignity of a power to "alter, amend, revoke, or terminate" the transfer. In *Kramer,* supra, we held that a substantially similar plan did not create section 2038(a)(1) powers. The facts here are not significantly different. Therefore, section 2038(a)(1) does not operate to compel inclusion of the death benefits in decedent's gross estate.

* * *

Notes

[¶ 19,067]

1. In Estate of Levin v. Commissioner, 90 T.C. 723 (1988), aff'd, 891 F.2d 281 (3d Cir.1989), the court confronted death benefits which were payable under the company plan to a company designated beneficiary, the spouse of the employee. The decedent was Chairman of the Board of Directors of the employer corporation and owned stock possessing more than 80 percent of the corporation's voting power. Based on the decedent's control of the corporate employer both as shareholder and officer, the court found the death benefits includible in decedent's estate under § 2038.

2. In Rev. Rul. 76–304, 1976–2 C.B. 269, the IRS indicated that where an executive had power to change beneficiaries, the death benefit paid by the employer under the employer's plan was includible in the employee's estate under § 2038.

D. RECIPROCAL TRUSTS

[¶ 19,073]

The reciprocal trust issue that was studied with respect to § 2036 (¶ ¶ 18,103; 18,188) is also of significance with respect to § 2038. The leading reciprocal trust cases in the § 2038 context are Estate of Green v. United States, 68 F.3d 151 (6th Cir.1995) and Estate of Bischoff v. Commissioner, 69 T.C. 32 (1977). In *Bischoff,* a husband and wife had separately created trusts

¶ 19,055

appointing each other as trustee of the trusts that each had established. The trusts were of equal value and were created one day apart. Husband's and wife's trust each designated the same parties as beneficiaries and vested the trustee with the discretion to accumulate trust income or distribute it and corpus to the beneficiaries. The Tax Court applied the reciprocal trust principles articulated by the Supreme Court in *United States v. Estate of Grace* (see ¶ 18,109) to tax the trust created by wife in husband's estate and that created by husband in wife's estate. As previously noted, the Sixth Circuit in *Estate of Green* (¶ 18,189) surprisingly has taken the position that *Bischoff* was wrongly decided and that the reciprocal trust doctrine cannot be applied to either § 2036(a)(2) or § 2038. However, the Court of Appeals for the Federal Circuit had previously indicated that it was of the opinion the doctrine applied to §§ 2036 and 2038 equally well. See Exchange Bank and Trust Co. of Fla. v. United States, 694 F.2d 1261 (Fed.Cir.1982).

Planning Note

[¶ 19,085]

The strategy disclosed under Planning Note at ¶ 18,199 is also worthy of consideration with respect to § 2038.

E. INCOMPETENCY

[¶ 19,091]

Unfortunately, a fair percentage of all elderly will confront incompetency. Its impact on the tax treatment of powers held by the incompetent can be significant. For example, assume that an individual, who established a trust under which she retained a power to revoke the trust, becomes incompetent and under state law may not during incompetency exercise the power to revoke. What are the estate tax consequences if she dies while incompetent, unable to exercise the power?

[¶ 19,097]

ROUND v. COMMISSIONER

United States Court of Appeals, First Circuit, 1964.
332 F.2d 590.

HARTIGAN, Circuit Judge.

* * *

The decedent [John J. Round] died on April 4, 1958 at the age of eighty-six. In 1934 and 1935 the decedent established three "spendthrift" trusts under which his five minor children were the principal beneficiaries. The first trust (hereinafter called the September trust) was established on September 14, 1934 by a trust agreement entered into between decedent and Old Colony Trust Company. The second trust (hereinafter called the August trust) was

¶ 19,097

established by a trust agreement entered into between decedent and State Street Trust Company of Boston on August 21, 1935. On December 31, 1935, the third trust (hereinafter called the December trust) was established by a trust agreement entered into between decedent and State Street Trust Company.

The August trust provided for the children to receive all of the income from their respective shares "so long as they shall live." It also allowed the trustees to advance or pay over portions of the principal held for the income beneficiary "if at any time in their sole discretion they shall deem such a distribution desirable." The September and December trusts gave the trustees the power to invade and advance principal "in case of emergency, from time to time and upon such conditions as in their sole discretion they shall determine to be for the best interests of said children."

[The August and September trusts gave the trustees power to accumulate income in their discretion. There was no such power with respect to the December trust.] John R. Round, the decedent and various financial institutions were appointed as co-trustees of the various trusts.

* * * All of the trusts provided that upon the decease, resignation or incapacity of decedent, the corporate trustee should act as the sole trustee of the particular trust.

In the latter part of 1955 or the early part of 1956 the decedent was unable to handle the details of his affairs. On April 6, 1956, he gave his son, John J. Round, Jr., a general power of attorney, and thereafter the son handled most of the decedent's affairs.

* * *

The decree of the Middlesex County Probate Court dated October 28, 1957, recited that "After a hearing of the matter of said petition, it appears to the Court that said John J. Round is incapable of caring properly for his property" and decreed that the Boston Safe Deposit and Trust Company be appointed conservator of the property of the decedent.

* * *

* * * Shortly after its appointment as conservator Boston forwarded to Old Colony Trust Company and to State Street Trust Company certified copies of its appointment. Both trust companies thereupon halted all compensation payments to decedent and took over sole responsibility for the trusts. There is no evidence that decedent took any action in regard to the trusts following the appointment of the conservator.

The trust property was not included in decedent's gross estate on the estate-tax return. The fair market value as of the date of decedent's death of the property held in the three trusts was $493,445.92. Included in this value was undistributed income totaling $131,109.21 which had been accumulated and added to the principal. The respondent included the value of the three trusts at $493,445.92 in the decedent's gross estate and determined a deficiency in the Federal estate tax of $162,072.88.

¶ 19,097

The Tax Court sustained the action of respondent. It held that decedent in establishing the trusts, retained sufficient powers as co-trustee to accumulate or distribute income and to invade and distribute corpus to make the trusts includible in his estate by reason of section 2036(a) and section 2038(a)(2) of the Internal Revenue Code of 1954. Petitioners do not here question this holding (except as to the income accumulations which will be discussed later) and, in any event, it is supported by well-established authority. E.g., Lober v. United States, 346 U.S. 335 (1953).

Petitioners' argument is that at the date of decedent's death, decedent no longer retained his powers as co-trustee; that under the terms of the trust decedent was removed as trustee upon his becoming incapacitated; further, the appointment of a conservator for decedent's property was a definitive act which extinguished all of the right, power and authority of decedent to act as co-trustee under the three instruments. The Tax Court held that decedent was not permanently removed from his trusteeship position and the appointment of a conservator was not the definitive act called for by Hurd v. Commissioner of Internal Revenue, 160 F.2d 610 (1st Cir.1947), affirming Estate of Edward L. Hurd, 6 T.C. 819 (1946).

The three trust instruments contained the following provision:

> "Upon the decease, resignation or incapacity of * * * [decedent, the corporate trustee] shall act as sole Trustee hereunder, and shall exercise all of the rights, privileges, immunities, discretions and duties hereunder."

Petitioners read this provision to provide that upon any of the three described contingencies, the corporate trustee would *become* sole trustee. It is reasoned that since upon resignation or death the corporate trustee would, in fact, become sole trustee rather than merely *act* as such, a harmonious construction of the provision requires the finding that upon incapacity as well, the corporate trustee would become sole trustee, extinguishing any powers decedent had over the trust.

While it is true that regardless of the words used in the trust instruments, the corporate trustee would, in fact, become sole trustee upon death or resignation of decedent, this fact is the necessary result of the permanent removal caused by those two events. Such a permanent removal does not necessarily follow from incapacity, which is often a temporary condition. Only an unusually strict construction of the provision could lead to the conclusion that upon the incapacity of a co-trustee his powers over the trust would be forever terminated. "Incapacity" is not defined in the trust instruments and if the word is given its common meaning, a two week hospital stay following an automobile accident would find a trustee sufficiently incapacitated and subject to removal within the contended-for meaning of the trust provision. It could not have been the intention of decedent, who as co-trustee maintained a large share of control over the trust, that he could be so easily ousted. Rather, it is more likely that the provision was drawn with the intention of decedent resuming his duties as co-trustee when the incapacity was at an end.

¶ 19,097

In Hurd v. Commissioner, supra, at 613, this court said "The statute is not concerned with the *manner* in which the power is exercised, but rather with the existence of the power." So long as the powers retained by decedent *still existed in his behalf* the trust property was includible in his estate. What is required, this court said, is "some definitive act correlating the decedent's actual incompetence with his incapacity to serve as trustee." The court suggested that besides resignation and removal, an adjudication of mental incompetency might be sufficient to extinguish a trustee's interest in the trust, undoubtedly following the belief that under the circumstances of that case a legal determination of insanity was the least that was necessary if the purpose of the statute was not to be defeated. The Tax Court, however, has gone even further and has held that a judicial declaration of a trustee's incompetence was insufficient to terminate for tax purposes a power held under a trust where the New York law "specifically grants the Supreme Court of New York jurisdiction over the care of the person and property of an insane person." Estate of Charles S. Inman, 18 T.C. 522, 526 (1952), rev'd on other grounds, 203 F.2d 679 (2d Cir.1953).

We do not need to go that far here. Suffice [it] to say that decedent was never declared mentally incompetent. The appointment of a conservator did not remove the possibility that decedent could have recovered and resumed his position as co-trustee. Mass. Laws Ann. ch. 201 § 18 (1955). A conservatorship "raises * * * no [conclusive] presumption of continued incapacity." Chase v. Chase, 216 Mass. 394, 396, 103 N.E. 857, 858 (1914). The trust instruments provided that upon incapacity the corporate trustee shall act as sole trustee, thus leaving decedent free to resume his duties as trustee upon the recovery of capacity. The definitive act required before a trustee's powers can be said to have been extinguished must certainly be more than an act which contains within it the possibility of a temporary incapacity. To this, it may be added, as the Tax Court noted, that the Probate Court's adjudication of decedent's capacity to file the petition for conservatorship makes clear that he "would have had capacity to resign at that time had it been his intention to abandon the trusteeship." 40 T.C. at 979. See Simons v. United States, 135 F.Supp. 461, 463 (E.D.N.Y.), aff'd per curiam, 227 F.2d 168 (2d Cir.1955), cert. denied, 350 U.S. 949 (1956).

[The discussion of the second issue in this case has been omitted; it related to the includibility in the gross estate of the accumulated income in the trusts. On this second issue, the First Circuit took the same position as was later confirmed by the Supreme Court in *O'Malley* ¶ 18,217.]

* * *

Judgment will be entered affirming the decision of the Tax Court.

Notes

[¶ 19,103]

1. Should a distinction have been made between the December trust with no power to accumulate income and the August and September trusts

which did contain such a power? Remember that contingent life estates and contingent powers are subject to § 2036, whereas § 2038 reaches only those powers exercisable at the time of death. Whether *Round* is an appropriate interpretation of § 2038 with respects to incapacity at the time of death of a grantor-powerholder is still something of a question.

2. Where a holder of a durable power of attorney uses the power to make gifts, unless the grantor of the power explicitly authorizes the holder to do so, the IRS has consistently challenged the authority of the holder to make gifts arguing that the holder in making gifts is acting ultra vires. The IRS asserts that gifts so made are revocable transfers, taxable in the estate of the grantor of the power at his or her death under § 2038. See, e.g. Priv. Ltr. Ruls. 8635007 and 9634004. The judiciary has often upheld the IRS position on this issue. See, e.g., Estate of Casey v. Commissioner, (¶ 3073); Wilkinson v. Commissioner, 66 T.C.M. (CCH) 270, T.C.M. (RIA) ¶ 93,336 (1993). Estate of Swanson v. United States, 46 Fed.Cl. 388 (2000), aff'd 10 Fed. Appx. 833, 2001–1 USTC ¶ 60,408, 87 A.F.T.R. 2d (RIA) 2345 (2001) Estate of Gaynor, 82 T.C.M. (CCH) 379, T.C.M. (RIA) ¶ 2001–206 (2001). However, where state law and the facts of the case are favorable, the courts have found authority for the holder of the power to make the gifts and have rejected the IRS position that such gifts are taxable under § 2038, or § 2036. See, e.g. Estate of Gagliardi v. Commissioner, 89 T.C. 1207 (1987); Estate of Bronston v. Commissioner, 56 T.C.M. (CCH) 550, T.C.M. (P–H) ¶ 88,510 (1988). Estate of Suzanne C. Pruitt, 80 T.C.M. (CCH) 348, T.C.M. (RIA) ¶ 2000–287 (2000).

Historically, state law, to protect grantors of powers of attorney, has typically insisted on an explicit grant of a power to make gifts before finding such power present. In recent years, to accommodate those seeking tax minimization, several states have thrown caution to the wind and have passed legislation which, under certain circumstances, vests a holder of a power of attorney with a limited power to make gifts from the wealth of the grantor of the power. See Va. Code Ann. § 11–9.5 (Michie 2005)(gifts must be consistent with grantor's gift giving history and with permission of court the holder can make gifts inconsistent with such history); Ala. Code § 26–1–2.1 (Michie Supp. 2005)(limited to gift tax annual exclusion). Lapping, License to Steal: Implied Gift—Giving Authority and Power of Attorney, 4 Elder L.J. 143 (1996).

Planning Note

[¶ 19,109]

Given the approach taken by the court in *Round* and the very real possibility of incompetence due to maladies such as stroke and Alzheimer's disease, estate planners who draft deeds of trust for taxpayers who wish to retain revocable powers now have something added to think about. It might be possible to avoid the problem produced in *Round* by providing that a power lapses at incompetence. Another way of dealing with the problem is by creating a durable power of attorney and granting the holder of the power the right to terminate a revocable power in the event of incompetency. In the

¶ 19,109

cases where a durable power is employed to avoid inclusion under *Round*, it is likely that, due to either § 2035(a) or the three-year rule of § 2038(a)(1), the former holder of the power would have to live for three years after the durable power was exercised to terminate the revocable power. In the case of lapse triggered by incompetence, as contrasted with the durable power, since the incompetent, or the incompetent's attorney, could claim that they neither "transferred" nor "relinquished" a revocable power, as required by statute, it does not appear that in order to avoid inclusion it is necessary that the former holder live three years after lapse. See Priv. Ltr. Rul. 9032002.

F. POWER SUBJECT TO STANDARD

[¶ 19,115]

As in the case of § 2036(a)(2), inclusion in the taxable estate does not result where the donor did not retain a discretionary power with respect to transferred property but merely retained a power subject to a fiduciary standard capable of being administered by a court of equity.

[¶ 19,121]

JENNINGS v. SMITH

United States Court of Appeals, Second Circuit, 1947.
161 F.2d 74.

SWAN, Circuit Judge.

This is an action by the executors of the will of Oliver Gould Jennings, a resident of Connecticut whose death occurred on October 13, 1936, to recover such part of the estate tax paid by them to the defendant collector as had been illegally collected.

[Decedent established identical trusts for the benefit of the families of each of his sons. Decedent and his two sons, B. Brewster and Lawrence K. Jennings, were named co-trustees with a majority vote required for all trustee actions. Under the terms of each trust, annual income was to be accumulated but the trustees were given power to distribute it for the benefit of each son and his family, provided "the trustees shall determine that such disbursement is reasonably necessary to enable the beneficiary in question to maintain himself and his family, if any, in comfort and in accordance with the station in life to which he belongs." Because of the financial situation of Lawrence, distributions of income were being made to him at decedent's death. The trustees also had the power to invade corpus for extraordinary medical or financial emergencies.]

Section 811(d)(2) [now § 2038] of the Code, which is applicable to transfers made before June 22, 1936, provides for inclusion in the gross estate of all property "To the extent of any interest therein of which the decedent has at any time made a transfer, by trust or otherwise, where the enjoyment thereof was subject at the date of his death to any change through the exercise of a power, either by the decedent alone or in conjunction with any person, to alter, amend, or revoke, * * *.''

[The Court rejected taxpayer's argument that § 811(d)(2), now § 2038, did not reach situations where the settlor retained a power to alter, amend or revoke where held by settlor in a fiduciary capacity.]

The next question is whether the powers conferred upon the trustees in the case at bar are powers of the character described in section 811(d)(2) [now § 2038], which requires that enjoyment of the trust property must be subject at the date of the decedent's death to change through the exercise of a power. The trustees' power to invade the capital of the trust property was exercisable only if the son or his issue "should suffer prolonged illness or be overtaken by financial misfortune which the trustees deem extraordinary." Neither of these contingencies had occurred before the decedent's death; hence enjoyment of the capital was not "subject at the date of his death to any change through the exercise of a power." In Commissioner v. Flanders, 111 F.2d 117, although decision was rested on another ground, this court expressed the opinion that a power conditioned upon an event which had not occurred before the settlor's death was not within the section. * * * The question has recently been explored by the Tax Court in Estate of Budlong v. Commissioner, 7 T.C. 756. There it was held in a convincing opinion that the power of trustees to invade corpus in case of "sickness or other emergency," which had not occurred before the decedent's death, was not a power to "alter, amend or revoke" within the meaning of the statute. The court reasoned that the trustees had not unlimited discretion to act or withhold action under the power, since the trust instrument provided an external standard which a court of equity would apply to compel compliance by the trustees on the happening of the specified contingency or to restrain threatened action if the condition were not fulfilled. In the case at bar the district judge was of opinion that even if the trustees found that the stated conditions had been fulfilled, "their finding created no enforceable rights in any of the beneficiaries." 63 F.Supp. 834 at 837. In this view we are unable to concur. The condition upon which the power to invade capital might arise is sufficiently definite to be capable of determination by a court of equity. As Judge L. Hand said in Stix v. Commissioner, 152 F.2d 562, 563 (2d Cir.), "no language, however strong, will entirely remove any power held in trust from the reach of a court of equity." Since the trustees were not free to exercise untrammeled discretion but were to be governed by determinable standards, their power to invade capital, conditioned on contingencies which had not happened, did not in our opinion bring the trust property within the reach of section 811(d)(2).

Similar reasoning leads to the same conclusion with respect to the trustees' power over net income. At the end of each calendar year they were to accumulate the net income of that year unless prior to its amalgamation into capital they exercised their power to disburse it to, or for the benefit of, the son or his issue. The power the trustees had with respect to disbursing income was exercisable year by year; and at the date of the decedent's death the only income of which the enjoyment was subject to change through exercise of a power was the income of the B. Brewster Jennings trust for the year 1936. But the exercise of this power was conditioned on the trustees' determination that disbursement of the income was necessary to enable the beneficiary to whom it might be allotted to maintain himself and his family "in comfort and in accordance with the station in life to which he belongs." The contingency which would justify exercise of the power had not happened before the decedent's death; consequently the 1936 net income of the B. Brewster Jennings trust was not subject at the date of the decedent's death "to any change through the exercise of a power." Hence it was not includible in the gross estate of the decedent under § 811(d). This conclusion is not inconsistent with Commissioner v. Newbold's Estate, 158 F.2d 694 (2d. Cir.), for there the trustees had unlimited discretion, the trust instrument expressly providing that no beneficiary should have any vested right to receive any payment from income.

There remains for consideration the question whether the value of the trust property is includible in the decedent's estate under § 811(c) [now § 2036] upon which the appellee also relies. This section, * * * provides for inclusion within the gross estate of all property "To the extent of any interest therein of which the decedent has at any time made a transfer by trust or otherwise, in contemplation of or intended to take effect in possession or enjoyment at or after his death, or of which he has at any time made a transfer, by trust or otherwise, under which he has retained for his life or for any period not ascertainable without reference to his death or for any period which does not in fact end before his death (1) the possession or enjoyment of, or the right to the income from, the property, or (2) the right, either alone or in conjunction with any person, to designate the persons who shall possess or enjoy the property or the income therefrom; * * *."

* * * The "right," referred to in clause (2), to designate the persons who shall possess or enjoy the property or the income therefrom, is not so limited and apparently overlaps the powers mentioned in § 302(d) as amended, § 811(d) [now § 2038] of the Code. See Art. 19, Treas. Reg. 80. At first glance it might seem that clause (2) covers the present case, because the decedent, for a period that did not in fact end before his death, "retained the right," in conjunction with another of the trustees, to designate the persons who should enjoy the trust property or the income therefrom. But for the reasons that moved us when considering the applicability of § 811(d) we think the decedent effectively put that "right" beyond his own control or retention by imposing conditions upon the exercise of it. A "right" so qualified that it becomes a duty enforcible in a court of equity on petition by the beneficiaries does not circumvent the obvious purpose of § 811(c) to prevent transfers akin to testamentary dispositions from escaping taxation. * * * In the Jennings trusts the rights of the beneficiaries were no more affected by the settlor's death in October 1936 than they would have been had he resigned as a trustee in January 1936. In either event the contingent power of the trustees to invade corpus or to disburse the net income of 1936 or any subsequent year would remain the same as before his death or resignation. Only when the interest of some beneficiary is enlarged or matured by the decedent's death, is § 811(c) applicable, in our opinion. In the case at bar the decedent's death had no such effect.

¶ 19,121

The judgment is reversed and the cause remanded with directions to enter judgment for the plaintiffs.

Planning Note

[¶ 19,127]

As in the case of § 2036(a)(2), the donor who wishes to make a gift that escapes under the "power subject to a standard" exception must be careful that the standard chosen is one that is enforceable by a court of equity. Moreover, it is wise to stay quite close to the most commonly chosen standards so as to minimize potential problems. Consequently, standards should be expressed in terms of support, maintenance, health and education while general language such as "best interests" or "as trustee deems advisable" should be eschewed. See ¶ 18,192 et seq. and ¶ 22,061 et seq.

G. UNIFORM TRANSFERS TO MINORS ACT

[¶ 19,133]

Where gifts are made to a minor under the Uniform Transfers to Minors Act (UTMA) or the Uniform Gifts to Minors Act (UGMA) and the donor appoints himself custodian and dies while the donee is under the age at which the custodianship terminates (typically 21), the IRS has two distinctly different theories whereby it can seek inclusion of the gifted property in the donor's gross estate. First, if the donor is also the parent of the donee and appoints himself as custodian under UGMA or UTMA, since the donor has the obligation to support the donee and as custodian has retained the power to use income from the gifted property to fulfill that obligation, inclusion in the taxable estate follows under § 2036(a)(1). See, e.g. Estate of Prudowsky v. Commissioner, 55 T.C. 890 (1971), aff'd 465 F.2d 62 (7th Cir.1972); Eichstedt v. United States, 354 F.Supp. 484 (N.D.Cal.1972). Second, regardless of whether the donor is a parent, if the donor appoints herself as custodian under UGMA or UTMA and dies prior to termination of the custodianship, because the donor, as custodian, has the power to bestow upon or withhold from the donee enjoyment of the income from the property (as well as this property itself), inclusion in the donor's taxable estate follows under either § 2036(a)(2) or § 2038. See, e.g., Stuit v. Commissioner, 452 F.2d 190 (7th Cir.1971), Rev. Ruls. 59–357, 1959–2 C.B. 212; and 57–366, 1957–2 C.B. 618.

On rare occasions, donor taxpayers who appoint themselves as custodians under UTMA or UGMA are able to avoid the grasp of both §§ 2036 and 2038. They do this by convincing the court that a completed gift had taken place and that the custodianship is merely nominal, or by convincing the court that under the particular facts of the case, the custodian did not possess normal custodial powers, and consequently, the custodian could not affect the minor's enjoyment of the property. See Estate of Chrysler v. Commissioner, 361 F.2d 508 (2d Cir.1966); Estate of Vogel v. Commissioner, 36 T.C.M. (CCH) 875, T.C.M. (P–H) ¶ 77,209 (1977). These cases are aberrations and should not be relied on by good estate planners.

Where two donors seek to avoid § 2036 or § 2038 problems by appointing each as custodian for the other's gift under UTMA or UGMA, they may run afoul of the reciprocal trust doctrine. See ¶¶ 18,103; 18,188; 19,073.

The IRS decreed in Rev. Rul. 74–556, 1974–2 C.B. 300, that, where an individual appoints a spouse as custodian for a gift under UGMA and that spouse joins in making a split gift, in the event of death of the custodian during minority there will not be an inclusion of one-half of the property in the gross estate of the deceased custodian spouse.

In Rev. Rul. 70–348, 1970–2 C.B. 193, a donor made a gift to minor children under UGMA, appointing his wife as custodian. At her death he was appointed successor custodian. At the donor's death the children were still in minority. No inclusion could be made under § 2036 since the deceased merely possessed, but had not retained, a § 2036(a)(2) power. Since § 2038 requires that the donor merely possess, not retain, the power to alter, amend, revoke, or terminate, the gift was included in the donor-custodian's gross estate under that section.

Rather than using the UTMA or UGMA to make gifts to minors, donors occasionally create "Totten Trust" bank accounts. Whether done for benefit of a minor or an adult, where the donor remains as trustee of a classic "Totten Trust" account, the value of such an account will be included in the estate of the donor. In Estate of Sulovich v. Commissioner, 587 F.2d 845 (6th Cir.1978), the taxpayer established savings bank accounts with himself as trustee for his niece and her children. Although he gave the passbooks to his niece, under the signature card contracts, withdrawals could be made only by him or with his approval. Based on this fact, the court found that the contents of the accounts were to be included in the estate of the settlor-trustee under both § 2036(a)(2) and § 2038.

H. POWER TO SUBSTITUTE TRUSTEE

[¶ 19,139]

Suppose that the settlor of a trust grants the trustee powers that, if retained by the settlor, would result in inclusion of trust corpus in the settlor's gross estate. Further suppose that the settlor retained the right to remove the trustee and replace him with the settlor or a trustee of the settlor's own choosing. Would inclusion result here, as it would under § 2036(a)(2)?

Regulation § 20.2038–1(a)(3) indicates that inclusion results under § 2038 where the decedent grantor had the unrestricted power to remove a trustee and replace the trustee with the decedent, and the trustee is invested with discretionary powers which if retained by the decedent would have resulted in inclusion under § 2038. See also Mathey v. United States, 491 F.2d 481 (3d Cir.1974). However, where the power of the decedent-grantor to appoint herself is limited to conditions not present at the time of death (e.g., death or resignation of the trustee) there is no inclusion under § 2038. See Reg. § 20.2038–1(a)(3) & (b). This is a critical distinction between § 2036, which applies to contingent retained powers and § 2038, which applies only to powers that are exercisable at death. See *Estate of Farrel* at ¶ 18,183. Except for this critical distinction, the contingent power issue should be resolved similarly under § 2036 and § 2038.

It would now be appropriate to review the materials on contingent powers in Chapter 18 at ¶ 18,183 through ¶ 18,186.

I. OVERLAP OF SECTIONS 2038 AND 2036(a)(2)

[¶ 19,157]

There is substantial overlap of § 2036(a)(2) and § 2038. In most cases involving overlap, the Internal Revenue Service will prefer to employ § 2036 since it typically results in the inclusion of a greater amount in the taxable estate. This is so for several reasons. When an inclusion is effected under § 2036, Reg. § 20.2036–1(a) indicates that the estate should include "the value of the entire property less only the value of any income interest which is not subject to the decedent's interest or right and which is actually being enjoyed by another person at the time of the decedent's death." In the case of § 2038, Reg. § 20.2038–1(a) indicates that "only the value of an interest in property subject to a power to which § 2038 applies is included in the decedent's gross estate under § 2038." The impact of these two rules and the Commissioner's preference for § 2036(a)(2) can be demonstrated as follows: Assume that X established a trust under which income was to be divided among his children as he designated until the youngest child reached age 25, at which time the corpus was to be divided equally among the children. Assume that X died long before his youngest child had reached 25 and that at his death the trust was worth $400,000, with the income interest worth $150,000 and the remainder interest worth $250,000. Under Reg. § 20.2038–1(a) only the value of the income interest ($150,000) would be included in X's estate, whereas under Reg. § 20.2036–1(a) the entire $400,000 value of the trust would be included in X's estate.

Much of the time a decedent who possesses a § 2036(a)(2) power will also possess a § 2038 power and vice versa. However, there are several circumstances where the two sections are not coextensive. For example, *Estate of Farrel* (¶ 18,183) indicates that, under § 2036, even a retained contingent power to designate enjoyment that is not presently exercisable will result in inclusion in the estate. Regulation § 20.2038–1(a)(3) and (b) indicates that unless such a power is presently exercisable at death, there will be no inclusion under § 2038.

There are other situations in which the two sections lack coextensiveness. Section 2036 taxes only "retained" powers to designate enjoyment whereas under § 2038, if the decedent-donor holds at death a power to designate enjoyment, taxation follows regardless of "when or from what source the decedent acquired such power." Thus, most commentators are of the opinion that if a settlor establishes a trust, vests powers to designate enjoyment of income in an independent trustee who dies and the settlor is appointed as successor trustee, an inclusion will be effected under § 2038. However, since the power to designate was not retained by the settlor, no inclusion results under § 2036. Recall, however, that in Rev. Rul. 84–179 (¶ 17,055) the IRS based its acceptance of the result and rationale in *Skifter* and its rejection of *Rose* and *Terriberry* on a belief that the "when and from what source" language of § 2038 was limited to essentially contrived situations where, for example, to avoid the technical application of § 2038 a power was temporarily vested in a third party before being "returned" to the grantor. This limited reading of the "when and from what source" language of § 2038 would, in the absence of collusive tax avoidance, make that section basically coextensive with § 2036 on the issue of non-retained powers.

There is an extremely significant situation in which § 2038 and not § 2036 will be the operative section where a power to designate enjoyment is present. This situation involves circumstances where the donor holds a power which, while it affects the enjoyment of wealth, does not affect the enjoyment of income during the donor's life. Section 2036(a)(2) is a parallel provision to § 2036(a)(1), including in the estate property with respect to which the decedent decided that, rather than enjoying "income" or the "use" of property during life (which would be taxed under § 2036(a)(1)), the decedent would prefer to determine who, or under what circumstances individuals should enjoy income or the use of property during the decedent's life. Consequently, where the donor has retained a power that affects wealth that the donor has transferred but does not affect its enjoyment during the donor's life, § 2038 and not § 2036 will be the operative section. For example, assume that X conveys property in trust with income to A for her life and the remainder to her estate and retains the power to terminate the trust, paying all of the corpus to A. Regulation § 20.2036–1(b)(3)(sentence 3 and the parenthetical) indicates that this property will not be includible in X's estate under § 2036 although it will be includible under § 2038. Having gone this far, it might be helpful to look back to *Struthers v. Kelm* (¶ 18,169) and ask how that case is distinguishable. What added power did the settlor in that case retain with respect to the right of the beneficiary to enjoy income?

For a good discussion of the overlap of these two sections you are referred to Bittker and Lokken, 5 Federal Taxation of Income Estates and Gifts, at ¶ 126.6.7 (2d ed. 1993).

J. REVOCABLE TRUSTS

[§ 19,159]

In recent years revocable trusts which make provision for distribution of trust assets at the death of the settlor-beneficiary have been increasingly used as will substitutes or supplements in modest to medium sized estates. A few examples of the advantages of revocable trusts will illustrate why they have been gaining increasing popularity. Wills are public documents, open to all as are other documents such as asset inventories filed by the estate in probate. Revocable trusts remain private even when used to dispose of property at death. Real property located out of state will result in expensive ancillary probate if disposed of by will or intestacy. Contribution of such realty to a revocable trust provides a means of avoiding ancillary probate. Revocable trusts also provide acceptable means of: (1) guarding against the glare of public proceedings regarding incompetency; and (2) avoiding probate fees and related expenses. In keeping with its descriptive title, the trust remains revocable by the settlor, thereby giving her the same flexibility that a will would provide. Add to this the fact that a revocable trust is at least as, if not more, easy to change as is a conventional will and it is easy to see why revocable trusts have been gaining popularity among estate planners and their clients.

Clearly, if a taxpayer places her wealth in a simple revocable trust, the corpus of the trust will be treated as part of her taxable estate at her death under § 2038. Accordingly, at death of the settlor the corpus of a revocable trust will qualify for a step up basis. The full tax treatment to be accorded joint revocable trusts was less clear until the release of Priv. Ltr. Rul. 200101021 which follows below. In the typical joint revocable trust a couple will contribute most of their property to a revocable trust that will provide them with either absolute or limited access to income and corpus of the trust during their lives. The trust will provide for disposition of some of the corpus at the death of the first to die and for disposition of all remaining property at the death of the survivor. Of acute interest to estate planners was how one would determine the basis of assets passing from the trust to the surviving settlor and to other heirs. Private Letter Ruling 200101021 provides the answer to that and several other questions.

[¶ 19,161]

PRIVATE LETTER RULING 200101021

January 5, 2001.

This is in response to your letter dated November 24, 1999, and subsequent correspondence, requesting a ruling concerning the estate and gift tax consequences of the creation of a proposed trust (Trust)under §§ 2033, 2038, 2041, 2501, and 2511 of the Internal Revenue Code.

The facts and representations submitted are summarized as follows: Grantor A and Grantor B, who are husband and wife, propose to create a joint trust ("Trust"). Grantor A will be the initial trustee of Trust. The Grantors will fund Trust with assets that they own as tenants by the entireties having a value of approximately $x.

Under the terms of Trust, during the joint lives of the Grantors, the trustee may apply income and principal of Trust as the trustee deems advisable for the comfort, support, maintenance, health and general welfare of the Grantors. The trustee may also pay additional sums to either or both of the Grantors or to a third person for the benefit of either or both Grantors as Grantor A directs, or if he is not capable of this decision, then as Grantor B directs. While both Grantors are living, either one may terminate Trust by written notice to the other Grantor. If Trust is terminated, the trustee will deliver the trust property to the Grantors in both their names as tenants in common. Either Grantor may also amend the trust will both grantors are living by delivering to the other Grantor the amendment in writing at least 90 days before the effective date of the amendment.

Upon the death of the first Grantor to die, he or she possesses a testamentary general power of appointment, exercisable alone and in all events, to appoint part or all of the assets of Trust, free of trust, to such deceased Grantor's estate or to or for the benefit of one or more persons or entities, in such proportions, outright, in trust, or otherwise as the deceased Grantor may direct in his or her will.

If the first Grantor to die fails to fully exercise his or his testamentary general power of appointment, and providing the surviving Grantor survives the first Grantor to die by at least six months, an amount of Trust property sufficient to equal the largest amount that can pass free of federal estate tax by reason of the unified credit, is to be transferred to an irrevocable Credit Shelter Trust. Any amount in excess of the amount needed to fully fund the Credit Shelter Trust that has not been appointed by the deceased Grantor will pass outright to the surviving Grantor.

The terms of the Credit Shelter Trust provide that during the life of the surviving Grantor, the trustee is to pay or apply for the benefit of the surviving Grantor any part of the income and/or principal of the trust as is reasonably necessary for the survivor's support and maintenance. The trustee shall also have the authority to pay or apply for the benefit of the joint descendants of the Grantors any portion of the income and/or principal of the trust as the trustee deems necessary for such descendants maintenance, support, and education. All distributions however, shall be limited by an ascertainable standard relating to health, education, support, or maintenance. Upon the death of the surviving Grantor, he or she shall have a limited power to appoint the Credit Shelter Trust assets to any one or more of the class consisting of the Grantor's joint descendants. Any assets not so appointed are to be divided into equal shares so as to provide one share for each living child of both Grantors and one share for the surviving issue collectively, per stirpes, of a deceased child of both Grantors.

* * *

Section 2001(a) of the Internal Revenue Code imposes a tax on the transfer of the taxable estate of every decedent who is a citizen or resident of the United States.

Section 2033 provides that the gross estate shall include the value of all property to the extent of the interest therein of the decedent at the time or his death.

Section 2038(a) of the Code provides that the value of the gross estate includes the value of all property of which the decedent has at any time made a transfer (except where there has been a bona fide sale for adequate and full consideration in money or money's worth) by trust or otherwise where the enjoyment thereof was subject at the date of death to any change through the exercise of a power by the decedent to alter, amend, revoke, or terminate the interest in the property or where the decedent relinquished this power within the three year period ending on the date of the decedent's death.

Section 2041(a)(2) provides for the inclusion in the gross estate of any property to which the decedent possesses, at the time of his death, a general power of appointment created after October 21, 1942.

Section 2041(b)(1) provides that the term "general power of appointment" means a power that is exercisable in favor of the decedent, the decedent's estate, the decedent's creditors, or the creditors of the decedent's estate, except that a power to consume property for the benefit of the decedent that is limited by an ascertainable standard relating to health, education, support, or maintenance of the decedent is not deemed a general power of appointment.

Section 20.2041–1 (b)(2) provides that the term power of appointment, does not include powers reserved by the decedent to himself within the concepts of sections 2036 to 2038.

Section 2501 imposes a tax for each calendar year on the transfer of property by gift during such calendar year by any individual, resident or nonresident.

Section 25.2511(2)(b) provides that as to any property, or part therein, of which the donor has so parted with dominion and control as to leave in him no power to change its disposition, whether for his own benefit or for the benefit of another, the gift is complete. Section 25.2511–2(c)provides that a gift is incomplete in every instance in which a donor reserves the power to revest the beneficial title to the property to himself or herself.

Section 2523 provides that where a donor transfers during the calendar year by gift an interest in property to a donee who at the time of the gift is the donor's spouse, there shall be allowed as a deduction in computing taxable gifts for the calendar year an amount with respect to such interest equal to its value.

Section 1014(a) provides that the basis of property in the hands of a person acquiring the property from a decedent or to whom the property passed from the decedent is the fair market value of the property at the date of the decedent's death (or alternate valuation date).

Section 1014(b)(9) provides that, for purposes of § 1014(a), property acquired from the decedent includes property acquired from the decedent by reason of death, form of ownership, or other conditions, including property acquired through the exercise or non-exercise of a power of appointment, if the property is required to be included in determining the value of the decedent's gross estate for federal estate tax purposes.

Section 1014(e), however, provides an exception to the general rule of section 1014(a). Under section 1014(e), if appreciated property was acquired by the decedent by gift during the one-year period ending on the date of the decedent's death and the property is acquired from the decedent by, or passes from the decedent to, the donor of such property, the basis of such property in the hands of the donor is the adjusted basis of the property in the hands of the decedent immediately before the death of the decedent.

Ruling #1. Grantor A and Grantor B propose to transfer property held as tenants by the entireties to Trust. The Grantors will each retain the power to terminate Trust by written notice to the other Grantor. If Trust is terminated, the trustee will deliver the trust property to the Grantors in both their names as tenants in common. We conclude that the initial contribution of assets to Trust as proposed will not constitute a completed gift by either Grantor under section 25.2511–2(c), since each will retain the right, exercisable unilaterally, to revoke their respective transfer, and revest title in themselves.

Ruling #2. If either Grantor exercises the right to terminate Trust, each Grantor will receive an undivided 50% interest in the remaining balance of the Trust corpus, as a tenant in common. Therefore, distributions of Trust property to either Grantor during their joint lives will constitute a gift by the other Grantor to the extent of 50% of the value of Trust assets distributed. The gift will qualify for the gift tax marital deduction under section 2523.

Ruling #3 and #4. Upon the death of the first Grantor to die, he or she will possess a testamentary power exercisable alone and in all events, to appoint part or all of the assets of the Trust, free of trust, to such deceased Grantor's estate or to or for the benefit of one or more persons or entities, in such proportions, outright, in trust, or otherwise as the deceased Grantor may direct in his or her will.

We conclude that, on the death of the first Grantor to die, the portion of the Trust property attributable to the property the deceased Grantor transferred to Trust will be includible in the deceased Grantor's gross estate under section 2038. The balance of the property attributable to the property the surviving Grantor contributed to Trust will be includible in the deceased Grantor's gross estate under section 2041.

Further, on the death of the first deceasing Grantor, the surviving Grantor is treated as relinquishing his or her dominion and control over the surviving Grantor's one-half interest in Trust. Accordingly, on the death of the first deceasing Grantor, the surviving Grantor will make a completed gift under section 2501 of the surviving Grantor's entire interest in Trust. This gift will qualify for the marital deduction under § 2523.

In addition, § 1014 (e) will apply to any Trust property includible in the deceased Grantor's gross estate that is attributable to the surviving Grantor's contribution to Trust and that is acquired by the surviving Grantor, either directly or indirectly, pursuant to the deceased Grantor's exercise, or failure to exercise, the general power of appointment. See, H. R. Rept. 97–201, 97th Cong., 1st Sess. (July 24, 1981).

Rulings #5 and #6. As discussed above, the surviving Grantor is treated as making a completed gift of his or her interest in Trust on the death of the first deceasing Grantor. Also, as discussed above, a portion of the Trust property will be subject to inclusion in the deceased Grantor's gross estate under section 2038, and a portion will be subject to inclusion under section

2041. Accordingly, to the extent the Credit Shelter Trust is funded, property passing to the trust is treated as passing from the deceased Grantor, and not from the surviving Grantor.

Similarly, any future payments from the Credit Shelter Trust to beneficiaries other than the surviving Grantor will not constitute a gift from surviving Grantor to those beneficiaries. None of the assets held in the Credit Shelter Trust will be includible in the surviving Grantor's gross estate, since the surviving Grantor will possess only a special power of appointment with respect to the assets in the Credit Shelter Trust.

Except as ruled above, we express or imply no opinion concerning the federal tax consequences of this transaction under the cited provisions of the Code or any other provision of the Code.

K.   POWER RELEASED WITHIN THREE YEARS OF DEATH

[¶ 19,163]

Section 2038 specifically provides that, where the decedent relinquishes a retained power "to alter, amend, revoke or terminate" within three years of the decedent's death, the property subject to this power is to be included in the decedent's estate. Given the general rule of § 2035 and the specific provision of § 2035(a), which refers to property that "would have been included in the decedent's gross estate under" § 2038, the specific inclusionary language in § 2038 for gifts made within three years of death can be viewed as a bit of legislative overkill.

A donor who has made a gift under which she has retained a power "to alter, amend, revoke or terminate" and who subsequently wishes to exclude such property from the gross estate should consequently be doubly mindful of the need to sever their taxable strings long before the "golden years." See Planning Note at ¶ 18,253.

L.   COMMUNITY PROPERTY AND POWERS

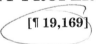 [¶ 19,169]

KATZ v. UNITED STATES

United States Court of Appeals, Ninth Circuit, 1967.
382 F.2d 723.

DUNIWAY, Circuit Judge:

Appellant [Sadie Katz] is the widow of Leroy Joseph Katz, who died a resident of California on February 27, 1960. * * *

On August 29, 1956, Title Insurance and Trust Company executed a Declaration of Trust, in which "Leroy Joseph Katz, a married man," was named Trustor. This paper acknowledged receipt by the Trust Company, without consideration, of real and personal property from Leroy, and that the property was to be held in trust for the benefit of Sadie and of Leroy's children, their surviving spouses and surviving issue. Sections One, Two and Three give the trustee the usual powers to manage the properties, collect income, and invest the trust's funds. * * *

Sadie claims that all of the assets conveyed to the trust were the community property of herself and Leroy. The government denies this, but the trial court, for the purpose of its decision, assumed that Sadie is right. * * *

Clearly, if Leroy placed his separate property in the trust, sections 2036 and 2038 would apply. But each section is limited by its express terms; property is to be included only "to the extent of any interest therein of which the decedent [Leroy] has at any time made a transfer." Here, assuming that the property conveyed to the trustee was community, acquired after 1927, Sadie and Leroy each had a "present, existing and equal" interest in it (Cal.Civ.C. § 161a). Leroy had certain powers of management and disposition (Cal.Civ.C. § 172), but he could not, without Sadie's written consent, "make a gift of such community personal property, or dispose of the same without a valuable consideration" (Cal.Civ.C. § 172) or convey community real property without her joinder (Cal.Civ.C. § 172a).

It seems clear to us that the interest in the property of which Leroy, the decedent, made a transfer was his one-half interest in the property. If he can be said at all to have made a transfer of Sadie's one-half interest, he did so only as managing agent for the two of them. What he did, being done without consideration required by Civil Code § 172, was voidable by her. Sadie's written approval, if it was a transfer at all, was in substance a transfer by her to the trustee, not to Leroy, of her one-half interest. This is even more clear, as to the real property. Leroy could not convey it. Both joined in the deeds; each transferred his or her one-half interest. Thus, the extent of the interest in the property that Leroy transferred is one-half, and that is the extent to which, under sections 2036 and 2038, the property is includible in his estate.

Nor can we accept the trial court's conclusion that by virtue of the execution of the Declaration of Trust, all of the property conveyed to the trustee became the separate property of Leroy. It is well settled in California that property acquired with community funds or property is also community property. We know of no case that holds that the equitable interests of a husband and wife in an inter vivos trust, created by them by conveyance of their community property to the trustee, cannot also be community property. We would not expect the California courts to so hold.

There is a statutory presumption that property acquired by the spouses during marriage is community property (Cal.Civ.C. § 164). The presumption is a strong one, which the California Supreme Court has characterized as fundamental to the community property system. It can be overcome only by clear and satisfactory proof. It is even stronger when the property was acquired with community property. It extends to every conceivable type of property, including insurance policies and their proceeds, Scott v. C.I.R., supra; United States v. Stewart, supra; a cause of action for the wrongful death of or injury to a minor child; a cause of action for injury to either spouse; * * * the interest of a spouse in a partnership; good will of a business; borrowed money; and leasehold interests; Why not to a retained equitable interest in a trust?

We find at least three California decisions that hold that such an interest can be community property. * * *

It is, however, well established that the spouses can, by agreement, change separate property to community, and vice versa. And the form of conveyance by which property is acquired may be inconsistent with its being community property, as in joint tenancies. Even in such a case, however, the spouses can agree that the property is community property. Here, there is, as the trial court found, no such collateral agreement as to the spouses' interest in the trust.

The trial court was of the opinion that the terms of the Declaration of Trust itself were inconsistent with there being community property. It treated the execution of the Declaration as, in substance, a conveyance by Sadie to Leroy. It said that the property became his separate property "since, under the terms of the trust, he was accorded the right solely to enjoy the income from the trust and was given the power to revoke, terminate or amend the trust. These rights and powers vested in the said decedent control of, and the beneficial enjoyment of, all of the trust property." 255 F.Supp. at 643.

We do not agree. In the first place, nothing that Sadie signed contains any express language whereby she conveyed anything to Leroy. In the second place, if she had conveyed all her rights when the Declaration was executed, why was her further approval of each amendment required? The Declaration does not require her approval of amendments. But if the property remained community, then Civil Code §§ 172 and 172a do require her consent or joinder, if the amendment would deprive her of any of her community interest. Absent such consent or joinder, she could have, at Leroy's death, set aside the trust as to her one-half of the community property. The fact that her consent was sought, each time, is some indication that the parties believed that she had a community property interest in the trust. In the third place, we do not find that the powers given to Leroy to "collect, receive, and disburse, without accounting to the trustee or any other person, all income" from the trust property (Section Four) and to "revoke, terminate or amend this trust" (Section Thirteen) are so inconsistent with the continued community character of the trust property as to overcome the presumptions to which we have referred.

* * *

We think that, whatever powers Leroy had under Section Four and Section Thirteen, they were held by him as manager of or agent for the community property and subject to his obligations as such manager. In this respect, we agree * * * [that] the trust was not created by Leroy with his property; it was created by Leroy and Sadie with their property.

Our views are reinforced by the peculiar nature of this trust. If ever a trust came close to being a "dry" trust, a mere agency, during Leroy's lifetime, and testamentary in character, this one does. See our discussion of this problem in Dessar v. Bank of America, 1965, 353 F.2d 468. There is far less substance to this trust than there was to the *Dessar* trust. We do not pass on the validity of this trust; we assume that it is valid. (The question was not argued in the trial court). We note its nature as a further aid to determining, from the instrument itself, the probable intent of the parties and the legal effect of what they did. In substance, and for all practical purposes, it left the management and control of the community property, during Leroy's life, exactly where it was before the trust was created, in Leroy. If it enlarged his managerial powers at all, it did so in but one respect—it permitted him to give away the community income. Its principal purpose is not to change, in any substantial way, the property rights of the parties during their joint lives, but to govern the disposition of those properties at death. We cannot find in it any intent on the part of either spouse to transmute their community property into Leroy's separate property. * * *

Alternatively, the government argues that the Declaration of Trust conferred upon Leroy a general power of appointment over Sadie's community interest, and that therefore that interest is includible under Int.Rev.Code of 1954 § 2041. See also Treasury Regulations on Estate Tax (1954 Code), 26 C.F.R. § 20.2041–1. The government relies on both Section Four and Section Thirteen of the Declaration. Section Four merely reserves to Leroy general powers of management, sale and investment of the trust property within the trust, and the right to collect, receive and disburse income. It is not a general power of appointment. Section Thirteen reserves to Leroy the power to revoke, terminate or amend. This, we have held, is a power as agent for the community. It is no more a general power of appointment than the powers that he had over the community property before the trust was created. It has never been held that those powers amount to a general power of appointment over the wife's interest.

As we have indicated, there remains a factual question as to whether the properties conveyed to the trustee were community property. That question remains to be tried. The judgment is therefore reversed, with instructions that the trial court take such further proceedings as are consistent with this opinion.

Problems

[¶ 19,175]

1. David established a trust for the benefit of his daughter, Claire. Under the terms of the trust, income was to be distributed to Claire as Valley Trust Co. determined to be "in her best interests" until Claire was 25 years old, at which time all accumulated income and corpus were to be distributed to Claire. David retained the right to remove the trustee and substitute for it another trustee, other than himself. David died when Claire was 22 years old and the trust corpus was worth $400,000. What are the tax consequences for David's estate?

2. Assume that in the prior problem David had vested the power to remove and appoint a new trustee in you, his estate planner. What would then be

the result? Assume further that David had created a joint power (held by you and him) to remove and appoint a new trustee (other than David). What would be the tax consequence of this action?

3. Patricia owns 75 percent of the stock of Acme, Inc. Patricia is the president of Acme, which has an employee death benefit under which "two times annual compensation is to be paid to the spouse of each employee who dies while employed by Acme." At Patricia's death, $200,000 was paid to her husband, Jerry. What are the tax consequences? Would your answer be any different if Patricia owned only 10 percent of the stock of Acme?

4. Morris established a trust for the benefit of his grandchildren, naming himself as trustee. Under the terms of the trust, income, in most circumstances, is to be distributed equally among the beneficiaries until the youngest reaches age 25, at which time the corpus is to be divided per stirpes among all grandchildren or their issue. The sole circumstance in which income is not to be divided equally arises when there is "a severe medical or other financial emergency." In such cases, the trustee is required to distribute income among beneficiaries so as to provide for the "support and maintenance of the individual experiencing the emergency." What are the tax consequences of this arrangement if Morris dies while the trust is still in operation?

5. Betty made a gift of stock to her 10–year-old son, Ben, under the Uniform Transfers to Minors Act, appointing herself as custodian. She died four years later when the stock was worth $30,000. What are the tax consequences to Betty's estate?

6. Calvin established a trust under which income was to be paid to his grandson, Ted, until Ted reached age 35, at which time the corpus of the trust was to be distributed to Ted. Calvin reserved to himself, acting in conjunction with Ted's mother, Lisa, the right to terminate the trust and accelerate Ted's enjoyment of the remainder. What are the tax consequences if Calvin dies while the trust is still in operation?

¶ 19,175

Chapter 20

TRANSFERS GEARED TO GRANTOR'S LIFE

(Section 2037)

A. INTRODUCTION

[¶ 20,001]

As mentioned in chapters 18 and 19, the original antecedent of § 2037 was § 202(b) of the Revenue Act of 1916, which brought into the gross estate transfers "intended to take effect in possession or enjoyment at or after" the grantor's death. Due to a series of Supreme Court decisions that gave this language an exceedingly narrow construction, § 202(b) did not reach the types of transfers that many believed a fair-minded reading of the statute would treat as subject to taxation under the section.

Congress responded to the situation with the passage of several pieces of legislation that were intended to compensate for the narrow readings given to § 202(b) by the Supreme Court. Section 2037 is one such addition to the Code. In its present form, it is the product of legislation passed by Congress in 1949, 1951 and 1954.

Under § 2037, property transferred during the decedent's life will be included in his or her estate if: (1) possession or enjoyment of the property, through ownership, can be obtained by an individual only by that individual or another party surviving the decedent; and (2) the decedent has retained a reversionary interest in the property, which immediately before the decedent's death, exceeds five percent of the value of such property. It is important to remember that, for inclusion to result under § 2037, both requirements must be satisfied. Moreover, in situations where a reversion is present, but one or both tests under § 2037 have not been met, taxation of the reversion in the decedent's estate under § 2033 should not be overlooked.

B. REMOTE AND UNINTENDED REVERSIONS

[¶ 20,007]

Since § 2037 requires both a reversion in the grantor and an interest that may pass to another only by surviving the grantor, an estate planner who wishes to put his client's transfer beyond its reach merely need insure that one of the two requirements of § 2037 is not present. This is often easier said than done.

Problems sometimes arise where the deed of conveyance contains no express reversion but one arises by operation of law because the deed did not effect a complete conveyance. For example, in Estate of Spiegel v. Commissioner, 335 U.S. 701 (1949), the taxpayer established a trust that provided that income was to be divided among his three children for his life, and if they did not survive him, the income was to be distributed among his grandchildren. On the taxpayer's death, the same pattern of distribution was to be employed to dispose of the corpus. The deed of trust failed to specify how the property was to be distributed if the taxpayer's children and grandchildren had all predeceased him. The Court found that, under Illinois law, the taxpayer's incomplete conveyance resulted in a reversion, albeit a remote one. Moreover, since the taxpayer's children and grandchildren could inherit the corpus that was transferred at his death only by surviving him, the Court found that, at the taxpayer's death, the corpus was to be included in his estate under the predecessor of § 2037.

Subsequent to the Supreme Court's decision in *Spiegel*, the Code was amended to provide that an inclusion under § 2037 results only where the value of the reversion exceeds five percent of the value of the property subject to the reversion. Occasionally this amendment serves to bail out taxpayers who, like the taxpayer in *Spiegel*, employed an estate planner with an inadequate understanding of state property law. As the materials in this chapter will illustrate, inclusions under § 2037 are often the result of sloppy or unskilled drafting of deeds of trust. The five-percent provision is a potential escape hatch for the unfortunate taxpayer and the estate planner who otherwise might be anxiously checking the limits on a malpractice policy. *Spiegel* and other cases like it are excellent illustrations of the fact that the able estate planner must be well versed in both tax and property law.

A classic example of a situation in which an unintended reversion was found to exist is Commissioner v. Estate of Marshall, 203 F.2d 534 (3d Cir.1953). There the decedent established a trust with income to his wife for life. At her death the corpus was to be paid as she had by will designated and, in default of such designation, to her then-heirs under Pennsylvania's intestate laws. Some time after establishment of the trust, Mrs. Marshall surrendered her right to designate by will the identification of the takers of the corpus at her death. The court decided that, as Mrs. Marshall's spouse at his death, Mr. Marshall, under Pennsylvania's intestacy laws which were incorporated by reference, had a potential reversion in a one-third share of the corpus on her death. The court then addressed the issue of whether the remaining requirement of § 2037 was satisfied, namely if it was possible for the Marshall children to take the reversionary interest of their father other than by surviving the decedent.

Undoubtedly then, in determining whether a transferred interest which might revert back to the settlor-decedent was intended to take effect in possession or enjoyment at or after his death, we must inquire whether it was possible, immediately prior thereto for some person who need not have survived him to take that interest. Or, otherwise stated, we must determine whether there was any other contingency, besides the settlor-decedent's death, upon the happening of which his reverter interest would be entirely cut off. If there was, and that contingency was "real", then the transfer was not intended to take effect in possession and enjoyment at or after his death.

At the moment preceding Marshall's death it was possible for beneficiaries to take the one-third interest without surviving him. This could have resulted (1) by a change in the intestate laws of Pennsylvania, mitigating or eliminating the surviving spouse's share; (2) under the present intestate laws if Marshall had divorced his wife or she had divorced him; (3) if Marshall either wilfully neglected or refused to provide for Mrs. Marshall for one year previous to her death, or if he wilfully and maliciously had deserted her for that period. Had any one of those things occurred, the one-third interest which decedent would otherwise have gotten, would have gone to persons (the children, if they survived their mother) who would not have had to survive the decedent.

Nor can these contingencies be disregarded on the ground that they are "unreal." They cannot be regarded as "sham", for, as the Tax Court said:

> "The indications are that the decedent was not thinking of himself or intending to provide that a part of the trust property was to revert to him and was not to pass to others save upon the condition that he predeceased his wife * * *. It seems unlikely that he had it in mind."

The possible contingencies taken together under which beneficiaries could have taken the interest without surviving Marshall cannot be regarded as so remote as to be "unreal."

Thus, there being another event (or events) upon which the beneficiaries could have taken the one-third interest without surviving the decedent, the transfer * * * is therefore not includible in Marshall's gross estate.

Assume that the beneficiary of the trust in *Estate of Marshall*, rather than being decedent's spouse, had been a child. Since the status of parent is not as legally fragile as that of spouse in an era in which divorce is commonplace, one should ponder if the same result would follow.

The injection of real conditions other than survivorship, whereby parties whose interests are otherwise conditioned on survivorship may take possession or enjoyment of the property, often provides a means by which an estate planner can snatch an interest from the jaws of § 2037.

As is the case under §§ 2036 and 2038, severance of a taxable string, if done earlier than three years prior to death, is a strategy to be considered in cases where the estate planner was not able to avoid inclusion in the first place.

C. VALUING THE REVERSION

[¶ 20,015]

1. ACTUARIAL VALUES AND CONDITION OF HEALTH

Regulation § 20.2037–1(c)(3) tells us that when determining if, immediately prior to death, the value of the decedent's reversion exceeds five percent, we are to ascertain the value of the reversion using recognized valuation principles for determining the value of conditional and future interests. Moreover, the regulation also indicates that the valuation shall be made without regard to whether the decedent's executor had elected the alternative valuation method under § 2032.

In § 7520 Congress delegated to the Treasury the authority, using a few legislatively mandated standards, to prescribe tables for determining the actuarial value of annuities, life estates, terms of years, remainders and reversions. Regulation § 20.2037–1(c)(3) indicates that in determining if, immediately prior to death, the value of the decedent's reversion exceeds five percent, one should employ the recognized valuation principles prescribed by Reg. §§ 20.2031–1, 20.2031–7 and 20.2031–9. The process of actuarial valuation required by the regulations is well explained in considerable detail in Chapter 10 of this volume, and it now might be helpful to review those materials paying special attention to the materials at ¶ 10,007. Under the valuation techniques required by the regulations, the tables provided in Reg. § 20.2031–7, in general, provide conclusive guidance for determining whether the value of decedent's reversion at the time of her death exceeds five percent.

Occasionally the question arises whether, in valuing decedent's reversion, it is appropriate to consider that taxpayer-decedent suffers from a terminal disease. Although Reg. § 20.7520–3(b)(3)(i) allows some modest wiggle room for consideration of the impact of the presence of a terminal condition on most actuarial calculations, Reg. § 20.7520–3(b)(3)(ii) specifically provides that "the value of a decedent's reversionary interest under section 2037(b) * * * shall be determined without regard to the physical condition, immediately before decedent's death, of the individual who is the measuring life." Were the regulations not to so provide, § 2037 would be almost exclusively restricted to situations involving sudden and unexpected deaths such as those which follow from accidents or coronaries in seemingly healthy individuals. In many other situations (such as death by cancer, stroke or, for that matter, most heart attacks) in the closing moments of the decedent-taxpayer's life few, if any, such individuals, regardless of their age, would have their reversionary interests valued in excess of five percent if one were to consider the medical condition of the decedent-taxpayer. For example, assume that A, while in good health, established a trust with income for life to husband B, and that at B's death, the corpus of the trust was to revert to A if she did not predecease B. If A predeceased B, the corpus was to be paid to their child C or her estate. Assume that A, survived by B and C, died in a plane crash six years after establishing this trust and that at the time of her death her reversionary interest was actuarially valued at 9.5% of the corpus of the trust, thereby, resulting in an inclusion in her estate of the value of the trust corpus minus the value of B's life estate. Next, assume that rather than dying in a plane crash, A had been diagnosed with advanced systemic esophageal cancer, had been given weeks to live and died several weeks after detection of her disease. Were we to consider the condition of A's health immediately prior to her death, the value of her reversion would be considerably less than five percent and there would be no inclusion under § 2037. Several courts which, prior to Congressional delegation under § 7520 to the Treasury of the power to issue "legislative" regulations and the Treasury's issuance of Reg. § 20.7520–3(b)(3)(ii), had considered the issue had concluded that to preclude § 2037 from being limited in application to totally unexpected deaths, it was necessary to disregard the status of decedent-taxpayer's health immediately prior to her death in determining the value of that party's reversionary interest. See, Robinson v. United States, 632 F.2d 822 (9th Cir.1980); Estate of Allen v. United States, 558 F.2d 14 (Cl.Ct.1977); Estate of Roy v. Commissioner, 54 T.C. 1317 (1970), but see Hall v. United States, 353 F.2d 500 (7th Cir.1965).

Although it may be inappropriate to consider the health of the decedent immediately prior to her death for the purpose of determining whether the value of decedent's reversion exceeds five percent, what of the health of other parties? Assume that, in the case of the previous example involving A, B and C, use of actuarial tables alone would result in A's reversion being assigned a value of 4.5% immediately prior to her death in the plane crash. If this were all that was to be considered, nothing would be included in her estate under § 2037. However, what result should prevail if B weeks earlier had been diagnosed as suffering from a terminal disease which would likely claim his life within six months and if this had been considered in valuing A's reversion, it would have been assigned a value of ninety percent? Strict adherence to the language of Reg. § 20.2037–3(b)(3)(ii) would seem to indicate that the condition of B's health, as well as that of A, should be ignored. It is worth noting that the court in the *Hall*, whose opinion is inconsistent with Reg. § 20.2037–3(b)(3)(ii), and which represents a distinct minority position, in reaching its conclusion had considered the pre-death health of all parties concerned.

[¶ 20,021]

2. OTHER FACTORS

Suppose that factors other than those dealing with death will impact on the value of the decedent's reversion. Should they be considered in determining if the value of the decedent's reversionary interest exceeds five percent?

Moreover, if they are to be considered, how is one to determine their relative weight? The issue of the impact of other factors is addressed by the case which follows.

[¶ 20,022]

ESTATE OF CARDEZA v. UNITED STATES

United States District Court, Eastern District of Pennsylvania, 1957.
57–1 USTC ¶ 11,681, 52 AFTR 1911, aff'd, 261 F.2d 423 (3d Cir.1958).

KIRKPATRICK, Ch. Judge:

The Technical Changes Act, 26 U.S. C., 1952 ed., Section 811(c)(2) [now § 2037], provides that inter vivos transfers made on or before October 7, 1949, and intended to take effect in possession or enjoyment at or after death need not be included in the gross estate unless the decedent had retained a reversionary interest of a value of more than 5% of the transferred property. In this estate, the decedent during her lifetime transferred property to a trust set up by her father's will, the terms of which provided that, in the event that the decedent survived all of her children and their issue, she would then become entitled to receive the income for life and to dispose of the principal by testamentary power of appointment. At the time of her death the decedent was 85 years old. She had one son then living who was 64 and married to a wife who was 59. The son had no children but was physically able to procreate. The decedent had no other children or lineal descendants.

The question for the Court is whether immediately before her death the decedent's reversionary interest had a value in excess of 5% of the value of the corpus or, stated in another way, whether it can be established that a woman 85 years old has a less than 5% chance of surviving a man of 64 married to a woman of 59 and also any child or children whom he may have in the future.

The taxpayer has the burden of proof, but that does not mean that he must come forward with evidence to prove the negative on which his case depends. The burden of proof in a case like this is the burden of convincing the Court, and the taxpayer has the risk of non-persuasion.

In this case statutory provisions govern the means of proof and define the issue. The Act provides that the value should be determined "by usual methods of valuation, including the use of tables of mortality and actuarial principles." The Conference Committee Report states that "The rule of Robinette v. Helvering (318 U.S. 184), under which a reversionary interest not having an ascertainable value under recognized valuation principles is considered to have a value of zero, is to apply." (1949–2 Cum. Bull. 295, 297) and a regulation issued under the Act by the Commissioner of Internal Revenue provides, "If a reversionary interest does not have an ascertainable value under the applicable valuation principles, it is considered to have a value of zero." (Reg. 105, Sec. 81.17(c).)

In the *Robinette* case, supra, the Court had before it a situation like the present one (except that the ages of the parties involved were different), namely, a deed of trust which provided for a life estate in a woman, remainder to her issue upon their reaching the age of 21 and, in default of issue, then to whomever she should appoint by will. The Court's ruling upon the point in which we are here interested is embodied in the following sentences: "Factors to be considered in fixing the value of this contingent reservation as of the date of the gift would have included consideration of whether or not the daughter would marry; whether she would have children; whether they would reach the age of 21; etc. Actuarial science may have made great strides in appraising the value of that which seems to be unappraisable, but we have no reason to believe from this record that even the actuarial art could do more than guess at the value here in question." Thus the taxpayer must demonstrate to the Court's satisfaction that the best that the actuarial art can do toward establishing the value of the reversion is no more than a guess, but if he can do that by the admitted facts and the defendant's evidence, he need not produce evidence and is entitled to judgment.

In Commissioner of Internal Revenue v. Cardeza's Estate, 173 F.2d 19, (another phase of the tax question arising in this estate, decided in 1949) the Court of Appeals for the Third Circuit followed the *Robinette* case, supra, and in Commissioner v. Sternberger's Estate, 348 U.S. 187, decided as late as January 1955, the Supreme Court had before it a case involving the same general scheme of devolution—an estate in trust during the joint lives of the decedent's wife and daughter, the principal payable to the then living descendants of the daughter upon the death of the survivor and, in default of such descendants, then over to designated relatives and charities. The question was the value of the part of the remainder bequeathed to charities. The Court had before it considerable [sic] more in the way of actuarial statistics than in the *Robinette* case, supra, and the data were more complete and up-to-date. The Court recognized that there had been advances in the actuarial art since the *Robinette* decision and that actuarial estimates are employed more widely than formerly. Nonetheless, the Court held that the amount of the bequest to the charity was incapable of ascertainment and disallowed the claim for a pro tanto deduction.

The Government relies upon several decisions including Brotherhood v. Pinkston, 293 U.S. 96, Commissioner of Internal Rev. v. State Street T. Co., 128 F.2d 618, and Commissioner of Internal Revenue v. Maresi, 156 F.2d 929, in all of which the possibility of ascertaining the likelihood of remarriage was accepted as a basis for the Court's decision. The distinction between these cases and the *Sternberger, Cardeza* and *Robinette* cases becomes clear when one considers the reasoning of the *Sternberger* opinion. The key is to be found in the following sentence: "The bequest, in fact, offers to the daughter an inducement . . . to remarry and leave a descendant." All the cases relied upon by the Government involved an interest in the life tenant which would cease upon her remarriage—a pension, a divorce settlement and payments to a widow during widowhood. In such cases the figures supporting the probability of remarriage in the whole population would naturally show a higher probability of remarriage than in a case in which remarriage would lead to the loss of income, and any error in the actuarial result would be on the safe side. On the other hand, in the cases cited by the taxpayer, as well as in the present case, there was a decided inducement to remarry so that the life tenant could

¶ 20,022

leave a descendant. This would tend to make the actuarial figures too low to apply to any case where such inducement existed, but no statistics can possibly even approximate how much too low. If the actuarial estimates of the probability of remarriage are too low, then the estimate of the value of the reversion must be too high, but again there is no possibility of saying how much too high.

Granted that the mere fact that an act is voluntary does not defeat the possibility of determining statistically the probability of its occurrence, yet, where inducements of widely varying potency and rewards of widely varying attractiveness are offered to people of widely varying personalities, it is manifestly impossible to arrive at a statistical analysis sufficiently accurate to permit of any intelligent valuation of reversion. Nor, in the nature of things, is any advance in the actuarial art conceivable, which would meet the difficulty.

My conclusion is that the reversionary interest in the present case does not have any ascertainable value under the applicable valuation principles and it, therefore, must be considered to have a valuation of zero.

I have carefully considered the argument of the Government that the conclusion of its actuary contained in his affidavit is an opinion as to a fact and that the taxpayer must offer evidence to show that it is unsound, thus creating a factual issue and preventing summary judgment. The actuary's valuation of the reversion was based on the assumption that the marriage between the son and his wife would not be dissolved except by death. Even accepting such assumption as a fact, the question is still whether the probability of the husband's remarriage can be ascertained [by] actuarial procedure in a case where the devolution of a large estate depends upon it and the birth of progeny offers substantial inducements to remarry. In such case, it seems to me, no results obtained by any kind of actuarial procedure can reach a higher level than a guess.

Judgment may be entered for the plaintiff.

AFFIRMED.

Notes

[¶ 20,023]

1.   Are the court in *Cardeza* and the Conference Committee Report on which the court based its opinion misreading the Supreme Court in *Robinette*, ¶ 14,007? In that case, the Court confronted a situation where three donors had contributed property to a trust and retained life estates for themselves with the remainder payable to the unborn issue of one of the donors, an unmarried young woman, when the unborn issue reach age 21. In the event of failure of this event, the corpus of the trust was to be distributed as designated by the will of the last survivor of the three donors. In determining the amount that was subject to the gift tax, the parties sought to have the gift tax imposed on the value that each transferred to the trust, less the value of their retained life estates and the value of their reversions. In a less than

clear opinion, the Court refused to fix a value for the reversions and allowed no exclusion from the gift tax for a value attributable to them. If *Robinette* is viewed as a burden of proof case, with the taxpayer having the burden of proof as the law then stood, then a different result should be obtained in *Cardeza*. It is possible to read *Robinette* as holding that, in computing the amount of the gift, no discount should be allowed for the value of potential reversionary interests because of the inability of the taxpayer to establish actuarially the value of the likelihood that the young unmarried female beneficiary would produce an issue who would survive until the age of 21. So construed, *Robinette* thus becomes a burden of proof case, that is to say, since the taxpayer could not meet his burden of proof in valuing a reversion, no discount was allowed with respect to it. Seemingly, the Court in *Robinette* would allow the taxpayer to meet his burden of proof in seeking a discount only by providing evidence that could be actuarially determined. This is far different from reading the case as holding, as the Conference Committee did, that in all cases where a reversionary interest does not have an ascertainable value, its value will be deemed to equal zero. Indeed, if *Robinette* is merely viewed as a burden of proof case, Cardeza's estate should have been deemed not to have met its burden of proof in establishing actuarially that the value of the decedent's reversion was less than five percent. Perhaps this reading of the authorities is what prompted the Senate Finance Committee in its report on § 2037 under the 1954 Code to comment:

> Where it is apparent from the facts that property could have reverted to the decedent under contingencies that were not remote, the reversionary interest is not to be regarded as having no value merely because the value thereof cannot be measured precisely. S. Rep. No. 1622, 83d Cong., 2d Sess. at 469.

It might be beneficial here to review and reconsider the materials dealing with contingent interests in Chapter 15 (¶ 15,085 et seq.).

2. Would it not have been appropriate for the court in *Cardeza* to have merely valued decedent's reversion using normal actuarial techniques and ignoring the possibility that her 59 year old daughter-in-law would produce a child or that taxpayer's 64 year old son might take up with another woman and that issue would result? If the court in *Cardeza* is correct, the five percent reversion requirement can always be defeated by injecting into the mix a non-actuarial wild card which is highly unlikely to disrupt the real world likelihood of decedent enjoying her reversion.

3. Even if valuation of a reversionary interest is to be based entirely on actuarially determinable factors (i.e., life expectancies), opportunities for dispute as to what that value should be still exist. For example, in Manufacturers Hanover Trust Co. v. United States, 775 F.2d 459 (2d Cir.1985), the court agreed that the IRS could use "gender based" mortality tables in calculating the value of retained reversionary interests under § 2037. The result in that case was to render taxable a reversionary interest retained by the female transferor—an interest that would have been nontaxable had a unisex mortality table been used. The Treasury, meanwhile, had nevertheless

issued new "gender neutral" tables based on a higher interest rate. See Reg. § 20.2031–7 applicable to decedents dying after November 30, 1983.

D. DETERMINATION OF AMOUNT INCLUDIBLE

[¶ 20,025]

Bear in mind that the value of the reversionary interest of the decedent-donor is calculated only to determine if we have met one of the two statutory requirements for inclusion under § 2037. If that requirement and the other requirement of § 2037 (an interest which is to be transferred only by surviving) have been met, inclusion results and the value included bears no relationship to the value of the reversionary interest of the decedent. Under § 2037, the value included is the value of those interests which pass to parties by virtue of their surviving the decedent. Illustration of the operation of this principle is provided by Reg. § 20.2037–1(e), Examples 3 and 4, and the ruling which follows.

[¶ 20,031]

REVENUE RULING 76–178

1976–1 C.B. 273.

Advice has been requested whether, under the circumstances described below, the interests transferred in trust are to be included in a decedent's gross estate under section 2037 of the Internal Revenue Code of 1954.

Pursuant to the terms of a trust agreement executed in 1961, the decedent (a male) gave *A* (a female) a life interest in Blackacre, a parcel of income-producing real property. The trust agreement provided that Blackacre would revert to the decedent if the decedent survived *A*; but, if *A* survived the decedent, then upon *A*'s death Blackacre should pass to the decedent's child or to the child's estate.

The decedent died on July 1, 1973, survived by *A* and decedent's child. At the date of decedent's death both the decedent and *A* were aged 88. The fair market value of Blackacre on such date was $100,000.

Section 2037(a) provides that the gross estate includes the value of a property interest that a decedent transferred by trust or otherwise, if (1) possession or enjoyment of the property can, through ownership of such interest, be obtained only by surviving the decedent, and (2) the decedent has retained a reversionary interest in the property, and the value of such reversionary interest immediately before the decedent's death exceeds 5 percent of the value of such property.

Section 2037(b) provides that the term "reversionary interest" includes a possibility that property transferred by the decedent (1) may return to the decedent or the decedent's estate, or (2) may be subject to a power of disposition by the decedent, but such term does not include a possibility that the income alone from such property may return to the decedent or become subject to a power of disposition by the decedent.

Section 20.2037–1(c)(3) of the Estate Tax Regulations provides that the value of the decedent's reversionary interest is computed without regard to whether or not the executor elects the alternate valuation method under section 2032 and without regard to the fact of the decedent's death. The value is ascertained in accordance with recognized valuation principles for determining the value, for estate tax purposes, of future or conditional interests in property under sections 20.2031–1, and 20.2031–10 of the regulations.

Section 20.2037–1(c)(4) of the regulations provides that in order to determine the value of the decedent's reversionary interest the value of the reversionary interest is compared with the value of the transferred property, including interests therein that are not dependent upon survivorship of the decedent.

Upon creation of the trust, A had immediate, absolute, and unconditional enjoyment of a life interest in Blackacre, which would be unaffected by the decedent's subsequent death. Consequently, the transfer of the life interest, does not come within the purview of section 2037. Compare Frank W. Thacher, 20 T.C. 474 (1953), acq., 1954–1 C. B. 7, which reached a contrary conclusion when a spouse's life interest was subject to divestment upon divorce and the property would revert to the decedent.

On the other hand, the vesting of the decedent's child's remainder interest in Blackacre is postponed until the decedent's death. Thus, with respect to the remainder interest the survivorship requirement of section 2037 is satisfied. Under the express terms of the trust agreement, the decedent retained a reversionary interest and includibility of the transferred property depends on whether the value of this reversionary interest meets the percentage requirement of section 2037.

The decedent's reversionary interest is described as the present worth of the right of the decedent (a male aged 88) to receive $100,000 upon the death of A (a female aged 88), provided the decedent survives. The actuarial factor representing this described reversionary interest is 0.43194. (This factor cannot be found in the tables contained in section 20.2031–10(f) of the regulations. Rather, it is a special factor that will be computed by the National Office upon submission of the information specified in section 20.2031–10(f) of the regulations.)

Using the factor of 0.43194 applicable in the present case the value of the decedent's reversionary interest is $43,194 ($100,000 x 0.43194). In determining whether the value of the decedent's reversionary interest exceeds 5 percent of the value of the transferred property, A's life estate is not excluded from such value for purposes of making this determination under section 20.2037–1(c)(4) of the regulations. Since the value of the decedent's reversionary interest exceeds 5 percent of the value of Blackacre, the percentage requirement of section 2037 is satisfied.

The value of the reversionary interest determines the applicability of section 2037, but this is not the interest includible in the decedent's gross estate. Since the decedent's child's possession or enjoyment of the underlying property, through ownership of the remainder interest, is dependent on surviving the decedent, the value of such property less the value of the outstanding life estate in *A* is includible in the decedent's gross estate. Klein v. United States, 283 U.S. 231 (1931), X–1 C.B. 462.

Accordingly, section 2037 requires the inclusion of the entire trust corpus at its date of death value of $100,000 less the value of *A*'s life estate; or using the remainder factor applicable to a female aged 88, as specified in Table A(2) of section 20.2031–10(f) of the regulations, the includible interest is the present worth of the right to receive $100,000 upon the death of a female aged 88 or $81,569 ($100,000 x 0.81569).

Problems

[¶ 20,055]

Note: For purposes of these problems, assume that all reversions in the settlor-decedent exceed five percent in value and that all transfers were made after October 8, 1949.

1. Tom established a trust under which income was to be paid to his wife, Sally, for her life and the remainder was to be distributed to their son, Nick. In the event that Nick dies first and Sally predeceased Tom, the corpus is then to revert to Tom. Tom was survived by both Sally and Nick and, at his death, the trust corpus was worth $750,000. What are the estate tax consequences?

2. John established a trust under which income was to go to a local charity for his life with the remainder to go to his daughter Barbara or her estate. John died four years later and was survived by Barbara. At his death, trust corpus was worth $400,000. What are the estate tax consequences?

3. Anne established a trust under which income was to go to a local charity for her life with the remainder to go to her brother, Bill, if living. Anne died eight years later, survived by Bill, when the value of the trust corpus was $1,200,000. What are the estate tax consequences?

4. Marsha established a trust under which income was to be paid to her husband Eric for his life with the remainder to be distributed to Marsha or if she predeceased Eric to their son Phil or his estate. Marsha died and was survived by Eric and Phil. At her death the trust corpus was worth $1,300,000 and Eric's life estate was worth $500,000. What are the estate tax consequences?

5. Gloria established a trust with $400,000 of corpus. Under the terms of the trust all income was to be accumulated until there was only one child of her father surviving, at which point the corpus and accumulated income were to be distributed to that child. Gloria died and was survived by her brother Macon and her sister Rose. At Gloria's death the trust corpus and accumulated income were worth $900,000. What are the estate tax consequences?

6. Maria established a trust under which income was to go to her husband, Norris, for his life with remainder to their daughter, Barbara, or her estate. In the event Norris divorced Maria, the trust was to terminate and the corpus was to be distributed to Maria. At Maria's death, she and Norris were still happily married and the trust corpus was worth $2,400,000. What are the estate tax consequences?

7. Ron established a trust with income to his wife, Paula, for her life, remainder to their son, Joe, or his estate. In the event that Paula divorced or predeceased Ron, the trust was to terminate and corpus was to be distributed to Ron. At Ron's death the entire trust corpus was worth $1,000,000 and Paula's life estate was actuarially determined to be worth $400,000. What are the estate tax consequences?

8. Under the intestate statutes in the State of Bliss, the property of an individual who dies without a will and who is survived by a spouse and issue is to be divided accordingly, one-third to the surviving spouse and the balance equally among issue. Where there is no surviving spouse and only issue, the property is to be divided equally among issue. Where there is a surviving spouse and no surviving issue, the surviving spouse will take all property under the intestate laws of Bliss. Where a child dies and is survived only by parents, that child's property is to be divided equally between the parents and, if the child is survived by only one parent, that parent will inherit all the child's property.

Martin established a trust under which income was to be distributed to his wife, Lisa, for her life with remainder to Lisa's heirs under the intestate law of the State of Bliss in effect at her death. Martin died and was survived by Lisa and their daughter, Nancy. At Martin's death the entire corpus of the trust was worth $900,000 and the actuarially computed value of Lisa's life estate was $300,000. What are the estate tax consequences?

9. Martin also established a second trust under which income was to go to his daughter, Nancy, for her life with remainder to go to her heirs under Bliss's intestate laws. As in the preceding problem, Martin died and was survived by both Lisa and Nancy. At Martin's death, the entire corpus of his trust was worth $1,200,000 and the actuarially computed value of Nancy's life estate was worth $800,000. What are the estate tax consequences?

Chapter 21

ANNUITIES AND RETIREMENT BENEFITS

(Section 2039)

A. THE NATURE AND IMPORTANCE OF ANNUITIES

[¶ 21,001]

The term "annuity" is derived from the Latin *annus*, for "year." The year reference is appropriate because the purchase of a traditional annuity involves the conversion of a lump sum into periodic (such as annual) payments. The purchaser of an annuity transfers a lump sum to an annuity or insurance company; in return, the company agrees to pay to the beneficiary a designated amount each year for an agreed period of years. The purchaser is said to "annuitize" the lump sum, and the beneficiary of the annual payments is called the "annuitant." (Although the year reference remains incorporated in these terms, in modern practice payments are more likely to be made monthly or quarterly.)

Annuities can offer unique advantages in appropriate circumstances. Assume, for example, that a childless 76–year old widow has finite resources of $200,000 to support her for the rest of her life. She could invest the $200,000 and live on the earnings—perhaps $10,000 per year. But this amount may be inadequate, and especially so if she encounters health problems. Furthermore, this approach essentially "wastes" the principal, which will not itself be used for the widow's benefit, but instead may go to a distant relative, friend, or charity at the widow's death. Alternatively, the widow could consume a portion of the principal each year, but this would decrease future income. Worse still, if the widow lives longer than expected, she may consume the entire principal and find herself destitute.

The solution is an annuity. The widow transfers $200,000 to an annuity or insurance company in exchange for the company's commitment to pay an agreed amount to the widow each year for as long as she lives. The company knows that the average life expectancy of a 76–year old is approximately 10 years. Therefore, the company is willing to commit to pay 10% of the principal, or $20,000, to the widow each year. In addition, the company will have the principal (beginning at $200,000 and gradually declining) to invest, yielding perhaps $60,000 over the expected 10–year period. After subtracting $10,000 for its profit, the company can commit to pay $50,000 in earnings to the widow—providing an additional $5,000 per year. Therefore, the company will commit to pay $25,000 to the widow each year for as long as she lives.

This is a perfect solution from the widow's viewpoint. She has raised her annual expendable resources from $10,000 to $25,000. She gets full benefit from the principal, and she is assured of the $25,000 annual amount regardless of how long she lives. The company may or may not make a profit, depending on whether the widow lives for fewer or more than 10 years. However, because the company will have entered into similar contracts with many other 76–year olds, the company can rely on the high probability that the average longevity of this group will be 10 years. Therefore, the company is likely to achieve the expected results for the group as a whole.

While traditional annuities of this kind remain important, the market has spawned numerous modifications and additional features designed to meet specific needs and objectives.

One of these is the "variable" annuity. Here the company does not guarantee a specific annual payment amount, but invests the principal in an agreed vehicle, such as a common stock fund. The return to the annuitant depends on the investment experience of the fund, including appreciation or depreciation as well as dividends. Hence the payment to the annuitant will vary over the years—a risk assumed by the annuitant.

A popular modification is the "refund" annuity. A parent purchasing an annuity for life may not want to take the risk arising from the parent's death shortly after the purchase, which would create a windfall for the annuity company and deprive the parent's children of assets they would have received had the annuity not been purchased. In response to this concern, the company will guarantee a refund to designated beneficiaries if the total payout to the parent does not reach a certain level. For example, the contract might provide that if the parent dies before receiving an amount equal to the original investment, the difference between the original investment and the amount actually received will be paid to a designated beneficiary, such as a child. Of course, this refund feature has a cost, and insertion of the refund feature will require a reduction in the periodic payments to be made during the life of the parent.

Another version of the refund feature is a contract guaranteeing payments for a minimum number of years, such as ten. If the annuitant dies before expiration of the ten-year period, his designated beneficiaries will continue to receive payments through the tenth year. Again, such a guaranteed term feature has a cost, and inclusion of this feature will require that the periodic payment amount be reduced.

¶ 21,001

An often used variant is the "survivor" annuity, whereby an annuity is paid to a survivor after the death of the original annuitant. For example, a wife might purchase an annuity providing $2,000 per month for herself during her life, and $1,500 per month for her husband throughout his life after the wife's death, should the husband survive.

By far the most important development is the adoption of the annuity as the preferred method for payment of retirement benefits. As retirement benefits have expanded dramatically since World War II, employers have typically chosen to make those benefits available in the form of periodic payments, rather than as lump sums. Even where employers have permitted retiring employees to elect either annuities or lump sums, a periodic payout is often elected. The same is true of payout patterns for retirement funds created by the employee or taxpayer herself, such as IRAs. Periodic payments are the vehicle of choice for tax qualified plans, primarily because they have the effect of perpetuating the income tax shelter as long as possible. For these reasons, the vast majority of retirement plan benefits are received in some form of periodic or "annuity" payment.

The expansion of the availability and attractiveness of tax qualified retirement plans, together with the long-term rise in equity values since World War II, has vastly expanded the amount invested in retirement funds. These are now a major wealth receptacle for American society. These plans, the great majority of which involve periodic or annuity payments of some kind, are increasingly important—often dominant—assets of the estates of our aging population.

B. GENERAL TAXATION PRINCIPLES

[¶ 21,009]

The taxation of annuities is governed by § 2039. An annuity is included in the gross estate if both of two tests (greatly simplified here) are met:

1. The decedent must have had an entitlement to payments—either current or prospective—during his life.

2. Another person must receive benefits by reason of surviving the decedent.

The application of these two rules produces results entirely consistent with the estate tax principles developed earlier, as is demonstrated by these examples:

1. Assume that the decedent was receiving a monthly payment of $1,000 at the time of his death. Under the annuity contract, the payments terminate at the decedent's death, and no one is entitled to payments after the decedent's death. Here the second test is not satisfied, and nothing will be included in the decedent's gross estate. There is no asset remaining after the decedent's death; hence there is no transfer and nothing to tax. This is consistent with the principle developed in

Chapter 15: the estate tax has no application to assets that terminate or disappear by reason of the decedent's death.

2. Assume that the decedent was not entitled to payments during his life. The annuity contract provides that beginning upon the decedent's death, and continuing for ten years thereafter, payments of $1,000 per month are to be made to a child of the decedent. Here the first test is not satisfied, and § 2039 is not applicable. The reason is that, at least on the facts given, there is no indication that the decedent retained an interest in the property until his death. Provisions other than § 2039, however, might cause the annuity to be subjected to gift or estate tax. If the decedent purchased the annuity prior to his death and retained no power to change the beneficiary, the purchase would have constituted a completed gift to the child, and a taxable gift would have occurred when the annuity was purchased. If, on the other hand, the decedent purchased the annuity prior to his death but reserved a power to control beneficial enjoyment (such as changing the beneficiary), the purchase would not have been a completed taxable gift, but the annuity would be included in the decedent's gross estate because of the decedent's retained power, pursuant to §§ 2036 and 2038.

3. Assume that the decedent was receiving payments of $1,000 per month at the time of death, and that the contract provides that beginning at the decedent's death and continuing for ten years thereafter, the decedent's daughter is to receive payments of $750 per month. Here both § 2039 tests are met, and the annuity will be included in the decedent's gross estate pursuant to § 2039. The amount included is the value of the annuity immediately after the decedent's death. As explained below, that value is the cost of an annuity of $750 per month for 10 years, under interest rates prevailing at the decedent's death.

The two tests described above state only the core of § 2039. Although § 2039 is mercifully short, it is packed with additional rules and qualifications, the most important of which are these:

1. The annuity is included in the decedent's gross estate only to the extent the decedent contributed the funds to purchase the annuity. § 2039(b). This rule is appropriate because there has been no transfer that can legitimately be taxed if the annuity does not ultimately derive from the decedent's resources. For example, if a mother purchases an annuity providing for payments for her daughter during the daughter's life, followed by payments to a son during his life, there would be no inclusion of the annuity in the daughter's gross estate at the daughter's death because the daughter did not purchase the annuity. If the daughter provided a part of the consideration for the annuity, that proportionate part of the total annuity value would be included in her gross estate. For example, if the daughter provided 40% of the total purchase cost, 40% of the total value would be included in the daughter's gross estate.

¶ 21,009

2. For purposes of the rule stated in the preceding paragraph, any contribution to the annuity by the decedent's employer or former employer is treated as if the employee herself made the contribution, provided the contribution is made by reason of the decedent's employment. § 2039(b). The rationale is that the contribution in essence constitutes additional compensation to the employee and should be viewed as first distributed to the employee, followed by contribution of that amount by the employee toward the annuity. This rule has immense importance because it subjects to estate tax the many noncontributory retirement plans, i.e., those purchased entirely with funds provided by the employer. It also causes inclusion in the gross estate of the entirety of retirement plans purchased jointly by the employer and employee.

3. The annuity is included in the decedent's gross estate if the survivor's entitlement to payments is based on "any form of contract or agreement * * * other than as insurance under policies on the life of the decedent." § 2039(a). This rule makes it clear that the nature of the contract or agreement makes no difference; any arrangement for payments (other than life insurance) is covered, whether or not denominated an annuity. Life insurance is entirely excluded from § 2039, leaving § 2033 and § 2042 to determine inclusion in the gross estate, as explained in Chapter 17.

4. The first core requirement—that the decedent be currently or prospectively entitled to payments—can be satisfied in either of two ways. One is current receipt of payments by the decedent at the time of his death. The other is entitlement to payments at a later date, such as subsequent to retirement. For example, assume that an employee dies while still employed, and that the employer has provided a plan that would have made payments to the employee after his retirement had he lived, with continuing payments to the employee's designated beneficiary upon the employee's death. The prospective entitlement to payments satisfies the first test, and the annuity will be included in the employee's gross estate. The issue becomes more complex, however, where there are conditions imposed on the employee's prospective entitlement, and those conditions might or might not be met at a later date. The Regulations resolve this issue by providing that the decedent will be treated as having satisfied the required conditions if he satisfies the conditions as of the date of death. Reg. § 20.2039–1(b)(1).

5. The fact that the decedent received payments at some point during his life is not sufficient to satisfy the first test. The annuity is included in the decedent's gross estate only if the decedent's entitlement is to payments "for his life or for any period not ascertainable without reference to his death or for any period which does not in fact end before his death." § 2039(a). This language replicates the retained life estate language of § 2036(a) and confirms that the annuity should be included in the decedent's gross estate only if the passage

of the annuity to the survivor beneficiary has a testamentary or death-related character. That is the case in the typical situation, where the annuity payments are to continue until the decedent's death. If, however, the annuity payments are to be made for a specific period, such as ten years, and the last payment is made prior to the decedent's death, the first test is not satisfied, and there is no inclusion by reason of § 2039. There might, however, be inclusion under another provision, such as § 2036 or § 2038, if the decedent had retained until his death the power to designate the recipient of the payments after his death.

6. The requirement that the decedent be entitled to payments during his life is satisfied even if he had only the right to receive payment jointly with another person. § 2039(a).

In many cases imposition of estate tax on annuities is prevented by the marital deduction, covered in Chapter 27. A typical example is the joint and survivor annuity, providing for payments to one spouse throughout that spouse's life, followed by payments to the surviving spouse. If no payments are to be made after the death of both spouses, the entire annuity will qualify for the marital deduction upon the death of the first spouse to die, and there will be nothing to tax at the death of the surviving spouse. Special marital deduction rules relating to annuities are discussed at ¶ ¶ 27,271 and 27,364.

Under current estate tax law there is no special exclusion for tax qualified plans or IRA's. The § 2039 Regulations are confusing because they continue to refer to § 2039(c), which generally exempted tax qualified retirement plans from inclusion in the gross estate under § 2039(a). That version of § 2039(c) was repealed in 1984. Similarly, the Regulations continue to refer to § 2039(e), which excluded IRA benefits from inclusion under § 2039(a). Section 2039(e) was repealed in 1986.

The following committee report that accompanied enactment of § 2039 provides a helpful summary of the § 2039 rules.

[¶ 21,017]

EXCERPTS FROM SENATE COMMITTEE REPORT ON THE REVENUE ACT OF 1954

Senate Report No. 1622, 83d Cong. 2d sess. at p. 470.

§ 2039. Annuities. * * * With certain limitations, this section requires the inclusion in the decedent's gross estate of the value of an annuity or other payments receivable by any beneficiary by reason of surviving the decedent under any form of contract or agreement (other than as insurance under policies on the life of the decedent) * * * if under the contract or agreement an annuity or other payment was payable to the decedent, or the decedent possessed the right to receive such annuity or payment, either alone or in conjunction with another for his life or for any period not ascertainable without reference to his death or for any period which does not in fact end before his death. * * * [T]he provisions of this section apply not only to cases

¶ 21,009

where an annuity was payable to a decedent but also to contracts or agreements under which a lump-sum payment was payable to the decedent or the decedent possessed the right to receive such a lump-sum payment in lieu of an annuity. For purposes of this section, the term "annuity" includes periodic payments for a specified period of time. The following are examples of contracts, but are not necessarily the only forms of contracts to which this section applies:

(1) A contract under which the decedent immediately before his death was receiving or was entitled to receive for the duration of his life an annuity, or other stipulated payment, with payments thereunder to continue after his death to a designated beneficiary if surviving the decedent.

(2) A contract under which the decedent immediately before his death was receiving or was entitled to receive, together with another person, an annuity, or other stipulated payment payable to the decedent and such other person for their joint lives, with payments thereunder to continue to the survivor following the death of either.

(3) A contract or agreement entered into by the decedent and his employer under which the decedent immediately before his death and following retirement was receiving or was entitled to receive an annuity or other stipulated payment, payable to the decedent for the duration of his life and thereafter to a designated beneficiary, if surviving the decedent, whether the payments after the decedent's death are fixed by the contract, or subject to an option or election exercised or exercisable by the decedent.

(4) A contract or agreement entered into by the decedent and his employer under which at decedent's death, prior to retirement or prior to the expiration of a stated period of time, an annuity or other payment was payable to a designated beneficiary if surviving the decedent.

(5) A contract or agreement under which the decedent immediately before his death was receiving or was entitled to receive an annuity for a stated period of time, with the annuity or other payment to continue to a designated beneficiary, upon the decedent's death prior to the expiration of such period, if surviving the decedent.

The amount to be included in the gross estate is the value at the decedent's death of the annuity or other payment receivable by the survivor of the decedent, and it is immaterial whether the payments to the survivor are payable in a lump sum, in installments, in the same, or in a greater or lesser amount than the annuity or payment to the decedent.

This section applies only to that part of the value of the annuity or other payment receivable by the surviving beneficiary which the decedent's contribution to the purchase price of the contract or agreement bears to the total purchase price thereof. For example, assume that the value of the annuity to the beneficiary at decedent's death is $20,000 and that the decedent contributed one half of the purchase price of the contract. In such case, $10,000 would be includible in the decedent's gross estate.

¶ 21,017

In determining the amount of the decedent's contribution to the purchase price of the contract, there shall be taken into account contributions made by his employer, if made by reason of decedent's employment * * *.

* * *

The provisions of this section shall not prevent the application of any other provision of law relating to the estate tax. For example, if a contract provides for a refund of a portion of the cost thereof, in the event of the decedent's premature death, payable to the decedent's estate the amount thereof shall be treated as any other property of the decedent. This section does not, however, apply to insurance under policies on the life of the decedent to which § 2042 is applicable.

The provisions of this section are applicable only to annuities or other payments payable to the decedent, or which the decedent possessed the right to receive, either alone or in conjunction with another for his life or for any period not ascertainable without reference to his death or for any period which does not in fact end before his death. The rules applicable under § 2036 in determining whether the annuity or other payment was payable to the decedent, or whether he possessed the right thereto, for his life or such periods shall be applicable under this section.

Note

[¶ 21,019]

The reach of § 2039(b) was tested in Estate of Shackleford v. United States, 98–2 USTC ¶ 60,320, 82 AFTR2d 98–5538 (E.D.Cal.1998), aff'd, 262 F.3d 1028 (9th Cir. 2001). In *Shackleford* the decedent had won a California lottery prize entitling him to twenty annual payments of $508,000 each. The decedent had received only three payments prior to his death. The executor contended that the right to receive seventeen additional payments constituted an annuity and was therefore controlled by § 2039. The executor further argued that § 2039(b) limited inclusion in the gross estate to the amount of the decedent's contribution—the one dollar the decedent had paid for the ticket. The court could find no convincing way to defeat this argument. Nevertheless, the court concluded that § 2039(b) should not be applied because "the lottery payments represent the accumulated wealth of the decedent." The court's alternative conclusion was that the prospective payments should be included as property owned under § 2033. As a result, the entire present value of the prospective payments was included in the decedent's estate, although valuation remained to be determined, as discussed at ¶ 10,019.

C. VALUATION

[¶ 21,021]

Valuation of an annuity that is included in a decedent's gross estate is entirely prospective. The age of the decedent and the payments to which the decedent was entitled prior to death are irrelevant. All that matters is the value to be received by the person or persons who become entitled to payments by reason of the decedent's death.

The general rule is that an annuity is valued using the §§ 20.2031–7 tables, applying the current § 7520 rate, as explained in Chapter 10. If, however, the annuity is issued by a company regularly engaged in the sale of annuities, the annuity is valued under Reg. §§ 20.2031–8 and 25.2512–6. Reg. §§ 20.2031–7(b) and 25.2512–5(b). Under these provisions, the value of such a "commercial annuity" is determined by the cost charged by the company for comparable contracts. §§ 20.2031–8(a)(1) and 25.2512–6(a).

Problem

[¶ 21,029]

Jane Treadway died at the age of 60, survived by her son, Wilfong, age 40. At the time of her death Jane was employed by Corbin, Inc., a manufacturer of hardware. Jane supervised the accounting department of Corbin, Inc.

Jane was a strong believer in annuities as an investment and estate planning device. For that reason she had invested a substantial amount of her savings in certain annuities, and Corbin, Inc. had joined her in purchase of one annuity. These annuity contracts are described below.

In the case of each annuity contract, indicate whether the annuity should be included in Jane's gross estate, whether under § 2039 or another section.

1. Jane purchased Annuity 1 with her own funds five years prior to her death, irrevocably naming Wilfong as the beneficiary. This annuity provides $10,000 per year for Wilfong throughout his life, beginning at Jane's death. Jane was not entitled to any payments during her life.

2. Jane purchased Annuity 2 with her own funds. It provides $10,000 per year for Jane throughout her life, beginning at age 55, and after Jane's death to Wilfong throughout his life. Jane was receiving annuity payments at the time of her death.

3. Jane purchased Annuity 3 with her own funds. It provides $10,000 per year for Jane throughout her life, beginning at age 70, and then throughout Wilfong's life as well. If Jane should die before attaining age 70, the annuity to Wilfong is to start immediately.

4. Jane purchased Annuity 4 with her own funds. It provides $10,000 per year for Jane throughout her life, beginning at age 55. The payments end at Jane's death. Jane was receiving the annuity at the time of her death.

5. Annuity 5 was purchased one-half with funds furnished by Jane and one-half with funds furnished by Corbin, Inc. It provides $10,000 per year for Jane throughout her life, beginning at age 65, and then throughout Wilfong's life as well. Jane and Wilfong would become entitled to the annuity only if, at the earlier of Jane's death or attainment of age 65, Jane was employed by Corbin, Inc. If Jane

¶ 21,029

should die while employed by Corbin, Inc. and before attaining age 65, the annuity to Wilfong would begin immediately.

D. COMBINING ANNUITIES WITH OTHER BENEFITS

[¶ 21,041]

ESTATE OF BAHEN v. UNITED STATES

Court of Claims of the United States, 1962.
305 F.2d 827.

DAVIS, Judge:

The estate of a former high-ranking officer of The Chesapeake and Ohio Railway Company claims that sums paid by the C. & O. to his widow on his death in 1955, under benefit plans unilaterally adopted by the railroad in 1952 and 1953, were improperly included in his gross estate for tax purposes.

* * *

After Mr. Bahen's death, the C. & O. made payments to his widow under two plans which it had earlier established for its employees. The first was the Death Benefit Plan, adopted in January 1952, which provided that, if a covered employee with more than 10 years' service died while in the company's employ and before becoming eligible for retirement, the C. & O. would pay, "in recognition of the services rendered by him", a sum equal to three months' salary to his widow or (if she died prior to payment) to the guardian of any of his minor children.

The more significant arrangement was the Deferred Compensation Plan adopted by the company in February 1953 for forty of its officers and executives. For a designated officer who was under 60 at that time, like Mr. Bahen, the C. & O. would pay a stated maximum sum ($100,000 in Mr. Bahen's case), at his death either before or after retirement, to his widow and to those of his surviving children under 21 the officer might specify (and in the proportions he designated), in 60 equal monthly installments. These payments were to be made only if a wife or minor child survived the officer and would continue only so long as there was a surviving wife or child under 21. However, if prior to retirement the officer became totally incapacitated, mentally or physically, for further performance of duty, the payments would be made to him in 60 equal monthly installments so long as he survived, any unpaid installment going to his widow or minor children. The president of the company was to notify each officer covered by the Plan of the benefits payable to him and was also "to represent that the Plan is irrevocable, not subject to later withdrawal by this Board [of Directors], and represents a firm commitment on the part of the company to extend benefits in accordance with the terms and conditions herein set forth." Mr. Bahen was immediately notified of this Deferred Compensation Plan and its irrevocability.

* * *

¶ 21,029

Section 2039 was a development of the earlier provisions of the estate tax which spoke of the decedent's "property" and of "transfers" by the decedent in contemplation of or taking effect at death. See § 811 of the Internal Revenue Code of 1939. The new section does not use that phraseology but frames its operative requirements more directly in terms of particular types of transactions or arrangements involving the decedent. This change is significant. We must pay heed to the precise new form in which Congress cast its net and not become entangled in the older meshes.

A. *The Deferred Compensation Plan*: We first consider the application of § 2039 (and the Regulations) to the C. & O's major plan, the Deferred Compensation Plan (of 1953) under which $100,000 was paid to Mrs. Bahen in a five-year span. As we read the section and the Regulations, they demand inclusion in the estate of the proceeds of this Plan. Every requirement is squarely met, not only in literal terms but in harmony with the legislative aim.

1. There is, initially, no doubt that the Plan, though adopted by the company unilaterally and without negotiation with the officers and employees, was a "form of contract or agreement" under the statute. This phrase is defined by § 20.2039–1(b)(1)(ii) of the Treasury Regulations on Estate Tax to include "any arrangement, understanding or plan, or any combination of arrangements, understandings, or plans arising by reason of the decedent's employment." A compensation plan unilaterally adopted by the employer, but made irrevocable and communicated to the employee, falls directly within this definition, at least where the employee continues in the company's service after the adoption of the plan.

2. There is likewise no doubt that Mrs. Bahen, the beneficiary, received "an annuity or other payment" under the statute when she was paid the $100,000 in sixty equal installments. The Regulations (Sec. 20.2039–1(b)(1)(ii)) appropriately say that this double term in § 2039, as used with respect to both the beneficiary and the decedent, "has reference to one or more payments extending over any period of time", and that the payments may "be equal or unequal, conditional or unconditional, periodic or sporadic." * * *

3. The next problem is whether at Mr. Bahen's death there was payable to him or he possessed the right to receive *"an annuity or other payment."* The Deferred Compensation Plan provided that, if Mr. Bahen became totally incapacitated for further performance of duty before retirement, the C. & O. would pay him the $100,000 in 60 equal monthly installments. Under both the normal understanding of the statutory words "annuity or other payment" and the broad definition given them by the Regulations (referred to above), these sums must be characterized as at least an "other payment." Stressing Congress's use of the singular ("payment") and a reference in the Senate Committee Report to a lump-sum payment in lieu of an annuity, plaintiff appears to urge that the *only* "payment" to a decedent covered by § 2039 is a lump sum paid or payable in the

place of a strict lifetime annuity (i.e., an annuity paid in the form of a lump sum). But we cannot confine the general language of § 2039, as interpreted by the Regulations, within the limits of one illustration given by the Committee as a reason for adding the all-inclusive words "other payment" to "annuity." As we point out more in detail below, the history and pattern of § 2039 fail to indicate that it deals only with true lifetime annuities (in installment form or in a commuted lump sum). The statute covers—as an "other payment", at least—disability compensation benefits of the type involved here.

4.   Were these benefit payments—assuming, as we have just decided, that they constituted an "annuity or other payment" within § 2039—"payable to" Mr. Bahen at his death or did he "possess the right to receive such annuity or payment"? The Regulations (Sec. 20.2039–1(1)(ii)) establish that amounts are "payable" to a decedent "if, at the time of his death, the decedent was in fact receiving an annuity or other payments, whether or not he had an enforceable right to have payments continue." Since Mr. Bahen was not receiving disability benefits when he died, this term of the statute is not satisfied.

We hold, however, that at his death Mr. Bahen did "possess the right" to receive the disability payments in the future if certain conditions were fulfilled, and therefore that the alternative requirement of § 2039 is met. The intentional juxtaposition in the statute of amounts "payable" and those the decedent "possessed the right to receive" indicates that the former relates to the present (i.e. at time of death) and the latter to the future. The Regulations make clear that, in circumstances like these, the decedent's interest in future benefits, even if contingent, is sufficient. Where the employer has offered a plan of this kind, the employee's compliance with his obligations to the company gives him "an enforceable right to receive payments in the future, whether or not, at the time of his death, he had a present right to receive payments." This provision of the Regulations both governs the Deferred Compensation Plan and faithfully reflects its essential characteristics. The arrangement may have been unilateral in inception but it was also irrevocable, and its irrevocability was deliberately communicated to the individuals covered. It thus became an integral article of Mr. Bahen's terms of employment by the C. & O. * * * There can be no doubt that he and the others relied upon the Plan, as they were expected to do. * * * The right they possessed may have been contingent but it was not at the whim of the employer. * * *

In answer, the plaintiff insists that the decedent cannot be considered to have "possessed the right to receive" these disability payments because they were contingent on his becoming totally disabled before retirement, and would never have been received had he lived healthily to retirement age. Only future payments which are sure to be paid if the decedent lives to a designated time are covered by § 2039, plaintiff says. However, as we have pointed out, in specifically covering amounts not payable to the decedent at the time of his death but which he then had merely the "right to receive", the statute and the Regulations obviously cover sums becoming due in the future; and there is no support in the statute's language for the distinction plaintiff makes between the different types of such future payments (at least if they are not forfeitable at the will of another). Both classes of payment are contingent and neither is sure. A benefit payable only if a man lives to a certain age is conditioned upon his living that long, just as a benefit payable only if he becomes disabled is conditional on his future disability. Any distinction between the types seems rejected by the Regulations which include "conditional" payments without qualification. * * * Moreover, the comparable term "right to income" in related earlier provisions of the estate tax (such as present § 2036, former § 811(c)(1)(B)) has been in effect read as including a contingent right to receive income. * * * The legislative history of § 2039 suggests that the rules applicable under § 2036, in this connection, should likewise control under the new provision. S. Rept. No. 1622, 83d Cong., 2d Sess., at p. 472; H. Rept. No. 1337, 83d Cong., 2d Sess., at p. A316. * * *

5. Another requirement of § 2039 is that the decedent's right to receive payments must be possessed "for his life or for any period not ascertainable without reference to his death or for any period which does not in fact end before his death." For the period from February 1953, when the Deferred Compensation Plan was adopted, to his death in November 1955, Mr. Bahen had the right to receive, under this Plan, $100,000 in 60 installments upon his total disability prior to retirement. He thus possessed the right to receive this "annuity or other payment" for a period which did not in fact end before his death—and, accordingly, this element of § 2039 is also present. The correctness of this conclusion is shown by the Regulations (Sec. 20.2039–1(b)(2)), Example (5) of which concerns a plan under which an employer-contributed fund is to be divided, on retirement at age 60, one-half in a lump sum to the employee and one-half to his beneficiary, the entire amount going to the beneficiary if the employee died before retiring. The Regulations state that if the employee dies before retirement the payment to the beneficiary is includible in gross estate under § 2039 because "the decedent possessed the right to receive a lump sum payment [at retirement] for a period which did not in fact end before his death [before retirement]." This regulation is consistent with the holdings, under older provisions of the estate tax, relating to the meaning of the phrase "for any period which does not in fact end before his death" * * *—rulings which Congress has indicated should be applied under § 2039. S. Rept. No. 1622, 83d Cong., 2d Sess., at p. 472; H. Rept. No. 1337, 83d Cong., 2d Sess., at p. A316.

6. The last element necessary for coverage by § 2039 is that Mr. Bahen must have "contributed" the "purchase price" of the "annuity or other payment" received by Mrs. Bahen which is to be included in the taxable estate. Subsection (b), which adds this requirement, provides:

"(b) *Amount includible.*—Subsection (a) shall apply to only such part of the value of the annuity or other payment receivable under such contract or agreement as is proportionate to that part of the purchase price therefor contributed by the decedent. For purposes of this section, any contribution by the decedent's employer or former employer to the purchase price of such contract or agreement (whether or not to an employee's trust or fund forming part of a pension, annuity, retirement, bonus or profit sharing plan) shall be considered to be contributed by the decedent if made by reason of his employment."

The second sentence of this subsection automatically attributes the employer's contribution to the employee "if made by reason of his employment." This phrase is given broad scope by the Senate Committee Report (S. Rept. No. 1622, 83d Cong., 2d Sess., at p. 471) which holds that it applies "if, for example, the annuity or other payment is offered by the employer as an inducement to employment, or a continuance thereof, or if the contributions are made by the employer in lieu of additional compensation or other rights, if so understood by employer and employee, whether or not expressly stated in the contract of employment or otherwise." The Deferred Compensation Plan, we have already noted, plainly meets this standard; it was an inducement to continued service with the C. & O. It is immaterial, we think, that the company did not formally make "contributions" to a separate fund, or actually purchase annuity or like contracts. Section 2039(b) does not use the words "contribution", "contributed", or "purchase price" in a narrow literal sense, any more than subsection (a) uses "contract or agreement" in that rigid fashion. The section deals, for the area it covers, with the substance of transactions, not with the mechanical way they happen to be formulated. The C. & O.'s undertaking to make payment under the Plan was its "contribution," made by reason of the decedent's employment. Congress did not demand that the company create a tangible fund as a condition to coverage of its employees under this new estate tax provision, and so far as we can see there would be no reason to impose that requirement in a taxing statute such as this.

7. To all of this the plaintiff—in addition to challenging the existence in this case of some individual elements of coverage—protests that despite its literal language § 2039 is applicable only where there is a true lifetime annuity payable to the decedent for life. Plaintiff correctly points out that the main impetus for the new section was the doubt in 1954 that the former estate tax provisions covered conventional joint and survivor annuities purchased wholly or partly *by the decedent's employer* (as distinguished from those purchased by the decedent himself). S. Rept. No. 1622, 83d Cong., 2d Sess., at p. 123; H. Rept. No. 1337, 83d Cong., 2d Sess., at p. 90. But the Committee Reports do not indicate that Congress, although using language in § 2039 which goes well beyond the precise situation which initially impelled the change, restricted the scope of the new provision to those very circumstances alone. We find nothing to show that Congress desired the broader words it carefully used in § 2039 not to have their normal significance and application; indeed some of the examples and words Congress used in the Committee Reports show

that wider coverage was plainly intended. And the Treasury Regulations, as our prior discussion explains, cover annuities and payments to a decedent other than a full lifetime annuity.

8. Finally, we note briefly that § 2039, as we construe it, is harmonious with the general objective of the federal estate tax to include in the decedent's estate (with designated exceptions) the valuable interests belonging to, accumulated by, or created by or for him, which pass to others at his death. Many such benefits promised, given, and paid for by an employer were specifically brought within this framework by the new section in 1954. In subsection (b), quoted above, Congress provides that contributions by the employer "shall be considered to be contributed by the decedent if made by reason of his employment." Phrased in terms of the earlier concepts of a decedent's "property" "transferred" at his death, Section 2039 declares that annuities or other payments payable by an employer to his employee, and on his death to a beneficiary, constitute his property—created by him through his employer as part of the employment arrangement and in consideration of his continued services—which is transferred to another at his death. * * * A new provision of the estate tax which attempts to apply these fundamental concepts to a fairly well understood set of concrete situations should not be grudgingly read so as to chip away at the specific rule and to continue (as in the past) to leave as much as possible to the ambiguities of the general sections.

* * *

B. *The Death Benefit Plan*: It is a more difficult question whether the Death Benefit Plan—under which the C. & O. paid Mrs. Bahen a sum equal to Mr. Bahen's salary for three months—is covered by § 2039. Under that arrangement no benefits were payable to the decedent during his life, and if the Plan were to be judged by itself it would fall outside the ambit of the section for lack of "an annuity or other payment" to the decedent. The defendant contends that this factor is present because the words "or other payment" can include the decedent-employee's regular salary; the Death Benefit Plan must be taken, defendant says, together with Mr. Bahen's entire employment arrangement including his ordinary compensation. We cannot agree. Since employees normally receive salary or wages, defendant's interpretation would effectively obliterate, for almost all employees, the express requirement in § 2039 of "an annuity or other payment" to the decedent. If Congress had intended that strange result, it would certainly have mentioned or referred to it. The Government's argument also runs counter to the theory and examples of the Regulations (Sec. 20.2039–1) which impliedly exclude ordinary salary from consideration.

But the Government makes another point which we do accept as bringing the Death Benefit Plan under § 2039. The suggestion is that this Plan should not be viewed in isolation but must be considered together with the Deferred Compensation Plan—as if both arrangements were combined into one plan, providing two types of benefits for beneficiaries after the employee's death but only one type of benefit (disability compensation) to the employee himself.

There is some factual support, if that be necessary, for looking at the two plans together, since the Death Benefit Plan was adopted in January 1952 and the Deferred Compensation Plan only a year later in February 1953. There appears to be a common genesis and a unifying thread.

The firmer legal basis is provided by the Regulations (Sec. 20.2039–1(b)(2), Example (6)) which provide: "All rights and benefits accruing to an employee and to others by reason of the employment (except rights and benefits accruing under certain plans meeting the requirements of section 401(a)(see § 20.2039–2)) are considered together in determining whether or not section 2039(a) and (b) applies. The scope of § 2039(a) and (b) cannot be limited by indirection." Effect must be given to this declaration, adopted pursuant to the Treasury's recognized power to issue regulations and not challenged by plaintiff, since it does not violate the terms or the spirit of § 2039. In view of the general purpose of the statute to cover a large share of employer-contributed payments to an employee's survivors, it is not unreasonable to lump together all of the employer's various benefit plans taking account of the employee's death (except those qualified under § 401(a), which are excepted by the statute, see footnotes 2 and 3, supra) in order to decide whether and to what extent § 2039 applies to his estate. There is no immutable requirement in the legislation that each plan separately adopted by a company must be considered alone. One good ground for rejecting that position is to prevent attempts to avoid the reach of the statute by a series of contrived plans none of which, in itself, would fall under the section.

This directive in the Regulations that all rights and benefits "are to be considered together"—read with another part of the same Regulation which defines "contract or agreement" under § 2039 to cover "any combination of arrangements, understandings, or plans arising by reason of the decedent's employment"—requires the two plans of the C. & O. to be deemed a coordinated whole for the purposes of § 2039. On that view the payments under the Death Benefit Plan were includible in the decedent's gross estate for the reasons given above with respect to the Deferred Compensation Plan. If the two Plans are integrated into one, each element required for coverage of all payments is present.

* * *

[¶ 21,049]

ESTATE OF SCHELBERG v. COMMISSIONER

United States Court of Appeals, Second Circuit, 1979.
612 F.2d 25.

FRIENDLY, Circuit Judge:

This appeal by a taxpayer from a decision of the Tax Court, 70 T.C. 690 (1978), raises a serious question with respect to the interpretation of § 2039, which was added to the Internal Revenue Code in 1954.

I.

Decedent William V. Schelberg was born on March 14, 1914 and died on January 6, 1974 from lung cancer after a week's illness. He was survived by his wife, Sarah, and two daughters, one aged 23 and the other 19. He had been employed by International Business Machines Corp. (IBM) since 1952. At his death he was serving as assistant director of international patent operations at a salary of $4,250 per month.

IBM maintained a variety of employee benefit plans, each adopted at a different time and separately administered. Those here relevant are the Group Life Insurance Plan, the Retirement Plan, the Sickness and Accident Income Plan, and the Total and Permanent Disability Plan. Schelberg was entitled to participate in each.

The Group Life Insurance Plan provided two basic benefits—a group term life insurance, which is not here at issue, and an uninsured and unfunded survivors income benefit, which is. This benefit, determined on the basis of the employee's compensation at the time of death and the amount of the aforementioned life insurance, was payable to a decedent's "eligible" survivors in an order of preference stated in the plan. Payment was to be made monthly, at the rate of one-quarter of the decedent's regular monthly compensation, until the total benefit was exhausted. Payments continued only so long as at least one eligible survivor remained.

The Retirement Plan was a qualified pension plan under I.R.C. § 401. Under IBM's general employment policy, Schelberg would have been required to retire at age 65 and would have been entitled to the retirement benefits provided in the plan.

Under the Sickness and Accident Plan all regular IBM employees were entitled to receive full salary (reduced by any workmen's compensation payments) while absent from work on account of sickness or accident for up to 52 weeks in any 24–month period. Benefits could be continued for more than 52 weeks at IBM's discretion in individual cases; these were known as "individual consideration" benefits.

The Disability Plan covered all IBM employees with more than five years' service. Eligibility was based on determination of "total and permanent disability" by a corporate panel on the basis of medical evidence. The quoted phrase was defined to mean that the employee was unable to perform any employment for pay or profit and had no reasonable expectation of becoming able to do so. Benefits were calculated on the basis of the employee's regular compensation prior to disability, taking account of eligibility for Social Security payments and workmen's compensation. They began on the expiration of the 52–week period of Sickness and Accident benefits plus any period of individual consideration benefits and continued until normal retirement date, at which time the employee became eligible for benefits under the Retirement Plan. During the period of disability an employee remained covered by a variety of other IBM employee plans and could, under certain conditions, accrue further credits under the Retirement Plan. If, contrary to expectation, the employee became able to work again, he was entitled to return, but few

¶ 21,049

did so. As of January 1, 1974, a total of 393 IBM employees out of 150,000 were receiving benefits under the Disability Plan.

At the time of his death Schelberg was not receiving benefits under any of these plans. By virtue of his decease his widow became entitled under the Group Life Insurance Plan to a death benefit of $23,666.67 under the group life insurance policy, and to a survivor's benefit of $1,062.50 per month. The value of the latter amount was not included in decedent's gross estate in his federal tax return, although its existence was reported. The Commissioner of Internal Revenue entered a notice of deficiency on the sole ground that the present value of the survivors annuity, which is stipulated to have been $94,708.83, was includible in the estate pursuant to I.R.C. § 2039. The Tax Court upheld the Commissioner * * *.

II.

The estate does not dispute that the survivors benefit constituted "an annuity or other payment receivable by any beneficiary by reason of surviving the decedent under any form of contract or agreement entered into after March 3, 1931 (other than as insurance under policies on the life of the decedent)" within the opening clause of § 2039(a). It is likewise indisputable that this alone would not suffice to make the survivors benefit includible in the gross estate. The Commissioner must also satisfy the condition that "under such contract or agreement, an annuity or other payment was payable to the decedent, or the decedent possessed the right to receive such annuity or payment, either alone or in conjunction with another for his life or for any period not ascertainable without reference to his death or for any period which does not in fact end before his death."

Not contending that he can satisfy this requirement within the four corners of the Group Life Insurance Plan, the Commissioner asserts that, as provided by the Treasury Regulations, 26 C.F.R. § 20.2039–1(b), he is entitled to consider "any arrangement, understanding or plan, or any combination of arrangements or plans arising by reason of the decedent's employment." Although this is a rather sharp departure from the letter of the statute, ... we accept it with the caveat that while the Commissioner is entitled to "consider" such arrangements, this does not mean that the mere possibility of an employee's receiving some benefit under an arrangement other than that giving rise to the survivors benefit necessarily satisfies the condition of § 2039(a). The Commissioner does not rely on either the Retirement Plan or the Sickness and Accident Plan to satisfy the condition that "an annuity or other payment" was payable to Schelberg. Apart from other considerations, any such reliance is precluded by previous revenue rulings. Revenue Ruling 76–380, 1976–2 C.B. 270, concluded that qualified plans, like the Retirement Plan, and non-qualified plans, like the Survivors Income Benefit Plan, were not to be considered together in determining the applicability of § 2039(a) and (b). [This ruling is based on the rationale that because § 2039 then excluded from the gross estate payments under qualified plans, payments from qualified plans could not be considered as one of the elements constituting "a combination of arrangements or plans" that satisfied the statutory conditions for taxation of other benefits under § 2039.] * * * Revenue Ruling

77–183, 1977–1 C.B. 274, held that benefits such as those Schelberg might have been entitled to under the Sickness and Accident Plan had he lived longer "were in the nature of compensation" and thus no more meet the test set out in the condition than would compensation payments themselves, * * *. This left as the Commissioner's sole reed the fact that, at the time of his death, Schelberg possessed the right that after 52 weeks (or more, if he qualified for "individual consideration") under the Sickness and Accident Plan, he might become entitled to payments under the Disability Plan. The estate contends that Schelberg's rights under the Disability Plan were too dissimilar in nature from an "annuity or other payment" and too contingent to meet the condition of § 2039(a). We agree.

It is worth repeating that the Commissioner's position here would apply to every IBM employee having more than five years' service who dies before attaining age 64 (or taking early retirement) although he neither received nor had any reasonable expectation of receiving anything under the Disability Plan. On the other hand, if he died after attaining age 64 but before taking retirement, the survivors benefit would not be includible since the first twelve months away from work would be covered by the Sickness and Accident Plan and he could never become eligible for the Disability Plan. And, of course, if he died after actually taking retirement, the most common case, the survivors benefit would not be includible by virtue of Revenue Ruling 76–380, 1976–2 C.B. 270. We find nothing in the language of § 2039, in its legislative history, or in the Treasury Regulations sufficient to justify a conclusion that the action of an employer in creating a plan whereby a handful of employees can receive disability benefits because of a rare health or accident syndrome should bring the survivors of all within § 2039.

As recognized by a learned commentator shortly after § 2039 was enacted, the statute was aimed at "annuity contracts under which the purchaser (alone or with a joint annuitant) was entitled to payments for his life, with payments to continue after his death at either the same or a reduced rate, to a survivor." Bittker, Estate and Gift Taxation under the 1954 Code: The Principal Changes, 29 Tul. L. Rev. 453, 469 (1955). While inclusion of the survivor's rights in the estate had been generally sustained, courts had differed as to the reason. Some courts had proceeded on the theory that purchase of the contract was in effect a transfer of property with the reservation of a life estate and thus taxable under the predecessors of I.R.C. § 2036. Others had proceeded on the theory that the transfer was intended to take effect at death. Id. A fundamental purpose of § 2039 was to supply an affirmative answer to the question of inclusion in such cases without further need to debate the theory.

A further purpose, as revealed by the relevant House and Senate Committee reports on what became § 2039 of the revised I.R.C. of 1954, H.R. Rep. No. 1337, 83d Cong. 2d Sess. 90–91, A 314–6 (1954); S. Rep. No. 1622, 83d Cong. 2d Sess. 123–24, 469–72 (1954); H.R. Rep. No. 2543 (Conference Report), 83d Cong. 2d Sess. 74 (1954), was to settle the question of includibility of a joint and survivor annuity where the annuity was purchased by the decedent's employer or both the decedent and the employer made contributions. Congress decided that such an annuity should be included except when the employer's contributions were made pursuant to "an approved trust, pension or retirement plan."

Both text and context show that § 2039 was conceived as dealing only with the problem of what in substance was a joint annuity, although to be sure in all its various ramifications, not with the whole gamut of arrangements under which an employee, his employer or both may create benefits for the employee's survivors. The new section applied only "if, under such contract or agreement, an annuity or other payment was payable to the decedent, or the decedent possessed the right to receive such annuity or payment, either alone or in conjunction with another for his life or for any period not ascertainable without reference to his death or for any period which does not in fact end before his death." If Congress had wished to legislate more broadly, it would have eliminated this clause or chosen more general language for it. The intended sphere of application is made quite clear by the illustrations given in the House and Senate reports "as examples of contracts, but ... not necessarily the only forms of contracts to which this section applies." Under all of these the decedent was receiving or entitled to receive at death what anyone would consider an "annuity or other payment" for the duration of his life or for a stipulated term. Furthermore, in each case the beneficiary succeeded to the interest of the decedent, as in the classic instance of a joint and survivor annuity, quite unlike the present case. Although the term "other payment" is literally broad, Congress was clearly thinking of payments in the nature of annuities—the same types of payments which, if made to the survivor, would be includible in the estate. * * * None of the examples is even close to payments receivable only if the deceased employee might have become totally and permanently disabled had he lived.

We do not consider the case to be altered in the Government's favor by the Treasury Regulations. While these contain some broad language, there is nothing to indicate that their framers addressed the problem here presented. The closest of the illustrations is example (6). While we have no quarrel with this, it is inapposite since the payments both to the employee and to the beneficiary were life annuities. Without endeavoring to be too precise, we deem it plain that, in framing the condition on § 2039(a), Congress was not going beyond benefits the employee was sure to get as a result of his prior employment if he lived long enough. Even more plainly Congress was not thinking of disability payments which an employee would have had only a remote chance of ever collecting had he lived. Not only are the disability payments in this case extremely hypothetical, they are also far from the "annuity or other payment" contemplated by Congress. Courts have, consistent with basic principles of statutory construction, recognized that "annuity or other payment" does not mean "annuity or any payment," but that the phrase is qualitatively limited by the context in which it appears. See Estate of Fusz, supra, 46 T.C. at 217–18. The Service itself has acquiesced in and furthered this view. See Rev. Rul. 77–183, supra. Thus, it seems clear to us that Congress did not intend the phrase to embrace wages, * * *; possible sickness and accident payments, which were a substitute for wages, * * *; or the disability payments involved in this case, which likewise were a partial continuation of wages when an employee's physical health deteriorated even further. The disability payments theoretically achievable here by the decedent in his lifetime are closer to the sickness benefits which he would have received at an early stage of his illness than they are to post-retirement benefits. The Tax Court's treatment of possible disability benefits as presupposing a post-retirement status linked to the widow's ultimate succession thereto seems to us to be unsupported in fact. * * *

III.

The final paragraph of the Tax Court's opinion, 70 T.C. at 705, * * * gives us some reason to think the able judge might have reached the same conclusion as we have if he had not deemed himself bound by authority. Of the cases cited by him, only one, All v. McCobb, 321 F.2d 633 (2 Cir.1963), is binding upon us. We think that he and others have given that decision a significance on the type of issues here presented that is unwarranted, and that most of the other cases are also distinguishable.

In *All* the decedent had been receiving annuities under a non-contributory non-qualified annuity plan and a partially contributory, non-qualified supplemental annuity plan of the Standard Oil Company of New Jersey. His widow received twelve monthly payments under a death benefit for such annuitants. The case for application of § 2039 would seem almost too clear for argument. The sole claim advanced against this by the taxpayer was that the payments were within the exception for insurance—a claim to which this court gave the short shrift that it deserved. The case thus has simply no bearing on the issue here before us.

The most influential decision on what the decedent must receive or be entitled to receive in order to trigger application of § 2039 is Estate of Bahen v. United States, 305 F.2d 827 (Ct.Cl.1962)(Davis, J.). The opinion is indeed a virtuoso performance which has tended to dominate the field to the extent that ... courts seem to look to the *Bahen* opinion rather than to the statute and the committee reports as indicative of the legislative intent. Beyond all this it is of peculiar importance here since it involved a sum payable only in the event of disability, and the Commissioner quite properly relies heavily upon it.

* * *

While * * * [*Bahen*] bears some resemblance to ours, there is a different flavor about it, at least so far as concerns the payments under the Deferred Compensation Plan. There was in fact a unitary right to receive deferred compensation of $100,000 in 60 equal monthly payments, this to be paid to Mrs. Bahen if Bahen died or to him if he became totally disabled prior to retirement. There was no question of grouping separate plans together, since both Mr. and Mrs. Bahen's rights were pursuant to the same Deferred Compensation Plan. Even more to the point, if payments were being made to Mr. Bahen due to his disability and he died prior to exhausting the fund, the remaining payments would be made to Mrs. Bahen. In this respect the Deferred Compensation Plan was much like the joint and survivor annuity at which § 2039 was aimed. Here, of course, Mrs. Schelberg had no rights to any

¶ 21,049

payments under the Disability Plan. The possible payments to Mr. Bahen were not, as under IBM's Disability Plan, true disability payments intended to cover a portion of previous salary; they were deferred compensation, as the plan's title indicates, payable by the railway in any event, to be made available to Mr. Bahen at a date earlier than death if his needs so required. They thus met the test * * * as IBM's disability benefits do not, of being of the same nature as the payments to the beneficiary. We are not sure that the distinction is sufficient or—what is more or less the same thing—that we would have decided *Bahen* as the Court of Claims did. For the moment we shall leave the matter that way.

* * *

We here decide only that to consider a deceased employee's potential ability to have qualified at some future time for payments under a plan protecting against total and permanent disability—a disagreeable feat that had been accomplished as of January 1, 1974, by only a quarter of one percent of IBM's employees—as meeting the condition in § 2039(a) that there must be a contract or agreement under which the decedent received or be entitled to receive "an annuity or other payment", is such a departure from the language used by Congress, read in the light of the problem with which it was intending to deal, as to be at war with common sense. The only decision by which we are bound, All v. McCobb, supra, 321 F.2d 633, does not come near to the problem here presented. Of the other decisions cited to us, there are clear grounds of distinguishing all with the possible exception of the leading one, Estate of Bahen, supra, 305 F.2d 827, and the certain exception of Gaffney [v. United States, 200 Ct. Cls. 744 (1972)]. Although we have been able to distinguish the cases other than Gaffney and possibly Bahen on grounds that seem to us sufficient, we would not wish to be understood as necessarily agreeing with all of them or with the general approach taken in Bahen, see 305 F.2d at 833. Some other case may require complete rethinking whether courts, under the influence of the Bahen opinion, have not unduly eroded the condition in § 2039(a), as is pointedly suggested by Judge Aldisert's dissent in Gray v. United States, [410 F.2d 1094, at 1112–14 (3d Cir.1969)]; on the other hand, Congress might decide to cast its net more widely and eliminate or broaden the condition, as it could have done in 1954. We simply decline to carry the erosion of the condition to the extent here urged by the Commissioner.

The judgment is reversed and the cause remanded with instructions to annul the determination of a deficiency.

Notes

[¶ 21,055]

1. The Sixth Circuit in Van Wye's Estate v. United States, 686 F.2d 425 (6th Cir.1982) fully accepted the rationale of the Second Circuit in *Schelberg* in disposing of a case involving comparable facts with a different employer. A district court, addressing facts virtually identical to those in *Schelberg*, reached the opposite conclusion. Looney v. United States, 569 F.Supp. 1569 (M.D.Ga.1983).

¶ 21,049

2. Regulation § 20.2039–1(b)(1) indicates that the decedent will be deemed to have"possessed the right to receive an annuity or other payment if immediately before his death, the decedent had an enforceable right to receive payments at some time in the future, whether or not, at the time of his death, he had a present right to receive payments." Although Schelberg was entitled to receive pension benefits from IBM at age 65, the court, acting pursuant to the direction of Rev. Rul. 76–380 refused to consider Schelberg's future retirement benefits for the purpose of being able to tax the survivors' income benefits payable under the Group Life Insurance Plan. The IRS, in Rev. Rul. 76–380, reasoned that to consider rights to retirement benefits under a qualified plan for the purpose of exposing other benefits to taxation would be inconsistent with the grant of tax exempt status to qualified plan benefits then granted to qualified plans. After qualified plans were stripped of their exemption under § 2039 in 1984, the IRS in Rev. Rul. 88–85, 1988–2 C.B. 333 declared Rev. Rul. 76–380 obsolete.

Thus it would appear that under present law, if an employee is presently receiving either qualified or unqualified pension benefits, or as indicated by Reg. § 20.2039–1(b)(1) has "an enforceable right to receive" such benefits in the future, these benefits may be considered for the purpose of subjecting to taxation other payments, whether periodic or lump sum, made to survivors under other employer provided benefit plans.

3. The IRS was unsuccessful in its attempts to tax the life insurance portion of an annuity-life insurance combination in the *Fidelity-Philadelphia Trust* case, ¶ 18,079, under the predecessor provisions to § 2036, as if a life estate had been reserved by the insured-decedent. However, since the advent of § 2039 in 1954, the IRS has often been successful in looking to § 2039 as a basis for including the proceeds of annuity-life insurance packages in the annuitant's gross estate. See e.g. Estate of Montgomery v. Commissioner, 458 F.2d 616 (5th Cir.1972).

E. INCOME TAXATION OF TAX QUALIFIED RETIREMENT PLANS AND IRA'S

[¶ 21,097]

Tax qualified retirement plans and Individual Retirement Accounts enjoy broad protection from income taxation until distribution to the beneficiary, as is fulsomely provided in §§ 401–420. Most contributions are made with pretax dollars, i.e., no tax is imposed on the funds contributed to the plan. Similarly, earnings on such plans are typically exempt from tax. The price the beneficiary pays for the privilege of tax-free contribution and compounding is that all payments from the plan to the beneficiary are taxed as income to the beneficiary, except to the extent nondeductible contributions were made. Typically there are no nondeductible contributions, with the result that all payments to the beneficiary are fully taxable.

Often the payments to the beneficiary are enhanced by appreciation of plan assets. Furthermore, as explained above, the entire plan will usually be included in the gross estate of the deceased owner. For that reason it would seem that upon the death of the owner the surviving beneficiaries should get the benefit of the step-up in basis at death pursuant § 1014, i.e., the beneficiaries should have a basis for the plan equal to its value at the date of death (or alternate valuation date, if elected). If that were the case, immediate distribution of the plan assets to the beneficiaries would produce no taxable gain to the beneficiaries, who would receive the assets entirely free of income tax.

Congress and the Treasury thought that result a bit much, reasoning that, in return for the immense advantages of the shelter from income taxes, *someone* should pay tax on the plan assets, which typically represent either untaxed compensation or untaxed earnings on those funds. Assurance of taxation of qualified plan and IRA proceeds is provided by treating such assets as "income in respect of a decedent," or "IRD." As more fully explained in Chapter 32, IRD is income "not properly includible in respect of the taxable period in which falls the date of [the decedent's] death or a prior period." § 691(a)(1). Qualified plan and IRA assets meet this definition because §§ 401–420 have the effect of deferring, but not forgiving, taxation on both contributions and earnings. Under § 691(a)(1), IRD, such as a qualified plan distribution, is taxed to the surviving plan beneficiary in the same manner and to the same extent as if the decedent had received the funds during her life. Any argument that the basis of the plan assets should step-up at death is prevented by § 1014(c), which expressly denies the step-up to IRD assets.

The ultimate result is that qualified plan and IRA assets, to the extent attributable to untaxed contributions and earnings, are fully subject to income tax when distributed to plan beneficiaries, including beneficiaries who receive payments by reason of surviving the original owner. Because most plans consist entirely of untaxed assets, the usual result is that all plan distributions will be taxed to the ultimate recipients—whoever the recipients may be and whenever the distributions are made.

Because of the heavy tax burden that might result from imposition of both estate tax and income tax on IRD items such as qualified plans and IRAs, some relief is provided by § 691(c). This subsection grants an income tax deduction for estate tax imposed on an IRD item. As a result, a portion of the qualified plan or IRA corresponding to the estate tax imposed can be received free of income tax, as more fully explained at ¶ 32,109.

Much of the value of a qualified plan or IRA lies in the "tax shelter," i.e., deferral of taxation of the plan earnings until distribution to the beneficiary. This permits tax-free compounding of earnings as long as the assets are in the plan. Because Congress intended qualified plans and IRA's to serve primarily as funding vehicles for retirement, and not as perpetual tax shelters, Congress has imposed minimum distribution rules that require the beneficiary to begin withdrawals at a certain age and to continue the withdrawals at a required level. In specified circumstances, the withdrawal period can extend beyond the original beneficiary's life and well into the lives of other beneficiaries. The result can be perpetuation of the tax shelter benefits for many years.

Because of the importance of perpetuating the income tax shelter, the designation of beneficiaries after the death of the original beneficiary typically involves both income tax and estate tax issues. Specifically, the designation of beneficiaries should be designed so as to produce the longest perpetuation of the tax shelter consistent with the minimum distribution rules, estate tax minimization, and the decedent's nontax objectives. Some of the complex rules governing these alternatives are discussed at ¶ 32,053.

Chapter 22

POWERS OF APPOINTMENT

(Section 2041)

A. INTRODUCTION

[¶ 22,001]

The property law concept of a power of appointment is a power of disposition over property that, typically, is given to a third person by deed or will by the owner of the property. The owner of the property who creates the power of appointment is usually called the donor, and the person who is given the power to designate the one who is to take the property or its enjoyment, i.e., the holder of the power, is called the donee. The person who receives the property or interest upon the exercise of the power is the appointee, and the person who would take the property in default of the exercise of the power is called the taker in default.

Powers of appointment are variously classified for property law purposes. However, for estate and gift tax purposes, powers are classified as either general powers or special powers. Special powers are those exercisable in favor of a limited group of persons. Generally speaking, neither exercise nor nonexercise of a special power of appointment has estate or gift tax consequences. Consider the following illustration:

Example: Abby is trustee of a trust established by her father for the benefit of her three sons. The trust provides that Abby is to receive all the income from the trust for her life and, at her death, the trust is to terminate and the trust property is to be distributed in equal shares to Abby's three sons. However, the trust provides that Abby is authorized to include a provision in her will changing the shares her sons are to receive. In fact, Abby has included such a provision in her will and, as a result, Abby's oldest child is to receive 70 percent of the trust and the two younger boys are to receive only 15 percent each. Abby's power to vary the share each of her sons is to receive in the trust at her death is referred to as a special power. However, despite the power vested in

¶ 22,001

Abby, no part of the trust property will be subject to estate tax at Abby's death.

General powers are different. General powers are those powers that may be exercised in favor of the powerholder, or the powerholder's estate, or the powerholder's creditors, or the creditors of the powerholder's estate. § 2041(b)(1). Because the holder of a general power can benefit directly from the power, the powerholder's exercise of such a power will result in the property subject to the power being included in the powerholder's estate if the power is exercised at death (or being subject to gift tax if the power is exercised during life). Similarly, failure to exercise a power will also generally have either estate or gift tax consequences, the reasoning being that forbearance to exercise is a decision committed to the powerholder and is truly effective control of the power property that ends only when the power can no longer be exercised.

Example: Bert is trustee of a trust established for his benefit by his father. As trustee, Bert is authorized by the terms of the trust to distribute to himself "so much or all of the income and principal" of the trust as he, as trustee, determines that he "needs for his welfare, happiness and comfort in life as well as advancement in business." In this case Bert will be deemed to have a general power of appointment—and even if he never takes a distribution from the trust, the trust property will be included in his estate at his death. See § 2041(a)(2).

In the early stages of the estate tax, unexercised general powers of appointment had no estate tax consequences, as was seen in the *Safe Deposit and Trust* case, ¶ 15,013. However, since 1918, there have been several developmental legislative revisions aimed at general powers of appointment.

Section 2041 is the current provision that sets forth the complex set of rules governing the taxation of property subject to a general power of appointment. This section has remained virtually unchanged since 1951. The present approach of § 2041 is to classify all general powers in accordance with their date of creation, between those existing on or before October 21, 1942 (the date of an interim revenue act dealing with powers), and those created thereafter. See § 2041(a).

Such pre-existing powers—"pre-October 21, 1942, powers"—are to be taxed only if the power is exercised (1) by will or (2) by a disposition that would have made the property includible if the disposition had been a transfer of property owned by the decedent. Accordingly, the nonexercise of such a power results in no estate tax; moreover, the release of such a power is permitted wholly tax free.

For the purpose of this division between pre–1942 and post–1942 powers, the Regulations point out that the date the power is created is controlled by the date when the instrument creating the power takes effect. Reg. § 20.2041–1(e).

As for post–1942 powers, under the statute, mere possession of such a power at death will cause inclusion of the property in the gross estate of the holder. Also, the inter vivos exercise or release of the post–1942 power will

¶ 22,001

result in estate taxation, provided that the transaction occurs under such circumstances as would have required the inclusion of the property in the gross estate if it had been a transfer of property owned by the deceased holder of the power. See § 2041(a)(2).

The foregoing guidelines for pre–1942 and post–1942 powers assume that the power falls within the definition of a general power. Any power that is not a general power (no matter when created) will not result in the inclusion in the gross estate of the property subject to the power, with a limited statutory exception for certain powers that are exercised to create a further power (§ 2041(a)(3)), and an exception for the nongeneral self-created power, i.e., the case where the powerholder holding a limited nongeneral power has created the limited nongeneral power. In the latter case, the power property is included in the powerholder's estate as a result of § 2038 and not § 2041.

> *Example*: Klalid is trustee of an irrevocable trust that he created for his three children. While Klalid cannot make distributions to himself, he can make distributions to his children—and he can be selective in amount and distribution, meaning that he can favor one of the children to the exclusion of the others. In this case, the trust property will be included in Klalid's estate at his death because he has transferred the trust property and, at his death, he has the power to control the enjoyment of that property by the trust beneficiaries. See § 2038.

An explicit definition of a general power was developed for the purpose of determining what powers should be treated as taxable. While the term "general power" is used for this purpose, the definition is really more closely allied to a beneficial power, i.e., a power that can be used to the economic advantage of the holder. See § 2041(b)(1). Thus, a general power is any power that is exercisable in favor of (1) the powerholder, or (2) the powerholder's creditors, or (3) the powerholder's estate, or (4) creditors of the powerholder's estate. Whether any other possible appointees are included within the group is immaterial if one or more of the foregoing can be an appointee.

There are two major exclusions from the definition of a general power. First, a power to "consume, invade, or appropriate" the property for the benefit of the donee is exempt if its exercise is subject to an ascertainable standard relating to the health, education, maintenance or support of the donee. § 2041(b)(1)(A). The fact that the power is subject to a fixed standard deprives it of the broad discretion inherent in a general or taxable power.

The second exception to general powers relates to jointly held powers. § 2041(b)(1)(C). Any jointly held power created on or before October 21, 1942, is not a general power. With respect to joint powers created thereafter, they are classed as general powers only if the other holder of the power is not the donor or if the other holder has no substantial adverse interest in the property which would be adverse to the exercise of the power in favor of the donee.

It is useful to note, too, that estate taxes attributable to the inclusion of power property in the power holder's gross estate can be recovered from the power property except in cases where the power holder's will otherwise

¶ 22,001

directs. § 2207. This relief opportunity is intended to prevent burdening the powerholder's other beneficiaries with the taxes on the power property where estate tax inclusion of the power property was not anticipated by the power-holder.

Sometimes the holder of a general power is viewed as having the practical equivalent of a fee simple interest in the power property. For example, a lifetime exercise or release of a post–1942 general power will result in inclusion of the power property in the powerholder's estate at death in those cases where a similar transfer by a decedent of non power property would be recaptured under §§ 2035 to 2038. § 2041(a)(2). As an illustration, suppose the trust created in Mom's will provided Dad with all trust income for life and also gave Dad a general power of appointment over the remainder. During life, Dad exercised the power in favor of Muleshoe. Under one analysis, the value of the power property at Dad's later death would be included in his gross estate because he made a transfer subject to a retained life estate. See § 2036(a)(1). Under another analysis, it is said to be arguable that § 2041(a)(2) does not reach the power property (so long as Dad lives three years after exercise) because Mom, rather than Dad, created the life estate enjoyed by Dad. If the latter position were to prevail, would Dad (or Muleshoe) be tax advantaged by his lifetime exercise of the power?

Problems

[¶ 22,007]

1. In the case of a revocable trust that creates a power, when should the power be considered to be created? On the date of the execution of the trust instrument? Or on the later date when it became irrevocable?

2. Assume that a post–1942 general power was partially released by an inter vivos act so that it was no longer a general power; upon the donee's death, without any further exercise of the now-special power, would the property subject to the power be included in the donee's gross estate? See Reg. § 20.2041–3(d)(1). Is this result supported by the statute?

B. WHAT IS A POWER OF APPOINTMENT?

[¶ 22,013]

KEETER v. UNITED STATES

United States Court of Appeals, Fifth Circuit, 1972.
461 F.2d 714.

GOLDBERG, Circuit Judge:

* * *

The decedent's husband, Daniel A. Shaw, died in 1930, the owner of an insurance policy on his own life in the amount of $100,000, which he had purchased in 1919. In 1926 Mr. Shaw (the "insured" or the "settlor") elected a settlement option which provided that the insurance proceeds should be held under four identical supplementary contracts, issued to the decedent, Mrs. Bessie Love Shaw, and their daughters in equal shares. By the terms of this settlement option decedent was to receive interest on her share of the proceeds for her life, and a supplementary contract in the amount of $25,000 was accordingly issued to the decedent. The settlement option also expressly provided that the principal and accrued interest from the proceeds were to be paid to "the executors or administrators" of the decedent at her death. Mrs. Shaw, domiciled in Florida, died in 1964, leaving a will, duly probated, that read in part:

> All the rest, residue and remainder of my property of every kind and description and wherever located, and any property over which I may hold the power of appointment or distribution, I give, devise, and bequeath in three equal portions for [her daughters].

Pursuant to the 1926 settlement election, the insurance company paid the $25,000 to the decedent's executor. The executor did not include that sum in the decedent's gross estate when he filed the estate tax return, and the Commissioner assessed a deficiency. * * *

General powers of appointment created on or before October 21, 1942, are includable in the gross estate of a decedent only if they are "exercised," * * * § 2041(a)(1). * * * The issue in this case is whether or not the settlor's election of annuities-cum-payments to the decedent's executor constitutes such a power of appointment for purposes of the estate tax. It is acknowledged by all parties that if the settlement option elected by the decedent's husband constituted a general power of appointment, the power was "created," for tax purposes, prior to 1942. * * * And it is also conceded by all that the power of appointment, if that is what it really was, was "exercised," for tax purposes, by a specific provision in the decedent's will that distributed any of her property held under power of appointment to her three daughters in equal shares.

We will look to applicable state law to determine whether the substance of the property interests created by the settlor fits within the federal tax law's definition of a power of appointment, but we emphasize that it is the substance of the state law that is relevant and not any labels that a state or the parties might attach to that substance. * * * see also Morgan v. Commissioner, 1940, 309 U.S. 78, 60 S.Ct. 424, 84 L.Ed. 585:

> State law creates legal interests and rights. The federal revenue acts designate what interests or rights, so created, shall be taxed.

The law in this case is as clear as the Internal Revenue Code and attendant regulations are ever wont to be. A general power of appointment is defined by the Code as "a power which is exercisable in favor of the decedent, *his estate*, his creditors, or the creditors of his estate," * * * § 2041(b)(1) [emphasis added]. The Code definition is cast in the disjunctive, so that the donee is in possession of a general power of appointment if he or she is able to exercise that power in favor of any one of the four groups of beneficiaries specified in the statute. * * * A donee possesses a general power of appointment when he or she holds

¶ 22,013

... such a power of control as to be able to apply it to his own benefit, or the benefit of his creditors, to dispose of it by will, or to appoint it to his estate or the creditors of his estate, or to consume it without restriction. Security–Peoples Trust Co. v. United States, W.D.Pa.1965, 238 F.Supp. 40 at 45. * * *

Mrs. Shaw's executor argues that the settlement option elected by Mrs. Shaw's husband was not a general power of appointment, resting his argument principally upon the assertion that Mrs. Shaw did not receive solely from that settlement option, and at the moment of the death of the insured, the unrestricted power to dispose of the insurance proceeds. Mrs. Shaw's power to distribute the funds came, the executor concludes, from the laws of Florida which empowered her to make a will and not from her husband's settlement option. In sum, the executor's argument is that because the proceeds would have to receive their direction under the will and not directly under the insurance clause, the option could not be called a power of appointment at the time of the insured's death. The executor's argument is unrealistic at best, conclusory at worst. We conclude that the making of a will was merely a conduit, not a rheostat, in the legal authority that ran between the decedent and the insurance option.

* * *

It appears to this court that Mrs. Shaw was granted at her husband's death an absolute power of appointment over the insurance proceeds, the power to be exercisable by her will at her death. We are aware of the fact that the Seventh Circuit was presented with a set of circumstances substantially similar to those we face, and that the court held for the taxpayer. Second National Bank of Danville v. Dallman, 7 Cir.1954, 209 F.2d 321. In *Dallman* the insured (the decedent's father) selected an insurance settlement option that required the insurance company to pay interest to the decedent for life and then gave to the decedent the right to designate a contingent beneficiary to take the proceeds at the decedent's death. If the decedent failed to designate her beneficiary expressly, the insurance company was to pay the proceeds to the decedent's "executors, administrators, or assigns." The decedent never designated a beneficiary. Her will provided that her entire residuary estate should be held in trust but did not mention specifically the insurance proceeds. In accordance with the contract with the decedent's father, the insurance company paid the funds to the decedent's testamentary trustee, and the government included the proceeds in the decedent's gross estate for estate tax purposes. The Seventh Circuit, reversing the district court, held that the proceeds were not includable in the decedent's gross estate:

> [T]he proceeds were payable at decedent's death *not by her direction but by that of her father as contained in the contract.*

209 F.2d at 324 [emphasis added]. We are unable to distinguish the *Dallman* case on its facts, and we are thus compelled to disagree with that case on the law. In essence, we hold that there is no substantive difference between directly granting the power to dispose of property and placing that same

property in such a position that the donee is able to dispose of it to her benefit by means of some power that existed prior to or separate from the settlor's grant.

It appears to this court that the settlors in *Dallman* and in our case granted absolute powers of appointment to their respective donees subject only to the proviso that the donees were to exercise their powers of appointment by means of a will. * * * Therefore, the substance of the settlement option was to grant an absolute power of appointment of the insurance principal and interest to Mrs. Shaw, exercisable at her death by her will. It is quite true that Mrs. Shaw could not dispose of the insurance proceeds to her own benefit immediately after the death of her husband. But a power of appointment need not be exercisable only immediately or only in favor of the donee. The power is also taxable if it is exercisable at some point in favor of the grantee's estate. * * *

In brief, Mrs. Shaw's husband directed the funds to Mrs. Shaw's executor, and Mrs. Shaw directed the executor. In practical terms, Mr. Shaw simply put the insurance proceeds into a receptacle from which his wife could appoint them, but it is Mrs. Shaw who substantively directed the funds to the ultimate recipients. And the fact that Mrs. Shaw spoke through her executor does not make her voice any less her own. For estate tax purposes, the critical question is whether the decedent directed her property after her death, not how that property got into the position from which she could direct it. In terms of the actual authority of direction over the insurance proceeds that was conferred and exercised, we see no substantive differences among an express grant of a general power of appointment, a grant utilizing a previously-existing trust with the donee as the sole trustee, an express grant of a general power of appointment exercisable only by will, and a grant employing a previously-existing law that allows the donee to distribute property freely by will. In each instance the power realistically conferred and exercised is the power to direct the fund as the donee sees fit at the point of her death, or in legalese the power to appoint. Abrasive as it may seem to the donees of the power, " ... that is precisely what the federal estate tax hits—an exercise of the privilege of directing the course of property after ... death." Estate of Rogers v. Helvering, 1943, 320 U.S. 410, 413 * * *. Mrs. Shaw exercised her general power of appointment by specifically directing her executors in her will, and her estate is therefore taxable on the value of the exercise.

Note

[¶ 22,019]

At one level it is appropriate to note that *Keeter* highlights the fact that no special words need by used to create a power of appointment. Regulation § 20.2041–1(b)(1) provides that the term includes "all powers which are in substance and effect powers of appointment regardless of the nomenclature used in creating the power and regardless of local property law connotations."

At another level, however, it is useful to compare *Keeter* with Estate of Margrave v. Commissioner, 618 F.2d 34 (8th Cir.1980), a case with an odd set of facts. Wife owned a policy of life insurance on Husband (Margrave) and had used her own property to pay the premiums. Bank, as trustee of a revocable trust created by Husband, was designated beneficiary of the policy proceeds—and Bank received those proceeds at the death of Husband. The court concluded that the policy proceeds were not included in Husband's estate at his death despite the IRS contention that Husband's unrestricted right to revoke or amend the trust constituted a general power of appointment taxable under § 2041. The court explained its decision in these terms (618 F.2d at 38–9):

> In order for such a power to result in the inclusion of an item in decedent's gross estate under § 2041, the decedent must at least (1) possess a power within this definition of "a general power of appointment," and (2) there must be a property interest to which this "general power of appointment" attaches.

> While it is clear that the decedent possessed a "general power of appointment" by virtue of his ability to modify or revoke the trust, * * * we do not believe that any property interest attached to that power.

> * * * Prior to his death, Margrave possessed only a power over an expectancy because the rights of the trustee to the proceeds were subject to Mrs. Margrave's power to change the designation of the trustee as beneficiary. Although the death of Mr. Margrave caused the trustee's right to the proceeds to vest and create a property interest to which Mr. Margrave's power of appointment might attach, Mr. Margrave's death simultaneously terminated his ability to modify or revoke the trust. Thus, Mr. Margrave's "general power of appointment" was at all times merely a power over an expectancy. In such circumstances, we do not believe the proceeds of the life insurance policy can be included in decedent's gross estate under § 2041.

Subsequently, the IRS acquiesced in *Margrave* in Rev. Rul. 81–166, 1981 C.B. 477. The ruling also expressed that Wife made a taxable gift of the insurance proceeds when the insurance proceeds were paid to the trust.

The court in *Margrave* noted approvingly the result reached in *Connecticut Bank and Trust Co.*, which follows. Part of the decision in *Connecticut Bank and Trust Co.* appears at ¶ 15,151 on the issue of what constitutes "property" for estate tax purposes. In that portion of the case, the government lost its argument that proceeds received from the settlement of a wrongful death action were "property owned at death" and thus includible in the decedent's taxable estate. The second part of the opinion follows, and the government fared no better on its argument that the proceeds were includible under Section 2041.

[¶ 22,022]

CONNECTICUT BANK AND TRUST CO. v. UNITED STATES

United States Court of Appeals, Second Circuit, 1972.
465 F.2d 760.

ROBERT P. ANDERSON, Circuit Judge:

* * *

As a second point on appeal, the Government argues that the wrongful death proceeds must also be included in the gross estate under § 2041, as "property with respect to which the decedent has at the time of his death a general power of appointment." This argument must actually assume that the wrongful death proceeds were not property owned by the decedent at death under § 2033, because § 2041 is concerned with the power to deal with property belonging to someone else, cf. Reg. § 20.2041–1(b)(2) (1972).

The Government claims that the wrongful death proceeds are subject to a § 2041 power of appointment because they are to be distributed under the terms of the decedents' wills as authorized by Connecticut General Statutes § 45–280. This, in effect, asserts that any property which is distributed according to a testamentary disposition is taxable as part of the gross estate, a view which enlarges the statute far beyond the purposes intended for it by Congress. A sufficient answer to the Government's position is that, at the very least, property subject to a § 2041 power of appointment must be in existence prior to the time of the decedent's death. * * *

Section 2041 was never intended to encompass within the gross estate what the Government now claims. If the Government were correct, then income earned during the administration of an estate and later distributed according to the terms of the will would be included in the value of the gross estate under § 2041, but it is abundantly clear that such income is not subject to the estate tax * * *.

Moreover § 2041(a)(2) provides that "[a] disclaimer or renunciation of such a power of appointment shall not be deemed a release of such power." "If a decedent exercises this right [to disclaim], the value of property as to which he has renounced the power will not be included in his gross estate," Jenkins v. United States, 428 F.2d 538, 550 (5 Cir.), cert. denied, 400 U.S. 829 (1970); see also, Reg. § 20.2041–3(d)(6). Under the Government's theory, however, it would be impossible for the decedent to renounce his "general power of appointment" over the wrongful death proceeds, because they did not exist prior to his death.

Note

[¶ 22,023]

In Tech. Adv. Mem. 9722001, the IRS concluded that the decedent did not have a general power of appointment. The trust provided the decedent with all the trust income and access to principal on the following terms:

I am desirous that the corpus hereof be liberally invaded in favor of my niece, [Decedent], to the fullest extent necessary or advisable to provide her with a secure and comfortable living and to provide her with ample funds for investment or business purposes. In the absence of potential tax savings in favor of her beneficiaries, I should prefer and, therefore, would have mandated that distribution be made to her upon my demise, but in view of potential benefits to her and to her estate and beneficiaries, I leave the matter on a discretionary basis with the trustee, but I am desirous that the same be paid and distributed to her in accord with her wishes.

The IRS said that contrasting the settler's use of precatory language ("I am desirous") when speaking of the decedent's access to the trust principal with her use of the language of imperative elsewhere in the will ("I hereby give and bequeath") made it clear that the decedent had not been given a general power of appointment over the trust principal.

C. DISTINGUISHING GENERAL AND SPECIAL POWERS

[¶ 22,024]

PRIVATE LETTER RULING 7903055

October 18, 1978.

* * * [Y]ou ask about the includibility in the gross estate [of B] of a power of appointment created by [H's] trust.

* * * The trustees are to pay;

[T]he net dividends and income to [B] for and during the term of her natural life. Upon her death the principal is given either outright or upon further trust, to her heirs-at-law and next of kin, in such manner, interests and proportions as she shall in and by her Last Will and Testament in that behalf direct, limit and appoint and in default of such appointment or insofar as the same shall fail effectually to dispose of said fund then unto the issue of [B] per stirpes.

* * * In exercising the power of appointment, [B, in her] will provided that the principal of the trust was to pass outright to her four children in equal shares.

Section 2041(a)(2) provides that the value of the gross estate shall include the value of all property with respect to which the decedent had, at the time of her death, a general power of appointment. Section 2041(b)(1) defines general power of appointment as a power which is exercisable in favor of the decedent, her estate, her creditors or the creditors of her estate.

[B] possessed the testamentary power to appoint the principal of the trust only to her heirs-at-law or next of kin. She could not exercise the power in favor of herself, her estate, her creditors, or the creditors of her estate. Thus, at death, [B] did not have a general power of appointment over the

¶ 22,024

principal * * *. The principal will not be includible in her gross estate under section 2041.

[¶ 22,038]

REVENUE RULING 69–342

1969–1 C.B. 221.

* * *

The decedent's husband, who died in 1950, devised and bequeathed the residue of his estate to his wife for her life "with power to mortgage, sell, assign, and convey the same, and use and dispose of the proceeds thereof to all intents and purposes as if she were the absolute owner thereof." Upon her death, the unconsumed portion of the husband's estate, if any, was to be distributed in fee to their daughter. The decedent died in 1968. Under the laws of the state in which the decedent's husband's will was probated the quoted language is not construed to include a power to dispose of the property by gift.

Under the state law applicable to the administration of the deceased wife's estate, an absolute power of disposition given to the owner of a particular estate for life creates a life estate absolute in respect to the rights of creditors and purchasers, but subject to any future estate provided by the grantor.

Section 2041(a)(2) provides that the value of the gross estate shall include the value of all property with respect to which the decedent has at the time of his death a general power of appointment created after October 21, 1942. A power of appointment created by will is, except as provided by section 2041(b)(3), considered to have been created on the date of testator's death.

Section 2041(b) defines the term "general power of appointment" as a power that is exercisable in favor of the decedent, his estate, his creditors, or the creditors of his estate. An exception is provided where a power to consume, invade, or appropriate property for the benefit of the decedent is limited by an ascertainable standard relating to the health, education, support, or maintenance of the decedent.

Section 20.2041–1(b) provides that the term "power of appointment" includes all powers which are in substance and effect powers of appointment regardless of the nomenclature used in creating the powers and regardless of local property law connotations.

The language of the husband's will giving his wife the power to mortgage, sell, assign, and convey the property and use and dispose of the proceeds as if she were the absolute owner thereof clearly manifests his intention that his wife was to have the unlimited right to consume and dispose of the estate (except by gift) without reference to her needs or to any other standard. The interests of the remainderman are entirely subordinate to the desires of the wife, the husband having provided only that the remainderman receive the balance of the estate, if any, at his wife's death.

¶ 22,024

A power possessed by a lifetime beneficiary to consume, invade, or appropriate the estate for his own benefit, which power is not limited by an ascertainable standard, is within the statutory definition of a general power of appointment for purposes of the estate tax, notwithstanding the beneficiary's lack of power to exercise testamentary control over any unconsumed portion of the estate. * * *

Accordingly, it is held that the deceased wife possessed a general power of appointment, notwithstanding her lack of power to exercise testamentary control over the unconsumed portion of her predeceased husband's estate and notwithstanding that she did not possess the power during her lifetime to dispose of the property by gift. The value of the remaining property of her husband's estate is includible in her gross estate under section 2041.

Note

[¶ 22,039]

In Gaskill v. United States, 561 F.Supp. 73 (D.Kan.1983), aff'd per curiam, 787 F.2d 1446 (10th Cir.1986), on facts relatively identical to those found in Rev. Rul. 69–342, the district court found that the surviving spouse did not have a general power of appointment. In reaching its conclusion in favor of the taxpayer, the court distinguished a number of cases reaching contrary results on the ground that the Gaskill will stipulated that "all of the remainder of my estate" was to be distributed to the decedent's children after the death of the surviving spouse, whereas the dispositive provisions found in the cases reaching contrary results indicated that the respective decedents:

> explicitly recognized the possibility that the property held by the life tenants would diminish in quantity and value before that property found its way into the hands of the remaindermen by the use of language such as "the remainder of such residue remaining," "such of my estate as shall remain," and "whatever of my said property, if any . . ." The Gaskill will, in strong contrast, unambiguously directs that all of the life estate property shall go to the remaindermen at the life tenant's death.

Contrast the use of the word "all" in *Gaskill* and the conclusion reached by the court with the operative words described in Rev. Rul. 69–342. Note that in Rev. Rul. 69–342, the IRS concludes that the "interests of the remainderman are entirely subordinate to the desires of the wife." The court in *Gaskill*, on the other hand, says that while the surviving spouse "had unlimited powers to dispose of the life estate property," state law "imposed a correlative duty on her to make any such dispositions for full consideration and to hold the proceeds as a quasi-trustee for the remaindermen."

In Tech. Adv. Mem. 9431004, the IRS concluded that a power to mortgage was a power of appointment when held by the holder of a life estate. In this case, husband mortgaged the ranch in which he held a life estate (provided him in the joint will he and his deceased first wife had executed). He then gifted the proceeds of the loan to his new spouse. Rejected was the argument that the power to mortgage enjoyed by the husband was administrative only. Reg. § 20.2041–1(b)(1). In the opinion of the IRS, husband's ability to "encumber or mortgage all or any part of" the ranch if he deemed it "necessary to essential for any purpose" was a power to consume or dispose of the property in favor of himself because the mortgage was "binding upon the remaindermen"–and was, in fact, subsequently assumed. Also the loan secured by the mortgage was repaid by the remaindermen. Even if the husband could not have consumed the property or disposed of it in favor of himself, the IRS the said husband could exercise the power in favor of his creditors–and that was sufficient taint.

D. INVASION POWERS

[¶ 22,055]

REVENUE RULING 76–368
1976–2 C.B. 271.

Advice has been requested whether under section 2041 a power of invasion not limited by an ascertainable standard, granted to an independent trustee, can be imputed to the decedent-income beneficiary of a trust under the circumstances described below.

The decedent's spouse, who died testate in 1965, created a testamentary trust under the terms of which the trust income was payable to the decedent for life, and the remainder payable to other named persons upon the decedent's death. The trustee, an independent bank, was authorized to invade the trust corpus and pay portions thereof to or for the use and benefit of the decedent in such manner as the trustee, in its sole and unfettered discretion, deemed advisable should the decedent be in need of funds in excess of the trust income for "health, comfort, maintenance, welfare, or for any other purpose or purposes." The trustee was directed to liberally exercise its discretionary power of invasion. Prior to the decedent's death in 1976, numerous requests had been made to the trustee for additional funds and all such requests of the decedent had been honored by the trustee.

* * *

Under section 20.2041–1(b), defining a power of appointment, it is provided that a power to consume or appropriate property is a power of appointment if, for example, a trust instrument provides that the beneficiary may appropriate or consume the principal of a trust.

* * *

In the instant case, * * * the independent trustee alone was expressly authorized to invade the trust corpus and pay portions thereof to or for the use and benefit of the decedent as the trustee, in its sole and unfettered discretion, deemed advisable for the stated purposes. The governing trust instrument did not give the decedent any supervening right or power, or even a conjunctive right or power, such as would indicate an intent by the testator to grant to the decedent the power to consume or appropriate the trust principal.

¶ 22,039

While the decedent had the power to invoke a process of judicial review had the trustee, in the judgment of the decedent, failed to liberally exercise its discretionary power of invasion on the decedent's behalf, this kind of power does not transfer a power of invasion granted an independent trustee to the beneficiary of the trust.

Accordingly, the power of invasion not limited by an ascertainable standard, granted to the independent trustee, cannot be imputed to the decedent so as to render the power taxable in the decedent's gross estate under section 2041.

Note

[¶ 22,058]

1. Revenue Ruling 79–353, 1979–2 C.B. 325, discussed at ¶ 18,184, was much criticized and was finally repudiated in Estate of Wall v. Commissioner, 101 T.C. 300 (1993), ¶ 18,185. (Subsequently the IRS reversed Rev. Rul. 79–353 in Rev. Rul. 95–58, 95–2 C.B. 191, ¶ 18,186.) The IRS claimed in Rev. Rul. 79–353 that a grantor's retained right to remove a corporate trustee and appoint a successor corporate trustee required inclusion of the trust property in the grantor's estate at death in cases where the distributions were left to the discretion of the trustee—even though the grantor was not a permissible distributee.

The IRS's repudiation of Rev. Rul. 79–353 may well be complete. In Priv. Ltr. Rul. 9746007, the IRS ruled that a trust beneficiary's power to remove and replace a corporate trustee with another corporate trustee or an individual unrelated to him did not constitute a general power of appointment even though the trustee had discretionary authority to make distributions of income and principal to the beneficiary.

The IRS position has obviously evolved since the rejection of Rev. Rul. 79–353 in *Wall* but, even so, it is worth noting Priv. Ltr. Rul. 8916032, released before *Wall* was decided, as an example of the IRS's aspirations, now apparently frustrated. In Priv. Ltr. Rul. 8916032, the IRS concluded that a wife had a general power of appointment over a trust created by her husband because of her right to remove the corporate trustee and appoint a successor corporate trustee for the trust. Under the terms of the trust, the trustee had discretion to make distributions to the wife's minor children whom the wife had an obligation to support under state law. Relevant was Reg. § 20.2041–1(c)(1), which provides that a power of appointment exercisable for purposes of discharging a legal obligation of the powerholder is "considered a power of appointment exercisable" in favor of the powerholder or the powerholder's creditors. If nothing else, Priv. Ltr. Rul. 8916032 is a reminder that the ability to discharge one's legal obligation is effectively a power of appointment exercisable in favor of the powerholder.

2. The typical tax planning will for married persons causes the so-called tax free amount, *i.e.,* the amount that can be sheltered by the applicable exclusion amount provided for in § 2010(a) ($2 million in 2006–08 but scheduled to rise to $3.5 million in 2009), to be set aside in a bypass trust for

the benefit of the surviving spouse. The testator's remaining property is then not uncommonly set aside in a trust also for the benefit of the surviving spouse, this second trust being designed to qualify for the marital deduction (§ 2056), the effect of which is to cause the marital trust to be subject to estate tax at the death of the surviving spouse. (Of course, the plan contemplates that the marital deduction will allow the marital trust property to escape estate tax at the death of the first spouse to die.) Naturally, from a tax planning perspective, it is advantageous to exhaust the marital trust (during the life of the surviving spouse) before making distributions from the tax free amount warehoused in the bypass trust. Needless to say, however, fears that the surviving spouse "will run out of money" or that "the trustee won't give needed monies" to the surviving spouse are common concerns in the planning process, leading to the inclusion of mechanisms that allow the surviving spouse access to the bypass trust without causing the tax free amount in the bypass trust to be taxed at the death of the surviving spouse. Careful, sophisticated drafting is the order of the day here. One example of the pitfalls is illustrated by Estate of Kurz v. Commissioner, 68 F.3d 1027 (7th Cir.1995), where the surviving spouse was given the right to withdraw 5 percent from the bypass trust annually—but the withdrawal right was exercisable only if the marital trust had first been exhausted. The court held that, at death, the surviving spouse held a general power of appointment over 5 percent of the bypass trust and that, as a result, that 5 percent was included in the surviving spouse's estate for tax purposes under § 2041. The court found that the spouse could have exhausted the marital trust by merely giving notice to the trustee of her intention to withdraw all of it. The fact that the surviving spouse had not given that notice was considered irrelevant inasmuch as she had the power to effect such a withdrawal.

E. ASCERTAINABLE STANDARD

[¶ 22,061]

The volume of reported cases and rulings suggest that a claim that an otherwise general power is tax sheltered because it meets the conditions of the ascertainable standard exception provided in § 2041(b) will often be disputed by the IRS. New ground is continually being plowed because few, if any, situations are identical. As an illustration consider the ruling set forth below and Reg. § 20.2041–1(c)(2).

[¶ 22,067]

REVENUE RULING 77–60

1977–1 C.B. 282.

Under the will of decedent's spouse, who died in 1970, the decedent was granted a life estate in certain properties, with the power to invade corpus as desired "to continue the donee's accustomed standard of living." Upon the death of the decedent, the corpus was to be distributed to other named beneficiaries. The decedent died in 1975. Under the state law applicable to the administration of the estate of decedent's spouse, the quoted language is not construed to impose an objective limitation on the exercise of the power of invasion granted by the donor, other than one of good faith.

* * *

The ascertainable standard set forth in section 2041(b)(1)(A) spells out the limited degree of economic control over property that Congress chose to exempt from the estate tax. The language of the Code is detailed, i.e., if the exercise of the power is restricted by definite bounds relating to the health, education, support, or maintenance of the donee, it is not a general power of appointment with the resulting tax consequence. Further, section 20.2041–1(c)(2) provides that the power must be limited to the donee's "needs for health, education, or support (or any combination of them)." While this ascertainable standard is not restricted to the bare necessities of life, the power must be exercisable only for the designated statutory purposes.

In determining whether property subject to a power is limited by an ascertainable standard within the meaning of section 2041, the test is the "measure of control" over the property by virtue of the grant of the power, i.e., whether the exercise of the power is restricted by definite bounds. That the amount of property that could be consumed for the benefit of the donee is not measurable or predictable is of no consequence. * * *

A power to use property to enable the donee to continue an accustomed mode of living, without further limitation, although predictable and measurable on the basis of past expenditures, does not come within the ascertainable standard prescribed in section 2041(b)(1)(A) since the standard of living may include customary travel, entertainment, luxury items, or other expenditures not required for meeting the donee's "needs for health, education or support." Nor does the requirement of a good faith exercise of a power create an ascertainable standard. Good faith exercise of a power is not determinative of its breadth.

Accordingly, the power possessed by the decedent to invade trust principal as desired to continue an accustomed standard of living was not limited by an ascertainable standard relating to health, education, support or maintenance. Therefore, the decedent possessed at death a general power of appointment requiring inclusion of the value of the trust property in the decedent's gross estate under section 2041.

[¶ 22,073]

ESTATE OF SOWELL v. COMMISSIONER

United States Court of Appeals, Tenth Circuit, 1983.
708 F.2d 1564.

WILLIAM E. DOYLE, Circuit Judge.

* * *

The issue is whether the Tax Court erred in holding that the power to invade the trust corpus, "in case of emergency or illness," constitutes a

¶ 22,073

general power of appointment and therefore the entire corpus should have been included in the gross estate of appellant's decedent pursuant to Section 2041. The appellant's argument states that in determining whether this invasion meets the requirements of section 2041(b)(1)(A) for exclusion from treatment as a power of appointment requires a two-step analysis. *First,* the standard of invasion must be ascertainable, that is, capable of being readily interpreted and applied by a court of law. Secondly, the standard of invasion must be related to or reasonably measurable in terms of the decedent's needs for health, support, or maintenance. Appellant urges that Mrs. Sowell's power of invasion is ascertainable and in addition is reasonably measurable in terms of her need for health and support. Accordingly, it does not constitute a general power of appointment within the meaning of the code.

* * *

Ida Maude Sowell was the surviving spouse of Thomas R. Sowell, who died in November of 1967. She was named Trustee of a testamentary trust established by her husband's will. By the terms of the trust the net income was payable to Mrs. Sowell during her natural life, and upon her death, the corpus of the trust and all accumulations were to be distributed to Mr. Sowell's sons and daughter-in-law. The Trustee was also given "the right to invade the corpus of said trust in cases of emergency or illness."

* * *

The first question is: What is the meaning of "the right to invade the corpus of said trust in cases of emergency or illness"? What is meant by the term "emergency"?

Bouvier's Legal Dictionary states that an emergency is "an unforeseen occurrence or condition; see accident." The term "accident" is defined as "an event which, under the circumstances, is unusual and unexpected; an event the real cause of which cannot be traced or is at least not apparent."

* * *

Appellee's contention boils down to the question whether the phrase "in cases of emergency or illness" is an ascertainable standard related to Mrs. Sowell's health, education and support or maintenance. The taxability of an interest or power possessed by the decedent is determined under federal law, according to appellee, and the extent of the decedent's interest is governed by state law. A more precise question then is whether the courts of New Mexico, the jurisdiction in which decedent's will was probated, would hold that the phrase "in cases of emergency or illness" constitutes an ascertainable standard relating solely to decedent's health, education, support or maintenance. New Mexico law provides that the intent and meaning of the testator must be ascertained from the will itself, according to appellee. In determining the testator's intention, the purpose is to ascertain not what he meant to express apart from the language used, but what the words used actually express. Certainly the New Mexico court could readily ascertain the meaning of the governing words here.

* * *

¶ 22,073

The appellee maintains that the term "emergency" is not one that is clearly limited in its exercise to matters relating to decedent's health, education, support or maintenance. As used, the term "emergency" is clear and unambiguous, they say. The use of such a general term creates a broad power that can be utilized for any purpose so long as an emergency exists. To relate the word "emergency" to decedent's health, education, support or maintenance would require the addition of words that would contradict the plain meaning of the will.

* * *

Our conclusion is that an emergency is an emergency, and it is not susceptible to the expansive application suggested.

In the case of Funk v. Commissioner of Internal Revenue, 185 F.2d 127, 130–32 (3d Cir.1950), * * * [the] court reviewed a decision of the Tax Court of the United States to determine whether the income of four trusts, of which the petitioner was the sole trustee, was taxable to the petitioner. The Court of Appeals held that the petitioner was not endowed in the trust instruments with such unfettered command that the income from the trusts was her own money. She was only entitled, therefore, to receive income in accordance with her "needs." The Court there said:

> The term "needs" is not, of course, one the content of which can be defined precisely. * * * If, as the Tax Court observed, the trusts are unambiguous and specific it can only be said of the term "needs" that it must [be] construed according to its ordinary meaning. While obviously it must include the essentials of life, it has been construed in New Jersey to mean that which is reasonably necessary to maintain a beneficiary's station in life. It is not indicative of an unqualified gift, nor is it dependent upon the fancy of the administrator. Thus, its use confined the trustee to limits objectively determinable, and any conduct on her part beyond those limits would be unreasonable and breach of trust; certainly it did not countenance extravagance, whim, or caprice. * * *

The case of Pittsfield National Bank v. United States, 181 F.Supp. 851, 854 (D.Mass.1960) involved the power to invade corpus on basis of "need" and it was held not to be a general power of appointment within the meaning of § 2041. In *Pittsfield*, the Court said:

> The word "need" according to its dictionary definition and the cases interpreting it, has an even narrower and explicit meaning than the words discussed above, i.e., "want to the means of subsistence, necessity." The principal case explaining the word ... requires a showing of "actual financial or physical necessity" before the life tenant could exercise a power to sell "if she should need to during her lifetime." * * *

The Court further said:

> * * * The grant of the power must be read in its entirety, and so read I (*sic*) rule that it was a grant of power to invade corpus only in the event the donee was in financial or physical need.

* * *

¶ 22,073

We have exhaustively researched this issue and have not discovered a case which broadly construes the term "emergency" so as to allow a general power of appointment, sufficient to render a fund taxable to an estate.

Our conclusion is that no such case exists; that the term "emergency" is a restricted term which would tolerate obtaining the money from the trust only if the situation was extraordinary.

Accordingly, the judgment of the Tax Court must be reversed, and the cause must be remanded for further proceedings.

It is so ordered.

Note

[¶ 22,079]

1.   Has the court in *Sowell* expanded the meaning of "health, education, maintenance and support" to include "emergency" or has it restricted the meaning of "emergency" as it relates to "health, education, maintenance and support"? If the latter is correct, does that mean that the outcome of similar cases will depend on the interpretation placed on "emergency" by applicable state law, i.e., that the outcome in similar cases will vary from state to state and case to case depending on what a court finds to be the decedent's intention in using the word "emergency," or by applicable state-supplied rules of construction in those cases where the decedent's intention cannot be determined?

2.   In Hyde v. United States, 950 F.Supp. 418 (D.N.H.1996), the court concluded that the decedent had a general power of appointment where she was authorized to use the income and principal of a trust "as in her sole discretion shall be necessary or desirable." By way of contrast, though, in Best v. United States, 902 F.Supp. 1023 (D.Neb.1995), the decedent's power of appointment was found to have satisfied the ascertainable standard exception even though, by its plain terms, it would seem to have flunked the test. In *Best*, the court concluded that the words "sole and absolute discretion" to make distributions of principal as may be "reasonably necessary for her comfort, support and maintenance" protected the trust from inclusion in the decedent's estate because "the Supreme Court of the state of Nebraska, if presented with this case at hand, would hold" these words to "create an invasionary power 'limited by an ascertainable standard relating to the health, education, support or maintenance' "of the decedent "consistent with" § 2041(b)(1)(A).

An interesting aspect of *Best* is the court's failure to be especially troubled by the presence of the word "comfort" in the trust. Most practitioners avoid the word "comfort" (as well as words such as "welfare", and "happiness") out of fear that its presence might jeopardize the protection of the ascertainable standard exception. Thus, the *Best* court's analysis is useful:

> Courts have held that use of the word "comfort," when used conjunctively with the other specified purposes permitting excludability from a decedent's gross estate, does not destroy an invasionary power limited by

¶ 22,073

an ascertainable standard in reference to "health, education, support, or maintenance of the decedent" pursuant to 26 U.S.C. § 2041(b)(1)(A). For instance, in Vissering v. Commissioner of Internal Revenue, 990 F.2d 578 (10th Cir.1993), the court examined the testamentary language in a trust which allowed an invasion "required for the continued comfort, support, maintenance, or education of said beneficiary." The trust assets, according to a decision by the United States Tax Court that was under review, were includable in the Estate of Norman Vissering, the deceased beneficiary of the trust. As observed by the Circuit Court in Vissering: "The appeal turns on whether decedent held powers permitting him to invade the principal of the trust for his own benefit unrestrained by an ascertainable standard relating to health, education, support, or maintenance." 990 F.2d at 578. In Vissering, the court also stated:

> "The Internal Revenue Service (IRS) and the Tax Court focused on portions of the invasion provision providing that the trust principal could be expended for the 'comfort' of decedent, declaring that this statement rendered the power of invasion incapable of limitation by the courts."

> ... The instant language states that invasion of principal is permitted to the extent "required for the continued comfort" of the decedent, and is part of a clause referencing the support, maintenance and education of the beneficiary. Invasion of the corpus is not permitted to the extent "determined" or "desired" for the beneficiary's comfort but only to the extent that it is "required." Furthermore, the invasion must be for the beneficiary's "continued" comfort, implying, we believe, more than the minimum necessary for survival, but nevertheless reasonably necessary to maintain the beneficiary in his accustomed manner of living. These words in context state a standard essentially no different from the examples in the Treasury Regulation, in which phrases such as "support in reasonable comfort," "maintenance in health and reasonable comfort," and "support in his accustomed manner of living" are deemed to be limited by an ascertainable standard. Treas.Reg. § 20.2041–1(c)(2).

> 990 F.2d at 579–81. See, also, Brantingham, [631 F.2d 542, 545 (7th Cir.1980)](power to invade life estate if necessary for "maintenance, comfort and happiness" is an invasionary power limited by an ascertainable standard); Hunter v. U.S., 597 F.Supp. 1293 (W.D.Penn.1984) (trustee's power to invade trust corpus "for the comfortable support and maintenance of any beneficiary therein, or should any emergency arise" is an invasionary power limited by an ascertainable standard); Toledo Trust Co. v. U.S., 1987 U.S.Dist. LEXIS 16111 [1987 WL 364077] (N.D.Ohio 1987) (power to invade trust corpus for "care, comfort and support" is an invasionary power limited by an ascertainable standard).

¶ 22,079

Problem

[¶ 22,081]

Sun is both trustee and beneficiary of a trust established by her father. Distributions from the income and principal of the trust are to be made to Sun. Which, if any, of the following dispositive provisions will result in the trust property's being included in Sun's estate for estate tax purposes at her death? See Reg. § 20.2041–1(c)(2).

(a) The trustee shall distribute so much or all of the income and principal of the trust estate as shall be needed by Sun for her health, education, maintenance and support?

(b) The trustee shall distribute so much or all of the income and principal of the trust estate as shall be needed by Sun for her health, education, maintenance and support in her accustomed manner of living?

(c) The trustee shall distribute so much or all of the income and principal of the trust estate as shall be needed by Sun for her welfare and happiness?

(d) The trustee shall distribute so much or all of the income and principal of the trust estate as shall be needed by Sun for her health, education, maintenance, support, welfare and happiness in her accustomed manner of living?

F.   COMPETENCY OF HOLDER OF POWER

[¶ 22,085]

ESTATE OF ALPERSTEIN v. COMMISSIONER

United States Court of Appeals, Second Circuit, 1979.
613 F.2d 1213.

FRIENDLY, Circuit Judge:

* * * Fannie Alperstein died intestate on December 3, 1972, after surviving her husband, Harry, who had died more than five years earlier on July 6, 1967. His will established a trust for the benefit of the decedent. * * * Fannie Alperstein was to receive all the net income from the trust payable at frequent intervals for the duration of her life, and was granted a testamentary power to appoint the principal of the trust free of any restrictions. If the decedent failed to exercise her testamentary power of appointment, Mr. Alperstein's children or their issue would take in default.

On January 16, some six months before Harry Alperstein's death, Fannie Alperstein had entered a nursing home where she remained until shortly before her death. On December 27, 1967, a New York court declared Fannie to be incompetent * * *. Although the judicial determination of the decedent's incompetence followed the death of Mr. Alperstein by almost six months, the parties have stipulated that from her husband's death until her own death, the decedent lacked the capacity to execute a will under New York law, did not purport to exercise the power of appointment granted by her husband's will, and was legally incapable of exercising that power.

Rosalind A. Greenberg, the decedent's executrix, filed a federal estate tax return that did not include in the decedent's gross estate the value of the property over which the decedent had been granted testamentary power of appointment by her husband's will. The Commissioner asserted a deficiency based on his determination that the decedent possessed at death a general power of appointment within the meaning of I.R.C. § 2041(a)(2), which required the inclusion of the entire value of the property subject to that power within her gross estate. The parties have stipulated that if the property subject to the power created by Mr. Alperstein's will is included in the decedent's gross estate, that property is to be valued at $242,167.17.

* * *

Appellant does not question that, so far as language is concerned, the power of appointment conferred by Article Fourth of Harry Alperstein's will met the statutory test. The claim is that, despite this § 2041(a)(2) is inapplicable because, under the stipulated facts, Fannie Alperstein was never able to exercise the power vested in her by her husband's will—a situation allegedly not present in any of the cases that have sustained the taxability of powers against attacks of the same general sort as that mounted here.

I.

We start, as always, with the words of the statute * * *. The operative verb in § 2041(a)(2) is "has." Beyond cavil Mrs. Alperstein "had" a general power of appointment at the time of her death. This had been granted by her husband's will and nothing done by the New York courts purported to take it away. Even if we assume that the judgment of Fannie Alperstein's incompetency conclusively established her inability to exercise this power, that judgment was subject to being vacated if her mental condition changed for the better. The argument is rather that although Mrs. Alperstein "had" such a power, it was not "exercisable" at the time of her death since she had long since been declared incompetent and in fact had been so ever since her husband had died. However, the word "exercisable" is found not in the operative portion of the statute but in a section addressed to how broad a power must be in order to be "general." The natural meaning of the words is that "exercisable" is shorthand for "which by its terms may be exercised," and does not mean that § 2041(a)(2) is limited to cases where the decedent could in fact exercise the power at the moment of death—something which, in the absence of a will or similar instrument could rarely occur.

II.

The meaning which thus emerges from the words of the statute is strongly reinforced by the legislative history.* * *

Prior to the 1942 legislation, estate taxation of powers of appointment had remained substantially unchanged since § 402 of the Revenue Act of

1918, 40 Stat. 1057, 1097, first imposed a federal estate tax on appointed property. Under pre–1942 law, such property was taxed "only if (1) the [decedent's appointive] power was general, (2) the power was exercised, and (3) the appointive property passed as a result of such exercise." Craven, Powers of Appointment Act of 1951, 65 Harv.L.Rev. 55, 55–56 (1951). The 1942 amendments dramatically altered this policy in response to a widespread belief that it had served as "an outstanding device for the avoidance of estate tax." S. Rep. No. 1631, 77th Cong., 2d Sess. 232 (1942). Dissatisfaction with the pre–1942 law by those interested in protecting the revenue focused on the opportunities it afforded to avoid taxation, either through deliberately failing to exercise a general power of appointment (in effect, retaining the power to choose other appointees by deciding in favor of the takers-in-default) or through eluding court-fashioned definitions of "general" powers of appointment with the aid of minor restrictions that transmuted a general power into an exempt "special" power. Both loopholes were plugged by the 1942 amendments, which taxed all powers of appointment created after the enactment of the amendments regardless of whether they were exercised, save for those powers that could only be exercised in favor of certain restricted classes of potential appointees. See 1942 amendments, supra, at § 403(a). In addition, the 1942 amendment fixed the time of death as the relevant moment for determining the existence of a taxable power. Id. § 403(a). Powers that lapsed prior to the decedent's death were treated as taxable releases by the post–1942 estate and gift tax regulations. See U.S. Treas. Reg. 105, § 81.24(b)(1) (1943); U.S. Treas. Reg. 108, § 96.2(b) (1943).

The 1942 amendments extended the policy of taxing powers, regardless of exercise, to general powers created before the enactment of the amendments. See 1942 amendments, supra, § 403(d)(1). However, the amendments sought to mitigate the retroactive impact of this by allowing a grace period in which all holders of general powers might release their power without estate tax consequences, id. § 403(d)(3), and by extending this grace period in the case of holders who were "under a legal disability to release such power" until six months after the termination of their disability, id. § 403(d)(2). * * * [T]he fact that the 1942 Congress felt it necessary to include this provision strongly suggests its belief that the existence of a legal disability by the holder of a general power would not prevent inclusion of property subject to that power in the estate. Although the provision in question related only to pre–1942 powers, there is no reason to suppose that Congress intended a different rule with respect to incompetency for post–1942 powers.

* * * [T]he 1951 Act continued the policy of taxing post–1942 general powers regardless of their exercise * * *.

This conclusion is also buttressed by one of the Act's broader purposes, namely, to provide "a test of taxability which is simple, clear-cut, and easy to apply." S. Rep. No. 382, 82nd Cong., 1st Sess. 2, [1951] U.S. Code Cong. & Ad. News 1530, 1531. Linking an interpretation of "exercisable" to decedents' disabilities under local law would hardly simplify the 1951 test, particularly since the Act provides no basis for distinguishing decedents adjudged to be legally incompetent from those who were otherwise barred from exercising their powers.

* * *

Further support for the construction that the 1951 Act embraced all general powers regardless of the donee's capacity to exercise them is furnished by a provision in the marital deduction * * * codified as amended in I.R.C. § 2056(b)(5). This provides that property passing in trust to a surviving spouse will qualify for exclusion from the decedent's estate, inter alia, if the surviving spouse is entitled to all income from the property for life; if the surviving spouse has the power to appoint such property in favor of herself or the estate; and if the power to appoint such property, "whether exercisable by will or during life, is exercisable by such spouse alone and in all events." The Internal Revenue Service has long held that competency under local law is irrelevant for determining whether a power is "exercisable" within the meaning of the marital deduction. Rev. Rul. 55–518, 1955–2 Cum. Bull. 384; Rev. Rul. 75–350, 1975–2 Cum. Bull. 367. This conclusion is virtually dictated by the consideration that "[o]therwise, in view of the possibility that any given person may become legally incompetent during his or her lifetime, no trust could ever qualify under section 2056(b)(5)." Rev. Rul. 75–350, supra, 1975–2 Cum. Bull. at 368. * * * Still more persuasive is the evidence that Congress intended the marital deduction as a deferral of the tax on property which, however, would eventually be subject to a gift or an estate tax paid by the surviving spouse or by her estate. See S. Rep. No. 1013, 80th Cong., 2d Sess. 16, [1948] U.S. Code Cong. & Ad. News 1163, 1238; * * *. Given that this purpose was served in 1948 by adopting the same use of "exercisable" in the marital deduction that had already existed in the corresponding powers of appointment provision, Congress cannot be thought to have abandoned Sub silentio the intended interaction between these two provisions a mere three years later and thereby to have created a situation, such as concededly would exist here if appellant were to prevail, wherein property escapes estate tax at the time of the death of the donor of the power because the competency of the donee is immaterial and also at the time of the death of the donee because competency is held to be crucial. The 1951 Powers of Appointment Act must be read not in isolation but as a part of a comprehensive statutory scheme.

III.

We find no basis for a contrary view in the Service's rulings and regulations.

The Service first addressed the relationship between incompetency and § 2041(a)(2) in Rev. Rul. 55–518, 1955–2 Cum. Bul. 384 (1955), which ruled on the estate of a surviving spouse who had enjoyed an unrestricted lifetime power of appointment over a testamentary trust created by her husband. In a dual holding, the Service determined that the husband's estate qualified for a marital deduction and the wife's estate was taxable for her power even though the wife was incompetent from the date of her husband's death until the time of her own death. Id. 385. The Service reasoned that the wife could have exercised her power with the aid of a local court and, therefore, "possessed" the power at the time of her death even if she could not have freely exercised it at any time. Id.

* * *

[The gift tax regulations relating to the circumstances under which transfers to minors of a future interest would qualify for the gift tax annual exclusion as provided in § 2503(c) are consistent. Reg.] § 25.2503–4(b) stated:

> if the minor is given a power of appointment . . . the fact that under local law a minor is under a disability to exercise an inter vivos power or to execute a will does not cause the transfer to fail to satisfy the conditions of section 2502(c) [2503(c)].

* * * Rev. Rul. 74–350, 1975–2 Cum. Bull. 367, the Service's most recent pronouncement on the relationship between incompetency and the possession of a general power within the meaning of § 2041, extends the Service's original determination of taxability to a legally incompetent holder of a testamentary power who is indistinguishable from Mrs. Alperstein in all relevant respects. This ruling abandons any reliance on the possibility that a legally incompetent holder of a power might be able to exercise his power with the aid of a court or anyone else. Instead, it concludes:

> [j]ust as incapacity or incompetency does not render property owned outright by a decedent exempt from estate taxation, neither is property subject to a general power of appointment exempt in such circumstances, unless *by the terms of the grant of the power* such circumstances have caused the existence of the power itself to cease prior to the decedent's death. [Emphasis original.]

Id. at 368.

IV.

Although appellant may be right in contending that no decision upholding the estate taxation of property subject to a general power of appointment has presented facts quite so humanly appealing in favor of the donee as this, the general thrust of the case law in appellate courts is decidedly unfavorable to her.

While the Supreme Court has not had occasion to rule on the effect of incompetency of the holder of a general power on taxability under § 2041, C.I.R. v. Estate of Noel, 380 U.S. 678 (1965), strongly indicated the Court's probable approach. Noel required a construction of I.R.C. § 2042, which provides inter alia that a decedent's estate is taxable for the proceeds of insurance policies on the life of the decedent "with respect to which the decedent possessed at his death any of the incidents of ownership, exercisable alone or in conjunction with any other person." Immediately before boarding a plane doomed to a fatal crash, the decedent in *Noel* purchased several flight insurance policies which he left with his wife on the ground. The decedent's estate contended that on these facts there had been no exercisable incidents of ownership within the meaning of the statute. While acknowledging that "there was no practical opportunity" to exercise ownership power, the Court concluded:

¶ 22,085

It would stretch the imagination to think that Congress intended to measure estate tax liability by an individual's fluctuating, day-to-day, hour-by-hour capacity to dispose of property which he owns. We hold that estate tax liability for policies "with respect to which the decedent possessed at his death any of the incidents of ownership" depends on a general, legal power to exercise ownership, without regard to the owner's ability to exercise it at a particular moment.

Id. at 684.

Three courts of appeals have considered the effect upon taxability under § 2041 of the inability of the holder of a power to exercise it; all have ruled in favor of the Government. [Discussion and citations omitted.] * * *

In sum we hold, on the basis of statutory language, legislative history (particularly the interaction of § 2041(a)(1) with the marital deduction, § 2056(b)(5)), administrative interpretation and case law, that when an instrument has conferred a testamentary power which by its terms can be exercised in favor of the donee's estate, the property subject to the power is part of the donee's gross estate even though the donee, by virtue of incompetency was unable to make a valid will at any time after the power was granted.

Affirmed.

Note

[¶ 22,087]

At death, Lillian Halpern held a testamentary general power of appointment over a certain trust and as a result the trust property was included in her estate for estate tax purposes. Estate of Halpern v. Commissioner, 70 T.C.M. (CCH) 229, T.C.M. (RIA) ¶ 95,352 (1995). All trust income was to be paid to Lillian. Principal could be invaded for her benefit at the discretion of the trustees in the event of illness or other emergency. While she lived, trust property was given to Lillian's loved ones by the trustees even though the trust authorized distributions only to Lillian. Gift tax returns were filed by Lillian reflecting these gifts. The transfers to Lillian's loved ones were made over a period of years, beginning in 1982 and ending in 1988, the year of Lillian's death. Lillian suffered a stroke in 1986 and was incompetent at all times thereafter. Lillian had consented in writing to the transfers made from the trust before she became incompetent. Other family members joined in the consents. The IRS claimed that all of the gifts should be included in Lillian's estate for estate tax purposes. It reasoned that the trustees could recover the transfers made from the trust because they were improper and, therefore, that property was included in Lillian's gross estate because it was subject to her general power of appointment. The court agreed as to the transfers made after Lillian became incompetent but concluded that the pre-incompetence transfers were not included in Lillian's estate. The IRS expressed concern that excluding the lifetime transfers from Lillian's estate "would undermine the federal transfer tax system." The court responded by effectively saying, "not to worry. Lillian reported these transfers for gift tax purposes." So far as impropriety is concerned, Lillian's consents to the transfers made prior to her incompetence would be considered effective family agreements under state law. The post-competency transfers were included in Lillian's estate because, under local law, Lillian had not effectively consented to those transfers and, as a result, either Lillian or her successors in interest could revoke them and recapture the transferred property either before or after her death.

G. RELEASE AND DISCLAIMER

[¶ 22,091]

A release of a post–1942 general power is considered an inter vivos exercise of the power. § 2514(b). Moreover, the property subject to the power will be included in the powerholder's gross estate if the power is released in such a way that the property would have been included in the powerholder's gross estate if it had been owned and so transferred by the powerholder, i.e., if the provisions of §§ 2035–2038 would apply to the transaction if nonpower property had been transferred. § 2041(a)(2). For example, if the life income beneficiary of a trust also had a general testamentary power of appointment over the trust property and this power was released by the life income beneficiary by an inter vivos conveyance, the release would likely bring the trust property into the life income beneficiary's gross estate at death because the release was the equivalent of a transfer of the trust property by the donee subject to a retained life estate under § 2036(a)(1). For discussion of related material, see ¶ ¶ 5007–5009.

Section 2518(c)(2) allows disclaimer of a power of appointment. Satisfying the statutorily imposed disclaimer requirements means that what would otherwise be a taxable release will have no transfer tax consequences. For further discussion of the disclaimer requirements, see ¶ ¶ 5001, 6001 and 6013.

H. LAPSE

[¶ 22,097]

1. INTRODUCTION

Section 2041(b)(2) equates a lapse of a power created after 1942 with a release of a power—and a release of a power triggers gift tax. However, § 2041(b)(2) carves out an exception whereby the lapse of certain powers of appointment will not be treated as a taxable release. This exception, commonly referred to as the "five-and-five power," provides that a lapse is not to be considered a taxable release to the extent that the property subject to the lapsing power, at the time of the lapse, did not exceed in value the greater of $5,000 or 5 percent of the value of the property out of which the exercise of the lapsed power could be satisfied. The plain meaning of this exception is to create, practically speaking, an exemption from tax for estate and gift tax purposes.

¶ 22,087

[¶ 22,103]

2. FIVE–AND–FIVE POWERS

The lapse exemption, or five-and-five power as it is more commonly referred to, is regularly used as a basis of a plan which gives trust beneficiaries the right to make annual withdrawals from the trust without adverse estate or gift tax consequences. Pure and simple, a right of withdrawal is a general power of appointment by another name—and property subject to a general power is included in the estate of the powerholder at death for estate tax purposes (or is subject to gift tax if the power is exercised during the lifetime of the powerholder). However, in cases where the trust is drafted to take advantage of the five-and-five lapse exemption, the trust beneficiary (or beneficiaries) can benefit from the trust without having the trust property included in the estate of the beneficiary at his or her subsequent death. In the typical case, the beneficiary may be given all of the trust income along with the right to withdraw from the trust on an annual noncumulative basis, for example, "the greater of $5,000 or 5 percent of the value of the property constituting the trust estate, the trust to be valued for these purposes as of the last calendar day of the year." The purpose of such a provision is to give the trust beneficiary the unfettered right to withdraw a limited amount from the trust, the goal being, perhaps, to give the beneficiary some discretionary funds, maybe an "Acapulco Fund" or a source of funds for some unanticipated needs.

The exercise or nonexercise of a five-and-five right of withdrawal power is generally estate and gift tax neutral. That is, neither estate nor gift taxes are triggered by the exercise or nonexercise of a five-and-five right of withdrawal power. One exception to this general proposition may be noted. In the year of death, the powerholder's estate will be deemed to include the amount eligible for withdrawal by the powerholder at the moment of death. Reg. § 20.2041–3(d)(3). In addition, the powerholder will be taxed under the income tax on the portion of the trust income attributable to the portion of the property that he or she could have withdrawn each year. For discussion, see ¶ 32,229 and § 678(a)(1) and (2). This latter point relates to the possibility that with each lapse or nonexercise of the powerholder's annual right of withdrawal, the powerholder will be treated as owner of an ever increasing share of the trust—and will be taxed on the trust income attributable to that portion in those cases where the powerholder does not receive that income or is not otherwise taxed on it.

Suppose, however, that a generous settlor provides that the income beneficiary of a trust may withdraw $20,000 per annum from the trust "with the right of withdrawal to lapse to the extent not exercised at the end of each calendar year during the continuance of the trust." In those years when the trust property has a value of less than $400,000, the failure of the beneficiary to exercise his or her right of withdrawal will result in a taxable transfer being made by the powerholder. Code § 2514(e). Furthermore, the failure to exercise the right of withdrawal will have estate tax consequences. For example, assume the trust consists of property having a value of $300,000 and the trust beneficiary is to receive all of the trust income quarterly. Failure to withdraw the $20,000 means that the beneficiary will have made a transfer of $5,000 ($20,000 minus $15,000 (5 percent of $300,000)), the lapse exclusion shielding $15,000 from gift tax. (Technically, the value of the $5,000 transfer, for gift tax purposes, would be reduced by the value of the beneficiary's retained right to the income from the transferred $5,000.) But that is not all. At the death of the powerholder, a portion of the trust property will be included in the estate of the powerholder. For estate tax purposes, the powerholder will be deemed to have made a transfer to the trust of the $5,000 that was not sheltered by the five-and-five lapse exclusion—and to have retained the right to the income from the transferred $5,000 for life. Section 2036(a)(1), relating to retained life estates, is then invoked to cause a fraction of the trust property, valued at the time of the death of the powerholder, to be included in the estate of the powerholder for estate tax purposes. In addition, the $20,000 eligible for withdrawal by the powerholder at death will be included in the powerholder's estate for estate tax purposes. Reg. § 20.2041–3(d)(3).

[¶ 22,109]

3. TAX SHELTER

Not only does the five-and-five lapse exception have positive planning possibilities, it can also have utility in sheltering property subject to a general power from estate taxation. Consider the case where a trust beneficiary has the right to withdraw from the trust all trust income annually but, to the extent that the trust income is not withdrawn at year-end, the portion of the income remaining in the trust is to be added to principal. Obviously, the power of withdrawal lapsed at year-end, meaning that the five-and-five lapse exemption is available to shelter the amount not withdrawn from the gift tax—and the estate tax. However, the question arises as to the application of the five-and-five lapse exception. That is, is the exempt amount five percent of the value of the trust corpus or is it five percent of the value of the trust income (inasmuch as it is only the income that can be withdrawn)? While the issue may appear to be esoteric, its resolution can have significant financial consequences and is presented all too frequently when it comes time for preparation of the estate tax return of the powerholder. The *Fish* case below considers this issue.

[¶ 22,115]

FISH v. UNITED STATES

United States Court of Appeals, Ninth Circuit, 1970.
432 F.2d 1278.

TAYLOR, District Judge:

* * * Clarence G. Blagen, the husband of Minnie C. Blagen, died on May 28, 1951. The residuary clause of his will established a trust, the terms of which provided that Minnie C. Blagen should have, during her lifetime, the right in any calendar year to demand payment to her of all or part of the net

¶ 22,103

income of the trust for that year, but that any income not so claimed by her would be added to the corpus of the trust. Upon the death of Minnie C. Blagen, the trust corpus, including such accumulated income added to the corpus, was to be distributed to the grandchildren of Clarence G. Blagen.

Minnie C. Blagen (decedent) never exercised or released her power over the income of the trust in any year from the inception of the trust until her death on July 13, 1960, except insofar as the annual lapse of the power, if any such lapse occurred, constituted a release of the power as a matter of law under Section 2041(b)(2) * * *. The Commissioner, in assessing the tax deficiency, included in the decedent's gross estate the net income of the trust, less allowable exemptions, for the years 1955, 1956, 1957, 1958 and 1959. The inclusion of accumulated income which had been added to the trust in those years resulted in an increase in the decedent's gross estate of $116,045.36. The taxpayer had not included this amount in the estate tax return which he had filed for the estate.

The Commissioner determined that the decedent possessed a general power of appointment over the trust income and that the failure of the decedent to exercise this power constituted a lapse of the power in each year in which it was not exercised. The Commissioner contends that the lapse constitutes a release of the power under Section 2041(b)(2) in such a way that, if it were a transfer of property owned by the decedent, the property would have been includible in the decedent's gross estate as a transfer with a retained life estate under Section 2036(a)(1). [The court explained in a footnote that "As income was added to the trust each year as a result of the decedent's inaction, that income generated additional income in following years which was subject to the decedent's lifetime power of appointment, and thus the 'transfer' each year by the decedent was one which left her with a lifetime interest in the property. Such a transfer, resulting from the exercise or release of a power of appointment, becomes includible in the gross estate of the decedent under the provisions of Section 2041(a)(2)."]

The taxpayer agrees that the decedent possessed a general power of appointment, and that the "transfer" each year, had the property been owned by the decedent, would be a transfer with a retained life estate. The taxpayer contends, however, that * * * the Commissioner and the District Court erred in computing the allowable exemption under Section 2041(b)(2) on the basis of five per cent of the net income of the trust instead of * * * five per cent of the total trust assets.

* * * [§ 2041(b)(2)] allows as an exemption to the amount includible in the taxable estate an amount equal to five per cent of "the aggregate value of the assets out of which, or the proceeds out of which, the exercise of the lapsed powers could be satisfied," or the sum of $5,000, whichever is the greater. The District Court, in determining the amount of the exemption, computed the exemption on the basis of five per cent of the trust income. Since for each year in question, the sum of $5,000 was greater than five per cent of the trust income, the District Court allowed an exemption of $5,000 for each year, as the Commissioner had done. The taxpayer argues that the exemption should be $5,000 or five per cent of the total trust assets, and since

five per cent of the total assets would exceed the net income for three of the five years in question and would nearly equal the net income in the other two years, the end result should be that the amount includible in the decedent's estate should be reduced to $15,858.47. The taxpayer argues that since the income payable to the decedent, had she demanded it, would have been payable either from corpus or income, the entire trust represents "assets out of which, or the proceeds out of which, the exercise of lapsed powers could be satisfied," and thus the entire trust assets should serve as the basis for the five per cent computation. We do not agree. Even if the trustee could have satisfied a demand for income out of either corpus assets or income funds, a point which we do not here decide, the distribution would necessarily have been a distribution of income as a matter of federal tax law or as a matter of trust accounting, since the decedent had no power whatever to invade the corpus of the trust.

While the language of Section 2041(b)(2)(B), like much of the statutory tax law, is hardly a model of precision and clarity on the point, we are satisfied from a reading of the statute together with its legislative history that the applicable basis for computation on the allowable exemption is the trust or fund in which the lapsed power existed. The District Court correctly determined that the power of appointment in the instant case existed only with respect to the trust income, and properly allowed an exemption of $5,000 for each year in question.

* * *

Note

[¶ 22,121]

While the court in *Fish* states that the Commissioner has included all of the net income of the trust in the decedent's estate as a result of the decedent's power to withdraw that income, the regulations suggest that, in a case like *Fish,* the correct amount to be included in the estate of the deceased powerholder is the sum of a series of fractions of the trust rather than the dollar amount that could have been withdrawn by the deceased powerholder. Reg. § 20.2041–3(d)(4). The numerator of each such fraction will be equal to the amount that could have been withdrawn by the powerholder in each year less the amount of the lapse exemption available to the powerholder that year. The denominator will be equal to the value of the fund out of which the right of withdrawal could have been satisfied, the fund being valued on the date that the right of withdrawal lapsed. Using the example given in the regulations, where the value of the trust is $800,000 and the powerholder had the right to withdraw $50,000, a taxable release of 1/80th of the total value of the trust resulted from the failure of the powerholder to exercise his or her right of withdrawal. The numerator of the fraction is determined by subtracting five percent of the value of the trust corpus ($800,000), or $40,000, from the amount that could have been withdrawn ($50,000). The denominator is the value of the corpus ($800,000). In the case where the trust beneficiary has an annual right of withdrawal of $50,000 that is not exercised and that lapses at year-end and the value of the trust corpus is a constant $800,000 over a seven-year period, 7/80ths of the value of the trust at the time of the death of the powerholder will be included in the powerholder's estate for estate tax purposes—provided, of course, that the powerholder retains or possesses a §§ 2036–2038 power over the trust, such as a right to receive all of the trust income during the seven-year period.

Problems

[¶ 22,127]

1. Review the facts in the *Fish* case and consider the following:

   (a) Could the controversy in *Fish* have been avoided if the power-holder had exercised her right of withdrawal each year?

   (b) Should the drafter of the will have anticipated the controversy that arose in *Fish* and suggested to the client that the will contain a provision requiring the trustee to distribute the trust income at least annually?

2. Suppose Mary has the power to withdraw $40,000 annually from a trust, the right of withdrawal to be exercised on or before year-end, and, to the extent not exercised, the $40,000 will be added to the principal of the trust. At the time of her death, Mary had not exercised the power for that year. Is it appropriate to conclude that the full $40,000 will be included in Mary's estate for estate tax purposes? See Reg. § 20.2041–3(d)(3).

I. STATE LEGISLATION TO LIMIT GENERAL POWER

[¶ 22,129]

State legislators routinely add default rules to the state's probate code or equivalent so as to effect a "best results" or "most likely results" outcome in cases where the text appearing in the governing instrument is susceptible of more than one meaning. Typically, the statutory interpretation is intended to prevail unless, in the specified instances, the governing instrument is found to otherwise provide. In more recent times, legislatures have taken to "fixing" instruments that might be construed to have a "bad tax result." An example follows in Priv. Ltr. Rul. 200530020. Should the likely presence of such legislation in the jurisdiction whose law governs embolden the inexperienced draftsperson, strong in resolve (to take the assignment) but weak in funda-mentals? Would it be helpful to recite, in the governing instrument, the desired tax benefit? What about the case where the draftsperson was not even aware of the peril and/or benefit that might result from certain choices? Suppose the document included text stating that the maker wanted "the best tax outcome possible and the instrument should be so construed or modified?" Is it possible that some instruments would contain text that, perhaps uninten-tionally, precluded application of a state statute aimed at providing the best tax outcome?

¶ 22,129

[¶ 22,130]

PRIVATE LETTER RULING 200530020

April 6, 2005.

Decedent died testate on Date 1, a date prior to September 25, 1985. At his death, Decedent was a resident of State and was survived by Spouse and three children.

Article 6 of Decedent's Will created Trust. Under the terms of Trust, until the death of Spouse, the trustees may accumulate the net income of the trust or pay to or apply so much thereof to the use of such one or more of Spouse, Decedent's children, and the then living issue of Decedent's children, in such amounts and proportions as the trustees in their sole and absolute discretion deem advisable from time to time without regard to equality of distribution. There is no power to distribute the principal of Trust during the lifetime of Spouse. At Spouse's death, Trust provides for distributions to Decedent's descendants.

In Article 7 of Decedent's Will, Decedent designated his father, his brother, and Spouse as original co-trustees of Trust. Spouse and sister of Spouse are the current trustees and have been serving as co-trustees since Year 6 of Trust.

Trust was irrevocable on September 25, 1985. * * *

In 1995, Statute was added to the State Code that provides, in part, that unless the terms of a trust refer specifically to this provision and provide to the contrary, a trustee shall not, on behalf of or for the benefit of a beneficiary who is also a trustee, make discretionary distributions of either principal or income for the benefit of the trustee, except to provide for the health, education, maintenance, or support of the trustee as described under §§ 2041 and 2514 of the Internal Revenue Code (Code). The Statute also provides that a trustee shall not, on behalf of or for the benefit of a beneficiary who is also a trustee, make discretionary distributions of either principal or income to satisfy any legal or support obligations of the trustee. This provision applies to all irrevocable trusts existing on July 7, 1995, unless all parties in interest elect affirmatively not to be subject to the application of this section.

It is represented that the parties in interest with respect to Trust have not elected affirmatively for Trust to be excluded from the application of Statute.

You have asked us to rule, as follows:

    1.   That, upon her death, no portion of trust income will be included in Spouse's gross estate under § 2041(b)(2).

    2.   That, during Spouse's lifetime, no distributions of trust income from Trust after the effective date of Statute will be subject to gift tax under § 2514(c)(1).

* * *

LAW AND ANALYSIS

* * *

While federal law controls what rights or interests shall be taxed after they are created, creation of legal rights and interests in property (such as the breadth and scope of a power of appointment over the corpus of a testamentary trust) is a matter of state law. United States v. Pelzer, 312 U.S. 399 (1941), 1941–1 C.B. 441; Morgan v. Commissioner, 309 U.S. 78 (1940), 1940–1 C.B. 229.

As referred to above, Statute provides that unless the terms of a trust refer specifically to the provision and provide to the contrary, a trustee shall not perform any of the following on behalf of or for the benefit of a beneficiary who is also a trustee: (1) make discretionary distributions of either principal or income for the benefit of the trustee, except to provide for the health, education, maintenance, or support of the trustee as described under §§ 2041 and 2514 of the Internal Revenue Code, as amended; (2) make discretionary allocations of receipts or expenses as between principal and income, unless the trustee has no power to enlarge or shift any beneficial interest except as an incidental consequence of the discharge of the fiduciary duties of the trustee; and (3) make discretionary distributions of either principal or income to satisfy any legal or support obligations of the trustee.

Statute provides, in part, that it applies to all irrevocable trusts existing on July 7, 1995, unless all parties in interest elect affirmatively not to be subject to the application of this section.

Rev. Proc. 94–44, 1994–2 C.B. 683, sets forth the Service's position regarding the transfer tax consequences of the enactment of Florida Statutes Annotated (F.S.A.) § 737.402(4)(a)(1). Under this statute, any fiduciary power conferred upon a trustee to make discretionary distributions of either principal or income to or for the trustee's own benefit cannot be exercised by the trustee, except to provide for that trustee's health, education, maintenance, or support, as described in §§ 2041 and 2514. The statute was effective with respect to trusts that were irrevocable on or after July 1, 1991. Pursuant to the revenue procedure, the Service will not treat the statute as causing the lapse of a general power of appointment for purposes of §§ 2041 and 2514, where the scope of a fiduciary power held by a beneficiary was restricted as a result of the statute.

In the present case, prior to the effective date of Statute, Spouse's unlimited power to distribute income to herself as a trustee-beneficiary constituted a general power of appointment over the income of Trust under §§ 2041(b)(1)(A) and 2514(c)(1). See § 20.2041–1(b)(1) and (3) and § 25.2514–1(b)(1) and (3). Consistent with the principles of Rev. Proc. § 94–44, the enactment of Statute will not be treated as causing a lapse of Spouse's general power of appointment over Trust income for transfer tax purposes. The statute will be treated as effective with respect to Trust on the effective date of Statute. Therefore, as of the effective date, Spouse, as trustee-beneficiary of Trust, will not have the power to appoint trust income for her own benefit except in satisfaction of any needs she may have for

¶ 22,130

health, education, maintenance, and support. Since Spouse's power to distribute income to herself is limited to an ascertainable standard as described in §§ 2041(b)(1)(A) and 2514(c)(1), Spouse will not possess a general power of appointment over the trust income for transfer tax purposes by virtue of any fiduciary power to distribute income. Accordingly, we conclude that no portion of trust income will be included in Spouse's gross estate under § 2041(b)(2) upon her death and that distributions of trust income to the trust beneficiaries after the effective date of Statute will not be subject to gift tax under § 2514(c)(1).

J. JOINT POWERS

[¶ 22,133]

A major exception to the rule that general powers of appointment held or exercised at death are included in the decedent's taxable estate relates to jointly held powers. As to powers created on or before October 21, 1942, any power that the decedent holds jointly with another party is not a general power and thus not subject to the estate tax. Jointly held powers created thereafter will escape taxation as general powers if: (1) the other holder of the power is the donor; or (2) the other holder has a substantial interest in the property adverse to that of the donee. As the *Towle* case illustrates, the other holder does not have a "substantial adverse interest" unless that holder somehow has a personal stake in seeing that the power is not exercised by the donee in the donee's own favor.

[¶ 22,139]

ESTATE OF TOWLE v. COMMISSIONER

United States Tax Court, 1970.
54 T.C. 368.

TANNENWALD, Judge: * * *

[At the death of Janet McNear Towle in 1964, she was the income beneficiary of three post–1942 settlement contracts of insurance on her deceased father's life. The contracts gave her two further rights: (1) a noncumulative privilege to withdraw $13,500 annually from principal and (2) the privilege (unexercised at her death) of withdrawing at any time all of the principal with the consent of the First National Bank, as trustee under the will of her father, Charles W. McNear. Upon the decedent's death, undistributed funds remaining with the insurance company were to be paid to the bank as trustee of a residuary trust set up in her father's will. The residuary trust provided that the income was to be paid to the decedent for life with the remainder to her son. The bank as trustee under the will was authorized to invade principal for the decedent if the net income from the residuary trust was insufficient for her support and maintenance.]

* * *

¶ 22,130

Petitioner makes a two-pronged argument to support its contention that the power of withdrawal by the decedent of the entire proceeds of the insurance settlement contracts was not a general power of appointment within the meaning of section 2041(b)(1) and that therefore the amount of those proceeds, in excess of that subject to the noncumulative annual right of withdrawal, is not includable in the decedent's gross estate under section 2041(a).

The first prong is developed along the following lines: (1) First National, albeit concededly as a trustee, held a direct remainder interest under the insurance settlement contracts and consequently had an "interest in the property, subject to the power"; (2) because of the fiduciary duty imposed upon First National to protect the interests of the remaindermen of the residuary trust under the will of Charles W. McNear, its "interest" was "substantial" and "adverse" within the meaning of subsection (C)(ii) of section 2041(b)(1); and (3) First National was simply an agent of the grandson remainderman whose interest was undeniably substantial and adverse to that of the decedent. We disagree.

As a general rule, the interest of a nonbeneficiary trustee is neither substantial nor adverse. Reinecke v. Smith, 289 U.S. 172 (1933), so holds with respect to the income tax and its principles are fully applicable to the estate tax. * * * This conclusion is further supported by the following statement in the committee reports which accompanied the original enactment of the pertinent portion of section 2041, as an amendment to section 811(f) of the 1939 Code, by the Powers of Appointment Act of 1951, 65 Stat. 91:

> a future joint power is totally exempt if it is not exercisable by the decedent except with the consent or joinder of a person having a substantial interest. In the property subject to the power, which is adverse to the exercise of the power in favor of the decedent, his estate, his creditors, or the creditors of his estate, a taker in default of appointment has an interest which is adverse to such an exercise. Principles developed under the income and gift taxes will be applicable in determining whether an interest is substantial and the amount of property in which the adversity exists. A coholder of the power has no adverse interest merely because of his joint possession of the power nor merely because he is a permissible appointee under a power, since neither the power nor the expectancy as appointee is an 'interest' in the property. * * * [See H. Rept. No. 327, to accompany H.R. 2084 (Pub. L. 58), 82d Cong., 1st Sess., pp. 5–6 (1951); S. Rept. No. 382 to accompany H.R. 2084 (Pub. L. 591), 82d Cong., 1st Sess., p. 5 (1951).]

In Reinecke v. Smith, supra, the Supreme Court stated:

> In approaching the decision of the question before us it is to be borne in mind that the trustee is not a trustee of the power of revocation and owes no duty to the beneficiary to resist alteration or revocation of the trust. Of course he owes a duty to the beneficiary to protect the trust res, faithfully to administer it, and to distribute the income; but the very fact that he participates in the right of alteration or revocation negatives any

¶ 22,139

fiduciary duty to the beneficiary to refrain from exercising the power. * * *[See 289 U.S. at pp. 176–177.]

Petitioner seeks to avoid the application of the principles announced in Reinecke v. Smith, supra, by claiming that First National had a direct remainder interest in the insurance proceeds and that its fiduciary obligations arose only under the will of Charles W. McNear after it had collected the insurance proceeds. In essence, petitioner asserts that First National was a beneficiary of those proceeds in its own right. But a beneficiary is one who has a beneficial interest of his own and not one who administers property for the benefit of others. * * * Clearly, First National fits the latter category. We do not think its status as the remainderman of the insurance proceeds so enlarged its interest as to place it outside the rationale of Reinecke v. Smith, supra. * * * Nor does petitioner's recital of numerous authorities under state law with respect to the requirement of good faith imposed upon the exercise of discretionary powers by a trustee or the ability of a beneficiary to enforce that requirement by injunction, surcharge, or otherwise have any bearing on the issue before us.

Petitioner admits that, "No provision in the Will of Charles W. McNear in express terms directs or controls the exercise of the Trustee's power to permit the withdrawal of the retained funds by Janice McNear Towle." Petitioner argues that the testamentary objective of Charles W. McNear was to assure that the principal of his estate would pass to his grandson or his heirs and that the trustee had a special duty to see that such objective was accomplished. But on this record it is at least equally, if not more, plausible to conclude that Charles W. McNear considered the insurance settlements to be separate from the residuary trust in order that the decedent would have funds adequate to meet her reasonable desires during her lifetime, as she saw them, and that the corporate trustee had merely the usual fiduciary responsibility to guard against the capricious exhaustion of the insurance principal.

We think that the phrase "substantial interest in the property, subject to the power, which is adverse to exercise of the power in favor of the decedent," as used in section 2041(b)(1)(C)(ii), was intended at the very least to require that the third person have a present or future chance to obtain a personal benefit from the property itself. * * * Compare also the provisions of section 2041(b)(1)(C)(iii), which exclude, on an allocable basis, a portion of property subject to a power which would otherwise be a general power of appointment, but which is exercisable "in favor of" a person whose consent is required.

As the final element in the first prong of its argument, petitioner asserts that First National was simply the agent of the grandson remainderman under the will of Charles W. McNear in granting or withholding its consent to the invasion of the insurance principal by decedent. We can find nothing in the record herein to support such an assertion. Clearly, First National's relationship to the grandson was simply that of a trustee to a beneficiary and, in this context, our previous analysis refutes petitioner's contention.

* * *

Decision will be entered for the respondent.

¶ 22,139

Problems

[¶ 22,145]

1. In 1940, Hatlake's father died leaving the residue of his estate (valued at $100,000) to a trust company "to pay the income to Hatlake for life and upon his death the trust corpus is to be distributed among Hatlake's then living children in equal shares." Under the terms of the testamentary trust, Hatlake was given a power to alter or amend the trust provisions.

   By will, Hatlake exercised his power of amendment over his father's trust by prescribing that the trust corpus was to be held in trust for 20 years after his death, with the income being divided among his then living children, and at the end of that period, the corpus to be divided among his then living children in equal shares. At Hatlake's death, the trust corpus was valued at $1,000,000.

   Was Hatlake well advised to exercise the power of amendment? What are the tax consequences? What were his alternatives?

2. Hatlake's mother died in 1964, leaving a will by which she directed that her 70–percent stock interest in Rumble Motors be placed in trust with Hatlake as sole trustee. Under the terms of the trust, the income was to be divided equally among Hatlake's children, with the remainder upon the death of the last survivor of such children to go to their issue then living. If such children died without issue, then the trust corpus was to be distributed to Hatlake or his estate. In addition, the trust provided that Hatlake was authorized to withdraw $10,000 per year from trust corpus "if his needs so required."

   At the time of Hatlake's death last year, the corpus of the trust was valued at $150,000, and the value of Hatlake's remainder interest was $5,000; Hatlake left two children surviving him.

   What are the estate tax consequences of Hatlake's powers?

3. Ma's will created a trust with Pa and her sons, Bo, Moe, and Luke as trustees. The trust's income and principal was to be distributed among Pa and the sons "as needed" by each of them for "health, education, maintenance and support in his accustomed manner of living taking into consideration any other property available" for these purposes. In addition, distributions could be made to any or more of the sons "to assist him in purchasing a home or starting a business." Undistributed income is to be added to principal. The trust is to terminate at Pa's death. Moe has died, survived by Pa, Bo and Luke. Is any part of the trust included in Moe's estate for estate tax purposes?

Chapter 23

TRANSFERS WITHIN THREE YEARS OF DEATH

(Section 2035)

A. INTRODUCTION

[¶ 23,001]

1. SECTION 2035 BEFORE 1976

Since the beginning of the federal estate tax in 1916, it has been recognized that the tax base had to be protected against lifetime transfers motivated by thoughts of death, estate taxes, or both. "Transfers in contemplation of death" were accordingly swept back into the estate tax base by what is now § 2035. But the question of whether the particular transfer was or was not in "contemplation of death" provided a field day for lawyers who litigated that issue, often in federal district court with juries, to the frequent advantage of estates, beneficiaries and those same lawyers.

Illustrative of the bizarre nature of evidence deemed relevant and germane to the question of a decedent's motives in making a transfer shortly prior to death is the case of Kniskern v. United States, 232 F.Supp. 7 (S.D.Fla.1964), involving a decedent who made substantial gifts at age 99 and died one year later at age 100. The IRS's attempt to include the transferred property, valued at date of death at $157,800, failed. Included in the findings of facts supportive of the court's conclusion that the patriarch was not contemplating death when he made his substantial gifts were the following: (1) he kept charge of and repaired the sprinkler system in his yard; (2) he worked on supports for fruit trees with a sledgehammer; (3) he took frequent automobile rides with the maid; (4) he played with his great-grandchildren, frequently bouncing them on his knees; (5) he frequently attended church and smoked his pipe before services; (6) he was greatly interested in radio and television; (7) he was proud of his age and condition and boasted of having the physique of a man 25 to 30 years his junior; (8) he had asserted that he was going to make the centennial mark and live even longer; and (9) his minister had testified that "he was full of the joy of living."

It has long been recognized that litigation of the contemplation of death issue was not very sensible or rewarding in a larger social sense. In 1926 Congress attempted to solve the problem with an irrebuttable presumption that gifts made in the last two years of life were in contemplation of death. However, the Supreme Court held that irrebuttable presumption to be unconstitutional in Heiner v. Donnan, 285 U.S. 312 (1932).

As a result, the feeble "contemplation of death" standard was often the lone legal defenseman that stood between octogenarians and the tax advantages of inter vivos gifts. Juries, which passed on the factual issue of whether a gift was in contemplation of death, seemed regularly to show their approval of the spunk of cocky oldsters, who thought they would go on forever, by rarely finding against those who lost the foot race with the grim reaper.

[¶ 23,007]

2. THE 1976 ACT CHANGES

The Tax Reform Act of 1976 changed all of this. Section 2035 was amended to provide that all transfers within the last three years of the decedent's life should be swept into the taxable estate as death-related transfers—along with the gift taxes paid on the gifts. This process of including the gift taxes paid, known as "grossing up," accomplishes the result of treating transfers during the last three years in the same way as the rest of the taxable estate, in the sense that the transfer tax money is included in the tax base. The old and bizarre practice of making gifts in contemplation of death to take the gift tax money out of the taxable estate, while retaining its use as a down payment on the estate tax through the credit for gift tax paid under § 2012, has thus been brought to a complete and deserved end.

[¶ 23,013]

3. THE 1981 ACT AND THE 1997 ACT CHANGES

Gradually there was awareness that the federal gift tax had truly been integrated by the 1976 Act into a unified transfer tax so that lifetime gifts enter into the computation of the tax payable on the final transfer at death. Thus, there was little need for a provision sweeping deathbed transfers into the taxable estate, since all post–1976 transfers are reflected in the final estate tax return in any case. The Economic Recovery Tax Act of 1981 accepted the view that § 2035 could be largely disarmed without adverse impact on the system. The Taxpayer Relief Act of 1997, with one exception mentioned later, reenacted the changes made to the substance of § 2035 by the 1981 Act and rearranged the various subsections of the statute to produce a sensibly ordered, more user friendly provision.

The general rule of § 2035, which under the Tax Reform Act of 1976 was a rule of automatic inclusion in the taxable estate, has been drastically altered. The statute now provides that except in certain limited situations there is no special rule of inclusion in the gross estate for deathbed transfers. All such transfers are subject to the gift tax and will, in addition, be reflected in the final estate tax return as lifetime transfers, affecting the tax rate to be applied to the property in the taxable estate. But the valuation of transfers within three years of death will occur at the date of the gift and not, as under former § 2035, at the date of death. Thus, there may be some leakage in terms of escape from transfer tax of the appreciation of the donated property between the date of gift and the date of the donor's death.

The three-year rule is preserved for certain gift tax inclusion transfers described by the language of § 2035(a) as transfers of property with respect to which "the value of such property (or an interest therein) would have been included in the decedent's gross estate under section 2036, 2037, 2038 or 2042 if such transferred interest or relinquished power had been retained by the decedent on the date of his death." In all such cases, the statute calls for inclusion in the deceased's gross estate of the value which would have been included, had the transfer within three years of death not been made.

Since a decedent can now make a large outright gift in the final year, the final month, or the final day of life, and the gift will not be subject to the old rule requiring inclusion of that transfer in the gross estate, one might wonder whether it is sensible to require inclusion in the gross estate when the original transfer was made, perhaps years earlier, and it is only in the final days of life that the retained taxable string is cut. The answer must be that Congress thought the opportunity to enjoy what amounts to constructive ownership of the property for an extended period should not also enable the decedent to avoid transfer tax on appreciation in value enjoyed, in a sense, by the decedent in the final years or days of life. Thus, the target seems to be appreciation of transferred property with respect to which the decedent retained, to within three years of death, enjoyment in some fashion.

It should be noted, as well, that the "grossing-up" rule that calls for putting the gift tax on transfers within three years of death back into the gross estate continues, under § 2035(b), to be operational. In addition, the three-year rule is retained to de-emphasize manipulations of property ownership during the final years of life to achieve certain income or transfer tax advantages under §§ 303, 2032A and 6166. A brief explanation of the revision of § 2035, as effected by the Economic Recovery Tax Act of 1981, appears in the House Committee Report on P.L. 97–34, as follows:

> In general, the bill provides that ... gifts made within 3 years of death will not be included in the decedent's gross estate, and the post-gift appreciation will not be subject to transfer taxes. Accordingly, such property will not be considered to pass from the decedent and the step-up basis rules of section 1014 will not apply.

> The committee bill contains exceptions which continue the application of [the old rule] to (1) gifts of life insurance and (2) interests in property otherwise included in the value of the gross estate pursuant to sections 2036, 2037, 2038, * * * or 2042 (or those which would have been included under any of such sections if the interest had been retained by the decedent).

> In addition, [under what is now § 2035(c)] all transfers within 3 years of death (other than gifts eligible for the annual gift tax exclusion)

will be included for purposes of determining the estate's qualification for special redemption, valuation, and deferral purposes (under secs. 303, 2032A, and 6166) and for purposes of determining property subject to the estate tax liens (under subchapter C of Chapter 64).

Section 2035(c) [now § 2035(b)], requiring the inclusion of all gift taxes paid by the decedent or his estate on any gift made by the decedent or his spouse after December 31, 1976, and within 3 years of death, will continue to apply to all estates.

Effective Date—This provision applies to the estates of decedents dying after December 31, 1981.

As previously mentioned, the 1997 Act rearranged the various subsections of § 2035 and provided clearer wording of the provision. While extremely helpful, this revision also means that considerable care must be exercised in referring to primary materials, such as cases, and to secondary materials, such as treatises, which may be referring to § 2035 subsections under the pre–1997 version of the law. The 1997 Act added § 2035(e); making a substantive change to the law which impacts transfers from revocable trusts. The significance of this change is discussed in detail at ¶ 23,092 through ¶ 23,096.

B. "GROSSING UP"

[¶ 23,019]

As noted above, under § 2035(b) gift taxes paid on gifts made during the last three years of the decedent's life are to be added to the gross estate of the decedent. This process of including the gift taxes paid in the gross estate is known as "grossing up" and has the effect of including the tax money, i.e., the money used to pay the transfer tax, in the tax base. That is the system as respects the estate tax. In contrast, the gift tax, even under the single uniform rate schedule that has prevailed since 1976, is imposed against the amount passing to the donee only, a very different (and favorable to the taxpayer) way of calculating the tax base. Under § 2035(b) the decedent who fails to live three years after the lifetime gift loses the advantage of excluding the transfer tax from the tax base. In other words, the donor who makes a taxed gift, pays the gift tax and lives three years pays no additional estate tax due to the gift. Were the taxpayer not to survive for three years after making the taxed gift, however, pursuant to § 2035(b) the amount of the gift tax paid would be included in that taxpayer's gross estate. In T.A.M. 200432016 the I.R.S. has ruled that where a taxpayer dies precisely on the same date as a gift made three years previously his gift will not be deemed to have been made "during the 3–year period ending on the date of decedent's death" as required by § 2035(b), with the result that "grossing up" is not called for in such situation.

The language of § 2035(b) provides for "grossing up" the amount of gift tax paid with respect to a gift within the last three years of life by the "decedent or his estate." In Estate of Sachs v. Commissioner, 88 T.C. 769 (1987), the Court was faced with a "net gift," whereby, under the terms of the gift, the gift tax was to be paid by the donee, and was, in fact, so paid. To the estate's argument that it did not have to include the gift tax paid by the donee, the Tax Court turned an unsympathetic ear. The Court was of the view that it was entitled to stretch the literal language of § 2035(b) to cover the gift tax payment by the donee to make the system work as Congress intended. A concurring opinion took the view that the donee's payment of the gift tax was really a payment on behalf of the donor who otherwise would have had to make the payment. Surely, the result is in accordance with congressional intent.

In Estate of Armstrong v. Commissioner, 119 T.C. 220 (2002) the court held that the grossing up feature of § 2035(c) violated neither the due process nor the equal protection requirements of the Fifth Amendment of the Constitution.

In Priv. Ltr. Rul. 9128009, the IRS dealt with a situation where a wife joined with her husband in effectively splitting a gift under § 2513, with the wife's one-half of the gift tax paid by the husband. The husband died within three years. The IRS ruled that the gross-up amount includible in the husband's estate consists of both the gift tax directly paid by the husband on his one-half and the gift tax indirectly paid by him on the wife's one-half of the gift. The same result was produced where an aged wealthy husband transferred to his wife money to fund a life insurance trust and sufficient funds to pay the resulting gift tax, with the couple electing to treat the gift of the policy as a split gift under § 2513 and the husband died within three years of making the transfer. The court held that despite the fact that the tax was technically paid by the wife, the step transaction doctrine dictated that the gift tax formally paid by the wife (but indirectly and practically speaking by the husband) be swept back into husband's estate. See, Brown v. United States, 329 F.3d 664 (9th Cir. 2003).

Where the estate is unable to pay estate tax because it has insufficient assets on hand, § 6324 (a)(2) imposes liability for the tax on the transferees of property included in the gross estate. Frank Armstrong, Jr. transferred most of his substantial wealth by gift to his issue, retaining little more than the $4.7 million needed to pay the federal gift tax. When Armstrong died near penniless within two years of his gift giving binge, his issue took the position that, because estate tax resulted under § 2035 from inclusion in Armstrong's estate of the gift tax paid to the government and not the $9–10 million in gifts made by Armstrong to them, they, as donees, should not be liable for unpaid estate tax under § 6324 (a)(2). The Tax Court rejected this contention in Frank Armstrong III, 114 T.C. 94 (2000) holding that, in such circumstances, donees whose gifts generate estate tax liability under the gross up provisions of § 2035 are to be deemed transferees under § 6324 (a)(2).

C. LIFE INSURANCE TRANSFERS WITHIN THREE YEARS OF DEATH

[¶ 23,025]

Along with gross-up situations, the areas described in § 2035(a) and (c) are the principal areas where the Commissioner and taxpayers will remain keenly concerned about whether a donor survives for three years after making a gift. Moreover, given the importance of life insurance as an asset of significant value in many estates, much interest will focus on the treatment of this asset under § 2035.

Quite clearly, where the decedent purchases from an insurer a life insurance policy and transfers all incidents of ownership in the policy to another individual within three years of death, the proceeds of the policy, and not merely the value of the interpolated terminal reserve, will be included in the gross estate of the decedent pursuant to § 2035(a). Of more interest are situations in which an individual taxpayer, within three years of death, strongly suggested to another person that he or she purchase a policy on the taxpayer's life and then proceeded to furnish that person with the funds necessary to pay the premiums on the policy.

1. PRE 1982 DEATHS

[¶ 23,031]

The courts have uniformly agreed that, based on statutory language which predates the present version of § 2035, the following rule applies to decedents dying on or before December 31, 1981. If the decedent was the propelling force in the acquisition of the policy (even if acquired by another) and provided for the payment of premiums, the decedent may be deemed the transferor of the policy with the result that, if death occurred within three years of a "deemed transfer" of a life insurance policy on decedent's life, the proceeds of the policy may be included in the decedent's estate under § 2035. See, e.g., Knisley v. United States, 901 F.2d 793 (9th Cir.1990); Estate of Schnack v. Commissioner, 848 F.2d 933 (9th Cir.1988). For example, in *Estate of Schnack*, the wife was the driving force behind her husband's purchasing a $500,000 life insurance policy on her life. She also purchased a policy of equal value on her husband's life. The premiums for both policies were paid from a joint bank account held by husband and wife. Wife died on August 9, 1979 shortly after issuance of the policies. The court decided that, since the decedent wife had been the propelling force for issuance of the policy on her life and through the joint bank account had provided the monetary consideration for issuance of the policy on her life, she should be deemed the transferor of that policy under § 2035, with the result that the full proceeds of the policy were included in her estate.

2. POST 1981 DEATHS

[¶ 23,043]

The different language employed by Congress in the 1981 Act under § 2035 with respect to transfers made by decedents who die after December 31, 1981, provided the courts with an opportunity to produce a different result.

As a result of the 1981 Act changes, the statute made explicit reference to § 2042 when dealing with the includibility of life insurance under § 2035. The judiciary was thereby given the opportunity to determine if the explicit statutory cross-reference meant that, in the case of life insurance policies, the incidents of ownership test of § 2042 would control. This would mean that, even though the decedent was the propelling force for the acquisition of a policy on her life, if she never possessed (and consequently never transferred) any of the incidents of ownership with respect to the policy within three years prior to her death, there could be no inclusion of policy proceeds in her estate under § 2035.

In a series of decisions handed down in the late 1980s and early 1990s, the judiciary served notice that the language employed by the 1981 Act with respect to decedents dying after 1981 was intended to represent a break with the "deemed transfer" rationale of the pre–1981 Act version of § 2035. See, e.g., Estate of Perry v. Commissioner, 927 F.2d 209 (5th Cir.1991); Estate of Headrick v. Commissioner, 918 F.2d 1263 (6th Cir.1990); and Estate of Leder v. Commissioner, 893 F.2d 237 (10th Cir.1989).

Most instructive of these cases is *Estate of Headrick*. There the decedent, a young tax attorney who had recently obtained an L.L.M. from the NYU Graduate Tax Program, had established and funded an irrevocable life insurance trust that acquired a policy on his life. The trustee of the trust held all incidents of ownership from the first moment of its issuance on January 8, 1980. The insured died in an accident on June 19, 1982, less than three years after issuance of the policy. The court held that, since the decedent had never held any of the incidents of ownership of the life insurance policy on his life, he could not and did not transfer them within three years of his death, and the proceeds of the policy were therefore not includible in his gross estate under § 2035. It asserted that the cross-reference to § 2042 in § 2035 with respect to post–1981 deaths indicates that the "incidents of ownership" test of that section is to apply in determining taxation under § 2035. In other words, only if decedent had held, and transferred within three years of his life, incidents of ownership on the policy on his life could the proceeds of the policy be included in his estate under § 2035 for post–1981 deaths. Thus, just as who is the propelling force for issuance of a policy and who provides consideration for payment of premiums is irrelevant under § 2042 (see Chapter 17), so too should it be irrelevant under § 2035. In brief, the cross-reference to § 2042 in the revised version of § 2035 provided by the 1981 Act was viewed as: (1) incorporating tests of that section for purposes of determining the tax treatment of transfers of life insurance under what is now § 2035(a); and (2) rejecting the "deemed transfer" test which applied to pre 1982 deaths. In

Tech. Adv. Mem. 9323002 the IRS threw in the towel on this issue with the result that the "deemed transfer" test saw its last with those taxpayers who also saw their last day on or before December 31, 1981.

[¶ 23,048]

TECHNICAL ADVICE MEMORANDUM 9323002

February 24, 1993.

ISSUE

Are the proceeds of a life insurance policy includible in a decedent's gross estate under section 2035 of the Internal Revenue Code?

FACTS

The decedent died on July 27, 1990, survived by her two sons, A and B.

On June 1, 1989, the decedent signed an application for a life insurance policy with a face value of $500,000. The decedent signed the application as the "Proposed Insured," designated her estate as the beneficiary, and left blank a space for the designation of a policy owner other than the insured.

Several lines above the decedent's signature, the application contains the printed statement, "I agree that any policy(ies) issued on this application shall take effect only if the first full premium is paid and such policy(ies) is issued and delivered to the owner."

Later in the summer of 1989, the decedent completed a printed form from the same insurance company, entitled "Supplementary Application," signing the form but leaving it undated. On this form, the decedent requested that the policy be split into two $250,000 policies; she named A as the beneficiary and owner of one policy and B as the beneficiary and owner of the other policy. The insurance company routinely uses supplementary applications for revising initial applications. The insurance company's records indicate that, when this "Supplemental Application" was executed, no policy or policies on the decedent's life had yet been issued or delivered, nor had any premiums been paid on such a policy.

On August 28, 1989, A wrote a check to the insurance company for $3,670 to cover the first two premium payments on the policies. On August 29, 1989, the check was delivered to the insurance company which issued the policies for which the decedent had applied. Each was a $250,000 policy naming one of the decedent's sons as both the beneficiary and the owner. Each policy also expressly named the decedent as successor owner if the designated owner died. Under the terms of the policies, as owner, each son could obtain, alone and in all events, the cash surrender value of his policy at any time before the decedent's death, as well as exercising all other ownership powers. [The policy is governed by Texas state law.]

Between the time that the decedent made her original application and the time the "Supplementary Application" was signed, the insurance company raised its rates. The insurance company did not view supplementary applications as new applications. Therefore, the policies on the decedent's life remained subject to the rates in effect when she made the initial application. If A and B had initially applied for the policies on the decedent's life at the time that the decedent executed the Supplementary Application, A and B would have been able to obtain premiums based upon the same life expectancy applicable to the decedent's first application; however, the new higher rates would have been applied.

A and B paid all of the premiums on the policies. At the decedent's death, all of the proceeds from each policy were paid to A and B, respectively, as beneficiaries.

LAW AND ANALYSIS

[With respect to post 1981 deaths, the Economic Recovery Tax Act of 1981 amended section 2035 to provide that in the case of transfers by the decedent within three years of death, there shall be included in decedent's estate the value of all property which would have been included under sections 2036, 2037, 2038 or 2042 had such transfers not been made.]

Under section 2042(2), the gross estate includes the proceeds of insurance on the decedent's life receivable by beneficiaries other than the decedent's estate under policies in which the decedent possessed at death any incidents of ownership that can be exercised either alone or in conjunction with any other person.

Section 20.2042–1(a)(2) of the Estate Tax Regulations provides that the term "incidents of ownership" is not limited to legal ownership but refers to the right to the "economic benefits" of the policy. The term includes the power to change the beneficiary, to surrender or cancel the policy, to assign the policy, to revoke an assignment, to pledge the policy for a loan, or to obtain a loan against the surrender value of the policy.

[Section 2035(a)] operate[s] to include a life insurance policy transferred by a decedent only if the policy would have been includible under section 2042 had the decedent "retained" the policy or incidents of ownership in the policy. Generally, the courts have concluded that, based on the statutory language, in order for a life insurance policy to be subject to inclusion under [section 2035(a)], the decedent must have actually owned the policy (or have had incidents of ownership in the policy) and must have actually transferred the policy. Estate of Perry v. Commissioner, 927 F.2d 209 (5th Cir.1991), aff'g., 59 T.C.M. 1990–123; Estate of Headrick v. Commissioner, 918 F.2d 1263 (6th Cir.1990), aff'g., 93 T.C. 171 (1989); Estate of Leder v. Commissioner, 893 F.2d 237 (10th Cir.1989), aff'g., 89 T.C. 235 (1987).

This is in contrast to cases involving decedents dying before 1982, subject to the provisions of section 2035 prior to amendment by ERTA [the 1981 Act]. In those cases, the government has successfully argued that if the decedent procured the policy and paid the premiums, but had the policy titled in the name of a third party, the decedent in substance, if not in form, transferred the policy. This deemed transfer was sufficient to cause inclusion under section 2035, prior to amendment. See, e.g., Knisley v. United States, 901 F.2d 793 (9th Cir.1990).

¶ 23,048

Accordingly, in situations involving decedents dying after 1981, in order for a transferred life insurance policy to be subject to inclusion under section 2035 . . . , it must be determined that the decedent actually held incidents of ownership in the policy and actually transferred those incidents of ownership. This is a question of state law as well as of federal tax law.

In the present case, within three years of her death, the decedent initially applied for an insurance policy, specifying in the application that she was to be designated as owner. Subsequently, on a supplementary application, the decedent revised the initial application and requested issuance of two policies to be owned by A and B. These policies were issued.

Under applicable state law, the policies issued did not become effective until the first full premium was paid and the policies were issued and delivered to the owners, as provided in the application for insurance completed by the decedent. An application for insurance, according to the state law, is an offer to the insurance company which does not become bound in an insurance contract until accepting the offer. As stated by the Texas Commission of Appeals in an opinion adopted by the Supreme Court of Texas:

> All of the authorities class insurance contracts, as such, as fundamentally the same as other contracts as regards to offer and acceptance. There is no contract unless and until the application for insurance is accepted by the insurance company. American Life Insurance Co. v. Nabors, 76 S.W.2d 497 (Tex.Com.App.1934, opinion adopted).

Further, Texas courts have long held that an insurer's express statement of the manner in which the insurer will accept the application for insurance places a valid limitation on the insurer's acceptance. * * *

In the present case, the decedent's June 1, 1989, application named the decedent as insured and owner and her estate as beneficiary. However, under state law, that application was a mere offer to the insurance company for an insurance contract. Under the terms of the application, any policies issued would not be effective until the first premium was paid and the policy was delivered to the owner. When the decedent signed the Supplementary Application, the insurer's conditions for accepting an offer had not yet occurred. The first premium had not been paid, and no policies had been delivered.

After the decedent submitted her Supplementary Application, the first premium payment was paid to the insurance company on August 29, 1989, and the insurance company issued and delivered the two policies designating A and B as owners and beneficiaries to A and B on that date. In so doing, the insurance company created a binding insurance contract between itself and the decedent's sons, based on the decedent's Supplementary Application. The policies issued on August 29, 1989, were the only policies issued on the decedent's life. Thus, A and B held all of the incidents of ownership in the policies from the date of issuance, and the decedent never actually held any economic, ownership, or contractual rights in the policies and, therefore, would not be subject to inclusion under section 2035. See Estate of Perry v. Commissioner, supra.

We recognize that, at the time the decedent filed the Supplementary Application designating A and B as policy owners, the insurance company agreed to use the same favorable premium rate applicable at the time of the decedent's first application. Thus, to this extent, the decedent succeeded in passing to A and B a benefit concerning the cost of the policies to be issued to A and B as the designated owners. If A and B had applied for initial policies on the decedent's life at the time when the decedent executed the Supplementary Application, A and B could have obtained premiums based upon the same life expectancy applicable to the decedent's first application but not the more favorable rate schedule.

However, we believe it is questionable whether the transfer of this favorable premium rate, which may have facilitated the *acquisition* of the policies by A and B, would constitute the transfer of an incident of ownership in a policy itself. Generally, the term "incidents of ownership" focuses on the right to control the economic benefits of the policy, and the mere right to apply for insurance coverage is not an incident of ownership. See, e.g., Rev. Rul. 76–421, 1976–2 C.B. 280. In any event, we do not believe the transfer of this favorable premium rate would take this case out of the purview of *Estate of Perry.*

CONCLUSION

The proceeds of the life insurance policies on the decedent's life are not includible in a decedent's gross estate under section 2035 of the Code.

D. REMAINING ISSUES UNDER SECTION 2035(a)

[¶ 23,055]

It should come as no surprise that, with the exception of the previously mentioned life insurance cases, to date there has not been much litigation shedding significant light on what is now § 2035(a). Nonetheless, in addition to consulting some of the recent authorities, it is possible to look to some of the pre–1981 § 2035 cases and authorities to gain some insight into what might still be deemed significant remaining issues under § 2035(a).

[¶ 23,061]

1. INDIRECT TRANSFERS

Where an individual controls an entity such as a corporation and the entity makes a gratuitous transfer that, had it been made by the controlling individual, would have been deemed covered by § 2035(a), should such transfer be deemed to have been made by the controlling individual?

In Rev. Rul. 82–141, 1982–2 C.B. 209, the IRS ruled that where the decedent owned 80 percent of the stock of a corporation that transferred ownership of a policy of insurance on his life within three years of death, the transfer was to be charged to the shareholder and included in his gross estate under § 2035. The ruling indicates that the result would be the same regardless of whether the transaction was covered by what is now § 2035(a) or the pre–1981 version of § 2035. Cases consistent with Rev. Rul. 82–141 involving deaths that occurred prior to 1981 are Estate of Porter v. Commissioner, 442 F.2d 915 (1st Cir.1971), and Haneke v. United States, 548 F.2d 1138 (4th Cir.1977).

In Rev. Rul. 90–21, 1990–1 C.B. 172, the IRS amplified Rev. Rul. 82–141. Here, the IRS ruled on two situations. The first situation involved a corporation that, within three years of the death of the decedent-insured, made a gift of a life insurance policy on the life of the insured. At the time of the gift, the insured held 80 percent of the stock of the corporation. Shortly before his death, the insured gave his controlling interest in the corporation to his child. The IRS ruled that the gift of stock did not change the result produced by Rev. Rul. 82–141 and the policy proceeds were included in the donor's estate. In the second situation, the insured-decedent, who also owned 80 percent of the stock of a corporation that owned a policy on the life of the insured payable to a child of the insured, gave most of his stock in the corporation to a third party within three years of his death. Piercing through the corporate veil, the IRS included in the decedent's taxable estate the full value of the policy proceeds.

[¶ 23,067]

2. AMOUNT INCLUDED

Where an inclusion in the gross estate results because of the application of § 2035(a), an issue may arise as to the value of the property to be included in the estate in a situation in which the transferred property was sold after the transfer and either the transferred property, or the property purchased as a replacement, fluctuated wildly in value. For example, assume that a taxpayer who had retained a life estate with respect to Blackacre subsequently transferred her life estate to her children and failed to live the required three years. Assume also that the children, who also owned the remainder interest, sold Blackacre immediately before it doubled in value and replaced it with bonds that did not change in value. What value is to be included in the taxpayer's estate? Similarly difficult issues are presented by income realized on transferred property, as well as stock dividends and redemptions.

[¶ 23,073]

ESTATE OF HUMPHREY v. COMMISSIONER

United States Court of Appeals, Fifth Circuit, 1947.
162 F.2d 1.

SIBLEY, Circuit Judge.

The case relates to the estate taxes of Albert P. Humphrey, who died testate February 23, 1942, the reported value of his estate being $185,475. On January 18, 1941, within two years prior to his death, decedent and his wife each made cash gifts to their two sons of $40,000. The Commissioner included this $40,000 in the gross estate of decedent and taxed it. The Tax Court sustained this action * * *

¶ 23,073

The Tax Court made no finding of the value at decedent's death of the property so transferred. The evidence is that the two sons took the $80,000 given by their parents and combined it with $80,000 of their own and by their operations prior to their father's death had lost about half of the $160,000 capital. It is therefore contended that $20,000 rather than $40,000 is to be included in this estate for taxation. I.R.C. § 811, supra, says that all included property, real or personal, tangible or intangible, is to be valued at the time of decedent's death. Regulation 105, Sec. 81.15, declares more specifically that *transferred property* in the estate is to be valued at the *date of decedent's death*. The evident purpose is to make the transferred property cause the same tax result as if the decedent had kept it till he died instead of transferring it. We do not accede to the argument that if the transferee injures or makes way with it, it shall be considered that he has acted as the agent of the decedent, or that he may substitute it by other property of less value. What is to be valued at the time of decedent's death is the very property which the decedent transferred. He transferred $40,000, and its money value was the same in 1942 as in 1941. No finding to that effect was needed. That the transferees may have lost some of it does not diminish the sum that was transferred. The Commissioner's inclusion of the $40,000 value was demanded as a matter of law.

Affirmed.

Notes

[¶ 23,079]

1. In a later ruling, Rev. Rul. 72–282, 1972–1 C.B. 305, the Treasury dealt with the situation where a gift two years before the death of the decedent consisted of shares of stock that was sold by the donee and reinvested with spectacular results. But the Treasury ruled that the value to be included in the decedent's gross estate was the value of the original shares transferred and not the value of the newly acquired stock purchased by the son with the proceeds of the sale of the original shares. The ruling states, "The value of stock acquired by subsequent independent actions of the donee is not that which is includible in the decedent's gross estate, despite the fact that the stock now owned by the donee can be attributed to the proceeds of the sale of the transferred property. Rather, what is includible is the present value of the property originally transferred by the decedent."

2. In Estate of DeWitt v. Commissioner, 68 T.C.M. (CCH) 1136, T.C.M. (RIA) ¶ 94,552 (1994), the Tax Court was called upon to determine the proper amount to be included under § 2035 where the decedent, prior to December 31, 1981, had funded a trust for the benefit of her son with $250,000 in cash and the trust had invested in assets which by decedent's death 17 months later had declined in value to $187,500. Since decedent had transferred to her son an interest in trust, and not $250,000, the Tax Court concluded that it was the value of that interest ($187,500) which was to be included in decedent's estate under § 2035.

¶ **23,073**

[¶ 23,085]

COMMISSIONER v. ESTATE OF GIDWITZ

United States Court of Appeals, Seventh Circuit, 1952.
196 F.2d 813.

SWAIM, Circuit Judge.

[The Tax Court found that the transfer by the decedent was in contemplation of death. Factors supporting this conclusion were the age of the decedent at the time of transfer (72), the circumstance that he had suffered a heart attack previously, the fact that under the transfer the beneficiaries could not enjoy the property during the life of the transferor, and the fact that the transfers were made so as to equalize the holdings of his sons. On appeal the Court of Appeals affirmed the Tax Court decision that the transfer was in contemplation of death. That portion of the Circuit Court's opinion is omitted here. Another question of some importance concerned the amount of property to be hauled back into the taxable estate under § 2035. That question was dealt with as follows:]

The Commissioner insists that the Tax Court erred in not including in the decedent's gross estate the income, together with property purchased by such income, which accrued in the trust prior to the decedent's death. When Gidwitz died the total assets in the trust had a value of $341,102.02. The original shares of stock transferred to the trust had a valuation of $140,610. The difference of $200,492.02 represented the value of accrued income and property purchased for the trust with accrued income.

The Commissioner, while admitting that the statute places in the gross estate only property *transferred* by the decedent, bases the Government's claim that the valuation of the gross estate should include all income received by the trust prior to the decedent's death on the theory that the property transferred to the trust in 1936 included not only the ownership of the 83 1/3 shares of stock but also a separate property right to receive the income on the stock. It is argued that the value of this property right to receive income is measured by the income accumulated in the trust prior to the decedent's death.

The same theory advanced by the Commissioner in this case was rejected by the Supreme Court in Maass v. Higgins, 312 U.S. 443. The *Maass* case involved two estates where the executors had elected to have the gross estates valued as of one year after the decedents' deaths, pursuant to 26 U.S.C.A. § 811(j) [now § 2032]. During the year after the decedents' deaths the executors had collected interest and dividends on bonds and stocks belonging to the estates. The Commissioner determined tax deficiencies against the estates for failures to include these collections as part of the gross estates. A Treasury regulation, then being enforced, required the return and inclusion of such income as a part of the gross estate. The Supreme Court, while recognizing that a bond embodies two promises to pay—one to pay the principal at maturity and the other to pay interest periodically—and while recognizing that the income factor affects the value of a security, said, at page 448:

> "But these elements are not separately valued in appraising the worth of the asset at any given time."

The Supreme Court there, at page 447, agreed with the taxpayer:

> " * * * that the Government's position is unreal and artificial; that it does not comport either with economic theory or business practice; and that the regulation is an unwarranted extension of the plain meaning of the statute and cannot therefore, be sustained."

In Humphrey's Estate v. Commissioner, 5 Cir., 162 F.2d 1, the donees of an *inter vivos* gift made in contemplation of death, by an improvident investment, lost one-half of the amount of the gift. It was contended that the half of the property lost should not be included in the decedent's gross estate. The Court held, however, that it was the *transferred* property which was to be valued at the time of the decedent's death. The Court said, at page 2:

> "What is to be valued at the time of decedent's death is *the very property which the decedent transferred.*" (Italics by court)

In Burns v. Commissioner, 5 Cir., 177 F.2d 739, affirming Estate of James E. Frizzell, 9 T.C. 979, a father established an irrevocable trust and, in contemplation of death, made an *inter vivos* gift of certain shares of the stock of the Coca Cola Company to the trust. The trustee invested part of the income from the trust in other stocks and bonds prior to the donor's death. The Court accepted the conclusion of the Tax Court that part of the corpus of the trust which represented income received prior to the death of the donor, or property acquired with such income, had not been *transferred* by the decedent and, therefore, should not be included in the decedent's gross estate for estate tax purposes. The Court said, at page 741:

> "The tax statute in question should be strictly construed in favor of the taxpayer, and since it does not expressly provide for the inclusion of income derived from the *transferred* property in the gross estate, it is not our prerogative, by judicial fiat, to give it that effect. Title 26 U.S.C.A., Sections 811(c), 811(j). (Citing cases.)" (Italics by court)

As against the principles announced in the above cases the Commissioner cites decisions involving other provisions of the Internal Revenue Code which admittedly deal with transfers intended to take effect in possession or enjoyment at or after death, or in which the grantor had retained until death the power to designate the persons who would enjoy the property, or in which the grantor had retained until death the power to alter, amend or revoke. The Commissioner admits that such transfers are included in the gross estate on the theory that such a transfer does not become complete and effective until death, whereas a transfer in contemplation of death is included because of the motive inducing it. The Commissioner argues that the same rules should apply in both classes of cases. Such an argument ignores the realities of the two types of transfers.

¶ 23,085

In transfers made in contemplation of death, such as in the instant case, the donor has made an actual transfer during his life. The transfer became effective at that time. The transfer was irrevocable. The terms of the trust agreement expressly prohibited any change in the provisions of the agreement which would in any manner effect a change relating to the distribution, disposition, possession or enjoyment of the trust property. Here the income was paid to the trust because it belonged to the trust, not to Gidwitz. The income was payable to the trust and belonged to the trust as an incident of the ownership by the trust of the stock transferred to the trust by Gidwitz in 1936. The Tax Court correctly held that such income and the property acquired with such income should not be included in the decedent's gross estate for estate tax purposes.

In both of these petitions for review the decision of the Tax Court is affirmed.

Notes

[¶ 23,091]

1. Regulation § 20.2035–1(e) accepts the result of *Gidwitz*. One might ask if the result in *Gidwitz* should prevail where, under § 2035(a), a "severed string" is involved under a provision such as § 2036 or 2038 and, had no gift been made, a different result would prevail under those sections with respect to retained income or property purchased with retained income? See United States v. O'Malley at ¶ 18,217. Should the result depend on whether the retained income was realized prior to, or after, the severance of the string? We all await judicial enlightenment on these issues.

2. In Rev. Rul. 80–336, 1980–2 C.B. 271, the IRS ruled that where a corporation, the stock of which was the object of a gift covered by § 2035, makes a one-for-two stock dividend, both the original stock and the dividend stock are included in the estate. In McGehee v. Commissioner, 260 F.2d 818 (5th Cir.1958), the court distinguished between stock dividends representing pre-and post-gift earnings, including only those reflective of the former.

E.   REVOCABLE TRUSTS

[¶ 23,092]

1. THE PARAMETERS OF THE PROBLEM

Nontax estate planning goals, such as avoidance of probate, protection of privacy or coping with incompetency, frequently result in individuals contributing a significant portion of their estates to revocable trusts. Often the grantors of such trusts are their sole beneficiaries. On other occasions the beneficiaries include not only the grantor but other individuals. In the past decade there was flurry of judicial decisions and administrative releases regarding how post–1981 transfers from such trusts should be treated under what is now § 2035(a). In 1997, Congress decided to weigh in on the topic with the passage of § 2035(e) which is described below at ¶ 23,096.

¶ 23,092

Prior to the passage of § 2035(e), decedents who had created revocable trusts designating themselves as beneficiaries, provided the IRS with the opportunity to argue that at their death, under what is now § 2035(a), all gratuitous transfers from the trust within three years of death were to be taxed as transfers described in § 2038. Had the IRS prevailed with this argument, it would have meant that decedents who had conveyed their assets to such a trust for the simple purpose of avoiding probate and then made gifts from the trust within three years of their death would have suffered adverse tax consequences when compared to decedents who had not transferred their assets to such a trust and had followed an identical pattern of gift giving in the three years prior to their death.

There would have been two important consequences for taxpayers had the IRS prevailed in including in decedent-grantor's estate (under what is now § 2035(a)) all transfers from such revocable trust under which the decedent-grantor had retained the power to revest title in herself. First, the benefit of the annual per donee exclusion would have been lost to the taxpayer. For example, assume that Grandma had placed all her assets in such a trust to avoid probate and made gifts of $10,000 from the trust to each of four grandchildren for two years prior to her death. Had the IRS position been accepted, the full $80,000 would have been swept back into her estate. Of course, had Grandma never been concerned about using a revocable trust to avoid probate and had she merely retained direct title to her property and made the same gifts to her grandchildren, the $80,000 so gifted would not have been swept back into her estate. Second, where the value of property gifted from such a revocable trust increased by the date of death, if what is now § 2035(a) could have been used to effect an inclusion of the gifted property in decedent-grantor's estate, the principles set fort in ¶ 23,067 through ¶ 23,079 would indicate that the increased amount be included in decedent's estate. For example, assume that Grandma, after placing all her assets in a revocable trust, decided to give, from trust assets, 100 shares of XYZ stock worth $10,000 to Grandson and that the stock increased in value to $30,000 by the date of Grandma's death. Ignoring the presence of the annual per donee exclusion, had the IRS prevailed in applying § 2035(a) to the transfer, the full $30,000 in value would have been included in Grandma's estate. As in the case of the previously mentioned gifts, had Grandma held the stock directly and gifted it to Grandson, nothing would have been included in her estate under § 2035.

The principal test of this IRS theory came in Estate of Jalkut v. Commissioner, 96 T.C. 675 (1991), acq. 1991-2 C.B.1. Lee Jalkut, the decedent, in 1971 conveyed most of his assets to a revocable trust designed to act as a will substitute. Jalkut was the trustee and sole beneficiary of the trust. Acting pursuant to powers he had retained, Jalkut subsequently amended the trust to provide that during his lifetime all income and so much of the principal as he requests shall be paid to him. In the event of Jalkut's incapacity, successor trustees were authorized to make distributions for Jalkut's benefit and for the benefit of his descendants and historically favored charities and private donees. In late 1984 Jalkut, after being diagnosed as having a terminal disease, made transfers from his revocable trust to various irrevocable trusts created for benefit of his issue. In early 1985, shortly after Jalkut was declared incapable of serving as trustee and several days prior to his death, Jalkut's successor trustees made additional gifts to these same irrevocable trusts.

The Tax Court refused to include in Jalkut's gross estate, under what is now § 2035(a), the transfers from the revocable trust made by Jalkut in 1984 on the theory that, because he was the sole permissible distributee from the trust, the transaction must be treated as a transfer from the trust to Jalkut followed by a transfer from him to the ultimate donees. Since the final transfer to the donees was not from a revocable trusts it could not be deemed described in § 2038 and consequently escaped tax under what is now § 2035(a).

In contrast, the Tax Court held the 1985 transfers made by the successor trustees were not required to be, and in fact could not be, treated as withdrawals made by Jalkut followed by transfers by him to the ultimate donees. The court held that these transfers must be deemed transfers described in § 2038 which occurred within three years of decedent's death with the result that they were to be taxed under what is now § 2035(a).

Despite the IRS's limited loss in *Jalkut* with respect to the 1984 transfers, the Tax Court's formalistic reading of the statute and especially its treatment of the 1985 transfers provided the IRS with encouragement to argue that, in a variety of circumstances which differed slightly from the 1984 transfers, it was appropriate to include within the estate, under what is now § 2035(a), transfers from revocable trusts where the power was retained to revest title in the decedent-grantor. It could and did argue that inclusion under what is now § 2035(a) was appropriate where: (1) as in the case of the 1985 transfers, appointment could be made to beneficiaries in addition to the decedent; (2) the decedent accomplished a transfer to others merely by relinquishing a power to revoke and did not actually withdraw property from the revocable trust to effect the transfer; or (3) the decedent exercised her power of revocation to create separate irrevocable accounts within the revocable trust for the benefit of her donees. The IRS met defeat with respect to a number of such endeavors. See, Kisling v. Commissioner, 32 F.3d 1222 (8th Cir.1994); McNeely v. United States, 16 F.3d 303 (8th Cir.1994); Estate of Barton v. Commissioner, 66 T.C.M. (CCH) 1547, T.C.M. (RIA) § 93,583 (1993). Nonetheless, taxpayers were uncertain as to precisely where the line would ultimately be drawn by the judiciary.

To quiet the issue Congress, in 1997, added to the Code § 2035(e) which addresses the taxation, under both § 2035(a) and § 2038, of transfers by decedent-grantors from revocable trusts where the right to revest the grantor in title has been retained.

[¶ 23,096]

2. THE STATUTORY SOLUTION

Section 2035(e) provides that, in the case of qualifying revocable trusts, a transfer from the trust to other parties shall be treated as a transfer made directly by the decedent. The revocable trusts which qualify for this benefit are those that, under § 676, are treated as owned by the decedent by reason of a power in the grantor to revest title of trust corpus in the grantor. The principal consequence of § 2035(e) is to insure that where a decedent had placed property in a trust, retaining the power to revest herself with title to the property, and within three years of her death made gifts from such trust, neither § 2035(a) nor § 2038 shall operate to include within her estate any such gifts to the extent excluded from the gift tax by the annual per donee exclusion. Another consequence of the addition of § 2035(e) is to repeal that portion of the *Jalkut* opinion which deals with the 1985 transfers. It is now irrelevant whether the decedent-grantor or a third party, such as a guardian or other fiduciary acting on decedent's behalf, made the transfers from the qualifying revocable trust and whether the trust allowed transfers to be made to beneficiaries other than decedent. In neither case shall they be included in decedent's estate under § 2035(a) or § 2038 solely because they were made within three years of death. It is also irrelevant whether the transfers were accomplished: (1) by withdrawal; (2) by relinquishment of a power to revoke; or (3) by creation of segregated irrevocable accounts within the trust. Moreover, the legislative history indicates that Congress intended that, in addition to not effecting an inclusion of gifts or a portion of gifts excluded from gift taxation by the annual per donee exclusion, § 2035(e) would operate to disregard post gift appreciation with respect to transfers from qualifying revocable trusts. S. Rep. No. 105–33 at 682–684 (1997). In the final analysis the principal impact of § 2035(e) is to treat property held by a revocable inter vivos trust, which is intended to function as a will substitute, as if the property were held directly by the decedent-grantor.

F. SECTION 1014(e)—AN INCOME TAX WRINKLE

[¶ 23,097]

Section 1014(e), which was added to the Code in 1981, is an interesting provision. Under § 1014, individuals who inherit property will, in general, receive a basis in inherited property equal to the value properly assigned to such property on the estate tax return. This means that, when an heir sells such property, the heir will account only for changes in value that take place in the heir's hands. Since we live in inflationary times, the rule of § 1014 is typically referred to as the "step-up in basis" rule. It should be kept in mind that the rule also results in a step-down in basis where property declines in value between acquisition and death and that § 1014 is scheduled for repeal for those dying after December 31, 2009 to be replaced by the limited step up basis rule of § 1022.

The step-up in basis rule provided relatively easy means whereby a family could escape income tax on built-in gain by transferring appreciated property to a family member on his or her deathbed. The burden of a gift tax followed by an estate tax was often sufficient to prevent use of this device for families with sufficient wealth to concern themselves with these taxes.

¶ 23,096

The unlimited marital gift and estate tax deductions that were brought to us by the 1981 Tax Act meant that married couples with one spouse at death's door could achieve a step-up in basis at no gift or estate tax cost. For example, assume that wife is on her deathbed and that husband has $300,000 worth of stock that he purchased for $50,000. If he were assured of his wife's loyalty and cooperation and if the simple step-up rule of § 1014 were available to him, he could give the stock to his wife and at her death acquire a basis in the stock equal to its then-fair market value. Section 1014(e) was added to the Code to bar that result.

In general, under § 1014(e), if a donor gives appreciated property to a donee who dies within one year of the gift, no step-up in basis is effected under § 1014 if the appreciated property is inherited by the donor or if such property is sold by the estate of the deceased and the donor is entitled to the proceeds of the sale.

Several observations are in order. First, a married couple that wishes to attempt to attain a step-up in basis in a situation in which death is imminent has everything to win, from a tax standpoint, and nothing to lose. If the ill spouse lives for a year and a day after the gift, the couple will attain a tax-free step-up in basis. If death comes earlier, the couple will have lost nothing from a tax standpoint. It is only under the Internal Revenue Code that an early death could be characterized as a no-loss situation.

Second, by the donee's leaving the gift property to other than the donor, § 1014(e) is easily avoided. For example, take the case of our previously mentioned couple with $300,000 of appreciated stock. Assume that husband gives the stock to wife and that wife's will provides for a credit shelter trust, a relatively common estate planning device. The credit shelter trust names the couple's children as the beneficiaries of that trust. The balance of the wife's estate is then left to her spouse. As its title implies, the credit shelter trust will be funded with an amount sufficient to exhaust wife's unused unified credit, which means that, in the absence of significant inter vivos gift giving by the wife, a considerable amount will be transferred to the trust for the benefit of the children. If wife's will provides that, in the event she dies within one year of the date of the gift, her credit shelter trust is to be funded with, among other things, the $300,000 of appreciated stock that husband gave to her, § 1014(e) will be rendered impotent and the family will reap an enormous potential income tax saving at no estate or gift tax cost. The same result could, presumably, be obtained even if wife's will contained no such direction with respect to the funding of her credit shelter trust so long as her executor decided to fund the trust with the appreciated gift property. About the only risk in all of this is that the wife, on her deathbed, might decide to disinherit the entire miserable bunch and either leave her estate to other individuals or buy her way past the pearly gates with substantial charitable gifts.

Planning Note

[¶ 23,103]

For some taxpayers, the failure of the post–1981 version of § 2035 to include within decedent's estate all gifts made by decedent within three years of death has the unhappy result of depriving them of a windfall step-up in basis which they otherwise would have realized under the pre–1981 statute. Prior to 1981, the automatic inclusion in the estate of all gifts made within three years of death resulted in a step-up in the basis for all such assets. The 1981 changes deprived taxpayers of this potential benefit unless inclusion in the estate results under § 2035(a). Since the step-up in basis rule has little to recommend it from a standpoint of sound tax policy, not even a single crocodile tear should be shed for these taxpayers. A clever estate planner who wishes to assist a terminally ill client in making an inter vivos gift that qualifies for the step-up in basis can cause the transfer to be taxed under § 2035(a) by creating a revocable transfer, which will thereby be includible in the taxable estate, as a transfer described in § 2038, thus assuring the client's donee of a step-up in basis so long as death comes within three years of any relinquishment of the power to revoke. For example, assume that an aged, ill taxpayer wishes to make an inter vivos gift of a vastly appreciated vacation home to a child. By making a revocable gift of the house to the child, the taxpayer can assure that the child will realize a step-up in basis upon the taxpayer's death so long as the power of revocation remains outstanding. Moreover, even if the power of revocation is surrendered, so long as the donor dies within three years of surrender, a step-up will be available. Care must be taken, of course, to avoid loss of step-up through application of the step transaction doctrine to the gift and subsequent surrender of the power of revocation.

Problems

[¶ 23,109]

1. Gloria made a gift of stock to Nora eighteen months ago. At the time of the gift, the stock was worth $50,000 and Gloria paid $15,000 of gift tax on the transaction. At Gloria's death six months ago, the stock was worth $60,000. What value is included in Gloria's estate.

2. Tony took out a $100,000 life insurance policy on his life 10 years ago. Last year, when the policy's interpolated terminal reserve was worth $40,000, Tony gave the policy to his son, Chuck. Tony paid $10,000 in gift tax on the transaction. At Tony's death last month, Chuck, who was both full owner of the policy and sole beneficiary, was paid $100,000. What amount is included in Tony's estate.

3. Monica, the mother of Dora, urged Dora, in the fall of last year, to purchase a $100,000 policy on Monica's life. Dora paid for the premiums on the policy with income from a trust that was funded by Monica. Monica died last week. Are the $100,000 in proceeds taxable in her estate?

4. Eight years ago, Charlie established a trust under which he retained income for his life with remainder to his son Ken. On finding that he had a terminal disease, Charlie transferred his life interest to Ken. The trust's sole asset then consisted of an apartment house. At the time of the transfer, Charlie's life estate was worth $150,000 and Ken's remainder interest was worth $100,000. Charlie paid $50,000 in gift tax on the transfer. At Charlie's death 15 months later, the value of the trust's

assets (the same apartment house) was $400,000. What value, if any, is includible in Charlie's taxable estate?

 Emma was sole shareholder of Acme, Inc., which held a $250,000 term insurance policy on Emma's life payable to her son Alex. Two years ago, when the stock of Acme was worth $1,000,000, Emma gave the stock to her son Alex and paid a gift tax of $400,000 on the transfer. At Emma's death last month Acme, exclusive of the insurance policy, was worth $1,300,000. Shortly after Emma's death Blitzkrieg Insurance paid Alex $250,000 in policy proceeds. What value, if any, is includible in Emma's estate?

Chapter 24

CONSIDERATION IN MONEY
OR MONEY'S WORTH

A. INTRODUCTION

[¶ 24,001]

In addition to the property owned by the decedent at the time of death (§ 2033), the federal estate tax reaches a variety of lifetime transfers, as have already been explored, that may serve as substitutes for testamentary disposition—joint tenancies, life insurance, some gifts within three years of death, retained life estates, certain reversionary interest trusts geared to the grantor's life and trusts amendable by the grantor while the grantor lives. These lifetime transfers have one element in common. They deplete the probate estate while serving as testamentary substitutes—hence their taxability.

In contrast, lifetime transfers for value do not deplete the prospective estate tax base and, therefore, such transfers are not subject to estate taxation. Similarly, with respect to claims deductible by the estate (§ 2053), a requirement that claims be based on a valuable consideration serves to protect the estate tax base from depletion by the deduction of claims enforceable at law (under seal or with formal consideration recited) but representing estate depleting testamentary substitutes. See § 2053(c)(1)(A).

To perform the function of separating the nondepleting transfers and claims for value from the estate-depleting type of gratuitous transfers or claims, the estate tax prescribes a test of "consideration in money or money's worth." This concept appears in a variety of settings. See § 2036, taxing certain transfers "except in the case of a bona fide sale for an adequate and full consideration in money or money's worth." The same language appears in § 2037. Similar language appears in § 2038 and § 2035. Again in § 2043 the rule is prescribed for transfers falling under §§ 2036, 2037 and 2038 that are only partially supported by a consideration in money or money's worth.

In § 2053(c)(1)(A), dealing with deductible claims, the consideration requirement is stated at length, and § 2043(b)(1) provides that "For purposes of this chapter, a relinquishment or promised relinquishment of dower or curtesy, or of a statutory estate created in lieu of dower or curtesy, or of other marital rights in the decedent's property or estate, shall not be considered to any extent a consideration 'in money or money's worth.' "

B. CONSIDERATION RECEIVED

[¶ 24,007]

ESTATE OF FROTHINGHAM v. COMMISSIONER

United States Tax Court, 1973.
60 T.C. 211.

The Commissioner determined a $103,046.62 deficiency in the estate tax of the Estate of C(harles) Mifflin Frothingham. As part of a compromise of a will contest [involving the will of decedent's cousin, George Mifflin] the decedent acquired a general power of appointment in respect of a property interest valued at $856,330.01 as of the date of his own death. He exercised that power by will without receiving any consideration, and the property subject to it was includable in his gross estate under section 2041 of the 1954 Code, unless rendered nontaxable by section 2043(a). The principal issue is whether section 2043(a) is applicable by reason of consideration *given* by the decedent in connection with the creation of the power, or whether the consideration referred to in section 2043(a) relates only to consideration *received* by the decedent.

* * *

RAUM, Judge:

There is no dispute between the parties that the decedent at his death had a "general power of appointment" over an asset having a value of $856,330.01, that he exercised that power of appointment, and that section 2041 calls for the inclusion of the amount in his gross estate unless some other provision of the statute requires a different result. Petitioner contends, however, that the property passing under the decedent's power is excludable from his gross estate by reason of section 2043(a) * * *.

It is petitioner's theory that the compromise agreement through which George's will was amended to grant the decedent the power of appointment here in issue represented a "bona fide sale for an adequate and full consideration in money or money's worth," and that therefore section 2043(a) renders section 2041(a) inoperative. The requisite consideration, the argument goes, is to be found in the decedent's bargained-for relinquishment of the interest he had sought as George's heir by intestacy. The Commissioner argues that whether the decedent *paid* any consideration for the power of appointment is irrelevant, that the "adequate and full consideration" clause in section 2043(a) refers only to consideration *received* by the decedent in connection with the property passing under the power at his death, that he received no consideration in that respect, and that section 2041(a) remains operative, unaffected by section 2043(a). We hold that the Commissioner is correct.

It is important that the structure of the estate tax statute and the part played therein by the "adequate and full consideration" clause be kept clearly in mind. Sections 2035–2038 deal with various types of inter vivos transfer that are regarded as testamentary in character and are therefore included in a decedent's gross estate—e.g., transfers in contemplation of death, transfers taking effect at death, and revocable transfers. In each case the property transferred is includable in the gross estate, but in each of the sections 2035–2038 there is a parenthetical clause rendering the provisions inoperative "in case of a bona fide sale for an adequate and full consideration in money or money's worth." This clause first appeared in the estate tax law in the Revenue Act of 1926. See, e.g., sec. 302(c) of that Act.

The obvious purpose of the clause was to relieve of estate tax those transfers, etc., in respect of which the decedent-transferor had *received* an equivalent amount of consideration. Thus, where the transferred property is replaced by other property of equal value received in exchange, there is no reason to impose an estate tax in respect of the transferred property, for it is reasonable to assume that the property acquired in exchange will find its way into the decedent's gross estate at his death unless consumed or otherwise disposed of in a nontestamentary transaction in much the same manner as would the transferred property itself had the transfer not taken place. Stated differently, the aim of the "consideration" provisions in the Federal gift and estate tax laws "was to prevent the depletion of the transferor's or decedent's estate, unless a tax was paid on the transfer, by requiring that the transferor or decedent receive in exchange something of the same money value." Commissioner v. Bristol, 121 F.2d 129, 134 (1st Cir.).

In short, unless replaced by property of equal value that could be exposed to inclusion in the decedent's gross estate, the property transferred in a testamentary transaction of the type described in the statute must be included in his gross estate. The only consideration involved is the consideration *received* by the decedent. The consideration, if any, given by the decedent is of no greater consequence than the amount, if any, that he may have paid for property which he owns at his death and which is included in his gross estate at its fair market value as of that time. It is with the foregoing as background that the meaning and scope of section 2043(a) must be examined.

* * * It was plainly designed to deal with the situation where the decedent has received some, but not "adequate and full," consideration for the transfer. In providing that there shall be included in the gross estate "only the excess of the fair market value at the time of death of the property * * * over the value of the consideration *received* therefor by the decedent" (emphasis supplied), Congress was obviously attempting merely to provide a measure of relief from double taxation of the same economic interest. We have found no support whatever for petitioner's contention that Congress may have intended to relieve from estate tax property passing under a general power of appointment that was "created" for a consideration supplied by the decedent himself.

Petitioner merely isolates the word "created" in section 2043(a) and assumes that since the power of appointment in issue was "created" for an "adequate and full" consideration furnished by the decedent at the time of the dispute with respect to George's will, the property passing under that power may not be included in his gross estate. Petitioner argues that a literal

¶ 24,007

reading of the statute requires that result. We disagree. The language of section 2043(a) certainly does not call for that interpretation. Section 2043(a) is concerned not only with powers of appointment but also with transfers of the character dealt with in sections 2035–2038, and it seems likely that the word "created" was intended to relate to "trusts" or "interests" involving such transfers for which the decedent received consideration, rather than to powers of appointment. The portion of section 2043(a) that more appropriately relates to "powers" is the language "exercised, or relinquished for a consideration in money or money's worth"—language that clearly contemplates the *receipt* of consideration by the decedent, not the payment of consideration by him. And finally, the last clause in section 2043(a) refers explicitly to "the consideration received therefor by the decedent."

* * *

Note

[¶ 24,011]

It would now be useful to refer back to *Estate of Maxwell* (¶ 18,009) to see how one court disposed of an attempt by the taxpayer to find consideration in a sale where the vendor apparently never intended to collect payment from the vendee.

C.   CHILD SUPPORT AS CONSIDERATION

[¶ 24,013]

As will be recalled from the discussion of support of dependents and other beneficial reservations beginning at ¶ 18,121, where the courts are dealing with trusts established by a noncustodial parent in a broken marriage for support of minor issue of the marriage, no inclusion is made under § 2036 on the ground that discharge of the support obligation provides the consideration necessary to put the trust beyond the reach of § 2036. Occasionally, settlors of such trusts will retain rights (e.g., a contingent life estate) or powers (e.g., a power to alter, amend or revoke) with respect to such trusts that will result in their being included in the settlor's estate. The question that then arises is how much of the value of the support trust is to be excluded because the discharge of the support obligation provided adequate consideration for establishment of all or a portion of the trust.

[¶ 24,019]

ESTATE OF MCDONALD v. COMMISSIONER
Tax Court of the United States, 1953.
19 T.C. 672.

TIETJENS, Judge:

[Decedent, on separation from his wife, created a trust (Trust 924) for the purpose of first providing support and maintenance for his children during

¶ 24,019

their minority. They were income beneficiaries thereafter and entitled to the corpus on reaching the age of 35. Decedent reserved the power to alter, amend and revoke the trust in conjunction with his divorced wife. The Commissioner took the position that the entire trust property should be included in the decedent's gross estate. The first issue, as to whether the trust assets had been community property and therefore not entirely owned by the decedent, was resolved against the decedent. Accordingly, the Tax Court now addresses the issue of whether the transfer in trust had been made for consideration.]

The parties are in apparent agreement that in the event we hold that decedent was the transferor of the assets to Trust 924, the value of such assets is includible in the gross estate unless the transfer of all or some part thereof was made for an adequate and full consideration in money or money's worth.

The question, then, is whether the transfer to Trust 924, or any part thereof, was made for "money's worth." In dealing with gift tax questions and questions involving claims deductible in determining gross estate where the statutory language is similar to the language used in section 811 (i) [now § 2043] it has been held and recognized that transfers of property or contracts entered into for the support of children by the father are made for "money's worth." On this point both parties cite Helvering v. United States Trust Co., 111 Fed. (2d) 576, (2d Cir.1940), reversing on another issue and remanding 39 B. T. A. 783, certiorari denied 311 U.S. 678. * * *

The *United States Trust Co.* case involved the question of whether any part of a trust fund was includible in the gross estate of decedent under the then equivalent of section 811 (d)(2) [now § 2038] of the Internal Revenue Code. In that case decedent had become estranged from his wife some years before he died, and in contemplation of a divorce he made an agreement with her on January 31, 1929, by which he agreed to pay her $2,500 a month during her life, out of which she was to support herself without further recourse to him, and, in addition, to support, maintain, and educate her daughter during the time the said daughter resided with her. The child was to spend half her time with her father and half with her mother, and the testator agreed to assume certain of her expenses while she was with her mother. The amount of $2,500 per month was fixed by the parties as the approximate amount reasonably required for the support of the wife and daughter in accordance with their station in life and with the decedent's ability to furnish such support. The stipulation upon which the case was tried declared that it was established and fixed by agreement of the parties that of the said sum of $2,500 it was contemplated that approximately one third thereof should be allocated and devoted to the support and maintenance of the daughter during her minority.

The agreement of 1929 also provided that the decedent might at any time commute the annuity by setting up a trust for $425,000, the income from which was to be paid to his wife for life, and which she should accept in satisfaction of any claims against him under the agreement. The parties were divorced in May 1929. In the following June the decedent exercised his option to discharge his obligations by setting up a trust, and transferred to trustees securities valued at about $414,000, the income from which was to be paid to the wife for life, she to have a power to appoint $200,000 of the principal by will. The balance of the corpus, or the entire corpus in case there was no valid exercise of the power of appointment, went to the daughter at the death of the wife or to her lawful issue, if any. If she left no issue, then the corpus went to decedent, or as he should appoint by will. Decedent reserved a joint power in himself and his wife at any time to terminate, modify, alter, or revoke the trust in whole or part. The property of the decedent in 1929 was worth more than $1,425,000. He died in May 1935. At the date of decedent's death the child was ten and one-half years of age.

The Board of Tax Appeals (now this Court) excluded the corpus from decedent's estate on the ground that the release by the wife was adequate and full consideration in money or money's worth. The Circuit Court of Appeals held that the release of the wife's marital right of support was not "money's worth," but that insofar as the trust was set up in consideration of a release of that part of the annuity for the support of the child, it was not set up in consideration of the release of a marital right, and was not includible in the gross estate.

* * *

The Circuit Court of Appeals also concluded that it was necessary to find the prospective yearly cost of the child's support when the trust was set up in 1929; then find the commuted value of the cost and what proportion it represented of the value of the trust fund when it was set up; and exclude from the gross estate that proportion of the value of the trust fund when the decedent died.

In the case before us both parties agree that the trust was for the primary benefit of the children and that no marital rights are involved. Nevertheless, in its essentials, it seems to us that the purposes and terms of the trust instrument executed by decedent here are substantially similar to those involved in Helvering v. United States Trust Co., supra, and that the question is what was the prospective value of the children's support.

Petitioners contend that the full value of the transferred assets is to be taken as "money's worth" since the settlement agreement and the terms of the trust were agreed upon at arm's length and only after bitter negotiations between decedent and Lenore and their attorneys. We cannot accept this contention. It is apparent that decedent went beyond his legal obligation to his children in creating the trust. At most, Delos was entitled to his father's support for about four years when the trust was established; Nedra for about 12 years. In 1931 the corpus of the trust was worth at least $220,000 and it produced net income ranging from some $28,000 in 1931 to $33,500 in 1943. In 1936 the income was $65,000 while in 1933 it amounted to but $8,578.90. That decedent thought this income alone was more than necessary for the support of the children is shown by the fact that provision was made for the accumulation of unused income in the event of Lenore's death before the children attained their majority. Furthermore, after majority, when decedent's obligation to support would cease, the children were still entitled to certain amounts of income and on reaching the age of 35 the trust corpus was distributable to them. Also, the recital in decedent's will in connection with bequests of $5 to each child that "my reason for such bequest is that I have previously made a settlement upon (them) from my estate," is evidence that decedent was doing more in setting up the trust then merely meeting his legal obligation of support. The arrangement had aspects of a testamentary disposition. Certainly, in these circumstances, we cannot say that the entire value of the trust assets was transferred for "money's worth." Only that portion of the value which represents the children's right to support is to be so treated. Helvering v. United States Trust Co., supra.

The question of the proper valuation of the children's support has given us pause. The evidence on this point is meager at best. Respondent argues that petitioners have failed in their burden of proof and that nothing whatever should be allowed. Nevertheless, it seems incumbent on the Court to place a reasonable prospective value on the children's support and after carefully considering the evidence, and "bearing heavily" on the petitioners "whose inexactitude" raises the problem, we have found that value to be $30,000. Cohan v. Commissioner, 39 F.2d 540, 544 Edith M. Bensel, et al., Executors, 36 B. T. A. 246, 255, affd. 100 F.2d 639.

Accordingly, pursuant to section 811 (i) [now § 2043], there should be included in the gross estate only "the excess of the fair market value at the time of death" of the assets of Trust 924 over the sum of $30,000 which we have found to be the value of the children's rights to support at the time the trust was set up.

* * *

Note

[¶ 24,025]

1. Should a trust set up for the support of minor children be regarded as a transfer for a valuable consideration to any extent? The taxpayer who retains property in his or her own name and supports children with the resulting income gets no deduction. Why should a formal trust arrangement make any difference? Is a trust that is classed as a retained life estate because it supports legal dependents different at all as regards "consideration?" Does the circumstance that only the income from the transfer is used for support indicate that the principal is being handed over eventually as a type of testamentary substitute to the natural objects of the grantor's bounty?

The Treasury fully accepts that a transfer in satisfaction of the support obligation can be consideration in money or money's worth. For example, see Rev. Ruls. 77–314, 1977–2 C.B. 349, and 79–363, 1979–2 C.B. 346.

2. It would now be appropriate to review Priv.Ltr.Rul. 9235032 (¶ 18,159) on the topic of alimony trusts and the consideration rule.

D. SALES OF REMAINDER INTERESTS

[¶ 24,031]

During the 1970's and early 1980's, the estate planning Bar became fascinated with planning devices involving sales of remainder interests. The devices employed relied on the fact that § 2036(a) excludes from taxation transfers involving bona fide sales for "adequate and full consideration." Owners of property, such as a ranch or stock in a closely held business were often advised to retain ownership of the asset for their life but to sell the remainder interest, to family members. At the death of the vendor, it was thought that, because of the "adequate and full consideration" exception, all that would remain to be taxed in the vendor's estate from such a transaction would be what remained of the consideration that the vendor received from the remaindermen on their purchase of the remainder interest.

Another variation on the above theme was the so called surviving spouses election, which in tribute to women's longevity is commonly called the widow's election. This estate planning devise, which first gained favor more than a decade before the conventional sales of remainders previously described, was quite popular in community property states, and in point of fact, was basically a sale of a remainder in family garb. In the community property version of the widow's election, the will of the first spouse to die, who in our example is the husband, gives the survivor-wife either her share of the community property or, if she elects, an income interest in both her spouse's and her interest in the community property with the will of the first spouse disposing of all community property in exchange for the survivor receiving the extra income from decedent's share of community property. Assuming that all the couple's assets are community assets and the survivor makes the election, the hoped for result is that the only assets that will be taxed in the estate of the husband will be his share of the community property and that at wife's death the only assets that will be taxed in her estate will be whatever property she did not consume from the income paid to her. As in the case of the sale of a remainder interest, the avoidance of any estate tax under § 2036, at the death of the surviving spouse, is predicated on the election qualifying under the "adequate and full consideration" exception of § 2036.

Although these devices have been described by some as providing a "taxpayer's utopia," in fact, like the private annuity, if they are properly priced, which they often were not, no abuse is present. In the conventional sale of a remainder interest, if the transaction is properly priced, if the vendor life tenant invests the sales proceeds in property which produces a rate of return equal to the modest rate of return used in the discount tables in pricing the sale and if the vendor life tenant lives to his or her projected life expectancy, the value of the sales proceeds so invested should, at the vendor's death, equal the fee simple value of the property sold. Moreover, although there will be some vendors who will not reach their normal life expectancies and will die with less accumulated than was projected, they will be offset by other vendors who will exceed their life expectancies and will die with more accumulated under the arrangement than was projected.

The two principal cases in this area are Gradow v. United States, 11 Cl. Ct. 808 (1987), aff'd 897 F.2d 516 (Fed.Cir.1990) and Estate of D'Ambrosio v. Commissioner, 101 F.3d 309 (3d Cir.1996) which reach contrary conclusions. *Gradow* is a widow's election case in which the court concluded that for the sale of a remainder to be deemed to be for adequate consideration, the purchasers of the remainder interest would have to pay the vendor-life tenant an amount equal to the amount which would be included in the vendor's estate had the sale not taken place. This, of course, produces the troubling possibility that by doing so the purchaser might be slapped with gift tax liability if the amount transferred in excess of full and adequate consideration does not qualify for the marital deduction. Although this deficiency of the result in *Gradow* was not addressed by the court in *D'Ambrosio*, a number of the other defects of the opinion in *Gradow* are discussed in the opinion which follows:

[¶ 24,037]

ESTATE OF D'AMBROSIO v. COMMISSIONER

United States Court of Appeals, Third Circuit, 1996.
101 F.3d 309.

NYGAARD, Circuit Judge.

[Decedent Rose D'Ambrosio was the owner of half the preferred stock of Vaparo, Inc. which had a fair market value of $2,350,000. In 1987, at age 80, she sold a remainder interest in her shares to a family owned corporation in exchange for an annuity of $296,039 per year and retained the income interest in her shares. The annuity had a value of $1,324,014 which the parties stipulate was the fair market value of D'Ambrosio's remainder interest in the stock. Decedent died in 1990 after having received a total of $592,078 under the annuity. Her executor included nothing in her estate with respect to the stock. The IRS issued a notice of deficiency including in decedent's estate, under § 2036(a)(1), $2,350,000 (the still then value of the stock) minus the payments received by decedent under the annuity. The executor brought suit in the Tax Court which decided that decedent's transfer of a remainder interest did not fall within the adequate consideration exception of § 2036(a)(1). Its opinion relied principally on two widow's election cases, Estate of Gregory v. Commissioner, 39 T.C. 1012 (1963) and Gradow v. United States, 11 Cl. Ct 808, (1987)aff'd 897 F.2d 516 (Fed.Cir.1990). It, however, did allow the estate to subtract, from the $2,350,000 value of the stock, as "inadequate consideration" the $1,324,014 value of the annuity, not the amounts actually paid to decedent. Taxpayer appealed to the Court of Appeals for the Third Circuit.

The Court of Appeals in its opinion found *Estate of Gregory* to be of little assistance in resolving how the issue before it should be decided since that case did not involve adequate consideration with the widow exchanging property worth almost $66,000 for a life estate with an actuarial value of about $12,000. It then turned its attention to an analysis of the claims Court's opinion in *Gradow*.]

The facts in *Gradow* were similar to those in *Gregory*; both are "widow's election" cases. That case is particularly significant, however, because the court focused on the statutory language of § 2036.

* * *

We examine first the *Gradow* court's construction of the statute. It opined that

> there is no question that the term "property" in the phrase "The gross estate shall include ... all property ... of which the decedent has at any time made a transfer" means that part of the trust corpus attributable to plaintiff. If § 2036(a) applies, all of [the electing widow's] former community property is brought into her gross estate. Fundamental principles of grammar dictate that the parenthetical exception which then follows— "(except in case of a bona fide sale ...)"—refers to a transfer of that same property, i.e. the one-half of the community property she placed into the trust.

Id. (ellipses in original). We disagree; although the *Gradow* court's rationale appears plausible, we note that the court, in quoting the statute, left out significant portions of its language. Below is the text of § 2036, with the omitted words emphasized:

> The *value of the* gross estate shall include *the value* of all property *to the extent of any interest therein* of which the decedent has at any time made a transfer (except in case of a bona fide sale for an adequate and full consideration in money or money's worth), by trust or otherwise, under which he has retained for his life * * * (1) the possession or enjoyment of, or the right to the income from, the property * * *

After parsing this language, we cannot agree with the *Gradow* court's conclusions that "property" refers to the fee simple interest and that adequate consideration must be measured against that value. Rather, we believe that the clear import of the phrase "to the extent of any interest therein" is that the gross estate shall include the value of the remainder *interest*, unless it was sold for adequate and fair consideration.

In addition to § 2036, Treas. Reg. § 20.2036–1 also addresses this issue. It provides, in pertinent part (emphases added):

> (a) In general. A decedent's gross estate includes under section 2036 the value of any *interest* in property *transferred* by the decedent ... except to the extent that the transfer was for an adequate and full consideration in money or money's worth if the decedent retained or reserved (1) for his life ...

> (i) The use, possession, right to the income, or other enjoyment of *the transferred property*, ...

Appellant refers us to the emphasized words "interest" and "transferred" in § 20.2036–1(a) and argues that "adequate and full consideration" must be measured against the interest transferred. The Commissioner, on the other hand, looks at the phrase "of the transferred property" in § 20.2036–1(a)(i) and concludes that, because one cannot retain any lifetime interest in a remainder, "property" must refer to the fee simple interest.

The regulation, unfortunately, is not exactingly drafted and does not parse "cleanly" under either party's interpretation. The Commissioner is of course correct that one cannot enjoy any sort of life interest in a remainder. On the other hand, appellant validly asks why, if the drafters of the regulation meant to include the full value of the property, they referred to the value of any "*interest* in property transferred." On balance, we believe that, if some words of the regulation must be construed as surplusage, it is more reasonable and faithful to the statutory text to render inoperative the word "transferred" in § 20.2036–1(a)(i) than it would be to strike "interest" in the first part of the section. We think it is likely that, although the choice of verbiage was less than precise, the drafters meant merely to refer to the "transferred" property so as to distinguish it from other property owned by the estate. It strains the judicial imagination, however, to conclude that the drafters used the term of art "interest in property" when they meant simply "property."

The *Gradow* court also believed that its construction of § 2036 was "most consistent" with its purposes. 11 Cl.Ct. at 813. The tax court in this case, although recognizing that the issue has spawned considerable legal commentary and that scholars dispute its resolution, 105 T.C. at 254, was persuaded that decedent's sale of her remainder interest was testamentary in character and designed to avoid the payment of estate tax that otherwise would have been due. *Id.* at 260. It noted particularly that the transfer was made when decedent was eighty years old and that the value of the annuity she received was over $1 million less than the fee simple value of the stock she gave up. *Id.* Again, we disagree.

We too are cognizant that techniques for attempting to reduce estate taxes are limited only by the imagination of estate planners, and that new devices appear regularly. There is, to be sure, a role for the federal courts to play in properly limiting these techniques in accordance with the expressed intent of Congress.

*   *   *

On the other hand, it is not our role to police the techniques of estate planning by determining, based on our own policy views and perceptions, which transfers are abusive and which are not. That is properly the role of Congress, whose statutory enactments we are bound to interpret. As stated *supra*, we think the statutory text better supports appellant's argument.

Even looking at this case in policy terms, however, it is difficult to fathom either the tax court's or the Commissioner's concerns about the "abusiveness" of this transaction. A hypothetical example will illustrate the point.

A fee simple interest is comprised of a life estate and a remainder. Returning to the widow's election cases, assume that the surviving spouse's share of the community property is valued at $2,000,000. Assuming that she decides not to accept the settlement and to keep that property, its whole value will be available for inclusion in the gross estate at death, but only as long as the widow lives entirely on the income from the property. If she invades principal and sells some of the property in order to meet living expenses or purchase luxury items, then at least some of that value will not be included in the gross estate. Tax law, of course (with the exception of the gift tax), imposes no burdens on how a person spends her money during life.

Next, assume that same widow decides to sell her remainder and keep a life estate. As long as she sells the remainder for its fair market value, it makes no difference whether she receives cash, other property, or an annuity. All can be discounted to their respective present values and quantified. If she continues to support herself from the income from her life estate, the consideration she received in exchange for the remainder, if properly invested, will still be available for inclusion in the gross estate when she dies,* * *. On the other hand, if her life estate is insufficient to meet her living expenses, the widow will have to invade the consideration she received in exchange for her remainder, but to no different an extent than she would under the previous hypothetical in which she retained the fee simple interest. In sum, there is simply no change in the date-of-death value of the final estate, regardless of which option she selects, at any given standard of living.

On the other hand, if the full, fee simple value of the property at the time of death is pulled back into the gross estate under § 2036(a), subject only to an offset for the consideration received, then the post-sale appreciation of the transferred asset will be taxed at death. Indeed, it will be double-taxed, because, all things being equal, the consideration she received will also have appreciated and will be subject to tax on its increased value. In addition, it would appear virtually impossible, under the tax court's reasoning, ever to sell a remainder interest; if the adequacy of the consideration must be measured against the fee simple value of the property at the time of the transfer, the transferor will have to find an arms-length buyer willing to pay a fee simple price for a future interest. Unless a buyer is willing to speculate that the future value of the asset will skyrocket, few if any such sales will take place.

Another potential concern, expressed by the *Gradow* court, is that, under appellant's theory, "[a] young person could sell a remainder interest for a fraction of the property's [current, fee simple] worth, enjoy the property for life, and then pass it along without estate or gift tax consequences." 11 Cl.Ct. at 815. This reasoning is problematic, however, because it ignores the time value of money. Assume that a decedent sells his son a remainder interest in that much-debated and often-sold parcel of land called Blackacre, which is worth $1 million in fee simple, for its actuarial fair market value of $100,000 (an amount which implicitly includes the market value of Blackacre's expected appreciation). Decedent then invests the proceeds of the sale. If the rates of return for both assets are equal and decedent lives exactly as long as the actuarial tables predict, the consideration that decedent received for his remainder will equal the value of Blackacre on the date of his death. The equivalent value will, accordingly, still be included in the gross estate. Moreover, decedent's son will have only a $100,000 basis in Blackacre, because that is all he paid for it. He will then be subject to capital gains taxes

¶ 24,037

on its appreciated value if he decides to ever sell the property. Had Blackacre been passed by decedent's will and included in the gross estate, the son would have received a stepped-up basis at the time of his father's death or the alternate valuation date. We therefore have great difficulty understanding how this transaction could be abusive.

On this appeal, the Commissioner likewise argues for the *Gradow* rule on the rationale that "the retained life interest is in closely held stock whose dividend treatment is subject to the control of decedent and her family. In such circumstances, the amount of the dividend income that decedent was to receive from her life income interest in the Vaparo preferred stock was susceptible of manipulation[.]" Commissioner's Brief at 33. There is no evidence, however, that the Vaparo dividends *were* manipulated, and the Commissioner directs us to no authority that we should presume so. In addition, implicit in her argument is the proposition that the life estate was overvalued by the executor and the remainder correspondingly undervalued. Such a position, however, is directly contrary to the Commissioner's own stipulation regarding the values of those interests.

The Commissioner also asserts that the D'Ambrosio estate plan is "calculated to deplete decedent's estate in the event that she should not survive as long as her actuarially projected life expectancy." Commissioner's Brief at 34–35. We note first that the Commissioner does not argue that decedent transferred her remainder in contemplation of imminent death under such circumstances that the tables should not be applied. Leaving aside the untimely death of Rose D'Ambrosio, any given transferor of a remainder is equally likely to *outlive* the tables, in which case she would collect more from her annuity, the gross estate would be correspondingly larger and the Commissioner would collect more tax revenue than if the remainder had never been transferred.

Because we conclude that the tax court erred as a matter of law when it determined that the consideration received by Rose D'Ambrosio for her remainder interest was not adequate and full, we will reverse and remand for it to enter judgment in favor of the estate.

Notes

[¶ 24,043]

1. Although the court's opinion in *D'Ambrosio* is well reasoned and is correct in its economic analysis, the ultimate judicial resolution of adequacy of consideration in situations involving sales of remainder issues may require Supreme Court intervention. Support for the *Gradow* approach can be found in Pittman v. United States, 878 F.Supp. 833 (E.D.N.C.1994), whereas the Fifth Circuit in Wheeler v. United States, 116 F.3d 749 (5th Cir.1997) (sale of remainder interest in ranch) and the Ninth Circuit in Estate of Magnin v. Commissioner, 184 F.3d 1074 (9th Cir. 1999) are supportive of the Third Circuit analysis in *D'Amrosio* as are several older cases. See Estate of Christ v. Commissioner, 54 T.C. 493 (1970), aff'd 480 F.2d 171 (9th Cir.1973) & Estate of Vardell v. Commissioner, 307 F.2d 688 (5th Cir.1962).

¶ 24,037

2.   In 1990 Congress added §§ 2701 and 2702 to the Code. These sections will have special meaning for parties contemplating a sale of a remainder interest. Section 2701 will impact on situations such as those involved in *D'Ambrosio* in which a remainder interest in a family corporation or partnership is transferred and an income interest is retained, whereas § 2702 will apply to transfers of other assets in trust or other transfers involving life or term interests. While these provisions, which are discussed in detail in Chapter 12, will not preclude taxpayers from engaging in sales of remainder interests for full and adequate consideration to avoid taxation under § 2036, the harshness of the zero valuation rule for retained interests for gift tax purposes will insure that most sales of remainder interests are structured so as to avoid the zero value rule. For example, if a taxpayer wishes to sell a remainder interest in a trust to a child, she will likely structure it as a sale of an interest in a qualified annuity or unitrust to avoid the zero valuation rule (¶ 12,079 through ¶ 12,091).

E.   INADEQUATE CONSIDERATION— AMOUNT INCLUDED

[¶ 24,049]

Assuming that the statute means what it says, and that the courts in *D'Ambrosio* and *Wheeler* are correct in their analysis and that the courts in *Gradow* and its progeny have misconstrued the law, we now turn our attention to the issue of the amount includible where inadequate consideration has been employed.

Where inadequate consideration has been used to effect the transfer of an interest, determination of the amount to be included in the estate presents an interesting issue. For example, assume that A, who owns Blackacre, which is worth $100,000, retains a life estate in Blackacre and sells the remainder to her nephew for $40,000. If the actuarially determined value of A's life estate was $60,000, at her death nothing should be included in her estate under § 2036 since she has made a transfer of the remainder interest "for an adequate consideration in money or money's worth," which is consequently excluded from taxation under the parenthetical consideration rule found in § 2036(a). Even if Blackacre doubles in value prior to A's death, there should be no inclusion since the transfer was for adequate consideration. Assume, however, that A sold the $40,000 remainder interest to the nephew for $20,000, what amount should be included in her estate? A literal reading of § 2043 indicates that, if A dies with Blackacre worth $100,000, the amount to be included would be determined by subtracting from Blackacre's $100,000 value the $20,000 paid, with the result that $80,000 in value would be included in her estate. Moreover, if Blackacre doubles in value, the same subtractional rule is applied and $180,000 in value is included in her estate. Theoretically, if she were to be a mere $1,000 short in the value assigned to the remainder interest and were to value it at $39,000, then $61,000 would be included in her estate if Blackacre did not increase in value and $161,000 would be included if it doubled in value. These results all follow from a literal reading of the subtractional nature of the cure provided by § 2043. Fortunately, the Courts do not expect exacting precision and are content with approximately equal valuations. In re Estate of Davis, 440 F.2d 896 (3d Cir. 1971); Estate of Carli v. Commissioner, 84 T.C. 649 (1985).

An interesting case in which a modest discrepancy in consideration cost the taxpayer mightily is Estate of Magnin v. Commissioner, 81 T.C.M. (CCH) 1126, T.C.M. (RIA) ¶ 2001–031 (2001). Taxpayer, who held a life interest in a trust which would be includible in his estate under § 2036 sold his interest in the trust for $43,878. He died shortly after the sale. Absent the sale of his interest $3,833,743 would have been included in his estate because of his retained life estate. The Tax Court in an earlier proceeding applied *Gradow* (¶ 24,031) and decided that since the taxpayer had not received $3,833,747 for his life interest, full and adequate consideration was lacking. The Ninth Circuit reversed the Tax Court (¶ 24,043) accepting the reasoning of the Third Circuit in *Estate of D'Ambrosio* (¶ 24,037). It remanded the case to the Tax Court to determine if full and adequate consideration was present. Judge Ruwe, the same judge who had been reversed by the Ninth Circuit, found that the value of taxpayer's life estate was between $90,000 and $110,000. He indicated that while the adequate consideration rule did not require pinpoint accuracy, this more than 2 to 1 disparity in values did not measure up. The result was that he included in taxpayer's estate $3,833,747 minus the $43,878 paid to taxpayer to purchase his life interest.

A better consideration rule is provided by the proportional consideration rule of § 2040, which taxes joint property. Under that rule, where the surviving joint tenant provided a part of the consideration, the amount to be included in the estate of the deceased joint tenant is that portion of the fair market value of the property that is reflective of the portion of the total consideration provided by the deceased joint tenant. For example, if the deceased joint tenant provided three-quarters of the consideration used to purchase Blackacre and the survivor provided the balance, only three-quarters of the value of Blackacre would be included in the decedent's estate, regardless of how value had changed by date of death.

Consider the question of why Congress should not consider changing the inadequate subtractional consideration rule of § 2043 into a proportional consideration rule such as is provided by § 2040? For example, where A sold the $40,000 life estate to her nephew for $20,000, under a proportional rule, one-half of the value of Blackacre would be included in her estate at death. Such an approach certainly seems to be more reflective of the economic realities. Had this been the rule in *Magnin* only a little more than one-half of the $3.8 million trust would have been included in the taxpayer's estate. As it turned out being about $50,000 short on consideration resulted in a $3.8 million inclusion.

F. INTRAFAMILY TRANSFERS AND ENTITIES

[¶ 24,051]

As discussed elsewhere (¶ ¶ 11,115 & 18,257) taxpayers in search of valuation discounts have, in recent years, made transfers to entities (typically

¶ 24,049

limited partnerships) for the purpose, or at very least having the effect, of reducing the valuation of transferred assets. The I.R.S. has seized upon the opportunity to impose estate tax on many such transfers on the grounds that they come within the scope of one of the basic inclusion sections such as § 2036 or § 2035. Where taxpayers are unable to escape the general reach of these sections, they find themselves falling back on the argument that the transfer is not covered by the provision in question because it is a "bona fide sale for an adequate and full consideration in money or money's worth." See, e.g. §§ 2035(d) & 2036(a). The cases discussing the requirements of this language in such situations are legion and final resolution of what these words mean must await further discussion and consideration by the courts. The case that follows probably represents the best assortment of food for thought on this issue.

[¶ 24,052]

ESTATE OF BONGARD v. COMMISSIONER

United States Tax Court, 2005.
124 T.C. 95.

GOEKE, Judge

[Wayne C. Bongard (Bongard) was a highly successful businessman who was a founder of Empak, Inc., a very successful business. Bongard was, until his death, the sole member of the board of directors of Empak and was also its CEO. In 1986 he transferred some of his shares of Empak to a trust (ISA Trust) for the benefit of his children and one other individual. In 1995 Bongard entered into serious discussions with financial advisers as to how best to secure an additional infusion of capital for Empak. Based on their advice, in January of 1996 he formed WBC Holdings, LLC (WBC Holdings) for the purpose of eventually positioning Empak "for a corporate liquidity event" (a primary issuance of additional stock to obtain added operating capital). Bongard's financial advisers asserted that outsiders would be more willing to invest in the company if the Bongard family interests in Empak were placed in a holding company. Wayne Bongard's son Mark was made the manager of WBC Holdings and was invested with significant decision making powers, although members who possessed the majority of the voting power (Bongard) were invested with the power to overrule a number of critical decisions made by the manager and their approval must be obtained for a number of actions such as sales of stock held by WCB Holdings in excess of $10,000 per year, purchases of new investments, borrowing even modest sums and voting stock held by WCB Holdings. In addition, those with majority voting power in WCB Holdings were authorized to take any action that the manager could take and were authorized to remove him at will. On December 28, 1996, Bongard and ISA Trust each transferred all their Empak stock to WCB Holdings with each receiving in exchange both class A and class B membership units in WCB Holdings. Class A units were voting units whereas class B units were nonvoting units. Based on his holdings in Empak, Bongard was issued an 86.39 percent ownership interest in each class of ownership units, making him alone the majority owner of WCB Holdings vested with the special powers noted. On the next day, at the behest of his estate planners, The Bongard Family Limited Partnership (BFLP) was formed with ISA Trust and Bongard each transferring all their WBC Holdings class B membership units to BFLP in exchange for interests in BFLP reflective of the value of the class B units each transferred. The court found that the formation of BFLP was part of Bongard's estate plan and was not part of the planning for the "liquidity event." In December of 1997, Bongard entered into a postmarital agreement with his wife Cynthia (his second wife with whom he had no children) and transferred to her a 7.72 percent limited partnership in BFLP as part of that agreement. On November 16, 1998, Bongard unexpectedly died at age 58 on a hunting trip to Austria. The estate sought valuation discounts from the value of the Empak shares based on: (1) the interposition of WBC Holdings between the Empak shares and Bongard's ownership interest; and (2) the added interposition of BFLP between Bongard's ownership and the underlying Empak shares. The I.R.S. countered ,asserting that there was an inclusion of Bongard's interests in Empak under § 2036. Prior to addressing the basic § 2036 issue, the Tax Court addressed whether it need not wade into those waters because both transfers had been made in a "bona fide sale for adequate and full consideration."]

In the context of family limited partnerships, the adequate and full consideration requirement is met where the record establishes the existence of a legitimate and significant nontax reason for creating the family limited partnership, and the transferors received partnership interests proportionate to the value of the property transferred.* * * The objective evidence must indicate that the nontax reason was a significant factor that motivated the partnerships creation. * * * A significant purpose must be an actual motivation, not a theoretical justification.

By contrast, the bona fide sale exception is not applicable where the facts fail to establish that the transaction was motivated by a legitimate and significant nontax purpose. * * * A list of facts that support such a finding includes the taxpayer standing on both sides of the transaction, the taxpayer's financial dependence on distributions from the partnership, the partners' commingling of partnership funds with their own and the taxpayer's actual failure to transfer the property to the partnership* * *.

A transaction between family members is, however, subjected to heightened scrutiny to ensure that it is not a sham or a disguised gift.* * *

     C.   Decedent's Transfer of Empak Stock to WCB Holdings

* * *

In 1995, decedent, while in good health, met with his advisers, Messers. Boyle, Bernards, and Eitel, to discuss how Empak could remain successful and competitive. These discussions determined that Empak needed to develop additional means for acquiring capital to remain successful and competitive. Mr. Bernards testified that for Empak to grow, "additional capital other than bank debt and through [reinvesting its] earnings" was needed. It was believed that positioning Empak for either a public or private offering (a corporate liquidity event) would accomplish this goal. Decedent and his advisers discussed how to facilitate a corporate liquidity event for Empak. Mr. Boyle drafted a memo and a checklist detailing the specific steps of the plan to position Empak for a corporate liquidity event.

Many of the steps in the checklist were completed.* * *

The positioning and structuring of Empak to facilitate a corporate liquidity event was also beneficial for decedent and ISA Trust. ISA Trust held a single asset, Empak stock. The value of the shares held by both decedent and ISA Trust was maximized by positioning Empak to attract potential investors. Moreover, the potential market for Empak shares was increased. These facts together support that positioning Empak for a corporate liquidity event was a legitimate and significant nontax reason that motivated the Empak shareholders to create WCBHoldings.

1. Bona Fide Sale

* * *

Respondent appears to assert that an arm's-length transaction cannot occur between related parties. An arm's-length transaction has been defined as "A transaction between two unrelated and unaffiliated parties" or alternatively, a transaction "between two parties, however closely related they may be, conducted as if the parties were strangers, so that no conflict of interest arises." * * * The bona fide sale exception has not been limited to transactions involving unrelated parties as respondent's argument implies. * * *

It is axiomatic that intrafamily transactions are subjected to a higher level of scrutiny, but this heightened scrutiny is not tantamount to an absolute bar. In that connection, we have already concluded that decedent and ISA Trust had mutual legitimate and significant nontax reasons for forming WCB Holdings. In addition, both decedent and ISA Trust received interests in WCB Holdings proportionate to the number of shares transferred. We believe that had this transaction occurred between two unrelated parties the majority interest holder in Empak would have received similar powers to those received via WCB Holdings' member control agreement. An important purpose for creating WCB Holdings was to position Empak for a corporate liquidity event, and the record does not contain any credible evidence that unrelated parties would not have agreed to the same terms and conditions. Given these facts, we cannot hold that the terms of the transaction differed from those of two unrelated parties negotiating at arm's length.

Respondent's final argument is that the formation of WCB Holdings was not a bona fide sale because there was not a true pooling of assets. WCB Holdings' purpose was to pool the Bongard family's Empak stock within a single entity, which decedent and ISA Trust satisfied through their respective contributions. WCB Holdings' creation was part of a much grander plan, to attract potential investors or to stimulate a corporate liquidity event to facilitate Empak's growth. Moreover, when WCB Holdings was capitalized, the members' capital accounts were properly credited and maintained, WCB Holdings' funds were not commingled with decedent's, and all distributions during decedent's life were pro rata. The amalgamation of these facts evidences that this transaction resulted in a true pooling of assets.

2. Full and Adequate Consideration

The factual circumstances of this case further establish that the decedent and ISA Trust each received an interest in WCB Holdings that represented adequate and full consideration reducible to money value. * * * Decedent and ISA Trust received interests in WCB Holdings proportionate to the number of Empak shares each contributed. Although by itself this may not be sufficient evidence to meet the adequate and full consideration requirement, two additional facts do support such a funding. We have determined that the respective assets contributed by the members were properly credited to the respective capital accounts of each contributing member, and distributions from WCB Holdings required a negative adjustment in the distributee member's capital account. Most importantly, we have found the presence of a legitimate and significant nontax business reason for engaging in this transaction.

Respondent nonetheless argues that decedent did not receive adequate and full consideration since decedent contributed 86.31 percent of Empak's outstanding stock without receiving a control premium for his contribution. Decedent did not need to receive a control premium because he retained effective control over Emak after he contributed his Empak stock to WCB Holdings. True, decedent was not the chief manager of WCB Holdings [Mark Bongard was], but the 86.31 percent interest in the class A governance units he received in the exchange provided him with the power to remove the WCB Holdings chief manager and replace him with himself as chief manager, to take any action the chief manager himself could take, and to approve any significant action the chief manager could take including selling more than $10,000 of any security in any 12–month period and the voting of any security held by WCB Holdings.* * *

3. Conclusion

We hold that decedent's transfer of Empak stock to WCB Holdings satisfies the bona fide sale exception of section 2036(a). Therefor, we need not determine whether decedent retained a section 2036(a) or (b) interest in the transferred property. * * *

D. BFLP

The estate argues that section 2036(a) is not applicable to decedent's transfer of WCB Holdings class B membership units to BFLP since the transfer was also a bona fide sale for adequate and full consideration. The estate contends that the creation of BFLP was motivated by nontax reasons. The BFLP agreement provides that BFLP was established to "acquire, own and sell from time to time stocks (including closely held stocks), bonds, options, mutual funds and other securities." At trial, Mr. Fullmer [one of Bongard's estate planners] testified that BFLP was established to provide another layer of credit protection for decedent. Additionally the estate assets that BFLP facilitated decedent's and Cynthia Bongard's postmarital agreement. Messers. Bernards and Fullmer [Bongard's attorneys] both also testi-

¶ 24,052

fied that BFLP was established, in part, to make gifts. On December 10, 1997, decedent made a gift of a 7.72 percent interest in BFLP to Cynthia Bongard. This gift was the sole transfer of a BFLP interest by decedent during his life. BFLP also never diversified its assets during decedent's life, never had an investment plan, and never functioned as a business enterprise or otherwise engaged in any meaningful economic activity.

* * *

Estate tax savings did play an important role in motivating the transfer to BFLP. The record does not support that the nontax reasons for BFLP's existence were significant motivating factors. The formation of WCB Holdings eliminated direct stock ownership in Empak and allowed decedent to make gifts without diversifying the direct ownership of Emapk. Messers Fullmer and Bernards testified that an impetus for forming BFLP was to continue decedent's gift giving. Decedent, in fact made numerous gifts after the formation of BFLP, but not of his BFLP interest ... except for the 7.72–percent limited partnership interest he gave to Cynthia Bongard in 1997. At the time of BFLP's formation and at the time of his death, any additional gifts decedent had contemplated were speculative and indefinite at best. There was no immediate plan for such gifts. Such intent is not sufficient to establish ... a significant nontax reason.

* * *

The estate's credit protection argument is also unpersuasive because WCB Holdings served this function for decedent. In fact, decedent via letter stated that "by holding a majority of my assets in the limited liability company or the limited partnership, I will be providing a greater amount of protection for those assets from both creditors and lawsuits." * * * Decedent's initial transfer of his Empak shares to WCB Holdings accorded him the credit protection he sought.

* * *

Our determination that the bona fide sale exception does not apply ... does not end our inquiry. [S]ection 2036(a) includes in a decedent's gross estate "all property to the extent of any interest therein" of which the decedent has made a transfer wherein he has "retained for his life" either "(1) the possession or enjoyment of, or the right to income from, the property, or (2) the right, either alone or in conjunction with any person, to designate the persons who shall possess or enjoy the property or the income therefrom." * * *

The decedent did not need the membership interest in WCB Holdings class B shares to continue his lifestyle. However, decedent retained ownership of more than 91 percent of his BFLP interest and did not make gifts of such interest prior to his death. More importantly, decedent controlled whether BFLP could transform its sole asset, the class B WCB Holdings membership units, into a liquid asset. Decedent as CEO and sole member of Empak's board of directors determined when Empak redeemed its stock in each of the seven instances of redemptions prior to his death, including the last redemption ... in 1998 after WCB Holdings was formed. * * * In order for BFLP to be able to diversify or take any steps other than simply holding the class B membership uints, decedent would have to cause the membership units and the underlying Empak stock to be redeemed. He chose not to do this. By not redeeming the WCB membership units held by BFLP, decedent ensured that BFLP would not engage in asset management. Thereby, decedent exercised practical control over BFLP and limited its function to simply holding title to the class B membership units. Whether decedent caused the WCB membership units held by BFLP and the underlying Empak stock to be redeemed or not, his ability to decide whether that event would occur demonstrates the understanding of the parties involved that the decedent retained the right to control the units transferred to BFLP.

The estate's argument that the general partner's fiduciary duties prevents a finding of an implied agreement is overcome by a lack of activity following BFLP's formation and BFLP's failure to perform any meaningful functions as an entity.

* * *

Under the circumstances of this case, an implied agreement existed that allowed decedent to retain the enjoyment of the property held by BFLP. Therefor, under section 2036(a)(1), decedent's estate includes the value of the WCB Holdings class B membership units held by BFLP on decedent's death that is proportionate to decedent's 91.28 percent limited partnership interest. Given this finding, it is unnecessary to determine whether the terms of the BFLP agreement provided decedent explicit rights to control the property.

* * *

[The parties had stipulated as to the discounts which would apply in the event that the court held that § 2036 did not apply to the transfer to WCB holdings and the transfer to BFLP. The court then entered a judgement consistent with its holding and the stipulation of the parties. The case also involved other issues, not relevant to our purposes.]

LARO, J., CONCURRING IN RESULT: I concur only because I am uncomfortable with the analysis used by the majority in arriving at its result. That analysis applies a new test that the majority has created to decide whether a transfer to a family limited partnership should be respected for Federal tax purposes. The majority applies its test in lieu of deeply ingrained caselaw that conditions satisfaction of the "bona fide sale for an adequate and full consideration in money or money's worth" exception of section 2036(a) (adequate and full consideration exception) on the transferor's receipt of property equal in value to that of the property transferred by the transferor. In other words, under that caselaw, the adequate and full consideration exception may apply only where the transferor's receipt of consideration is of a sufficient value to prevent the transfer from depleting the transferor's estate.

The majority states its test as follows: "In the context of family limited partnerships, the bona fide sale for adequate and full consideration exception

¶ 24,052

is met where [1] the record establishes the existence of a legitimate and significant nontax reason for creating the family limited partnership, and [2] the transferors received partnership interests proportionate to the value of the property transferred." * * * I disagree with both prongs of this test. I believe that a transferor satisfies the adequate and full consideration exception in the context of a transfer to a partnership only when: (1) The record establishes either that (i) in return for the transfer, the transferor received a partnership interest and any other property with an aggregate fair market value equal to the fair market value of the transferor's transferred property, or (ii) the transfer was an ordinary commercial transaction (in which case, the transferred property and the consideration received in return are considered to have the same fair market values), and (2) the transfer was made with a business purpose or, in other words, a "useful nontax purpose that is plausible in light of the taxpayer's [transferor's] conduct and useful in light of the taxpayer's economic situation and intentions."

* * *

HALPERIN, J., CONCURRING IN PART AND DISSENTING IN PART

[Judge Halperin concurred with the majority's decision to allow a discount for the WCB Holdings units but dissented from the decision not to allow a discount for the BFLP holdings.]

I believe that the majority has strayed from the traditional interpretation of the bona fide sale exception by incorporating into the exception an inappropriate motive test ("a legitimate significant nontax reason"), and by concluding that a partnership interest "proportionate" to the value of the property transferred constitutes adequate and full consideration in money or money's worth.

* * *

I would approach the question of whether the value of property transferred by the decedent is included in the gross estate on account of section 2036 by, first, determining whether the decedent retained lifetime possession, enjoyment, income, or control of transferred property. Only after answering that question in the affirmative would I proceed to determine whether the bona fide sale exception applies to the transfer. In determining whether the bona fide sale exception applies, I would first determine whether the transfer was made in the ordinary course of business, as that term is used in section 25.2512–8, Gift Tax Regs. If not, I would determine whether the transfer was made for full value (i.e., whether the value of the transferred property at most equaled the cash value of the consideration received therefor). If not, I would find that the value of the transferred property was included in the value of the gross estate pursuant to section 2036. Motive would only play the limited role I have outlined above (i.e., determining donative intent for purposes of the ordinary-course-of-business test).

¶ 24,052

Problem

[¶ 24,055]

Early in his career Strawbridge married Martha, whom he later divorced. In connection with this divorce he entered into a settlement agreement, not conditioned on the entry of a divorce decree; but subsequently the agreement was incorporated verbatim in the divorce decree and was thus approved by the court. By its terms, the agreement provided that Strawbridge would transfer to Martha all property then held in the spouses' joint names, worth $200,000, and Martha would relinquish all dower and other marital rights in his property. He also agreed to pay her $3,000 per year for life and to keep up the annual premiums of $300 on an ordinary life insurance policy in the face amount of $40,000. The policy was transferred to Martha as owner, and she was named as the primary beneficiary, but if he should survive her the policy would revert to him. Strawbridge kept up his payments on the policy until the time of his death. He was at that time $6,000 behind on the alimony payments. Martha survived him.

What impact will the gift tax have on the settlement? How does the estate tax apply to the foregoing?

Chapter 25

EXPENSES, DEBTS, CLAIMS, AND STATE DEATH TAXES

(Sections 2053 and 2058)

A. DEDUCTIONS

[¶ 25,001]

The United States estate tax is imposed on "net" transfers rather than "gross" transfers. Accordingly, while the gross estate is built up under §§ 2031 through 2045, a number of deductions are permitted to bring the gross estate down to a net taxable figure, called the "taxable estate."

§ 2051. The estate tax is imposed only on this net amount, after reduction of the gross estate by the amounts allowed as deductions under §§ 2053 through 2058.

The § 2055 deduction for charitable transfers is covered in Chapter 26, and the § 2056 deduction for marital transfers is covered in Chapter 27. Section 2058 allows a deduction for state death taxes.

Section 2054 allows a deduction for casualty and theft losses incurred during "settlement" of the estate. The idea is that the estate tax should not be imposed on value that is destroyed by casualty or theft prior to its distribution to the beneficiary. The deduction is not allowed if the loss occurs after distribution of the asset to a beneficiary. Reg. § 20.2054–1. Casualty and theft losses may also be deductible for income tax purposes under § 165(c)(3) as limited by § 165(h), but double deductions are prohibited. The executor may elect to deduct the loss for either income or estate tax purposes, but not both. § 642(g); Reg. §§ 1.642(g)–1 and 20.2054–1.

Section 2053 provides a deduction for four classes of expenses, debts, and claims:

1. Funeral expenses.

2. Administration expenses.

3. Claims against the estate.

4. Unpaid mortgages encumbering property included in the gross estate, but only if the property is included in the gross estate at its full value, without reduction for the mortgage.

The statute and regulations, however, impose specific requirements that must be met for deductibility of these items. These requirements are described below.

[¶ 25,002]

1. ADEQUATE AND FULL CONSIDERATION

As explained in Chapter 24 on consideration, § 2053(c)(1)(A) provides that, in the case of claims, debts, and unpaid mortgages, where based on a promise or agreement, the consideration therefor must be "adequate and full consideration in money or money's worth." The purpose of this rule is to assure that the gross estate is not reduced by obligations that were essentially gratuitous, i.e., obligations that reduce the decedent's assets without any offsetting receipt of value. For example, assume that a father makes a promise, under seal, to transfer $100,000 to his son at the father's death, and that under local law a promise under seal is binding despite the absence of consideration. Without the § 2053(c)(1)(A) "adequate and full consideration" rule, the $100,000 would be deductible as a claim, and $100,000 would pass to the son free of transfer tax.

The "adequate and full consideration" rule has special application to transfers arising from marital relationships. Section 2043(b)(1) provides that relinquishment of marital rights is not deemed to be adequate and full consideration. Assume, for example, that a wife, in consideration of her husband's agreement to surrender his right to receive a portion of the wife's property at her death, agrees to pay $200,000 to the husband at the wife's death. Section 2043(b)(1), in conjunction with § 2053(c)(1)(A), renders the husband's claim nondeductible (although the $200,000 transfer could qualify for the marital deduction if it meets the requirements of § 2056). Where the obligation arises from divorce, a special rule applies. As explained at ¶ 3121, above, a claim arising from divorce is treated as made for full and adequate consideration if the requirements of § 2516 are met. § 2043(b)(2).

Also, if any claim against the estate is founded on a promise by the decedent to make a gift to charity, the statute permits the deduction as if the promise were a bequest to charity under § 2055. § 2053(c)(1)(A).

[¶ 25,003]

2. ALLOWABLE UNDER LOCAL LAW

The second limitation on the deductibility of the four classes of items listed above is that they must be "allowable by the laws of the jurisdiction." § 2053(a). The Regulations expand on this language by requiring that the amounts also be "allowable out of property subject to claims," undoubtedly a logical extension of the statutory clause "allowable by the laws of the jurisdiction." Reg. § 20.2053–1(c).

¶ 25,001

The statute does not require that the amount actually be allowed under the local law. Apparently, so long as the item is of the kind and in the amount that would hypothetically be allowable under the local law, it will be deductible. Furthermore, actual allowance of the claim by the local probate court is not conclusive, as evidenced by *Hibernia*, ¶ 25,013, below. See First Nat'l Bank of Ft. Worth v. United States, 301 F.Supp. 667 (N.D.Tex.1969)(attorney's fees of $125,000 ruled not "reasonable" in amount and, therefore, not allowable under the local law, even though the court had approved the payment in a friendly nonadversary probate proceeding).

This requirement of "allowability" would appear to result in denying an estate tax deduction for any amount incurred in administering nonprobate assets (such as joint tenancy or revocable trust property), because such amounts are not "allowable" under the local law, i.e., they are not payable out of the probate estate. However, § 2053(b) expressly permits a deduction for administration expenses incurred in connection with nonprobate assets that are included in the gross estate. The expenses of administering nonprobate assets are deductible to the same extent as the normal administration expenses incurred with respect to, and payable out of, the probate estate. There are two requirements that such expenses must meet in order to be deductible: (1) the expense must be of the type that would be deductible under the basic rule if the expense were incurred in connection with probate assets; and (2) the expense must actually be paid within the period for assessment of the tax, which is normally three years from the date on which the estate tax return was filed.

With regard to the first requirement, the regulations limit the scope of the applicable expenses as follows: "The only expenses in administering property not subject to claims which are allowed as deductions are those occasioned by the decedent's death and incurred in settling the decedent's interest in the property or vesting good title to the property in the beneficiaries." Reg. § 20.2053–8(b). Examples of deductible expenses are set forth in Reg. § 20.2053–8(d).

[¶ 25,004]

3. LIMITED TO VALUE OF PROBATE ESTATE

The third major limitation on the § 2053(a) deductions, § 2053(c)(2), provides that the total amount within the four classes above may not be deducted to the extent it exceeds the value of the property subject to claims *unless* the amounts are paid by the date prescribed for the filing of the estate tax return (or any extension of time granted therefor). This limitation, however, is made inapplicable to expenses incurred in administering nonprobate assets deductible under § 2053(b).

[¶ 25,005]

4. NECESSARILY INCURRED

The Regulations provide that administration expenses are deductible only if "necessarily incurred in preserving and distributing the estate." Reg.

§ 20.2053–3(d)(1). Expenses of sale of estate assets, for example, are deductible only if the sale is "necessary in order to pay the decedent's debts, expenses of administration, or taxes, or to preserve the estate, or to effect distribution." Reg. § 20.2053–3(d)(2). If the executor (or successor trustee, in the case of a revocable trust) borrows funds to pay death taxes, the IRS may question whether the interest on the loan is "necessarily incurred." In Rupert v. Commissioner, 2004–2 USTC ¶ 60,492, (M.D. Pa. 2004), the court stated the test is whether assets could be sold to provide the tax payments without damage to the estate assets. In PLR 200449031 the IRS ruled that interest could be deducted if a loan was necessary to prevent a forced sale of estate assets. In TAM 200513028, the IRS ruled that interest could not be deducted where there were adequate liquid assets to provide funds for payment of death taxes.

B. STATE DEATH TAXES

[¶ 25,007]

Any death tax imposed by a state or by the District of Columbia with regard to property included in the decedent's gross estate is deductible in determining the taxable estate. § 2058(a). The tax must actually be paid and the deduction claimed within a limited time period specified in § 2058(b), generally four years after the estate tax return is filed.

The § 2058 deduction is available only with respect to deaths that occur on or after January 1, 2005. § 532(b), P.L. 107–16. In the case of decedents who died prior to 2005, § 2011 provided a limited credit against the United States Estate Tax to the extent death taxes were paid to a state or the District of Columbia. This credit is more fully explained at ¶ 28,009.

Because the deduction is allowed for the full amount of the state death tax, the amount of the state death tax must be determined before the United States Estate Tax can be determined. If the amount of the state death tax is determined by the amount of the United States Estate Tax, a simultaneous equation is necessary to determine these interrelated numbers.

C. ADMINISTRATION EXPENSES

1. ALLOWABILITY UNDER LOCAL LAW

[¶ 25,013]

HIBERNIA BANK v. UNITED STATES

United States Court of Appeals, Ninth Circuit, 1978.
581 F.2d 741.

WALLACE, Circuit Judge:

* * * This appeal squarely presents an important issue of estate tax law which had engendered a crisp conflict among the circuits. We affirm.

¶ 25,005

I.

In May 1965, Celia Tobin Clark died testate, leaving an estate worth several million dollars. Mrs. Clark's will provided for several specific bequests of personal property. The will also directed that the residue, which included the bulk of the estate, be divided among four testamentary trusts. The income of each trust was to be paid to one of Mrs. Clark's children with the remainder to be divided equally among Mrs. Clark's grandchildren. The residue of Mrs. Clark's estate included two principal components: a mansion situated on 240 acres in Hillsborough, California, and approximately 10,000 common shares of Hibernia Bank stock.

Mrs. Clark's will named Hibernia as trustee for the four testamentary trusts. * * * Hibernia was appointed administrator with the will annexed of the Clark estate.

On June 2, 1965, Mrs. Clark's will was admitted to probate. By December 1967, all of the specific bequests and virtually all claims against the estate had been paid. Apparently, at this time, Hibernia, acting as the administrator, could have sought permission to distribute the remaining assets, including the mansion and the Hibernia stock, to the testamentary trusts and to close the estate. Rather than do so, however, Hibernia elected first to liquidate the Hillsborough mansion.

Hibernia encountered substantial difficulty in disposing of the mansion, and it was not finally sold until the spring of 1972. During this period, the administrator was required to spend some $60,000 per year in order to maintain the residence. Thus, Hibernia believed that it was necessary either to sell the estate's share of Hibernia stock or, alternatively, to borrow the funds required to maintain the mansion. Hibernia elected to borrow.

In each of the years from 1966 through 1969, Hibernia executed a substantial loan from a commercial bank. The net proceeds from these loans equaled $775,000. Hibernia itself acted as lender for two of the four loans, the proceeds of which totaled $625,000. The interest payments for the four loans totaled $196,210.

In June 1971, Hibernia filed with the Commissioner a claim for a refund of part of the estate taxes paid on the Clark estate. As part of this claim, Hibernia asserted that it was entitled to deduct from the gross estate as expenses of administration the amount it had paid in interest on the four bank loans. The Commissioner disallowed the claimed deduction for the interest and denied the corresponding refund.

* * *

II.

Hibernia's argument is straightforward. Section 2053(a)(2) provides:

> For purposes of the [estate] tax ... the value of the taxable estate shall be determined by deducting from the value of the gross estate such amounts ... for administration expenses ... as are allowable by the laws

¶ 25,013

of the jurisdiction, whether within or without the United States, under which the estate is being administered.

In addition, Treas. Reg. § 20.2053–1(b)(2) provides in part:

> The decision of a local court as to the amount and allowability under local law of a claim or administration expense will ordinarily be accepted if the court passes upon the facts upon which deductibility depends.

Therefore, the essence of Hibernia's argument is that the deductibility of administration expenses is exclusively a question of state law. Since in this case the California probate court expressly approved the $196,210 interest payments as administration expenses, Hibernia contends that the Commissioner was required to permit a corresponding deduction.

* * * [T]he dispute centers around whether or not the interest payments were expenses of administration within the meaning of federal estate tax law. In order to resolve this issue, the district judge focused on Treas. Reg. § 20.2053–3(a), which provides in part:

> The amounts deductible from a decedent's gross estate as "administration expenses" ... are limited to such expenses as are actually and necessarily incurred in the administration of the decedent's estate; that is, in the collection of assets, payment of debts, and distribution of property to the persons entitled to it. The expenses contemplated in the law are such only as attend the settlement of an estate and the transfer of the property of the estate to individual beneficiaries or to a trustee.... Expenditures not essential to the proper settlement of the estate, but incurred for the individual benefit of the heirs, legatees, or devises, may not be taken as deductions.

Viewing the issue in this light, the district judge found that the estate had been kept open much longer than necessary, thereby rendering the loans and interest payments made during the excess period also unnecessary. Specifically, the judge found as a matter of fact that "[w]ithin fifteen months of the testator's death [Hibernia], in its capacity as administrator of the estate, had sold all the assets of the estate except the mansion with its surrounding acreage and the Hibernia Bank stock." In addition, the district judge concluded that Hibernia had failed "factually [to] demonstrate an existing necessity to keep the Clark estate open for seven years." The district judge reasoned that since it was wholly unnecessary to keep the estate open during the period of the loans, the loans and interest payments were therefore also unnecessary to the administration of the estate. The implication is that the estate was left open in order to sell the mansion not because the sale was necessary for the administration of the estate, but rather because the heirs preferred to have cash distributed to the trusts rather than an undivided interest in the mansion. Thus, the expenses were not deductible.

III.

We agree with the district judge that allowability under state law is not the sole criterion for determining the deductibility of a particular expenditure under section 2053(a)(2).

In Pitner v. United States, 388 F.2d 651 (5th Cir.1967), the Fifth Circuit held that

> [i]n the determination of deductibility under section 2053(a)(2), it is not enough that the deduction be allowable under state law. It is necessary as well that the deduction be for an "administration expense" within the meaning of that term as it is used in the statute, and that the amount sought to be deducted be reasonable under the circumstances. These are both questions of federal law and establish the outside limits for what may be considered allowable deductions under section 2053(a)(2).

Id. at 659. * * *

We agree with the Fifth Circuit. We cannot read section 2053(a)(2) as permitting the deduction of expenditures which simply are not expenses of administration within the meaning afforded that term by federal estate tax law. Our holding is firmly supported by prior decisions as well as sound principles of policy.

* * *

Policy considerations also militate in favor of our holding. The federal estate tax is not a tax on the decedent's property, but rather a tax on the transfer of that property. * * * The mechanics of the estate tax give meaning to this distinction by permitting deductions from the decedent's gross estate for debts, administration expenses, and certain other liabilities. The resulting "taxable estate" on which the estate tax is calculated is the amount actually transferred to the heirs. Although fairness dictates that the taxable estate not include assets which will not be available for transfer to the heirs, fairness does not require the deduction of amounts which are not true liabilities of the estate. Thus, "[e]xpenditures not essential to the proper settlement of the estate, but incurred for the individual benefit of the heirs, legatees, or devises" are not expenses of administration within the meaning of section 2053. 26 C.F.R. § 20.2053–3(a).

The district judge's conclusion that the Clark estate was left open much too long is amply supported by the record. * * * Since it was unnecessary to leave the estate open during the period of the loans, it is clear that the loans were not necessary to the administration of the estate. Accordingly, the district judge was correct in disallowing an administration expense deduction for the amount of the interest payments.

AFFIRMED.

Note

[¶ 25,033]

The Second, Fourth, and Fifth Circuits have concurred with the Ninth Circuit on this issue. See, e.g., Estate of Love v. Commissioner, 923 F.2d 335 (4th Cir.1991). The Sixth Circuit, however, has held that state law controls, i.e., allowance by the probate court is conclusive. Estate of Park v. Commissioner, 475 F.2d 673 (6th Cir.1973).

¶ 25,033

[¶ 25,039]

2. PROHIBITION AGAINST DOUBLE DEDUCTION

Administration expenses are deductible for income tax purposes as well as estate tax purposes. § 212; Reg. § 1.212–1(i). Section 642(g), however, prohibits deduction of the same expenses for both income and estate tax purposes. The prohibition is achieved by conditioning the income tax deduction on execution of a waiver of the deduction for estate tax purposes. The procedure is described in Reg. § 1.642(g)–1.

D. UNENFORCEABLE CLAIMS

[¶ 25,043]

REVENUE RULING 78–271

1978–2 C.B. 239.

The decedent, D, owned and operated a business as a sole proprietorship from 1945 until death. In 1956, D's spouse, A, began to actively render substantial services to the business on a full-time basis and continued to do so until D's death in 1976. D and A had no understanding, express or implied, that A would be compensated for the services. No compensation was paid to A during the time that A rendered the services.

At D's death, A submitted a claim to the executor of the estate for 200x dollars, the value of the services rendered to the business. The executor limited payment to A to 30x dollars, the value of the services rendered within the applicable time allowed by the statute of limitations for bringing an action for recovery. The decedent's federal estate tax return includes a deduction of 30x dollars with respect to the claim made by A for the value of A's services.

Applicable local law recognizes a married person's right to recover for services rendered to the spouse's business provided that the services were rendered pursuant to a contract between the spouses. Local law provides that, in the absence of a bona fide agreement to compensate the spouse, the services of the spouse are deemed to have been gratuitously rendered to the business. * * *

The specific question presented is whether A's claim for the value of services rendered to D's business qualifies as a deduction against D's estate for purposes of section 2053(a) of the Code.

The payment of a claim by an executor does not, of itself, establish the claim as being enforceable against the estate. * * * A deductible claim, within the meaning of section 2053(a), must represent a debt of the decedent that is recognized by state law. * * * A claim may be deducted from the decedent's gross estate only if the claimant had a valid right under state law to enforce the claim against the estate. * * *

In the present situation, A's claim is not enforceable under local law since there was no agreement between the spouses that A would be compensated. A

¶ 25,039

is deemed, under applicable local laws, to have gratuitously rendered the services to D's business. Consequently, A's claim does not represent a personal obligation of D existing at the time of D's death.

Accordingly, A's claim for services rendered to D's business fails to meet the requirement of section 2053(a) that the claim be enforceable under local law. Therefore, the amounts paid by the executor in satisfaction of A's claim are not deductible from D's gross estate. In other cases, where there is a claim founded upon an agreement between the spouses, the claim will be allowed under section 2053(a) only if it is determined that, based on all the facts and circumstances, the agreement is bona fide and was contracted for an adequate and full consideration in money or money's worth.

E. CONSIDERATION AND DEBTS

[¶ 25,045]

ESTATE OF FLANDREAU v. COMMISSIONER

United States Court of Appeals, Second Circuit, 1993.
994 F.2d 91.

LOKEN, Circuit Judge:

* * * I.R.C. § 2053(a)(3) provides an estate tax deduction "for claims against the estate." A deduction "founded on a promise or agreement," however, is "limited to the extent that [the claims] were contracted bona fide and for an adequate and full consideration in money or money's worth." I.R.C. § 2053(c)(1). In this case, the Estate claims a $102,000 deduction for the face amounts of fourteen non-interest bearing, unsecured promissory notes executed by decedent in December 1970, January 1971, and January 1972 payable to her two sons and their wives.

Each note was preceded by a gift of the same amount from decedent to the purported lender. Decedent reported each of these transfers on a gift tax return but paid only $126 in federal gift taxes as all but two of the transfers were within the then-applicable gift tax exclusion. The recipients then transferred the gifted amounts back to decedent and received the notes in question. The notes were payable in 1995, when decedent would be 95 years old, or upon her death.

Mrs. Flandreau died on February 20, 1986, without having repaid any portion of the notes. The Estate claimed a deduction of $102,000 for the full amount due. The Commissioner issued a Notice of Deficiency denying the deduction on the ground that, "The debts were not bona fide debts contracted for adequate and full consideration under Section 2053 of the Internal Revenue Code." The tax court ... concluded that "these were merely circular transfers of money from decedent to her children and back to decedent." As such, the notes did not represent debts, but were rather "unenforceable gratuitous promises to make a gift, based upon neither money nor money's worth," and therefore did not qualify as deductible claims under § 2053. * * *

¶ 25,045

We have consistently rejected taxpayer's attempts to use gifts to family members followed by loans back to the taxpayer to avoid federal taxes that would otherwise be imposed.

* * * The gifts, loans, and notes were exchanged contemporaneously, and the amounts of the gifts were identical to the amounts subsequently loaned. The Estate argues that the tax court improperly considered the source of the funds that decedent's sons and daughters-in-law "loaned" to her in exchange for the notes. However, * * * it is appropriate to look beyond the form of the transactions and to determine, as the tax court did here, that the gifts and loans back to decedent were "component parts of single transactions." * * *

As the Supreme Court has observed, "the family relationship often makes it possible for one to shift tax incidence by surface changes of ownership without disturbing in the least his dominion and control over the subject of the gift or the purposes for which the income from the property is used." Commissioner v. Culbertson, 337 U.S. 733, 746 (1949). For this reason, courts examine such intrafamily transactions with heightened scrutiny; when the bona fides of promissory notes is at issue, the taxpayer must demonstrate affirmatively that "there existed at the time of the transaction a real expectation of repayment and an intent to enforce the collection of the indebtedness." Estate of Van Anda v. Commissioner, 12 T.C. 1158, 1162 (1949), aff'd per curiam, 192 F.2d 391 (2d Cir.1951). * * *Here, the tax court expressly found that the sons and daughters-in-law never expected that the money they transferred to decedent would be repaid.

Having carefully considered the entire transaction, we agree with the tax court that the Estate failed to carry its burden of showing the notes were "contracted bona fide and for an adequate and full consideration in money or money's worth."

* * * The judgment of the tax court is affirmed.

F.   UNFILED CLAIMS

[¶ 25,073]

REVENUE RULING 75–24

1975–1 C.B. 306.

Advice has been requested concerning the deductibility under section 2053 of the Internal Revenue Code of 1954, and section 20.2053–4 of the Estate Tax Regulations, of a claim against a decedent's estate that was valid and enforceable at the time of decedent's death but was not probated, under the circumstances described below.

A died domiciled in Mississippi and left real and personal property in that state. Letters testamentary were issued in Mississippi.

At his death, A owed B, a resident of Mississippi, an unsecured debt. The claim was not probated. Three months after A's death, B informally asserted his claim against the executor and his claim was promptly paid out of the

Mississippi property. Payment of the claim was approved by the beneficiaries of the estate. The claim was deducted on the Federal estate tax return filed on behalf of A's estate.

Section 2053(a) of the Code provides that the value of the taxable estate shall be determined by deducting from the value of the gross estate such amounts for claims against the estate as are allowable by the laws of the jurisdiction under which the estate is being administered. Section 20.2053–4 of the regulations states that only claims enforceable against the decedent's estate may be deducted.

Title 91–7–151 of the Mississippi Code 1972, Annotated, requires that all claims against the estate of a decedent be registered, probated and allowed in the court having jurisdiction over the administration of the estate within six months after publication of notice to creditors. The purpose of the Mississippi statute is to protect the executor or administrator (hereinafter fiduciary) in his payment of the obligations of the estate. The statute requires creditors to present evidence of their claims and gives the fiduciary an opportunity to contest them if he feels the claims to be unwarranted. * * *

The Mississippi Code charges the fiduciary with the duty of promptly paying all claims against the estate, but he is prohibited from paying any claim that has not been properly registered, probated and allowed. Compliance with the statute is mandatory * * * and the fiduciary may be surcharged if a claim is paid without complying with the requirements of State law * * *. Nevertheless, in Townsend v. Beavers, 185 Miss. 312, 188 So. 1 (1939), it was held that the payment of promissory notes that were not probated could not be surcharged against the fiduciary where the distributees of the estate had consented to their payment. Also, in Riegelhaupt v. Ostroffsky, 237 Miss. 521, 115 So.2d 331 (1959), it was held that the statute does not affect the right of the devisee of encumbered real property to have his claim against the property satisfied out of the other property in the decedent's estate where the devisee's claim was not probated.

Based on Mississippi statutory law, as construed by the Supreme Court of Mississippi, it is concluded that where payment is made within the six-month bar period of a valid but unprobated claim that was approved by all the beneficiaries of the estate within such period—that is, during the time in which the claim was enforceable—the claim is allowable as a section 2053 deduction. Rev. Rul. 60–247, 1960–2 C.B. 272, recognizes an exception to the enforceability requirement of section 20.2053–4 of the regulations where that requirement would compel a useless act, e.g., where the creditor is the sole beneficiary of the estate.

However, if the payment of a valid but unfiled claim renders the fiduciary subject to surcharge after the period for filing has terminated, either because the payment was not approved by all the beneficiaries of the estate within such period or because such approval would not bar a surcharge, no deduction is allowable under section 2053, whether or not the fiduciary is actually surcharged. If the fiduciary is later surcharged, the claim would not be deductible because there is no economic loss to the estate, and if the fiduciary

¶ 25,073

is not surcharged, the gratuitous forbearance of the beneficiaries does not render the claim enforceable.

Accordingly, it is held that payment of B's valid claim is deductible under section 2053 of the Code, because it was made and approved by all the beneficiaries of the estate during the period in which the claim was enforceable and such approval rendered the probating of the claim unnecessary to prevent surcharge of the executor.

G. VALUATION OF CLAIMS

[¶ 25,079]

ESTATE OF VAN HORNE v. COMMISSIONER

United States Court of Appeals, Ninth Circuit, 1983.
720 F.2d 1114, cert. denied, 466 U.S. 980 (1984).

REINHARDT, Circuit Judge:

This case concerns the proper method of valuing certain assets and liabilities for estate tax purposes. The tax court determined that under I. R. C. § 2053(a)(3)(1976) the estate is entitled to a deduction for the full date of death actuarial value of a life time spousal support obligation even when the spouse of the decedent dies prior to the filing of the estate tax return. The government appeals. * * * We affirm the tax court in all respects.

* * *

At the time of her death, the decedent was obligated, pursuant to an interlocutory judgment of dissolution of marriage, to pay $5,000 per month for spousal support to her surviving ex-husband, James Van Horne, for the remainder of his life. The judgment provided that the award could not be modified, notwithstanding either his remarriage or her death. In the event of the latter, the judgment provided that all payments thereafter falling due would become payable by the estate. The ex-husband filed a creditor's claim against the estate on October 29, 1976. The executors filed a petition for court approval of this claim on November 29, 1976, and it was approved on December 27, 1976.

The ex-husband died on April 20, 1977, having received only $35,000 from the estate in support payments. At the time of decedent's death, the ex-husband was aware that he had a liver ailment but had no reason to suspect that he was terminally ill with cancer. His fatal condition was not diagnosed until March of 1977.

The estate claims a deduction of $596,386.58 for the value of the ex-husband's claim. This amount was calculated by reference to the actuarial tables included in Treas. Reg. § 20.2031–10 (1983). The parties have stipulated that the amount computed is correct, if actuarial valuation is proper. The government contends that actuarial valuation is not proper here because the claim was actually extinguished after payment of only $35,000.

* * *

The general principle that a claim against a decedent's estate is to be valued at the time of the decedent's death, and that events subsequent to death do not alter this valuation, was first announced by the Supreme Court in Ithaca Trust Co. v. United States, 279 U.S. 151 (1929). We recently reaffirmed this principle in Propstra v. United States, 680 F.2d 1248 (9th Cir.1982). In *Propstra*, the petitioner's estate included two parcels of real estate which were encumbered by liens for past dues and penalties owing to a local water users' association. The Government contested petitioner's claim that the liens were to be valued at the time of decedent's death. Because the amount of the liens was reduced by the association prior to the time the tax return was filed, the Government argued that their actual value rather than their value as of the date of death, should be deducted for estate tax purposes. We held that because the claims were certain and enforceable, we would not consider post-death events. Rather, "as a matter of law, when claims are for sums certain, and are legally enforceable as of the date of death, post-death events are not relevant in computing the permissible deduction." Id. at 1254.

The government argues both that *Propstra* was wrongly decided and that it is distinguishable on the ground that petitioner's spousal support obligation was not a "sum certain" and is therefore outside the rationale of *Propstra*. It contends that "[h]ere the spousal support obligation amounted in effect to a series of monthly claims each of which was contingent upon James' survival to a particular date."

In deciding *Propstra*, we carefully considered and rejected many of the arguments which the Government sets forth here. We said that Congress clearly intended that post-death events be disregarded when valuing legally recognized and enforceable claims against an estate. We see no reason to reconsider *Propstra* or to distinguish spousal support obligations from other allowable claims.

The fact that it is necessary to refer to an actuarial table in order to value a support obligation does not justify our reaching a different result here than we did in *Propstra*. A claim that is actuarily [*sic*] valued is not uncertain for estate tax purposes. We have recently approved the use of actuarial tables to value assets for purposes of estate tax deduction in Bank of California v. U.S., 672 F.2d 758 (9th Cir.1982). After reexamining this method of valuation we concluded that "actuarial tables provide a needed degree of certainty and administrative convenience in ascertaining property values." Id. at 760.

Moreover, the charitable trust at issue in *Ithaca Trust Co.*, also required actuarial valuation. Justice Holmes, writing for the Court, specifically considered whether post-death events are relevant when lifetime interests are at issue, and concluded that they are not:

> "The first impression is that it is absurd to resort to statistical probabilities when you know the fact. But this is due to inaccurate thinking. The estate so far as may be is settled as of the date of the testator's death. ...Tempting as it is to correct uncertain probabilities by the now certain fact, we are of opinion that it cannot be done, but that the value of the [wife's] life interest must be estimated by the mortality tables."

Id. at 155.

We hold that legally enforceable claims valued by reference to an actuarial table meet the test of certainty for estate tax purposes. Because decedent's

¶ 25,079

spousal support obligation meets that test, it is subject to the *Propstra* rule. We affirm the tax court's determination that the date of decedent's death was the proper time for valuation of the claim.

* * *

Note

[¶ 25,087]

The rule that claims must be valued at the date of death, and without consideration of subsequent events, has been implemented by the 10th and 11th circuits as well. Estate of McMorris v. Commissioner, 243 F.3d 1254 (10th Cir. 2001); Estate of O'Neal v. United States, 258 F.3d 1265 (11th Cir. 2001).

Problem

[¶ 25,091]

Herman Brown died on March 3 of this year, survived by his daughter, Mildred, and his son, Timothy. Herman's gross estate had a value of $3,000,000 on the date of his death. This included a tract of undeveloped real estate (Sunny Acres) owned entirely by Herman. The value of Sunny Acres without taking into account any mortgage encumbering the property was $200,000, and this amount was included in Herman's gross estate. Sunny Acres was encumbered by a mortgage securing a note made by Alice Wilson and payable to the Tenth National Bank in the amount of $75,000. Herman had bought Sunny Acres from Alice two years before his death. He purchased the property subject to the mortgage, i.e., Alice simply deeded the property to Herman, and Herman did not assume personal liability under the Tenth National Bank note.

Mildred is serving as executor and will decline any fee. She has retained Tammy Larson, a lawyer, to represent Mildred (as executor) in the estate proceeding. Tammy's fee will be $20,000, and Mildred will not make the election described in § 642(g) as to this fee.

Herman belongs to the Bigtown Country Club, which sends bills every four weeks for Herman's membership dues for the prior four weeks. Herman received a bill for $400 for dues and meals through the date three weeks prior to his death, but because of his ill health he did not pay the bill prior to his death. One week after Herman's death Mildred received a bill for $300 for dues for the three weeks ending at Herman's death.

Four months before his death Herman bought a parcel of land (Cloudy Acres) from Elinor Sheridan. The purchase price was $300,000. Herman made a down payment of $40,000 in cash at the time of the purchase and agreed to pay the remaining $260,000 in three years. Herman's promise was not secured by an interest in Cloudy Acres.

Five years before his death Herman promised to pay his nephew, Artemis *doesn't matter* Gordon, $5,000 if Artemis completed a bachelor's degree. Artemis completed the degree in January of this year, but Herman had not yet paid Artemis at the time Herman died.

Herman was divorced from his wife, Agatha, in 1999. A divorce decree was entered on February 1, 1999, and the decree incorporated a property settlement agreement entered into between Agatha and Herman on November 2, 1998. The decree required Herman to transfer $50,000 to Agatha upon Herman's death.

What is the amount of Herman's taxable estate?

Chapter 26

CHARITABLE BEQUESTS

(Section 2055)

A. "SWEET CHARITY"

[¶ 26,001]

From the outset the federal estate tax was friendly to charitable dispositions. In sharp contrast to the income tax, where § 170 limits to a percentage of income the amount that may be claimed as an income tax deduction, the deduction provided for charitable bequests and includible transfers for estate and gift tax purposes is unlimited. An easy and complete escape from the federal estate tax is simply to leave all one's property to a qualified charity, and, it may be noted, the federal government itself is just such a charity.

A Treasury study of estate tax returns has revealed several interesting patterns of charitable giving. In 1989 decedents gave almost $5.8 billion to charities. Examination of the estates of decedents with net worths of $500,000 or more revealed married individuals to be least generous with only 8.1 percent of them having left anything to charities, and those that did make gifts to charities left only 10.1 percent of their net worth. Single decedents were most likely to make charitable bequests with 54.7 percent of the single women and 33.5 percent of the single men having remembered charities in their wills. Single females who gave to charities left them on average 37 percent of their net worth, and single male decedents with charitable impulses left about 49 percent of their net worth to charity. Widows and widowers fell somewhere in between with 25.1 percent of the widowers making charitable bequests which constituted 26 percent of their net worth. Twenty-nine percent of all widows made charitable bequests which constituted about 21 percent of their net worth. In general, this data lets us conclude that, although the charitable deduction is used by only a minority of all estates, it is of extreme importance to most of those that employ it. See, Johnson, Estate Tax Returns, 1989–1991, Statistics of Income Bulletin, Spring 1993, 76, 78–80.

Section 2055 authorizes a deduction for transfers to three basic types of recipients: (1) the federal government, state governments or subdivisions thereof; (2) corporations operated exclusively for religious, charitable, scientific, literary, or educational purposes, which do not attempt to influence elections and are not substantially engaged in carrying on propaganda or influencing legislation; and (3) certain fraternal and veterans organizations. Court battles over the status of recipients under § 2055 are hotly waged not only by the donors and their descendants seeking deductions, but also by the recipients themselves whose contribution inflow often depends on the deductibility of the gifts.

The vast number of decisions on this issue have produced paradoxical results. The Bar Association of St. Louis is a qualified charity, see St. Louis Union Trust Co. v. United States, 374 F.2d 427 (8th Cir.1967), but the St. Louis Medical Society is not, see Hammerstein v. Kelley, 349 F.2d 928 (8th Cir.1965). The self-governing Zuni Indian Tribe of Zuni, New Mexico, failed to qualify as a governmental subdivision because its political powers stemmed from "original sovereignty" rather than from an act of Congress. Rev. Rul. 74–179, 1974–1 C.B. 279. However, the Indian Tribal Government Status Act provides that Indian tribes are to be treated as state governments for federal tax purposes thereby changing that result. See 26 USCA § 7871(a)(6). See Rev. Proc. 84–36, 1984–1 C.B. 10, listing Indian tribes and approved agencies and Rev. Rul. 86–44, 1986–1 C.B. 376.

The types of eligible recipients enumerated in § 2055 are the only types that may receive deductible bequests—no matter how "charitable" the donor's intent. Thus, a bequest to an indigent acquaintance or to an individual orphan or invalid will not produce an estate tax deduction. Can you see what possible abuses Congress was trying to prevent?

B.   CHARITABLE?

[¶ 26,007]

DULLES v. JOHNSON

United States Court of Appeals, Second Circuit, 1959.
273 F.2d 362.

WATERMAN, Circuit Judge.

[William Nelson Cromwell, a prominent New York attorney, died leaving portions of the residue of his estate to the New York County Lawyers Association, to the Association of the Bar of the City of New York and to the New York State Bar Association. His executors claimed charitable deductions for such bequests, but they were denied by the Commissioner. Upon bringing suit for refund in the District Court, relief was denied. The executors appealed.]

In order to secure a deduction for the bequests made to the Bar Associations plaintiffs must demonstrate that these bequests come within the language of Section 812(d) [now § 2055] of the 1939 Internal Revenue Code which permits as a deduction from the value of the gross estate "[t]he amount of all bequests, legacies, devises, or transfers * * * to or for the use of any corporation organized and operated exclusively for religious, charitable, scientific, literary or educational purposes * * * and no substantial part of the activities of which is carrying on propaganda, or otherwise attempting to influence legislation * * *." The district court held that the executors failed to carry this burden, Dulles v. Johnson, 155 F.Supp. 275. That court concluded that the Associations "exist primarily to benefit members of the legal profession, and to provide a method whereby their views and recommendations as a body on legislation of various kinds is made known to the legislators." Supra, at page 279. The court appears to have based its conclusion on the following Association activities as they existed on July 19, 1948: (1) regulation of the unauthorized practice of law; (2) institution of disciplinary measures for professional misconduct of members of the bar and judiciary; (3) recommendations with respect to judicial administration and procedure and the endorsement of candidates for judicial office; and (4) activities in support of or in opposition to various legislative proposals.

The New York County Lawyers Association (sometimes referred to as "County Lawyers") was incorporated in 1908 under the New York Membership Corporations Law (Chapter 559, Laws of 1895). The Certificate of Incorporation provided:

> "The purposes for which said Association is to be formed are, the cultivation of the science of jurisprudence; the promotion of reforms in the law; the facilitation of the administration of justice; the elevation of the standards of integrity, honor and courtesy in the legal profession; the cherishing of the spirit of brotherhood among the members of said Association."

County Lawyers owns its own four-story building in New York City which contains a large auditorium, a library (some 85,000 volumes as of April 1948), and a number of rooms used for conference and staff purposes. As of April 1948 there were approximately 7,000 members. The auditorium and the other facilities have been used by the Practising Law Institute for courses and lectures available to members of the bar generally. In addition, there were many other lectures and forums so available. County Lawyers publishes a magazine entitled "Bar Bulletin" which is mailed to its members and various law libraries throughout the country, and which contains articles relating to various phases of the law. Its standing and special committees comprehensively deal with a wide range of legal matters.

The Association of the Bar of the City of New York (sometimes referred to as the City Bar) was incorporated in 1871 by a Special Act of the New York Legislature (Chapter 819, Laws of 1871)(amended Chapter 134, Laws of 1924)

> " * * *for the purposes of cultivating the science of jurisprudence, promoting reforms in the law, facilitating the administration of justice, elevating the standards of integrity, honor and courtesy in the legal profession, and cherishing the spirit of brotherhood among the members thereof."

¶ 26,007

The City Bar owns a four-story building in the City of New York, in which there is a large auditorium, a library of some 268,000 volumes, conference rooms, and staff and legal referral offices. The City Bar sponsors numerous lectures on a wide variety of legal subjects. The City Bar's Committee of Legal Education has sponsored a symposium on this subject at which some 45 law schools were represented. Just as in the case of the County Bar, committees are annually appointed to deal with all important phases of the law, both State and Federal. The City Bar aids in combating election frauds and actively supports legal aid work. The City Bar also publishes a magazine, entitled "The Record," which contains articles of interest both to lawyers and the public.

The New York State Bar Association (sometimes referred to as the State Bar) was incorporated in 1877 by a Special Act of the New York Legislature (Chapter 210, Laws of 1877):

> "And the said association is formed to cultivate the science of jurisprudence, to promote reform in the law, to facilitate the administration of justice, to elevate the standard of integrity, honor and courtesy in the legal profession, and to cherish the spirit of brotherhood among the members thereof."

It has offices in Albany, New York. Because of the large State Law Library located in that City, the State Bar maintains only a small library. Its committees, however, cover the same wide range as the County Lawyers and City Bar committees. State Bar publishes a magazine known as "The Bulletin." In addition, it publishes pamphlets containing summaries of recent developments in the law, legislative circulars containing analyses of important bills, and a year book.

The district court conceded that much of the activity of the Associations fulfilled the requirements of Section 812(d). However, in holding that bequests to the Associations could not be deducted from the gross estate under Section 812(d) it would appear from the stipulated facts it enumerated that the court emphasized four activities in which the Associations engage. Each activity will be considered in turn.

1. Regulation of the Unauthorized Practice of Law

The three associations maintain committees to receive and investigate complaints dealing with unauthorized practice of law. The committees also present cases for prosecution to state or federal authorities, bring actions in behalf of the organizations, and initiate and support legislation—in order to prohibit the practice of the law by persons not admitted to the bar. We cannot say that this program does not benefit the public or that it does not serve charitable and educational purposes. Recognizing the need to protect the public, New York law makes it a misdemeanor for unauthorized persons to practice or hold themselves out as authorized to practice law. And the Bar Associations are empowered to commence proceedings for the punishment and restraint of such behavior. * * * If these activities were not undertaken by the Associations, the cost of this necessary regulation would descend upon the public. Hence we conclude that as to regulation of the unauthorized practice of law the Associations must be deemed "charitable."

2. Disciplining of the Profession

The Associations maintain committees on discipline and grievance. The work of these committees has consisted of considering complaints filed against members of the bar by laymen and attorneys, of presenting to the courts charges against some of these attorneys, and of submitting requests to the Presiding Justice of the Appellate Division to appoint attorneys designated by the Bar Associations to prosecute disciplinary proceedings. Here again we think that the district court misconceived the purpose of these activities. Lawyers play a unique and important role in our society. In its dealings with lawyers the public must often act on faith. It is the function of bar associations to see that this faith is not misplaced. New York recognizes the need for this public service and confers upon bar associations statutory powers and obligations in connection therewith. While increased public esteem for lawyers may result in material advantage to members of the legal profession, the true benefit from a disciplined and socially responsive bar accrues directly to the public. Accordingly the present case is readily distinguishable from Better Business Bureau v. United States, 326 U.S. 279 (1945), cited by the Government, and relied upon by the court below. There it was "apparent beyond dispute that an important if not the primary pursuit of petitioner's organization [was] to promote not only an ethical but also a profitable business community." Supra at 283. We agree with the case of Rhode Island Hospital Trust Co. v. United States, 159 F.Supp. 204, 205 (D.R.I.1958), wherein a bequest to the Rhode Island Bar Association "to be used and employed by it for the advancement and upholding of those standards of the profession which are assumed by the members upon their admission to the Bar, and for the prosecution and punishment of those members who violate their obligations to the court and to the public," was held to be a gift to be used for charitable purposes within the meaning of Section 812(d).

3. Improving Court Procedure and Endorsement of Judicial Candidates

There is no dispute but that the associations have taken an active interest in improving legal and litigation procedure and judicial administration, and have probed into the qualifications of candidates for judicial office. In the past, for example, committees of the Associations have reported to the Judicial Council on a proposed revision of the procedure to review tax assessments on real property; they have made recommendations with respect to the Appellate Division rules, they have furthered proposals to unify and consolidate certain New York courts and proposals to increase the number of judges in New York and Federal courts. Although such complaints have been happily few, committees of the Associations have investigated complaints of misconduct by judicial officers and employees. Recommendations concerning judicial candidates have been non-partisan and reflect primarily an evaluation of the professional experience and technical ability of the candidates. Here the committees perform a most valuable function, for lawyers are peculiarly well equipped to seek out and remedy flaws in the judicial machinery and to assess the performances and capabilities of judges. In today's immensely complex society they alone, perhaps, are alert to watch for and attempt correction of manifest defects prior to the time when malfunctions become apparent to everyone. These activities clearly constitute a public service, and we fail to discern that they indicate that the Associations seek to achieve a selfish professional benefit thereby.

4. INFLUENCING LEGISLATION

Finally, we must consider those activities which concern or affect legislation, a subject highlighted by the district court and upon which it would appear to have placed considerable emphasis. Through their various committees the Associations study and report on proposed and existing legislation. Often they send copies of their reports and resolutions to the legislative, executive and judicial branches of the federal and state governments. The major portion of this work is of a technical nature involving the adequacy of proposed and existing legislation in terms of its form, clarity of expression and its effect on and relation to other law. The Associations' work has been expressed in expert reports on matters uniquely within the fields of experts and has avoided questions which are outside those fields, i.e., questions which turn largely on economic or political decisions.

These activities serve no selfish purpose of the legal profession—rather they constitute an expert's effort to improve the law in technical and non-controversial areas. In our opinion these activities are scientific, educational and charitable.

The Government argues that these activities constitute propaganda and represent a substantial part of all the activities of the Associations. The cases upon which the Government relies are inapposite. Those cases involved organizations whose principal purpose was to implement legislative programs embodying broad principles of social amelioration. Here, on the other hand, approval of or opposition to proposed legislation constitutes but a small portion of the total activity of the Associations. * * * Moreover, the legislative recommendations of the Associations, insofar as these recommendations do not involve matters the responsibility for which has been entrusted to the Associations by the Legislature, are designed to improve court procedure or to clarify some technical matter of substantive law. They are not intended for the economic aggrandizement of a particular group or to promote some larger principle of governmental policy. These two factors lead us to the conclusion that the recommendations of the Associations concerning impending legislation are not such as to cause the forfeiture of charitable status under Section 812(d).

Other activities of the Associations which the district court did not refer to and yet which are substantial in nature include maintaining libraries for legal research, sponsoring lectures and forums on the law, providing free legal service through participation in legal aid, and providing low cost legal service through participation in a legal referral system. All of these activities are, in our opinion, educational and charitable. The Associations do engage in certain other incidental activities, but these activities, some social in nature, are merely auxiliary to the charitable and educational purposes we have discussed.

"Organized and operated exclusively" means only that these unconforming activities be incidental in nature. Seasongood v. C.I.R., 227 F.2d 907 (6th Cir.1955); 1 Paul, Federal Estate and Gift Taxation 668 (1946); cf. Better Business Bureau v. United States, 326 U.S. 279, 283 (1945). Such is the situation here.

Looking at the total operations of the three Bar Associations we hold that they are "charitable, scientific * * * [and] educational" within the meaning of Section 812(d) [now § 2055] and that the district court erred in disallowing deductions for the bequests to them. The judgment is reversed with respect to the disallowance of the deductions.

Note

[¶ 26,013]

In Association of Bar of City of N.Y. v. Commissioner, 858 F.2d 876 (2d Cir.1988), the Court of Appeals for the Second Circuit held that the Association of the Bar of the City of New York lacked exempt status. The court based its holding on the ground that the ranking of candidates for judicial office as acceptable or unacceptable constituted an impermissible attempt to influence the electoral process given the elective nature of the New York judiciary. This should be contrasted with the Second Circuit's holding in *Dulles* involving gifts to the same organization, which the Second Circuit then found to be exempt. Is this a better result?

In Fulani v. League of Women Voters Education Fund, 882 F.2d 621 (2d Cir.1989), the Second Circuit held that mere sponsorship of major party candidate debates did not constitute disqualifying political activity.

Planning Note

[¶ 26,019]

Organizations with a significant base of charitable activities but with a political agenda that can result in disqualification can often have their cake and eat it too. This is frequently done by creating a second "action organization" that limits its activities to those of the impermissible political sort. The nonpolitical charitable activities are then confined to the original organization, which often has a similar name and some overlap with the board of directors of the action organization. Donors who are concerned about tax-exempt status can then focus their contributions on the exempt organization and unconcerned donors can make their gifts to the action organization. The National Association for the Advancement of Colored People, Inc. (nonexempt action organization) and the NAACP Legal Defense and Educational Fund, Inc. (exempt public interest legal defense organization) were, in part, originally formed as separate organizations for this very reason. See National Ass'n for the Advancement of Colored People v. N.A.A.C.P. Legal Defense and Ed'l Fund, Inc., 753 F.2d 131 (D.C.Cir.1985), cert. denied, 472 U.S. 1021 (1985), which explains the relationship between the two organizations and indicates that total harmony does not always prevail between a charity and an action organization. In more recent years the NAACP itself has once again divided into an action and an exempt organization to secure tax-exempt status for the principal organization.

[¶ 26,025]

CHILD v. UNITED STATES

United States Court of Appeals, Second Circuit, 1976.
540 F.2d 579.

OAKES, Circuit Judge:

[Decedent bequeathed a large portion of her estate to two nonprofit cemetery associations. Her executor claimed a deduction under § 2055(a)(2) on the ground that the associations are charitable or religious. The Commissioner rejected the claim and the executor brought suit in district court where his claim was again rejected. Appeal was then taken to the Court of Appeals which, in the following opinion, affirmed the decision of the district court.]

* * * The 1939 Internal Revenue Code did not expressly provide for either income or estate tax deductions for donations to cemetery associations. In 1954, however, the Code was amended to provide an express exemption from the *income* tax for "[c]emetery companies owned and operated exclusively for the benefit of their members or which are not operated for profit. . . ." 26 U.S.C. § 501(c)(13). [Emphasis in original.] But it is significant that this was done as a *special* exemption, wholly outside the rubric of "charitable" or "religious" status under § 501(c)(3).

* * *

No similar *estate* tax provision expanding deductibility for bequests to cemeteries either specially or as "charitable" or "religious" contributions has been made by Congress. The estate tax provision regarding such bequests in the 1939 and 1954 Codes is identical in content to the old income tax charitable contribution provision, see 26 U.S.C. § 170(c)(2), which the 1954 Congress felt did not extend to include gifts or bequests to cemetery associations. Under the congressional understanding and the prior case law, it appears that a per se rule allowing deduction for bequests to cemetery associations would be "beyond [that] allowed under present law. . . ." S.Rep. on Int.Rev.Code of 1954, supra.

In this situation, the executor is constrained to argue that the two cemetery association beneficiaries involved in this case serve in the traditional sense as charitable or religious enterprises. As was stated in Gund's Estate v. Commissioner, 113 F.2d 61, 62 (6th Cir.1940)(bequest to association not deductible where no free burial space provided or less than fair value charged for burial or upkeep), cert. denied, 311 U.S. 696 (1940), "[a] cemetery association doubtless could be so organized and operated as to be a charitable organization within the meaning of the [Internal Revenue Code]. . . ."

¶ 26,025

* * * As the district court found, however, "[t]he Cemetery Associations did not make it a practice of providing free burial to indigents, nor is it their usual custom to provide any plots at reduced prices." Here, as in Bank of Carthage v. United States, 304 F.Supp. 77, 80 (W.D.Mo.1969), "[i]t appears the rich, the poor, and the in-between are treated alike." While some of the various functions claimed to be charitable by the cemetery may in fact be so, here as in *Bank of Carthage* "the conclusion is inescapable that the [cemetery's] funds are not used *exclusively for charitable purposes*," as the statute requires. Id. (emphasis original).

We cannot accept the broad view of Dulles v. Johnson, 273 F.2d 362 (2d Cir.1959), cert. denied, 364 U.S. 834 (1960), espoused by the executor, that if the activity of burying the dead were not undertaken by these and like associations, the cost would devolve upon the public, thereby rendering the associations "charitable" in purpose. * * * In *Dulles*, however, it is clear that substantial "charitable" and "educational" activities of a more traditional sort were continuously being performed by the beneficiary associations: "maintaining libraries for legal research, sponsoring lectures and forums on the law, providing free legal service through participation in legal aid, and providing low cost legal service through participation in a legal referral system." 273 F.2d at 367–68. In our view, *Dulles* should be read for the proposition that public dedication of services by an organization may be colored by a history of that organization's performance of more traditional charitable activities to such an extent that the entire enterprise, or the "total operations" of the association, id. at 368, assume the aspect of charitable service to the community. The activities which are not charitable or educational, e.g., social or economic, must be merely "auxiliary" or "incidental in nature." Id. By concentrating solely on the factor of relieving public expense, we believe the executor has overlooked the complex of factors upon which the *Dulles* opinion was based. Relief of general tax burdens alone, in a society with some progressivity in its tax structure, cannot be deemed a single, inalienable mark of charity.

* * *

[The court below] was also correct in holding that the two cemetery associations do not qualify as "religious" entities under § 2055. Here, as in the case of "charitable" status, it must again be assumed that a cemetery could be so organized as to constitute a "religious" entity under the estate tax provisions, 26 U.S.C. § 2055(a). In fact, we have been informed on argument of this case that many cemeteries directly associated with and under the supervision of particular churches have been treated by the Commissioner as "religious" activities for purposes of § 2055, even though church or church-owned burial plots are not given free of charge except to occasional indigents. See also Estate of Elizabeth L. Audenried, 26 T.C. 120 (1956). The executor claims that Grove Cemetery and Watertown Cemetery [the object of the decedent's bounty] should be similarly treated, despite their lack of religious affiliation, because burial in general serves a religious purpose. While burial may, in many or most instances, serve a religious function, the fact remains that the cemetery associations in this case do not themselves perform that function. Accordingly, we affirm the judgment of the district court, leaving to congressional wisdom the apparent anomaly establishing different treatment of nonprofit cemetery associations for income and estate tax purposes.

Judgment affirmed.

Notes

[¶ 26,031]

1.   In First Nat'l Bank of Omaha v. United States, 681 F.2d 534 (8th Cir.1982), the court rejected the approach of the *Child* decision and took the view that a bequest to a cemetery association could qualify for a charitable deduction—if the bequest was directed to a qualified charitable purpose. But the court found that, since the particular fund was first to be used for maintenance of the decedent's family plot, the bequest did not qualify for a charitable deduction under § 2055.

2.   The question of whether educational institutions (and perhaps other forms of charitable institutions as well) could qualify as charities, exempt from income tax and eligible for tax deductible contributions, notwithstanding the practice of discrimination based on race, has had something of a checkered history. After a long period of nonconcern on this front, the Treasury in 1970 announced that discriminating educational institutions could not qualify as tax-exempt institutions and, thus, would not be qualified recipients for deductible contributions or bequests. IRS News Release, July 7, 1970. This followed a ruling in 1967, Rev. Rul. 67–325, 1967–2 C.B. 113, denying deductibility of contributions to a recreational organization that barred use of its facilities by members of a nonfavored race. The ground of the ruling was the common-law definition of a charity for legal purposes. In Rev. Rul. 71–447, 1971–2 C.B. 230 the IRS issued a formal public revenue ruling which was in accord with its July 7, 1970 News Release.

In Bob Jones University v. United States, 461 U.S. 574 (1983), the Supreme Court decided, in the context of an income tax question about the university's tax-exempt status, that Rev. Rul. 71–447 was valid, reinforced by unsuccessful efforts to change the rule by congressional legislation. Accordingly, the Court sustained the action of the Commissioner in revoking the university's tax-exempt status. The case is good precedent, of course, for estate and gift tax as well as income tax purposes.

The Bob Jones case involved an educational institution. What of the tax status of other types of charities? May any of them practice discrimination and still qualify for favorable tax treatment? What of institutions discriminating against women? Can McCoy v. Schultz, 73–1 USTC ¶ 12,906, 31 AFTR 2d 73–858 (D.D.C.1973), holding that the Portland City Club denying admission to women was nevertheless tax-exempt, continue to stand? What of single sex schools?

¶ **26,031**

C. WHOSE CHARITABLE TRANSFER?

[¶ 26,037]

ESTATE OF PICKARD v. COMMISSIONER

United States Tax Court, 1973.
60 T.C. 618, aff'd, 503 F.2d 1404 (6th Cir.1974).

TANNENWALD, Judge:

[Decedent bequeathed her residuary estate to the Pickard Trust in which her stepfather had a vested remainder. Her stepfather, who died shortly before her, in his will left his residuary estate to the Peterson Trust, which, in its deed of trust, provided that two qualified charities were to receive the corpus upon the death of certain family members. In filing the estate tax return for the decedent, her executor claimed a charitable deduction for the amount of her estate that passed to the Pickard Trust and then to the Peterson Trust under her stepfather's will and that would in turn be received by the two charities through their remainder interests in the Peterson Trust. The Commissioner disallowed the deduction.]

Section 2055 provides, among other things, that "the value of the taxable estate shall be determined by deducting from the value of the gross estate the amount of all bequests, legacies, devises, or transfers * * * to or for the use of any corporation organized and operated exclusively for religious, charitable, scientific, literary, or educational purposes."

The parties herein are in agreement as to the exempt character of the two organizations involved and as to the amount of the deduction, if found to be allowable. Additionally, no question has been raised whether the provisions of any of the instruments involved or the possibility of claims against either the Pickard or Peterson estates or trusts might operate in such a way as to make the interests of those organizations unascertainable or subject to the so-remote-as-to-be-negligible possibility that the transfers would not become effective. See sec. 20.2055–2, Estate Tax Regs.

The sole question to be decided herein is whether the provisions of decedent's will and the Pickard Trust are operative within the framework of the above-quoted statutory language. Petitioner asserts that there are three elements contained in section 2055, all of which are satisfied in this case, namely, (1) decedent made a transfer, (2) of property includable in her gross estate, and (3), by virtue of her stepfather's death and the provisions of his will and the Peterson Trust, to or for the use of a qualified entity. Such assertion is premised upon the assumption that each of three elements is independent of each other and that section 2055 can therefore be fragmented in order to determine whether a deduction is allowable. Under petitioner's reasoning, the route of devolution is immaterial; it is enough if there is a transfer of includable property which must, because of the surrounding circumstances, inevitably find its way into the coffers of an exempt organization.

¶ 26,037

In our opinion, such separation of the three elements is improper. We believe that the first and third elements are mutually interdependent and that the "transfer * * * to or for the use of" such organization must be manifest from the provisions of the decedent's testamentary instrument.

The impact of the route of devolution has been considered in a variety of contexts. Thus, in Senft v. United States, 319 F.2d 642 (3d Cir.1963), property of the decedent, who died intestate, escheated to the Commonwealth of Pennsylvania. In denying the decedent a deduction under section 2055, the Court of Appeals emphasized decedent's failure to make the transfer, as opposed to the property passing to the qualified recipient by another force, i.e., by operation of law.

In Cox v. Commissioner, 297 F.2d 36 (2d Cir.1961), affirming a Memorandum Opinion of this Court, a deduction under the predecessor of section 2055 was denied where the testatrix, with full knowledge of all relevant facts and her express approval of the ultimate recipient of the bequest, bequeathed part of her estate to her son, a priest, who had, prior to her death but subsequent to the making of the testatrix's will, taken solemn vows of poverty and renounced all his interests in property (including donations and legacies) in favor of the Society of Jesus, a qualified entity under the statute.

Similar reasoning formed the underpinning of the Supreme Court's decision in Taft v. Commissioner, 304 U.S. 351 (1938), where the decedent died with an outstanding but unfulfilled pledge of a charitable contribution which constituted a binding contractual obligation under local law. The Supreme Court denied a deduction for estate tax purposes on the grounds that the claim was not supported by adequate and full consideration as required by then existing law and that there was no bequest, legacy, devise, or transfer within the meaning of the predecessor of section 2055.

In each of the foregoing cases, the fact that the designated portion of the decedent's estate inevitably inured to the benefit of the charity did not save the day. To be sure, they can be distinguished on their facts, but the common element which forms the foundation for decision is that the transfer to or for the use of the charity was not effectuated by a testamentary transfer on decedent's part but rather by the operation of an external force. The same is true herein, where it was the testamentary disposition of decedent's stepfather via the Peterson Trust which accomplished the transfer.

Concededly, the charities herein would not have received decedent's property if the decedent had not made the testamentary disposition to her stepfather. The lesson from the decided cases, however, is that a simple "but for" test is not, as petitioner would have us hold, sufficient. There must be something more, namely, the testamentary facts as gleaned from the decedent's own disposition must manifest the transfer to the charity. Commissioner v. Noel's Estate, 380 U.S. 678 (1965). In so stating, we do not imply that the decedent must specify the charitable recipient in so many words. But, at the very least, the instrument of testamentary disposition must sufficiently articulate, either directly or through appropriate incorporation by reference of another instrument, the manifestation of decedent's charitable bounty. See

Y.M.C.A. v. Davis, 264 U.S. 47, 50 (1924). Such a situation simply does not obtain herein and, accordingly, the claimed deduction is not allowable.

* * *

Notes

[¶ 26,043]

1. Regulation § 20.2055–2(c) states that a deduction is allowable for an amount "falling into" a charitable bequest as a result of a disclaimer by a beneficiary; for example, if the residue of an estate were donated to charity, and a legatee renounced his interest under the will, the bequest would "fall into" the charitable gift and would be deductible. To qualify, the disclaimer must be irrevocable and must be made before the estate tax return is due. The disclaimer must also be made voluntarily; the beneficiary can receive no consideration in return for a disclaimer. Can the policy behind this regulation be reconciled with the *Pickard* case, above, and the *Senft* and *Cox* cases cited therein? It should be noted that the regulation in question was based squarely on statutory language that was contained in the first sentence of § 2055(a) prior to its deletion by the Tax Reform Act of 1976, which inserted the general provision governing disclaimers for estate and gift tax purposes. See § 2518.

2. In Estate of Lamson v. United States, 338 F.2d 376 (Ct.Cl.1964), it was held that a bequest to an individual, who was a member of a religious order subject to a vow of poverty, did not qualify as a charitable deduction. This was so despite the fact that the religious order might have rights under contract with the member that would insure transfer of the bequest to it. See also Estate of Barry v. Commissioner, 311 F.2d 681 (9th Cir.1962), Rev. Ruls. 55–760, 1955–2 C.B. 607, and 55–759, 1955–2 C.B. 607 and Priv. Ltr. Rul. 200437032.

In Estate of Hubert v. Commissioner, 66 T.C.M. (CCH) 1064, T.C.M. (RIA) ¶ 93,482 (1993), the Tax Court upheld the deductibility of bequests to trusts to support the missionary work of a charity through a named individual for his life, including support for the named missionary during retirement with remainder interests to be distributed to the charity.

D. SPLIT GIFTS

[¶ 26,047]

Taxpayers who have the opportunity to give an interest in an asset to a charity while retaining also an interest in the asset provide a special challenge to the Treasury. By retaining an interest in the property, a portion of which is being conveyed to charity, these individuals create opportunities for abuse, yet it is hardly appropriate to prevent abuse by denying them a deduction of their generosity. The materials below discuss how Congress has, and has not, met this challenge.

¶ 26,037

[¶ 26,049]

1. THE BASIC STATUTORY SOLUTION

Prior to the passage of the Tax Reform Act of 1969, the split gift was a popular form of charitable donation. If a trust was created or property was transferred for both a private and a charitable purpose, a deduction was allowed for the value of the charitable interest. The regulations imposed two limitations on deductibility. First, the value of the charitable interest had to be "presently ascertainable," that is, subject to reasonably precise valuation. Reg. § 20.2055–2(a). Second, the charity had to be assured of eventually taking its interest. A contingent gift to charity was deductible only if the conditions imposed were "so remote as to be negligible." Reg. § 20.2055–2(b).

These two tests produced a multitude of problems in their application. The courts were forced to reinterpret the valuation and contingency language under the widely varying circumstances of each case. Some taxpayers took advantage of the imprecision in the language to obtain a deduction for a larger amount than the charity actually received. The following excerpt from the House Ways and Means Committee Report on the Tax Reform Act of 1969 outlines Congress' concerns in revamping the law in this area. H. Rep. No. 91–413, 91st Cong., 1st Sess. at 58–59 (1969).

> *General reasons for change*—The rules of present law for determining the amount of a charitable contribution deduction in the case of gifts of remainder interests in trust do not necessarily have any relation to the value of the benefit which the charity receives. This is because the trust assets may be invested in a manner so as to maximize the income interest with the result that there is little relation between the interest assumptions used in calculating present values and the amount received by the charity. For example, the trust corpus can be invested in high-income, high-risk assets. This enhances the value of the income interest but decreases the value of the charity's remainder interest.

> Your committee does not believe that a taxpayer should be allowed to obtain a charitable contribution deduction for a gift of a remainder interest in trust to a charity which is substantially in excess of the amount the charity may ultimately receive.

> Your committee's attention also was called to the fact that in some cases charitable contributions deductions have been allowed for gifts of charitable remainder interests in trust even though it is not probable that the gift will ultimately be received by the charity. An example of this is a situation where the charity has only a contingent remainder interest in a trust (for example, a $5,000 annuity to A for life, remainder to his children, or to charity if A has no children). Another example is the situation where a charity has a remainder interest and the trust permits invasion of the charitable share for the benefit of a noncharitable intervening interest which is incapable of reasonably certain actuarial valuation (for example, a $5,000 annuity to A for life, remainder to a charity, but the trust provides that the trustee may pay A amounts in excess of $5,000 in order to maintain his standard of living).

¶ 26,049

In the Tax Reform Act of 1969, Congress took its initial steps to correct these abuses. Section 2055(e), which has been amended on several occasions since, represents Congress's principal endeavor to protect the integrity of the estate tax against such abuses. Under § 2055(e), when interests in the same property pass to both a private party and a charity, no charitable deduction will be allowed unless the gift is, in general, in one of the forms prescribed below:

1. Charitable Remainder Annuity Trust—A taxpayer may establish a trust from which a private person or persons will receive a sum of money at least once a year, not less than 5 nor more than 50 percent of the value of the initial value of the corpus. The payments may extend for life or for a term not over 20 years. Following the termination of these payments, the remainder must be transferred to or held in trust for a charity, and it must equal or exceed 10 per cent of the initial fair market value of the property initially transferred to the trust. See § 664(d)(1).

2. Charitable Remainder Unitrust—This structure is similar to the annuity trust except that, instead of a fixed sum, the private beneficiaries must receive a fixed percentage (not less than 5 nor more than 50 percent) of the fair market value of the trust assets, valued annually. See § 664(d)(2).

3. Pooled Income Fund—This is a trust established by a charity to which each of several donors contributes property, retaining income interests for private beneficiaries and leaving the remainder interests to the charity. All property contributed to the trust will be commingled to form a single fund. The amount of each private beneficiary's annual payment will be determined by the rate of return on the entire fund. See § 642(c)(5).

4. Remainder Interest in a Farm or Personal Residence—These split interests may still be donated to charity outright and a charitable deduction allowed therefor.

5. Guaranteed Annuity or Fixed Percentage Income Interest—An income interest can be donated to charity in the form of a guaranteed annuity, or a fixed percentage of the assets to a trust. See § 2055(e)(2)(B). Although the Code does not specify that the property must be in trust, the regulations state that the donor must either establish an annuity trust or a unitrust or make the income interests payable by an organization engaged in issuing annuity contracts (e.g., an insurance company). See Reg. § 20.2055–2(e)(2)(v) and (vi).

6. Undivided Interest—A taxpayer may donate an undivided fractional interest in property to a charity and retain a fractional interest in the property. See § 170(f)(3)(B)(ii).

7. Qualified Conservation Contribution—Interests, such as scenic easements, in real property conveyed to qualified charities exclusively for prescribed conservation purposes may qualify for a charitable deduc-

tion despite the fact that the donor retains rights to the property subject to the conveyed interest. See § 170(f)(3)(B)(iii).

The amount of the deduction allowed from the gross estate will equal the fair market value of the interest given to charity. The regulations are quite specific as to how the fair market value of the interests is to be figured. For the charitable remainder interests, the basic notion behind the rules is that the value of the stream of income payments to be received by the life beneficiary must be deducted from the fair market value of the property placed in the trust. Reg. §§ 1.664–2(c), 1.664–4 and 1.642(c)–6. The value of a charitable income interest is figured on the present value of the series of payments that the charity will receive. (Reg. §§ 20.2031–7.) The regulations leave nothing to the imagination as to how the precise calculations are to be made. A glance at the extensive formulas and tables found in the regulations should convince the student that the taxpayer has no room left for argument.

Note that Congress has solved the problems of prior law by requiring taxpayers to follow a prearranged scheme in their gift giving that simply excludes the troublesome factors altogether. The new rules do not allow any invasions of the corpus by the trustee, or any contingent gifts to charity, no matter how certain the chances of taking may be. The problem of the trustee manipulating investments and allocations to favor the individual life beneficiary is eliminated by making the individual's share dependent on total trust assets rather than trust income.

Congress replaced the uncertainties of prior law with a set of complex and inflexible rules that must be carefully followed to avoid complete loss of the charitable deduction. The intricacies of this area are now so formidable that the Treasury has broken precedent and has issued forms which, if followed with religious zeal, will assure the availability of the charitable deduction for annuity trusts and unitrusts. For the road map, see Rev. Procs. 89–20, 1989–1 C.B. 841; 89–21, 1989–1 C.B. 842; 90–30, 1990–1 C.B. 534; 90–31, 1990–1 C.B. 539; and 90–32, 1990–1 C.B. 546.

A corresponding revision of the gift tax charitable deduction provision was made in § 2522(c) by the Tax Reform Act of 1969.

The second important revision under the Tax Reform Act of 1969 affecting the charitable deduction for estate and gift tax purposes was the denial of the deduction for transfers to private foundations that have engaged in willful and repeated acts subjecting them to the new penalty taxes imposed by Chapter 42, relating to private foundations involved in acts of self-dealing, substantial income accumulations, excessive business holdings, improper investments, and forbidden expenditures. See § 508(d).

[¶ 26,052]

2. THE EXCLUSION FOR QUALIFIED CONSERVATION EASEMENTS

In the Taxpayer Relief Act of 1997 Congress provided an exclusion for the estates of taxpayers that hold realty subject to qualified conservation easements, which are defined broadly to include permanent environmental, recreational, educational, scenic and historic dedications of interests in property. See § 2031(c). Although in form an exclusion, § 2031(c) has the effect of providing an added deduction for such easements, many of which will also qualify for charitable contribution deduction under § 2055(f) noted above. This and the close coordination of § 2031(c) with many charitable contribution concepts make it appropriate to discuss this provision in this chapter.

Section 2031(c) is very technical and the benefit provided taxpayers is of limited importance in a general estate and gift tax course, consequently the discussion which follows is restricted to the provision's most salient features.

The land which is subject to a qualifying easement must be owned by the decedent (or a member of his family or controlled entity) at all times during the three years prior to death. Moreover, if the property is debt financed, the exclusion is only available to the extent of the equity interest in the property.

The amount which qualifies for the exclusion is capped at the lesser of: (1) a dollar figure which increases annually in $100,000 increments from $100,000 in 1998 to $500,000 in 2002; or (2) 40% of the value of the land calculated without regard to the easement, reduced by the value of any charitable deduction allowed under § 2055(f) to the estate because of creation of the easement.

Section 2031(c)(2) provides a phase out mechanism for the 40% exclusion for the purpose of limiting the value of the exclusion in the case of easements which, relatively speaking, effect only modest reductions in the value of the land.

One of the more interesting features of § 2031(c) is that it applies regardless of when a qualified conservation easement was donated and once land is subject to such an easement the exclusion is available to subsequent decedent-holders of the land as long as they are members of the original donor's family. Seemingly this will enable who inherit land subject to an conservation easement to claim benefit of § 2031(c) when they die and for them to pass the benefit on to their issue or others satisfying the § 2032A(e)(2) definition of family.

Qualifying conservation easements can provide taxpayers with extraordinary tax benefits for several reasons. First, if given during life the donor may, when calculating her income tax, obtain a charitable deduction for the reduction in value of the land that results from the easement (¶ 26,141). Second, at the donor's death her executor lists as an estate asset the value of the property reduced by the easement. Third, under § 2031(c) an estate tax exclusion will also be allowed to the donor's estate. In some cases the value of all of the resulting tax savings can exceed the reduction in value caused by the easement. And finally, as the *pièce de résistance* the donor-decedent's heirs, if they remain as holders of the property, will also be able to claim the exclusion and list only the value of the property reduced by the easement thereby resulting in not only conservation of nature but also conservation of wealth.

¶ 26,052

Planning Note

[¶ 26,055]

The charitable remainder trust is a favorite device of estate planners for two principal reasons: (1) since the corpus (as contrasted with the income interest) belongs to a tax-exempt charity, trust holdings can generally be sold without income tax liability; and (2) in the case of a gift in trust of an income interest to a private party and the remainder interest to a charity, the income from a charitable remainder trust will be taxed to the income beneficiary who may be in a low tax bracket. These advantages can be illustrated by the following examples. First, take the case of a middle-aged founder of a highly successful corporation who has a very low basis in that company's stock which pays little or no dividends, and who wishes to sell out and spend the rest of his life on the beach and on the ski slopes. A cash sale of his stock will leave him with only the after-tax proceeds to invest in income producing assets to fund his life of leisure. If, on the other hand, our friend were to give his stock to a charitable remainder trust, he would get the stock out of his estate, have a nice income tax deduction equal to the value of the charity's remainder interest, receive the thanks of the charity of his choice and the acclaim of his community and, since the remainder interest is held for the benefit of a tax-exempt charity, the stock could be sold by the trust with no income tax liabilities and the entire sales proceeds invested in income producing assets for the benefit of our entrepreneur, thereby leaving him with the income for his life on the full fair market value of his stock. Second, consider the case of someone like our entrepreneur friend, who in this instance is in a high tax bracket and is concerned about providing for a family member, such as a retarded child, who has little or no prospect of income during her or his life. If the entrepreneur were to contribute assets to a charitable remainder trust, with income to the child for life, remainder to an appropriate charity, the annual income from the trust would be taxed to the child at her or his lower rates and not those of the high bracket entrepreneur, who would also benefit from an income tax deduction equal to the value of the charitable remainder. The advantage of the first scenario, avoidance of income tax on sale of appreciated assets contributed to the trust, can also be combined with the income assignment benefits of this second scenario.

E. UNASCERTAINABILITY OF IDENTITY OF CHARITY OR AMOUNT OF CHARITABLE GIFT; AND CONDITIONAL GIFTS

[¶ 26,097]

Testators, with occasional unfortunate results, sometimes leave open the identification of the charitable beneficiary or the amount passing to an identified charity. The creation of conditional charitable bequests is also another potentially hazardous venture.

1. FAILURE TO IDENTIFY CHARITY

[¶ 26,110]

REVENUE RULING 69–285

1969–1 C.B. 222.

A, a resident of Massachusetts, died testate. Paragraph One of his will provided bequests for several persons including *B*. Paragraph Two named *B* as executrix of the estate. Paragraph Three of the will reads:

> "All the rest and residue of my estate of whatsoever kind and nature and wheresoever situated, I bequeath to said *B* to be distributed to whatever charities she may deem worthy."

Two years after *A*'s death a Massachusetts probate court issued a decree which recited that *B* had selected several organizations to receive the residue. The organizations selected were charitable within the meaning of section 2055(a).

The basic question is whether under the terms of the will the local law would (1) impose a trust upon the residuary assets and (2) require the trustee to distribute the assets to organizations that are charitable within the meaning of section 2055. If local law would not infer an intent to establish a trust relationship over the residuary estate, the property could be diverted to noncharitable uses by the voluntary act of the residuary legatee, *B*. And, even if the Commonwealth of Massachusetts would impose a trust upon the residuary estate, it must be determined whether the local law definition of "charities" is restricted to organizations that are charitable within the meaning of section 2055. No deduction is allowed if local law merely imposes a trust upon the residue but fails to restrict the trustee's choice to organizations that are deemed charitable within the meaning of section 2055.

Section 2055(a)(3) provides in part that the value of a decedent's taxable estate shall be determined by deducting from the value of the gross estate the amount of all bequests "to a trustee or trustees, * * * but only if such contributions or gifts are to be used by such trustee or trustees, * * * exclusively for religious, charitable, scientific, literary, or educational purposes * * * and no substantial part of the activities of such trustee or trustees * * * is carrying on propaganda, or otherwise attempting to influence legislation."

A state court decree is considered to be conclusive in the determination of the Federal tax liability of an estate only to the extent that it determines property rights, and if the issuing court is the highest court in the state. Commissioner v. Estate of Herman J. Bosch, et al., 387 U.S. 456 (1967), Ct. D. 1915, C.B. 1967–2, 337. Therefore, the fact that the State probate court in this case placed a stamp of approval on *B*'s appointment of the property to charity is not determinative of whether a charitable deduction is allowable.

In Delaney v. Gardner, 204 F.2d 855 (1953), the decedent bequeathed $100,000 to the executors " * * * not subject to any trust, but in the hope that they will dispose of it at their absolute discretion and according to their own judgment, but giving due weight to any memoranda I may leave or any oral expressions by me to them made during my life." The probate court admitted as part of the will a memorandum that was dated the same day as the will. The memorandum contained a list of charitable organizations to which the executors ultimately appointed the residue. The deduction was disallowed because the executors were held to have discretion under the terms of the will to withhold part or all of the bequest from charity. Amounts so withheld would have passed to noncharitable beneficiaries.

The charitable deduction was also denied in Mississippi Valley Trust v. Commissioner, 72 F.2d 197 (1934). The decedent had devised all of his property in equal shares to his wife and two sons. The will stated: "I have heretofore expressed to my sons my wishes as to certain charitable gifts, and I therefore make no such bequests herein, preferring that my sons shall make such donations within their sole discretion as shall seem to them to be best." The court held that the provision was not mandatory, but was merely an expression of desire.

Charitable deductions have been allowed where the terms of the bequest would be construed to impose a trust on the subject property by operation of local law. In Lincoln National Bank & Trust Company of Fort Wayne v. United States, 6 A.F.T.R. 2d 6142 (1960), the decedent's bequest of a portion of her estate "to such corporations, foundations, or organizations organized and operated exclusively for religious, charitable, or educational purposes, as may be selected by my said nieces, Venette Marie Sites and Mabel Margaret Sites, or the survivor of them," qualified for a charitable deduction. Charitable deductions were also allowed based on similar language in George Beggs, Executor of the Estate of Edward Farmer v. United States, 27 F.Supp. 599 (1939).

It is clear that the above-quoted provision in A's will placed a fiduciary obligation on B to distribute the residue to organizations that are charitable within the meaning of Massachusetts law. Gill v. Attorney General, 83 N.E. 676 (1908); Reilly v. McGowan, 166 N.E. 766 (1929). The intention to establish a trust may be derived from the instrument, even though the testator does not use the word "trust" or "trustee." Gordon v. Gordon, 124 N.E.2d 226 (1955), Sherwin v. Smith, 185 N.E. 17 (1933).

The fact that B might have refused to appoint the residue to charity would not have prevented the property from passing to charity. It is ordinarily to be inferred that the testator's primary purpose was that the property should be devoted to charitable uses, and the selection of those uses is a secondary matter. Scott on Trusts, section 397 (3d Ed. 1967). Scott cites Minot v. Baker, 17 N.E. 839 (1888), as "the leading case" on this point. In that case the will appointed one John Healy executor, and gave the residue to Healy, "to be disposed of by him for such charitable purposes as he shall think proper." Healy died, having disposed of only a small portion of the residuary estate in his hands for charitable purposes. In denying the claim of the first decedent's heirs the court stated at page 845:

> "The first point to be determined, therefore, is a matter of construction, whether the limitation to charities was conditional upon Healy's making

¶ 26,110

an appointment, or whether it should be construed as a gift to charitable uses out and out with a super-added power to Healy to specify them if he saw fit; and on this part of the question, we are of the opinion that the gift is an unconditional gift for charitable purposes."

Section 2055(a)(3) of the Code requires that bequests to trustees must be used by the trustee for purposes that are exclusively charitable. Some jurisdictions characterize as charitable certain purposes that are not deemed charitable within the meaning of the Federal statute. * * *

Decisions by the Massachusetts Supreme Court indicate that the Massachusetts definition of "charitable" is at least as restrictive as the Federal definition of that term under section 2055. See Boston Chamber of Commerce v. Assessors, 54 N.E.2d 199 (1944); Garden Cemetery Corporation v. Baker, 105 N.E. 1070 (1914); Massachusetts Medical Society v. Assessors, 164 N.E.2d 325 (1960); Workman's Circle Educational Center v. Assessors, 51 N.E.2d 313 (1943). In these cases the court excluded from the definition of charity trade associations, nonreligious cemetery associations, professional organizations, and lobbying activities.

The executrix in this case had a fiduciary duty to use the net residuary estate for purposes which are exclusively charitable within the meaning of section 2055 of the Code. Accordingly, it is held that the charitable deduction is allowable for the value of the net amount of the residuary estate.

[¶ 26,115]

REVENUE RULING 78–101

1978–1 C.B. 301.

On December 30, 1976, the donor transferred property in trust under the terms of which the trustee is directed to pay a charitable lead unitrust an amount equal to 4 percent of the net fair market value of the trust property, determined annually, to such organizations described in sections 170(c) and 2522(a) of the Internal Revenue Code of 1954, as the trustee may select. The trust is to terminate at the expiration of ten years and one month, at which time the trust corpus is to revert to the donor if living; and if the donor is not living, then to the donor's estate.

Section 25.2522(c)–3(c)(2)(vi)(e) of the Gift Tax Regulations provides that, with certain exceptions not relevant here, a charitable lead unitrust interest will be considered a qualifying unitrust interest provided no amount other than the unitrust amount may be paid by the trust for a private purpose; that is, a purpose other than a charitable purpose described in section 2522(a).

Rev. Rul. 76–371, 1976–2 C.B. 305, holds that a charitable *remainder* unitrust interest will not be disallowed under section 25.2522(c)–3(c)(2)(iv) of the regulations where the trustee possessed the power to add or substitute charitable remaindermen but was required to select only organizations that qualified under section 2522(a).

Held, the failure to designate the specific charitable recipients of a charitable lead interest in the form of a unitrust interest will not disqualify the interest for the charitable deduction where the trustee is empowered to select the charitable beneficiaries and the governing instrument requires that only charitable organizations that meet the requirements of section 2522(a) can be selected.

Note

[¶ 26,118]

1. In Priv. Ltr. Rul. 9634025 the taxpayer died with all his property held in a New York revocable trust which at his death became irrevocable. The trust provided that, with respect to certain assets, eighty percent was to pass to Catholic charities, ten percent to Protestant charities, and ten percent to Jewish charities "as shall be chosen by the trustee." As it did in Rev. Rul. 69–285, the IRS ruled that since New York state law imposed a definition of charity which was at least as restrictive as § 2055(a), the gifts in question were valid charitable contributions under § 2055.

2. In Rev. Rul. 71–200, 1971–1 C.B. 272, a decedent left property to be distributed by a trustee "to or for the use of those organizations to which gifts of income or principal shall qualify as tax-free under the laws relating to income, estate, inheritance, *or* gifts, of the United States, *or* of any state having jurisdiction * * *." The IRS ruled that a valid charitable estate tax deduction was not present. First, it noted that since Federal income (§ 170), gift (§ 2522) and estate (§ 2055) tax definitions of charity are not identical, it was possible that property might be left to a valid charity under the income or gift taxes which did not qualify under § 2055. Second, there was a possibility that the trustee would distribute property to a charity that, while valid under state law, would not qualify as a charity under § 2055.

Planning Note

[¶ 26,120]

Careful estate planners often include language in wills and other dispositive documents, such as revocable trusts that act as wills substitutes, conditioning intended charitable bequests on an organization qualifying under § 2055(a) and providing for appropriate alternative donees in the event of failure to so qualify. For example, in Priv. Ltr. Rul. 200019011 decedent's will left the residue of her estate to six organizations but provided that if any failed to qualify as a charity under § 2055(a) that organization shall not share in the bequest and the residue shall be divided among the remaining organizations which do qualify as charities under § 2055(a). In Priv. Ltr. Rul. 200202032 the I.R.S. gave its blessing to a bequest of paintings to a museum conditioned on its remaining qualified under § 2055(a). The decedent's will also empowered his executors to select a substitute § 2055 charity in the event the museum declined to accept the bequest.

¶ 26,120

2. UNASCERTAINABILITY OF AMOUNT

[¶ 26,123]

ESTATE OF MARINE v. COMMISSIONER

United States Court of Appeals, Fourth Circuit, 1993.
990 F.2d 136.

CHAPMAN, Senior Circuit Judge:

[David N. Marine executed a will that made a number of specific bequests to designated individuals and left the residue of his estate to be divided equally between his alma maters, Princeton University and Johns Hopkins University. A little more than one year later he executed a codicil that empowered his personal representatives to compensate individuals who had contributed to his well-being or otherwise been helpful to him during his life by transferring to them such property as the representatives deemed to be a fair bequest based on the services rendered. No single person was to receive an amount in excess of one percent of Marine's gross probate estate. Marine died about two years after executing the codicil and his personal representatives, acting under the power granted by the codicil, distributed $10,000 to one individual and $15,000 to another. Marine's estate tax return reported a gross estate of about $2.6 million and a deduction of about $2.1 for the residue bequeathed to Princeton and Johns Hopkins. The IRS disallowed the claimed charitable deduction on the ground that the amount of the charitable bequest was unascertainable since the personal representatives could have used their power under the codicil to distribute the entire estate to private parties. The Tax Court upheld the Commissioner's determination and taxpayer appealed.]

Any testamentary gift to "any corporation organized and operated exclusively for ... scientific ... or educational purposes" may be deducted from the gross taxable estate. 26 U.S.C. § 2055(a)(2) (1988).

There is no dispute that Princeton University and the Johns Hopkins University are both legitimate recipients of § 2055(a)(2) gifts. To be deductible as a charitable gift, the value of a testamentary remainder interest must be "presently ascertainable, and hence severable from the non-charitable interest." Treas. Reg. § 20.2055–2(a)(as amended in 1986).

The Supreme Court addressed the question of ascertainability in Ithaca Trust Co. v. United States, 279 U.S. 151 (1929), and upheld a deduction for the remainder of a trust dedicated to charity even though the trustees were authorized to invade the corpus if necessary to "maintain [the widow] in as much comfort as she now enjoys."

Justice Holmes writing for the Court stated:

The principal that could be used was only so much as might be necessary to continue the comfort then enjoyed. The standard was fixed in fact and capable of being stated in definite terms of money. It was not left to the widow's discretion. The income of the estate at the death of the testator, and even after debts and specific legacies had been paid, was more than sufficient to maintain the widow as required. There was no uncertainty

¶ 26,120

appreciably greater than the general uncertainty that attends human affairs.

Id. at 154. Because there was a fixed standard, the Court found that the remainder was ascertainable at the date of death and the charitable remainder was deductible.

Ascertainability at the date of death of the amount going to charity is the test. To be "presently ascertainable" the power of the trustee to divert the corpus from the charities must be restricted by a fixed standard. In Merchants Nat. Bank of Boston, Executor v. Commission of Internal Revenue, 320 U.S. 256 (1943), the Court was faced with a will which created a trust, with the income going to the widow for her life, and upon her death all but $100,000 of the principal was to pass to certain charities. The trustee was authorized to invade the corpus,

> at such time or times as my said trustee shall in its sole discretion deem wise and proper for the comfort, support, maintenance, and/or happiness of my said wife, and it is my wish and will that in the exercise of its discretion with reference to such payments from the principal of the trust fund to my said wife, May L. Field, my said trustee shall exercise its discretion with liberality to my said wife, and consider her welfare, comfort and happiness prior to claims of residuary beneficiaries under this trust. Id. at 257–58.

The Court held that the extent to which the principal might be used was not restricted by a fixed standard, and

> Introducing the element of the widow's happiness and instructing the trustee to exercise its discretion with liberality to make her wishes prior to the claims of residuary beneficiaries brought into the calculation elements of speculation too large to be overcome, notwithstanding the widow's previous mode of life was modest and her own resources substantial. We conclude that the Commissioner properly disallowed the deduction for estate tax purposes. 320 U.S. at 263.

There is no fixed standard that can be applied to the discretion given to Marine's personal representatives. They had "sole and absolute discretion, to compensate persons who have contributed to my well-being or who have been otherwise helpful to me during my lifetime." There is no limit as to the number of persons who may be compensated, and there are no standards for determining and measuring such imprecise elements as "contribution," "my well-being" and "have been otherwise helpful to me during my lifetime." What would be considered a "contribution" to Marine's "well-being?" How large must the contribution be, and over what period of time must it have been made? How would the personal representatives define "helpful?" Would helpfulness during his last illness be rewarded at a higher rate than helpfulness during his infancy or childhood? Dr. Marine lived 60 years and there must have been many persons "helpful" to him in different degrees throughout his life. The number of such individuals has no limit and a standard for measuring "contribution," "well-being" and "helpful" does not exist. This is similar to the problem created by the "widow's happiness" in *Merchant's*

¶ 26,123

Bank, supra. These elements are uncertain and cannot be measured with any precision, and therefore they make the amount going to charity unascertainable at the time of death. The fact that only two persons received payments under [Marine's codicil] is of no moment, because this could not be determined at the time of death so as to affect ascertainability. Henslee, Collector of Internal Revenue v. Union Planters National Bank & Trust Co., 335 U.S. 595 (1949).

* * *

We hold that the language of the codicil, giving the personal representatives "sole and absolute discretion" to reward those who had been helpful to Marine during his life, established no real standards. The personal representatives had virtually unlimited authority as to the number of gifts, although the amount of each bequest was limited to one percent of the corpus. Since the number of such bequests was unlimited and a standard for determining the amount of a bequest was uncertain, the amount of the charitable bequest could not be ascertained at the time of death and the deduction is not available. The tax court was correct in its determinations.

AFFIRMED.

Note

[¶ 26,129]

Had decedent limited the total amount of noncharitable discretionary gifts that could be made by his personal representatives to an amount such as $200,000, seemingly, only that amount (which presumably would have been excluded from taxation by the unified credit) would have failed to qualify for charitable contribution status. Note that the real losers in *Marine* are the very charities which decedent sought to benefit.

[¶ 26,131]

3. CONDITIONAL GIFTS

Under Reg. § 20.2055–2(b), if, at decedent's death, a transfer to a qualifying charity is conditional, no charitable deduction is allowed, unless the likelihood that the charity will not receive the bequest is so remote as to be considered negligible.

[¶ 26,133]

Revenue Ruling 71–442
1971–2 C.B. 336.

Advice has been requested whether a deduction is allowable under section 2055 of the Internal Revenue Code of 1954 (prior to amendment by the Tax Reform Act of 1969, P.L. 91–172, C.B. 1969–3, 10) with respect to a remainder interest in a trust payable to charity under the circumstances described below.

The decedent, a resident of North Carolina, died testate in 1968. He bequeathed his entire residuary estate in trust and provided that the entire net income of the trust be paid to his son for life. At the son's death, the remainder is to be distributed to his children then living. If the son should die without children surviving him, the trust assets are to be distributed to specified charitable organizations. At the decedent's death, his son was 56 years of age and had no children.

Section 2055(a)(2) provides that a deduction from the gross estate is allowable in the amount of bequests to or for the use of any corporation organized and operated exclusively for religious, charitable, scientific, literary or educational purposes. Section 20.2055–2(b) of the Estate Tax Regulations provides that if, as of the date of a decedent's death, a transfer for charitable purposes is dependent upon the performance of some act or the happening of a precedent event in order that it might become effective, no deduction is allowable unless the possibility that the charitable transfer will not become effective is so remote as to be negligible.

Section 48–23(3) of the General Statutes of North Carolina provides:

> From and after the entry of the final order of adoption, the words "child," "grandchild," "heir," "issue," "descendant," or an equivalent, or the plural forms thereof, or any other word of like import in any deed, grant, will or other written instrument shall be held to include any adopted person, unless the contrary plainly appears by the terms thereof, whether such instrument was executed before or after the entry of the final order of adoption and whether such instrument was executed before or after the enactment of this section.

Although at the date of the decedent's death his son had no children, the possibility remained that he might be survived by children since:

1. children might be born to him at some time in the future, or

2. he might adopt a person at some future time.

In Estate of Cardeza v. Commissioner, 173 F.2d 19 (1949), it was held that men are presumed capable of fathering children until death. In City Bank Farmers' Trust Co. v. United States, 5 F.Supp. 871 (1934), the court held that the possibility of a 53–year-old, childless man having issue surviving was sufficient to require that a charitable deduction for the contingent remainder interest be disallowed. See also Revenue Ruling 68–336, C.B. 1968–1, 408.

Inasmuch as the decedent's will does not evidence a clear intent that an adopted child should not share in the class gift to his son's children, North Carolina law, as set forth in the statute cited above, would require distribution of the remainder interest, or the appropriate share thereof, to any adopted child or children surviving at the son's death, rather than to charity.

Accordingly, it is held that the bequest of a remainder interest to charitable organizations subject to defeasance by the survival at the life tenant's death of a natural-born or adopted child of such life tenant does not qualify for the deduction provided by section 2055 of the Code.

¶ 26,133

Notes

[¶ 26,138]

1.   In Estate of De Foucaucourt v. Commissioner, 62 T.C. 485 (1974), the Tax Court held that where a gift to a charity was contingent on decedent's nephew dying without issue, the age (65), poor physical condition, existing lengthy marriage and unlikelihood of the nephew's adopting to create issue should all be considered to decide that there was only a remote contingency that the charity would not realize its bequest. A charitable deduction was therefore allowed. To the contrary is Priv. Ltr. Rul. 8010011 where the IRS disallowed a deduction for a charitable bequest conditioned on decedent's 60–year-old, medically disabled, unmarried son dying without issue. The possibility of adoption alone was deemed sufficient by the IRS to bar deduction under § 2055.

2.   In Rev. Rul. 59–143, 1959–1 C.B. 247, the IRS, in a sporadic display of realism, ruled that a charitable contribution deduction would stand where a bequest to a charity was contingent on the death without bodily issue of two women over 55 years of age.

F.   WHEN TO GIVE: NOW, LATER OR NEVER

[¶ 26,141]

Estate planners frequently suggest to their clients that, if they can afford doing so, it is often preferable from a tax standpoint to make gifts to charities during the donor's life. Property given during the donor's life is out of her estate at death and in essence gives the donor the benefit of the estate tax deduction accorded a charitable bequest. Moreover, the donor has the added advantage of an income tax deduction for her lifetime gift to the charity of her choice. To be added to the tax advantages of lifetime giving are a number of intangible benefits. The donor during her life gets to see her charity benefit from her gift. She also has the opportunity to bask in the sunlight of public recognition, if this is of importance to her. In addition, lifetime gifts are far less likely to be set aside by courts than are bequests, should disapproving heirs institute wills contests.

With the possibility of permanent disappearance of the estate tax waiting in the wings, taxpayers are presented with an additional consideration. For taxpayers whose generosity to a charity is solely motivated by the consideration that they would rather see a large part of their wealth pass to a charity than see it pass in part to the government and in part to their heirs, there now is the possibility of living until repeal and leaving their wealth in its entirely to their heirs. Single individuals who wish to wait out the clock will have to hope for good health and good luck while also hoping that Congress decides to make repeal permanent or at least last until their death. Married couples whose generosity is motivated solely by the availability of an estate tax deduction for bequests to charities can play a somewhat different waiting game. The presence of an unlimited marital deduction for bequests to spouses

¶ 26,138

allows them to have two opportunities to run the clock. For example, if Dad dies while the estate tax is in effect, if his will (after taking full advantage of the unified credit to provide for their issue) leaves the remainder of his estate to Mom, the couple has a second chance to allow their wealth to pass free of the estate tax. If Mom is concerned about the fact that she might die before repeal of the estate tax and would rather pass a portion of her wealth to a charity to cut back on the government's tax bite, she can provide by will that, if she dies while the estate tax is in effect, some portion of her estate will pass to charity.

Problems

[¶ 26,143]

1. The client owns a farm on which he does not live. He proposes to leave the farm to his wife for life with remainder to a qualified charity. He wishes, in addition, to provide for invasions of principal for the benefit of the wife to the maximum extent permissible consistent with retaining a deduction for the charitable remainder. Prepare a proposed standard to govern invasion of principal for the benefit of the wife.

2. You are counsel for a university and are commonly asked to advise potential donors with respect to charitable dispositions in their wills. Will you recommend a unitrust, an annuity trust or the pooled income fund for those who would like to leave their property to the widow for life with remainder to the university? Will your recommendation be the same for all cases or will it vary with the circumstances of the donor? If so, what factors will affect the nature of the advice to be given?

Chapter 27

MARITAL DEDUCTION

(Section 2056)

A. INTRODUCTION

[¶ 27,001]

1. HISTORICAL PERSPECTIVE

One of the most significant features of the estate tax is the marital deduction, enacted in 1948. Its importance is two-fold: the large tax savings possible through the skillful use of the marital deduction and the radical effect its availability has on the drafting of wills and trusts when the goal is to maximize the inherent tax savings potential.

The marital deduction provisions initially were introduced into the estate tax as part of the overall program of Congress to equalize the burden of married couples in the common law states with those in the community property states. From the beginning of the estate tax in 1916, and of the income tax in 1913, the local community property laws of the eight western or southwestern states were accepted in determining the tax treatment of married couples residing in those states. As a result, the combined earnings of a married couple were taxed 50 percent to the husband and 50 percent to the wife, without regard to the respective contributions of each spouse to the earnings pool. This determination reflected the community property rule that each spouse is deemed to own one-half of the community—and that earnings received during marriage are community property. Also, in some states, such as Texas, income from separate property is community property, while in others income from separate property is the separate property of the spouse whose property produced the income. Extending this analysis for federal estate tax purposes resulted in a determination that only one-half of the value of community property was includible in the gross estate of the first spouse to die. For example, if a spouse in a noncommunity property state died with an estate that included accumulated earnings of $1,000,000, the entire $1,000,000 would be includible in that spouse's federal gross estate. But in a community property state, only the spouse's one-half community interest, or

$500,000, would be includible in the deceased spouse's gross estate. A similar effect was applicable in the case of the gift tax; where married persons made a gift of their community property, the husband and wife were each treated as having individually made a separate gift of one-half of the property transferred.

The disparity in the impact of the federal income, gift, and estate taxes as a result of this automatic splitting of the family property for couples residing in community property states as compared with their counterparts in the common-law states was very substantial and became increasingly preferential as the tax rates were raised to meet the revenue needs of the war years. Some states, in an effort to ease the burden on their respective citizens, adopted community property laws.

[¶ 27,007]

2. LIMITED MARITAL DEDUCTION BEGINNING IN 1948

In 1948 Congress attempted to reconcile the differing tax consequences that resulted from ownership of community and noncommunity property and the receipt of income while resident in a community property rather than a noncommunity property jurisdiction. The income tax solution was to permit the splitting of income between husband and wife through the use of special tax tables for married couples filing joint returns. See § 1. The gift tax cure was accomplished at two levels: first, any gift made by a married person could be divided between husband and wife and thus be treated as a separate gift by each to the extent of one-half of the gift (§ 2513), and, second, with respect to any gift between husband and wife, a marital deduction was allowed to the extent of one-half of the gift (§ 2523). As to the estate tax, the correction was made through a marital deduction for property passing to the surviving spouse, the amount of the deduction being limited to the lesser of one-half of the decedent's adjusted gross estate or the amount actually passing to the surviving spouse.

While there is a tendency to believe that the effect of the marital deduction was to bring about equal tax treatment for community property and noncommunity property, the Senate Finance Committee expressly rejected any such notion in the report accompanying the 1948 changes. The Senate Finance Committee explained that the "inherent differences between community property and noncommunity property" preclude "complete equalization." However, the Committee Report concluded that the gift tax and estate tax marital deduction "will result in equality in the important situations." S. Rep. No. 1013, 88th Cong., 2d Sess., reprinted in 1948–1 C.B. 285, 305. As may be readily imagined, this lack of complete equalization occasionally has resulted in different tax consequences for community property and noncommunity property—and, in particular, frustrated taxpayers who have difficulty appreciating the subtle distinctions that are involved.

After Congress acted in 1948 to minimize the differing federal tax consequences that resulted from community property and separate property, the states that had adopted community property laws reversed course and returned to separate property systems.

¶ 27,007

[¶ 27,013]

3. UNLIMITED MARITAL DEDUCTION AFTER 1981

In 1981, Congress eliminated completely the original 50–percent ceiling on the amount to be deducted for both the gift and the estate taxes, the result being the present-day unlimited marital deduction for transfers between spouses. § 2056. The 1981 marital deduction provisions were based on the policy that interspousal transfers should not be subject to taxation, rather than on the former policy that attempted to equalize the estate and gift tax treatment of noncommunity property with community property. According to the legislative history, Congress "believed that a husband and a wife should be treated as one economic unit for purposes of estate and gift taxes, as they generally are for income tax purposes. Accordingly, no tax should be imposed on transfers between a husband and wife." Senate Finance Committee, S. Rep. No. 97–144, Economic Recovery Tax Act of 1981, 97th Cong., 1st Sess. at 127 (1981). Despite the appealing simplicity of this policy, qualification for the marital deduction is subject to strict rules, the interpretation of which continues to be encrusted by considerations of an earlier time. Guiding notions include the axiom that deductions are a matter of legislative grace—that is, are to be strictly construed—and the idea that property that escapes tax at the death of the first spouse to die is to be taxed at the death of the surviving spouse. While the second idea reflects an over generalization and does not take into account the leakage contemplated by the effort to harmonize to a certain extent the marital deduction and community property, it remains a consideration. See ¶ 27,025.

[¶ 27,019]

4. INTERIM CHANGES TO MARITAL DEDUCTION

While no longer significant, it may sometimes be useful to bear in mind that Congress, in 1976, attempted a modification of the marital deduction that persisted until 1981. From 1977 until 1982, § 2056 allowed a marital deduction of the greater of $250,000 or one-half of the decedent's adjusted gross estate. The gift tax marital deduction allowed during this period was equal to the greater of $100,000 or one-half of the value of the transferred property. And, for the first time, both the estate tax and the gift tax marital deductions were allowed as to community property in a limited sense, i.e., to the extent of the first $250,000 and $100,000, respectively, of property transfers. Keeping in mind these special rules, which prevailed from 1977 until 1982, will sometimes be important in reading cases and rulings from that era that make reference to the marital deduction.

B. REQUIREMENTS FOR MARITAL DEDUCTION—OVERVIEW

[¶ 27,025]

Section 2056 specifies the conditions that must be satisfied for the allowance of the marital deduction. Inasmuch as deductions are a matter of legislative grace, the marital deduction will be allowed only in cases where the taxpayer strictly complies with these conditions. However, with one notable exception to be discussed below, namely Qualified Terminable Interest Property (commonly known by the acronym "QTIP"), the marital deduction is not elective, i.e., it is mandatory in those instances where the conditions for its allowance have been satisfied.

Fundamentally, the marital deduction is available only for property passing to the decedent's surviving spouse—and passing in such a way as to be included in the surviving spouse's estate, unless the surviving spouse has disposed of the property prior to death. § 2056(c). As noted above, these overly simplistic premises have been implemented by stringent requirements for qualification for the marital deduction. For example, as will be seen in subsequent portions of this chapter, there are numerous cases where the marital deduction has been denied although the property for which the marital deduction had been sought was to be included in the estate of the surviving spouse, resulting in what could be simplistically referred to as double taxation.

> *Example*: Chastity's will provided that her $5 million estate was to be placed in trust for the life of her husband, Buck. The trustee was instructed to distribute to Buck "so much or all of the income and principal of the trust as was necessary for Buck's support in his accustomed manner of living." At Buck's death, the trust was to be distributed to "those persons or institutions selected by Buck by provision in his will which makes specific reference to this provision of this trust." While Buck has a general power of appointment over Chastity's trust (which results in the inclusion of the trust property in Buck's estate at his death on the authority of § 2041), the peculiarities of § 2056 bar a marital deduction for the property Chastity placed in trust for Buck. (While full consideration of § 2056 is premature, be reminded of the cardinal principle that deductions are a matter of legislative grace and, if not expressly permitted, are not allowed.) Thus, the $5 million was taxed to Chastity at her death (with no marital deduction being allowed) and taxed again in Buck's estate at the time of his death (at its then fair market value).

In passing, note that Chastity's trust for Buck's benefit would have qualified for the marital deduction if the trustee had been required to distribute all the trust income to Buck at least annually. § 2056(b)(7).

Problem

[¶ 27,031]

Should the person who drafted Chastity's will (described above) be subject to a claim for malpractice? Suppose Chastity's lawyer, in defense, reports that Chastity was told that the gift in trust for Buck would not qualify for the marital deduction but that Chastity insisted on the terms that were included in the trust. In such a case, what should the lawyer have done as protection against a later claim for malpractice?

¶ 27,031

C. CITIZENSHIP REQUIREMENT

[¶ 27,055]

The marital deduction is available only if the decedent was a citizen or resident of the United States. Moreover, except in limited circumstances, the decedent's spouse must be a U.S. citizen if the marital deduction is to be allowed for property passing from the decedent to the surviving spouse; i.e., under § 2056(d), enacted in 1988, property passing to a surviving spouse who is not a U.S. citizen does not qualify for the marital deduction. An exception is made for property passing to the noncitizen spouse in the form of a "qualified domestic trust." § 2056(d)(2)(A). A qualified domestic trust is defined in § 2056A(a), which requires that at least one trustee be a U.S. citizen or domestic corporation, that no distribution be made from the trust without the approval of that trustee (except in cases where the U.S. trustee has the authority to withhold estate tax generated by the distribution), that the trust meet the requirements of regulations prescribed to ensure the collection of estate tax imposed in the trust, and that an election be made by the executor of the decedent's estate. The general rule of § 2056(d)(1) does not apply if the surviving spouse becomes a citizen of the United States before the date of filing the estate tax return and the spouse was a U.S. resident at all times after the decedent's death and before becoming a U.S. citizen. § 2056(d)(4).

The marital deduction is denied in cases where the decedent's surviving spouse is not a citizen so as to insure collection of the estate tax that was avoided when the marital deduction was claimed by the decedent's estate for the property passing to the surviving spouse. Congress apparently believed that there were too many instances where estate taxes were not being collected because noncitizen surviving spouses were leaving the United States—and dying elsewhere—with property for which a marital deduction had been claimed. While there was nothing illegal about the actions of such surviving spouses, the revenue opportunity lost to the United States as a result of such movements must have been too much for Congress to accept.

Example: Marie, a United States citizen and resident, died in 1987 survived by her husband, Pierre, a Canadian citizen but a resident of the United States at the time of Marie's death. As a result of Marie's will, Pierre received all Marie's $3 million estate. No estate taxes were paid at Marie's death, her executor having claimed the marital deduction for the $3 million that passed to Pierre. (Note that Marie died prior to 1988 and the advent of restrictions of the availability of the marital deduction for gifts to surviving spouses who were not citizens of the United States.) Upon receipt of the $3 million, Pierre returned to Canada on a permanent basis where he died in 2001. Since Pierre was a noncitizen nonresident of the United States at his death, no United States estate tax was ever paid on the $3 million (despite the tax benefit enjoyed as a result of the marital deduction at the time of Marie's death in 1987).

The qualified domestic trust authorized in § 2056(d) provides a means by which the marital deduction may be made available if the decedent's surviving spouse is not a citizen. At the death of the surviving spouse, all the property then in the trust will be subject to estate tax as if it had been taxed to the deceased spouse at the earlier death of the deceased spouse, with the rate of tax being determined by reference to the estate of the decedent rather than to the estate of the surviving spouse. § 2056A(b). Furthermore, any distributions from the qualified domestic trust to the surviving spouse during the lifetime of the surviving spouse in excess of the trust income (or for reasons other than hardship or reimbursement of the spouse for federal income tax on undistributed trust income) are to be subjected to the federal estate tax and taxed as if they were a part of the estate of the deceased spouse (at the marginal rate of tax applicable to the deceased spouse). The federal estate tax on such distributions is to be paid on April 15th of the year following the date of the taxable distribution. The trustee of the qualified domestic trust is personally liable for the estate tax on the qualified domestic trust and distributions from it. § 2056A(b)(6).

Obviously, there will be cases where property passes free of trust from a deceased citizen to a noncitizen surviving spouse with the resulting payment of estate taxes at the death of the citizen spouse. Clearly, harshness would result if the noncitizen surviving spouse did the unexpected and remained a resident of the United States until his or her death inasmuch as the property that the surviving spouse received from the decedent would be subject to estate tax at the death of the surviving spouse to the extent that the surviving spouse had not consumed it or disposed of it. Accordingly, a credit is available to the surviving spouse for the estate tax paid at the death of the first spouse to die. § 2056(d)(3).

Also, property passing to a noncitizen surviving spouse free of trust could be placed in a Qualified Domestic Trust by the surviving spouse. § 2056(d)(2)(B). Moreover, nothing prevents a surviving spouse from creating a Qualified Domestic Trust for this purpose (in cases where the deceased spouse had not provided for such a trust). Furthermore, a nonqualifying trust can be reformed to qualify as a Qualified Domestic Trust. § 2056(d)(4).

D. PART OF GROSS ESTATE

[¶ 27,061]

The property given to the surviving spouse for which the marital deduction is claimed must be included in determining the value of the deceased spouse's gross estate. § 2056(a). The marital deduction is not allowed for property not included in the decedent's gross estate.

E. SURVIVING SPOUSE

[¶ 27,067]

1. LEGAL STATUS

The decedent must have left a surviving spouse who takes the property for which the marital deduction is claimed. The term "surviving spouse" has been defined by the IRS as "a legal status that arises from the termination of a lawful marital union by the death of the other mate." Rev. Rul. 76–155, 1976–1 C.B. 286. Status as a surviving spouse is to be determined "from the best evidence available." Thus, the IRS ruled that the marital deduction was not available for payments made to a person claiming to be the surviving spouse of the decedent where the payments were made in compromise of a dispute as to whether a valid common law marriage existed. The alleged spouse claimed a dower interest in the decedent's property. The IRS concluded that "evidence submitted does not support the conclusion that the alleged spouse was decedent's legal surviving spouse" despite the fact that the payments were made as a result of a good faith, arm's-length compromise of the claim.

The Defense of Marriage Act bars recognition of same sex marriage for federal tax purposes. 1 USC Chap. 1, § 7.

[¶ 27,073]

2. VALIDITY OF DIVORCE WITH RESPECT TO STATUS AS SPOUSE

It is not uncommon for the availability of the marital deduction to depend on the validity of a divorce decree obtained by either the deceased spouse or the surviving spouse. For example, a marriage of persons who are not validly divorced from their previous spouses is invalid for both tax and nontax purposes. As a result, in such cases, for example, the "true" surviving spouse is the spouse from whom the decedent is invalidly divorced and not the person to whom the decedent is invalidly married. Estate of Goldwater, 539 F.2d 878 (2d Cir.), cert. denied sub nom., Lipkowitz v. Commissioner, 429 U.S. 1023 (1976). Moreover, the validity of the divorce for federal estate tax purposes will be determined by the law applicable in the jurisdiction in which the decedent was domiciled at his or her death. The test was set out in Estate of Steffke, 538 F.2d 730 (7th Cir.), cert. denied sub nom., Wisconsin Valley Trust Co. v. Commissioner, 429 U.S. 1022 (1976), where the court said:

> When there are conflicting judicial decrees regarding the validity of a divorce, the decision should be followed for federal estate tax purposes that would be followed by the state which has primary jurisdiction over the administration of a decedent's estate, i.e., the jurisdiction in which the decedent was domiciled at the time of his death.

[¶ 27,079]

3. CLOSE ORDER OF DEATHS AND PRESUMPTIONS OF SURVIVORSHIP

In cases where two persons both die and it cannot be determined which of them died first, state law will ordinarily supply a presumption as to the order of deaths, which will be recognized for purposes of the marital deduction. See, e.g., Reg. § 20.2056(c)–2(e); Rev. Rul. 66–60, 1966–1 C.B. 221 (simultaneous death of joint tenants). Many states presume that where there is no sufficient evidence of the order of deaths, each decedent will be presumed to have survived the other decedent. (Under the Uniform Probate Code, unless there is clear and convincing evidence that one decedent survived the other decedent by 120 hours, each decedent is presumed to have survived the other.) For purposes of the marital deduction, in cases where there is uncertainty as to the order of deaths, a presumption of survivorship included in the will of one of the decedents will be respected (unless a provision of the applicable state law bars such a provision). See Reg. § 20.2056(c)–2(e). To illustrate, if both Tony and Marsha die and there is uncertainty as to the order of their deaths, a gift to Marsha in Tony's will is eligible for the marital deduction if Tony's will states, for example, that "Marsha shall be deemed to survive me where the order of our deaths cannot be determined without reference to judicial proceedings."

F. PASSING TO SURVIVING SPOUSE

[¶ 27,085]

The marital deduction is available only as to property that "passes or has passed" to the surviving spouse from the decedent in a manner contemplated by § 2056. § 2056(a). Section 2056(c) purports to list the types of transfers from the decedent that satisfy the passing requirement. Note, too, Reg. § 20.2056(c)–2(a), which, perhaps, could be viewed as broadening the scope of passing. In the meantime, as you consider the alternatives presented below that qualify for the marital deduction, remember that an outright and unconditional bequest or devise of property has always been available as a completely secure way of obtaining the marital deduction.

1. POST MORTEM SURRENDER OF JOINT PROPERTY, SURVIVOR'S STATUTORY SHARE

[¶ 27,091]

SCHROEDER v. UNITED STATES

United States Court of Appeals, Tenth Circuit, 1991.
924 F.2d 1547.

PER CURIAM.

This is a case of first impression in the area of federal estate tax. A surviving spouse surrendered her survivorship rights to property held in joint tenancy with her husband, and her statutory-election rights to the decedent's property, in settlement of a controversy with decedent's daughters from a previous marriage concerning her entitlement to the property. At issue is whether that property nevertheless "passed" to her within the meaning of the marital deduction statute, § 2056(a), (d). The District Court for the Western District of Oklahoma determined on summary judgment that such property in these circumstances does not pass to the surviving spouse and accordingly disallowed the marital deduction. Schroeder v. United States, 696 F.Supp. 1426 (W.D.Okla.1988). We agree with the district court and affirm.

I.

Thomas J. Woodmansee (Thomas) was married to Peggy Woodmansee (Peggy) for approximately eighteen years, and had two adult daughters from a previous marriage, Martha Schroeder (Martha) and Lou Ann Waters (Lou). On July 6, 1981, Thomas created a substantial stock account, naming himself and Peggy as joint tenants with a right of survivorship. Neither of his daughters was aware of the creation of this account. On July 16, 1981, Thomas signed a will providing that his property be placed in a trust, the income from which was to be used to provide for Peggy for the remainder of her life. After Peggy's death, the corpus of the trust was to be divided equally between Martha and Lou, or their issue, keeping the property in the family. On the same day, Thomas deeded the family farm over to Martha and Lou. Both of the daughters stated by affidavit that they knew of the provisions of the will and of their father's intent and that both intended to honor their father's wishes. In addition, both daughters stated that Thomas was mentally competent at all times during his life.

Thomas died two months later. At the time of his death, the fair market value of the stock account was approximately $229,843. Later that month, Martha and Lou learned for the first time that Thomas had created the joint stock account, which was wholly and independently owned by Peggy and would not pass through Thomas' will. Relations between Peggy and Thomas' daughters were strained by this revelation. In their affidavits, Martha and Lou stated that they thought Peggy had a "moral duty" to leave the principal of the stock account to them and their children.

The will was admitted to probate and Harry D. Schroeder (Schroeder), Martha's husband, was named executor. Martha and Lou were advised by an attorney to negotiate with Peggy concerning the stock account, and their attorney entered into discussions with Peggy's attorney. In February 1982, in settlement of these discussions, Peggy placed the stock account into a trust account with a neutral trustee. Quarterly income from the trust is divided among the three women, one-fourth to Peggy and three-fourths divided equally between Martha and Lou, or their issue, until Peggy's death. At that time, the principal in the trust account is to be distributed equally to Martha and Lou, or their issue.

In April 1982, Peggy filed her election to take the statutory spousal share of the estate rather than take under the will. At the time of Thomas' death, the spousal election, one-third of the estate, had a fair market value of $77,121. Peggy deposited the spousal share into the trust account, under the conditions for distribution set forth for the stock account.

When Schroeder filed the estate tax return, he included the joint stock account and the spousal election share in the estate, pursuant to §§ 2033, 2040(a). He also claimed them as part of the federal marital deduction, pursuant to § 2056. The IRS issued Schroeder a notice of deficiency after it disallowed the marital deduction with respect to the stock account and Peggy's statutory share of the estate. Schroeder paid the deficiency and claimed a refund, which the IRS denied. Schroeder then brought this action.

* * *

¶ 27,091

* * * [I]nterpretive regulations provide that property surrendered by a surviving spouse in settlement of a controversy over a decedent's will is constructively deemed not to have "passed" to such spouse. Treas. Reg. § 20.2056(e)–2(d)(1)(will contest regulation). This regulation is consistent with the legislative history of the code section:

> If the surviving spouse takes under the decedent's will, the interest passing to her is determined from the will. In this connection proper regard should be given to interpretations of the will rendered by a court in a bona fide adversary proceeding. If as a result of a controversy involving a bequest or devise to the surviving spouse, such spouse assigns or surrenders an interest in property pursuant to a compromise agreement in settlement of such controversy, the amount so assigned or surrendered is not deductible as an interest passing to such spouse.

S. Rep. No. 1013 Part 2, 80th Cong., 2d Sess. 4 (1948), reprinted in 4 Rabkin & Johnson at 5344.

This statutory and regulatory scheme is built upon the fundamental rule that state law determines what property interest individuals hold, and federal law determines how that property shall be taxed. * * * Thus, federal law controls whether property "passes" from the estate of a deceased individual for the purposes of the federal estate tax.

The IRS and the district court relied heavily on United States Trust Co. v. Commissioner, 321 F.2d 908 (2d Cir.1963), and Citizens & Southern Nat'l Bank v. United States, 451 F.2d 221 (5th Cir.1971). These cases involved situations in which the surviving spouse and a beneficiary reached an agreement modifying the estate which would have otherwise passed to the surviving spouse.

* * *

These two cases invoked policy to expand the reach of Treas. Reg. § 20.2056(e)–2(d)(1) well beyond its plain language. *Citizens & Southern* defined "the decedent's will, or involving any bequest or devise thereunder" to include transfers of property at death under intestacy statutes or spousal election. Both cases expanded the terms "will contest" or "controversy" to include arm's-length negotiations conducted between parties who have potentially adverse positions. Under this view, no litigation is required, much less court adjudication of various parties' rights to the property of the deceased.

Peggy's rights in the present case to a statutory share of the probate estate and to the joint account do not arise under Thomas' will. It is undisputed that Peggy surrendered this property in settlement not of a will contest, but of a more general controversy over the rightful passing of Thomas' property considered as a whole. [The court explained, in a footnote, that Peggy's rights "derive from state law" that gave Peggy a statutorily determined spousal share notwithstanding her husband's will.] By its plain terms, therefore, the will contest regulation is not dispositive here. In the absence of an applicable regulation, we must look directly to the relevant provisions of the Internal Revenue Code.

¶ 27,091

As previously discussed, section 2056(a) requires that property "pass" from the decedent to his or her surviving spouse to claim the marital deduction. The meaning of this term is dispositive of this appeal. Clearly, transfers of property under spousal election statutes and by survivorship rights concerning joint interests may "pass" within the meaning of the marital deduction provision. See § 2056(d)(3) and (5). The issue in this case is whether the *rationale* for the Secretary's regulatory gloss on the passing requirement in the context of a will contest mandates a similar result based on an analysis of the term "passes" in the marital deduction statute.

In *United States Trust Co.*, the court noted that the statutory "passing" requirement is "crucial in qualifying property for a marital deduction." 321 F.2d at 910. It held that "[w]hen the resolution of a controversy between the beneficiaries regarding the decedent's property culminates in an agreement by which the surviving spouse relinquishes property which qualifies for the marital deduction in return for property which does not so qualify, [the will-contest regulation] is applicable." Id. In essence, the court defined "passing" to mean property to which the surviving spouse retains her rights after resolution of all disputes concerning the decedent's property. The court in *Citizens & Southern* agreed with this definition of passing in concluding that "the medium by which the decedent's property passes * * * is immaterial." 451 F.2d at 227.

Both courts also properly disregarded the significance of the surviving spouse's acquisition of "vested" rights under state law in determining whether the property "passed" for purposes of the marital deduction. See United States Trust, 321 F.2d at 910 (vesting under state law has no bearing on interpretation of federal passing requirement); Citizens & Southern, 451 F.2d at 228 ("acquisition and subsequent relinquishment of 'vested' rights in no way renders the 'will controversy' regulation inapplicable"). Indeed, a contrary view arguably would transgress the Supreme Court's holding in Lyeth v. Hoey, 305 U.S. 188, 193–94 (1938), that federal law controls the incidence of federal taxation of property acquired under state law.

Unlike the district court and the courts in *United States Trust* and *Citizens & Southern*, we believe the will-contest regulation is inapplicable to property passing to a surviving spouse by statutory election or under the law of survivorship because the regulation speaks only in terms of a controversy involving a bequest or devise under decedent's will. Nonetheless, we find the reasons those courts articulated to broaden the reach of the regulation to be persuasive in our own analysis of what Congress intended by the "passing" requirement in the marital deduction statute. To the extent a surviving spouse surrenders her share of the decedent's property to other beneficiaries not entitled to the marital deduction to avoid litigation concerning her rights, it defies common sense to conclude that this property "passed" to the surviving spouse. Not only is the ultimate recipient of the property a person other than the surviving spouse, but the transfer comprising the settlement could altogether escape taxation applying to gratuitous transfers of wealth.

In creating the marital deduction, Congress envisioned a scheme in which interspousal transfers of wealth would not result in a taxable event. See S.

Rep. No. 97–144, 97th Cong., 1st Sess. 126, reprinted in 1981 U.S. Code & Cong. Admin. News 105, 228 ("a husband and wife should be treated as one economic unit for purposes of estate and gift taxes, as they generally are for income tax purposes. Accordingly, no tax should be imposed on transfers between a husband and wife."). The marital deduction was designed to eliminate the "double-taxation" that would result when the same property became subject to tax upon the death of each spouse. Once property passes outside of the interspousal unit, however, this exception no longer applies. Under Schroeder's proposed interpretation, property may exit the spousal unit without ever creating a taxable event. Congress clearly did not intend to replace double-taxation with tax avoidance.

Accordingly, we hold that the property comprising Peggy's statutory election and the joint account did not "pass" to her within the meaning of the marital deduction statute. Instead, Peggy surrendered her entitlement to this property in settlement of a bona fide controversy concerning her rights to the property in the decedent's gross estate for federal estate tax purposes. We therefore AFFIRM the district court.

Note

[¶ 27,094]

The *Schroeder* court noted that Peggy's transfer could "altogether escape taxation applying to transfers of wealth" if she were allowed the marital deduction. In a footnote, the court noted Peggy's claim that she had no gift tax liability for the transfer in settlement of the controversy because the "avoidance of litigation over her rights was appropriate consideration for the transfer." Do you agree? Similarly, the court noted, Peggy claimed that she realized neither gain nor loss on sale "when she transferred the joint tenancy account to the trust even though the premise of [the] * * * argument here is that the property 'passed' to her prior to transfer." Does this position make sense?

[¶ 27,097]

2. INTERESTS ACQUIRED POST-MORTEM REQUIRE ENFORCE-ABLE RIGHTS SURRENDER

In Estate of Brandon v. Commissioner, 91 T.C. 829 (1988), the Tax Court concluded that the marital deduction was limited to $25,000, the amount of the pecuniary bequest to the decedent's surviving spouse, Chanoy. The marital deduction had been claimed for $90,000, the amount actually paid to Chanoy by the decedent's estate in settlement of litigation that arose over Chanoy's election to take a surviving spouse's share under the applicable Arkansas statute rather than under the decedent's will. The Tax Court denied the marital deduction for the full $90,000 on the ground that Chanoy did not have an enforceable right to a surviving spouse's share at the time of the settlement because the Arkansas statute on which Chanoy premised her claim was unconstitutional. Thus, the Court reasoned, any property passing to Chanoy—other than the $25,000 legacy to her in the decedent's will—passed to her as a result of the litigation settlement and not under the decedent's will as required for the marital deduction. At the time of the settlement agreement, the Arkansas statute on which Chanoy had based her claim had not been declared unconstitutional. However, in an earlier decision on the same case, Estate of Brandon v. Commissioner, 828 F.2d 493 (8th Cir.1987), an appeal from an even earlier Tax Court decision in the same case (reported at 86 T.C. 327 (1986)), the Eighth Circuit decided that "either a good faith settlement or a judgment of a lower state court must be based on an enforceable right, under state law properly interpreted, in order to qualify as 'passing' pursuant to the estate tax marital deduction." The Eighth Circuit specifically rejected the notion that the appropriate test was "whether or not the settlement agreement was made as the result of good faith, arm's-length negotiations." Looking to the *Bosch* case (¶ 1,107), the Eighth Circuit relied on the result reached in Ahmanson Foundation v. United States, 674 F.2d 761 (9th Cir.1981), explaining its decision and describing the facts of *Ahmanson* in these terms:

> * * * In that case the decedent left a trust agreement giving his surviving spouse the sum of $5,000,000. Following his death, the surviving spouse argued that she also was entitled to an additional amount in satisfaction of her community property rights. This claim was negotiated and settled for the additional sum of $750,000. As in the present case, the estate claimed the full settlement payment as part of the estate tax marital deduction. The government disallowed deduction of the settlement payment, arguing that under state law the surviving spouse did not have an enforceable right to receive any amount of property beyond the $5,000,000 left to her under the terms of decedent's trust. The estate argued, however, that where a private good faith settlement of the surviving spouse's claims against the estate is the result of a genuine adversary proceeding and is approved by the state court, then the settlement agreement should be considered a bona fide recognition of enforceable rights of the surviving spouse and binding for federal estate tax purposes.

> In considering the enforceability issue raised by the government, the Ninth Circuit carefully examined the holding of *Bosch*, noting that "the majority [of the Supreme Court] concluded that the test of 'passing' for estate tax purposes should be whether the interest reaches the spouse pursuant to state law, correctly interpreted [by the federal court]—not whether it reached the spouse as a result of a good faith adversary confrontation." Id. at 774. The court agreed with the government that if a state court adjudication as a result of a good faith adversary proceeding is not binding for estate tax purposes pursuant to *Bosch*, then a private good faith settlement cannot be either. The court found that under *Bosch* the issue of deductibility turned on whether the settlement payment was made pursuant to an enforceable right, i.e., whether state law entitled the surviving spouse to at least $750,000 of property above and beyond the $5,000,000 given to her under decedent's trust. The court opined that the evidence did not support any conclusion that the settlement payment was based upon an enforceable right under state law. The court therefore

remanded the case to the district court for a determination of whether state law supported the additional payment made to the surviving spouse.

We agree with the Ninth Circuit's analysis and application of the principles set forth in *Bosch* with respect to good faith settlements of a surviving spouse's claims against the estate. * * *

Bosch and *Ahmanson* support the conclusion that the Tax Court was required, in this instance, to make an independent determination as to the enforceability of Chanoy Brandon's dower claims against the estate under state law at the time the settlement was reached. Specifically, the Tax Court was required to consider the constitutionality of the Arkansas dower statute at the time of settlement * * *.

Turn, now, to a different situation. Suppose that the surviving spouse and other will beneficiaries decide not to probate the decedent's will and, as a result, all the decedent's property passes to the surviving spouse under the applicable intestate statute (rather than to the spouse and other beneficiaries under the will). Would the property passing to the spouse in such an eventuality qualify for the marital deduction? Not in the opinion of the IRS. Technical Advice Memorandum 9610004 concludes that the marital deduction must be denied in these circumstances because the property passed to the spouse not "from the decedent" but by virtue of the agreement among the will beneficiaries not to probate the will and the subsequent approval of that agreement by the probate court having jurisdiction. The marital deduction is allowed in such circumstances only if the agreement not to probate resulted from settlement of a controversy based on an underlying legally enforceable claim that the will beneficiaries planned to assert. In the situation considered by the IRS, there was no allegation that the agreement was the result of such a conflict. See Reg. § 20.2056(c)–2(d)(2).

By way of contrast, the marital deduction was allowed for an amount distributed free of trust to the surviving spouse who had surrendered her interest in a trust created for her benefit by her deceased spouse. Priv. Ltr. Rul. 9733017. The payment resulted from an agreement in compromise with those challenging the testator's will on grounds he lacked testamentary capacity, the IRS explaining that the surviving spouse had an enforceable right to the value of the trust that would have been created for her benefit under the will of the deceased spouse. The claim was described as having been asserted in good faith and the settlement resulted from an arm's length negotiation—even though it was arrived at without court action. Similarly, the marital deduction was allowed for amounts set aside in trust for the surviving spouse as a result of an agreement compromising her claim that the premarital agreement she signed 12 days prior to marriage was invalid. Priv. Ltr. Rul. 9251002. However, the marital deduction was limited to the value of the property she would have received had she exercised her right to elect against the decedent's will (even though the value of the property placed in trust for the surviving spouse exceeded the value of the property she would have received had she exercised her statutory rights).

¶ 27,097

Problem

[¶ 27,099]

Beth is preparing Dick's estate tax return and worries that the marital deduction may not be allowed for the gift to Jane, Dick's surviving spouse. The cause of her worry is an *in terrorem* clause in the will, *i.e.,* a clause that cancels the gift of each beneficiary who participates in any contest of Dick's will, regardless of probable cause, good faith, or subsequent withdrawal of the contest. Another clause provides that if a court rules the *in terrorem* clause to be invalid, any expenses incurred in defending any such contest are to be paid from the amounts that would have been paid to the contestants. Can you put Beth's mind at ease? See *Mackie v. Commissioner*, 64 T.C. 308 (1975), *aff'd,* 545 F.2d 883 (4th Cir.1976); Priv. Ltr. Ruls. 9036040, and 8936009; Tech. Adv. Mems. 8735003 and 8727002.

[¶ 27,103]

3. MARITAL DEDUCTION PROPERTY NOT DISTRIBUTED TO SPOUSE

Distribution of the property included in the estate of a decedent to the estate's beneficiaries is not often accomplished prior to the completion of the audit of the federal estate tax return (in cases where a federal estate tax return is required). Moreover, in many states, policing the distribution of the decedent's property is left to the estate's beneficiaries (rather than to the courts, as in some states). As a result, there are isolated instances in which the distribution called for by the decedent's will is not made—usually with the acquiescence of the beneficiary. For example, from the standpoint of the surviving spouse, not claiming the property for which the marital deduction was allowed may appear to be a means of keeping the marital property out of the surviving spouse's gross estate at the surviving spouse's death. However, in Rev. Rul. 84-105, 1984-2 C.B. 197, the IRS has concluded that the surviving spouse, in such a case, will be deemed to have made a taxable gift of the unclaimed amount—but the marital deduction itself will not be impaired.

G. NONDEDUCTIBLE TERMINABLE INTERESTS

[¶ 27,115]

The most troublesome of all the requirements for allowance of the marital deduction is the statutory provision that the interest for which the marital deduction is claimed must not be a nondeductible terminable interest, with its several complex exceptions. In view of the fact that the half interest of the surviving spouse in the community property of the couple is an outright interest, it was the general plan of the Congress to restrict the marital deduction to outright bequests, i.e., nonterminable interests. However, in effectuating this objective, Congress quickly lost sight of this concept of equivalence. Section 2056(b)(1) provides that the interest going to the surviving spouse must not be one which may terminate or fail on the lapse of time or on the occurrence or nonoccurrence of an event or contingency; thus, a life estate, a term for years, a patent or copyright, or a conditional interest would be terminable and subject to disallowance. However, the statute does not disallow all terminable interests; it disallows only those terminable interests which are coupled with either of the following conditions:

1. Another interest in the same property, in which the surviving spouse holds his or her interest, is given or has been given to a third party by the decedent, and by reason of such interest, the third party may possess or enjoy the property after the termination or failure of such spouse's interest, or

2. The terminable interest of the surviving spouse was directed by the decedent to be acquired by the executor or by a trustee.

The first condition would bar all life estates or conditional interests to the spouse in property in which others are given a remainder interest by the decedent that may be enjoyed after the spouse's interest ceases. The second condition strikes down all terminable interests that the decedent directs his or her executor or a trustee to acquire for the surviving spouse, such as the purchase of a life estate or an annuity, without regard to whether interests in the property are held by others.

From an historical standpoint, it is useful to note that the nondeductible terminable interest rule was necessary to accomplish rough equivalence between community property and separate property for transfer tax purposes while allowing persons with separate property to control the disposition of that property while claiming the marital deduction (a privilege not available to person's dying with community property). See ¶ 27,007. With the advent, in 1981, of the rule permitting tax free transfers between spouses, the nondeductible terminable interest rule continues to be of importance in preventing "leakage" by denying the marital deduction in cases where the property will not be included in the estate of the surviving spouse at his or her later death.

[¶ 27,121]

1. SPOUSAL AWARD

Most, if not all, states make provision for the surviving spouse by way of an allowance to be paid from the estate of the decedent before distribution of the decedent's property pursuant to the decedent's will. Normally, this statutory allowance or award is in addition to any provision in favor of the spouse in the decedent's will or provided to the spouse by the intestate laws in cases where the decedent has died intestate. In many states, payment of the spousal award or allowance is conditioned upon the spouse making claim to the award and the court having jurisdiction over the estate entering an order setting the amount of the award. Whether such awards qualify for the marital deduction is an almost never-ending controversy as the litigation marches through the states.

¶ 27,121

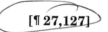

[¶ 27,127]

JACKSON v. UNITED STATES

Supreme Court of the United States, 1964.
376 U.S. 503.

MR. JUSTICE WHITE delivered the opinion of the Court.

Since 1948 § 812(e)(1)(A) [1986 Code § 2056(a)] of the Internal Revenue Code of 1939 has allowed a "marital deduction" from a decedent's gross taxable estate for the value of interests in property passing from the decedent to his surviving spouse. Subsection (B) adds the qualification, however, that interests defined therein as "terminable" shall not qualify as an interest in property to which the marital deduction applies. The question raised by this case is whether the allowance provided by California law for the support of a widow during the settlement of her husband's estate is a terminable interest.

Petitioners are the widow-executrix and testamentary trustee under the will of George Richards who died a resident of California on May 27, 1951. Acting under the Probate Code of California, the state court, on June 30, 1952, allowed Mrs. Richards the sum of $3,000 per month from the corpus of the estate for her support and maintenance, beginning as of May 27, 1951, and continuing for a period of 24 months from that date. Under the terms of the order, an allowance of $42,000 had accrued during the 14 months since her husband's death. This amount, plus an additional $3,000 per month for the remainder of the two-year period, making a total of $72,000, was in fact paid to Mrs. Richards as widow's allowance.

On the federal estate tax return filed on behalf of the estate, the full $72,000 was claimed as a marital deduction under § 812(e) of the Internal Revenue Code of 1939. The deduction was disallowed, as was a claim for refund after payment of the deficiency, and the present suit for refund was then brought in the District Court. The District Court granted summary judgment for the United States, holding * * * that the allowance to the widow was a terminable interest and not deductible under the marital provision * * *. The Court of Appeals affirmed * * *. For the reasons given below, we affirm the decision of the Court of Appeals.

* * * The issue * * * is whether the interest in property passing to Mrs. Richards as widow's allowance would "terminate or fail" upon the "lapse of time, upon the occurrence of an event or contingency, or upon the failure of an event or contingency to occur." [1939 Code § 812(e)(1)(B); 1986 Code § 2056(b)(1)]

We accept the Court of Appeals description of the nature and characteristics of the widow's allowance under California law. In that State, the right to a widow's allowance is not a vested right and nothing accrues before the order granting it. The right to an allowance is lost when the one for whom it is asked has lost the status upon which the right depends. If a widow dies or remarries prior to securing an order for a widow's allowance, the right does not survive such death or remarriage. The amount of the widow's allowance which has accrued and is unpaid at the date of death of the widow is payable to her estate but the right to future payments abates upon her death. The remarriage of a widow subsequent to an order for an allowance likewise abates her right to future payments. 317 F.2d 821, 825.

In light of these characteristics of the California widow's allowance, Mrs. Richards did not have an indefeasible interest in property at the moment of her husband's death since either her death or remarriage would defeat it. If the order for support allowance had been entered on the day of her husband's death, her death or remarriage at any time within two years thereafter would terminate that portion of the interest allocable to the remainder of the two-year period. As of the date of Mr. Richards' death, therefore, the allowance was subject to failure or termination "upon the occurrence of an event or contingency." That the support order was entered in this case 14 months later does not, in our opinion, change the defeasible nature of the interest.

Petitioners ask us to judge the terminability of the widow's interest in property represented by her allowance as of the date of the Probate Court's order rather than as of the date of her husband's death. The court's order, they argue, unconditionally entitled the widow to $42,000 in accrued allowance of which she could not be deprived by either her death or remarriage. It is true that some courts have followed this path, but it is difficult to accept an approach which would allow a deduction of $42,000 on the facts of this case, a deduction of $72,000 if the order had been entered at the end of two years from Mr. Richards' death and none at all if the order had been entered immediately upon his death. Moreover, judging deductibility as of the date of the Probate Court's order ignores the Senate Committee's admonition that in considering terminability of an interest for purposes of a marital deduction "the situation is viewed as at the date of the decedent's death." S.Rep. No. 1013, Part 2, 80th Cong., 2d Sess., p. 10. We prefer the * * * [view which] is in accord with the rule uniformly followed with regard to interests other than the widow's allowance, that qualification for the marital deduction must be determined as of the time of death.

Our conclusion is confirmed by § 812(e)(1)(D) [1986 Code § 2056(b)(3)], which saves from the operation of the terminable interest rule interests which by their terms may (but do not in fact) terminate only upon failure of the widow to survive her husband for a period not in excess of six months. The premise of this provision is that an interest passing to a widow is normally to be judged as of the time of the testator's death rather than at a later time when the condition imposed may be satisfied; hence the necessity to provide an exception to the rule in the case of a six months' survivorship contingency in a will. A gift conditioned upon eight months' survivorship, rather than six, is a nondeductible terminable interest for reasons which also disqualify the statutory widow's allowance in California where the widow must survive and remain unmarried at least to the date of an allowance order to become indefeasibly entitled to any widow's allowance at all.

Petitioners contend, however, that the sole purpose of the terminable interest provisions of the Code is to assure that interests deducted from the estate of the deceased spouse will not also escape taxation in the estate of the survivor. This argument leads to the conclusion that since it is now clear that

¶ 27,127

unless consumed or given away during Mrs. Richard's life, the entire $72,000 will be taxed to her estate, it should not be included in her husband's. But as we have already seen, there is no provision in the Code for deducting all terminable interests which become nonterminable at a later date and therefore taxable in the estate of the surviving spouse if not consumed or transferred. The examples cited in the legislative history make it clear that the determinative factor is not taxability to the surviving spouse but terminability as defined by the statute. Under the view advanced by petitioners all cash allowances actually paid would fall outside § 812(e)(1)(B) [1986 Code § 2056(b)(1)]; on two different occasions the Senate has refused to give its approval to House-passed amendments to the 1954 Code which would have made the terminable interest rule inapplicable to all widows' allowances actually paid within specified periods of time.

We are mindful that the general goal of the marital deduction provisions was to achieve uniformity of federal estate tax impact between those States with community property laws and those without them. But the device of the marital deduction which Congress chose to achieve uniformity was knowingly hedged with limitations, including the terminable interest rule. These provisions may be imperfect devices to achieve the desired end, but they are the means which Congress chose. To the extent it was thought desirable to modify the rigors of the terminable-interest rule, exceptions to the rule were written into the Code. Courts should hesitate to provide still another exception by straying so far from the statutory language as to allow a marital deduction for the widow's allowance provided by the California statute. The achievement of the purposes of the marital deduction is dependent to a great degree upon the careful drafting of wills; we have no fear that our decision today will prevent either the full utilization of the marital deduction or the proper support of widows during the pendency of an estate proceeding.

Affirmed.

Note

[¶ 27,133]

1. Under *Jackson*, the spousal award or allowance provided by the laws of most states will be disallowed as a marital deduction because of the contingency of remarriage or death. Similarly, where the state statute is designed to provide support to the surviving spouse for the period of administration, as is the usual case, a major change in the circumstances of the surviving spouse, such as subsequent remarriage or death, would affect the amount or the continuance of the payments, thus constituting a terminable interest. However, the marital deduction has been allowed for the spousal allowance in several cases. Estate of Green v. United States, 441 F.2d 303 (6th Cir.1971); Estate of Watson v. Commissioner, 94 T.C. 262 (1990). In both cases, under applicable state law (Michigan and Mississippi, respectively), the spousal allowance could have been lost if the spouse had failed to petition the court for the allowance. Moreover, the amount of the allowance was not fixed, the court having authority to set the amount of the allowance in each case.

¶ 27,127

Both courts rejected the argument that the allowances awarded to the respective spouses were terminable interests. Judge Hamblen of the Tax Court explained in *Watson*:

> * * * We agree with the Sixth Circuit that "To hold that an interest is terminable only because legal procedures are invoked to enforce an interest which is otherwise vested at the date of the husband's death, is to hold that all elective rights, such as the widow's allowance and the statutory interest in lieu of dower, are disqualified as marital deductions." Estate of Green v. United States, 441 F.2d at 308. Without a clear expression of intent from Congress that all rights such as the Mississippi widow's allowance should be considered terminable interests, we will not treat the necessity of invoking legal procedures as a condition or contingency making the Mississippi widow's allowance a terminable interest for purposes of section 2056. Accordingly, we hold that the requirement under Mississippi law that the chancellor make a final determination of the amount of the allowance and the possibility that the widow may lose her right to the allowance by failing to take some action to request the allowance are not conditions or contingencies that make the Mississippi widow's allowance a terminable interest. Consequently, we hold that the widow's allowance paid to the decedent's widow qualifies for the marital deduction provided in section 2056(a).

2.   Practice varies but states sometimes offer the surviving spouse dower (perhaps a life estate in one-third of the deceased spouse's real estate) or homestead (perhaps a right to occupy the principal residence for life). Whether these interests qualify for the marital deduction—or are nondeductible terminable interests—is sometimes in dispute. See, e.g., First National Exchange Bank of Roanoke v. United States, 335 F.2d 91 (4th Cir.1964)(marital deduction allowed for commuted value of Virginia dower interest where spouse could not be divested of interest once awarded); Estate of Kyle v. Commissioner, 94 T.C. 829 (1990)(marital deduction denied for Texas homestead right where homestead will be lost upon abandonment by spouse at any time).

Problems

[¶ 27,139]

1.   Will the state court's construction of its own spousal award statute be determinative of the issue as to the nature of the award, i.e., whether vested or contingent at death? See *Bosch* (¶ 1,107) and Molner v. United States, 175 F.Supp. 271 (N.D.Ill.1959)(court concluded from Illinois cases that the Illinois spousal award became unconditionally vested at death).

2.   Does the *Jackson* case have implications, as to the vesting of the surviving spouse's interest, that are broader than the spousal award? For example, if the executor has the power to vary the size of the spouse's bequest through electing the alternate valuation date under § 2032 or by taking administration expenses as deductions for income tax purposes rather than on the estate tax return under § 642(g), will such power make the spouse's bequest so contingent as to prevent it from qualifying under the

Jackson rule as to vesting at death? See Rev. Rul. 85–100 1985–2 C.B. 200 (¶ 27,157); ¶ 31,388. Or does this carry the vesting rule too far?

[¶ 27,145]

2. ESTATE TRUST

The so-called "estate trust" is a scheme that qualifies for the marital deduction. See § 20.2056(c)–2(b)(1); Rev. Rul. 68–554, 1968–2 C.B. 412. The challenge, of course, is that the trust is a nondeductible terminable interest. To illustrate, suppose Delbert's will creates a trust for his bride, Kendra, for life. All distributions of income and principal to Kendra are at the discretion of the trustee. The trust terminates at Kendra's death at which time all the undistributed trust property—both income and principal—are to be paid to Kendra's estate for distribution under her will (or to her intestate takers if she has no will). The estate trust is not a nondeductible terminable interest because "no interest" in the trust property passes to anyone other than the surviving spouse or her estate—and, accordingly, Delbert's trust for Kendra qualifies for the marital deduction.

For the controlling spouse, the estate trust has appeal. It qualifies for the marital deduction but the surviving spouse enjoys the trust benefits only at the discretion of the trustee. While there is risk that the surviving spouse by will can make a disfavored disposition of the trust property, that is a risk that the controlling spouse may accept as the price of the marital deduction. Furthermore, prior to 1986 (when the income tax rates were restructured), the estate trust often yielded income tax savings since any undistributed income was taxed to the trust and not the surviving spouse. Today, warehousing income in a trust is normally tax disadvantageous. Usually, income tax savings can be realized by distributing the trust income to the surviving spouse who is likely to be in a lower income tax bracket than the trust. See ¶ 31,235.

[¶ 27,150]

3. ALTERNATE VALUATION DATE

As the Supreme Court made clear in Jackson v. United States, 376 U.S. 503 (1964), 1964–2 C.B. 522, which appears at ¶ 28,127, qualification of an interest for the marital deduction is determined at the time of the decedent's death, based on the facts at that time. What then in the situation where the alternate valuation date is elected? Section 2032 allows property to valued as of the "alternate valuation date", i.e., the date in the sixth month following death that numerically corresponds with the date of death. Consider Rev. Rul. 85–100, 1985–2 C.B. 200 where the marital deduction was denied even though the property would be included in the surviving spouse's estate at the spouse's later death. Here are the facts. Call the players Mom, Dad, and child, Bunny. Mom is dead. Her estate includes an annuity contract. Dad is sole beneficiary of the annuity. However, if he dies before Bunny reaches 18, Bunny is substituted for Dad as beneficiary. If Bunny reaches 18 and Dad is still living, she is denied benefits of the annuity and, at Dad's death, any unpaid annuity benefits are paid to Dad's estate. Four months after Mom died, Bunny reached 18—and her contingent right to annuity benefits terminated since Dad was then living. Does the annuity qualify for the marital deduction? Had Bunny predeceased Mom, the annuity for the benefit of Dad would have qualified. However, since Bunny survived, her contingent interest disqualified the annuity for the marital deduction. *But wait*. Mom's executor elected to value Mom's estate as of the date 6 months following Mom's death as permitted using the alternate valuation date rule set out in § 2032(a). Since Bunny had forfeited all rights in the annuity several months before the alternate valuation date—when she reached 18—it was argued that the marital deduction was available to the annuity since it was now clear—as of the valuation date elected—that Dad was the sole beneficiary. Nonetheless, the IRS concluded that Dad's interest in the annuity was a nondeductible terminable interest because Bunny's contingent interest existed at the date of Mom's death. One effect of Rev. Rul. 85–100 is to reaffirm—as if it were necessary—that terminability is determined as of the date of the decedent's death.

[¶ 27,157]

4. LIFE INSURANCE SETTLEMENT OPTIONS

As a general rule—subject to what are known as the exceptions to the nondeductible terminable interest rule, which are set out in § 2056(b) and developed in part later in these materials (beginning at ¶ 27,181)—qualification for the marital deduction turns on: (1) whether any person other than the surviving spouse has an interest in the property for which the marital deduction is claimed; and (2) whether that interest is to take effect in possession and enjoyment after the expiration of the interest of the surviving spouse. The dispute in Meyer v. United States, 364 U.S. 410 (1960), involved an insurance policy—and related to the first requirement. The case is illustrative of the technical requirements of the marital deduction and the difficulty sometimes encountered in satisfying these requirements. In *Meyer*, the insurance company was obligated to make equal monthly payments to the wife for life, with 240 payments guaranteed. If the wife died before receiving all 240 payments, the remaining guaranteed payments would be made to the wife's child. Thus, the child's interest followed the wife's—making the interest of the wife a nondeductible terminable interest. However, the husband's executor, seeking qualification for the marital deduction, advanced a cleaver argument. The executor's argument was based on the insurance company action in making internal bookkeeping entries to reflect the actuarially determined likelihood that payments beyond the guaranteed 240 would be made to the wife. The Court explained (364 U.S. at 411):

> Two policies of life insurance are involved, but since they are in all material respects identical, we need deal with only one of them. The policy obligated the insurer to pay a death benefit of $25,187.50, and that sum was included by the executors in the federal estate tax return and the tax thereon was paid. The decedent had selected an optional mode of settlement which provided for the payment of equal monthly installments

to his wife for her life, with 240 installments guaranteed, and further provided that if the wife should die before receiving the 240 installments his daughter would receive the remainder of them, but if both the wife and the daughter died before receiving the 240 installments the commuted value of those unpaid was to be paid in one sum to the estate of the last one of them to die.

Of the total proceeds of the policy of $25,187.50, the insurer determined that $17,956.41 was necessary to fund the 240 monthly payments to the wife, the daughter, or to the estate of the last survivor of them, and that the remaining $7,231.09 was necessary to fund the monthly payments to the wife so long as she might live beyond the 240 months. Accordingly, the insurer made such entries on its books.

The executor claimed the marital deduction for the $7,231.09, the amount "which the insurer had shown upon its books as necessary to fund the monthly payments to the wife for her actuarial expectancy beyond the 240 months certain, on the theory that the insurer's treatment of that sum on its books created a separate 'property' or fund payable to the wife alone, and hence it qualified for the marital deduction under § 812 (e) (1) [1986 Code § 2056(b)(1)]." However, despite the executor's creativity—and the insurer's bookkeeping entries, the marital deduction was denied on the ground that there was but one property and the interest of the child followed that of the wife in the *same property* and, as a result, the interest of the wife was a nondeductible terminable interest. See § 2056(b)(1). The Court expressed its conclusion that (364 U.S. at 415–16):

> The allocations made were merely actuarial ones—mere bookkeeping entries—made by the insurer on its own books for its own convenience after the insured, the other party to the contract, had died. The wife and the daughter were, respectively, primary and contingent beneficiaries of the policy alone. Neither of them had any title to, nor right to receive, any special fund, and indeed none was actually created. The bookkeeping entries made by the insurer no more created or measured their rights than the insurer's erasure of those entries—which it was free to make at any time—would destroy their rights. Their rights derive solely from the policy. It, not the insurer's bookkeeping entries, created and constitutes the property involved. Any action by the beneficiaries to enforce their rights against the insurer would have to be upon the policy, not upon the entries the insurer had made on its books for its own actuarial information and convenience. * * *
>
> * * * It follows that the "interest passing to the surviving spouse [may] terminate or fail" and that a "person other than [the] surviving spouse * * * may possess or enjoy [a] part of such property after such termination or failure of the interest so passing to the surviving spouse; * * * "and hence the property is disqualified for the marital deduction by the express provisions of § 812 (e)(1)(B) [§ 2056(b)(1)(B)]* * *.

Meyer, if for no other reason, is notable as one of what seem to be too many cases that make it to the Supreme Court for determination as to whether the technical requirements of the marital deduction have been

¶ 27,157

satisfied. The fact specificity of these cases and their number may suggest that the nondeductible terminable interest rule is not only complicated but perhaps too complicated—and that, perhaps, the goal of excusing property from tax at the death of the first spouse to die on condition that it be taxed at the death of the surviving spouse unless consumed or disposed of (by gift) could be otherwise accomplished. Despite the appeal of this observation, note that no part of the policy proceeds in *Meyer* would be includible in the estate of the wife at her later death whether she died before or after receiving the guaranteed 240 payments.

Problem

[¶ 27,161]

Sumi owned a $1 million life insurance policy. The policy stipulated that, at Sumi's death, the policy proceeds would be held by the insurance company for the life of her husband, Denzel, during which time he would be paid interest on the $1 million at market rates. After his death, the $1 million would be paid to his estate for distribution under his will (or to his intestate takers if he had no will). Does the $1 million qualify for the marital deduction at Sumi's death?

H. EXCEPTIONS TO NONDEDUCTIBLE TERMINABLE INTEREST RULE

[¶ 27,181]

Due to the breadth of the rule forbidding nondeductible terminable interests and its serious effect on prior patterns of estate planning, the following important exceptions have been incorporated into the statute.

[¶ 27,187]

1. SURVIVORSHIP

A frequently used provision in pre–1948 wills was a clause designed to avoid multiple administration of estates upon the death of the beneficiary "hard upon the heels" of the testator. Thereunder, a beneficiary dying in a common accident with the testator or within a period of, say, six months of the death of the testator would be considered as having predeceased the testator and thus would not take the gift provided in the will. Inasmuch as such a clause, when applied to the surviving spouse, would result in a nondeductible terminable interest, whether or not the actual deaths occurred as feared, Congress wanted to permit the free use of such a clause. Accordingly, § 2056(b)(3) provides that an interest that will fail if the surviving spouse dies within six months of the decedent's death will not be considered a terminable interest, provided that the deaths do not occur.

However, it should also be noted that a survivorship clause can result in loss of the marital deduction. In Estate of Shepherd v. Commissioner, 58

T.C.M. (CCH) 671, T.C.M. (P–H) ¶ 89,610 (1989), the marital deduction was denied because the surviving spouse was required to survive until the decedent's will was "admitted to probate." The spouse did, in fact, survive until the will was probated, but the marital deduction was denied because

> the possibility existed at the time of the decedent's death that the will might have been admitted to probate beyond the 6–month exception to the terminable interest rule contained in § 2056(b)(3) and that the surviving spouse's interest might have terminated and passed to someone else at a point in time thereafter.

The Court said that "the probate of a will has substantive significance and cannot be considered as merely a ministerial act or a method of perfecting title." And, in Rev. Rul. 88–90, 1988–2 C.B. 335, the IRS denied the marital deduction where the spouse was required to survive until a trust provided for in the will was funded. The IRS said that, "due to the requirements of local probate law, the possibility exists at the time of the decedent's death that the funding may occur more than 6 months after the decedent's death."

> By way of contrast, in Priv. Ltr. Rul. 8809003, the marital deduction was allowed where the surviving spouse was required to survive "for a sufficient length of time to receive" the decedent's property. The IRS explained that the "surviving spouse was competent to serve as Independent Executrix upon the decedent's death, and did in fact assume the position" and for this reason, the surviving spouse:

> > had the unqualified right to initiate and complete probate proceedings immediately under local law without the need for the probate court to respond or take any further action with respect to the acts of the surviving spouse.

Important to the IRS's determination was the freedom from court supervision that an independent executor enjoyed under Texas law after probating the will and filing the inventory and list of claims in cases such as this where the decedent's will specifically states that no further action is needed in the probate court.

> Examples of results adverse to taxpayers seeking to have the marital deduction allowed for gifts conditioned on survivorship are numerous. Witness Tech. Adv. Mem. 8834002 where a clause providing that a decedent's wife was to receive property only if she survived distribution of the estate was ruled to be a contingent interest that did not qualify for the marital deduction. See Reg. § 20.2056(b)–3(d), Example (4). But cases like Estate of Bond v. Commissioner, 104 T.C. 652 (1995), cause hope to spring eternal in the breast of the creatively assertive taxpayer. There, state property law rules saved the marital deduction despite the will's requirement that the spouse "survive distribution." Looking to Washington law, the Tax Court concluded that, since title to real property vests at death, the words "survive distribution" are, practically speaking, without meaning. To the court, there can be no distribution of that which has already vested. Thus, so long as the testator

¶ 27,187

intended Washington law to apply, in the case of gifts of real property, presence of the words "survive distribution" will not bar the marital deduction. Contrasted, though, is personal property which the Tax Court found did not vest in Washington until actual distribution. (Interestingly, the Tax Court found inapplicable a Washington statute—one claimed to be shared with California—that banned application of any survivorship requirement "in excess of six months" for gifts "passing under a marital deduction." Fatal to the statute's application in *Bond* was the absence of any reference to the marital deduction in the decedent's will.)

Problem

[¶ 27,193]

1. Consider whether the result reached in Rev. Rul. 88–90, 1988–2 C.B. 335, would have been different had the decedent's will been probated in a state with laws similar to those described in Priv. Ltr. Rul. 8809003.

2. Josh is perplexed. Meeting with Isabel to prepare her will, she tells him (1) she does not want a trust "no how"; (2) she wants to make a substantial cash bequest to her husband, Hobart ("he needs it to live on"), even though she knows that Hobart will give "whatever is left" to his girl friend when he dies; and (3) Josh is to "make certain that Hobart does not get his hands on my money until everything is wrapped up with the probate" after her death ("maybe he'll die in the meantime and won't need it and *that woman* won't get it"). Suggest how Josh should draft the gift to Hobart.

[¶ 27,199]

2. LIFE ESTATE WITH POWER OF APPOINTMENT

Prior to 1948 and the advent of the marital deduction, the common type of provision for a family of some means was a life estate for the surviving spouse with a remainder to the children. Rather than discourage the use of the life estate device, Congress created an exception, sometimes referred to as the "life estate/power of appointment" exception (LEPA), to the nondeductible terminable interest rule—but only if five basic conditions are met. § 2056(b)(5).

[¶ 27,205]

a. The "Income" Requirement

The surviving spouse must be entitled for life to all income from the property or to all income from a specific portion of the property as a condition for allowance of the martial deduction under the life estate/power of appointment exception. § 2056(b)(5). While the property is not required to be held in trust as a condition for allowance of the marital deduction, this is the usual form in which the bequest is found.

[¶ 27,211]

WISELY v. UNITED STATES

United States Court of Appeals, Fourth Circuit, 1990.
893 F.2d 660.

JAMES C. FOX, District Judge:

* * * The principal question for our determination is whether the district court properly granted summary judgment for the government in holding that the deceased's will, as drafted, failed to qualify the marital trust for the marital estate tax deduction under * * * § 2056(b)(5). Having concluded that the district court's disposition was proper, we affirm.

* * *

The decedent, William H. Wisely, died testate on November 9, 1982, leaving his Last Will and Testament which he had executed on April 22, 1982. The will named the decedent's wife, Hazel S. Wisely, as the executor of the Estate.

The will contained provisions for the creation of two trusts, the William H. Wisely Family Trust created under Article V, and the marital trust created under Article VI. The portion of the will which is pertinent to this appeal concerns the payment of income from the marital trust and is found in paragraph 2 of Article VI, which states:

> My trustees shall pay to my said wife so much, or all, of the net income of the said trust as my Trustees shall, in their sole discretion, deem necessary to provide for her care and support in the style and manner of living to which she has been accustomed, and to provide for her medical or other emergency needs. Any income not so used shall be accumulated and added to the corpus. Such payments may also be made from the corpus at any time or times in the event of any illness of my said wife or any other emergency, physical or financial.

The will also granted Mrs. Wisely a general testamentary power of appointment over the marital trust corpus. * * *

On its federal estate tax return, the Estate claimed a marital deduction in the amount of $281,575, representing the full value of the property transferred to the marital trust pursuant to Article VI of the will. The Internal Revenue Service disallowed the marital deduction on the ground that the marital trust did not fully comply with the requirements of Section 2056(b)(5). * * **

Code Section 2056(a) generally permits a deduction from the gross estate for the value of an interest in property passing to the surviving spouse. Section 2056(b), however, limits marital deductions of "terminable interests." A terminable interest is one "where on the lapse of time, on the occurrence of a contingency, or on the failure of an event or contingency to occur, an interest passing to the surviving spouse will terminate or fail. . . . " Included in such "terminable interests" is property transferred as a life estate to the surviving spouse. § 2056(a), Treas. Reg. § 20.2056(b)–1(b).

An exception to the general rule barring a marital deduction for a terminable interest is contained in Section 2056(b)(5). In order to fall within this exception, the bequest must meet the five separate requirements set forth in Section 20.2056(b)–5(a) * * *.

Under Section 20.2056(b)–5(a)(1), the value of the life estate passing to the surviving spouse with a general power of appointment qualifies for the marital deduction if the surviving spouse is entitled for life either: (1) to all the income from the entire interest; (2) to all the income from a specific portion of the entire interest; or (3) to a specific portion of all the income from the entire interest.

The district court concluded that the terms of the marital trust, as found in Article VI, paragraph 2 of the will, did not meet any of these three requirements because the will failed to expressly state that Mrs. Wisely was entitled to either all the income outright or to some lesser specific portion expressed as a "fractional or percentile share" of the marital trust income. We agree with the district court's conclusion.

Under Article VI paragraph 2 of the will, the trustees may, in their *sole discretion*, decide to accumulate any income they do not deem necessary for Mrs. Wisely's support, medical, or emergency expenses. Moreover, Mrs. Wisely is not entitled, under the terms of the trust, to demand that the trustees distribute income to her. On the contrary, the trustees' affirmative action is required in order for the trust to distribute income to Mrs. Wisely. In short, the consent of persons other than Mrs. Wisely is required as a condition precedent to distribution of the marital trust income. Likewise, it is within the discretion of persons other than Mrs. Wisely to accumulate the trust income rather than to pay it to her, if they should determine that the income is not necessary to maintain her standard of living. We agree with the district court's reasoning that the "sole discretion" language in the trust does not entitle Mrs. Wisely to all of the income from the entire interest for life. Furthermore, we affirm the district court's finding that the language of the trust fails to satisfy the second or third conditions of Section 20.2056(b)–5(a)(1). We rely on the district court's reasoning that the language allowing the trustees to pay Mrs. Wisely income in their "sole discretion" fails to designate either a specific portion of the entire interest or a specific portion of all of the income from the entire interest.

Accordingly, we conclude that the district court did not err in finding that the marital trust failed to meet the requirement of Section 20.2056(b)–5(a)(1).

* * *

The Estate argues that the district court erred in concluding that the marital trust did not qualify for the marital deduction under §§ 20.2056(b)–5(a)(1) & (2) because the district court failed to refer to extrinsic evidence in construing the terms of the will.

¶ 27,211

The Estate contends that the two-trust structure of the will (i.e., Family Trust and Marital Trust) when juxtaposed with the discretionary income standard used in the marital trust, creates an ambiguity in the will itself requiring reference to extrinsic evidence of the decedent's intent to qualify the marital trust for the marital deduction.

As the district court correctly noted, the property interests bequeathed in the will are to be interpreted pursuant to Virginia law. * * * While the intention of the testator is the "polar star" of construction, intention must be found in the testator's expressed words. The meaning of the words as used by the testator are the equivalent of his legal intention—the intention which the law recognizes as dispositive. A court may not speculate upon what the testator may have intended to do, but rather must give strict effect to the testator's words. Consequently, the true inquiry is not what the testator meant to express, but what the words he has used do actually express. In short, in the construction of a will in Virginia, the intent of the testator rests in the words he uses. The courts may only give the words actually used the meanings and definitions which the testator possibly could have intended. * * *

Here, the Estate's contention that "[t]he decedent's use of a two-trust structure is tantamount to a flat declaration by the decedent that he intended . . . [the Marital Trust to be construed so as to qualify for the marital deduction]" is conjectural. The Estate has not pointed to any language in the will from which it can be concluded that the testator's paramount intention was to qualify the marital trust for a marital deduction, particularly where it requires the court to disregard the decedent's expressed intention that the trustees should use their sole discretion to determine the amount of marital trust income necessary for his wife's support. Because words are not to be rejected unless they manifestly conflict with the plain intention of the testator, * * * there is nothing in the law that would permit reformation of the will to overcome the specific language used in Article VI, paragraph 2, bequeathing marital trust income to decedent's wife in amounts that "the trustees in their sole discretion, deem necessary."

Indeed, the sole discretion vested in decedent's trustees with respect to the marital trust income is likewise vested in the trustees with respect to the Family Trust income, thereby confirming that the decedent intended his words expressed in both Articles V and VI, paragraphs 2. * * *

Here, the decedent did not bequeath the appropriate property interest in the marital trust to his wife to qualify for the marital deduction. Deductions are a matter of legislative grace, and the taxpayer seeking the benefit of a deduction must show that every condition which Congress has seen fit to impose has been fully satisfied. The taxpayer may not haggle with Congress; he either fits squarely within the statute in every particular or the deduction is unavailable. We know of no rule by which the foregoing doctrine is any less applicable to the estate tax than to the income tax. We decline to rewrite Article VI, paragraph 2, to give effect to what the estate contends, based on the will's structure to have been the decedent's intent, when to do so would require ignoring decedent's express intention, stated in two separate places in the will, of granting his trustees sole discretion in determining the amount of income necessary for his wife's support. [Citations omitted.] * * *

Notes

[¶ 27,212]

1. The *Wisely* trust agreement called for distribution to Mrs. Wisely of so much or all of the trust income as the trustees, "in their sole discretion" deemed "necessary to provide for her care and support in the style and manner of living to which she has been accustomed." Suppose that, as a practical matter, there could be no disagreement that the trust income was required to maintain Mrs. Wisely in the specified manner. Should the trust, in these circumstances, thus qualify for the marital deduction? Could the distinction be expressed in terms not of her "need" but of her "right" to the income? Which is it?

2. Creating a trust is a time honored and legislatively permitted technique whereby a spousal gift can qualify for the marital deduction while allowing the donor spouse to establish a measure of control over the trust property by restricting the spouse's enjoyment of the trust property. Most practitioners—but not all—know that the surviving spouse must be entitled to all the income from the trust during life. Despite that knowledge, all too many stumble in fleshing out the trust terms, sometimes including restrictions that inadvertently compromise the spouse's income right. The following IRS memorandum opinion illustrates how an option to purchase property at less than fair market value may disqualify a trust for the marital deduction.

[¶ 27,214]

TECHNICAL ADVICE MEMORANDUM 9147065

July 12, 1991.

ISSUE

If a trust for the benefit of the surviving spouse is required to be funded, in part, with closely-held stock subject to specified restrictions and purchase options described below, does that portion of the trust qualify for the marital deduction under section 2056(b)(5)?

FACTS

At the time of his death, the decedent owned 561 shares of stock in the Company, a closely held corporation. The shares owned by the decedent constituted approximately 95 percent of the outstanding shares. The remaining 5 percent were owned by the decedent's family. * * *

The decedent was survived by his spouse and four sons. The decedent's will provides for a preresiduary bequest in trust for the benefit of the surviving spouse. The trust is to be funded with a pecuniary amount equal to the maximum allowable federal estate tax marital deduction, with specified adjustments that would result in no federal estate tax.

¶ 27,214

During her lifetime, the surviving spouse will be paid all income from the trust at least quarterly and principal, in the trustee's discretion, for her health, maintenance, and best interests. The surviving spouse has the power to appoint by will, to any person including her estate, the trust assets remaining at her death. Any unappointed assets will pass to a residuary trust for the benefit of the decedent's lineal descendants. Unless the surviving spouse directs otherwise in her will, before distribution is made to the residuary trust, trust principal will be used to pay any death taxes attributable to the inclusion of the surviving spouse's trust in her gross estate.

The will states that "[u]nproductive property shall not be held as an asset of the Trust for more than a reasonable time during the lifetime of [the surviving spouse] without her written consent."

The will also specifically provides that the spouse's trust is to be funded with the Company stock only to the extent that other assets are unavailable. One of the decedent's sons is named in the will as trustee of the spouse's trust and the residuary trust. Another son is expressly authorized to manage the corporation, vote the Company stock in the trusts, and determine the price or any other conditions concerning any sale of these shares. The trustee is expressly prohibited from exercising these responsibilities during the life of the authorized son. In addition, the will states, "The Trustee shall sell the securities only as and when [the authorized son] shall direct and shall follow his direction as to price and other terms and conditions of sale."

Thus, although the will contains a general provision to the effect that nonproductive property cannot be held in the spouse's trust for more than a reasonable time, the will specifically precludes the trustee from disposing of the (nonproductive) Company stock at any time unless directed by the son authorized to dispose of the Company stock. Under ordinary rules of construction, subsequent and specific directions prevail over preceding and general directions in a will.

Immediately following the provision prohibiting the trustee from selling the Company stock, the will provides, "[n]otwithstanding anything in the above to the contrary * * * "each of the decedent's sons is granted an option to purchase from the executor or the trustee a specified percentage (totaling 100 percent) of the total Company shares at a specified price of $1,000 per share. Each son must exercise his option within 24 months after the decedent's death. The option price can be paid with a note due not more than 60 months after issuance and bearing interest of 9 percent per year.

On the federal estate tax return, the estate included the 561 shares in the gross estate at a value of approximately $11,000 per share. The return indicates that the spouse's trust was funded, but the residuary trust was not. The return * * * also indicates that, before it was filed, and well before the 24–month period for exercising the options expired, options were exercised on 29.746 of the shares. A marital deduction was claimed for the value of the spouse's trust. The Schedule M indicates that the trust was funded with the proceeds paid to the estate when the options were exercised, the remaining 531.254 shares, and some incidental miscellaneous assets. In computing the marital deduction claimed for the spouse's trust, the estate reported the

531.254 shares at the same $11,000 per share value reported in the gross estate, for a total of more than 5.8 million. This value constituted the major part of the marital deduction claimed. For purposes of the marital deduction, the miscellaneous assets in the spouse's trust were reported at a value of about $1 million.

* * *

Section 20.2056(b)–5(f)(1) of the regulations provides, in part, that if an interest is transferred in trust, the surviving spouse is regarded as "entitled for life to all the income" from the property only if the spouse has that degree of beneficial enjoyment of the property which is accorded to a person who is unqualifiedly designated as a life beneficiary. The requisite degree of enjoyment is given only if it was the decedent's intention, as manifested by the instrument and surrounding circumstances, that the property should produce for the surviving spouse, during life, such an income, or that the spouse should have such use of the property as is consistent with the value of the corpus and with its preservation.

Section 20.2056(b)–5(f)(4) provides, in part, that a trustee's power to retain trust assets which consist substantially of unproductive property will not disqualify the spouse's lifetime income interest if the applicable rules for the trust administration require, or permit the spouse to require, that the trustee either make the property productive or convert it into productive property within a reasonable time.

Section 20.2056(b)–5(f)(5) provides, in part, that the spouse's lifetime income interest will be disqualified if the primary purpose of the trust is to safeguard the property without providing the spouse with the required beneficial enjoyment. Such trusts include those which expressly provide for the accumulation of income and those which indirectly accomplish a similar purpose. The example is given in which the corpus of a trust consists substantially of property unlikely to be income producing during the spouse's life and the spouse cannot compel the trustee to convert or otherwise deal with the property as described in section 20.2056(b)–5(f)(4). Such a trust would not meet the requisite standards for deductibility.

Qualification of an interest for the marital deduction is determined at the time of the decedent's death, based on the facts at that time. Jackson v. United States, 376 U.S. 503 (1964), 1964–2 C.B. 522. See also Rev. Rul. 79–14, 1979–1 C.B. 309.

In the present case, no marital deduction can be allowed with respect to the portion of the spouse's trust that is required to be funded with the Company stock.

First, by giving his sons an option to purchase the Company stock at $1,000 a share, the decedent effectively divided the value of the stock between his sons and the spouse's trust. At the decedent's death, the fair market value of the stock was $11,000 per share. This was nearly 11 times the option price. The fair market value during the 24 months after the decedent's death could be expected to change due to a variety of factors. There was almost no possibility as of the date of decedent's death that the fair market value of the

¶ 27,214

stock would equal the option price when the option was exercised. (Indeed, there must be presumed to be a greater likelihood of exercise where the fair market value exceeds the option price.) Thus, viewed as of the decedent's death, each son held a right, exercisable during the spouse's life, to make a bargain purchase of the Company stock. The effect of the bargain purchase would be to substantially deplete the value of the trust corpus.

Each son's option right is, effectively, a right to appoint to himself the excess of the fair market value of a share on the option exercise date over the option price. The sons' rights to purchase Company stock confers upon them a power to withdraw property with a substantial value from the spouse's trust for less than adequate and full consideration. This right is a "power in any other person to appoint any part of the interest, or such specific portion, to any person other than the surviving spouse" as that phrase is used in section 2056(b)(5). Because of this power, the amount of the marital deduction for the property passing to the spouse's trust must be reduced by the value of the stock passing to the trust.

In this regard, at the decedent's death, it was not certain that the spouse's trust would receive even $1,000 upon the exercise of an option. The will entitled a son to pay the option price with a note bearing annual interest of nine percent. At decedent's death, the date that an option might be exercised certainly could not be predicted nor could the applicable interest rates for most of the 24–month period. If the rate of interest prescribed under section 7872 on the date of exercise is below nine percent, the trust would actually receive value greater than the $1,000 face amount of the nine percent note. (But a son would presumably not borrow from the trust at a rate that was higher than otherwise available from other sources.) Conversely, if the section 7872 rate exceeds nine percent, the trust would receive less than the equivalent of $1,000 on the nine percent note. In view of this financing arrangement prescribed by the will, at the decedent's death no minimum value that the trust would receive upon a son's exercise of his option can be determined. Therefore, for purposes of the marital deduction, we cannot attach even a $1,000 per share minimum value to the stock.

* * *

Under the will, unproductive property generally cannot be held for more than a reasonable time during the spouse's life without her written consent. However, the will expressly prohibits the trustee from selling the Company stock, unless so directed by the son authorized to sell it (except if a son exercises his option). Thus, effectively, neither the spouse nor the trustee have any legal right to establish an adequate income flow for the spouse from the Company stock. Consequently, under section 20.2056(b)–5(f)(4) of the regulations, the spouse is not entitled to "all the income for life" from the stock.

The spouse has a qualifying power of appointment over and income interest in a specific portion of the spouse's trust, the portion funded with miscellaneous assets of about $1 million in value, and this portion qualifies for a marital deduction under section 2056(b)(5). However, we cannot conclude

¶ 27,214

that she has a qualifying income interest in the trust viewed as a whole, because of the relatively large value of the nonproductive portion of the trust funded with the Company stock. * * *

That portion of the spouse's trust that is funded with the Company stock (and the proceeds of Company stock sold pursuant to the exercise of the option) does not qualify for the marital deduction under section 2056(b)(5). Viewed as of the date of the decedent's death, a person other than the spouse has power to appoint trust corpus, the spouse has no right to income from or a power of appointment over that portion of the trust represented by the value of the Company stock. Further, the spouse's income interest attributable to the value of the Company stock fails to satisfy the requisite standard under section 2056(b)(5). Therefore, the marital deduction is allowable only with respect to the specific portion of the spouse's trust that is represented by the trust assets other than the Company stock.

[¶ 27,217]

b. The "Specific Portion" Possibility

A fractional or percentile interest in a property may qualify for the marital deduction. § 2056(b)(10). That is, a partial interest in a property is treated as a "specific portion" within the meaning of § 2056(b)(5) for purposes of allowing the marital deduction for that partial interest so long as the surviving spouse's partial interest in the property constitutes a fractional or percentage share of the entire property interest. That means that the surviving spouse's partial interest must share, proportionally, in "the increase or decrease in the value of the entire property." Reg. § 20.2056(b)–5(c)(2).

Problem

[¶ 27,220]

Zeke's will provided that his widow, Alma, was to receive $300 per month for life from the trust that he provided for her in his will. If the trust income was insufficient, corpus could be invaded to make the trust payments. Consider whether Alma has a qualifying income interest in a specific portion of the property for purposes of § 2056(b)(5). See Reg. § 20.2056(b)–5(c)(2) through (5). Cf. Northeastern Pa. Nat'l Bank & Trust Co. v. United States, 387 U.S. 213 (1967).

[¶ 27,235]

c. The "Payable Annually" Requirement

The income must be payable at least annually. While the statute specifically requires the income to be payable to the spouse "annually or at more frequent intervals." Regulation § 20.2056(b)–5(e) suggests that silence in the will or trust as to the time for payment is not a failure to meet the statute unless local law permits periodic payments to be delayed more than a year.

[¶ 27,247]

d. The "Power of Appointment" Requirement

A broad power of appointment must be given to the surviving spouse. The surviving spouse must have a power of appointment over the property (or a specific portion thereof) pursuant to which the property can be appointed to the surviving spouse or to the surviving spouse's estate. However, the necessary power is not defined in terms of a general power of appointment taxable under § 2041; rather, § 2056(b)(5) is explicit as to the requirements that will lead to the allowance of the marital deduction. As a result, there are instances where a trust may not qualify for the marital deduction, even though the gross estate of the surviving spouse may include the trust property because the surviving spouse has a general power of appointment over the trust property as described in § 2041. See, e.g., Reg. § 20.2056(b)–5(g); Estate of Pipe v. Commissioner, 241 F.2d 210 (2d Cir.), cert. denied, 355 U.S. 814 (1957). In *Pipe*, the marital deduction was denied despite the spouse's power during life to use, enjoy, sell or dispose of the trust property "for such purposes or in such manner, as she in her uncontrolled discretion may choose, it being [decedent's] * * * desire to place no restraint on her in any respect concerning the absolute right of full disposition and use * * * [of the trust property] except that she shall have no power over the disposition of such part thereof as remains unexpended at the time of her death." See also ¶ 27,343.

[¶ 27,253]

e. The "All Events" Requirement

The power of appointment held by the surviving spouse must be exercisable freely by the spouse, and by the spouse alone, and in all events if the marital deduction is to be allowed pursuant to the life estate/power of appointment exception to the nondeductible terminable interest rule. This requirement is strictly applied. For example, in Starrett v. Commissioner, 223 F.2d 163 (1st Cir.1955), the marital deduction was denied the decedent's estate for property placed in trust by the decedent despite the fact that trust property would be includible in the gross estate of the surviving spouse at the spouse's subsequent death. While the spouse had the unlimited right to withdraw all trust property, her right of withdrawal terminated in the event of her incapacity. As a result, the court concluded that the surviving spouse's right of withdrawal was not exercisable "in all events," as required for the marital deduction. The decedent's estate had argued that the will's prohibition on withdrawals by the spouse (or a guardian for the spouse) during a period of incompetency was no different than the similar limitation imposed by applicable state law. The court distinguished the cases on the ground that state law prohibited withdrawals by the spouse only during the period of incompetency, while the will caused the withdrawal right to terminate if the spouse became incompetent.

Might the *Starrett* court have reached a different result if only the testator made clearly known his intention to qualify his gift for the marital deduction? Not likely. On similar facts, the marital deduction was disallowed in Estate of Walsh v. Commissioner, 110 T.C. 393 (1998), where the testator stated "his intention" that the trust "qualify for the marital deduction" and that the trust "provisions shall be so construed and questions pertaining" to the trust "shall be resolved accordingly." The court said the possibility that the "surviving spouse could lose power over the corpus upon the happening of a contingent event; namely incompetency" was the "critical fact," this despite the fact that the spouse had, pursuant to authority given her in the trust, withdrawn the trust corpus shortly after the testator's death—and before any period of incompetency.

Disputes are commonplace when wills are professionally prepared let alone when "home brewed." Stanley Carpenter did his own trust and created a question as to whether his spouse's broad powers of disposition over the trust property constituted a general power of appointment as contemplated by § 2056(b)(5), warranting the allowance of the marital deduction. Estate of Carpenter v. Commissioner, 52 F.3d 1266 (4th Cir.1995). Pointing to the decedent's own words, the court denied the marital deduction, concluding that the spouse's powers were not exercisable "alone and in all events." The trust provided (52 F.3d at 1268):

> My wife is to select the Trust Dept. She is also to take an equal part as an executor with the Trust in all decisions regarding this trust [sic].

> This Trust is to work with my wife + to give her all money necessary to give her a good life and happiness.

> I chose to use a Trust so that no one can dominate or take advantage of her for her entire life.

> I love my wife dearly and she has given me the happiest years of my life and I am concerned that people may try to influence her if she should be depressed or ill.

> The Trust working with my wife may sell any property at anytime if necessary for cash for the Trust in case my wife wants cash for her personal health, needs, trips or anything relating to my wife.

[¶ 27,259]

f. Forbidden Powers

Qualification for the life estate/power of appointment exception to the nondeductible terminable interest rule depends on the absence of so-called forbidden powers. Forbidden powers are those powers that, if held by a person other than the spouse, could be exercised so as to effectively deny the surviving spouse all the income from the property for which the marital deduction is claimed or in some way limit the exercise of the general power of appointment the surviving spouse must receive. Reg. § 20.2056(b)–5(f)(8). A prime example is a spendthrift clause. The IRS claims that the marital deduction cannot be allowed where the governing instrument "requires the trustee to accumulate all income of the trust during the period of any attachment, assignment, etc., to or by any creditor rather than pay the income to the surviving spouse." Priv. Ltr. Rul. 8248008. Under these circumstances, the IRS believes, "the surviving spouse is not entitled for life to all the income," as is required for allowance of the marital deduction under the life estate/power of appointment exception.

By way of contrast, purely administrative powers held by a trustee will not disqualify a trust for the marital deduction under the life estate/power of appointment exception. Examples of permitted powers include the ability to apportion items of income and expense between successive beneficial interests where applicable state law requires the trustee's determination to be made fairly so as to balance the interests of the successive beneficiaries; the ability to treat capital gain dividends received from mutual funds as principal; the right to maintain reasonable reserves for depreciation; and the right to charge fiduciary and professional fees to either income or principal, to make distributions in cash or in kind at current values and to make reasonable determinations as to current values. Rev. Rul. 69–56, 1969–1 C.B. 224.

A fairly comprehensive discussion of the permitted discretions appears in Reg. § 20.2056(b)–5(f)(8).

Problem

[¶ 27,265]

Shalandria knows that, by giving all her property to her spouse, Al, free of trust, the gift will qualify for the marital deduction. However, in the interest of protecting Al from himself (and other predators), she wants her property to pass to Al in trust for his use for life—and she wants the gift to qualify for the marital deduction. Because of her interest in protecting Al, list for Shalandria the possible limitations that could be placed on the trust for Al's benefit without compromising the marital deduction.

[¶ 27,271]

3. LIFE INSURANCE SETTLEMENT OPTIONS

Another exception to the nondeductible terminable interest rule permits the use of certain life insurance settlement options which would otherwise be disallowed as terminable interests. § 2056(b)(6). This exception is hedged with five requirements which are similar in purpose and in structure to the requirements discussed in connection with the life estate-power of appointment exception.

Also note that the result reached in *Meyer*, ¶ 27,157, where the marital deduction was denied for proceeds of a life insurance settlement option left with an insurance company, is not inconsistent with the exception from the terminable interest rule described in § 2056(b)(6) for the proceeds of life insurance left with the insurance company under the circumstances specified in § 2056(b)(6). However, note, too, that the facts in *Meyer* would not allow the surviving spouse to take advantage of the exception provided in § 2056(b)(6) for the proceeds of life insurance and thereby qualify those proceeds for the marital deduction. Why not? What are the operative facts present in *Meyer* that make the shelter of § 2056(b)(6) unavailable to the taxpayer in *Meyer*?

¶ 27,259

[¶ 27,275]

4. QUALIFIED TERMINABLE INTEREST PROPERTY

The most commonly used exception currently is the exception in § 2056(b)(7) for Qualified Terminable Interest Property (sometimes called QTIP). The QTIP exception permits a marital deduction for property that passes from the decedent so long as:

1. All the income generated by the property is payable at least annually to the surviving spouse for life, and

2. Distribution of part or all of the property to anyone other than the surviving spouse is barred during the lifetime of the surviving spouse, and

3. The decedent's executor claims the marital deduction on the decedent's estate tax return.

a. The "Income" Requirement

Regulation § 20.2056(b)–7(d)(2) states that all the principles expressed in Reg. § 20.2056(b)–5(f)(as to the life estate/power of appointment exception to the nondeductible terminable interest rule) apply to the QTIP income entitlement requirement.

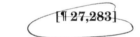

[¶ 27,283]

ESTATE OF NICHOLSON v. COMMISSIONER

United States Tax Court, 1990.
94 T.C. 666.

GERBER, Judge:

* * *

The decedent died testate in 1983. His will provided that his share of community property was to be distributed to an existing inter vivos trust. The trustees were directed to pay the income of the trust to the decedent's surviving spouse "as * * * [she] may from time to time require to maintain * * * [her] usual and customary standard of living." Additionally, "in this regard the Trustees may also invade the corpus of the Trust for these purposes." The decedent further granted the trustees "full and complete independent authority to invest, sell, assign, transfer, trade, mortgage, lease or otherwise deal with the property of this Trust as they may deem to be in the best interests of Dorothy Nell Nicholson."

In 1984, the trustees and beneficiary of the trust sought and obtained an "Order of Modification" from a Texas State court. Pursuant to that order, the trust instrument was changed to provide that, at the decedent's death, the trustees were to "pay the net income of the Trust estate to * * * [decedent's wife] in quarterly or more frequent installments."

We must decide whether, at the time of the decedent's death, his wife's interest in the trust qualified for an estate tax marital deduction as * * *

"qualified terminable interest property," or "QTIP" interests. QTIP interests are those in which a decedent passes to the surviving spouse a "qualifying income interest for life." Generally, when the surviving spouse has a "qualifying income interest for life" she is entitled to "all the income from the property, payable annually or at more frequent intervals," and, while she is alive, no one else can appoint any part of the property to anyone but her. Sec. 2056(b)(7)(B).

The legislative history underlying the QTIP provisions indicates that a QTIP interest must meet the requirements of section 20.2056(b)-5(f). See H. Rept. 97-201 (1981), 1981-2 C.B. 352, 378. Under that regulation, a surviving spouse is entitled to "all the income from the property" if she has the equivalent "beneficial enjoyment" of the trust estate as one who is "unqualifiedly designated as the life beneficiary ." Generally, absent indications to the contrary, the "designation of the spouse as sole income beneficiary for life * * * will be sufficient." Sec. 20.2056(b)-5(f)(1)* * *.

A determination of the nature of the interest which passes to the surviving spouse is made under the law of the jurisdiction under which the interest passes. * * * Here, we look to the law of Texas. Under that law, the issue of whether a beneficiary is entitled to a particular interest in the trust estate depends upon the intention of the settlor. The settlor's intention as it existed at the time the trust was created is determinative. * * *

While we will look to local law in order to determine the nature of the interests provided under a trust document, we are not bound to give effect to a local court order which modifies that document after respondent has acquired rights to tax revenues under its terms.* * * "[N]ot even judicial reformation can operate to change the federal tax consequences of a completed transaction." Van Den Wymelenberg v. United States 397 F.2d 443, 445 (7th Cir.1968), cert. denied 393 U.S. 953 (1968). The reformation of an instrument has retroactive effect as between the parties to the instrument, but not as to third parties who previously acquired rights under the instrument. * * * As the Court of Appeals explained in Van Den Wymelenberg v. United States, supra at 445—

> As to the parties to the reformed instrument the reformation relates back to the date of the original instrument, but it does not affect the rights acquired by non-parties, including the Government. Were the law otherwise there would exist considerable opportunity for "collusive" state court actions having the sole purpose of reducing federal tax liabilities. Furthermore, federal tax liabilities would remain unsettled for years after their assessment if state courts and private persons were empowered to retroactively affect the tax consequences of completed transactions and completed tax years.

Under the terms of the trust at issue, the decedent's wife is not "entitled to all the income from the property, payable annually or at more frequent intervals" as is required by section 2056(b)(7). Instead, the unambiguous language of the trust only allows her "so much of the net income * * * as * * * [she] may from time to time require to maintain * * * [her] usual and customary standard of living." * * *

¶ 27,283

In the context of the trust instrument at issue, the provision for "so much of the net income * * * as * * * [she] may from time to time require" gives Mrs. Nicholson only such income as she may reasonably *need*, but not necessarily all the income that she may *demand*. The trust instrument reveals clearly the decedent's intention that his children, as trustees, were to determine, and provide, the amounts Mrs. Nicholson required to maintain her "usual and customary" standard of living. As long as they carried out their duties, Mrs. Nicholson had neither the obligation, nor the right, to demand "all the income," or any particular amount of income, from the trust.

Consideration of the trust document as a whole reveals no internal inconsistencies with limiting Mrs. Nicholson's income to that which she "may from time to time require." To be sure, nowhere in that document did the decedent make specific provision for the disposition of income in excess of his wife's requirements. That failure, however, does not establish his intention that there would be no excess income. Instead, the trust instrument provides that, when both the decedent and his wife have died, "this irrevocable Trust shall then terminate, and the Trustee or Trustees shall then distribute the Trust estate to SALLY LYNN NICHOLSON MILLER and WILLIAM B. NICHOLSON, equally, share and share alike * * *." This bequest of the remainder interest, unlike the support bequest for Mrs. Nicholson, makes no distinction between trust corpus and trust income. It is therefore clear that the decedent intended a gift of both the corpus component and the undistributed income component of "the Trust estate" to his children after his wife died.

We are aware that respondent's regulations provide a broad scope for interpreting a trust instrument. Those provisions, however, do not permit us to rewrite the trust instrument. The instrument here, as executed by the decedent, and as in existence at the time of his death, fails to establish that Mrs. Nicholson is "unqualifiedly designated as the life beneficiary." Nor does it otherwise designate her as "sole income beneficiary for life." Sec. 20.2056(b)–5(f) * * *. It instead limits Mrs. Nicholson's trust income to amounts she would "require." Any excess would go to the remaindermen. Plainly, then, under the trust instrument at issue, Mrs. Nicholson is not "entitled to all the income" from the property within the meaning of section 2056(b)(7)(B)(ii), and her interest in the trust fails to qualify for the marital deduction.

Petitioner, however, urges that the language of the trust document is ambiguous. It is contended that we must therefore look to the circumstances surrounding the establishment of the trust to determine the decedent's intent. Petitioner then points to the decedent's awareness that the trust assets, at the date of his death, would not generate sufficient income to support Mrs. Nicholson in the manner to which she was accustomed. Petitioner concludes that the decedent must have intended that his wife would receive "all the income" from the trust, plus some amount from the invasion of the corpus. In support of these contentions, petitioner relies heavily upon the Court of Appeals' decision in Estate of Mittleman v. Commissioner, 522 F.2d 132 (D.C.Cir.1975) * * *.

¶ 27,283

Even if petitioner were correct, and we were permitted to look at the circumstances surrounding the execution of the trust, those circumstances do not compel a finding that the decedent "entitled" his wife to all the income from the trust. The extrinsic evidence shows instead that the decedent wished only to provide support to his wife in the manner to which she was accustomed. He especially wished to spare her the concerns of providing for herself, because she was not familiar with business operations. A bequest of all the potential trust income would have been inconsistent with this intention.

Additional extrinsic evidence shows that the decedent's grant of "so much of the net income * * * as [she] may from time to time require" was, in effect, a bequest of some $50,000 to $60,000 annually. That bequest, however, does not constitute an automatic entitlement to all the trust income. Although the trust as originally constituted did not generate that amount of income, it easily could have yielded more than that amount. The value of the trust principal at the decedent's death amounted to more then $1 million dollars. If these assets were converted to income-producing assets in this amount, a return on the trust principal of 6 percent or more would surpass the amount needed to maintain Mrs. Nicholson's "usual and customary standard of living." In other words, such a return would generate more trust income than that to which she was entitled.

Moreover, Mrs. Nicholson was entitled to only so much of the trust's income as she may "from time to time" require to maintain her usual and customary standard of living. The implication of this language is that Mrs. Nicholson's requirements for income from the trust were to be evaluated in light of income from other sources that she might have—such as, perhaps, her share of the community property assets. The availability of income from such other sources would lower the amount of trust income that she might otherwise need, again indicating that she was not "entitled to all the income" from the trust.

The extrinsic evidence further shows that the trustees, consistent with the settlor's intent, might well have managed the trust in a way that would generate more income than the sole beneficiary needed to maintain her standard of living. Reinvestment in income-producing property was a very real possibility. The decedent, in fact, contemplated that some of the trust principal would have to be sold. He specifically confided to his son that his ranch "would probably" be among the trust assets that would be sold, "the reason being that it was a drain rather than a benefitting asset." His son, within the scope of his authority as trustee, thereafter sold some of the trust's real estate, foreclosed upon certain notes that were also part of the trust principal, and attempted to negotiate the payment of other such notes. Nothing prohibited him, as trustee, from selling any of the trust properties; to the contrary, the decedent contemplated such sales. Nor was there any requirement that the proceeds of a sale of property not be invested in income-producing assets; to the contrary, the decedent appeared to favor "benefitting" assets.

¶ 27,283

Accordingly, even a consideration of the extrinsic evidence fails to show that the decedent intended that his wife be "entitled to all the income" from the trust.

The opinion of the Court of Appeals in Estate of Mittleman v. Commissioner, 522 F.2d at 133 n.1, upon which petitioner relies, is not inconsistent with our opinion here. In that case, a decedent left his residuary estate to a trust for the following purposes:

a. To provide for the proper support, maintenance, welfare and comfort of my beloved wife, HENRIETTA MITTLEMAN, for her entire lifetime.

b. To invade the corpus of the trust estate from time to time in the sole and exclusive discretion of the Trustees and to use all or any portion of the said corpus for the proper support, maintenance and welfare of my wife, HENRIETTA MITTLEMAN.

Respondent argued that the above language failed to provide that "all of the income" of the trust be payable "annually or at more frequent intervals" to the surviving spouse, for purposes of section 2056(b)(5). Respondent initially prevailed in a Memorandum Opinion, Estate of Mittleman v. Commissioner, T.C. Memo. 1973–112.

In reversing, the Court of Appeals noted that the Mittleman will made no mention of income from the trust. To the court, the will placed no restriction—either "expressly" or "impliedly"—on the amount of income to be spent on behalf of the beneficiary. The only limitation upon trust expenditures were those restricting expenditures from the corpus to those expenditures made in the "sole and exclusive discretion of the [t]rustees." From this, the Court of Appeals concluded that the "compelling inference" was that the decedent intended to make an unqualified disposition of the income to the wife. The court rejected the notion that the decedent's specific provisions for "the proper support, maintenance, welfare and comfort" of his wife established any limit upon the amount of income she would receive. To the Court of Appeals, that language was "a mere declaration of the purpose of the trust." *Estate of Mittleman v. Commissioner*, 522 F.2d at 138. The court further found the language as to the disposition of income "ambiguous," thus justifying an examination of "surrounding circumstances." The court determined that these surrounding circumstances supported its conclusion that the wife was "entitled to all of the income." It pointed out that the corpus of the trust was "not large" and that the anticipated income, without invasions of the trust, would produce yields "far short of the family income before Mr. Mittleman died." Estate of Mittleman v. Commissioner, 522 F.2d at 139. The court also took into account the decedent's explicit wish that his estate be able to claim the marital deduction.

This case is factually distinguishable. The trust at issue here, unlike the trust in *Mittleman*, contains explicit language limiting the amount of income that would be paid to the surviving wife. Here, the trustees are directed to pay only "so much of the net income" of the trust to the decedent's surviving spouse "as * * * [she] may from time to time require to maintain * * * [her] usual and customary standard of living." That language is not ambiguous, and no examination of "surrounding circumstances" is indicated. Were the situation otherwise, however, this case is still not *Mittleman*. The "surrounding circumstances" here show that the estate was capable of yielding income in excess of that needed to maintain the beneficiary in her accustomed standard of living. Accordingly, she was not necessarily entitled to "all the income." Moreover, here the decedent specifically did not draft his trust with an intention to maximize the marital deduction. There is, accordingly, no reason for us to contort the language he used in order to achieve that result.

Finally, we do not believe that the modification to the trust instrument made in 1984, after the decedent's death, affects the result we have reached. We have not been provided with the evidence presented to the Texas court; we have only the decree allowing the modification. The new language in that modification provides specifically that the trustees "shall pay the net income of the Trust estate to Dorothy Nell Nicholson in quarterly or more frequent installments." The modified trust instrument appears to meet the requirements for the marital deduction set forth in section 2056(b)(7). As indicated above, however, we have found that respondent is entitled to estate taxes on the basis of the trust provisions that existed at the time of the decedent's death. The attempt to claim an estate tax deduction by means of a post-mortem modification to the trust instrument therefore fails. We will not give effect to a local court order or decree that alters or modifies a trust instrument after respondent has acquired rights to tax revenues under its provisions. * * *

Petitioner, in fact, does not now claim that the language of the 1984 modification is controlling. It is instead urged that the 1984 modification is merely a "clarification" of the decedent's original intention that all the trust income be distributed to his wife at least annually. We do not agree that the 1984 modification serves only to clarify the original instrument. The original document did not require that all the income go to Mrs. Nicholson; rather it restricted the payment of income to situations where some income is needed to maintain Mrs. Nicholson's standard of living. The modification, however, requires all income to go to her. The original instrument required payments of income only "from time to time." The 1984 modification, however, mandates quarterly payments of all the income. The original trust instrument indicates that accumulated but undistributed income would go to Mrs. Nicholson's children as part of the "Trust estate." The modification, however, provides that any accumulated but undistributed income would go to "her personal representative as part of her probate estate." The 1984 modification is thus more than a mere clarification; it is instead a substantial change in the trust instrument made after respondent had secured rights under the original instrument. As such, we will not give it effect.

We are mindful of the statement of the Texas State court that its modification of the 1984 trust instrument "would be in keeping with the intent of the settlors when the Trust was created." That statement, however, does not affect our opinion here. "Although this reformation may comply with the original intentions of the grantor as disclosed by * * * evidence at the

¶ 27,283

hearing in that proceeding, it is not an interpretation of the original instrument." M.T. Straight Trust v. Commissioner, 24 T.C. at 74. Moreover and as we have found, decedent was not concerned with obtaining the maximum estate deduction. He was concerned with taking care of his wife's needs.

We are not unsympathetic to the contention that the decedent herein would have wished to establish a QTIP trust, but the fact is that he did not do so. There may well have been an opportunity for him to do so; the QTIP provisions were effective for estates of decedents dying after December 31, 1981, and decedent died in 1983. The evidence, however, does not disclose whether he was informed of the possibility of establishing a QTIP trust. Moreover, the decedent wished to spare his widow concerns about providing for her own support. We cannot dismiss the possibility that he might have preferred to have the trustees determine the amount of trust proceeds she required, rather than to force all income to be paid to her, as his adoption of a QTIP trust would mandate.

It follows that the decedent's desire that the trust "not create a tax problem" does not absolve his failure to take advantage of a possible QTIP marital deduction that Congress made available only in 1981, several years after he established the trust at issue. For estate taxes, as for income taxes, "Deductions are a matter of legislative grace, and a taxpayer seeking the benefit of a deduction must show that every condition which Congress has seen fit to impose has been fully satisfied." * * *

Note

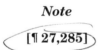

1. In Ellingson v. Commissioner, 964 F.2d 959 (9th Cir.1992), the marital deduction was allowed, based on a QTIP election, in a case where the trustee was expressly allowed to accumulate the trust income if (1) the trust income exceeded the amount which the trustee deemed to be necessary for the "needs, best interests and welfare" of the surviving spouse and (2) the trustee deemed such an accumulation "advisable." The court concluded:

> The Commissioner argues that it would make bad law to read a trust agreement as creating an interest which qualifies for a QTIP deduction solely because the settlor expressly declared in the trust that he intended that effect. We agree. However, this case does not implicate the Commissioner's concern. Certainly, the Trust Agreement could have been more clearly drafted. Nevertheless, the choice for this court is between two plausible readings of the agreement, only one of which effectuates the settlors' clearly manifested intent. If the Accumulation Proviso could plausibly be read only as granting the trustee unlimited discretion, the QTIP deduction would be lost. That is not the case here, however.

The governing instrument in *Ellingson* was laced with references to the decedent's intention that the spousal gift qualify for the marital deduction. Such references were not present in Estate of Davis v. Commissioner, 394 F.3d 1294 (9th Cir. 2005), where the marital deduction was denied. A significant feature in *Davis* was a California's statute aimed at curing drafting deficiencies. That statute, California Probate Code § 21552, at the time provided as follows:

If an instrument contains a marital deduction gift:

(a) The provisions of the instrument, including any power, duty, or discretionary authority given to a fiduciary, shall be construed to comply with the marital deduction provisions of the Internal Revenue Code.

(b) The fiduciary shall not take any action or have any power that impairs the deduction as applied to the marital deduction gift.

(c) The marital deduction gift may be satisfied only with property that qualifies for the marital deduction.

That statute might well have saved the marital deduction in *Davis* but the decedent did not expressly state that his gift to his spouse was to qualify for the marital deduction. In fact, the marital deduction was not mentioned. While reference to the marital deduction is not a condition of eligibility, such reference is helpful in cases where the language of the marital gift fails to satisfying the statutory requirements for qualification for the marital deduction. In *Davis*, the disqualifying language was as follows:

[T]he trustee shall pay to or apply for the benefit of the surviving spouse, in quarter annual or more frequent installments, all of the net income from the trust estate as the trustee, in the trustee's reasonable discretion, shall determine to be proper for the health, education, or support, maintenance, comfort and welfare of grantor's surviving spouse in accordance with the surviving spouse's accustomed manner of living.

Davis is consistent with Estate of Walsh v. Commissioner, 110 T.C. 393 (1998), discussed at ¶ 27,253, where the testator's expressed intent—to qualify for the marital deduction—was said to be insufficient to overcome the words found in the testator's will that limited the surviving spouse's control over the marital deduction property in the event of incompetency, a possibility that ran afoul of the "all events" requirement for allowance of the marital deduction under § 2056(b)(5), the life estate/power of appointment safe harbor.

2. Estate of Howard v. Commissioner, 910 F.2d 633 (9th Cir.1990), the so-called stub income case, is a reminder of the careful attention that must be given to statutory requirements when the marital deduction is the object. It also emphasizes the differences between the QTIP exception to the nondeductible terminable interest rule (§ 2056(b)(7)) and the life estate/power of appointment exception to that rule (§ 2056(b)(5)). *Howard* presented an unusual fact situation that turned on a particular provision in the trust established in the will of the decedent. The IRS had concluded that the trust qualified for the marital deduction, but the decedent's estate argued that the trust did not qualify! The provision in question specified that all trust income should be distributed to the surviving spouse at quarterly intervals for life but that any trust income accrued between the date of the death of the surviving spouse and the immediately preceding quarterly payment date was to be distributed not to the spouse's estate but to the remaindermen, i.e., to those who were to enjoy the trust property after the death of the surviving spouse. The dispute related to this "stub income" and presented the question of

¶ 27,285

whether the trust qualified as a QTIP, since the surviving spouse was not entitled to all trust income for life. The court held that the trust was eligible for QTIP treatment, finding congressional intent by looking to legislative history (which was silent as to stub income) and by contrasting the provisions in Section 2056(b)(7) relating to QTIPs with those in Section 2056(b)(5) applicable to cases where the marital deduction is claimed on the ground that the surviving spouse has a life estate and a general power of appointment over the property for which the marital deduction is claimed. The life estate/power of appointment provision of Section 2056(b)(5) is construed as requiring the stub income to be paid to the surviving spouse's estate. Reg. § 20.2056(b)–5(f)(8). By way of contrast, the court pointed to then-proposed Reg. § 20.2056(b)–7(c)(ii) relating to QTIPs, which specifically concluded that a trust was eligible for the marital deduction as a QTIP even though the surviving spouse was not entitled to the stub income. See Reg. §§ 20.2056(b)–5(f)(8)(life estate/power of appointment) and 20.2056(b)–7(d)(4)(QTIP). It should be noted that Reg. § 20.2044–1(d)(2) provides that the stub income is included in the gross estate of the surviving spouse for estate tax purposes even if not distributed to the spouse or to the spouse's estate.

3. The stub income problem considered in *Howard* might seem to be a tempest in a tea pot but it has given rise to more controversy, controversy that nicely illustrates taxpayer ambition contrasted with efforts to protect the fisc. In Estate of Shelfer v. Commissioner, 86 F.3d 1045 (11th Cir.1996)—a case that gave rise to the expression *"Shelfer* Shuffle"—Louise Shelfer had been entitled to all but the stub income from a trust established by her husband, Elbert, in his will. Louise Shelfer's executor contended that a trust created by the will of Louise's husband, Elbert, was not included in Louise's estate at her death. The executor's claim became the subject of an IRS challenge when the IRS took note that Elbert's estate had been allowed the marital deduction for the trust property at his earlier death and, as a condition of such allowance, § 2044 required the inclusion of the trust property in Louise's estate at her death. (Recall that the basic premise of the marital deduction is that the marital deduction is allowed where the property for which the deduction is claimed will be included in the estate of the surviving spouse at his or her subsequent death unless consumed or disposed of by that spouse during life). Listening in on the meeting between Louise's executor and the IRS agent examining Louise's estate tax return, Louise's executor might have been heard to retort, "Yes, we acknowledge that the marital deduction was allowed Elbert's estate but the allowance was improper—because Louise was not entitled to the stub income from the trust! That is, Louise was not entitled to all the trust income for life as required by § 2056(b)(7)(B)(ii)(I) and, therefore, allowance of the marital deduction at the time of Elbert's death was wrong. Sorry. We'd like to be accommodating but it's out of our hands—and if we volunteer the tax (by including the trust property in Louise's estate for tax purposes) 'to make it right, so-to-speak', we'd have liability to the estate's beneficiaries for paying out money we didn't owe." Interestingly, a bank, Quincy State, was executor of both estates. Perhaps it can said that "strange bedfellows tax doth make" for it appears

¶ 27,285

that the American Bar Association filed an amicus brief in support of the IRS position. The ABA position was that the statute is satisfied if the surviving spouse has all the income which has been distributed—even if the stub income goes elsewhere. Undertaking the tedious task of statutory construction, the 11th Circuit stepped from word to word and from comma to comma and concluded that it was necessary to look beyond the "plain language" of the statute to its history and purpose—but that, too, was found deficient. The court next turned to policy considerations and said:

> [W]e must decide which interpretation of the statute best comports with the two general goals discussed above: expanding the marital deduction to provide for the spouse while granting the decedent more control over the ultimate disposition of the property, and treating a husband and wife as one economic entity for the purposes of estate taxation.
>
> Under the Commissioner's interpretation of the statute, the decedent would gain the tax benefit, retain control of the trust corpus, and provide the spouse with all of the periodic payments for her personal support. The stub income, which accrues after her death and is thus not used for her maintenance, could be appointed to someone else. This result is consistent with the statutory goals of expanding the deduction while providing for the spouse's support. In contrast, the Tax Court's reading of the statute would condition the tax benefit for the entire trust corpus on ceding control over a much smaller amount that is not needed for the spouse's support.
>
> The statute's second goal, treating a married couple as one economic entity, was effected in a comprehensive statutory scheme. In addition to the QTIP provisions of § 2056(b)(7), Congress added § 2044, which requires the estate of the surviving spouse to include all property for which a marital deduction was previously allowed, and § 2056(b)(7)(B)(v), which states that a QTIP "election, once made, shall be irrevocable." Taken together, these sections * * * provide that assets can pass between spouses without being subject to taxation. Upon the death of the surviving spouse, the spouse's estate will be required to pay tax on all of the previously deducted marital assets. The Commissioner's position comports with the statutory scheme because it compels the surviving spouse to abide by the irrevocable election of a QTIP trust and to pay taxes on property that had previously been subject to a deduction.

The court concluded that the "goals" of the marital deduction favor a "broad interpretation of the statute that would allow the QTIP election" to Elbert's estate and the resulting inclusion of the trust property in Louise's estate as required by § 2044. Notably the court commented that "a broad reading of the marital deduction provisions benefits the federal Treasury and furthers Congressional intent to ensure taxation of all previously deducted property." Here, more than $1 million of taxes and deficiencies were at stake. The windfall that would result from a finding for the taxpayer in this case, the court said, would be a "substantial windfall, encouraging other executors of wills to disclaim previously taken deductions."

¶ 27,285

While the *Shelfer* outcome might be explained as simple justice, the case speaks volumes about the interpretive issues that routinely develop.

4. Cavenaugh v. Commissioner, 51 F.3d 597 (5th Cir.1995), is another case where the surviving spouse looked to *Howard* and, as a result, might have been heard to say, "Sorry, but the marital deduction was improperly claimed at my spouse's death 'cause I don't get all the income" and, as a result, "§ 2044 cannot be invoked to cause the marital deduction property to be included in my estate at my death." The Fifth Circuit disagreed with the taxpayer (saying that the technical argument advanced by the taxpayer—"I don't get all the income"—had to yield to the court's finding that the deceased spouse *intended* the survivor to receive all the trust income—and *intent* governs).

In Tech. Adv. Mem. 9548002, the IRS advanced the "duty of consistency doctrine" as an appropriate solution. Here, too, the marital deduction was claimed and allowed by the IRS at Husband's death. At Wife's later death, her executor made the standard claim that the Wife did not have a qualifying income interest for life as required by § 2044—because, in this case, Wife's income interest was subject to a spendthrift clause. The IRS explained application of the "consistency doctrine" in these terms:

> In this case the Decedent's estate and the Spouse's estate are closely related in that the Decedent's estate derives a direct benefit from the marital deduction taken by the first estate. See, Estate of Shelfer v. Commissioner, 103 T.C. 10, 19 (Parr, J. dissenting)(1994). ("The legislative history shows that the intent of Congress was that a husband and wife should be treated as one economic unit for purposes of estate and gift taxes.")

Concluding, the IRS described, in the following terms, the rather untenable position in which taxpayers attempt to place the IRS—and said, effectively, "We won't play"!

> The taxpayer argues that equitable principles should not apply in this case. The taxpayer contends that the Service was placed on notice that the trust might not qualify under § 2056(b)(7) because a copy of the trust instrument was filed with the Spouse's estate tax return. However, we note that there was no specific indication on the return that the qualification of the trust was at issue. Thus, we doubt that attaching a multipage trust instrument containing numerous paragraphs, one of which, a "boilerplate" provision, raises an issue regarding qualification, constitutes sufficient notice. This is especially the case since the return itself is prepared on the basis that no such issue is presented.

Lending support to the IRS "duty of consistency" argument is Estate of Letts v. Commissioner, 109 T.C. 290 (1997), where the court carefully worked through the elements of the duty of consistency argument, including the claimed lack of privity between the first and second decedent's estates, and concluded that the duty of consistency mandated inclusion in the estate of the second spouse to die of the property for which the marital deduction was allowed at the death of the first spouse to die. The *Letts* facts were interesting. James Letts was the first to die. His wife, Mildred, survived. While the marital deduction was claimed on James' estate tax return in the amount of $1,000,264 for what was described on Schedule M of the Form 706 as a "qualified marital trust," James' executor (1) placed an "x" in the "No" box in response to the question, "Do you elect to claim a marital deduction for qualified terminable interest property (QTIP) under Section 2056(b)(7)"; (2) listed no property on Schedule M as QTIP even though the instructions stated that the property for which the QTIP election is being made must be listed on Schedule M and marked as "qualified terminable interest property"; and (3) failed to include a copy of James' will with his estate tax return as required. Subsequently, as part of the estate tax return for Mildred's estate (which did not include the property for which the marital deduction was enjoyed at James' death), Mildred's executor explained that the James' "executor did not elect to treat" the trust (for which the marital deduction was enjoyed) as "qualified terminable interest property." Neat, huh? The Letts' son, as executor, signed both returns (although they were prepared by different professionals, one a CPA and the other, an attorney). While development of the duty of consistency in *Letts* is a factual journey beyond the scope of these materials, it is worth noting that the court found three elements necessary to its application, namely, (1) that the taxpayer made a representation of fact or reported an item for tax purposes in one year; (2) that the Commissioner acquiesced in or relied upon the fact for that year; and (3) the taxpayer desires to change the representation made in a later year after the earlier year has been closed by the statute of limitations. Bottom line? The court applied the duty of consistency to include the subject property in the estate of Mildred at her later death, finding a "sufficient identity of interests" between the estates of James and Mildred to cause them to be a "single economic unit" and for the doctrine to apply (despite taxpayer claims that applying the doctrine circumvented the statute of limitations).

Cases like *Letts* are obviously growing in number, resulting in at least one proposal for a legislative solution, it being explained that the purpose of the QTIP rules was to "permit deferral of taxation" and not to "provide an exemption from estate and gift tax." See Joint Committee on Taxation, *Description of Revenue Provisions Contained in the President's Fiscal Year 1999 Budget Proposal* (JCS–4–98), February 24, 1998, at 184–85 (where marital deduction is allowed for QTIP property, inclusion in estate of surviving spouse is proposed to be mandatory).

Problem

[¶ 27,289]

Taxpayers frequently miss a step when they attempt to secure the benefits of the marital deduction. Could many of these missteps be avoided by including a provision such as the following in all dispositive instruments where the donor intends that the marital deduction be claimed?

> Notwithstanding any other provision in this instrument to the contrary, each and every provision is to be construed so as to permit the

property passing to my spouse to qualify for the marital deduction for federal estate tax purposes and any provision which cannot be so construed will be limited or modified so that the property passing to my spouse qualifies for the marital deduction.

[¶ 27,319]

b. *The Distribution Limitation*

QTIP treatment will be denied if distributions from the trust can be made to a person other than the surviving spouse before the death of the surviving spouse. § 2056(b)(7)(B)(ii)(II). While taxpayer compliance with this requirement so as to insure the marital deduction would seem relatively easy to accomplish, all too frequently it results in the loss of the marital deduction by the innocent, the uninformed, and the well intentioned. In Estate of Bowling v. Commissioner, 93 T.C. 286 (1989), the marital deduction was denied because the will allowed the trustee to invade the trust "for any emergency needs which effect [sic] the support, maintenance and health needs of any beneficiary" of the trust. The surviving spouse was to receive the income for life and, after the death of the wife, the income was to be distributed to the decedent's son, who was institutionalized because of his mental retardation. The court denied the marital deduction after concluding that, during the lifetime of the spouse, the trustee could make distributions for the emergency needs of the institutionalized child. The court rejected the argument that the "emergency needs" authorization was limited to the needs of the current income beneficiary, namely, the surviving spouse during her lifetime. The court pointed to the severely disabled condition of the child as the reason why it was unlikely that the decedent would have intended to prohibit distributions to the son to meet emergency needs. See also Estate of Manscill v. Commissioner, 98 T.C. 413 (1992)(trustee's power to distribute corpus to the child of the surviving spouse invalidated QTIP election).

The IRS, too, specifically says it will not allow the marital deduction for any part of the trust where the surviving spouse, as sole trustee, holds the power to appoint part of the trust property ("up to $5,000 annually" in the IRS's example) to a minor child for "maintenance and support"—even though all trust income is payable to the surviving spouse for life. § 20.2056(b)–7(h), Example 4. Contrast, though, Tech. Adv. Mem. 8943005, which follows—and then note that Example 4 of the regulations was published in 1994 and Tech. Adv. Mem. 8943005 was published in 1989. The clear suggestion is that the IRS, by publishing Example 4, has changed it mind about its conclusion in Tech. Adv. Mem. 8943005. Is the effect to exalt form over substance? What is the IRS afraid of here?

[¶ 27,325]

TECHNICAL ADVICE MEMORANDUM 8943005

July 9, 1989.

* * *

Is the Decedent's estate entitled to a marital deduction under § 2056(b)(7) * * * even though the Spouse, in her individual capacity, was

¶ 27,325

given a general power to annually appoint up to $5,000 or 5 percent of the trust corpus annually?

FACTS

The Decedent died testate on December 20, 1985. On the Decedent's estate tax return the estate elected to claim a marital deduction for qualified terminable interest property passing to a residuary trust for the benefit of the surviving spouse.

Paragraph FOURTH: (c) of Decedent's will provides in part:

> My wife, during her lifetime, is hereby given a general power to appoint from the principal of this trust to whomsoever she may designate, including herself, during each taxable year of the trust, an amount or amounts not exceeding Five Thousand Dollars ($5,000.00) in the aggregate, and, in addition, ... an amount, if any, by which Five Percent (5%) of the then fair market value of the net principal of this trust, ... exceeds the amount or amounts previously appointed by my wife for such year....

* * *

The issue presented in this case is whether the Spouse's power to appoint property "to whomsoever she may designate" violates section 2056(b)(7)(B)(ii)(II) [which allows a marital deduction for Qualified Terminable Interest Property], in that the Spouse has a power to appoint part of the property to a person other than the surviving spouse.

Since enactment of the marital deduction provisions in 1948, the philosophy behind this deduction has evolved from an attempt to equate community property with noncommunity property states towards recognition of the marital unit as a single taxpayer. Thus, the Code currently provides fewer restrictions on the availability of the deduction for interspousal transfers. However, one aspect of the deduction that has remained constant over the years is that no deduction is available unless a transfer tax will be imposed when the property is transferred outside the marital unit. The restriction imposed by the terminable interest rule of section 2056(b)(1) was enacted in recognition of the fact that many terminable interest arrangements will not be subject to tax when the surviving spouse's interest, in fact, terminates. In general, the exceptions to the terminable interest rule (such as section 2056(b)(7)) are available to taxpayers only in those cases where the nature of the interest passing to the spouse is such that any enjoyment by any person other than the surviving spouse will result in estate or gift tax liability with respect to the surviving spouse.

The legislative history underlying section 2056(b)(7) states, in part:

> "... [T]here must be no power in any person (including the spouse) to appoint any part of the property subject to the qualifying income interest to any person other than the spouse during the spouse's life. This rule will ... insure that the value of the property not consumed by the

spouse is subject to tax upon the spouse's death (*or earlier disposition*)."
[Emphasis added.]

H.R. Rep. No. 201, 97th Cong., 1st Sess., 161 (1981), 1981–2 C.B. 352 at 378.

While it is true that the first parenthetical phrase in the committee report literally precludes a power in the surviving spouse exercisable in favor of any person other than the surviving spouse, we believe such a reading would be unnecessarily restrictive, and, as a practical matter, meaningless. It is axiomatic that a power to appoint exclusively to oneself includes the power to exercise such dominion and control over the property that one may give it to whomsoever one wishes. Thus, it is reasonable to believe that Congress intended that a spouse would be able to give the property away, especially in view of the second (emphasized) parenthetical.

Consistent with this understanding of legislative history, and recognizing that the philosophy of section 2056 requires the imposition of the transfer tax only once during the lives of a husband and wife, we believe the better reading of the legislative history would preclude a spousal power of appointment only where the exercise of the power would not be subject to transfer taxation; i.e., where the power is not a general power of appointment as defined in section 2514.

An interpretation requiring that a spouse must first take physical possession of the property prior to a transfer to a third party would focus too much attention on the form of the transaction. It is sufficient that the exercise of the power by the spouse in favor of a third party would be subject to transfer taxation.

CONCLUSION

Because the power held by the Spouse in this case is a general power of appointment as defined in section 2514, we conclude that the Decedent's estate is entitled to a marital deduction under section 2056(b)(7) * * *.

Problem

[¶ 27,329]

Amy's will provided a trust for the benefit of her husband, Slim. Amy appointed Slim trustee. The trust's income was to be paid to Slim at least quarterly. Distributions from principal not to exceed $5,000 annually could be made by the trustee to Amy's child, Ned, if needed for his education. The IRS claims that no part of Amy's trust qualifies for the marital deduction. Slim, as executor of Amy's estate, disagrees and claims the marital deduction is available "at least for everything in excess of the $5,000." Who should prevail? See § 20.2056(b)–7(h), Example 4.   *Need to disclaim Ned's interest.*

[¶ 27,331]

c. *QTIP Election*

As a further condition of qualifying the QTIP for the marital deduction, the decedent's executor must make an election on the decedent's estate tax

¶ 27,331

return, and such election is irrevocable. § 2056(b)(7)(B)(v). The election is available for separate properties as well as for specific portions of property. The election is also available to the donor spouse in the case of gifts made to the other spouse while both spouses are living. § 2523(f)(4).

With the availability of the QTIP, the decedent's will need not provide any broad taxable power of appointment in the surviving spouse, so long as no one has the power to appoint the property to anyone else during the spouse's life. This feature, in conjunction with the flexibility of election after death as to the amount of property to be deducted, makes the QTIP an extremely useful tool for the estate planner.

Inasmuch as the QTIP would not be includible in the gross estate of the surviving spouse upon the surviving spouse's subsequent death because the spouse has only a life estate and no taxable power, a special provision, § 2044, brings the QTIP property into the gross estate of the surviving spouse. This is to satisfy the premise on which the marital deduction is based, i.e., that the amount deducted in the first estate will eventually be taxed in the second estate.

Since making the QTIP election will mean that the estate of the surviving spouse will be inflated by the amount of the QTIP property at the death of the surviving spouse, § 2207A provides for recovery of the tax from the QTIP property itself unless the will of the surviving spouse otherwise directs.

The procedure for making the QTIP election has proved challenging. Currently, IRS Form 706 provides that the QTIP election is deemed to have been made as to qualifying property that is listed on Schedule M. While that sounds simple enough, earlier versions of Form 706 have challenged some taxpayers, resulting in litigation. So far as the standard is concerned, one court was moved to say that a "clear manifestation of an affirmative intent to elect qualified terminable interest treatment" is required and "the election must be unequivocally communicated on the estate tax return of the spouse who dies first." Estate of Higgins v. Commissioner, 897 F.2d 856 (6th Cir.1990). Understandably, then, the marital deduction was appropriately denied where a typewritten "X" appeared in the "No" box on the decedent's federal estate tax return in response to the question "Do you elect to claim a marital deduction for an otherwise nondeductible terminable interest under § 2056(b)(7)?" even though Schedule M, the schedule used to claim the marital deduction on the federal estate tax return, showed property passing to the surviving spouse and an actual deduction was claimed for that property in making the computation of the estate's tax liability in the summary portion of the tax return. Notably, the estate did not designate any of the property listed on Schedule M as QTIP property. The court commented (897 F.2d at 860) that § 2056(b)(7):

> was not enacted to allow the taxpayer to take a "wait and see" approach. As in the case of other elective provisions, the policy of the section is "furthered by requiring a clear manifestation to the government of taxpayer's election"; any other rule "would leave room for the taxpayer to argue later that it had never intended to make an election."

IRS Form 706 has been changed to eliminate the "yes/no" question that proved troublesome in *Higgins*.

Adding to the complexity, though, is § 2056(b)(7)(C) which provides for an automatic QTIP election in the case of an annuity includible in the decedent's gross estate under § 2039. The QTIP election is automatic when only the surviving spouse has the right to receive payments so long as he or she is alive. An "election out" option is available to the decedent's executor and his or her decision is to be reflected on Schedule M of the Form 706 in the form of a "yes/no" question. See Priv. Ltr. Rul. 9822031.

[¶ 27,337]

d. *QTIP Compared to Life Estate/Power of Appointment*

Section 2056(b)(7), providing for Qualified Terminable Interest Property (QTIP), is probably the most important exception, from a planning perspective, to the nondeductible terminable interest rule. The QTIP differs from the life estate/power of appointment exception in two principal respects. First, the decedent's executor has the option whether to elect to claim the marital deduction for the QTIP property or allow the QTIP property to be taxed at the death of the deceased spouse (while the marital deduction is mandatory as to property qualifying for the life estate/power of appointment exception). Second, the marital deduction is available as to the QTIP property even though the surviving spouse has no right to control the disposition of the QTIP property at the subsequent death of the surviving spouse (as contrasted with the life estate/power of appointment exception, the core of which is the general power of appointment which the surviving spouse must have as one of the conditions for qualification for the life estate/power of appointment exception). Thus, as a result of the QTIP exception, a prospective decedent can defer estate taxes until the death of his or her spouse, allow the spouse to enjoy the property during life, while all the while controlling the ultimate disposition of the property.

The QTIP provisions allow the executor to elect to deduct any property passing from the decedent provided: (1) the income is payable to the surviving spouse for life; and (2) no one has any power during the life of the surviving spouse to appoint any part of the property to anyone other than the surviving spouse. Moreover, the election has the added flexibility, comparable to what has been observed with regard to the disclaimer provision under § 2518 (see Chapter 6), of being applicable to all or "a specific portion of property," thus permitting an accurate and careful computation of the tax upon the death of the first to die with a better appraisal of the possible tax upon the estate of the survivor.

The Report of the House Ways and Means Committee, which accompanied the Economic Recovery Tax Act of 1981 in its legislative passage, describes the QTIP provision, as follows (Rep. 97–201, p. 159–160).

> [T]he committee believes that the present limitations on the nature of interests qualifying for the marital deduction should be liberalized to permit certain transfers of terminable interests to qualify for the marital

¶ 27,337

deduction. Under present law, the marital deduction is available only with respect to property passing outright to the spouse or in specified forms which give the spouse control over the transferred property. Because the surviving spouse must be given control over the property, the decedent cannot insure that the spouse will subsequently pass the property to his children. Because the maximum marital deduction is limited under present law to one-half of the decedent's adjusted gross estate, a decedent may at least control disposition of one-half of his estate and still maximize current tax benefits. However, unless certain interests which do not grant the spouse total control are eligible for the unlimited marital deduction, a decedent would be forced to choose between surrendering control of the entire estate to avoid imposition of estate tax at his death or reducing his tax benefits at his death to insure inheritance by the children. The committee believes that the tax laws should be neutral and that tax consequences should not control an individual's disposition of property. Accordingly, the committee believes that a deduction should be permitted for certain terminable interests.

Note

[¶ 27,343]

Had the QTIP exception been available prior to 1981, the court would have reached the same result in the *Starrett* case, ¶ 27,253, and no marital deduction would have been allowed because the income interest was not for life. By way of contrast, the income interest available to the surviving spouse in *Estate of Pipe*, ¶ 27,247, would have been sufficient to qualify as a QTIP.

[¶ 27,349]

e. *Partial QTIP Elections*

Partial QTIP elections are often made as part of postmortem estate planning. Fractional or percentile interests can qualify for the marital deduction. See § 2056(b)(10); ¶ 27,217. In the typical case, the decedent's will provides that all the decedent's property is to pass in trust for the benefit of the surviving spouse, that the surviving spouse is to receive all the trust income, and that no one except the spouse is to receive any distribution from the trust so long as the spouse survives. Such a trust obviously meets the requirements for the QTIP election. See § 2056(b)(7). However, making the QTIP election for the entire trust causes the entire trust to be included in the estate of the surviving spouse—and will also often mean that the decedent has not utilized the opportunity to shelter from estate tax, at the death of the spouse, the applicable exclusion amount available to the decedent under § 2010(c) ($1 million in 2002 but scheduled to increase to $3.5 million in 2009). A partial QTIP election can sometimes be utilized to rectify such a development, as can be seen in the following letter ruling.

¶ 27,337

[¶ 27,353]

PRIVATE LETTER RULING 8301050

September 30, 1982.

This is in reference to your letter dated July 13, 1982, requesting rulings concerning the federal estate tax consequences of a proposed election under section 2056(b)(7)(B)(v) * * *. More specifically, you request rulings that: (1) the fractional share of the property subject to the proposed election will constitute qualified terminable property, and (2) the value of the decedent's taxable estate shall be determined, in part, by deducting from the gross estate an amount equal to the value of the fractional share of the property subject to the proposed election.

Your proposed election states as follows: that specific portion, represented by a fractional share up to 100% of all trust property, that is required to reduce the federal estate tax on [the decedent's] estate to zero based on finally determined federal estate tax values, after taking into consideration all other items deducted on the federal estate tax return, the allowable state death tax credit (to the extent it does not increase the amount of death taxes payable to any state) and unified credit.

The submitted information indicates that the decedent died testate after December 31, 1981, survived by a wife and two children. The decedent had previously executed a will in which he bequeathed to his wife an amount equal to 50 percent of his adjusted gross estate as finally determined for federal estate tax purposes, less property which passed to her either by specific bequest or outside the will and which qualifies for the marital deduction. The remainder of his estate passed to an inter vivos family trust of which the decedent was the grantor. * * * The trust provided that, upon the decedent's death, * * * (1) the trustee is to pay all the income of the trust to the wife during her life, at least annually. Any undistributed net income upon the wife's death would be distributed to her estate. (2) The trustee has discretion to pay to the wife all or part of the corpus in order to maintain her in her usual manner and style of living or for illness or other emergency. (3) Upon the death of the wife, the balance of the trust corpus will be divided into separate trusts for the benefit of the decedent's children.

* * *

Section 2056(b)(7)(B) defines qualified terminable interest property as property which passes from the decedent, in which the surviving spouse has a qualifying income interest for life, and as to which an election has been made. In order for the income interest to qualify under section 2056(b)(7)(B), the surviving spouse must be entitled to all the income from the property, payable at least annually, and no person may have the power to appoint any part of the property of any person other than the surviving spouse during the spouse's life. In addition, an irrevocable election must be made by the executor on the estate tax return with respect to such property. Section 2056(b)(7)(B)(iv) provides that a specific portion of property shall be treated as separate property.

¶ 27,353

The trust * * * provides that all the income is paid solely to the wife for her life, at least annually, and that no person other than the wife has an interest in the trust corpus during her life. You intend to elect for treatment as qualifying terminable interest property, a fractional share of the trust property defined by means of a formula and computed in a manner necessary to reduce the decedent's federal estate tax liability to zero. The temporary regulation under section 2056, section 22.2056–1, provides that such a partial election is valid. The fractional share will be determined in the following manner. The numerator of the fraction will be the smallest amount of the deduction under section 2056(b)(7) that will, after taking into account the allowable unified credit and any other allowable credits and deductions, result in no federal estate tax being imposed on the decedent's estate. The denominator of the fraction will be the value of the trust corpus as finally determined for federal estate tax purposes less any amounts paid out of the trust fund (such as specific bequests, estate taxes, inheritance taxes, any other debts of the estate, decedent, or beneficiaries that are paid out of the trust fund).

The proposed election of the interest of the trust passing to the surviving spouse will result in determination of a specific portion, after final valuation of the decedent's gross estate and taking into account all allowable deductions and credits. Since the surviving spouse has a qualifying income interest in the trust for life, payable at least annually, no other person has an interest in the trust during the spouse's life, and no one has the power to appoint any part of the trust to anyone other than the spouse, the requirements of section 2056(b)(7) are satisfied as to the fractional share subject to the election. Accordingly, the fractional share subject to the election will be treated as qualifying terminable interest property described in section 2056(b)(7) for which a marital deduction will be allowable under section 2056(a).

The value of the decedent's taxable estate shall be determined, in part, by deducting from the value of the gross estate an amount equal to the value of the specific portion (fractional share) of the trust property subject to the election. That same fractional share of the trust will be taxable to the surviving spouse or the surviving spouse's estate under section 2519 or 2044, as the case may be.

If all property included in the decedent's gross estate which does not qualify for the marital deduction, excluding the family trust, does not exceed all allowable credits and other deductions, the fractional share of the trust treated as qualified terminable interest property as described above will reduce the decedent's federal estate tax to zero.

[¶ 27,355]

f. Spousal Gift Contingent on QTIP Election

Consider Mei Ling's will. It provides that all her property is to be placed in trust. Her husband, George, is to receive all the income for life from the trust (and no one other than George is eligible to receive distributions from the trust while George lives). However, these provisions for the benefit of Mei Ling's husband, George, are to apply if, and only if, Mei Ling's executor makes the QTIP election for the trust property. The executor is also authorized to make a partial QTIP election, and the will provides that Mei Ling's sister (not husband, George) is to receive all the income from the portion of the trust for which the QTIP election is not made. (Practically speaking, the executor's refusal to make the QTIP election would mean that Mei Ling's sister is substituted for George as beneficiary of the entire trust.)

Sound pretty straight forward so far? Hestitatingly you think, almost aloud, "Well, I *guess* so," wondering, "but, why would the executor ever *not* make the QTIP election. The answer is that "not making the election may well be good tax planning." The portion of Mei Ling's estate for which the QTIP election is made will be included in George's estate at his subsequent death. This might not be desirable (for a number of reasons) and allowing Mei Ling's executor discretion to make this election allows for a "last look" at the effectiveness of the tax plan contemplated when the will was drafted.

So far, so good, right? Certainly from the taxpayer's standpoint. What about the IRS? Its initial reaction—as expressed in Reg. § 20.2056(b)–7(d)(3)—was negative. Its view was that an income interest that is contingent upon the QTIP election being made does not qualify for the marital deduction. However, the Fifth, Sixth, and Eighth Circuits and, most recently, the Tax Court, have taken a different approach, concluding that the marital deduction is not lost where the spousal gift is contingent on the QTIP election being made. See, e.g., Estate of Clayton v. Commissioner, 976 F.2d 1486 (5th Cir.1992); Estate of Robertson v. Commissioner, 15 F.3d 779 (8th Cir.1994); Estate of Spencer v. Commissioner 43 F.3d 226 (6th Cir.1995); Estate of Clack v. Commissioner, 106 T.C. 131 (1996). The *Clayton* court reasoned that the making of the QTIP election is an essential part of the statutory definition of what constitutes the qualified terminable interest property. That is, the court concluded that "property" in the statutory definition means that property which the executor identified by making the QTIP election. The court said that evaluation of whether the interest qualifies for the marital deduction begins only after the QTIP election is made. As for the position of the IRS, the court said to disallow the QTIP election in these cases because of the "circular reasoning advanced by the Commissioner" defies "logic, common sense, and the purpose for which QTIP was designed and implemented." 976 F.2d at 1501.

In 1998, the IRS conceded the issue and published new Reg. § 20.2056(b)–7(d)(3)(ii), which provides that an otherwise qualifying income interest that is contingent on an executor's election will not be precluded from QTIP status under the requirements of § 2056(b)(7).

[¶ 27,356]

g. *Spousal Gift Contingent on Tax Payment or Other Election*

It goes without saying that producing a will or trust is a complex undertaking and that it would be uneconomical as well not in the interest of the client for each instrument to be produced from scratch for each client. Boilerplate makes it possible to address myriad issues using techniques that have been refined through repeated use in common situations. Not only do such practices effect economies in the delivery of legal services at prices that

clients are willing and able to afford but the client gets the benefit of the
draftspersons experience and sophistication. Sometimes, though, the draftsperson is unsuccessful in reconciling custom provisions and boilerplate—or
as the draftsperson probably would have explained, "No matter how many
times I read it, I would never have foreseen that conflict!" "Good intentions,
notwithstanding," the Internal Revenue Service might well have said when it
claimed in Patterson v. United States, 181 F.3d 927 (8th Cir. 1999) that the
QTIP election was compromised by the tax payment clause that appear in the
governing instrument. Fortunately, for the taxpayer, the court believed itself
able to provide the needed harmonization by extending what it said was the
common sensical rationale of *Clayton* and its progeny. *Quere: Was that
extension appropriate, i.e., was Patterson really a Clayton-like situation?*
Perhaps, too, as an alternative analysis, consider whether *Patterson* might
well be more than a failed drafting case; perhaps it represents an IRS testing
of some relatively common provisions found in boiler plate documents. Whatever the explanation, it illustrates the perils of boilerplate, a necessary
ingredient in the will and trust drafting process.

Mr. Patterson had executed both a will and a trust. The will provided
that the residue of his probate estate—the property passing under his will—
was to be added to the trust, as is common. The will included a relatively
common tax allocation clause, calling on the executor to pay all death taxes
from Mr. Patterson's residuary probate estate. But, again, as is relatively
common, the will also provided that all or part of Mr. Patterson's death taxes
could, at the discretion of the trustee, be paid from the trust. For its part, the
trust authorized the trustee to pay death taxes from the trust if the trustee
believed such payment to be "expedient and in the best interests" of the trust
beneficiaries. The death taxes were, in fact, paid from the trust.

The dispute in *Patterson* related to the amount of the marital deduction
allowable for estate tax purposes. The trust provided that ten percent of the
trust estate "computed before any reduction for ... death taxes" would be set
aside in a separate trust that would qualify for the QTIP election. The
executors made the QTIP election. The IRS then did its arithmetic and
concluded that payment of the death taxes—more than $4 million—from the
probate estate *rather than from the trust estate* would, under the terms of the
will and trust taken together, require the payment of additional death taxes.
(Why? Using this assumption, the marital deduction would be less than
claimed by the taxpayer because the death taxes would be subtracted before
applying the ten percent.) The IRS relied on Jackson v. United States, 376
U.S. 503 (1964), which appears at ¶ 27,127, for the proposition that the value
of the probate estate must be fixed at the date of death and not when, as in
Patterson, the trustee exercises his discretion to pay the death taxes or not
pay them (thus leaving that task to the executor who would be obligated to
pay the death taxes from the probate estate). It was this discretion that the
IRS claimed to be an impermissible power of appointment, impermissible in
the sense that its exercise could either bring about, post mortem, either an
increase or a decease in the marital deduction. Rejecting the IRS claim, and
finding for the taxpayer, the court first looked approvingly to *Clayton* and
then borrowed the words "counter-intuitive and against common sense" from

¶ 27,356

Spencer and used them inferentially to describe the IRS position in *Patterson*. For additional discussion, see ¶ 27,357.

[¶ 27,357]

h. *Postmortem Rehabilitation*

Postmortem attempts to rehabilitate gifts to a spouse that do not otherwise qualify for the marital deduction have not generally met with success. There are several illustrations. First consider Estate of Rapp v. Commissioner, 140 F.3d 1211 (9th Cir.1998), where Bert Rapp's will created a discretionary pay trust for the benefit of his surviving spouse. Alleging that Mr. Rapp intended the trust to qualify for the marital deduction, his executor petitioned the probate court to modify the trust so that it would qualify for the marital deduction. The probate court obliged and ordered that the trust income be paid to the surviving spouse. The claimed marital deduction on Mr. Rapp's subsequently filed estate tax return was denied, the Ninth Circuit concluding that the will was unambiguous and therefore the probate court was without authority to modify the trust. Conceding that the probate court's decision to reform the trust was erroneous, the executor nonetheless attached great significance to the fact that the probate court order had become final and was unappealable and argued that, as of the date of the filing of the federal estate tax return, the trust, as reformed, then satisfied the requirements for QTIP property for marital deduction purposes. Relying on Commissioner v. Bosch, 387 U.S. 456 (1967), reprinted at ¶ 1107, the Ninth Circuit concluded that the federal court could make an independent determination as to the merits of the case presented to the probate court by Mr. Rapp's executor and was not bound by the state court determination unless that determination had been made by the highest court of the state. That the probate court order had become final and unappealable did not make it a determination of the state's highest court so as to bar the federal court from making an independent determination as to the state property rules that should be applied. From this perspective, the court noted that reference to *Spencer*, *Clayton*, and *Robertson* was misplaced as the issue in *Rapp* was not "the correct measuring date for QTIP election" as it had been in those cases.

The executor used a nonjudicial approach in Estate of Rinaldi v. United States, 38 Fed.Cl. 341 (1997), with a similar lack of success. Again the marital deduction was claimed for property passing to the surviving spouse which was clearly ineligible for the marital deduction at decedent's death. However, the executor claimed the property became eligible for the marital deduction as a result of postmortem developments initiated by him to remove the taint that precluded the property from qualifying for the marital deduction. Clyde Rinaldi willed stock in his printing company to a trust for his surviving spouse, Nelle, expressly authorizing but not requiring that the QTIP election be made for this gift. However, the company stock was subject to an unusual provision that made it ineligible for the marital deduction. By the trust terms, the company stock was required to be offered to son William Rinaldi at a bargain price if son William ever ceased day-to-day management of the printing company. The stock was, thus, ineligible for the marital deduction

¶ **27,357**

because a bargain sale to William—which would diminish the value of the trust—is seen, effectively, as a power to appoint the QTIP property to someone other than the surviving spouse and barred by § 2056(b)(7)(B)(ii)(II). Nonetheless, the executor asserted that the marital deduction was available for the gift to the spouse because the taint of the possible bargain sale was removed from the gift because the shares were redeemed at fair market value by the corporation prior to the filing of the federal estate tax return. Thus, at the time of the filing of the federal estate tax return, son William no longer had the ability to effect the bargain sale (that would result in diminishing the value of the trust). The court explained:

> The initial question for the court, then, is to determine the point at which property must be statutorily eligible for QTIP treatment. If eligibility must be attained at the time of the testator's death, then the court in this case need only look to the terms of the will, and to the right granted thereunder giving the son the opportunity to purchase the Trust's shares at a price below fair market value. Under this approach, the inquiry would end at that point, as the property would clearly fall short of the QTIP non-diminution requirements. If, however, property's QTIP eligibility should not be judged until the estate's executor elects such treatment, then the court's inquiry will expand to include those events occurring subsequent to the testator's death that, according to plaintiff, cured the property's ineligibility.

> A long line of cases echoes the principle that, in general, "qualification for the marital deduction must be determined as of the time of death." Jackson v. United States, 376 U.S. 503, 508, 84 S.Ct. 869, 872, 11 L.Ed.2d 871 (1964). * * * If the trust does not satisfy the statutory requirements at the time of the relevant transaction—usually the death of the decedent—"deductibility of the bequest in controversy cannot hang suspended pending later events." Estate of Weisberger v. Commissioner, 29 T.C. 217, 221–22 (1957).

> Defendant's reliance on this line of cases, though well-founded, does not adequately address the circumstances presented by the QTIP election in this case. Because courts in cases like *Jackson* "ruled on the proper determination date for an interest which is not an exception to the [terminable] interest rule, and not subject to a later election, we do not think [they are] dispositive of this issue." Estate of Spencer v. Commissioner, 43 F.3d 226, 231 (6th Cir.1995). In most situations in which a marital deduction is sought, the final event of any relevance will be the testator's death. In contrast, when QTIP treatment is sought by a taxpayer's estate, one of the prerequisites is that an election have been made on the estate tax return—an event which naturally cannot take place until after the testator's death. Several courts have recognized this event as being of significance sufficient to justify postponing the QTIP eligibility determination until its occurrence.

> In *Spencer*, the taxpayer's will did not designate specific property to receive QTIP treatment, but rather granted his executor the authority to decide what amount of property would be subject to QTIP treatment

when the time came to make the election. The IRS argued that because the executor had the power to decide how much property would go to the QTIP trust, she "possessed an impermissible power to appoint property away from the surviving spouse for the interim period from decedent's death until the date of the QTIP election." Id. at 227.

The court rejected this argument, noting first that "[i]t is often impossible to prudently designate what should be committed as QTIP far in advance of death." Id. at 228. Further, because "no property meets the definition of QTIP until the proper election is made, and no QTIP election can be made until the estate tax form is filed," id. at 231, then logically "no property anywhere can meet the definition of [QTIP] until after the decedent's death." Id. at 228. As such, the court reasoned, it would be "contrary to the policy and meaning of the statute, as well as counter-intuitive and against common sense, to apply the definition before the election can be satisfied." Id. Therefore, the court held that "the date of election is the proper date for deciding if property meets the requirements set out under § 2056(b)(7)." Id.

As to the nature of the QTIP election itself, the court expressed its view as follows:

> The IRS would have us adopt an interpretation that would force property to satisfy every requirement for the QTIP counter-exception on the date of decedent's death except the requirement of election. This would effectively reduce the election requirement to a mere formality, defeat its apparent purpose and its most reasonable interpretation.

Other courts have also refused to invalidate a QTIP election when the subject property is not explicitly defined at the time of the testator's death. In Estate of Clayton v. Commissioner, 976 F.2d 1486, 1490 (5th Cir.1992), the testator's will provided that any property for which a QTIP election was not made would go into a non-QTIP trust. The IRS took the position that this power of the executor to divert part of the estate's property away from a QTIP trust was " 'tantamount' to a power of appointment to the testator's children." Id. at 1497. The court disagreed, finding the IRS's argument to be "flawed logic and deliberate disregard of the plain wording of [the statute]," id., and noting "the overarching truism that many acts must be done and many facts must be determined after the death of the testator in order to determine the taxable estate." Id. at 1498. See also Estate of Robertson v. Commissioner, 15 F.3d 779, 781 (8th Cir.1994) ("We believe the [executor's] right to make or refrain from making a QTIP election is not a prohibited 'power to appoint.' ").

The logic of this line of cases is readily apparent in light of the policies underlying the QTIP legislation. Congress enacted § 2056(b)(7) primarily to allow a testator to provide for a surviving spouse while maintaining control over the ultimate disposition of his or her property following the surviving spouse's death. See H.R.Rep. No. 97–201, at 159–60 (1981), U.S. Code Cong. & Admin. News at 105, 258–59. Under prior law, a testator was forced to choose between leaving property outright to his or her surviving spouse, in which case the property would not be included in the taxable estate, and leaving the property to his or her surviving children, in which case it would be taxed at the testator's death. Under the enacted QTIP provision, a testator may give the surviving spouse the benefit of the property for his or her lifetime without also granting the discretion to direct the ultimate disposition of the property away from the testator's intended beneficiaries.

In offering this tax-deferral opportunity, Congress was careful to include several important conditions within the statutory framework. Most important to our inquiry was its requirement that no person have the "power to appoint any part of the property to any person other than the surviving spouse." § 2056(b)(7)(B)(ii)(II). This provision does not reflect a congressional purpose of ensuring the financial stability of the surviving spouse, for "[i]f the intention had been to dangle the carrot of deductibility in front of testators to induce them to ensure the financial well-being of the surviving spouse, Congress would surely have given the power to make the QTIP election to the surviving spouse, not the executor." *Clayton*, supra, at 1498. Rather, the restriction's inclusion is to ensure that QTIP property does not escape taxation in the surviving spouse's estate, apart from that portion of the corpus used in furtherance of the surviving spouse's well-being. Congress was not concerned with that portion of the estate's property that, for whatever reason, is ineligible for QTIP treatment because "that property is taxed right where the Commissioner and Congress want it taxed—in the estate of the first spouse to die." Id.

There is no compelling reason to prohibit QTIP treatment for those assets whose election is left up to the discretion of the executor. If the executor includes a particular asset in the QTIP trust established by the testator's will, then the asset will be taxed in the estate of the surviving spouse. If the executor declines to elect QTIP status for an asset, then it will be taxed in the testator's estate. Congressional objectives thus do not require that the status of a particular asset be determined at the time of the testator's death. As long as property's QTIP eligibility is ascertainable when the executor elects such treatment in the estate tax return, postponing the eligibility determination until that time runs afoul of neither the plain meaning of the statute's language, nor its underlying objectives.

* * * The factual circumstances on which the reasoning of *Spencer* and its progeny were based differ dramatically from the circumstances presented by the case at hand. In *Spencer*, for example, the terms of the testator's will clearly established a valid QTIP trust—the only ambiguity stemmed from the discretion granted to the executor to decide what amount of property to contribute to the trust. See 43 F.3d at 227.

In this case, by contrast, the trust established by the terms of Rinaldi's will was clearly ineligible for QTIP treatment–the will explicitly subjected the trust's value to diminution through the potential sale of its assets at a bargain price to someone other than the surviving spouse. It is only because the terms of the will apparently no longer dictate the make-up of the trust that plaintiff now can assert QTIP eligibility. * * *

The difficulty with accepting plaintiff's characterization stems from the means by which the trust's defect was allegedly remedied. The trust may indeed have rid itself of the troublesome stock in question; what remains unchanged, however, are the terms of the will that rendered the trust ineligible for QTIP treatment in the first place. There exists no legal impediment to the trust's ownership of the printing company's stock. * * * [T]here is nothing to prevent the trust from reacquiring shares of the company. In the event of such a reacquisition, the terms of Rinaldi's will presumably would still govern. Under those terms, the shares potentially would be subject once again to a bargain sale to Rinaldi's son or a third party, thereby diminishing the corpus of the trust. The portion of the trust's corpus lost in the bargain sale would have escaped taxation in both Rinaldi's and his surviving spouse's estates–the very potentiality which the statutory QTIP requirements were implemented to avoid.

* * *

This potential reemergence of the trust's defect reflects an even more fundamental problem with the approach to QTIP eligibility advocated by plaintiff. Plaintiff is asking this court to judge property's QTIP eligibility solely on the basis of the factual circumstances in place at the time of the executor's election, regardless of the specific terms of the testator's will. Under plaintiff's approach, ad hoc measures enacted after the testator's death by the executor would effectively negate the memorialized intent of the testator, no matter how contrary that intent was to the letter and spirit of the QTIP requirements. In *Spencer*, *Clayton*, and *Robertson*, the testators' memorialized intent was to allow their executors to decide whether or not to elect QTIP status as to a particular asset–importantly, however, every aspect of their wills' terms was consistent with QTIP eligibility. Here, in contrast, Rinaldi's explicit intent was to allow his wife's trust to operate in a manner clearly inconsistent with § 2056(b)(7)'s criteria. To say the least, it would take a generous reading of tax law by the court to extract a legally viable QTIP trust from the facially invalid framework set forth by the testator. Such a reading, in this court's view, is not feasible.

* * *

In addition to requiring precision in the crafting of a will's terms, courts interpreting QTIP provisions place an unmistakable emphasis on the expressed intent of the testator. * * *

When measured against these twin strains of judicial analysis—emphasizing the will's language and the testator's intent—Rinaldi's will falls short. The terms of the will are precise, but their precision sets forth a framework directly contradictory to the statutory requirements for QTIP eligibility. And Rinaldi clearly intended to establish the trust with a condition that would render it ineligible for QTIP treatment. Regardless of his motivation, he did not want his wife's trust to be made up of the printing company's stock in the event that his son no longer participated in the company's management. To bring this about, he was willing to arrange a bargain sale of the shares to his son—an arrangement that violates both the letter and spirit of § 2056(b)(7).

Plaintiff would have us ignore both the terms of the will and the intent of the testator, and focus solely on the factual circumstances as they happened to exist at the time of the QTIP election. The court, however, does not believe that the inquiry into a trust's QTIP eligibility can be divorced from the testamentary framework from which it arose. It is one thing to allow the testator—as the court did in *Spencer*, for example—to defer the identification of particular QTIP assets until after his or her death, when an account of the estate can be made. In those situations, recognizing the validity of the resulting QTIP trust is consistent with the terms and underlying tax policies of § 2056, as well as the intentions and instructions of the testator. It is quite another matter to allow the executor to step in and point to a post-mortem, circumstantial change in the QTIP trust as a remedy for an obvious flaw created by the terms of the trust itself, as set forth in the will.

Does *Patterson*, ¶ 27,356, impact *Rinaldi*? Certainly the *Patterson* court never mentioned *Rinaldi* despite *Rinaldi* having been decided two years earlier. A possible explanation is that it was only the post mortem rehabilative steps taken in *Rinaldi* to eliminate the effect of the tainting language in the will that even made it possible for the executor to attempt to claim the marital deduction for the *Rinaldi* gift. In *Patterson*, by way of contrast, paying the death taxes was just one of "many acts [that] must be done and many facts [that] must be determined *after* the death of the testator in order to determine the taxable estate". 181 F.3d at 930.

Problem

[¶ 27,359]

1. Nick is to receive all of the income from the trust established by his deceased wife, Joanna, in her will. No one else is permitted to receive distributions from the trust while Nick lives. However, if Joanna's executor does not elect QTIP treatment for part or all of Nick's trust, the part for which QTIP is not elected is to be distributed to Sonny, Joanna's son from her first marriage. Is the marital deduction allowed for Nick's entire trust if Joanna's executor makes the QTIP election? For 40 percent of the trust if the executor makes the election for only 40 percent?

2. Refer to ¶ 27,357 and give Bert Rapp's executor some advise. Tell him whether the failure to carry-the-day for marital deduction purposes with the reformed trust means that the trust reverts to its prior terms and is once again a discretionary pay trust—or must it continue to be administered as reformed by the probate court?

[¶ 27,360]

i. Valuation Discounts

Fractionalizing ownership in property not susceptible of ready division is avoided, typically, in planning. Sometimes, though, it becomes reality—with, perhaps, surprisingly favorable consequences to the taxpayer.

ACTION ON DECISION 1999–006

1999–35 IRB 314.

Subject: Estate of Mellinger v. Commissioner, 112 T.C. 26 (1999)

Issue: Whether, for estate tax valuation purposes, a minority interest in a closely-held corporation held in a Qualified Terminable Interest Property (QTIP) trust, which is includible in the gross estate under § 2044, is aggregated with a minority interest in the same corporation that is includible in a decedent's gross estate under other provisions of the Code.

Discussion: Harriet R. Mellinger (decedent) died on April 18, 1993. Decedent's predeceased spouse, Frederick N. Mellinger, died on June 20, 1990. Under the terms of Mr. Mellinger's inter vivos revocable trust, shares comprising 27.861 percent of Fredericks of Hollywood (FOH) passed to a QTIP trust for the benefit of decedent. Mr. Mellinger's estate elected to claim a marital deduction under § 2056(b)(7) for this bequest. Accordingly, on decedent's death, the QTIP trust was includible in decedent's gross estate under § 2044.

Decedent's revocable inter vivos trust also held 27.861 percent of the outstanding shares of FOH. This property was otherwise includible in decedent's gross estate. In a statutory notice of deficiency, the Service determined that the FOH shares held by the QTIP trust and the revocable trust should be aggregated and valued as a controlling interest. In the Tax Court, the Service argued that, under § 2044(a) and (c), the decedent should be treated as the owner of the QTIP trust for valuation purposes. Therefore, the FOH shares held in the QTIP trust should be aggregated with the FOH shares held in the revocable trust and valued as a single block of stock for estate tax purposes.

Under § 2056(b)(7), a decedent's estate is entitled to a marital deduction for transfers of QTIP to the surviving spouse. In order to qualify as QTIP, the surviving spouse must receive a qualifying income interest for life in the property. Upon the death of the surviving spouse, the property usually passes to beneficiaries designated by the decedent or by the spouse pursuant to a limited power of appointment. Accordingly, the first spouse to die can postpone federal estate tax that would otherwise be due on the QTIP trust while also retaining partial or total control over the ultimate disposition of that property.

Under § 2044, the gross estate includes the value of property in which the decedent had a qualifying income interest for life and for which a deduction was allowed under § 2056(b)(7). Section 2044(c) provides that, for purposes of chapters 11 and 13, property includible in the gross estate of the decedent under § 2044(a) will be treated as property passing from the decedent.

The Tax Court rejected the Service's position that the FOH shares includible in the gross estate under § 2044(a) should be aggregated with the FOH shares includible in the gross estate held in the revocable trust. The Tax Court noted that an analysis of § 2044, and the regulations thereunder, does not indicate that Congress intended that property interests includible under § 2044 should be aggregated with interests includible under other Code sections for purposes of determining federal estate tax value. Although § 2044(c) treats QTIP as "passing from the decedent," the court noted that the statute does not provide that the decedent should be treated as the owner of such property for valuation purposes.

Upon further consideration, we agree with the Tax Court's opinion that closely-held stock held in a QTIP trust should not be aggregated, for valuation purposes, with stock in the same corporation held in a revocable trust and includible in the decedent's gross estate. The Tax Court's decision in this case is consistent with the Service's position regarding the valuation of minority interests passing to QTIP trusts. The proper funding of the QTIP trust should reflect, for example, the value of minority interests in closely-held entities or fractional interests in real estate that are used in satisfying the marital bequest. Cf. Estate of Chenoweth v. Commissioner, 88 T.C. 1577 (1987); see also Rev. Rul. 84–105, 1984–2 C.B. 197.

Note

[¶ 27,361]

1. Harriett Mellinger's executor valued each of her shares in Frederick's of Hollywood (FOH) at $4.79 on her estate tax return when filed. The IRS objected, claiming each share had a value of $8.46. The IRS valuation reflected its aggregation of Harriett's 27.8671 percent of FOH with the 27.8671 percent of the shares that her husband, Frederick, had placed in trust for her benefit at the time of his earlier death. Not only did the court reject this aggregation theory—and resulting control premium the IRS placed on the shares—it also allowed Harriett's shares a 25–percent discount for lack of marketability. The effect was to reduce the value of Harriett's FOH shares for estate tax purposes by $8 million.

The IRS and Harriett's executor were able to agree that without aggregation—and without the control premium the IRS claimed—Harriett's shares each had a value of $6.9375. They also agreed that a lack of marketability discount was appropriate if the shares were not to be aggregated. Harriett's executor claimed a 31–percent discount; the IRS claimed a 15–percent discount. Both relied on expert opinion, in each case drawing on one or more experts from the itinerant cadre who travel the country serving as expert witnesses in case-after-case like this. In concluding that the appropriate discount was 25–percent and valuing Harriett's shares at $5.2031 for estate tax purposes, the court explained (112 T.C. at 39):

Petitioner has the burden of proof as to the correctness and amount of the discount. This burden is a burden of persuasion, requiring petitioner to prove the merits of its claim by at least a preponderance of the evidence.

Both parties rely extensively on expert testimony to establish the amount of the discount. Expert opinions are admissible if they will assist the trier of fact to understand evidence that will determine a fact in issue. We evaluate the opinions of experts in light of the demonstrated qualifications of each expert and all other evidence in the record. However, we are not bound by the opinion of an expert witness, especially when such opinions are contrary to our judgment. Where experts offer divergent estimates of fair market value, we decide what weight to give those estimates by examining the factors used by those experts to arrive at their conclusions. While we may accept the opinion of an expert in its entirety, we may be selective and use only part of such an opinion. We may also reach a determination of value based on our own examination of the evidence in the record.

2. The *Mellinger* court followed the conclusion reached in Estate of Bonner v. United States, 84 F.3d 196 (5th Cir.1996). In *Bonner*, a trust created by Mrs. Bonner's will for the benefit of Louis, her husband, owned 37.5% of "the ranch" and 50% of "the New Mexico property" and 50% of a $30,000 boat. Louis Bonner owned the other portions free of trust. Mrs. Bonner's trust was included in Louis' estate under § 2044 because the QTIP election had been made for the trust at Mrs. Bonner's death. Effectively, thus, 100% of each of the three properties were included in Louis' estate for tax purposes at his death. Nonetheless, the court determined that Louis' estate was entitled to a fractional interest discount in valuing each of the parcels for estate tax purposes. (The estate claimed a discount of 45%.) The court explained (84 F.3d at 198):

> In *Estate of Bright v. United States,* [658 F.2d 999 (5th Cir.1981), ¶ 11,037] * * *, this Court, sitting *en banc,* rejected a similar argument, there termed the "doctrine of family attribution." In that case, Bright held a 27 1/2% interest in an asset as executor of his deceased wife's estate, while simultaneously holding an additional 27 1/2% interest in the same asset in his individual capacity. This Court rejected the government's contention that Bright's interests for estate tax purposes should be treated as one 55% interest in the asset.

* * *

The question before us is controlled by the holding in *Bright.* Although § 2044 contemplates that the QTIP property will be treated as having passed from Bonner for estate tax purposes, the statute does not require, nor logically contemplate that in so passing, the QTIP assets would merge with other assets. The assets in the QTIP trust could have been left to any recipient of Mrs. Bonner's choosing, and neither Bonner nor the estate had any control over their ultimate disposition. We are precluded from considering evidence submitted by the government regarding who actually received the assets. An estate tax is an excise tax on the transfer of property at death and accordingly the valuation is made as of the moment of death and must be measured by the interest that passes, as contrasted with the interest held by the decedent before death or the interest held by the legatee after death. *Bright,* 658 F.2d at 1006.

      In addition to arguing that § 2044 mandates merging of the Bonners' fractional interests in the assets, the government also argues that public policy dictates that the Bonners not use the QTIP device to avoid paying taxes on the unified value of the property. In fact, public policy mitigates in favor of the estate's position in this litigation. The estate of each decedent should be required to pay taxes on those assets whose disposition that decedent directs and controls, in spite of the labyrinth of federal tax fictions. In this case, Mrs. Bonner controlled the disposition of her assets, first into a trust with a life interest for Bonner and later to the objects of her largesse. The assets, although taxed as if they passed through Bonner's estate, in fact were controlled at every step by Mrs. Bonner, which a tax valuation with a fractional interest discount would reflect. At the time of Bonner's death, his estate did not have control over Mrs. Bonner's interests in the assets such that it could act as a hypothetical seller negotiating with willing buyers free of the handicaps associated with fractional undivided interests. The valuation of the assets should reflect that reality.

Fractional interest discounts were considered at ¶ 11,066.

Problem

[¶ 27,362]

      " * * * and give the house free of trust to your wife," said Bobbye to her wealthy client, Jonathan. "No," said Luis, the other lawyer. "What Jonathan should do is put part of the house in the bypass trust for the benefit of his wife and give her only part of it free of trust." Bobbye looks surprised and asks, "Why?" His quick reply is, "Look at *Mellinger* and *Bonner! Got it?*" Is his strategy viable? Explain.

[¶ 27,364]

j. Retirement Plan Benefits

      Taxpayers who are participants in tax qualified retirement plans are specially benefitted. "Tax qualification" means that earnings experienced by such plans remain untaxed—for income tax purposes—until distributed to plan participants. And, generally speaking, contributions to such plans are (income) tax deductible by the contributor (and free of income taxes to the plan participant until received by the plan participant). Although most often the plan participant's employer is the source of such contributions, many taxpayers, when eligible, elect to establish tax qualified individual retirement accounts (IRAs). ¶ 21,097.

      As for estate taxes, the value of the benefits held in tax qualified retirement plans, with few, few exceptions, are included in the gross estate of

¶ 27,361

each plan participant at death and are subject to estate tax at that time. § 2039. Qualification of such plans for the marital deduction, though, is sometimes at issue on the grounds that the plan benefits passing to the surviving spouse constitute a nondeductible terminable interest. Near virtual compliance with "the specs" set out in Revenue Ruling 2000–2, ¶ 27,365, is an essential minimum in cases where the plan benefits are payable to a trust. The critical elements are that both the receiving trust and the retirement plan must satisfy the QTIP income requirements and distribution limitations and, for both, the QTIP election must be made. The emphasis is on making certain, at a minimum, that the surviving spouse is entitled to at least annually claim or not claim, at the spouse's option, all of the income from both the receiving trust and the retirement plan.

It should be noted that income tax deferral on plan benefits is ordinarily longest when plan benefits are payable to individuals rather than to a trustee. Sometimes, though, nontax considerations such as control of the ultimate enjoyment of the plan benefits by the plan participant warrants naming a trust as the beneficiary of the plan benefits. In those instances, the marital deduction may well be important. Generally speaking, though it should be kept in mind that naming the surviving spouse as plan beneficiary—rather than a trust—is tax optimum because it allows the surviving spouse to roll the plan benefits over to his or her own IRA, §§ 402(c)(9) and 408(d)(3)(C), and postpone distributions until 70 ½ at which time the "minimum distributions" that must be made from the IRA will be based on the joint life expectancy of the spouse and the spouse's oldest designated beneficiary. § 401(a)(9)C). When distributions are being made to the trust, "minimum distributions" must begin the year following the plan participant's death and the "minimum" will be based on the single life expectancy of the spouse. § 401(a)(9).

[¶ 27,365]

REVENUE RULING 2000–2

2000–3 I.R.B. 305.

* * *

May an executor elect under § 2056(b)(7) of the Internal Revenue Code to treat an individual retirement account (IRA) and a trust as qualified terminable interest property (QTIP) if the trustee of the trust is the named beneficiary of decedent's IRA and the surviving spouse can compel the trustee to withdraw from the IRA an amount equal to all the income earned on the IRA assets at least annually and to distribute that amount to the spouse?

Facts

A died in 1999 at the age of 55, survived by spouse, B, who was 50 years old. Prior to death, A established an IRA described in § 408(a). The IRA is invested only in productive assets. A named the trustee of a testamentary trust established under A's will as the beneficiary of all amounts payable from the IRA after A's death. A copy of the testamentary trust and a list of the trust beneficiaries were provided to the custodian of A's IRA within nine months after A's death. As of the date of A's death, the testamentary trust was irrevocable and was a valid trust under the laws of the state of A's domicile. The IRA was includible in A's gross estate under § 2039.

Under the terms of the testamentary trust, all trust income is payable annually to B, and no one has the power to appoint trust principal to any person other than B. A's children, who are all younger than B, are the sole remainder beneficiaries of the trust. No other person has a beneficial interest in the trust. Under the terms of the trust, B has the power, exercisable annually, to compel the trustee to withdraw from the IRA an amount equal to the income earned on the assets held by the IRA during the year and to distribute that amount through the trust to B. The IRA document contains no prohibition on withdrawal from the IRA of amounts in excess of the annual minimum required distributions under § 408(a)(6).

In accordance with the terms of the IRA instrument, the trustee of the testamentary trust elects, in order to satisfy § 408(a)(6), to receive annual minimum required distributions using the exception to the five year rule in § 401(a)(9)(B)(iii) for distributions over a distribution period equal to a designated beneficiary's life expectancy. Because B's life expectancy is the shortest of all the potential beneficiaries of the testamentary trust's interest in the IRA (including remainder beneficiaries), the distribution period for purposes of § 401(a)(9)(B)(iii) is B's life expectancy. Because B is not the sole beneficiary of the testamentary trust's interest in the IRA, the trustee elected to have the annual minimum required distributions from the IRA to the testamentary trust begin no later than December 31 of the year immediately following the year of A's death. The amount of the annual minimum required distribution for each year is calculated by dividing the account balance of the IRA as of the December 31 immediately preceding the year by the remaining distribution period. On B's death, any undistributed balance of the IRA will be distributed to the testamentary trust over the remaining distribution period.

Law and Analysis

Section 2056(a) provides that the value of the taxable estate is, except as limited by § 2056(b), determined by deducting from the value of the gross estate an amount equal to the value of any interest in property that passes from the decedent to the surviving spouse.

Under § 2056(b)(1), if an interest passing to the surviving spouse will terminate, no deduction is allowed with respect to the interest if, after termination of the spouse's interest, an interest in the property passes or has passed from the decedent to any person other than the surviving spouse (or the estate of the spouse).

Section 2056(b)(7) provides that QTIP, for purposes of § 2056(a), is treated as passing to the surviving spouse and no part of the property shall be treated as passing to any person other than the surviving spouse. Section 2056(b)(7)(B)(i) defines QTIP as property that passes from the decedent, in which the surviving spouse has a qualifying income interest for life, and to which an election applies. Under § 2056(b)(7)(B)(ii), the surviving spouse has a qualifying income interest for life if (I) the surviving spouse is entitled to all the income from the property, payable annually or at more frequent intervals, or has a usufruct interest for life in the property, and (II) no person has a power to appoint any part of the property to any person other than the surviving spouse.

Section 20.2056(b)–7(d)(2) of the Estate Tax Regulations provides that the principles of § 20.2056(b)–5(f), relating to whether the spouse is entitled for life to all of the income from the entire interest, apply in determining whether the surviving spouse is entitled for life to all of the income from the property for QTIP purposes.

Section 20.2056(b)–5(f)(1) provides that, if an interest is transferred in trust, the surviving spouse is entitled for life to all of the income from the entire interest, if the effect of the trust is to give the surviving spouse substantially that degree of beneficial enjoyment of the trust property during the surviving spouse's life which the principles of the law of trusts accord to a person who is unqualifiedly designated as the life beneficiary of a trust.

Section 20.2056(b)–5(f)(8) provides that the terms "entitled for life" and "payable annually or at more frequent intervals" require that under the terms of the trust the income referred to must be currently (at least annually) distributable to the spouse or that the spouse must have such command over the income so that it is virtually the spouse's. Thus, the surviving spouse will be entitled for life to all of the income from the interest, payable annually, if, under the terms of the trust instrument, the spouse has the right exercisable annually (or more frequently) to require distribution to the spouse of the trust income, and otherwise the trust income is to be accumulated and added to corpus.

In the present situation, the IRA is payable to a trust the terms of which entitle B to receive all trust income, payable annually. In addition, no one has a power to appoint any part of the property in the trust or the IRA to any person other than B. Therefore, whether A's executor can elect to treat the trust and the IRA as QTIP depends on whether B is entitled to all the income for life from the IRA, payable annually.

Under the terms of the testamentary trust, B is given the power, exercisable annually, to compel the trustee to withdraw from the IRA an amount equal to all the income earned on the assets held in the IRA and pay that amount to B. If B exercises this power, the trustee must withdraw from the IRA the greater of the amount of income earned on the IRA assets during the year or the annual minimum required distribution. Nothing in the IRA instrument prohibits the trustee from withdrawing such amount from the IRA. If B does not exercise this power, the trustee must withdraw from the IRA only the annual minimum required distribution.

B's power to compel the trustee's action meets the standard set forth in § 20.2056(b)–5(f)(8) for the surviving spouse to be entitled to all the income for life payable annually. Thus, B has a qualifying income interest for life within the meaning of § 2056(b)(7) in both the IRA and the testamentary

¶ 27,365

trust. Furthermore, B has a qualifying income interest for life in the IRA and the testamentary trust for purposes of §§ 2519 and 2044. Because the trust is a conduit for payments equal to income from the IRA to B, A's executor needs to make the QTIP election under § 2056(b)(7) for both the IRA and the testamentary trust.

The result would be the same if the terms of the testamentary trust require the trustee to withdraw from the IRA annually an amount equal to all the income earned on the IRA assets and pay that amount to the surviving spouse.

HOLDING

An executor may elect under § 2056(b)(7) to treat an IRA and a trust as QTIP when the trustee of the trust is the named beneficiary of the decedent's IRA, the surviving spouse can compel the trustee to withdraw from the IRA an amount equal to all the income earned on the IRA assets at least annually and to distribute that amount to the spouse, and no person has a power to appoint any part of the trust property to any person other than the spouse.

[¶ 27,368]

5. SPLIT GIFTS

A marital deduction is also available for the value of an income interest payable to the surviving spouse under a qualified charitable remainder trust as defined under § 664. See § 2056(b)(8). Thereunder, if the surviving spouse is the only noncharitable beneficiary of a charitable remainder annuity trust or unitrust, the value of the annuity or fixed payment payable to the surviving spouse is allowable as a marital deduction. And, of course, the value of the remainder interest destined to go to the charitable organization is deductible under § 2055(e)(2)(A).

In Roels v. United States, 928 F.Supp. 812 (E.D.Wis.1996), the surviving spouse was given all the income from her dead husband's trust until her death or remarriage. The trust was then to terminate and all the remaining trust property was to be distributed to charity. The marital deduction was denied the dead husband's estate because (1) the surviving spouse's interest was terminable upon remarriage and, thus, did not qualify as QTIP as provided in § 2056(b)(7); and (2) the trust did not qualify as a charitable remainder annuity or unitrust as provided in § 2056(b)(8) because the charitable remainder was not determinable at the decedent's death. The charitable deduction, too, would be unavailable to the dead husband's estate (because it was not in a form specified for split interest gifts with both noncharitable and charitable beneficiaries). See ¶ 26,049.

Note

[¶ 27,370]

The taxpayer's rejected argument in *Roels* might have gone something like this: "This is the way I look at it. The marital deduction and/or the charitable deduction should be allowed because it all either goes to the spouse or to charity—and transfers to both are tax deductible. What's the harm?" And getting no reply, one can only imagine the taxpayer walking off, muttering, "The 'law' must be 'an ass' after all." Is it?

I. BARGAINED BEQUESTS

[¶ 27,372]

Sometimes a decedent will put the surviving spouse to an election by making a provision in the will that the surviving spouse may claim only if the spouse allows a portion or all of the spouse's property to pass under the will of the decedent. This technique is commonly referred to as the "widow's election" and not only has nontax aspects but sometimes offers positive tax advantages. However, the device is not often used because of uncertainty as to some of its income tax consequences.

[¶ 27,373]

UNITED STATES v. STAPF

Supreme Court of the United States, 1963.
375 U.S. 118.

MR. JUSTICE GOLDBERG delivered the opinion of the Court.

* * * The Court of Appeals for the Fifth Circuit held that respondents were entitled to certain marital deductions under § 812(e) [1986 Code § 2056(a)] * * *.

Lowell H. Stapf died testate on July 29, 1953, a resident and domiciliary of Texas, a community property jurisdiction. At the time of his death he owned, in addition to his separate estate, a substantial amount of property in community with his wife. His will required that his widow elect either to retain her one-half interest in the community or to take under the will and allow its terms to govern the disposition of her community interest. If Mrs. Stapf were to elect to take under the will, she would be given, after specific bequests to others, one-third of the community property and one-third of her husband's separate estate. By accepting this bequest she would allow her one-half interest in the community to pass, in accordance with the will, into a trust for the benefit of the children. It was further provided that if she chose to take under the will the executors were to pay "all and not merely one-half" of the community debts and administration expenses.

The relevant facts and computations are not in dispute. The decedent's separate property was valued at $65,100 and the community property at $258,105. The only debts were community debts totaling $32,368. The administration expenses, including attorneys' fees, were $4,073. If Mrs. Stapf had not elected to take under the will, she would have retained her fully vested one-half interest in the community property ($129,052) which would have been charged with one-half of the community debts ($16,184) and 35% of the administration expenses ($1,426). Thus, as the parties agree, she would have received a net of $111,443.

In fact Mrs. Stapf elected to take under the will. She received, after specific bequests to others, one-third of the combined separate and community property, a devise valued at $106,268, which was $5,175 less than she would have received had she retained her community property and refused to take under the will.

In computing the net taxable estate, the executors claimed a marital deduction under § 812(e)(1) of the Internal Revenue Code of 1939 [1986 Code § 2056(a)] for the full value of the one-third of decedent's separate estate ($22,367) which passed to his wife under the will. The executors also claimed a deduction for the entire $32,368 of community debts as "claims against the estate" under § 812(b)(3) [1986 Code § 2053(a)(3)] and for the entire $4,073 of expenses as "administration expenses" under § 812(b)(2) [1986 Code § 2053(a)(2)]. The Commissioner of Internal Revenue disallowed the marital deduction and the deductions for claims and administration insofar as these represented debts (50%) and expenses (35%) chargeable to the wife's one-half of the community. Respondents then instituted this suit for a tax refund. * * * For reasons stated below, we hold that the Commissioner was correct and that none of the disputed deductions is allowable.

* * *

By electing to take under the will, Mrs. Stapf, in effect, agreed to accept the property devised to her and, in turn, to surrender property of greater value to the trust for the benefit of the children. This raises the question of whether a decedent's estate is allowed a marital deduction under § 812(e)(1)(E)(ii) of the 1939 Code [1986 Code § 2056(b)(4)(B)] where the bequest to the surviving spouse is on the condition that she convey property of equivalent or greater value to her children. The Government contends that, for purposes of a marital deduction, "the value of the interest passing to the wife is the value of the property given her less the value of the property she is required to give another as a condition to receiving it." On this view, since the widow had no net benefit from the exercise of her election, the estate would be entitled to no marital deduction. Respondents reject this net benefit approach and argue that the plain meaning of the statute makes detriment to the surviving spouse immaterial.

Section 812(e)(1)(a) [1986 Code § 2056(a)] provides that "in general" the marital deduction is for "the value of any interest in property which passes * * * from the decedent to his surviving spouse." Subparagraph (E) [1986 Code § 2056(b)(4)] then deals specifically with the question of valuation:

* * *

> (ii) where such interest or property is encumbered in any manner, or where the surviving spouse incurs any obligation imposed by the decedent with respect to the passing of such interest, such encumbrance or obligation shall be taken into account in the same manner as if the amount of a gift to such spouse of such interest were being determined.

¶ 27,373

The disputed deduction turns upon the interpretation of (1) the introductory phrase "any obligation imposed by the decedent with respect to the passing of such interest," and (2) the concluding provision that "such ... obligation shall be taken into account in the same manner as if the amount of a gift to such spouse of such interest were being determined."

* * * First, § 812(e) [1986 Code § 2056(a)] allows a marital deduction only for the decedent's gifts or bequests which pass "to his surviving spouse." In the present case the effect of the devise was not to distribute wealth to the surviving spouse, but instead to transmit, through the widow, a gift to the couple's children. * * * What the statute provides is a "marital deduction"—a deduction for gifts to the surviving spouse—not a deduction for gifts to the children or a deduction for gifts to privately selected beneficiaries. The appropriate reference, therefore, is * * * to the net value of the gift received by the surviving spouse.

Second, the introductory phrases of § 812(e)(1)(E)(ii) [1986 Code § 2056(b)(4)(B)] provide that the gift-amount determination is to be made "where such interest or property is encumbered in any manner, or where the surviving spouse incurs any obligation imposed by the decedent with respect to the passing of such interest.... " The Government, drawing upon the broad import of this language, argues: "An undertaking by the wife to convey property to a third person, upon which her receipt of property under the decedent's will is conditioned, is plainly an 'obligation imposed by the decedent with respect to the passing of such interest.' " * * * Finally, to arrive at the real value of the gift "such * * * obligation shall be taken into account.... " In context we think this relates the gift-amount determination to the net economic interest received by the surviving spouse.

This interpretation is supported by authoritative declarations of congressional intent. The Senate Committee on Finance, in explaining the operation of the marital deduction, stated its understanding as follows:

> If the decedent bequeaths certain property to his surviving spouse *subject*, however, *to her agreement*, or a charge on the property, for payment of $1,000 to X, the value of the bequest (and, accordingly, the value of the interest passing to the surviving spouse) is the value, reduced by $1,000, of such property. S. Rep. No. 1013, 80th Cong., 2d Sess., Pt. 2, p. 6. (Emphasis added.)

* * * Reg. 105, § 81.47c(b)(1949)[Reg. § 20.2056(b), Example (3)] * * * specifically includes an example of the kind of testamentary disposition involved in this case:

> A decedent bequeathed certain securities to his wife in lieu of her interest in property held by them as community property under the law of the State of their residence. The wife elected to relinquish her community property interest and to take the bequest. For the purpose of the marital deduction, the value of the bequest is to be reduced by the value of the community property interest relinquished by the wife.

We conclude, therefore, that the governing principle, approved by Congress and embodied in the Treasury Regulation, must be that a marital deduction is allowable only to the extent that the property bequeathed to the surviving spouse exceeds in value the property she is required to relinquish.

Our conclusion concerning the congressionally intended result under § 812(e)(1) [1986 Code § 2056(a)] accords with the general purpose of Congress in creating the marital deduction. The 1948 tax amendments were intended to equalize the effect of the estate taxes in community property and common-law jurisdictions. Under a community property system, such as that in Texas, the surviving spouse receives outright ownership of one-half of the community property and only the other one-half is included in the decedent's estate. To equalize the incidence of progressively scaled estate taxes and to adhere to the patterns of state law, the marital deduction permits a deceased spouse, subject to certain requirements, to transfer free of taxes one-half of his non-community property to his surviving spouse. Although applicable to separately held property in a community property state, the primary thrust of this is to extend to taxpayers in common-law States the advantages of "estate splitting" otherwise available only in community property States. The purpose, however, is only to permit a married couple's property to be taxed in two stages and not to allow a tax-exempt transfer of wealth into succeeding generations. Thus the marital deduction is generally restricted to the transfer of property interests that will be includible in the surviving spouse's gross estate. Respondents' construction of § 812(e)(1) [1986 Code § 2056(a)] would, nevertheless, permit one-half of a spouse's wealth to pass from one generation to another without being subject either to gift or estate taxes. We do not believe that this result, squarely contrary to the concept of the marital deduction, can be justified by the language of § 812(e)(1). Furthermore, since in a community property jurisdiction one-half of the community normally vests in the wife, approval of the claimed deduction would create an opportunity for tax reduction that, as a practical matter, would be more readily available to couples in community property jurisdictions than to couples in common-law jurisdictions. Such a result, again, would be unnecessarily inconsistent with a basic purpose of the statute.

* * * We conclude that, for estate tax purposes, the value of a conditional bequest to a widow should be the value of the property given to her less the value of the property she is required to give to another. In this case the value of the property transferred to Mrs. Stapf ($106,268) must be reduced by the value of the community property she was required to relinquish ($111,443). Since she received no net benefit, the estate is entitled to no marital deduction. * * *

J. JOINT AND MUTUAL WILLS

[¶ 27,379]

While not commonplace, all too frequently spouses are found to have executed a joint and mutual will, i.e., a single will signed by both spouses and purporting to be the will of both of them containing, usually, reciprocal provisions with a disposition of all the property owned by the last of them to die. Sometimes separate wills are found to be "contractual," i.e., executed in consideration of each other. Contractual wills raise many of the practical issues associated joint and mutual wills Such endeavors are characterized, at best, as well-intentioned efforts at self-help that invariably raise questions as to the ability of the surviving spouse to make a different disposition than that contemplated by the joint and mutual will or the separate will of the contracting party first to die. Joint and mutual wills and contractual wills also raise questions as to whether such wills allow the property passing to the survivor to qualify for the marital deduction.

1. PROBATE PROPERTY

[¶ 27,385]

ESTATE OF ABRUZZINO v. COMMISSIONER

United States Tax Court, 1973.
61 T.C. 306.

TIETJENS, Judge.

* * * [T]he only question remaining for decision is whether the estate is entitled to a marital deduction under section 2056 for the value of the interest in real estate and stock in Community Super Markets, Inc., passing to Barbara Abruzzino (hereafter Barbara) pursuant to the terms of the joint last will and testament of Barbara and Robert Abruzzino (hereafter decedent). [Robert was survived not only by wife, Barbara, but also by two daughters, and a son, William Abruzzino. The will provided:]

* * *

SECOND: In case my husband, Robert Abruzzino, survive me, I Barbara Abruzzino, give, devise and bequeath to my husband, Robert Abruzzino, all property (real, personal and mixed) of whatever kind and description and wherever located, of which I may die seized or possessed * * *.

THIRD: In case my wife, Barbara Abruzzino, survive me, I, Robert Abruzzino, hereby give, devise and bequeath to my son William Abruzzino forty percent (40%) of my stock in Community Super Markets, Inc.; I give, devise and bequeath * * * to my wife, Barbara Abruzzino, all the balance and residue of all property (real, personal and mixed) of whatever kind and description and wherever located, of which I may die seized or possessed * * *.

FOURTH: * * * In case Barbara Abruzzino survive [sic], she agrees not to dispose of the real estate or the stock in Community Super Markets, Inc. except as provided in the will of the survivor set out below.

FIFTH: The survivor of us * * * gives, devises and bequeaths all the balance and residue of all property (real, personal and mixed) of whatever kind and description and wherever located of which the survivor of us may die seized or possessed to our son, William Abruzzino.

The Commissioner determined that decedent's estate was not entitled to a marital deduction for the value of the real estate and stock in Community

Super Markets, Inc., devised and bequeathed to Barbara. He argues that, because Barbara is contractually bound to hold the real estate and stock for her life and to give them to her son at her death, her interests are terminable and not deductible under section 2056(b)(1).

* * *

Petitioner and the Commissioner recognize the necessity of looking to the law of West Virginia to determine the nature of Barbara's interests in the real estate and stock. * * *

The Supreme Court of Appeals of West Virginia has held that a joint will or mutual wills may represent a contract which entitles its beneficiaries to its enforcement in equity once the survivor has accepted benefits under the will of the first to die. See, for example, Underwood v. Myer, 107 W.Va. 57, 146 S.E. 896 (1929). The Supreme Court of Appeals follows a rule attributed to Underwood v. Myer, supra, that "reciprocal provisions of * * * [a joint] will prima facie evidence a contractual relationship between the makers." Wilson v. Starbuck, 116 W.Va. 554, 182 S.E. 539 at 540 (1935). In Wilson v. Starbuck, supra, the rationale of the *Underwood* rule was explained (182 S.E. at 540):

The reasoning upon which this holding is based seems to be that the fact of execution of a joint will is of itself proof positive that both of the parties had full knowledge of the terms and provisions of the will, that the reciprocal dispositions show a consideration moving from each to the other, and hence that it must be supposed that they entered into the agreement in a contractual sense.

Considering the reasoning on which the *Underwood* rule is based, we believe that the provisions of the joint will of Barbara and decedent are sufficiently reciprocal for us to conclude that those provisions contractually bind Barbara after decedent's death. The joint will is "proof positive" that both Barbara and decedent had full knowledge of its terms. Although not strictly reciprocal, the dispositions show "a consideration moving from" decedent to Barbara. Accordingly, we are convinced that a West Virginia court would hold that Barbara and decedent entered into an agreement "in a contractual sense" since the fully stipulated record contains nothing to disprove the prima facie contract established by the will.

The language of the second sentence of Article Fourth supports our conclusion that the provisions of the will are contractually binding. That sentence states: "In case Barbara Abruzzino survive, she *agrees* not to dispose of the real estate or the stock in Community Super Markets, Inc., except as provided in the will of the survivor set out below." [Emphasis supplied.] We believe that the language of that sentence indicates a contract. * * *

Accordingly, we construe the second sentence of Article Fourth as restricting Barbara's disposition of the real estate and stock whenever she received that real estate and stock by surviving the decedent. We note that sentence logically precedes Article Fifth which gives the terms of the disposition.

* * *

¶ 27,385

Since we have concluded that Barbara is contractually bound to hold the real estate and stock for her life and to give it to her son at her death, [we] hold that Barbara's interests in the real estate and stock are terminable [and do not qualify for the marital deduction]. * * *

2. NONPROBATE PROPERTY

[¶ 27,391]

ESTATE OF AWTRY v. COMMISSIONER

United States Court of Appeals, Eighth Circuit, 1955.
221 F.2d 749.

VAN OOSTERHOUT, Circuit Judge.

* * * The Commissioner and The Tax Court denied petitioner a marital deduction as to certain property * * * held by decedent and his spouse as joint tenants. The court based its decision upon its conclusion that the interest of the surviving spouse, Nellie Awtry, in the joint tenancy property was a terminable interest.

* * *

[The estate would be free of estate tax if the marital deduction was available for the joint tenancy property. The will provided:]

"Whatever property we own, real or personal, we jointly own whether or not so recorded, and we have agreed and do hereby agree that the survivor of us shall have the full use and income and control of all our property as long as the survivor of us shall live.

"ARTICLE THREE.

"After the death of the survivor of us all our property, real and personal, shall be sold by our trustees hereinafter named and the net proceeds shall be divided into two equal parts to be distributed amongst our nephews and nieces hereinafter named, to-wit: * * * * "

* * *

We are convinced after a careful consideration of the authorities above cited that Nellie Awtry received complete and absolute fee simple title to the joint tenancy real estate, the joint bank deposits, and the jointly-held Government bonds by virtue of the deeds and contracts creating such joint tenancies. No interest in any of such property ever reached the estate of Emmet Awtry. Emmet Awtry's death terminated all interest that he had in the joint tenancy property. A will only operates upon such property as a decedent may own at the time of his death. We conclude that so far as the involved joint tenancy properties are concerned there was nothing for Mr. Awtry's will to operate upon, and this is true even if it be conceded that the will by its terms was broad enough to include the joint tenancy property.

* * *

¶ 27,391

The joint will of Mr. and Mrs. Awtry is the separate will of each of them. To make the wills effective, separate probate upon the death of each of them is required. Each will passes the property owned by each testator at the time of his death. All the usual and ordinary rules pertaining to wills and the property passing thereunder prevail. It appears to us that there was nothing which Mr. Awtry by his will as a testamentary instrument could do to affect the complete title in the joint tenancy property which had passed to Mrs. Awtry by survivorship.

We wish to emphasize again that the effect of Mr. Awtry's will upon the property owned by Mr. Awtry at the time of his death is in no way involved in this case. As to such property it may be conceded for the purposes of this case that Mrs. Awtry's interest is a terminable interest.

It now becomes necessary to determine whether the contractual features of the joint will are such as to make the interest acquired by Mrs. Awtry in the joint tenancy property a terminable interest within the meaning of § 812(e)(1)(B) [1986 Code § 2056(a)].

* * *

As a * * * reason for refusing to deny the marital deduction as to the jointly owned property, we note that so far as the record discloses the survivor voluntarily surrendered the right to revoke her will. Any restriction which may have been placed upon her right to revoke could, under the circumstances of the case, only be imposed upon her by her voluntary act. The husband was without any power or right to restrict the wife's right to deal with property she might own at the time of her death. The estate tax involved here is that due from the husband's estate. It seems unreasonable to hold that by his contract the husband could, for estate tax purposes, reduce his wife's independently acquired fee simple title to what is defined in the estate tax law as a terminable interest. The contractual restrictions now relied upon by the Commissioner were not imposed by Mr. Awtry in connection with the creation of the various joint tenancies. If the contract now relied on was part of the consideration for the joint tenancies, there would be more merit in the Commissioner's present position. Such, however, is not the case under this record.

* * *

We will now consider the question of the meaning of the words "passing from the decedent" in section 812(e)(1)(B), [1986 Code § 2056(a)] * * *. We do not believe that there is anything which requires us to give these words any strained or artificial construction. The natural construction should prevail. Section 812(e)(3) [1986 Code § 2056(c)] defines the situations where interests are to be considered as passing from the decedent. There is nothing in such definitions which requires us to hold that a restriction voluntarily placed by a beneficiary upon her own property turns an absolute interest into a terminable one. * * *

We conclude that Mrs. Awtry acquired absolute title to the joint tenancy property through the joint tenancy contracts, that the will as a testamentary instrument in no way affects the title to the joint tenancy property, and that the joint tenancy property did not by reason of anything done by Mr. Awtry pass to others than his surviving spouse. The estate is entitled to the marital deduction on the property passing to Mrs. Awtry by the joint tenancy contracts.

The judgment of the Tax Court is reversed.

Notes

[¶ 27,397]

1. The IRS accepted the position of *Awtry* in Rev. Rul. 71–51, 1971–1 C.B. 274. Similarly, the IRS concluded that the proceeds of life insurance payable to the surviving spouse qualified for the marital deduction despite the fact that they were subject to the joint and mutual will. The IRS explained:

> [T]he proceeds of life insurance pass to the named beneficiary by reason of the designation in the insurance contract and not under the will or pursuant to any contractual provision in the will. Any restriction limiting the surviving tenant's (beneficiary's) interest to a life estate is not placed on the property by the decedent but arises out of the contract voluntarily entered into by the survivor.

The IRS also concluded, in the following terms, that the surviving spouse made a transfer subject to a retained life estate under § 2036(a)(1):

> The surviving wife's survivorship interest in the jointly held property * * * ripened into absolute ownership upon the death of her husband. However, under the contractual aspects of the joint and mutual will that were irrevocable at the death of the husband, the wife's fee interest in the property was reduced to a life estate, the remainder interest passing to the children. Thus, the wife is deemed to have made a transfer * * * [at the time of the husband's death] of the entire value of the property, under which she retained for her life the right to the income from the property.
>
> Accordingly, * * * the entire value of the remainder of the property held jointly with her husband * * * is includible in the deceased wife's gross estate under section 2036 * * *.

2. The IRS may be suggesting in Rev. Rul. 71–51 that there was a taxable gift made by the surviving spouse at the time the mutual will became contractually binding on her to leave the remainder interest in the joint property to their children.

3. For a discussion of the consequences with regard to the marital deduction of joint and mutual wills, see Hess, "The Federal Transfer Tax Consequences of Joint and Mutual Wills," 24 Real Prop. Prob. & Trust J. 469, 495 (1990).

Problem

[¶ 27,403]

Charlie and Jeanne had shared life and wanted to share a will, the result being that they both executed the following simple writing, complying fully with all requirements for the execution of wills:

WILL

We direct that the survivor of us shall have all our property of every kind and character and wherever the same may be situated of which either of us or both of us may die possessed, to be used, occupied, enjoyed, sold, conveyed and expended and disposed of by such survivor as such survivor shall desire, fee simple title. Upon the death of the second of us to die, any property remaining shall be distributed to our children. In the event that we shall be killed by an accident or die from the infirmities of old age or any other cause bringing death to each of us at or near the same time, then, in that event ONLY, we give all our property to our beloved children, share and share alike, in fee simple.

Jeanne has died. Her property consisted of a ranch with a value of $1 million. Is the marital deduction available to Jeanne's estate for the ranch? See § 2056(b)(7)(relating to QTIP); Reg. § 20.2056(c)–2 (relating to the "passing" requirement).

K. PLANNING FOR MARITAL DEDUCTION

[¶ 27,409]

1. OVERMARITALIZATION

One of the objectives in planning the estates of a married couple is, of course, the minimization of the estate taxes on the two estates. This involves a consideration of the amount of property to be left to the surviving spouse as a part of the marital deduction. Overuse of the marital deduction in the estate of the first member of the couple to die can result in a much heavier overall tax by reason of the second estate's being placed in the higher tax brackets through the addition of too much property from the first estate. With the unlimited marital deduction readily available, one may be encouraged to do exactly that, i.e., to over utilize the marital deduction and give the surviving spouse more property than necessary to eliminate all tax in the first estate, even though the second estate may wind up in substantially higher brackets. It is difficult to conceive of a situation where over utilization of the marital deduction is warranted even if the surviving spouse contemplates an aggressive gift-giving program to take advantage of the $10,000 per-donee exclusion provided for in § 2503(b). The estate planner may try to meet this problem in advance through a careful use of the marital deduction formula in spelling out the spouse's bequest. At this point, if the projection misses the mark by a substantial amount, a qualified disclaimer filed by the surviving spouse under § 2518 may be extremely useful in making a more appropriate division of the estate between the taxable and nontaxable portions. Note that the disclaimer may be operative upon all of an interest in property or upon an undivided portion thereof. For consideration of disclaimers, see Chapter 6.

2. FORMULA MARITAL DEDUCTION CLAUSES AND RELATED PROVISIONS

[¶ 27,415]

a. Use of the Bypass Trust

With the unlimited marital deduction, all estate tax upon the death of the first spouse can be eliminated merely by leaving all the estate to the surviving spouse. However, it is at the death of second spouse that the aggregate property—that of both spouses—will be taxed and, this time, without benefit of any marital deduction (unless the surviving spouse has remarried and has made a gift to the new spouse) and with only *one* applicable exclusion amount available to shelter the aggregate property. (The applicable exclusion amount increased to $2 million in 2006 and is scheduled to increase to $3.5 million in 2009. § 2010(c)) The availability of only *one* applicable exclusion amount at the death of the second spouse results because Congress has not seen fit to provide for transferability of a decedent's unused applicable exclusion amount.

In the case of larger estates, so long as there is an estate tax, responsible planning dictates securing the benefits of the applicable exclusion amount for the estate of the first spouse to die. Otherwise, the concentration of the family's property in the estate of the surviving spouse will lead to unnecessary estate taxes. A married couple with $4 million in 2006, for example, would want to see that each estate used fully the available applicable exclusion amount, without having the property covered by the applicable exclusion amount in the first estate added to the second estate to be there taxed. Instead a trust is typically created that benefits the surviving spouse but "bypasses" the estate of the surviving spouse for tax purposes.

> *Example*: If Hapless and Willful each had estates of $2 million, upon the death of the first (whether it be Hapless or Willful), the deceased spouse's will should give to a so-called "bypass" trust—which is not intended to qualify for the marital deduction—an amount equal to the applicable exclusion amount (then available) with the balance of the decedent's estate being given to the surviving spouse. In this fashion, no tax would be payable upon the death of either spouse (assuming the value of survivor's property remains at or below the applicable exclusion amount available at that person's death).

The bypass trust is sometimes referred to as the "credit shelter trust" or even, less descriptively, as the "family trust". It will provide benefits (income or principal or both) for the surviving spouse or others but will not be taxable in the estate of the surviving spouse unless the surviving spouse is found to have a general power of appointment over the trust—a condition to be scrupulously avoided if the tax sheltering promise of the bypass trust is to be realized. See § 2041. (Alternatively the bypass vehicle could be an outright

¶ 27,415

bequest to persons other than the surviving spouse, thus accomplishing the same tax sheltering effect.)

Taxpayers planning to shelter the applicable exclusion amount in a bypass trust will normally use a formula to bring about the division of the estate between the bypass trust and the gift to the surviving spouse designed to qualify for the marital deduction. While the following provisions could be further refined, they are examples of what might be found in a so-called tax-planning will:

(a) To my spouse I give the smallest amount necessary to eliminate federal estate tax at my death;

(b) The balance of my estate I give to my trustee to pay the income to my spouse for life and, at the death of my spouse, the trust shall terminate, and the trustee shall distribute the property then constituting the trust estate per stirpes to my then-living lineal descendants.

The basic concept, however, is a rather simple one: to set aside a portion of the estate—the portion that would go free of tax by reason of the unified credit—such portion then being disposed of in such a way as not to fall into the gross estate of the survivor. The balance of the estate then can go to the survivor in a form that will qualify for the marital deduction.

Nontax considerations complicate use of the formula driven bypass trust. With the scheduled increase in the unified credit to $3.5 million in 2009 (and the scheduled repeal of the estate tax for those dying in 2010), the formula commonly employed will, in many estates, cause all the decedent's property to flow to the bypass trust, leaving the surviving spouse with none of the decedent's property *free of trust*. Care will need to taken to make certain that taxpayers *really* want such a result and, for those who do not, special drafting will be required to make clear the intention of the will maker to give some or all property to the surviving spouse *free of trust* where estate taxes are not thereby increased. Among the possible solutions is a will giving everything to the surviving trust free of trust but, to the extent the surviving spouse disclaims part or all of the gift, the disclaimed share falls back into a bypass trust provided for in the decedent's will. Obviously, this places "control" in the surviving spouse, a situation not welcomed by every testator. Another alternative is to provide a certain "minimum" gift to the surviving spouse free of trust, the minimum gift being determined by making projections as to the likely value of the estate of the surviving spouse at the spouse's later death. Such projections are necessarily fraught with uncertainty and risk disappointing one or more expectant beneficiaries.

In the smaller estates, it might seem that less care would need be exercised with respect to securing the applicable exclusion amount. For example, § 2010(c)'s applicable exclusion amount completely shelters estates aggregating less than $2 million in 2006. With scheduled increases to $3.5 million in 2009, a relatively large amount of property can be concentrated in the estate of the surviving spouse free of estate taxes at the death of that spouse. However, there are no assurances that one spouse will survive until the applicable exclusion amount is increased to $3.5 million (or the estate tax is repealed in 2010 as scheduled). In anticipation of that possibility, responsible planning calls for securing to the first spouse to die the sheltering benefits of the applicable exclusion amount. That means, causing to be subject to tax at the death of the first spouse to die, an amount up to but not greater than the applicable exclusion amount.

[¶ 27,421]

b. *Division of Estate Before Death*

Lifetime transfers between spouses often must be considered. For example, in the case where one spouse has an estate of $2 million or more in 2006 but the other spouse's estate is negligible, lifetime interspousal transfers to increase the estate of the poorer spouse may well be warranted to lock in the sheltering effect of the unified credit that is available to each spouse. Otherwise, if the poorer spouse dies first, without such transfers from the richer spouse, little or no property would be available to be sheltered from estate tax at the death of the surviving spouse. By increasing the estate of the poorer spouse, full benefit of the unified credit for each spouse will be obtained without regard to which dies first. And here, too, the assumption is made that the amount of the property measured by the unified credit formula goes into a bypass vehicle.

[¶ 27,427]

c. *Estate Equalization*

In past years, some estate planners, who had already seen to it that the spouses' property was divided sufficiently to assure a full use of the credit in each estate, would go further and provide for an equal division between the two spouses at the death of the first of them to die, taking account of values at the death of the first spouse to die. In some cases, such a strategy meant paying estate tax at the death of the first spouse to die (effectively ignoring the right to eliminate all estate taxes at the death of the first to die through use of the marital deduction). Under certain facts such a strategy would result in lower total estate taxes for persons married to each other even though it meant paying estate tax at the death of the first spouse to die. However, with the announced repeal of the estate tax effective as to decedents dying in 2010, any strategy that contemplates payment of estate tax that is otherwise deferrable is likely flawed. Moreover, even without repeal, the strategy is flawed because of the virtually flat rate estate tax of 45 percent beginning in 2007.

[¶ 27,439]

d. *Transition to Unlimited Marital Deduction*

There are many pre–1982 wills that used one of the then-customary marital deduction formula clauses "expressly providing that the spouse is to receive the maximum amount of property qualifying for the marital deduction allowable by federal law." For this reason, Congress felt it unwise to allow the unlimited marital deduction amendment to enlarge such marital bequests automatically without a clear indication that it was the testator's intent to do so. Accordingly, the amendment removing the ceiling on the marital deduction was made inapplicable to wills executed before September 13, 1981, or to trusts created before that date, if such instruments contained maximum marital deduction clauses that had not been amended after that date "to refer specifically to an unlimited marital deduction." Thus, almost invariably, pre–1982 wills and trusts should be reviewed carefully with this transition rule in mind.

[¶ 27,445]

3. EQUALIZATION CLAUSES

Taxpayers unafraid of complexity and committed to tax minimization sometimes resorted to including "estate equalization" clauses in a will or trust in anticipation of close order of deaths of husband and wife. Such a clause might provide, for example, that:

> If the decedent's surviving spouse dies within six months of the decedent, the property distributed to the surviving spouse from the decedent's estate is not to exceed that amount necessary to reduce the combined federal estate taxes imposed on the estates of the decedent and the spouse to the least possible amount and shall be zero if the combined federal estate taxes imposed on the estates of the decedent and the spouse are not reduced by the distribution of property from the decedent to the surviving spouse.

While such clauses are less likely to be used in the coming years, they will be found in existing wills. That said, it is worth noting that the IRS has challenged equalization clauses in the past using its traditional "snapshot" approach to the marital deduction, *i.e.,* all events relative to the allowance of the marital deduction must be resolved at the instant of death. The leading case is Estate of Smith (C.W.) v. Commissioner, 565 F.2d 455 (7th Cir.1977), where the court rejected the IRS' argument that the use of a so-called estate equalization clause created a nondeductible terminable interest for marital deduction purposes. In *Smith,* the executor was authorized to value the property on the alternate valuation date under § 2032. The IRS had argued, on the authority of the Supreme Court's decision in *Jackson,* ¶ 27,127, that, as of the date of the decedent's death, the presence of the estate equalization clause made it impossible to know whether any property would pass from the decedent to his spouse and that the spouse's interest in the property passing from the decedent was contingent, or subject to divestment, upon an event, namely the valuation of the spouse's estate that would occur after the death of the decedent. The court reasoned, however, that, although the value of the interest passing to the spouse "would remain unknown until a later time, the spouse was nevertheless indefeasibly vested in the interest" in the property passing to the surviving spouse upon the decedent's death.

The IRS has announced that it will follow the result in *Smith.* Rev. Rul. 82–23, 1982–1 C.B. 139. However, it might be ventured that no two equalization clauses are alike and that, as a result, IRS challenges are not foreclosed.

4. FUNDING THE MARITAL BEQUEST

[¶ 27,451]

a. *Fractional Formula Clauses*

Determination of the amount is the starting point for thinking about the marital deduction. Even in cases where the marital deduction amount is determined by a formula clause, very complex issues relating to funding the marital deduction gift are often presented during the administration of the estate. For example, in cases where the marital gift is expressed as a fraction of the decedent's property (e.g., "1/2 of my estate") or where the marital gift is expressed as in terms of formula that results in a fraction (e.g., "smallest fraction of my estate necessary to eliminate federal estate tax"), questions often arise as to whether the decedent intended to give the surviving spouse a fraction of every item of property in the estate or merely a fraction of the residue of the estate. Similarly, the question will invariably arise as to whether a non-pro rata distribution can be effected (to avoid fractionalization of the items of property making up the fund against which the fraction is applied), and, even in cases where a non-pro rata distribution is permitted, the question arises as to whether a non-pro rata distribution will trigger recognition of gain or loss in cases where estate property is distributed in kind.

> *Example*: Snerdly, the lawyer, and Elizabeth, his client, are in the 5th hour of their meeting to review the will he prepared for her. Lets pick up on the conversation with Elizabeth saying, "What's this provision saying that 'My executor is authorized to make non-pro rata distributions in kind.'?" Barely holding back a yawn, Snerdly resolves to get-himself-up for a response one more time and begins with. "Glad you asked that. Shows that you are a careful reader. I like that in clients." Looking at Elizabeth approvingly, he adds, "currently your estate has a value of $2 million–and, as a result it will be fully sheltered for estate tax purposes by the applicable exclusion amount." § 2010(c). He goes on to say, however, that suppose Elizabeth dies in 2009 when the applicable exclusion amount is $3.5 million and her estate has a then value of $4 million. Suppose, further, that her estate then consists of three parcels of real estate, the first parcel having a value of $3.5 million, the second a value of $300,000 and the third a value of $200,000. Her will provides that her husband, Philip, is to receive the "smallest fraction" of her estate "necessary to eliminate federal estate tax" at her death, with the balance going to a bypass trust for Philip's benefit for life. Taking into account the $3.5 million applicable exclusion amount available to Elizabeth's estate in 2009 under § 2010(c), the fraction of the residue passing to Philip will be 25 percent ($500,000/$4,000,000). Snerdly asks, "should Philip receive a 12.5 percent interest in all three parcels? Or what if Philip is given the second and third parcels, having an aggregate value of $500,000," as of the date of Elizabeth's death? Continuing, "Furthermore, what if the value of each of the parcels changes" after Elizabeth's death (and the projected date for the distribution to Philip) so that the

first parcel then has a value of $500,000 (down from its date of death value of $3.5 million), the second, a value of $500,000 and, the third, a value of $1.2 million? (Presently the third parcel is swampland, its value is inflated because a modern day "dot.com" plans to build it new headquarters on the adjacent parcel, leading to speculation that the "dot.com" will want to acquire the third parcel for expansion after it goes public.) Assume that, under these circumstances, Philip is given the second parcel with a date-of-distribution value of $500,000. That is, he says, "assume, in other words, that a non-pro rata distribution is made, meaning that Philip has given up his fractional interest in the first and third parcels in return for all of the second." Generally speaking, Snerdly says, "this is a sale and exchange," and sales and exchanges have income tax consequences, the seller recognizing gain or loss to the extent of the difference between the value of the interest given up and the value of the interest obtained. However, if local law or the governing instrument authorizes non-pro rata distributions in satisfaction of a fractional bequest, a taxable sale or exchange will not result. Rev. Ruls. 83–61, 1983–1 C.B. 78 and 69–486, 1969–2 C.B. 159; Priv. Ltr. Rul. 8119040. "It is for the latter reason that we inserted that non-pro rata authorization clause in your will." At this point, Snerdly asks, looking over at Elizabeth somewhat apprehensively, "Are you with me?" And Elizabeth, eyes beginning to glaze over, says, hesitatingly, "I think so." After a moment staring at the copy of the will she is holding, she says, "actually I don't think that I have any more questions. When can we sign the will?" Snerdly sighs. He'd enjoyed explaining marital deduction funding issues to Elizabeth and hoped that she would have been inclined to engage him further.

[¶ 27,457]

b. Pecuniary Formula Clauses

Different issues are presented in cases where the marital gift is expressed as a pecuniary amount (e.g., "$300,000 to my spouse") or a formula clause is used to produce a pecuniary amount (e.g., "to my spouse, I give the smallest amount necessary to eliminate federal estate tax at my death"). Few problems are presented in such a case where cash is available to satisfy the claim of the surviving spouse. However, in cases where appreciated property is used to satisfy the gift to the surviving spouse, gain or loss recognition is often triggered.

> *Example*: Assume the same facts as in the case of the example at ¶ 27,451, except that the formula marital gift was expressed in terms of "the smallest pecuniary amount." If Elizabeth dies in 2009, satisfaction of the marital gift of $500,000 with the second parcel, which had appreciated from $300,000 to $500,000, will result in the estate of the decedent recognizing gain to the extent of $200,000. This assumes that the property distributed in kind was valued as of the date of distribution (even though the property was valued as of the date of death for estate tax purposes).

¶ 27,451

In an effort to avoid not only gain recognition when a pecuniary bequest is satisfied with appreciated property but also the need for a second valuation as of the date of distribution, taxpayers have undertaken to utilize a number of different stratagems. One short-lived stratagem called for any distribution in kind to be valued as of the date of the decedent's death without regard for the value of the property as of the date of distribution.

Example: George's will called for his wife, Barbara, to receive a bequest of $400,000. George's estate consisted of three parcels, to wit:

Valuation

	Date of Death	*Date of Distribution*
Parcel X	$400,000	$100,000
Parcel Y	$100,000	$400,000
Parcel Z	$500,000	$500,000
	$1,000,000	$1,000,000

Inasmuch as Barbara is entitled to $400,000 from George's estate using date-of-death values, George's executor proposes to distribute parcel X to Barbara in full satisfaction of Barbara's claim. Barbara wonders whether the executor "can get away with" ripping her off in this way? For his part, George's executor says that Barbara should look on the bright side and appreciate the fact that funding her $400,000 claim with depreciated property will cause her estate to be smaller for estate tax purposes (assuming parcel X never regains its lost value). In essence, George's executor says, George's estate enjoyed an estate tax deduction of $400,000, while Barbara will need to include only the depreciated value of parcel X in her estate at her later death (assuming it does not increase in value in the meantime). Without regard to George's executor's ability under the governing instrument or applicable state law to do or not do as he proposes, the IRS will disallow the full marital deduction to George's estate under the authority of Rev. Proc. 64–19, discussed below.

[¶ 27,463]

c. *Rev. Proc. 64–19*

Rev. Proc. 64–19, 1964–1 C.B. 682, is one of the best-known IRS pronouncements. In it, the IRS announced that the marital deduction will not be allowed where a gift of a pecuniary amount is made to the surviving spouse and the gift, under either applicable state law or the governing instrument, could be satisfied by a distribution in kind valued using date-of-death values. It is the position of the IRS that where a pecuniary bequest could be satisfied by a distribution in kind using other than date-of-distribution values, the full marital deduction will be allowed only if the fiduciary must distribute property in satisfaction of the pecuniary amount that: (a) has "an aggregate fair market value at the date, or dates, of distribution amounting to no less than the amount of the pecuniary bequest or transfer, as finally determined for Federal estate tax purposes"; or (b) is "fairly representative of appreciation or depreciation in the value of all property" that is available for distribution in satisfaction of the pecuniary bequest.

As a result of Rev. Proc. 64–19, wills and trusts that provide for pecuniary bequests commonly include a stipulation specifying the valuation procedure to be followed in satisfying pecuniary bequests in kind. The governing instrument will provide either that property distributed in kind must be valued using date-of-distribution values or that any property distributed in kind in satisfaction of the pecuniary bequest must have a value of not less than the pecuniary bequest or that the property will have an aggregate value that is fairly representative of the appreciation and depreciation experienced by the estate during administration.

Rev. Proc. 64–19, by its terms, does not apply in the following cases:

(1) In a bequest or transfer in trust of a fractional share of the estate, under which each beneficiary shares proportionately in the appreciation or depreciation in the value of assets to the date, or dates, of distribution.

(2) In a bequest or transfer in trust of specific assets.

(3) In a pecuniary bequest or transfer in trust, whether in a stated amount or an amount computed by the use of a formula, if:

    (a) The fiduciary must satisfy the pecuniary bequest or transfer in trust solely in cash, or

    (b) The fiduciary has no discretion in the selection of the assets to be distributed in kind, or

    (c) Assets selected by the fiduciary to be distributed in kind in satisfaction of the bequest or transfer in trust are required to be valued at their respective values on the date, or dates, of their distribution.

[¶ 27,466]

d. *Upfront Credit Shelter Clauses*

Consider Jack, a born pessimist. Jack's lawyer told him that the optimum tax plan calls for him to give his bride, Jill, "the smallest amount necessary to eliminate estate tax" at his death with the balance to pass to a bypass trust (perhaps for the benefit of Jill or perhaps for the benefit of his children). Jack, unsure of his longevity, "just knows" that amount passing to the bypass trust will not be greater than the $2 million applicable exclusion amount available to persons dying in 2006. § 2010(c). Even so, Jack believes that Jill will be "put off" by a gift of the "smallest amount" and wonders whether there is a drafting alternative. Musing, his lawyer, says, "What if we provide for an upfront credit shelter gift and write the will so that it says, first, 'I give $2 million to the trustee of the bypass trust' and, second, 'All the rest of my property I give to my beloved Jill.' " Jack says, "Hey, I like that." The will is prepared and Jack signs it—and dies survived by Jill. At Jack's death, say in 2006 (much as he had predicted), his estate has a value of $2.3 million. During administration, however, one of his investments "goes South" and his estate

¶ 27,463

has a value of only $800,000 at the time of distribution. In this case, possibly much to Jill's chagrin, the $800,000 flows into the bypass trust and Jill receives nothing—even though the marital deduction was claimed for $300,000 on Jack's federal estate tax return.

Jill is, in fact, found to be more than chagrined; she is profoundly unhappy about the above result. What about the IRS? In Rev. Proc. 64–19, involving a pecuniary formula gift to the spouse, the IRS concluded that the marital deduction must be denied if the pecuniary gift to the spouse could be satisfied by a distribution in kind using date-of-death values. In such cases, the opportunity for the executor to engage in postmortem planning was too great. It would be all too easy for the executor to fund the marital gift with depreciated property, thereby increasing the likelihood that the value of the surviving spouse's estate at the spouse's later death would be smaller.

By way of contrast, an upfront credit shelter clause like that used by Jack was examined in Rev. Rul. 90–3, 1990–1 C.B. 175, and it was concluded that the availability of the marital deduction was in no way affected by the decline in value experienced by the estate during administration. Regrettably the explanation provided in the ruling was limited, consisting, in pertinent part, of the following:

> In the present case, the residuary bequest is considered as having passed from D to the surviving spouse within the meaning of [Reg. §] 20.2056(e) * * *. The fact that estate assets decline in value before the property is distributed does not affect this conclusion. Further, the residuary bequest is not a "terminable interest" as defined in [Reg. §] 20.2056(b)–1(b).

Problem

[¶ 27,475]

Bill has an $2.2 million all cash estate. His wife, Hillary, has $400,000 of cash and Roaring Fork, a real estate parcel having a market value of $800,000. They each answer "my spouse and then my children" when asked, in conjunction with preparing their wills, "Who do you want to get your property at your death." However, they also say that they are "hooked" on tax planning schemes and want to minimize death taxes. How should the spousal gift be expressed in the wills of Bill and Hillary?

L. DISCLAIMERS

[¶ 27,481]

Section 2518 is designed to govern the recognition of disclaimers of property under the entire transfer tax system. Pursuant to this provision, if the disclaimer qualifies, the property interest disclaimed will be treated as if the interest had never been transferred to the disclaimant. Accordingly, as for the marital bequest, if the surviving spouse disclaims an interest transferred, no deduction will be allowed. Cf. § 20.2056(d)-(2). Similarly, if others disclaim

¶ 27,481

an interest and, thereby, the surviving spouse becomes entitled to the disclaimed interest, then such interest will be considered as passing to the surviving spouse from the decedent for purposes of the marital deduction. See § 2518. Several requirements must be met before a disclaimer will be considered as qualified for special treatment. For a detailed discussion of the requirements for qualification, see ¶ 6001 and 6013.

Problems

[¶ 27,487]

1. Henry's father died in 1990, leaving $100,000 in trust "to pay the income to my son, Henry, for life and upon his death to deliver the entire corpus to such of his blood relatives or to his spouse or to such charity as Henry might by will appoint." Henry died last year, leaving a will in which he exercised the power of appointment by appointing the trust corpus to his wife for her life with the remainder to her estate. Is Henry's estate entitled to a marital deduction with respect to any part of the trust property?

2. Hortense by will directed her executor to convert the residue of her estate into cash and distribute it equally between two trusts: Trust A provides for the payment of "all net income (excluding gains from the sale of securities) to my husband for his life." A further provision authorizes her husband to withdraw such portion or all of the corpus as he may desire. Upon his death the corpus of Trust A is to go to such beneficiaries as he and the Solid Granite Trust Company, as Trustee, may designate; in default of appointment, the corpus is to be divided among Hortense's then-surviving children. Trust B is an accumulation trust for the benefit of the children of Hortense with distribution to be made upon her husband's death, dividing the accumulated income and corpus equally among her then living children. Is either of the Trusts entitled to marital deduction treatment? To take optimum advantage of the marital deduction and the unified credit, how should the will divide the property of Hortense's estate between the two trusts in lieu of the "equally" standard? For this purpose, assume that Hortense's estate amounts to $2.5 million and, at the time of her death, her husband's separate property amounts to $3 million.

3. Howard, age 90, has investments valued at $2.5 million; his wife, Wilma, has no appreciable assets. They have three adult children who are doing moderately well in their respective vocations. In 1948, Howard executed a will under which he left all his property to the Solid Granite Trust Company, as Trustee, to pay the income from the corpus to Wilma for life, and upon her death to distribute the corpus to their children in equal shares. Howard gave the Trustee power to pay over to Wilma any part of the corpus that the Trustee in its uncontrolled discretion deemed necessary for her support and maintenance. Howard also gave Wilma power to appoint by will the trust property among their issue in such shares and in such manner as she may determine. Does Howard's gift to Wilma qualify

¶ 27,481

for the marital deduction? What revisions would you suggest for Howard's will?

4. Helen owned one-fourth of the outstanding capital stock of General Micro; her three brothers owned the rest of the outstanding stock in equal shares. Helen and her brothers have been employed with General Micro and have been receiving substantial salaries for their services. General Micro has never paid dividends. Helen's will left her shares in General Micro in trust with instructions to pay the trust income to her husband, Horatio, for her life; she also gave Horatio a power to consume the corpus and to appoint any remaining corpus among their children. Will this trust qualify for the marital deduction?

5. Jasper's will now contains the following trust provision for his wife:

"If my wife, Kate, survives me, I give to the Solid Granite Trust Company, as Trustee, for her benefit, an amount equal to the excess value of the property disposed of by this will over the sum of (1) the value of the property passing under other articles of this will, plus (2) a sum equal to the largest amount which could pass free of federal estate tax under this will by reason of the unified credit and the state death tax credit after taking into account property passing under other articles of this will, property passing outside of this will, and all principal charges not deductible in computing my federal estate tax, plus (3) all my debts, expenses of administration and other principal charges, including all death taxes; the foregoing trust property shall be held in trust to pay all the income therefrom to my wife for her life and upon her death to distribute the corpus to such person or persons as she may designate by will. And the residue of my estate shall be distributed to my issue surviving at the time of my death per stirpes."

Jasper's estate is estimated at about $1.5 million; his attorney is considering the addition of the following clauses to the above trust provision in Jasper' will:

(a) My trustee may from time to time make such distribution from the corpus of the trust as may be necessary to provide for the support, maintenance or needs of my wife and of such of my children as may be minors.

(b) If my wife fails to exercise her power to designate the persons who shall take the trust corpus upon her death, I direct that the trust corpus shall be distributed among my issue per stirpes.

(c) When any of my children shall marry for the first time, I direct that my trustee (with the consent of my wife) shall pay over to each such child $10,000 out of the trust corpus.

(d) I authorize my trustee to invest the trust assets in such corporate securities, mortgages and interests in real estate as its judgment may dictate from time to time without being limited to any rule of law concerning trust investments and without regard to the prior or anticipated earnings from such investments.

Consider the estate tax consequences of each one of the above will clauses, including the testamentary trust provision.

¶ 27,487

Chapter 28

ESTATE TAX CREDITS, RETURNS, PAYMENT, AND APPORTIONMENT

A. CREDITS

[¶ 28,001]

Several important credits are allowed against the estate tax liability as determined under § 2001. Credits constitute the final step in the tax computation process.

First the assets to be included in the gross estate are determined in accord with §§ 2031 and 2033–2046, taking into account the exclusion provided by §§ 2031(c). Those assets are valued in accord with §§ 2031, 2032, 2032A, and 2701–2704 to produce a total value for the gross estate. Then, in accord with § 2051, the deductions provided by §§ 2053–2056 and § 2058 are subtracted to produce the taxable estate amount, and § 2001 is applied to determine the estate tax liability.

At this point the credits provided in §§ 2010 and 2012–2015 are applied. One of these, the § 2010 unified credit, has the effect of eliminating any tax liability for the vast majority of estates. If liability remains after application of the unified credit, the other credits may significantly reduce the amount actually due.

[¶ 28,005]

1. UNIFIED CREDIT

Section 2010 provides a unified credit of a fixed amount that varies with the year of death. As explained at ¶ 7001, the credit originated in 1977 and gradually rose to the $192,800 level over the period 1977 through 1987. The credit remained at $192,800 through 1997 but rose again beginning in 1998. The 2001 Act raised the unified credit for 2002 and 2003 to $345,800—equal to the tax on a taxable gift or taxable estate of $1,000,000. Beginning in 2004 the credit was no longer "unified," and the estate tax credit rose above the gift tax credit. The gift tax credit was capped at $345,800—the tax on $1,000,000 of taxable gifts. The estate tax credit, however, rose dramatically.

The estate tax credit amounts (and the corresponding amounts effectively excluded from tax) are as follows:

Year	Applicable Credit Amount	Applicable Exclusion Amount
2004–2005	$ 555,800	$1,500,000
2006–2008	$ 780,800	$2,000,000
2009	$1,455,800	$3,500,000

The effect of the credit is to shelter from tax the "applicable exclusion amount" for the year of death, assuming no taxable gifts were made by the decedent during the decedent's life. For example, in 2006 the estate tax credit offsets the $780,800 tax that would otherwise be imposed on the first $2,000,000 of a decedent's taxable estate.

Section 2010 can lead to confusion because it allows the full credit at death without regard to how much of the § 2505 credit the decedent might have used during her life. This appears to permit duplication of the credit. As explained at ¶ 2007, however, that is not the case because § 2001(b)(2) has the effect of increasing the tax at death in the amount of any credit used during life, thereby offsetting the benefit of the gift tax credit and effectively preventing any duplication of the §§ 2505 and 2010 credits.

The Internal Revenue Code currently provides that the estate tax is to be repealed as to deaths after 2009. § 2210. Section 901 of the Economic Growth and Tax Reconciliation Act of 2001, however, provides that the estate tax provisions are to be restored on January 1, 2011, in the form in which they existed prior to the 2001 Act. If this "sunset" provision is not eliminated by Congress, the estate tax unified credit will be restored in the amount of $345,800–the tax on a $1,000,000 taxable estate.

[¶ 28,009]

2. CREDIT FOR STATE DEATH TAXES

Until 2004 § 2011 provided a credit against the United States estate tax in the amount of certain state death taxes. Effective beginning in 2005, the § 2011 credit was replaced by the § 2058 deduction for state death taxes, discussed above at ¶ 25,007. Although the § 2011 credit no longer applies for purposes of the United States estate tax, some states impose a death tax based on the amount formerly allowed as the § 2011 credit. In those states some knowledge of the operation of the § 2011 credit is important.

In the 1920's, when the estate tax was in its infancy, inheritance taxes were a significant revenue source for a number of states. Officials in those states became concerned that the United States might expand the federal estate tax in such a way as to preempt the field, making it politically impossible for states to obtain substantial revenue from death taxes. The result was a compromise, originally enacted in 1924 and modified to its present form in 1926, that assured the states of the opportunity to preserve a portion of death tax revenues.

The compromise survived until 2004 in the form of § 2011, which granted a credit for state death taxes. The credit was allowed for any "estate, inheritance, legacy, or succession taxes actually paid" to a state or the District of Columbia, but the credit was limited to a dollar maximum that varied with the size of the taxable estate, as determined under § 2011(b). The computation of the maximum credit derives from the 1926 political compromise and had a curious aspect. As provided in the last sentence of § 2011(b), a fixed amount of $60,000 was first subtracted from the taxable estate to produce the "adjusted taxable estate." The credit was then determined by applying the § 2011(b) rate table to the adjusted taxable estate. For example, if the taxable estate was $2,000,000, the adjusted taxable estate was $1,940,000, and the maximum credit was $99,600.

The entirety of the maximum credit amount was available until 2002. The 2001 Act mandated a phaseout of the credit, beginning in 2002. For deaths in 2002, the credit allowed was 75% of the maximum. In 2003 50% was allowed, and in 2004 only 25% was allowed. § 2011(b)(2). The credit was repealed as to deaths in 2005 and later years. § 2011(g).

Many states imposed an estate tax in the exact amount of the maximum state death tax credit. Such a tax was often called a "pickup tax" or "sponge tax" because its purpose was to preserve for the state a portion of the taxes that would otherwise go to the United States. Such a tax was politically attractive because it simply diverted the credit amount from the United States to the state and therefore imposed no additional tax burden on the state's citizens. Some states retain such a tax, typically referring to the § 2011 credit as it existed prior to the 2001 Act.

[¶ 28,013]

3. CREDIT FOR GIFT TAX

The Section 2012 credit for gift tax has very limited importance. It applies only to gift tax paid with respect to a gift made prior to 1977, and then only to a gift that is included in the decedent's gross estate.

For example, assume that in 1970 the decedent had made a transfer to a trust but reserved a power to change beneficial enjoyment. Further assume that the power to change beneficial enjoyment could be exercised only with the consent of a person who held a trust interest adverse to exercise. Such a transfer would have been considered a completed gift for gift tax purposes, pursuant to Reg. § 25.2511–2(e), with the result that gift tax might have been paid. Upon the decedent's later death, the trust property would nevertheless be included in the decedent's gross estate pursuant to § 2038. In such a case, the decedent's estate is entitled to a credit for gift tax paid with respect to the 1970 gift, but subject to various limitations described in §§ 2012(a), (b), and (d).

The § 2012 credit has no application to gifts after 1976 because such gifts are fully addressed under the unified gift and estate tax regime adopted in

1976. Specifically, § 2001(b)(2) reduces the estate tax by the amount of gift tax payable with respect to gifts made after 1976.

[¶ 28,017]

4. CREDIT FOR TAX ON PRIOR TRANSFERS

The deaths of members of successive generations within a short period of time could have devastating tax consequences for a family. For example, assume that a widowed mother dies with a large estate that is subjected to an overall estate tax burden of 45%. Assume further that the mother bequeaths the entirety of her estate to her unmarried son, who dies a year later, when another tax of 45% is imposed on what is left after payment of tax at the mother's death. The family's resources are reduced by 70% within a single year.

Congress has responded to such circumstances by adopting the § 2013 credit for tax on prior transfers. If the son dies within two years after the mother, the entirety of the estate tax paid by the mother's estate can be credited against the tax that would otherwise be imposed at the son's death, largely preventing double taxation. The credit is subject to important limitations relating to both the mother's estate and the son's estate, as described in §§ 2013(b) and (c), and fully explored in Reg. §§ 20.2013–2, 20.2013–3, and 20.2013–6.

A credit is available if the son's death occurs at any time up to 10 years after the mother's death, but is progressively limited in amount. If the son dies within two years after the mother's death, a full credit (subject to the §§ 2013(b) and (c) limitations) is allowed. If the son dies during the third or fourth year after the mother's death, the credit is reduced to 80% of the amount otherwise allowable, and the credit is ultimately reduced to 20% if the son's death occurs in the 9th or 10th year.

The credit is also available at 100% if the son dies during the two years *before* the mother's death. This rule would apply in circumstances such as these. A mother creates a trust, with income to daughter and a vested remainder to son at daughter's death. The mother retains a power to change beneficial enjoyment that causes the trust to be included in her gross estate under § 2038. The son dies first, and the value of the vested remainder is taxed in his gross estate. One year later the mother dies, and the entire trust is taxed in her gross estate. Under § 2013(a), and subject again to the § 2013(b) and (c) limitations, a credit would be available to the son's estate for a portion of the tax paid at the mother's death.

There is no requirement of family or other relationship between the two decedents. Section 2013 may apply if there is any passage of property from one decedent to another. The example of mother and son above is used only for illustrative purposes.

B. WHEN A RETURN IS REQUIRED

[¶ 28,025]

Form 706, United States Estate Tax Return, must be filed by the executor for the estate of every U.S. citizen or resident whose gross estate exceeds the "applicable exclusion amount" for the year in which the decedent dies. § 6018(a)(1). The applicable exclusion amount is the amount of taxable estate that is sheltered from tax by the unified credit for the year of death. § 2010(c). For example, in 2006 the applicable exclusion amount is $2,000,000.

If the decedent made taxable gifts after 1976, estate tax might be payable even if the gross estate is less than the applicable exclusion amount. Adjusted taxable gifts are added to the taxable estate for purposes of determining the estate tax under § 2001. § 2001(b)(1)(B). For this reason § 6018(a)(3)(A) requires that the applicable exclusion amount be reduced by adjusted taxable gifts in determining whether a return must be filed. For example, assume that the decedent dies in 2006, when the applicable exclusion amount is $2,000,000. She has a gross estate of only $1,800,000 but made adjusted taxable gifts, as defined in § 2001(b), in the amount of $300,000. Although her gross estate is less than the § 2010(c) applicable exclusion amount, § 6018(a)(3)(A) requires that the filing threshold be reduced by $300,000 to $1,700,000. Because the $1,800,000 gross estate exceeds this amount, a return is required.

Form 706 is reproduced in Appendix A. Appendix A also sets forth an Estate Tax Return Problem providing facts on the basis of which a Form 706 may be completed.

C. WHO MUST PAY AND WHEN

[¶ 28,029]

It is the executor of the decedent's estate who is directed to pay the estate tax. § 2002. However, "if there is no executor or administrator appointed, qualified and acting within the United States, then any person in actual or constructive possession of any property of the decedent" is considered the "executor" for purposes of § 2002. § 2203. For example, if the decedent's property is entirely in joint tenancy, so that there is no need for probate and hence no executor, the surviving joint tenant is the "executor" for purposes of § 2002 and is responsible for paying the estate tax. Similarly, if the entirety of the decedent's property is owned by the trustee of a revocable trust, the trustee will be the "executor" for purposes of § 2002.

The Regulations explain that the requirement of payment by the executor pertains to the whole tax without regard to the fact that the gross estate may consist in part of property not included in the probate estate or probate property that is not within the possession of the executor. Reg. § 20.2002–1. For example, a life insurance policy on the life of the decedent may be payable to a person other than the executor, despite inclusion of the policy proceeds in the gross estate. Hence the executor has a liability for tax relating to an asset entirely beyond the executor's control. The solution for this problem is discussed at ¶ 28,073, below.

In general, the estate tax shown on the return is due and payable at the time fixed by statute for the filing of the return, without regard to any extension of time obtained for the filing of the return. § 6151(a). Thus, payment of the estate tax must be made within nine months after the date of the decedent's death. § 6075.

D. EXTENSIONS OF TIME FOR PAYMENT

[¶ 28,031]

1. DEFERRAL BY CONSENT

Section 6161(a)(1) authorizes the IRS to extend the time for payment of tax shown on any return for a period not in excess of six months from the date fixed for payment. This applies to both the estate and gift taxes, except that the period of extension for the estate tax may be as long as 12 months.

In addition, in the case of the estate tax, the IRS may grant an extension not in excess of 10 years from the original due date where reasonable cause is demonstrated. Regulation § 20.6161–1(a)(1) provides these illustrations of "reasonable cause" for an extension:

1. An estate includes sufficient liquid assets to pay the estate tax when otherwise due. The liquid assets, however, are located in several jurisdictions and are not immediately subject to the control of the executor. Consequently, such assets cannot readily be marshaled by the executor, even with the exercise of due diligence.

2. An estate is comprised in substantial part of assets consisting of rights to receive payments in the future (i.e., annuities, copyright royalties, contingent fees, or accounts receivable). These assets provide insufficient present cash with which to pay the estate tax when otherwise due and the estate cannot borrow against these assets except upon terms which would inflict loss upon the estate.

3. An estate includes a claim to substantial assets which cannot be collected without litigation. Consequently, the size of the gross estate is unascertainable as of the time the tax is otherwise due.

4. An estate does not have sufficient funds (without borrowing at a rate of interest higher than that generally available) with which to pay the entire estate tax when otherwise due, to provide a reasonable allowance during the remaining period of administration of the estate for the descendent's widow and dependent children, and to satisfy claims against the estate that are due and payable. Furthermore, the executor has made a reasonable effort to convert assets in his possession (other than an interest in a closely held business to which § 6166 applies) into cash.

¶ 28,031

Regulation § 20.6161–1 still includes references to deferral for "undue hardship." This is no longer operative, as the "undue hardship" basis for deferral was deleted from the statute in 1976.

[¶ 28,033]

2. DEFERRAL BY RIGHT

The executor is entitled to defer payment of tax allocable to a reversionary or remainder interest that is not yet possessory. § 6163(a). For example, assume that a mother creates a trust at her death, giving a life estate to a daughter and a vested remainder to a son. Assume further that the son predeceases the daughter, in which case the son's remainder would be taxed in the son's estate, although it will not be possessory until the daughter's death—perhaps many years later. The executor of the son's estate could defer payment of the tax allocable to the son's remainder until six months after the daughter's death, but the Commissioner could require posting of adequate security as a condition of the extension. §§ 6163(c) and 6165.

A further opportunity for deferral of payment of the estate tax is granted by § 6166 where a substantial portion of the gross estate is represented by a closely held business. The statute provides explicit and detailed rules for the determination of what constitutes a closely held business. If the estate qualifies under these rules, the estate tax attributable to the interest in the closely held business included in the gross estate may be paid, at the election of the executor, in as many as 10 equal installments beginning five years after the original return due date, i.e., nine months after death. Interest must be paid annually until principal payments begin. Assuming maximum deferral, the payment pattern operates in this fashion:

1. On the return due date (nine months after death) the executor pays the entire estate tax that is not allocable to the qualifying closely held business.

2. On each of the anniversary dates one, two, three, four, and five years after the return due date, the executor pays interest on the deferred tax outstanding during the prior year. On the anniversary date five years after the return due date, the executor also pays one-tenth of the deferred tax.

3. On each of the anniversary dates six years after the return due date through fourteen years after the return due date, the executor pays one-tenth of the deferred tax. Also on each of these anniversary dates the executor pays interest on the deferred tax outstanding during the prior year.

This election to pay in installments is limited to estates in which the value of the closely held business exceeds 35 percent of the adjusted gross estate. For this purpose, the adjusted gross estate is the gross estate reduced by deductions under §§ 2053 and 2054, such as claims, administration expenses, and losses. § 6166(b)(6).

The term "closely held business" is defined in the statute as a trade or business: (1) carried on by the decedent as a proprietor; (2) carried on by the

¶ 28,031

decedent as a partner in a partnership of which the decedent owned 20 percent or more of the capital interest or in which there were 45 or fewer partners; or (3) operated by a corporation in which the decedent owned 20 percent or more of the voting stock or in which there were 45 or fewer shareholders. § 6166(b)(1). Deferral is not available for "passive assets," and the deferral amount is reduced to the extent an otherwise qualifying business holds "passive assets." § 6166(b)(9). The Tax Court has jurisdiction to render a declaratory judgment as to qualification for deferral under § 6166. § 7479.

The tax originally deferred under § 6166 may become due and payable prior to the end of the elected installment period where substantial portions of the closely held business are sold or distributed or where substantial assets are withdrawn from the business. See § 6166(g) for the detailed rules and exceptions in this regard.

In general, the interest rate imposed on the deferred tax is 45% of the underpayment rate established under § 6621(a)(2), which changes quarterly. § 6601(j)(1)(B). A special 2% rate, however, is available for a portion of the deferred tax. The 2% portion is (1) the tax on the applicable exclusion amount for the year of death plus $1,000,000 (indexed after 1998) less (2) the unified credit for the year of death. § 6601(j)(2).

For example, in 2006 the indexed value of the $1,000,000 amount stated in § 6601(j) is $1,200,000. Rev. Proc. 2005–70, 2005–47 I.R.B. 979. Also in 2006, the applicable exclusion amount is $2,000,000. § 2010(c). The tax before credits on the total of $1,200,000 and $2,000,000, or $3,200,000 is $1,332,800. Subtracting the 2006 unified credit of $780,800 from this amount produces the portion of the tax that qualifies for the 2% rate: $552,000. Therefore, in the case of a decedent dying during 2006, the first $552,000 of deferred tax qualifies for the 2% rate, and the remainder of the deferred tax bears interest at 45% of the § 6621(a)(2) underpayment rate.

The benefits of the very favorable interest rates on § 6166 deferred tax are diminished because interest on § 6166 deferral is not deductible for either income or estate tax purposes. §§ 163(k), 2053(c)(1)(D).

Problem

[¶ 28,036]

Norman Wilson died on March 20, 2006, with a gross estate of $4,050,000. Funeral and administration expenses deductible under § 2053(a) totaled $50,000. A charitable deduction of $100,000 was available. Assume that the total estate tax payable is $800,000 after all credits. Further assume that the § 6601(j)(2)(A)(i) indexed dollar amount for 2006 is $1,200,000. A total of $3,200,000 of Norman's gross estate consists of shares in a closely held corporation that is actively involved in a manufacturing business. At his death Norman owned 40% of the stock in the corporation, and six unrelated parties owned the remaining 60%. The remaining assets of Norman's estate consist of readily marketable securities. Norman's executor wishes to defer payment of tax as long as possible.

Is deferral available under § 6166? If § 6166 deferral is available, what amounts of taxes and interest would have to be paid on December 20 of each of the years 2006 through 2012, assuming Norman's executor elects to defer payment as long as possible and assuming the § 6621(a)(2) underpayment rate throughout the period 2005 through 2011 is 7% per annum? (Ignore the daily compounding requirement of § 6622(a).)

E. PAYMENT THROUGH STOCK REDEMPTIONS

[¶ 28,039]

Even with deferral under § 6166, obtaining cash for payment of estate taxes may be very difficult for the decedent's family. That is especially so if the family's assets consist largely of a closely held business in corporate form. If the corporation has not made the election to be taxed as an S Corporation pursuant to § 1361 *et seq.*, the general rule is that withdrawal of funds from the business is treated as an ordinary income dividend to the extent of the corporation's "earnings and profits"—essentially its retained earnings. §§ 301(c)(1), 316. This can make provision of cash for payment of estate taxes an expensive proposition. For example, if the amount needed for estate taxes is $300,000, there might have to be a distribution of $350,000 to the executor, approximately $50,000 of which would be used to pay income taxes. Although there are exceptions to this dividend rule, they are narrow and difficult to satisfy in the case of most closely held businesses. (In the case of an S Corporation, it may be possible to withdraw part or all of the necessary funds without income tax cost.)

This problem is greatly alleviated by § 303, which permits withdrawal of an amount sufficient to pay death taxes (including the United States estate tax), as well as funeral and administration expenses, with much more favorable income tax treatment. Under § 303, a redemption of stock for consideration up to this amount is treated as a "sale or exchange" of the stock by the owner—typically the executor. Therefore, the dividend rule does not apply, and the estate realizes income from the distribution only to the extent the amount received in the redemption exceeds the estate's basis for the stock. Because the estate's basis will be the value of the stock at the date of death (or alternate valuation date), and not the decedent's possibly much lower original cost basis, the taxable gain will usually be very small. § 1014(a). Furthermore, any realized gain will usually constitute long-term capital gain taxed at a lower rate than dividend income. § 1223(11).

Section 303 redemption treatment is available only if the stock in the redeeming corporation included in the decedent's gross estate has a value greater than 35% of the decedent's gross estate less §§ 2053 and 2054 deductions. In some cases the stock of multiple corporations may be aggregated to meet the 35% threshold. § 303(b)(2)(B). Although the qualification requirements for § 303 redemption and for § 6166 deferral (¶ 28,033) both incorporate 35% thresholds, the § 303 requirement is much less demanding because under § 303 there is no requirement that the decedent's stock constitute 20% of all stock outstanding or that the corporation have 45 or fewer shareholders, as is the case under § 6166. § 6166(b)(1).

F. NONCOMPLIANCE WITH FILING AND PAYMENT OBLIGATIONS

1. PENALTIES

[¶ 28,043]

a. *Failure to File and Failure to Pay Tax*

The Treasury has an array of unpleasant medicines to administer for noncompliance with the filing and payment obligations imposed by the estate, gift, and generation-skipping taxes. First, there are penalties for failure to file estate and gift tax returns. For such an unintended transgression there is a civil penalty imposed under § 6651(a)(1) of five percent of the tax owing added for the first month of delinquency, and an additional five percent for each delinquent month thereafter—but only up to a total penalty of 25 percent. Similar penalties apply in the case of underpayment of tax. § 6651(a)(2). Furthermore, an additional penalty is imposed where the taxpayer fails to pay the tax after notice and demand have been made on the taxpayer by the IRS. § 6651(a)(3).

Whether one is liable for an addition to tax for the untimely filing of a return is essentially a question of fact. Because the decision in each case depends upon its particular circumstances, specific rules capable of easy application are nearly impossible to formulate. However, it is useful to note that the United States Supreme Court has held that a late filing penalty applies even in cases where the executor relies on his attorney to file the estate tax return and the attorney, through no fault of the executor, is delinquent. United States v. Boyle, 469 U.S. 241 (1985). In another case, Estate of Buring v. Commissioner, 51 T.C.M. (CCH) 113, T.C.M. (P–H) ¶ 85,610 (1985), the Tax Court distinguished *Boyle*. In *Buring*, on the advice of an accountant, the donor did not file gift tax returns. When it was later determined that a gift tax return was due, the IRS asserted a late-filing penalty. Holding that no penalty applied, the Tax Court said that reliance on a tax professional in concluding that no tax return is required is "reasonable cause" for not filing the return.

[¶ 28,049]

b. *Negligence and the Wages of Fraud—Heavier Penalties*

1. *Civil Penalties.* Under § 6662, if the underpayment of estate or gift tax is due to negligence or disregard of the rules and regulations, a penalty of 20 percent of the underpayment is imposed. (No penalty will be imposed upon a showing that the taxpayer acted with good faith and for reasonable cause. § 6664(c).) If the underpayment is due to fraud, the penalty jumps to 75 percent of the underpayment. § 6663(a). Similarly, the penalty for fraudulent failure to file an estate, gift or generation-skipping tax return is 15 percent per month of the net tax due (rather than five percent per month where failure to file is not fraudulent), up to a maximum of 75 percent. § 6651(f).

Negligence, for purposes of the 20–percent penalty, means a failure to make a reasonable attempt to comply with the applicable rules and regulations. § 6662(c).

    2. *Criminal Penalties.* Strong criminal sanctions are in place to chasten persons who willfully or fraudulently endeavor to avoid paying estate and gift taxes. Straightforward and willful refusal to file or pay these taxes is chargeable as a misdemeanor, subject to imprisonment for not more than one year or a fine up to $25,000 or both. § 7203. But for tax evasion, such as purposeful nondisclosure of taxable assets, § 7201 provides for imprisonment for up to five years and a fine of up to $100,000 or both. Tax evasion is a felony. The line between willful refusal and fraud or tax evasion thus has serious consequences.

[¶ 28,055]

2. INTEREST

    Section 6601 imposes interest on tax underpayments, payments under extended time arrangements (such as § 6166) and nonpayments. This interest is imposed on any tax not paid on or before the last date prescribed for payment.

    In general, interest on tax underpayments, nonpayments, and extended payments is nondeductible for income tax purposes. § 163(h). However, interest is deductible for income tax purposes if payment of the estate tax is deferred under § 6163 (reversionary interests). § 163(h)(2)(E).

    Interest paid with respect to the estate tax is generally deductible for estate tax purposes under § 2053(a)(2) as an administration expense. Rev. Rul. 80-250, 1980-2 C.B. 278. However, as with other administration expenses, the deduction may be not be taken for both income and estate tax purposes. § 642(g). See ¶ 25,039, above.

    As explained above at ¶ 28,033, interest on tax deferred under § 6166 is not deductible for either income or estate tax purposes. §§ 163(k), 2053(c)(1)(D).

[¶ 28,061]

3. LIENS

    There is provision in the Internal Revenue Code for a general lien for unpaid federal taxes. § 6321. The subject of the general lien for unpaid federal taxes is beyond the scope of these materials.

    There is, in addition to the general lien for unpaid federal taxes under § 6321, a special lien for estate and gift taxes provided by § 6324. The special lien, unlike the general lien, attaches immediately when the tax liability arises. It lasts, moreover, for 10 years.

¶ 28,049

G. PERSONAL LIABILITY OF EXECUTOR

[¶ 28,067]

It is a bit curious that the personal liability of the executor for payment of federal taxes, to the extent that property has come into the executor's hands, is not based on a provision of the Internal Revenue Code, but on a general provision of federal law protecting governmental claims. See Reg. § 20.2002–1, describing the extent of the Treasury's claim of personal liability. Accordingly, executors are well advised to make distributions only after payment or provision for payment of taxes owing.

Fortunately for the fiduciary, there are procedures available for securing release from personal liability. Section 2204 offers the executor and other fiduciaries an opportunity to request early determination of the tax liability and release from personal liability after payment of the stated amount.

H. APPORTIONMENT: WHO BEARS THE ESTATE TAX BURDEN

[¶ 28,073]

Although the executor is personally liable for the estate tax, the executor will not pay the tax out of her own pocket (unless she has prematurely and inadvisedly distributed the assets to beneficiaries who have left for parts unknown). The estate tax liability is an obligation of the decedent's estate. It is a debt—like any other—to be charged against the decedent's assets.

But several problems complicate the executor's charging of the tax against estate assets. One is the sheer size of the tax obligation. With estate tax rates reaching 45% or more, the tax can effectively wipe out a large portion of the decedent's assets. Another problem is the presence of bequests qualifying for estate tax deductions, such as bequests to a spouse or charity. The spouse or charity may expect to receive the bequest free of any estate tax burden. Furthermore, to the extent the estate tax is actually charged against a marital or charitable bequest, the marital or charitable deduction will be concomitantly reduced, in turn increasing the tax due. §§ 2055(c) and 2056(b)(4)(A). Finally, there may be substantial assets that are beyond the executor's control but nevertheless subject to estate tax, such as life insurance and property in trusts as to which the decedent retained interests or powers. The tax on such nonprobate assets may be large and, if charged against the assets owned outright by the decedent, could wipe out the probate assets, perhaps destroying or dramatically reducing the value of bequests the decedent thought important.

As a result, the question of who will bear the United States estate tax (as well as state death tax) should be a central part of any estate plan and must not be left to chance. The prospective decedent should have a well conceived plan as to who will bear the burden of death taxes, and that plan should be

¶ 28,073

clearly stated in the appropriate documents, especially the will or revocable trust that dictates disposition of the primary assets.

In planning for payment of the estate tax, the planner should take into account these principles:

1. The decedent has the power to dictate where the tax burden will fall, in effect preempting any or all of the rules described below. This is done primarily by including a specific directive in the will or revocable trust that is the decedent's primary dispositive document. Of course, if the tax exceeds the assets designated as the source of funds, the executor will have no choice but to charge the tax against other assets, in accordance with the principles that follow.

2. The Internal Revenue Code empowers the executor to charge an appropriate share of the tax against certain nonprobate assets that are included in the gross estate. In each case the executor's power to charge the nonprobate asset may be negated by the decedent's will.

    (a) If insurance on the life of the decedent is included in the gross estate, the executor may recover the allocable estate tax from the beneficiary of the life insurance. § 2206. The portion of the tax to be recovered is determined by the ratio of the included life insurance to the taxable estate. For example, assume that the estate tax due is $500,000, the life insurance included in the gross estate is $300,000, and the taxable estate is $3,000,000. The executor would be entitled to recover 300,000/3,000,000 x $500,000, or $50,000, from the life insurance beneficiaries.

    (b) If by reason of § 2041 the gross estate includes a trust over which the decedent had a general power of appointment, the executor can recover the allocable estate tax from the trustee of that trust. § 2207. The allocable tax is determined in the same way as with life insurance.

    (c) If the gross estate includes trust property by reason of § 2036, because of the decedent's retention of a power or interest, the executor can recover the allocable estate tax from the trust. § 2207B. Again, the allocable tax is determined in the same way as with life insurance.

    (d) If the gross estate includes property as to which a qualified terminable interest property (QTIP) election under § 2523(f) or § 2056(b)(7) was made, with the result that the property is included in the surviving spouse's gross estate under § 2044, the executor can collect an allocable share of the tax from the QTIP property. § 2207A(a). The tax allocable to the QTIP property is not a pro rata portion, as with life insurance, powers of appointment, and retained life estates. Instead, the tax recoverable by the executor is the incremental tax, i.e., the amount by which the estate tax is increased by reason of inclusion of the QTIP property in the decedent's gross estate. § 2207A(a)(1). Hence the highest applicable tax rates are in effect assigned to the QTIP property, maximizing the amount the executor can recover.

3. If none of the recovery provisions described in Paragraph 2 apply, and the will or revocable trust is silent as to the tax burden, the law of the state governing administration of the estate will determine who bears the tax. The United States Supreme Court has held that for this purpose the estate tax is like any other debt of the decedent, and state (rather than federal) law will determine the assets against which the tax is to be charged. Riggs v. Del Drago, 317 U.S. 95 (1942).

   (a) A minority of states apply the "burden-on-the-residue rule," i.e., the tax is charged against the residuary estate until it is exhausted, after which it is charged against specific and pecuniary bequests as determined by local law. This rule can prove very damaging because it may cause the tax to be charged against property going to a spouse or charity, thereby reducing the marital or charitable deduction, which will further increase the tax due, and so on. In some states the courts have created common law exceptions to the residue rule, freeing the marital residue share (and sometimes even a charitable residue share) from tax.

   (b) Most states have rejected the residue rule and have adopted "apportionment" statutes that specifically allocate the tax burden in the absence of direction by the decedent. Typically such statutes charge the tax only against interests that are not deductible for estate tax purposes; in other words, marital and charitable beneficiaries have no responsibility to pay any of the tax unless other assets are insufficient. The Uniform Estate Tax Apportionment Act (2003) (Part 9A of the Uniform Probate Code) is a typical apportionment statute of this kind.

The presence of a tax burden provision in the will or revocable trust does not guarantee the optimum result unless it clearly resolves all issues. Such a provision should be absolutely clear and take into account the possibility of dispute over interpretation, as occurred in the following case.

[¶ 28,079]

FIRST NAT'L BANK OF ATLANTA v. UNITED STATES

United States Court of Appeals, Fifth Circuit, 1981.
634 F.2d 212.

PER CURIAM:

In this will construction case, the district court held that federal estate taxes are to be paid out of the residue of the testator's estate, including the marital trust property. Although plaintiffs vigorously argue on appeal that the testator intended to maximize his marital deduction and thereby minimize estate taxes, that intent is not clear on the face of the document and, absent such a showing, the unambiguous provision of the will that all estate taxes should be paid from the residue of the estate will govern.

Daniel L. McWhorter died testate on June 16, 1972. His will provides for certain specific bequests and then for the residue of his estate to be divided equally between a marital trust and a family trust. Item Three specifically provides:

> If my wife survives me, I direct my Executors (after paying all of the above bequests, and after paying all debts, taxes and expenses other than Estate Taxes) to divide the residue of my estate into two parts, which (after adjusting for the insurance and other property payable to my wife hereinafter mentioned) shall be equal in size. I hereby designate these as Parts A and B. There shall be regarded as a portion of my estate assigned to Part A, for the purpose of this calculation only, the following: (1) any insurance on my life which is so payable to my wife as to be lawfully the subject of a marital deduction for Federal Estate Tax purposes, and (2) the value of any other property passing to my wife either outside this Will or under any other Item of this Will in such manner as to qualify as a part of such marital deduction. . . . There shall not be included in Part A any property as to which such a marital deduction would not be allowed.

Regarding payment of estate taxes, Item Seven of the will states that all estate taxes shall be paid from the residue:

> All estate taxes shall be paid from the residue of my estate, and no claim shall be made against any life insurance beneficiaries for payment of any pro rata part of such taxes. Notwithstanding the foregoing, my Executor shall make claim against the appointee, if permitted by law, for any such estate taxes assessed because of any power of appointment which I may have.

An estate tax return was filed which calculated the marital deduction as one-half of the residue before payment of estate taxes. The Internal Revenue Service determined that the deduction should have been calculated after payment of estate taxes and assessed a deficiency. The co-executors of the estate paid the tax and then brought this suit for a refund.

Section 2056 of the Internal Revenue Code allows a deduction from the gross estate for "the value of any interest in property which passes or has passed from the decedent to his surviving spouse," up to fifty percent of the adjusted gross estate [as to decedents dying before 1982]. 26 U.S.C.A. § 2056. The value of any interest passing to the surviving spouse for which a deduction is allowed, however, is the net value of such interest after payment of any estate taxes charged against it under the will. 26 U.S.C.A. § 2056(b)(4). The sole issue on appeal is whether the district court correctly ruled as a matter of law that the McWhorter will requires the estate taxes to be paid out of the residue before division, and thus paid in part out of the marital bequest, or whether the taxes should be paid after division and only out of the non-marital bequest.

¶ 28,079

Proper construction of a will is determined by reference to state law, Riggs v. Del Drago, 317 U.S. 95, 97–98, 63 S.Ct. 109, 110, 87 L.Ed. 106 (1942), in this case the law of Georgia. * * *

The cardinal rule of will construction under Georgia law is to ascertain the intention of the testator by looking at the document and giving consideration to all of its parts. * * * Plaintiffs argue that the language used by the testator in setting up the marital trust evidences his intent to maximize the marital deduction. They contend that the provision in Item Three that the residue be divided, after payment of taxes other than estate taxes, shows the testator did not intend for the taxes to be paid out of the marital portion. They suggest that the language in Item Seven that all estate taxes be paid from the residue of the estate was mistakenly added as part of a "formbook" provision designed to instruct executors on whether to seek estate taxes from life insurance beneficiaries and appointees of any powers of appointment.

The difficulty with plaintiffs' position is that there is no provision for payment of estate taxes only out of the non-marital portion of the estate, even if the residue were to be divided prior to payment of such taxes. In essence, plaintiffs ask this Court to either eliminate Item Seven, or rewrite it to read "[a]ll estate taxes shall be paid from Part B of the residue of my estate," or otherwise define the word "residue" in Item Three and Item Seven in two different ways.

Item Seven, however, clearly provides that estate taxes are to be paid out of the "residue" of the estate, which includes the marital trust property. Item Three provides that the "residue" will be divided into two parts. Neither part is thereafter referred to any place in the will as the "residue." Nothing in the will suggests that the word "residue" as used in Item Three is to have any different meaning when used in Item Seven. While one of the purposes of the will clearly is to take advantage of the marital deduction, nothing therein suggests the testator's intention to maximize that deduction. Even if plaintiff's interpretation of the will were correct, the marital deduction would not be used to the maximum. To the contrary, the specific bequests to siblings which are to be paid before dividing the residue into the marital and family trusts deprives the arrangement of any maximization of the marital deduction. Finally, even though the parenthetical in Item Three that the residue is to be divided "after paying all debts, taxes and expenses other than Estate Taxes" would indicate that McWhorter might provide that the estate taxes be paid in some manner other than out of the residue, the language of Item Seven is unambiguous, and "if the clause as it stands may have effect, it shall be so construed, however well satisfied the court may be of a different testamentary intention." Ga. Code Ann. § 113–806 (1975). * * *

AFFIRMED.

[¶ 28,097]

Problem

Tammy Larson died this year, domiciled in a state that does not impose a death tax. Her husband, Wilmer, had died three years earlier. Tammy's daughter, Linda, was appointed executor of Tammy's estate. Tammy's will bequeaths the entirety of her estate to Linda.

At the time of her death Tammy owned only one asset (other than the Aetna insurance policy described below): IBM stock worth $1,050,000. The cost of administering Tammy's estate was $50,000, and all of this was paid from Tammy's probate assets. Tammy's administrator elected to deduct the $50,000 for estate rather than income tax purposes.

Tammy was the insured under an Aetna Life Insurance Co. policy with a face value of $1,000,000. Tammy owned the policy at the time of her death. The beneficiary was Tammy's nephew, Sam.

Ten years before her death Tammy had transferred $300,000 to the Larson Trust. At the time of the transfer Tammy's age was 72. The trust provided that Tammy was to receive all income from the trust until her death, at which time the principal was to be paid to Tammy's uncle, Horatio. On the date of Tammy's death there was no accrued income and the value of the trust assets was $1,000,000.

Fifteen years before Tammy's death, Tammy's mother, Agatha, had created a trust that provided income for life to Tammy, with remainder to Tammy's brother, Wilbur. The trust provided that until Tammy's death Tammy had the power to appoint trust assets to herself to the extent necessary for Tammy's support, health, or comfort. Tammy had never exercised this power. On the date of Tammy's death this trust had a value of $1,000,000.

How much estate tax must be paid as a result of Tammy's death? How much, if any, of the tax will ultimately be borne, respectively, by Linda, Sam, Horatio, and Wilbur?

Part V

GENERATION–SKIPPING TAX

(Chapter 13 of the Internal Revenue Code)

Chapter 29

GENERATION–SKIPPING TRANSFER TAX

(Sections 2601–2664)

A. INTRODUCTION

[¶ 29,001]

After a half-century of experience with the gift and estate taxes, it became apparent that taxpayers with substantial resources and astute advisers could dramatically reduce or entirely eliminate the impact of these taxes by "skipping" generations. Typically, this involved use of trusts that provided economic benefits for younger generation family members without causing the trust assets to be included in the gross estates of those younger generation family members.

For example, at her death Mother would create a trust for the benefit of Daughter throughout Daughter's life, with remainder to Granddaughter at Daughter's death. Daughter would be named trustee of the trust, would receive the income from the trust, and would have a power to invade the trust principal limited by an ascertainable standard. This arrangement would permit Daughter to manage the trust investments, thereby both preserving family control of the trust assets and permitting Daughter to control the amount of income produced. Yet none of the trust assets—other than income or principal actually distributed to Daughter—would be included in Daughter's gross estate for estate tax purposes. Although an estate tax would have been paid at Mother's death, the trust assets would pass to Granddaughter entirely free of gift or estate tax at Daughter's death. For transfer tax purposes, Daughter's generation would be "skipped."

This "generation-skipping" strategy could be extended much further if desired. Mother could provide for the trust to continue not just throughout Daughter's life, but also throughout the life of Granddaughter, and then throughout the life of Great Granddaughter, and so on. At each generation the living descendant would manage the property, receive its income, and have a limited opportunity to invade principal—but with no inclusion in her gross estate. Hence multiple generations could be "skipped" for tax purposes, enabling a family of substantial resources to control its assets (such as a closely held business), enjoy the income from the property, and have access to principal when needed, yet avoid estate tax exposure for many decades subsequent to Mother's death. Such "generation-skipping trusts" became standard practice for families of substantial wealth.

The only limitation on the longevity of these arrangements was the Rule Against Perpetuities, which required that the trust property eventually vest in specific individuals, thereby ultimately exposing the property to gift or estate tax. Even so, trusts lasting more than 100 years could readily be devised without running afoul of the Rule Against Perpetuities. Also, as explained at ¶ 29,036, a number of states have eliminated or relaxed the Rule Against Perpetuities by statute.

As a practical matter, generation-skipping trusts were available only to the most prosperous of families—those that could keep their assets locked up in trusts and that could afford the sophisticated planning and drafting involved. As a result, those who should have been most directly impacted by the gift and estate taxes were often effectively shielded from taxation for several generations.

Congress responded in 1976, adding to the Code Chapter 13, which imposed an entirely new tax on generation-skipping transfers. This early version of the tax proved to be so complex in comprehension and computation that Congress was confronted with two alternatives: repeal it or substantially revise it. With the Tax Reform Act of 1986, Congress took the latter alternative, and with the support of the Treasury completely revised Chapter 13, keeping the same objectives but designing provisions intended to be simpler in application and understanding. In the process, Congress repealed the original version of Chapter 13 retroactively and provided for the new version to become effective, generally, with respect to transfers to generation-skipping arrangements made after October 22, 1986.

The Ways and Means Committee Report accompanying the Tax Reform Act of 1986 explained Congress' reasoning:

> The committee believes, as it stated when the generation-skipping transfer tax originally was enacted in 1976, that the purpose of the three transfer taxes (gift, estate, and generation-skipping) is not only to raise revenue, but also to do so in a manner that has as nearly as possible a uniform effect. This policy is best served when transfer tax consequences do not vary widely depending on whether property is transferred outright to immediately succeeding generations or is transferred in ways that skip generations. The committee determined that the present generation-skipping transfer tax is unduly complicated. Therefore, the committee determined that this tax should be replaced with a simplified tax, determined at a flat rate. The bill accomplishes the committee's goal of simplified administration while ensuring that transfers having a similar substantial effect will be subject to tax in a similar manner.

¶ 29,001

H.R. Rep. No. 99–426, 99th Cong., 1st Sess. at 824 (1985), reprinted in 1986–3 CB 824 (Vol. 2).

As noted above, the generation-skipping tax applies only to transfers to generation-skipping arrangements made after October 22, 1986. It is important to note that the transfer referred to is the *original* transfer in trust, such as Mother's transfer in trust in the example above. Therefore, the generation-skipping tax has no application to generation-skipping trusts that were irrevocably created and funded before October 23, 1986, regardless of how long those trusts last. As a result, many "old wealth" and funded families who created generation-skipping trusts before October 23, 1986, will be protected from both the estate tax and the generation-skipping tax throughout the existence of the trusts, which may last for many decades. By contrast, "new wealth" entrepreneurs accumulating resources since 1986 do not have this opportunity and will in general see their property fully taxed at each and every generation.

From a reasonably attentive reading of the turgid prose of Chapter 13, it will be clear that of the narrow range of estates actually subject to the estate tax only a small fraction will ever encounter the tax on generation-skipping transfers. However, few lawyers can afford to ignore the generation-skipping tax, because its potential application is universal. For example, as discussed at ¶ 29,025, any gift of more than the § 2503(b) and (e) exclusion amounts to a grandchild will, at a minimum, use up a portion of the donor's generation-skipping tax exemption. While it may not be desirable to attempt to plumb the depths or scale the heights of this subject in the basic course in estate and gift taxation, an acquaintance with the general nature of the generation-skipping tax and especially its plainly marked escape hatches should be assimilated by anyone interested in estate planning.

As explained above, the purpose of the generation-skipping tax is to prevent avoidance of the estate tax. Repeal of the estate tax in 2010 will eliminate the rationale for the generation-skipping tax. Therefore, under the Economic Growth and Tax Relief Reconciliation Act of 2001, the generation-skipping tax will be repealed simultaneously with repeal of the estate tax—on January 1, 2010. § 2664. It should be remembered, however, that the 2001 Act also includes a "sunset" section stating that all provisions of the 2001 Act will be null and void as of January 1, 2011. § 901, Economic Growth and Tax Relief Reconciliation Act of 2001. Therefore, unless Congress takes contrary action in the interim, on January 1, 2011, the generation-skipping tax will be revived and fully operative.

B. OPERATION OF THE GENERATION–SKIPPING TAX

[¶ 29,013]

1. TAXABLE EVENTS

The generation-skipping tax ("GST") is imposed on each of three events: taxable terminations, taxable distributions, and direct skips; all three are considered generation-skipping transfers. §§ 2611, 2612. Each involves a transfer of income or principal (or a beneficial interest in either) to at least one beneficiary who is two or more generations younger than the transferor. For example, a transfer by a donor to her child is not subject to tax; a transfer by the donor to her grandchildren or descendants of her grandchildren, however, is subject to tax.

A *taxable termination* is the termination of an interest in a trust (whether by reason of death, passage of time, or cessation of a power) under which a "skip person" receives an interest in the trust property. § 2612(a). A skip person is defined as one who is two or more generations younger than the transferor. § 2613(a)(1). An example of such a taxable termination would involve a trust established by a parent to provide life income for a child and then upon the child's death to distribute the principal free of trust to the child's children; the taxable termination occurs upon the child's death.

A *taxable distribution* is a distribution of income or principal from a trust to a skip person, other than by reason of termination of the trust. § 2612(b). An example of a taxable distribution is a trust created by a parent for children and grandchildren; any distribution from the trust to a grandchild would be a taxable distribution.

The third type of taxable event is the *direct skip*. This is a transfer that is subject to either the estate or gift tax and that gives an interest in the transferred property to a skip person. This would include a transfer in trust, subject to the estate or gift tax, where no one has an interest in the property other than a skip person. §§ 2612(c), 2613(a)(2). The simplest example of a direct skip, however, would be a transfer of property outright by a grandparent to a grandchild.

The following illustration, taken from the Ways and Means Committee Report accompanying the Tax Reform Act of 1986, is useful:

> A single trust may provide for transfers to more than one generation of generation-skipping beneficiaries. For example, a trust may provide for income payments to the grantor's child for life, then for such payments to the grantor's grandchild, and finally for distribution of the trust property to the grantor's great-grandchild. Were such property left outright to each such generation, the property would be subject to gift or estate tax a total of three times. Under the bill, the property likewise is subject to transfer tax a total of three times—gift or estate tax on the original transfer and generation-skipping transfer tax on the transfers to the grandchild and the great-grandchild.

H.R. Rep. No. 99–426, 99th Cong., 1st Sess. at 825–26 (1985), reprinted in 1986–3 CB 825–26 (Vol. 2).

[¶ 29,017]

2. GENERATION ASSIGNMENT

As indicated above, the GST does not apply unless property goes to a "skip person." Although certain trusts can constitute skip persons under § 2613(a)(2), the most important definition applies to human beings: a skip person is "a natural person assigned to a generation which is 2 or more generations below the generation assignment of the transferor." § 2613(a)(1).

A typical example of a gift to a skip person is a gift from grandfather to grandson. This is an easy case because the grandson is obviously two generations below the grandfather. The statute provides elaborate mechanisms for determining the generation where relationships are more complex.

Where the recipient is a lineal descendant of a grandparent of the transferor, the relative generation levels are determined by simply counting generations. § 2651(b)(1). For example, assume the following family structure. The transferor is William III, one of whose grandparents was William I. Joseph I is another grandchild of William I, and Joseph's father was Albert, brother of William III's father. Assume further that Joseph I has a child (Joseph II), and that Joseph II has a child (Joseph III). Joseph I is assigned to the same generation as William III; if William III makes a gift to Joseph I, Joseph I is not treated as a skip person. Similarly, Joseph II is only one generation below William III, and if William III makes a gift to Joseph II, Joseph II is not treated as a skip person.

Joseph III, however, is a skip person with respect to William III. Joseph III is four generations below William I, the grandfather of the transferor, William III. William III is only two generations below William I. Hence Joseph III is two generations below William III. A gift from William III to a descendant of Joseph III would likewise be a gift to a skip person.

Note that the tax is imposed only on gifts *to* younger generations. Under § 2612, a skip person must be two or more generations *below* the transferor. A gift by Joseph III to William III is not subject to the tax although Joseph III and William III are two generations apart.

If the gift is a to a more distant relative, i.e., a person who does not have a common grandparent with the transferor, or to an unrelated person, arbitrary age ranges are used. § 2651(d). For example, assume that Alice, age 56, gives property to Jane, age 36, and that the two are not related. Because the difference in their ages is between 12–1/2 and 37–1/2 years, Jane is assigned to the generation immediately below Alice, and Jane is not a skip person. By contrast, if Alice gives property to Emily, age 12, the age difference is 44 years, and Emily is treated as being two generations below Alice. Hence Emily is a skip person, and the tax applies.

If the recipient is or has been married to the transferor at any time, the recipient is treated as being in the same generation as the transferor, without regard to their relative ages. § 2651(c)(1).

In some circumstances, the generation assignment is modified to reflect the death of a person in the intervening generation. For example, if a grandparent makes a gift to a grandchild at a time when the parent of the grandchild who was a child of the grandparent is deceased, the intervening generation is ignored, and the grandchild will not be treated as a skip person. § 2651(e).

¶ 29,017

[¶ 29,019]

3. AMOUNT SUBJECT TO TAX

The taxable amount for a *taxable termination* is the fair market value, at the time of termination, of the property with respect to which the termination occurs, decreased by expenses, debts, and taxes attributable to the property, similar to the deductions allowable under § 2053 of the estate tax. § 2622. One result of this formulation is that the amount taxed will necessarily include the amount used to pay the generation-skipping tax. In this sense, the tax on a taxable termination can be described as "tax-inclusive." In that respect the tax on taxable terminations is analogous to the estate tax.

The taxable amount in the case of a *taxable distribution* is the value of the property received by the distributee, less any expense incurred by the distributee in connection with the determination of the generation-skipping tax on the transfer. § 2621. Because the generation-skipping tax is imposed on the distributee, the tax will in effect be paid from the amount received by the distributee. Therefore, the amount subject to tax will include the tax itself–a "tax inclusive" result. In this respect the tax on taxable distributions is analogous to the estate tax. If the tax is paid by the trust, rather than by the distributee, the payment of tax is treated as an additional taxable distribution to the distributee. § 2621(b).

In the case of a *direct skip*, the amount subject to the tax is the amount received by the donee skip person. § 2623. The liability for the tax is imposed on the transferor (§ 2603(a)(3)), and the amount of the tax is not included in the taxable amount of the direct skip. In this sense, the tax on a direct skip is "tax-exclusive." In that respect the tax on a direct skip is analogous to the gift tax. But there is a secondary tax on direct skips. Under § 2515 the generation-skipping tax paid by the transferor is treated as an additional gift for *gift tax* purposes, and the gift amount is "grossed-up" accordingly. As a result, in the case of a direct skip it is entirely possible for the total tax paid (both generation-skipping tax and gift tax) to equal a large portion of the amount actually received by the donee. Section 2515 applies only to direct skips by gift; it does not apply to direct skips at death.

Distributions of income are fully subject to the generation-skipping tax. Put another way, there is no exemption from tax because the distribution comes from income rather than principal.

[¶ 29,025]

4. NONTAXABLE GIFTS

In general, the GST does not apply to any inter vivos direct skip that would be exempt from the gift tax by reason of the annual exclusion under § 2503(b) or the exclusion under § 2503(e) for certain educational or medical expenses. § 2642(c).

The exemption of § 2503(b) annual exclusion gifts for GST purposes, however, is available only where the person identified as the donee when the exclusion was claimed is the sole beneficiary of the trust. More specifically, the exclusion is available only in cases where: (1) during the lifetime of the person identified as the donee, distributions from the trust can be made only to that person; and (2) if the person identified as the donee dies before the trust terminates, the property in the trust at that person's death will be included in the gross estate of such person for estate tax purposes. § 2642(c)(2). The most important practical effect of this rule is to deny the exclusion for GST purposes in the case of a *Crummey* withdrawal right if the trust has beneficiaries other than the holder of the withdrawal right. *Crummey* withdrawal rights are addressed beginning at ¶ 7071.

[¶ 29,031]

5. GST EXEMPTION

Every transferor is allowed an exemption from the generation-skipping tax. The exemption amount was $1,000,000 from 1986 until 1998 and was then indexed for inflation through 2003. Beginning in 2004 and since then the GST exemption has been the same amount as the § 2010 unified credit for gift tax purposes. For example, in 2006 the GST exemption is $2,000,000. § 2631(a) and(c).

The exemption may be allocated to any property that is transferred during life or at death; any such allocation is irrevocable. § 2631(b). An allocation of the exemption may be made by the individual (or the individual's executor) at any time before the date prescribed for the filing of the transferor's estate tax return. § 2631(a)(1).

The Ways and Means Committee Report provides this example of the practical effect of the exemption:

> Assume a grantor transfers $1 million in trust for the benefit of his or her children and grandchildren. If the grantor allocates $1 million of exemption to the trust, no part of the trust will ever be subject to generation-skipping transfer tax—even if the value of the trust property appreciates in subsequent years to $10 million or more. On the other hand, if the grantor allocates only $500,000 of exemption to the trust, one-half of all distributions to grandchildren will be subject to tax and one-half of the trust property will be subject to tax on termination of the children's interest. If, after creation of the trust, the grantor allocates an additional $250,000 of exemption to the trust, the exempt portion of trust will be redetermined, based upon the values of the trust property at that time. This new inclusion ratio applies to future distributions and terminations, but generally does not change the tax treatment of any past events.

H.R. Rep. No. 99–426, 99th Cong., 1st Sess. at 826 (1985), reprinted in 1986–3 C.B. 826 (Vol. 2).

If a donor makes a direct skip gift during her life, any unused portion of the donor's exemption is automatically allocated to the direct skip gift unless the donor elects otherwise. § 2632(b). In certain cases any unused exemption is automatically allocated to an "indirect skip" gift made during the donor's life. In general, an "indirect skip" is a transfer to a trust, later transfers from

¶ 29,025

which might constitute generation-skipping transfers. § 2632(c)(1)–(3). Again, the donor can elect out of such an automatic allocation. § 2632(c)(5).

[¶ 29,035]

6. ALLOCATION OF EXEMPTION TO SPOUSE'S TRANSFERS

A special rule allows a decedent to both: (1) claim the marital deduction for property passing to a trust for the benefit of the decedent's spouse and (2) allocate part or all of the decedent's GST exemption to that trust. This rule applies only where the trust qualifies for the marital deduction as Qualified Terminable Interest Property (QTIP) under § 2056(b)(7), discussed at ¶ 27,275, above.

An example: Sam dies when the amount of the GST exemption is $2,000,000. Sam's will gives his $2,000,000 residuary estate to a trust for the benefit of Sam's wife, Gloria, for life, with remainder to Sam's grandchildren. Sam's executor could claim the marital deduction by making the QTIP election authorized by § 2056(b)(7)(B)(v). At the same time, on the authority of § 2652(a)(3), Sam's executor could decline to have the QTIP election be effective for generation-skipping tax purposes. As a result, while § 2044 will cause all of the QTIP property in the trust to be included in Gloria's estate for estate tax purposes at her death, the trust property flowing to Sam's grand-children will be sheltered by Sam's $2,000,000 GST exemption. This becomes important in the case where Gloria has used her $2,000,000 GST exemption to shield other transfers. From a technical standpoint, this rule, known as the "reverse QTIP election," achieves this effect by preventing Gloria from being treated as the "transferor" of the QTIP property for generation-skipping tax purposes under § 2652(a)(1)(A) (although she remains the "transferor" of the QTIP property for estate tax purposes).

[¶ 29,036]

7. SIGNIFICANCE OF THE EXEMPTION

The exemption described in ¶ 29,031 has great importance for estate planning. The reason is that the exemption, although limited in dollar amount when allocated to a transfer, can shelter an unlimited amount of property from later exposure to GST.

Take the case of Donna, who transfers $2,000,000 to a trust in 2006, paying gift tax of $435,000. The GST exemption for 2006 is $2,000,000, and Donna allocates $2,000,000 of her exemption to the trust. The result is that the entire trust–regardless of its later value—is forever free of GST. This occurs because under § 2642, as explained in ¶ 29,037, the trust has a permanent "inclusion ratio" of zero.

Donna can also effectively prevent the trust from being subject to estate tax at the deaths of her descendants. For example, she can give each generation only a right to income, accompanied by a right to invade limited by an ascertainable standard. As explained at ¶ 22,061, the ascertainable standard prevents inclusion of any of the trust property in the gross estates of the descendants holding the power to invade.

The result is that Donna can make available to her descendants much of the economic benefit of the property, including a right to invade in case of serious need, while entirely avoiding future exposure to estate tax or GST. Although the trust may be worth only $2,000,000 when Donna creates it, it may be worth many times that at the deaths of Donna's successive descendants. As a result, allocation of the maximum exemption amount to such a "generation-skipping trust" has become customary estate planning for prosperous families.

The "catch" is that there are property law limits on the period during which property can be held in trust. The most important, of course, is the traditional common law Rule Against Perpetuities, which requires that any interest vest within 21 years after a life in being at the creation of the interest. Although astute drafting can produce trusts that might well last more than a century without transgressing the Rule, some families want tax protection for an even longer period—preferably forever.

The response has been statutory modification or, in some cases, outright abolition of the common law Rule Against Perpetuities in a number of states. In such states, a true "dynastic trust" can be created, protecting the trust assets from estate tax and GST in perpetuity. The number of states repealing the Rule Against Perpetuities has expanded rapidly in recent years, encouraged in part by the aggressive sales efforts of banks and trust companies located in the repealing states.

[¶ 29,037]

8. COMPUTATION OF THE TAX

The language expressing the procedure for determining the tax is obtuse. We are told that the generation-skipping tax is the taxable amount multiplied by the applicable rate (§ 2602), and that the applicable rate is the maximum estate tax rate times the inclusion ratio. § 2641. The inclusion ratio is determined by subtracting the applicable fraction from 1; and in turn the applicable fraction is made up of a numerator consisting of the generation-skipping exemption allocated to the trust or the direct skip and a denominator consisting of the value of the property placed in trust or the property subject to the direct skip, reduced by any estate tax attributable to the property in trust and any charitable gift involved. § 2642. The general purport of the inclusion ratio is to exempt from GST the portion of the transfer that is covered by the exemption allocated to the transfer.

The computation may be illustrated by the establishment of a trust in a parent's will to provide income to a child for life , with remainder outright to a grandchild upon the child's death. Assume that the GST exemption at the parent's death is $2,000,000, and that the trust is funded with $3,000,000 from the parent's estate after the payment of all death taxes. The child dies a number of years later, when the trust has a value of $5,000,000. The parent had not used any part of her $2,000,000 GST exemption prior to her death. At the child's death, there is a taxable termination, and the taxable amount will be the $5,000,000 value of the trust property at that time. The trustee must pay the generation-skipping tax out of the trust assets, and the taxable

¶ 29,036

amount will include the funds used to pay the tax. The parent's $2,000,000 exemption was automatically allocated to the trust at the parent's death. § 2632(e)(1). The inclusion ratio will be 1 minus a fraction with a numerator of $2,000,000 (the allocated exemption) and a denominator of $3,000,000 (the value of the property placed in trust); this results in an inclusion ratio of 1/3. If the maximum estate tax rate at the child's death is 45%, the generation skipping tax imposed is 1/3 x 45% x $5,000,000, or $750,000. In effect, 2/3 of the trust is sheltered by the exemption, and the remaining 1/3 of the trust— whatever its value when the trust terminates—is subject to the 45 percent tax.

Because the GST rate is the same as the highest estate tax rate, the GST rate is 46% in 2006 and declines to 45% in 2007, 2008, and 2009. §§ 2001(c)(2), 2641(a)(1).

[¶ 29,041]

9. BASIS

Because the GST is intended to approximate the results that would occur if property were held outright rather than in trust, some aspects of the § 1014 step-up in basis at death are applied to certain generation-skipping transfers. If a taxable termination occurs at the same time and as a result of the death of an individual, the basis of the property subject to the termination is stepped up (or down) to its date of death value. §§ 2654(a)(2), 1014(a). This rule, however, applies only to the portion of the property subject to GST. For example, if the inclusion ratio is one-fourth, the basis of the property would be increased by only one-fourth of the total step-up (or step-down).

In the case of other generation-skipping transfers, there is an effort to replicate the addition to basis provided for gift tax under § 1015(d). The basis for the property involved in the transfer is increased by the portion of the GST allocable to the excess of the fair market value of the property over its basis immediately prior to the transfer. § 2654(a)(1). For example, if the property has a basis of $400,000 and a fair market value of $1,000,000, and a GST of $300,000 is imposed, the basis increase would be 60% of $300,000, or $180,000.

C. PRACTICAL IMPACT OF THE GENERATION–SKIPPING TAX

[¶ 29,043]

It might appear that the GST affects only families of great wealth. In fact, its impact is much broader, and attention must be given to the GST in all but the simplest estate planning circumstances.

The GST can be an expensive trap for the unwary because no unified credit is available. For example, assume that Father created an irrevocable trust in 1990, having exhausted his GST exemption with prior transfers. The result would be an inclusion ratio of 100% for the trust. Assume further that the trust provides income for Son throughout Son's life, with a remainder outright to Grandson at Son's death. If Son died in 2006, there would be a taxable termination at that time, and no unified credit is available under the GST. If the value of the trust were $2,000,000 at the time of the Son's death, the GST would be 46% of $2,000,000, or $920,000. The Grandson would receive only $1,080,000.

By contrast, if Father had given the property outright to Son in 1990, Son's estate tax unified credit could be used to shelter the property from tax at Son's death. If Son has no other property, the $2,000,000 would be entirely sheltered from estate tax at Son's death, and Grandson would receive $2,000,000 tax-free.

The lesson here is that creation of any trust arrangement can be expensive unless there is sufficient GST exemption to shelter the trust from GST. So the GST should be considered whenever trusts are created.

This bad news is offset by the good news that the GST exemption, although limited in amount at the outset, can shelter an unlimited amount of property from tax in later years. For example, assume that Mother transfers $2,000,000 to a trust in 2006 and assigns her entire $2,000,000 GST exemption to the trust. The trust will have an inclusion ratio of zero throughout its existence, regardless of the later value of the trust property. Although the trust might have a value of $6,000,000 at Daughter's later death, the entire amount of the trust would be sheltered from both estate tax and GST. Although the trust might have a value of $15,000,000 at Granddaughter's later death, the entire trust will still be sheltered from estate tax and GST. This 100% sheltering will be available in subsequent generations as well, and in perpetuity if the Rule Against Perpetuities has been abrogated.

The lesson for prosperous families is clear. There are great advantages in creation of generation-skipping trusts fully utilizing the available GST exemption. This can create an important and growing reservoir of family resources that is likely to be protected from both estate tax and GST for several generations—and perhaps forever.

Finally, there is the exemption of § 2503(b) annual exclusion gifts and § 2503(e) tuition and medical expense gifts provided by § 2642(c). These exemptions can be used to transfer very substantial amounts to grandchildren and great-grandchildren without exposure to gift tax or GST, and without using any of the donor's GST exemption. The planner must remember, however, that the exemption for § 2503(b) exclusion gifts is very limited where the transfer is in trust. § 2642(c)(2).

Problems

[¶ 29,049]

1. George Perkins, whose wife died five years ago, made a cash gift this year of $5,012,000 to his grandson, George Perkins III. Assume that the § 2503(b) exclusion amount for this year is $12,000. The father of George Perkins III, George Perkins, Jr., was alive at the time of this gift and is the son of George Perkins. George Perkins had not previously made any

¶ 29,043

taxable gifts and had not previously used any of his unified credit. Nor had he used any of his GST exemption. George allocated the entirety of his GST exemption to this gift. George is not married.

How much, if any, does George owe the United States in gift tax and generation-skipping tax, respectively?

Note: For purposes of the GST, the portion of the transfer that qualifies for the § 2503(b) annual per donee exclusion is treated as a separate transfer to which an inclusion ratio of zero is applied, pursuant to § 2642(c)(1).

2. (a) On March 12, 1998, Maynard Collins, whose wife died in 1989, transferred $3,000,000 to the Collins Trust, naming the Tenth National Bank as trustee. The trust provides that the income is to be paid to Maynard Collins, Jr. (son of Maynard Collins) throughout the life of Maynard Collins, Jr. Upon the death of Maynard Collins, Jr., the trust is to terminate, and the trust property is to be paid outright to Maynard Collins III (son of Maynard Collins, Jr.). Earlier in 1998 Maynard Collins made a $10,000 outright cash gift to Maynard Collins, Jr. Assume that the § 2503(b) exclusion amount is $10,000 in 1998, and that Maynard Collins applied the entirety of the § 2503(b) exclusion against this cash gift. Assume that in 1998 the § 2631 GST exemption amount was $1,000,000.

Maynard Collins filed a gift tax return reporting the $3,010,000 of transfers and electing to allocate the entirety of his GST exemption to the Collins Trust.

Maynard Collins, Jr., dies in 2006, when the trust property is worth $6,000,000. The entirety of the trust property after payment of taxes is paid to Maynard Collins III at that time.

How much generation skipping tax, if any, must Maynard Collins pay with respect to the transfer in 1998?

How much estate tax, gift tax, and generation-skipping tax, if any, is imposed with respect to the 2006 trust termination?

(b) Assume the same facts as in Part (a) except that the Collins Trust provides that upon the death of Maynard, Jr., the property is to remain in trust throughout the life of Maynard III, and Maynard III is to receive all income during this period. Upon Maynard III's death the trust property is to be distributed outright to Maynard III's descendants, per stirpes.

Maynard Jr. dies in 2006, when the trust property is worth $6,000,000. Maynard III dies in 2009, when the trust property (after payment of any generation-skipping tax due in 2006) is worth $10,000,000.

How much generation-skipping tax, if any, must Maynard Collins pay with respect to the transfer in 1998? How much generation-skipping tax and estate tax, if any, will be imposed upon the deaths of Maynard, Jr., and Maynard III?

(c) Assume the same facts as in Part (b), with the following changes:

(i) The Collins Trust permits the Tenth National Bank to make discretionary distributions of corpus to Maynard Collins III at any time.

¶ 29,049

(ii) In 2003 the Tenth National Bank distributes $1,200,000 from the trust to Maynard Collins III.

(iii) Any generation-skipping tax imposed in 2003 is paid by Maynard Collins III as distributee.

How much generation-skipping tax and estate tax, if any, will be imposed on Maynard Collins III in 2003?

3. Alfonso Muraty is age 65. His wife, Winifred, died ten years ago. Alfonso's only child, Helen, is still alive. Helen has three children, Artemis, Boyd, and Callender, ages 5, 7, and 10.

Alfonso made no gifts whatever until 2006. In 2006 he gave $2,012,000 in cash to Mortimer, the grandson of Alfonso's brother, Samuel. Mortimer's father is Theodore, son of Alfonso. Theodore is still alive. Alfonso allocated the entirety of his GST exemption to this gift. Assume that the § 2503(b) annual exclusion amount for 2006 is $12,000.

In 2006 Alfonso created the Muraty Trust and transferred $36,000 to it, naming the Tenth National Bank as trustee. The Muraty Trust provides that until Artemis attains age 30 the trustee has discretionary power to distribute income and principal to Artemis according to the best interests of Artemis as determined by the trustee. When Artemis attains age 30 the entire trust property is to be transferred to Artemis. If Artemis dies before reaching age 30, the entire trust property is to be transferred outright in equal shares to Boyd and Callender.

The Muraty Trust also provides that notice of any contribution to the trust is to be given to Artemis, Boyd, Callender, and their guardians. Each of Artemis, Boyd, and Callender, or his or her guardian, has power to withdraw from the trust a maximum of $12,000 of the amount contributed, provided the request for withdrawal is made within 30 days after the notice.

How much gift tax and generation-skipping tax, if any, does Alfonso owe the United States as a result of the $36,000 transfer to the Muraty Trust?

¶ 29,049

Part VI

TRUST AND ESTATE INCOME AND INCOME FROM DECEDENTS

(Subchapter J of the Internal Revenue Code)

Chapter 30

INCOME TAXATION OF ESTATES AND TRUSTS

(Sections 641–667)

A. INTRODUCTION

[¶ 30,001]

Trusts and estates, like corporations and individuals but unlike partnerships, are income taxpaying entities. Like corporations, which make distributions to their shareholders in the form of dividends, trusts and estates make distributions to the beneficiaries of the trust or estate. However, these distributions will often be tax deductible by the trust or estate, whereas, generally speaking, no deduction can be taken by a corporation for the dividends it pays its noncorporate shareholders.

Subchapter J of the Internal Revenue Code (§§ 641 through 692) contains the specialized provisions relating to the income taxation of estates and trusts and related matters. Included are both inter vivos and testamentary trusts and decedents' estates. The rules are designed to minimize or eliminate any income tax advantage to having income received by a trust or estate, i.e., to render the trust and estate income tax neutral so that persons who receive distributions of income from trusts or estates do not enjoy any income tax advantage from having had the income flow through the trust or estate.

The function of the trustee is, by nature, to hold property and manage it for the benefit of the beneficiaries of the trust. The fruit of that management, whether it be income or appreciation realized on the sale of trust property, inures to the benefit of the trust beneficiaries. In the meantime, it may be accumulated by the trustee and added to the other trust property under management by the trustee.

In the case of an estate, the function of the decedent's executor or administrator is to collect the decedent's property and distribute it to the beneficiaries of the decedent's estate. During the course of this collection and distribution process, the estate will normally continue to receive income on the decedent's property, and the decedent's property may well grow in value, pending distribution.

As a means of minimizing or eliminating any income tax advantage to the ultimate recipient of the property that is under management in an estate or trust, Congress has adopted a number of rather specific rules. One rule provides that every distribution from an estate or trust will carry out the income of the estate or trust to the persons who receive that distribution. Thus, the recipient of a distribution from an estate or trust will be taxed on the portion of that distribution that represents the income earned by the estate or trust—and the estate or trust making the distribution will receive an income tax deduction for the amount of that distribution.

It is worth noting that Congress has created a series of descriptive terms to facilitate the implementation of the foregoing rule. For example, "distributable net income" or DNI refers to the amount of income of an estate or trust that is deemed to be available for distribution to the estate or trust's beneficiaries under the rules of Subchapter J. § 643(a). Thus, it can be said, subject to certain limitations, that every distribution from an estate or trust will carry out the income of the estate or trust to the extent of the estate or trust's DNI.

The income tax rates applicable to trusts and estates are described as having been "compressed" relative to those applicable to individuals. The effect of "rate compression" is that the maximum annual benefit (in the form of income tax savings) to be derived from having income taxed to a trust or an estate rather than to a high-income beneficiary of the trust or estate—where it would likely also be taxed at the top rate—is roughly $922.

Another rule aimed at minimizing the income tax benefits of using trusts requires the consolidation of certain trusts for income tax purposes. § 643(f). However, it is the grantor trust rules that probably supply the most important limitation. §§ 671–678. These rules identify certain trusts as "grantor trusts" and then stipulate that the person who created the trust (or, in some cases, a person who is deemed to have created the trust)—the grantor—will be taxed on the trust income even though that person does not receive the income. The grantor trust rules are the subject of Chapter 31.

Planning Note

[¶ 30,007]

Despite the efforts to minimize or eliminate any income tax advantages that could result from the use of a trust, oftentimes there are advantages to be realized. For example, generally speaking, unless the trust beneficiary has a general power of appointment over the trust property, the beneficiary will be able to have the benefit of the trust property without having the trust property included in his or her estate for federal estate tax purposes. See Chapter 22. This powerful incentive may well be sufficient to encourage income to be warehoused in the trust—and taxed at the highest marginal income tax rate to the trust rather than be distributed to the beneficiary where it might very well be taxed at a lower marginal rate.

¶ 30,007

As a means of adding perspective to possible debate on the merits of income tax rate compression as applied to estates and trusts, consider the possible adverse economic consequences to trusts that accumulate income for nontax reasons. For example, in the case where the trust beneficiary is legally disabled and is not competent to manage income distributed from the trust, nontax considerations mandate that the trust accumulate any income not needed by the beneficiary. Yet that accumulated income will be burdened by the compressed income tax rates applicable to trusts.

Not to be ignored, too, is the phenomenon commonly referred to as the "kiddie tax." § 1(g). The kiddie tax is part of a continuing effort by Congress to limit the ability of taxpayers to shift income within the family unit or family-controlled entities. The effect of the kiddie tax is to tax the unearned income of each child under the age of 14 to that child but at the marginal income tax rate of the child's parents. Obviously, the kiddie tax, when considered together with income tax rate compression noted above as applied to income warehoused in trusts, can discourage trust creation for beneficiaries under 14 years of age. Why? Because warehoused trust income may be taxed at the highest marginal income tax rates and, if distributed to the under–14 year old beneficiary, the trust income will be taxed to the beneficiary at income tax rates applicable to the beneficiary's parents, possibly also in a high marginal income tax rate bracket. (In appraising the need for the kiddie tax—which was adopted in 1986—and the increase in complexity that resulted, it may be useful to note that the Treasury reported that, in 1981, 612,000 persons who filed returns reporting unearned income were claimed as dependents on another taxpayer's return. "This represents less than one percent of the number of children claimed as dependents in that year." 2 Treasury Dept. Rep. to the President, Tax Reform for Fairness, Simplicity, and Economic Growth 95 (1984).)

B. BASIC CONCEPTS

[¶ 30,013]

1. INTRODUCTION

The provisions of Subchapter J reflect Congress's effort to resolve the fundamental questions of taxing What, to Whom, and When in cases where property is held by an estate or trust. The "What" has to do with determinations as to what receipts by a trust or an estate are income in a constitutionally permissible sense. The "to Whom" has to do with determinations as to whether income should be taxed to the trust or estate itself or to some other taxpayer. The "When" relates to the concept of matching revenues and expenses within different tax years so as to avoid distorting income tax liability.

[¶ 30,019]

2. WHAT IS INCOME?

Section 641 provides that receipts which constitute gross income when received by an individual will constitute gross income when received by an estate or trust. Thus, the traditional exclusions apply. For example, gratuitous transfers of property to the trust ordinarily will not constitute gross income. § 102(a). But if the subject of a transfer is the right to income from property, the income when earned will be taxable to the recipient, in this case, the trust. See § 102(b)(2); Irwin v. Gavit, 268 U.S. 161 (1925).

Example: Slim established a trust for his granddaughter, Bunny, by delivering $5,000 to his neighbor, Tim. Concurrently with the transfer and as a condition of it, Slim asked Tim to hold the property in trust for Bunny for life and, upon her death, to terminate the trust and distribute the remaining trust property to Bunny's then living lineal descendants per stirpes. Slim's transfer is excluded from Tim's income and from Bunny's income because it constituted a gift from Slim to Tim for the benefit of Bunny and her descendants. § 102.

Example: Saul was the beneficiary of a trust that stipulated that Saul was to be paid all of the trust income at least quarterly. In 1985 Saul transferred his right to the income to a trust that he established for his son, Chip, for a period of 32 years and one month. The income received by Chip's trust is taxable to the trust and the value of the right to receive the income constituted a gift from Saul for federal gift tax purposes. For discussion, see ¶ 31,211.

In addition, a further distinction is made between income in a trust accounting sense (sometimes referred to as "fiduciary accounting income") and income in a tax accounting sense. The former is determined according to state law and the provisions of the governing instrument. Reg. § 1.643(b)–1. The latter is as defined by § 641(b), which provides that the taxable income of an estate or trust is to be computed in the same manner as for an individual, subject to certain exceptions. See also § 63(a) and (b) defining taxable income for an individual. For example, state law or the governing instrument may direct that gains from the sale of trust property be allocated to the principal of the trust rather than to the income beneficiary. Such an allocation, however, will not change the federal tax consequences of the sale. To the extent gain is realized on the sale or exchange, the gain will be recognized as gross income except to the extent it qualifies for nonrecognition pursuant to one of several provisions developed by Congress to cover instances where Congress felt that imposition of a tax would contravene social policy. See § 1001; Reg. § 1.61–6(a) and (b).

Example: Shortly after he agreed to act as trustee of Slim's gift to Bunny, Tim invested all $5,000 of the trust property in Belchfire common stock. Six months later Belchfire common had tripled in value and Tim sold all the Belchfire stock that he held as trustee. Tim was required to include the $10,000 gain in the income tax return that he filed for the trust.

Bunny claimed the $10,000 gain realized on the sale of the Belchfire stock because the trust agreement provided that "all of the trust income shall be paid to Bunny annually." However, Tim, over Bunny's protests, properly allocated the realized gain to principal. In so doing Tim relied on the following provision which Slim had included in Bunny's trust:

¶ 30,019

"The Trustee shall allocate receipts, gains, losses and expenditures to income and principal in accordance with generally accepted principles of trust accounting and applicable law governing the trust estate as the same may exist from time to time; but the Trustee is directed to allocate to principal all distributions representing capital gains and losses received from the sale of securities held by regulated investment companies, real estate investment trusts, or mutual funds owned by the Trust as well as all other realized capital gains and losses, and to allocate to income all current expenses and amortize out of income premiums paid on bonds, debentures or other money obligations."

3. WHO IS THE TAXPAYER?

[¶ 30,025]

a. *Trusts Distinguished From Corporations*

Trusts, unlike corporations, lack most of the attributes of separate juristic existence. Scott, Scott on Trusts § 2.4. This is because, conceptually, a trust is a relationship rather than an entity. Title to property transferred in trust is held by the trustee (and not the trust), subject, of course, to the trustee's duties to the beneficiary of the trust. Restatement of Trusts (Second) § 2. For federal tax purposes, however, the trust is treated as a taxpaying entity. § 641(a). It is distinguished from a corporation, however, in the sense that the trust is allowed a deduction in computing its taxable income for amounts of income distributed to its beneficiaries. §§ 651(a), 661(b). Correspondingly, the recipient of the distribution must include the income received in gross income. § 61(a)(15).

A corporation, on the other hand, cannot deduct the dividends it pays to its noncorporate shareholders in computing its taxable income. The obvious incentive to operate a business in trust form, however, is limited by the IRS's power to tax trusts as corporations where the trust has been created for the conduct of a business for profit. See Morrissey v. Commissioner, 296 U.S. 344 (1935). Trust-like tax treatment is limited to arrangements vesting in trustees "responsibility for the protection and conservation of property for beneficiaries." Reg. § 301.7701–4(a).

Controversy with respect to when trusts are properly taxed as corporations sometimes arises. In Priv. Ltr. Rul. 8552010, the IRS concluded that an irrevocable trust created by a father for the lifetime benefit of his son was an association taxable as a corporation. Ruling that the trustee's powers went beyond merely protecting and conserving trust assets, the IRS pointed to the trustee's broad powers, including the power to engage in such businesses as he deemed prudent; the fact that the trustee had purchased real property from the son and made periodic loans to the son; and the fact that the son acted on behalf of the trust in negotiating sales and other transactions that were coordinated with the son's own real estate activities. However, in Priv. Ltr. Rul. 8624015, the IRS concluded that an irrevocable trust for the benefit of the grantor and his family was properly classified as a trust (and not a

¶ 30,019

corporation) for income tax purposes. In reaching this conclusion, the IRS pointed to a provision in the trust agreement specifically prohibiting the trustee from engaging in any business enterprise or operating any business if such activity would constitute the carrying on of a business under Reg. § 301.7701–2.

In Bedell v. Commissioner, 86 T.C. 1207 (1986), the court concluded that a testamentary trust for the benefit of the surviving spouse and children of the decedent was not "an association taxable as a corporation" under Reg. § 301.7701–4 because the beneficiaries were not "associates and their trust is not an association." *Bedell* is significant, in part, because of three observations made by the court in its opinion (86 T.C. at 1222):

> [T]he Government regarded this case as a test case in respect of testamentary trusts and trusts engaged in the conduct of a business, and that high levels in the IRS were active in pressing the matter;

> [I]t is difficult to imagine a more unsuitable vehicle than this case [for arguing that the trust was an association taxable as a corporation], and we think it regrettable that extensive misguided efforts were exerted to such a fruitless end in this litigation; and

> [T]he case should not be regarded as authority for the conclusion that no testamentary trust can be classified as an association.

[¶ 30,031]

b. Governing Principle

The governing principle applied in determining who is to be taxed on the income of trusts and estates can be stated this way: income retained by the trust or estate will be taxed to the trust or estate; income distributed to a beneficiary will be taxed to the beneficiary. However, to avoid manipulation by the trustee or executor, any distribution from an estate or trust to a beneficiary eligible to receive an income distribution is treated as having carried out income from the trust or estate to the beneficiary to the extent of the trust's or estate's distributable net income (DNI). §§ 651(b) and 661(a).

> *Example*: Ben was a beneficiary of a trust established by his father, Sam. The trustee was authorized "to distribute so much or all of the income and principal of the trust as the trustee determines to be appropriate to Ben's welfare." Although Ben was in a high-income tax bracket this year, he needed cash to make the down payment on a new personal residence. To make it possible for Ben to purchase the house, the trustee distributed $60,000 to Ben. In the same year, the trust had income of $26,000. Ben is required to report the receipt of $26,000 on his personal income tax return this year, and the trustee can deduct the $26,000 on the trust's income tax return.

[¶ 30,037]

4. DISTRIBUTABLE NET INCOME (DNI)

A trust is oftentimes merely a conduit insofar as income tax accounting is concerned. That is, to the extent income is retained by the trust, it is taxed to the trust. However, to the extent it is distributed by the trust, it is taxed to the beneficiary.

To limit the role of taxation in motivating distribution decisions, Congress also established the principle that, with certain exceptions, every distribution to a beneficiary would constitute taxable income to the extent of the trust's "distributable net income" (DNI). Mechanically speaking, the trust is entitled to a deduction in computing its taxable income to the extent of the lesser of (a) the amounts actually distributed or (b) DNI. §§ 651(b) and 661(b). The amount constituting the distribution deduction allowable to the trust will correspondingly constitute gross income to those recipients who receive the distribution. §§ 652(a) and 662(a).

DNI is a legislatively created concept (§ 643(a)) designed to limit the trust's deduction for distributions to beneficiaries (§§ 651(b), 661(a)) and, correspondingly, limit the amount and fix the character of such income to be taxed to the distributee (§§ 652(a) and 662(a)). Practically speaking, the role of DNI is to limit the deduction and inclusion to amounts actually available for distribution by the trust. For example, recalling the capital gains illustration noted earlier at ¶ 30,019, the governing instrument or state law may mandate that such gains be held in trust as a part of principal, thus rendering them unavailable for immediate distribution. Nonetheless, the gain continues to be recognized for federal income tax purposes by the trust. § 61(a)(3); Reg. § 1.641(a)–2. Moreover, but for the limitation of DNI, the governing principle applied in determining who is to be taxed on the income of the trust would dictate that a distribution to a beneficiary of that trust, which would otherwise be a nontaxable distribution of principal, would constitute taxable income to the beneficiary of that trust! See Reg. § 1.643(a)–3.

Example: A trust is created to pay the income to LaVonda for life, with a discretionary power in the trustee to invade principal for LaVonda's benefit. In one taxable year the trust had $5,000 of dividend income and realized $10,000 from the sale of securities at a profit. Before year end the trustee distributed $15,000 to LaVonda. No other cash was received or on hand during the taxable year. The trustee allocated the capital gain to principal. Accordingly, the capital gain will not ordinarily be included in distributable net income. However, if the trustee follows a regular practice of distributing the exact net proceeds of the sale of trust property, capital gains will be included in distributable net income. Reg. § 1.643(a)–3(d).

Strictly speaking, the statute approaches distributable net income from the standpoint of the "taxable income of the estate or trust computed with" certain indicated modifications. § 643(a). The computational scheme is described in the following terms:

First, the amount of taxable income is increased by (1) all distribution deductions, (2) the deductions allowed of the trust or estate in lieu of the personal exemption, (3) tax-exempt interest, (4) and any excluded interest or dividends. Second, the amount of taxable income is then reduced by certain capital gains, and in the case of simple trusts, stock dividends and extraordinary dividends, which are not distributed to beneficiaries. Finally, additional modifications are required in the case of foreign trusts.

H.R. Rep. No. 99–426, 99th Cong., 1st Sess. at 805 (1985), reprinted in 1986–3 C.B. 805 (Vol. 2).

The statute's approach is confusing in that the trust's taxable income cannot be determined until the trust's distribution deduction is determined. It might be easier to start by developing a conceptual model based on adjusted gross income (even though "adjusted gross income" is computed only for limited purposes in the case of trusts) and then make the appropriate modifications to determine exactly how much is available for distribution. In fact, the Fiduciary Income Tax Return (Form 1041) uses this approach in directing the determination of DNI, using the term "adjusted total income" in place of "adjusted gross income." Thus, it can be said that distributable net income is determined by adding to what could be called "adjusted gross income" the tax-exempt interest received by the trust and then reducing so-called adjusted gross income by the amount of capital gains, extraordinary dividends, and taxable stock dividends which are allocated to the principal of the trust pursuant to state law or the governing instrument and which accordingly are not available for distribution to the beneficiaries.

The concept of "availability for distribution" is central to the concept of DNI and understanding DNI and how it serves as a limitation on the governing principle is critical to understanding Subchapter J. Equally important is recognizing that the governing principle—every distribution from an estate or trust carries out the income of the estate or trust—is Congress's effort to limit the role of taxation in motivating distribution decisions.

5. FIDUCIARY ACCOUNTING INCOME

[¶ 30,043]

a. State Law Deference

Important to understanding distributable net income (DNI) is to recognize, first, that while DNI and "fiduciary accounting income" are not necessarily the same, fiduciary accounting income is the scheme used in the Internal Revenue Code for establishing the competing rights of income beneficiaries and remaindermen. Thus, while fiduciary accounting income is determined by the governing instrument and applicable local law (Reg. § 1.643(b)–1), the concept significantly impacts the trust's adjusted total income, which is the base utilized for computing the trust's DNI. The capital gains illustration presented at ¶ 30,019 illustrates this proposition.

Moreover, wherever the term "income" appears in Subchapter J and is not preceded by words such as "Taxable," "Distributable Net," "Undistributed Net," or "Gross," it refers to fiduciary accounting income. This is defined by the statute to be the amount of income of the estate or trust for the taxable year determined "under the terms of the governing instrument and applicable local law." § 643(b). This deference to state law is a keystone of federal taxing policy. Thus, exercise of discretion by a fiduciary in allocating between principal and income will be binding if the fiduciary acts in good faith. Thornton v. Commissioner, 5 T.C. 1177 (1945)(acq.), 1946–2 C.B. 4. Where a trustee abused his discretion and allocated ordinary dividends to principal, the IRS refused to be bound. Doty v. Commissioner, 148 F.2d 503 (1st Cir.1945). The only limitation on this deference to state law and the governing instrument is that the federal courts reserve the right to make an independent determination of what "the state law rule" will be in a particular case in those instances in which the highest court of the state has not yet ruled on the issue. Commissioner v. Estate of Bosch, 387 U.S. 456 (1967) which appears at ¶ 1107; Case v. Commissioner, 8 T.C. 343 (1947).

[¶ 30,045]

b. Total Return Trusts, Unitrust Amount, and Equitable Adjustments

Over time widespread agreement has developed as to what generally constitutes "fiduciary accounting income". Recently though changes in the financial markets are forcing a reexamination of these notions. At one level, the situation can be illustrated by reference to the once common provision requiring "all trust income is to be distributed at least annually" to one or more named trust beneficiaries and that "no distributions from principle are to be made". This worked acceptably in an economy where corporations were inclined to distribute corporate profits in the form of dividends. That changed in recent years because of the disparity in the income tax rates applicable to dividends (so-called "ordinary income") and those applicable to appreciation realized when a stock is sold (so called "capital gains"). Until 2003, dividends were taxed as ordinary income at a maximum rate verging on 40 percent (or more, effectively, in some cases) while appreciation—capital gains—were taxed at a maximum rate of 20 percent and not taxed at all until the gain is realized when the property is disposed of. Currently, however, a maximum income tax rate of 15 percent is applicable to both dividends and capital gains. Despite this seeming equality, the enterprise manager, deciding to distribute or not distribute earnings in the form of dividends, may well take into account the income taxation of those earnings first to the corporation at corporate tax rates of 35 percent followed by taxation to shareholders at 15 percent—and decide against an earnings distribution in the form of a dividend, choosing, instead to reinvest the corporate earnings in the enterprise. As the argument goes, shareholders needing or wanting cash, can sell shares, shares likely to have appreciated (reflecting the reinvested earnings)—and pay tax on the realized appreciation at a maximum capital gains rate of 15 percent. §§ 61(a)(3); 1001(a). And, to encourage share appreciation, corporations not infrequently maintain "stock buyback" programs, i.e., use corporate cash to buy company stock. These buybacks suck out cash that might otherwise go to shareholders in the form of dividends. "Everybody wins," so it might be claimed—except the trust beneficiary limited to receiving distributions of trust income! There does not appear to be an organized lobby of trust beneficiaries and, thus, it is not uncommon to see dividends reduced with the explanation that cash is being conserved to increase stock price.

¶ 30,043

Obviously restrictive dividend policies work a major hardship on shareholders looking only to distributions of trust income for support and to facilitate lifestyle choices. While one rarely hears of trust beneficiaries "living under a bridge" because of dividend cuts (that have lead to a reduction in trust income), it is not hard to imagine that trust income in many trusts is lagging trust valuation (or at least it was most profoundly during the bull market of the late 1990's). To address this situation, state legislatures and persons creating new trusts are turning to new concepts of trust income. Talk is of "total return trusts" and making distributions of a "unitrust" amount; trustees fulfilling their duty of impartiality between income and remainder beneficiaries by making "equitable adjustments between income and principal" in cases where the trustee invests and manages the trust property under the state's "prudent investor standard"; or capital gains being allocated to income in a consistent fashion by a trustee exercising discretionary authority pursuant to state law or the governing instrument. In Prop. Reg. § 1.643(b)(1), the IRS said that it would "respect" allocations between income and principal based on these concepts to the extent applicable local law permitted their utilization. Examples are provided in Prop. Reg. § 1.643(a)–3.

The effect of the state law changes is to increase the amount distributable to so-called income beneficiaries of the trust. In turn, the effect of the IRS acceptance of these state law changes—sometimes referred to as "ordering" rules—is to cause the tax liability to follow the income to the beneficiary, thereby avoiding an anomalous situation where "income" flows to a beneficiary but tax liability for that income is stuck at the trust level because the IRS based its regulations on an antiquated definition of "fiduciary accounting income".

[¶ 30,049]

6. DISTRIBUTIONS

A trust is entitled to a deduction for amounts distributed to its beneficiaries to the extent of the portion of the trust's distributable net income (DNI) which is not tax exempt, provided such distributions are not merely distributions of specific property or payments of a sum of money (in not more than three installments) which were required by the governing instrument. §§ 651(a), 661(a) and 663(a)(1). Thus, it will not be uncommon for a distribution of corpus to be eligible for the distribution deduction and, thereby, constitute taxable income in the hands of the recipient. That could happen, for instance, where a trustee elects to make a distribution to a beneficiary eligible for distributions of corpus only, makes no other distributions that tax year, and the trust has distributable net income. Reg. § 1.661(a)–2(c). Conversely, distributions from whatever source in excess of DNI will not be deductible by the trust or taxable to the distributee.

Example: Mary Margaret established a trust for her son, Sean, which provided that:

> "The trustee shall distribute so much or all of the trust income to Sean as the trustee determines to be in Sean's best interest. Any income not so distributed is to be accumulated in the trust until Sean

reaches maturity at which time the trust is to terminate and the accumulated income is to be distributed to Sean but in no event shall the trust terminate before Sean attains 55 years of age."

When Mary Margaret established Sean's trust she thought it unlikely that her daughter, Stretch, a professional basketball player, would ever "come upon hard times." However, in anticipation of the unexpected, Mary Margaret included the following provision in Sean's trust:

"The trustee may make distributions of principal for the benefit of my daughter, Stretch, if, in the opinion of the trustee, such distributions would be in the best interests of Stretch."

Stretch was unexpectedly "cut" by her team and found herself destitute. The trustee, recognizing Stretch's plight, distributed $6,000 to Stretch from the trust. No distributions were made to Sean from the trust during that year.

The same year the trust had $4,000 of interest income and $10,000 of capital gain, which it realized from securities transactions. Pursuant to the terms of the trust agreement, the realized capital gain was allocated to principal and was not available for distribution. The trust had no other expenses during this year. Accordingly the trust had Distributable Net Income (DNI)(income available for distribution) of $4,000.

Stretch will be deemed to have received $4,000 of taxable income from the trust this year as well as a $2,000 nontaxable distribution of corpus.

Problem

[¶ 30,055]

Under the terms of a trust it is provided that all income, including capital gains, shall be distributed annually to Ben. The trust income for the year includes (1) $10,000 cash dividends on stock of domestic corporations and (2) $10,000 in long term capital gains realized from the sale of trust property. Trustee's fees totaled $1,200. The trust instrument provides that all expenses are to be charged to income.

(a) What is the income of the trust as a matter of fiduciary accounting? Note the deduction for the personal exemption in § 642(b). See ¶ 30,079.

(b) What is the taxable income of the trust determined without consideration of distributions to beneficiaries?

(c) What is the "distributable net income" of the trust? Compute DNI by applying the statutory formula. § 643.

(d) How would Ben report his share of the trust income? See §§ 652.

(e) What, if any, income would be taxable to the fiduciary? § 651.

(f) What would be the tax consequences if the trust instrument provided that gains realized on the sale or exchange of trust property should be added to corpus and that all expenses should be charged against principal?

[¶ 30,061]

7. SPECIFIC BEQUEST RULE

Section 663 provides that a distribution in satisfaction of a qualified specific bequest will not constitute a distribution deduction to the trust nor will it constitute taxable income to the distributee. § 663(a)(1). To qualify for this specific bequest exclusion, the amount of money or the identity of the specific property must be ascertainable as of the date of the inception of the trust or estate. Reg. § 1.663(a)–1(b)(1). The following are examples of gifts which qualify for the exclusion: (1) "I give $10,000 to Jane"; (2) "All my stock in Z Corporation. I give to Martin"; (3) a bequest through a testamentary trust of all corporate securities owned by the decedent at death; and (4) a bequest of household items and personal effects, automobiles and jewelry. Cf. Reg. § 1.663(a)–1(c)(2), Example (1)(ii) and (c)(2)(i); see 4 Bowe–Parker, Page on Wills §§ 33.5, 33.6 (1961).

On the other hand, a bequest of the residue of a decedent's estate or a stated portion or fraction of the residue does not qualify as specific within the meaning of § 663, because it is not possible to determine the amount of the residue or the property comprising it until the decedent's death. Reg. § 1.663(a)–1(b)(2)(iii).

In addition, in order to meet the requirements of § 663, the gift or bequest must be payable pursuant to the terms of the trust or estate in not more than three installments. This is an arbitrary rule designed to separate a gift of income (akin to an annuity) from a gift of the property. The will or trust instrument governs, not what the trustee or executor actually does. If the trust or will requires four installment payments, then all flunk the specific bequest rule, and the distribution rules apply. However, the three-installment rule is applied to each beneficiary. Moreover, for this purpose, a trust is a separate beneficiary even though the beneficiary of the three installments from the estate is also a beneficiary of the trust. Thus, three qualified distributions from an estate can be made to a single beneficiary and that same beneficiary can receive three more qualified distributions from each trust into which pour assets from the same estate.

It is irrelevant whether the components of the installment are money or property. However, specific bequests of household items and personal effects, including the family automobile, are not counted in the three-installment test. Reg. § 1.663(a)–1(c). Also excluded is specifically devised real estate that passes directly from the decedent to the beneficiary under local law.

[¶ 30,067]

8. WHEN TRUST INCOME IS TAXABLE

Trusts and estates are required to report their income on an annual basis like other taxpayers. § 441(a). However, estates may elect to report income on a fiscal-year basis (§ 441(b)(1)), while trusts generally must report on a calendar-year basis. § 644(a).

An estate's ability to elect a fiscal year for tax purposes provides a distinct income tax planning device for distributions from the estate to a beneficiary. That is, income distributed to a beneficiary will be recognized as such only in the beneficiary's taxable year in which the last month of the estate's taxable year falls. Suppose, for example, the estate elects a January 31st fiscal year (beginning February 1, 2006, and ending January 31, 2007). Assume further that on February 1, 2006, the estate distributes income to a beneficiary. Assuming that the beneficiary is a calendar-year taxpayer, the income will not be taxed to that beneficiary until the beneficiary's taxable year ending December 31, 2007, and, thus, the tax attributable to that income will not be payable until April 15, 2008 (although quarterly estimated payments may be required of the beneficiary during 2007). Thus, the beneficiary has tax-free use of the 2006 distribution for slightly over two years.

This deferral opportunity is permitted because the estate's DNI cannot be calculated until the end of the estate's fiscal year (January 31, 2007); accordingly, the distribution on February 1, 2006, cannot be characterized as income or principal before January 31, 2007.

C. "SIMPLE" TRUSTS

[¶ 30,073]

1. INTRODUCTION

It is commonplace to describe trusts, for income tax purposes, as either "simple" or "complex." While these terms do not appear in the Internal Revenue Code, they are used in the implementing Treasury regulations.

Simple trusts are those described in §§ 651 and 652. Complex trusts are those described in §§ 661 and 662.

A trust will be characterized as "simple" if it is required to distribute all of its income "currently," has no charitable beneficiaries, and does not make any distributions of corpus. In those years when the trust makes distributions of corpus, it will be considered a complex trust. Thus, in one year a trust may be a simple trust and, in the next, it may be a complex trust. Crucial to eligibility for classification as a simple trust is that the trust stipulate that all of its income be distributed "currently." The trust does not lose its status as a simple trust merely because the trustee did not, in fact, make the required distribution.

Section 651 describes the tax treatment of simple trusts. These trusts enjoy a tax deduction for the amounts that are "required to be distributed currently." However, the tax deduction is limited by § 651(b) to the trust's distributable net income (DNI).

Section 652 describes the tax consequences to beneficiaries of simple trusts. These beneficiaries will have the trust income "required to be distributed currently" included in their gross income whether or not the income is in fact distributed to the beneficiaries. However, the amount actually included in the beneficiaries' gross income cannot exceed the trust's DNI.

[¶ 30,079]

2. PERSONAL EXEMPTION FOR SIMPLE TRUSTS

Trusts that are required to distribute all of the trust's income annually enjoy a $300 exemption for federal income tax purposes. § 642(b). Trusts that are not required to distribute all of the trust's income annually enjoy only a $100 exemption. (Estates enjoy a $600 exemption.) (These exemptions, unchanged in amount since 1954, originally were intended to spare estates and trusts with trivial amounts of income from the burden of filing income tax returns. Spared, too, was the IRS from having to process such returns. See H.R. Rep. No. 1860, 75th Cong., 3d Sess. (1938), reprinted in 1939–1 (Part 2) CB 728, 761. Failure to adjust these exemptions for inflation—personal exemptions are automatically adjusted, § 151(d)(4)—suggests that, today, Congress declines to act to increase trust and estate exemptions as part of a plan to limit the tax avoidance incentive that results from being able to warehouse, tax free—or at low tax rates—even small amounts of income in trusts and estates.)

There is a tendency to say that trusts entitled to a $300 exemption are "simple" trusts and that trusts not entitled to the $300 exemption are "complex" trusts. Such labels are misleading. A trust required by the governing instrument to distribute all of its income is entitled to the $300 exemption even in years when it is classified as a complex trust because corpus was distributed from the trust in that particular year. See Reg. § 1.642(b)–1; § 651 (last sentence). Classification as a complex trust means that the rules set out in §§ 661–662 apply to the trust rather than those set out in §§ 651–652.

[¶ 30,085]

3. WHAT IS INCOME?

A trust is classified as simple if it is required by the terms of its governing instrument to distribute all its "income." For purposes of this classification system, "income" refers to the trust's fiduciary accounting income, i.e., the trust's income determined not for income tax purposes but for trust accounting purposes. See ¶ 30,043.

What about the case where the beneficiary has the use of the trust property, i.e., resides rent free in a dwelling house owned by the trust? Is the reasonable value of the use of the dwelling treated as an income distribution to the beneficiary? Consider the following Letter Ruling and the *duPont Testamentary Trust* case which follows.

[¶ 30,091]

TECHNICAL ADVICE MEMORANDUM 8341005
June 24, 1983.

[The issue considered in this ruling was whether the rent-free use of trust property by the income beneficiary was taxable income to that beneficiary under § 652. The trust was created by Grantor and funded with shares of stock. All trust income was to be paid to Grantor's Spouse. Using trust property, the trustees purchased residential premises in a resort area ("Resort Home") and Grantor's Spouse occupied Resort Home, rent-free. (The trustees had been given "the power to invest in such property, either real or personal, as may to them, in their absolute and uncontrolled discretion, seem advisable.") Resort Home produced no income. Hence, the trustees used trust income from the trust property to pay the real property taxes on Resort Home and to provide a year-round caretaker. None of the income was used to pay for electricity, heating or the personal expenses of Grantor's Spouse.]

In its income tax return for * * * Trust treated the real property taxes and the cost of the caretaker as its own expenditures. It did not regard those expenditures as distributions to Grantor's Spouse. Instead, Trust deducted the real property taxes. Trust did not deduct the cost of the caretaker but did pay the income tax on the earnings it retained and used for that purpose.

* * *

In Plant v. Commissioner, 30 B.T.A. 133 (1934), acq. 1976–1 C.B. 1, aff'd, 76 F.2d 8 (2d Cir.1935), a settlor created a residuary testamentary trust to pay over specified shares of its net income to his widow and two sons during their lives. The trust instrument provided further that the trustees were to maintain the settlor's elaborate estate in Connecticut so long as Henry, one of the settlor's sons, "may wish to occupy the same as a permanent or summer residence and to charge the expense of such maintenance proportionately against the income of the trusts hereby created for the benefit of my wife and sons before ascertaining the net income from such trusts." 76 F.2d at 9. During [the tax years in question] * * * the trustees expended (exclusive of taxes) $14,754.47 and $37,221.98, respectively, in the maintenance of the Connecticut estate, and charged the amounts against the income of the testamentary trust. The trustees treated the amounts as undistributable income, and paid income taxes thereon. The Commissioner determined that the trustees' expenditures constituted taxable income to Henry.

The Board of Tax Appeals held that the income collected by the trustees and used in maintaining the Connecticut estate did not represent income distributed or distributable to Henry. The Second Circuit agreed with the Board of Tax Appeals and reasoned that the expenditures of the Connecticut estate were not applied to the use of Henry, but were employed in maintaining a capital asset of the testamentary trust. Therefore, in spite of the fact that Henry received some benefit from the expenditures, the income so used was not distributed to him.

[The IRS concluded that the questioned expenditures "were not applied to the use of Grantor's Spouse, but were employed in maintaining a capital asset of Trust" and, accordingly, "Grantor's Spouse was not taxable on the income of Trust used to pay the real property taxes and the caretaker."]

¶ 30,091

[¶ 30,097]

duPONT TESTAMENTARY TRUST v. COMMISSIONER

United States Court of Appeals, Fifth Circuit, 1975.
514 F.2d 917.

CLARK, Circuit Judge:

The Commissioner disallowed deductions claimed by the taxpayer, a testamentary trust created under the will of Alfred I. duPont, in the tax years 1966 and 1967 for expenses of maintaining an estate owned by the taxpayer but which was then being used as Mrs. duPont's home. The expense deductions were claimed to be ordinary and necessary expenses under § 212 because the estate was rental property or alternatively because the estate was part of an income producing entity comprised of the estate and securities owned by taxpayer. * * *

About 1910 Alfred I. duPont built a mansion on a 300 acre tract in Brandywine Hundred, New Castle County, Delaware which he named "Nemours." Mr. duPont lived at Nemours with his wife, Jessie Ball duPont * * *

In 1925 Mr. duPont organized Nemours, Inc. (the corporation) and transferred to it full title to the mansion house and grounds in exchange for all of the corporation's stock. Subsequently Mr. and Mrs. duPont leased Nemours for the term of their joint lives plus the life of the survivor. The agreed rental was one dollar a year. The duPonts were required by the lease agreement to pay all taxes and the expense of the upkeep of the buildings and grounds. In January 1929 Mr. duPont transferred to the corporation 20,000 shares of preferred stock of Almour Securities, Inc. valued at 2,000,000 dollars. In exchange for this transfer, the lease agreement was amended to provide that the corporation would pay taxes and expenses of upkeep.

* * *

Mr. duPont died in 1935 survived by his wife. His will vested title to the stock of the corporation in his executors who were instructed by the will to set up a trust to continue the maintenance of the grounds. The stock of the corporation was to comprise the corpus of this testamentary trust along with large blocks of other securities. Mrs. duPont was a trustee and the principal income beneficiary for her life. The trust was to pay her 200,000 dollars plus any income remaining after the payment of specified annuities. The trustees were directed to organize a charitable foundation at the death of Mrs. duPont and to transfer to it the trust assets.

* * *

During 1966 and 1967, the tax years in question, the gross income of the trust was 13,000,000 dollars. Of this sum 11,000,000 dollars was distributed to Mrs. duPont. The trust spent 255,753 dollars in 1966 and 274,451 dollars in 1967 for general maintenance of the Nemours estate. An additional 114,284 dollars was expended during 1967 for repaving existing paved roadways and walkways; paving existing unpaved roadways; rehabilitating various structures such as a classical temple, ornamental balustrades, steps, fountains, terraces, flagstones, and urns; and purchasing a jeep and a dump truck. The Commissioner disallowed all of these deductions. The reasons given were that (1) the property was not held for the production of income; (2) the expenditures did not qualify as administration expenses * * *. Alternatively he contended that the 114,284 dollar outlay represented capital expenditures which were not allowable as deductions.

PREPAID RENT

The taxpayer maintains that the deductions were proper under * * * § 212(1), which provides a deduction for "all the ordinary and necessary expenses paid or incurred during the taxable year . . . for the production or collection of income . . ."

Taxpayer contends that under the 1929 amendment to the 1925 lease to the duPonts, the transfer of the 2,000,000 dollars worth of Almour securities constituted prepaid rent, and therefore that, insofar as the corporation and the trust were concerned, Nemours was income producing rental property.

The attempt to characterize the transfer of the Almour securities as prepaid rent was correctly rejected by the Tax Court both as a matter of form and of substance. No part of these assets or the dividends therefrom were ever reported as taxable rental income on the corporation's income tax returns. The 1929 agreement clearly establishes that Mr. duPont conveyed the Almour securities to the corporation which he continuously owned and controlled until the time of his death, to enable it to pay taxes and maintenance expenses he had previously borne personally. The only payment specified as rent in the initial agreement and in the 1929 amendment was a token 1 dollar a year. The record contains no other indication that the conveyance of Almour stock was intended to constitute prepaid rent. Neither the documentation or the conduct of the parties indicates that the securities were transferred for any purpose other than to relieve the duPonts of the day-to-day burdens of administering the estate.

No attempt was made to show what the anticipated expenses of maintaining the estate might be as compared to the income produced by or the total value of Almour securities. In short, the taxpayer trust simply failed to carry its burden of proving that Nemours was rental property in these tax years. This failure of affirmative proof controls our decision here. * * *

PROPERTY HELD FOR THE PRODUCTION OF INCOME

Alternatively, the taxpayer urges the upkeep and maintenance expense was deductible under § 212(2) which allows a deduction for "all the ordinary and necessary expenses paid or incurred . . . for the management, conservation or maintenance of property held for the production of income. . . ."

To support this argument before us, taxpayer relies principally on Bingham's Trust v. Commissioner of Internal Revenue, 325 U.S. 365, 65 S.Ct. 1232, 89 L.Ed. 1670 (1945) in which the Court held that legal fees incurred to contest an income tax deficiency were deductible since they were funds expended for the conservation of trust property which was held for the

¶ 30,097

production of income. The taxpayer asserts that *Bingham's* rationale covers the expenses incurred in maintaining Nemours even though Nemours was not strictly property held for the production of income.

The thrust of the argument is that the taxpayer trust, an entity for the production of income comparable to a business enterprise, could deduct these expenses as maintenance expenses even though Nemours did not directly produce income, because payment of the maintenance and upkeep expense was a fundamental duty of the trustees in the administration of the trust. This interpretation glosses over the fact that a threshold determination in *Bingham* was that the property which the expenditure protected was held for the production of income. Although it was the duty of the trustees to maintain Nemours, Nemours was not property held for the production of income. * * * In the case at bar, the question which concerned the Court in *Bingham*—whether the expense incurred was connected with, or proximately resulted from, the management of property held for production of income—is never reached.

Despite the lease agreement between the wholly owned corporation and the duPonts and the controlling terms of Mr. duPont's testamentary trust, Nemours remained the duPonts' personal residence. It was the antithesis of income producing property. The expenses incurred in the maintenance and upkeep of this private residence never were deductible expenses relating to property held for the present or future production of income. [The court, in a footnote, commented that the trust itself was not invalid nor was it the result of "sham, fraud, purpose of tax avoidance or other lack of bona fides" and that it had "a real and viable purpose: to hold the property for the benefit of the spouse of testator during her lifetime and for the ultimate disposition to a charitable foundation at her death. This is an entirely proper purpose for the creation and funding of a trust."]

* * *

We agree with the Tax Court that the trustees were entitled to no deduction for the expenses incurred in the maintenance and upkeep of Nemours during Mrs. duPont's life * * *.

Affirmed in part and remanded.

Note

[¶ 30,103]

On remand, the Tax Court in duPont Testamentary Trust v. Commissioner, 66 T.C. 761 (1976), considered whether the maintenance expenses for the "Nemours" estate were deductible by the trust under §§ 651 or 661 as distributions includible in the widow's gross income. On this issue, the Court concluded that, since the expenses were incurred by the trust pursuant to a contractual obligation, the expenditures could not be deemed to be distributions to the beneficiary under the terms of the trust.

The court also considered the question as to whether the maintenance expenditures, even if required by the trust, could properly be treated as distributions taxable to the beneficiary. On this point, it is of interest to note that the government argued that the *Plant* decision cited in Tech. Adv. Mem. 8341005 (¶ 30,091) was controlling and that such expenditures were expenses "employed in maintaining a capital asset of the trust estate." Commissioner v. Plant, 76 F.2d 8, 9–10 (2d Cir.1935), aff'g, 30 B.T.A. 133 (1934). The Tax Court answered by stating that it "did not feel completely comfortable" with the decision in *Plant* and was not relying on that case. (Curiously it was only in 1976 that the IRS announced its acquiescence in the decision in *Plant*. 1976–2 C.B. 2.)

Problem

[¶ 30,109]

What is the proper tax treatment of income of a trust that is required to be applied to the maintenance of a residence held in trust for occupancy by a surviving spouse or other designated beneficiary of a trust?

D. COMPLEX TRUSTS

[¶ 30,115]

With one exception, the income tax deduction for distributions from complex trusts and estates is mandatory up to the amount of the trust or estate's distributable net income determined under § 643(a), that is the amount of income available for distribution to the beneficiaries. ¶ 30,037. The exception is as to distributions in satisfaction of a specific bequest. § 663; ¶ 30,061. This is the same rule that applies in the case of simple trusts. ¶ 30,073.

H.R. REP. NO. 99–426

99th Cong., 1st Sess. at 806 (1985), reprinted in 1986–3 C.B. 806 (Vol. 2).

The complex trust rules apply to all trusts that are not simple trusts and all estates. Thus, the complex trust rules apply, for example, if there are distributions of corpus during the year, if the trust has any charitable beneficiaries for the taxable year, if any part of the income of the trust is not distributable that year, or if the trustee has discretion as to whether or not to distribute income that year.

Under the complex trust rules, the trust or estate is allowed a deduction for amounts of income that are required to be distributed that year (whether or not actually distributed during that taxable year) and for all other amounts that are properly paid, credited, or required to be distributed for that taxable year....

¶ 30,103

E. ESTATES

[¶ 30,121]

Estates enjoy a $600 exemption while complex trusts enjoy only a $100 exemption. § 642(b). However, in other respects for income tax purposes, estates are treated as complex trusts. That means, as a general proposition, that every distribution from the estate carries out the income of the estate unless the distribution is in satisfaction of a specific bequest. §§ 661(a); 663(a); ¶ ¶ 30,037; 30,049; and 30,061.

[¶ 30,124]

1. SPOUSAL ALLOWANCE

Statutes in most jurisdictions authorize payment or set off of a "spousal allowance" from a decedent's property notwithstanding the absence of any authorization in the decedent's will. This is an amount thought necessary by the court to support the surviving spouse for a short period following the death of the other spouse, usually one year. Tax accounting for this payment is not intuitive. On its face, payment of the spousal allowance would appear to be made out of principal rather than income? Is that to suggest that it is free of income taxes in the hand's of the surviving spouse. One widow, Dorothy, was heard to make this claim. Dorothy received $7,000 in one year and $12,000 the next from her husband's estate as a result of the court's award of a widow's allowance to be paid, as permitted under local law. These amounts were paid out of the estate's principal as ordered by the court—and not out of the estate's income. Despite Dorothy's claims that the distribution should be free of income tax consequences, the estate was required to deduct the amount of the distribution (to the extent of the estate's DNI) and Dorothy had taxable income to the extent of the deduction claimed by the estate. Reg. §§ 1.661(a)–2(e) and 1.662(a)–3(b); Estate of McCoy v. Commissioner, 50 T.C. 562 (1968)(unnecessary to trace source of spousal award to income or principal in determining distribution deduction required by § 661(a)). The *McCoy* court explained that "a widow's allowance ordered by a Probate Court, whether payable from income or corpus is '[an amount] properly paid * * * or required to be distributed' "as described in § 661(a) and is, as such, a deduction in computing the estate's taxable income.

[¶ 30,128]

2. ELECTIVE SHARE

The "spousal allowance" should be compared to the situation where the surviving spouse has claimed his or her "elective share", i.e., exercised the option state law typically gives the surviving spouse to reject the will of the deceased spouse and claim a statutorily prescribed share of the property otherwise passing under the will of the deceased spouse. Typically "elective share" statutes allow the surviving spouse to claim as much as 50 percent of the deceased spouse's property—and, as a result, disappoint the beneficiaries under the will who, as a result of the spouse's election, will receive a corresponding lesser amount. One income tax issue generated by these facts is whether satisfaction of the elective share carries out the income of the estate to the surviving spouse.

The position of the IRS is quite clear. Beginning with decedents who die after 1999—§ 663(c)'s "separate share" rule was extended to estates in 1998 (¶ 30,175)—none of the estate's income is carried out to the surviving spouse when the elective share is satisfied. Reg. § 1.663(c)–5, Example 7. This conclusion assumes that the surviving spouse, as is quite common under the elective share statutes of the various states, is not entitled to any of the estate's income and does not participate in appreciation or depreciation of the estate's assets.

Problem

[¶ 30,139]

Doug died June 1. His will, after providing for the payment of debts, claims, administration expenses and death taxes, devised and bequeathed all the rest, residue and remainder of his estate to Wilda, his surviving spouse. The executor elected the cash method and calendar year for reporting the income of the estate. During the period from June 1 to December 31, the following transactions were consummated:

Receipts

Cash dividends	$15,000
Interest on corporate bonds	15,000
Total receipts	$30,000

Payments and distributions

Debts and funeral expenses	$5,000
Miscellaneous administration expenses	2,500
Distributions to Wilda:	
Cash award to Wilda as surviving spouse by Probate Court	10,000
Family auto (fair market value)	3,000
Total payments and distributions	$20,500

What are the income tax consequences of these transactions to Doug's estate and to Wilda?

F. THE TIER SYSTEM

[¶ 30,145]

Trusts having more than one beneficiary present additional tax accounting issues relating to the allocation of distributable net income (DNI) among those beneficiaries. Those issues are resolved by the rules provided in §§ 652(a) and 662(a), rules typically referred to as the "tier" rules.

> *Example*: Maria Elena was entitled to all of the income from a trust established by her deceased spouse, Luis. The trustee was also authorized

to make distributions of principal to Juan, Maria Elena's child, if needed by Juan for his education. This year, at a time when the trust had $12,000 of DNI, the trustee distributed $12,000 to Maria Elena and $4,000 to Juan. As a result of the tier rules, Juan is treated as having received a tax-free distribution of capital and Maria Elena as having received all of the DNI. Reg. § 1.662(a)–3(d), *Example.*

The issues are further complicated when distributions of both cash and property are made from the trust in the same year.

[¶ 30,151]

1. MANDATORY ALLOCATION OF DNI

Technically speaking, the so-called "tier system" of allocating DNI among multiple distributees from the same trust or estate refers to the mandatory allocation of DNI whenever there are (1) both mandatory and discretionary income recipients and/or (2) multiple recipients of mandatory payments and/or discretionary payments. (Normally, all distributions from estates are "second tier" distributions because usually there is no requirement in the governing instrument that such distributions be made currently.)

The "first tier" recipients are those who have a legally enforceable right, using fiduciary accounting rules, to a current distribution of income from the trust. §§ 652(a) and 662(a)(1). The available DNI will be prorated among these beneficiaries, with each beneficiary taking his or her pro rata share of dividends, interest, and tax-exempt income, as well as other income included in the DNI of the trust (even including gains realized from the sale or exchange of property in those few cases where such gains are required to be included in DNI).

The "second tier" distributees are all others who receive distributions but have no legally enforceable right to a distribution of income. § 662(a)(2). Distributions to second tier beneficiaries will constitute taxable income only to the extent that the first tier beneficiaries did not exhaust the available DNI. The DNI remaining after the allocation to the first tier beneficiaries is prorated among the second tier beneficiaries with each one taking his or her proportionate share of dividend income, interest, tax-exempt interest, etc. § 662(a)(2) and (b).

The distribution rules are quite inflexible, the inflexibility resulting from a determination to deny fiduciaries the opportunity to manipulate income tax consequences by allocating income among the distributees of the estate or trust in a fashion designed to minimize income taxes for the estate and beneficiaries as a whole. Instead, as noted above, DNI, to the extent distributed, is annually prorated, first, among "first tier" recipients of distributions from the estate or trust according to the aggregate distribution each receives, and, second, whatever remains of the DNI, to the extent distributed, is prorated among "second tier" recipients of distributions from the estate or trust, here too, according to the aggregate distribution each receives in that tax year.

¶ 30,151

Example: Ben and Jerry are beneficiaries of their father's trust. Bank, as trustee, is authorized to make distributions to either or both of them "when, Bank, deems it in the proposed distributee's best interest". Last year, Ben needed money and Bank distributed $1,000 to him. No distribution was made to Jerry last year. The trust's DNI last year was $800. In this instance, accordingly, all $800 of the trust's income was taxed to Ben last year (and Ben was deemed to have received a $200 nontaxable distribution from the trust).

Problem

[¶ 30,163]

Smedley is trustee of two trusts, the Bigge Family Trust and the Little Family Trust. Each trust has $10,000 of distributable net income this year.

(a) The Bigge Family Trust is required to distribute all its income to Mrs. Bigge. In addition, the trustee is authorized to make distributions of principal to Mrs. Bigge and to the Bigge children in such amounts as the trustee "deems appropriate to their respective circumstances." The trustee has distributed $6,000 to the Bigge's son, Thad, this year. Mrs. Bigge received a total of $12,000 from the trust this year. What is the trust's distribution deduction this year? §§ 651 and 661. What are the income tax consequences to Thad and his mother from the trust distributions they received this year? §§ 652 and 662.

(b) The trustee of the Little Family Trust is authorized to distribute to Mrs. Little and the Little lineal descendants so much of the income and principal of the trust as the trustee determines to be in the "best interests of the income beneficiaries" but with "due regard for the interests of the remainderman." This year, the trustee distributed $20,000 to Mrs. Little's son, Fred, and $20,000 to Mrs. Little. §§ 651, 652, 661 and 662. What are the income tax consequences to Mrs. Little and Fred this year?

[¶ 30,169]

2. PROPERLY PAID, CREDITED, OR REQUIRED TO BE DISTRIBUTED

Sections 661(a)(2) and 662(a)(2) speak in terms of second-tier distributions being "properly paid, credited, or required to be distributed to all beneficiaries." Each of those words is important in determining whether the trust is entitled to a distribution deduction and whether a distribution constitutes taxable income to the recipients.

For an amount to be determined "paid" or "credited," an actual payment or specific credit to the beneficiary must occur. That is, in determining whether an amount has been "paid," accrual notions are not utilized, nor are ideas of constructive receipt. See McCauley v. United States, 193 F.Supp. 938 (E.D.Ark.1961)(not considered "paid" where the executor, as sole beneficiary of the estate, deposited estate funds to her own bank account, intending thereby merely to repay herself for advances to the estate). However, there will be a payment, within the meaning of the statute, when the trustee uses trust funds to discharge a legal obligation of the beneficiary. Reg. § 1.662(a)–4; cf. Old Colony Trust Co. v. Commissioner, 279 U.S. 716 (1929). In such cases, the beneficiary is deemed to have taxable income to the extent that his or her legal obligation is discharged. Rev. Rul. 58–69, 1958–1 C.B. 254. When an amount is "credited" to a beneficiary, actual payment need not be made. However, a mere bookkeeping entry is not sufficient, because the amount must be subject to immediate enjoyment by the beneficiary. This becomes a question of fact for the courts. Harris v. United States, 370 F.2d 887 (4th Cir.1966).

Determination of whether a payment is "properly" made turns on applicable local law and the governing instrument. See, e.g., Kennedy v. Commissioner, 38 B.T.A. 1307 (1938)(distribution is deductible by the trust in computing its income only if the payment is proper); cf. Bohan v. United States, 456 F.2d 851 (8th Cir.1972)(Nonacq.) and Rev. Rul. 72–396, 1972–2 C.B. 312.

[¶ 30,171]

BUCKMASTER v. UNITED STATES

United States Court of Appeals, Tenth Circuit, 1993.
984 F.2d 379.

LOGAN, Circuit Judge.

* * *The only issue on appeal is whether the estate is entitled to claim a deduction under I.R.C. § 661 for income it distributed to estate beneficiaries during two of the estate's tax years. The disbursements were made without explicit authority under the will and without any prior order from the state probate court in Oklahoma; but the distributions were approved as part of the final accounting in the probate court's order of final settlement and again later by a nunc pro tunc order specifically referencing the payments.

I

Daisy Murphy died testate on February 9, 1984, leaving a will that gave her entire estate to her niece, Sylvia M. Buckmaster, and to her nephew, Jesse Murphy, in equal shares. Murphy was named as executor. * * * The estate contained valuable mineral interests that earned significant royalties during the course of the estate's administration. Choosing for the estate a tax year ending January 31, 1985, Murphy distributed during that year $437,000 of the estate's income to himself and to Buckmaster in equal shares, and the estate took a deduction for this amount, plus Oklahoma gross production taxes and federal windfall profits taxes relating to that income, on the estate's income tax return. The estate remained open for another year during which it distributed $155,649.51 to the beneficiaries, again claiming similar deductions on the estate's income tax return. In neither year did the estate secure an order from the probate court authorizing the distributions before they were

¶ 30,171

made, but the estate was closed out on February 20, 1986. At that time the probate court issued an order of final settlement in which it approved all actions taken by the personal representative without the order itself referencing the specific disbursements to the beneficiaries. These distributions, however, apparently were shown on the executor's final accounting filed with the petition for final settlement * * * and the probate court's order referenced the final accounting.

When the IRS notified the estate after an August 1987 audit that it was disallowing the deductions taken by the estate, the personal representative obtained from the probate court an order nunc pro tunc to reflect explicit approval of the disbursements. This did not satisfy the IRS, which issued a deficiency assessment disallowing the deductions as unlawful because there was no probate court approval before they were made. * * *

* * *

II

The federal income tax law recognizes the estate of a decedent as a separate tax entity entitled to choose its own tax year ending at the end of any month not exceeding one year after the decedent's death. I.R.C. §§ 441(b), 443(a)(2), 641; Treas. Reg. § 1.443–1(a)(2). It also recognizes the right of the representative of the estate, when acting properly, to spread the income otherwise taxable to the estate between the estate and the beneficiaries. This is accomplished by allowing deductions on the estate's income tax return for income required to be distributed currently or in fact "properly paid" during the tax year to beneficiaries of the estate. I.R.C. § 661(a)(2). It is common practice for personal representatives of decedents' estates to make distributions of income during the estate's tax year either for the support or convenience of the beneficiaries or to obtain the advantages of having the income taxed in the lowest possible rates.

The only question in the instant case is the correctness of the district court's determination that the distributions from the estate were not "properly paid" unless the probate court approved them before they were made. It is acknowledged that the will did not require the payments. The law is that the determination of what is properly paid is a matter governed by local law. See Freuler v. Helvering, 291 U.S. 35, 44–45, 54 S.Ct. 308, 311–312, 78 L.Ed. 634 (1934). * * * We review the district court's determination of local law de novo. * * *

The United States Supreme Court has considered the issue before us in the context of distributions from a trust under California law. In *Freuler*, the Supreme Court found no meaningful distinction between pre-distribution and post-distribution orders: "[I]f the order of the state court does in fact govern the distribution, it is difficult to see why, whether it antedated actual payment or was subsequent to that event, it should not be effective to fix the amount of the taxable income of the beneficiaries." 291 U.S. at 44–45, 54 S.Ct. at 311–312. * * *

¶ 30,171

A number of state court decisions have upheld post-payment approvals of personal representative's payments to beneficiaries. * * *

The government claims and the district court found that the law in Oklahoma is contrary to these other decisions, * * *.

* * *

Our task is to determine how the Oklahoma Supreme Court, if presented with the issue before us, would rule. * * * The probate laws were not drafted with the income tax laws in mind. Rather, they exist to facilitate resolution of a decedent's affairs and distribution of the estate to the proper beneficiaries. Of course it would be better if the personal representative would secure advance probate court approval of distributions of income from the estate. But these decisions often must be made near the end of the tax year of the estate, when the amount of its income can be estimated reasonably. There may not be time to follow the normal procedures for probate court approval. In such cases the personal representative acts on his own at some peril. Nevertheless, a disbursement that operates to reduce the net tax liability of the estate and the beneficiaries and that does not contravene provisions of the will would almost certainly meet with the approval of the probate court, as it did here.

We hold that the Oklahoma Supreme Court, if presented with the issue, would consider distributions of estate income by an executor or administrator made without prior probate court approval but subsequently ratified by that court to be "properly paid" within the definition of I.R.C. § 661(a)(2). This is the position of every appellate court that has directly considered the question, including the United States Supreme Court. The decision of the district court is therefore reversed, and the cause remanded for further proceedings consistent with this opinion.

[¶ 30,175]

3. SEPARATE SHARE RULE

A single trust or estate may have multiple beneficiaries with differing interests in the trust or estate. Accordingly, § 663(c) provides that distinctly separate shares of a trust or estate will be treated as separate trusts or separate estates for purposes of determining the distributable net income of each separate share when computing the distribution deduction available to each such separate share. The separate share rule applies whenever the trust or estate provides for "substantially separate and independent shares" for different beneficiaries. The rule is mandatory and not elective. § 1.663(c)–1(d).

[¶ 30,176]

a. *Funding Pecuniary and Fractional Formula Gifts*

It was only beginning in 1998 that the separate share rule was extended to estates. This happy development allowed for Reg. § 1.663(c)–4 in which the IRS takes the position that "pecuniary formula" and "fractional formula" bequests are separate shares. For an illustration of the significant impact of this decision, consider the relief potential in a case like Harkness v. United States, 469 F.2d 310 (Ct.Cl.1972), a case decided before the separate share rule applied to estates. There, the executors claimed that the surviving spouse should be treated as having received only 50 percent of the estate's 1955 DNI despite having received approximately 76 percent of the total property distributed to all of the beneficiaries of the estate in 1955. In finding for the IRS and concluding that the surviving spouse is taxable on 76 percent of the DNI, the court deemed irrelevant the executors' claim that the disproportionate distribution in favor of the surviving spouse was made purely for reasons of convenience in administering the decedent's estate—and not because of tax considerations.

Noting only the conclusion in *Harkness* illustrates the inflexibility of the distribution rules but it does not say enough about the importance of the case generally or its importance in indicating how application of the separate share rule to estates can be meaningful. The considerations that gave rise to the controversy in *Harkness* are quite commonly encountered. The difficulty in such cases may be said to have stemmed from the provisions of the testator's will, provisions that were undoubtedly carefully crafted (in as much as similar provisions are common in wills). The testator's goal was to minimize estate taxes by taking advantage of the marital deduction available for property passing to his spouse. The provision for the spouse was "fractional" rather than "pecuniary", *i.e.*, the testator gave his spouse a gift of a fraction of his estate (*e.g.*, "1/2") rather than a pecuniary amount (*e.g.*, "$300,000") and in good tax planning fashion he barred his executor from charging any death taxes (that might be paid) to his spouse's gift. (Freeing the spouse's gift from death taxes is commonly provided as a means of avoiding a complicated calculation that might otherwise result.) So, in *Harkness*, you had a situation where the spouse is to receive 1/2 of the testator's property and all death taxes that become payable are to be paid out of the share passing to beneficiaries other than the surviving spouse.

Enter now the executors engaged in collecting and distributing the testator's property. They are, practically speaking, keeping two accounts, one for the spouse's 1/2 and another for the 1/2 passing to the other beneficiaries. In normal course, death taxes are paid—and charged against the 1/2 not passing to the spouse. At this point, the executors come to a crossroads. Up until now, practically speaking, receipts and disbursements received in the course of administration of the estate had been charged 1/2 to the spouse's account and 1/2 to the other beneficiaries' account. This was all relatively simple—but it was about to change because the 1/2 belonging to the other beneficiaries had been dramatically reduced by the death tax payment—in this case, some $36 million! The executors then came upon a scheme that they believed would facilitate the estate accounting. Rather than adjust the fraction that was to be applied in dividing receipts and disbursements by the estate subsequent to the death tax payment (as would be required to correctly reflect the interests of the spouse relative to those of the other beneficiaries), the executors determined to make a distribution to the surviving spouse of that part of the estate necessary to allow the executors to continue to charge receipts and disbursements 1/2 to the spouse and 1/2 to the other beneficia-

¶ 30,176

ries. This resulted in a distribution to the spouse of $27 million in 1955 and, while it may seem hard to feel sorry for the spouse, this decision meant that the spouse received 76 percent of the property distributed to beneficiaries by the executor in 1955—and as a result the IRS claimed that she was taxable on 76 percent of the income earned in 1955 by the estate.

The spouse protested. She said that estate and trust accounting principles entitled her to only 1/2 the estate's income (since she was beneficiary of only 1/2 the testator's estate)—and only 1/2 the income was credited to her account by the executors—and, therefore, it is, as she might have said privately, "plain wrong" that she should be taxed on 76 percent of the income solely because she received 76 percent of the total property distributed in 1955.

The executors, for their part, reiterated that they were only trying to simplify the accounting for the estate. The court's response was unmistakable (469 F.2d at 315):

> There can be no doubt but that plaintiff's situation falls squarely within the literal provisions of Section 662(a)(2)(B), and plaintiff is not understood to contend otherwise. The nub of her contention is that the payments here involved should not be treated as being covered by the statute because the executors' actions were not tax motivated. Even so, the section applies. Clear statutory coverage of this kind, based upon a presumption that any distribution is deemed to be a distribution of the estate's income to the extent of its income for the year, does not and cannot be made to depend on such intangible factors as the subjective intent of executors.
>
> Section 662(a)(2)(B) was specifically intended, for the purposes of that section, "to avoid the necessity for tracing of income." [H.R. Rep. No. 1337, 83d Cong., 2d Sess. A199, 3 U.S.C. Cong. & Adm. News 4017, 4339 (1954); S. Rep. No. 1622, 83d Cong., 2d Sess. 349, 3 U.S.C. Cong. & Adm. News 4621, 4990 (1954)]. Such tracing was required by the 1939 Code, which provided that distributions by an estate or trust to its beneficiaries were taxed to the beneficiaries for the taxable year in which they received the distributions only if the distributions were made from the current income of the estate or trust. As shown, this lent itself to various kinds of manipulations by executors in the labeling of estate moneys as "income" or "principal." To eliminate such manipulations and tax consequences based upon such estate tax accounting designations of what was "principal" and "income" and from which source a distribution had been made, the "tracing" requirement was, for such distribution purposes, eliminated.

Instead, the court, citing 3 U.S.C. Cong. & Adm. News, supra n. 6, at 4340, 4990, noted that "[t]he beneficiary's proportionate share of the distributable net income * * * is determined by taking the same fractional part of [the] distributable net income as the * * * amounts * * * distributed to him * * * bear to the total of [the] amounts * * * distributed to all beneficiaries." Then, taking note, figuratively speaking, that the executors claimed to be between 'the rock and the hard place', the court might have been heard to say "maybe not" when it explained (469 F.2d at 316–17):

¶ 30,176

The fact nevertheless remains that, by making the discretionary "balancing" distributions as they did—required neither by the will nor state law—plaintiff received, under their estate accounting, less of the distributable net income than she probably otherwise would have. There is no showing that—either by not making distributions until the estate was wound up finally, or otherwise—the residuary estate could not have been so managed as to produce the same result as the statutory formula. Thus, in that sense (and not in the sense of tax avoidance), the distributions were "manipulated" so that plaintiff, who received over 75 percent of the 1955 payments, is nevertheless said to have received in that year only 50 percent of the taxable distributable net income. On its face and as its purpose is shown by its development and legislative history, the statute was designed to prevent such a result for tax purposes. Indeed, the statutory formula could be considered as providing the more natural and logical result—income earned during the administration of the residuary estate is allocated to the beneficiaries in the same ratio as their interests in the corpus of such estate. Generally, of course, various percentages of corpus will produce like percentages of income. It is thus plain that plaintiff's situation is, by the unambiguous provisions thereof, covered by the statute and although recognizing, of course, the difficulties involved in envisaging every specific situation that could arise under general statutory language, it would nevertheless appear to constitute the type of situation that Congress intended should be covered.

Applying the separate share rule in cases such as *Harkness* will provide significant relief for those who administer wills and trusts containing complex marital deduction formula clauses. The saga of separate share, however, is more than just formula clauses. As noted in ¶ 30,121, for example, separate share is an issue in the commonest of situations such as distributions in satisfaction of the elective share of a surviving spouse, *i.e.*, where the spouse ignores the decedent's will and exercises an option provided by state law to claim a statutorily determined share of the decedent's estate.

[¶ 30,177]

b. *Two-or-more Beneficiaries*

The IRS has determined that separate shares are created where the residuary estate passes to several beneficiaries. Reg. § 1.663(c)–1(a). This is an important development for it means that residuary beneficiaries such as Zero and Yacko will not be at odds over distributions from Dad's estate. Zero needs $5,000; Yacko does not; the estate's available cash is limited to $5,000; the estate is, at least for a time, otherwise illiquid. Dad's executor distributes the $5,000 to Zero in a year when the estate has $3,000 of taxable income. Prior to the extension of the separate share rule to estates, all $3,000 would be taxable income to Zero. With the separate share rule extended to estates, only $1,500 of the $5,000 distributed to Zero will be taxable income to him; the remaining $1,500 will be taxable income to the estate.

¶ 30,176

Problem

[¶ 30,179]

Sweetie and Savannah, Harry's adult children, were the sole beneficiaries under his will. Winsome, Harry's 19 year old widow, elected against the will, claiming her statutory share. Harry's estate was valued at $100,000; Winsome's statutory share had a monetary value of $30,000. This year, a year in which the estate had $2,000 of DNI, the executor distributed $30,000 to Winsome in satisfaction of her claim. Immediately after the end of the year, on January 1st, the executor distributed the balance of the estate to Harry's children. The children received a total of $72,000, consisting of the $70,000 remaining after the distribution to Winsome plus $2,000 earned during administration of Harry's estate.

(a) Assuming Winsome is in the top income tax bracket and taking into consideration the separate share rule of § 663(c) having been extended to estates, suggest the likely income tax consequences to Winsome, and to Savannah and Sweetie, the latter two being the estate's beneficiaries in both tax years.

(b) What difference would it make, if any, if the elective share in Harry's state of domicile was equal to a (i) fixed dollar amount; or (ii) percentage or fraction of Harry's estate and, if the latter, expressly provided the surviving spouse with a share in the appreciation or depreciation experienced by the estate during the course of administration (and of the income earned by the estate during the course of administration) as is common in certain situations?

G. TAX–EXEMPT INTEREST IN ESTATE OR TRUST

[¶ 30,181]

Interest on certain state and local government obligations is free from federal income taxation. § 103 ("gross income does not include interest on any State or local bond").

Normally the presence of tax-exempt interest in a trust or an estate means that a portion of the expenses of administration becomes nondeductible. Regulation § 1.265–1(c) requires the allocation of indirect expenses to be made "in the light of all facts and circumstances in each case." The portion that is nondeductible is the portion that is attributed to the tax-exempt interest. Obviously, controversy can arise as to the portion of the expenses that is attributed to the tax-exempt interest and the method of calculation, as can be seen in the following case.

¶ 30,181

[¶ 30,187]

MANUFACTURERS HANOVER TRUST CO. v. UNITED STATES

United States Court of Claims, 1963.
312 F.2d 785.

DAVIS, Judge.

* * * [Plaintiff was trustee of a trust required to distribute all of its income to Millicent Rogers during her lifetime. The facts given in the court's opinion suggests that the trustee's accounting might have been presented to the court as follows:

Gross income items allocable to income:			
Domestic dividends		$26,245.95	
Foreign dividends		150.00	
Interest		468.75	
Total		$26,864.70	(A)
Gross income items allocable to principal:			
Taxable stock dividends	$162.25		
Long term capital gain	71,205.24		
Short term capital loss	(171.10)	$71,196.39	(B)
Tax-exempt interest		8,370.85	(C)
TOTAL		$106,431.94	(D)
In addition during 1954 the trustee incurred the following expenses:			
Trustee fees	$3,350.68		
Legal fees	49,015.25	$52,365.93	(E)
N.Y. Corporate Profits Tax		1,658.88	
Total expenses		$54,024.81	
TENTATIVE TAXABLE INCOME		$52,407.13	

The court was faced with deciding what portion, if not all of the $52,365.93 in the legal and trustee fees was income tax deductible. The dispute arose because the trustee and the IRS differed as to the formula to be used in determining the portion of the legal and trustee fees that should be allocated to tax exempt interest and thereby rendered nondeductible. The litigants used the following formulas, respectively, with the taxpayer determining that $4,121.20 should be nondeductible and the IRS determining that $12,442.14 should be nondeductible:

Trustee:	*Internal Revenue Service:*
$\dfrac{C}{D} \times E = \$4{,}121.20$	$\dfrac{C}{A + C} \times E = \$12{,}442.14$

In broader terms, the dispute raised the question of whether 'apples and oranges' were being mixed. The taxpayer claimed that the IRS, in its allocation of indirect expenses between tax exempt interest and taxable income, was inappropriately relying on the rules applied by § 643(a)(5) in determining distributable net income (DNI), DNI being a legislatively created concept meant only as an upper limit to the distribution deduction available to the trust in its determination of taxable income. The taxpayer claimed the true test for the required allocation was to found in § 265 and the regulations thereunder. The court's opinion continues:]

* * * [The IRS] allocated the indirect expenses (legal fees and commissions) between tax-exempt interest, on the one hand, and dividends and taxable interest, on the other, but, in so doing, excluded from the allocation base capital gains and taxable stock dividends, both of which, although elements of the trust's taxable income, were allocable to the principal of the trust under local law and the trust indenture. By the exclusion of these elements of taxable income from the base, the portion of the indirect expenses allocable to tax-exempt interest, and hence not deductible, was significantly increased. It is this refusal of the Internal Revenue Service to consider all the elements of the trust's taxable income, in making the allocation, which prompts plaintiff's complaint.

* * *

[The taxpayer, plaintiff in this case, claimed] that, by excluding capital gains and taxable stock dividends from the allocation base used in determining the amount of administration expenses deductible, the Commissioner of Internal Revenue followed Special Instruction 39 of the instructions to Form 1041, the fiduciary income tax return. Instruction 39 applies to the separate schedule on the form to be used for the computation of "distributable net income," and says that for this purpose tax-exempt interest is to be reduced by

"any amounts which, but for the provisions of Section 265, would be deductible in respect of disbursements, expenses, losses, etc., of the trust or estate, directly or indirectly allocable to such interest. The amount of the indirect disbursements, etc., allocable to tax-exempt interest is that amount which bears the same ratio to the total disbursements, etc., of the trust or estate not directly attributable to other items of income as the total tax-exempt interest received bears to the total of all the items of gross income (including tax-exempt interest * * *) entering into *distributable net income*" (Emphasis added).

By including only those items of gross income which enter into distributable net income, this instruction excludes capital gains and taxable stock dividends (both allocable to corpus). The plaintiff says that the Commissioner also presumably relied on the examples in [Reg. § 1.652(c)–4] * * * which similarly determine the amount of administration expenses allocable to tax-exempt interest. The argument is that the instruction and the regulation are unreasonable in arbitrarily ignoring large classes of income, and that this exclusion will result, through the years, in the over-collection of tax. Plaintiff urges that, although the "artificial concept" of distributable net income may be suited to the determination of the maximum amount of income taxable to beneficiaries, "it is peculiarly ill-adapted to answer the far more simple and truly unrelated question of what general administration expenses are allocable to tax-exempt interest."

The [IRS's] reply is that Instruction 39 to Form 1041, and the examples set forth in various regulations under subchapter J, are irrelevant to the question of allocation of deductions by the trust; they relate to the computation of distributable net income, and "although in such computation capital gains and losses are also excluded, this has only an indirect bearing upon the reasonableness of the allocation under Section 265(1) which is here involved."
* * *

[W]e cannot agree with the [IRS's] assertion that Instruction 39 and the regulations under subchapter J are irrelevant to the reasonableness of the allocation of trust expenses under Section 265(1). * * * [Reg.] § 1.652(c)–4, to which taxpayer refers, furnishes an example of the application of the rules for trust required to distribute all income currently. Subparagraph (e) of this example consists of a computation of the taxable income of a trust, and the allocation of indirect expenses to the taxable and nontaxable portions of the trust's income is made, without discussion, on a distribution base from which capital gains allocable to corpus have been excluded. This is a plain enough indication, which we cannot ignore, of the specific method the Commissioner has chosen, *by regulation*, for the allocation of the expenses of trusts. Instruction 39, which by its terms purports to operate within the boundaries of Section 265, simply follows suit. More generally, the overall regulation on allocation of expenses between taxable and tax-exempt income (Section 1.265–1(c) * * *) requires that allocation of indirect expenses should be made "in the light of all facts and circumstances in each case." When the income of a trust is involved, the concept of distributable net income, as well as the special system of taxation in subchapter J, is an important component "of all the facts and circumstances." That concept and system are, as we have said, the primary mechanisms by which the income of a trust is taxed but once, either to the trust or to its beneficiaries; * * * they should not be disregarded in applying the general allocation provisions of Section 265 to the particular problems of trust income. * * *

Since the challenged regulation and instruction are thus applicable, we are controlled by their provisions unless we can agree with plaintiff that they are unreasonable as applied to the case before us. * * * But in the present circumstances—where the deductible expenses fall short of absorbing the distributable net income—the regulation and the instruction do not unfairly ignore large classes of income in making the expense allocation. The income beneficiaries are taxable only to the extent of distributable net income, which excludes gains attributable to corpus. It is not out of key, therefore, to insist that the allocation of expenses between taxable and tax-exempt income should be restricted to the same type of non-corpus gains. This is all the more so since, under Section 652(b), the amounts included in the income beneficiary's gross income have the same character in his hands—e.g., as taxable dividends or tax-exempt interest—as in the hands of the trust. Moreover, under the 1954 Code, as a result of the structure of distributable net income (which has as its starting point the taxable income of the trust), the tax benefit of deductions allocable to corpus is generally shifted to the income beneficiaries. * * * The challenged regulation and instruction allowably balance this incongruity—that the income beneficiary, not the corpus beneficiary, receives the tax benefit of expenses allocable to corpus—by providing that those indirect expenses which are usually chargeable against capital gains must be allocated by the income beneficiary to all the income (both taxable and tax-exempt) required to be distributed to him. All the income required to be distributed currently by the trust and "included" in gross income by the beneficiary (particularly tax-exempt income), rather than just the taxable elements, bears the burden of the expenses attributable to capital gain. The tax benefit of the portion of these expenses assigned to tax-exempt income is lost, but this is not unfair to a taxpayer who has the special advantage of deductions attributable to gains he does not receive. Perhaps there may be other trust situations in which the Commissioner's regulations on allocation are unreasonable, but they are not so in the circumstances we have here. Plaintiff cannot recover the tax computed under those regulations.

* * *

Problems

[¶ 30,193]

1. Refer to ¶ 30,055; assume that the trust had $10,000 of interest from municipal bonds that was tax exempt under § 103 and make the determinations requested. Consider especially the impact of the tax-exempt interest on the deduction for trustee fees and the increased importance of the personal exemption.

2. Does the potential loss of a part of the tax deduction for expenses incurred by a trust holding tax-exempt income-producing property suggest that such property should not be included in a trust? Also, when an estate is found to include tax-exempt income-producing property, could the executor do some effective postmortem planning by distributing the tax-exempt income-producing property before the estate incurred any administration expenses? By so doing, could you not avoid prorating administration expenses between taxable and tax-exempt income, thereby rendering such expenses fully deductible?

H.   CAPITAL GAINS IN ESTATE OR TRUST

[¶ 30,199]

While it is important to note that capital gains enjoy special income tax treatment—a maximum tax rate of 15 percent generally speaking—there are also oftentimes questions as to whether such gains are to be taxed to the estate or trust or distributed to the beneficiaries of the estate or trust. Generally speaking, state law or the governing instrument determines whether capital gains are part of DNI and, thus, available for distribution to the beneficiaries, or whether such gains are corpus and retained in the trust (and are not a part of DNI since they are unavailable for distribution). See ¶ 30,037. Regulation § 1.643(a)–3(a) sets out standards to be followed in making this determination—and is the subject of the following letter ruling.

[¶ 30,205]

PRIVATE LETTER RULING 8324002

February 16, 1983.

* * *

A, a resident of S, died on October 26, 1980. The executors of X, B and C, elected a fiscal year ending on January 31 of each year. B and C filed X's income tax return for the first fiscal year ending January 31, 1981.

A's Will made no specific provision concerning the payment of income earned by the estate. Under the terms of the Will and applicable state law, capital gains are allocated to corpus. During the first fiscal year of the estate, capital gains in the amount of $550,444.42 were realized from the sale of securities, the net proceeds of which amounted to $5,012,758.62. A separate account was maintained for capital gains and losses from all transactions. On January 30, 1981, an amount equal to the net capital gain for the year was segregated for the benefit of two residuary trusts. On the same day this net capital gain was actually distributed equally to the trustees of the two residuary trusts.

In filing the return for the estate, the net capital gain was included in distributable net income. The result was that the residuary trust beneficiaries reported the net capital gain as income. The agent believes the net capital gain should not be included in distributable net income, and thus, is taxable income to the estate.

* * *

Generally, capital gains are excluded from distributable net income unless they are paid, credited or required to be distributed to any beneficiary during the taxable year or are paid, set aside or used for charitable purposes. Section 643(a)(3). * * *

Gains from the sale or exchange of capital assets are not ordinarily considered as paid, credited, or required to be distributed to any beneficiary unless they are (1) allocated to income under the terms of the governing instrument or local law, (2) allocated to corpus and actually distributed to beneficiaries, or (3) utilized (pursuant to the terms of the governing instrument or the practice followed by the fiduciary) in determining the amount which is distributed or required to be distributed. Section 1.643(a)–3(a) * * *.

The first instance, under section 1.643(a)–3(a), for including capital gains in distributable net income is not satisfied because capital gains are allocated to principal under the terms of the Will and local law.

The second instance, under this regulation, for including capital gains in distributable net income requires that capital gains be allocated to corpus and actually distributed to beneficiaries during the taxable year. As illustrated by Examples (3), (4) and (5) of section 1.643(a)–3(d), this provision regarding the inclusion of capital gains in distributable net income applies only where there is a distribution required by the terms of the governing instrument upon the happening of a specified event. In the instant case, such a condition for including capital gains in distributable net income is not present. See also Rev. Rul. 68–392, 1968–2 C.B. 284.

The third instance, under this regulation, for including capital gains in distributable net income indicates there are two separate methods that capital gains may be utilized in determining the amount which is distributed or required to be distributed. One is to utilize capital gains pursuant to the terms of the governing instrument to determine the amount distributed or required to be distributed. The second method is to utilize capital gains pursuant to the practice followed by the fiduciary in determining the amount distributed or required to be distributed. In the present case, A's Will contains no instructions as to the treatment of capital gains in determining the amount of any discretionary distribution made by the executors. Thus, capital gains are not utilized pursuant to the terms of the Will. Therefore, capital gains will not be included in distributable net income of the estate under the first method described in section 1.643(a)–3(a)(3).

The second method described in section 1.643(a)–3(a)(3) requires an examination of whether a practice followed by the fiduciary is established in determining the amount which is distributed or required to be distributed. In this regard, Rev. Rul. 68–392 addressed the issue of whether a practice followed by a fiduciary may be established in the first taxable year of a trust, and reasoned that since this is the first taxable year of the trust, capital gains are not utilized pursuant to the practice followed by the fiduciary in determining the amount that is distributed or required to be distributed. Accordingly, since the year involved in the present case is the first taxable year of the estate, capital gains are not utilized pursuant to a practice followed by the fiduciary in determining the amount that is distributed or required to be distributed. Thus, capital gains will not be included in distributable net income of the estate under the second method described in section 1.643(a)–3(a)(3) * * *.

The distributable net income of X does not include the capital gains recognized by X upon the sale of securities held by X.

Planning Note

[¶ 30,211]

1. Taxpayers continually search for techniques by which to manipulate the tax consequences of transactions. In that sense, Priv. Ltr. Rul. 8324002 is particularly illustrative. The taxpayer had obviously determined that a tax advantage would be gained if the capital gains could "flow through" to the estate's beneficiaries rather than be taxable to the estate. With that in mind, consider how wills should be drafted to give the decedent's executor the maximum postmortem planning opportunity. For example, would it be appro-

priate to provide that "my executor shall have complete discretion in allocating capital gains to income or principal during the administration of my estate"? In reflecting upon this suggestion, consider whether the answer would be different if the estate's beneficiary was also the executor of the estate. In such a case, could it be argued that the beneficiary would be in "constructive" receipt of the capital gains even if they were not distributed to him or her?

Keep in mind that, in Priv. Ltr. Rul. 8627043, the IRS took the position that the parties to a trust could not agree that any distributions from a trust would first come from the tax-exempt income of the trust. The IRS concluded that the claimed allocation of the tax-exempt income had no economic effect independent of tax consequences and, therefore, could not be given effect for income tax purposes.

2.   Many years ago, H.L. Hunt, the famous oil man, created a trust for the benefit of his daughter, Caroline, the trust to last for her life plus 21 years. On the trust's income tax return for a recent year, the trust claimed that capital gains realized by the trust and distributed to Caroline were a part of DNI. The trust's claim was based on the decision by the trust's auditor to allocate the gains to income rather than corpus for trust accounting purposes. The claim was that trust accounting income is the starting point for determination of DNI and, thus, treating the capital gains as trust accounting income means that the capital gains were part of DNI. The IRS claimed that the auditor's decision was wrong. The dispute, involving millions of dollars in taxes, played out in Crisp v. United States, 34 Fed.Cl. 112 (1995), a case useful to illustrate the interplay of trust accounting determinations based on state law and the governing instrument and tax accounting considerations. The IRS noted that the trust prohibited distributions of corpus to Caroline and, therefore, argued that the auditor's allocation of capital gains to income was manifestly incorrect. The court did not agree. It concluded that the trustee's decision to distribute the capital gains to Caroline was proper and, accordingly, for trust accounting purposes, the capital gains could not be corpus for trust accounting purposes (in as much as the trustee did not have authority to distribute corpus to Caroline). The court reasoned that whether receipts are income or corpus is determined by state law and, according to the state law applicable in this case (Texas), the trust instrument is looked to for this determination. While the trust barred corpus distributions, it permitted distributions of "net profits" and "net earnings" at the discretion of the trustee. (The trust was purely "discretionary" in the sense that it did not require that the trustee make any distributions whatsoever to Caroline.) The capital gains represented the profit realized by the trust as a limited partner in a partnership engaged in active stock market trading. In the court's opinion, the creator of the trust intended these profits to constitute "net profits" or "net earnings." Thus, for trust accounting purposes, the capital gains were income even though the capital gains were entitled to preferential income tax treatment. Now, here is the rub. The court admitted that had the securities that produced the profits been owned directly by the trust—rather than the limited partnership—the realized profits would be corpus for trust accounting purposes as well as for tax purposes. It rejected the notion,

¶ 30,211

however, that making the distinction meant that taxpayers could manipulate income tax consequences by creating a partnership and generating "profits" rather than capital gains. Instead the court concluded that the creator intended that the trustee have broad discretion in making investments and would in no way have wanted the form of investment to have dictated whether income was available for distribution to the trust beneficiary. And since the trustee thought that the limited partnership investment was the most efficient investment vehicle, that decision should not dictate tax results.

Did you get that? If not, read it again and consider whether you agree with the court? Or is this, as the IRS suggests, an opportunity to manipulate tax consequences. For example, if the *Crisp* capital gains were not part of DNI, these gains would have been taxed to the trust and the amounts distributed to Caroline would have been a nontaxable distribution (to the extent the amount distributed exceeded DNI). By including the capital gains in DNI, DNI was inflated by the amount of the gains, allowing the trust a bigger distribution deduction.

It is possible that the decisions taken by the *Crisp* trustees were part of a tax management scheme perhaps in a year when Caroline, the trust beneficiary, had no other taxable income. Getting the capital gains to her for income tax purposes—and out of the trust—may have resulted in those gains being partially or completely sheltered from income tax because of other losses Caroline had in that tax year.

I. THE CHARACTER RULES

[¶ 30,217]

Sections 652(b) and 662(b) set forth the "character" rules. According to these rules, the amount deemed distributed to beneficiaries of a trust or estate will have the same "character" in the hands of the beneficiaries as it had in the hands of the trust or estate. That is, if the estate's or trust's income was composed of 25–percent dividend income and 75–percent interest income, the beneficiary would be deemed to have received a distribution of dividend income and a distribution of interest income in the same proportions. If there was more than one beneficiary, each of them would be deemed to have received his or her proportionate share of the dividend and interest income. See §§ 652(b) and 662(b). As a result of these "character" rules, the trust's role as merely a "conduit" is readily apparent.

Similarly, tax-exempt interest is included in distributable net income (DNI) and, as such, flows through to the estate or trust beneficiaries . Reg. § 1.643(a)–5.

The "character" rules also provide principles to be used in allocating, among the items of distributable net income, items of deduction entering into the computation of distributable net income. Expenses such as property taxes on rental properties which can be directly attributed to rental income are to be allocated to the rental income for purposes of determining the character of the distributions made to beneficiaries.

Example: The Smith Trust, which requires all income to be distributed currently to Billy Bob and Clint in equal shares, has the following items of income: $25,000 in rental income; $50,000 in dividend income; $25,000 in tax-exempt interest. The trust has $10,000 in rental expense and $4,000 in trustee's fees. The allocation of taxable income is computed as follows:

Trust Accounting Income:
Rents $25,000
Rental expense... (10,000)
Dividends 50,000
Tax-exempt interest 25,000
Trustee's fees .... (4,000)
$86,000

Federal Gross Income:
Rent $25,000
Dividends 50,000
$75,000

Tentative Taxable Income:
Gross Income $75,000
Section 642(b) exemption .... (300)
Rental expense... (10,000)
Trustee's fees (Because tax-exempt interest constituted one-fourth of total trust income, one-fourth of indirect expense—$4,000 of trustee fees—was allocated to that interest and is disallowed as a deduction.) .... (3,000)
61,700

DNI:
Tentative taxable income $61,700
Personal exemption 300
Tax-exempt interest 25,000
Trustee's fees allocable to tax-exempt interest (Reg. § 1.643(a)–5(a)) .... (1,000)
$86,000

Distribution Deduction:
DNI.. $86,000
Tax-exempt interest less deduction .... (24,000)
$62,000

Because amounts required to be distributed currently do not exceed DNI, Billy Bob and Clint each receive $43,000 and include that amount in their gross income. The income retains the same character in the hands of the beneficiaries as it had in the trust. Thus, in the above example, Billy Bob and Clint each have received $7,000 in rental income [(25,000–10,000–1,000) ÷ 2]; $24,000 in dividend income [(50,000–2,000) ÷ 2]; and $12,000 in tax-exempt interest income [(25,000–1,000) ÷ 2]. See Reg. § 1.652(b)–3(b).

¶ 30,217

J. TRUST AND ESTATE TAXABLE INCOME

[¶ 30,223]

1. COMPUTATIONAL SCHEME

Taxable income is computed for estates and trusts in the same manner as for individuals, subject to certain modifications. §§ 67(e) and 641(b). For individuals, gross income is reduced by the cost of producing that income to determine adjusted gross income, and adjusted gross income, in turn, is reduced by certain other deductions specifically authorized by Congress for policy reasons. § 63. The result is "taxable income," against which is applied the tax table or rate schedule, whichever is appropriate. § 1. The amount of tax thus determined is further reduced by credits specifically allowed by law. §§ 21–53.

When these concepts are applied to estate and trust income taxation, receipts that will be gross income to an individual will be gross income to the estate or trust. Reg. § 1.641(a)–2. Similarly, expenditures that would be deductible by individuals are, generally speaking, deductible by estates and trusts. § 641(b). Examples include court costs, attorney and fiduciary fees, taxes, etc. See Reg. § 1.212–1(i), § 164, and Reg. § 1.641(b)–1, respectively. Adjusted gross income, in the case of a trust, is only computed for limited purposes under § 67(e), but, even so, it is determined in the same manner as that prescribed for determining the adjusted gross income of individuals.

The scheme for taxing trust and estate income is as follows (tracking here for, convenience of reference, the U.S. Fiduciary Income Tax Return—Form 1041 (Appendix B), assuming an estate with $1,000 of dividend income, $100 of attorney fees, and a distribution of $200 to a beneficiary):

Trust Accounting Income:

Rents	$25,000
Rental expense	(10,000)
Dividends	50,000
Tax-exempt interest	25,000
Trustee's fees	(4,000)
	$86,000

Federal Gross Income:

Rent	$25,000
Dividends	50,000
	$75,000

Tentative Taxable Income:

Gross Income	$75,000
Section 642(b) exemption	(300)
Rental expense	(10,000)
Trustee's fees (Because tax-exempt interest constituted one-fourth of total trust income, one-fourth of indirect expense—$4,000 of trustee fees—was allocated to that interest and is disallowed as a deduction.)	(3,000)

	61,700

DNI:

Tentative taxable income	$61,700
Personal exemption	300
Tax-exempt interest	25,000
Trustee's fees allocable to tax-exempt interest (Reg. § 1.643(a)–5(a))	(1,000)
	$86,000

Distribution Deduction:

DNI...	$86,000
Tax-exempt interest less deduction	(24,000)
	$62,000

Among the rules peculiar to taxing the income from trusts and estates are the following:

1. Trusts required to distribute all their income currently are entitled to a deduction for a personal exemption of $300. § 642(b). For all other trusts, the personal deduction is limited to $100. Estates get a $600 exemption.

2. The standard deduction is expressly denied to estates and trusts. § 63(c)(6)(D).

3. As a general rule, distributions made to beneficiaries are required to be deducted by both trusts and estates in determining taxable income, but only to the extent that the estate has "distributable net income" as determined under § 643(b). See ¶¶ 30,037; 30,049.

4. While the charitable deduction under § 170 is not available to trusts, amounts "paid" pursuant to the terms of the governing instrument for public charitable purposes are deductible by both estates and trusts, and amounts "permanently set aside" are deductible by estates and certain (not all) trusts. § 642(c). See ¶ 30,490.

[¶ 30,225]

2. TWO PERCENT "HAIRCUT"

As in the case of individuals, estates and trusts may deduct "miscellaneous itemized deductions" to the extent that such deductions exceed 2 percent of the estate's or trust's adjusted gross income. § 67(a). However a special exception applies to estates and trusts. This rule provides that, while the adjusted gross income of an estate or trust is "computed in the same manner as in the case of an individual," an estate or trust, in arriving at adjusted gross income, is entitled to a deduction for 100 percent of the "costs which are paid or incurred if the property were not held in such trust or estate." § 67(e). Four cases of note have been reported. The latest, *Rudkin*, appears below; the others, *O'Neill*, *Mellon Bank*, and *Scott* are discussed in *Rudkin*. Certainly there was agreement in *O'Neill* and *Mellon Bank* "that trustee fees were not subject to the 2 percent "haircut" and were fully deductible. (And, it is fair to say, that all the courts would agree that the personal exemption deduction available to trusts and estates under § 642(b) and the distribution deduction under §§ 651 and 661, respectively, for amounts distributed to beneficiaries are fully deductible and not subject to the 2–percent "haircut.") In dispute is the full deductibility of the fees incurred for investment advisory services provided the fiduciary whose task, typically, was to "make the trust property productive." The argument is that these fees are subject to the 2 percent haircut. (*Query*: Whether the dispute could be avoided if the trustee increased his or her fees by an amount sufficient to cover the investment advisory fees incurred by the trust and, on the trustee's personal income tax return, claimed a business expense deduction for the fees paid to the investment advisor. Or are there ethical implications—and, possibly, legal—implications for such a strategy?)

[¶ 30,226]

RUDKIN TESTAMENTARY TRUST v. COMMISSIONER

United States Tax Court, 2005.
124 T.C. 304.

WHERRY, J.

Respondent determined a Federal income tax deficiency in the amount of $4,448 with respect to the 2000 taxable year of the William L. Rudkin Testamentary Trust (the trust). The sole issue for decision is whether investment advisory fees paid by the trust are fully deductible under the exception provided in § 67(e)(1) or whether the fees are deductible only to the extent that they exceed 2 percent of the trust's adjusted gross income pursuant to § 67(a).

FINDINGS OF FACT

* * *

The trust was established under the will of Henry A. Rudkin on April 14, 1967. Henry A. Rudkin's family was involved in the founding of Pepperidge Farm, a food products company. Pepperidge Farm was sold to Campbell Soup Company in the 1960s, and the trust was initially funded primarily with proceeds from that sale.

* * * In general, income and principal of the trust were to be applied for the benefit of Henry A. Rudkin's son, William L. Rudkin, and the son's spouse, descendants, and spouses of descendants. Principal distributions were also subject to a special power of appointment held by William L. Rudkin. The trustee and other fiduciaries of Henry A. Rudkin's estate were provided with broad authority in the management of property, including the authority "to invest and reinvest the funds of my estate or of any trust created hereunder in such manner as they may deem advisable without being restricted to investments of the character authorized by law for the investment of estate or trust funds" and "to employ such agents, experts and counsel as they may deem advisable in connection with the administration and management of my estate and of any trust created hereunder, and to delegate discretionary

powers to or rely upon information or advice furnished by such agents, experts and counsel".

The trustee engaged Warfield Associates, Inc., to provide investment management advice for the trust. During the taxable year 2000, Warfield Associates, Inc., was paid $22,241.31 for its services.

A Form 1041, U.S. Income Tax Return for Estates and Trusts, for the 2000 year was timely filed on behalf of the trust. Thereon the trust reported total income of $624,816. The Form 1041 also reflected, among other things, a deduction of $22,241 on line 15a for "Other deductions not subject to the 2% floor", further described on an attached statement as "INVESTMENT MANAGEMENT FEES". No deduction was claimed on line 15b for "Allowable miscellaneous itemized deductions subject to the 2% floor".

On December 5, 2003, respondent issued to the trust a statutory notice of deficiency determining the aforementioned $4,448 deficiency for the taxable year 2000. Respondent disallowed full deduction of the $22,241 in investment fees and instead permitted a deduction of $9,780, the amount by which $22,241 exceeded 2 percent of adjusted gross income of $623,050 (i.e., $12,461).

The trustee filed the underlying petition in this case disputing respondent's determination on grounds that the investment advisory fees should not be subject to the 2–percent limitation. * * *

Opinion

I. General Rules

As a general rule, the Internal Revenue Code imposes a Federal tax on the taxable income of every individual and trust. § 1. Taxable income is defined as gross income less allowable deductions. § 63(a). Gross income broadly comprises "all income from whatever source derived," § 61(a), and allowable deductions are calculated through application of a multi-tiered process. First, certain enumerated deductions may be subtracted from gross income to arrive at adjusted gross income. § 62(a). Itemized deductions may then be subtracted from adjusted gross income in arriving at taxable income. § 63(d).

Itemized deductions, however, are further segregated into two categories that impact on their deductibility. § 67(b) sets forth a list of itemized deductions allowed without further limitation to the extent permitted under the appropriate statutory section authorizing the deduction. For individual taxpayers, the remaining itemized deductions are characterized as "miscellaneous itemized deductions" and are allowed under § 67(a) only to the extent that they exceed 2 percent of adjusted gross income. For estates and trusts, § 67(e) mandates application of the rule of § 67(a), with specified modifications. Specifically, § 67 provides as follows in relevant part:

§ 67. 2–PERCENT FLOOR ON MISCELLANEOUS ITEMIZED DEDUCTIONS.

(a) General Rule.—In the case of an individual, the miscellaneous itemized deductions for any taxable year shall be allowed only to the extent that the aggregate of such deductions exceeds 2 percent of adjusted gross income.

* * *

(e) Determination of Adjusted Gross Income in Case of Estates and Trusts.—For purposes of this section, the adjusted gross income of an estate or trust shall be computed in the same manner as in the case of an individual, except that—

> (1) the deductions for costs which are paid or incurred in connection with the administration of the estate or trust and which would not have been incurred if the property were not held in such trust or estate * * *

* * *

shall be treated as allowable in arriving at adjusted gross income. * * *

Hence, the statutory text of § 67(e)(1) creates an exception allowing for deduction of trust expenditures without regard to the 2–percent floor where two requirements are satisfied: (1) The costs are paid or incurred in connection with administration of the trust, and (2) the costs would not have been incurred if the property were not held in trust. Otherwise, deductibility is limited to the extent it would be for individual taxpayers.

In that vein, regulations promulgated under § 67 list examples of expenses that, in the context of individuals, are subject to the 2–percent floor. Temp Reg. § 1.67–1T(a)(1). Included are expenses incurred "for the production or collection of income for which a deduction is otherwise allowable under § 212(1) and (2), such as *investment advisory fees,* subscriptions to investment advisory publications, certain attorneys' fees, and the cost of safe deposit boxes". Temp. Reg. § 1.67–1T(a)(1)(ii)(emphasis added).

II. *Contentions of the Parties*

Against this backdrop, the trustee contends that the investment management fees in dispute here are properly deductible under the exception set forth in § 67(e)(1). The trustee maintains that the fees were paid in connection with administration of the trust and would not have been incurred if the property were not held in trust. In reaching this conclusion, the trustee relies largely on the fiduciary duties imposed on trustees. According to the trustee, while an individual may make a voluntary and personal choice to seek investment advice, fiduciary duties render such professional advice a necessary and "involuntary" component of trust administration.

In contrast, it is respondent's position that the § 67(e)(1) exception does not apply to the expenses at issue. Respondent does not dispute the expenditures were made in connection with the administration of the trust. However, respondent alleges that because investment advisory fees are commonly incurred by individual investors outside the context of trust administration, the fees fail to satisfy the requirement that they would not have been incurred if the assets were not held in trust. It is also respondent's view that neither

State law nor the governing trust instrument imposed a legal obligation on the fiduciary to obtain professional investment management services.

III. *Analysis*

The deductibility of investment advisory fees by a trust under § 67(e)(1) is not a matter of first impression. This Court and three Courts of Appeals have ruled on the question. Scott v. United States, 328 F.3d 132 (4th Cir.2003); Mellon Bank, N.A. v. United States, 265 F.3d 1275 (Fed.Cir.2001); O'Neill v. Commissioner, 994 F.2d 302 (6th Cir.1993), revg. 98 T.C. 227 (1992). The result has been a split in authority on the issue.

This Court in O'Neill v. Commissioner, 98 T.C. at 230–231, held that investment advice costs were not deductible under § 67(e), reasoning as follows:

> We believe that the thrust of the language of § 67(e) is that only those costs which are *unique* to the administration of an estate or trust are to be deducted from gross income without being subject to the 2–percent floor on itemized deductions set forth at § 67(a). Examples of items unique to the administration of a trust or estate would be the fees paid to a trustee and trust accounting fees mandated by law or the trust agreement. Individual investors routinely incur costs for investment advice as an integral part of their investment activities. Consequently, it cannot be argued that such costs are somehow unique to the administration of an estate or trust simply because a fiduciary might feel compelled to incur such expenses in order to meet the prudent person standards imposed by State law.

The Court of Appeals for the Sixth Circuit reversed in O'Neill v. Commissioner, 994 F.2d at 304–305. Although the Court of Appeals concurred that "certain expenditures unique to trust administration are excepted from the two percent floor", the Court disagreed with our analysis as to why the costs in dispute were not unique. Id. at 303–304. Noting our statement that individual investors routinely incur costs for investment advice, the Court of Appeals opined: "Nevertheless, they are not required to consult advisors and suffer no penalties or potential liability if they act negligently for themselves. Therefore, fiduciaries uniquely occupy a position of trust for others and have an obligation to the beneficiaries to exercise proper skill and care with the assets of the trust." Id. at 304.

Subsequently, the Courts of Appeals for the Federal and Fourth Circuits in Mellon Bank, N.A. v. United States, supra, and Scott v. United States, supra, respectively, diverged from the position taken by the Court of Appeals for the Sixth Circuit. These latter rulings were consistent in their rationale and result, summarized as follows by the Court of Appeals for the Fourth Circuit:

> the second requirement of § 67(e)(1) does not ask whether costs are commonly incurred in the administration of trusts. Instead, it asks whether costs are commonly incurred outside the administration of trusts. As the Federal Circuit decided in *Mellon Bank,* investment-advice fees are commonly incurred outside the administration of trusts, and they

are therefore subject to the 2% floor established by § 67(a). * * * [Scott v. United States, supra at 140.]

See also Mellon Bank, N.A. v. United States, supra at 1281 ("the second requirement treats as fully deductible only those trust-related administrative expenses that are unique to the administration of a trust and not customarily incurred outside of trusts").

In construing § 67(e)(1), the Courts of Appeals for both the Federal and Fourth Circuits emphasized the importance of not interpreting the statute so as to render superfluous any portion thereof. Scott v. United States, supra at 140; Mellon Bank, N.A. v. United States, supra at 1280. Moreover, both courts explicitly rejected the taxpayers' arguments premised on fiduciary duties as running afoul of this principle of construction. Scott v. United States, supra at 140; Mellon Bank, N.A. v. United States, supra at 1280–1281. In the words of the Court of Appeals for the Fourth Circuit:

> we would, by holding that a trust's investment-advice fees were fully deductible, render meaningless the second requirement of § 67(e)(1). All trust-related administrative expenses could be attributed to a trustee's fiduciary duties, and the broad reading of § 67(e)(1) urged by the taxpayers would treat as fully deductible any costs associated with a trust. But the second clause of § 67(e)(1) specifically limits the applicability of § 67(e) to certain types of trust-related administrative expenses. To give effect to this limitation, we must hold that the investment-advice fees incurred by the Trust do not qualify for the exception created by § 67(e). Rather, they are subject to the 2% floor established by § 67(a). [Scott v. United States, supra at 140.]

The Court of Appeals for the Fourth Circuit characterized the contrary analysis in this regard of the Court of Appeals for the Sixth Circuit in O'Neill v. Commissioner, 994 F.2d at 304, as containing "a fatal flaw". Scott v. United States, supra at 140. The Court of Appeals for the Federal Circuit similarly branded the taxpayer's attempts to bolster its interpretation through legislative history as "unpersuasive." Mellon Bank, N.A. v. United States, supra at 1281. To wit, the Court of Appeals for the Federal Circuit, tracing the genesis of § 67(e), noted that to premise full deduction of all trust expenses on fiduciary duties would run counter to

> legislative intent to equate the taxation of trusts with the taxation of individuals, limit the ability of sophisticated taxpayers to use trusts or other complex arrangements to lower their tax burden compared to similarly situated individuals, and to minimize the impact of the tax code on economic decision making. [Id.]

Having reviewed our initial construction of § 67(e) and the ensuing judicial developments detailed above, this Court concludes that the interpretation set forth in O'Neill v. Commissioner, 98 T.C. at 230–231, and expressed by the Courts of Appeals in Scott v. United States, 328 F.3d at 139–140, and Mellon Bank, N.A. v. United States, 265 F.3d at 1280–1281, remains sound. The trustee here, in support of full deductibility, relies on concepts rejected in the foregoing decisions. Appeal in the instant case, barring stipulation to the contrary, would be to the Court of Appeals for the Second Circuit, which has not ruled on the issue. See Golsen v. Commissioner, 54 T.C. 742, 757, 1970 WL 2191 (1970), affd. 445 F.2d 985 (10th Cir.1971). The Court therefore holds that the investment advisory fees paid by the trust are not fully deductible under the exception provided in § 67(e)(1) and are deductible only to the extent that they exceed 2 percent of the trust's adjusted gross income pursuant to § 67(a).

[¶ 30,229]

3. PASSIVE ACTIVITY LOSS LIMITATIONS

Section 469 generally limits deductions and credits derived from passive activities to the amount of income derived from all passive activities.

The passive activity loss limitations apply to estates and trusts. However, there are several rules relating to the passive activity loss limitations which are peculiar to estates and trusts.

Generally, an activity is deemed to be passive if it involves the conduct of any trade or business and the taxpayer does not materially participate in the activity. § 469(c)(1). Passive activities do not include working interests in oil and gas properties "which the taxpayer holds directly or through an entity which does not limit the liability of the taxpayer with respect to such interest." § 469(c)(3).

An estate or trust is treated as materially participating in an activity if an executor or fiduciary, in his or her capacity as such, is involved in operations of the activity on a regular, continuous, and substantial basis. However, in the case of a grantor trust, material participation is determined at the grantor level.

Rental activities are considered to be passive activities, whether or not the taxpayer materially participates. However, in the case of tax years of an estate ending less than two years after the date of death of the decedent, up to $25,000 of the passive activity losses attributable to all rental real estate activities in which the decedent actively participated prior to death are allowed as deductions. § 469(i). Any unused losses and/or credits are deemed "suspended" passive activity losses for the year and are carried forward indefinitely. However, it should be noted that the $25,000 offset for rental real estate activities is to be reduced by the amount of the exemption "allowable to the surviving spouse of the decedent for the taxable year ending with or within the taxable year of the estate." § 469(i)(4)(B).

Losses from passive activities are first subject to the at-risk rules. When the losses are deductible under the at-risk rules, the passive activity rules then apply.

Portfolio income of an estate or trust must be accounted for separately and may not be offset by losses from passive activities. Portfolio income generally includes interest, dividends, royalties not derived in the ordinary course of business, and income from annuities. § 469(e).

¶ 30,226

If a trust or estate distributes its entire interest in a passive activity to a beneficiary, the basis of the property is increased (no deduction allowed) by the amount of any suspended losses generated by that passive activity. Gain or loss to the trust or estate and the basis of the property to the beneficiary is then determined under the rules set forth in § 643(e). § 469(j)(12).

[¶ 30,235]

4. TAX RATE SCHEDULE

To discourage the use of trusts—and estates—as income tax shelters, the income tax rates applied to income that is retained by the trust—or estate—and not distributed to the beneficiaries could be described as "compressed" compared to the tax rates applicable to individuals. For example, for tax years beginning in 2006, adjusted for inflation, the first $30,650 of income received by an unmarried taxpayer (and the first $61,300 of income received by married taxpayers filing jointly) is taxed at a rate of 15 percent or less (the first $7,550 and $15,100 respectively, at 10 percent), § 1(a), (c), and (i); Rev. Proc. 2005–70, 2005–47 I.R.B. 979. By way of contrast, compare the 2006 inflation adjusted income tax rate schedule applicable to trusts and estates (§ 1(e) and (i); Rev. Proc. 2005–70, 2005–47 I.R.B. 979):

Not over $2,050	15%
Over $2,050 but not over $4,850	25%
Over $4,850 but not over $7,400	28%
Over $7,400 but not over $10,050	33%
Over $10,050	35%

As a general rule, net long term capital gains as well as most dividends are taxed at a maximum rate of 15 percent. § 1(h).

Planning Note

[¶ 30,241]

Possible planning may include accumulating income in a trust rather than distributing it to a beneficiary in those cases where the income will be taxed to the beneficiary at the top rate (if the income is distributed) but taxed to the trust at a lower rate (if not distributed). For example, in 2006, an annual income tax savings of $922 ($957 taking account of the $100 exemption) could be realized by accumulating income in a trust in lieu of distributing that income to a beneficiary where it would be taxed at the top rate. However, in many such cases, the income savings may well be more than offset by the expenses of trust administration. For that reason, only a few taxpayers will look at the trust as a vehicle to accomplish income tax savings. Instead, trusts will be used either for nontax reasons or because of estate tax and generation-skipping tax considerations. Certainly, from an income tax perspective, the application of the compressed rates constitutes a tax penalty to estates and for the use of trusts, a penalty that will need to be balanced against the nontax benefits of the trust or the estate tax and/or generation-skipping tax savings benefits of the trust.

[¶ 30,247]

5. TAX RETURN OBLIGATIONS

An executor must file Form 1041, U.S. Fiduciary Income Tax Return, for the estate if the estate has gross income for its tax year of $600 or more. § 6012(a)(3).

A trustee must file Form 1041 for the trust for each year in which the trust has "any taxable income" or "gross income of $600 or over, regardless of the amount of taxable income." § 6012(a)(4).

The executor may elect to file the estate's income tax returns on a calendar or fiscal year basis. § 441(b)(1). However, new and existing trusts must use a calendar year.

Certain trusts revocable by the decedent at the time of the decedent's death may elect to be treated and taxed as part of the decedent's estate for income tax purposes for two years after the decedent's death if no federal estate tax return is necessary or for a period ending six months after the conclusion of any proceeding relating to the decedent's federal estate tax return. § 645. Where the decedent has created more than one revocable trust, all can be combined with the decedent's estate. A consolidated income tax return *as an estate* is filed for the combined entities. Both the executor and trustee must indicate that consolidated reporting has been elected. § 645(a). An election to consolidate is irrevocable once made. § 645(c).

[¶ 30,253]

6. ALTERNATIVE MINIMUM TAX

The alternative minimum tax applies to trusts and estates, the minimum tax rate being 26 percent and the maximum, 28 percent. § 55(b)(1)(a). Trusts and estates are entitled to a $22,500 exemption. § 55(d)(1)(C)(ii). However, the exemption is phased out in cases where the trust or estate has alternative minimum taxable income (AMTI) in excess of $75,000, the phase-out being at a rate of $.25 per $1 of AMTI in excess of $75,000. § 55(d)(3)(C).

[¶ 30,259]

7. ESTIMATED INCOME TAX PAYMENTS

Trusts and estates must make quarterly estimated income tax payments in the same manner as individuals except that estates and revocable trusts are exempt from making such payments, generally speaking, during the first two taxable years of the estate. § 6654(*l*). More specifically, estates are required to make quarterly estimated income tax payments for those taxable years "ending two or more years after the date of the death" of the decedent. This special rule allowing estates an exemption from the burden of making estimated income tax payments extends to revocable trusts in cases where the revocable trust is to receive the grantor's residuary estate under a pour-over will or, if no will is admitted to probate, the special rule extends to the revocable trust primarily responsible for paying the decedent's debts, taxes and administration expenses. § 6654(*l*)(2).

¶ 30,247

Example: Antonio Lopez died on December 12, 2005. His will, dated April 10, 1986, provided, in pertinent part, as follows: "I give all of my property to the Trustee of the Lopez Family Revocable Living Trust, which I created on April 10, 1986."

The trust reports its income on a calendar year basis but Antonio's executor elected to report the estate's income on a fiscal year ending November 30th. As far as estimated tax payments are concerned, no estimated income tax payments are required of Antonio's executor for the fiscal years ending on November 30, 2006 and November 30, 2007. As for the trust, estimated income tax payments are not required for the trust tax years ending December 31, 2005 and December 31, 2006, but such payments are required for the trust tax year ending December 31, 2007.

Understandably, the penalties for underpayment of quarterly estimated income tax are applicable to fiduciaries as well as individuals.

In the case of trusts, "the trustee may elect to treat any portion of a payment of estimated tax made by such trust for any taxable year of the trust as a payment made by a beneficiary of such trust." § 643(g)(1)(a). The trustee's election must be made "on or before the 65th day after the close of the taxable year of the trust." Estates may also make this election but only in the "taxable year reasonably expected to be the last taxable year" of the estate. Thus, an estate may find itself in the position of claiming a refund of an overpayment of estimated taxes in a year other than its final year while the estate's beneficiaries will incur an underpayment penalty in the same year as a result of receiving a distribution from the estate during that year and not taking the distribution into account for estimated income tax purposes.

From the standpoint of the beneficiary, in cases where the trust elects to attribute the estimated income tax payment to the trust beneficiary, the payment made by the trust is "treated as a payment of estimated tax made by such beneficiary on January 15 following the taxable year." § 643(g)(1)(C)(ii). In such a case, the amount of tax attributed to the beneficiary is treated as a distribution by the trust (and is deductible by the trust in computing its income tax liability) and as taxable income to the beneficiary. §§ 651 and 661.

K. TERMINATION OF ESTATES AND TRUSTS

[¶ 30,265]

1. TIMING

From and after the date on which administration of an estate is deemed completed or a trust is deemed terminated for federal income tax purposes, the income of the estate or trust is taxable to the beneficiaries even though it has not been distributed to those beneficiaries.

In the case of a trust, termination depends on whether the trust property has in fact been distributed to the beneficiaries of the trust—and not on the happening of the event by which the trust's duration is to be measured. Reg. § 1.641(b)-3(b). However, the Treasury says "the winding up of a trust cannot be unduly postponed and if the distribution of the trust corpus is unreasonably delayed, the trust is considered terminated for Federal income tax purposes after the expiration of a reasonable period for the trustee to complete the administration of the trust."

In the case of an estate, for income tax purposes, the period of administration of an estate is the "period actually required * * * to perform the ordinary duties of administration" (Reg. § 1.641(b)–3(a)), the duties being principally to collect and distribute the decedent's property while discharging obligations to creditors and taxing authorities. However, the Treasury claims that the "period of administration of an estate cannot be unduly prolonged." On the other hand, taxpayers have argued that the "period of administration" referred to in § 641(a)(3) is the period actually consumed rather than a reasonable time, as the Treasury asserts in Reg. § 1.641(b)–3(a).

[¶ 30,271]

BROWN v. UNITED STATES

United States Court of Appeals, Fifth Circuit, 1989.
890 F.2d 1329.

KING, Circuit Judge:

* * *

[Fourteen years after his mother died, Earl A. Brown Jr., principal beneficiary and executor of her estate had not closed the estate and filed a final income tax return. Brown was also the principal beneficiary and executor of his father's estate and 13 years after the father's death the father's estate remained open. The IRS claimed the income earned by the respective estates was properly reportable on Brown's personal income tax return for at least 5 of the tax years in question (rather than on the income tax returns filed for the estates for those years). In dispute was almost $700,000 in additional income taxes.]

We are concerned in this case with the application of section 641(a)(3) [which imposes the federal income tax on "the taxable income of estates or of any kind of property held in trust, including— * * * income received by estates of deceased persons during the period of administration or settlement of the estate."] The pivotal issue for Taxpayers is the meaning of the term "period of administration." Congress has never provided a statutory definition for this term; therefore, the IRS has long interpreted the broad language of section 641(a)(3) in its regulations. The Treasury Regulations promulgated under the 1939 Internal Revenue Code, interpreting the same statutory language, provided that the period of administration is the time actually required by the executor or administrator to perform the ordinary duties pertaining to administration, "whether longer or shorter than the period specified in the local statute for the settlement of estates." Treas. Reg. § 19.162–1 (1940).

In 1956, the IRS promulgated new regulations under the 1954 Code. The IRS reissued the above-quoted regulation—renumbered to correspond to the

¶ 30,265

1954 Code—incorporating the substance of the former version, but clarifying the meaning of "period of administration." Two pertinent sentences were added:

> However, the period of administration of an estate cannot be unduly prolonged. If the administration of an estate is unreasonably prolonged, the estate is considered terminated for Federal income tax purposes after the expiration of a reasonable period for the performance by the executor of all the duties of administration.

Treas. Reg. § 1.641(b)–3(a)(1956).

Under the plain language of the amended regulation, the Commissioner has authority to determine whether an estate's administration has been "unduly prolonged" and to deem the estate closed for federal income tax purposes once a reasonable time has elapsed for the administrator to have performed all the ordinary duties of administration. Taxpayers * * * contend that we must interpret the statutory term "period of administration," * * * to mean the period that an administrator actually consumes before closing the estate, regardless of a determination by the Commissioner that a reasonable time has passed for the estate's termination. Taxpayers also argue that, in any event, a 1982 Texas probate court order, authorizing Brown to continue administration of the Estates at his discretion, was conclusive on the issue of whether the period of administration had terminated under section 641(a)(3) * * *.

We construe Taxpayers' arguments as a challenge to the validity of Treasury Regulation § 1.641(b)–3(a) * * *. The Government, in turn, contends that the regulation is a valid and reasonable interpretation of section 641(a)(3) * * *. The Government also asserts that under the teaching of Commissioner v. Estate of Bosch, 387 U.S. 456 (1967), a lower state court ruling cannot be controlling in a federal tax dispute; therefore, the IRS and the district court acted properly in conducting an independent review of whether the Estates had terminated for federal income tax purposes.

* * *

We must determine whether Treasury Regulation § 1.641(b)–3(a), as expanded in 1956, validly vests the Commissioner with authority to deem an estate's administration terminated for purposes of taxing the estate's income to the beneficiaries, even in cases, such as this one, where administration might legally be continued under state law. The broad language of section 641(a)(3) is open to different interpretations, and the legislative history prior to the 1954 Code is unenlightening. However, in the absence of statutory language to the contrary, the Supreme Court has advised that a provision of the Internal Revenue Code should be read "so as to give a uniform application to a nationwide scheme of taxation." * * * Although state probate laws would, of course, be pertinent in the Commissioner's determination of what the ordinary duties of administration entailed in a particular case, the existence of an estate as a *taxable* entity is a question of federal, not state, law. * * * [S]ection 641(a)(3) can be fairly read to require a uniform federal standard by which the Commissioner may deem an estate closed if the reasonable period of time required to perform the ordinary administrative duties has passed, and the administrator is unduly prolonging the estate's termination.

In the committee reports accompanying the enactment of the 1954 Code, both the House and Senate Reports describe the period of administration as

the period actually required by the administrator or executor to perform the ordinary duties of administration, such as the collection of assets and the payment of debts, legacies, and bequests, whether this period is longer or shorter than the period specified under local law for the settlement of estates.

H.R. Rep. No. 1337, 83d Cong., 2d Sess., reprinted in 1954 U.S. Code Cong. & Ad. News 4017, 4331; S. Rep. No. 1622, 83d Cong., 2d Sess., reprinted in 1954 U.S. Code Cong. & Ad. News 4621, 4980–81. This language adopts the substance of the Treasury Regulation promulgated under the Internal Revenue Code of 1939 interpreting "period of administration," and thus indicates congressional endorsement of the then-existing regulation. Taxpayers do not dispute the validity of the predecessor to Treasury Regulation § 1.641(b)–3(a).

As described above, the IRS added a caveat to the regulation in 1956 that emphasizes the Commissioner's authority to ascertain whether an estate's administration has been unreasonably prolonged for federal income tax purposes. Taxpayers contend that this revision "is not binding on the taxpayer or this Court." However, we find that this change does not contradict the prior regulation, apparently approved by Congress, but merely makes explicit what was formerly implicit. If Congress intended that an estate's period of administration for purposes of section 641(a)(3) should not turn on "local law for the settlement of estates," it appears to us obvious that the period must turn on a federal factual standard, as ascertained by the federal agency charged with enforcement of the Code.

This interpretation of section 641(a)(3) and its accompanying regulation, that the Commissioner is clothed with the authority to deem an estate terminated for income tax purposes if it has been unduly prolonged, has been consistently espoused by the Commissioner—both before and after the amendment to the regulation in 1956—and consistently accepted by the courts. * * * Moreover, the IRS promulgated Treasury Regulation § 1.641(b)–3(a) less than two years after Congress's enactment of the 1954 Code; therefore, the regulation "represents a substantially contemporaneous construction of Subchapter J's conduit principles by those with the expertise to appreciate and define the intent and purposes" of the statute. United States Trust Co. v. IRS, 803 F.2d 1363, 1370 (5th Cir.1986). The amended regulation has now been in effect for over 30 years, yet Congress has left section 641(a)(3) unchanged despite several amendments to the 1954 Code and the enactment of the Internal Revenue Code of 1986. This acquiescence strongly suggests congressional approval of the longstanding interpretation of section 641(a)(3) by the Commissioner. * * *

Taxpayers' position is that "period of administration" should be read to mean the actual period an administrator keeps the estate open, irrespective of

¶ 30,271

whether all ordinary duties actually required for the estate's existence have been completed except for the transfer of the estate's corpus to the legal beneficiaries. We do not believe that Congress intended a rule such as Taxpayers propose that would result both in nonuniform benefits to taxpayers and potential detriment to the Treasury. The increasing popularity of independent estate administrations, for example, in which an administrator operates free of court intervention and under which an estate might legally remain open indefinitely, creates the potential for prolonging an estate to achieve income-splitting and tax avoidance goals, a strategy not available to those estates administered under court supervision. The risk to the Government of lost revenues is most pronounced in cases where the estate fiduciary is also the sole or principal beneficiary of the estate's assets, a not uncommon situation.

Even if we believed Taxpayers' position to be a logical and reasonable interpretation of section 641(a)(3), a conclusion we cannot endorse, Taxpayers could not prevail on that point alone. The issue is whether the Commissioner's interpretation of the statute is a reasonable one, not whether it is the only, or even the best, one. * * * We conclude, as has every other court faced with this issue, that Treasury Regulation 1.641(b)–3(a) is a reasonable and valid interpretation of section 641(a)(3).

* * *

In March 1982, shortly after the IRS sent deficiency notices to Taxpayers notifying them of the termination of the Estates for income tax purposes, Brown filed petitions in the probate court of Dallas County, Texas, requesting the court to find that the Estates required ongoing management and administration. The United States was not a party to this action. In a nonadversary proceeding in April 1982, the probate court entered an order authorizing Brown to continue to manage the assets of the Estates as independent executor until such time as he determined "in his sole discretion" that it would be in the best interest of the beneficiaries to terminate the Estates. Taxpayers argued below, and maintain on appeal, that this probate court decree was binding on both the IRS and the district court * * *. We reject Taxpayers' argument.

Because the United States was not made a party to the probate court proceeding, the ensuing order was not "binding" on the Commissioner in the sense of res judicata or collateral estoppel; see Commissioner v. Estate of Bosch, 387 U.S. 456, 462–63 (1967). * * * The issue, therefore, is what degree of deference the district court should have accorded this state judgment.

It is axiomatic that federal law controls the interpretation of federal statutes and regulations. In the field of federal taxation, however, federal and state law are tightly intertwined. The Internal Revenue Code does not operate in a vacuum; it attaches tax significance to legal rights and transactions that are created under state law.

When a taxpayer's federal tax liability clearly turns on the characterization under state law of a property interest, a state court's determination of that interest is obviously relevant in a subsequent federal tax controversy.

¶ 30,271

* * * In *Bosch*, * * * the Court held that in such cases, federal authorities are to give "proper regard" to a lower state court's adjudication of the relevant issue, but need not accept such rulings as conclusive. 387 U.S. at 465. Unless the highest court in the state has spoken to the issue, a federal court is to make its own inquiry into state law. Id. When a federal tax law establishes a uniform criterion for taxing certain transactions or situations—irrespective of how state law might label those transactions or situations—the decision of a state probate court as to an underlying issue a fortiori should not be controlling. Thus, regardless of whether section 641(a)(3) creates a uniform federal criterion—as we have concluded in this opinion—or defers to a state's local characterization of the statute's terms, the Supreme Court holds that a federal court must make its own inquiry into relevant issues previously decided by a lower state court.

On the other hand, because state law pervades every tax issue, it would not be accurate to say that a federal court is free to simply ignore a state court's adjudication of relevant underlying facts. The relevance of a state court's judgment to the resolution of a federal tax question will vary, depending on the particular tax statute involved as well as the nature of the state proceeding that produced the judgment. An examination of the state court's judgment will usually be a relevant factor for the federal court's determination of whether "ordinary duties" required under state probate law are "actually required." However, the issue of whether administration has been unduly prolonged for purposes of section 641(a)(3) is ultimately one of federal, not state, law. * * * We next consider the nature of the local proceeding and the resulting decree to evaluate the judgment's relevance to this tax refund case and to determine whether the district court should have accorded it greater weight as an evidentiary factor.

We note first the nonadversary quality of the Texas probate court proceeding instituted by Brown. The United States was not a party. Moreover, Brown and the putative remaindermen agreed that Brown's administration of the Estates should continue, and it was apparently to their economic benefit to do so. Under these circumstances, the court was not presented with all the relevant facts and differing views that would have afforded the basis for a full analysis of the estate administration issue. In addition, the natural tendency of a busy probate court is to accede to a proposed order without great deliberation when all known interested parties are in agreement and when state interests are not adversely affected.

It is evident that Texas state interests were not affected—or even implicated—as a result of the probate court proceeding in question. Not only was there no genuine controversy involved, the probate court's order was unnecessary under the Texas probate Code provisions relating to independent administrations. An independent executor such as Brown has authority to determine when to terminate the administration of an estate free of any court intervention. * * * Absent objection from a person interested in the estate, there is no statutory requirement regarding the period within which independent administration must be closed. The Dallas County Probate Court merely placed official approval on actions that Brown could have legally pursued

¶ 30,271

without the court's direction. Thus, the judgment had no practical consequences apart from this federal tax controversy, and was consequently entitled to little weight in the district court.

* * *

Taxpayers argue in the alternative that, assuming Treasury Regulation
§ 1.641(b)–3(a) is a valid interpretation of section 641, and one to which this
court must defer, the IRS nevertheless acted contrary to the regulation
because the Estates were not unduly prolonged. In this case, the IRS determined after its 1981 audit of the Estates that administration had continued
for over 12 years and, based on the duties performed and yet to be performed,
a reasonable time had passed for terminating the Estates. The district court
reviewed that determination and agreed. The court found that by the end of
1976:

> [a]ll papers necessary to probate the wills such as the inventories and
> appraisals were filed and approved. The inheritance taxes and the federal
> estate tax returns were filed. All the debts and expenses of the estates
> were paid. All assets were located and collected. There were no outstand-
> ing claims, will contests, or property title disputes. No litigation was
> pending regarding claims to the assets or claims by the estates. No federal
> income tax disputes or litigation were pending. . . .

Taxpayers do not dispute that these duties were completed well before
December 31, 1976. However, they argue that the IRS should not have
deemed the Estates terminated because Brown's continued administration
was necessary to * * * disburse legacies to beneficiaries.

* * *

* * * We do not find this argument convincing.

Earl Brown Sr.'s will provided a lifetime income to his secretary, Lucille
Cathey, from a $30,000 investment, which was deposited among three savings
and loan institutions. The will directed that the savings and loan institutions
were to pay the income directly to Ms. Cathey and to return the funds to the
estate after her death [in 1979]. We agree with the district court that it is
generally unreasonable to continue an estate until the death of a beneficiary.
This is particularly true when a bequest is small in relation to the size of the
total estate. "The administration of an estate is concerned primarily with the
collection of assets and payment of claims, and not with the more or less
permanent custody of property for the protection of a legatee." Williams, 16
T.C. at 904. * * *

This reasoning applies with equal force to the purported legacies to Susan
Brown Barry—Brown's only child—and her children. Moreover, we agree with
the district court that such payments during Brown's lifetime were not
specifically mandated by the wills [the court considering such payments, at
best, "a moral obligation"].

* * * [T]he question of whether the administration of an estate has been
unduly prolonged is one of fact. However, "the facts in a given case may be so
clear that reasonable men could not differ on the question of whether the

¶ **30,271**

administration was or was not unduly prolonged, in which case, the question is one of law." [Wylie v. United States, 281 F.Supp. 180, 190 (N.D.Tex.1968).] We agree with the district court in this case that, as a matter of law, the continuing payments of federal income taxes and of the legacies described above were insufficient reasons to prolong the administration of the Estates for federal tax purposes.

Note

[¶ 30,277]

1. *Brown* is a case that can be appropriately given close scrutiny because the facts detail some of the practical aspects of estate administration. Apparently the taxpayer in *Brown*, the executor, had concluded that it was advantageous for income tax purposes to continue the estates as income tax paying entities, the alternative being to conclude the respective estate administrations, whereupon the income would be taxable to the estate's beneficiary, namely himself. Likely only a few taxpayers today would see much practical advantage in warehousing income in an estate because taxing estate income at the estate level (rather than to the beneficiaries) would have yielded what some would say are relatively insignificant tax savings. (In 2005, for example, only $754 of income tax savings would be realized from taxing the income at the estate level rather than to the estate's beneficiaries.) Nonetheless an aggressive executor might be tempted to keep an estate open as a means of attempting to claim income tax deductions for the expenses incurred in managing the estate property, expenses that would be personal and nondeductible if the property were distributed to the beneficiaries. See, e.g., Hibernia Bank v. United States, 581 F.2d 741 (9th Cir.1978), which appears at ¶ 25,013. And there is always the possibility that a beneficiary's creditors cannot reach property held in an estate during the period of administration, a possibility that might cause a sympathetic executor to postpone distribution to the affected beneficiary. Finally, see Estate of Berger v. Commissioner, T.C. Memo 1990–554, which appears at ¶ 30,491, where an estate was claimed to be "open" as a means of claiming a charitable deduction.

2. In Turner v. United States, 306 F.Supp.2d, 668 (D. Tex. 2004), a charitable deduction had been claimed on the estate tax return for a $10 million pecuniary amount gift. Because the executor was uncertain as to whether the gift qualified for the charitable deduction, payment of the $10 million to the organization was delayed for 2 ½ years pending receipt of the estate tax closing letter—thereby, extending the period of estate administration. As a result of the delayed distribution, the organization was paid more than $1 million interest on its gift (because state law mandated payment of six percent interest on pecuniary amount gifts not satisfied within one year of death). The estate was held able to claim an estate tax administration expense deduction as an administration expense for estate tax purposes under § 2053 because the payment delay was "necessarily incurred" and was not incurred "for a longer period than" the executor "was reasonably required to retain the property." The court discussed the role of the estate tax closing letter (*Turner*, 675–76):

* * * Turner prudently withheld funding the bequest until the estate received an IRS closing letter and resolved any estate tax audit. Receipt of a closing letter prior to distributing estate assets is, in the general practice of estate administration, not an imprudent exercise of an executor's fiduciary duties. *See* IRS Field Service Advisory, 1997 WL 33313776 (Sept. 5, 1997) ("[A] reasonably, prudent person would not make distributions until they were in receipt of an estate tax closing letter ...”). An estate tax closing letter from the IRS provides assurance to an executrix that issues such as the payment of estate tax and valuation of estate assets have been fully resolved, thus making it safe to distribute the assets of the estate to the beneficiaries. See, *e.g., Estate of Cameron Bommer v. Commissioner of Internal Revenue,* 69 T.C.M. (CCH) 2541 at n. 9, 1995 WL 258415 (U.S.Tax Ct.1995) ("[C]losing letters are normally issued in estate cases to provide a measure of assurance that the estate's Federal tax liabilities have been satisfied and, thus, to permit the closing of the probate estate at the local level."). Professors Richard Schmalbeck & Jay A. Soled observe the following:

> Many executors choose not to make estate distributions until they receive a closing letter from the Service that verifies the accuracy of the estate tax return. Because estate tax returns are not due until nine months after the death of a taxpayer (fifteen months if the executors file for an extension), and because the IRS usually does not issue an estate tax closing letter until six months after submission of the return, this precautionary stance [taken by executors often means that estates are kept open an extra] fifteen months to two years from the date of the decedent's death.

Richard Schmalbeck & Jay A. Soled, *Many Unhappy Returns: Estate Tax Returns of Married Decedents,* 21 Va. Tax Rev. 361, 366 (2002) (footnotes omitted). Turner prudently followed this practice but promptly paid the * * * bequest two weeks after receiving the IRS closing letter, albeit 2 1/2 years after the decedent's death. * * * In light of these circumstances, the court is satisfied that Turner was properly acting within her fiduciary duty to the beneficiaries of the Will by awaiting the receipt of a closing letter.

3. *Brown* involved an estate that stayed open too long. For many a fiduciary, the goal is wind up the estate or trust at the earliest possible time, effect distribution—and be released from personal liability (1) to the beneficiaries for his or her stewardship as fiduciary; and (2) income and gift taxes due from the decedent (in the case of an estate) or on account of income taxes owed by the fiduciary *as fiduciary.* Obtaining releases from the beneficiaries for liability for stewardship decisions is beyond the scope of these materials but, suffice it to say, that absent some consideration flowing to the beneficiaries for the release, there is some question as to the effectiveness of such releases. As for tax liability, § 6501(d) provides that the personal representative, upon request, is entitled to receive within 18 months of filing the request, a prompt assessment of any income and gift taxes due from the decedent, including penalties. Section 6905(a) provides that a personal repre-

sentative, upon request, is entitled to be released or notified of any taxes dues within nine months of making the request. Rare though is the fiduciary who makes either request, it being commonly believed that the making of either request will trigger "an audit or even an arbitrary assessment." Jerry A. Kasner, Post Mortem Tax Planning, 2–46 (3rd ed. 1998)

[¶ 30,283]

2. EXCESS DEDUCTIONS UNDER SECTION 642(h)

The term "excess deductions" refers to the amount by which the tax deductible expenses incurred by an estate or trust in its last tax year exceed the income of the estate or trust in that final year. § 642(h)(2). Specifically excluded from the definition of these so-called excess deductions is the personal exemption otherwise available to estates and trusts and the charitable deduction. The excess deductions in the final year flow through to the beneficiary or beneficiaries of the estate or trust and are available as deductions on the income tax return of the beneficiaries. However, the excess deductions are available to the beneficiary only as itemized deductions and only in the tax year of the beneficiary in which the estate or trust tax year ended.

Planning Note

[¶ 30,289]

While estate administration expenses are deductible in computing the federal estate tax (pursuant to § 2053(a)(2)) or the estate's income tax, such expenses are not deductible for both purposes. § 642(g). In deciding whether to claim these deductions on the federal estate tax return or on the estate's income tax return, the fiduciary must compare the marginal tax brackets that are applicable for estate tax purposes and income tax purposes to the particular trust or estate. Ordinarily, the deductions will be claimed on the return that provides the greatest dollar amount reduction in tax. Inasmuch as the estate tax rate is 46 percent in 2006 (when the applicable exclusion amount is $2 million) and the effective income tax rates for the great majority of taxpayers are 30 percent or less (despite higher brackets of 33 percent and 35 percent in 2006), in most instances where an estate has federal estate tax liability, it makes economic sense to claim the deduction for administration expenses on the federal estate tax return rather than on the estate's income tax return. However, in smaller estates and estates that have no federal estate tax liability, the deduction for fiduciary administration expenses should be claimed on the income tax return.

In the case of many smaller estates that have little income, wise tax planning calls for the executor to postpone payment of estate administration expenses until the final year of the administration. By such postponement, to the extent possible, the expenses are bunched in the final year of the estate administration and will generally exceed the estate's income in that final year, particularly if the final year is a short tax year, as is so often the case. Thus, excess deductions are generated and, where the beneficiary or beneficiaries of the estate are in higher income tax brackets than the estate, the pass through of these excess deductions can be economically advantageous. However, whether the beneficiary can actually use the excess deductions will depend on whether the beneficiary itemizes deductions for federal income tax purposes. It also depends on whether these excess deductions exceed two percent of the beneficiary's adjusted gross income. As a result of § 67(a), the deduction of the excess deductions from an estate or trust by the beneficiary of the estate or trust is limited to the amount by which these excess deductions exceed two percent of the beneficiary's adjusted gross income.

Income tax returns should be filed even in small estates where the estate's income is negligible. Filing such returns will give both the IRS and the estate beneficiaries the necessary information concerning the existence and amount of excess deductions.

[¶ 30,295]

3. NET OPERATING LOSS AND CAPITAL LOSS CARRYOVER

As in the case of excess deductions, § 642(h) permits an estate or trust to pass on to its beneficiaries any net operating loss carryover and capital loss carryover in the year in which the estate or trust terminates. While the loss need not be generated in the final year of the estate or trust (Reg. § 1.642(h)–1), the loss must have been generated at the estate or trust level. Losses sustained by the decedent prior to death or losses sustained by the creator of the trust cannot be carried into the estate or trust and then out to the beneficiaries. See Frank, "Termination Deductions and Carryovers: Timing, Classifications," 24 N.Y. Inst. on Fed. Taxation 411, 418 (1966). Similarly, the beneficiary can utilize the loss only currently or carry it forward; the loss cannot be carried back to a prior tax year by the beneficiary.

In cases where the terminating year of the estate or trust is the last year for using the operating loss, any amount not utilized by the estate or trust in that last year will qualify as an excess deduction and may be carried out to the beneficiaries under § 642(h)(2). With this exception, neither net operating losses nor capital losses can be considered both a loss carryover and an excess deduction. Reg. § 1.642(h)–2(b). Moreover, a deductible item used to compute the loss cannot also qualify as a component of "excess deductions" available to the beneficiaries of the estate or trust. Reg. § 1.642(h)–2(c).

[¶ 30,301]

4. TWO–PERCENT "HAIRCUT"

As noted above, in the hands of the beneficiary, "excess deductions" in the final year of an estate or trust would appear to be "miscellaneous itemized deductions" as that term is defined in § 67(b)(even though these deductions are not subject to the two-percent haircut in the hands of the estate or trust). Section 67(a) provides that "in the case of an individual, the miscellaneous itemized deductions for any year shall be allowed only to the extent that the aggregate of such deductions exceeds 2 percent of adjusted gross income." Accordingly, it is possible that a beneficiary to whom "excess deductions" are allocated would be required to subject those deductions to the two-percent rule. Whether the "safe harbor" of § 67(e) would be available to the beneficiary is unclear. Section 67(e) states that the two-percent rule is not applicable to "deductions for costs which are paid or incurred in connection with the administration of an estate or trust and would not have been incurred if such property were not held in trust or estate." For related materials, see ¶ 30,225.

Problems

[¶ 30,307]

1. A trust provided that income should be distributed to Bob until December 31 of the current year. At that time, the trust was to terminate and the corpus was to be distributed to Chuck. During the year, the trust received dividends of $32,000 and sustained capital losses of $16,000. Capital gains and losses were allocable to corpus under the terms of the trust. The trustee's current fees were $2,000, of which $1,500 was chargeable to income and $500 chargeable to corpus. In addition, there was a trustee's termination fee of $10,000. The trust was duly terminated and the corpus distributed to Chuck on December 31. How will the various items of income and expense be reported by the trustee, Bob, and Chuck? §§ 642(h) and 1212.

2. Novice, the trustee of a trust that has terminated, wants to postpone distribution of a "holdback" amount until he gets the "all clear" from the IRS for the income tax returns that he has filed (and those that were filed by the prior trustee). Ben, one of the beneficiaries, objects, saying "it's my money and I want it *now!*" Novice, young and inexperienced as a trustee, had succeeded, under the terms of the trust agreement, to the trusteeship when Dad abruptly resigned as trustee because of ill health. Dad, the trust's sole beneficiary while he was alive, has now died. By its terms, the trust "terminates" when Dad dies. Novice is about the task of distributing the trust property to the trust beneficiaries (including himself, Ben, several cousins, and several half-brothers, each taking somewhat different shares of the trust property). Novice was challenged by the income tax accounting he had to prepare for the trust. Uncertainty as to basis (of trust property sold after Dad's death), ¶ 30,313, as well as computation of "the 691(c) deduction" for estate taxes paid at Dad's death, ¶ 32,109, have prompted Novice, with the consent of all cousins (except Ben) and stepbrothers, to seek to defer final distribution of a "holdback amount" until the statute of limitations related to the income tax returns he has filed for the trust has expired. Novice worries that the trust will be deemed to have terminated for tax purposes in the year Dad died, Reg. § 1.641(b)–3(b), ¶ 30,265, and the expenses he incurs (including his trustee fees) during this likely "3–year period waiting for the statute of limitations to run" will be (1) rendered not deductible by the trust, or (2) deemed to have been incurred by him as agent for the trust beneficiaries and, as a result, effectively, "somehow subject to the two-percent haircut", ¶ 30,301. Pointing to *Brown*, ¶ 30,271, and *Berger*, ¶ 30,491, Novice wonders whether the IRS could argue that the expenses should appear on

¶ 30,301

the personal income tax returns of the respective beneficiaries (rather than the trust) and that those expenses were not necessary to the trust administration, claiming that it was unduly prolonged. Novice, for his part, retorts that he finds support in *Turner*, ¶ 30,277 (where the estate was held open for 2 ½ years pending receipt of a estate tax closing letter from the IRS). Is it possible to responsibly balance these interests and give Novice advice on which he can rely?

L. BASIS CONSIDERATIONS

[¶ 30,313]

1. INTRODUCTION

When it comes to basis, trusts and estates are treated like any other taxpayer. More specifically, property purchased by the trustee has its cost as its basis. § 1012. Property acquired from the settlor or creator of the trust has for its basis the grantor's basis if the trust was created inter vivos, § 1015, or, if testamentary, the estate tax value at date of death or at alternate valuation date. § 1014(a).

Technically speaking, property included in the estate of a decedent has, for its basis in the hands of a recipient, its estate tax value at the decedent's date of death or at alternate valuation date. Thus, in cases where property was transferred to a trust during the life of the transferor and is subsequently included in the transferor's gross estate for estate tax purposes, that property will have as its basis in the hands of the trustee its estate tax value at the death of the transferor.

[¶ 30,315]

2. CARRY OVER BASIS

In 2010, carry over basis is scheduled to replace the new-basis-at-death rule. § 1022. The basis of property acquired from decedents dying in 2010 will, in principle, carry over to the recipient of that property. However, the new-basis-at-death rule will automatically be revived as to decedents dying in 2011 and subsequent years—unless Congress acts to bring about a different result in the meantime.

As for that carry over basis year—2010—a number of exceptions and modifications will apply in determining basis in the hands of recipients. First, basis in the hands of the recipient will be the *lower* of the decedent's basis or fair market value of the transferred property at the decedent's death. § 1022(a). Second, a $1.3 million aggregate basis increase is available to be allocated among the different items of property included in the decedent's estate. § 1022(b). Third, an additional $3 million aggregate basis increase is available to be allocated among items acquired by a surviving spouse from the decedent. § 1022(c) The $3 million spousal basis increase is available for qualified terminable interest property held in trust. § 1022(c)(3)(B). Notwithstanding the foregoing, worth noting, is that resulting basis in the hands of recipients cannot exceed the date of death value of that property. § 1022(d)(2).

[¶ 30,319]

3. ADJUSTMENTS TO BASIS OF TRUST AND ESTATE PROPERTY

Depreciation deductions are allowable to both estates and trusts with respect to income-producing or business property (§ 167(a)(1) and (2)) held by the estate or trust. However, the depreciation deduction will be shared with the beneficiaries in proportion to the income distributed to the beneficiaries and the income retained by the estate or trust. §§ 642(e) and 167(h); Reg. § 1.167(h)–1. Furthermore, regardless of the allocation of the depreciation deduction, the basis of property in the hands of the fiduciary is required to be adjusted downward to take account of depreciation.

[¶ 30,322]

4. DISTRIBUTIONS RECEIVED BY A BENEFICIARY AFTER DEATH

Section 1014 provides that property "passed" or "acquired" from a decedent receives a new basis at the decedent's death. The meaning of the word "acquire" was litigated in Connecticut Nat'l Bank v. United States, 92–1 USTC ¶ 60,102, 71 AFTR2d 93–4454 (D.Conn.1992) on remand from 937 F.2d 90 (2d Cir.1991). The husband had died, leaving his wife as beneficiary of the marital trust. The wife received an income interest in and held a general power of appointment (GPA) over the corpus of the trust. However, at the time of the wife's death, the husband's executor had not distributed to the trust the property to which the trust was entitled. While the trust remained unfunded at the wife's death, the value of the property subject to the GPA but not yet distributed to the trust was included in her gross estate. Furthermore, the wife had exercised the GPA to pass the trust property at her death to an inter vivos trust in favor of her grandchildren. After the wife's death, the husband's estate sold a substantial portion of the trust property, computed a taxable gain based on the fair market value (FMV) of the property at the date of the wife's death and paid the related capital gains tax. The IRS concluded that the estate erroneously computed the income tax payable because the estate was not entitled to use the FMV at the wife's death as the basis of the property sold. It determined that the correct basis for the sold property was the FMV at the date of the husband's death because the property had not been distributed to the trust and therefore the estate did not "acquire" the property at the wife's death. It argued that the correct basis to compute the taxable gain on the fiduciary income tax return was the FMV at the date of the husband's death even though the property would be included in the wife's estate at the FMV at her death for estate tax purposes (because of the general power of appointment). § 2041.

The Second Circuit, nonetheless, agreed with the estate and held that the correct basis to determine the tax payable on the sale was the FMV of the property at the date of the wife's death regardless of whether the property was ever distributed to the trust. The court found under § 1014(b)(4) that the trust was entitled to a new basis in computing any capital gains realized on the sale. The Second Circuit, in its holding, denounced the strict interpretation the IRS advanced and invoked a more liberal reading of the terms "acquired" and "passed" in § 1014.

M. DISTRIBUTION IN KIND

[¶ 30,325]

1. BASIS

Section 643(e) provides that the basis of property distributed in kind is to be "the adjusted basis of such property in the hands of the estate or trust immediately before the distribution, adjusted for * * * any gain or loss recognized to the estate or trust on the distribution." However, whether gain or loss is recognized by the estate or trust is optional, with the election to be made by the estate or trust. As § 643(e) reads, the estate or trust apparently has the option of treating a distribution in kind "as if such property had been sold to the distributee at its fair market value." This means that the estate or trust recognizes gain if the property has appreciated. Where the property has depreciated in value, estates may recognize the loss. However, § 267(b) bars trusts from deducting such losses. If the estate or trust does not choose—or is unable—to recognize gain or loss on the distribution in kind, the distributee assumes the basis of the property to the estate or trust—essentially "carryover" basis.

Any election made under § 643(e) "shall apply to all distributions made by the estate or trust" during the taxable year and "shall be made on the return of such estate or trust for such taxable year." § 643(e)(3)(B). Section 643(e) does not apply in cases where there is no DNI or the cash distributed from the estate or trust "soaks up" the DNI.

> *Example*: Assume that a trust which held appreciated property also provided that all distributions shall be at the sole discretion of the trustee. More specifically, assume that the trust has $500 of distributable net income, that it has an asset with a fair market value of $500 and a basis of $100, and that the trustee plans to exercise his discretion to distribute $500 to the beneficiary. If the trustee distributes $500 in cash, the trust will enjoy a distribution deduction of $500 and the beneficiary will have ordinary income of $500. See §§ 661(a) and 662(a).
>
> If the trustee elects to distribute the appreciated asset to the beneficiary, he will be put to an election. He can elect to claim a distribution deduction of $500. If he does claim a $500 distribution deduction, the beneficiary will have taxable income of $500 and the property will have a basis of $500 in the hands of the beneficiary. In addition, the trust will be required to recognize gain of $400 (fair market value of $500 less basis of $100) on the distribution.
>
> In lieu of claiming the $500 distribution deduction, the trustee could be content with claiming only a $100 distribution deduction. In that case,

¶ **30,325**

the beneficiary will be deemed to have received taxable income of only $100 and the beneficiary's basis in the distributed property would only be $100. If the beneficiary then sells the distributed property for $500, he or she would experience a $400 taxable gain.

If the estate includes property that has depreciated in value, i.e., has a fair market value below its basis in the hands of the estate, distribution of that loss property carries out DNI only to the extent of the property's fair market value. However, the distributee will assume the basis of the property in the hands of the estate unless the estate elects to recognize the loss. In the ordinary case, it would seem that loss recognition would be warranted because it has the effect of reducing DNI and providing income tax relief without any immediate tax cost. Of course, if the property is to be sold, the determination of whether the loss should be claimed by the estate or the distributee will depend on the relative tax brackets of the estate and the distributee.

Example: The Jones Estate plans to distribute 100 shares of stock to Ted, the estate beneficiary. The shares had a value of $2,000 at the time of acquisition but have declined in value to $1,200. Both Ted and the estate are in the 31–percent income tax bracket. The estate can elect to recognize the loss on the stock when the stock is distributed to Ted. His basis in the distributed stock will then be $1,200. If the estate does not elect to recognize the loss, Ted's basis in the distributed stock will be $2,000.

Note that § 643(e) does not apply in cases where there is no DNI. Similarly, § 643(e) would not apply in cases where the cash distributed from the estate or trust "soaks up" the DNI, inasmuch as DNI is first allocated to cash when both cash and property are distributed. Reg. § 1.661(a)–2(f)(3). And, finally, by way of contrast, remember that § 643(e) does not apply to property distributed in kind in satisfaction of a specific bequest that meets the requirements of § 663(a). § 643(e)(4).

Example: In her will, Allison first provided that all her tangible personal property was to be distributed to her husband, Lennie; next, she provided that the property that she was using for residential purposes at the time of her death was to be distributed to Lennie; and, finally, she provided that "my husband, Lennie, is to receive the rest and residue of my property not otherwise disposed of under this will." Except for Allison's 1987 automobile, nothing was distributed to Lennie in the 12–month period following Allison's death. The automobile had a $3,000 income tax basis in the hands of Allison's executor and a $2,500 fair market value at the date of distribution. The automobile's basis is $3,000 in the hands of the decedent's husband, inasmuch as it was distributed to Lennie pursuant to the specific bequest in Allison's will.

Example: Claire's will provided simply that "all my property is to be distributed to my husband, Dennie." As in the case of Allison's estate, the only distribution from Claire's estate during the 12–month period following her death was Claire's 1988 automobile, which was distributed to her husband, Dennie. Claire's automobile had a $5,000 income tax basis in the hands of Claire's executor and a $4,500 fair market value at the date of distribution. While Claire's executor has the option of recognizing as a loss the $500 depreciation in the value of Claire's automobile between the date of her death and the date the automobile was distributed (§ 643(e)(1)), perhaps the more significant point is that the distribution of Claire's automobile will have the effect of carrying out to Dennie only $4,500 of DNI.

The obvious purpose of the two examples immediately preceding is to demonstrate that distributions from an estate or trust carry out the estate or trust's DNI, often to the surprise of the recipient who thought that he or she was getting a "car" and not "taxable income." The lesson, obviously, is to draft the document so as to include specific bequests of those items that are likely to be distributed early in the estate administration. § 663(a)(1); ¶ 30,061. Otherwise, these distributions will "catch" all of the estate's DNI.

Problem

[¶ 30,331]

Pedro's will stipulated that "My friend, Antonio, is to receive all my property at my death." During the year following Pedro's death, Pedro's estate had $5,600 of income. The only distribution from the estate was Pedro's automobile, which was distributed to Antonio. Although the automobile had a value of $3,900 at the time of Pedro's death, its value was $3,000 at the time of distribution to Antonio. What is the income tax basis of the automobile in the hands of Antonio? See § 643(e).

[¶ 30,337]

2. SPECIFIC BEQUESTS

Section 643(e) does not apply to property distributed in kind in satisfaction of a specific bequest that meets the requirements of § 663(a). § 643(e)(4). That is, the property received from the estate has the same basis in the hands of the beneficiary as it did in the hands of the estate. For a discussion of the specific bequest rule, see ¶ 30,061.

3. SALE OR EXCHANGE

[¶ 30,343]

a. *Pecuniary Bequest*

Recognition of gain is not elective in cases where appreciated property is distributed in satisfaction of a pecuniary bequest. In such cases, the distribution in kind will be treated as a sale or exchange by the trust or estate inasmuch as the trust or estate is satisfying a specific dollar obligation with appreciated property. Reg. § 1.661(a)–2(f)(1). It is as if the trustee distributed cash and the beneficiary purchased the property with the cash distributed.

Recognition of loss is denied except when the loss is incurred in connection with a distribution by an estate–but not a trust–in satisfaction of a pecuniary bequest. §§ 267(a)(1) and (b)(13). Thus, loss recognition is prevented in that all too common situation where the decedent has funded a revocable trust during life and directs that the trustee shall distribute to the surviving spouse a pecuniary bequest intended to qualify for the marital deduction. The alternative, of course, is for the trustee to sell the loss property, realize the loss for income tax purposes, and satisfy the spouse's pecuniary gift with cash.

[¶ 30,349]

KENAN v. COMMISSIONER

United States Court of Appeals, Second Circuit, 1940.
114 F.2d 217.

AUGUSTUS N. HAND, Circuit Judge.

The testatrix, Mrs. Bingham, died on July 27, 1917, leaving a will under which she placed her residuary estate in trust and provided in item "Seventh" that her trustees should pay a certain amount annually to her niece, Louise Clisby Wise, until the latter reached the age of forty, "at which time or as soon thereafter as compatible with the interests of my estate they shall pay to her the sum of Five Million ($5,000,000.00) Dollars." The will provided in item "Eleventh" that the trustees, in the case of certain payments including that of the $5,000,000 under item "Seventh", should have the right "to substitute for the payment in money, payment in marketable securities of a value equal to the sum to be paid, the selection of the securities to be substituted in any instance, and the valuation of such securities to be done by the Trustees and their selection and valuation to be final."

Louise Clisby Wise became forty years of age on July 28, 1935. The trustees decided to pay her the $5,000,000 partly in cash and in securities. The greater part of the securities had been owned by the testator and transferred as part of her estate to the trustees; others had been purchased by the trustees. All had appreciated in value during the period for which they were held by the trustees, and the Commissioner determined that the distribution of the securities to the niece resulted in capital gains * * *.

The taxpayers contend that * * * they realized neither gain from the sale or exchange of capital assets nor income of any character by delivering the securities to the legatee pursuant to the permissive terms of the will. The Commissioner contends that gain was realized by the delivery of the securities but that such gain was ordinary income not derived from a sale or exchange and therefore taxable in its entirety.

* * *

In support of their petition the taxpayers contend that the delivery of the securities of the trust estate to the legatee was a donative disposition of property pursuant to the terms of the will, and that no gain was thereby realized. They argue that when they determined that the legacy should be one of securities, it became for all purposes a bequest of property, just as if the cash alternative had not been provided, and not taxable for the reason that no gain is realized on the transfer by a testamentary trustee of specific securities or other property bequeathed by will to a legatee.

We do not think that the situation here is the same as that of a legacy of specific property. The legatee was never in the position occupied by the recipient of specific securities under a will. She had a claim against the estate of $5,000,000, payable either in cash or securities of that value, but had no title or right to the securities, legal or equitable, until they were delivered to her by the trustees after the exercise of their option. She took none of the chances of a legatee of specific securities or of a share of a residue that the securities might appreciate or decline in value between the time of the death of the testator and the transfer to her by the trustees, but instead had at all times a claim for an unvarying amount in money or its equivalent.

If there had merely been a bequest to the legatee of $5,000,000 and she had agreed with the trustees to take securities of that value, the transaction would have been a "sale or other disposition" of the securities * * *.

In the present case, the legatee had a claim which was a charge against the trust estate for $5,000,000 in cash or securities and the trustees had the power to determine whether the claim should be satisfied in one form or the other. The claim, though enforceable only in the alternative, was * * * a charge against the entire trust estate. If it were satisfied by a cash payment securities might have to be sold on which (if those actually delivered in specie were selected) a taxable gain would necessarily have been realized. Instead of making such a sale the trustees delivered the securities and exchanged them pro tanto for the general claim of the legatee, which was thereby satisfied.

It is said that this transaction was not such a "sale or other disposition" as is intended by Section 111(a) [1986 Code § 1001] * * * because it was effectuated only by the will of the trustees and not through a mutual agreement between trustee and legatee. * * *[W]e are not inclined to limit thus the meaning of the words "other disposition" used in Section 111(a), or of "exchange" used in Section 117. The word "exchange" does not necessarily have the connotation of a bilateral agreement which may be said to attach to the word "sale." Thus, should a person set up a trust and reserve to himself the power to substitute for the securities placed in trust other securities of equal value, there would seem no doubt that the exercise of this reserved power would be an "exchange" within the common meaning of the word, even though the settlor consulted no will other than his own, although, of course, we do not here advert to the problems of taxability in such a situation.

* * *Under circumstances like those here, where the legatee did not take securities designated by the will or an interest in the corpus which might be more or less at the time of the transfer than at the time of decedent's death, it seems to us that the trustees realized a gain by using these securities to settle a claim worth $5,000,000 * * *.

It seems reasonably clear that the property was not "transmitted at death" or "acquired by bequest * * * from the decedent." Section 113(a)(5). [1986 Code § 1014(b)]. It follows that the fears of the taxpayers that double taxation of this appreciation will result because the legatee will take the basis of the decedent * * * are groundless. It is true that under Section 113(a)(5) [1986 Code § 1014(a)] the basis for property "acquired by bequest, devise, or inheritance" is "the fair market value of such property at the time of such acquisition" and * * * the date of acquisition has been defined as the date of death of the testator. But the holding of the present case is necessarily a determination that the property here acquired is acquired in an exchange and not "by bequest, devise or inheritance," since Sections 117 and 113(a)(5) seem to be mutually exclusive. The legatee's basis would seem to be the value of the claim surrendered in exchange for the securities.

* * *

[¶ 30,355]

b. Legal Obligation

For tax purposes, distributions in kind in satisfaction of a legal obligation of the trust will be treated as distributions in kind in satisfaction of a pecuniary bequest. A typical example arises where a trust provision calls for distribution of all trust income at least annually. Distributions of appreciated property in satisfaction of the beneficiary's right to income results in recognition of taxable gain to the trust equal to the difference between the basis of the property distributed and the fair market value on the date of distribution. Reg. § 1.661(a)–2(f)(3).

In a similar factual posture, the IRS has ruled (Rev. Rul. 67–74, 1967–1 C.B. 194) that such a transaction is:

> treated as though the trustee had actually distributed to the beneficiary cash in an amount equal to the trust income required to be distributed currently, and if the beneficiary had purchased the stock from the trustee with cash. The trust is allowed a deduction under § 651(a) limited by the distributable net income of the trust, for the amount of income required to be distributed currently, and the beneficiary must report a like amount in gross income under § 652(a). The instant transfer, involving stock having a fair market value equal to the trust income for the year in question which the trustee was required to distribute to the beneficiary, resulted in a capital gain to the trust equal to the difference between the basis of the stock in the hands of the trustee and the amount of the obligation satisfied by the transfer. Further, the basis of the stock in the hands of the beneficiary is his cost, that is, the price he is deemed to have paid for it.

Problems

[¶ 30,361]

1. Mr. Tweede, trust officer at Accumulation National Bank, is responsible for a number of accounts that hold shares in Belchfire Automobile, Inc. The shares of Belchfire have risen dramatically in value, but Mr. Tweede believes that the "bloom is off the rose" and he wants to "dump the shares at the top of the market." However, if he sells the shares for his

various accounts, the gain to be realized is significant. Instead, he proposes that he distribute the shares to the account beneficiaries and let them decide whether to sell.

He cites the case of the Arthur Dawg Estate. Mr. Dawg's will stipulates that his spouse is to receive "the smallest amount necessary to eliminate all federal estate tax" from his estate. That amount, as finally determined, is equal to $50,000. The Belchfire stock in Arthur's estate has a current market value of $50,000 and Mr. Tweede proposes to distribute the stock to Mrs. Dawg in satisfaction of Arthur's gift. The estate's basis in the shares is $10,000. The estate has $80,000 of distributable net income this year.

    a.   What are the income tax consequences to the estate if it makes this distribution? § 661(a), Reg. § 1.663(a)–1(b)(I) and Rev. Rul. 60–87, 1960–1 C.B. 286.

    b.   What are the tax consequences to Mrs. Dawg upon receipt of the shares? § 662.

    c.   What is her basis if she sells the shares upon receipt? Reg. § 1.1014–4(a)(3).

2. In the following cases Mr. Tweede proposes to distribute Belchfire stock rather than cash. Indicate the income tax consequences to each trust if the stock is distributed in kind. Also indicate the income tax consequences to the beneficiary of each trust. Determine the basis of the shares to each beneficiary. Then consider the tax consequences to the trust if the trustee sold the shares and distributed cash to each beneficiary. In making your analysis, assume each beneficiary is effectively in the top income tax bracket; that the trust has $20,000 of DNI for this tax year; the trustee proposes to distribute either cash or Belchfire stock having a market value of $10,000 and a basis of $2,000. § 643(e).

    a.   The Able Trust requires the trustee to distribute all the income of the trust.

    b.   The Baker Trust requires the trustee to distribute so much or all of the principal and income of the trust as shall be required for the "maintenance, care, and support" of the trust beneficiary.

    c.   The Charlie Trust permits the trustee to make distributions of income and principal whenever the trustee determines such distributions to be in the "best interests" of the beneficiary.

N. INTEGRATED PLANNING FOR ESTATE ADMINISTRATION

[¶ 30,367]

1. STATE PROPERTY LAW CONSIDERATIONS

The federal income tax treatment of the income generated by a decedent's property after the decedent's death is complicated not only by the distribution rules of Subchapter J of the Internal Revenue Code but also by questions of title and possession.

In the majority of states, title to real property, and, in some states, title to personal property, vests immediately in those persons who are the beneficiaries under the will of the decedent or, if the decedent dies intestate, title vests in the heirs of the decedent. This means that even though the decedent's executor may collect and hold the decedent's property during administration, legal title to that property is in the indicated beneficiary. Ohio would be one of the states where legal title to real estate vests in the beneficiaries or heirs.

In the majority of states, title to the decedent's personal property vests in the decedent's personal representative.

For income tax purposes, it can be said that, as a general rule, the fruit follows the tree. Accordingly, income earned by the decedent's property after the decedent's death will be taxable to the person who has title to that property at the time the income is generated. Thus, rental income generated by the decedent's real property will be taxable to the ultimate recipient of that property as determined by the decedent's will or the applicable intestate statute. On the other hand, applying the general rule, income from personal property will be taxable to the decedent's estate.

Some states, particularly those adopting the Uniform Probate Code, stipulate that, while title is in the beneficiaries, the decedent's personal representative is to have possession of the decedent's property—both real and personal—during administration of the decedent's estate. In these states, there is some agreement that title is not determinative of income tax liability and the fruit does not follow the tree. In these states income generated by the decedent's property after the decedent's death is to be taxed to the decedent's estate. Texas is one of these states. See Jones v. Whittington, 194 F.2d 812 (10th Cir.1952).

In addition to these considerations of title, estate administration is often complicated by the receipt after the decedent's death of income that was earned before death. An example would be the decedent's final wages, received after death, for work performed before death. These wages—referred to as income in respect of a decedent (IRD)—are an asset of the decedent's estate for federal estate tax purposes but they are also income! ¶ 32,001.

An additional factor is the need to file a final federal income tax return for the decedent reflecting the income the decedent earned that year before death.

Another factor in some estates is the presence of community property. Community property refers to the peculiar system of rules that determine the rights of married persons in property acquired by them during marriage. Most of the western states and Wisconsin have adopted the community property system. However, the rules of no two states are exactly alike.

Under the community property system, the term "separate property" refers to property acquired before marriage or property acquired after marriage by gift, devise, bequest or inheritance. By way of contrast, community property is property acquired after marriage that is not separate property. In

¶ 30,367

addition, in Texas, Idaho, and Louisiana, income from separate property is community property. In all other states, income from separate property is also separate property.

Under community property rules generally, each spouse can dispose of his or her 50% of the community property by will at death and any portion of the decedent's one-half that is not effectively disposed of by will passes by intestacy. Generally, no survivorship is associated with community property.

[¶ 30,373]

2. RELATIONSHIP OF ESTATE TAX AND INCOME TAX

Estate administration is complicated by the need to take into account not only provisions of the decedent's will and state property law but also the federal income tax, the federal estate tax, the federal gift tax and the federal generation-skipping tax as well as state income and death taxes. Of particular importance is the relationship of the requirements imposed by these different elements.

In the typical estate, the executor must be concerned about whether items of income are includible on (1) the decedent's final income tax returns because the decedent was in constructive receipt of that item, (2) on the estate's income tax returns, or (3) on the beneficiary's income tax returns because the item was received by the executor as agent for the beneficiary (as can happen in the case of rental income from real property in those states where title to real estate passes to the beneficiary immediately at the death of the decedent). See ¶ 30,367. The executor must also be concerned about whether any of these items of income are also subject to state and federal death taxes, i.e., as income in respect of a decedent (which would mean that the recipient of this item of IRD would be entitled to an income tax deduction for the estate tax attributable to the item of IRD). See ¶ 32,109. Not to be ignored are the basis rules. See ¶ 30,313.

Thus, after death, there are three potential taxpayers and three taxes to be considered. The taxes are the federal estate tax, the federal generation-skipping tax, and the federal income tax. The potential taxpayers are the decedent's estate, which is subject to the estate tax, the generation-skipping tax, and the income tax; the beneficiaries of the decedent's estate, who are also potential income taxpayers; and the decedent, for whom a final federal income tax return may be required. Similarly, in the case of expenditures by the executor, questions arise as to whether the expenditure is a deduction: (1) on the decedent's final income tax return; (2) by the executor on the estate's income tax return; or (3) by the beneficiary on his or her income tax return (because the executor was acting only as agent of the beneficiary in making the expenditure) and whether any of these items are deductions on the decedent's state and federal death tax returns, perhaps even being deductible for both income tax and estate tax purposes. Reg. § 1.212–1(i). The matter is complicated because some disbursements are deductible for one tax and not for another. Others are deductible for both taxes but only by certain taxpayers. For example, funeral expenses are deductible for estate tax purposes but not for income tax purposes. On the other hand, the medical expenses incurred by the decedent in the final illness and unpaid at the time of death are deductible for estate tax purposes and for income tax purposes but only on the decedent's final income tax return and then only if it is agreed that the estate tax deduction will not be claimed. Such expenses are not deductible by the decedent's beneficiaries or by the estate for federal income tax purposes. § 642(g). An example of a deduction available for both federal income tax and federal estate tax purposes would be real property taxes that become a lien at the beginning of the calendar year but are not paid (nor payable) until the end of the calendar year. By way of further contrast, administration expenses, such as attorney fees, are deductible for both taxes but not by the decedent on the final federal income tax return.

And, as noted earlier, generation-skipping taxes paid as the result of the death of the transferor on items of gross income of a trust are deductible for income tax purposes in cases where those items of gross income "were not properly includible in the gross income of the trust for the period before the date" of the taxable termination or direct skip that gave rise to the imposition of the generation-skipping tax. § 691(c)(3).

a. Final Medical Expenses

[¶ 30,379]

REVENUE RULING 77-357
1977–2 C.B. 328.

Advice has been requested whether, under the circumstances described below, a Federal estate tax deduction is allowable under section 2053(a) * * * for the three percent portion of medical expenses that is not deductible for Federal income tax purposes. [After 1976, only medical expenses exceeding 7.5% of adjusted gross income are deductible. § 213(a).]

The decedent died on December 31, 1974, after a six-month illness during which decedent incurred doctor and hospital expenses in the amount of $20,000. These medical expenses were paid by the decedent's representative in 1975. For the 1974 taxable year, the decedent had an adjusted gross income of $100,000. The decedent's representative deducted $5,000 as a claim against the decedent's estate under section 2053 * * *. The necessary statement and the waiver indicating that the balance of the expenses, or $15,000, had not been allowed and would not be allowed at any time as a deduction under section 2053 were filed with the decedent's final income tax return.

* * *

The Senate Finance Committee Report, S. Rep. No. 1983, 85th Cong., 2d Sess., p. 27, 1958–3 C.B. 922, 948, accompanying the Technical Amendments Act of 1958, Pub. L. 85–866, 1958–3 C.B. 254, reads in part as follows:

> Present law (sec. 213(d)) * * * permits the deduction in the last year of a decedent of expenses for his medical care which are paid out of his estate during the 1–year period after his death. These expenses are treated as if they had been paid by the taxpayer at the time they were

incurred. This deduction is not available unless a statement is filed that the amount has not been claimed or allowed as a deduction for estate-tax purposes and a waiver of the right to this amount as an estate-tax deduction has been filed. . . .

This provision conforms the language in section 213(d)(2)(a) relating to the deduction of the expenses in the last year of the decedent with the language in section 642(g) which allows other expenses as deductions to the estate. * * *

Section 2053(a)(3) provides that the value of the taxable estate shall be determined by deducting from the value of the gross estate such amounts for claims against the estate as are allowable by the laws of the jurisdiction under which the estate is being administered. [Reg. § 20.2053–4] * * * states that the amounts that may be deducted as claims against a decedent's estate are such only as represent personal obligations of the decedent existing at the time of decedent's death, whether or not then matured, and interest thereon which has accrued at the time of death.

The medical expenses of a decedent's last illness are a deductible claim against the estate within the meaning of section 2053(a)(3) and, thus, medical expenses are deductible on the estate tax return or on the decedent's final income tax return under section 213(a)(1).

Certain other deductions allowable for income tax purposes are also allowable as deductions for estate tax purposes. For example: section 2053 provides for the deduction, among other things, of administration expenses in determining the value of the taxable estate for estate tax purposes. Such expenses would also constitute allowable deductions as expenses for the production of income under section 212 in determining the net income of the estate for Federal income tax purposes.

However, with respect to the allowance of a deduction in computing the taxable income of the estate, section 642(g) provides [that the deductions allowable under §§ 2053 or 2054 in computing the taxable estate of a decedent are not allowed as a deduction in computing the taxable income of the decedent's estate or that of any other person, unless a written waiver of the right to claim those deductions for estate tax purposes is filed with the IRS] * * *.

The purpose of section 642(g) is to prevent an estate from obtaining a double deduction with respect to the same items of administration expenses. Administration expenses are, therefore, not allowable deductions under section 212 unless there is filed a statement that the items representing such expenses have not been allowed as deductions in the estate tax return, and a waiver of the right to have such items allowed at any time as deductions in the estate tax return. In the event that administration expenses are such that they would be allowable for either income or estate tax purposes, the taxpayer may allocate the expenses to either the estate tax return or the income tax return for the year in which payment is made, provided there is no duplication of deduction and provided the terms of section 642(g) are complied with. See Rev. Rul. 70–361, 1970–2 C.B. 133.

¶ 30,379

Similarly, with respect to medical expenses, as long as there is no duplication of a deduction and the provisions of section 213(d) are complied with, there is nothing to prevent a decedent's representative from taking a deduction for certain items of the medical expenses of a decedent's last illness in computing the net estate under section 2053 and also taking a deduction for other items of such expenses on the decedent's final income tax return under section 213.

The issue of the deductibility of the three percent portion of medical expenses on the estate tax return pivots on the construction of section 213(d)(2). If the intent of Congress in enacting section 213(d)(2) was simply to prohibit the allowance of a double deduction as might be inferred from its reference to section 642(g) in the 1958 amendment to 213(d)(2)(a), then the three percent portion might arguably be available as an estate tax deduction since such portion is not actually deducted on the decedent's final income tax return but rather is used in computing the allowable amount of the deduction. However, a literal interpretation of section 213(d)(2) requires that section 213(d)(1) not apply if the "amount paid" is allowable under section 2053 as a deduction, unless the requisite waiver and statement are filed to the effect that the "amount paid" has not been nor will be at any time allowed on a 2053 deduction. In the instant case, the "amount paid" for purposes of section 213(d)(2) is $15,000 (total medical expenses of $20,000 less $5,000 deducted as a claim against the decedent's estate). The application of subsection (d)(2) to the portion of medical expenses ($15,000) deemed paid at the time incurred, without consideration of the three percent of adjusted gross income limitation, is clear and unambiguous from the language used by Congress in the enactment of this section.

Accordingly, the three percent portion of medical expenses ($3,000) not allowable as a deduction for income tax purposes is not deductible from the gross estate under section 2053(a). Thus, of the total medical expenses of $20,000 in the instant case, $5,000 is deductible from the decedent's gross estate under section 2053 and $12,000 is deductible on the decedent's final income tax return under section 213.

Note

[¶ 30,381]

Income received by an estate during administration must be included in the estate's gross income for income tax purposes rather than the gross estate for estate tax purposes. Administration expenses, however, can be taken as a deduction on either the estate's income or estate tax return, but not both. § 642(g).

[¶ 30,388]

b. *Marital Deduction and Deduction of Administration Expenses*

The interplay of the estate tax marital deduction under § 2056 and the availability of an income tax deduction for administration expenses has given rise to a controversy of such significance that it was considered by the Supreme Court in Commissioner v. Estate of Hubert, 520 U.S. 93 (1997), a decision that was followed by a change in course by the IRS. In sum, the issue is whether the estate tax marital deduction otherwise allowable under § 2056 must be reduced by administrative expenses—and interest accruing on federal estate tax and state inheritance tax deficiencies—if a deduction is taken on the estate's income tax return for these items.

Taxpayers see the issue in these terms. Because of the easy availability of § 2056's unlimited marital deduction for gifts to a surviving spouse, estate taxes can easily be—and *are* routinely—eliminated by the planning expedient of causing the decedent's will to make a gift to the surviving spouse of at least the amount or share necessary to reduce estate taxes to zero. See ¶ 27,415. With estate taxes, thus, at zero, practitioners are inclined to claim a deduction on the estate's income tax return for the estate administration expenses—*"where it will do some good."*

For its part, currently—that is post-*Hubert*—the IRS begins by insisting that administration expenses be classified either as "estate transmission expenses" or "estate management expenses". Reg. § 20.2056(b)–4(d)(1). It then concludes, in Reg. § 20.2056(b)–4(d)(2), that the estate tax marital deduction is to be "reduced by the amount of the estate transmission expenses paid from the marital share." (Estate transmission expenses, in the view of the IRS, are those expenses that would not have been incurred but for the death of the decedent and the resulting need for collecting and distributing the decedent's property. Reg. § 20.2056(b)–4(d)(1)(ii). Examples include attorney fees, court costs—and "any administration expense that is not a management expense." Reg. § 20.2056(b)–4(d)(1)(ii).) "Marital share" is defined as the property for which the marital deduction is allowed for estate tax purposes under § 2056(a) and is further defined as including the income produced by that property during the period of administration. Reg. § 20.2056(b)–4(d)(1)(iii).

The IRS position is illustrated in a series of examples given in Reg. § 20.2056(b)–4(d)(5), the conclusion from which is that the governing instrument—the will or trust—or applicable state law must impose the burden of the estate transmission expenses on the portion of the decedent's property *not* passing to the surviving spouse. This is the crucial point and it bears emphasis. The governing instrument or applicable state law must impose the actual burden of the estate transmission expenses on the share of the decedent's property passing to others than the surviving spouse. To the extent that these expenses are imposed on the share passing to the surviving spouse, the marital deduction will be reduced. In the latter case, unless the estate transmission expenses are claimed as a deduction of the estate tax return, the estate will not be "zeroed out" for estate tax purposes—and estate tax may well be payable! (Whether estate tax is actually payable depends on whether § 2010(c)'s applicable exclusion amount ($1M in 2002 and 2003) is available to shelter the taxable estate that is thus determined by this process.)

As an illustration, consider Sing and Lotus. Sing's will provides a gift to Lotus of $3 million followed by a gift of the residue to their child, Chi–Hsi.

¶ 30,388

The will provides that all debts, taxes and administration expenses are to be paid out of the residuary estate. In this case estate transmission expenses can be claimed on the estate's income tax return without impairing the marital deduction for the full $3 million. See Reg. § 20.2056(b)–4(d)(5), *Example 7*.

Contrast the situation of Horatio and Lucky. Lucky's will provides gift of § 2010(c)'s applicable exclusion amount as of the date of her death (which occurred in 2002) to her child, Sunny. The residue is to pass to a trust for the benefit of Lucky's spouse, Horatio, after payment of debts, taxes and administration expenses. Lucky's estate has a date of death value of $3M; estate transmission expenses are $200,000; the applicable exclusion amount is $1M. Sunny gets the $1M. But only $1.8M is available for distribution to Horatio ($2M minus $200,000, estate transmission expenses) even if the estate transmission expenses are paid out of income earned during estate administration. Hence, Lucky's marital deduction is limited to $1.8M. If the estate transmission expenses are deducted on Lucky's estate tax return, the taxable estate is zero ($3M minus $1M applicable exclusion amount minus $1.8M marital deduction minus $200,000 estate transmission expenses). However, if the estate transmission expenses are deducted on income tax return for Lucky's estate, the net value of the property passing to Horatio—and, thus, qualifying for the marital deduction—in the view of the IRS is $1,657,874 ($1.8M minus $142,106 of estate taxes that become payable). (Claiming a marital deduction for $1,657,874 will result in a taxable estate of $1,342,106 and the payment of $142,106 of estate taxes. (This computation involves an interdependent variable, *i.e.*, the amount of the marital deduction depends upon the amount of the estate tax and the amount of the estate tax depends upon the amount of the marital deduction. Supplemental instructions are available from the IRS for purposes of making this computation, although it can be easily made using an electronic spreadsheet.)) Reg. § 20.2056(b)–4(d)(5), *Example 6*.

The IRS says that estate management expenses—estate preservation and management expenses such as investment advisory fees—are deductible on the income tax return for the estate without impairing the marital deduction *even if paid from the marital gift.* Reg. § 20.2056(b)–4(d)(3).

Not surprisingly the current regulations on estate administration expenses are referred to as the *"Hubert* Regs". *Hubert* considered an earlier version of Reg.§ 20.2056(b)–4(a) which, at the time, stated that, in "determining the value of the interest in property passing to the spouse, account must be taken of the effect of any material limitations upon her right to income from the property." An example given in the regulation of a "material limitation" was the use of income from property bequeathed to a spouse to pay administration expenses from the time of death until distribution.

The courts were divided as to the interpretation of this regulation. In Estate of Street v. Commissioner, 974 F.2d 723 (6th Cir.1992), aff'g in part and rev'g in part, 56 T.C.M. (CCH) 774, T.C.M. (P–H) ¶ 88,553 (1988), the Sixth Circuit determined that administrative expenses accrue at the decedent's death, and therefore, if the administrative expenses are taken as a deduction on the estate's income tax return, the marital deduction must be reduced by the same amount. The Sixth Circuit said that Reg.

§ 20.2056(b)–4(a) requires that "expenses from income must operate to reduce the size of the marital deduction, otherwise the spouse would receive a deduction which exceeded the amount which was actually in the estate." 974 F.2d at 727. (The court reasoned that the spouse enjoyed a two deductions for the same property. That is, the spouse would have received a deduction for 100 percent of the allowable marital deduction even though a lesser amount was actually distributed to her, to wit, the allowable marital deduction reduced by the expenses incurred in administration. By claiming an income tax deduction for the administration expenses, the court reasoned the spouse was getting a second deduction for the same items.)

The Sixth Circuit's decision in *Street* had the effect of increasing the taxes payable by many estates. However, despite *Street*, the Tax Court continued to insist that the marital deduction is not reduced by administration expenses paid out of income. The Tax Court's position was upheld by the Eleventh Circuit in Estate of Hubert v. Commissioner, 63 F.3d 1083 (11th Cir.1995). On appeal, a plurality of the Supreme Court—there was no majority for any one view—while not resolving the dispute, changed the focus of the debate even though it upheld the Tax Court in *Hubert* in result. Commissioner v. Estate of Hubert, 520 U.S. 93 (1997). At best, perhaps, it can be said that the Supreme Court held in *Hubert* that it was not a "material limitation" (as contemplated by Reg. § 20.2056(b)–4(a)) on the right of the surviving spouse to the income from the marital gift for the personal representative to charge $1.5 million of estate administration expenses (38 percent of the income earned during administration) against the share of the estate passing to the surviving spouse for which the marital deduction was claimed. (A charitable gift was also affected. See ¶ 30,497.) Beyond knowing that siphoning off 38 percent of the income attributable to the marital share is not a "material limitation" so as to compromise the availability of the marital deduction, not much else can be said about *Hubert* (except, perhaps, to speculate that the Court, given the disparate opinions expressed by the Justices, probably wished *Hubert* had never been accepted for review).

The IRS response to its defeat in *Hubert* was to abandon the "material limitation" standard litigated in *Hubert* and substitute its current rule requiring that estate administration expenses be classified as either an estate transmission expense or an estate management expense. Practically speaking the IRS abandoned the "material limitation" standard and introduced a black-and-white rule, namely that estate transmission expenses reduce the marital share! *And that's final!* Or at least the IRS would appear to hope. What the IRS has done, in abandoning the "material limitation" standard of its earlier regulation, is attempt to prevent courts from deciding, on a case-by-case basis, whether the marital deduction gift should be reduced when so-called estate transmission expenses are claimed on the estate's income tax return.

Among the remaining questions is whether the use of income to pay interest on unpaid estate taxes would impose a "material limitation" on the surviving spouse's right to income from the property for which the marital deduction was claimed. Almost surprisingly—after its aggressive prosecution

¶ 30,388

of its case in *Hubert*—it is the IRS position, expressed in Rev. Rul. 93–48, 93–2 C.B. 270, that interest on unpaid estate taxes taken as a deduction on the fiduciary income tax return does not reduce the estate tax marital deduction! The IRS view, expressed in Rev. Rul. 93–48, is in accord with a number of judicial decisions. The court, in one of those decisions, Estate of Richardson v. Commissioner, 89 T.C. 1193 (1987), explained that it found a material difference between administrative expenses which accrue at death and interest on unpaid taxes which accrue after death. The *Richardson* court, in explaining the difference in treatment (and finding that the marital deduction was not reduced by interest on unpaid estate taxes taken as a deduction of the fiduciary income tax return), said that to insist upon a reduction in the marital deduction would be to "reduce the principal of the estate as it existed at the time of decedent's death by interest that has accrued since decedent's death." It concluded that to pay the interest on the deferred taxes out of income of the estate would neither increase nor decrease the principal of the estate as it was at the time of the decedent's death (and, therefore, the marital deduction should not be affected).

How did the Supreme Court feel about interest paid on unpaid taxes (and the impact of such payments on the marital deduction)? Several of the Justices (O'Connor and Scalia) in opinions in *Hubert* mentioned Rev. Rul. 93–48 but could not agree as to the effect to be given it in the *Hubert* context.

[¶ 30,389]

c. *Income from Community Property*

The presence of community property in an estate complicates the tax accounting. The complication results from the fact that both halves of the community are subject to administration at the death of the first spouse to die. Thus, although only one-half of the community property is subject to disposition under the will of the first spouse to die, both halves become subject to the estate administration process in the estate of the first spouse to die. Application of state property law produces this result. For federal tax purposes, however, the decedent's one-half of the community is seen as belonging to his or her estate while the survivor's one-half is treated as belonging to the survivor. Practically speaking, the survivor is taxed on the income generated by the survivor's one-half of the community—even though that income is collected by the decedent's executor and is subject to administration in the decedent's estate—and the income generated by the decedent's one-half of the community is taxed to the decedent's estate. Mrs. Grimm, the taxpayer in Grimm v. Commissioner, 894 F.2d 1165 (10th Cir.1990), used a novel approach in an attempt to avoid this result. She claimed that her one-half of the income generated by community property being administered as part of her husband's estate was not taxable to her until distributed to her (in as much as she is restricted in her enjoyment of the her one-half of the community income until the estate administration is completed during which period her half of the community property—and income—could be exhausted by community debts for which she is responsible). The court rejected Mrs. Grimm's claim and explained:

¶ 30,388

Grimm's share of the community property accumulated during her marriage and her share of the income from such property is her own. It does not pass to her as part of her husband's estate. * * * [Grimm received her] portion of the community assets and community income as fiduciaries for Grimm herself, not as fiduciaries of the estate; the estate never has title to Grimm's interest in these assets.* * *

The administrative restrictions placed on Grimm's use and disposition of her share of community property during the liquidation procedure do not defeat her ownership interest in that property and do not effectively negate her receipt of the same. * * * Judge Rives, concurring with the court's opinion [in Sneed v. Commissioner, 220 F.2d 313, 316 (5th Cir.1955)], reasoned: "In every real sense the widow's ownership acquired during the marriage continues uninterruptedly, and the executor has title to that half only of the community property belonging to his decedent. It does not follow from the fact that the executor has control and possession of the community and its income during administration that the income is not taxable to the widow. It is said that the widow may have received no funds with which to pay the tax. I apprehend that under state law it would be the executor's fiduciary duty to provide the widow with such necessary funds."

894 F.2d at 1168–69. Furthermore, the court offered, the community property is "immediately available for the purpose of satisfying community debts" for which the surviving spouse is "personally responsible along with her husband's estate." Id.

[¶ 30,390]

d. *Community Property and Deduction of Administration Expenses*

Taxpayers routinely deduct estate administration expenses. Reg. § 1.212–1(i). Special allocation problems are usually present where the decedent's estate includes community property. While both halves of the community—that of the decedent and that of the surviving spouse—are subject to administration at the death of the first of the spouses to die, only those administration expenses allocable to the decedent's one-half of the community are deductible by the decedent's executor (on his or her estate tax return or, alternatively, on the estate's income tax return). Nonetheless, while it is a perfectly logical to assume that only fifty percent of estate administration fees are thus likely to be deductible (where those fees are attributable to the presence of community property in the decedent's estate), practically speaking, a case for virtually 100 percent deductibility can often be effectively made. For example, in Ray v. United States, 385 F.Supp. 372 (S.D.Tex.1974), all but 5 percent of attorney fees were found to be attributable to the decedent's 50 percent of the community (based on testimony that 75 percent of the attorney fees were incurred in the process of determining estate and income taxes of the decedent's estate and the court's finding that another 20 percent was attributable to the routine probating of the decedent's will (rather than to the management or division of the community as a whole)) and were, thus, deductible; and 100 percent of appraisal fees were deductible (because of testimony that an appraisal was required only because it was needed in conjunction with preparation of the decedent's estate tax return).

Problem

[¶ 30,391]

Assume that it is now February 15th and that Herb Shark died five (5) months ago on September 29th. Fearful of lawyers, he made his own will which provided: "I give all my worldly goods to my beloved wife, Wanda." Wanda, or W as she was called by Herb, survived Herb. Herb's estate included the following property:

	Cost	Market Value Date of Death
Dwelling house	$21,000	$ 58,000
Cash (certificate of deposit at 10%)		20,000
Life insurance (proceeds payable to W)		20,000
Automobile	8,000	3,000
General Microcomputers common stock ("GM") (200 shares)	6,000	9,000
Household goods	26,000	10,000
		$120,000

The following schedule sets forth the transactions completed by Herb's executor, W, in the administration of Herb's estate during the period beginning with his death and ending on December 31st of the year of his death.

	Receipts	Disbursements
Interest on Certificate of Deposit (10%)(CD)	$1,000	
General Microcomputers dividend ("GM")	170	
Court costs		$ 100
Decedent's medical expenses		3,000
State death taxes		4,000
Funeral expenses		2,000
Auto distributed to W		3,000

There were no transactions with respect to Herb's estate during the January following his death. However, shortly after February 1st, the following transactions were accomplished:

1. W, as executor, sold 100 shares of GM stock for $50 per share.

2. W, as executor, distributed to herself cash in the amount of $20,000.

Wanda projects that, during the balance of this second year, the GM stock will produce dividends of $680 and the certificate of deposit will earn interest in the amount of $2,000.

Wanda's attorney has quoted her a fee of $4,000. She does not foresee that the estate will incur any other expenses. After paying the lawyer, she plans to distribute the balance of the estate property to herself.

¶ 30,390

Wanda is also beginning to prepare Herb's final federal income tax return. She and Herb have always filed joint returns and she expects to do so for the year in which Herb died. See § 6013. Wanda's earnings from her employment are sufficient to put her into the highest income tax bracket.

Wanda has not filed any income tax returns for Herb's estate. She does not think such a return is required since the expenses of the estate exceed its income.

Do you agree with Wanda? Give her your suggestions as to the most efficient method of managing Herb's estate for maximum estate and income tax economy. Indicate how each of the transactions described above should be treated for estate and income tax purposes. Sketch out any tax computations necessary to implement your recommendations so as to demonstrate the merits of your recommendations. Show the estate's tentative taxable income, its DNI, and its distribution deduction.

In considering these questions, it might be helpful to keep in mind the following:

(1) Governing Principle

(a) Income earned by an estate or trust is taxable to the estate or trust except to the extent distributed to beneficiaries of the estate or trust.

(b) How is that principle given effect? Each and every distribution from an estate or trust constitutes a distribution of taxable income to the recipient to the extent of the entity's distributable net income (DNI). § 661(a).

> (i) Distributable net income (DNI)(§ 643) is a legislatively created concept designed to limit a fiduciary's postmortem tax planning. How does it do that?

> (ii) Distributions from an estate or trust are treated as deductions in computing an estate's taxable income. § 661(a). Does that raise any questions in your mind? Does that suggest that distribution of the auto to W might constitute taxable income to W in year 1? See ¶ 30,049 and 30,325. What provision should H have included in his will to avoid this result? See § 663(a)(1). See also ¶ 30,061.

(2) Double Deductions and Choice of Taxpayer

Consider carefully the deductibility of disbursements for state death taxes, funeral expenses, decedent's final medical bills, and court costs associated with the decedent's estate. To which taxpayer are these deductions available? The decedent on the final return? The decedent's estate for income tax purposes? §§ 212(b), 213(d), 642(g) and 2053.

(3) Choice of Tax Year

(a) Wanda proposes to close Herb's estate and distribute all of the remaining property in the estate. Can you suggest any reason why an extended administration period may be desirable? Consider the tax savings potential of having three tax years. See § 441. So what? Those tax years mean

¶ 30,391

two personal exemptions. § 642(b). Ever hear of tax shelters? Even Herb's estate can enjoy one! (Why not three tax years? See below.)

(b) How about choosing a tax year other than one that coincides with that of the beneficiaries? Sure, but why? See § 652(c). See also ¶ 30,247.

(4) Capital Gains by an Estate or Trust

One hundred shares of GM stock were sold in Year 2. The gain must be taxed to somebody? The entity? The beneficiaries of the estate? Taxpayer's choice! You bet! See Reg. § 1.643(a)(3). Code and Regulations not clear, you say? Perhaps, but what rule would you suggest? Why should it matter? Moreover, is the rule consistent with the DNI concept (§ 643) discussed above? See Priv. Ltr. Rul. 8324002 at ¶ 30,205.

(5) The Short Last Tax Year

Can you suggest why it would be to Wanda's advantage to defer paying all of the expenses of the estate until the last tax year of the estate? Another exemption? Nah! See Reg. § 1.642(h)(2). (Is Reg. § 1.642(h)(2) inconsistent with § 642(b)? See ¶ 30,283. Wouldn't it be great if the exemption were available in the last year also?)

(6) Two–Percent Limitation on Deductions

Is any portion of the expenses incurred in conjunction with the administration of Herb's estate rendered nondeductible because of the two-percent rule of Section 67(a) or are all of these expenses fully deductible as within the Section 67(e) "safe harbor"? See ¶ 30,223.

O. ACCUMULATION TRUSTS

[¶ 30,397]

Worth noting if nothing more than as an virtual historical curiosity are the "throwback rules". Although of little current application, these rules appear as §§ 665–667.

The purpose of the throwback rules was to tax "warehoused" trust income as if it had been distributed to the trust beneficiary in the year it was initially received by the trust. Congress also developed a multiple trust penalty, designed to impose a special income tax burden on taxpayers who are the recipients of accumulated or "warehoused" income from more than two trusts. § 667(c). The penalty applied only to those tax years in which more than two trusts accumulated income for the same beneficiary. That having been said, beginning with tax year 1998, the throwback rules (and multiple trust penalty rules) only apply to foreign trusts, domestic trusts that were once treated as foreign trusts, and domestic trusts created before March 1, 1984, that would be treated as "multiple trusts" under § 643(f). § 665(c). (Section 643(f) treats multiple trusts created by the same grantor for the same beneficiaries for tax avoidance purposes as a single trust for income tax purposes. See ¶ 30,469.) Trusts to which the throwback rules no longer apply

¶ 30,391

are described as "qualified trusts." § 665(c)(1). Effectively, thus, the throwback rules are history, eliminating one of the disadvantages of accumulating income in a trust. (The principal disadvantage to income accumulations is the relatively small amount of income that can be taxed at income tax rates less than the current maximum (35 percent in 2005, § 1(i)). See ¶ 30,235.)

The throwback rules reflected Congressional concern about the potential for income distortion inherent in the use of trusts. As Congress understands it, income generated by trust property can be taxed to the trust and warehoused there if not needed by the trust's beneficiaries. By taxing the income to the trust, the ultimate recipients of that income will have the benefit of "riding up" the progressive income tax brackets applicable to the trust's income, thereby taking advantage of the opportunity to have more income taxed at lower rates than would have been the case had the ultimate recipients received the income in the year in which it was earned. Needless to say, this opportunity could discriminate against those with modest resources because their circumstances do not permit them the luxury of using a trust to shelter any of their income.

In 1997 Congress was moved to effect a practical repeal of the throwback rules after more than ten years experience with its "rate compression" strategy. Introduced in 1986, the tax brackets applied to estates and trusts are compressed, resulting in estate and trust income, when warehoused, being taxed to the estate or trust for the most part at the top income tax rate. § 1(e); ¶ 30,235; ¶ 30,241. Since only a relatively few beneficiaries are in the top income tax bracket, Congress apparently thinks that trustees will opt to minimize income taxes by distributing trust income to lower bracket beneficiaries rather than warehousing it in the estate or trust where it will be taxed at the maximum rate. (While that is a likely result in many cases, in some instances trustees, perhaps with the concurrence of the trust beneficiaries, will warehouse income in the trust knowing that the warehoused income will escape the federal estate tax at the death of the beneficiaries. This strategy, of course, only has appeal in those instances where the income distributions are likely to go unconsumed by the trust beneficiaries and the trust itself bypasses the beneficiaries' estates for death tax purposes–a likely result where the trust beneficiaries have not been given a general power of appointment over the trust property. § 2041; ¶ 22,201; ¶ 30,007.)

Despite repeal of the throwback rules, Congress continues to insist on consolidation, for income tax purposes, of certain trusts having "substantially" the same grantor and "substantially" the same beneficiary. § 643(f); ¶ 30,469.

The throwback rules do not and have never applied to estates.

P. CONSOLIDATION OF MULTIPLE TRUSTS

[¶ 30,469]

Section 643(f) is an attempt by Congress to further limit the use of multiple trusts as income tax shelters. It provides that trusts having substan-

¶ 30,469

tially the same grantor or grantors and substantially the same primary beneficiary or beneficiaries are to be consolidated for income tax purposes in cases where the principal purpose of the trusts is the avoidance of income tax. Moreover, for purposes of applying the trust consolidation rule, a husband and wife are to be treated as one person.

The exact text of § 643(f) is important because Congress had the option of copying Reg. § 1.641(a)–0(c) but chose to use other, perhaps more far-reaching, language to accomplish its objective. Regulation § 1.641(a)–0(c) provides that multiple trusts will be consolidated for tax purposes if the trusts have (1) no substantially independent purposes (such as independent dispositive purposes), (2) the same grantor and substantially the same beneficiary, and (3) the avoidance or mitigation of taxes as their principal purpose.

Section 643(f) is obviously broader than Reg. § 1.641(a)–0(c) inasmuch as it dispenses with the "no substantially independent purposes" test of the regulation and provides that it (§ 643(f)) is applicable when "the trusts have substantially the same grantor or grantors." The regulation spoke in the singular and was applicable only if the trusts had "the same grantor." As a result, the IRS has a stronger tool to use in reaching multiple trusts.

The IRS had been less than successful in using Reg. § 1.641(a)–0(c) to consolidate trusts for income tax purposes and ultimately the case law has generally considered trusts with common grantors, terms and beneficiaries to be separate taxpayers if they were administered as separate trusts. See Morris Trusts v. Commissioner, 51 T.C. 20 (1968), aff'd per curiam, 427 F.2d 1361 (9th Cir. 1970). The validity of 20 family trusts created by the same grantors for the same beneficiaries was upheld even though their primary purpose was to avoid tax. They were upheld because they were administered separately. Moreover, in Edward L. Stephenson Trust v. Commissioner, 81 T.C. 283 (1983), the Tax Court held Reg. § 1.641(a)–0(c) unconstitutional.

With the compression of the income tax rates applicable to trusts, fewer trusts will be able to realize any income tax savings as a result of accumulating income within the trust. Accordingly, the trust consolidation rules may be infrequently invoked since it will be easier to show that the nontax purposes of the trust outweighed any possible tax considerations.

Section 643(f) may possibly apply to separate bypass trusts established by husband and wife for the benefit of their lineal descendants. Clearly, these trusts for the benefit of the same persons would be treated as separate trusts under the consolidation regulation but, according to § 643(f), "husband and wife shall be treated as 1 person." However, it could be argued that § 643(f) is actually more limiting than the regulation that it replaces. The regulation applied to trusts that had as "their principal purpose" the "avoidance or mitigation of * * * the progressive rates of tax (including mitigation as a result of deferral of tax)." Section 643(f) applies to trusts that have as "a principal purpose" the avoidance of tax. Thus, the question is, must the IRS prove "more" under § 643(f) to bring about consolidation than under the old regulation inasmuch as proving that the grantor had "avoidance" in mind would seem harder to accomplish than merely proving that the grantor

¶ 30,469

wanted to "mitigate" the progressive rates of tax as the regulation contemplated?

Section 643(f) applies only to that portion of a trust that is attributable to contributions to the trust made after March 1, 1984.

Q. CHARITABLE BENEFICIARIES

[¶ 30,481]

1. INTRODUCTION

Although trusts and estates are generally taxed in the same manner as individuals, one exception provided by § 642(c) is an unlimited deduction for charitable contributions paid or (in certain cases) for amounts permanently set aside for charity out of taxable gross income.

There are several limitations on this general rule. First, to the extent the contribution is paid from tax-exempt income, there is no deduction. Second, in the absence of a specific provision in the trust instrument, charitable contributions are deemed to have been made pro rata from all the several classes of income received by the fiduciary.

Charitable contributions also affect the determination of DNI inasmuch as they are not taken into account in determining DNI for the purpose of ascertaining the amount of income taxable to first-tier beneficiaries. § 662(a)(1). However, to the extent that charitable contributions are made from income, they are deducted in determining the amount of DNI allocable to second-tier beneficiaries. Reg. § 1.662(b)–2.

[¶ 30,490]

2. PAID OR PERMANENTLY SET ASIDE

Two frequent observations are "deductions are a matter of legislative grace" and "deductions are strictly construed." Nothing could be more true when it comes to the charitable deduction. Section 170 provides for deductions for charitable contributions by individuals and corporations; § 170 does not apply to contributions by estates or trusts. Section 642(c) relates to deductions for amounts paid or permanently set aside for charitable purposes by estates or certain trusts specifically described in § 642(c). Sometimes an estate will be entitled to a deduction whereas a trust would be denied a deduction if it were to make the claim. Hence, it matters who is seeking the deduction. *Berger*, below, is an illustration raising the spectre that, in some instances, amounts ending up with charities are not tax deductible. Consider whether there was any way for the taxpayer in *Berger* to have structured the transaction to produce the desired tax deduction. There, prolonging the estate administration proved to be an unsuccessful strategy to qualify for having "permanently set aside" an amount for charity, the statutory requirement imposed by § 642(c) for the charitable deduction where the amount was not "paid" that year.

[¶ 30,491]

ESTATE OF BERGER v. COMMISSIONER

United States Tax Court, 1990.
T.C. Memo 1990-554

CLAPP, JUDGE:

Respondent determined a deficiency in the Federal income tax of the Estate of Helen Barrow Berger in the amount of $15,351.53 for the year 1982. The issues are (1) whether petitioner is an estate or a trust for Federal income tax purposes; and (2) whether petitioner is entitled to a charitable deduction under either § 170 or 642(c) for the portion of a capital gain ultimately designated for charities. * * *

* * *

Decedent was married to Berger, and in her will, which was executed on October 18, 1976, she * * * provided that on Berger's death, the residue was to be liquidated and distributed as follows: 45 percent to various relatives; 20 percent to Catholic Charities of the Roman Catholic Diocese of Joliet, Illinois; 25 percent to Our Lady of Lourdes Roman Catholic Church of Gibson City, Illinois; and 10 percent to the Missionaries of Our Lady of Lasalette of Olivet, Illinois.

The will was admitted to probate on December 7, 1976, and Letters of Office as executor were granted to Berger. Berger filed a probate inventory, which included the second farm. On May 17, 1977, the court granted Berger possession of all realty of the estate. * * * At the time this case was submitted, the probate proceeding in Illinois state court had not been closed.

On February 17, 1982, Berger sold the second farm that was part of the residue of the estate for $354,000. This sale resulted in a capital gain of $140,650.50, which petitioner reported on its 1982 Federal fiduciary income tax return. The return claimed a charitable deduction of $30,943.11, representing 55 percent of the capital gain (after the gain was reduced by the long-term capital gain deduction). The proceeds from the sale of the second farm were deposited in bank accounts, the income from which has been distributed to Berger.

The basic question for consideration is whether petitioner is entitled to a deduction for the taxable portion of the capital gain realized on the sale of the second farm which is permanently set aside for charities under the terms of decedent's will. * * *

Charitable deductions are allowed under §§ 170 and 642(c). Section 170 provides for deductions for charitable contributions by individuals and corporations, and the provisions of § 170 do not apply to contributions by estates or trusts. § 1.170A–1(h)(1), Income Tax Regs. Section 642(c) relates to deductions for amounts paid or permanently set aside for charitable purposes by estates or certain trusts specifically described in § 642(c). Section 642(c)(1) relates to amounts of gross income actually paid during the taxable year by an estate or trust and specifically provides that a deduction is 'in lieu of the deduction allowed by § 170(a).' Section 642(c)(2) allows a deduction for any amount of gross income permanently set aside by an estate or by, generally, a trust created on or before October 9, 1969. If a trust does not meet the requirements of § 642(c)(2), then the trust will receive no deduction under § 642(c) for amounts of gross income permanently set aside for charities. Such a post-October 9, 1969, trust must then look to § 664, and if it qualifies as a charitable remainder annuity trust or a charitable remainder unitrust under § 664(d), it will be exempt from income taxes under § 664(c). If the trust is exempt, gross income is not taxable and, therefore, deductions for any amounts of gross income permanently set aside for charities become academic. In summary, an estate will get a deduction for any amount of gross income paid under § 642(c)(1) or for any such amounts permanently set aside for charities under § 642(c)(2). A trust which is not exempt under § 664 will get a deduction for amounts of gross income paid during the taxable year or, in the limited cases of pre-October 9, 1969 trusts, for amounts permanently set aside. If a trust does not qualify as a pre-October 9, 1969, trust under § 642(c)(2), it will get relief for amounts permanently set aside only if it qualifies for tax exemption under § 664 as an annuity trust or a unitrust. Thus, deductions for amounts of gross income permanently set aside for charity are effectively disallowed except for the limited pre-October 9, 1969 exception.

With that background in mind, we return to the facts before us to see whether there is any basis for a deduction by petitioner for the taxable portion of the capital gain realized on the sale of the second farm, which is permanently set aside for charities.

We first address whether petitioner is an estate or a trust for Federal income tax purposes. Section 1.641(b)–3(a), Income Tax Regs., provides:

> The income of an estate * * * is that which is received by the estate during the period of administration * * *. The period of administration * * * is the period actually required by the * * * executor to perform the ordinary duties of administration, such as the collection of assets and the payment of debts, taxes, legacies, and bequests * * * the period of administration * * * cannot be unduly prolonged. If the administration of an estate is unreasonably prolonged, the estate is considered terminated for Federal income tax purposes * * *.

Whether the administration of an estate has been unduly prolonged is a question of fact. If the estate has been essentially fully administered, the residuary bequest, including a bequest in the form of a legal life estate with remainder, will continue as a trust for Federal tax purposes. * * *

Petitioner contends that it is an estate, while respondent asserts petitioner should be treated as a trust. We agree with respondent. On August 1, 1978, an Order Approving First Account and Report for the estate was entered. By such date all assets had been collected, all taxes, debts, and bequests payable by reason of decedent's death had been paid, a Federal estate tax return had been filed, and the estate tax paid. The residue of the estate had not been formally distributed to Berger as trustee by or during 1982, but this is not sufficient to keep the estate open for Federal income tax purposes. The

¶ 30,491

remainder interests did not require estate administration, such as the collection of assets and payment of debts, taxes, and legacies, but rather any administration necessary was in the nature of trust administration. We hold that the estate was terminated for Federal income tax purposes prior to 1982, and that during 1982 petitioner was a trust for Federal income tax purposes.

We will next consider whether petitioner is entitled to a deduction under § 170(a). As already noted above, § 170 provides for deductions for charitable contributions by individuals and corporations and does not apply to contributions by trusts or estates. The Internal Revenue Code deals with deductions for charitable contributions by estates and trusts in § 642(c). * * * Thus, § 170 is inapplicable to the present case without regard to whether petitioner is an estate or a trust, and petitioner is not entitled to a deduction under that section.

We next turn to § 642(c) as it applies to trusts, since we have concluded that petitioner is a trust for tax purposes. Since no amount was paid to a charitable beneficiary during 1982, § 642(c)(1) does not apply, and no deduction is allowable under that section. Section 642(c)(2) applies only to trusts which were created on or before October 9, 1969, or established by a will executed on or before October 9, 1969. In the instant case, the trust was established by a will executed on October 18, 1976, and decedent died on November 1, 1976. Both dates are well after the cutoff date set forth in § 642(c)(2)(A) and (B), and hence petitioner is not entitled to a deduction under § 642(c)(2) for any amounts of gross income permanently set aside for charitable purposes.

We next look to § 664 to see whether petitioner might be entitled to exempt status, which would allow the capital gain here in question to go untaxed with the same net result as allowing a deduction. Petitioner has not made this argument, nor has either party addressed it on brief. This inattention appears to be with good cause, as the residuary trust here involved would not qualify as either a charitable remainder annuity trust or a charitable remainder unitrust under § 664(d).

Based on the foregoing, we conclude that petitioner is not entitled to a deduction for the taxable portion of the capital gain which is permanently set aside for charitable purposes. * * *

3. DEDUCTION FOR BOTH ESTATE AND INCOME TAX PURPOSES

[¶ 30,493]

UNITED STATES TRUST CO. v. INTERNAL REVENUE SERVICE

United States Court of Appeals, Fifth Circuit, 1986.
803 F.2d 1363.

ROGER MADDEN HILL, Circuit Judge:

In this appeal we are asked to determine whether an estate taxpayer which has been allowed a deduction from its federal estate tax return for the amount of a bequest made to a charitable organization is also entitled to a deduction for the amount of the bequest from its income tax return during the taxable year that the bequest was made. * * *

The facts in this case are not in dispute. Alexander F. Chisholm (Chisholm), a resident of Mississippi, died on March 12, 1974, leaving a valid will dated May 17, 1967. * * * In article three of his will, Chisholm made a specific bequest to the Chisholm Foundation (Foundation), a New York-based charity organization. The bequest provided:

> I give to the Chisholm Foundation, a New York membership corporation, a sum equal to ten percent (10%) of the value of my gross testamentary estate as finally determined in the Federal estate tax proceeding relating to my Estate, provided that such bequest is deductible from my gross Estate in determining my taxable Estate for Federal Estate tax purposes.

Ten percent of Chisholm's gross testamentary estate was later calculated to be $2,473,719.

From Chisholm's death in March to December 31, 1974, no part of the specific bequest to the Foundation was paid. During 1975 $1,505,000 in cash and $512,635 in stock was distributed to the Foundation in partial satisfaction of the specific bequest. The cash payments were made in twelve monthly payments from a bank account containing monies derived from the original corpus of Chisholm's estate and the income that had accrued in 1974 and 1975. The remaining balance of the bequest to the Foundation was paid in 1976.

On its 1976 federal estate tax return, the taxpayer claimed an estate tax deduction, as allowed by section 2055(a)(2), for the entire $2,473,719 bequest which had been distributed to the Foundation during 1975 and 1976. The deduction was allowed by the IRS for the full amount of the distributions.

In 1976 the taxpayer also filed an income tax return for the year 1975. On this return the taxpayer claimed an income tax deduction for a part of the cash distributions made to the Foundation. Of the $1,505,000 in cash distributed to the Foundation in 1975, the taxpayer deducted $1,240,467 from its gross income as a deduction for distributions to a beneficiary under section 661(a)(2). These distributions could not qualify for a deduction as distributions to a charitable organization under section 642(c) because Chisholm's will did not direct that the distributions come from gross income. After auditing the 1975 income tax return, the IRS disallowed the deduction.

* * *

The issue as stated before is: May the taxpayer claim an income tax deduction for distributions of present income to a charitable beneficiary under section 661(a)(2) when the distributions did not otherwise qualify as a section 642(c) deduction and the taxpayer had already claimed and received a federal estate tax deduction for the same distributions? In answering this question we decide whether treasury regulation § 1.663(a)–2 is valid.

* * * We recognize that the purpose of tax benefits or deductions arising from charitable distributions is to encourage the making of charitable be-

¶ 30,493

quests. Several tax benefits are given to an estate that includes a charitable bequest. * * *

One such benefit is the estate tax deduction embodied in section 2055(a)(2). Section 2055(a)(2) allows an estate to reduce its federal estate tax liability by deducting from the gross value of the estate the amount it pays to satisfy a charitable bequest that is to be funded by property owned by the decedent at death. In this case, the taxpayer was allowed a section 2055(a)(2) deduction for the full amount of its distributions to the Foundation, and the IRS concedes the validity of this deduction.

Another tax benefit conferred upon estates which contain charitable bequests is contained in section 642(c) [which provides an income tax deduction for "any amount of the gross income without limitation, which pursuant to the terms of the governing instrument is, during the taxable year, paid for" a charitable purpose specified in § 170(c)] * * *. Thus, the deduction under section 642(c) is allowed only if the relevant governing instrument provides that the bequest be funded solely from the "gross income" of the estate.

As the plain language of §§ 2055(a)(2) and 642(c) demonstrates, Congress intended that the benefit for a charitable bequest be conferred only once— either as an offset against the gross value of the estate or as an offset against income. This intent is accomplished by limiting section 2055(a)(2) deductions to the value of the property that is included in the gross estate at the time of decedent's death. Thus, no estate tax deduction is available for amounts that are paid to a charitable organization at the direction of the governing instrument from estate income. The tax benefit for income distributions is then bestowed by section 642(c) which allows deductions for amounts payable out of gross income.

In light of these beneficial tax provisions for charitable bequests, the apparent exclusion of charitable distributions from the conduit taxing rules is reflected in [§ 663(a) which provides that any "amount paid or permanently set aside or otherwise qualifying for the deduction provided in Section 642(c)" shall not be included as an amount "falling within Section 661(a) or 662(a)"] * * *. Therefore, if an estate may take a section 642(c) deduction for a distribution to a charitable organization, it cannot also take a section 661(a)(2) deduction for the same distribution. As one court has noted, the relevant provisions of the Code reflect a "symmetry which insures that all charitable contributions result in a tax benefit, but precludes a double benefit." Pullen v. United States, 45 A.F.T.R.2d 80–381, 80–383 (D.Nev. Nov. 29, 1979), aff'd, No. 80–1034 (8th Cir. Sept. 29, 1980)(mem.).

Furthermore, the committee reports accompanying the enactment of the Code support the conclusion that Congress did not intend the general conduit taxation rules to apply to charitable distributions. * * * Both the House and Senate Reports state:

> Paragraph (3) provides that any amount paid, permanently set aside or to be used for the purposes specified in section 642(c) is excluded from the provisions of section 661 and 662. Since the estate or trust is allowed a deduction under section 642(c) for these amounts, *they are not allowed as*

an additional deduction for distributions nor are they treated as amounts distributed for purposes of section 662 in determining the amounts includible in the gross income of beneficiaries.

H.R. Rep. No. 1337, at 4344; S. Rep. No. 1622, at 4995 (emphasis added).

One final fact bolstering our observation that charitable distributions are not considered in the conduit principles of sections 661 and 662 is that Congress has expressly refused to incorporate charitable distributions into the taxing scheme of section 661. In 1960 House Bill 9662 would have amended section 661(a) to encompass all charitable distributions, while eliminating the deduction under section 642(c). See H.R. 9662, 86th Cong., 2d Sess. §§ 102(b), 103(g), 106(a), 107, 108(a) (1960). The House committee report accompanying the bill expressly recognized that deductions for charitable distributions under existing law required tracing and that such distributions therefore fell outside sections 661 and 662 since they did not. H.R. Rep. No. 1231, 86th Cong., 2d Sess. 9–10 (1960). This modification to include all charitable distributions in the conduit taxation scheme was rejected.

* * *

Note

[¶ 30,497]

In Burke v. United States, 994 F.2d 1576 (Fed.Cir.1993), cert. denied, 510 U.S. 990 (1993), the Federal Circuit upheld the decision of the Court of Federal Claims (previously known as the Claims Court) that an estate cannot effectively increase the amount of a residuary charitable deduction by using postmortem income to pay administrative expenses. (This conclusion is premised on the same reasoning used by the Sixth Circuit in deciding *Street*, noted at ¶ 30,388.) The testator's will directed that her entire residuary estate pass to a charitable foundation named after herself, provided that all taxes and administration expenses must first be deducted from the residuary. The executor petitioned the Florida probate court to interpret the testator's will so as to allow payment of the administrative expenses from income earned by the estate, rather than from the principal of the gross estate. The probate court entered an order allowing payment from the income; subsequently, a fiduciary income tax return was filed, claiming a deduction for administrative expenses of $144,441. The estate tax return was filed thereafter claiming a charitable deduction for the amount actually received by the charity but not diminished by taxes and administration expenses paid out of income earned during administration.

The Federal Circuit Court found that the value of the gross estate was indirectly increased by deducting the administration expenses from the estate's income rather than the gross estate. This accounting method allows the estate "to claim two deductions for the exact same portion of the gross estate as being both an administrative expense deductible under § 2053, which Burke, the executor of the estate, elected to claim on the estate's income tax return, and a charitable donation deductible under § 2055, which Burke claimed on the estate tax return." 994 F.2d at 1582.

¶ 30,497

Using a "snapshot" approach, the *Burke* court said (Id. at 1581–82):

In sum, when a decedent dies, a finite amount known as the gross estate is legally created. Any deductions for expenses incurred in administering the estate are theoretically derived from this amount and, regardless of the actual source of payment, must be accounted for within the gross estate. * * *

Burke argues that the only relevant provision of the tax code is § 2055 which allows a deduction from the decedent's gross estate of amounts given to a qualifying charity. Per Burke, for purposes of the § 2055 deduction, the only requirement is that the charity actually receive the amount claimed as the deduction. Burke argues that since the Foundation received more than the amount claimed as a deduction under § 2055 over the probate period, the requirements for claiming a deduction are satisfied.

However, the fact that the charitable deduction taken on Burke's federal estate tax return was less than the actual amount received by the charity over the seven-year probate period is not determinative. The relevant inquiry is the amount received by the charity *under the will*, i.e., the amount of the gross estate that passed to the charity. That the charitable donation was augmented by post-mortem income, resulting in an overall charitable donation of an amount greater than the estate tax deduction claimed, does not increase the amount of the charitable bequest under the will.

Under Williams' will, the Foundation received the residue of the estate. Therefore, the value of the gross estate that passed to the Foundation for which the estate may claim a charitable deduction under section 2055, is the amount remaining in the estate after Burke had accounted for all of the obligations of the estate accruing at the time of death. These obligations included payment of the administrative expenses for which the estate claimed a deduction, albeit on the estate's income tax return. In calculating the residue, the amount of the gross estate passing to charity under the will, Burke failed to take into account the reduction necessitated by administrative expenses. This was error because, for purposes of federal estate taxation, the gross estate is obligated to pay those expenses. In essence, Burke would have us indirectly increase the value of the gross estate by allowing him to use post-mortem income to pay the obligations of the gross estate. While, as we have previously noted, it may be beneficial or convenient to pay such obligations out of post-mortem income, the post-mortem income so used does not itself become part of the gross estate. The result Burke seeks would allow the estate to claim two deductions for the exact same portion of the gross estate as being both an administrative expense deductible under section 2053, which Burke elected to claim on the estate's income tax return, and a charitable donation deductible under section 2055, which Burke claimed on the estate tax return.

The amount of the charitable deduction claimed by Williams' estate was properly reduced by the amount of administrative expenses claimed as a deduction on the estate's fiduciary income tax return because, for federal estate taxation purposes, only this lesser amount was paid to the charity from the gross estate. The additional amount paid to charity over the probation period was post-mortem income for which estate received a deduction on its federal income tax returns.

Subsequent to the decision in *Burke* and the decision in Commissioner v. Estate of Hubert, 520 U.S. 93 (1997), discussed at ¶ 30,388, the IRS published new regulations applicable in cases where administration expenses are claimed as a deduction on the estate's income tax return. These regulations, appearing as Reg. § 20.2055–3(b), follow the model of similar regulations applicable when the marital deduction is claimed. For discussion, see ¶ 30,388. These regulations require that estate administration expenses be classified as either estate transmission expenses or estate management expenses. Estate transmission expenses where paid from the charitable share and claimed on the estate's income tax return are viewed by the IRS as reducing the value of the charitable gift and, thus, reduce the estate tax deduction for the gift to charity. Estate management expenses paid from the charitable share do not reduce the charitable gift deduction.

[¶ 30,499]

4. INCOME INTERESTS GIVEN TO CHARITY

Special rules apply to charitable gifts of income interests in trust. With respect to such gifts, a charitable contribution deduction is allowed to the settlor only if the settlor is taxable on the trust income under the grantor trust rules set out in §§ 671–678 and the income interest of the charity is a guaranteed annuity or a fixed percentage of the value of the trust corpus determined yearly. § 170(f)(2)(B). In this case, however, the settlor is allowed a charitable contribution deduction for the present value of the charitable income interest in the year the trust is established but is taxed each year thereafter on the trust income. Moreover, the trust is not allowed a deduction for the income subsequently distributed to the charity. § 170(f)(2)(C) and Reg. § 1.170A–6(d)(1). By way of contrast, though, and as an example of the complex rules that determine the tax deductibility of amounts distributed to charity, consider the revenue ruling at ¶ 30,505 relating to a charitable trust created for a term in excess of ten years.

By way of contrast, where no income tax deduction is available to the settlor when the trust is established, § 642(c)(1) provides the trust with an income tax deduction, without limitation, for any amount of income that, pursuant to the trust agreement, is paid for any purpose specified in § 170(c).

[¶ 30,505]

REVENUE RULING 79–223
1979–2 C.B. 254.

ISSUE

Is a trust allowed a deduction for amounts of gross income paid out to charitable beneficiaries under the circumstances described below?

¶ 30,505

FACTS

Y, a bank holding company, created an irrevocable trust that will not terminate before ten years and one month after the date of its creation. The governing instrument of the trust provides that no additional property may be contributed to the trust after it is created.

The net income of the trust is to be distributed to organizations described in section 170(c)(1), (2), and (3). All income is to be distributed before the close of the year succeeding the year in which the income is received. Capital gains are to be added to corpus.

Y has reserved the power to designate recipients of income. Such designation is to be made at any time before or after the income is received. If Y fails to designate by the time income is required to be distributed, the trustee is required to select charitable beneficiaries. Distributions are to be made only from income received by the trust.

The trust agreement provides that all powers reserved by Y shall be exercised by Y in a fiduciary capacity and that none of the powers will be construed to permit the trustee to lend any of the principal or income of the trust property, directly or indirectly, to the grantor without adequate interest or security or to borrow directly or indirectly from the grantor at more than adequate interest or other consideration. Except in the case of permitted distributions, Y is prohibited from dealing with or disposing of the principal of the trust property or the income therefrom for less than an adequate consideration. Y is precluded from designating any distribution in satisfaction of its own obligation to a charitable organization.

Upon the termination of the trust, all of the property comprising the principal of the trust will be distributed to Y. All of the then undistributed income of the trust will be distributed to or for the use of the charitable organizations described above.

LAW AND ANALYSIS

Because the terms of the trust require the capital gains of the trust to be accumulated for future distribution by Y, Y will be treated as the owner of the income of the trust with respect to capital gains. See section 677(a). Other items of gross income and deductions and credits attributable to the ordinary income portion of the trust will be subject to the provisions of subparts a through D (section 641 and following), part I, subchapter J, of the Code. See section 1.671–3 of the Income Tax Regulations. Thus, no deduction will be allowed to Y for any amounts of the trust's income paid to charitable organizations. The capital gains allocable to the corpus portion of the trust will be includible in Y's gross income when realized by the trust. See Rev. Rul. 66–161, 1966–1 C.B. 167.

Section 170(a) generally allows a deduction for charitable contributions paid during the taxable year. Section 170(f)(2)(B) provides, with respect to charitable transfers in trusts of income interests, that no deduction under subsection (a) is allowed unless the interest is in the form of a guaranteed annuity or the trust instrument specifies that the interest is a fixed percentage distributed annually, and the grantor is treated as the owner of such interest for purposes of applying section 671.

No income tax deduction was allowable to Y at the time of the creation of the trust since the income interest given to charity did not meet the requirements of section 170(f)(2)(B).

Section 642(c)(1) provides, in part, that in the case of a trust, there shall be allowed as a deduction in computing its taxable income any amount of gross income, without limitation, which pursuant to the terms of the governing instrument is, during the taxable year, paid for a purpose specified in section 170(c). If a charitable contribution is paid after the close of such taxable year and on or before the last day of the year following the close of such taxable year, then the trustee may elect to treat such contribution as paid during such taxable year.

HOLDING

Accordingly, * * * the trust will be allowed a deduction in accordance with section 642(c)(1) for amounts of gross income paid out to charitable beneficiaries described in section 170(c) during its taxable year, or by the close of the following taxable year.

[¶ 30,511]

5. CHARITABLE REMAINDER TRUSTS AND POOLED INCOME FUNDS

Special rules govern the taxation of charitable remainder trusts and pooled income funds. See § 664. These are trusts that have remainder interests held by charitable organizations. See ¶ 26,049 for a discussion of these rules.

[¶ 30,517]

6. SELECTION OF TAX YEAR

Also, trusts exempt from tax under § 501(a) and charitable trusts described in § 4947(a)(1) are not required to use a calendar year for income tax reporting purposes.

¶ 30,517

Chapter 31

GRANTOR TRUSTS

(Sections 671–678)

A. INTRODUCTION

[¶ 31,001]

Generally speaking, the income of each trust and estate will be taxed to either the trust or estate or the beneficiaries of the trust or estate who receive distributions from the trust or estate. Much of the discussion in Chapter 31 was concerned with determining, in a particular case, whether the income should be taxed to the estate or trust or to the beneficiaries and, as among the beneficiaries, to which beneficiary the income should be attributed.

This portion of these materials will be devoted to determining under what circumstances the income of a trust will be taxed to either the settlor of the trust or one of the beneficiaries even though the person to whom the income is taxed may not have received it! Sections 671–677 determine the circumstances in which trust income will be taxed to the settlor of the trust.

> *Example*: Mr. Slowe established a trust during his lifetime which provided that all of the income from the trust would be paid to his child, Borne, age fourteen. He funded the trust with $100,000 cash. The trust was to continue for Borne's lifetime and, at Borne's death, any property that remained in the trust was to be distributed to Borne's then living lineal descendants *per stirpes*. Mr. Slowe believed the trust would be a good way to shift income from himself to Borne who was in a much lower income tax bracket than Mr. Slowe. In addition, Mr. Slowe believed that any of the trust income not taxed to Borne would be taxed to the trust. Taxing some of the income to the trust would effect even greater income tax savings because it means the income would be taxed to several taxpayers, all of whom are, at least initially, low bracket income taxpayers. Mr. Slowe was, indeed, proud of his son, but not knowing what kind of a person Borne would become as he grew to adulthood, Mr. Slowe reserved the right to revoke the trust at any time by written notice to the trustee, Accumulation National Bank.

Under these circumstances should Mr. Slowe be permitted to shift the income from the trust property to Borne or to the trust or should it continue to be taxed to Mr. Slowe since he had the power to revoke the trust whenever he determined to do so? See § 676.

The foregoing is an "easy case" but it provides an illustration of the kind of features that can characterize trusts as taxpayers attempt to shift income tax liability to others within the family unit while, at the same time, retaining control, not only of the property that produces the income, but also of the income itself. Sections 671–677 identify those features which, if included in a particular trust, will cause the income of that trust to be taxed to the settlor or "grantor" of the trust.

If it is the grantor to whom the trust income is to be taxed, then, obviously, the grantor trust rules apply only during the lifetime of the settlor (inasmuch as the grantor ceases to be a taxpayer for income tax purposes at death).

However, trust income may be taxed to someone other than the grantor even though that other person did not receive the trust income. That is possible when the nongrantor has such control over the trust income that to allow the nongrantor to avoid income tax liability for that income would—in the opinion of Congress—impair the integrity of the tax system. Section 678 determines the circumstances in which trust income will be taxed to someone other than the settlor even though that other person did not receive the income!

Example: Mr. Quick's will provided that an amount equal to the exemption equivalent of the unified credit for estate tax purposes be placed in a trust for his wife, Bea. Bea was made the trustee of the trust and, as trustee, she had the power to distribute to herself so much or all of the income of the trust as she "deems appropriate." She also had the power to make distributions of income to Mr. Quick's children in "such amounts as she deems appropriate." Any income not distributed in a particular year was to be added to the principal of the trust. During the last calendar year, Bea made no distributions from the trust to anyone. To whom should the trust income for last year be taxed? Bea says the trust should be taxed on all of the trust income since the income was kept in the trust. Do you agree with her? See § 678.

The concept of "owner" is used as an organizational technique in §§ 671–678. The grantor of the trust will be deemed its "owner" if the trust contains any of the features identified in §§ 673–677. If the grantor is deemed to be the "owner" of the trust, the income from the trust will be taxed to the grantor as if the trust never existed. § 671.

Procedurally speaking, the trustee of a grantor trust will report the trust's status as a grantor trust to the IRS by filing the normal fiduciary income tax return—Form 1041—and declaring on that return that the trust is a grantor trust and that all of the income and expenses of the trust are to be reported on the grantor's personal federal income tax return. The trustee will not actually complete the form but will file a blank form to which is attached

¶ 31,001

a schedule reflecting the information that is to be reflected on the grantor's personal income tax return. Reg. § 1.671–4. As a technical matter, it may be worth noting that not even a Form 1041 is required in the case of a grantor trust in which the grantor is either trustee or co-trustee. In those cases, the grantor may report all the trust income on Form 1040, the grantor's personal income tax return. Reg. § 1.671–4(b)(1) and (2).

Finally, there are two special caveats that should be noted. First, the grantor trust rules expressly contemplate that, in some cases, only a portion of the trust's income will be taxed to the grantor, while the remainder of the trust income is taxed to the trust or to the trust beneficiaries. § 671. That is, the rules recognize that only a portion of a trust's income may be subject to one of the features that have been identified as requiring the trust income to be taxed to the grantor of the trust.

Second, § 671 expressly provides that the income of a trust will not be taxed to the grantor of a trust solely because the grantor has "dominion and control over the trust." Section 671 states that the grantor will be taxed on trust income not received only if the trust contains one or more of the features identified in §§ 673–677. This is a significant concession by Congress inasmuch as it limits the courts from determining on a case-by-case basis when the grantor of a trust has such substantial dominion and control over the trust to warrant taxing the trust income to the grantor.

The "dominion and control" test was used by the Supreme Court in Helvering v. Clifford, 309 U.S. 331 (1940). In *Clifford*, the Court established general rules for taxing grantor trusts. These general rules were then endorsed by the IRS in the form of Treasury regulations. Later these regulations were codified as §§ 671–678. The grantor trust rules of §§ 671–678 are commonly referred to as the *Clifford* rules and, despite the congressional decision to reject the "dominion and control" test, Helvering v. Clifford remains a landmark case.

[¶ 31,007]

HELVERING v. CLIFFORD

Supreme Court of the United States, 1940.
309 U.S. 331.

Mr. Justice DOUGLAS delivered the opinion of the Court:

In 1934 respondent declared himself trustee of certain securities which he owned. All net income from the trust was to be held for the "exclusive benefit" of respondent's wife. The trust was for a term of five years, except that it would terminate earlier on the death of either respondent or his wife. On termination of the trust the entire corpus was to go to respondent, while all "accrued or undistributed net income" and "any proceeds from the investment of such net income" was to be treated as property owned absolutely by the wife. During the continuance of the trust respondent was to pay over to his wife the whole or such part of the net income as he in his "absolute discretion" might determine. And during that period he had full power (a) to exercise all voting powers incident to the trusteed shares of stock; (b) to "sell, exchange, mortgage, or pledge" any of the securities under the declaration of trust "whether as part of the corpus or principal thereof or as investments or proceeds and any income therefrom, upon such terms and for such consideration" as respondent in his "absolute discretion may deem fitting"; (c) to invest "any cash or money in the trust estate or any income therefrom" by loans, secured or unsecured, by deposits in banks, or by purchase of securities or other personal property "without restriction" because of their "speculative character" or "rate of return" or any "laws pertaining to the investment of trust funds"; (d) to collect all income; (e) to compromise, etc., any claims held by him as trustee; (f) to hold any property in the trust estate in the names of "other persons or in my own name as an individual" except as otherwise provided. Extraordinary cash dividends, stock dividends, proceeds from the sale of unexercised subscription rights, or any enhancement, realized or not, in the value of the securities were to be treated as principal, not income. An exculpatory clause purported to protect him from all losses except those occasioned by his "own wilful and deliberate" breach of duties as trustee. And finally it was provided that neither the principal nor any future or accrued income should be liable for the debts of the wife; and that the wife could not transfer, encumber, or anticipate any interest in the trust or any income therefrom prior to actual payment thereof to her.

It was stipulated that while the "tax effects" of this trust were considered by respondent they were not the "sole consideration" involved in his decision to set it up, as by this and other gifts he intended to give "security and economic independence" to his wife and children. It was also stipulated that respondent's wife had substantial income of her own from other sources; that there was no restriction on her use of the trust income, all of which income was placed in her personal checking account, intermingled with her other funds, and expended by her on herself, her children and relatives; that the trust was not designed to relieve respondent from liability for family or household expenses and that after execution of the trust he paid large sums from his personal funds for such purposes.

Respondent paid a federal gift tax on this transfer. During the year 1934 all income from the trust was distributed to the wife who included it in her individual return for that year. The Commissioner, however, determined a deficiency in respondent's return for that year on the theory that income from the trust was taxable to him. The Board of Tax Appeals sustained that redetermination (38 B.T.A. 1532). The Circuit Court of Appeals reversed (105 F. (2d) 586). We granted certiorari because of the importance to the revenue of the use of such short term trusts in the reduction of surtaxes.

Sec. 22(a) of the Revenue Act of 1934 (48 Stat. 680) [1986 Code § 61] includes among "gross income" all "gains, profits, and income derived ... from professions, vocations, trades, businesses, commerce, or sales, or dealings in property, whether real or personal, growing out of the ownership or use of or interest in such property; also from interest, rent, dividends, securities, or the transaction of any business carried on for gain or profit, or gains or profits and income derived from any source whatever." The broad sweep of this

¶ 31,007

language indicates the purpose of Congress to use the full measure of its taxing power within those definable categories. * * * Hence our construction of the statute should be consonant with that purpose. Technical considerations, niceties of the law of trusts or conveyances, or the legal paraphernalia which inventive genius may construct as a refuge from surtaxes should not obscure the basic issue. That issue is whether the grantor after the trust has been established may still be treated, under this statutory scheme, as the owner of the corpus. * * * In absence of more precise standards or guides supplied by statute or appropriate regulations, the answer to that question must depend on an analysis of the terms of the trust and all the circumstances attendant on its creation and operation. And where the grantor is the trustee and the beneficiaries are members of his family group, special scrutiny of the arrangement is necessary lest what is in reality but one economic unit be multiplied into two or more by devices which, though valid under state law, are not conclusive so far as § 22(a) is concerned.

In this case we cannot conclude as a matter of law that respondent ceased to be the owner of the corpus after the trust was created. Rather, the short duration of the trust, the fact that the wife was the beneficiary, and the retention of control over the corpus by respondent all lead irresistibly to the conclusion that respondent continued to be the owner for purposes of § 22(a).

So far as his dominion and control were concerned it seems clear that the trust did not effect any substantial change. In substance his control over the corpus was in all essential respects the same after the trust was created, as before. The wide powers which he retained included for all practical purposes most of the control which he as an individual would have. There were, we may assume, exceptions, such as his disability to make a gift of the corpus to others during the term of the trust and to make loans to himself. But this dilution in his control would seem to be insignificant and immaterial, since control over investment remained. If it be said that such control is the type of dominion exercised by any trustee, the answer is simple. We have at best a temporary reallocation of income within an intimate family group. Since the income remains in the family and since the husband retains control over the investment, he has rather complete assurance that the trust will not effect any substantial change in his economic position. It is hard to imagine that respondent felt himself the poorer after this trust had been executed or, if he did, that it had any rational foundation in fact. For as a result of the terms of the trust and the intimacy of the familial relationship respondent retained the substance of full enjoyment of all the rights which previously he had in the property. That might not be true if only strictly legal rights were considered. But when the benefits flowing to him indirectly through the wife are added to the legal rights he retained, the aggregate may be said to be a fair equivalent of what he previously had. To exclude from the aggregate those indirect benefits would be to deprive § 22(a) of considerable vitality and to treat as immaterial what may be highly relevant considerations in the creation of such family trusts. For where the head of the household has income in excess of normal needs, it may well make but little difference to him (except income-tax

¶ 31,007

wise) where portions of that income are routed—so long as it stays in the family group. In those circumstances the all-important factor might be retention by him of control over the principal. With that control in his hands he would keep direct command over all that he needed to remain in substantially the same financial situation as before. Our point here is that no one fact is normally decisive but that all considerations and circumstances of the kind we have mentioned are relevant to the question of ownership and are appropriate foundations for findings on that issue. Thus, where, as in this case, the benefits directly or indirectly retained blend so imperceptibly with the normal concepts of full ownership, we cannot say that the triers of fact committed reversible error when they found that the husband was the owner of the corpus for the purposes of § 22(a). To hold otherwise would be to treat the wife as a complete stranger; to let mere formalism obscure the normal consequences of family solidarity; and to force concepts of ownership to be fashioned out of legal niceties which may have little or no significance in such household arrangements.

The bundle of rights which he retained was so substantial that respondent cannot be heard to complain that he is the "victim of despotic power when for the purpose of taxation he is treated as owner altogether." See Du Pont v. Commissioner, 289 U.S. 685, 689.

* * *

B. SPOUSAL ATTRIBUTION RULE

[¶ 31,013]

All powers and interests of the grantor's spouse are treated as being held by the grantor. § 672(e)(1). Moreover, a spouse's powers and interests are attributed to the grantor even in cases where the parties marry after the power or interest was created. However, persons legally separated from each other under a decree of divorce or of separate maintenance are not considered as married. § 672(e)(2).

C. REVOCABLE TRUSTS (SECTION 676)

[¶ 31,025]

1. GENERAL RULE

The ability of the grantor of a trust to revoke it is a plain example of a case in which the trust income should be taxed to the grantor even though the income is received by someone other than the grantor. The United States Supreme Court reached this conclusion very early in the history of the income tax and long before the grantor trust rules formally entered the Internal Revenue Code.

¶ 31,025

[¶ 31,031]

CORLISS v. BOWERS

Supreme Court of the United States, 1930.
281 U.S. 376.

Mr. Justice HOLMES delivered the opinion of the Court.

* * * In 1922 [petitioner] transferred the fund from which arose the income in respect of which the petitioner was taxed, to trustees, in trust to pay the income to his wife for life with remainder over to their children. By the instrument creating the trust the petitioner reserved power "to modify or alter in any manner, or revoke in whole or in part, this indenture and the trusts then existing, and the estates and interests in property hereby created." It is not necessary to quote more words because there can be no doubt that the petitioner fully reserved the power at any moment to abolish or change the trust at his will. The statute referred to provides that "when the grantor of a trust has, at any time during the taxable year, . . . the power to revest in himself title to any part of the corpus of the trust, then the income of such part of the trust for such taxable year shall be included in computing the net income of the grantor." § 219(g) with other similar provisions as to income in § 219(h). There can be no doubt either that the statute purports to tax the plaintiff in this case. But the net income for 1924 was paid over to the petitioner's wife and the petitioner's argument is that however it might have been in different circumstances the income never was his and he cannot be taxed for it. The legal estate was in the trustee and the equitable interest in the wife.

But taxation is not so much concerned with the refinements of title as it is with actual command over the property taxed—the actual benefit for which the tax is paid. If a man directed his bank to pay over income as received to a servant or friend, until further orders, no one would doubt that he could be taxed upon the amounts so paid. It is answered that in that case he would have a title, whereas here he did not. But from the point of view of taxation there would be no difference. The title would merely mean a right to stop the payment before it took place. The same right existed here although it is not called a title but is called a power. The acquisition by the wife of the income became complete only when the plaintiff failed to exercise the power that he reserved. * * * Still speaking with reference to taxation, if a man disposes of a fund in such a way that another is allowed to enjoy the income which it is in the power of the first to appropriate it does not matter whether the permission is given by assent or by failure to express dissent. The income that is subject to a man's unfettered command and that he is free to enjoy at his own option may be taxed to him as his income, whether he sees fit to enjoy it or not. We consider the case too clear to need help from the local law of New York or from arguments based on the power of Congress to prevent escape from taxes or surtaxes by devices that easily might be applied to that end. Judgment affirmed.

Problems

[¶ 31,037]

1. Aaron, at the time of his divorce, created a trust for the benefit of Hyman, an adult son of the marriage. Under the terms of the trust, Aaron may revoke the trust at any time with the consent of his divorced spouse, the mother of Hyman. Is Aaron taxable on the income of the trust?

2. There are cases where someone other than the grantor has the power to revoke a trust. Or, at least, some enterprising grantor (with the assistance of counsel) could conceivably craft an instrument that would give someone who is ostensibly independent of the grantor the power to revoke the grantor's trust and cause the trust property and income to be returned to the grantor. In circumstances like this, should the income be taxable to the grantor prior to the exercise of the power of revocation? Should the answer depend on whether the person holding the power of revocation is truly independent of the grantor?

   (a) What standards should be included in the statute by which true independence could be determined? Are the provisions of § 676(a), which provide that the trust is considered revocable if the power is exercisable by the grantor or "nonadverse party or both," satisfactory? (The terms "adverse party" and "nonadverse party" are defined in § 672(a) and (b)).

   (b) Is a life income beneficiary an adverse party for purposes of § 676(a)?

(c) Is the grantor's attorney an adverse party?

[¶ 31,043]

2. LIMITED POWERS OF REVOCATION

Section 676(b) describes circumstances in which the presence of a power of revocation in the grantor of the trust will not cause the trust income to be taxed to the grantor. These circumstances are limited and are designed to correlate with § 673, which allows the grantor of a trust to retain a reversionary interest in a trust but have the income taxed to the recipient of the income. These reversionary trusts are discussed at ¶ 31,217.

D. TRUSTS FOR BENEFIT OF GRANTOR

[¶ 31,049]

1. GENERAL RULE

The trust grantor will be taxed on the trust's income in cases where that income is to be: (1) distributed to the grantor or to his or her spouse; (2) held or accumulated for future distribution to the grantor or to his or her spouse; or (3) applied to pay the premiums on policies of life insurance on the life of the grantor or his or her spouse. § 677(a). The grantor is taxed, too, on that trust income if it may be used for any of these purposes at the discretion of the grantor or some other person who is not considered an adverse party for these purposes (applying the statutory definition). An adverse party is a person having a substantial beneficial interest in the trust which would be adversely affected by the exercise or nonexercise of the power which he or she possesses. § 672(a).

The rationale for taxing trust income to the grantor where he or she has the benefit of that income is obvious. Consider Leeza. She created an irrevocable trust, funded it with income producing securities, and stipulated in the trust agreement that the trust income was to be used to pay the premiums on insurance on her life. After her death, the insurance proceeds were to continue in trust for the benefit of her son, Bubba. In just such a case, Burnet v. Wells, 289 U.S. 670 (1933), the Supreme Court concluded that it was constitutionally permissible to tax the trust income to the trust grantor where it was used to pay premiums on insurance on the life of the grantor. In reaching its conclusion, the Court noted that "there has been a progressive endeavor by the Congress and the courts to bring about a correspondence between the legal concept of ownership and the economic realities of enjoyment or fruition." The Court explained further:

The controversy is one as to the boundaries of legislative power. It must be dealt with in a large way, as questions of due process always are, not narrowly or pedantically, in slavery to forms or phrases. "Taxation is not so much concerned with the refinements of title as it is with the actual command over the property taxed—the actual benefit for which the tax is paid." Corliss v. Bowers, [281 U.S.] 378. * * * Refinements of title have at times supplied the rule when the question has been one of construction and nothing more, a question as to the meaning of a taxing act to be read in favor of the taxpayer. Refinements of title are without controlling force when a statute, unmistakable in meaning, is assailed by a taxpayer as overpassing the bounds of reason, an exercise by the lawmakers of arbitrary power. In such circumstances the question is no longer whether the concept of ownership reflected in the statute is to be squared with the concept embodied, more or less vaguely, in common law traditions. The question is whether it is one that an enlightened legislator might act upon without affront to justice. Even administrative convenience, the practical necessities of an efficient system of taxation, will have heed and recognition within reasonable limits. * * * Liability does not have to rest upon the enjoyment by the taxpayer of all the privileges and benefits enjoyed by the most favored owner at a given time or place. * * * Government in casting about for proper subjects of taxation is not confined by the traditional classification of interests or estates. It may tax not only ownership, but any right or privilege that is a constituent of ownership. * * * Liability may rest upon the enjoyment by the taxpayer of privileges and benefits so substantial and important as to make it reasonable and just to deal with him as if he were the owner, and to tax him on that basis. A margin must be allowed for the play of legislative judgment. To overcome this statute the taxpayer must show that in attributing to him the ownership of the income of the trusts, or something fairly to be dealt with as equivalent to ownership, the lawmakers

¶ 31,049

have done a wholly arbitrary thing, have found equivalence where there was none nor anything approaching it, and laid a burden unrelated to privilege or benefit. * * * The statute, as we view it, is not subject to that reproach.

The Court explained that life insurance, to many, is thought of as a "pressing social duty", that life insurance is "a common item in the family budget, kept up very often at the cost of painful sacrifice", and that "[t]rusts for the preservation of policies of insurance involve a continuing exercise by the settlor of a power to direct the application of the income along predetermined channels." Thus, the Court concluded that "Congress does not play the despot in ordaining that trusts for such uses * * * shall be treated for the purpose of taxation as if the income of the trust had been retained by the grantor."

So as to put to rest any notion that there was unanimity on the *Wells* Court, note the dissenting opinion (which follows in pertinent part). Keep in mind, that the argument advanced in the dissent has long since been put to rest as a matter of legislative policy development as expressed in § 677(a). For the antiquarians, here is the other side of the coin:

> The powers of taxation are broad, but the distinction between taxation and confiscation must still be observed. So long as the Fifth Amendment remains unrepealed and is permitted to control, Congress may not tax the property of A as the property of B, or the income of A as the income of B.

> * * *

> It is not accurate, we think, to say that these trusts involve the continuing exercise by the settlor of a power to direct the application of the income along predetermined channels. The exertion of power on the part of the settlor to direct such application begins and ends with the creation of the irrevocable trusts. Thereafter, the power is to be exercised automatically by the trustee under a grant which neither he nor the settlor can recall or abridge. The income, of course, is taxable, but to the trustee, not to the settlor.

Problems

[¶ 31,061]

1. It should be noted that § 677 was amended by the Tax Reform Act of 1969 to require taxation of the settlor if the trust income may be distributed to or is accumulated for distribution to the settlor's spouse or may be applied to the maintenance of life insurance on the life of the settlor's spouse. Does this change square with the rationale of the *Wells* decision?

2. From a policy standpoint, would it be consistent to expand § 677 to tax the settlor on the income of a trust created for the benefit of a "family" member (ancestor, descendant, brother, or sister)? See Amabile v. Commissioner, 51 T.C.M. (CCH) 963, T.C.M. (P–H) ¶ 86,180 (1986)(grantor treated as owner of trust where trustee had discretion to distribute income to grantor's spouse).

¶ 31,061

3.   Pedro purchased income-producing real estate, financing 60 percent of the purchase price with a purchase-money mortgage. He thereupon transferred the property subject to the mortgage to an irrevocable trust for the benefit of his son, Kenny, for life, remainder as Kenny might appoint by will; in the absence of appointment by Kenny, the property is to be distributed in equal shares to Kenny's children. Under the terms of the trust, the income is to be applied first to the payment of principal and interest due on the purchase-money mortgage. Is Pedro taxable to any extent on the income of the trust? Rev. Rul. 54–516, 1954–2 C.B. 54; Loeb v. Commissioner, 159 F.2d 549 (7th Cir.1946) and Hays' Estate v. Commissioner, 181 F.2d 169 (5th Cir.1950).

4.   Sarah plans to create a substantial irrevocable trust for the benefit of, and ultimate distribution to, her children and grandchildren. It is Sarah's plan to grant broad powers to the independent trustee to apply trust income to the purchase of life insurance contracts on her life. Sarah would, of course, cooperate with the trustee in the acquisition of such contracts as assets of the trust. How would such a power affect the taxability of the trust income to Sarah? Would it make any difference whether the trustee exercised the power?

[¶ 31,067]

2.   FAMILY TRUSTS

Some taxpayers have undertaken to create trusts for their own benefit that are expressly irrevocable in the hope that the income from the trust will not be taxed to them (and that the trust property will not be included in their gross estates for estate tax purposes despite § 2036(a)(1)). These trusts are variously referred to within the trust documents as "a Constitutional Trust," "a Pure Equity Trust," even "a Family Trust." In and of themselves the names have no meaning, but the presence of such words in a trust should be enough to compel closer review of the document. Naturally, such broad-brush classifications do a disservice to the many trusts that are not designed to frustrate the fair and impartial administration of the tax system but that, coincidentally, bear the same descriptive titles.

Typically, so-called family trusts that are abusive will follow a similar pattern. Usually the settlor of the trust will transfer all of the property—both real and personal—to the trust, including the "exclusive right" to the settlor's "services and future earnings." While the beneficiaries of the trust are usually the settlor's children, normally the trustee is obligated to pay the living expenses of the settlor. The settlor's spouse is often the trustee, and distributions from the trust beneficiaries are totally discretionary with the trustee.

In Notice 97–24, 1997–16 I.R.B. 6, the IRS "warns taxpayers" about abusive trust arrangements and describes some of them in detail.

[¶ 31,073]

HOLMAN v. UNITED STATES

United States Court of Appeals, Tenth Circuit, 1984.
728 F.2d 462.

PER CURIAM.

* * *

Plaintiffs, husband and wife, sought to form a trust (the "Bruce Holman Family Estate") which would hold as corpus all personal and real property owned by plaintiffs. In addition, the trust acquired the exclusive right to plaintiff Bruce Holman's services and future earnings. The trust originally named plaintiffs and Bruce Holman's mother, Addie Duncan, as trustees. Approximately five months later, Addie Duncan resigned as trustee leaving plaintiffs as sole trustees. Plaintiffs were also named as officers of the trust for which they were to be paid consulting fees. Plaintiffs, their four children and the "Bruce Holman Educational and Research Trust" were named as beneficiaries. Plaintiffs continued to use their property in the same manner as they had prior to the creation of the trust. The trust was obligated to pay various living expenses for plaintiffs and their family, such as "rent" and maintenance on plaintiffs' home, utilities, automobile expenses such as gas, oil, maintenance, insurance premiums, as well as other miscellaneous expenses.

Under the terms of the trust, the beneficiaries were entitled to receive only what the trustees, in their discretion, decided to distribute. The trustees had the power to fix and pay compensation for themselves in their capacity as trustees. The trustees' powers were "construed as general powers of citizens of the United States of America, to do anything any citizen may do in any state or country," and essentially to take any action that they may "deem advantageous." The duration of the trust was stated as "twenty-five years from date, unless the trustees shall unanimously determine upon an earlier date."

In January 1974 plaintiffs received a letter from the Internal Revenue Service informing them that the Service would not recognize the trust for federal income tax purposes. Nevertheless, the Bruce Holman Family Estate (a Trust) filed a fiduciary income tax return for the tax years 1973 and 1974. Plaintiffs also filed a joint return for those years. The trust included in income the earnings of Dr. Holman and took deductions for various expenses such as payments to the plaintiffs as consultants, officers and trustees of the trust as well as other personal living expenses of plaintiffs.

Upon the filing of the returns in 1973 and 1974, plaintiffs were audited and their income was increased by the amounts reported by the trust. This amount was then decreased by deducting the amounts reported by plaintiffs as consulting fees and distributions from the trust, together with allowable deductions. As a result of the increase in income, plaintiffs were assessed

¶ 31,073

deficiencies for the tax years 1973 and 1974 for taxes, interest, and negligence penalties.

Plaintiffs paid the deficiency and brought the instant action for refund claiming that the trust was valid and that plaintiffs should not have been taxed on the trust's income.

* * *

Although this circuit has not yet considered the tax consequences of this type of "family trust," three circuits and the United States Tax Court have considered the issue and have uniformly applied the assignment of income doctrine and the grantor trust provisions in holding that trusts virtually identical to the one in question are mere shams designed for tax avoidance purposes. [Citations omitted.]

The assignment of income doctrine originated with the Supreme Court decision of Lucas v. Earl, 281 U.S. 111 (1930), which stands for the principle that income is taxed to the one who earned it. The Bruce Holman Family Estate Trust is a transparent attempt to assign the income earned by Dr. Holman. An examination of the terms of the trust reveals that the trust neither supervises Dr. Holman's employment nor determines his compensation. Vnuk, 621 F 2d at 1321. Furthermore, Dr. Holman is under no legal duty to earn money or perform services for the trust. Id. Dr. Holman is no less the earner of the income than he was before simply because he now purports to act as an "employee" or "servant" of the trust.

Under § 671, the grantor of a trust is treated as the owner of that trust if certain conditions specified in §§ 672–679 exist. Critical to the discussion here is § 674(a) which provides that:

> [T]he grantor shall be treated as the owner of any portion of a trust in respect of which the beneficial enjoyment of the corpus or the income therefrom is subject to a power of disposition, exercisable by the grantor or a nonadverse party, or both, without the approval or consent of any adverse party.

"Adverse party" is defined in § 672(a) as "any person having a substantial beneficial interest in the trust which would be adversely affected by the exercise or nonexercise of the power which he possesses respecting the trust." Section 677 * * * provides that the grantor is to be treated as the owner of any portion of a trust whose income could, in the discretion of the grantor or a nonadverse party or both, be distributed to, or accumulated for, the grantor's spouse. The regulations promulgated by the Treasury Department under § 677 specifically exclude the grantor's spouse as an adverse party. * * * § 1.677(a)–1(b)(2). It was on this basis that the district court ruled that the "grantor trust" provisions apply to the Holman Trust.

For the majority of the tax years in question, Bruce Holman and his wife, Audrey, were the sole trustees of the trust. In an attempt to circumvent the grantor trust provisions both Bruce and Audrey held beneficial interests in the trust assets. In this way, plaintiffs sought to be considered as adverse parties to each other thereby avoiding the effects of §§ 671–679. The only way

¶ 31,073

Audrey could be considered adverse would be if she exercised her power as trustee so as to prevent income from being distributed to herself as beneficiary. As pointed out in Vercio, 73 T.C. at 1248–49 and Luman v. Commissioner, 79 T.C. 846 (1982), it is inconceivable that the grantor's spouse would be motivated to prevent income from being distributed for her benefit. Therefore, Audrey cannot be an adverse party as to Bruce. Bruce and Audrey Holman were properly taxed on the income conveyed to the trust under §§ 671–79.

* * *

The Bruce Holman Family Estate (a Trust) is a mere sham, lacking any economic substance. See Hanson, 696 F.2d at 1234. The district court properly applied the assignment of income doctrine and the grantor trust provisions of * * * §§ 671–679 in determining that plaintiffs are not entitled to a refund for overpayment of taxes for the years 1973 and 1974.

* * *

[¶ 31,085]

3. OBLIGATIONS OF SUPPORT

The general rule of § 677 is plainly written and seems to leave little doubt as to its reach. However, § 677(b), while also apparently plainly written, has provoked much controversy. It appears to say that, if trust income is used for the "support or maintenance" of a person that the grantor is "legally obligated to support or maintain," the income "so applied" would be taxable to the grantor. The controversy has arisen over whether the distributions of income from a trust that are used for "support and maintenance" are taxable to the grantor only if the grantor was legally obligated to provide the particular items of support and maintenance for which the trust distributions were applied. See A. James Casner, Estate Planning 228, fn. 79 (4th ed. 1979). A taxpayer's legal obligation may arise out of contract or as a result of a duty imposed by state law.

What is included in the obligation of support is much debated. Is it only the necessaries of life or does it include college education?

Gift tax implications of transfers for the support or maintenance of a child are noted at ¶ 3125.

[¶ 31,090]

WYCHE v. UNITED STATES

United States Court of Claims Trial Judge's Report, 1974.
36 A.F.T.R. 2d (P–H) 75–5816.

WOOD, Trial Judge: * * *

The first issue is whether or not the income from the corpus of three * * * trusts established by plaintiff for the benefit of his three children is, to the extent used to pay for private school tuition and music and dancing lessons for the children, includible in plaintiff's income for the said years. The facts relating to this issue follow.

Plaintiffs have three children, all of whom were minors throughout the period 1963–67. In 1957, 1960, and 1963, respectively, plaintiff, a successful practicing attorney in Greenville, South Carolina, established three separate trusts, each for the benefit of all of the children, and each extending for more than 10 years, with Mrs. Wyche as trustee. The corpus of each trust consisted of rental real property in Greenville.

Under each trust, the trustee was required, after collecting rentals and paying expenses, to distribute to each of the beneficiaries, in equal shares, all of the current income of each trust, at least annually, on or before April 1 following the preceding calendar year. Under the terms of each trust, the distribution of income could be made directly to the beneficiaries or by "depositing the same in a bank or savings account in the beneficiaries' names, or by purchasing securities in the beneficiaries' names, or the expending of said sums for the education of said beneficiaries."

During each of the years in issue, a portion of the current income of the trusts (administered, at all times here relevant, as a single trust, with all receipts or disbursements processed through a bank account in the name of Mrs. Wyche as trustee) was used to pay for tuition at a private day school, and for certain music and dancing lessons, for plaintiffs' children. The total amount of all such payments, for the years 1963–67, amounted to some $8,500. Plaintiff was financially able to make all such payments from his own funds.

Plaintiffs' children began to attend Christ Church Episcopal School in 1960, at which time plaintiffs' son was in the fourth grade, one daughter was in the first grade, and one daughter was in kindergarten. For two of the children plaintiff, and for one of the children Mrs. Wyche, signed an application form (essentially an information sheet) in connection with their commencement of such attendance. Thereafter, however, plaintiffs did not execute any document with or for the School.

The School had elected as a matter of policy not to enter into contractual arrangements with parents (or others) desirous of having a child attend the School. Instead, tuition charges and enrollment fees (the latter to reserve a place for a current student during the next school year) were payable in advance of school attendance. Tuition charges and enrollment fees for plaintiffs' children were paid from trust funds in advance of any due date. Thus, their accounts were never delinquent, and no bills for tuition were ever sent to plaintiffs, the trustee, or the children.

Payments to the School were made by use of a check printed "Harriet S. Wyche, Trustee." Such checks were made payable to one of plaintiffs' children, and endorsed by the child. Mrs. Wyche then either took the check, or cashed it and took the proceeds, to the School. In the latter event, Mrs. Wyche advised the School representative receiving the money (normally the Church Treasurer or a clerk in that office) that the cash payment was being made from trust funds.

During the years 1963 through 1967, free elementary and secondary public schools, primarily supported by local property taxes, were available in

¶ 31,090

Greenville County, South Carolina, and plaintiffs' children might have attended such public schools at no cost to plaintiffs. Throughout at least most of that period, if not all of it, attendance of a child at any school (public, private, or parochial) was not compulsory under South Carolina law.

During the years 1963–67, a portion of the income of the trusts was also used to pay for music and dancing lessons for one or more of plaintiffs' children. Again, there were no written contracts. Both the music teacher and the ballet teacher were informed by Mrs. Wyche that the trusts were the source of funds for such lessons, and payments, from trust funds, were generally made in essentially the same manner as were payments to the School. On some occasions, however, a check on the trustee account was drawn in favor of the appropriate teacher.

Except for his execution of application forms for two of the children in connection with their commencement of attendance at the School, plaintiff had no contact with either the School or the music and dancing teachers. Plaintiffs' children were not required to attend private school, or to take lessons in music or dancing. One child ultimately decided to, and did, attend public school, and one or more children did not take music or dancing lessons during some of the years in suit.

Under Section 677(a) * * * the grantor "shall be treated as the owner of any portion of a trust * * * whose income without the approval or consent of any adverse party is, or, in the discretion of the grantor or a nonadverse party, or both, may be * * * "distributed to the grantor. Under Section 677(b), however, trust income "shall not be considered taxable to the grantor under subsection (a) * * * merely because such income in the discretion of * * * the trustee * * * may be applied or distributed for the support or maintenance of a beneficiary whom the grantor is legally obligated to support or maintain, except to the extent that such income is so applied or distributed. * * * "

Rev. Rul. 56–484, 1956–2 Cum. Bull. 23, provides, in effect, that trust income "used in the discharge or satisfaction, in whole or in part, of a legal obligation of any person to support or maintain a minor is, to the extent so used, taxable to such person * * *. However, the amount of such income includible in the gross income of a person obligated to support or maintain a minor *is limited by the extent of his obligations under local law*." (Emphasis supplied.)

The injection into the decisional process of the utilization of state law to determine Federal income tax consequences in a case such as this has rightfully been said to pose difficult problems in terms of tax equity and inequity. * * * It is clear, however, that "local law" is here determinative.

Under South Carolina law, plaintiff had (in broad terms) a statutory obligation to provide for his children "the actual necessaries of life. * * *." It is not disputed that obligation extended (notwithstanding the absence of any state statute making school attendance compulsory throughout most if not all of the period here relevant) to education of plaintiff's minor children. * * * Plaintiff's position is, rather, that, under South Carolina law, he had no legal obligation whatever to send his children to private day school, or to provide music and dancing lessons for them, and that, accordingly, the taxing of trust income so used to plaintiff is erroneous and unlawful.

Defendant agrees that the primary issues on this phase of the matter are whether plaintiff was legally obligated under South Carolina law to send his children to private day school, or to afford them such private lessons, but contends that under South Carolina law plaintiff plainly had a legal obligation to do both. Defendant also asserts, alternatively, that plaintiff impliedly obligated himself to pay the amounts in question actually paid from trust income, and that those amounts are accordingly taxable to plaintiff under Section 677 in any event.

In Brooke v. United States, 300 F.Supp. 465 (D.C.Mont.1969), the court, equating a court-administered guardianship with a trust for purposes of Section 677, considered whether payments by the "trustee" from "trust" income for, inter alia, private school tuition and music, swimming, and public speaking lessons for his minor children were in discharge of his legal obligations under Montana law. Under Montana law, a parent must give his child "support and education suitable to his circumstances." Plaintiff in Brooke, in the years there relevant, had income ranging from $26,000 to $30,000.

With plain cognizance of "the result that should happen as a matter of tax equality," the court nonetheless held squarely that the amounts expended for private school tuition and lessons were "not items which plaintiff was legally required to provide for the support and maintenance of the children," and, accordingly, were not includible in the parent's income. Brooke v. United States, supra, 300 F.Supp. at 466–67. That holding was unanimously affirmed on appeal. Brooke v. United States, 468 F.2d 1155 (9th Cir.1972).

Defendant urges that the decision in Brooke reflects a narrow, minority, view of the obligation of a parent to support his minor children, and that, in other jurisdictions (indeed, defendant says, in a majority of the states), a different rule would apply. * * *

These arguments are wide of the mark. The determinative consideration here is South Carolina law, and upon a careful consideration of the record and the briefs and arguments of the parties, together with extensive independent research, it is concluded that, for the years here relevant, plaintiff had no legal obligation under South Carolina law to send his children to private day school or to afford them music and dancing lessons.

* * *

Defendant alternatively contends that plaintiff had an implied contractual obligation to pay the cost of his children's tuition at private day school, and the costs of their music and dancing lessons. Relying on Morrill v. United States, 228 F.Supp. 734 (D.C.Me.1964), defendant asserts that since the

¶ 31,090

amounts here in issue were used to satisfy such an obligation, they are accordingly taxable to plaintiff under Section 677(a).

* * *

Insofar as here relevant, that holding rested on a finding that the schools believed Mr. Morrill responsible for payment of bills incurred on behalf of his children, and the "settled principle of contract law that when one renders services to another at the request, or with the knowledge and consent, of the others, and the surrounding circumstances make it reasonable for him to believe that he will receive payment therefor from the other, and he does so believe, a promise to pay will be inferred, and there is an implied contract." Ibid. Thus, it was held, Mr. Morrill alone was legally liable for payment of the amounts there in issue. On the facts of this cause, however, that "settled principle" is clearly inapplicable.

There being no valid basis for attribution to plaintiff of the trust income in question, plaintiffs are entitled to recover on this issue.

* * *

Note

[¶ 31,097]

In Stone v. Commissioner, T.C. Memo 1987–454, the court, looking to California divorce cases as precedent, concluded that a parent's affluence rendered "private" high school education furnished his child a part of his legal obligation of support—and, accordingly trust dollars expended for this purpose were taxable to the parent having the obligation rather than to the trust. Furthermore, in *Braun*, below, the court looked at New Jersey divorce cases as precedent, and also concluded that parent's affluence rendered his child's college expenses a part of his legal obligation of support—and, again, trust dollars expended for this purpose were taxable to the parent having the obligation rather than to the trust. Reconciling *Wyche* with *Stone* and *Braun* may well turn on the precedental value of legal obligation of support determinations made in the context of divorce. Despite the *Braun* court's statement, should support and maintenance be relative, i.e., one standard, perhaps taking into account parental affluence, applies when parents are divorcing, and another standard, perhaps one more modest in aspiration, when divorce and division of parental financial responsibility are not at issue? However, *Stone*, like *Braun*, relying on divorce precedents, did not recognize a different standard and, in a footnote, quickly differentiated Brooke v. United States, 468 F.2d 1155 (9th Cir. 1972), a case arising under Montana law, (and cited approvingly in Wyche) where the court found that expenditures for private schooling were not legal obligations of the taxpayer. The *Stone* court explained that "few facts were reported" in *Brooke*, and those reported were "markedly different", and that the "similar" Montana statute "was not identical to the California statute."

[¶ 31,098]

BRAUN v. COMMISSIONER

United States Tax Court, 1984.
48 T.C.M. (CCH) 210, T.C.M. (P–H) ¶ 84,285.

WHITAKER, Judge:

* * * [Dr. Frederick Braun and his wife, Marjorie, jointly established one trust for the benefit of three of their children (Trust I) and another trust for the benefit of their other three children (Trust II). Dr. and Mrs. Braun and "a friend," Mr. Torres, were the trustees. The terms of each trust provided that "the entire net income is to be distributed to the three children for whom the trust was established."]

* * * All of the distributed income was used for educational purposes. In 1976, 1977 and 1978, from Trust I the disbursements were for college tuition, room and board for Cynthia and Fred, two of the three beneficiaries of that trust. Both children were over 18 years of age in 1976. In 1976 the income from Trust II was used for tuition at the private high school attended by two of that trust's beneficiaries, Stephen and Christopher. In 1977 and 1978, a portion of the Trust II income was used for tuition, room and board of Stephen at college and a portion for Christopher at the private high school. During these years, none of the income was used for one beneficiary of each trust. Stephen became 18 in December of 1976, whereas Christopher did not become 18 until 1979.

* * *

Under section 677(b), the income of a trust is taxable to the grantor to the extent that such income is applied or distributed for the support or maintenance of a beneficiary whom the grantor is legally obligated to support or maintain. Petitioners argue that under New Jersey law the petitioners had no obligation to pay college tuition and room and board expenses of an unmarried child over 18 or to pay private school expense for an unmarried child under 18. Petitioners further argue that this issue has come up in New Jersey only in controversies between divorced parents and that such cases are inapplicable to this situation. We do not agree.

The recent decision of Newburgh v. Arrigo, 88 N.J. 529, 443 A.2d 1031 (1982), fully reviews the obligation of parents to continue to provide educational expenses for unmarried children over the age of 18. The Supreme Court of New Jersey held that necessary education is a flexible concept that can vary in different circumstances.

In general, financially capable parents should contribute to the higher education of children who are qualified students. In appropriate circumstances, parental responsibility includes the duty to assure children of a college and even of a post-graduate education such as law school. [Newburgh v. Arrigo, supra at 1038.]

In an adversarial situation, courts in New Jersey consider all relevant factors, which include 12 which were enumerated in Newburgh v. Arrigo, supra. It is obvious that many of these factors would have no bearing except

¶ 31,098

in a controversy between divorced parents or between a child and a noncustodial parent. But the support rule is not limited to such divorced parent context. Sakovits v. Sakovits, 178 N.J.Super. 623, 429 A.2d 1091, 1095 (1981). While many of these factors described by the New Jersey Supreme Court are not directly applicable to the instant facts, the import to our facts is clearly that petitioners retained the obligation to provide their children with a college education. They were both able and willing to do so, a college education was imminently reasonable in the light of the background, values and goals of the parents as well as the children, and petitioners have brought forward no facts or arguments which would militate against the recognition of this obligation on the part of these particular parents. Newburgh v. Arrigo, supra. With respect to private high school education, the law of New Jersey is less clear. There is dictum in the case of Rosenthal v. Rosenthal, 19 N.J. Super, 521, 88 A.2d 655 (1952), to the effect that a father is not required to provide his son with private school, college or professional training, or with any education beyond public schools, but that dictum as to college and professional education is certainly obsolete. Khalaf v. Khalaf, 58 N.J. 63, 275 A.2d 132, 137 (1971), refers with approval to Annot. 56 A.L.R.2d 1207 (1956). While that court's reference to the annotation was with respect to college expenses, the annotation also recognizes the existence of a parental obligation in similar circumstances to provide for private or boarding school education. It would be an anomaly to find a support obligation for college tuition for an emancipated child but none for private high school expense for a younger child in the same family. In view of the recent New Jersey cases cited, we do not think the dictum in Rosenthal v. Rosenthal, supra, represents the current view of the New Jersey courts. We believe that private high school education in appropriate cases would be held by the New Jersey courts to be within the scope of parental obligation. Accordingly, we hold that the income of these two trusts, to the extent actually utilized for tuition, room and board for four of the six children of petitioners was used to discharge Dr. Braun's legal support obligations and is therefore taxable to him under section 677(b).

Problems

[¶ 31,103]

Golda transferred property to Granite Trust Co. on trust with the direction that the income shall be distributed annually and applied to the maintenance and support of her grandson, Joel, until Joel attains age 25. At that time the trust is to terminate and the corpus distributed to Joel. Joel is 15 years old and is attending an exclusive preparatory school. During the current year, the income of the trust was applied to defray all of Joel's expenses.

(a) Is the income of the trust taxable to Milton, the father of Joel? §§ 662 and 677; Reg. § 1.662(a)–4.

(b) Would the result be different if the trust provided that Joel was to receive all of the trust income during the continuance of the trust? § 662.

(c) What would be the result if Milton were trustee with discretionary power to distribute income to Joel for Joel's support and maintenance? §§ 674, 677, and 678; see *Wyche* at ¶ 31,091.

Note

[¶ 31,109]

The Uniform Gifts to Minors Act (UGMA)—as well as the Uniform Transfers to Minors Act (UTMA), the successor act which has been adopted by the vast majority of states—provides a simplified procedure by which property can be held for the benefit of a person under 18 (or 21 years) of age without the formality of a trust or a formal guardianship proceeding in the state courts. The benefits (and burdens) of UTMA are obtained by titling property as "(name) as custodian under the Uniform Transfers to Minors Act as adopted by (state) for the benefit of (name of child)."

Income earned by property held in a custodianship is taxed directly to the child, the custodianship not being recognized as an income taxpaying entity (unlike a trust, which is an income taxpaying entity). Rev. Rul. 56–484, 1956–2 C.B. 23. However, in cases where custodianship income is used to discharge the legal obligation of support of another person, the custodianship income will be taxable to the person whose legal obligation was so discharged but only to the extent the custodianship income was applied to discharge that obligation. Thus, if the custodianship generated $1,000 of income but only $450 was used to discharge a parent's obligation of support, then only $450 would be taxed to the parent and the balance of the custodianship income that year would be taxed to the child. Rev. Rul. 59–357, 1959–2 C.B. 212, reprinted at ¶ 7127.

4. ADVERSE PARTY EXCEPTION

[¶ 31,115]

An adverse party is defined as any person having a substantial beneficial interest in the trust which would be adversely affected by the exercise or nonexercise of a power which he possesses. § 672(a). A trustee is not an adverse party merely because he is a fiduciary with respect to the trust. Reg. § 1.672(a)–1. However, the holder of a general power of appointment over the trust property is considered an adverse party.

Consider Michael. He was brain damaged at birth as a result of negligence. A substantial sum of money was awarded him in the resulting litigation. The damages were ordered to be placed in trust for Michael's benefit. The trust is not subject to revocation by Michael but is subject to amendment, modification, or revocation at any time by the court. The trust is to terminate when Michael attains 21 or dies. In the meantime, Bank, as trustee, has discretion to distribute income and principal to Michael for his health, education, support and maintenance. To date the trust income has always exceeded the amounts Bank has distributed to Michael. The IRS position is that all the trust income is taxable to Michael under the grantor trust rules in the year it is earned by the trust even though some of that income is warehoused in the trust and not distributed to Michael. Rev. Rul. 83–25, 1983–1 C.B. 116. While the damages themselves are excluded from Michael's income by § 104(a)(29), as owner of the damages Michael is considered the grantor of the trust. Both the distributed and the undistributed income is taxable to Michael under § 677(a) because it is either distributed to him or held and accumulated for future distribution to him at the discretion of a nonadverse party.

Problem

[¶ 31,121]

Does the IRS position in Rev. Rul. 83–25, ¶ 31,115, suggest that it is impossible to create a trust for your own benefit yet cause the income to be taxed to the trust to the extent that the income is not needed by you? Or can you suggest techniques by which such a trust can be created by taking advantage of the adverse party exception? See § 672.

E. POWER TO CONTROL BENEFICIAL ENJOYMENT

[¶ 31,127]

1. GENERAL RULE

Section 674(a) provides that the grantor of a trust will be taxed on the income generated by the trust to the extent that "the beneficial enjoyment of the corpus or the income therefrom is subject to a power of disposition, exercisable by the grantor or a nonadverse party, or both, without the approval or consent of any adverse party." The theory is, obviously, that a person should not be able to shift income to another while controlling the enjoyment of that income.

[¶ 31,133]

BRAUN v. COMMISSIONER

United States Tax Court, 1984.
48 T.C.M. (CCH) 210, T.C.M. (P–H) ¶ 84,285.

[The facts are set forth at ¶ 31,097.]

Respondent assumes that Mr. Torres is not an adverse party. The term "adverse party" is defined in § 672 to mean "any person having a substantial beneficial interest in the trust which would be adversely affected by the exercise or nonexercise of the power which he possesses respecting the trust." A nonadverse party means any party who is not an adverse party. We agree with respondent that Mr. Torres is not an adverse party. Thus, under § 674(a), the issue is whether or not the grantors as trustees, along with Mr. Torres, retained the power to sprinkle the income among the three beneficiaries of each of the two trusts.

¶ 31,133

The trust instrument does not prescribe the shares of each of the three beneficiaries of each trust in the income. While one might tend to assume that each beneficiary was entitled to an equal share, New Jersey follows the rule that extrinsic evidence may be considered to interpret the terms of a trust which is ambiguous. * * * The extrinsic evidence in this case illustrating intent, which under New Jersey law can be looked to, is the contemporaneous action by the parties, that is, the grantor-trustees in making distributions from the two trusts. In each trust, during each of the years, one of the beneficiaries was ignored altogether and income which was distributed was utilized in varying amounts for the benefit of the other two beneficiaries without any apparent pattern. This clearly evidences a sprinkling of the income among the beneficiaries. On the basis of the New Jersey cases cited, we conclude that the trust instrument must be construed as permitting such sprinkling. We agree with respondent that this is not a case such as Bennett v. Commissioner, 79 T.C. 470, 487 (1982), where the grantor-trustees misadministered the express directions of the trust instrument. Based on this interpretation of these trust instruments, we hold that the income of the two trusts is taxable to petitioners under section 674(a).

[¶ 31,139]

2. EXCEPTIONS TO GENERAL RULE

There are numerous exceptions to the general rule that the grantor is treated as the owner of a trust, regardless of its duration, where the beneficial enjoyment of the trust property or income is subject to a power of disposition exercisable by the grantor or by a nonadverse party. Whether a power is "excepted" from the reach of the general rule depends on the identity of the holder of that power. For example, some powers are excepted only if they are held by a trustee or trustees other than the grantor or a spouse living with the grantor. And some powers are excepted if they are held by a trustee or trustees who are other than the grantor and at least half of whom are independent. § 674(c) and Reg. § 1.674(a)–1(a).

[¶ 31,145]

a. Exception: Power to Apply Income of Dependent

A power to apply income to the support or maintenance of the grantor's dependents, exercisable by the grantor as trustee or by another person as trustee or otherwise, will only cause the income of the trust to be taxed to the grantor to the extent that such income is so applied and distributed. §§ 674(b)(1) and 677(b). In other words, the presence of this power alone will not attract tax to the grantor—it is the exercise of this power that is a taxable event for the grantor.

[¶ 31,151]

b. Exception: Power Exercisable Only by Will

In general, the grantor is not taxable on trust income if the grantor's power to control disposition is exercisable only by will. However, this exception is not applicable where the grantor, or a nonadverse party, or both, also has the power to accumulate trust income for disposition by will, without the approval or consent of any adverse party. § 674(b)(3). For example, if the grantor provides in the trust that the income is to be accumulated during the grantor's life and that the grantor may appoint the accumulated income in the will, the grantor is subject to income tax on the trust income.

[¶ 31,157]

c. Exception: Power to Withhold Income During Minority of Beneficiary

A power to pay or apply income to or for a beneficiary or to accumulate and add the income to the corpus, which is exercisable only while an income beneficiary is under age 21 or under some other legal disability, will not subject the grantor to tax. § 674(b)(7). Such a power is excepted even though the accumulated income will not be paid to the beneficiary from whom it is withheld. Accumulated income may be added to corpus and ultimately be distributed to others. Reg. § 1.674(b)–1(b)(7).

[¶ 31,163]

d. Exception: Powers Exercisable by Independent Trustees

A broader exception is made for certain powers exercisable solely by independent trustees. § 674(c). Trustees are often given the power to distribute, apportion or accumulate income to or for one or more beneficiaries or within a class of beneficiaries, or to pay out corpus to or for them. Such power will not subject the grantor to tax if it is solely exercisable by a trustee or trustees (without the consent of any other person), none of whom is the grantor, and no more than half of whom are related or subordinate parties who are subservient to the wishes of the grantor. Thus, in the ordinary sprinkling or spray trust, the co-trustees may be a corporate fiduciary and a family member (even the decedent grantor's spouse).

Technically speaking, a "related or subordinate party" means any nonadverse party who is the grantor's spouse, if they are living together; a parent, issue, brother or sister, or employee of the grantor; a corporation or any employee thereof in which the stock holdings of the grantor and the trust are significant from the viewpoint of voting control; or a subordinate employee of a corporation in which the grantor is an executive. There is a rebuttable presumption that a related or subordinate party is subservient to the grantor. § 672(c).

[¶ 31,169]

e. Exception: Power to Allocate Income Limited by Standard

A power to distribute, apportion or accumulate income to or for one or more beneficiaries or within a class of beneficiaries, but limited to a standard such as the reasonable needs of the beneficiaries, is excepted from the reach of the general rule. Such a power will not subject the grantor to tax if it is solely exercisable by a trustee or trustees, none of whom is the grantor or a spouse living with the grantor, provided such power is exercisable without the consent of any other person and is limited by a reasonably definite external standard that is set forth in the trust instrument. The exception applies even though the power is held by a related or subordinate trustee (other than the grantor's spouse living with the grantor), who is subservient to the grantor.

This power is not an excepted power, however, if any person has a power to add trust beneficiaries, except where the power is limited to providing for after-born or after-adopted children. § 674(d). Moreover, the power is not an excepted power if the grantor has an unrestricted power to remove the trustee, unless the grantor is under a duty to substitute another independent trustee. Reg. § 1.674(d)–2(a).

Unlike § 674(b)(6), § 674(d) permits distributions to remaindermen as well as to current income beneficiaries, and it makes no effort to insure that accumulated income will eventually be placed at the disposition of the beneficiary for whom it was withheld.

[¶ 31,175]

f. Other Exceptions

There are a number of other exceptions to the general rule that should be noted by reviewing § 674.

F. ADMINISTRATIVE POWERS

[¶ 31,181]

All the income of a trust will be taxed to the grantor—rather than to the trust or to the person to whom the income is distributed—if under the terms of the trust the trust is or can be administered for the benefit of the grantor. Section 675 provides specifically for cases in which the grantor or a nonadverse party has the power to deal with or dispose of the trust property for less than adequate and full consideration; or has the power to borrow trust funds without adequate interest or adequate security; or has the power to control trust investments or reacquire the trust property by substituting property of an equivalent value (except in cases where these powers of administration are exercisable by the grantor or nonadverse party only when serving in a fiduciary capacity).

[¶ 31,187]

REVENUE RULING 85–13

1985–1 C.B. 184.

* * *

In 1980, A, an individual, created an irrevocable trust, T. W., A's spouse, is the trustee of T. The trust instrument of T provides that all income of T is to be paid semiannually to C, A's child, for a term of 15 years. Upon

¶ 31,169

expiration of the trust term, or if C dies before the trust term expires, the corpus of T will be distributed to C's child or to the estate of C's child. Neither A nor any other person has a power over or an interest in T that would cause A to be treated as the owner of T under the grantor trust provisions , section 671 and following.

A funded T with a contribution of 100 shares of stock in Corporation Z. When A funded T, a's basis in the shares was $20x.

On December 27, 1981, when the fair market value of the Corporation Z shares was $40x, W, as trustee, transferred the 100 shares to A. In exchange, A gave W A's unsecured promissory note with a face amount of $40x, bearing an adequate annual rate of interest, payable semiannually, beginning six months following the date on which the shares were transferred to A. Principal payments on the note were scheduled to be paid in 10 equal annual installments, the first installment being due 3 years following the date on which the 100 shares were transferred to A, December 27, 1984.

On January 20, 1984, A sold the 100 shares to an unrelated party for $50x. Corporation Z did not make any distributions with respect to the 100 shares at any time before the sale of those shares to the unrelated party.

LAW AND ANALYSIS

Under section 675(3), a grantor will be treated as the owner of any portion of a trust in respect of which the grantor has directly or indirectly borrowed the trust corpus or income and has not completely repaid the loan, including any interest, before the beginning of the taxable year, unless the loan (1) provides for adequate interest, (2) is adequately secured, and (3) is not made by the grantor or by a related or subordinate trustee who is subservient to the grantor.

* * * [Reg. §] 1.675–1 * * * explains that, in effect, section 675 treats the grantor as the owner of a trust if under the terms of the trust instrument, or the circumstances attendant to its operation, administrative control is exercisable primarily for the benefit of the grantor rather than the beneficiaries of the trust. Section 675(3) differs from the other provisions of section 675 which provide rules for determining grantor ownership of a trust, because it requires an affirmative act (borrowing) rather than a retained power, before it applies. Nevertheless, the same theme underlies section 675(3) as underlies the other provisions of section 675 which treat the grantor as owning the trust. In all of these cases the justification for treating the grantor as owner is evidence of substantial grantor dominion and control over the trust.

* * *

In this case, A has acquired control over and use of the entire trust corpus, the 100 shares of Corporation Z stock, in exchange for A's unsecured note. If A, instead of giving W a note in exchange for the 100 shares, had made a cash payment of $40x to W and subsequently borrowed that cash, giving W the unsecured note to evidence the borrowing, section 675(3) * * * would be applicable and a would be the owner of T. Although A did not engage in this kind of direct borrowing, A's acquisition of the entire corpus of

¶ 31,187

T in exchange for an unsecured note was, in substance, the economic equivalent of borrowing trust corpus. Accordingly, under section 675(3), A is treated as the owner of the portion of T represented by A's promissory note. Further, because the promissory note is T's only asset, A is treated as the owner of the entire trust.

Because A is treated as the owner of the entire trust, A is considered to be the owner of the trust assets for federal income tax purposes. [Citations omitted.] In this case, A is considered to be the owner of the promissory note held by the trust. Therefore, the transfer of the Corporation Z shares by T to A is not recognized as a sale for federal income tax purposes because A is both the maker and the owner of the promissory note. A transaction cannot be recognized as a sale for federal income tax purposes if the same person is treated as owning the purported consideration both before and after the transaction. See Dobson v. Commissioner, 1 B.T.A. 1082 (1925).

A's basis in the shares received from T will be equal to A's basis in the shares at the time he funded T because the basis of the shares was not adjusted during the period that T held them. See Rev. Rul. 72–406, 1972–2 C.B. 462, a ruling involving the determination of a grantor's basis in property upon reversion of that property to the grantor at the expiration of a trust's term.

In Rothstein v. United States, 735 F.2d 704 (2d Cir.1984), the court considered a transaction that is in substance identical to the facts described in this ruling. The court held that the grantor was the owner of a trust under section 675(3) because by exchanging an unsecured note for the entire trust corpus, the grantor had indirectly borrowed the trust corpus. The court held further, however, that although the grantor must be treated as the owner of the trust, this means only that the grantor must include items of income, deduction, and credit attributable to the trust in computing the grantor's taxable income and credits, and that the trust must continue to be viewed as a separate taxpayer. The court held, therefore, that the transfer of trust corpus to the grantor in exchange for an unsecured promissory note was a sale and that the taxpayer acquired a cost basis in the assets.

In *Rothstein*, as in this case, section 671 requires that the grantor includes [sic] in computing the grantor's tax liability all items of income, deduction, and credit of the trust as though the trust were not in existence during the period the grantor is treated as the owner. Section 1.671–3(a)(1). It is anomalous to suggest that Congress, in enacting the grantor trust provisions * * *, intended that the existence of a trust would be ignored for purposes of attribution of income, deduction, and credit, and yet, retain its vitality as a separate entity capable of entering into a sales transaction with the grantor. The reason for attributing items of income, deduction, and credit to the grantor under section 671 is that, by exercising dominion and control over a trust, either by retaining a power over or an interest in the trust, or, as in this case, by dealing with the trust property for the grantor's benefit, the grantor has treated the trust property as though it were the grantor's property. The Service position of treating the owner of an entire trust as the

¶ 31,187

owner of the trust's assets is, therefore, consistent with and supported by the rationale for attributing items of income, deduction, and credit to the grantor.

The court's decision in *Rothstein*, insofar as it holds that a trust owned by a grantor must be regarded as a separate taxpayer capable of engaging in sales transactions with the grantor, is not in accord with the views of the Service. Accordingly, the Service will not follow *Rothstein*.

HOLDINGS

(1) A's receipt of the entire corpus of the trust in exchange for A's unsecured promissory note constituted an indirect borrowing of the trust corpus which caused a to be the owner of the entire trust under section 675(3).

(2) At the time A became the owner of the trust, A became the owner of the trust property. As a result, the transfer of trust assets to A was not a sale for federal income tax purposes and A did not acquire a cost basis in those assets. Accordingly, when A sold the shares of Corporation Z stock on January 20, 1984, A recognized gain of $30x (amount realized of $50x less adjusted basis of $20x). Further, this holding would apply even if the trust held other assets in addition to A's promissory note if A, under any of the grantor trust provisions, was treated as the owner of the portion of the trust represented by the promissory note because A would be treated as the owner of the purported consideration (the promissory note) both before and after the transaction. See § 1.671–3(a)(2).

Problems

[¶ 31,193]

1. Refer to §§ 674 and 675 (and the other sections of the grantor trust rules) and make a list of all powers that can be included in a trust without causing the income from the trust property to be taxed to the person who establishes the trust.

2. Similarly, make a list of all limitations that must be placed on the trust if the grantor is to avoid being taxed on the trust income during his or her lifetime.

3. Describe the additional limitations that must burden the trust if the trustee is the person who establishes the trust.

[¶ 31,199]

REVENUE RULING 86–82

1986–1 C.B. 253.

ISSUE

If the grantor of a trust borrows the entire trust corpus and makes complete repayment of principal and interest within the same year, is that grantor treated as owner of the trust under section 675(3)?

FACTS

On May 11, 1985, A created an irrevocable trust for the benefit of A's children. The trust instrument names A trustee and gives a power to borrow trust corpus or income at the market rate of interest with adequate security. On June 11, 1985, A borrowed 100x dollars from the trust in compliance with these requirements. The borrowed funds comprised the entire trust corpus. On November 3, 1985, A repaid the loan plus interest. Both A and the trust are calendar year taxpayers.

LAW AND ANALYSIS

Section 671 provides that if any section of subpart E of subchapter J treats the grantor as the owner of any portion of the trust, then the grantor must include in computing taxable income those items of income, deductions, and credits which are attributable to that portion of the trust.

Section 675(3) provides that, generally, the grantor of a trust will be treated as the owner of any portion of a trust in respect to which the grantor has borrowed the corpus or income and has not completely repaid the loan, including any interest, before the beginning of the taxable year.

In Mau v. United States, 355 F.Supp. 909 (D.Haw.1973), the taxpayer established five separate trusts, with the taxpayer designated trustee of each. In 1965, the taxpayer borrowed money from each of the trusts. These amounts were not repaid until 1969. The taxpayer argued that section 675(3) did not cause the taxpayer-grantor to be liable for federal income tax on the trusts' 1965 income because the loans were not outstanding at the beginning of the year. The court rejected this interpretation of the statute, reasoning that section 675(3) was enacted to prevent the shifting of taxable income in situations where a grantor retained control and use of trust properties through borrowing. Therefore, the court held that the borrowing of trust corpus or income by a grantor at any time during a taxable year would result in the grantor being taxed on trust income for that entire year under section 675(3). The court concluded that the taxpayer was taxable on income of the trusts in 1965, the year the borrowing occurred, even though the loans were made after the beginning of the year. If section 675(3) otherwise applies for a given year, its effect is not avoided by making repayment before the year closes. *Mau* therefore stands for the principle that section 675(3) applies for any year during any part of which a loan by a trust to the grantor-trustee is outstanding.

In the present case, A borrowed the entire trust corpus during calendar 1985. Accordingly, A is treated as the owner of the entire trust under section 675(3) in spite of the fact that A made full payment of principal and interest before the close of 1985. See section 1.671–3(b)(3). Hence, under section 671, A must include in gross income all income earned by the trust in 1985.

* * *

¶ 31,199

Note

[¶ 31,205]

In Pvt. Ltr. Rul. 8802004, a taxpayer, in his capacity as trustee of an irrevocable trust that he had created, failed to enforce the terms of a promissory note held by him as trustee. As a result, the trust was determined to be a grantor trust and the trust income was taxed to the taxpayer personally on the ground that the failure to enforce the repayment terms of the note constituted a borrowing by the taxpayer from the trust under § 675(3). The facts were unusual. The note, secured by real estate, had been given by a partnership in which the taxpayer was a partner. After the taxpayer placed the note in trust, the partnership terminated and the taxpayer became the sole obligor on the note. Essentially the taxpayer, in his individual capacity, was obligated to himself as trustee. When the cash flow from the encumbered property proved to be less than the obligation on the note, the taxpayer passed through to the trust only the amount of the cash flow despite his obligation under the note to pay a greater amount. The IRS concluded that the taxpayer, in effect, extended credit to himself on terms different from those contained in the mortgage note. This new extension of credit was the economic equivalent of a transaction in which the borrower renegotiates a loan with a lender and substitutes a new note for a preexisting one. In each instance, there is a new borrowing for purposes of § 675(3).

The IRS pointed to the regulations and legislative history and commented that "section 675 was enacted to ensure that ownership of a trust is attributed to a grantor in those situations where a trust is administered in a manner that primarily benefits the grantor."

G. REVERSIONARY INTERESTS

[¶ 31,211]

1. INTRODUCTION

Generally speaking, a grantor will be taxed on the income from each trust in which the grantor retains a reversion. More specifically, reversionary trusts—trusts providing benefits to persons other than the grantor but followed by a reversion in the grantor at the death of the nongrantor beneficiary or after a term of years—are effective income-shifting devices only in cases where the value of the grantor's reversionary interest, at the inception of the trust, is valued at five percent or less of the value of that portion of the trust in which the grantor has the reversionary interest. § 673(a).

Example 1: Lazlo established an irrevocable trust with Accumulation National Bank. Lazlo funded the trust with $100,000 and provided that the trust was to continue until the first to occur of the following events: (a) the death of his son, Boris, age twenty at the time the trust was created; or (b) the 46th anniversary of the creation of the trust. During the continuance of the trust, all trust income is to be paid to Boris. Upon termination of the trust, the property then constituting the trust is to be paid over to Lazlo. In this case, the trust income is taxable to Boris and not to Lazlo since the value of Lazlo's reversion is only $4,996 (using Table S prescribed in Reg. § 20.2031–7, and assuming an applicable interest rate of 6.8 percent). Had the trust been created for only 45 years (and its duration was in no way related to Boris' age), the trust income would be taxable to Lazlo rather than Boris even though Boris received that income because the value of Lazlo's reversion (using Table B prescribed in Reg. § 20.2031–7 and assuming an applicable interest rate of 6.8 percent) would be $5,179.60, which is more than five percent of the value of the trust corpus at the inception of the trust. Similarly, if Boris was 21 at the trust's creation and the trust was to last for his life, the trust income would be taxable to Lazlo because the value of Lazlo's reversion (using Table B) would be $5,217, which is more than five percent of the value of the trust corpus at the inception of the trust.

Example 2: Margaret established an irrevocable trust with Rockhard Bank & Trust. Margaret funded the trust with $100,000 and provided that the trust was to continue until the first to occur of the following events: (a) the death of her mother, Gert, age 60 at the time the trust was created; or (b) the 60th anniversary of the creation of the trust. During the continuance of the trust, all trust income is to be paid to Gert. Upon termination of the trust, the property then constituting the trust is to be paid over to Margaret. In this case, the trust income is taxable to Margaret and not to her mother, Gert, since the value of Margaret's reversion, $32,963 (determined using Table S provided by Reg. § 20.2031–7, and assuming an applicable interest rate of 6.8 percent) is greater than 5 percent of the value of the trust corpus. Note that using Table B would have provided a reversionary value of only $1,930.70, well within the five-percent limit. However, Table S, relating to life expectancy, must be used since it causes a higher value to be placed on Margaret's reversionary interest.

It should be noted, too, that, in determining the value of any reversionary interest, it is assumed that any discretionary powers over the trust, by whomsoever possessed, will be exercised for the maximum benefit of the grantor. § 673(c).

[¶ 31,217]

2. INTERESTS TAKING EFFECT AT DEATH OF MINORS

Oftentimes taxpayers make gifts in trust for the benefit of a child, the trust to last only until the child attains 21 years of age, at which time the trust is to terminate and the property then constituting the trust estate is to be distributed to the child. This can be a tax-favored arrangement in the sense that the $10,000 per donee per annum gift tax exclusion will be available to shelter such a gift if the trust otherwise satisfies the requirements of § 2503(c). Section 673(b) anticipates that the grantor of such a trust may wish to retain, in that trust, a reversion that will be triggered only in the case where the child dies before attaining age 21. If the grantor retains a reversion in such a case, that retention alone will not cause the trust income to be taxed to the grantor (rather than to the child or to the trust itself) even though the value of the retained reversion may be greater than five percent of the trust property in which the grantor has the reversion.

[¶ 31,223]

3. "CLIFFORD" OR 10–YEAR TRUSTS

Reversionary trusts created before March 2, 1986—sometimes referred to as short-term trusts or 10–year trusts or even "Clifford trusts," after the case by the same name, Helvering v. Clifford, reproduced at ¶ 31,007—are subject to different rules. See Tax Reform Act of 1986, § 1402(c)(1). For trusts that qualify, the trust income is taxed to the trust or to the recipient of the trust income—rather than to the grantor. Reversionary trusts that qualify are those in which the reversion could not reasonably have been expected to take effect in possession and enjoyment in the grantor for more than 10 years after the transfer of the property to the trust. (Section 673(a), as it was then written, was the legislative authority for this tax preference.)

During the years when 10–year trusts offered income tax shifting opportunities, such trusts became almost commonplace. Taxpayers would establish a trust to last for 10 years and 1 day (or perhaps longer), during which time the trust income was to be paid to someone other than the grantor—such as the grantor's child or an elderly parent—with the result that the trust income would be taxed to the recipient of the income and not to the grantor. At the end of the trust term, the trust property would revert to the grantor. In cases where the child or elderly parent looked to the grantor for support, and the child or elderly parent was in a lower income tax bracket than the grantor, these so-called 10–year trusts were attractive income-shifting devices.

H. MALLINCKRODT TRUSTS

[¶ 31,229]

Section 678 describes the circumstances in which someone other than the grantor of a trust will be taxed on the income of the trust even though that other person does not receive that income. At first look, this rule appears harsh. However, since the circumstances under which it is applied are limited, it is principally a trap for many taxpayers who are attempting to shelter income in a trust while giving a beneficiary of the trust substantial control over the enjoyment of the trust income.

Section 678 is sometimes referred to as the *Mallinckrodt* rule in deference to the principal case—Mallinckrodt v. Nunan, 146 F.2d 1 (8th Cir.1945), cert. denied, 324 U.S. 871 (1945), reh'g denied, 325 U.S. 892 (1945)—which imposed liability upon a nongrantor nonrecipient. In *Mallinckrodt*, the taxpayer and an independent trust company served as co-trustees of an inter vivos trust created by taxpayer's father. The trust was for the benefit of the taxpayer, his wife, and their descendants, and the taxpayer was given a testamentary power of appointment over the corpus. After payment of $10,000 to his wife, taxpayer had the power to withdraw the balance of the annual trust income. In the absence of such withdrawal, the excess income was added to corpus. At any time, the taxpayer, with the consent of the co-trustee, could terminate the trust and receive the corpus. Although the taxpayer did not exercise any of these powers, he was held taxable as owner of the annual trust income in excess of $10,000.

Problems

[¶ 31,235]

1. Lotus was the sole trustee of three trusts, each established by the respective wills of her former husbands, who had predeceased Lotus. The trusts were the same in the sense that each trust was to continue for the life of Lotus and, upon her death, to terminate, the property then constituting the respective trusts to be distributed to the children born to Lotus and the spouse who had created that particular trust. The trusts differed, however, as to the distribution provisions during the lifetime of Lotus. Consider whether the trust income should be taxed to Lotus or to the respective trusts in the circumstances presented below. Note that Lotus believed that she had more than adequate resources for her support and, as a result, no distributions had ever been made from any of the trusts to Lotus. See § 678(a)(1).

    (a) Under the terms of the trust established by Lotus's first husband, all trust income was to be distributed to Lotus quarter-annually or more often.

    (b) Under the terms of the trust established by Lotus's second husband, Lotus, as sole trustee, had discretion to distribute to herself "such amounts of income and principal as she, in her sole discretion, shall determine to be essential to her well-being."

    (c) Under the terms of the trust established by Lotus's third husband, Lotus, as sole trustee, had discretion to distribute to herself "such amounts of income and principal as was necessary for health, education, maintenance, and support in her accustomed manner of living."

2. Refer to the immediately preceding problem and note that the trust established by Lotus's second husband provided that any income not distributed to Lotus at the end of each calendar year was to be added to the corpus of the trust. Note, too, that last year, Lotus resigned as trustee of the trust established by her second husband and was replaced as trustee by Accumulation National Bank. Accumulation National made no distributions from the trust to Lotus this year. Is the trust income taxable to the trust or to Lotus? The trust had $15,000 of income last year and $20,000 this year. The value of the trust corpus on December 31 of last year was $300,000; on December 31, this year, it was $400,000. See § 678(a)(2).

Chapter 32

INCOME IN RESPECT OF A
DECEDENT

(Section 691)

A. INTRODUCTION

[¶ 32,001]

Generally speaking, income in respect of a decedent (IRD) is taxable income received after a taxpayer has died. § 691. More specifically, it is income earned by the taxpayer prior to death but not properly includible on the taxpayer's final income tax return because the taxpayer was not eligible, for one reason or another, to collect the income prior to death. For example, if Daisy, a salaried employee compensated on a monthly basis, dies on a day other than the last day of the month, she will have earned wages for the period of the month she worked but, in many cases, will be ineligible to receive those wages until the end of the month. Accordingly, if Daisy is a cash-basis taxpayer (as distinguished from an accrual-basis taxpayer), the earned but uncollected income is not properly included on Daisy's final income tax return. Instead, that income, known as income in respect of a decedent (IRD) for federal income tax purposes, becomes income belonging to Daisy's estate. See § 691(a).

Other important illustrations of IRD are accrued vacation and leave pay; billed but uncollected fees; renewal commissions on sales of life insurance policies; lawyer's contingent fees; post death employer provided bonuses; distributions from tax-qualified retirement plans; and accrued interest on Series E and Series EE United States savings bonds.

It is important to note that IRD is subject to two taxes: the federal income tax and the federal estate tax. For example, consider the typical tax-qualified retirement plan. Established by an employer for the benefit of employees, subject to specified limits, the employer will be allowed an income tax deduction for plan contributions on behalf of employees in the year in which contributions are made. During the continuance of the plan, plan property is invested but no income taxes are imposed on the earnings of the plan property. However, distributions from the plan to the plan beneficiaries—usually the employee and the employee's spouse—constitute taxable income to the recipients of the distribution in the year of receipt. In addition, amounts that are included in the plan at the death of a plan beneficiary and become payable to the beneficiary's survivors are subject to federal estate tax at the time of the plan beneficiary's death. See Chapter 21. When the undistributed plan benefits—IRD—are paid to the survivors of the plan beneficiary, those distributions constitute taxable income to the recipients in the year of receipt.

The situation is similar with respect to accrued interest on widely held Series E and Series EE United States savings bonds. Savings bonds are sold at a discount from face value, i.e., a $100 bond sells for $50. Interest accrues on each bond while it remains outstanding and, when it is surrendered, the accrued interest constitutes taxable income (unless the owner of the bond has elected to be taxed on the interest as it annually accrues on the bond, even though the interest is not paid until the bond is surrendered). If the bond owner dies before surrendering the bond, the accrued interest is subject to federal estate tax in the bond owner's estate and, when the bond is surrendered by the owner's survivors, the accrued interest—IRD—constitutes taxable income to the recipient.

A distinction should be made between items of income that are earned but not yet payable, which constitute IRD, and items of income that are earned and payable but not collected by the decedent at the time of death. The latter items are deemed to have been constructively received and are included in the decedent's final income tax return. An example would be wages that the employee could have collected before death by simply demanding them from the employer. Bob is an example. Bob failed to pick up his paycheck when he left work–and died later that night. The amount of the paycheck is not IRD but income to be reported on Bob's final income tax return (and as an item of property on his Federal estate tax return).

Similarly, items of deductible expense may be incurred prior to death but not be paid until after death. These items are not properly deductible on the decedent's final income tax return. To the extent that they are deductible for federal income tax purposes, they are referred to as deductions in respect of a decedent (DIRD). See § 691(b) and ¶ 32,085. An example would be real property taxes that become a lien on January 1st in many states but are not payable until the following January. Ethel's death during the year means that these real property taxes are deductible as a debt of hers for Federal estate tax purposes *and* constitute a deduction as DIRD on the income tax return filed for Ethel's estate.

B. HISTORICAL DEVELOPMENT

[¶ 32,007]

While IRD, for federal income tax purposes, is merely income by another name, it is specially identified because it is also subject to the federal estate tax at the time of the decedent's death. IRD is a claim and, in that sense, is like any other item of property belonging to the decedent at the time of death. However, because IRD is subject to the federal estate tax, its treatment for income tax purposes presents special problems. Those problems relate to the question of whether the IRD acquires a basis because it is subject to the federal estate tax.

Congress has adhered to the principle that IRD is income and that income is income until it is taxed to someone as income. As a result, IRD is subject to both income tax and estate tax—but IRD receives no basis as a result of being included in the decedent's estate for federal estate tax purposes. § 1014(c). The recipient of the IRD is, however, entitled to a deduction for the federal estate tax attributed to the IRD as a result of the inclusion of the IRD in the decedent's estate. See § 691(c) and ¶ 32,109.

Another approach—rejected by Congress—is that IRD, as an item of property at the death of the decedent, acquires a new basis at the decedent's death as a result of § 1014, much like other items of property included in the decedent's estate for federal estate tax purposes. Implicit in this rejected approach is the notion that the IRD would escape income taxation because the amount of the IRD, when received, would be offset by its basis.

The present approach to IRD came about in 1942 legislation. See H.R. Rep. 2333, 77th Cong., 1st Sess., reprinted in 1942–2 C.B. 372, 435–39; S. Rep. 1631, 77th Cong., 2nd Sess., reprinted in 1942–2 C.B. 504, 579–83; H.R. Rep. 2586, 77th Cong., 2nd Sess., reprinted in 1942–2 C.B. 701, 706. Between 1934 and 1942, each decedent's final income tax return was effectively required to be filed on an accrual basis (even though the decedent may have been a cash basis taxpayer). This approach quite naturally proved unsatisfactory because it resulted in a bunching of income on the final return, pushing some taxpayers into higher tax brackets. This interim step was an effort to cure problems inherent in the taxation scheme that had prevailed earlier when no legislation applied specifically to IRD. In that earlier period, basis was assigned to income rights equal to the fair market value of those rights at death. When the IRD was collected, the recipient would offset the receipt, for income tax purposes, by the basis of the IRD, thereby effectively freeing the IRD from income taxes. Apparently, at the time, though, it was thought inappropriate to impose both estate taxes and income taxes on what some might argue was the same transaction, namely the collection of the income. Upon closer examination, it becomes apparent that fears of "double taxation" are conceptually unwarranted because the estate tax applies to "transfers" and the income tax applies to "income" (or, as someone might suggest in an effort at clarification, to "receipts", a term used advisedly when it comes to taxation of income).

C. TO WHOM IRD IS TAXED AND BY WHOM DIRD MAY BE CLAIMED

[¶ 32,013]

Income earned by the decedent that would have been received if the decedent had lived is to be taxed to the actual recipient in the year of actual receipt, provided the recipient is entitled to receive the IRD under applicable state property law principles. The recipient may be the decedent's estate, a legatee, devisee, or next of kin. For example, if the decedent's executor collects renewal commissions due on insurance policies sold by the decedent prior to death but not payable unless the policies are renewed by the buyers in later years, the commissions, when earned and payable, are items of gross income to the decedent's estate. § 691(a)(1). However, where the estate administration has been completed and the decedent's property has been distributed, the proper recipients of the IRD are the decedent's beneficiaries. IRD is never reported on the decedent's final income tax return.

Deductions in respect of a decedent (DIRD) are allowed to whoever actually pays the expense, provided that person is obligated to make the expenditure.

D. WHICH RECEIPTS CONSTITUTE IRD?

1. VOLUNTARY PAYMENTS

[¶ 32,019]

ROLLERT RESIDUARY TRUST v. COMMISSIONER

United States Court of Appeals, Sixth Circuit, 1985.
752 F.2d 1128.

WEICK, Senior Circuit Judge.

[Prior to his death, the decedent's employer, General Motors Corporation, had made a "tentative decision" to award bonuses to a group of employees, including the decedent, who was an executive vice-president. However, it was not until more than three months after the decedent's death that the bonus was formally awarded to the decedent. The taxpayer complained that the decedent had no legal right to the bonus at the time of his death and, therefore, the bonus was not income in respect of a decedent (IRD) "within the meaning of Section 691." In holding that the bonus was IRD, the court said:]

"Income in respect of a decedent" is not defined in the Code. However, the Service's regulations do provide a definition. 26 C.F.R. § 1.691(a)–1(b) states that, in general, "the term refers to those amounts to which a decedent was entitled as gross income but which were not properly includible in computing his taxable income for the taxable year ending with the date of his death or for a previous taxable year. . . ." More specifically, the term includes

¶ 32,013

three categories of income: (1) all accrued income of the decedent who reported his income by use of the cash receipts and disbursements methods; (2) income accrued solely by reason of the decedent's death in case of a decedent who reports his income by use of the accrued method of accounting; and (3) income to which the decedent had a contingent claim at the time of his death. It is not clear from this definition whether the term "entitled" means legally entitled, as appellant contends, or whether it simply means substantial likelihood of receiving the income, as the Commissioner argues.

Our circuit has, on two previous occasions, attempted to clarify this definition. In Keck v. Commissioner, 415 F.2d 531 (6th Cir.1969), the court held that "entitled", as used in the regulation, contemplated that the decedent was required to have a "right" to the income. However, the court failed to definitively answer whether this "right" had to be legally enforceable or whether the substantial likelihood that the decedent would receive the income would suffice. Twelve years later, in Claiborne v. United States, 648 F.2d 448 (6th Cir.1981), the court was again faced with this issue. In *Claiborne*, the government asked the court to overrule *Keck* to the extent that it implied that legal enforceability was required. The court, in an opinion written by Judge Edwards, concluded that the decedent had a legally enforceable right to the income at issue in the case and, therefore, it need not address the issue of whether a lesser standard, such as the "economic activities'" test suggested by the government, would be sufficient. This issue is squarely presented in this case, however, because the parties have agreed that the decedent did not have a legally enforceable right to receive the post-mortem bonus.

The Second Circuit held, in O'Daniel's Estate v. Commissioner, 173 F.2d 966 (2d Cir.1949), a case factually identical to the instant case, that as long as the decedent had provided services from which he had a reasonable expectation that he would be rewarded, any bonuses awarded subsequent to his death for those prior services would constitute income in respect of the decedent, notwithstanding that he did not have a legally enforceable right to the bonus. Other circuits have expressed their approval of this holding.

O'Daniel's Estate should be followed in this case. The key test for determining whether the decedent had a "right" or was "entitled" to the post-mortem bonus should be based on the likelihood, at the time of his death, that he would receive the bonus, not on his legal rights to it. The alternative interpretation "would permit parties to avoid taxation simply by failing to embody obligations incurred by reason of decedent's services into a binding contract even in situations where benefits were otherwise paid to discharge these obligations." Halliday v. United States, 655 F.2d 68, 71 (5th Cir.1981). If Congress had intended such a result, it could have expressly adopted the legal enforceability test. Similarly, the Service could have done the same, through its regulatory powers, if it had believed that this was Congress' intent. Given their failure to do so, we believe it is unwise for the courts to impose such a requirement.

There was a substantial certainty, at the time of decedent's death, that he would be awarded a bonus for his work for G.M. in 1969. G.M. had consistently awarded bonuses to its executive vice-presidents and it had already made a

¶ **32,019**

tentative decision, even prior to his death, to award bonuses to decedent and its other vice-presidents for their 1969 labors. Accordingly, the decedent had a "right" to the post-mortem bonus, within the meaning of § 691, and the bonus, therefore, constituted income in respect of the decedent.

[¶ 32,023]

2. EXECUTORY CONTRACTS

Determining whether a sale is completed prior to death can often have significant income tax consequences. If the sale is not deemed completed, the property will assume a new basis equal to its estate tax value. Subsequent sale at a price equal to the new basis will result in no taxable gain. However, if the sale is deemed completed prior to death—because only ministerial acts remain to be performed after the death—taxable gain (or loss) will be determined by the basis of the property in the hands of the decedent during life. Estate tax will be based on the value of the property at death.

Consider Saul's predicament (or at least the predicament in which Winifred, Saul's executor, finds herself). Saul died February 6th. On January 15th, Saul had signed a contract to sell his vacation condo for $235,000 to Butch. (Saul had paid $85,000 for the condo 10 years earlier.) The transaction was scheduled to close on February 15th. Closing, however, was conditioned on Butch selling his existing vacation home. Come February 15th, the scheduled closing date, Butch had not sold his existing property—but he was willing to waive the condition. However, it was not until March 10th that Saul's will was admitted to probate and Winifred appointed as executor of his estate.

Winifred is drawn to Priv. Ltr. Rul. 9023012. There, according to the IRS:

A entered into a real estate sales contract containing a clause making the contract cancellable by either party if the buyer did not obtain a mortgage commitment within 45 days. The contract also provided that the contract could be extended in writing. A died before the mortgage commitment was obtained and within the 45–day period. The mortgage commitment was not obtained within the 45–day period, but the buyer and the executor continued to closing without extending the contract in writing.

The IRS concluded that the gain realized by A's executor on the sale was income in respect of a decedent (IRD) within the meaning of § 691(a). The IRS explained that Reg. § 1.691(a)–1(b) "includes income to which the decedent had a contingent claim at the time of his death."

Application of Priv. Ltr. Rul. 9023012 to Saul's sale would result in Saul's executor having taxable income of $150,000 ($235,000—$85,000). Of course, the full $235,000 is subject to estate tax in Saul's estate.

Winifred, for her part, rejects the application of Priv. Ltr. Rul. 9023012. She says that Saul's condo has an income tax basis of $235,000 at Saul's death—applying the new-basis-at-death-rule of § 1014(a)—and there is no gain realized for income tax purposes (and, thus, no IRD).

¶ 32,019

Winifred relies on two distinct arguments, drawing upon the standards set out in Estate of Peterson v. Commissioner, 667 F.2d 675 (8th Cir. 1981), below. She says that the financing contingency in Saul's contract of sale was "economically material" because it could have disrupted the sale of the condo and, as set out in *Peterson,* that fact alone means the sale proceeds could not be IRD.

Winifred's argument is based on favorably reconciling two cases, Keck v. Commissioner, 415 F.2d 531 (6th Cir. 1969) and Estate of Sidles v. Commissioner, 65 T.C. 873, *acq.*, 1976–2 C.B. 12, *aff'd mem.*, 553 F.2d 102 (8th Cir. 1977), *Keck* burdened by "economically material contingencies" (resulting in a finding of no IRD) and *Sidles,* not (resulting in a finding of IRD).

Keck concluded that there was no IRD where, prior to the decedent's death, the decedent's corporation had (1) contracted to sell its assets—a sale that required approval of the Interstate Commerce Commission; and (2) settled on a plan for liquidating the corporation after the asset sale. The decedent had even delivered his shares to an escrow agent before his death. In rejecting the claim that the gain was IRD, the Sixth Circuit, in *Keck,* approvingly quoted Judge Featherstone who had written the dissenting opinion in the Tax Court's decision in *Keck*:

> 'The proper test for determining whether gain from the sale of property is to be treated as income in respect of a decedent is the status of the transaction at decedent's death, not who carried on the 'economic activity' which brought it to that status....'

It was further pointed out by Judge Featherston that at the time of decedent's death, his stock had not been converted to an item of income 'in respect of a decedent under section 691,' because of the fact that the sale of the stock was subject to a number of contingencies; that it was, at that time, subject to the approval of the Interstate Commerce Commission, a condition precedent which was not met until eighteen months after decedent's death, and that such approval was neither routine or perfunctory; that, at the time of his death, neither the decedent nor the other stockholders were contractually committed to the plan to liquidate the corporation; that ... the majority stockholder, for reasons of his own, might have decided not to liquidate the corporations....

It should be emphasized that *Keck*, in rejecting use of an "economic activities" test, was joining the Fifth Circuit which had announced its position in Trust Company of Georgia v. Ross, 392 F.2d 694 (5th Cir. 1967), *cert. denied,* 393 U.S. 830 (1968), in these terms:

Although it is pertinent to inquire whether the income received after death was attributable to activities and economic efforts of the decedent in his lifetime, these activities must give rise to a right to that income. And the right is to be distinguished from the activity which creates the right. Absent such a right, no matter how great the activities or efforts, there would be no taxable income under § 691. 392 F.2d 694, 695 (1967)

¶ **32,023**

The *Keck* court added:

> We agree with the United States Court of Appeals for the Fifth Circuit in holding [in *Trust Company of Georgia*] that the right to income, under the provision of the statute here pertinent, is to be distinguished from the economic activities that create that right and that, absent such a right, no matter how great the activities, there is no taxable income under Section 691.

By way of contrast, consider *Sidles* which also involved the need to adopt a plan of liquidation.

> The *Keck* case is clearly distinguishable on its facts. Unlike *Keck*, the decedent, as Bi–State's sole shareholder, possessed the power to compel payment of the liquidating distribution, as well as the right to that payment, when he died. His right to the liquidation distribution was not subject to the many contingencies involved in *Keck*. The transaction was not subject to the approval of any Government agency; there was no other stockholder who could vote note to liquidate the corporation. The distribution made to the Estate of Harry B. Sidles, was clearly 'income in respect of a decedent' within the meaning of section 691

In sum, Winifred's position is that the financing contingency in Saul's contract makes her case more like *Keck* than *Sidles*.

Winifred's other basis for her position is her claim that getting herself appointed as executor of Saul's estate is more than a "ministerial act" and, as a consequence, the proceeds of sale realized under Saul's contract are not IRD. Winifred's position that accomplishing the probate of Saul's will and her appointment as his executor were not minor or ministerial tasks, at least, certainly not in the context of the opinion in *Peterson* or in the context of Estate of Napolitano v. Commissioner, T.C. Memo. 1992–316, 63 T.C.M. (CCH) 3092, T.C.M. (RIA) 92,316, 1992 RIA TC Memo 92,316.

In *Napolitano*, seller had agreed to remove, prior to closing, existing housing code violations that burdened the property. The violations had not been cleared at seller's death, the day preceding the scheduled closing. Subsequently, seller's attorney is noted as having spent 3 hours negotiating final settlement of the violations with the city and brought about a closing by offering the buyer a $2,250 reduction in the purchase price to offset those violations that were not cleared at the time the sale was finally closed. Because these acts were considered "not ministerial" by the court, the seller was found not to have had a right or entitlement to the proceeds of sale at the time of his death and, thus, there was no IRD. The court said this about the the work of the seller's lawyer: "[T]his type of decision-making and negotiating demanded judgment and discretion, and cannot be considered "ministerial", perfunctory, routine, or insubstantial.

In sum, Winifred argues that proceeds of sale cannot be IRD in any case where the seller has tasks to accomplish to effect delivery—in Saul's case, securing probate of the will and appointment of Winifred as executor—because, before those tasks have been accomplished, the seller has no right to the income. (Saul had no right to the income at the time of death because delivery had yet to be effected and, subsequent to his death, Winifred, as

¶ 32,023

executor of Saul's estate, had no right to the income until the court proceedings necessary to probate the will and appoint her as executor.) That is, it is Winifred's argument that without delivery there can be no right or entitlement to income; she claims that, on the authority of *Keck* and *Peterson*, delivery is never ministerial or minor where court proceedings must be completed in order to effect delivery.

In Priv. Ltr. Rul 9319005, prior to the grantor's death, a revocable trust entered into a contract to sell stock short, pledging the trust's own shares in the same company. The grantor died before the trust closed the sale. The IRS said that the proceeds of the short sale did not constitute income in respect of a decedent because "delivery of property is more than a ministerial act." In Priv. Ltr. Rul. 9436017, an individual, prior to death, sold stock short, pledging personal shares in the same company. The IRS concluded that, if death occurred prior to the closing of the sale, the proceeds would not constitute income in respect of a decedent, "since the delivery of property to close the short sale is more than a ministerial act."

What should Winifred do? Obviously, the predicament she finds herself in is likely to come up for some estate virtually everyday. Consider both of Winifred's arguments and determine the course that you would recommend to her as she threads her way through this murky area. Is the definitive answer found in *Peterson*?

[¶ 32,025]

ESTATE OF PETERSON v. COMMISSIONER

United States Court of Appeals, Eighth Circuit, 1981.
667 F.2d 675.

McMILLIAN, Circuit Judge.

This is an appeal from the decision of the Tax Court holding that the sale proceeds received by the estate of Charley W. Peterson from the sale of 2,398 calves did not constitute "income in respect of a decedent" under § 691(a)(1) * * *.

* * * The decedent, Charley W. Peterson, was in the business of raising and selling cattle. On July 11, 1972, he entered into a "livestock sales contract" * * *. Under the terms of this contract, the decedent was to raise and sell to the Max Rosenstock Co. "approximately 3,300 calves" at $0.49 per pound, with the date of delivery to be designated by the decedent upon five days notice. One group of calves (the Brown County calves) was to be delivered no later than November 1, 1972; the other group (the Holt County calves) was to be delivered no later than December 15, 1972. The calves were to be from three to eleven months old and in "merchantable condition" when delivered. * * * The risk of loss was on the decedent until delivery.

The decedent did not designate a delivery date or deliver any calves by the November 1 delivery date. * * * The decedent died on November 9, 1972. The estate (the taxpayer) assumed responsibility for the calves, designated several December delivery dates, and delivered a total of 2,929 calves, 2,398

¶ 32,025

owned by the estate and 531 owned by the decedent's sons, * * *. As found by the Tax Court, approximately two-thirds of the calves were in a "deliverable" condition as of the date of the decedent's death. The remaining calves were not "deliverable" on that date because they were too young.

The estate reported the sale of the calves on its fiduciary income tax return and computed the gain from the sale by subtracting the fair market value of the calves on the date of the decedent's death from the sale proceeds. The Commissioner, however, determined that the gain from the sale constituted "income in respect of a decedent" under § 691(a)(1) and recomputed the estate's gain on the sale by subtracting the decedent's adjusted basis in the calves from the sale proceeds. See §§ 691(a)(1), 1014(a)(basis of property acquired from decedent is the fair market value at date of decedent's death), 1014(c)(§ 1014(a) does not apply to property which constitutes a right to receive an item of income in respect of a decedent under § 691). The characterization of the sales transaction thus determines whether the estate uses the decedent's adjusted basis or a stepped-up basis (fair market value on date of death) in calculating the gain from the sale. The amount of income tax deficiency at issue is $185,384.10.

The Tax Court decided that the sale proceeds did not constitute "income in respect of a decedent" under § 691(a)(1). 74 T.C. at 641. After noting that § 691 does not itself define "income in respect of a decedent," the Tax Court reviewed the history of the section, referred to the applicable regulations, § 1.691(a)(1)–(3)(1981), examined the case law, and distilled a four-factor test for determining whether sale proceeds constitute "income in respect of a decedent": (1) whether the decedent entered into a legally significant arrangement regarding the subject matter of the sale, (2) whether the decedent performed the substantive (nonministerial) acts required as preconditions to the sale, (3) whether there existed at the time of the decedent's death any economically material contingencies which might have disrupted the sale, and (4) whether the decedent would have eventually received the sale proceeds if he or she had lived. 74 T.C. at 639–41.

The Tax Court concluded that the decedent had entered into a legally significant agreement to sell the calves on the basis of the livestock sales contract. The Tax Court also found that there were no economically material contingencies which could potentially have disrupted the sale; the transaction was not contingent upon the actions or approval of third parties. * * * Further, the decedent, if he had lived, would have received the sale proceeds; the transaction was not effective only at death. * * * The Tax Court, however, concluded that the decedent had not performed the substantive acts required under the livestock sales contract. 74 T.C. at 644. At the date of the decedent's death one-third of the calves were not in "deliverable" condition; all the calves required care and feeding until actually delivered. The estate assumed responsibility for the care and feeding of all the calves until delivery (for approximately one month). The Tax Court concluded that the activities performed by the estate were not perfunctory or ministerial and that these activities were sufficient to remove the sale proceeds from the scope of § 691(a)(1). Id. at 644–45.

¶ 32,025

On appeal the Commissioner does not disagree with the four-factor test developed by the Tax Court. The Commissioner argues that the Tax Court misapplied the test and that, under a proper application of the test, that portion of the sale proceeds attributable to the calves which were "deliverable" at the date of the decedent's death constitute "income in respect of a decedent" under § 691(a)(1). See 74 T.C. at 646 (Simpson, J., concurring). This argument was not raised below by either party. Ordinarily we do not consider questions of law which were not presented to the court * * *. However, in order to determine whether the Tax Court misapplied its four-factor test, we necessarily reach the Commissioner's apportionment or allocation argument. We think that the apportionment or allocation argument incorrectly emphasizes the condition or character of the subject matter of the sale instead of the status of the transaction itself at the time of the decedent's death. For the reasons discussed below, we affirm the decision of the Tax Court.

Stated in misleadingly simple terms, whether income is considered income in respect of a decedent under § 691 depends upon whether the decedent had a right to receive income at the time of his or her death. The focus is upon the decedent's *right or entitlement to income* at the time of death.

* * *

The leading commentators have proposed the following as a "tentative working definition" of income in respect of a decedent:

> Items of income in respect of a decedent ... are payments received toward satisfaction of a right or expectancy created almost entirely through the efforts or status of the decedent and which, except for his death and without further action on his part, the decedent would have realized as gross income. Two observations should be made. First, the concept is manifestly broader than the mere accrued earnings of a cash basis decedent. Second, despite the breadth of this tentative definition, § 691 does not reach the income potential in a decedent's appreciated property, even if that appreciation is due to the decedent's own efforts. Further action on the decedent's part (e.g., a sale) would have been required for such appreciation to be realized as income. Within this definition farm produce inventories grown, harvested, and processed for market, but not delivered by the decedent before his death, even though they come very close to representing ordinary income actually realized, are "property" rather than a bare right to income until they are sold. * * *

M. Ferguson, J. Freeland & R. Stephens, Federal Income Taxation of Estates and Beneficiaries 146 (1970)(footnote omitted). [In a footnote, the court quoted the following from Ferguson, Freeland & Stephens, Id. at 146–8, for purposes of describing the "four salient characteristics" of IRD:

> First, the item of income must have been taxable to the decedent had he survived to the time the income was realized. This is to say, the income

must have been attributable to his services, his sales, or his income-producing property.

Second, although the decedent must have become "entitled" to the income by his death, his rights must not have matured sufficiently to require inclusion of the income in his final income tax return under the accounting method employed by him. This return, normally filed by the executor, is prepared on the decedent's regular method of accounting without references to any items which might have become accruable solely because of death. . . .

Third, what is transferred at death must be a passive right to receive income, as distinguished from "property" entitled to a fair market value basis under § 1014(a). Although the gross estate for Federal estate tax purposes includes, along with all other kinds of property rights, the value of any rights to future income, §§ 691 and 1014(c) force a differentiation between income rights and other assets for income tax purposes. Here, too, generalization is difficult. . . . Regardless of the nature of the asset, § 691 applies only when the decedent performed all substantial acts within his control necessary to convert prior efforts or property into an intangible right to receive income.

Fourth, the recipient of the right to the income in question must have acquired it solely by reason of the death of the taxpayer who created it. This characteristic subjects income in respect of a decedent to two important limitations, each of which sheds further light upon the basic concept: First, § 691 presupposes a gratuitous transfer from a decedent at death of a right to income. Second, the ultimate proceeds must be received solely because of the taxpayer's passive status as the decedent's transferee of the specific right.]

* * * For example, items of income attributable to the decedent's services are generally income in respect of a decedent. Characterization of items attributable to sales proceeds, as in the present case, however, is less clear, particularly because of the operation of the basis rules of § 1014. Id. at 177–78.

[I]t may be difficult to determine whether the decedent's steps prior to his death had proceeded sufficiently to treat sales proceeds received after death as income in respect of a decedent. The test here is not quite whether the decedent "closed" the sale or transferred title and possession of an asset before death. Rather, it is whether his successor acquired a right to receive proceeds from an asset's disposition on the one hand, or acquired the asset itself on the other. Depending upon the subject and the terms of a sale, death may interrupt the transaction at a number of stages which do not fall clearly on either side of this murky distinction.

Id. at 178–79.

As noted by Ferguson, Freeland and Stephens, "the definitional problem under § 691(a) is complicated by the general rule of § 1014(a) according to a basis equal to estate tax value to the decedent's 'property' other than such § 691(a) 'rights'." Id. at 180. As illustrated by the present case, the tax consequences of characterizing a particular item of income may be substan-

¶ 32,025

tial. Ferguson, Freeland and Stephens apparently do not favor characterizing sales proceeds from sales transactions substantially "incomplete" at the time of the decedent's death as income in respect of a decedent:

> [W]here there is a contract of sale which would have been completed during the decedent's life but for his death, the proceeds received upon culmination of the sale by the decedent's transferee will be taxed as income in respect of a decedent if no substantial conditions remained to be performed by the decedent at his death. Thus, if the executor had only a passive or ministerial role to play in completing the sale, the proceeds should be taxed as income in respect of a decedent.
>
> . . . Whenever the decedent negotiates a contract enforceable by his executor after death, the profit may properly be attributed to the decedent's bargaining and other efforts, which would seem to suggest income treatment for a part of the post-death receipts. On the other hand, the basis rules of § 1014(a) suggest that, wherever the risks inherent in ownership remain with the decedent until death, adjustments to the property's basis (and hence variations in the amount of gain or loss under the contract) remain possible until actual disposition by the decedent's successor.

Id. at 183–84 (footnote omitted).

Here, the task remaining to be performed by the estate was performance of the contract. We agree with the conclusion of the Tax Court that performance of the contract, which, under the circumstances, involved care and feeding of livestock and delivery, cannot be characterized as a ministerial or minor act. However, we think that characterization of the tasks which remain after the death of the decedent should not necessarily depend upon the nature of the subject matter of the sales transaction. For example, the subject matter of the sales transaction in the present case was livestock, which obviously required care and feeding. What if the subject matter was not livestock but logs or refrigerators? It would still be the task of the decedent's transferee to deliver or otherwise dispose of the logs or refrigerators, even though that type of property does not require the care that livestock does.

We recognize that the analysis followed by the Tax Court emphasizes delivery or disposal of the subject matter of the sales transaction and, to a certain degree, discounts the significance of the sales contract. * * * After all, the decedent in a sales case does not prearrange his death in order to shift the responsibility for delivering the subject matter of the sale transaction to his executor or to take advantage of the fair market value basis rule of § 1014(a) and thus avoid the reach of § 691.

Accordingly, the decision of the Tax Court is affirmed.

Note

[¶ 32,031]

Revenue Ruling 64–289, 1964–2 C.B. 173, deals with farm crops. The decedent had leased two parcels of land and was due to receive a percentage of the crops grown on the land as rent. At the decedent's death, the crops had been planted but not yet harvested. Relying on Estate of Davison v. United States, 292 F.2d 937 (Ct.Cl.1961), cert. denied, 368 U.S. 939 (1961), the IRS concluded that a decedent who used the cash-basis method of accounting and received or had a right to receive livestock or crop shares prior to death is to be deemed to have received income in respect of a decedent. Proceeds attributed to the portion of rent accrued after death to the end of the rental period are ordinary income to the estate. Livestock or crop shares received in kind as rentals and held by the lessor at the decedent's death and later disposed of by the executor are to be allocated between ordinary income and income in respect of a decedent applying the following formulas:

Income in respect of a decedent

$$\text{Proceeds} \times \frac{\text{no. of days in rental period up to death}}{\text{total no. of days in rental period}}$$

Ordinary income

$$\text{Proceeds} \times \frac{\text{no. of days in rental period up to death}}{\text{total no. of days in rental period}}$$

Problem

[¶ 32,037]

Tammy sold the assets of three corporations she owned with the intention of subsequently liquidating the corporations. At the time of Tammy's death, the sale of the corporations were subject to a number of contingencies, including the requirements that: (1) federal regulatory approval was given for the sale; and (2) none of the stockholders was contractually committed to the liquidation plan. Before the approval was obtained, Tammy died. Eventually, the liquidations took place and the proceeds were distributed to the stockholders, including Tammy's surviving spouse. Tammy's spouse claims that, at the date of Tammy's death, Tammy was not entitled to receive any proceeds from the contemplated liquidation and, therefore, the amounts eventually received by him after Tammy's death were not income in respect of a decedent. Is Tammy's spouse correct? If so, does that suggest that the IRD test applied in *Rollert* (¶ 32,019) is limited to cases where the payments are made in conjunction with employment? Keck v. Commissioner, 415 F.2d 531 (6th Cir.1969).

3. SELF–CANCELING INSTALLMENT NOTES (SCINS)

[¶ 32,041]

"Installment sale" refers to a method of property disposition whereby the proceeds of sale are received over a period of more than one year. § 453(b)(1). Installment sale reporting is assumed for income tax purposes in such cases unless the seller makes a timely election to treat the disposition as a noninstallment sale. § 453(d). One advantage of the installment sale is that the seller is permitted to recognize the gain on the sale as payment is received

¶ 32,031

(rather than in the year of the sale itself). This deferral opportunity is often prized.

A self-canceling installment note (SCIN)—sometimes referred to as "death-terminating installment note" (because the death is the mechanism that triggers cancellation)—is not much different from a regular installment note except that the purchaser's obligation is canceled if the seller dies before the note is fully paid. Often the seller will receive an above market interest rate as a premium for including the self-cancellation feature in the note. Use of the premium is designed to eliminate gift tax on the transfer in as much the SCIN is primarily used for estate planning purposes. For example, where the seller dies before the note is paid, his or her estate is reduced by the amount of the canceled note. See § 15,061.

It is obvious from the *Frane* case that follows that the seller's advisors and the IRS have different views as to the income tax treatment accorded SCINs. Has the SCIN lost any of its appeal as a result of *Frane*? And what of taxing the gain to the seller's estate rather than the seller?

[¶ 32,043]

FRANE v. COMMISSIONER

United States Court of Appeals, Eighth Circuit, 1993.
998 F.2d 567.

JOHN R. GIBSON, Circuit Judge.

In this case we examine the income tax consequences of an estate planning device known as the "death-terminating installment note." Janet Frane and the estate of Robert Frane, her late husband, appeal from a Tax Court decision holding that they were required to report income resulting from the cancellation of notes from the Franes' children upon Robert Frane's death. On appeal the Franes argue that no one should have to recognize income from the cancellation of the notes or, in the alternative, that if anyone does, it should be the estate and not Mr. Frane himself. We affirm the judgment of the Tax Court in part and reverse in part.

At the age of fifty-three, Robert Frane sold stock in his company, the Sherwood Grove Co., to his four children by four separate stock purchase agreements. Each child signed a note for the appraised value of the stock payable in annual installments over twenty years for a total principal amount of $141,050. Key to this litigation is the self-cancellation clause in the stock purchase agreements, which required the notes to provide "that in the event of [Robert Frane's] death prior to the final payment of principal and interest under said note, the unpaid principal and interest of such note shall be deemed canceled and extinguished as though paid upon the death of [Robert Frane]." * * * The notes so provided, and the Franes contend they also included an above-market interest rate (twelve percent) meant to compensate Robert Frane for assuming the risk that he would die before twenty years passed and thus not receive full payment on the notes. At the time of the sale,

¶ 32,043

Frane's life expectancy (as determined from United States Department of Commerce statistics) exceeded the twenty year term of the promissory notes.

Frane lived to receive two of the installments, recognizing income on each installment according to the ratio between Frane's basis in the stock and the amount he would receive under the contracts if he lived the full twenty years. * * * § 453–1(b)(2). After Frane died in 1984, his children made no further payments. * * * In 1986, Sherwood liquidated its assets. Two of the children reported a capital loss from the transaction, claiming as their basis in the stock only the amount they actually paid for it (rather than the face amount of the note). The two other children did not report a gain or a loss.

Neither Frane's last income tax return nor the estate's income tax return reported any income resulting from the self-cancellation of the notes. The Commissioner issued a notice of deficiency. * * * The Tax Court upheld the Commissioner's position that gain was recognized upon Frane's death and the cancellation of the notes, but concluded that the gain was taxable to Frane himself, rather than to the estate.

The Franes' principal argument is that the automatic cancellation of the note upon Frane's death did not generate taxable income. This is an uphill battle, since the Internal Revenue Code specifically provides that "if any installment obligation is canceled or otherwise becomes unenforceable," and the obligee and obligor are related persons, it shall cause the obligee to recognize income equal to the difference between the basis of the obligation and its face value. § 453B(a), (f). A similar provision applies to estates, requiring "cancellation" of an installment obligation to be treated as a transfer of the obligation, which causes the estate to recognize income in respect of a decedent in the face amount of the obligation less its basis in the hands of the decedent. § 691(a)(2), (4) & (5).

The Franes argue that the automatic self-cancellation of the notes is not the sort of "cancellation" covered by sections 453B and 691(a)(5). The Franes first argue that the word "cancellation" does not, in ordinary usage, cover their death-terminating installment note, and second, they argue that since the code sections were drafted to prevent abuses that occur when an obligation is canceled by an act subsequent and extraneous to the contract, they were not meant to apply to cancellation resulting from an integral term of the contract itself.

The Franes contend that the word "cancellation" describes an action occurring "after the original transaction and independently from it." While we agree with the Franes that there is a distinction to be made between cancellation by act subsequent to the contract and cancellation upon a contingency pursuant to the contract's terms, the term "cancellation" can be used to describe both situations. To establish this we need go no further than point to the commonly used name for the very estate planning device used here: "self-canceling installment notes." * * * Most telling, however, is the use of the words "canceled and extinguished" in the Franes' notes. The Franes' argument is answered by the very words the Franes used.

¶ 32,043

As for Congressional intent, sections 453B(f) and 691(a)(5) were indeed drafted to prevent an abuse involving after the fact cancellations. In Miller v. Usry, 160 F.Supp. 368 (W.D.La.1958), a father transferred property to his son in exchange for an installment note payable in twenty annual installments. The father had a low basis in the property and the note was for a much higher amount. Id. at 369. The father later canceled the note. Id. The government collected income tax from the father on the difference between his basis and the unpaid balance on the note, but the court held that the father could only be taxed on the amount he actually realized from the sale. Id. at 370–72. The unstated result of the *Miller* case was that the appreciation of the property could never be taxed at all, since the son's basis in the property was the face amount of the note, even though the son had not had to pay the note. Thus, the father avoided recognizing income on the property and the son obtained a stepped-up basis in the property without paying for it.

To close this loophole, Congress enacted sections 453B(f), which provides that when an installment loan between family members is canceled the obligee recognizes as income the difference between his basis in the obligation and the face amount of the note. The legislative history makes it clear that this is the purpose of section 453B(f):

* * *

　　Under present law, some have argued that the installment obligation disposition rules can be avoided by making gift cancellations of the obligation or the installments as they come due. In other words, by making an installment sale and then canceling the obligation or a number of installment payments, it is argued that the seller will incur no income tax liability, but possibly some gift taxes, and the buyer will have a cost basis in the property sold although no income tax cost will have been incurred on the transaction. If a direct gift is made, the donee's basis is generally the same as the donor's basis rather than a "cost" basis which reflects future payments which will never be made.

* * *

The committee believes that present law should be clarified to make it clear that the installment obligation disposition rules cannot be circumvented by canceling the obligation.

* * *

　　The bill makes it clear that the cancellation of an installment obligation is treated as a disposition of the obligation. In the case where the obligor is a related party, the amount taken into account as a disposition triggering recognition of unreported gain attributable (sic) to the obligation is not to be less than the face amount of the installment obligation.

S. Rep. No. 1000, 96th Cong., 2d Sess., at 25–26 (1980), reprinted in 1980 U.S.C.C.A.N. 4696, 4720–21. The legislative history gives a similar explanation for section 691(a)(5). See id. at 26–27.

The Franes argue that sections 453B(f) and 691(a)(5) were not meant to apply to death-terminating installment notes because in such notes the actual price depends on when the obligee dies and the obligor's basis in the property acquired is thus the amount he actually paid on the note, not its face value. The Franes claim that the abuse addressed by the statutes is not possible with death-terminating installment notes, because there is no step-up in the obligor's basis in the property; consequently, there is no reason to adjust the basis on the obligee's side, as there would be in a gratuitous cancellation.

In addressing "Death Terminating Installment Sales," the IRS General Counsel acknowledges that generally a taxpayer may not increase its basis in property "to reflect obligations it assumed in acquiring the property which are contingent or indefinite." Gen. Couns. Mem. 39,503 (May 7, 1986). This reasoning would lead to the conclusion that the Frane childrens' basis in the property is the principal they actually paid. However, the memorandum concludes that the obligor of a self-canceling installment note has a basis in property purchased with the note equal to the note's face value. Interestingly, the General Counsel's reasoning is that since section 453B will tax the obligee on the amount of appreciation, the obligor should get the benefit of an increased basis. This argument is, of course, circular in our case, for the Franes have tried to establish that section 453B cannot tax the obligee because the obligor will not receive the benefit of an increased basis. The General Counsel's reasoning is nevertheless instructive, because the injustice the Franes complain of only occurs if the treatments accorded the obligor and obligee are inconsistent. The General Counsel's memorandum shows that the plain language of sections 453B and 691(a)(5) can be applied to make the obligee recognize gain, a consistent treatment can be afforded the obligor, and no injustice results.

Therefore, the Franes lose their uphill battle to adopt a specialized meaning for the word "canceled" in sections 453B and 691(a)(5), and we affirm the Tax Court's result.

Next, we must decide whether the income should be taxed to Robert Frane individually or to his estate. The Code provides that income in respect of a decedent which is not properly included in the decedent's last tax return shall be taxed to his estate. § 691(a)(1). "Transfer" of the right to receive such income by the estate would be a taxable event for the estate under section 691(a)(2). Section 691(a)(5)(iii) provides that "any cancellation of [an installment] obligation occurring at the death of the decedent shall be treated as a transfer by the estate of the decedent."

The Tax Court reasoned that the cancellation constituted a "disposition," which 453B(f) provides is taxed to the individual under 453B, rather than a "transmission of installment obligations at death," which section 453B provides is covered under section 691 and thus taxed to the estate. 98 T.C. at 3512.

This reasoning appears to us quite nebulous in comparison with the unambiguous language in section 691(a)(5)(iii) that cancellation occurring at the death of obligee shall be treated as a transfer by the estate, taxable under section 691(a)(2). This language covers the case before us. * * *

¶ 32,043

We affirm the Tax Court's decision that income was recognized on Robert Frane's death, but reverse the holding that the income was recognizable by Frane himself and hold that instead the estate was responsible for it.

Note

[¶ 32,049]

When speaking of income tax considerations, it is useful to distinguish cases where an installment note is subject to a self-cancellation feature and cases where the installment note, unencumbered by a self-cancellation feature, passes to the maker of the note at the death of the holder of the note either by intestacy or under the holder's will. In the latter cases, while the previously unrecognized gain becomes taxable, the taxable event occurs only when the note is distributed from the estate to the maker. See Priv. Ltr. Rul. 8806048.

Problem

[¶ 32,050]

Four years before his death, Doug sold certain farm land to Sam, his son, for $250,000, the fair market value. Doug's basis for the land was $50,000. Under the contract of sale, payment was to be made in 10 equal annual installments of $25,000 each, with interest on the unpaid balance. Prior to Doug's death, Sam made four payments, leaving a balance of $150,000. By a provision in his will, Doug canceled Sam's remaining obligation under the contract. What are the estate and income tax consequences of this transaction? § 691(a)(2), (a)(5), and (c); § 2033; ¶¶ 15,061, 15,073 and 32,043.

4. TAX DEFERRED RETIREMENT BENEFITS

[¶ 32,051]

Income tax deferred property is the stuff of tax qualified retirement accounts and individual retirement accounts (IRAs). At death of the account owner, the value of the account is part of the owner's estate for estate tax purposes. § 2039. In addition, the account's value is income in respect of a decedent (IRD) and thus subject to income taxation not later than when distributed to the account's beneficiary (to the extent it exceeds the value of previously taxed property that might be included in the account). § 72. The amount of the estate tax is deductible for income tax purposes by the recipient of the account balance. § 691(c); ¶ 32,109. In addition, amounts passing to the surviving spouse may well qualify for the marital deduction. See § 2056; ¶ 28,364.

[¶ 32,052]

REVENUE RULING 92–47

1992–1 C.B. 198.

ISSUE

What are the federal income tax consequences to the non-spouse beneficiary of an individual retirement account (IRA) of a decedent on receipt of a lump sum distribution from the IRA?

FACTS

A died owning an IRA. As of A's death, the IRA held assets that had appreciated since they were acquired by the IRA. Some of the contributions by A to the IRA had been nondeductible contributions. The designated beneficiary of the IRA was A's child, B. The entire balance in the IRA, including appreciation and income accruing before and after a's death, was distributed to B in a lump sum shortly after A's death.

LAW AND ANALYSIS

Section 1.691(a)–1(b) provides that the term "income in respect of a decedent" refers to those amounts to which a decedent was entitled as gross income but that were not properly includible in computing taxable income for the taxable year ending with the date of death or for a previous taxable year under the method of accounting employed by the decedent.

Section 408(d)(1) provides that, except as otherwise provided in section 408(d)(relating to rollover contributions), any amount paid or distributed out of an IRA is included in gross income by the payee or distributee in the manner provided under section 72. Under section 72, nondeductible contributions to an IRA are not included in the gross income of the payee or distributee.

Section 408(e)(1) provides that an IRA is exempt from income taxation.

Section 1.408–4(a)(2) provides that notwithstanding section 1015(d) or any other provision * * *, the basis (or investment in the contract) of any person in an IRA is zero. This regulation has been superseded by changes in the law to the extent that an individual does have basis in his IRA equal to his nondeductible contributions.

Section 691(c)(1)(a) provides that a person who includes an amount in gross income under section 691(a) is allowed, for the same taxable year, as an income tax deduction an amount determined by reference to the estate tax attributable to the amount included in gross income under section 691(a). Section 691(c) and section 1.691(c)–1(a) * * * provide rules for determining the amount of the deduction.

In Rev. Rul. 69–297, 1969–1 C.B. 131, an employee died designating his estate the beneficiary of his interest in a qualified profit-sharing trust. His interest in the trust, which included appreciated securities of the employer corporation, was distributed to his estate within one taxable year of his death.

Rev. Rul. 69–297 holds that for the taxable year in which the distribution was made, the estate is required by section 402(a) to include in its gross income an amount equal to the cost or other basis to the trust of the employer securities (thus excluding any net unrealized appreciation in the employer securities), plus an amount equal to the cash and the fair market value of any other property received as part of the distribution, minus the amount of the employee's contributions. Rev. Rul. 69–297 characterizes this income as income in respect of a decedent under section 691(a), and holds that the estate is allowed a deduction under section 691(c) for that portion of the estate tax attributable to the inclusion in the decedent's estate of the distribution from the employee's trust. Rev. Rul. 69–297 further holds that the net unrealized appreciation in the securities of the employer is includible in gross income as income in respect of a decedent in the taxable year of their disposition by either the executor or the residuary legatees in a taxable transaction and that the transferor will be allowed the deduction provided under section 691 for any estate tax paid attributable to the net unrealized appreciation.

In Rev. Rul. 75–125, 1975–1 C.B. 254, a retired employee received from a qualified trust a lump sum distribution consisting entirely of securities of his corporate employer. The securities had a basis to the qualified trust of 5x dollars and a fair market value on the date of distribution of 10x dollars. Under section 402(a)(2), as in effect at the time of the distribution, the 5x dollars net unrealized appreciation in the securities was not taxed to the employee upon distribution. Following the distribution, the employee died leaving the securities to his surviving spouse. Rev. Rul. 75–125 holds that the net unrealized appreciation of 5x dollars attributable to the employer securities constitutes income in respect of a decedent under section 691(a) to be included in gross income by the surviving spouse when she disposes of the securities. Rev. Rul. 75–125 also holds that the surviving spouse is entitled to a deduction under section 691(c) for that portion of the federal estate tax attributable to the amount of the net unrealized appreciation included in the decedent's estate.

Amounts in A's IRA that were not distributed to A prior to A's death are not includible on A's final income tax return. If distributions from the IRA had been made to A prior to A's death, the distributions would have been taxable to A to the extent required under section 72. Upon A's death, the value of the IRA was included in A's estate and the entire balance in the IRA was distributed to B as designated beneficiary.

Under the above facts, the amount of the distribution that equals the balance in the IRA at A's death less A's nondeductible contributions to the IRA constitutes income in respect of a decedent and is includible in B's gross income for the taxable year in which B receives the distribution. The balance of the distribution, which represents appreciation and income accruing between the date of death and the date of distribution, is taxable to B under sections 408(d) and 72. In computing income tax for the taxable year of inclusion of the income in respect of a decedent, B may claim a deduction for any federal estate tax on A's estate attributable to that income in respect of a decedent.

* * *

Planning Note

[¶ 32,053]

Post death income tax deferral opportunities are sometimes available to recipients of tax qualified retirement plan accounts and recipients of IRA balances. For the most part, the complexities of qualifying for tax deferral are beyond the scope of these materials. Suffice it to say that, in specified circumstances, e.g., where the beneficiary is the plan participant's "designated beneficiary" (and not just "any" beneficiary qualifies as a "designated beneficiary" (DB)), distribution of account balances can be made over the lifetime of the account beneficiary—and, in those cases, the account balance becomes taxable for income tax purposes only upon distribution to the beneficiary. However, using mandated "minimum" distribution rules (MRD), a certain percentage of the account balance must be distributed annually and taken into income by the beneficiary in that year. § 401(a)(9)(B). A 50 percent penalty applies for failing to take the required minimum distribution. § 4974.

Having the plan benefits payable to the plan participant's estate at death is a likely "worst case" scenario for income tax minimization purposes (where tax deferral is viewed as "tax minimization") because the estate, while a "beneficiary", does not qualify as a "designated beneficiary", Reg. § 1.401(a)(9)–4, A–3; PLR 200126041, the effect being that all plan benefits, as a general rule, are subject to income tax in the year following death (in cases where death occurs after the plan participant's required beginning date (RBD), i.e., normally 70 ½). By way of contrast, tax deferral is sometimes possible even if the plan benefits are payable to a trust. Such deferral is possible when the trust beneficiary is recognized as a DB, a status not easily obtained. Reg. § 1.401(a)(9)–4, A–5.

In the case where the beneficiary is the surviving spouse, the spouse can roll the account balance over into his or her own IRA and defer income tax until actual distribution, § 408(d), distribution being required to begin in the year that the surviving spouse attains 70 ½, again, using prescribed minimum distribution rules. § 401(a)(9).

Qualification of plan benefits for the estate tax marital deduction is considered in ¶ 27,364.

From the foregoing, it should be clear that naming a qualifying "designated beneficiary" is critical to effective tax planning for plan benefits.

For a complete examination of extraordinarily complicated rules, see Natalie B. Choate, Life and Death Planning for Retirement Benefits (5th ed. 2003).

[¶ 32,054]

5. OTHER EXAMPLES

Annuities constitute IRD. In Rev. Rul. 2005–30, 2005–20 I.R.B. 1015, the IRS said:

> If the owner-annuitant of a deferred annuity contract dies before the annuity starting date, and the beneficiary receives a death benefit under the annuity contract, the amount received by the beneficiary in a lump sum in excess of the owner-annuitant's investment in the contract is includible in the beneficiary's gross income as IRD within the meaning of § 691. If the death benefit is instead received in the form of a series of periodic payments in accordance with § 72(s), the amounts received are likewise includible in the beneficiary's gross income (in an amount determined under § 72) as IRD within the meaning of § 691.

Furthermore, (1) the IRS said, in accordance with § 1014(c), discussed in ¶ 32,055, and reiterating Rev. Rul. 79–335, 1979–2 C.B. 292, the beneficiary does not receive a basis adjustment in the contract; and (2) the beneficiary is entitled to a deduction under § 691(c), discussed in ¶ 32,103, if estate tax was due by reason of the owner-annuitant's death. The result would be the same whether the beneficiary receives the death benefit in a lump sum or as periodic payments.

Rent and interest accrued prior to the decedent's death but not properly included in the decedent's final income tax return is also IRD. See Richardson v. United States, 177 F.Supp. 394 (E.D.Mich.1959), aff'd, 294 F.2d 593 (6th Cir.1961), cert. denied, 369 U.S. 802 (1962).

E.   BASIS OF IRD

[¶ 32,055]

Section 1014(c) plainly states that § 1014(a) does not apply to provide a new basis for income in respect of a decedent. Nonetheless, in the following case, the taxpayer creatively invoked—for naught—the rules applicable to distributions from trusts and estates that appear in §§ 661 and 662.

[¶ 32,061]

ROLLERT RESIDUARY TRUST v. COMMISSIONER

United States Tax Court, 1983.
80 T.C. 619, aff'd, 752 F.2d 1128 (6th Cir.1985).

WHITAKER, Judge:

[Some of the facts are set forth at ¶ 32,019. In addition, note that the right to receive the bonus installments became part of the residue of the decedent's estate, passing under his will to the Edward D. Rollert Residuary Trust. Both the estate and the legatee treated the distribution of the rights as a distribution of the estate's distributable net income even though the bonus installments would constitute income in respect of a decedent when paid. In the year the rights were distributed, the legatee reported as income under § 662 the date-of-distribution fair market values of the rights, and the estate took a corresponding deduction under Section 661(a). Under Reg. § 1.661(a)–2(f), the legatee took the date-of-distribution values as its basis in the rights, and in the subsequent years when the bonus installments were paid to it, the legatee reported as income only the difference between such basis and the amount received.]

We must determine now whether the estate's distribution to petitioner of the rights to receive bonus installments in subsequent years gave petitioner a basis in these rights equal to their fair market values when distributed and whether such basis could be used by petitioner to reduce the income it received when the bonus installments were actually paid to it. This is a question of first impression.

* * *

In resolving this case, we must analyze the relationship between the rules of section 691 for the taxation of income in respect of a decedent and those of subchapter J, part I, governing the income taxation of estates. In general, the provisions of subchapter J, part I, are designed to allocate between the estate and its beneficiaries taxable income received by the estate, so that income will be taxed at only one level. For an estate that may accumulate income, such as Mr. Rollert's estate, this general allocation scheme is accomplished through the distribution rules of sections 661 through 663. Section 691 serves a totally different purpose. It is designed to deal with the problem of how to tax income that has been earned but not received by an individual as of the date of his or her death. Under section 691, income that has accrued to a decedent prior to death but has not yet been received is not included in the decedent's final income tax return, even though the right to such income may be included on the estate's estate tax return. Instead, the income is reported when received by the person who actually receives the income. * * *

Here, petitioner used the distribution rules of section 662 in an attempt to reduce the income taxed to it under section 691. In effect what petitioner did here was to report part of the payments of income in respect of a decedent as income under section 662, even before the payments were made by General Motors. When the payments were actually made in subsequent years, petitioner excluded the previously reported amounts from its section 691 income. Because the treatment of payments of income in respect of a decedent in this manner would completely undermine the mandate of section 691 that the recipient of such income report it for the year when received, we agree with respondent that petitioner had no right to reduce its income in respect of a decedent in the year it received the bonus payments by the amounts it had previously reported as income under section 662.

Section 691(a)(1) provides that the amount of all items of income in respect of a decedent shall be included in gross income, for the taxable year when received. This rule applies to income in respect of a decedent received by (a) the decedent's estate if it has acquired from the decedent the right to receive such income; (B) a person who has acquired, by reason of the decedent's death, the right to receive such income if the right to receive such income was not acquired by the decedent's estate from decedent; and (c) a person who has acquired the right to receive the amount by bequest, devise or inheritance from the decedent, after a distribution by the decedent's estate of such right. See also section 1.691(a)–2(a), * * *. In this case, subparagraph (a) required Mr. Rollert's estate to include in income amounts received with respect to those rights to bonus installments that it did not distribute to petitioner, and subparagraph (c) required petitioner to include those bonus installments that it received with respect to rights the estate had distributed to it.

Under section 661(a), an estate deducts in computing its taxable income (1) any amount of income required to be distributed currently and (2) "any other amounts properly paid or credited or required to be distributed for such taxable year." However, the total amount of these deductions may not exceed the estate's distributable net income. Under section 662, the beneficiary to whom these distributions are made must include in gross income a corresponding amount. Sections 661(b) and 662(b) are designed to assure that the character of the amounts deducted by the estate and taken into income by the beneficiary is proportionate to the character of items entering into the computation of distributable net income.

Petitioner and the estate applied the distribution rules of sections 661 and 662 to the distribution of the rights to receive subsequent bonus installments. With respect to each bonus right it distributed, the estate deducted the entire fair market value of the right as a distribution of its distributable net income. Petitioner took this same amount into income and used it as its basis in the right to the bonus installment. The character of petitioner's income was determined under sections 661(b) and 662(b) by reference to the character of the estate's distributable net income rather than by reference to the character of the bonus itself.

Petitioner treated section 691 as coming into play only when the actual payments of the bonus installments were made. It treated each bonus payment as income when received but only to the extent, if any, that the amount paid to it exceeded the basis it had previously assigned the bonus right.

Petitioner claims that the distribution to it of the rights to the bonus installments falls squarely within the literal language of sections 661(a)(2) and 662(a)(2) as "amounts properly paid or credited." Since the rights were irrevocably transferred to petitioner and had an acknowledged value to it at the time of distribution, which was taken into income as a distribution from the estate, the distribution appears on its face to fall within the ambit of these provisions. However, the terms "amounts properly paid or credited" would be excessively broad if read literally. Thus, these words must be interpreted in the light of the statutory framework and overall legislative objectives of subchapter J. * * *

In characterizing the distribution of the rights to the bonus installments as amounts properly paid or credited, petitioner placed particular reliance upon sections 1.661(a)–2(c) and (f), * * *. Section 1.661(a)–2(c) specifies that the term "any other amounts properly paid or credited or required to be distributed" includes a distribution of property in kind, which petitioner believes includes the distribution here of the rights to the bonus installments. Section 1.661(a)–2(f)(2)* * * states that, in determining the amount deductible by the estate and includable in gross income of the beneficiary, the property distributed in kind is taken into account at its fair market value at the time it was distributed, credited, or required to be distributed. There is no dispute in this case as to the fair market values of the rights on the dates of distribution. Section 1.661(a)–2(f)(3) provides that to the extent the fair market value of the property is included in a beneficiary's gross income, the beneficiary takes such amount as its basis for the property.

Respondent points out that the assigning of tax basis to the rights to income in respect of a decedent has enabled petitioner to escape income taxation on much of the income payable under those rights. In each year in which the rights to the bonus installments were distributed, the estate had distributable net income consisting primarily of bonus payments actually received by it in that year. The estate retained part of this income, but offset this action by distributing to petitioner rights to bonus installments that had not yet been paid to the estate. Because it treated the transfers of the rights as distributions of distributable net income, the estate's deduction for distributions of distributable net income included the date-of-distribution values of the bonus rights. The estate thereby reduced its taxable income by carrying its distributable net income out to petitioner, even though it retained much of the income it had received. Petitioner increased its income in the years of distribution by taking into income the date-of-distribution values of the bonus rights, in other words the discounted value of the future installments of income. However, by assigning basis under section 1.661(a)–2(f)(3), to these rights, its income was reduced by the same amounts in the later years when the bonus installments were actually paid, except with respect to two installments of stock which had declined in value between the date the rights were awarded and the dates the installments were paid, in which case the reduction in income was limited by the value of the stock when the installments were paid. Thus, for the bonus rights that increased in value between the dates of distribution and receipt, the net effect of the treatment of the bonus rights by petitioner and the estate was to reduce the aggregate taxable income of the estate and petitioner by the fair market values of the bonus rights as of the dates of distribution. For the two stock installments that declined in value during this period, aggregate taxable income was reduced by the values of the stock when paid to petitioner.

We therefore agree with respondent that the approach taken by petitioner and the estate allowed substantial sums of income to escape taxation. Section 691 and its legislative history evince a clear purpose to tax income in respect of a decedent in the same manner as if it had been received by the decedent. Allowing the escape from taxation suggested by petitioner would undermine this purpose. In this respect, we believe the following language from Commissioner v. Linde, 213 F.2d 1, 5–6 (9th Cir.1954), * * * is instructive:

¶ 32,061

[T]here is nothing in the legislative history or in the text of Sec. 126 [the 1939 I.R.C. predecessor to section 691] to indicate that it was intended to be anything other than an improved device to accomplish the general purpose of the internal revenue code that all income should pay a tax and that death should not rob the United States of the revenue which otherwise it would have had. * * *

* * *

[I]t is our view that section 126 was but an improved method adopted by Congress in aid of its continuing effort to avoid the loss of tax upon income merely because of the death of the decedent who would have paid a tax upon the same economic returns had he lived to receive them.

Petitioner would have us accept its taking into income under section 662(a) the value of the bonus rights when distributed as satisfying the objective of section 691 to tax all income in respect of a decedent to the actual recipient of the income. Petitioner is correct that the overall amount of income reported by it under either section 662(a) or section 691 was similar to the amount it would have reported had it not treated the receipt of the rights to future bonus installments as distributions of the estate's distributable net income. However, as we have explained above, the aggregate amount of income reported by the estate and petitioner was substantially reduced by petitioner's approach since the distributions of the rights to future bonus installments were treated as carrying out to petitioner the estate's distributable net income. The estate thereby reduced its reported income and was able to accumulate funds, which could subsequently be paid out, tax-free, to petitioner, the residuary legatee.

For this reason, we do not believe that petitioner's reporting income under section 662 when it received the rights to subsequent bonus installments should be treated as satisfying the requirement that the recipient report all income in respect of a decedent. Furthermore, even if we were to assume that petitioner's treatment of the bonus rights and installments satisfied the requirement of section 691 that income in respect of a decedent be taxed to the recipient of such income, we see no way that it could also satisfy the timing and characterization rules of that section.

Section 691(a)(1) requires income in respect of a decedent to be included in income "for the taxable year when received." It is designed to defer taxation of these amounts until actual receipt. Were we to accept petitioner's view that its reporting income when the rights to bonus installments were distributed satisfied the objective that it be taxed on the income in respect of a decedent, it would be apparent that the timing rule had been violated. Under petitioner's approach, the only income deferred until actual receipt would be the excess of the amount received over the amount reported in the year the right was distributed.

Section 691(a)(3) requires the character of income in respect of a decedent to be the same as it would have been in the hands of the decedent if the decedent had lived and received such income. Here, however, only that income actually reported in the year of receipt as income in respect of a decedent took

¶ 32,061

its character under section 691(a)(3). The character of the rights to income in respect of a decedent that were distributed was determined under section 662(b) by reference to the character of the estate's distributable net income. Thus, it is apparent that petitioner's approach would also cripple the characterization rule for income in respect of a decedent.

It is a well accepted principle of law that a specific statute controls over a general one even if the latter might otherwise appear to govern. * * * As we have explained, there is an apparent conflict between section 691 and the distribution rules of sections 661 and 662. In view of the nature of section 691 as a specific statutory scheme for the taxation of income in respect of a decedent, which would be largely defeated were rights to income in respect of a decedent allowed to acquire basis under the distribution rules, we believe section 691 must take precedence here.

Although the legislative history of section 691 and the regulations under that section do not specifically address the issue presented in this case, they do tend to support our conclusion that sections 661 and 662 should not be applied to an estate's distribution of rights to income in respect of a decedent. Example 1 of section 1.691(a)–2(b) * * * which illustrates the application of the general principle of taxing income in respect of decedent when received, involves a fact situation quite similar to that now before us. A decedent was entitled to salary payments in five annual installments after his death. The estate collected the first two payments and then distributed to the residuary legatee the right to the remaining three installments. The example states that the estate must include the first two installments in its gross income and the legatee must include the subsequent three installments in his gross income. This example does not even refer to the possibility of the right to the final three installments being treated as distribution governed by sections 661 and 662. If the distribution rules were meant to apply to distributions of rights to income in respect of a decedent, the absence of any reference to this effect in the regulation is incomprehensible.

The current rules in section 691 for the taxation of income in respect of a decedent are derived primarily from section 126 of the 1939 I.R.C. * * * The legislative history of that provision clearly states Congress' intent that amounts of income in respect of a decedent—* * *

> be treated, in the hands of the persons receiving them, as income of the same nature and to the same extent as such amounts would be income if the decedent remained alive and received such amounts. [S. Rept. 1631, 77th Cong., 2d Sess., 1942–2 C.B. 504, 580.]

At several points, the Senate report indicates the provision was designed to place the recipient of the income in respect of a decedent in the same position as the decedent with respect to both the amount and character of income. Nothing in the legislative history of the 1954 I.R.C., which introduced the distribution rules of sections 661 and 662, indicates any congressional desire to change the requirement that income in respect of a decedent be taxed in the same manner as it would have been treated if it had been received by the decedent himself. The decedent would normally report for tax purposes each installment as received, with the full installment being included

¶ 32,061

as income. The provisions of the legislative history cited by petitioner do not indicate otherwise. All that these provisions are concerned with is the general rule of sections 661 and 662 that all distributions are deductible by the estate and includable by the beneficiary when distributed. They do not deal, however, with the question before us now of whether a distribution of rights to income in respect of a decedent is a distribution subject to sections 661 and 662.

Contrary to petitioner's contention, the changes made when the 1954 I.R.C. was enacted actually support respondent. * * * Congress extended section 691(a)(1) so that it applies to rights to income in respect of a prior decedent that are acquired by a beneficiary from a second decedent. As an example of how this provision works, the committee reports mention a widow who was entitled to receive insurance renewal commissions but who died before receiving such commission income. Under the pre–1954 law, the fair market value of the right to receive the commissions had to be included in the widow's final income tax return, even though she left to her son the right to receive the commissions. Congress explained that section 691 was being expanded so that no income would be realized on the transfer to the widow's estate of the right to income from the prior decedent. The commissions earned by the prior decedent should be taxed to the recipient upon receipt and their character determined by reference to the prior decedent. These results outlined in the reports under the post–1954 law could not be obtained if petitioner's theory were accepted, since petitioner would treat the distribution from the estate of the prior decedent to the widow as a distribution of a right to income in respect of a decedent, which would require the widow to recognize income and would create a basis in the right to receive future commissions. The rights to the commission income had necessarily been distributed from the estate of the prior decedent to the widow, and under petitioner's theory the widow would have reported the fair market value of such rights when they were distributed to her and taken such value as her basis in the rights. Nowhere do the committee reports even intimate that this might be the proper treatment.

We address finally petitioner's contention that its treatment of the bonus rights did not defeat the overall scheme of section 691 since section 1.661(a)–2(f) * * * forgives any income tax on the appreciation in value of property in kind distributed by an estate or trust. It is apparent that this regulation does cause the nonrecognition of some unrealized appreciation. However, there are several key distinctions between the nonrecognition sanctioned by this regulation and the situation before us now. First of all, petitioner has assumed that the difference between the value of a right to income in respect of a decedent and its basis can properly be labeled as appreciation. However, the right to income in respect of a decedent is the right to compensation income, which was already earned by the decedent and became nonforfeitable upon his death. This is simply income that has been earned but not yet reported, and thus cannot be seen as constituting appreciation in the value of property. Any increase in the value of bonus rights resulted from the fact that they were initially discounted because of the delay

¶ 32,061

that had to be borne until the recipient could actually enjoy receipt of the income.

More importantly, petitioner's analogy to appreciated property is misplaced because it fails to consider that section 1014(a) generally allows a step-up in basis to the date-of-death valuation for property acquired from a decedent, while section 1014(c) denies a basis step-up for rights to income in respect of a decedent. Petitioner's approach would allow an escape from income taxation for all income in respect of a decedent represented by the value of the right to such income when distributed. This would have the effect of allowing a step-up in basis for increases in value of rights to income in respect of a decedent occurring before the decedent's death, as well as those occurring between the date of death and the date of distribution. Thus, petitioner's interpretation of section 1.661(a)–2(f) * * * sees respondent as having allowed by regulation what was specifically denied by statute under section 1014(c), i.e., a step-up basis to the date-of-death value for rights to income in respect of a decedent.

We hold as a general principle that section 691 overrides sections 661 and 662 and precludes the assignment of a basis to a right to income in respect of a decedent when that right is transferred by an estate to a legatee. Therefore, we find in this case that petitioner improperly offset against its income in respect of a decedent basis previously assigned to the rights to the bonus installments. Because the lifetime bonus installments were included in the gross estate, in computing petitioner's income tax liability relative to the contested bonus installments, a deduction under section 691(c) should be allowed for the Federal estate tax the estate paid with respect to the rights to these installments.

F. RELATIONSHIP OF IRD TO DISTRIBUTION RULES

[¶ 32,067]

In *Rollert* (¶ 32,061), the estate had claimed a distribution deduction for the IRD distributed to the estate's beneficiaries. However, the Tax Court refused to allow the recipients of the IRD to claim that the IRD had a basis for income tax purposes in their hands. Implicit in Rollert is the notion that the taxpayer acted improperly in claiming a distribution deduction pursuant to § 661 for the distributed IRD.

Similarly, in Estate of Dean v. Commissioner, 46 T.C.M. (CCH) 184, T.C.M. (P–H) ¶ 83,276 (1983), the Tax Court refused a distribution deduction under § 661 for the distribution of IRD, in this case, an installment note.

In affirming *Rollert*, the Sixth Circuit stated (752 F.2d at 1133):

Accordingly, in the absence of § 691, the distribution of the bonus rights would have been governed by §§ 661 and 662 and the regulations thereunder.

However, section 691 does exist and it specifically applies to the transaction at issue here—the distribution of income in respect of a decedent. Sections 661 and 662 apply to a wider range of property interests, including income which would not qualify under section 691. It is a basic rule of statutory construction that a specific statute controls over a general statute. * * *. If we were to hold that the more general statute controls over the specific one, we would effectively eliminate the specific statute. Congress did not enact section 691 merely to have it subsumed by §§ 661 and 662.

Thus, with the decision in *Rollert*, IRD joins specific bequests in being disengaged or exempted from the distribution rules of Sections 661 and 662. See § 663(a)(1) and ¶ 30,061.

G. WHEN IRD IS INCLUDIBLE IN TAXPAYER'S GROSS INCOME

[¶ 32,073]

Generally, IRD is included in the gross income of the taxpayer in the taxable year it is received, without regard to the taxpayer's usual method of accounting. § 691(a)(1); *Rollert Residuary Trust*, ¶ 32,019 and 32,061. Thus, the decedent's estate or successor in interest is placed on a cash method of accounting with respect to the taxation of IRD amounts. The recipient's tax bracket (not the decedent's) determines the tax liability.

H. CHARACTER OF IRD

[¶ 32,079]

The character of the IRD to the estate or successor in interest is considered the same as it would have been to the decedent had the decedent lived and received the income. § 691(a)(3) and Reg. § 1.691(a)–3(b).

Example: David sold Blackacre on November 15, 1998. The terms of the contract provided that David would receive all cash on or before January 15, 1999. David died on December 15, 1998, however, and the gain from the sale was not properly includible in David's 1998 income tax return. Had the gain been reported, however, it would have been capital gain from the sale or exchange of an asset held for longer than one (1) year (and entitled to preferential income tax treatment under the rules then applicable to capital gains). Thus, to the extent the proceeds are received by David's estate or successor in interest, such income (IRD) would be long-term capital gain, because it is treated in the same manner as if David's estate or successor had held the property for the period David held it and had made the sale. See Reg. § 1.691(a)–3(b).

I. ALLOWANCE OF DEDUCTIONS

[¶ 32,085]

Section 691(b) permits certain items of expense that would have been allowed as deductions to the decedent had the decedent lived to pay them to be allowed as deductions to the decedent's estate or to the person who is obliged to pay them and in fact does pay them. These deductions are known as deductions in respect of a decedent (DIRD).

[¶ 32,091]

1. DIRD ALLOWED

DIRDs are allowed for expenses, interest and taxes under §§ 162, 163, 164, and 212, for the foreign tax paid credit under § 33, and for the § 611 depletion allowance (only to whomever receives income to which the depletion allowance relates).

[¶ 32,097]

2. LIMITATIONS ON DIRD

The DIRD is allowed to the estate of the decedent except in those cases where (1) the DIRD is properly allowable to the decedent, or (2) the estate itself is not liable to discharge the obligations to which the deduction or credit relates. In the latter case, the items of DIRD are allowed to the person who, by reason of the death of the decedent, acquires, subject to the obligation, an interest in the property of the decedent, which is liable for these obligations of the decedent.

[¶ 32,103]

3. DOUBLE DEDUCTIONS

Section 642(g), which generally disallows deductions on both the federal estate tax return and the fiduciary income tax return, does not apply to DIRD.

Example: At Louise's death on July 30, 2005, the taxes imposed for 2005 on her real property by the city, county, and school district in which she resided had not been paid. Moreover, as of the date of Louise's death, the tax bills were not even required to have been mailed by the respective taxing entities nor, for that matter, was there any requirement that the tax rate for 2005 even be established by the respective taxing districts prior to October 1, 2005. However, under the law applicable in Louise's state—and in many other states—Louise's real property taxes for 2005 became a lien on January 1, 2005, even though payment could be made as late as January 15, 2006, without penalty. Accordingly, the real property taxes, when paid by Louise's executor, would be deductions in respect of a decedent (DIRD)—and would also be deductible on Louise's federal estate tax return as one of Louise's debts. See § 2053(a).

J. RELIEF FROM "DOUBLE" TAXATION

[¶ 32,109]

A right to income possessed by a decedent at death (IRD) will be included in the decedent's gross estate and will be subject to the estate tax. §§ 2033,

2035, 2036, 2038, 2039, and 2043. In order to avoid what may be perceived as double taxation, i.e., when the item of IRD is later collected by the decedent's estate or successor in interest, the recipient may claim an income tax deduction for the amount of the estate and inheritance taxes that were paid as a result of the inclusion of the IRD item in the decedent's gross estate. § 691(c). Similarly, any generation-skipping tax paid on an item of income may be claimed as an income tax deduction. § 691(c)(3).

The mechanics of the IRD computation are described in Rev. Rul. 67–242, 1967–2 C.B. 227, as follows:

> To determine the deduction allowable, it is first necessary to compute the net value of the items which are to be treated as income in respect of a decedent under the provisions of section 691(a). This net value is the value in the gross estate of all items of income in respect of a decedent, less the claims deductible for Federal estate tax purposes which represent the deductions and credits in respect of the decedent described in section 691(b).

> The estate tax attributable to such net value is an amount equal to the excess of the estate tax over the estate tax computed without including in the gross estate such net value. The recomputation of the estate tax to arrive at the latter figure is effected by excluding from the value of the gross estate the net value of all items of income in respect of the decedent. The difference between the estate tax and the estate tax as so recomputed is the total deduction allowed under section 691(c).

While this general statement of the arithmetic model is easily understood, there is disagreement as to the procedure for determining the § 691(c) amount when either or both the marital (§ 2056) and charitable (§ 2055) deductions have been claimed on the decedent's Federal estate tax return. See Estate of Cherry v. United States, 133 F. Supp.2d 949 (W.D. Ky. 2001); Estate of Kincaid v. Commissioner, 85 T.C. 25 (1985); Chastain v. Commissioner, 59 T.C. 461 (1972); C. J. Langstraat & A.M Cagle, Deduction Offsets 'Double Tax' on Inherited Income, 67 Prac. Tax Strategies 86 (2001). At issue is whether the marital deduction and/or the charitable deduction need be recalculated once the IRD has been removed from the value of the gross estate as called for by § 691(c).

A more detailed description of the controversy is beyond the scope of these materials, but it is worthy of note that, fortunately, the uncertainty that produces the controversy is eliminated in those instances where the governing instrument—the decedent's will or trust—earmarks the IRD either (1) as part of the property to pass to the spouse (in the case where the marital deduction has been claimed) or to the charity (in the case where the charitable deduction has been claimed), or (2) as part of the property to pass to the other beneficiaries. The ultimate choice of a final destination for the IRD is a function of *other* criteria, *i.e.*, criteria unrelated to the § 691(c) deduction. That is, in earmarking the IRD during the will or trust drafting stage, both tax and nontax factors, for example, affect whether the IRD should be specifically earmarked as part of the gift to the surviving spouse that qualifies for the marital deduction or whether it should be earmarked as part of the share that is to pass to the bypass trust that the decedent has asked to be established after death for the benefit of the children. Identifying these factors, too, is beyond the scope of these materials. Suffice it to say, that earmarking, simply put, *should eliminate* the uncertainty—and controversy with the IRS (and possible) litigation that can result—when making the § 691(c) computation.

K. SERIES E, EE AND I SAVINGS BONDS

[¶ 32,133]

1. INTRODUCTION

Series E United States Savings Bonds were bonds sold by the government at a discount from face value. For example, a $25 bond was sold for $18.75. At maturity, the bond was redeemable at face value. Originally, Series E bonds matured on the 10th anniversary of the purchase date. Given the time to maturity, the rate of return on the original investment was not great. Accordingly, as interest rates rose and the American public became more sophisticated, sales of Series E bonds declined. To combat this decline, in recent years the Treasury stopped selling Series E bonds and began the sale of Series EE bonds, Series EE bonds being priced in terms of discount and time to maturity so as to make the rate of return on the investment more competitive. Currently, I bonds are also offered. Interest on I bonds are inflation adjusted.

In the meantime, the dollar value of outstanding Series E, EE and I bonds is enormous. More importantly, many of the outstanding E and EE bonds have been outstanding for 20–40 years. They were not redeemed because the government offered to extend the maturity date of the outstanding bonds and to continue to credit the bonds with interest. Thus, many of the outstanding bonds can be redeemed for an amount that greatly exceeds the face value of the bonds.

The maturity date on Series E and EE bonds will not, however, be extended beyond 40 years. (I bonds and recently issued EE bonds have maturities limited to 30 years.) For example, a bond purchased in May 1941 did not earn interest after April 30, 1981. More importantly, perhaps, is the fact that any unreported interest on such bonds becomes taxable on the 40th anniversary of the bond's purchase even if the bond is not then redeemed.

For tax purposes the difference between purchase price and the amount received upon redemption is taxable income at ordinary income tax rates. Taxpayers have the option of annually reporting for income tax purposes the interest income as it accrues, or deferring recognition of that income until the bonds are redeemed. Taxpayers also have an intermediate position available to them. They may defer recognition for a number of years and then report for income tax purposes all of the deferred interest in a particular year without redeeming the bonds. Once having elected to report the accrued interest on a Series E, EE or I bond, the taxpayer must thereafter report annually each subsequent year's interest accrual. When a taxpayer dies

¶ 32,109

holding such bonds, important postmortem planning elections should be considered.

[¶ 32,139]

2. SECTION 454(a) ELECTION

If the taxpayer dies holding Series E, EE or I bonds, their full value, including all accrued interest, would be includible in the gross estate. The accrued interest is also IRD. The executor of the estate may elect to report all interest accrued to the date of death as income on the decedent's final income tax return, or on the subsequent estate income tax returns. However, the executor is not obligated to report the accrued income currently (from the date of purchase through the year in which the decedent died). Instead, reporting the accrued interest for income tax purposes can be put off until the bonds are redeemed. § 454(a).

[¶ 32,145]

3. TIMING

Assume a decedent dies this year on October 15. If the executor elects a short calendar year for the estate income tax return rather than a full fiscal year, the estate will have only 2½ months of income to report from sources other than Series EE bonds (e.g., bank accounts, cash dividends). By electing to report all accrued interest from the Series E, EE and I bonds in the short year, the estate can take advantage of what may be lower marginal income tax rates. See Rev. Rul. 68–145, 1968–1 C.B. 203.

[¶ 32,151]

a. *Later Recognition of Income*

The election of § 454(a), once made, will require annual current income recognition thereafter. Because the tax attributable to such income may be substantial, the costs should be considered by the executor prior to making the election.

[¶ 32,157]

b. *Inclusion in Decedent's Final Return*

The decedent's executor may elect to include all accrued interest from Series E, EE and I bonds in the decedent's final income tax return. For example, consider Melvin, a person of modest circumstances and modest income, all his income coming from his wages as a stenographer. If Melvin died this year on January 15, income for his final tax year would probably be insubstantial, as would be the tax thereon. Furthermore, increases in income taxes payable as a result of the inclusion of accrued interest on saving bonds in Melvin's return will increase the debt deduction on his estate tax return, if any. (The income tax liability shown on Melvin's final income tax return is viewed as Melvin's tax deductible debt for estate tax purposes. § 2053(a).)

¶ 32,157

[¶ 32,163]

c. *Distribution to Beneficiaries*

Series E, EE and I bonds can be distributed to the estate's beneficiaries and reissued in their names. The beneficiaries can then dispose of the bonds and recognize all accrued income at that time. Alternately, the beneficiaries can, at any time before disposition of the bonds, elect to report all accrued interest not previously reported and pay the income tax thereon. § 454(a). In either event, the accrued interest income is not included on the decedent's or fiduciary's income tax return. The executor should determine which of these procedures, or combination of procedures, will result in the least income tax.

Appendix A

ESTATE TAX RETURN PROBLEM

The following information should be used in preparing the United States Estate Tax Return, Form 706, for Melissa Lenore "Missy'" Sanchez, M.D., who died this year on April 14.

Missy, who was born 70 years ago on April 1, had always been a United States citizen and, at the time of her death, was a resident of Massey City in Thorp County. Her address was known for street numbering purposes as 2036 Copulsky Way. Missy died at the Massey Hospital after an illness of three weeks, her death certificate stating that carcinoma was the cause of death. Her physician was P.D. Quick, M.D., 2056 Lindblad Street, Massey.

Missy's social security number was 209–06–1843. The Federal Tax Identification Number issued to her estate is 75–1234567. Her estate is being administered in the Thorp County Probate Court as Case No. P–9113.

Missy's will was admitted to probate on April 30, and letters testamentary were granted on that day to her son, Chad Van Swelt (SSN 678–67–8901), age 45, as executor. Chad resides at 2033 Citera Avenue, in Massey City.

In addition to Chad, Missy was survived by her daughter, Ann "Buffy" Van Swelt Takenaka (SSN 109–06–1879), age 40; Chad's 10–year-old child, Zeb; Ann's 11 children, ranging in age from 8 to 19; and Missy's husband, Hector Sanchez (SSN 456–56–6789), now 84 years old. Hector and Missy were married on April 2, two years ago, shortly after the death of Missy's first husband, Bickford P. "Bick" Van Swelt. Bick died on January 8, two years ago.

In her will, Missy:

1. Provided for a gift of $60,000 to State Ag & Tech Medical School; and

2. Directed her executor to divide the remainder of her estate into two separate funds, one fund to be known as Fund A and the other as Fund B. Her executor was directed to allocate to Fund A "the smallest amount necessary to reduce the federal and state death taxes imposed on my estate to the least possible amount." The balance of her estate was to be placed in Fund B. Under the terms of Missy's will, Fund A was to be placed in trust for the benefit of her husband, Hector, for life. During the continuance of the trust, Hector was to receive all of the income from the trust. Upon termination of the trust, the trust property was to be distributed free of trust to Missy's grandchildren who were living at that time. As to Fund B, Missy directed that the property allocated to Fund B was to be distributed free of trust in equal shares "per capita and not per stirpes" to Missy's grandchildren who were living at the time of her death. Any

state or federal death taxes payable as a result of Missy's death were to be paid from the portion of Missy's property allocated to Fund B.

At the time of her death, Missy was a medical doctor under contract with Doc-in-a-Box, Inc., a publicly owned business offering walk-up medical services from kiosks located in shopping malls in a three state area. The business address of Doc-in-a-Box was 2042 Barton–Coven Bank Building, Massey. The taxpayer identification number of Doc-in-a-Box was 75–7654321.

The following additional facts have been developed:

1. *Gifts.* Five years ago, Missy gave her son and daughter $25,000 each.

2. *Investments.* Stocks and bonds, in Missy's name alone, having a value of $1,990,000 were found in safe deposit box 231 at Granite Bank, Massey. The safe deposit box was jointly owned by Missy and Hector. Reg. § 20.2033–1.

3. *Residence.* Missy's residence was owned, according to the deed, by "Hector and Melissa Lenore Sanchez, husband and wife" which under state law created a tenancy to the entireties. Missy paid $40,000 from her separate property for the property in 1958 and took title in her own name, where it remained until she married Hector. At that time, Missy signed a deed placing the property in her name and that of Hector. The property was valued at $600,000 at Missy's death. See § 2040(b).

4. *Insurance on Missy's Life.* Missy was the insured on two insurance policies, both issued by HAHA (Honest American Hodcarriers Mutual Benefit Society). The $100,000 proceeds of one, Policy No. 456456, owned by Missy, were payable in equal shares to her children, Chad and Buffy. The $100,000 proceeds of the other, Policy No. 678678, taken out and owned by her son, Chad (who worked as a hodcarrier), were payable to Chad. See § 2042.

5. *Insurance on Lives of Others.* Missy also owned $60,000 policies of life insurance on the lives of each of her children. The policy on Chad's life HAHA Policy No. 123123, had a cash value at Missy's death of $32,000 and the policy on Buffy's life, HAHA Policy No. 345345, had a surrender value of $28,000. See § 2033.

6. *Claims Owned by Missy.* After Missy died, the executor of her estate received $8,626 from the Internal Revenue Service. The payment constituted the refund of Missy's income tax overpayment for last year. Missy had filed last year's income tax return prior to her death and claimed the refund at that time.

7. *Retirement Plans.* At her death, Missy was receiving benefits from a qualified pension plan established by Doc-in-a-Box, Inc., for her benefit (and that of other employees). At the time of her death, the value of Missy's account in the plan was $800,000. Under the terms of the beneficiary designation made by Missy during her lifetime, the plan benefits continued to be paid to her husband, Hector, for life. See § 2039.

8. *KidsTrust #1.* In 1968, Missy transferred property to a trustee "to pay the income to my children during my life." The trust was to

terminate at Missy's death and, upon termination, the trust property was to be distributed to those of Missy's children who survived her. Within the family, the trust was referred to as the KidsTrust #1. If no child survived Missy the corpus was to be paid to the estates of all deceased children. The property in the trust had a value of $60,000 at Missy's death. While Missy's brother, Snerd, was the original trustee, Missy became the trustee of the trust when Snerd died ten years ago. Reg. § 20.2038–1.

9. *Kids Trust #2.* Missy also established an irrevocable trust in 1973. The trust, known as the Kids Trust #2, provided that all of the trust income would be paid quarterly to those children of Missy who were living on the date set by the trustee for each quarterly payment. Kids Trust #2 was to terminate upon the death of the last to die of Missy's children. Upon termination, the property constituting Kids Trust #2 was to be distributed to those persons selected by Missy from among her grandchildren and their issue. In default of effective exercise of the power of appointment by Missy, the trust property was to be distributed to Missy's issue pcr stirpes. The trust corpus was valued at $100,000 at Missy's death. Reg. § 20.2038–1.

10. *BickTrust.* Missy's first husband, Bick, created a testamentary trust for the benefit of Missy (which was referred to within the family as the BickTrust. At Bick's death, his executor claimed the marital deduction for the property then constituting the BickTrust which, at the time, had a value of $250,000. During her lifetime, all of the trust income was to be paid to Missy. At her death, the trust provided that Missy could appoint the property then constituting the trust estate to one or more of her children (or to the exclusion of one or more of them), as she might designate in her will. As noted above, Missy exercised the power by designating her son, Chad, as the recipient of the trust property upon her death. At Missy's death BickTrust had a value of $300,000. See §§ 2041 and 2044; Reg. §§ 20.2041–3 and 20.2044–1.

11. *Mom'sTrust.* Upon her marriage to Hector, Missy established a trust to pay the income to herself for life, remainder to such persons, including herself, as she might appoint by her will. This trust was referred to as the Mom'sTrust. While Missy retained the right to revoke the trust at any time, it had not been revoked at the time of her death and had a value of $80,000 at that time. Reg. § 20.2038–1.

12. *Expenses.* Missy's debts at her death were funeral expenses of $15,000 and administration expenses of $25,000. In addition, the $4,200 real property taxes imposed on Missy's residence became a lien this year on January 1, even though the taxes will not be billed to Missy until October and will not be required to be paid under applicable state law until next January 31. Missy's executor will pay these taxes next year when due. Reg. § 20.2053.

Form **706**	**United States Estate (and Generation-Skipping**		
(Rev. August 2005)	**Transfer) Tax Return**		OMB No. 1545-0015
Department of the Treasury Internal Revenue Service	Estate of a citizen or resident of the United States (see separate instructions). To be filed for decedents dying after December 31, 2004, and before January 1, 2006.		

Part 1.—Decedent and Executor

1a	Decedent's first name and middle initial (and maiden name, if any)	1b Decedent's last name	2 Decedent's Social Security No.
3a	County, state, and ZIP code, or foreign country, of legal residence (domicile) at time of death	3b Year domicile established	4 Date of birth	5 Date of death
6a	Name of executor (see page 3 of the instructions)	6b Executor's address (number and street including apartment or suite no. or rural route; city, town, or post office; state; and ZIP code) and phone no.	
6c	Executor's social security number (see page 3 of the instructions)		Phone no. ( )
7a	Name and location of court where will was probated or estate administered		7b Case number
8	If decedent died testate, check here ▶ ☐ and attach a certified copy of the will.	9 If you extended the time to file this Form 706, check here ▶ ☐	
10	If Schedule R-1 is attached, check here ▶ ☐		

Part 2.—Tax Computation

1	Total gross estate less exclusion (from Part 5, Recapitulation, page 3, item 12)	1	
2	Total allowable deductions (from Part 5, Recapitulation, page 3, item 22)	2	
3a	Tentative taxable estate (before state death tax deduction) (subtract line 2 from line 1)	3a	
b	State death tax deduction	3b	
c	Taxable estate (subtract line 3b from line 3a)	3c	
4	Adjusted taxable gifts (total taxable gifts (within the meaning of section 2503) made by the decedent after December 31, 1976, other than gifts that are includible in decedent's gross estate (section 2001(b)))	4	
5	Add lines 3c and 4	5	
6	Tentative tax on the amount on line 5 from Table A on page 4 of the instructions	6	
7	Total gift tax payable with respect to gifts made by the decedent after December 31, 1976. Include gift taxes by the decedent's spouse for such spouse's share of split gifts (section 2513) only if the decedent was the donor of these gifts and they are includible in the decedent's gross estate (see instructions)	7	
8	Gross estate tax (subtract line 7 from line 6)	8	
9	Maximum unified credit (applicable credit amount) against estate tax .	9	
10	Adjustment to unified credit (applicable credit amount). (This adjustment may not exceed $6,000. See page 5 of the instructions.)	10	
11	Allowable unified credit (applicable credit amount) (subtract line 10 from line 9).	11	
12	Subtract line 11 from line 8 (but do not enter less than zero)	12	
13	Credit for foreign death taxes (from Schedule(s) P). (Attach Form(s) 706-CE.)	13	
14	Credit for tax on prior transfers (from Schedule Q)	14	
15	Total credits (add lines 13 and 14)	15	
16	Net estate tax (subtract line 15 from line 12)	16	
17	Generation-skipping transfer taxes (from Schedule R, Part 2, line 10)	17	
18	Total transfer taxes (add lines 16 and 17)	18	
19	Prior payments. Explain in an attached statement	19	
20	Balance due (or overpayment) (subtract line 19 from line 18)	20	

Under penalties of perjury, I declare that I have examined this return, including accompanying schedules and statements, and to the best of my knowledge and belief, it is true, correct, and complete. Declaration of preparer other than the executor is based on all information of which preparer has any knowledge.

Signature(s) of executor(s) _____   Date _____

Signature of preparer other than executor _____   Address (and ZIP code) _____   Date _____

For Privacy Act and Paperwork Reduction Act Notice, see page 27 of the separate instructions for this form.   Cat. No. 20548R   Form **706** (Rev. 8-2005)

* The above form is the most recent version of Form 706 which was available when this edition was published. A current version of it and other forms can be found in libraries, at local IRS offices or on the internet at the IRS website (www.irs.gov).

Form 706 (Rev. 8-2005)

Estate of:

Part 3—Elections by the Executor

Please check the "Yes" or "No" box for each question. (See instructions beginning on page 6.)		Yes	No
1	Do you elect alternate valuation? **1**		
2	Do you elect special-use valuation? . . . . If "Yes," you must complete and attach Schedule A–1. **2**		
3	Do you elect to pay the taxes in installments as described in section 6166? . . . . If "Yes," you must attach the additional information described on page 9 of the instructions. **3**		
4	Do you elect to postpone the part of the taxes attributable to a reversionary or remainder interest as described in section 6163? **4**		

Part 4—General Information (Note: *Please attach the necessary supplemental documents.* **You must attach the death certificate.)** *(See instructions on page 10.)*

Authorization to receive confidential tax information under Regs. sec. 601.504(b)(2)(i); to act as the estate's representative before the IRS; and to make written or oral presentations on behalf of the estate if return prepared by an attorney, accountant, or enrolled agent for the executor:

Name of representative (print or type)	State	Address (number, street, and room or suite no., city, state, and ZIP code)

I declare that I am the ☐ attorney/ ☐ certified public accountant/ ☐ enrolled agent (you must check the applicable box) for the executor and prepared this return for the executor. I am not under suspension or disbarment from practice before the Internal Revenue Service and am qualified to practice in the state shown above.

Signature	CAF number	Date	Telephone number

1   Death certificate number and issuing authority (attach a copy of the death certificate to this return).

2   Decedent's business or occupation. If retired, check here ► ☐ and state decedent's former business or occupation.

3   Marital status of the decedent at time of death:
    ☐ Married
    ☐ Widow or widower—Name, SSN, and date of death of deceased spouse ►.....................
    ....
    ☐ Single
    ☐ Legally separated
    ☐ Divorced—Date divorce decree became final ►

4a Surviving spouse's name	4b Social security number	4c Amount received (see page 10 of the instructions)

5   Individuals (other than the surviving spouse), trusts, or other estates who receive benefits from the estate (do not include charitable beneficiaries shown in Schedule O) (see instructions).

Name of individual, trust, or estate receiving $5,000 or more	Identifying number	Relationship to decedent	Amount (see instructions)

All unascertainable beneficiaries and those who receive less than $5,000 . . . . ►

Total . . . .

Please check the "Yes" or "No" box for each question.		Yes	No
6	Does the gross estate contain any section 2044 property (qualified terminable interest property (QTIP) from a prior gift or estate) (see page 10 of the instructions)?		
7a	Have Federal gift tax returns ever been filed? . . . . If "Yes," please attach copies of the returns, if available, and furnish the following information:		

7b Period(s) covered	7c Internal Revenue office(s) where filed

(continued on next page)   **Page 2**

Form 706 (Rev. 8-2005)

Part 4—General Information (continued)

If you answer "Yes" to any of questions 8–16, you must attach additional information as described in the instructions.	Yes	No
8a Was there any insurance on the decedent's life that is not included on the return as part of the gross estate?		
b Did the decedent own any insurance on the life of another that is not included in the gross estate?		
9 Did the decedent at the time of death own any property as a joint tenant with right of survivorship in which (a) one or more of the other joint tenants was someone other than the decedent's spouse, and (b) less than the full value of the property is included on the return as part of the gross estate? If "Yes," you must complete and attach Schedule E		
10 Did the decedent, at the time of death, own any interest in a partnership or unincorporated business or any stock in an inactive or closely held corporation?		
11 Did the decedent make any transfer described in section 2035, 2036, 2037, or 2038 (see the instructions for Schedule G beginning on page 13 of the separate instructions)? If "Yes," you must complete and attach Schedule G		
12a Were there in existence at the time of the decedent's death any trusts created by the decedent during his or her lifetime?		
b Were there in existence at the time of the decedent's death any trusts not created by the decedent under which the decedent possessed any power, beneficial interest, or trusteeship?		
c Was the decedent receiving income from a trust created after October 22, 1986 by a parent or grandparent?		
If "Yes," was there a GST taxable termination (under section 2612) upon the death of the decedent?		
d If there was a GST taxable termination (under section 2612), attach a statement to explain. Provide a copy of the trust or will creating the trust, and give the name, address, and phone number of the current trustee(s).		
13 Did the decedent ever possess, exercise, or release any general power of appointment? If "Yes," you must complete and attach Schedule H		
14 Was the marital deduction computed under the transitional rule of Public Law 97-34, section 403(e)(3) (Economic Recovery Tax Act of 1981)?		
If "Yes," attach a separate computation of the marital deduction, enter the amount on item 20 of the Recapitulation, and note on item 20 "computation attached."		
15 Was the decedent, immediately before death, receiving an annuity described in the "General" paragraph of the instructions for Schedule I? If "Yes," you must complete and attach Schedule I		
16 Was the decedent ever the beneficiary of a trust for which a deduction was claimed by the estate of a pre-deceased spouse under section 2056(b)(7) and which is not reported on this return? If "Yes," attach an explanation		

Part 5—Recapitulation

Item number	Gross estate		Alternate value	Value at date of death
1	Schedule A—Real Estate	1		
2	Schedule B—Stocks and Bonds	2		
3	Schedule C—Mortgages, Notes, and Cash	3		
4	Schedule D—Insurance on the Decedent's Life (attach Form(s) 712).	4		
5	Schedule E—Jointly Owned Property (attach Form(s) 712 for life insurance)	5		
6	Schedule F—Other Miscellaneous Property (attach Form(s) 712 for life insurance)	6		
7	Schedule G—Transfers During Decedent's Life (att. Form(s) 712 for life insurance)	7		
8	Schedule H—Powers of Appointment	8		
9	Schedule I—Annuities	9		
10	Total gross estate (add items 1 through 9).	10		
11	Schedule U—Qualified Conservation Easement Exclusion	11		
12	Total gross estate less exclusion (subtract item 11 from item 10). Enter here and on line 1 of Part 2—Tax Computation	12		

Item number	Deductions		Amount
13	Schedule J—Funeral Expenses and Expenses Incurred in Administering Property Subject to Claims	13	
14	Schedule K—Debts of the Decedent	14	
15	Schedule K—Mortgages and Liens	15	
16	Total of items 13 through 15	16	
17	Allowable amount of deductions from item 16 (see the instructions for item 17 of the Recapitulation)	17	
18	Schedule L—Net Losses During Administration	18	
19	Schedule L—Expenses Incurred in Administering Property Not Subject to Claims	19	
20	Schedule M—Bequests, etc., to Surviving Spouse	20	
21	Schedule O—Charitable, Public, and Similar Gifts and Bequests	21	
22	Total allowable deductions (add items 17 through 21). Enter here and on line 2 of the Tax Computation.	22	

Page 3

Form 706 (Rev. 8-2005)

Estate of: _____

SCHEDULE A—Real Estate

- For jointly owned property that must be disclosed on Schedule E, see the instructions on the reverse side of Schedule E.
- Real estate that is part of a sole proprietorship should be shown on Schedule F.
- Real estate that is included in the gross estate under section 2035, 2036, 2037, or 2038 should be shown on Schedule G.
- Real estate that is included in the gross estate under section 2041 should be shown on Schedule H.
- If you elect section 2032A valuation, you must complete Schedule A and Schedule A-1.

Item number	Description	Alternate valuation date	Alternate value	Value at date of death
1				
	Total from continuation schedules or additional sheets attached to this schedule			
	TOTAL. (Also enter on Part 5, Recapitulation, page 3, at item 1.)			

(If more space is needed, attach the continuation schedule from the end of this package or additional sheets of the same size.)
(See the instructions on the reverse side.)

Schedule A—Page 4

Form 706 (Rev. 8-2005)

Instructions for Schedule A—Real Estate

If the total gross estate contains any real estate, you must complete Schedule A and file it with the return. On Schedule A, list real estate the decedent owned or had contracted to purchase. Number each parcel in the left-hand column.

Describe the real estate in enough detail so that the IRS can easily locate it for inspection and valuation. For each parcel of real estate, report the area and, if the parcel is improved, describe the improvements. For city or town property, report the street and number, ward, subdivision, block and lot, etc. For rural property, report the township, range, landmarks, etc.

If any item of real estate is subject to a mortgage for which the decedent's estate is liable; that is, if the indebtedness may be charged against other property of the estate that is not subject to that mortgage, or if the decedent was personally liable for that mortgage, you must report the full value of the property in the value

column. Enter the amount of the mortgage under "Description" on this schedule. The unpaid amount of the mortgage may be deducted on Schedule K.

If the decedent's estate is NOT liable for the amount of the mortgage, report only the value of the equity of redemption (or value of the property less the indebtedness) in the value column as part of the gross estate. Do not enter any amount less than zero. Do not deduct the amount of indebtedness on Schedule K.

Also list on Schedule A real property the decedent contracted to purchase. Report the full value of the property and not the equity in the value column. Deduct the unpaid part of the purchase price on Schedule K.

Report the value of real estate without reducing it for homestead or other exemption, or the value of dower, curtesy, or a statutory estate created instead of dower or curtesy.

Explain how the reported values were determined and attach copies of any appraisals.

Schedule A Examples

In this example, alternate valuation is not adopted; the date of death is January 1, 2005.

Item number	Description	Alternate valuation date	Alternate value	Value at date of death
1	House and lot, 1921 William Street NW, Washington, DC (lot 6, square 481). Rent of $2,700 due at end of each quarter, February 1, May 1, August 1, and November 1. Value based on appraisal, copy of which is attached			$108,000
	Rent due on item 1 for quarter ending November 1, 2004, but not collected at date of death			2,700
	Rent accrued on item 1 for November and December 2004			1,800
2	House and lot, 304 Jefferson Street, Alexandria, VA (lot 18, square 40). Rent of $600 payable monthly. Value based on appraisal, copy of which is attached. . . .			96,000
	Rent due on item 2 for December 2004, but not collected at date of death . . .			600

In this example, alternate valuation is adopted; the date of death is January 1, 2005.

Item number	Description	Alternate valuation date	Alternate value	Value at date of death
1	House and lot, 1921 William Street NW, Washington, DC (lot 6, square 481). Rent of $2,700 due at end of each quarter, February 1, May 1, August 1, and November 1. Value based on appraisal, copy of which is attached. Not disposed of within 6 months following death	7/1/05	90,000	$108,000
	Rent due on item 1 for quarter ending November 1, 2004, but not collected until February 1, 2005	2/1/05	2,700	2,700
	Rent accrued on item 1 for November and December 2004, collected on February 1, 2005	2/1/05	1,800	1,800
2	House and lot, 304 Jefferson Street, Alexandria, VA (lot 18, square 40). Rent of $600 payable monthly. Value based on appraisal, copy of which is attached. Property exchanged for farm on May 1, 2005	5/1/05	90,000	96,000
	Rent due on item 2 for December 2004, but not collected until February 1, 2005.	2/1/05	600	600

Schedule A—Page 5

Form 706 (Rev. 8-2005)

Instructions for Schedule A-1. Section 2032A Valuation

The election to value certain farm and closely held business property at its special-use value is made by checking "Yes" to line 2 of Part 3, Elections by the Executor, Form 706. Schedule A-1 is used to report the additional information that must be submitted to support this election. In order to make a valid election, you must complete Schedule A-1 and attach all of the required statements and appraisals.

For definitions and additional information concerning special-use valuation, see section 2032A and the related regulations.

Part 1. Type of Election

Estate and GST Tax Elections. If you elect special-use valuation for the estate tax, you must also elect special-use valuation for the GST tax and *vice versa.*

You must value each specific property interest at the same value for GST tax purposes that you value it at for estate tax purposes.

Protective Election. To make the protective election described in the separate instructions for line 2 of Part 3, Elections by the Executor, you must check this box, enter the decedent's name and social security number in the spaces provided at the top of Schedule A-1, and complete line 1 and column A of lines 3 and 4 of Part 2. For purposes of the protective election, list on line 3 all of the real property that passes to the qualified heirs even though some of the property will be shown on line 2 when the additional notice of election is subsequently filed. You need not complete columns B–D of lines 3 and 4. You need not complete any other line entries on Schedule A-1. Completing Schedule A-1 as described above constitutes a Notice of Protective Election as described in Regulations section 20.2032A-8(b).

Part 2. Notice of Election

Line 10. Because the special-use valuation election creates a potential tax liability for the recapture tax of section 2032A(c), you must list each person who receives an interest in the specially valued property on Schedule A-1. If there are more than eight persons who receive interests, use an additional sheet that follows the format of line 10. In the columns "Fair market value" and "Special-use value," you should enter the total respective values of all the specially valued property interests received by each person.

GST Tax Savings

To compute the additional GST tax due upon disposition (or cessation of qualified use) of the property, each "skip person" (as defined in the instructions to Schedule R) who receives an interest in the specially valued property must know the total GST tax savings on all of the interests in specially valued property received. This GST tax savings is the difference between the total GST tax that was imposed on all of the interests in specially valued property received by the skip person valued at their special-use value and the total GST tax that would have been imposed on the same interests received by the skip person had they been valued at their fair market value.

Because the GST tax depends on the executor's allocation of the GST exemption and the grandchild exclusion, the skip person who receives the interests is unable to compute this GST tax savings. Therefore, for each skip person who receives an interest in specially valued property, you must attach worksheets showing the total GST tax savings attributable to all of that person's interests in specially valued property.

How To Compute the GST Tax Savings. Before computing each skip person's GST tax savings, you must complete Schedules R and R-1 for the entire estate (using the special-use values).

For each skip person, you must complete two Schedules R (Parts 2 and 3 only) as worksheets, one showing the interests in specially valued property received by the skip person at their special-use value and one showing the same interests at their fair market value.

If the skip person received interests in specially valued property that were shown on Schedule R-1, show these interests on the Schedule R, Parts 2 and 3 worksheets, as appropriate. Do not use Schedule R-1 as a worksheet.

Completing the Special-Use Value Worksheets. On lines 2–4 and 6, enter -0-.

Completing the Fair Market Value Worksheets. *Lines 2 and 3, fixed taxes and other charges.* If valuing the interests at their fair market value (instead of special-use value) causes any of these taxes and charges to increase, enter the increased amount (only) on these lines and attach an explanation of the increase. Otherwise, enter -0-.

Line 6—GST exemption. If you completed line 10 of Schedule R, Part 1, enter on line 6 the amount shown for the skip person on the line 10 special-use allocation schedule you attached to Schedule R. If you did not complete line 10 of Schedule R, Part 1, enter -0- on line 6.

Total GST Tax Savings. For each skip person, subtract the tax amount on line 10, Part 2 of the special-use value worksheet from the tax amount on line 10, Part 2 of the fair market value worksheet. This difference is the skip person's total GST tax savings.

Part 3. Agreement to Special Valuation Under Section 2032A

The agreement to special valuation by persons with an interest in property is required under section 2032A(a)(1)(B) and (d)(2) and must be signed by all parties who have any interest in the property being valued based on its qualified use as of the date of the decedent's death.

An interest in property is an interest that, as of the date of the decedent's death, can be asserted under applicable local law so as to affect the disposition of the specially valued property by the estate. Any person who at the decedent's death has any such interest in the property, whether present or future, or vested or contingent, must enter into the agreement. Included are owners of remainder and executory interests; the holders of general or special powers of appointment; beneficiaries of a gift over in default of exercise of any such power; joint tenants and holders of similar undivided interests when the decedent held only a joint or undivided interest in the property or when only an undivided interest is specially valued; and trustees of trusts and representatives of other entities holding title to, or holding any interests in the property. An heir who has the power under local law to caveat (challenge) a will and thereby affect disposition of the property is not, however, considered to be a person with an interest in property under section 2032A solely by reason of that right. Likewise, creditors of an estate are not such persons solely by reason of their status as creditors.

If any person required to enter into the agreement either desires that an agent act for him or her or cannot legally bind himself or herself due to infancy or other incompetency, or due to death before the election under section 2032A is timely exercised, a representative authorized by local law to bind the person in an agreement of this nature may sign the agreement on his or her behalf.

The Internal Revenue Service will contact the agent designated in the agreement on all matters relating to continued qualification under section 2032A of the specially valued real property and on all matters relating to the special lien arising under section 6324B. It is the duty of the agent as attorney-in-fact for the parties with interests in the specially valued property to furnish the IRS with any requested information and to notify the IRS of any disposition or cessation of qualified use of any part of the property.

Schedule A-1—Page 6

Form 706 (Rev. 8-2005)

Checklist for Section 2032A Election.

If you are going to make the special-use valuation election on Schedule A-1, please use this checklist to ensure that you are providing everything necessary to make a valid election.

To have a valid special-use valuation election under section 2032A, you must file, in addition to the Federal estate tax return, **(a)** a notice of election (Schedule A-1, Part 2), and **(b)** a fully executed agreement (Schedule A-1, Part 3). You must include certain information in the notice of election. To ensure that the notice of election includes all of the information required for a valid election, use the following checklist. The checklist is for your use only. Do not file it with the return.

1. Does the notice of election include the decedent's name and social security number as they appear on the estate tax return?

2. Does the notice of election include the relevant qualified use of the property to be specially valued?

3. Does the notice of election describe the items of real property shown on the estate tax return that are to be specially valued and identify the property by the Form 706 schedule and item number?

4. Does the notice of election include the fair market value of the real property to be specially valued and also include its value based on the qualified use (determined without the adjustments provided in section 2032A(b)(3)(B))?

5. Does the notice of election include the adjusted value (as defined in section 2032A(b)(3)(B)) of **(a)** all real property that both passes from the decedent and is used in a qualified use, without regard to whether it is to be specially valued, and **(b)** all real property to be specially valued?

6. Does the notice of election include **(a)** the items of personal property shown on the estate tax return that pass from the decedent to a qualified heir and that are used in qualified use and **(b)** the total value of such personal property adjusted under section 2032A(b)(3)(B)?

7. Does the notice of election include the adjusted value of the gross estate? (See section 2032A(b)(3)(A).)

8. Does the notice of election include the method used to determine the special use value?

9. Does the notice of election include copies of written appraisals of the fair market value of the real property?

10. Does the notice of election include a statement that the decedent and/or a member of his or her family has owned all of the specially valued property for at

least 5 years of the 8 years immediately preceding the date of the decedent's death?

11. Does the notice of election include a statement as to whether there were any periods during the 8-year period preceding the decedent's date of death during which the decedent or a member of his or her family did not **(a)** own the property to be specially valued, **(b)** use it in a qualified use, or **(c)** materially participate in the operation of the farm or other business? (See section 2032A(e)(6).)

12. Does the notice of election include, for each item of specially valued property, the name of every person taking an interest in that item of specially valued property and the following information about each such person: **(a)** the person's address, **(b)** the person's taxpayer identification number, **(c)** the person's relationship to the decedent, and **(d)** the value of the property interest passing to that person based on both fair market value and qualified use?

13. Does the notice of election include affidavits describing the activities constituting material participation and the identity of the material participants?

14. Does the notice of election include a legal description of each item of specially valued property?

(In the case of an election made for qualified woodlands, the information included in the notice of election must include the reason for entitlement to the woodlands election.)

Any election made under section 2032A will not be valid unless a properly executed agreement (Schedule A-1, Part 3) is filed with the estate tax return. To ensure that the agreement satisfies the requirements for a valid election, use the following checklist.

1. Has the agreement been signed by each and every qualified heir having an interest in the property being specially valued?

2. Has every qualified heir expressed consent to personal liability under section 2032A(c) in the event of an early disposition or early cessation of qualified use?

3. Is the agreement that is actually signed by the qualified heirs in a form that is binding on all of the qualified heirs having an interest in the specially valued property?

4. Does the agreement designate an agent to act for the parties to the agreement in all dealings with the IRS on matters arising under section 2032A?

5. Has the agreement been signed by the designated agent and does it give the address of the agent?

Form 706 (Rev. 8-2005)

Decedent's Social Security Number

Estate of:

SCHEDULE A-1—Section 2032A Valuation

Part 1. Type of Election (Before making an election, see the checklist on page 7.):

☐ **Protective election (Regulations section 20.2032A-8(b)).** Complete Part 2, line 1, and column A of lines 3 and 4. (See instructions.)

☐ **Regular election.** Complete all of Part 2 (including line 11, if applicable) and Part 3. (See instructions.)

Before completing Schedule A-1, see the checklist on page 7 for the information and documents that must be included to make a valid election.

The election is not valid unless the agreement (i.e., Part 3—Agreement to Special Valuation Under Section 2032A)—
- Is signed by each and every qualified heir with an interest in the specially valued property, and
- Is attached to this return when it is filed.

Part 2. Notice of Election (Regulations section 20.2032A-8(a)(3))

    Note. All real property entered on lines 2 and 3 must also be entered on Schedules A, E, F, G, or H, as applicable.

1   Qualified use—check one ▶   ☐ Farm used for farming, or

                        ▶   ☐ Trade or business other than farming

2   Real property used in a qualified use, passing to qualified heirs, and to be specially valued on this Form 706.

A Schedule and item number from Form 706	B Full value (without section 2032A(b)(3)(B) adjustment)	C Adjusted value (with section 2032A(b)(3)(B) adjustment)	D Value based on qualified use (without section 2032A(b)(3)(B) adjustment)

Totals

Attach a legal description of all property listed on line 2.

Attach copies of appraisals showing the column B values for all property listed on line 2.

3   Real property used in a qualified use, passing to qualified heirs, but not specially valued on this Form 706.

A Schedule and item number from Form 706	B Full value (without section 2032A(b)(3)(B) adjustment)	C Adjusted value (with section 2032A(b)(3)(B) adjustment)	D Value based on qualified use (without section 2032A(b)(3)(B) adjustment)

Totals

If you checked "Regular election," you must attach copies of appraisals showing the column B values for all property listed on line 3.

(continued on next page)   **Schedule A-1—Page 8**

Form 706 (Rev. 8-2005)

4 Personal property used in a qualified use and passing to qualified heirs.

A Schedule and item number from Form 706	B Adjusted value (with section 2032A(b)(3)(B) adjustment)	A (continued) Schedule and item number from Form 706	B (continued) Adjusted value (with section 2032A(b)(3)(B) adjustment)
		"Subtotal" from Col. B, below left	....

Subtotal . . . .   Total adjusted value . . .

5 Enter the value of the total gross estate as adjusted under section 2032A(b)(3)(A). ▶ _____

6 Attach a description of the method used to determine the special value based on qualified use.

7 Did the decedent and/or a member of his or her family own all property listed on line 2 for at least 5 of the 8 years immediately preceding the date of the decedent's death? . . . . ☐ **Yes** ☐ **No**

8 Were there any periods during the 8-year period preceding the date of the decedent's death during which the decedent or a member of his or her family:

	Yes	No
a Did not own the property listed on line 2 above?		
b Did not use the property listed on line 2 above in a qualified use?		
c Did not materially participate in the operation of the farm or other business within the meaning of section 2032A(e)(6)?		

If "Yes" to any of the above, you must attach a statement listing the periods. If applicable, describe whether the exceptions of sections 2032A(b)(4) or (5) are met.

9 Attach affidavits describing the activities constituting material participation and the identity and relationship to the decedent of the material participants.

10 Persons holding interests. Enter the requested information for each party who received any interest in the specially valued property. **(Each of the qualified heirs receiving an interest in the property must sign the agreement, and the agreement must be filed with this return.)**

	Name	Address
A		
B		
C		
D		
E		
F		
G		
H		

	Identifying number	Relationship to decedent	Fair market value	Special-use value
A				
B				
C				
D				
E				
F				
G				
H				

You must attach a computation of the GST tax savings attributable to direct skips for each person listed above who is a skip person. (See instructions.)

11 Woodlands election. Check here ▶ ☐ if you wish to make a Woodlands election as described in section 2032A(e)(13). Enter the schedule and item numbers from Form 706 of the property for which you are making this election ▶ ....
You must attach a statement explaining why you are entitled to make this election. The IRS may issue regulations that require more information to substantiate this election. You will be notified by the IRS if you must supply further information.

Schedule A-1—Page 9

Form 706 (Rev. 8-2005)

Part 3. Agreement to Special Valuation Under Section 2032A

Estate of:	Date of Death	Decedent's Social Security Number

There cannot be a valid election unless:

- The agreement is executed by each and every one of the qualified heirs, and
- The agreement is included with the estate tax return when the estate tax return is filed.

We (list all qualified heirs and other persons having an interest in the property required to sign this agreement)

_____

_____ ,

being all the qualified heirs and _____

_____ ,

being all other parties having interests in the property which is qualified real property and which is valued under section 2032A of the Internal Revenue Code, do hereby approve of the election made by _____ ,

Executor/Administrator of the estate of _____

pursuant to section 2032A to value said property on the basis of the qualified use to which the property is devoted and do hereby enter into this agreement pursuant to section 2032A(d).

The undersigned agree and consent to the application of subsection (c) of section 2032A of the Code with respect to all the property described on line 2 of Part 2 of Schedule A-1 of Form 706, attached to this agreement. More specifically, the undersigned heirs expressly agree and consent to personal liability under subsection (c) of 2032A for the additional estate and GST taxes imposed by that subsection with respect to their respective interests in the above-described property in the event of certain early dispositions of the property or early cessation of the qualified use of the property. It is understood that if a qualified heir disposes of any interest in qualified real property to any member of his or her family, such member may thereafter be treated as the qualified heir with respect to such interest upon filing a Form 706-A and a new agreement.

The undersigned interested parties who are not qualified heirs consent to the collection of any additional estate and GST taxes imposed under section 2032A(c) of the Code from the specially valued property.

If there is a disposition of any interest which passes, or has passed to him or her, or if there is a cessation of the qualified use of any specially valued property which passes or passed to him or her, each of the undersigned heirs agrees to file a Form 706-A, United States Additional Estate Tax Return, and pay any additional estate and GST taxes due within 6 months of the disposition or cessation.

It is understood by all interested parties that this agreement is a condition precedent to the election of special use valuation under section 2032A of the Code and must be executed by every interested party even though that person may not have received the estate (or GST) tax benefits or be in possession of such property.

Each of the undersigned understands that by making this election, a lien will be created and recorded pursuant to section 6324B of the Code on the property referred to in this agreement for the adjusted tax differences with respect to the estate as defined in section 2032A(c)(2)(C).

As the interested parties, the undersigned designate the following individual as their agent for all dealings with the Internal Revenue Service concerning the continued qualification of the specially valued property under section 2032A of the Code and on all issues regarding the special lien under section 6324B. The agent is authorized to act for the parties with respect to all dealings with the Service on matters affecting the qualified real property described earlier. This authority includes the following:

- To receive confidential information on all matters relating to continued qualification under section 2032A of the specially valued real property and on all matters relating to the special lien arising under section 6324B;

- To furnish the Internal Revenue Service with any requested information concerning the property;

- To notify the Internal Revenue Service of any disposition or cessation of qualified use of any part of the property;

- To receive, but not to endorse and collect, checks in payment of any refund of Internal Revenue taxes, penalties, or interest;

- To execute waivers (including offers of waivers) of restrictions on assessment or collection of deficiencies in tax and waivers of notice of disallowance of a claim for credit or refund; and

- To execute closing agreements under section 7121.

(continued on next page)

Schedule A-1— Page 10

Form 706 (Rev. 8-2005)

Part 3. Agreement to Special Valuation Under Section 2032A *(Continued)*

Estate of:	Date of Death	Decedent's Social Security Number

- Other acts (specify) ▶ _____

By signing this agreement, the agent agrees to provide the Internal Revenue Service with any requested information concerning this property and to notify the Internal Revenue Service of any disposition or cessation of the qualified use of any part of this property.

Name of Agent	Signature	Address

The property to which this agreement relates is listed in Form 706, United States Estate (and Generation-Skipping Transfer) Tax Return, and in the Notice of Election, along with its fair market value according to section 2031 of the Code and its special use value according to section 2032A. The name, address, social security number, and interest (including the value) of each of the undersigned in this property are as set forth in the attached Notice of Election.

IN WITNESS WHEREOF, the undersigned have hereunto set their hands at _____ ,

this _____ day of _____ .

SIGNATURES OF EACH OF THE QUALIFIED HEIRS:

Signature of qualified heir	Signature of qualified heir
Signature of qualified heir	Signature of qualified heir
Signature of qualified heir	Signature of qualified heir
Signature of qualified heir	Signature of qualified heir
Signature of qualified heir	Signature of qualified heir
Signature of qualified heir	Signature of qualified heir

Signatures of other interested parties

Signatures of other interested parties

Schedule A-1—Page 11

Form 706 (Rev. 8-2005)

Estate of:

SCHEDULE B—Stocks and Bonds

(For jointly owned property that must be disclosed on Schedule E, see the instructions for Schedule E.)

Item number	Description including face amount of bonds or number of shares and par value for identification. Give CUSIP number. If closely held entity, give EIN.		Unit value	Alternate valuation date	Alternate value	Value at date of death
		CUSIP number				
1						
	Total from continuation schedules (or additional sheets) attached to this schedule . . .					
	TOTAL. (Also enter on Part 5, Recapitulation, page 3, at item 2.)					

(If more space is needed, attach the continuation schedule from the end of this package or additional sheets of the same size.)

(The instructions to Schedule B are in the separate instructions.)   **Schedule B—Page 12**

Form 706 (Rev. 8-2005)

Estate of:

SCHEDULE C—Mortgages, Notes, and Cash

(For jointly owned property that must be disclosed on Schedule E, see the instructions for Schedule E.)

Item number	Description	Alternate valuation date	Alternate value	Value at date of death
1				
	Total from continuation schedules (or additional sheets) attached to this schedule . .			
	TOTAL. (Also enter on Part 5, Recapitulation, page 3, at item 3.)			

(If more space is needed, attach the continuation schedule from the end of this package or additional sheets of the same size.)
(See the instructions on the reverse side.)

Schedule C—Page 13

Form 706 (Rev. 8-2005)

Instructions for Schedule C— Mortgages, Notes, and Cash

Complete Schedule C and file it with your return if the total gross estate contains any:

- mortgages,
- notes, or
- cash.

List on Schedule C:

- Mortgages and notes payable **to the decedent** at the time of death.
- Cash the decedent had at the date of death.

Do not list on Schedule C:

- Mortgages and notes payable **by the decedent.** (If these are deductible, list them on Schedule K.)

List the items on Schedule C in the following order:

1. mortgages,
2. promissory notes,
3. contracts by decedent to sell land,
4. cash in possession, and
5. cash in banks, savings and loan associations, and other types of financial organizations.

What to enter in the "Description" column:

For mortgages, list:

- face value,
- unpaid balance,
- date of mortgage,
- date of maturity,
- name of maker,
- property mortgaged,
- interest dates, and
- interest rate.

Example to enter in "Description" column:

"Bond and mortgage of $50,000, unpaid balance: $24,000; dated: January 1, 1985; John Doe to Richard Roe; premises: 22 Clinton Street, Newark, NJ; due: January 1, 2005; interest payable at 10% a year—January 1 and July 1."

For promissory notes, list:

- in the same way as mortgages.

For contracts by the decedent to sell land, list:

- name of purchaser,
- contract date,
- property description,
- sale price,
- initial payment,
- amounts of installment payment,
- unpaid balance of principal, and
- interest rate.

For cash in possession, list:

- such cash separately from bank deposits.

For cash in banks, savings and loan associations, and other types of financial organizations, list:

- name and address of each financial organization,
- amount in each account,
- serial or account number,
- nature of account—checking, savings, time deposit, etc., and
- unpaid interest accrued from date of last interest payment to the date of death.

Note. If you obtain statements from the financial organizations, keep them for IRS inspection.

Form 706 (Rev. 8-2005)

Estate of:

SCHEDULE D—Insurance on the Decedent's Life

You must list **all** policies on the life of the decedent and attach a Form 712 for each policy.

Item number	Description	Alternate valuation date	Alternate value	Value at date of death
1				

Total from continuation schedules (or additional sheets) attached to this schedule . .

TOTAL. (Also enter on Part 5, Recapitulation, page 3, at item 4.) . . . . . .

(If more space is needed, attach the continuation schedule from the end of this package or additional sheets of the same size.)

(See the instructions on the reverse side.)

Schedule D—Page 15

Form 706 (Rev. 8-2005)

Instructions for Schedule D—Insurance on the Decedent's Life

If you are required to file Form 706 and there was any insurance on the decedent's life, whether or not included in the gross estate, you must complete Schedule D and file it with the return.

Insurance you must include on Schedule D. Under section 2042 you must include in the gross estate:

- Insurance on the decedent's life receivable by or for the benefit of the estate; and
- Insurance on the decedent's life receivable by beneficiaries other than the estate, as described below.

The term "insurance" refers to life insurance of every description, including death benefits paid by fraternal beneficiary societies operating under the lodge system, and death benefits paid under no-fault automobile insurance policies if the no-fault insurer was unconditionally bound to pay the benefit in the event of the insured's death.

Insurance in favor of the estate. Include on Schedule D the full amount of the proceeds of insurance on the life of the decedent receivable by the executor or otherwise payable to or for the benefit of the estate. Insurance in favor of the estate includes insurance used to pay the estate tax, and any other taxes, debts, or charges that are enforceable against the estate. The manner in which the policy is drawn is immaterial as long as there is an obligation, legally binding on the beneficiary, to use the proceeds to pay taxes, debts, or charges. You must include the full amount even though the premiums or other consideration may have been paid by a person other than the decedent.

Insurance receivable by beneficiaries other than the estate. Include on Schedule D the proceeds of all insurance on the life of the decedent not receivable by or for the benefit of the decedent's estate if the decedent possessed at death any of the incidents of ownership, exercisable either alone or in conjunction with any person.

Incidents of ownership in a policy include:

- The right of the insured or estate to its economic benefits;
- The power to change the beneficiary;
- The power to surrender or cancel the policy;
- The power to assign the policy or to revoke an assignment;
- The power to pledge the policy for a loan;
- The power to obtain from the insurer a loan against the surrender value of the policy; and
- A reversionary interest if the value of the reversionary interest was more than 5% of the value of the policy immediately before the decedent died. (An interest in an insurance policy is considered a reversionary interest if, for example, the proceeds become payable to the insured's estate or payable as the insured directs if the beneficiary dies before the insured.)

Life insurance not includible in the gross estate under section 2042 may be includible under some other section of the Code. For example, a life insurance policy could be transferred by the decedent in such a way that it would be includible in the gross estate under section 2036, 2037, or 2038. (See the instructions to Schedule G for a description of these sections.)

Completing the Schedule

You must list every policy of insurance on the life of the decedent, whether or not it is included in the gross estate.

Under "Description" list:

- Name of the insurance company and
- Number of the policy.

For every policy of life insurance listed on the schedule, you must request a statement on Form 712, Life Insurance Statement, from the company that issued the policy. Attach the Form 712 to the back of Schedule D.

If the policy proceeds are paid in one sum, enter the net proceeds received (from Form 712, line 24) in the value (and alternate value) columns of Schedule D. If the policy proceeds are not paid in one sum, enter the value of the proceeds as of the date of the decedent's death (from Form 712, line 25).

If part or all of the policy proceeds are not included in the gross estate, you must explain why they were not included.

Form 706 (Rev. 8-2005)

Estate of:

SCHEDULE E—Jointly Owned Property
(If you elect section 2032A valuation, you must complete Schedule E and Schedule A-1.)

PART 1.—Qualified Joint Interests—Interests Held by the Decedent and His or Her Spouse as the Only Joint Tenants (Section 2040(b)(2))

Item number	Description For securities, give CUSIP number.	Alternate valuation date	Alternate value	Value at date of death
	Total from continuation schedules (or additional sheets) attached to this schedule			
1a Totals	**1a**		
1b Amounts included in gross estate (one-half of line **1a**)	**1b**		

PART 2.—All Other Joint Interests

2a State the name and address of each surviving co-tenant. If there are more than three surviving co-tenants, list the additional co-tenants on an attached sheet.

Name	Address (number and street, city, state, and ZIP code)
A.	
B.	
C.	

Item number	Enter letter for co-tenant	Description (including alternate valuation date if any). For securities, give CUSIP number.	Percentage includible	Includible alternate value	Includible value at date of death
		Total from continuation schedules (or additional sheets) attached to this schedule			
2b Total other joint interests	**2b**		
3 Total includible joint interests (add lines 1b and 2b). Also enter on Part 5, Recapitulation, page 3, at item 5	**3**		

(If more space is needed, attach the continuation schedule from the end of this package or additional sheets of the same size.)
(See the instructions on the reverse side.)   **Schedule E—Page 17**

Instructions for Schedule E—Jointly Owned Property

If you are required to file Form 706, you must complete Schedule E and file it with the return if the decedent owned any joint property at the time of death, whether or not the decedent's interest is includible in the gross estate.

Enter on this schedule all property of whatever kind or character, whether real estate, personal property, or bank accounts, in which the decedent held at the time of death an interest either as a joint tenant with right to survivorship or as a tenant by the entirety.

Do not list on this schedule property that the decedent held as a tenant in common, but report the value of the interest on Schedule A if real estate, or on the appropriate schedule if personal property. Similarly, community property held by the decedent and spouse should be reported on the appropriate Schedules A through I. The decedent's interest in a partnership should not be entered on this schedule unless the partnership interest itself is jointly owned. Solely owned partnership interests should be reported on Schedule F, "Other Miscellaneous Property."

Part 1—Qualified joint interests held by decedent and spouse. Under section 2040(b)(2), a joint interest is a qualified joint interest if the decedent and the surviving spouse held the interest as:

- Tenants by the entirety, or
- Joint tenants with right of survivorship if the decedent and the decedent's spouse are the only joint tenants.

Interests that meet either of the two requirements above should be entered in Part 1. Joint interests that do not meet either of the two requirements above should be entered in Part 2.

Under "Description," describe the property as required in the instructions for Schedules A, B, C, and F for the type of property involved. For example, jointly held stocks and bonds should be described using the rules given in the instructions to Schedule B.

Under "Alternate value" and "Value at date of death," enter the full value of the property.

Note. You cannot claim the special treatment under section 2040(b) for property held jointly by a decedent and a surviving spouse who is not a U.S. citizen. You must report these joint interests on Part 2 of Schedule E, not Part 1.

Part 2—Other joint interests. All joint interests that were not entered in Part 1 must be entered in Part 2.

For each item of property, enter the appropriate letter A, B, C, etc., from line 2a to indicate the name and address of the surviving co-tenant.

Under "Description," describe the property as required in the instructions for Schedules A, B, C, and F for the type of property involved.

In the "Percentage includible" column, enter the percentage of the total value of the property that you intend to include in the gross estate.

Generally, you must include the full value of the jointly owned property in the gross estate. However, the full value should not be included if you can show that a part of the property originally belonged to the other tenant or tenants and was never received or acquired by the other tenant or tenants from the decedent for less than adequate and full consideration in money or money's worth, or unless you can show that any part of the property was acquired with consideration originally belonging to the surviving joint tenant or tenants. In this case, you may exclude from the value of the property an amount proportionate to the consideration furnished by the other tenant or tenants. Relinquishing or promising to relinquish dower, curtesy, or statutory estate created instead of dower or curtesy, or other marital rights in the decedent's property or estate is not consideration in money or money's worth. See the Schedule A instructions for the value to show for real property that is subject to a mortgage.

If the property was acquired by the decedent and another person or persons by gift, bequest, devise, or inheritance as joint tenants, and their interests are not otherwise specified by law, include only that part of the value of the property that is figured by dividing the full value of the property by the number of joint tenants.

If you believe that less than the full value of the entire property is includible in the gross estate for tax purposes, you must establish the right to include the smaller value by attaching proof of the extent, origin, and nature of the decedent's interest and the interest(s) of the decedent's co-tenant or co-tenants.

In the "Includible alternate value" and "Includible value at date of death" columns, you should enter only the values that you believe are includible in the gross estate.

Form 706 (Rev. 8-2005)

Estate of:

SCHEDULE F—Other Miscellaneous Property Not Reportable Under Any Other Schedule

(For jointly owned property that must be disclosed on Schedule E, see the instructions for Schedule E.)
(If you elect section 2032A valuation, you must complete Schedule F and Schedule A-1.)

		Yes	No
1	Did the decedent at the time of death own any articles of artistic or collectible value in excess of $3,000 or any collections whose artistic or collectible value combined at date of death exceeded $10,000? . . . . If "Yes," submit full details on this schedule and attach appraisals.		
2	Has the decedent's estate, spouse, or any other person, received (or will receive) any bonus or award as a result of the decedent's employment or death? . . . . If "Yes," submit full details on this schedule.		
3	Did the decedent at the time of death have, or have access to, a safe deposit box? . . . . If "Yes," state location, and if held in joint names of decedent and another, state name and relationship of joint depositor.		

If any of the contents of the safe deposit box are omitted from the schedules in this return, explain fully why omitted.

Item number	Description For securities, give CUSIP number.	Alternate valuation date	Alternate value	Value at date of death
1				
	Total from continuation schedules (or additional sheets) attached to this schedule . .			
	TOTAL. (Also enter on Part 5, Recapitulation, page 3, at item 6.)			

(If more space is needed, attach the continuation schedule from the end of this package or additional sheets of the same size.)
(See the instructions on the reverse side.)

Schedule F—Page 19

Form 706 (Rev. 8-2005)

Instructions for Schedule F—Other Miscellaneous Property

You must complete Schedule F and file it with the return.

On Schedule F, list all items that must be included in the gross estate that are not reported on any other schedule, including:

- Debts due the decedent (other than notes and mortgages included on Schedule C);
- Interests in business;
- Any interest in an Archer medical savings account (MSA) or Health Savings Account (HSA), unless such interest passes to the surviving spouse; and
- Insurance on the life of another (obtain and attach Form 712, Life Insurance Statement, for each policy).

Note (for single premium or paid-up policies). In certain situations, for example where the surrender value of the policy exceeds its replacement cost, the true economic value of the policy will be greater than the amount shown on line 59 of Form 712. In these situations, you should report the full economic value of the policy on Schedule F. See Rev. Rul. 78-137, 1978-1 C.B. 280 for details.

- Section 2044 property (see *Decedent Who Was a Surviving Spouse* below);
- Claims (including the value of the decedent's interest in a claim for refund of income taxes or the amount of the refund actually received);
- Rights;
- Royalties;
- Leaseholds;
- Judgments;
- Reversionary or remainder interests;
- Shares in trust funds (attach a copy of the trust instrument);
- Household goods and personal effects, including wearing apparel;
- Farm products and growing crops;
- Livestock;
- Farm machinery; and
- Automobiles.

If the decedent owned any interest in a partnership or unincorporated business, attach a statement of assets and liabilities for the valuation date and for the 5 years before the valuation date. Also attach statements of the net earnings for the same 5 years. Be sure to include the EIN of the entity. You must account for goodwill in the valuation. In general, furnish the same information and follow the methods used to value close corporations. See the instructions for Schedule B.

All partnership interests should be reported on Schedule F unless the partnership interest, itself, is jointly owned. Jointly owned partnership interests should be reported on Schedule E.

If real estate is owned by the sole proprietorship, it should be reported on Schedule F and not on Schedule A. Describe the real estate with the same detail required for Schedule A.

Line 1. If the decedent owned at the date of death articles with artistic or intrinsic value (e.g., jewelry, furs, silverware, books, statuary, vases, oriental rugs, coin or stamp collections), check the "Yes" box on line 1 and provide full details. If any one article is valued at more than $3,000, or any collection of similar articles is valued at more than $10,000, attach an appraisal by an expert under oath and the required statement regarding the appraiser's qualifications (see Regulations section 20.2031-6(b)).

Decedent Who Was a Surviving Spouse

If the decedent was a surviving spouse, he or she may have received qualified terminable interest property (QTIP) from the predeceased spouse for which the marital deduction was elected either on the predeceased spouse's estate tax return or on a gift tax return, Form 709. The election was available for gifts made and decedents dying after December 31, 1981. List such property on Schedule F.

If this election was made and the surviving spouse retained his or her interest in the QTIP property at death, the full value of the QTIP property is includible in his or her estate, even though the qualifying income interest terminated at death. It is valued as of the date of the surviving spouse's death, or alternate valuation date, if applicable. Do not reduce the value by any annual exclusion that may have applied to the transfer creating the interest.

The value of such property included in the surviving spouse's gross estate is treated as passing from the surviving spouse. It therefore qualifies for the charitable and marital deductions on the surviving spouse's estate tax return if it meets the other requirements for those deductions.

For additional details, see Regulations section 20.2044-1.

Form 706 (Rev. 8-2005)

Estate of:

SCHEDULE G—Transfers During Decedent's Life
(If you elect section 2032A valuation, you must complete Schedule G and Schedule A-1.)

Item number	Description For securities, give CUSIP number.	Alternate valuation date	Alternate value	Value at date of death
A.	Gift tax paid by the decedent or the estate for all gifts made by the decedent or his or her spouse within 3 years before the decedent's death (section 2035(b))	X X X X X		
B. 1	Transfers includible under section 2035(a), 2036, 2037, or 2038:			

Total from continuation schedules (or additional sheets) attached to this schedule . .

TOTAL. (Also enter on Part 5, Recapitulation, page 3, at item 7.) . . . . . .

SCHEDULE H—Powers of Appointment
(Include "5 and 5 lapsing" powers (section 2041(b)(2)) held by the decedent.)
(If you elect section 2032A valuation, you must complete Schedule H and Schedule A-1.)

Item number	Description	Alternate valuation date	Alternate value	Value at date of death
1				

Total from continuation schedules (or additional sheets) attached to this schedule . .

TOTAL. (Also enter on Part 5, Recapitulation, page 3, at item 8.) . . . . .

(If more space is needed, attach the continuation schedule from the end of this package or additional sheets of the same size.)
(The instructions to Schedules G and H are in the separate instructions.)

Schedules G and H—Page 21

Form 706 (Rev. 8-2005)

Estate of:

SCHEDULE I—Annuities

Note. Generally, no exclusion is allowed for the estates of decedents dying after December 31, 1984 (see page 15 of the instructions).

A Are you excluding from the decedent's gross estate the value of a lump-sum distribution described in section 2039(f)(2) (as in effect before its repeal by the Deficit Reduction Act of 1984)?
If "Yes," you must attach the information required by the instructions.

			Yes	No

Item number	Description Show the entire value of the annuity before any exclusions.	Alternate valuation date	Includible alternate value	Includible value at date of death
1				

Total from continuation schedules (or additional sheets) attached to this schedule

TOTAL. (Also enter on Part 5, Recapitulation, page 3, at item 9.)

(If more space is needed, attach the continuation schedule from the end of this package or additional sheets of the same size.)

Schedule I—Page 22   (The instructions to Schedule I are in the separate instructions.)

Form 706 (Rev. 8-2005)

Estate of:

SCHEDULE J—Funeral Expenses and Expenses Incurred in Administering Property Subject to Claims

Note. Do not list on this schedule expenses of administering property not subject to claims. For those expenses, see the instructions for Schedule L.

If executors' commissions, attorney fees, etc., are claimed and allowed as a deduction for estate tax purposes, they are not allowable as a deduction in computing the taxable income of the estate for federal income tax purposes. They are allowable as an income tax deduction on Form 1041 if a waiver is filed to waive the deduction on Form 706 (see the Form 1041 instructions).

Item number	Description	Expense amount	Total amount
1	**A. Funeral expenses:**		
	Total funeral expenses ▶		
	B. Administration expenses:		
1	Executors' commissions—amount estimated/agreed upon/paid. (Strike out the words that do not apply.)		
2	Attorney fees—amount estimated/agreed upon/paid. (Strike out the words that do not apply.)		
3	Accountant fees—amount estimated/agreed upon/paid. (Strike out the words that do not apply.)		
4	Miscellaneous expenses:	Expense amount	
	Total miscellaneous expenses from continuation schedules (or additional sheets) attached to this schedule		
	Total miscellaneous expenses ▶		
	TOTAL. (Also enter on Part 5, Recapitulation, page 3, at item 13.) ▶		

(If more space is needed, attach the continuation schedule from the end of this package or additional sheets of the same size.)
(See the instructions on the reverse side.)

Schedule J—Page 23

Form 706 (Rev. 8-2005)

Instructions for Schedule J—Funeral Expenses and Expenses Incurred in Administering Property Subject to Claims

General. You must complete and file Schedule J if you claim a deduction on item 13 of Part 5, Recapitulation.

On Schedule J, itemize funeral expenses and expenses incurred in administering property subject to claims. List the names and addresses of persons to whom the expenses are payable and describe the nature of the expense. **Do not list expenses incurred in administering property not subject to claims on this schedule. List them on Schedule L instead.**

The deduction is limited to the amount paid for these expenses that is allowable under local law but may not exceed:

1. The value of property subject to claims included in the gross estate, plus

2. The amount paid out of property included in the gross estate but not subject to claims. This amount must actually be paid by the due date of the estate tax return.

The applicable local law under which the estate is being administered determines which property is and is not subject to claims. If under local law a particular property interest included in the gross estate would bear the burden for the payment of the expenses, then the property is considered property subject to claims.

Unlike certain claims against the estate for debts of the decedent (see the instructions for Schedule K in the separate instructions), you cannot deduct expenses incurred in administering property subject to claims on both the estate tax return and the estate's income tax return. If you choose to deduct them on the estate tax return, you cannot deduct them on a Form 1041 filed for the estate. Funeral expenses are only deductible on the estate tax return.

Funeral Expenses. Itemize funeral expenses on line A. Deduct from the expenses any amounts that were reimbursed, such as death benefits payable by the Social Security Administration and the Veterans Administration.

Executors' Commissions. When you file the return, you may deduct commissions that have actually been paid to you or that you expect will be paid. You may not deduct commissions if none will be collected. If the amount of the commissions has not been fixed by decree of the proper court, the deduction will be allowed on the final examination of the return, provided that:

- The Estate and Gift Tax Territory Manager is reasonably satisfied that the commissions claimed will be paid;
- The amount entered as a deduction is within the amount allowable by the laws of the jurisdiction where the estate is being administered; and
- It is in accordance with the usually accepted practice in that jurisdiction for estates of similar size and character.

If you have not been paid the commissions claimed at the time of the final examination of the return, you must support the amount you deducted with an affidavit or statement signed under the penalties of perjury that the amount has been agreed upon and will be paid.

You may not deduct a bequest or devise made to you instead of commissions. If, however, the decedent fixed by will the compensation payable to you for services to be rendered in the administration of the estate, you may deduct this amount to the extent it is not more than the compensation allowable by the local law or practice.

Do not deduct on this schedule amounts paid as trustees' commissions whether received by you acting in the capacity of a trustee or by a separate trustee. If such amounts were paid in administering property not subject to claims, deduct them on Schedule L.

Note. Executors' commissions are taxable income to the executors. Therefore, be sure to include them as income on your individual income tax return.

Attorney Fees. Enter the amount of attorney fees that have actually been paid or that you reasonably expect to be paid. If on the final examination of the return the fees claimed have not been awarded by the proper court and paid, the deduction will be allowed provided the Estate and Gift Tax Territory Manager is reasonably satisfied that the amount claimed will be paid and that it does not exceed a reasonable payment for the services performed, taking into account the size and character of the estate and the local law and practice. If the fees claimed have not been paid at the time of final examination of the return, the amount deducted must be supported by an affidavit, or statement signed under the penalties of perjury, by the executor or the attorney stating that the amount has been agreed upon and will be paid.

Do not deduct attorney fees incidental to litigation incurred by the beneficiaries. These expenses are charged against the beneficiaries personally and are not administration expenses authorized by the Code.

Interest Expense. Interest expenses incurred after the decedent's death are generally allowed as a deduction if they are reasonable, necessary to the administration of the estate, and allowable under local law.

Interest incurred as the result of a Federal estate tax deficiency is a deductible administrative expense. Penalties are not deductible even if they are allowable under local law.

Note. If you elect to pay the tax in installments under section 6166, you may not deduct the interest payable on the installments.

Miscellaneous Expenses. Miscellaneous administration expenses necessarily incurred in preserving and distributing the estate are deductible. These expenses include appraiser's and accountant's fees, certain court costs, and costs of storing or maintaining assets of the estate.

The expenses of selling assets are deductible only if the sale is necessary to pay the decedent's debts, the expenses of administration, or taxes, or to preserve the estate or carry out distribution.

Form 706 (Rev. 8-2005)

Estate of:

SCHEDULE K—Debts of the Decedent, and Mortgages and Liens

Item number	Debts of the Decedent—Creditor and nature of claim, and allowable death taxes	Amount unpaid to date	Amount in contest	Amount claimed as a deduction
1				

Total from continuation schedules (or additional sheets) attached to this schedule . . . .

TOTAL. (Also enter on Part 5, Recapitulation, page 3, at item 14.) . . . .

Item number	Mortgages and Liens—Description	Amount
1		

Total from continuation schedules (or additional sheets) attached to this schedule . . . .

TOTAL. (Also enter on Part 5, Recapitulation, page 3, at item 15.) . . . .

(If more space is needed, attach the continuation schedule from the end of this package or additional sheets of the same size.)
(The instructions to Schedule K are in the separate instructions.)　　　　　　　　　　**Schedule K—Page 25**

Form 706 (Rev. 8-2005)

Estate of:

SCHEDULE L—Net Losses During Administration and
Expenses Incurred in Administering Property Not Subject to Claims

Item number	Net losses during administration (**Note.** Do not deduct losses claimed on a Federal income tax return.)	Amount
1		

Total from continuation schedules (or additional sheets) attached to this schedule . . . .

TOTAL. (Also enter on Part 5, Recapitulation, page 3, at item 18.) . . . .

Item number	Expenses incurred in administering property not subject to claims. (Indicate whether estimated, agreed upon, or paid.)	Amount
1		

Total from continuation schedules (or additional sheets) attached to this schedule . . . .

TOTAL. (Also enter on Part 5, Recapitulation, page 3, at item 19.) . . . .

(If more space is needed, attach the continuation schedule from the end of this package or additional sheets of the same size.)

Schedule L—Page 26   (The instructions to Schedule L are in the separate instructions.)

Form 706 (Rev. 8-2005)

Estate of:

SCHEDULE M—Bequests, etc., to Surviving Spouse

Election To Deduct Qualified Terminable Interest Property Under Section 2056(b)(7). If a trust (or other property) meets the requirements of qualified terminable interest property under section 2056(b)(7), and

a. The trust or other property is listed on Schedule M, and

b. The value of the trust (or other property) is entered in whole or in part as a deduction on Schedule M,

then unless the executor specifically identifies the trust (all or a fractional portion or percentage) or other property to be excluded from the election, the executor shall be deemed to have made an election to have such trust (or other property) treated as qualified terminable interest property under section 2056(b)(7).

If less than the entire value of the trust (or other property) that the executor has included in the gross estate is entered as a deduction on Schedule M, the executor shall be considered to have made an election only as to a fraction of the trust (or other property). The numerator of this fraction is equal to the amount of the trust (or other property) deducted on Schedule M. The denominator is equal to the total value of the trust (or other property).

Election To Deduct Qualified Domestic Trust Property Under Section 2056A. If a trust meets the requirements of a qualified domestic trust under section 2056A(a) and this return is filed no later than 1 year after the time prescribed by law (including extensions) for filing the return, and

a. The entire value of a trust or trust property is listed on Schedule M, and

b. The entire value of the trust or trust property is entered as a deduction on Schedule M,

then unless the executor specifically identifies the trust to be excluded from the election, the executor shall be deemed to have made an election to have the entire trust treated as qualified domestic trust property.

		Yes	No
1	Did any property pass to the surviving spouse as a result of a qualified disclaimer? **1**		
	If "Yes," attach a copy of the written disclaimer required by section 2518(b).		
2a	In what country was the surviving spouse born? _____		
b	What is the surviving spouse's date of birth? _____		
c	Is the surviving spouse a U.S. citizen? **2c**		
d	If the surviving spouse is a naturalized citizen, when did the surviving spouse acquire citizenship? _____		
e	If the surviving spouse is not a U.S. citizen, of what country is the surviving spouse a citizen? _____		
3	**Election Out of QTIP Treatment of Annuities**—Do you elect under section 2056(b)(7)(C)(ii) **not** to treat as qualified terminable interest property any joint and survivor annuities that are included in the gross estate and would otherwise be treated as qualified terminable interest property under section 2056(b)(7)(C)? (see instructions) **3**		

Item number	Description of property interests passing to surviving spouse	Amount
1		
	Total from continuation schedules (or additional sheets) attached to this schedule	

4	**Total** amount of property interests listed on Schedule M	**4**	
5a	Federal estate taxes payable out of property interests listed on Schedule M . .	**5a**	
b	Other death taxes payable out of property interests listed on Schedule M . .	**5b**	
c	Federal and state GST taxes payable out of property interests listed on Schedule M	**5c**	
d	Add items 5a, b, and c	**5d**	
6	Net amount of property interests listed on Schedule M (subtract 5d from 4). Also enter on Part 5, Recapitulation, page 3, at item 20	**6**	

(If more space is needed, attach the continuation schedule from the end of this package or additional sheets of the same size.)
(See the instructions on the reverse side.)

Schedule M—Page 27

Form 706 (Rev. 8-2005)

Examples of Listing of Property Interests on Schedule M

Item number	Description of property interests passing to surviving spouse	Amount
1	One-half the value of a house and lot, 256 South West Street, held by decedent and surviving spouse as joint tenants with right of survivorship under deed dated July 15, 1957 (Schedule E, Part I, item 1)	$132,500
2	Proceeds of Gibraltar Life Insurance Company policy No. 104729, payable in one sum to surviving spouse (Schedule D, item 3)	200,000
3	Cash bequest under Paragraph Six of will	100,000

Instructions for Schedule M—Bequests, etc., to Surviving Spouse (Marital Deduction)

General

You must complete Schedule M and file it with the return if you claim a deduction on item 20 of Part 5, Recapitulation.

The marital deduction is authorized by section 2056 for certain property interests that pass from the decedent to the surviving spouse. You may claim the deduction only for property interests that are included in the decedent's gross estate (Schedules A through I).

Note. The marital deduction is generally not allowed if the surviving spouse is **not** a U.S. citizen. The marital deduction is allowed for property passing to such a surviving spouse in a "qualified domestic trust" or if such property is transferred or irrevocably assigned to such a trust before the estate tax return is filed. The executor must elect qualified domestic trust status on this return. See the instructions that follow, on pages 29–30, for details on the election.

Property Interests That You May List on Schedule M

Generally, you may list on Schedule M all property interests that pass from the decedent to the surviving spouse and are included in the gross estate. However, you should not list any "Nondeductible terminable interests" (described below) on Schedule M unless you are making a QTIP election. The property for which you make this election must be included on Schedule M. See "Qualified terminable interest property" on the following page.

For the rules on common disaster and survival for a limited period, see section 2056(b)(3).

You may list on Schedule M only those interests that the surviving spouse takes:

1. As the decedent's legatee, devisee, heir, or donee;

2. As the decedent's surviving tenant by the entirety or joint tenant;

3. As an appointee under the decedent's exercise of a power or as a taker in default at the decedent's nonexercise of a power;

4. As a beneficiary of insurance on the decedent's life;

5. As the surviving spouse taking under dower or curtesy (or similar statutory interest); and

6. As a transferee of a transfer made by the decedent at any time.

Property Interests That You May Not List on Schedule M

You should not list on Schedule M:

1. The value of any property that does not pass from the decedent to the surviving spouse;

2. Property interests that are not included in the decedent's gross estate;

3. The full value of a property interest for which a deduction was claimed on Schedules J through L. The value of the property interest should be reduced by the deductions claimed with respect to it;

4. The full value of a property interest that passes to the surviving spouse subject to a mortgage or other encumbrance or an obligation of the surviving spouse. Include on Schedule M only the net value of the interest after reducing it by the amount of the mortgage or other debt;

5. Nondeductible terminable interests (described below); or

6. Any property interest disclaimed by the surviving spouse.

Terminable Interests

Certain interests in property passing from a decedent to a surviving spouse are referred to as *terminable interests*. These are interests that will terminate or fail after the passage of time, or on the occurrence or nonoccurrence of some contingency. Examples are: life estates, annuities, estates for terms of years, and patents.

The ownership of a bond, note, or other contractual obligation, which when discharged would not have the effect of an annuity for life or for a term, is not considered a terminable interest.

Nondeductible terminable interests. A terminable interest is **nondeductible**, and should not be entered on Schedule M (unless you are making a QTIP election) if:

1. Another interest in the same property passed from the decedent to some other person for less than adequate and full consideration in money or money's worth; and

2. By reason of its passing, the other person or that person's heirs may enjoy part of the property after the termination of the surviving spouse's interest.

This rule applies even though the interest that passes from the decedent to a person other than the surviving spouse is not included in the gross estate, and regardless of when the interest passes. The rule also applies regardless of whether the surviving spouse's interest and the other person's interest pass from the decedent at the same time.

Property interests that are considered to pass to a person other than the surviving spouse are any property interest that: **(a)** passes under a decedent's will or intestacy; **(b)** was transferred by a decedent during life; or **(c)** is held by or passed on to any person as a decedent's joint tenant, as appointee under a decedent's exercise of a power, as taker in default at a decedent's release or nonexercise of a power, or as a beneficiary of insurance on the decedent's life.

For example, a decedent devised real property to his wife for life, with remainder to his children. The life interest that passed to the wife does not qualify for the marital deduction because it will terminate at her death and the children will thereafter possess or enjoy the property.

However, if the decedent purchased a joint and survivor annuity for himself and his wife who survived him, the value of the survivor's annuity, to the extent that it is included in the gross estate, qualifies for the marital deduction because even though the interest will terminate on the wife's death, no one else will possess or enjoy any part of the property.

The marital deduction is not allowed for an interest that the decedent directed the executor or a trustee to convert, after death, into a terminable interest for the surviving spouse. The marital deduction is not allowed for such an interest even if there was no interest

Page 28

Form 706 (Rev. 8-2005)

in the property passing to another person and even If the terminable interest would otherwise have been deductible under the exceptions described below for life estate and life insurance and annuity payments with powers of appointment. For more information, see Regulations sections 20.2056(b)-1(f) and 20.2056(b)-1(g), Example (7).

If any property interest passing from the decedent to the surviving spouse may be paid or otherwise satisfied out of any of a group of assets, the value of the property interest is, for the entry on Schedule M, reduced by the value of any asset or assets that, if passing from the decedent to the surviving spouse, would be nondeductible terminable interests. Examples of property interests that may be paid or otherwise satisfied out of any of a group of assets are a bequest of the residue of the decedent's estate, or of a share of the residue, and a cash legacy payable out of the general estate.

Example: A decedent bequeathed $100,000 to the surviving spouse. The general estate includes a term for years (valued at $10,000 in determining the value of the gross estate) in an office building, which interest was retained by the decedent under a deed of the building by gift to a son. Accordingly, the value of the specific bequest entered on Schedule M is $90,000.

Life Estate With Power of Appointment in the Surviving Spouse. A property interest, whether or not in trust, will be treated as passing to the surviving spouse, and will not be treated as a nondeductible terminable interest if: **(a)** the surviving spouse is entitled for life to all of the income from the entire interest; **(b)** the income is payable annually or at more frequent intervals; **(c)** the surviving spouse has the power, exercisable in favor of the surviving spouse or the estate of the surviving spouse, to appoint the entire interest; **(d)** the power is exercisable by the surviving spouse alone and (whether exercisable by will or during life) is exercisable by the surviving spouse in all events; and **(e)** no part of the entire interest is subject to a power in any other person to appoint any part to any person other than the surviving spouse (or the surviving spouse's legal representative or relative if the surviving spouse is disabled. See Rev. Rul. 85-35, 1985-1 C.B. 328). If these five conditions are satisfied only for a specific portion of the entire interest, see the section 2056(b) regulations to determine the amount of the marital deduction.

Life Insurance, Endowment, or Annuity Payments, With Power of Appointment in Surviving Spouse. A property interest consisting of the entire proceeds under

a life insurance, endowment, or annuity contract is treated as passing from the decedent to the surviving spouse, and will not be treated as a nondeductible terminable interest if: **(a)** the surviving spouse is entitled to receive the proceeds in installments, or is entitled to interest on them, with all amounts payable during the life of the spouse, payable only to the surviving spouse; **(b)** the installment or interest payments are payable annually, or more frequently, beginning not later than 13 months after the decedent's death; **(c)** the surviving spouse has the power, exercisable in favor of the surviving spouse or of the estate of the surviving spouse, to appoint all amounts payable under the contract; **(d)** the power is exercisable by the surviving spouse alone and (whether exercisable by will or during life) is exercisable by the surviving spouse in all events; and **(e)** no part of the amount payable under the contract is subject to a power in any other person to appoint any part to any person other than the surviving spouse. If these five conditions are satisfied only for a specific portion of the proceeds, see the section 2056(b) regulations to determine the amount of the marital deduction.

Charitable Remainder Trusts. An interest in a charitable remainder trust will **not** be treated as a nondeductible terminable interest if:

1. The interest in the trust passes from the decedent to the surviving spouse; and

2. The surviving spouse is the only beneficiary of the trust other than charitable organizations described in section 170(c).

A "charitable remainder trust" is either a charitable remainder annuity trust or a charitable remainder unitrust. (See section 664 for descriptions of these trusts.)

Election To Deduct Qualified Terminable Interests (QTIP)

You may elect to claim a marital deduction for qualified terminable interest property or property interests. You make the QTIP election simply by listing the qualified terminable interest property on Schedule M and deducting its value. You are presumed to have made the QTIP election if you list the property and deduct its value on Schedule M. If you make this election, the surviving spouse's gross estate will include the value of the "qualified terminable interest property." See the instructions for line 6 of Part 4, General Information, for more details. **The election is irrevocable.**

If you file a Form 706 in which you do not make this election, you may not file an amended return to make the election

unless you file the amended return on or before the due date for filing the original Form 706.

The effect of the election is that the property (interest) will be treated as passing to the surviving spouse and will not be treated as a nondeductible terminable interest. All of the other marital deduction requirements must still be satisfied before you may make this election. For example, you may not make this election for property or property interests that are not included in the decedent's gross estate.

Qualified terminable interest property. Qualified terminable interest property is property **(a)** that passes from the decedent, and **(b)** in which the surviving spouse has a qualifying income interest for life.

The surviving spouse has a *qualifying income interest for life* if the surviving spouse is entitled to all of the income from the property payable annually or at more frequent intervals, or has a usufruct interest for life in the property, and during the surviving spouse's lifetime no person has a power to appoint any part of the property to any person other than the surviving spouse. An annuity is treated as an income interest regardless of whether the property from which the annuity is payable can be separately identified.

Amendments to Regulations sections 20.2044-1, 20.2056(b)-7 and 20.2056(b)-10 clarify that an interest in property is eligible for QTIP treatment if the income interest is contingent upon the executor's election even if that portion of the property for which no election is made will pass to or for the benefit of beneficiaries other than the surviving spouse.

The QTIP election may be made for all or any part of qualified terminable interest property. A partial election must relate to a fractional or percentile share of the property so that the elective part will reflect its proportionate share of the increase or decline in the whole of the property when applying sections 2044 or 2519. Thus, if the interest of the surviving spouse in a trust (or other property in which the spouse has a qualified life estate) is qualified terminable interest property, you may make an election for a part of the trust (or other property) only if the election relates to a defined fraction or percentage of the entire trust (or other property). The fraction or percentage may be defined by means of a formula.

Qualified Domestic Trust Election (QDOT)

The marital deduction is allowed for transfers to a surviving spouse who is not a U.S. citizen only if the property passes to the surviving spouse in a "qualified domestic trust" (QDOT) or if

Page 29

Form 706 (Rev. 8-2005)

such property is transferred or irrevocably assigned to a QDOT before the decedent's estate tax return is filed.

A QDOT is any trust:

1. That requires at least one trustee to be either an individual who is a citizen of the United States or a domestic corporation;

2. That requires that no distribution of corpus from the trust can be made unless such a trustee has the right to withhold from the distribution the tax imposed on the QDOT;

3. That meets the requirements of any applicable regulations; and

4. For which the executor has made an election on the estate tax return of the decedent.

Note. For trusts created by an instrument executed before November 5, 1990, paragraphs 1 and 2 above will be treated as met if the trust instrument requires that all trustees be individuals who are citizens of the United States or domestic corporations.

You make the QDOT election simply by listing the qualified domestic trust or the **entire value** of the trust property on Schedule M and deducting its value. You are presumed to have made the QDOT election if you list the trust or trust property and deduct its value on Schedule M. **Once made, the election is irrevocable.**

If an election is made to deduct qualified domestic trust property under section 2056A(d), provide the following information for each qualified domestic trust on an attachment to this schedule:

1. The name and address of every trustee;

2. A description of each transfer passing from the decedent that is the source of the property to be placed in trust; and

3. The employer identification number (EIN) for the trust.

The election must be made for an entire QDOT trust. In listing a trust for which you are making a QDOT election, unless you specifically identify the trust as not subject to the election, the election will be considered made for the entire trust.

The determination of whether a trust qualifies as a QDOT will be made as of the date the decedent's Form 706 is filed. If, however, judicial proceedings are brought before the Form 706's due

date (including extensions) to have the trust revised to meet the QDOT requirements, then the determination will not be made until the court-ordered changes to the trust are made.

Line 1

If property passes to the surviving spouse as the result of a qualified disclaimer, check "Yes" and attach a copy of the written disclaimer required by section 2518(b).

Line 3

Section 2056(b)(7) creates an automatic QTIP election for certain joint and survivor annuities that are includible in the estate under section 2039. To qualify, only the surviving spouse can have the right to receive payments before the death of the surviving spouse.

The executor can elect out of QTIP treatment, however, by checking the "Yes" box on line 3. Once made, the election is irrevocable. If there is more than one such joint and survivor annuity, you are not required to make the election for all of them.

If you make the election out of QTIP treatment by checking "Yes" on line 3, you cannot deduct the amount of the annuity on Schedule M. If you do not make the election out, you must list the joint and survivor annuities on Schedule M.

Listing Property Interests on Schedule M

List each property interest included in the gross estate that passes from the decedent to the surviving spouse and for which a marital deduction is claimed. This includes otherwise nondeductible terminable interest property for which you are making a QTIP election. Number each item in sequence and describe each item in detail. Describe the instrument (including any clause or paragraph number) or provision of law under which each item passed to the surviving spouse. If possible, show where each item appears (number and schedule) on Schedules A through I.

In listing otherwise nondeductible property for which you are making a QTIP election, unless you specifically identify a fractional portion of the trust or other property as not subject to the election, the election will be considered made for all of the trust or other property.

Enter the value of each interest before taking into account the federal estate tax or any other death tax. The valuation dates used in determining the value of the gross estate apply also on Schedule M.

If Schedule M includes a bequest of the residue or a part of the residue of the decedent's estate, attach a copy of the computation showing how the value of the residue was determined. Include a statement showing:

● The value of all property that is included in the decedent's gross estate (Schedules A through I) but is not a part of the decedent's probate estate, such as lifetime transfers, jointly owned property that passed to the survivor on decedent's death, and the insurance payable to specific beneficiaries;

● The values of all specific and general legacies or devises, with reference to the applicable clause or paragraph of the decedent's will or codicil. (If legacies are made to each member of a class; for example, $1,000 to each of decedent's employees, only the number in each class and the total value of property received by them need be furnished);

● The date of birth of all persons, the length of whose lives may affect the value of the residuary interest passing to the surviving spouse; and

● Any other important information such as that relating to any claim to any part of the estate not arising under the will.

Lines 5a, b, and c. The total of the values listed on Schedule M must be reduced by the amount of the federal estate tax, the federal GST tax, and the amount of state or other death and GST taxes paid out of the property interest involved. If you enter an amount for state or other death or GST taxes on lines 5b or 5c, identify the taxes and attach your computation of them.

Attachments. If you list property interests passing by the decedent's will on Schedule M, attach a certified copy of the order admitting the will to probate. If, when you file the return, the court of probate jurisdiction has entered any decree interpreting the will or any of its provisions affecting any of the interests listed on Schedule M, or has entered any order of distribution, attach a copy of the decree or order. In addition, the IRS may request other evidence to support the marital deduction claimed.

Form 706 (Rev. 8-2005)

Estate of:

SCHEDULE O—Charitable, Public, and Similar Gifts and Bequests

		Yes	No
1a	If the transfer was made by will, has any action been instituted to have interpreted or to contest the will or any of its provisions affecting the charitable deductions claimed in this schedule?		
	If "Yes," full details must be submitted with this schedule.		
b	According to the information and belief of the person or persons filing this return, is any such action planned? If "Yes," full details must be submitted with this schedule.		
2	Did any property pass to charity as the result of a qualified disclaimer?. . . . . If "Yes," attach a copy of the written disclaimer required by section 2518(b).		

Item number	Name and address of beneficiary	Character of institution	Amount
1			

Total from continuation schedules (or additional sheets) attached to this schedule . . . .

3	Total	**3**	
4a	Federal estate tax payable out of property interests listed above	**4a**	
b	Other death taxes payable out of property interests listed above	**4b**	
c	Federal and state GST taxes payable out of property interests listed above	**4c**	
d	Add items 4a, b, and c	**4d**	
5	Net value of property interests listed above (subtract 4d from 3). Also enter on Part 5, Recapitulation, page 3, at item 21	**5**	

(If more space is needed, attach the continuation schedule from the end of this package or additional sheets of the same size.)
(The instructions to Schedule O are in the separate instructions.)

Schedule O—Page 31

Form 706 (Rev. 8-2005)

Estate of:

SCHEDULE P—Credit for Foreign Death Taxes

List all foreign countries to which death taxes have been paid and for which a credit is claimed on this return.

If a credit is claimed for death taxes paid to more than one foreign country, compute the credit for taxes paid to one country on this sheet and attach a separate copy of Schedule P for each of the other countries.

The credit computed on this sheet is for the ....
(Name of death tax or taxes)

.... imposed in ....
(Name of country)

Credit is computed under the..
(Insert title of treaty or "statute")

Citizenship (nationality) of decedent at time of death

(All amounts and values must be entered in United States money.)

1	Total of estate, inheritance, legacy, and succession taxes imposed in the country named above attributable to property situated in that country, subjected to these taxes, and included in the gross estate (as defined by statute)	**1**
2	Value of the gross estate (adjusted, if necessary, according to the instructions for item 2)	**2**
3	Value of property situated in that country, subjected to death taxes imposed in that country, and included in the gross estate (adjusted, if necessary, according to the instructions for item 3)	**3**
4	Tax imposed by section 2001 reduced by the total credits claimed under sections 2010 and 2012 (see instructions)	**4**
5	Amount of Federal estate tax attributable to property specified at item 3. (Divide item 3 by item 2 and multiply the result by item 4.)	**5**
6	Credit for death taxes imposed in the country named above (the smaller of item 1 or item 5). Also enter on line 13 of Part 2, Tax Computation	**6**

SCHEDULE Q—Credit for Tax on Prior Transfers

Part 1—Transferor Information

	Name of transferor	Social security number	IRS office where estate tax return was filed	Date of death
A				
B				
C				

Check here ▶ ☐ if section 2013(f) (special valuation of farm, etc., real property) adjustments to the computation of the credit were made (see page 20 of the instructions).

Part 2—Computation of Credit (see instructions beginning on page 20)

Item	Transferor			Total A, B, & C
	A	B	C	
1 Transferee's tax as apportioned (from worksheet, (line 7 ÷ line 8) × line 35 for each column) . .				
2 Transferor's tax (from each column of worksheet, line 20)				
3 Maximum amount before percentage requirement (for each column, enter amount from line 1 or 2, whichever is smaller)				
4 Percentage allowed (each column) (see instructions)	%	%	%	
5 Credit allowable (line 3 × line 4 for each column)				
6 TOTAL credit allowable (add columns A, B, and C of line 5). Enter here and on line 14 of Part 2, Tax Computation				

Schedules P and Q—Page 32 (The instructions to Schedules P and Q are in the separate instructions.)

Form 706 (Rev. 8-2005)

SCHEDULE R—Generation-Skipping Transfer Tax

Note. To avoid application of the deemed allocation rules, Form 706 and Schedule R should be filed to allocate the GST exemption to trusts that may later have taxable terminations or distributions under section 2612 even if the form is not required to be filed to report estate or GST tax.

The GST tax is imposed on taxable transfers of interests in property located **outside the United States** as well as property located inside the United States.

See instructions beginning on page 21.

Part 1—GST Exemption Reconciliation (Section 2631) and Section 2652(a)(3) (Special QTIP) Election

You no longer need to check a box to make a section 2652(a)(3) (special QTIP) election. If you list qualifying property in Part 1, line 9, below, you will be considered to have made this election. See page 23 of the separate instructions for details.

1 Maximum allowable GST exemption	**1**	
2 Total GST exemption allocated by the decedent against decedent's lifetime transfers	**2**	
3 Total GST exemption allocated by the executor, using Form 709, against decedent's lifetime transfers	**3**	
4 GST exemption allocated on line 6 of Schedule R, Part 2	**4**	
5 GST exemption allocated on line 6 of Schedule R, Part 3	**5**	
6 Total GST exemption allocated on line 4 of Schedule(s) R-1	**6**	
7 Total GST exemption allocated to *inter vivos* transfers and direct skips (add lines 2–6)	**7**	
8 GST exemption available to allocate to trusts and section 2032A interests (subtract line 7 from line 1)	**8**	

9 Allocation of GST exemption to trusts (as defined for GST tax purposes):

A Name of trust	B Trust's EIN (if any)	C GST exemption allocated on lines 2–6, above (see instructions)	D Additional GST exemption allocated (see instructions)	E Trust's inclusion ratio (optional—see instructions)

9D Total. May not exceed line 8, above **9D**		
10 GST exemption available to allocate to section 2032A interests received by individual beneficiaries (subtract line 9D from line 8). You must attach special use allocation schedule (see instructions).	**10**	

(The instructions to Schedule R are in the separate instructions.)　　　　　　　　　　　**Schedule R—Page 33**

Form 706 (Rev. 8-2005)

Estate of:

Part 2—Direct Skips Where the Property Interests Transferred Bear the GST Tax on the Direct Skips

Name of skip person	Description of property interest transferred	Estate tax value

1 Total estate tax values of all property interests listed above	1	
2 Estate taxes, state death taxes, and other charges borne by the property interests listed above.	2	
3 GST taxes borne by the property interests listed above but imposed on direct skips other than those shown on this Part 2 (see instructions)	3	
4 Total fixed taxes and other charges (add lines 2 and 3).	4	
5 Total tentative maximum direct skips (subtract line 4 from line 1)	5	
6 GST exemption allocated	6	
7 Subtract line 6 from line 5	7	
8 GST tax due (divide line 7 by 3.127659)	8	
9 Enter the amount from line 8 of Schedule R, Part 3.	9	
10 **Total GST taxes payable by the estate** (add lines 8 and 9). Enter here and on line 17 of Part 2—Tax Computation, on page 1.	10	

Schedule R—Page 34

Form 706 (Rev. 8-2005)

Estate of:

Part 3—Direct Skips Where the Property Interests Transferred Do Not Bear the GST Tax on the Direct Skips

Name of skip person	Description of property interest transferred	Estate tax value

1 Total estate tax values of all property interests listed above	1	
2 Estate taxes, state death taxes, and other charges borne by the property interests listed above	2	
3 GST taxes borne by the property interests listed above but imposed on direct skips other than those shown on this Part 3 (see instructions)	3	
4 Total fixed taxes and other charges (add lines 2 and 3).	4	
5 Total tentative maximum direct skips (subtract line 4 from line 1)	5	
6 GST exemption allocated	6	
7 Subtract line 6 from line 5	7	
8 GST tax due (multiply line 7 by .47). Enter here and on Schedule R, Part 2, line 9	8	

Schedule R—Page 35

SCHEDULE R-1	**Generation-Skipping Transfer Tax**	
(Form 706)	Direct Skips From a Trust	OMB No. 1545-0015
(Rev. August 2005) Department of the Treasury Internal Revenue Service	Payment Voucher	

Executor: File one copy with Form 706 and send two copies to the fiduciary. Do not pay the tax shown. See the separate instructions.
Fiduciary: See instructions on the following page. Pay the tax shown on line 6.

Name of trust	Trust's EIN

Name and title of fiduciary	Name of decedent	
Address of fiduciary (number and street)	Decedent's SSN	Service Center where Form 706 was filed
City, state, and ZIP code	Name of executor	
Address of executor (number and street)	City, state, and ZIP code	
Date of decedent's death	Filing due date of Schedule R, Form 706 (with extensions)	

Part 1—Computation of the GST Tax on the Direct Skip

Description of property interests subject to the direct skip	Estate tax value

1	Total estate tax value of all property interests listed above	1
2	Estate taxes, state death taxes, and other charges borne by the property interests listed above	2
3	Tentative maximum direct skip from trust (subtract line 2 from line 1)	3
4	GST exemption allocated	4
5	Subtract line 4 from line 3	5
6	GST tax due from fiduciary (divide line 5 by 3.127659). **(See instructions if property will not bear the GST tax.)**	6

Under penalties of perjury, I declare that I have examined this return, including accompanying schedules and statements, and to the best of my knowledge and belief, it is true, correct, and complete.

Signature(s) of executor(s)	Date
	Date
Signature of fiduciary or officer representing fiduciary	Date

Schedule R-1 (Form 706)—Page 36

Form 706 (Rev. 8-2005)
_____

Instructions for the Trustee

_____

Introduction   Schedule R-1 (Form 706) serves as a payment voucher for the Generation-Skipping Transfer
(GST) tax imposed on a direct skip from a trust, which you, the trustee of the trust, must pay.
The executor completes the Schedule R-1 (Form 706) and gives you 2 copies. File one copy
and keep one for your records.

_____

How to pay   You can pay by check or money order.
- Make it payable to the "United States Treasury."
- Make the check or money order for the amount on line 6 of Schedule R-1.
- Write "GST Tax" and the trust's EIN on the check or money order.

_____

Signature   You must sign the Schedule R-1 in the space provided.

_____

What to mail   Mail your check or money order and the copy of Schedule R-1 that you signed.

_____

Where to mail   Mail to the Service Center shown on Schedule R-1.

_____

When to pay   The GST tax is due and payable 9 months after the decedent's date of death (shown on the
Schedule R-1). You will owe interest on any GST tax not paid by that date.

_____

Automatic   You have an automatic extension of time to file Schedule R-1 and pay the GST tax. The
extension   automatic extension allows you to file and pay by 2 months after the due date (with
extensions) for filing the decedent's Schedule R (shown on the Schedule R-1).
   If you pay the GST tax under the automatic extension, you will be charged interest (but no
penalties).

_____

Additional   For more information, see Code section 2603(a)(2) and the instructions for Form 706, United
information   States Estate (and Generation-Skipping Transfer) Tax Return.

_____

Form 706 (Rev. 8-2005)

Estate of:

SCHEDULE U. Qualified Conservation Easement Exclusion

Part 1—Election

Note. *The executor is deemed to have made the election under section 2031(c)(6) if he or she files Schedule U and excludes any qualifying conservation easements from the gross estate.*

Part 2—General Qualifications

1   Describe the land subject to the qualified conservation easement (see separate instructions) _____

2   Did the decedent or a member of the decedent's family own the land described above during the 3-year period ending on the date of the decedent's death? . . . .   ☐ **Yes**   ☐ **No**

3   Describe the conservation easement with regard to which the exclusion is being claimed (see separate instructions).

Part 3—Computation of Exclusion

4 Estate tax value of the land subject to the qualified conservation easement (see separate instructions).		**4**
5 Date of death value of any easements granted prior to decedent's death and included on line 10 below (see instructions)	**5**	
6 Add lines 4 and 5.	**6**	
7 Value of retained development rights on the land (see instructions) .	**7**	
8 Subtract line 7 from line 6	**8**	
9 Multiply line 8 by 30% (.30)	**9**	
10 Value of qualified conservation easement for which the exclusion is being claimed (see instructions)	**10**	
Note: *If line 10 is less than line 9, continue with line 11. If line 10 is equal to or more than line 9, skip lines 11 through 13, enter ".40" on line 14, and complete the schedule.*		
11 Divide line 10 by line 8. Figure to 3 decimal places (e.g., .123) .	**11**	
If line 11 is equal to or less than .100, stop here; the estate does not qualify for the conservation easement exclusion.		
12 Subtract line 11 from .300. Enter the answer in hundredths by rounding any thousandths up to the next higher hundredth (i.e., .030 = .03; but .031 = .04)	**12**	
13 Multiply line 12 by 2	**13**	
14 Subtract line 13 from .40	**14**	
15 Deduction under section 2055(f) for the conservation easement (see separate instructions)	**15**	
16 Amount of indebtedness on the land (see separate instructions) .	**16**	
17 Total reductions in value (add lines 7, 15, and 16)		**17**
18 Net value of land (subtract line 17 from line 4)		**18**
19 Multiply line 18 by line 14		**19**
20 Enter the smaller of line 19 or the exclusion limitation (see instructions). Also enter this amount on item 11, Part 5, Recapitulation, page 3		**20**

Form 706 (Rev. 8-2005)   (Make copies of this schedule before completing it if you will need more than one schedule.)

Estate of: _____

CONTINUATION SCHEDULE

Continuation of Schedule _____

(Enter letter of schedule you are continuing.)

Item number	Description For securities, give CUSIP number.	Unit value (Sch. B, E, or G only)	Alternate valuation date	Alternate value	Value at date of death or amount deductible

_____ **TOTAL.** (Carry forward to main schedule.) . . . .

See the instructions on the reverse side.

Continuation Schedule—Page 39

Form 706 (Rev. 8-2005)

Instructions for Continuation Schedule

When you need to list more assets or deductions than you have room for on one of the main schedules, use the Continuation Schedule on page 39. It provides a uniform format for listing additional assets from Schedules A through I and additional deductions from Schedules J, K, L, M, and O.

Please keep the following points in mind:

• Use a separate Continuation Schedule for each main schedule you are continuing. Do not combine assets or deductions from different schedules on one Continuation Schedule.

• Make copies of the blank schedule before completing it if you expect to need more than one.

• Use as many Continuation Schedules as needed to list all the assets or deductions.

• Enter the letter of the schedule you are continuing in the space at the top of the Continuation Schedule.

• Use the *Unit value* column **only** if continuing Schedule B, E, or G. For all other schedules, use this space to continue the description.

• Carry the total from the Continuation Schedules forward to the appropriate line on the main schedule.

If continuing	Report	Where on Continuation Schedule
Schedule E, Pt. 2	*Percentage includible*	*Alternate valuation date*
Schedule K	*Amount unpaid to date*	*Alternate valuation date*
Schedule K	*Amount in contest*	*Alternate value*
Schedules J, L, M	*Description of deduction continuation*	*Alternate valuation date* **and** *Alternate value*
Schedule O	*Character of institution*	*Alternate valuation date* **and** *Alternate value*
Schedule O	*Amount of each deduction*	*Amount deductible*

Continuation Schedule—Page 40

Printed on recycled paper

*

Appendix B

FORM 1041

Form 1041 — Department of the Treasury—Internal Revenue Service
U.S. Income Tax Return for Estates and Trusts — 2005   OMB No. 1545-0092

A Type of entity (see instr.):
- [ ] Decedent's estate
- [ ] Simple trust
- [ ] Complex trust
- [ ] Qualified disability trust
- [ ] ESBT (S portion only)
- [ ] Grantor type trust
- [ ] Bankruptcy estate–Ch. 7
- [ ] Bankruptcy estate–Ch. 11
- [ ] Pooled income fund

For calendar year 2005 or fiscal year beginning , 2005, and ending , 20

Name of estate or trust (If a grantor type trust, see page 12 of the instructions.)

Name and title of fiduciary

Number, street, and room or suite no. (If a P.O. box, see page 12 of the instructions.)

City or town, state, and ZIP code

C Employer identification number

D Date entity created

E Nonexempt charitable and split-interest trusts, check applicable boxes (see page 13 of the instr.):
- [ ] Described in section 4947(a)(1)
- [ ] Not a private foundation
- [ ] Described in section 4947(a)(2)

B Number of Schedules K-1 attached (see instructions) ▶

F Check applicable boxes:
- [ ] Initial return
- [ ] Final return
- [ ] Amended return
- [ ] Change in fiduciary
- [ ] Change in fiduciary's name
- [ ] Change in trust's name
- [ ] Change in fiduciary's address

G Pooled mortgage account (see page 14 of the instructions): [ ] Bought [ ] Sold Date:

Income

1	Interest income	1
2a	Total ordinary dividends	2a
b	Qualified dividends allocable to: (1) Beneficiaries _____ (2) Estate or trust _____	
3	Business income or (loss) (attach Schedule C or C-EZ (Form 1040))	3
4	Capital gain or (loss) (attach Schedule D (Form 1041))	4
5	Rents, royalties, partnerships, other estates and trusts, etc. (attach Schedule E (Form 1040))	5
6	Farm income or (loss) (attach Schedule F (Form 1040))	6
7	Ordinary gain or (loss) (attach Form 4797)	7
8	Other income. List type and amount	8
9	**Total income.** Combine lines 1, 2a, and 3 through 8 ▶	9

Deductions

10	Interest. Check if Form 4952 is attached ▶ [ ]	10
11	Taxes	11
12	Fiduciary fees	12
13	Charitable deduction (from Schedule A, line 7)	13
14	Attorney, accountant, and return preparer fees	14
15a	Other deductions **not** subject to the 2% floor (attach schedule)	15a
b	Allowable miscellaneous itemized deductions subject to the 2% floor	15b
16	Add lines 10 through 15b ▶	16
17	Adjusted total income or (loss). Subtract line 16 from line 9 [17]	
18	Income distribution deduction (from Schedule B, line 15) (attach Schedules K-1 (Form 1041))	18
19	Estate tax deduction (including certain generation-skipping taxes) (attach computation)	19
20	Exemption	20
21	Add lines 18 through 20 ▶	21

Tax and Payments

22	Taxable income. Subtract line 21 from line 17. If a loss, see page 20 of the instructions	22
23	**Total tax** (from Schedule G, line 7)	23
24	Payments: **a** 2005 estimated tax payments and amount applied from 2004 return	24a
b	Estimated tax payments allocated to beneficiaries (from Form 1041-T)	24b
c	Subtract line 24b from line 24a	24c
d	Tax paid with Form 7004 (see page 20 of the instructions)	24d
e	Federal income tax withheld. If any is from Form(s) 1099, check ▶ [ ]	24e
	Other payments: **f** Form 2439 _____ ; **g** Form 4136 _____ ; Total ▶	24h
25	**Total payments.** Add lines 24c through 24e, and 24h ▶	25
26	Estimated tax penalty (see page 20 of the instructions)	26
27	**Tax due.** If line 25 is smaller than the total of lines 23 and 26, enter amount owed	27
28	**Overpayment.** If line 25 is larger than the total of lines 23 and 26, enter amount overpaid	28
29	Amount of line 28 to be: **a** Credited to 2006 estimated tax ▶ ; **b** Refunded ▶	29

Sign Here — Under penalties of perjury, I declare that I have examined this return, including accompanying schedules and statements, and to the best of my knowledge and belief, it is true, correct, and complete. Declaration of preparer (other than taxpayer) is based on all information of which preparer has any knowledge.

Signature of fiduciary or officer representing fiduciary — Date — EIN of fiduciary if a financial institution

May the IRS discuss this return with the preparer shown below (see instr.)? [ ] Yes [ ] No

Paid Preparer's Use Only

Preparer's signature — Date — Check if self-employed [ ]

Preparer's SSN or PTIN

Firm's name (or yours if self-employed), address, and ZIP code ▶ — EIN — Phone no. ( )

For Privacy Act and Paperwork Reduction Act Notice, see the separate instructions.   Cat. No. 11370H   Form **1041** (2005)

* The above form is the most recent version of Form 1041 available when this edition was published. A current version of it and other forms can be found at local IRS offices, libraries or on the internet at the IRS website (www.irs.gov).

Form 1041 (2005)   Page **2**

Schedule A   Charitable Deduction. Do not complete for a simple trust or a pooled income fund.

1	Amounts paid or permanently set aside for charitable purposes from gross income (see page 21)	**1**
2	Tax-exempt income allocable to charitable contributions (see page 21 of the instructions)	**2**
3	Subtract line 2 from line 1	**3**
4	Capital gains for the tax year allocated to corpus and paid or permanently set aside for charitable purposes	**4**
5	Add lines 3 and 4	**5**
6	Section 1202 exclusion allocable to capital gains paid or permanently set aside for charitable purposes (see page 21 of the instructions)	**6**
7	**Charitable deduction.** Subtract line 6 from line 5. Enter here and on page 1, line 13	**7**

Schedule B   Income Distribution Deduction

1	Adjusted total income (see page 22 of the instructions)	**1**
2	Adjusted tax-exempt interest	**2**
3	Total net gain from Schedule D (Form 1041), line 15, column (1) (see page 22 of the instructions)	**3**
4	Enter amount from Schedule A, line 4 (reduced by any allocable section 1202 exclusion)	**4**
5	Capital gains for the tax year included on Schedule A, line 1 (see page 22 of the instructions)	**5**
6	Enter any gain from page 1, line 4, as a negative number. If page 1, line 4, is a loss, enter the loss as a positive number	**6**
7	**Distributable net income (DNI).** Combine lines 1 through 6. If zero or less, enter -0-	**7**
8	If a complex trust, enter accounting income for the tax year as determined under the governing instrument and applicable local law **8**	
9	Income required to be distributed currently	**9**
10	Other amounts paid, credited, or otherwise required to be distributed	**10**
11	Total distributions. Add lines 9 and 10. If greater than line 8, see page 22 of the Instructions	**11**
12	Enter the amount of tax-exempt income included on line 11	**12**
13	Tentative income distribution deduction. Subtract line 12 from line 11	**13**
14	Tentative income distribution deduction. Subtract line 2 from line 7. If zero or less, enter -0-	**14**
15	**Income distribution deduction.** Enter the smaller of line 13 or line 14 here and on page 1, line 18	**15**

Schedule G   Tax Computation (see page 23 of the instructions)

1	Tax: **a** Tax on taxable income (see page 23 of the instructions)	**1a**	
	b Tax on lump-sum distributions (attach Form 4972)	**1b**	
	c Alternative minimum tax (from Schedule I, line 56)	**1c**	
	d Total. Add lines 1a through 1c	▶ **1d**	
2a	Foreign tax credit (attach Form 1116)	**2a**	
b	Other nonbusiness credits (attach schedule)	**2b**	
c	General business credit. Enter here and check which forms are attached: ☐ Form 3800 ☐ Forms (specify) ▶	**2c**	
d	Credit for prior year minimum tax (attach Form 8801)	**2d**	
3	**Total credits.** Add lines 2a through 2d	▶	**3**
4	Subtract line 3 from line 1d. If zero or less, enter -0-		**4**
5	Recapture taxes. Check if from: ☐ Form 4255 ☐ Form 8611		**5**
6	Household employment taxes. Attach Schedule H (Form 1040)		**6**
7	**Total tax.** Add lines 4 through 6. Enter here and on page 1, line 23	▶	**7**

Other Information

		Yes	No
1	Did the estate or trust receive tax-exempt income? If "Yes," attach a computation of the allocation of expenses. Enter the amount of tax-exempt interest income and exempt-interest dividends ▶ $		
2	Did the estate or trust receive all or any part of the earnings (salary, wages, and other compensation) of any individual by reason of a contract assignment or similar arrangement?		
3	At any time during calendar year 2005, did the estate or trust have an interest in or a signature or other authority over a bank, securities, or other financial account in a foreign country? See page 25 of the instructions for exceptions and filing requirements for Form TD F 90-22.1. If "Yes," enter the name of the foreign country ▶		
4	During the tax year, did the estate or trust receive a distribution from, or was it the grantor of, or transferor to, a foreign trust? If "Yes," the estate or trust may have to file Form 3520. See page 25 of the instructions		
5	Did the estate or trust receive, or pay, any qualified residence interest on seller-provided financing? If "Yes," see page 25 for required attachment		
6	If this is an estate or a complex trust making the section 663(b) election, check here (see page 25) . ▶ ☐		
7	To make a section 643(e)(3) election, attach Schedule D (Form 1040), and check here (see page 25) . ▶ ☐		
8	If the decedent's estate has been open for more than 2 years, attach an explanation for the delay in closing the estate, and check here ▶ ☐		
9	Are any present or future trust beneficiaries skip persons? See page 26 of the instructions		

Form **1041** (2005)

Form 1041 (2005)   Page **3**

Schedule I   Alternative Minimum Tax (see pages 26 through 32 of the instructions)

Part I—Estate's or Trust's Share of Alternative Minimum Taxable Income

1	Adjusted total income or (loss) (from page 1, line 17)	1	
2	Interest	2	
3	Taxes	3	
4	Miscellaneous itemized deductions (from page 1, line 15b)	4	
5	Refund of taxes	5 (	)
6	Depletion (difference between regular tax and AMT)	6	
7	Net operating loss deduction. Enter as a positive amount	7	
8	Interest from specified private activity bonds exempt from the regular tax	8	
9	Qualified small business stock (see page 27 of the instructions)	9	
10	Exercise of incentive stock options (excess of AMT income over regular tax income) . . .	10	
11	Other estates and trusts (amount from Schedule K-1 (Form 1041), box 12, code A)	11	
12	Electing large partnerships (amount from Schedule K-1 (Form 1065-B), box 6)	12	
13	Disposition of property (difference between AMT and regular tax gain or loss)	13	
14	Depreciation on assets placed in service after 1986 (difference between regular tax and AMT)	14	
15	Passive activities (difference between AMT and regular tax income or loss)	15	
16	Loss limitations (difference between AMT and regular tax income or loss)	16	
17	Circulation costs (difference between regular tax and AMT)	17	
18	Long-term contracts (difference between AMT and regular tax income)	18	
19	Mining costs (difference between regular tax and AMT)	19	
20	Research and experimental costs (difference between regular tax and AMT)	20	
21	Income from certain installment sales before January 1, 1987	21 (	)
22	Intangible drilling costs preference	22	
23	Other adjustments, including income-based related adjustments	23	
24	Alternative tax net operating loss deduction (See the instructions for the limitation that applies.)	24 (	)
25	Adjusted alternative minimum taxable income. Combine lines 1 through 24	25	

Note: *Complete Part II below before going to line 26.*

26	Income distribution deduction from Part II, line 44	26		
27	Estate tax deduction (from page 1, line 19)	27		
28	Add lines 26 and 27		28	
29	Estate's or trust's share of alternative minimum taxable income. Subtract line 28 from line 25		29	

If line 29 is:

- $22,500 or less, stop here and enter -0- on Schedule G, line 1c. The estate or trust is not liable for the alternative minimum tax.
- Over $22,500, but less than $165,000, go to line 45.
- $165,000 or more, enter the amount from line 29 on line 51 and go to line 52.

Part II—Income Distribution Deduction on a Minimum Tax Basis

30	Adjusted alternative minimum taxable income (see page 30 of the instructions)	30	
31	Adjusted tax-exempt interest (other than amounts included on line 8)	31	
32	Total net gain from Schedule D (Form 1041), line 15, column (1). If a loss, enter -0- . . .	32	
33	Capital gains for the tax year allocated to corpus and paid or permanently set aside for charitable purposes (from Schedule A, line 4)	33	
34	Capital gains paid or permanently set aside for charitable purposes from gross income (see page 30 of the instructions)	34	
35	Capital gains computed on a minimum tax basis included on line 25	35 (	)
36	Capital losses computed on a minimum tax basis included on line 25. Enter as a positive amount	36	
37	Distributable net alternative minimum taxable income (DNAMTI). Combine lines 30 through 36. If zero or less, enter -0-	37	
38	Income required to be distributed currently (from Schedule B, line 9)	38	
39	Other amounts paid, credited, or otherwise required to be distributed (from Schedule B, line 10)	39	
40	Total distributions. Add lines 38 and 39	40	
41	Tax-exempt income included on line 40 (other than amounts included on line 8)	41	
42	Tentative income distribution deduction on a minimum tax basis. Subtract line 41 from line 40	42	
43	Tentative income distribution deduction on a minimum tax basis. Subtract line 31 from line 37. If zero or less, enter -0-	43	
44	**Income distribution deduction on a minimum tax basis.** Enter the smaller of line 42 or line 43. Enter here and on line 26	44	

Form **1041** (2005)

Form 1041 (2005)   Page **4**

Part III—Alternative Minimum Tax

45	Exemption amount	**45**	$22,500 00

46	Enter the amount from line 29	46	
47	Phase-out of exemption amount	47	$75,000 00
48	Subtract line 47 from line 46. If zero or less, enter -0-	48	

49	Multiply line 48 by 25% (.25)	**49**	
50	Subtract line 49 from line 45. If zero or less, enter -0-	**50**	
51	Subtract line 50 from line 46	**51**	
52	Go to Part IV of Schedule I to figure line 52 if the estate or trust has qualified dividends or has a gain on lines 14a and 15 of column (2) of Schedule D (Form 1041) (as refigured for the AMT, if necessary). Otherwise, if line 51 is—		
	• $175,000 or less, multiply line 51 by 26% (.26).		
	• Over $175,000, multiply line 51 by 28% (.28) and subtract $3,500 from the result	**52**	
53	Alternative minimum foreign tax credit (see page 30 of the instructions)	**53**	
54	Tentative minimum tax. Subtract line 53 from line 52	**54**	
55	Enter the tax from Schedule G, line 1a (minus any foreign tax credit from Schedule G, line 2a)	**55**	
56	**Alternative minimum tax.** Subtract line 55 from line 54. If zero or less, enter -0-. Enter here and on Schedule G, line 1c	**56**	

Part IV—Line 52 Computation Using Maximum Capital Gains Rates

Caution: *If you did not complete Part V of Schedule D (Form 1041), the Schedule D Tax Worksheet, or the Qualified Dividends Tax Worksheet, see page 32 of the instructions before completing this part.*

57	Enter the amount from line 51	**57**	
58	Enter the amount from Schedule D (Form 1041), line 22, line 13 of the Schedule D Tax Worksheet, or line 4 of the Qualified Dividends Tax Worksheet, whichever applies (as refigured for the AMT, if necessary) — 58		
59	Enter the amount from Schedule D (Form 1041), line 14b, column (2) (as refigured for the AMT, if necessary). If you did not complete Schedule D for the regular tax or the AMT, enter -0- — 59		
60	If you did not complete a Schedule D Tax Worksheet for the regular tax or the AMT, enter the amount from line 58. Otherwise, add lines 58 and 59 and enter the **smaller** of that result or the amount from line 10 of the Schedule D Tax Worksheet (as refigured for the AMT, if necessary) — 60		
61	Enter the **smaller** of line 57 or line 60	**61**	
62	Subtract line 61 from line 57	**62**	
63	If line 62 is $175,000 or less, multiply line 62 by 26% (.26). Otherwise, multiply line 62 by 28% (.28) and subtract $3,500 from the result ▶	**63**	
64	Maximum amount subject to the 5% rate — 64	$2,000 00	
65	Enter the amount from line 23 of Schedule D (Form 1041), line 14 of the Schedule D Tax Worksheet, or line 5 of the Qualified Dividends Tax Worksheet, whichever applies (as figured for the regular tax). If you did not complete Schedule D or either worksheet for the regular tax, enter -0- — 65		
66	Subtract line 65 from line 64. If zero or less, enter -0- — 66		
67	Enter the **smaller** of line 57 or line 58 — 67		
68	Enter the **smaller** of line 66 or line 67 — 68		
69	Multiply line 68 by 5% (.05) ▶	**69**	
70	Subtract line 68 from line 67 — 70		
71	Multiply line 70 by 15% (.15) ▶	**71**	
	If line 59 is zero or blank, skip lines 72 and 73 and go to line 74. Otherwise, go to line 72.		
72	Subtract line 67 from line 61 — 72		
73	Multiply line 72 by 25% (.25) ▶	**73**	
74	Add lines 63, 69, 71, and 73	**74**	
75	If line 57 is $175,000 or less, multiply line 57 by 26% (.26). Otherwise, multiply line 57 by 28% (.28) and subtract $3,500 from the result	**75**	
76	Enter the **smaller** of line 74 or line 75 here and on line 52	**76**	

Form **1041** (2005)

*

Appendix C

FORM 709

Form **709**	United States Gift (and Generation-Skipping Transfer) Tax Return		OMB No. 1545-0020
Department of the Treasury Internal Revenue Service	(For gifts made during calendar year 2005) ▶ See separate instructions.		**2005**

Part 1—General Information

1 Donor's first name and middle initial	2 Donor's last name	3 Donor's social security number
4 Address (number, street, and apartment number)		5 Legal residence (domicile) (county and state)
6 City, state, and ZIP code		7 Citizenship

		Yes	No
8	If the donor died during the year, check here ▶ ☐ and enter date of death _____		
9	If you extended the time to file this Form 709, check here ▶ ☐		
10	Enter the total number of donees listed on Schedule A. Count each person only once. ▶		
11a	Have you (the donor) previously filed a Form 709 (or 709-A) for any other year? If "No," skip line 11b .		
11b	If the answer to line 11a is "Yes," has your address changed since you last filed Form 709 (or 709-A)?		
12	**Gifts by husband or wife to third parties.** Do you consent to have the gifts (including generation-skipping transfers) made by you and by your spouse to third parties during the calendar year considered as made one-half by each of you? (See instructions.) (If the answer is "Yes," the following information must be furnished and your spouse must sign the consent shown below. **If the answer is "No," skip lines 13–18 and go to Schedule A.**) .		
13	Name of consenting spouse **14** SSN		
15	Were you married to one another during the entire calendar year? (see instructions)		
16	If 15 is "No," check whether ☐ married ☐ divorced or ☐ widowed/deceased, and give date (see instructions) ▶		
17	Will a gift tax return for this year be filed by your spouse? (If "Yes," mail both returns in the same envelope.) . . .		
18	**Consent of Spouse.** I consent to have the gifts (and generation-skipping transfers) made by me and by my spouse to third parties during the calendar year considered as made one-half by each of us. We are both aware of the joint and several liability for tax created by the execution of this consent.		

Consenting spouse's signature ▶   Date ▶

Part 2—Tax Computation

1	Enter the amount from Schedule A, Part 4, line 11	**1**		
2	Enter the amount from Schedule B, line 3	**2**		
3	Total taxable gifts. Add lines 1 and 2	**3**		
4	Tax computed on amount on line 3 (see *Table for Computing Gift Tax* in separate instructions) .	**4**		
5	Tax computed on amount on line 2 (see *Table for Computing Gift Tax* in separate instructions) .	**5**		
6	Balance. Subtract line 5 from line 4	**6**		
7	Maximum unified credit (nonresident aliens, see instructions)	**7**	345,800	00
8	Enter the unified credit against tax allowable for all prior periods (from Sch. B, line 1, col. C) .	**8**		
9	Balance. Subtract line 8 from line 7	**9**		
10	Enter 20% (.20) of the amount allowed as a specific exemption for gifts made after September 8, 1976, and before January 1, 1977 (see instructions)	**10**		
11	Balance. Subtract line 10 from line 9	**11**		
12	Unified credit. Enter the smaller of line 6 or line 11	**12**		
13	Credit for foreign gift taxes (see instructions)	**13**		
14	Total credits. Add lines 12 and 13	**14**		
15	Balance. Subtract line 14 from line 6. Do not enter less than zero	**15**		
16	Generation-skipping transfer taxes (from Schedule C, Part 3, col. H, Total) . . .	**16**		
17	Total tax. Add lines 15 and 16	**17**		
18	Gift and generation-skipping transfer taxes prepaid with extension of time to file . . .	**18**		
19	If line 18 is less than line 17, enter **balance due** (see instructions)	**19**		
20	If line 18 is greater than line 17, enter **amount to be refunded**	**20**		

Sign Here

Under penalties of perjury, I declare that I have examined this return, including any accompanying schedules and statements, and to the best of my knowledge and belief, it is true, correct, and complete. Declaration of preparer (other than donor) is based on all information of which preparer has any knowledge.

▶ Signature of donor	Date

Paid Preparer's Use Only

Preparer's signature ▶	Date	Check if self-employed ▶ ☐
Firm's name (or yours if self-employed), address, and ZIP code ▶		Phone no. ▶ ( )

For Disclosure, Privacy Act, and Paperwork Reduction Act Notice, see page 12 of the separate instructions for this form.   Cat. No. 16783M   Form **709** (2005)

Attach check or money order here.

* The above Form is the most recent version of Form 709 available when this edition was published. A current version of this and other IRS forms may be found in libraries, at local IRS offices, or on the internet at the IRS website (www.irs.gov).

Page **2**

Form 709 (2005)

| **SCHEDULE A** | **Computation of Taxable Gifts** (Including transfers in trust) (see instructions) |

A　Does the value of any item listed on Schedule A reflect any valuation discount? If "Yes," attach explanation . . . . . . Yes ☐ No ☐

B　☐　◄ Check here if you elect under section 529(c)(2)(B) to treat any transfers made this year to a qualified tuition program as made ratably over a 5-year period beginning this year. See instructions. Attach explanation.

Part 1—Gifts Subject Only to Gift Tax. Gifts less political organization, medical, and educational exclusions. See instructions.

A Item number	B · Donee's name and address · Relationship to donor (if any) · Description of gift · If the gift was of securities, give CUSIP no. · If closely held entity, give EIN	C	D Donor's adjusted basis of gift	E Date of gift	F Value at date of gift	G For split gifts, enter ½ of column F	H Net transfer (subtract col. G from col. F)
1							
*Gifts made by spouse—complete **only** if you are splitting gifts with your spouse and he/she also made gifts.*							

Total of Part 1. Add amounts from Part 1, column H . . . . ▶

Part 2—Direct Skips. Gifts that are direct skips and are subject to both gift tax and generation-skipping transfer tax. You must list the gifts in chronological order.

A Item number	B · Donee's name and address · Relationship to donor (if any) · Description of gift · If the gift was of securities, give CUSIP no. · If closely held entity, give EIN	C 2632(b) election out	D Donor's adjusted basis of gift	E Date of gift	F Value at date of gift	G For split gifts, enter ½ of column F	H Net transfer (subtract col. G from col. F)
1							
*Gifts made by spouse—complete **only** if you are splitting gifts with your spouse and he/she also made gifts.*							

Total of Part 2. Add amounts from Part 2, column H . . . . ▶

Part 3—Indirect Skips. Gifts to trusts that are currently subject to gift tax and may later be subject to generation-skipping transfer tax. You must list these gifts in chronological order.

A Item number	B · Donee's name and address · Relationship to donor (if any) · Description of gift · If the gift was of securities, give CUSIP no. · If closely held entity, give EIN	C 2632(c) election	D Donor's adjusted basis of gift	E Date of gift	F Value at date of gift	G For split gifts, enter ½ of column F	H Net transfer (subtract col. G from col. F)
1							
*Gifts made by spouse—complete **only** if you are splitting gifts with your spouse and he/she also made gifts.*							

Total of Part 3. Add amounts from Part 3, column H . . . . ▶

(If more space is needed, attach additional sheets of same size.)　　　　　　　Form **709** (2005)

Form 709 (2005)   Page **3**

Part 4—Taxable Gift Reconciliation

1	Total value of gifts of donor. Add totals from column H of Parts 1, 2, and 3	**1**	
2	Total annual exclusions for gifts listed on line 1 (see instructions)	**2**	
3	Total included amount of gifts. Subtract line 2 from line 1	**3**	

Deductions (see instructions)

4	Gifts of interests to spouse for which a marital deduction will be claimed, based on items .... of Schedule A	**4**		
5	Exclusions attributable to gifts on line 4	**5**		
6	Marital deduction. Subtract line 5 from line 4	**6**		
7	Charitable deduction, based on items .... less exclusions . .	**7**		
8	Total deductions. Add lines 6 and 7		**8**	
9	Subtract line 8 from line 3		**9**	
10	Generation-skipping transfer taxes payable with this Form 709 (from Schedule C, Part 3, col. H, Total) .		**10**	
11	Taxable gifts. Add lines 9 and 10. Enter here and on line 1 of the Tax Computation on page 1 . . .		**11**	

12 Terminable Interest (QTIP) Marital Deduction. (See instructions for Schedule A, Part 4, line 4.)

If a trust (or other property) meets the requirements of qualified terminable interest property under section 2523(f), and:

a. The trust (or other property) is listed on Schedule A, and

b. The value of the trust (or other property) is entered in whole or in part as a deduction on Schedule A, Part 4, line 4, then the donor shall be deemed to have made an election to have such trust (or other property) treated as qualified terminable interest property under section 2523(f).

If less than the entire value of the trust (or other property) that the donor has included in Parts 1 and 3 of Schedule A is entered as a deduction on line 4, the donor shall be considered to have made an election only as to a fraction of the trust (or other property). The numerator of this fraction is equal to the amount of the trust (or other property) deducted on Schedule A, Part 4, line 6. The denominator is equal to the total value of the trust (or other property) listed in Parts 1 and 3 of Schedule A.

If you make the QTIP election, the terminable interest property involved will be included in your spouse's gross estate upon his or her death (section 2044). See instructions for line 4 of Schedule A. If your spouse disposes (by gift or otherwise) of all or part of the qualifying life income interest, he or she will be considered to have made a transfer of the entire property that is subject to the gift tax. See *Transfer of Certain Life Estates Received From Spouse* on page 4 of the instructions.

13 Election Out of QTIP Treatment of Annuities

☐ ◄ Check here if you elect under section 2523(f)(6) **not** to treat as qualified terminable interest property any joint and survivor annuities that are reported on Schedule A and would otherwise be treated as qualified terminable interest property under section 2523(f). See instructions. Enter the item numbers from Schedule A for the annuities for which you are making this election ►

SCHEDULE B   Gifts From Prior Periods

If you answered "Yes" on line 11a of page 1, Part 1, see the instructions for completing Schedule B. If you answered "No," skip to the Tax Computation on page 1 (or Schedule C, if applicable).

A Calendar year or calendar quarter (see instructions)	B Internal Revenue office where prior return was filed	C Amount of unified credit against gift tax for periods after December 31, 1976	D Amount of specific exemption for prior periods ending before January 1, 1977	E Amount of taxable gifts

1	Totals for prior periods	**1**	
2	Amount, if any, by which total specific exemption, line 1, column D, is more than $30,000	**2**
3	Total amount of taxable gifts for prior periods. Add amount on line 1, column E and amount, if any, on line 2. Enter here and on line 2 of the Tax Computation on page 1	**3**

(If more space is needed, attach additional sheets of same size.)

Form **709** (2005)

SCHEDULE C	Computation of Generation-Skipping Transfer Tax

Note: *Inter vivos direct skips that are completely excluded by the GST exemption must still be fully reported (including value and exemptions claimed) on Schedule C.*

Part 1—Generation-Skipping Transfers

A Item No. (from Schedule A, Part 2, col. A)	B Value (from Schedule A, Part 2, col. H)	C Nontaxable portion of transfer	D Net Transfer (subtract col. C from col. B)
1			
Gifts made by spouse (for gift splitting only)			

Part 2—GST Exemption Reconciliation (Section 2631) and Section 2652(a)(3) Election

Check box ▶ ☐ if you are making a section 2652(a)(3) (special QTIP) election (see instructions)

Enter the item numbers from Schedule A of the gifts for which you are making this election ▶ . . . .

1	Maximum allowable exemption (see instructions)	1
2	Total exemption used for periods before filing this return	2
3	Exemption available for this return. Subtract line 2 from line 1	3
4	Exemption claimed on this return from Part 3, col. C total, below	4
5	Automatic allocation of exemption to transfers reported on Schedule A, Part 3 (see instructions)	5
6	Exemption allocated to transfers not shown on line 4 or 5, above. **You must attach a Notice of Allocation.** (see instructions)	6
7	Add lines 4, 5, and 6	7
8	Exemption available for future transfers. Subtract line 7 from line 3	8

Part 3—Tax Computation

A Item No. (from Schedule C, Part 1)	B Net transfer (from Schedule C, Part 1, col. D)	C GST Exemption Allocated	D Divide col. C by col. B	E Inclusion Ratio (subtract col. D from 1.000)	F Maximum Estate Tax Rate	G Applicable Rate (multiply col. E by col. F)	H Generation-Skipping Transfer Tax (multiply col. B by col. G)
1					47% (.47)		
2					47% (.47)		
3					47% (.47)		
4					47% (.47)		
5					47% (.47)		
6					47% (.47)		
					47% (.47)		
					47% (.47)		
					47% (.47)		
					47% (.47)		
					47% (.47)		
					47% (.47)		

Total exemption claimed. Enter here and on line 4, Part 2, above. May not exceed line 3, Part 2, above	**Total generation-skipping transfer tax.** Enter here; on Schedule A, Part 4, line 10; and on line 16 of the Tax Computation on page 1 . . . .

(If more space is needed, attach additional sheets of same size.)   Form **709** (2005)

*

Topical Index

All references are to paragraph numbers

961

DISTRIBUTABLE NET INCOME (DNI), 30,037; 30,151
Allocation among beneficiaries, 30,151
Capital gains, 30,199; 30,211
Chronological order, 30,427
Complex trusts, 30,115
Elective share, 30,121
Estates, 30,121—30,133; 30,171
First-tier recipients, 30,151
Second-tier recipients, 30,151; 30,169
Simple trusts, 30,073
Specific bequest rule, 30,061
Spousal Award, 30,121
Tier system of priorities, 30,145; 30,151

DISTRIBUTION IN KIND
Basis, 30,325
Legal obligation, 30,355
Sale or exchange,
Pecuniary bequest, 30,343; 30,349
Specific bequests, 30,337

DONATIVE INTENT, 3001
Antenuptial agreement, 3007

E

ECONOMIC RECOVERY TAX ACT OF 1981 (ERTA), 1025
Annual gift exclusion, 7013
Marital deduction, 28,337
Reduction in tax rates, 1025; 1163
Spousal joint tenancies, 16,007

EDUCATIONAL INSTITUTIONS
Charitable gifts to, 26,031

ELECTIONS
Alternate valuation date, 9013
Deduction of administration expenses, 25,039
Spousal, 24,031—24,043

ELECTIVE SHARE, 30,121; 30,175; 30,177

EMPLOYEE DEATH BENEFITS
See also Annuities
Amount includible, 15,127; 15,133
Deferred compensation payments, 15,133; 21,013
Maximum excludable from gross estate, 21,097
Retirement plans qualified for special income tax treatment, 21,043; 32,051—32,053
Spouse's benefits, 15,115; 27,364
Transfer with power retained to alter, amend, modify, or revoke, 19,061

EMPLOYEE GROUP INSURANCE
Incidents of ownership in, 17,075—17,085

EQUALIZATION CLAUSES, 27,445

EQUITABLE ADJUSTMENTS, 30,045

ESTATE ADMINISTRATION
Income tax aspects—see Income tax
Integrated planning,
Relationship of estate tax and income tax, 30,373—30,388
State property law, 30,367

ESTATE AND GIFT TAX
See also specific topics
Computation methods during life and at death, 2007
Deferment, 28,013
Final, 2007
Impact of Tax Reform Act of 1976, 1013—1031
Introduction, 1001
Legislative history, 1013
1976 revolution in, 1019
Pre–1976, 1013
Reasons for, 1120—1135
Reduction in rates, 1025
Reform, 1120—1135
Repeal of estate tax, 1033
Statutory mechanics for achieving integrated system of, 2007
Taxable estate, 2001
Tentative, 2007
Trust and estate income, 1145
Unification of system of, 1019
Unified credit—see Unified credit
Valuation for purposes of—see also Valuation, 9001—9025

ESTATE EQUALIZATION CLAUSES, 27,427

ESTATE TAX
See also Estate and gift tax, 2001; 2007
Complex trusts, 30,115
Credits, 28,001—28,017
Extensions of time for payment, 28,031—28,036
Integration with gift tax, 15,001
Payment of, 28,029—28,067
Stock redemptions, 28,039
When a return is required, 28,025
Who must file and when, 28,029
Who must pay and when, 28,007

ESTATE TRUST, 27,145

ESTATES, 30,121—30,133
Estate and gift tax on—See Estate and gift tax and other specific topics
Income tax on—see Income tax

ESTIMATED INCOME TAX PAYMENTS, 31,259

EVOLUTION OF GIFT TAX, 2001

EXCLUSION FOR EDUCATIONAL AND MEDICAL EXPENSES, 7157

EXECUTORS
See Fiduciaries

EXPENSES, DEBTS AND CLAIMS, 25,001—25,079
Administration expenses, 25,013—25,039
Consideration and debts, 25,045
Unenforceable claims, 25,043
Unfiled claims, 25,073
Valuation of claims, 25,079

F

FAIR MARKET VALUE
See Valuation

LIFE INSURANCE—Cont'd

Decedent as transferor of proceeds, 18,085; 18,097

Decedent's acquiring' policy on own life, 17,001

Incidents of ownership, 17,050—17,060

Capacity in which held, 17,005

Defined, 17,005

Group life policies, 17,075

Indirect control, 17,100

Partner in partnership holding, 17,100; 17,110

Sole or controlling shareholder of corporation, 17,100; 17,110

Trustee as owner, 17,061

Incomplete gift, 17,045

Irrevocable beneficiary designation, 17,035

Joint power of appointment over proceeds, 22,133; 22,139

Ownership determination,

Assignment of incidents, 17,035

Policy facts, 17,030

Payable to other beneficiaries, 17,001

Payment of premiums test, 17,001

Property settlement agreement provision for payment, 25,049

Receivable by executor, 17,001

Statutory provisions governing taxability of, 17,001; 17,010; 23,025

Stock exchange gratuity fund, 17,020

Valuation, 9025; 17,010

LIFETIME TRANSFERS

See also Gifts and other specific topics, 1019; 24,001

LIQUIDATION, RESTRICTIONS ON, 11,111

LIVESTOCK SALES, 32,025

LOCAL LAW

See State law

LOW–INTEREST LOANS, 3019—3037

M

MALLINCKRODT TRUSTS, 31,229

MARITAL DEDUCTION, 7163; 27,001

Administration expenses, 30,388

Alternative valuation date, 27,150

Bargained bequests, 27,367; 27,373

Beginning in 1948, 27,007

Bypass trust, 27,415

Ceiling, 27,013

Citizenship requirement, 27,055

Community property, 7163; 27,001

Consistency, duty of 27,285

Contingencies, 27,355; 27,356

Defined, 27,001

Disclaimers, 27,481

Discounts, 27,360

Division of estate before death, 27,415

Dower, 27,157

Economic Recovery Tax Act of 1981, 1025; 27,013

Election, QTIP, 27,331; 27,349; 27,356

Contingent, 27,359

Estate equalization clauses, 27,427; 27,445

MARITAL DEDUCTION—Cont'd

Estate splitting, 27,361

Estate trust, 27,145

Five-and-five powers, 27,325

Formula clauses, 27,415; 27,451; 27,457

Gross estate, 27,061

Historical background, 27,001

Importance, 27,001

Intention, 27,283; 27,285

Interim changes, 27,019

Joint wills and joint tenancies, 27,379

Nonprobate property, 27,391; 27,397

Probate property, 27,385

Jointly held property, 7163, 27,091

Life estate with power of appointment, 7163; 27,199; 27,247

Life insurance settlement options, 27,157; 27,271

Nature, 7163; 27,001

Nature of interest in property, 27,103; 27,109

Noncommunity property transfers, 7163

Nondeductible terminable interest requirement, 7163; 27,115; 27,181

Estate trust, 27,145; 27,151

Exceptions, 27,181

Spousal award, 27,121; 27,133

Overuse, consequences of, 27,409

Part of gross estate, 27,061

Passing to surviving spouse, 27,085—27,109

Planning,

Formula clauses, 27,415—27,439

Overmaritalization, 27,409

Post mortem planning, 27,091; 27,349; 27,356—57; 27,481

Purpose, 27,001

Qualified terminable interest property, 1025; 7163; 27,181; 27,275

Retirement benefits, 27,313

Specific portion, 27,217

Split gifts, 27,361

Spousal award, 27,091, 27,121; 27,133

Statutory requirements, 27,025

Stub income, 27,285

Surviving spouse, 27,067—27,109

Testamentary trust 27,385

Unlimited, 27,013

Valuation date determination, 27,175

Valuation discounts, 27,360

Value of interest passing, 27,391

Widow's award or allowance—see spousal award, this heading

Will contest, 27,091

MARKETABILITY DISCOUNTS, 11,071

MARRIED COUPLES

See Husband and wife

MECHANICS OF GIFT TAX, 2007

MINORITY DISCOUNTS, 11,037

MINORS

See also Children

Gifts to, 7039—7133

Sec. 2503(c) trusts, 7109—7121

Support, 18,121—18,151; 24,013—24,025

†